THE HOLY GEETA

Commentary by

SWAMI CHINMAYANANDA

CENTRAL CHINMAYA MISSION TRUST
Mumbai-400 072

•

Reprint - 1992 - 15,000 copies
New Edition - 1996 - 15,000 copies
Reprint - December 1999 - September 2008 - 58,000 copies
Reprint - May 2011 - 15,000 copies
Reprint - July 2013 - 15,000 copies

•

Published by:
Chinmaya Prakashan
The Publications Division of
Central Chinmaya Mission Trust
Sandeepany Sadhanalaya
Saki Vihar Road, Mumbai 400072, India
Tel.: +91-22-2857 2367, 2857 5806
Fax: +91-22-2857 3065
Email: ccmtpublications@chinmayamission.com
Website: www.chinmayamission.com

•

Distribution Centre in USA:
Chinmaya Mission West
Publications Division
560 Bridgetown Pike
Langhorne, PA 19053, USA
Tel.: 1-888-CMW-READ, (215) 396-0390 Fax: (215) 396-9710
Email: publications@chinmayamission.org
Website: www.chinmayapublications.org

•

Printed by:
Jayant Printery

•

Price: ₹ 400/-

•

ISBN: 978-81-7597-074-8

CTP

PUBLISHER'S NOTE

"When Param Pujya Gurudev Chinmayananda attained *Mahasamadhi,* Sri Krishna must have welcomed him into his abode saying, "Come, come, my beloved one. You outdid me, for I taught *Geeta* to one Arjuna, and you awakened many Arjunas round the globe", remarked a devotee fondly. Such was the profound influence of Gurudev's *Geeta* discourses on the audience.

His talks have been compiled in this commentary - The Holy *Geeta.* This text of Gurudev is so popular that it has made its entry into corporate houses and five-star hotels.

This edition owes its prim look to a very assiduous team – Joseph, Raju Nair, Pradeep Kharwal for executing the tedious but unavoidable task of DTP; Mr KS Rindani, Mrs Savita Chakravarty for relentless proof reading; Ramona Singh for the appealing cover design and book mark; Thomson Press for its commitment to fine details and technical execution.

Revamped from cover to cover, we now present the latest edition, for your joy, solace and guidance.

Mumbai **Central Chinmaya Mission Trust**
September 3, 2008

We take the opportunity to thank
Shri Badri Venkata Reddi of Badhri Spinning Mills Pvt Ltd
for having sponsored the printing of this book
and ensuring that this timeless wisdom
reaches the hands of seekers galore.

CONTENTS

THE ONE SONG IN MANY TONGUES

SANSKRIT

सर्व धर्मान्परित्यज्य मामेकं शरणं व्रज ।
अहं त्वा सर्वपापेभ्यो मोक्षयिष्यामि मा शुचः ॥

१८-६६

ENGLISH

Abandoning all Dharmas (of the body, mind and intellect), take refuge in Me alone; I will liberate thee from all sins: grieve not.

XVIII-66

FRENCH

En renconcant à tous les "dharmas"-c'est à dire-toutes les passions du corps, de l'esprit et de l'intelligence, cherche l'abri seulement en moi. Je te délivrerai, de tous tes péchés:
Ne te désole pas.

GERMAN

Gib das Ich auf (körperlich, geistig und intellektuell), suche Obdach nur in mir; ich will Dich von allen Sünden befreien: kränke Dich nicht.

SPANISH

Dejando a un lado todos (tus otros) deberes (como secundarios) búscame a MI solo como tu refugio; yo te libraré de todos tus pecados- no tengas pena!

POLISH

Zrzeknij sie wszelkich powinności
I bez wahania do mnie wróć,
A od wszelkiej uwolnie ciebie skazy.

SWEDISH

Uppge all Dharma* (i kropp, sinne och förstand) tag tillflykt i mig allena; Jag skall befria dig fran allt ont, sörj icke.

'Sanskritordet "Dharmas" betyder förmodligen här att man skall avsta fran all yttre paverkan och istället försöka utveckla självlakttagelse.

GREEK

Άφησε κάθε άγχος και εύρε σε μένα μόνο καταφύγιο· θα σε ελευθερώσω από όλες τις αμαρτίες! μη θλίβεσαι.

NORWEGIAN

Oppgi alle hellige Handlinger, og sok tilflugt hos meg alene! Jeg vil frelse deg fra alle Onder; sørg ikke!

DANISH

Opgiv alle hellige Handlinger, og tag Din Tilflugt til mig alene! Jeg vil frelse Dig fra alle Onder; sørg ikke!

BULGARIAN

Otrechi vsichki dostoinstva/na tialoto uma i intelekta/potarsi spasenie pri men: as ste te osvobodia ot vsichki grehove: nedei taguva.

ITALIAN

Liberandoti da ogni vincolo dei sensi,
delle percezioni, delle idee, rifugiati in me solo:
Io ti libererò da tutti i peceati: non crucciarti.

HIJNGARIAN

Megszabadulva tested, eszed ertelmed minden
vágyától, egyedül Hozzám menekülj;
én megszabaditalak teged minden büntől;
ne bánkodj.

RUSSIAN

Покинув все дхармы
(все религии тела, ума и интеллекта),
иди ко мне, я один твое прибежище;
не печалься,
я освобожу тебя от всех грехов.

CZECH

Zanechej vsechny bludy
a uchyl se ke mně!
Já tě osvobodim od všech hříchů,
netrap se.

DUTCH

Doe afstand van alle dharma's (van het lichaam, het verstand, en het intellect), neem toevlucht tot mij alleen; Ik zal U van alle zonden bevrijden: treur niet.

FINNISH

Jätä kaikki ruumiiseen, mieleen ja älyyn liittyvät ulkonaiset pyrkimykset, turvaudu yksin minuun: minä vapautan sinut kaikista synneistä: älä murehdi.

ROMANIAN

Părăsindu-ți toate tentațiile trupului, minții și gîndirii, caută-ți scăpare doar în mine;
Te voi elibera de toate păcatele:
Nu te întrista.

Hindi

सब धर्मों को त्यागकर केवल एक मेरे (सच्चिदानन्द धन वासुदेव परमात्मा की) ही अनन्यशरण में आओ । मैं तुम्हें संपूर्ण पापों से मुक्त कर दूंगा । शोक मत करो ।

Tamil

எல்லா தர்மங்களையும் பற்றற விட்டொழித்து
என்னை ஒருவனையே சரண் புகுவாய் :
நான் உன்னை எல்லாப் பாவங்களினின்றும்
விடுவிப்பேன். வருந்தாதே.

Malayalam

സർവ്വധർമ്മാൻ പരിത്യജ്യ മാമേകം ശരണം വ്രജ
അഹം ത്വാ സർവ്വപാപേഭ്യോ മോക്ഷയിഷ്യാമി മാശുചഃ
സർവ്വ ധർമ്മങ്ങളും പരിത്യജിച്ചിട്ട്, എന്നെ മാത്രം ശരണം
പ്രാപിക്കുക. .ാൻ നിന്നെ സകല പാപങ്ങളിൽ നിന്നും
മുക്തനാക്കും. വ്യസനിക്കേണ്ട.

Telugu

సర్వ ధర్మ పరిత్యాగ
సరణి మొటిసి పొలుపు గానన్ను శరణము
బొందు మయ్య ఏను నీ సర్వ పాపవి
తాన మోక్షణమ్ము గూర్తును నీవు
శోకమ్ము వీడు.

Kannada

ಎಲ್ಲಾ ಧರ್ಮಗಳನ್ನೂ ಬಿಟ್ಟು,
ನನ್ನೊ ಬ್ಬನನ್ನೇ ಶರಣು ಹೊಂದು.
ನಾನು ನಿನ್ನನ್ನು ಎಲ್ಲಾ ಪಾಪಗಳಿಂದ
ಬಿಡಿಸುವೆನು ಮರುಗಬೇಡ.

Punjabi

ਸਭ ਧਰਮਾਂ ਦਾ ਕਰ ਤੂੰ ਤਯਾਗ, ਮੇਰੀ ਸਰਨ ਲੈ. ਪਰ ਵੈਰਾਗ,
ਸੋਚ ਨ ਕਰ ਤੁਧ ਲਵਾਂ ਛਡਾਇ ਸਭ ਪਾਪਾਂ ਤੋਮੁਕਤ ਕਰਾਇ। ੬੬

Marathi

सर्व धर्मांचा त्याग करून मलाच
शरण ये. मी तुला सर्व पापांपासून
मुक्त करीन. शोक करू नकोस.

Gujarati

સર્વે ધર્મોને (શારીરિક, માનસિક અને
બૌધ્ધિક ધર્મોને) ત્યજીને તું મારે
એકલાનેજ શરણે આવ. તને સર્વે
પાપોથી હું મુકત કરીશ : શોક ન કર

Oriya

ସର୍ବ ଧର୍ମ ତେଜି ଆସ ଏକା ମୋ ଶରଣ
ସର୍ବ ପାପୁ ଉରିବି ନକର ଶୋଚନ ।

Bengali

সকল ধর্ম পরিত্যাগ করিয়া একমাত্র
আমার শরণ লও:
আমি তোমাকে সকল পাপ হইতে
মুক্ত করিব । দুঃখ করিও না ।

Urdu

ہر مذہب کو الوداع کہہ کر میری پناہ میں آجاؤ
ہو دِل نہ شکستہ رنج و غم سے میری رحمت میرے کرم سے
ہو جائیں گے پاپ دُور سارے (باقی نہ رہیں گے دُکھ تمہارے)

Assamese

তুঁমি সকল ধৰ্ম পৰিত্যাগ কৰি একমাত্ৰ
মোৰ শৰণ লোৱা, তোমাক মই
সমুদায় পাপৰ পৰা মুক্ত কৰিম:
শোক নকৰিবা ।

The Geeta as others see it

The *Geeta* is the universal mother. She turns away nobody. Her door is wide open to anyone who knocks. A true votary of the *Geeta* does not know what disappointment is. He ever dwells in perennial joy and 'peace that passeth all understanding'. But that peace and joy comes not to the sceptic or to him who is proud of his intellect or learning. It is reserved only for the humble in spirit who brings to her worship a fullness of faith and an undivided singleness of mind. There never was a man who worshipped her in this spirit and went back disappointed.

I find a solace in the *Bhagawad Geeta* that I miss even in the sermon on the Mount. When disappointment stares me in the face and all alone, I see not one ray of light, I go back to the *Bhagawad Geeta.* I find a verse here and a verse there, and I immediately begin to smile in the midst of overwhelming tragedies - and if they have left no visible, no indelible scare on me, I owe it all to the teaching of the *Bhagawad Geeta.*

- Mahatma Gandhi

* * *

What is the message of the *Geeta* and what is its working value, its spiritual utility to the human mind of the present day, after the long ages that have elapsed since it was written and the great subsequent transformations of thought and experience? The human mind always moves forward, alters its viewpoint and enlarges its thought-substance, and the effect of these changes is to render past systems of thinking obsolete, or when they are preserved; to extend, to modify and subtly or visibly, to alter their value. The vitality of ancient doctrine consists in the extent to which it naturally lends itself to such a treatment; for that means that whatever may have been the limitations or the obsolescence of the form of its thought, the truth of substance, the truth of living vision and experience on which its system was built, is still sound and retains a permanent validity and significance.

The *Geeta* is a book that has worn extraordinarily well, and it is almost as fresh and still in its real substance quite as new, because always renewable in experience, as when it first appeared in or was written into the frame of the 'Mahabharata'. It is still received in India as one of the great bodies of doctrine that most authoritatively govern religious thinking; and its teaching is acknowledged as of the highest value if not wholly accepted by almost all shades of religious belief and opinion. Its influence is not merely philosophic or academic but immediate and living, an influence both for thought and action and its ideas are actually at work as a powerful shaping factor in the revival and renewal of a nation and a culture. It has even been said recently by a great voice that all the needs for a spiritual life are to be found in the *Geeta*. It would be, to encourage the superstition of the book to take too literally that utterance. The truth of the Spirit is infinite and cannot be circumscribed in that manner. Still it may be said that most of the main clues are there and that after all the later developments of spiritual experience and discovery, we can still return to it for inspiration and guidance. Outside India too, it is universally acknowledged as one of the world's great scriptures, although in Europe its thought is better understood than its secret of spiritual practice.

- Aurobindo Ghose

The *Geeta* was not preached either as a pastime for persons tired out after living a worldly life in the pursuit of selfish motives, nor as a preparatory lesson for living such worldly life, but in order to give philosophical advice as to how one should live one's worldly life with an eye to Release, *Moksha* and as to the true duty of human beings in worldly life. My last prayer to everyone, therefore, is that one should not fail to thoroughly understand this ancient science of the life of a householder, or of worldly life, as early as possible in one's life.

- Lokmanya Tilak

* * *

Among the priceless teachings that may be found in the great Hindu poem Mahabharata, there is none so rare and precious as this 'The Lord's Song'. Since it fell from the divine lips of Shri Krishna on the field of battle, and stilled the surging emotions of His disciple and friend, how many troubled hearts has it quietened and strengthened, how many weary souls has it led to Him! It is meant to lift the aspirant from the lower levels of renunciation, where objects are renounced, to the loftier heights where desires are dead, and where the *Yogi* dwells in calm and ceaseless contemplation while his body and mind are actively employed in discharging the duties that fall to his lot in life. That the spiritual man need not be a recluse, that union with divine life may be achieved and maintained in the midst of worldly affairs, that the obstacles to that union lie, not outside us but within us, such is the central lesson of the *Bhagawad Geeta*.

It is a scripture of *Yoga*; now *Yoga* is literally union; and it means harmony with the Divine law, becoming one with the Divine life, by the subdual of all outward-going energies.

To reach this, balance must be gained, as also equilibrium, so that self, joined to the Self, shall not be affected by pleasure or pain, desire or aversion, or any of the 'pair of opposites' between which untrained selves swing backwards and forwards. Moderation is therefore, the keynote of the *Geeta* and the harmonising of all the constituents of man, till they vibrate in perfect attunement with the One, the Supreme Self. This is the aim the disciple is to set before him. He must learn not to be attracted by the attractive nor repelled by the repellant, but must see both as manifestations of the Lord, so that they may be lessons for his guidance, not fetters for his bondage. In the midst of turmoil, he must rest in the Lord of Peace, discharging every duty to the fullest, not because he seeks the results of his actions, but because it is his duty to perform them. His heart is an altar of love to his Lord, the flame burning upon it; all his acts, physical and mental, are sacrifices offered at the altar, and once offered, he has with them no further concern.

As though to make the lesson more impressive, it was given on a field of battle. Arjuna, the warrior-prince, was to vindicate his brother's title, to destroy an usurper who was oppressing the land. It was his duty as prince, as warrior, to fight for the deliverance of his nation and to restore order and peace. To make the contest more bitter, loved comrades and friends stood on both sides, wringing his heart with personal anguish, and making the conflict of duties as well as physical strife. Could he slay those whom he owed love and duty, and trample on ties of kindred? To break family ties was a sin; to leave the people in cruel bondage was a sin; where was the right way? Justice must be done, else law would be disregarded; but how to slay without sin? The answer is the burden of the book. Have no personal interest in the event; carry out the duty imposed by the position in life, realise that *Ishvara*, at once Lord and Law, is the doer working out the mighty evolution that ends in Bliss and Peace; be identified with Him by devotion and then perform duty as duty, fighting without passion or desire without anger or hatred Thus activity forges no bonds, *Yoga* is accomplished, and the soul is free.

Such is the obvious teaching of this sacred book. But as all the acts of an *Avatara* are symbolical, we may pass from the outer to the inner planes, and see in the fight of Kurukshetra, the battlefield of the soul, and in the sons of Dhritarashtra, enemies it meets in its progress; Arjuna becomes the type of struggling soul of the disciple, and Shri Krishna is the Logos of the soul. Thus, the teaching of the ancient battlefield gives guidance in all later days, and trains the aspiring soul in treading the steep and thorny path that leads to peace. To all such souls in the East and the West come these divine lessons for, the path is one, though it has many names, and all souls seek the same goal, though they may not realise their unity.

- Dr. Annie Besant

* * *

The *Geeta* is a bouquet composed of the beautiful flowers of spiritual truths collected from the *Upanishads.*

- Swami Vivekananda

* * *

I believe that in all the living languages of the world, there is no book so full of true knowledge, and yet so handy as the *Bhagawad Geeta.....* It brings to men the highest knowledge, the purest love and the most luminous action. It teaches self-control, the threefold austerity, non-violence, truth, compassion, obedience to the call of duty for the sake of duty and putting up a fight against unrighteousness (*Adharma*)... To my knowledge, there is no book in the whole range of the world's literature so high above all as the *Bhagawad Geeta* which is treasure-house of *Dharma* not only for Hindus but for all mankind.

- Madan Mohan Malaviya

* * *

The *Geeta* is one of the clearest and most comprehensive summaries of the Perennial Philosophy ever to have been done. Hence its enduring value not only for Indians, but for all mankind.... The *Bhagawad Geeta* is perhaps the most systematic spiritual statement of the Perennial Philosophy.

- Aldous Huxley

* * *

The Esssence of the Bhagawad Geeta

Direct Guidance For Your Problems

	Topic	Chapter	Verses
1.	Who is God?	IX	17
		XVIII	61
2.	What is God's nature?	IV	6
		X	20
3.	What is God's function?	IV	7, 8
4.	What are God's manifestations?	VII	4
		X	41
5.	Where is God?	VI	30
		XV	15
6.	What is Om?	VIII	11, 13
		XVII	23, 24
7.	How does confusion affect us?	I	29
		VII	27
8.	What does delusion do to us?	II	7, 63
9.	How does desire destroy us?	II	62
		XVI	21

Topic	Chapter	Verses
10. How do passions bind us?	III	38,39
	XVI	16
11. How do we control our passion?	II	61
	VI	24, 25
12. How do we control anger?	V	23
	VI	14
13. How do we console the bereaved?	II	27
	VI	40
14. How do we help the disillusioned?	II	28
	IV	35
15. How do we help the disappointed?	XIII	8
	XVIII	62
16. How do we help those who have morally slipped?	IV	36
	IX	30
17. How do we help those who have spiritually fallen?	VI	43
	XVI	22
18. Guidance to politicians	II	38
	III	21
19. Guidance to businessmen	IV	31
	XVII	20
20. Guidance to teenagers	IV	39
	VI	5
21. Grand Vision of Universe	XV	1, 2, 3

Topic	Chapter	Verses
22. Right Action	II	48
	XVIII	23
23. Increasing Efficiency	III	30
	XII	16
24. Inner Peace	II	71
	V	12
25. Concentration	VI	25, 26
26. Usefulness to others	VI	32
	XII	4
27. Joy to Oneself	II	64
	XVIII	37
28. Object of Meditation	VI	25
	XVIII	57
29. Preparation for Meditation	VI	11, 13
30. Reward of Meditation	VI	15, 22
31. Mind in Meditation	VI	19, 20
32. Daily Life and Meditation	VI	16, 17
33. Way to Meditation	VI	24, 25
34. Perfect Person	II	55
	XIV	25
35. Spiritually Evolved Person	V	10, 18

Topic	Chapter	Verses
36. Signs of Spiritual Growth	XVII	14, 15, 16
37. Signs of Spiritual Fall	XIV	8, 13
38. Spiritual Stagnation	XVIII	32, 35
39. Nature of Matter	XIII	5, 6
40. Nature of Spirit	XIII	12, 17
41. Approaches to Meditation	VI	23
	XII	8
42. Relation with God	XI	43, 44
43. Way to Reach the Divine Goal	IX	34
	XVIII	66
44. Glory of the *Geeta*	XVIII	68, 70
45. Devotion	IX	26, 27
46. Surrender	VII	19
	IX	22
47. Service	III	19
	IV	20
48. Wisdom	XIII	27, 29
49. Self-control	II	58
	VI	4
50. Right Food	XVII	8
51. Right Speech	XVII	15

PS. : Verse numbers in Chapter XIII are as per the version of the *Geeta* with 700 verses.

What Says The Geeta?

Chapter - III

KARMA YOGA

Chapter - IV

THE *YOGA* OF RENUNCIATION OF ACTION IN KNOWLEDGE

Chapter - V

THE *YOGA* OF TRUE RENUNCIATION

Chapter - VI

THE YOGA OF MEDITATION

Chapter - VII

THE *YOGA* OF KNOWLEDGE AND WISDOM

Chapter - VIII

THE *YOGA* OF IMPERISHABLE *BRAHMAN*

Chapter - IX

THE *YOGA* OF ROYAL SECRET

Chapter - X

THE *YOGA* OF DIVINE GLORIES

Chapter - XI

THE *YOGA* OF COSMIC FORM

Chapter - XII

THE *YOGA* OF DEVOTION

Chapter - XIII

THE *YOGA* OF FIELD AND ITS KNOWER

Chapter - XIV

THE *YOGA* OF *GUNA*

Chapter - XV

THE *YOGA* OF THE SUPREME SPIRIT

Chapter - XVI

THE *YOGA* OF DIVINE AND DEVILISH ESTATES

Chapter - XVII

THE *YOGA* OF THREEFOLD FAITH

Chapter - XVIII

THE *YOGA* OF LIBERATION THROUGH RENUNCIATION

* * *

General Introduction to The Bhagawad Geeta

IF the *Upanishads* are the textbooks of philosophical principles discussing man, world and God, the *Geeta* is a handbook of instructions as to how every human being can come to live the subtle philosophical principles of *Vedanta* in the actual work-a-day world.

Shrimad Bhagawad Geeta, the Divine Song of the Lord, occurs in the Bhishma Parva of the Mahabharata, and comprises eighteen chapters, from the 25th to the 42nd. This great handbook of practical living marked a positive revolution in Hinduism and inaugurated a Hindu renaissance for the ages that followed the *Puranic* Era.

In the Song of the Lord, the *Geeta,* the Poet-Seer Vyasa has brought the *Vedic* truths from the sequestered Himalayan caves into the active fields of political life and into the confusing tensions of an imminent fratricidal war. Under the stress of some psychological maladjustments, Arjuna got shattered in his mental equipoise and lost his capacity to act with true discrimination. Lord Krishna takes in hand that neurotic mind of Arjuna for a Hindu treatment with *Vedic* truths.

Religion is philosophy in action. From time to time an ancient philosophy needs intelligent reinterpretation in the context of new times, and men of wisdom, prophets, and seers guide the common man on how to apply effectively the ancient laws in his present life.

If we try to digest properly the implications of the *Geeta's* advice in the light of *Vedic* lore, it becomes amply clear how actions performed without egocentric desires purge the mind of its deep-seated impressions and make it increasingly subtle in its purification and preparation for greater flights into the Infinite Beyond. To explain this, we will just try to review a little the conception of the mind and its functions in our day-to-day life.

Mind is man. As the mind, so is the individual. If the mind is disturbed, the individual is disturbed. If the mind is good, the individual is good. This mind, for purposes of our study and understanding, may be considered as constituted of two distinct sides - one facing the world of stimuli that reach it from the objects of the world, and the other facing the 'within' which reacts to the stimuli received. The outer mind facing the object is called the objective mind; in Sanskrit we call it the *Manas,* and the inner mind is called the subjective mind; in Sanskrit, the *Buddhi.*

That individual is whole and healthy in whom the objective and subjective aspects of the mind work in unison, and in moments of doubt, the OBJECTIVE MIND readily comes under the disciplining influence of the SUBJECTIVE MIND. But unfortunately, except for a rare few, the majority of us have minds that are split. This split between the SUBJECTIVE and the OBJECTIVE aspects of our mind is mainly created by the layer of egoistic desires in the individual. The greater the distance between these two aspects of the mind, the greater the inner confusion in the individual, and the greater the egoism and low desires which the individual comes to exhibit in life.

Through the five 'gateways of knowledge', the organs-of-perception, all of us experience the world of objects around us at all moments of our waking state. The innumerable stimuli that react with our sense-organs (receptors), create impulses which reach the OBJECTIVE MIND and these impulses filter deep down to the subjective stratum through the intervening layers of individual egocentric desires. These impulses, thus reaching the SUBJECTIVE MIND of a person, react with the existing impressions of his own past actions that are carefully stored away in the subjective layer and express themselves in the world outside through the five organs of action (effectors).

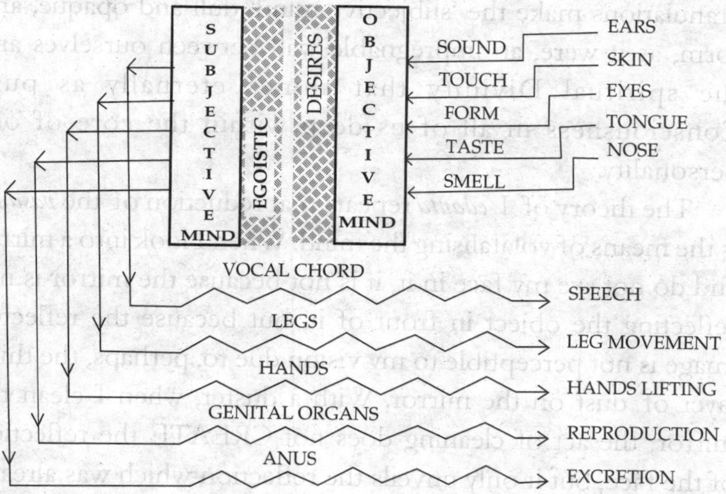

DIAGRAM "A"

The Diagram 'A' gives figuratively the design of each activity that man performs in the world outside when he consciously comes to react with a given set of stimuli.

At each moment, man meets with different patterns of these stimuli, and thus constantly gathers new impressions in the 'subjective mind'. Every set of impulses reaching it not only adds to the existing layers of impressions already in it, but also gets coloured by the quality of these *vasanas* hoarded within. When they are translated into action, the actions carry a flavour of the existing *vasanas* in the 'subjective mind'.

All of us live constantly meeting a variety of experiences; and at each incident, we perceive, react with the perceived, and come to act in the outer field. In this process, we unwittingly come to hoard in ourselves more and more dirt of new impressions. The 'subjective mind' gets increasingly granulated by overlapping signatures of our past moments. These granulations make the 'subjective mind' dull and opaque, and form, as it were, an impregnable wall between ourselves and the spiritual Divinity that shines eternally as pure Consciousness in all of us deep within the core of our personality.

The theory of *Vedanta* repeats that reduction of the *vasanas* is the means of volatalising the mind. When I look into a mirror and do not see my face in it, it is not because the mirror is not reflecting the object in front of it, but because the reflected image is not perceptible to my vision due to, perhaps, the thick layer of dust on the mirror. With a duster, when I clean the mirror, the act of cleaning does not CREATE the reflection of the face, but it only unveils the reflection which was already there. Similarly, man is not aware today of his divine spiritual nature because the 'subjective mind' reflecting it is thickly coated with dull *vasanas* gathered by it during its egocentric, passionate existence in the world.

To bring the subjective and the objective aspects of the mind together into a happy marriage where the 'objective mind' is well-disciplined to act faithfully as per the guidance of the 'subjective', is the *Yoga* pointed out in the *Geeta*. This is accomplished only by the removal of the dividing factor-the egocentric desires. The typical word used in the *Geeta* to indicate this practical implication of *Yoga* is self-explanatory-*Buddhi Yoga*.

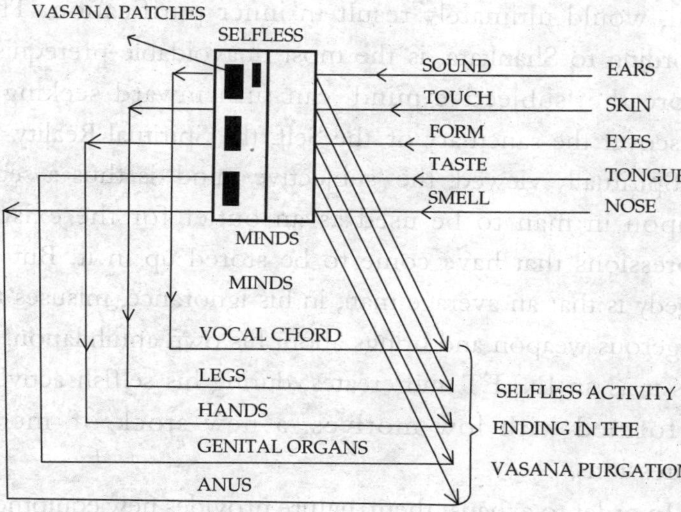

DIAGRAM "B"

As represented in Diagram 'B', when this happy marriage between the subjective and the objective aspects of the mind has taken place, thereafter that equanimous *Yogin* becomes skilled in action,* and he, with his 'objective-mind', reacts intelligently and faithfully to the external stimuli; his actions become, as it were, a purgation of the already existing *vasanas* in his 'subjective mind'. Thus, through intelligent action, an individual can exhaust his existing impressions and ultimately redeem his 'subjective-mind' from the granulations and make it more clear and crystalline.

* *'Yogah Karmasu Kousalam'* – 'Dexterity in action is *Yoga*' – II,50

This idea has been emphasised by great commentators like Shankara, who tirelessly repeat that selfless activity, performed in a spirit of egoless adoration and reverence to the divine ideal, would ultimately result in inner purification. This, according to Shankara, is the most unavoidable prerequisite before the 'subjective mind' can turn inward seeking to rediscover the sanctuary of the Self, the Spiritual Reality.

Spiritually viewed, the 'subjective mind' is thus a secret weapon in man to be used as an outlet for the existing impressions that have come to be stored up in it. But the tragedy is that an average man, in his ignorance, misuses this dangerous weapon and brings about his own annihilation. He uses it as an INLET and creates, during his selfish activities performed with low motives, a new stock of mental impressions.

In order to exhaust them, nature provides new equipments (bodies), in which the same ego comes to live, repeatedly, life after life. The message of the *Geeta* clearly points out that actions are not to be avoided and the world-of-objects is not to be denied. On the contrary, by making use of them intelligently, we must strive selflessly, and force the very *samsara* to provide us with a field for exhausting our mental dirt.

An unhealthy mind divided in itself, as we explained earlier, becomes an easy prey to a host of psychological diseases. Weakened in its constitution, it easily becomes a victim to all contagions. Arjuna was an average educated man, and from the details of the Mahabharata, we know the environments in which he grew up. But for the entire Mahabharata, we would not appreciate so fully Arjuna's mental condition, without which Krishna's message would have fallen flat upon the readers.

Therefore, the *Geeta* is an intrinsic part of the entire Mahabharata and the classic would have been a hotchpotch story, without pith and dignity, if *Srimad Bhagawad Geeta* was not in it - and the *Geeta* would have been a mere philosopher's riddle-poem without the Mahabharata background. The story and the poem together are an organic whole; each devoid of the other would be ineffectual and empty.

Modern psychology exhausts volumes in describing to us the dreary results of suppression and repression of emotions. There are many moments in our lives when we KNOWINGLY suppress many of our emotions; but more often in our day-to-day life, we, UNCONSCIOUSLY, repress many of our sentiments. Repressed emotions accumulate a tremendous amount of dynamic energy which must necessarily seek a field for expression. Unless these energies are properly guided they would boomerang back to destroy the very individual. Though there are no direct explanations of any repressions of emotion in Arjuna, a careful student of the story can easily diagnose that the great hero on the battlefield came under the influence of his repressed conditions and behaved as a victim of perfect neurosis.

The causes for his emotional repressions are not far to seek. A great hero, confident of his own strength, was made to live amidst the unjust tyranny of his Machiavellian cousins. At the same time, the great archer could not give vent to his nature because of the righteous policy of 'peace at all costs' of his eldest brother, Yudhishthira. These repressed emotions found a healthy field for expression in the severe *tapas* which he performed during his life in the jungles.

During the last year of their lives INCOGNITO, the Pandava family had to serve as menials in the palace of the *Raja* of Virata. The carping injustice and the cruel indignities of the situation caused, no doubt, a lot of repression in Arjuna's mind. But even these found a healthy field of expression in the battle that he had to wage against Duryodhana's forces that came to challenge the Virata-might.

After their long and strenuous trials, when the Pandavas at last reached their native kingdom, their tyrant cousin, with no rhyme or reason, denied them not only their right to half of the kingdom, but also all terms of conciliation.

The shrewd, blind Dhritarashtra, father of the Kauravas, probably understood the psychological condition of the great warrior, Arjuna. Hence on the day previous to the great war, he sent Sanjaya, his emissary, to Arjuna with a secret message. This message, full of mischievous import, sowed the seeds of dangerous ideas in the mind of Arjuna, directing his repressed energies into wrong channels, so that he became a hapless neurotic in the face of the great challenge. We shall read in the First Chapter the very same arguments and ideas repeated faithfully by Arjuna from the message he had received the previous day from his uncle.

On that fateful day when both the armies were getting into formation, Arjuna asks his charioteer, Lord Krishna, to drive the chariot to a point between the two forces, so that he may review the enemy lines. Larger in number, better equipped, more liberal in supplies and commanded by well-known personalities, the Kaurava formation, expanding itself like an 'eagle' stood poised to swoop down upon the smaller army of the Pandavas. This was a sight severely challenging the mental stamina of the Pandava hero. His 'objective-mind' under the impact of the stimuli, could not find any reaction from its 'subjective-mind' (*Buddhi*), because the shattering of these two aspects was complete due to the intervening layers of his egocentric assumptions and desire-prompted anxieties. The dynamic forces released in his mind due to the repressions were not properly channelised, but were misdirected by the suggestions of Dhritarashtra's words, and therefore, the greatest hero of the times, Arjuna, suddenly became a despondent, bewildered, neurotic patient.

The 'Krishna-treatment' of this patient of psychological derangement was certainly a specific cure, inasmuch as, in the last chapter we definitely hear Arjuna declaring that all his 'delusions have ended'. The rest of the story of how, having come into his own, he became a rejuvenated warrior of tremendous strength and valour, is quite well-known to all students of this great classic.

In varying degrees, every man is a victim of this 'Arjuna-Disease' and the 'Krishna-cure' being specific, is available to all of us at all times in the philosophy of the *Geeta.*

In the Second Chapter, which is almost a summary of the entire *Geeta,* Krishna indicates the two main lines of treatment. One is a 'treatment of Idealism' wherein Arjuna is directed to a greater Reality than his mind, ego and intellect and thereby the divorce between the 'subjective' and the 'objective' aspects of his mind is eliminated to some extent. In the second half of the same chapter, we shall read and come to understand how selfless activity will purge the existing *vasanas* in the individual. Arjuna being a *Kshatriya*, his mind was coloured by the impression of *Rajo-guna* (activity), and so he needed a battlefield to exhaust those impressions.

Thus, we find Krishna repeatedly goading his friend with the words, "Get up and fight". This need not necessarily mean that the *Geeta* is a war-mongering scripture of the ruling-class. It is a call to each one of us to get up and fight the battle of our own life, according to our own *vasanas* (*Swadharma*), so that we may exhaust them and thus gain inner purity. As we take it up stanza by stanza, for a close study of the entire Song, we shall try to see how Krishna indicates the same truth from different angles of vision and explains it in different words.

OM OM OM

I

Arjuna-Grief Introduction

NO other race in the world had ever harnessed so successfully the scintillating possibilities of the drama in literature for the purposes of philosophical exposition as the ancient Hindus. The *Upanishads* were recorded in the form of conversations between the teacher and the taught, in the quiet atmosphere of the silent and peaceful Himalayan valleys. In the *Geeta*, however, the highest and the best in Hindu philosophy have been reiterated, in a more elaborate and detailed dramatic layout amidst the din and roar of a total-war. Krishna gives his message of manly-action to Arjuna amidst the breathing, palpitating environment of the clash and carnage of a battlefield.

The Kauravas, hundred in number, represent the innumerable ungodly forces of negative tendencies within man's bosom, and the Pandavas, no doubt, represent the divine impulses in him. A constant Mahabharata war is being waged within every one of us at all our crucial moments of action; and in all cases, the negative forces in each one of us are larger in number and usually mightier in their effectiveness, while the inner divine army is ever lesser in number and apparently, comparatively weaker in efficiency. Therefore, every single individual, at the moment of his inward checking up, must necessarily feel the desperations of Arjuna.

The story of the Mahabharata sounds an optimistic note of hope to man that, even though the diviner impulses are seemingly less in number, if the same are organised fully and brought under the guidance of the Supreme Lord, Krishna, the Self; then, under His guidance, they can easily be ushered into a true and permanent victory over the outnumbering forces of lust and greed.

The Kauravas, representing the negative tendencies and the sinful motives in a mortal's bosom, are born as children to the old king, Dhritarashtra, a born-blind prince. He was wedded to Gandhari, who had voluntarily blinded herself by putting bandages over her eyes! Commentators are tempted to see in this, a very appropriate significance. Mind is born-blind to truth, and when it is wedded to an intellect, which has also assumed blindness, the negative instincts yoked with low motives can only beget a hundred criminalities and sins!

When, upon the spiritual field of self-development within (*Dharmakshetra*), the lower instincts and the higher ideals array themselves, ready to fight, a true seeker (the captain of the latter), under the guidance of his divine discriminative intellect, takes himself to a point on no-man's land between the two forces for the purpose of reviewing the enemy lines, without identifying himself with either the good or the evil in him. At that moment of his introspective meditations, the egoistic entity comes to feel a morbid desperation and feels generally incapacitated to undertake the great spiritual adventure of fighting his inner war with any hope of victory.

This peculiar mental condition of a seeker is beautifully represented in the vivid picture of Arjuna's dejection in the opening chapter.

In Sanskrit works, it is a recognised tradition that the opening stanza should generally indicate the whole theme of the text. The bulk of the book, then discusses at length, the different views and gives all possible arguments, until in its concluding portion, the last stanza generally summarises the final conclusions of the *shastra* on the theme indicated in the opening section of the book. In this way, when we consider the *Geeta,* we find that the Divine Song starts with the word *'Dharma'* and concludes with the term 'Mine'(*Mama*); and therefore, the contents of the *Geeta* - we may conclude - are nothing but 'My *Dharma'* (*Mama Dharma*).

The term *Dharma* is one of the most intractable terms in Hindu philosophy. Derived from the root *'dhar'* (*Dhri*) to uphold, sustain, support, the term *Dharma* denotes "that which holds together the different aspects and qualities of an object into a whole".* Ordinarily, the term *Dharma* has been translated as religious code, as righteousness, as a system of morality, as duty, as charity, etc. But the original Sanskrit term has a special connotation of its own which is not captured by any one of these renderings. The best rendering of this term *Dharma* that I have met with so far is, the law-of-Being meaning, "that which makes a thing or being what it is". For example, it is the *Dharma* of the Fire to burn, of the Sun to shine, etc.

* *"Dharanat dharmam ityahu, dharmena vidhritah prajah".*

Dharma means, therefore, not merely righteousness or goodness but it indicates the essential nature of anything, without which it cannot retain its independent existence.

For example, a cold, dark Sun is impossible, as heat and light are the *Dharma* of the Sun. Similarly, if we are to live as truly dynamic men in the world, we can only do so by being faithful to our true nature, and the *Geeta* explains to me 'my *Dharma*'.

In using thus the first person possessive noun, this scripture perhaps indicates that the Song Divine sung through the eighteen chapters is to be subjectively transcribed, lived, and personally experienced by each student in his own life.

Dhritarashtra said:

1. *What did the sons of Pandu and also my people do, when, desirous to fight, they assembled together on the holy plain of Kurukshetra, O Sanjaya?*

In the entire *Geeta* this is the only verse which the blind old king Dhritarashtra gives out. All the rest of the seven hundred stanzas are Sanjaya's report on what happened on the Kurukshetra battlefield, just before the war.

The blind old king is certainly conscious of the palpable injustices that he had done to his nephews, the Pandavas.

धृतराष्ट्र उवाच
धर्मक्षेत्रे कुरुक्षेत्रे समवेता युयुत्सवः।
मामकाः पाण्डवाश्चैव किमकुर्वत सञ्जय ॥ १ ॥

dhṛtarāṣṭra uvāca
dharmakṣetre kurukṣetre samavetā yuyutsavaḥ
māmakāḥ pāṇḍavāścaiva kimakurvata sañjaya 1.

Dhritarashtra knew the relative strength of the two armies, and therefore, was fully confident of the larger strength of his son's army. And yet, the viciousness of his past and the consciousness of the crimes perpetrated seem to be weighing heavily upon the heart of the blind king, and so he has his own doubts on the outcome of this war. He asks Sanjaya to explain to him, what is happening on the battlefield of Kurukshetra. Vyasa had given Sanjaya the powers to see and listen to the happenings in far-off Kurukshetra even while he was sitting beside Dhritarashtra in the palace at Hastinapura.

Sanjaya said:

2. *Having seen the army of the Pandavas drawn up in battle array, King Duryodhana then approached his teacher (Drona) and spoke these words.*

From this stanza onwards, we have the report of Sanjaya upon what he saw and heard on the warfront at Kurukshetra. When Duryodhana saw the Pandava-forces arrayed for battle, though they were less in number than his own forces, yet the tyrant felt his self-confidence draining away. As a child would run to its parents in fright, so too, Duryodhana, unsettled in his mind, runs to his teacher, Dronacharya. When our motives are impure and our cause unjust, however well equipped we

---

सञ्जय उवाच
दृष्ट्वा तु पाण्डवानीकं व्यूढं दुर्योधनस्तदा ।
आचार्यमुपसङ्गम्य राजा वचनमब्रवीत् ॥ २ ॥

sañjaya uvāca
dṛṣṭvā tu pāṇḍavānīkaṁ vyūḍhaṁ duryodhanastadā
ācāryamupasaṅgamya rājā vacavamabravīt 2.

may be, our minds should necessarily feel restless and agitated. This is the mental condition of all tyrants and lusty dictators.

3. *Behold, O Teacher! This mighty army of the sons of Pandu arrayed by the son of Drupada, thy wise disciple.*

It is indeed stupid of Duryodhana to point out to Drona the army formation of the Pandavas. Later on also, we shall find Duryodhana talking too much and that is a perfect symptom indicating the inward fears of the great king over the final outcome of the unjust war.

4. *Here are heroes, mighty archers, equal in battle to Bhima and Arjuna, Yuyudhana, Virata and Drupada, each commanding eleven-thousand archers.*

5. *Dhrishtaketu, Chekitana, and the valiant king of Kashi, Purujit and Kuntibhoja and Saibya, the best of men.*

पश्यैतां पाण्डुपुत्राणामाचार्य महतीं चमूम् ।
व्यूढां द्रुपदपुत्रेण तव शिष्येण धीमता ॥ ३ ॥
paśyaitāṁ pāṇḍuputrāṇāmācārya mahatīṁ camūm
vyūḍhāṁ drupadaputreṇa tava śiṣyaṇa dhīmatā 3.
अत्र शूरा महेष्वासा भीमार्जुनसमा युधि ।
युयुधानो विराटश्च द्रुपदश्च महारथः ॥ ४ ॥
atra śūrā maheṣvāsā bhīmārjunasamā yudhi
yuyudhāno virāṭaśca drupaśca mahārathaḥ 4.
धृष्टकेतुश्चेकितानः काशिराजश्च वीर्यवान् ।
पुरुजित्कुन्तिभोजश्च शैब्यश्च नरपुङ्गवः ॥ ५ ॥
dhṛṣṭaketuścekitānaḥ kāśirājaśca vīryavāna
purujitkuntibhojaśya śaibyaśca narapuṅgavaḥ 5.

6. *The strong Yudhamanyu and the brave Uttamaujas, the son of Subhadra and the sons of Draupadi, all of them, divisional commanders.*

In these three stanzas, we have a list of names of all those who were noted personalities in the Pandava army. Duryodhana, reviewing his enemies standing in formation, recognises very many noted men of war functioning as *maharathas* in the Pandava forces. A *maharathi* was in charge of a group of 11,000 archers, which formed a division in the ancient Hindu army.

Arjuna and Bhima were accepted men of war, noted for archery and strength. These enumerated heroes were, says Duryodhana, each as great as Arjuna and Bhima, the implication being that though the Pandava forces were less in number, their total effectiveness was much greater than that of the larger and better equipped army of the Kauravas.

7. *Know also, O best among the twice-born, the names of those who are the most distinguished amongst ourselves, the leaders of my army; these I name to thee for thy information.*

युधामन्युश्च विक्रान्त उत्तमौजाश्च वीर्यवान् ।
सौभद्रो द्रौपदेयाश्च सर्व एव महारथाः ॥ ६ ॥

yudhāmanyuśca vikrānta uttamaujāśca vīryavān
saubhadro dropadeyāśca sarva eva mahārathāḥ 6.

अस्माकं तु विशिष्टा ये तान्नि बोध द्विजोत्तम ।
नायका मम सैन्यस्य संज्ञार्थं तान्ब्रवीमि ते ॥ ७ ॥

asmākaṁ tu viśiṣṭā ye tānnibodha dvijottama
nāyakā mama sainyasa sañjñārtha tānbravīmi te 7.

Addressing his master as 'the best among the twice-born', Duryodhana now repeats the names of the distinguished heroes in his own army. A weak man, to escape from his own mental fears, will whistle to himself in the dark. The guilty conscience of the tyrant king had undermined all his mental strength. The more he realised the combined strength of the great personalities arrayed in the opposite enemy camp, the more abjectly nervous he felt, in spite of the fact that his own army was also manned by highly competent heroes. In order to revive himself, he wanted to hear words of encouragement from his teachers and elders. But when Duryodhana met Drona, the *Aacharya* chose to remain silent and the helpless king had to find for himself new means of encouragement to revive his own drooping enthusiasm. Therefore, he started enumerating the great leaders in his own army.

When a person has thus, completely lost his morale due to the heavy burden of his own crimes weighing on his conscience, it is but natural that he loses all sense of proportion in his words. At such moments of high tension, an individual clearly exhibits his true mental culture. He addresses his own teacher as 'the best among the twice-born'.

A *Brahmana* is considered as 'twice-born' because of his inner spiritual development. When born from his mother's womb man comes into the world only as the animal called man. Thereafter, through study and contemplation, he gains more and more discipline, and a cultured Hindu is called a *Brahmana* (*Brahmin*).

After all, Drona is a *Brahmana* by birth and as such, he must have a greater share of softness of heart. Moreover, the enemy lines are fully manned by his own dear students. As a shrewd dictator, Duryodhana entertained shameless doubts about the loyalty of his own teacher.

This is but an instinctive fear, which is natural with all men of foul motives and crooked dealings. When we are not ourselves pure, we will project our own weaknesses and impurities on others who are working around us as our subordinates.

8. *Yourself and Bhishma, and Karna and also Kripa, the victorious in war; Aswatthama, Vikarna, and so also the son of Somadatta.*

Though Duryodhana, in his mental hysteria, got slightly upset at the subjective onslaught of his own brutal motives and past crimes, like the true dictator that he was, he regained his balance in no time. The moment he had spilt out in his insulting arrogance, the term 'twice-born' in addressing his teacher, he realised that he had overstepped the bounds of discretion. Perhaps the cold silence of the revered *Acharya* spoke amply to Duryodhana.

भवान्भीष्मश्च कर्णश्च कृपश्च समितिंजय: ।
अश्वत्थामा विकर्णश्च सौमदत्तिस्तथैव च ॥ ८ ॥
bhavānbhīṣmaśca karṇaśca kṛpaśca samitiñjayaḥ
aśvatthāmā vikarṇaśca saumadattistathaiva ca 8.

9. *And many other heroes also who are determined to give up their lives for my sake, armed with various weapons and missiles, all well-skilled in battle.*

The incorrigible vanity of the dictatorial tyrant is amply clear when he arrogates to himself the stupendous honour that such a vast array of heroes had come ready to lay down their lives for 'MY SAKE'. To all careful students of the Mahabharata, it cannot be very difficult to estimate how many of these great veterans would have thrown in their lot with Duryodhana, had it not been for the fact that Bhishma, the grandsire, was fighting in the ranks of the Kauravas.

10. *This army of ours defended by Bhishma is insufficient, whereas that army of theirs defended by Bhima is sufficient. Or, this army of ours protected by Bhishma is unlimited, whereas that army of theirs protected by Bhima is limited.*

In the art of warfare, then known among the ancient Hindus, each army had, no doubt, a commander-in-chief, but it also had a powerful man of valour, courage and intelligence, who functioned as the 'defender'. In the Kaurava

---

अन्ये च बहवः शूरा मदर्थे त्यक्तजीविताः ।
नानाशस्त्रप्रहरणाः सर्वे युद्धविशारदाः ॥ ९ ॥
anye ca bahavaḥ śūra madartha tyaktajīvitāḥ
nānāśastraprharaṇāḥ sarve yuddhaviśāradāḥ 9.

अपर्याप्तं तदस्माकं बलं भीष्माभिरक्षितम् ।
पर्याप्तं त्विदमेतेषां बलं भीमाभिरक्षितम् ॥ १० ॥
apayārptaṁ tadasmākaṁ balaṁ bhīṣmābhirakṣitam
payārptaṁ tvidameteṣāṁ balaṁ bhīmābhirakṣitam 10.

forces, Bhishma officiated as the 'defender', and in the Pandava forces Bhima held the office.

11. *Therefore do you all, stationed in your respective positions in the several divisions of the army, protect Bhishma alone.*

After thus expressing in a soliloquy, his own estimate of the relative strength and merit of the two forces, now arrayed, ready for a total war, the king in Duryodhana rises above his mental clouds of desperation to shoot forth his imperial orders to his army officers. He advises them that each commander must keep to his position and fight in disciplined order, and all of them should spare no pains to see that the revered Bhishma is well protected. Perhaps, Duryodhana suspects that the lusty force that he had mobilised is an ill-assorted heterogeneous army constituted of the various tribal chieftains and kings of distant lands and that the strength of such an army could be assured, only when they hold on to a united strategy in all their various manoeuvres. Synchronisation of the different operations is the very backbone of an army's success, and in order to bring this about, as a true strategist, Duryodhana is instructing his various commanders working in different wings to work out the single policy of protecting Bhishma.

अयनेषु च सर्वेषु यथाभागमवस्थिताः ।
भीष्ममेवाभिरक्षन्तु भवन्तः सर्व एव हि ॥ ११ ॥

ayaneṣu ca sarveṣu yathābhāgamavasthitāḥ
bhīṣmamevābhirakṣantu bhavantuḥ sarva eva hi 11.

12. *His glorious grandsire (Bhishma), the oldest of the Kauravas, in order to cheer Duryodhana, now sounded aloud a lion's roar and blew his conch.*

All the while, that Duryodhana was busy making a fool of himself and in his excitement putting all the great officers of his army into an uncomfortable mood of desperate unhappiness, Bhishma was standing, not too far away, observing the pitiable confusions of the tyrant. The revered grandsire noticed, intelligently, in Dronacharya's silence, the outraged temper of a man of knowledge and action. He realised that the situation could be saved only if all those assembled were jerked out of their mental preoccupations. The more they were let alone with their revolting thoughts against Duryodhana, the more they would become ineffectual for the imminent battle. Understanding this psychology of the officers under his command, the great Marshall Bhishma took up his war-bugle (conch) and blew it, sending forth roaring waves of confidence into the hearts of the people manning the array.

This action of Bhishma, though performed by him out of pity for Duryodhana's mental condition, amounted to an act of aggression almost corresponding to the 'first-bullet-shot' in modern warfare. With this lion-roar, the Mahabharata war was actually started, and for all historical purposes, the Kauravas had thereby, become the aggressors.

तस्य संजनयन्हर्षं कुरुवृद्धः पितामहः ।
सिंहनादं विनद्योच्चैः शङ्खं दध्मौ प्रतापवान् ॥ १२ ॥
tasya sañjanayanharṣaṁ kuruvṛddhaḥ pitāmahaḥ
siṁhanādaṁ vinadyoccaiḥ śaṅkhaṁ dadhmau pratāpavān 12.

13. *Then (following Bhishma), conches and kettledrums, tabors, drums and cow-horns blared forth quite suddenly and the sound was tremendous.*

All the commanders were, no doubt, in high tension, and as soon as they heard the marshal's bugle, individually, each one of them took up his instrument and sounded the battle-cry. Thus, conches and kettledrums, tabors and trumpets, bugles and cow-horns, all burst forth into a challenging war-call, which Sanjaya, half-heartedly, describes as 'tremendous'. Later on, we shall find that when this challenge was replied to by the Pandavas, the sound was described by Sanjaya as 'terrific', resounding throughout heaven and earth, and rending the hearts of the Kauravas. Here is another instance to prove that Sanjaya was, evidently, a moral objector to the war-aim of Duryodhana. Therefore, we have in him, a most sympathetic reporter of the message of the Lord at the battlefront, as given out in His Song Divine.

14. *Then, also Madhava and the son of Pandu, seated in their magnificent chariot yoked with white horses, blew their divine conches.*

ततः शङ्खाश्च भेर्यश्च पणवानकगोमुखाः ।
सहसैवाभ्यहन्यन्त स शब्दस्तुमुलोऽभवत् ॥ १३ ॥

tataḥ śaṅkhāśc bheryasch 0paṇvānakagomukhaḥ
sahasaivābhyahanyanta sa śabdastumulo'bhavat 13.

ततः श्वेतैर्हयैर्युक्ते महति स्यन्दने स्थितौ ।
माधवः पाण्डवश्चैव दिव्यौ शङ्खौ प्रदध्मतुः ॥ १४ ॥

tataḥ śvetairhayairyukte mahati syandane sthitau
mādhavaḥ pāṇḍavaścaiva divyau śaṅkhau pradadhmatuḥ 14.

The wealth of detail that has been so lavishly squandered in expressing a simple fact that, from the Pandava-side, Krishna and Arjuna answered the battle-cry, clearly shows where Sanjaya's sympathies lay. Here, the description - sitting in the magnificent chariot, harnessed with white horses, Madhava and Arjuna blew their conches divine - clearly echoes the hope lurking in the heart of Sanjaya that due to the apparent contrast in the two descriptions; perhaps, even at this moment Dhritarashtra may be persuaded to withdraw his sons from the warfront.

15. *Hrishikesha blew the Panchajanya and Dhananjaya (Arjuna) blew the Devadatta and Vrikodara (Bhima), the doer of terrible deeds, blew the great conch, named Paundra.*

In his description of the Pandava array, Sanjaya is very particular to mention even the name of each warrior's special conch. Panchajanya was blown by Krishna.

Hrishikesha is the name of the Lord and it has often been described as meaning the "Lord of the Senses". But this is according to an old derivation: *Hrishika* + *Isha* = Lord of the Senses. But the word *'Hrishika'* is an obscure one. Modern commentators prefer to explain it as *Hrish* + *kasha* = Having short hair.

पाञ्चजन्यं हृषीकेशो देवदत्तं धनञ्जयः ।
पौण्ड्रं दध्मौ महाशङ्खं भीमकर्मा वृकोदरः ॥ १५ ॥

pāñcajanyaṁ hṛṣīkeśo devadattaṁ dhanañjanyaḥ
pauṇḍraṁ dadhmau mahāśaṅkhaṁ bhīmakamār vṛkodaraḥ 15.

16. *King Yudhisthira, the son of Kunti, blew the Anantavijaya; Nakula and Sahadeva blew the Sughosha and the Manipushpaka.*

17. *The king of Kashi, an excellent archer, Shikhandi, the mighty commander of eleven thousand archers, Dhristadyumna and Virata and Satyaki, the unconquered;*

18. *Drupada and the sons of Draupadi, O Lord of the Earth, and the son of Subhadra, the mighty armed, blew their respective conches.*

In the above verses, we have the enumeration of the great *Maharathas*, battalion-commanders, who, with enthusiasm, loudly blew their conches, again and again, in an ascending cadence. The arrow that ultimately felled Bhishma in the Mahabharata-war came from Shikhandi. The charioteer of Krishna, who was also a battalion-commander in the Pandava army, was called Satyaki.

अनन्तविजयं राजा कुन्तीपुत्रो युधिष्ठिरः ।
नकुलः सहदेवश्च सुघोषमणिपुष्पकौ ॥ १६ ॥
anantavijayaṁ rājā kuntīputro yudhiṣṭhiraḥ
nakulaḥ sahadevaśca sughoṣamaṇipuṣpakau 16.

काश्यश्च परमेष्वासः शिखण्डी च महारथः ।
धृष्टद्युम्नो विराटश्च सात्यकिश्चापराजितः ॥ १७ ॥
kāśyaśca parameṣvāsaḥ śikhaṇḍī ca mahārathaḥ
dhṛṣṭadyumno virāṭaśca sātyakiścāparājitaḥ 17.

द्रुपदो द्रौपदेयाश्च सर्वशः पृथिवीपते ।
सौभद्रश्च महाबाहुः शङ्खान्दध्मुः पृथक्पृथक् ॥ १८ ॥
drupado draupadeyāśca sarvaśaḥ pṛthivīpate
saubhadraśca mahābāhuḥ śaṅkhāndadhmu pṛthakpṛthak 18.

The report is being addressed to Dhritarashtra and it is indicated by Sanjaya's words, "Oh Lord of the earth".

19. *That tumultuous sound rent the hearts of (the people of) Dhritarashtra's party and made both heaven and earth reverberate.*

From the fourteenth stanza onwards, Sanjaya gives us in all detail, an exhaustive description of the Pandava forces, and he spares no pains to bring into the mind of Dhritarashtra a vivid understanding of the superiority of the Pandava forces. Perhaps, the minister hopes that his blind king will realise the disastrous end and, at least now, will send forth a command to stop the fratricidal war.

20-21. *Then, seeing the people of Dhritarashtra's party standing arrayed and the discharge of weapons about to begin, Arjuna, the son of Pandu, whose ensign was a monkey, took up his bow and said these words to Krishna (Hrishikesha), O Lord of the Earth!*

स घोषो धार्तराष्ट्राणां हृदयानि व्यदारयत् ।
नभश्च पृथिवीं चैव तुमुलो व्यनुनादयन् ॥ १९ ॥
sa ghoṣo dhārtarāṣṭrāṇāṁ hṛdayāni vyadārayat
nabhaśca pṛthiavī caiva tumulo vyanunādayan 19.

अथ व्यवस्थितान्दृष्ट्वा धार्तराष्ट्रान्कपिध्वजः ।
प्रवृत्ते शस्त्रसंपाते धनुरुद्यम्य पाण्डवः ॥ २० ॥
atha vyavasthitāndṛṣṭvā dhārtarāṣṭrānkapidhvajaḥ
pravṛtte śastra-sampāte dhanurudyamya pāṇḍavaḥ 20.

हृषीकेशं तदा वाक्यमिदमाह महीपते ।
hṛṣīkeśaṁ tadā vākyamidamāh mahīpate

In these one and a half verses we have a description of the arrival of the hero of the Mahabharata war, Arjuna, on the battlefield. The exact time and nature of his entry are noted here. The shooting had not yet started, but it was imminent. It was the most tense moment; the crisis had risen to its highest pitch. It was at this moment that Arjuna, whose ensign was that of Hanuman, said the following words to Lord Krishna.

In those ancient days of chivalrous warfare, each honoured hero had his own personal flag, carrying on it conspicuously, and a well-recognised symbol. By the flag flying on the chariot, the enemy could recognise who was the occupant of the chariot. A hero was not generally shot at by an ordinary soldier, but each fought with his equal on the battlefield. This system of carrying a symbol to recognize individuals in the battlefield is faithfully followed even in modern warfare. A high official's vehicle carries insignia of the officer's rank on its very number-plate; on the very uniform enough details are pinned on to recognize the wearer and identify him. Arjuna's ensign was that of a monkey.

The stanza also gives us, in hasty strokes, the information that Arjuna was impatient to start the righteous war. He had raised his instrument of war, his bow, indicating his readiness to fight.

Arjuna said:

21. In the midst of the two armies, place my chariot, O Achyuta.

अर्जुन उवाच
सेनयोरुभयोर्मध्ये रथं स्थापय मेऽच्युत ॥ २१ ॥
arjuna uvāca
senayorubhayormadhye rathaṁ sthāpaya me'cyuta 21.

22. *That I may behold those who stand here desirous of fighting and, on the eve of this battle, let me know with whom I must fight.*

Here, we hear Arjuna's soldier-like command to his charioteer to drive and place the vehicle between the two armies so that he might see and recognise the various heroes whom he has to meet and fight in the Great War. In expressing thus, a wish to review the enemy lines, the great hero is showing his daring and chivalry, his great courage and firm determination, his adventurous readiness and indomitable energy. Up to this point in the story, Arjuna, the invincible hero of the Mahabharata, was in his own true element unaffected by any mental hysteria.

23. *For I desire to observe those who are assembled here for the fight, wishing to please in battle, the evil-minded sons of Dhritarashtra.*

The verse only reinforces our impression of Arjuna gathered in the previous lines. He is giving the reason why he wants to review the enemy lines. As a man of action, he did not want to take any undue risk and so wanted to see for

---

यावदेतान्निरीक्षेऽहं योद्धुकामानवस्थितान् ।
कैर्मया सह योद्धव्यमस्मिन्रणसमुद्यमे ॥ २२ ॥

yāvadetānnirīkṣe'haṁ yoddhukāmānavasthitāv
kairmayā saha yoddhavyamasmainraṇasamudyame 22.

योत्स्यमानानवेक्षेऽहं य एतेऽत्र समागताः ।
धार्तराष्ट्रस्य दुर्बुद्धेर्युद्धे प्रियचिकीर्षवः ॥ २३ ॥

yotsyamānānavekṣe'haṁ ya ete'tra samāgatāḥ
dhārtarāṣṭrasya durbuddheyu'ddhe priyacikīrṣavaḥ 23.

himself who were the low-minded, power-mad, greed-ridden men who had joined the forces of the Kauravas, supporting the palpably tyrannical and evidently unjust cause of the unscrupulous Duryodhana.

As we read the stanza, we can almost hear the great warrior's teeth grinding, as he spits out these hot words, which express his mental estimate of his relentless cousins.

Sanjaya said:

24. *Thus addressed by Gudakesha, O Bharata, Hrishikesha, having stationed the best of chariots between the two armies;*

25. *In front of Bhishma and Drona, and all the rulers of the earth, he said, "O Partha, behold these Kurus gathered together".*

At a point facing Bhishma, Drona and all the rulers of the earth, the Divine Charioteer pulled up the reins and brought the royal chariot to a halt. As a dutiful driver, Krishna says to Arjuna, "Behold, O Partha! All the Kauravas gathered together". These are the only words that Krishna has spoken in the entire first chapter; and these represent the sparks that

---

सञ्जय उवाच
एवमुक्तो हृषीकेशो गुडाकेशेन भारत ।
सेनयोरुभयोर्मध्ये स्थापयित्वा रथोत्तमम् ॥ २४ ॥

sañjaya uvāca
evamukto hṛṣīkeśo guḍākeśena bhārata
senayorubhayormadhye sthāpayitvā rathottamam 24.

भीष्मद्रोणप्रमुखतः सर्वेषां च महीक्षिताम् ।
उवाच पार्थ पश्यैतान्समवेतान्कुरूनिति ॥ २५ ॥

bhīṣmadroṇapramukhataḥ sarveṣāṁ ca mahīkṣitām
uvah pārtha paśyaitānsamavetānkuruniti 25.

set fire to and brought down the egoistic edifice of false valuations, which the great hero had built for himself as a splendid dwelling place for his personality. Hereafter, we shall find how Arjuna reacted to this great challenge and ultimately got his entire 'within' wrecked and shattered.

Partha means 'Son of Pritha' – it is a name of Arjuna; 'Pritha' was another name of Kunti; the Sanskrit term Partha also carries a flavour of the term *Parthiva* meaning 'clay-made' - 'earth-formed'. The suggestive implication of this term is very striking inasmuch as it connotes that the *Geeta* is the Song-of-Truth sung by the Immortal to the mortal Arjuna, man's all-time representative.

26. *Then Partha saw stationed there in both the armies, fathers, grandfathers, teachers, maternal uncles, brothers, sons, grandsons and friends too.*

27. *(He saw) Fathers-in-law and friends also in both the armies. Then the son of Kunti, seeing all these kinsmen thus standing arrayed, spoke thus sorrowfully, filled with deep pity.*

तत्रापश्यत्स्थितान्पार्थः पितॄनथ पितामहान् ।
आचार्यान्मातुलान्भ्रातॄन्पुत्रान्पौत्रान्सखींस्तथा ॥ २६ ॥
tatrāpaśyatthitānpārtha pitṝnatha pitāmahān
ācāyārnmātulānbhrātṝnputrānpautrāsakhīṁstatha 26.

श्वशुरान्सुहृदश्चैव सेनयोरुभयोरपि ।
तान्समीक्ष्य स कौन्तेयः सर्वान्बन्धूनवस्थितान् ॥ २७ ॥
śvāśurānsuhṛdaścaiva senayorubhyorapi
tānsamīkṣya sa kaunteyaḥ savārnbandhūnavasthitān 27.

Thus shown by Shri Krishna, Arjuna recognised in his enemy lines, all his kith and kin, near and dear family members, brothers and cousins, teachers and grandsires, and almost all his acquaintances and friends. He recognized such intimate relations not only in the enemy lines, but even in his own army. This sight perhaps, brought to his mind, for the first time, the full realisation of the tragedies of a fratricidal war. As a warrior and a man of action, he did not, perhaps until then, fully realize the extent of sacrifice that society would be called upon to make in order that his ambition might be fulfilled and Duryodhana's cruelties avenged.

Whatever might have been the cause, the sight brought into his mind a flood of pity and compassion.

Evidently, this was not an honest emotion. Had it been honest, had his pity and compassion been Buddha-like, natural and instinctive, he would have, even long before the war, behaved quite differently. This emotion which now Sanjaya glorifies as 'pity' in Arjuna, is a misnomer. In the human heart, there is always a great tendency to glorify one's own weaknesses with some convenient angelic name and divine pose. Thus, a rich man's vanity is misnamed as charity when he builds a temple in his own name with the secret aim of immortalising himself. Here also we find that the feeling of desperation that came in Arjuna's mind due to the complete shattering of his mental equilibrium has been misnamed and glorified as 'pity'.

Arjuna had a long life of mental repressions, which had created an infinite amount of dynamic energies seeking a field for expression. His mind got split up because of his egoistic evaluation of himself as the greatest hero of his time, and because of his anxious desire for a victorious end of the war. The preoccupation of his mind, dreaming intensively, about the ultimate end of the war brought about a complete divorce between the 'subjective' and the 'objective' aspects of his mind.

Later on, in this chapter, we shall discover the various symptoms of this neurotic condition in him and his hysterical blabbering which are typical of such a mental patient. The endeavour in Chapter I of the *Geeta* is to give the complete 'case-history' of a patient suffering from the typical 'Arjuna-disease'. The *Bhagawad Geeta* gives, as I said earlier, an extremely efficient 'Krishna-cure' for this soul-killing 'Arjuna-disease'.

Arjuna said:

28. *Seeing these my kinsmen, O Krishna, arrayed, eager to fight,*

29. *My limbs fail and my mouth is parched, my body quivers and my hair stand on end.*

कृपया परयाविष्टो विषीदन्निदमब्रवीत् ।
kṛpayā parayāviṣṭo viṣīdannidamabravīt

अर्जुन उवाच
दृष्ट्वेमं स्वजनं कृष्ण युयुत्सुं समुपस्थितम् ॥ २८ ॥
arjuna uvāca
dṛṣṭvemaṁ svajanaṁ kṛṣṇa yuyutsuṁ samupasthitam 28.

सीदन्ति मम गात्राणि मुखं च परिशुष्यति ।
वेपथुश्च शरीरे मे रोमहर्षश्च जायते ॥ २९ ॥
sīdanti mama gātrāṇi mukhaṁ ca pariśuṣyati
vepathuśca śarīre me romaharṣaśca jāyate 29.

In these two stanzas, there is an exhaustive enumeration of the symptoms that the patient could then recognise in his own physical body as a result of his mental confusions. That which Sanjaya had glorified as 'pity', when coming out of Arjuna's own mouth, gains a more realistic expression. Arjuna says "seeing my kinsmen gathered here anxiously determined to fight, my limbs shiver" etc.

All these symptoms are described in the textbooks of modern psychology as typical symptoms of the mental disease named 'anxiety-neurosis'.

30. *The Gandiva-bow slips from my hand and my skin burns all over; I am also unable to stand and my mind is whirling round, as it were.*

Here Arjuna is adding some more details of the symptoms of his disease. Earlier we had a list of symptoms that manifested on the physical body. Now in this stanza, Arjuna tries to report recognised-symptoms of the maladjustments at his mental level.

Not only is his mind unsteady, agitated and chaotic, but it has lost all its morale. It has come down to the stupid level of accepting and recognising superstitious omens portending disastrous failures and imminent consequences.

गाण्डीवं स्रंसते हस्तात्त्वक्चैव परिदह्यते ।
न च शक्नोम्यवस्थातुं भ्रमतीव च मे मनः ॥ ३० ॥
gāṇḍīvaṁ sraṁsate hastāttvakcaiva paridahyate
na ca śaknomyavasthātuṁ bhramatīva ca me manaḥ 30.

Not only does the following stanza vividly picture to us his mental confusions, but it also shows how far his discrimination has been drained off, and his morale destroyed.

31. *And I see adverse omens, O Keshava. Nor do I see any good in killing my kinsmen in battle.*

In this state of mental confusion, when his emotions have been totally divorced from his intellect, the 'objective-mind', without the guidance of its 'subjective-aspect', runs wild and comes to some unintelligent conclusions. He says, "I desire neither victory, nor empire, nor even pleasure". It is a recognised fact that a patient of hysteria, when allowed to talk, will, in a negative way, express the very cause for the attack. For example, when a woman, hysterically raving, repeatedly declares with all emphasis, that she is not tired of her husband that she still respects him, that he still loves her, that there is no rupture between them, etc., she, by these very words, clearly indicates the exact cause of her mental chaos.

Similarly, the very denials of Arjuna clearly indicate to all careful readers how and why he got into such a state of mental grief. He desired victory. He urgently wanted the kingdom. He anxiously expected to win pleasures for himself and his relations. But the challenging look of the mighty Kaurava forces and the great and eminent warriors standing

---

निमित्तानि च पश्यामि विपरीतानि केशव ।
न च श्रेयोऽनुपश्यामि हत्वा स्वजनमाहवे ॥ ३१ ॥

nimittāni ca paśyāmi viparītāni keśava
na ca śreyo'nupaśyāmi hatvā svajanamāhave 31.

ready to fight, shattered his hopes, blasted his ambitions, and undermined his self-confidence and he slowly developed the well-known 'Arjuna-disease', the cure for which is the theme of the *Geeta*.

32. *For, I desire not victory, O Krishna, nor kingdom, nor pleasures. Of what avail, is dominion to us, O Govinda? Of what avail are pleasures or even life itself?*

33. *They for whose sake we desire kingdom, enjoyment and pleasures stand here in battle, having renounced life and wealth.*

34. *Teachers, fathers, sons and also grandfathers, maternal uncles, fathers-in-law, grandsons, brothers-in-law and other relatives.*

Arjuna continues his arguments to Krishna against the advisability of such a civil war between the two factions of the same royal family. A *Dharma*-hunting Arjuna is here mentally manufacturing a case for himself justifying his cowardly retreat from the post of duty where destiny has called upon him to act.

न काङ्क्षे विजयं कृष्ण न च राज्यं सुखानि च ।
किं नो राज्येन गोविन्द किं भोगैर्जीवितेन वा ॥ ३२ ॥
na kāṅkṣe vijayaṁ kṛṣṇa na ca rāpyaṁ sukhāni ca
kiṁ no rājyena govinda kiṁ bhogaurjīvitena vā 32.

येषामर्थे काङ्क्षितं नो राज्यं भोगाः सुखानि च ।
त इमेऽवस्थिता युद्धे प्राणांस्त्यक्त्वा धनानि च ॥ ३३ ॥
yeṣamārthe kāṅikṣatam no rājyaṁ sukhāni ca
ta ime'vasthitā yuddhe prāṇaṁstkvā dhanāni ca 33.

आचार्याः पितरः पुत्रास्तथैव च पितामहाः ।
मातुलाः श्वशुराः पौत्राः श्यालाः संबन्धिनस्तथा ॥ ३४ ॥
ācāyārḥ pitaraḥ putrāstathaiva ca pitāmahāḥ
mātulāḥ śvaśurāḥ pautrāḥ śyālāḥ sambandhinastathā 34.

He repeats what he had said earlier because Krishna, with his pregnant silence, is criticizing Arjuna's attitude. The provocatively smiling lips of the Lord are whipping Arjuna into a sense of shame. He wants the moral support of his friend and charioteer to come to the conclusion that what he is feeling in his own mind is acceptable and just. But the endorsement and the intellectual sanction are not forthcoming from either the look of Krishna or the Lord's words.

35. *These I do not wish to kill, though they may kill me, O Madhusudana, even for the sake of dominion over the three worlds; how much less for the sake of the earth.*

Feeling that he had not expressed his case strongly enough to Krishna, to make him come to this conclusion, and, assuming that it was because of this that the Lord had not given his assent to it, Arjuna therefore, decided to declare with a mock spirit of renunciation, that he had so much large-heartedness in him that he would not kill his cousins, even if they were to kill him. The climax came when Arjuna, with quixotic exaggeration, declared that he would not fight the war, even if he were to win all the three worlds of the universe, much less so, for the mere Hastinapura-kingship.

एतान्न हन्तुमिच्छामि घ्नतोऽपि मधुसूदन ।
अपि त्रैलोक्यराज्यस्य हेतोः किं नु महीकृते ॥ ३५ ॥
etānna hantumicchāmi ghnato'pi madhusūdana
api trailokyarājyāsya hetoḥ kiṁ nu mahīkṛte 35.

36. *Killing these sons of Dhritarashtra, what pleasure can be ours, O Janardana? Sin alone will be our gain by killing these felons.*

In spite of all that Arjuna said so far, Krishna is as silent as a sphinx. Therefore, Arjuna gives up his melodramatic expression and assumes a softer, a more appealing tone and takes the attitude of explaining in vain, a serious matter to a dull-witted friend. The change of strategy becomes conspicuously ludicrous when we notice Krishna's continued silence!!

In the first line of the stanza he explains to Krishna that no good can arise out of killing the sons of Dhritarashtra... still the wooden-smile of Krishna does not change and the Pandava hero, his intelligence shattered, tries to find a cause for Krishna's attitude. Immediately, he remembers that the Kaurava brothers were behaving towards the Pandavas as felons. *Atatayinah* means felons, who deserve to be killed according to the *Artha Shastra*.*

निहत्य धार्तराष्ट्रान्न : का प्रीतिः स्याज्जनार्दन ।
पापमेवाश्रयेदस्मान्हत्वैतानाततायिनः ॥ ३६ ॥
nihatya dhārtarāṣṭrannaḥ kā pritiḥ syājjanārdana
pāpamevāśrayedasmān hatvaitānātatāyinaḥ 36.

*"Whether he be a preceptor, an old man, or a *Veda*-knowing *Brahmana*, if he comes in front as an *Atatai* (felon) he should be killed on the spot without a thought. There is no sin involved in killing a felon". (Manu.VIII-350-351)

Sin is only a mistake committed by a misunderstood individual ego against its own Divine Nature as the Eternal Soul. To act as the body, the mind, or the intellect is not to act up to the responsibilities of a man but it becomes an attempt to behave under the impulses of an animal. All those acts performed and motives entertained, which create grosser mental impressions and thereby, build stronger walls between us and our cognition of the Real Divine Spark in ourselves, are called sins.

Arjuna's seemingly learned objection to killing enemies is a misinterpretation of our sacred texts (*shastra*), and to have acted upon it would have been suicidal to our very culture. Therefore, Krishna refuses to show any sign either of appreciation or criticism of Arjuna's stand. The Lord understands that his friend is raving hysterically and the best policy is to allow a mental patient first of all to bring out everything in his mind and thus exhaust himself.

37. *Therefore, we shall not kill the sons of Dhritarashtra, our relatives; for how can we be happy by killing our own people, O Madhava?*

Here, Arjuna concludes his seemingly logical arguments which have got a false look of Hindu scriptural sanction. More than deliberate blasphemers of a scripture, the unconscious misinterpreters of a sacred text are the innocent criminals

---

तस्मान्नार्हा वयं हन्तुं धार्तराष्ट्रान्स्वबान्धवान् ।
स्वजनं हि कथं हत्वा सुखिनः स्याम माधव ॥ ३७ ॥

tasmānnahār vayaṁ hantuṁ dhārtarāṣṭrānsvabāndhavān
svajanaṁ hi kathaṁ hatvā sukhinaḥ syāma mādhava 37.

who bring about the wretched downfall of its philosophy. Purring with the satisfaction of a cat in the kitchen, Arjuna, in this verse, is rounding up his arguments and coming to the dangerous conclusion that he should not kill the aggressors, nor face their heartless challenge! Even then, Krishna is silent.

Arjun's discomfiture makes him really quite conspicuous in his ugliness. In the second line of the stanza, he makes a personal appeal to Krishna and almost begs of him to think for himself and endorse Partha's own lunatic conclusions.

With the familiarity born out of his long-standing friendship, Arjuna addresses his charioteer with affection as Madhava, and asks him how one can come to any happiness after one has destroyed one's own kinsmen... Still, Krishna remains silent.

38. *Though these, with their intelligence clouded by greed, see no evil in the destruction of the families in the society, and no sin in their cruelty to friends...*

39. *Why should not we, who clearly see evil in the destruction of the family-units, learn to turn away from this sin, O Janardana?*

यद्यप्येते न पश्यन्ति लोभोपहतचेतसः ।
कुलक्षयकृतं दोषं मित्रद्रोहे च पातकम् ॥ ३८ ॥
yadyapyete na paśyanti lobhopahatacetasaḥ
kulakṣayakṛtaṁ doṣaṁ mitradrohe ca pātakam 38.

कथं न ज्ञेयमस्माभिः पापादस्मान्निवर्तितुम् ।
कुलक्षयकृतं दोषं प्रपश्यद्भिर्जनार्दन ॥ ३९ ॥
kathaṁ na jñeyamasmābhiḥ pāpādasmānnivartitum
kulakṣayakṛtaṁ doṣaṁ prapaśyadibharjanārdana 39.

No doubt, the Kauravas, grown blind in their greed for power and wealth, cannot see the destruction of the entire social structure by this war. Their ambition has so completely clouded their intelligence and sensibility that they fail to appreciate or understand the cruelty in annihilating their own friends.

But Arjuna seems to retain his reasoning capacity and can clearly foresee the chaos in which society will get buried by this fratricidal war. Now his argument amounts to this; if a friend of ours, in his drunkenness, behaves nastily, it would be worse than drunkenness in us, if we were to retaliate; for, we are expected to know that our friend, with his fumed-up intelligence, does not entertain enough discriminative awareness of what he is doing. At such moments, it would be our duty to forgive the mischief and overlook the impudence.

Similarly, here, Arjuna argues: "If Duryodhana and his friends are behaving as blind aggressors, should the Pandavas not retire quietly and suffer the ignominy of a defeat, and consider it their dutiful offering at the altar of peace?" How far this philosophy is dangerous in itself will be seen as we read more and more the passages of the *Geeta* and come to appreciate the pith of its philosophy which is the very kernel of our Hindu way-of-living. "Active resistance to evil" is the central idea in the doctrine expounded by Krishna in the *Geeta*.

40. *In the destruction of a family, the immemorial religious rites of that family perish; on the destruction of spirituality, impiety overcomes the whole family.*

Just as a storyteller comes to add new details each time he narrates the same old story, so too, Arjuna seems to draw new inspiration from his foolishness, and each time his creative intelligence puts forth fresh arguments in support of his wrong philosophy. As soon as he finishes a stanza, he gets, as it were, a new lease of arguments to prattle, and takes refuge behind their noise.

He indicates here that, when individual families are destroyed, along with them the religious traditions of the society will also end, and soon an era of impiety will be ushered in.

Cultural experiments were the preoccupations of our fore fathers and they knew that the culture and tradition of each family was a unit of the total culture and integrity of the whole nation. Hence the importance of the family-*Dharma* so seriously brought forth by Arjuna as an argument against this civil war.

कुलक्षये प्रणश्यन्ति कुलधर्माः सनातनाः ।
धर्मे नष्टे कुलं कृत्स्नमधर्मोऽभिभवत्युत ॥ ४० ॥
kulakṣaye praṇśyanti kuladhamārḥ sanātanāḥ
dharme naṣṭe kulaṁ kṛtsvamadharmoa'bhibhavatyuta 40.

41. *By the prevalence of impiety, O Krishna, the women of the family become corrupt; and women being corrupted, O descendent of the Vrishni-clan, there arises 'intermingling of castes' (VARNA-SAMKARA).*

Continuing the argument of the previous verse, Partha declares the consequences that will follow when the true moral integrity of the families is destroyed. Slowly the morality in the society will wane and there will be an 'admixture of castes'.

Caste is a word, which, in its perverted meaning, has recently come in for a lot of criticism from the educated; and they, no doubt, are all justified, if caste, in reality means what we understand it to be in our society today. But what we witness around us, in the name of caste, is the ugly decadence into which the Hindu way-of-living has fallen. Caste, in those days, was conceived of as an intelligent division of the available manpower in the community on the basis of intellectual and mental capacities of the individuals.

Those who were intellectuals and had a passion for research and study were styled *Brahmanas* (*Brahmins*); those who had political ambitions for leadership and took upon themselves the risky art of maintaining peace and plenty and saving the country from internal and external aggressions, were called the *Kshatriyas*; those who served the community

---

अधर्माभिभवात्कृष्ण प्रदुष्यन्ति कुलस्त्रियः ।
स्त्रीषु दुष्टासु वार्ष्णेय जायते वर्णसंकरः ॥ ४१ ॥
adhamārbhibhavātkṛṣṇa praduṣyanti kulastriyaḥ
strīṣu duṣṭāsu vārṣṇeya jāyate varṇasaṅkara 41.

through agriculture and trade were the *Vaishyas* and, lastly, all those who did not fall in any of the above categories were styled as *shudras*, whose duties in society were service and labour. Our modern social workers and officials, agricultural and industrial labourers all must fall under this noble category!

In the largest scope of its implication, when we thus understand the caste-system, it is the same as today's professional groups. Therefore, when they talk so seriously about the inadvisability of 'admixture of the castes', they only mean what we already know to be true in our own social pattern. An engineer in charge of a hospital and working in the operation-theatre as a doctor would be a social danger, as much as a doctor would be if he is appointed as an officer for planning, guiding and executing a hydroelectric scheme!

When the general morality of society has decayed; the young men and women, blinded by uncontrolled passion, start mingling without restraint. And lust knows no logic and cares least for better evolution or better culture. There will be thereafter, unhealthy intermingling of incompatible cultural traits.

42. *'Confusion of castes' leads the slayer of the family to hell; for their forefathers fall, deprived of the offerings of PINDA (rice-ball) and water (libations).*

सङ्करो नरकायैव कुलघ्नानां कुलस्य च ।
पतन्ति पितरो ह्येषां लुप्तपिण्डोदकक्रियाः ॥ ४२ ॥
saṅkro narakāyaiva kulaghnānāṁ kulasya ca
patanti pitaro hyeṣāṁ luptapiṇḍodakakriyāḥ 42.

The argument is still continued and Arjuna points out the consequences of 'caste-admixture'. When confusion of the castes has taken place, both, outside in the moral life of true discipline and in one's own inner temperament, then the family tradition gets flouted and ruined.

In the context of our discourses, we must understand that to the dead, it is bread-and-water; to see that their survivors maintain and continue the cultural purity that they themselves had so laboriously cultivated and inculcated into the minds of their children. In case the society squanders away its culture, so laboriously built up as a result of the slow blossoming of the social values of life through generations of careful cultivation, we will be insulting the very labours of our ancestors. It is attractive and poetic, indeed, to conceive of the dead as watching over their survivors and observing their ways of living from the balcony of their heavenly abode! It would certainly be as painful as the pains of hunger and thirst to them if they were to find that their survivors were deliberately making a jungle of their laboriously laid gardens. Understood thus, the entire stanza appears to be very appropriate.

Each generation passes down the torch of its culture to the next generation, its children, and it is for them to preserve, tend and nourish that torch and hand it over carefully to the succeeding generation, if not more, at least no less bright, than when they got it.

In India, the sages discovered and initiated a culture that is spiritual, and this spiritual culture is maintained and worked out through religious practices, and therefore, culture and religion are, to the Hindu, one and the same. Very rarely we find any mention of the term culture, as such, in our ancient literature. More often we meet with the insistence on and the mention of our religious practices.

In fact, the Hindu religion is a technique by which this spiritual culture can be maintained and worked out in the community. Therefore, we find in these stanzas, and in similar contexts, always an enthusiastic emphasis upon the religious life, whether it be in the family or in the society. *Dharma* comprises those divine values of life by living which we manifest more and more the essential spiritual being in us. Family-*Dharma* (*Kuladharma*) is thus nothing but the rules of living, thinking, and acting in a united, well-planned family. By strictly following these rules we soon come to learn in the prayer-rooms of our homes, how to live as better citizens of the Aryan-culture.

43. *By these evil deeds of the 'destroyers of the family', which cause confusion of castes, the eternal religious rites of the caste and the family are destroyed.*

What was said in the discourse upon the last stanza will become amply clear by this statement of Arjuna. Here also he bemoans that as a result of the civil war, the religious traditions of the family will all be lost and when he says so, as I have said earlier, if we understand religion as the 'spiritual culture of India', the training for which was primarily given

---

दोषैरेतैः कुलघ्नानां वर्णसङ्करकारकैः ।
उत्साद्यन्ते जातिधर्माः कुलधर्माश्च शाश्वताः ॥ ४३ ॥
doṣairetaiḥ kulaghnānāṁ varṇasaṅkarakārakaiḥ
utsādyante jātidhamārḥ kuladhamārśca śāśvatāḥ 43.

in the individual homes, then the stanza becomes self-explanatory. We also know that after a war there is a sudden cracking up of the existing cultural values in any society. Our modern world which is panting and sighing under the burden of its own immoralities and deceits, is an example of how war brings about not only disabled men with amputated limbs, but also deeper ulcers and uglier deformities in their mental make-up.

In these words, we can detect in Arjuna almost the world's first conscientious objector to war! In these passages he offers a splendid series of pacifist arguments good for all times!!

44. *We have heard, O Janardana, that it is inevitable for those men, in whose families the religious practices have been destroyed, to dwell in hell for an unknown period of time.*

Krishna still refuses to speak. Arjuna has come to a point where he can neither stop talking nor find any more arguments. Strangely compelling is the grace of the Lord's dignified silence. Here in this stanza, Arjuna almost concludes his arguments and mentions the tradition which he had heard that "men whose family-religion has broken down will go to hell".

But, on the other hand, when we understand the statement in all its scientific implications, even the worst of us will feel the immediate urgency for revolutionising our

---

उत्सन्नकुलधर्माणां मनुष्याणां जनार्दन ।
नरकेऽनियतं वासो भवतीत्यनुशुश्रुम ॥ ४४ ॥
utsannkuladhamārṇāṁ manuṣyāṇaṁ janārdana
narake'niyataṁ vāso bhavatityanuśuśruma 44.

point of view. We have already seen that the family-*Dharma* means only the cultural purity in the family, which is the unit of the community. We also found that since their culture is essentially spiritual, to the Hindus 'religion is culture'.

So, Arjuna implies that when the unity of home-life is shattered, and when purity of living and sanctity of thought are destroyed in the individual home-life, the generation that has caused such a shattering is ordering for itself and for others, a melancholy era of hellish sorrows and sufferings.

45. *Alas! We are involved in a great sin, in that we are prepared to kill our kinsmen, from greed for the pleasures of the kingdom.*

Though pitiable, it is indeed pleasantly ludicrous to watch Arjuna's intellectual exhaustion and emotional weariness as expressed in this verse. In his effeminate lack of self-confidence he bemoans here, "Alas! We are involved" etc. These words clearly show that instead of becoming a master of the situation, Arjuna is now a victim of it. He has not the virile confidence that he is the master of the circumstances and therefore, with a creeping sense of growing inner cowardice, he feels almost helplessly persecuted.

This unhealthy mental weakness drains off his heroism and he desperately tries to put a paper-crown upon his cowardice, to make it look divine and angelic, and to parade it as 'pity'. Thus, he deliberately misconstrues the very aim

---

अहो बत महत्पापं कर्तुं व्यवसिता वयम् ।
यद्राज्यसुखलोभेन हन्तुं स्वजनमुद्यताः ॥ ४५ ॥

aho bata mahatpāpaṁ kartuṁ vyavasitā vayam
yadrājyasukhalobhena hantuṁ svajanamudyatāḥ 45.

of the war and imputes a low motive to the righteous war simply because he wants to justify his pacifist idea, which does not instinctively gurgle out from his known strength, but which oozes out from his ulcerated mind.

46. *If the sons of Dhritarashrta weapons-in-hand, slay me in battle, unresisting and unarmed, that would be better for me.*

Here, Arjuna declares his FINAL opinion that, under the circumstances narrated during his long-drawn limping arguments, it is better for him to die in battle unresisting and unarmed, even if the Kauravas were to shoot him down, like a hunted deer, with a dozen arrows piercing his royal body!

The word that Arjuna uses here is particularly to be noted. The texture of the word used is, in itself, a great commentary upon the thought in the mind of the one who has made the statement... *Kshema* is the material and physical victory, while *Moksha* is the spiritual Self-mastery. Though Arjuna's arguments were all labouring hard to paint the idea, that to have fought that war was against the spiritual culture of the country (*Moksha*), he himself stated in his conclusions that not to fight this war would be a material blessing (*Kshema*) inasmuch as an escape from the battlefield now is to gain, perhaps, sure physical security !!

यदि मामप्रतीकारमशस्त्रं शस्त्रपाणयः ।
धार्तराष्ट्रा रणे हन्युस्तन्मे क्षेमतरं भवेत् ॥ ४६ ॥
yadi māmapratīkāramaśastraṁ śastrapāṇayaḥ
dhārtarāṣṭrā raṇe hanyustanme kṣemataraṁ bhavet 46.

In short, anxiety for the fruit-of-his-action (victory in battle) demoralised Arjuna and he got himself into an 'anxiety-state-neurosis'.

Sanjaya said:

47. *Having thus spoken in the midst of the battlefield, Arjuna sat down on the seat of the chariot, casting away his bow and arrow, with a mind distressed with sorrow.*

The concluding stanza of this chapter contains the words of Sanjaya in which he gave the running commentary of what he saw on the battlefield. Exhausted by his weary arguments, Arjuna, completely shattered within, sank back on the flag-staff in the open chariot, throwing down his kingly weapons.

This is the scene at which we shall leave Arjuna in the First Chapter of the *Geeta*.

Thus, in the UPANISHADS of the glorious Bhagawad Geeta, in the Science of the Eternal, in the scripture of YOGA, in the dialogue between Sri Krishna and Arjuna, the first discourse ends entitled:

The *Yoga* of the Arjuna-Grief

In the scriptural textbooks of ancient times, the end of a chapter was indicated by some sign or symbol. In modern days, this is not necessary, in as much we have the passages

---

सञ्जय उवाच

एवमुक्त्वार्जुनः संख्ये रथोपस्थ उपाविशत् ।

विसृज्य सशरं चापं शोकसंविग्नमानसः ॥ ४७ ॥

sañjaya uvāca

evamuktvārjunaḥ saṅkhye rathopastha upāviśat

visṛjya saśaraṁ cāpa śokasaṁvignamānasaḥ 47.

in print before us and we can see that one section or chapter has ended and another has begun. Even here, the printers have to mark the end of one chapter and, by a separate title, indicate the beginning of the next.

In olden days, it was much more difficult, since books were not printed, and each student got during his study a new edition of the scripture printed on the memory-slabs of his own mind. Since scripture-study was in those days from mouth to mouth, the students had to memorise whole textbooks and chant them daily. In such a case, it was necessary to have some word or words to inform both the reciter and the listeners as to the ending of a section and the fresh beginning of another. This was done by some conventional symbol.

In the *Upanishads*, the accepted method was to recite the last *Mantra* or the concluding portion of the last *Mantra* of the chapter twice. In the *Geeta*, however, we have the repetition of a statement, which may be considered as an epilogue, in Sanskrit called a *Sankalpa Vakya*. The same *Sankalpa* is repeated at the end of each chapter, the difference being only that at the end of each chapter, the chapter-number is mentioned along with the special title of that chapter.

The *Geeta Sankalpa Vakya* (Epilogue) is a beautiful statement of pregnant words conveying a wealth of details regarding the very textbook. *Sreemad Bhagawad Geeta* has been considered here as an *Upanishad* - nay, each chapter in the *Geeta* is considered as an *Upanishad*; and among the eighteen *Upanishads*, together constituting the Divine Song, we here end the first of them, entitled "THE YOGA OF ARJUNA'S DESPONDENCY". These chapters are called *Upanishads* because they are declarations concealing such deep significance that a hasty reader will miss their full import, unless he does long and intense meditation over the wealth of suggestive meaning that lies concealed behind the simple-looking stanzas. As in the *Upanishads,* here also we need the help of a sympathetic teacher who can train us in the art of opening the seven hundred lockers in the treasure chamber of the *Geeta.*

Upanishad is a word indicating a literature that is to be studied by sitting (*shad*), near (*upa*) a teacher, in a spirit of receptive meekness and surrender (*ni*). The contents of the scriptural textbooks are all over the world always the same. They teach us that there is a changeless Reality behind the ever-changing phenomenal world of perceptions, feelings and understanding. This great *ADVAITIC* TRUTH as declared in the Hindu scriptural textbooks is termed the *Brahman* and, therefore, the textbook that teaches us the nature of *Brahman* and shows us the means of realising it is called *Brahman*-knowledge (*Brahma-Vidya*).

Unlike western philosophy, among the Aryans, a theory is accepted as a philosophy only when the philosopher prescribes for us a practical technique by which all seekers can come to discover and experience for themselves the goal indicated in that philosophy. Thus, in all Hindu philosophies there are two distinct sections: one explains the theory and the other describing the technique of practice. The portion that explains the technique of living the philosophy and coming to a close subjective experience is called *Yoga Shastra.*

The word *Yoga* comes from the root *Yuj* = to join. Any conscious attempt on the part of an individual to lift his present available personality and attune it to a higher, perfect ideal is called *Yoga and* the science of *Yoga* is called *Yoga Shastra*. Since in this epilogue, the *Geeta* is called a *Yoga Shastra*, we must expect to discover in the SONG OF THE LORD, not only airy philosophical expositions of a Truth - too subtle for the ordinary man to grasp, but also instructions by which, every one of us can hope to reach, step by step, the giddy heights of the Divine pinnacles, that stand eternally swathed in the transcendental glory of Absolute Perfection.

The theme of philosophy and *Yoga* cannot be very attractive to the ordinary men of the world because it is so scientific and it deals with imperceptible ideologies. Mathematics cannot be thrilling reading except for a mathematician; and mathematics can very well afford to ignore those who have no taste for it. But religion tries to serve all and the anxiety of all prophets is to serve every one in all generations. Thus, in order to tame a difficult theme and to contain it within the ambit of a textbook of universal acceptance, the teachers of olden times had to discover methods by which the subjective ideologies could be given an appealing look of substantial objectivity. This was done by giving a detailed picture of the teacher, so that in our mental image he is so much familiarised, that we feel his words also as something very familiar to us.

In the tradition of the Hindu textbooks, the great *Rishis* worked out the subtle ideas containing the crystallised truths into an easily digestible capsule called *Dharma*. In the *Upanishads*, we have a complete picture of a teacher and a taught, painted with hasty strokes, unfinished, and rough. In the *Geeta,* on the other hand, it being a philosophical discourse embedded in the mythology of the nation, we find a finished picture, palpitating with life, against a scintillating situation, wherein the very same ancient truths have been reasserted.

Lord Krishna is now made to repeat the *Upanishadic* Truths in the context of a great conflict, to serve his life-long friend Arjuna, who is shown as seriously suffering from a total mental rupture. Therefore, we shall expect in the *Geeta* a much more sympathetic explanation and guidance than when the same truths came out from the inspired saints, who were not as much in contact with the weaknesses of ordinary mortals. This glory of the *Geeta* has been indicated here when the *Sankalpa Vakya* says that it is a conversation between the Lord and a mortal.

This chapter is called by a self-contradicting title. It is named as the *"Yoga* of ARJUNA'S GRIEF". If 'grief' could be *Yoga*, almost all of us, without a choice, are already *Yogins*. In the commentary of this chapter, I indicated that the Arjuna-condition of utter despair is the auspicious mental attitude wherein the *Geeta*-seeds are to be sown, and the flowers of Krishna-perfection gathered. Be it in an individual or a society, in a community or a nation, religion and philosophy will be in demand only when the heart has come to experience the Arjuna-grief.

To the extent that the world of today has felt its incompetence to face the battle of life, not daring to destroy their near and dear values of economic expansion and industrial lust, to that extent it is fit for listening to the message of the *Geeta*. Just as the act of cooking, by itself, is not fulfilled without the eating that follows, so also, in spite of the best that may be available in life, a sense of incompleteness is felt and a deep hunger to gain a better awareness and a fuller existence in the world is experienced. The scriptural texts cannot, in themselves, help any one. Since this mental condition is so unavoidable before the actual *Yoga* is started, even the initial mental condition is called by a wishful anticipation, as *Yoga*. For learning and living the *Geeta*, the Arjuna-condition is the initial *sadhana*.

Om Om Om Om Om

ॐ तत्सदिति श्रीमद् भगवद् गीतासूपनिषत्सु ब्रह्मविद्यायां
योगशास्त्रे श्रीकृष्णार्जुनसंवादे अर्जुनविषादयोगो नाम
प्रथमोऽध्याय:

Oṁ tatsaditi śrīmadbhagavadgītāsū ūpaniṣatsu brahmavidyāyāṁ yogaśāstre śrī kṛṣṇārjuna saṁvāde arjunaviṣādayogo nāma prathamo'dhyāyaḥ

II

Yoga of Knowledge

Introduction

IN this Chapter, entitled *'Sankhya Yoga'*, we get an exhaustive summary, as it were, of the whole philosophical content of the *Geeta*. Roughly, we may say, that the first ten stanzas explain the circumstances under which Arjuna totally surrenders to the 'Krishna-influence'.

From stanza 11 to stanza 46, we have a digest of the *Sankhya*, meaning here not so much a repetition of the *Sankhyan* philosophy, but as a word denoting 'the logic of thought in a philosophy'. From stanzas 47 to 60, we have an exhaustive, though hasty, sketch of the *Yoga*-of-Action as adumbrated in the entire *Geeta*. From stanzas 61 to 70, the Path-of-Love (*Bhakti Yoga*), has been indicated, and in 71 and 72, the Path-of-Renunciation *(Sannyasa Yoga)*, has been slightly suggested. Thus, the second chapter of the *Geeta* can be taken as an epitome of the entire *Geeta*.

We find in the *Geeta* all the known Paths-to-Perfection sketched out in the *Vedas namely, Jnana, Bhakti*, and *Karma*, by which *Upanishadic* realisation is reached when one has fully purified oneself by the pursuit of ritualism, *Karma Kanda*, and has spent a period of time in living the *Upasana Kanda*. People believed that these three are irreconcilable factors, and so many schools rose up, and each started quarrelling with all the others. This was the chaotic condition in which Vyasa found Hinduism, during the *Puranic* Age. In the *Geeta* he has tried to find for the Aryan children of the *Vedas* reconciliation and a synthesis in which all can walk hand in hand.

Sanjaya said:

1. *To him who was thus overcome with pity and despondency, with eyes full of tears and agitated, Madhusudana spoke these words.*

The second chapter opens with an announcement from Sanjaya which, with a few rightly chosen words, gives a complete picture of Arjuna's sad mental state of desperation. His mind had become overwhelmed with pity and sorrow. The very expression clearly indicates that Arjuna was not the master of the situation at that time, but on the contrary, the situation had Arjuna as its victim! To get ourselves over-ridden by life's circumstances is to ensure disastrous failures on all occasions. Only a weakling, who allows himself to be overpowered by circumstances, can be victimised by the outer happenings. Arjuna, in his present neurotic condition, has become a slave to the outer challenges.

The estimate of Sanjaya not only describes to us the

सञ्जय उवाच
तं तथा कृपयाविष्टमश्रुपूर्णाकुलेक्षणम् ।
विषीदन्तमिदं वाक्यमुवाच मधुसूदनः ॥ १ ॥
sañjaya uvāca
taṁ tatha kṛpayāviṣṭaṁ aśrupūrṇakulekṣaṇam,
viṣīdantanmidaṁ vākyamuvāca madhusūdanaḥ 1.

mental condition of Arjuṇa but also pointedly gives us a hint that the cracking of the inner personality of Arjuna has made deep fissures into the character of the great hero. The greatest archer of his time, Arjuna has been so totally impoverished within, that he has come to weep like a simple maiden!

To Arjuna, thus overwhelmed by an emotion of misplaced pity and tearless weeping, Madhusudana (slayer of the demon -Madhu), Lord Krishna spoke the following words. Here, it is to be noted that modern psychology has also observed and recorded that a tearless weeping is the climax in an attack of hysteria.

The Blessed Lord said:

2. *Whence is this perilous condition come upon thee, this dejection, un-Aryan-like, heaven-excluding, disgraceful, O Arjuna?*

The Lord of the Hindus is surprised to see that a king, claiming to be an Aryan, is feeling so flabbergasted on the battlefield. The instinct of a true Aryan is to be balanced and equipoised in all conditions of life and to face situations diligently, compelling them to change their threatening attitude and make them favourable to himself. When life is

---

श्रीभगवानुवाच
कुतस्त्वा कश्मलमिदं विषमे समुपस्थितम् ।
अनार्यजुष्टमस्वर्ग्यमकीर्तिकरमर्जुन ॥ २ ॥
śrī bhagavān uvāca
kutastvā kaśmalamidaṁ viṣame samupasthitam,
anāryajuṣṭamasvargyamakīrtikaramarjuna 2.

courted properly, even the ugliest situation can be transformed into a charming smile of success. Everything depends upon the intelligent man's dexterity in steering himself along the bumping roads of life. Thus, Lord Krishna characterises Arjuna's behaviour as un-Aryan. The Aryans are extremely sensitive to the higher calls of life, righteousness and nobility, both in thought and action.

The Divine Charioteer is quite surprised at discovering such an attitude of his friend, whom he had known for years through thick and thin. The mood of dejection was in fact, quite alien to the mental make-up and intellectual nature of Arjuna. Thus, we have here an expression of wonder and the Lord asks, "Whence comes upon thee this dejection, etc..."

It is believed by the Hindus that to die fighting for righteousness is the duty of one, born in a family of kings and by so sacrificing his life on the battlefield for a noble cause; he reaches and enjoys the Heaven of the Heroes (*Veera-Swarga*).

3. *Yield not to impotence, O Partha! It does not befit thee. Cast off this mean weakness of heart! Stand up, O Parantapa (O scorcher of foes)!*

In stinging reproachful words, Krishna is deliberately

क्लैब्यं मा स्म गमः पार्थ नैतत्त्वय्युपपद्यते ।
क्षुद्रं हृदयदौर्बल्यं त्यक्त्वोत्तिष्ठ परंतप ॥ ३ ॥

klaibyaṁ mā sma gamaḥ pārtha naitat tvayyupapadyate,
kṣudraṁ hṛdayadaurbalyaṁ tyaktvottiṣṭha paraṁtapa 3.

lashing out at the anxiety-state-neurosis in Arjuna. Krishna, who was silent so far, is now bursting forth into an eloquence, in which every word is a chosen missile, a pounding hammer-stroke that can flatten any victim.

The word *'Klaibyam'* means, the mental attitude of one who is neither masculine enough to feel a passionate courage and daring, nor womanly enough to feel the soft emotions of hesitation and despair. In modern parlance, sometimes friends wonder at the impotency of another friend and express their surprise with such an exclamation as, "Is he a man or a woman?" - indicating that from his behaviour it is not very easy to decide which characteristic is predominant in him. Emotionally therefore, Arjuna is behaving now as a contradiction; effeminately - manly and masculinely-effeminate; just like an eunuch of the Indian royal courts who looks like a man but dresses as a woman, talks like a man but feels like a woman, physically strong but mentally weak !

So far Krishna was silent and the silence had a deep meaning. Arjuna, overwhelmed with compassion, had taken the decision not to fight and was all along mustering arguments in support of it. As a diplomat, Krishna knew that it would have been useless to contradict his friend earlier when he was inspired to argue eloquently in support of his own wrong estimate of things. But the tears in the eyes of Arjuna indicated that his inward confusion had reached a climax.

In the tradition of religious devotion, it is very truly said and firmly believed all over the world, that the Lord in His high seat keeps mum and is almost deaf so long as we are arguing and asserting our maturity as intellectual beings. But when we come down to live and act as emotional beings, when tears of desperation trickle down the cheeks of true devotees, then, the LORD OF COMPASSION rushes forward to reach the lost souls, and guides them out of their inward darkness to the resplendent LIGHT OF WISDOM. A soul identifying with the intellect can seek and discover itself; but when it identifies with the mind, it needs the help and guidance of the Lord.

When the touch of the Lord's grace descends upon His devotees, it is invariably felt by the seekers more as an avalanche than as a refreshing shower of Divine Mercy. Spiritual Grace must necessarily reorientate the heart and burn away its negativities before the Spirit can radiate its sway upon matter. True to this great principle observed everywhere and experienced by every true seeker, in the *Geeta* too, we find that when the silent Lord started speaking from the Charioteer's seat, His words gleamed and landed like lightning on Arjuna, to burn his wrong mental tendencies in the fire of shame.

Soft words of sympathy could not have revived Arjuna's drooping mind to vigour. Thus, Krishna rightly lashed out at his friend with these stinging arrows of ridicule, dipped in the acid of satire! Krishna ends his 'word-treatment' with an appeal to Arjuna to "Get up and act". [1]

Arjuna said:

---

1 On a similar occasion, Christ said to Job, "Gird up your lions like a man," Bible: Job-38:3

4. *How, O Madhusudana, shall I in battle fight with arrows against Bhishma and Drona, who are fit to be worshipped, O destroyer of enemies !*

The motive-hunting cowardice in Arjuna has come to pick up a great argument, seemingly quite convincing to the undiscriminating. On the other hand, to one who has not lost his balance and who knows perfectly the art of evaluating such a situation, this is no problem at all, and Arjuna's arguments are quite hollow. The war that is imminent is not between individuals due to any personal rivalry. Arjuna has no personality apart from the Pandava-forces. The pair, namely Drona and Bhishma is also not mere individual entities. In their identification, they are the Kaurava-forces. The two forces are arrayed to fight for certain principles. The Kauravas are fighting for their policy of *Adharma*. The Pandavas are fighting for the principles of *Dharma* as enunciated in the ancient lore of the Hindus.

So glorious being the cause, when the two armies representing the will of the people have marshalled themselves, Arjuna, the hero had no individual right to accept any personal honour or dishonour, or to insist upon any

---

अर्जुन उवाच
कथं भीष्ममहं संख्ये द्रोणं च मधुसूदन ।
इषुभि: प्रति योत्स्यामि पूजार्हावरिसूदन ॥ ४ ॥
arjuna uvāca
kathaṁ bhīṣmamahaṁ saṅkhye droṇaṁ ca madhusūdana,
iṣubhiḥ pratiyotsyāmi pūjārhārvarisūdana 4.

respect or disrespect, while meeting the individuals who were champions of the wrong side. Without taking this total viewpoint of the situation, Arjuna made the mistake of arrogating and observed the problems through the glasses of his individual ego. He recognised himself to be the disciple of Drona and the grandson of Bhishma. The very same teacher and grandsire were also seeing Arjuna in the opposite camp, but they felt no compunction because they had no such egoistic misconceptions. They drowned their individuality in the cause they were championing. In short, Arjuna's egoism was the cause of his terrible moral confusions and misconceptions.

I have often discussed this portion with some of the best men of our country and have found all of them justifying Arjuna's argument! That is to say, this is a very subtle point to be decided upon, and perhaps Vyasa thought of solving this riddle for the society with the very principles of Hinduism for the guidance of future generations. The more we identify ourselves with the little 'I' in us, the more will be our problems and confusions in life. When we expand ourselves through our larger identifications -- with an army, a cause or a principle or a nation, or an age -- we shall find our moral confusions dwindling into almost nothingness. Perfect morality can be declared and lived up to only by him who has sought to live and discover his real identity with the Self, which is ONE-WITHOUT-A-SECOND, EVERYWHERE, IN ALL BEINGS AND FORMS. Later on, we shall find Krishna advising this TRUTH as a philosophical treatment for Arjuna's mental rehabilitation.

5. *Better indeed in this world, is to eat even the bread of 'beggary',*

than to slay the most noble of teachers. But, if I kill them, even in this world all my enjoyments of wealth and desires will be stained with blood.

Continuing his high sounding but futile arguments, due to his false estimate of himself and his problem, Arjuna poses here as a martyr of his own morality and ethical goodness.

His *gurus* meaning both Drona and Bhishma, are characterised here as *Mahanubhavah* - men who were the ideals of their age, symbolising the best in our culture, who, in their broad-mindedness and courage of conviction, had themselves offered many a sacrifice at the altars of the *Sanatana Dharma*, the Hindu Science of Perfect-living. Such noble men, who formed the very touchstones of our culture in that era, were not to be eliminated from life, merely for the fulfilment of an individual's appetite for power and position. Not only in their own age, but for future millennia, the world would be impoverished by the heartless squandering of such precious lives.

Thus, Arjuna says that it would be nobler for himself and

गुरूनहत्वा हि महानुभावान्
श्रेयो भोक्तुं भैक्ष्यमपीह लोके ।
हत्वार्थकामांस्तु गुरूनिहैव
भुञ्जीय भोगान्रुधिरप्रदिग्धान् ॥ ५ ॥

gurūnahatvā hi mahānubhāvān
śreyo bhoktuṁ bhaikṣyamapīha loke,
hatvārthakāmāṁstu gurūnihaiva
bhuñjīya bhogān rudhirapradigdhān 5.

the Pandava-brothers to live upon the bread of beggary than to gain kingship after destroying all the glorious flowers in the garden of our culture. After annihilating them all, elders and teachers, even supposing the Pandavas actually got their kingdom back, Arjuna points out, how his noble Aryan-heart would neither be able to enjoy the kingdom nor its wealth; for everything would be smeared with the bitter memories of the precious blood that would have been spilt in the war.

Once we misread a situation, sentiments cloud our understanding and then we too act in life as Arjuna did in his. This is clearly indicated here in the detailed narration of the incident by Vyasa.

6. *I can scarcely say which will be better; that we should conquer them or that they should conquer us. Even the sons of Dhritarashtra, after slaying whom we do not wish to live, stand facing us.*

The two earlier stanzas from Arjuna, undoubtedly indicate to us the state of perplexity and confusion in his 'objective-mind'. That the state of hysteria within has now developed to attack even his intellectual composure is indicated in this stanza. The stimuli coming from the array of the enemy-lines,

---

न चैतद्विद्मः कतरन्नो गरीयो
यद्वा जयेम यदि वा नो जयेयुः ।
यानेव हत्वा न जिजीविषामः
तेऽवस्थिताः प्रमुखे धार्तराष्ट्राः ॥ ६ ॥

na caitadvidmaḥ kataranno garīyo
yadvā jayema yadi vā no jayeyuḥ,
yāneva hatvā na jijīviṣāmaḥ
te'vasthitāḥ pramukhe dhārtaraṣṭrāḥ 6.

as they touched his 'objective-mind', created therein a problem, to solve which, he needed the guidance of the rational capacities of his intellect - the 'subjective-mind'. Split as he was within, his mental personality divorced from his intellect, could not easily come to any definite decision. His egoistic self-evaluation and the ego-created intense anxieties for the fruits of the Great War stood, as it were, between his mind and intellect, separating them and creating between them, an almost unbridgeable gulf. Hence, Arjuna's confusions are indicated here.

The mind generally functions as an efficient 'receiving-and-despatching-clerk'. It receives the information of the perceptions conveyed to it by the sense organs. After the mind arranges these perceptions in order, it conveys them to the intellect for its judgement. The intellect, with reference to its stored-up memories of similar experiences in the past comes to final decisions. They are conveyed to the mind for execution and the mind in its turn, issues the necessary orders for the organs-of-action to act upon. All these activities are happening at every moment, throughout our waking-state, in our intelligent existence, in the midst of the objects of the world.

Where these equipments are not functioning co-operatively with a perfect team spirit, the personality of the individual is shattered and he becomes inefficient in meeting life as a victorious mortal. Rehabilitation of that individual is the readjustment and re-education of his inner world. Once his personality is tuned up and adjusted, he comes to exhibit better efficiency in life.

Poor Arjuna victimised not so much by the external world

as by his own mental condition, is therefore seen here as being incapable of judging whether he should conquer his enemy, or by an ignoble retreat allow them to conquer him. In this stanza, Vyasa is indicating to us that the hysteria in Arjuna was not only mental, but was also at the level of the intellect.

7. *My heart is overpowered by the taint of pity; my mind is confused as to duty. I ask Thee. Tell me decisively what is good for me. I am Thy disciple. Instruct me, who has taken refuge in Thee.*

In this stanza, when Arjuna has completely realised the helpless impotency within himself to come to any decision, he surrenders totally to Krishna. In his own words he admits the psychological shattering felt and lived by him in his bosom. He has instinctively and correctly diagnosed even the cause of it to be 'an uncontrollable amount of overwhelming pity'. Of course, Arjuna does not realise that it is his misplaced compassion; whatever it may be, the patient is now under the mental stress of extreme confusion and bewilderment.

Arjuna confesses that his intellect (*chetas*) is obstructed

कार्पण्यदोषोपहतस्वभाव:
पृच्छामि त्वां धर्मसंमूढचेता: ।
यच्छ्रेय: स्यान्निश्चितं ब्रूहि तन्मे
शिष्यस्तेऽहं शाधि मां त्वां प्रपन्नम् ॥ ७ ॥

kārpaṇyadoṣopahatasvabhāvaḥ
pṛcchāmi tvāṁ dharmasammuḍhacetāḥ,
yacchreyaḥ syānniścitaṁ brūhi tanme
śiṣyaste'haṁ śādhi māṁ tvāṁ prapannam 7.

by a cloud of confusions regarding what *Dharma* and *Adharma* are at that moment for him. The problem whether to fight and conquer the enemies, or not to fight and allow the enemies to conquer him - which needed an urgent solution - could not be rationally judged with the depleted mental capacities of Arjuna.

We have already explained *Dharma* and found that the *Dharma* of a thing is the Law of its being. A thing cannot remain itself without faithfully maintaining its own nature, and THAT NATURE, WHICH MAKES A THING WHAT IT IS is called its *Dharma*. Hinduism insists upon the *Manava Dharma*, meaning, it insists that men should be true to their own essential nature, which is godly and divine, and therefore, all efforts in life should be directed towards maintaining themselves in the dignity of the Soul and not merely to plod on through life like helpless animals.

Here Arjuna indicates that he is quite ready to follow all the instructions of the Lord and maintain perfect faith in the wisdom of his Divine Charioteer. The Pandava must also be considered to have indicated, that if he, in his foolishness were to raise doubts, even for the thousandth time, Krishna should have the large-heartedness, compassion and kindness, to clarify them patiently yet again to his disciple. All through the *Geeta* we come across many occasions when Arjuna punctuates Krishna's message with his own doubts. Never does Krishna grow impatient with his disciple. On the other hand, each question as it were, is seen to have added more enthusiasm and interest to the discourses on the battlefield.

---

* In the concluding portion of the Introduction of Chapter I.

8. *I do not see that it would remove this sorrow that burns up my senses, even if I should attain prosperous and unrivalled dominion on earth, or even Lordship over the gods.*

Arjuna is indicating here to Krishna the urgency for guidance but for which he would be left to suffer the voiceless agonies of an inward pain. The patient is unable to explain or even to indicate even vaguely, the source from which the pain is rising within him.

This mental sorrow in Arjuna is blasting even his sense-organs! Under the heavy burden of his sorrows, he finds it very difficult even to see or hear things properly. Even his *Indriyas* (sense-organs) are being blasted by the overheated sorrows within him.

It is natural for any reasonable human being to feel an intellectual impatience to solve a problem of the mind and thereby make it quiet and peaceful. Poor Arjuna has also tried his best to bring some consolation to himself through his own intellectual discrimination. The sorrow that he felt was not for the acquisition and possession of any sensuous object in the outer world because, as his own words indicate, he has

---

न हि प्रपश्यामि ममापनुद्याद्
यच्छोकमुच्छोषणमिन्द्रियाणाम् ।
अवाप्य भूमावसपत्नमृद्धं
राज्यं सुराणामपि चाधिपत्यम् ॥ ८ ॥

na hi prapaśyāmi mamāpanudyād
yacchokamucchoṣaṇamindriyāṇām,
avāpya bhūmāvasapatnamṛddhaṁ
rājyāṁ surāṇāmapi cādhipatyam 8.

already thought over them and found that even an empire comprising the whole earth, flourishing under his kingship - nay, even a lordship over the gods - would not have wiped off his sense of sorrow.

The urgency felt by Arjuna, as is evident from his own words, may be considered as amounting to his burning aspiration for liberating himself from the limitations of being a mortal. All that he needed to make himself perfect was right discrimination (*viveka*) which the LORD OF THE SENSES (*Hrishikesha*) gives him throughout the DIVINE SONG.

Sanjaya said:

9. *Having spoken thus to Hrishikesha, Gudakesha, the destroyer of foes, (he) said to Govinda: "I will not fight"; and became silent.*

This and the next stanza together constitute the running commentary of Sanjaya - the faithful reporter of the *Geeta*. He says that after surrendering himself to Krishna and seeking the Lord's guidance, Arjuna who was the great CONQUEROR OF SLEEP and the SCORCHER OF HIS FOES, declared to Krishna, the Lord of the senses that he would not fight, and then became silent.

सञ्जय उवाच
एवमुक्त्वा हृषीकेशं गुडाकेशः परंतप ।
न योत्स्य इति गोविन्दमुक्त्वा तूष्णीं बभूव ह ॥ ९ ॥

sanjaya uvāca
evamuktvā hrṣīkeśaṁ gudākeśaḥ parantapaḥ,
na yotsya iti govindamuktvā tūṣṇīṁ babhūva ha 9.

No single individual alive during that period of time had the authority to call back the armies from the field of Kurukshetra, except the blind old uncle of the Pandavas. He had the necessary status and the weight of opinion for ordering a truce even at a time when it looked as though the time had slipped through the fingers. Sanjaya hoped that Dhritarashtra would understand the futility of their fighting against Arjuna, who would certainly conquer the Kaurava forces; since this 'Knotted-haired' warrior (*Gudakesha*) had surrendered himself to the Lord of the senses (*Hrishikesha*), the 'Winner of the World' (*Govinda*). But Dhritarashtra was born blind, and had grown deaf to the words of warning uttered by the good, due to his infinite attachment to his children.

10. *To him who was despondent in the midst of the two armies, Hrishikesha as if smiling, 'O Bharata', spoke these words.*

Thus standing between the two forces, (the good and the bad), arrayed for a battle to death, Arjuna (the *Jeeva*) surrenders completely to the Lord (the subtler discriminative intellect), his Charioteer, who holds the five horses (the five senses) yoked to his chariot (the body), under perfect control. When the stunned and confused ego – Arjuna totally surrenders to Krishna, the Lord with a smile reassures the *Jeeva* of its final victory, and declares the entire message of spiritual redemption, the *Geeta*. In this sense, we analyse the picture as painted in Sanjaya's words, while borrowing our sanction from the *Upanishads*.

तमुवाच हृषीकेशः प्रहसन्निव भारत ।
सेनयोरुभयोर्मध्ये विषीदन्तमिदं वचः ॥ १० ॥

tamuvāca hṛṣīkeśaḥ prahasanniva bhārata,
senayorubhayormadhye viṣīdantamidaṁ vacaḥ 10.

Once we agree to read this *Upanishad*-sense in the picture as painted here by the words of Sanjaya, we can discover in it an Eternal Truth. The ego (Arjuna) in its dejection sits back in the body (chariot), after throwing down all the instruments of egocentric activities (*Gandiva*). The sense-organs (the white horses) are held back well under control by the pulled-in reins (the mind). Then the Charioteer (the Pure Intellect) would lend to the ego a divine strength, and guide it to the ultimate victory over the forces of *Adharma*, with the help of the dynamism of *Dharma*; even though the former may seem much stronger in force than the simple-looking dynamism in the latter.

The Blessed Lord said:

11. *You have grieved for those that should not be grieved for; yet, you speak words of wisdom. The wise grieve neither for the living nor for the dead.*

When we rightly diagnose Arjuna's dejection, it is not very difficult for us to realise that though its immediate cause is the challenge of the war, his condition of mental torture is only a symptom of a deeper disease. Just as a true doctor will try to eradicate a disease, not by curing the symptoms but by removing the CAUSE of the disease, so too here, Lord Krishna is trying to remove the very source of Arjuna's delusion.

श्रीभगवानुवाच
अशोच्यानन्वशोचस्त्वं प्रज्ञावादांश्च भाषसे ।
गतासूनगतासूंश्च नानुशोचन्ति पण्डिताः ॥ ११ ॥

śrī bhagavanuvāca
aśocyānanvaśocastvaṁ prajñāvādāṁśca bhāṣase,
gatāsūnagatāsūṁśca nānuśocanti paṇḍitāḥ 11.

The ego rises when the PURE SELF is not recognised; this deep-seated ignorance in man not only veils his Divine Nature from himself, but also projects on the REALITY a positive misconception. The egocentric-idea, that he is conditioned by his own body, mind and intellect, is the true seed of Arjuna's delusory attachments with his own relations and the consequent deep compassion that has risen in his bosom to make him so impotent and helpless. Grief and dejection are the price that delusion demands from its victim. To rediscover ourselves to be really something higher than our own ego is to end all the sorrows that have come to us, through our false identifications.

Thus, the ETERNAL SPIRIT in man asserting its false relationships with his body comes to feel bound by a thousand relationships with the world of things and beings. The same PERFECT PRINCIPLE IN LIFE playing on the field of the mind comes to experience the imperfections of the emotional world as its own. Again, the DIVINE SPARK OF LIFE as it often does, a false identity with the intellect comes to sob and suffer for its hopes and desires, its ambitions, and ideologies, which are the characteristic preoccupations of the intellect.

The SELF, thus getting reflected in the intellect, the body and the senses is the ego, which is the victim of the world of objects, feelings, and ideas. To this ego, belong all the sad destinies of life as well as its fleeting thrills of acquisition and possession. The ego in Arjuna suffered a neurosis, goaded by its own delusions and the consequent misapprehensions. Krishna, in his INFINITE WISDOM knew that MIS-APPREHENSION OF REALITY can take place only because of a pitiable NON-APPREHENSION OF REALITY. Therefore, to cure the very source of Arjuna's delusion, Krishna is here teaching him the cream of knowledge, as declared in the immortal books of the Hindus, the *Upanishads*.

A re-education of the mind through metaphysical and psychic methods is the last word in psychotherapy which the East gave it to the world many thousand years ago. Krishna starts his entire *Geeta* lesson with this attempt at the re-education of Arjuna.

True to that traditional cultural concept of education here, the Great Master Krishna starts his instructions to Arjuna with a direct discourse upon the ETERNAL REALITY.

The inner equipments of both Bhishma and Drona allowed through them a glorious expression of the LIFE PRINCIPLE or the Soul in them. These great men were incomparable due to this Divine shine that beamed out through them. In this clashing of weapons, to consider that the cultural soul of Bhishma will be wounded, or that the life of Drona, the master-archer and military genius, will be ended, is a delusory concept of an uninitiated intellect. By this statement Krishna has indicated to Arjuna a greater Self than the ego in every embodiment.

At every level of our personality, we view Life and come to our own conclusions about things. Thus, we have a PHYSICAL ESTIMATE of the world from the body level, which is quite distinct from the EMOTIONAL PICTURE of life from the mental level and also an INTELLECTUAL CONCEPT of life that is from the level of the intellect.

Physically, what I see as a woman, is mentally my mother and intellectually, the same sacred feminine form is a bundle of cells. Each has in its protoplasmic content a nucleus that presides over all its functions. The imperfections that I see in a physical object will fail to give me misery, if I successfully gild it with my emotional appreciation. Similarly, an object which is physically abhorrent and mentally shameful will still fail to provide me with any sorrow, if I can appreciate it from my intellectual level.

Hence, that which gives me despondency and dejection at the physical, mental and intellectual levels can yield a thrilling inspiration if I review it from the spiritual level. Krishna is advising Arjuna to renounce his physical, emotional and intellectual estimates of his teacher and his grandsire and those of the whole battlefield problem, and to re-evaluate the situation through his spiritual understanding.

This great and transcendental Truth has been so suddenly expounded here that it has, on Arjuna the stunning effect of a sudden unexpected blast. Later on, we shall understand how this subtle, psycho-physical shock-therapy did an immeasurable good to the hysterical condition of Arjuna.

"WHY DO THEY DESERVE NO GRIEF? IT IS BECAUSE THEY ARE ETERNAL. HOW IS THAT SO?" THE LORD SAYS:

12. *It is not that at any time (in the past), indeed was I not, nor were you, nor these rulers of men. Nor verily, shall we all ever cease to be hereafter.*

न त्वेवाहं जातु नासं न त्वं नेमे जनाधिपा: ।
न चैव न भविष्याम: सर्वे वयमत: परम् ॥ १२ ॥

na tvevāhaṁ jātu nāsaṁ na tvaṁ neme janādhipāḥ,
na caiva na bhaviṣyāmaḥ sarve vayamataḥ param 12.

Krishna here declares in unequivocal terms, that the embodied Self in every one is set on a great pilgrimage in which It comes to identify itself with varied forms temporarily to gain a limited but determined set of experiences. He says that neither Himself, nor Arjuna, nor the great kings of the ages that have assembled in both the armies, are mere accidental happenings. They do not come from nowhere and, at their death, do not become mere non-existent nothingness. Correct philosophical thinking guides man's intellect to the apprehension of a continuity from the past – through the present -- to the endless future. The Spirit remaining the same, it gets seemingly conditioned by different body-equipments, and comes to live through its self-ordained environments.

It is this conclusion of the Hindu philosophers that has given us the most satisfactory THEORY OF REINCARNATION. The most powerful opponents of this idea do not seem to have studiously followed their own scriptures. Christ Himself has, if not directly, at least indirectly, proclaimed this doctrine when He told His disciples: "John, the Baptist, was Elijah". Origen who was the most learned of the Christian Fathers, has clearly declared "Every man received a body for himself according to his deserts in former lives".

There was no great thinker in the past who had not, or any in the present who has not accepted, expressly or tacitly, these logical conclusions about the DOCTRINE OF REINCARNATION. Buddha constantly made references to his previous births. Virgil and Ovid regarded the doctrine as perfectly self-evident. Josephus observed that the belief in reincarnation was widely accepted among the Jews of his era. Solomon's BOOK OF WISDOM says: "To be born in sound body with sound limbs is a reward of the virtues of the past lives".

And who does not remember the famous saying of the learned son of Islam who declared, "I died out of the stone and I became a plant; I died out of the plant and became an animal; I died out of the animal and became a man. Why then should I fear to die? When did I grow less by dying? I shall die out of man and shall become an angel!!"

In the later times, this most intelligent philosophical belief has been accepted as a doctrine by the German philosophers Goethe, Fichte, Schelling, and Lessing. Among the recent philosophers, Hume, Spencer, and Max Mueller, have recognised this doctrine as incontrovertible. Among the poets of the West also, we find many burnished intellects soaring into the cloudless sky of imagination. Within their poetic flights, they too have intuitively felt the sanction behind this immortal doctrine – Browning, Rossetti, Tennyson and Wordsworth, to mention but a few names.

The REINCARNATION THEORY is not a mere dream of the philosophers, and the day is not far off, when with the fast developing science of Psychology, the West will come to rewrite its scriptures under the sheer weight of observed phenomena. An uncompromising intellectual quest for understanding life cannot satisfy itself if it is thwarted at every corner by 'observed irregularities'. We cannot, for long ignore them all as mere 'chances'. The prodigy Mozart is a spectacular instance, which cannot be explained; to be logical we must accept the idea of the continuity of the embodied souls. This genius wrote sonatas at the age of four, played in public at the age of five, and composed his first opera at the age of seven! Without the REINCARNATION THEORY, we will have to label this wondrous incident as an accident, and throw it into the dustbin off chance, and bury it there!

Examples are often noticed, but rarely recorded as evidences to prove this great THEORY OF REINCARNATION. The modern world, as I said, has yet to discover this great and self-evident LAW OF LIFE.

Therefore, to an uninitiated student, this theory may seem too staggering for quiet appreciation. When Krishna declared that "none of them, (including himself, Arjuna and the great kings) even after their deaths on the battlefield shall cease to exist in future", Arjuna who was a typical man-of-the-world could not grasp it as a self-evident fact. His questioning eyes made the Lord explain again this idea through an example in the following stanza.

"WHY DO THEY DESERVE NO GRIEF? FOR THEY ARE ETERNAL IN ESSENCE. HOW?"..... THE LORD SAYS:

13. *Just as in this body the embodied (soul) passes into childhood, youth and old age, so also does he pass into another body; the firm man does not grieve at it.*

देहिनोऽस्मिन्यथा देहे कौमारं यौवनं जरा ।
तथा देहान्तरप्राप्तिर्धीरस्तत्र न मुह्यति ॥ १३ ॥

dehino'sminyathā dehe kaumāraṁ yauvnaṁ jarā,
tathā dehāntaraprāptirdhīrastatra na muhyati 13.

It is the law of memory that the experiencer and the memoriser must both be the same entity; then alone can memory-power function. I cannot remember any of YOUR experiences nor can YOU remember any of MY experiences; I can remember my experiences as readily and easily as you can remember your experiences.

In old age, every one of us can remember the main incidents of our own childhood and youth. In the progress of growth, childhood dies away and youth appears, and youth dies before old age can assert itself. In the old man, it is self-evident that neither his childhood nor his youth is with him, and yet, he can remember his own early days. Applying the principle of memory, it becomes quite clear then that SOMETHING in us is common in all the different stages of our growth so that the same entity remembers the experiences gained by it in the past through the childish body, and later, through the youthful structure.

Thus, youthfulness may be considered as a birth, when childhood has met with its death. So too, old age is born when youth is dead. And yet, none of us is the least disturbed by these changes. On the other hand, we feel, in fact, happier due to the wealth of experiences we have gained as the status of the body rose from innocent childhood to mature old age.

Using this subjective experience of every one in the world as a standard of comparison, Krishna is trying to bring home to Arjuna the fact that wise men do not worry when they leave one body for the purpose of taking another one.

This stanza is again asserting in unequivocal terms, the truth behind the Reincarnation Theory. And thus viewed, death can no more be a threat to a wise man. We do not moan the death of childhood, following which alone can we come to experience youth. We are confident in our knowledge that though youth is entered into and childhood has ended, there is a continuity of existence of the same one only, so that a child has now become a youth. So too, at the moment of death, there is no extinction of the individuality; but the embodied-ego of the dead-body leaves its previous structure, and according to the *vasanas* (mental impressions) that it had gathered during its embodiment, it gets identified with a physical equipment, where it can express itself completely, and seek its perfect fulfilment.

14. *The contacts of senses with objects, O son of Kunti, which cause heat and cold, pleasure and pain, have a beginning and an end; they are impermanent; endure them bravely, O descendant of Bharata.*

According to the accepted theory of perception in *Vedanta*, an object is perceived not BY the sense-organs but THROUGH them. The *Indriyas* are instruments through which the perceiving-ego gathers the knowledge of the various objects. If the perceiver is not actually contacting the objects through the sense-organs, the objects as such cannot bring any perception to him.

That the same objects can give two different types of experiences to two different individuals is very well known.

मात्रास्पर्शास्तु कौन्तेय शीतोष्णसुखदुःखदाः ।
आगमापायिनोऽनित्यास्तांस्तितिक्षस्व भारत ॥ १४ ॥

mātrāsparśās tu kaunteya śītoṣṇasukhaduḥkhadāḥ,
āgamāpāyino 'nityāḥ tāṁstitikṣasva bhārata 14.

If the object while remaining the same can give different experiences, it is evident that it is because of the difference in the mental composition of the individuals. It is also observed that objects of one's intense fancy during a certain stage in one's life become a nuisance to the same individual after a time, for, as time passes on, the mental constitution of each individual also changes. In short, it is very clear that the external objects can convey their stimuli and give us an experience only when our minds come in contact with the objects through the sense-organs.

He who can understand that the objects of the world are in a state of flux, (are constantly coming into existence, and perishing) will not allow himself to be tossed about by the existence or non-existence of the finite things of the world. In the flood of time, things, incidents, circumstances, and environments flow up to our present from the unknown future, to give us vivid experiences of varied intensity. They, in their very nature, cannot remain permanently, but out of necessity must pass on to become one with the entire past. Nothing can remain the same even for a short period, in the world-of-objects where change alone is the changeless law.

Having understood this finite nature of the changeable objects of the world, wherein every one of them has a beginning and an end, on no occasion need a wise man despair the least of things THAT ARE, or of things THAT ARE NOT. Heat and cold, success or failure, pain or joy – none of these can be permanent.

Since every situation of its own nature must keep on changing, it would be foolish of us to get upset at every change we notice. It is wisdom to suffer them meekly with the comfort and consolation of the knowledge of their finite nature. It is the attitude of the wise to go through life, both in joy and sorrow, in success and failure, in pain and joy, with the constant awareness: "Even this will pass away".

The external world of challenges is finite inasmuch as it has a beginning and an end. Not only that; Krishna adds, "They are impermanent by their very nature". By the term 'impermanent' used here, the Lord means that the same object which gives pleasure at one moment starts yielding at another moment, pain to the experiencer. This inconsistency is indicated by the term *'anitya'* in the stanza.

WHAT GOOD WILL ACCRUE TO HIM WHO IS INDIFFERENT TO HEAT AND COLD AND THE LIKE? LISTEN:

15. *That firm man to whom, surely these afflict not, O chief among men, to whom pleasure and pain are the same, is fit for realising the Immortality of the Self.*

Calm endurance, both in pleasure and pain, is a condition necessary for the right knowledge of the true Self; this is the technique of Self-realisation, as explained in the *Upanishadic* lore. Based upon this fact, here Lord Krishna explains that the one who has found in himself a mental equipoise, wherein he is not afflicted or disturbed by circumstances of pain and pleasure, he alone IS FIT FOR ATTAINING IMMORTALITY.

यं हि न व्यथयन्त्येते पुरुषं पुरुषर्षभ ।
समदुःखसुखं धीरं सोऽमृतत्वाय कल्पते ॥ १५ ॥

yaṁ hi na vyathayantyete puruṣaṁ puruṣarṣabha,
samaduḥkhasukhaṁ dhīraṁ so 'mṛtatvāya kalpate 15.

When the TRANSCENDENTAL TRUTH or the ETERNAL PERFECTION has been indicated by the term Immortality, the term is not used in its limited sense of 'deathlessness' of the body. Here the term 'death' not only indicates the destruction of the physical embodiment but also includes and incorporates within its significance, the entire range of finite experiences, whereby in each one of them there is an extinction-experience. No experience gained through the body, the mind, or the intellect is permanent.

In other words, each experience is born to live with us for a short period and then to die within us. These chains of finite experiences stretch out in front of us as the paths of sorrow and pain in our life. The term 'Immortality', used by the *Rishis* to indicate the 'Supermanhood', indicates a state wherein the one walking the path of endless sorrows, as the individual ego, transcends that state, to attain the Infinite experience of THE ETERNAL AND THE PERMANENT.

Through the *Geeta*, our poet-seer Vyasa is making Lord Krishna declare that the purpose of life for every one is the attainment of PERFECTION and, to evolve one must make use of every little chance in one's allotted span of life. To endure meekly with magnanimous joy the little pinpricks of life - heat and cold, success and failure, pain and joy – is the highest training that life can provide to all of us.

An incompetent idler's hapless endurance of life is not in itself what is indicated here. It is especially said that the equipoise of the mind, both in pleasure and sorrow entertained by a 'wise-man' (*dheerah*) makes him fit for the highest cultural self-development. That is to say, the equanimity should not flow from the dark caves of one's stupidity and inertia, but it must gurgle forth from the open sunny fields of wisdom and understanding. When one understands the essential nature of the objects of the world to be finite, out of that realised knowledge one gains enough balance for calm endurance, and feels neither exalted in pleasure nor is dejected in pain.

So long as we live 'in the body, as the body', we are not able to ignore or calmly endure the sorrows of the body. But when we are fired by a sentiment of love or hatred, we invariably make ready sacrifices of bodily pleasures. Because of my love for my son, I am ready to make any sacrifice of my physical needs, so that I may give him a good education, etc. When one gets fired up intellectually by some idea or ideology, for the satisfaction of it one readily ignores and overlooks the comforts and pleasures of one's body and mind. The martyrs and revolutionaries in the world could with pleasure, face physical persecutions and mental agonies for the satisfaction of their intellectual lives and for the fulfilment of their ideals and ideologies.

FOR THE FOLLOWING REASONS ALSO, IT IS PROPER THAT YOU SHOULD ABANDON YOUR GRIEF AND DISTRESSING DELUSION, AND SHOULD CALMLY ENDURE HEAT AND COLD, ETC. FOR:

16. *The unreal has no being; there is no non-being of the Real; the truth about both these has been seen by the Knowers of the Truth (or the Seers of the Essence).*

नासतो विद्यते भावो नाभावो विद्यते सतः ।
उभयोरपि दृष्टोऽन्तस्त्वनयोस्तत्त्वदर्शिभिः ॥ १६ ॥

nāsato vidyate bhāvo nābhāvo vidyate sataḥ,
ubhayorapi dṛṣṭo 'ntaḥ tvanayostattva darśibhiḥ 16.

In *Vedantic* literature the Real and the Un-real are very scientifically distinguished. These two categories are not considered as indefinables in our ancient scriptures; though they do not declare these to be definables. The *Rishis* have clearly indicated what constitutes the REAL, and what are the features of the UN-REAL. "That which was not in the past and which will not be in the future, but that which seemingly exists only in the present is called the UN-REAL". In the language of the *Karika,** "That which is non-existent in the beginning and in the end, is necessarily non-existent in the intermediate stages also; objects that we see are illusory, still they are regarded as real".

Naturally, the REAL is "that which defies all changes and remains the same in all the periods of time: past, present and future". Thus, in an ordinary example, when one misunderstands a post in the dark to be a ghost, the ghost-vision is considered unreal as compared to the post; because, the hallucination cannot be permanent and it does not remain, after the rediscovery of the post. Similarly, on waking up from our dream, we do not get anxious to provide for our dream-children. That is; because, as soon as we wake up, we realise that the dream was unreal. Before we went to bed, the dream-children were not with us, and after waking up, our dream-children are no more with us; thus, we understand and realise that our dream-children, whom we loved and tended as real during our dream, are, in fact, unreal. By significance, therefore, the REAL is that which exists at all times: in the past, the present and the future. The post is relatively real - it was, it is, and it will be.

---

* Refer to Swamiji's Discourses on *'Mandukya* and *Karika'*, II-6

The life in our matter envelopments, we know is finite, inasmuch as every little experience, at all the three levels of our existence - among the objects, with our sentiments, and in the company of our ideas – is finite. The body changes at every moment; the mind evolves, and the intellect grows. All changes, evolutionary movements, and growths are indicated by a constant-death of their previous state, in order that the thing concerned may change, evolve or grow. The body, the mind, and the intellect are ever changing in us, and all of them therefore, according to our definition, cannot be Real.

But is there a REAL entity behind it all? In order that change may take place, no doubt, a changeless substratum is necessary. For the waters of the river to flow, a motionless riverbed must exist. Similarly, in order to hold together the millions of experiences at the levels of our body, mind, and intellect, and to give us the experience of a synchronised whole - which we call life, we must necessarily have some substratum that is changeless and real, which is common to all three.

Something in us remains as it were, unchanged all through our changes, holding the vivid experiences together, just as a thread holds the beads in a necklace. On closer analysis, it becomes clear that it can be nothing other than the Self in us, the Pure Awareness. Experiences that have come under one's awareness do not constitute any vital aspect of one's own Self; life is the sum total of experiences that have been devised by the touch of one's illuminating Consciousness. In childhood, I was conscious of my childhood-life; in my youth, I was conscious of my youthful life; and in my old age, I am again conscious of my present experiences. The Consciousness remaining the same, endless experiences came under it, got illumined, and died away. This Awareness by which I become conscious of things in my life – because of which I am considered as alive, without which I will have no more existence in this given embodiment - 'That' Spiritual Entity, Eternal, All-Pervading, Unborn, Undying, and the One Changeless Factor, is the Infinite in me. And this *Atman* is the Real Self.

Men of knowledge and wisdom have known the essence, the meaning, and the implication of both these; the Self and the non-Self, the Real and the Unreal, which in their mysterious combination constitute the strange phenomenon called the world.

WHAT THEN IS THAT WHICH IS EVER REAL? LISTEN:

17. *Know That to be Indestructible by which all this is pervaded.*
None can cause the destruction of That – the Imperishable.

The REAL is that which envelops everything that exists, and which is the very stuff and substance of all the worlds of perceptions, which we experience. Different mud-pots, each different in form, shape, and colour, may have different names according to the things they contain, or according to the purpose for which they are used. Though each of them

---

अविनाशि तु तद्विद्धि येन सर्वमिदं ततम् ।
विनाशमव्ययस्यास्य न कश्चित्कर्तुमर्हति ॥ १७ ॥

avināśi tu tadviddhi yena sarvamidaṁ tatam,
vināśamavyayasyāsya na kaścitkartumarhati 17.

has thus a different name, yet all of them are; we may say; enveloped by, or permeated with one and the same stuff, the mud, without which none of the pots can exist. From mud they came; in mud they exist and when they are destroyed, their names and forms shall merge back to become mud. All the mud-pots are enveloped by mud; which is the Reality holding the world of mud-pots together.

Similarly, the world of finite changes is entirely permeated through and through and enveloped by the REAL; the Changeless and *Bhagawan* adds that there is no possibility of this REAL; even for a moment, ever getting destroyed, even by a fraction.

WHAT THEN IS THE UNREAL (*ASAT*) WHOSE EXISTENCE IS NOT CONSTANT? LISTEN :

18. *They have an end, it is said, these bodies of the embodied-Self.*
The Self is Eternal, Indestructible, Incomprehensible.
Therefore fight, O Bharata.

The physical forms, constituted of matter envelopments, are all perishable equipments for the indwelling. This Self which is the Eternal Factor, ever in Its nature, changeless, indestructible, and incomprehensible. By the term EVER CHANGELESS, the Supreme is indicated as Eternal because the non-eternals; by their nature must be ever-changing, change being the insignia of the finite. Here, by using the

---

अन्तवन्त इमे देहा नित्यस्योक्ता: शरीरिण: ।
अनाशिनोऽप्रमेयस्य तस्माद्युध्यस्व भारत ॥ १८ ॥
antavanta ime dehā nityasyoktāḥ śarīriṇaḥ,
anāśino 'prameyasya tasmādyudhyasva bhārata. 18

two terms: Eternal (*Nityah*) and Indestructible (*Anashinah*), the Lord is indicating that neither a total nor a partial destruction is possible in the Supreme.

By qualifying the Eternal as UNKNOWABLE, it is not, in any sense, intended to indicate that the Supreme is 'unknown'. Here, the term 'unknowable' is only meant to express that it is not knowable through the usual organs-of-perception. The sense organs are the instruments through which the Consciousness beams out and in ITS awareness objects get illumined. These instruments of cognition, whether they are sense organs, or the mind or the intellect, are in themselves inert and they can have their knowledge of perception only when they are dynamised by the Consciousness, the spark-of-Life. As such, these organs cannot make the Consciousness an object of their apprehension. Therefore, in terms of our most common source of knowledge – the direct perception – the *shastra* says here that the Supreme is 'unknowable', since It is self-determined (*Swatah siddhah*).

THEREFORE, FIGHT O DESCENDANT OF BHARATA!—This is, really not a command to fight. A religion that is built upon the concept of extreme forgiveness and large-hearted tolerance, as envisaged in the principle of 'non-violence', could not have raised a slogan of chaos or revolutionary bloodthirstiness in its very scripture. Such an interpretation is the unintentional mischief of a commentator, who does not read the *Geeta* in the context of the Mahabharata.

The words: "Fight, O Son of India" means that it is a religious call to every Hindu to discard his defeatist mentality and face whole-heartedly and sincerely the situations in every given field of his life, at every given moment of his existence.

Active resistance to evil is the Krishna-creed in the *Geeta.*

THE LORD NOW QUOTES TWO *VEDIC MANTRAS*, TO CONFIRM THE VIEW THAT *GEETA SHASTRA* IS INTENDED TO REMOVE THE CAUSE OF *SAMSARA*, SUCH AS GRIEF AND DELUSION. "IT IS ONLY A FALSE NOTION OF YOURS," SAYS THE LORD, "THAT YOU THINK THUS: BHISHMA AND OTHERS, WILL BE KILLED BY ME IN THE BATTLE; I WILL BE THEIR SLAYER..." HOW?

19. *He who takes the Self to be the slayer and he who thinks He is slain; neither of them knows. He slays not, nor is He slain.*

The Self being Immutable is neither slain nor can It be the slayer. Those who think that they have been slain when the body is slain and those who feel that they are the slayers, are both of them ignorant of the Real Nature of the Self, and hence they simply prattle meaningless assertions. That which is killed is the perishable body and the delusory arrogation; the notion "I am slain" belongs to the ego-centre. The Self is that which is beyond the body and the ego, since the Pure Consciousness is the Illuminator of both; the body and the ego. In short, being Immutable, the Self can neither be the agent nor the object of the action of slaying.

HOW IS THE SELF IMMUTABLE? THIS IS ANSWERED IN THE NEXT VERSE.

य एनं वेत्ति हन्तारं यश्चैनं मन्यते हतम् ।
उभौ तौ न विजानीतो नायं हन्ति न हन्यते ॥ १९ ॥

ya enaṁ vetti hantāraṁ yaścainaṁ manyate hatam,
ubhau tau na vijānīto nāyaṁ hanti na hanyate 19.

20. *He is not born, nor does He ever die; after having been, He again ceases not to be; Unborn, Eternal, Changeless and Ancient, He is not killed when the body is killed.*

This stanza labours to deny in the Self all the symptoms of mutability that are recognised and experienced by the body. The body is prone to different changes and these modifications are the sources of all sorrows in every embodiment. These six changes are common to all and they may be enumerated as: birth, existence, growth, decay, disease and death. These changes are the common womb of all pains in a mortal's life. All these are denied in the Self in this stanza, to prove the immutability of the Self.

Unlike the physical body, the Self is not born; It being the Eternal Factor that exists at all times. Waves are born and they die away but the ocean is not born with the waves; nor does it die when the waves disappear. Since there is no birth, there is no death, things that have a beginning alone can end; the rising waves alone can moan their dying conditions. Again, it is explained that like the birth of a child who was not in existence before, and who has come to exist after the birth, the *Atman* is not something that has come to

---

न जायते म्रियते वा कदाचित्
नायं भूत्वा भविता वा न भूय: ।
अजो नित्य: शाश्वतोऽयं पुराणो
न हन्यते हन्यमाने शरीरे ॥ २० ॥

na jāyate mriyate vā kadācit,
nāyaṁ bhūtvā bhavitā vā na bhūyaḥ,
ajo nityaḥ śāśvato 'yam purāṇo
na hanyate hanyamāne śarīre 20.

be born due to or because of the body. Thus the Self is Unborn, Eternal, Birthless, and Deathless (*Ajah, Nityah*).

HAVING THUS STATED THE PROPOSITION THAT THE SELF IS NEITHER AN AGENT, NOR AN OBJECT OF THE ACTION OF SLAYING, AND HAVING ESTABLISHED, BY ARGUMENTS THE IMMUTABILITY OF THE SELF, LORD KRISHNA HERE CONCLUDES THE PROPOSITION AS FOLLOWS:

21. *Whosoever knows Him to be Indestructible, Eternal, Unborn, and Inexhaustible, how can that man slay O Partha, or cause others to be slain?*

Summarising what is said so far as the Law-of-Being (*Dharma*) of the Self, which indicated rather than defined the Eternal, Immutable Reality, in this stanza we have in the form of an interrogation an assertion that those who know this shall have thereafter, no dejection or sorrow in facing life's realities.

Having known the Self to be Indestructible, Eternal, Unborn, and Inexhaustible, Krishna asks Arjuna, "How can one arrogate to oneself the stupid idea of agency?" The Lord says that neither can such an individual cause someone to slay nor himself be a slayer. In the context of the given situation, Krishna advises thus. It is interesting to note that He means both Himself and Arjuna by His words. If this knowledge of the Reality has come to the intellectual

---

वेदाविनाशिनं नित्यं य एनमजमव्ययम् ।
कथं स पुरुषः पार्थ कं घातयति हन्ति कम् ॥ २१ ॥

vedāvināśinaṁ nityaṁ ya enam-ajam-avyayam,
kathaṁ sa puruṣaḥ pārtha kaṁ ghātayati hanti kam 21.

appreciation and acceptance of Arjuna, he will have no more justification to consider himself to be the killer of the Unborn.

IN WHAT WAY IS THE SELF INDESTRUCTIBLE? HERE IN THE FOLLOWING VERSE, IS AN EXPLANATORY EXAMPLE:

22. *Just as a man casts off his worn out clothes and puts on new ones, so also the embodied-Self casts off its worn out bodies and enters other which are new.*

This is one of the oft-quoted famous stanzas in the *Geeta.* which by a very striking example explains to us how the egocentric entity in an individual readily leaves its associations with one set of equipments, and arrogates to itself another conducive envelopment for living a new set of its required experiences. The example that Vyasa uses is so universal that from the Lord's own mouth it rings with a note of irresistible appeal.

Just as an individual changes his clothes to suit the convenience of the occasion, so too the ego-centre discards one physical form and takes on another, which will be most suited for it to gain the next required type of experiences. No one will plan to go to his office wearing his nightgown; nor will he, in his stiff-collar, feel happy while playing tennis in the evening. He changes his dress according to the field where

---

वासांसि जीर्णानि यथा विहाय
नवानि गृह्णाति नरोऽपराणि ।
तथा शरीराणि विहाय जीर्णानि
अन्यानि संयाति नवानि देही ॥ २२ ॥

vāsāṁsi jīrṇāni yathā vihāya
navāni gṛhṇāti naro 'parāṇi,
tathā śarirāṇi vihāya jīrṇāni
anyāni saṁyāti navāni dehī 22.

he is intending to work for the time being. Similar is 'the why and wherefore' of death and thereafter.

This striking example, which comes within the comprehension of every one, is made use of by the Lord so that not only Arjuna, but even those who are overhearing these eighteen discourses even at this distant time, may come to understand the idea clearly.

Changing of our clothes that have become worn out, cannot be a pain to anyone of us, especially when it is for the purpose of putting on a new set of clothes. Similarly, when a mind-intellect-equipment finds that its embodiment in a given form can no longer help it to earn, from its available environments, experiences that would facilitate its evolutionary pilgrimage, it feels that this particular form is worn out (*Jeerna*). This 'worn out' condition of a body is to be decided neither by its age, nor by its biological condition. Nor can anybody other than its wearer, the ego, decide it.

Critics rise up in hosts however against the truth of this stanza and their main platform of arguments is built upon the observed facts of young people dying away in the bloom of their life. In the observers' opinion, the individual was young and his body was not worn out (*Jeerna*), but from the standpoint of the evolutionary necessity of the ego concerned, that body was already useless for it. A rich man for example feels like changing his house or a vehicle almost every year, and he invariably finds ready purchasers. As far as the rich owner is concerned, the thing has become useless for him, while for the purchaser it is 'as good as new'. Similarly, here nobody else can decide, whether a given body is worn out or not, except its 'wearer'.

In short, the stanza emphasizes the doctrine of reincarnation which we have already explained in an earlier stanza.*

On the whole, it must have definitely conveyed to Arjuna the idea that death grins only at those who have no understanding, and that it has no pain for those who understand its implications and working. Just as changing of the dress is no pain to the body, so too, when the dweller in the body leaves the envelopment, there is no pain possible; again, undressing does not mean that thereafter, we will ever live naked, so too, the embodied Self before long discovers an appropriate equipment from which to function, and to earn for itself new sets of experiences. Evolution and change are all for the mind-and-intellect and not for the Self. The Self is perfect and changeless, and needs no evolution.

WHY IS THE SELF CHANGELESS? THE LORD SAYS:

23. *Weapons cleave It not, fire burns It not, water moistens It not, wind dries It not.*

The unseen is always explained in terms of the seen, and thereby the unknown becomes fully indicated, rather than defined; for, any unknown thing merely defined in itself remains as unknown as before. Similarly here the Changeless, Immutable Self is being described by Lord Krishna in terms

---

नैनं छिन्दन्ति शस्त्राणि नैनं दहति पावकः ।
न चैनं क्लेदयन्त्यापो न शोषयति मारुतः ॥ २३ ॥

nainaṁ chindanti śastrāṇi nainaṁ dahati pāvakaḥ,
na cainaṁ kledayantyāpo na śoṣayati mārutaḥ 23.

*Ibid., stanza 12

of the mutable and ever-changing world, which is very familiar to Arjuna and all the people like us. In the world-of-change, objects come to their annihilation either through instruments of death, are consumed by fire, destroyed by water, or dried up by air. These are the various cosmic means and methods by which the objects of the world come to their destruction. All these means are declared as impotent in bringing about the destruction of the Self.

WEAPONS CLEAVE IT NOT—It is very well known that with an axe one can cut down a thing and with a bullet one can shoot some other object, but one cannot wound water, fire, air, or space with a sword, however sharp it might be. The principle is that no instrument can hit or destroy an element subtler than itself. Naturally therefore, *Atman,* the Self , the very cause of the subtlest element space and necessarily therefore subtler than space, cannot be cut asunder by the gross instruments.

FIRE CANNOT BURN IT— Fire can generally burn things other than the fire, but it cannot burn itself. The burning capacity of fire is the very Essence, the Truth within it, and therefore, fire cannot burn its own Essence, viz. its fiery nature. Wherever there is fire, it can consume things only in space and yet, space is never consumed by fire. Things are consumed by fire in space. If space itself cannot be consumed by fire, how impotent it must feel when it tries to consume the cause of space – the Self?

WATER CANNOT MOISTEN IT—Things get soaked only when they have got interspace within themselves. A piece of bread can be soaked in water or milk, but a piece of iron cannot be soaked, as iron has no interspace within. When the substance is one homogeneous mass containing nothing other than itself to condition it, water cannot enter the substance and therefore, cannot soak it. Another method of destruction observed is either through the quick effects of water in drowning, etc., or through the slow effects of moisture, such as corroding, etc. Even these cannot destroy the Truth.

WIND DRIES IT NOT—Dehydration is possible only when there are some traces of water in the substance dehydrated. Every crystal has its own water of crystallisation, which when removed, causes the crystals to lose their distinct shapes and forms and get pulverised into fine powder. These are days when vegetables and food materials are dehydrated for the purpose of preservation. This is possible because these substances contain moisture-molecules within them. The Supreme Consciousness contains nothing other than Itself and therefore, annihilation through the process of dehydration is not possible.

Apart from this direct word meaning, on the whole the stanza indicates deeper significances which are better brought out in the next stanza, where Lord Krishna gives out how and why the truth is Eternal.

FOR WHAT REASON, WHY, AND HOW CAN WE RECOGNISE THE SELF TO BE ETERNAL?

24. *This Self cannot be cut, nor burnt, nor moistened, nor dried up. It is eternal, all-pervading, stable, immovable and ancient.*

अच्छेद्योऽयमदाह्योऽयमक्लेद्योऽशोष्य एव च ।
नित्यः सर्वगतः स्थाणुरचलोऽयं सनातनः ॥ २४ ॥

acchedyo'yamadāhyo'yam akledyo' śoṣya eva ca,
nityaḥ sarvagataḥ sthāṇur acalo 'yaṁ sanātanaḥ 24.

It is amply clear that if a thing cannot be annihilated by any of the known methods of destruction of nature, or by those invented and perfected by man, then that given object must be everlasting.

Here in the second line, we have a series of qualities listed, indicating the Truth; they are not a haphazard collection of terms picked up at random and used in haste. Each word is chosen as a sequence to the previous one. That which has indestructibility, as indicated in the first line, should necessarily be everlasting (*nityah*). That which is thus Eternal must necessarily be All-Pervading (*sarvagatah*).

ALL-PERVADING is a short term of inconceivable depth of significance. ALL-PERVADING is that which pervades everywhere and therefore, there is nothing that is not pervaded by the ALL-PERVASIVE. The Eternal truth envelops all. The ALL-PERVADING has no shape, since that which has a shape is conditioned all along its outline by something other than itself.

A man with a head, a trunk, and limbs has a shape because all around him along his outline is space, which is something other than the carbon-material of his skull and bones. A thing conditioned should necessarily have a form of its own. By the term ALL-PERVADING, it is meant that it has only Itself all round It and at all places, and that It is unconditioned by anything other than Itself.

A truth that is thus Eternal (*nityah*), Homogeneous, and All-Pervading (*sarvagatah*), must necessarily be 'Stable' (s*thanuh*), because no change can ever take place in it. That which is thus stable must be 'Firm' (*achalah*); for, it cannot shake or move, since movement implies the transfer of a thing from one set of time and place to another set of time and place, where it was not. Since the Self is All-pervading, there is no spot in space, or period in time, where It is not already, and therefore, just as I cannot move myself in myself, the Self cannot move anywhere. A motionless thing is indeed 'Firm' (a*chalah*).

Here the two terms 'Stable' (*sthanuh)* and 'Firm' (*achalah*) may seem to be a tautology; both having almost the same meaning. But the former means stability at the base, as in the case of a banyan-tree. At the base of the trunk it is stable and yet at the top it is moving. Truth is 'stable' at the 'base' and 'firm' at the 'top'. In Its Infinite glory, It has no movement anywhere.

Sanatanah means that which is ancient. The implication of this term can fall under two categories, the obvious and the suggestive. The OBVIOUS meaning indicates that the Self is not new (*nutanah*) but it is ancient and therefore, we as students of *Brahma-Vidya* need not hesitate to accept it, because we necessarily would, if the theory was a modern ideology which was yet to be verified by observed experimental data. In its suggestiveness, the term *Sanatanah* implies that the Self is unconditioned by time and place. Perfection gained, whether it is in India or at the North Pole, in the present generation, or in the chaste periods of the *Vedic* culture, in all places and at all times, by all seers, in all the religions of the world, the Self-experience at the time of God-realisation, can only be one and the same.

MOREOVER, BHAGAWAN ADDS:

25. *This (Self) is said to be Unmanifest, Unthinkable and Unchangeable. Therefore, knowing This to be such, you should not grieve.*

This Eternal, All-Pervading Self is certainly Unmanifest, Unthinkable, and Unchangeable, and therefore, having known this truth in Its essential nature, Krishna argues that it is neither possible to kill nor to get really killed. Each of these terms is quite expressive of certain logical truths.

UNMANIFEST—The five Great Elements that we know, when they become subtler, they lose their capacity to impinge themselves upon our sense perceptions; considered from Earth to Air, we find the elements progressively getting subtler for our perceptions and finally Ether or Space by itself cannot be perceived directly by our senses at all. However, the five Great Elements can, to some extent be perceived through our sense organs. But the CAUSE of Ether, the subtlest of the five Elements, is too subtle for our perception, and therefore we will have to assume that it is Unmanifest.

A thing is called manifest when we can perceive it through one or the other of our sense-organs. That which is beyond all the five sense-organs is called Unmanifest. I cannot see, smell, hear, taste or touch a full-grown mango tree in a mango seed, and yet I know that the seed is the cause for the tree. Under the circumstances, the tree is said to be in an

---

अव्यक्तोऽयमचिन्त्योऽयमविकार्योऽयमुच्यते ।
तस्मादेवं विदित्वैनं नानुशोचितुमर्हसि ॥ २५ ॥

avyakto 'yamacintyo 'yam avikāryo 'yamucyate,
tasmādevaṁ viditvainaṁ nānuśocitumarhasi 25.

'unmanifest' condition within the seed. Similarly, when they say that Truth is Unmanifest, they only mean that It cannot be perceived through any of our sense organs. In the *Upanishads,* we have exhaustive explanations of why our senses cannot have the Eternal as an object of sense perceptions. It is the very subject because of which the sense organs can perceive.

UNTHINKABLE—After denying the sense-organs any play in the field of Truth, we are told that the human mind also cannot think, nor can the human intellect ruminate over, and comprehend the Infinite. The Self being the very life that energises the mind and the intellect, which by themselves are inert and insentient; it becomes obvious that the mind and intellect cannot make the Self an object of their comprehension. A telescope-gazer cannot see himself with his telescope; he cannot be at once the seer and the seen. Thus, here the Lord's word 'Unthinkable' is to be understood as meaning 'Incomprehensible' by the mind and the intellect of the seeker.

UNCHANGEABLE—This term indicates that the Self is without parts because things that have parts in themselves are things which have 'form' and those that have 'form' must necessarily come under the category of the FINITE, and exhibit in themselves various modifications and changes.

By these terms, Truth is declared as Immutable, Unmanifest, Unthinkable, and Unchangeable.

Krishna thus advises Arjuna to end his grief. He who understands the Eternal nature of the Self can have neither the occasion to perceive himself as the slayer, nor recognise others as the slain.

GRANTING THAT THE SELF IS NOT EVERLASTING, THE LORD PROCEEDS TO GIVE THE MATERIALISTS' POINT OF VIEW:

26. *But even if you think of Him as being constantly born and constantly dying, even then, O mighty-armed, you should not grieve.*

This and the following stanzas are arguments in which the materialists' point of view has been -- for the purpose of argument -- presented here by Krishna. According to them, direct perception alone is an authority for belief. With this standard for their knowledge, when they try to measure life, they have to accept it as a constant flux of infinite-births and infinite-deaths. Things are born, and they die away. This whirl of birth and death is constant. And this constant change is life to them. Krishna argues that if life is but a constant repetition of births and deaths, then also – the hero (*Mahabahu*) that you are – you do not deserve to grieve on this occasion.

ACCORDINGLY:

27. *Indeed, certain is death for the born, and certain is birth for the dead; therefore, over the inevitable, you should not grieve.*

अथ चैनं नित्यजातं नित्यं वा मन्यसे मृतम् ।
तथापि त्वं महाबाहो नैवं शोचितुमर्हसि ॥ २६ ॥

atha cainam nityajātaṁ nityaṁ vā manyase mṛtam,
tathāpi tvaṁ mahābāho naivaṁ śocitum arhaśi 26.

जातस्य हि ध्रुवो मृत्युर्ध्रुवं जन्म मृतस्य च ।
तस्मादपरिहार्येऽर्थे न त्वं शोचितुमर्हसि ॥ २७ ॥

jātasya hi dhruvo mṛtyur dhruvaṁ janma mṛtasya ca,
tasmādaparihārye 'rthe na tvaṁ śocitumarhasi 27.

That which is born must die and after death things are born again. Here, Krishna continues to view the whole situation from the materialist's angle. The materialists take life to be a constant flood of appearances of forms arising from nowhere, and disappearing into nowhere. The theists believe that the embodiments are taken up by the individual-ego in order that it may eke out its experiences and learn to grow in its understanding of life and ultimately realise the Truth behind it all. Thus, this is a common meeting point of both the theists and the atheists; that both of them believe life to be a continuous chain of birth and death.

Thus, if life being in its very nature a stream of births and deaths against this inevitable arrangement, no intelligent man should moan. Standing out in the blazing summer sun, one must indeed be stupid to complain against its heat and glare. Similarly, having come to life, to complain against the very nature of life is indeed an inexcusable stupidity.

On this score also, to weep is to admit one's own ignorance. Krishna's life on the whole is a message of cheer and joy. His doctrine of life is an insistence upon, 'to weep is folly and to smile is wisdom'. "Keep smiling" seems to be Krishna's philosophy put in two words, and that is why upon seeing his dear friend weeping in life, the Lord gets whipped up, as it were, to an enthusiasm to save Arjuna from his delusions, and bring him back to the true purpose of life.

THE FOLLOWING TEN VERSES GIVE THE COMMON-MAN'S VIEW. SHANKARA SAYS, "NEITHER IS IT PROPER TO

GRIEVE OVER BEINGS WHICH ARE MERE COMBINATIONS OF (MATERIAL) CAUSES AND EFFECTS, FOR":

28. *Beings unmanifest in the beginning, and unmanifest again in their end seem to be manifest in the middle, O Bharata. What then is there to grieve about?*

From this stanza onwards, we have a beautiful presentation of the whole problem of Arjuna, from the standpoint of the man-of-the-world. In these ten verses, Krishna explains the problem as viewed through the goggles of a common man of the world and valued by his intellectual judgement.

The material world of objects strictly follows the law of causation. The world of 'effects' arises from the world of 'causes'. In a majority of cases, the effects are manifest and the causes are unmanifest. To project from the unmanifest to the manifest is the programme of creation of a thing, strictly following the law-of-Causation.

Thus, the manifest-world of today was unmanifest before its creation; and now for the time being it is available for cognition as fully manifest, only to fade away soon into the unmanifest again. It amounts to saying that the present came from the UNKNOWN and shall return to the UNKNOWN. Even if viewed thus, why should one moan? For, the spokes of a wheel that turns eternally must COME DOWN only to RISE UP again.

अव्यक्तादीनि भूतानि व्यक्तमध्यानि भारत ।
अव्यक्तनिधनान्येव तत्र का परिदेवना ॥ २८ ॥

avyaktādīni bhūtāni vyakta madhyāni bhārata,
avyakta nidhanāny eva tatra kā paridevanā 28.

Again, the dream-children who were unmanifest before, and which came to manifestation during the dream, become unmanifest again upon waking up. Why moan, O you bachelor for a wife whom you had never married, who had disappeared with your dream, with the children unborn, who dissolved away with your dream?

If there be, as Krishna says, an Infinite, Eternal Truth which is Changeless and Deathless, in which alone this drama of change occurs, this whirl of birth-and-death spins, how is it that we are not able to realise It even though it is explained to us repeatedly? According to Sankara, Lord Krishna here feels that He should not blame Arjuna for his incapacity to understand the Self.

SHANKARA SAYS, "THE SELF JUST SPOKEN OF IS VERY DIFFICULT TO REALISE. WHY SHOULD I BLAME YOU ALONE WHILE THE CAUSE that is IGNORANCE, IS COMMON TO ALL?" ONE MAY ASK: "HOW IS IT THAT THE SELF IS SO DIFFICULT TO REALISE?" THE LORD SAYS:

29. *One sees This as a wonder; another speaks of This as a wonder; another hears of This as a wonder; yet, having heard none understands This at all!*

आश्चर्यवत्पश्यति कश्चिदेनम्
आश्चर्यवद्वदति तथैव चान्यः ।
आश्चर्यवच्चैनमन्यः श्रृणोति
श्रुत्वाप्येनं वेद न चैव कश्चित् ॥ २९ ॥

āscaryavatpaśyati kaścidenam
āścaryavad vadati tathaiva cānyaḥ,
āścaryavac cainam anyaḥ śṛṇoti
śrutvāpyenaṁ veda na caiva kaścit 29.

The Eternal Absolute is explained to us as Infinite, All-knowing, and All-blissful. Our experience of ourselves is that we are finite, ignorant, and miserable. Thus, between the Reality which is our Self, and what we experience ourselves to be, there seems to be as much of a difference as between heat and cold, light and darkness. Why is it that we are not able to recognise the Self, which is our Real Nature?

In our ignorance when we try to perceive the Truth, it seems to be a goal to be reached at some distant place, during a distant period of time. But in fact, if we are to believe the Lord's words, the Self being our essential nature, we are never far from It. A mortal is as far away from Immortality as the sinner is as far removed from a Saint; as the imperfect is as far removed from Perfection; as a dreamer is from the waker.

Man awakened to the Self's Glory is God; God forgetful of His own glory is the deluded man!

To the ego, the very existence of the subtler Self beyond the body, the mind, and the intellect is an idea that cannot even be conceived of. When a mortal, through the techniques of self-perfection comes to recognise himself to be the Self, he is struck with a wondrous ecstasy of that supra-sensuous experience.

The emotion of wonder when arises in the mind, has the capacity to blackout for the time being, all cognitions. The individual, who has been struck with wonder forgets himself and becomes for the moment, one with the very emotion. As an experiment, try to completely surprise somebody, and quietly watch his attitude. With the mouth open and his unseeing eyes protruding out, every nerve in him stretched to the highest tension, the victim of wonderment stands fixed to the spot, as a statue carved in moist cold flesh. The same is the thrilled hush of lived joy in the Temple of Experience, when the Self, all alone, comes to live as the Self. And therefore, the great *Rishis* of old times borrowed the term 'wonderment' to indicate to the student what exactly would be the condition of his personality layers at the moment when his ego drops off from the resplendent Infinite Form of the Self.

The true knowledge makes a man realise that he is 'The Soul with a body', but now in his ignorance, he thinks that he is a 'body with a soul'. Those who LISTEN well are encouraged to REFLECT upon what they have heard and to MEDITATE until they realise the Self. The unintelligent listeners also feel encouraged by the very same statement expressing the rarity of this knowledge, to make repeated attempts at listening (*shravana*), continuous reflection (*manana*), and long contemplation (*nididhyasana*).

HERE THE LORD CONCLUDES THE SUBJECT OF THIS SECTION THUS:

30. *This – the Indweller in the body of everyone is ever indestructible, O Bharata; and, therefore, you should not grieve for any creature.*

The subtle Reality in each body that is the indwelling Spirit in every creature is Eternal and Indestructible. All that is

---

देही नित्यमवध्योऽयं देहे सर्वस्य भारत ।
तस्मात्सर्वाणि भूतानि न त्वं शोचितुमर्हसि ॥ ३० ॥

dehī nityamavadhyo' yaṁ dehe sarvasya bhārata,
tasmātsarvāṇi bhūtāni na tvaṁ śocitumarhasi 30.

destroyed is only the container, the finite matter envelopment. Therefore, Arjuna has been advised that he should not grieve upon facing his enemies and in the great battle even killing them, if need be. To bring out this idea, the entire earlier section has been used by Krishna wherein he argued so well to establish the Eternal nature of the soul and the finite nature of the bodies. Sankara rightly concludes that this stanza winds up the entire section opened in verse 11.

IN THIS VERSE, IT HAS BEEN SHOWN THAT FROM THE STANDPOINT OF ABSOLUTE TRUTH, THERE IS NO OCCASION FOR GRIEF AND ATTACHMENT. NOT ONLY FROM THE STANDPOINT OF ABSOLUTE TRUTH, BUT ALSO:

31. *Further, looking at thine own duty thou ought not to waver, for there is nothing higher for a KSHATRIYA than a righteous war.*

Arjuna's personal call-of-character (*Swadharma*) is that of a leader of his generation (*Kshatriya*) and as such, when his generation is called upon to answer a challenge of an organised un-Aryan force (*adharma*), it is his duty not to waver but to fight and defend his sacred national culture.

स्वधर्ममपि चावेक्ष्य न विकम्पितुमर्हसि ।
धर्म्याद्धि युद्धाच्छ्रेयोऽन्यत्क्षत्रियस्य न विद्यते ॥ ३१ ॥

svadharmamapi cāvekṣya na vikampitumarhasi,
dharmyāddhi yuddhācchreyo'nyat kṣatriyasya na vidyate 31.

* Mahabharata, Udyoga Parva – 72-18 says: "The sin that is committed by killing one who does not deserve to be killed is as great as the sin of NOT killing one who deserves to be killed."

To the leaders of people, there can be nothing nobler than to get a glorious chance to fight for a righteous cause. Here Arjuna has been called upon to fight a righteous war wherein his enemies are the true aggressors. Therefore, it is said that such a chance comes indeed, only to a lucky few. That a king must fight on such an occasion is vividly brought out in the Mahabharata.*

REGARDING THE OTHER REASONS WHY THE BATTLE SHOULD BE FOUGHT, THE LORD SAYS:

32. *Happy indeed are the KSHATRIYAS, O Partha, who are called to fight in such a battle, that comes of itself as an open door to heaven.*

As used here, *Kshatriya* is not the name of a caste. It merely indicates a certain quality of the mental *vasanas* in the individual. Those who have an ever-bubbling enthusiasm to defend the weak and the poor, besides their own national culture from all threats of aggression are called *Kshatriyas*. Such leaders of men are not allowed to be tyrants and aggressors, according to the code of morality of the Hindus. But at the same time a cold, feminine, and cowardly non-resistance is not the spirit of the Hindu tradition. In all cases where the Hindu nation is forced to wage a war on the principles of righteousness (*upapannam*), leaders of India are ordered to fight in defence of their culture and to consider

---

यदृच्छया चोपपन्नं स्वर्गद्वारमपावृतम् ।
सुखिनः क्षत्रियाः पार्थ लभन्ते युद्धमीदृशम् ॥ ३२ ॥

yadrchayā copapannaṁ svarga-dvāram-apāvṛtaṁ,
sukhinaḥ kṣatriyāḥ pārtha labhante yuddham-īdṛśam. 32

themselves fortunate to get the chance to serve the country. Such battlefields are the wide-open gates to Heaven for the defending heroes who fight diligently on the side of *Dharma*.

It is interesting to note how Lord Krishna, in the scheme of his exhortations comes down slowly from the highest pinnacles of *Vedantic* ideologies to the lower plane of material philosophy, and still lower down to the point of view of an average worldly man. From all these different levels, he views the problem and presents Arjuna with the same logical conclusion that the war must be fought.

IT IS INDEED A FACT THAT IT IS YOUR DUTY, AND NOW IN CASE YOU RENOUNCE IT AND RUN AWAY FROM THE BATTLEFIELD, THEN:

33. *But if you will not fight this righteous war, then having abandoned your own duty and fame, you shall incur sin.*

In case you refuse to engage yourself in this glorious war, then not only will you be renouncing your own 'personal call-of-character' (*swadharma*) and honour, in not having fulfilled your noble duty, but will also incur a positive sin. Not to face this army of un-Aryan forces is as much sinful as to murder those who do not deserve such a treatment.

Dharma, as we have already explained is the Law-of-Being. Every living creature has taken up its form and has come into the world of objects for one great purpose, which is to

---

अथ चेत्त्वमिमं धर्म्यं संग्रामं न करिष्यसि ।
ततः स्वधर्मं कीर्तिं च हित्वा पापमवाप्स्यसि ॥ ३३ ॥

atha cettvamimaṁ dharmyaṁ saṁgrāmaṁ na kariṣyasi,
tataḥ svadharmaṁ kīrtiṁ ca hitvā pāpamavāpṣyasi 33.

gain an exhaustion of its existing mental impressions. The bundle of *vasanas* with which an individual has arrived into a particular incarnation is called his 'personal call-of-character' (*swadharma*). When classified thus, Arjuna falls within the group of the 'kingly' (*Kshatriya*), who are characterised by adventurous heroism and an insatiable thirst for honour and fame.

Not to make use of the evolutionary chances provided by life is to reject and refuse the chances provided for a *vasana*-catharsis. By not exhausting the old *vasanas*, one will be living under a high *vasana*-pressure when the existing tendencies are crowded out by the influx of new tendencies. Not fighting the war, Arjuna may run away from the field, but he will certainly come to regret his lost chances, since his mind is so composed that he can find complete relief and solace only by living the intensely dangerous life of the battlefield. A boy with tendencies for art cannot be successfully trained to become a businessman or an economist, since these are contrary to his nature. If an over-anxious parent in the name of love projects upon a growing child his own intentions and plans, we invariably find that the young boy will have a crushed personality.

Examples of this type are seen everywhere in the world, especially in the spiritual field. There are many seekers with over-enthusiasm for spiritual development, who, at the mere appearance of a misery, or at the threat of a sorrow, decide to run away into the jungles 'seeking God'. They invariably end up in a lifelong tragic disaster. They have within them sensuous *vasanas* which can be satisfied only in the embrace of a family under the roof of their own tenement, but rejecting them all, they reach the Himalayan caves and then all day through, they can neither meditate upon the Lord, nor find a field for sensuous enjoyment. Naturally they entertain more and more agitations in their minds, otherwise called sin (*papa*).

Sin in Hinduism is "a mistake of the mind in which it acts contrary to its essential nature as the Self". Any act of sensuousness which the mind pants for in the world-of-objects, hoping to get thereby a joy and satisfaction, creates necessarily within itself increasing agitations and this type of a mistake of the mind is called a sin.

CONTINUING THUS, NOT ONLY WILL YOU HAVE GIVEN UP YOUR DUTY AND FAME BUT ALSO:

34. *People too, will recount your everlasting dishonour and to the one who has been honoured, dishonour is more than death.*

To a famous hero, dishonour is worse than death. This is another argument that Krishna brings forth to persuade his friend to give up his hesitation in fighting the Great War. The general import is that if Arjuna were to abandon the fight, he could do so only because of his cowardice, since the cause of the war is righteous. Certainly, there is an under-current of sympathy in Krishna's words as he realises that however great a hero Arjuna might be, even he could be weakened by wrong emotionalism.

अकीर्तिं चापि भूतानि कथयिष्यन्ति तेऽव्ययाम् ।
संभावितस्य चाकीर्तिर्मरणादतिरिच्यते ॥ ३४ ॥

akīrtiṁ cāpi bhūtāni kathayiṣyanti te 'vyayām,
saṁbhāvitasya cākīrtir maraṇādatiricyate 34.

MOREOVER:

35. *The great battalion commanders will think that you have withdrawn from the battle through fear; and you will be looked down upon by those who had thought much of you and your heroism in the past.*

Continuing the common man's point of view arguments, Krishna says here that not only will the world blame him and history recount his infamy, but immediately the great warriors and battalion commanders (*Maharathas*) in the enemy lines will also start ridiculing him. They will laugh and say that the great archer Arjuna ran away from the battlefront because of sheer cowardice. They will interpret his conscientious objections against the fratricidal war as an act of cowardice of a hero during a weak moment in his life. No soldier can stand such dishonour, especially when it comes from one's own equals among the enemy lines.

MOREOVER:

36. *And many unspeakable words will your enemies speak caviling about your powers. What can be more painful than this?*

Finding that Arjuna is conspicuously reacting well to these arguments, Krishna drives home to him the folly of running

---

भयाद्रणादुपरतं मंस्यन्ते त्वां महारथा: ।
येषां च त्वं बहुमतो भूत्वा यास्यसि लाघवम् ॥ ३५ ॥
bhayādraṇād uparataṁ mansyante tvāṁ mahārathāḥ,
yeṣāṁ ca tvaṁ bahumato bhūtvā yāsyasi lāghavam 35.

अवाच्यवादांश्च बहून्वदिष्यन्ति तवाहिता: ।
निन्दन्तस्तव सामर्थ्यं ततो दु:खतरं नु किम् ॥ ३६ ॥
avācyavādāṁś ca bahūn vadiṣyanti tavāhitāḥ,
nindantas tava sāmarthyaṁ tato duḥkhataraṁ nu kim 36.

away from the battlefront. It will be intolerable when his enemies scandalize his glorious name and his chivalry in foul language, too indecent even for words. Not only will history record for all times his cowardly retreat but even while he lives, he will be pointed out and laughed at as a 'hero' who ran away from the battlefield.

37. *Slain, you will obtain heaven; victorious, you will enjoy the earth; therefore, stand up O son of Kunti, determined to fight.*

In case he has to give up his life on the warfront while fighting for such a noble cause, he shall certainly enter the 'Heaven of the Heroes' (*Veera-swarga*) to stay and to enjoy there for aeons. In case he wins, he shall certainly come to rule over the kingdom and enjoy in the world, and thereafter he shall go to Heaven to enjoy there the status of a mighty hero who fought championing the cause of *Dharma*. Either way he will gain because he was on the side of the good, with the war aims of the Pandavas being stoutly righteous.

Therefore, meaning, for all the reasons so far enumerated,[1] "ARISE, RESOLVED TO FIGHT". Earlier on, Arjuna, after expressing his feelings of grief and despair had sat inert and motionless upon throwing down his weapons.[2] Krishna asks his friend to come out of this moodiness and dejection, and be determined to fight the noble war.

हतो वा प्राप्स्यसि स्वर्गं जित्वा वा भोक्ष्यसे महीम् ।
तस्मादुत्तिष्ठ कौन्तेय युद्धाय कृतनिश्चयः ॥ ३७ ॥

hato vā prāpsyasi svargaṁ jitvā vā bhokṣyase mahīm,
tasmāduttiṣṭha kaunteya yuddhāya kṛtaniścayaḥ 37.

1 *Shlokas* 30-37, apart from the philosophical arguments given from *shloka* 11 onwards.

2 Refer Ch.I *shloka* 47; Ch.II *shloka* 9

The call to war is justified because of the particular situation in the Mahabharata wherein the *Geeta* was given out. Generalising the call of Krishna, we may say that it is a divine call to Man to discard his melancholy dejections in the face of life's challenges and to come forward to play as best as he can 'the game of life', with a firm determination to strive and to win. In this line, we have the universality of the *Geeta* explicitly brought out for those who understand and find its vast application to the community of man.

NOW LISTEN TO THE ADVICE I OFFER TO YOU ON YOUR INNER ATTITUDE, WHILE YOU FIGHT THE BATTLE:

38. Having made pleasure and pain, gain and loss, victory and defeat the same, engage in battle for the sake of battle; thus, you shall not incur sin.

From this stanza onwards we have a slight hint about the technique of *Karma Yoga* as explained in the *Geeta*. In the introduction we have stated that the second chapter is almost a summary of the whole *Geeta*. Later on, we shall see how the path of Devotion is also indicated in brief in this very chapter.

In this stanza we have Krishna's first direct statement on the technique of Self-Perfection and as such, a very careful study of it will be extremely fruitful to all students of the *Geeta.*

सुखदुःखे समे कृत्वा लाभालाभौ जयाजयौ ।
ततो युद्धाय युज्यस्व नैवं पापमवाप्स्यसि ॥ ३८ ॥
sukhaduḥkhe same kṛtvā lābhālābau jayājayau,
tato yuddhāya yujyasva naivaṁ pāpamavāpsyasi 38.

The three pairs-of-opposites mentioned here are distinct experiences at the three levels of our mortal existence. PLEASURE AND PAIN are the 'intellectual' awareness of experiences favourable and unfavourable; GAIN AND LOSS conceptions indicate the 'mental' zone where we feel the joys of meeting and the sorrows of parting. CONQUEST AND DEFEAT indicate the 'physical' fields wherein at the level of the body, we ourselves win or let others win. The advice that Krishna gives is that, one must learn to keep oneself in equilibrium in all these different vicissitudes at the respective levels of existence.

If one were to enter the sea for a bath, one must know the art of sea-bathing or else the incessant waves will play rough on the person, and may even sweep him off his feet and drag him to a watery grave. But he who knows the art of saving himself by ducking beneath the mighty waves, or by riding over the lesser ones alone can enjoy a sea-bath. To hope for all the waves to end, or to expect the waves not to trouble one while one is in the sea, is to order the sea to be something other than itself for one's convenience! This is exactly what a foolish man does in life. He expects life to be without waves, but life is ever full of waves. Pleasure and pain, gain and loss, conquest and defeat must arise in the waters of life or else it is a complete stagnation - it is almost a death.

If life be thus a tossing, stormy sea at all times, and it should be so, then we, who have entered life, must know the art of living it, being unaffected either by the rising crests, or by the sinking hollows in it. To identify ourselves with any of them is to be tossed about on the surface, and not just to stand astride like a lighthouse which has its foundations built on the bedrock of the very sea. Here Krishna advises Arjuna while inviting him to fight, that he should enter the contest and keep himself unaffected by the usual dissipating mental tendencies that come to everyone, while in activity. This equanimity of the mind alone can bring out the beam of inspiration, and give to one's achievements the glow of a real success.

It is very well known that in all activities, inspired work gathers to itself a texture of divine perfection which cannot be imitated or oft-repeated. Be he a poet or an artist, a doctor or a speaker; irrespective of his profession, whenever an individual is at his best, his masterpiece is always accepted by all as a 'work of inspiration'. When we thus work with the thrilled ecstasy of an unknown mood called 'inspiration', the ideas, thoughts, and activity that come out of us have a ringing beauty of their own, which cannot be otherwise mechanically repeated by us. Thus Da Vinci could not repeat for a second time and copy on another piece of canvas the enigmatic smile of his Mona Lisa. Keats' pen could no more recapture for a second time the song of the Nightingale in its flight. Beethoven could never again beat out of his faithful piano a second Moonlight Sonata. Lord Krishna himself, when requested by Arjuna after the war to repeat the *Geeta* admitted his inability to do so!!

To the Western mind and understanding, 'inspiration' is an accidental and mysterious happening over which the mortal has no control at all. To the eastern *Rishis* inspired living is the real godly destiny of man, when he lives in perfect unison with the Self within. A balanced life – wherein we live as unaffected witnesses of even our own mind and intellect - is the realm of self-forgetfulness, where instead of becoming inefficient, our profession gathers the scintillating glow of a new dawn. This extra aura in any achievement is that, which raises an ordinary success to an 'inspired achievement'.

The *Yogis* of ancient Hindu-lore discovered a technique whereby the mind and intellect could be consciously brought to a steadiness and poise. This technique is called *Yoga*. The Hindus of the *Vedic* period knew, practised, and lived it. With their incomparable achievements, they provided for their country the golden era of the Hindus.

The philosophy of a country like India during the *Vedic* period must necessarily be Theistic, but it has its applications in all walks of life. If it fails in its all-round application, it cannot be a philosophy. A theory of life which has no universal application can at best be appreciated as the noble opinion of an individual, which may have its own limited application; but it can never be accepted as a philosophy.

In the entire scheme of *Bhagawan's* arguments so far, He has provided Arjuna with all the necessary reasons which a healthy intellect should discover for itself, before it comes to a reliable judgment upon the outer happenings. A mere spiritual consideration should not be the last word in the evaluation of all material situations. Every challenge should be estimated from the spiritual standpoint, as well as from the intellectual standpoint of reason, from the emotional level of ethics and morality, and from the physical level of tradition and custom. If all these considerations, without any contradiction, indicate a solitary truth, then that is surely the Divine Path that one should pursue at all costs..

Arjuna came to the delusory miscalculation of the situation because he evaluated the war only from the level of his sentiments. The opposing forces were teeming with his relations; to kill and exterminate them was indeed against the ethical point of view. But this emotionalism overpowered him, and at this moment of his total inward chaos, he completely lost sight of the other considerations that would have helped him to regain his balance. He surrendered, as a mind should, to Krishna, the inner discriminative capacity. Therefore, the Lord having undertaken to guide Arjuna provides him with all the available data gathered from different points of view. Throughout the *Geeta*, Krishna plays the part of the 'discriminative intellect' in an individual, a true charioteer in the *Upanishad*-sense* of the term.

After thus placing all the possible points of view about the problem – the spiritual, the intellectual, the ethical and the traditional for Arjuna's consideration – Krishna concludes in the earlier stanza that Arjuna must fight. In this stanza Krishna tries to explain how he should conduct himself in this undertaking. It has been said that he should fight the war with perfect detachment from all anxieties which generally come to an individual, when he identifies himself with the non-Self (*Anatma*); meaning that at the level of his intellect with the concept of pain and pleasure, at the level of his mind with the fears of gain and loss, and at his body-level with the restlessness of conquest and defeat.

---

* Refer 'General Introduction'.

Equanimity in all such mental challenges is a factor that ensures true success in life. We have explained earlier how the human mind is to be kept open while working in its given field of life, so that while living in the midst of life's battle, it can exhaust the *vasanas* that are already in it. This purgation i.e. catharsis of the Soul is the compelling purpose for which every living creature has arrived on the platform of manifested life. Viewed thus, each individual living creature, plant, animal or human, is but a bundle of *vasanas*.

The equanimity in the face of all situations as advised here is the secret method of keeping the mind ever open for its outflow. When it gets clouded by the ego-sense and the egoistic desires, the outflow is choked, and new tendencies start flooding in. The ego is born when an individual starts getting upset at all these pairs-of-opposites (*Dwandwas*), such as joy and sorrow, etc. The attempt to keep equanimous is successful, only if action is detached from the ego. Thus, mental purification (*vasana*-catharsis) is the benign result of real living and right action, and this is *Yoga*. This is explained in the next chapter of the *Geeta* in full detail, as *Karma Yoga*.

The philosophical theory of truth was described in the very opening of the Lord's message, and in order to drive home those conclusions into the practical mind of a man of action namely, Arjuna, Lord Krishna gave arguments from the standpoint of the common man. Ultimately, he concluded that Arjuna must fight and also explained as to what attitude he should fight with. Practical religion consists in living the philosophy one has understood.

HEREAFTER, THE SCHEME OF THE *GEETA* IN THE CHAPTER IS TO EXPLAIN THE TECHNIQUES OF LIVING

THE *VEDANTIC* PHILOSOPHY IN, AND THROUGH KARMA *YOGA*. HENCE SAYS THE LORD:

39. *This, which has been taught to thee, is wisdom concerning SANKHYA. Now listen to the wisdom concerning YOGA, having known which, O Partha, you shall cast off the bonds-of-action.*

What is so far taught consists of the '*Sankhya*', meaning, the logic of reasoning, by which the true nature of the Absolute Reality is comprehended, which can end for you all sorrows arising from grief, attachment, and the like. Krishna promises that hereafter he will try to explain the technique of attaining the wisdom (*Buddhi*), which is otherwise called *Buddhi-Yoga*, "devotion through work".

FRUITS OF ACTION (*Karma-phala*) that is the law-of-*Karma*, which is often misunderstood as the law-of-Destiny, forms a cardinal creed of the Hindus and a right understanding of it is absolutely essential to all students of the Hindu way-of-Life. If I am now justly punished in Delhi for a crime committed last year by Sri Ramana Rao in Madras, then certainly there must be something common between the criminal Ramana Rao previously in Madras and the saintly Chinmaya now in Delhi! The long arm of the law of the country discovering the identity of Ramana Rao in Chinmaya must have slowly crept from Madras to Delhi and ultimately booked the 'Swami' for the crime of Rao that he was!!

एषा तेऽभिहिता सांख्ये बुद्धिर्योगेत्विमां श्रृणु ।
बुद्ध्या युक्तो यया पार्थ कर्मबन्ध प्रहास्यसि ॥ ३९ ॥

eṣā te'bhihitā sāṅkhye buddhiyoge tvimāṁ śṛṇu
bud dhyā yukto yayā pārtha karmabandhaṁ prahāsyasi 39.

Similarly, the nature's justice is always perfect and therefore, if the Hindu philosophers accept that each of us individually suffers because of our crimes committed in another form, in a different locality, at a different period of time in the past, certainly there must be some identity between the sinner of the past and the sufferer in the present. This identity, the *shastra* says, is the mind-intellect-equipment in each one of us.

Each act willfully performed leaves an impression upon the mind of the actor according to the texture of the motive entertained. In order to work out and remove these impressions (*vasanas*-catharsis), each individual arrives at his specific field of activity in life. Sin-impressions in the mind can be wiped away only with the water of tears acting upon the mind, in an atmosphere of sobs and sighs. Thus every one gets his quota of chances to weep, which in many cases comes to be discovered later on as not so sorrowful, after all. A mind which has thus been completely purified, fails to see a situation really worth weeping for. Weeping in fact, is not ordered by the circumstances, but by the '*papa*-tendencies' in the mind of the miserable.

Merely because there is a record in my gramophone box, I will have no music. Even when it is placed on its disc and revolved at the required speed, it will not and cannot sing. Music can come out of it only when the needle is in contact with it. The unmanifest music in the disc can be brought to expression only through the sound-box. Similarly here, the mental impressions cannot by themselves bring either disaster or reward unless they are connected with the external world through the needle-point of our egocentric self-assertion.

The one, who lives, as we found in the earlier verse, in perfect equanimity in all conditions, must necessarily come to live in a realm of his own, away from the pleasure and pain of the INTELLECT, the sobs of success and failure of the MIND, and the fears of loss and gain in the FLESH. To the degree, an individual detaches himself from his own body, mind and intellect; to that degree his ego is dead. Therefore, since the 'sufferer' is no longer available, there cannot be any more fruits-of-action for him to suffer.

When rightly understood, we shall realise during our discussions on this chapter, how this theory of Krishna has not the novelty of an original idea. The more intimately we understand it, the more we shall realise that Krishna has only given new vesture to an ancient idea. But due to this re-statement in the *Geeta,* of a cardinal truth of ancient Hinduism, a religion that was dying revived itself. From the days of its origin five thousand years before Christ was born, it is beckoning us today, even two thousand years after the Nazarene's death.

MOREOVER:

40. *In this there is no loss of effort, nor is there any harm (production of contrary results). Even a little of this knowledge, even a little practice of the YOGA, protects one from the great fear.*

नेहाभिक्रमनाशोऽस्ति प्रत्यवायो न विद्यते ।
स्वल्पमप्यस्य धर्मस्य त्रायते महतो भयात् ॥ ४० ॥

nehābhikramanāśo'sti pratyavāyo na vidyate
svalpamapyasya dharmasya trayāte mahato bhayāt 40.

Unfinished ritualistic acts will yield no fruits, just as ploughing and sowing are not fulfilled, if the sequence of actions as ploughing, watering, sowing, weeding, guarding, harvesting, etc. are not kept up exactly in that order. Similarly, some ritualistic acts, when not performed faithfully following all the strict injunctions, the chances are that the very same meritorious acts might result in sins accrued through the non-performance, or imperfect performance of enjoined acts. This sin is called in the language of ritualistic literature a *'Pratyavaya'*. In the material world also, we can find corresponding instances wherein a medicine misused may bring about a calamitous end for the patient.

These are the two dangers in the field of activities by which we are cheated of all our expected results. Krishna here as a *pukka** publicity agent of his own philosophy vigorously asserts that his technique of Action i.e. *Karma Yoga*, guarantees safety from these two main dangers.

THE WISDOM CONCERNING *SANKHYA* AND *YOGA* THUS FAR DESCRIBED IS OF THE FOLLOWING NATURE:

41. *Here, O Joy of the Kurus, Kurunandana, there is but a single-pointed determination; many-branched and endless are the thoughts of the irresolute.*

व्यवसायात्मिका बुद्धिरेकेह कुरुनन्दन ।
बहुशाखा ह्यनन्ताश्च बुद्धयोऽव्यवसायिनाम् ॥ ४१ ॥

a vyavasāyātmikā buddhirekeha kurunandana
bahuśākhā hyanantāśca buddhiyo'vyavasāyinām 41.

*Shrewd, seasoned or established – Ed.

In *Karma Yoga* which the Lord is now explaining, even the highest achievement of Self-realisation is possible, because here, the man works with one resolute determination, with a single-pointed mind. Those who perform actions while labouring under endless desires for results get their inner personality disintegrated. With a shattered, thousand-pronged mind, they are not able to consistently apply themselves to any line of action. Therefore, their endeavours invariably end in disastrous failures.

In this stanza lies the secret of Hindu success which is briefly hinted at, in hasty words. With a single-pointed mind, if an individual can entertain any single resolute-determination, and an action consistently directed towards its success, achievement must certainly result. But invariably, man when victimised by his ego entertains hundreds of desires that are often mutually contradictory, and therefore he comes to play upon these fields with an impoverished and exhausted mental strength. This is psychologically what we call 'self-cancellation of thoughts'. When this activity comes to plague the mental zone, it exhausts all the potentialities of man and loots away all his chances of success.

42. *Flowery speech is uttered by the unwise, taking pleasure in the eulogising words of VEDAS, O Partha, saying, "There is nothing else".*

यामिमां पुष्पितां वाचं प्रवदन्त्यविपश्चितः ।
वेदवादरताः पार्थ नान्यदस्तीति वादिनः ॥ ४२ ॥
yāmimāṁ puṣpitāṁ vācaṁ pravadantyavipaścitaḥ ।
vedavādaratāḥ pārtha nānyadastīti vādinaḥ 42.

43. *Full of desires, having heaven as their goal, they utter flowery words, which promise new birth as the reward of their actions, and prescribe various specific actions for the attainment of pleasure and Lordship.*

44. *For, those who cling to joy and Lordship, whose minds are drawn away by such teaching, are neither determinate and resolute nor are they fit for steady meditation and SAMADHI.*

Vyasa was one of the first daring revolutionaries in Hinduism who ever came up; to win back the Hindu culture from the decadence it had fallen into, in his time. The Bible of the Revolution that he created was the *Geeta*. His vigorous criticism is reflected in the words of Krishna, when he characterises the ritualistic portion of the *Vedas* as 'the flowery words of the unwise'. We have to live mentally in the orthodox atmosphere of that age to appreciate the daringness with which Vyasa then had to put up this criticism so strongly.

The ritualistic sections of the *Vedas* address those who are deeply attached to pleasure and power, whose

---

कामात्मान:स्वर्गपरा जन्मकर्मफलप्रदाम् ।
क्रियाविशेषबहुलां भोगैश्वर्यगतिं प्रति ॥ ४३ ॥
kāmātmānaḥ svargaparā janmakarmaphalapradām |
kriyāviśeṣabahulāṁ bhogaiśvaryagatiṁ prati 43.

भोगैश्वर्यसक्तानां तयापहृतचेतसाम् ।
व्यवसायात्मिका बुद्धि: समाधौ न विधीयते ॥ ४४ ॥
bhogaiśvaryaprasktānāṁ tayāpahṛtacetasām
vyavasāyātmikā buddhiḥ samadhau na vidhīyate 44.

discriminative power, the capacity to distinguish the Real from the Unreal, is stolen away from them, because they are concerned about the results and rewards of *Karma*. They were involved in the ritualism as such and not concerned with the Higher, to reach which these (rituals) are but the means.

These *Karmas* which promised the performer a post-mortem heavenly existence with supra-sensuous carnal pleasures are to be undertaken and laboriously pursued. In all these activities, man's inner personality has no time or chance to get integrated and evolved. Therefore, from the spiritual standpoint, Vyasa feels that they are methods of impotent religion. The ritualist gets involved in the means, without aspiring for the Real Goal!

Thus, as an expounder of the transcendental and the infinite, Krishna is here laughing at those who mistake the means for the end. The ritualistic portion is the means and the *Vedantic* portion dealing with realisation through meditation is the end. The *Karma Kanda* prepares the mind to single-pointedness, when it is pursued without specific desires (*Nishkama*). Such a prepared mind alone is fit for steady contemplation over the *Upanishadic* declarations.

The passage is concluded with the declaration that such persons who are tossed about by their desires shall never discover any experience of tranquillity in their inner life.

THE LORD NOW SPEAKS ABOUT THE RESULT ACCRUING TO THOSE LUSTFUL PERSONS

WHO ARE THUS WANTING (LACKING) IN DISCRIMINATION:

45. *The VEDAS deal with the three attributes; be you above these three attributes (GUNAS) O Arjuna, free yourself from the pairs-of-opposites, and ever remain in the SATTVA (goodness), freed from all thoughts of acquisition and preservation, and be established in the Self.*

The three inseparable *gunas* always remain in the inner constitution of every living creature, in varying proportions. The mind and the intellect are constituted of this triple-stuff. To go beyond these three temperaments is literally to go beyond the mind. If there is an alloy constituted of copper, zinc, and tin, and a pot is made of that alloy, then to remove all the tin, the zinc, and the copper from the pot is to destroy the pot completely. Tea is made up of hot water, tea leaves, sugar and milk. From a cup of tea if you are asked to remove these four components, it amounts to saying 'empty the cup'. In the direct language of the *Upanishads*, man has been advised to transcend the mind and the intellect, and they promise that the individual shall thereby rediscover himself to be God. This direct explanation came to frighten away the Hindu folk out of the *Aryan*-fold. Hence the 'call of the renaissance' here though meaning the same, puts it in different words when it says: "Arjuna, transcend the *gunas*".

त्रैगुण्यविषया वेदा निस्त्रैगुण्यो भवार्जुन ।
निर्द्वन्द्वो नित्यसत्त्वस्थो निर्योगक्षेम आत्मवान् ॥ ४५ ॥
traiguṇyaviṣayā vedā nistraiguṇyo bhavārjuna
nirdvandvo nityasattvastho niryogakṣema ātmavān 45.

If a medical doctor were to prescribe a medicine which is nowhere in the catalogue of any pharmaceutical company in the world and therefore not available in any bazaar, that prescription is certainly useless. Similarly, it may be a great prescription for Self-perfection when the Lord advises: "Be free from the triad of the *gunas*". However, it is useless, unless a student is practical-minded and adventurous enough to try to live this advice, and can be instructed as to how he can go beyond these instinctive temperaments in man, viz., unactivity (*sattva*), activity (*rajas*), and inactivity (*tamas*).

The second line in the stanza gives us a very practical and direct method of transporting ourselves from the realm of imperfection to the boundless regions of Bliss and Beatitude. Earlier, Krishna had indicated how Arjuna should enter the field and wage the war. The same mental equanimity is being advised here in a different language.

Pairs-of-opposites are the experiences in our life - such as joy and sorrow, health and disease, success and failure, heat and cold, etc. Each of them can be experienced and known only with reference to, and as a contrast to its opposite. Therefore the term 'pairs-of-opposites' (*Dwandwas*) envisages in its comprehensive meaning all the experiences of man in his life. Krishna advises Arjuna to be free from all the pairs-of-opposites (*Dwandwas*).

NITYA-SATTVA-STHAH: 'Ever established in purity' – The purity, *sattva*, the subtlest of the three *gunas*, often becomes impure by its contact with attachments and the consequent agitations (*rajas*) that attack the intellect with delusion and grief, and veil it from the right cognition of the Real Nature of things (*tamas*). To be established in purity (*sattva*) would, therefore, mean keeping ourselves least agitated, and so, least deluded in our perceptions of things and beings, and in our estimation of their true nature.

Yoga and *Kshema* in their meanings include all the activities of every living being in the universe. These are the two urges* which goad every one in all of one's activities. '*Yoga*' means 'to acquire' for the purposes of possessing; and *Kshema* means 'all efforts at preserving the acquired'. Thus the two terms *Yoga* and *Kshema* encompass all of our egocentric activities motivated by selfish desires to acquire, and compelled by the equally selfish wishes, to hoard and preserve what has been acquired. To renounce these two temperaments is to get away immediately from the two main fields that yield the poisonous harvest of extreme restlessness and sorrow in life.

It is very easy for a spiritual master to advise an aspirant to be "free from the pairs-of-opposites, remain ever pure and free from the natural appetites for acquisition, and from the usual greed for preservation". But the philosophy will be practical only when the seeker is advised as to HOW he can do so. This 'how' of it all has been indicated by the last

---

*These ideas should not be misunderstood and misinterpreted to mean that we the Hindus should not strive to embetter our conditions and diligently guard our national wealth, both secular and spiritual. By misreading our scriptures, we only have perpetrated many a sad crime against our own national responsibilities and social duties. A superficial study of this stanza may give us a delusory concept that Hinduism is 'a religion of the coward, for the coward, given out by a coward'. But historically it is clear that this assumption is a big lie.

As I said earlier, the *Geeta* is to be read against the background of its first chapter. If the terms in this chapter called '*Sankhya Yoga*' are to be understood properly, we must not forget that these were given out as an advice to Arjuna - a great hero on the battlefield, in order to redeem his potentialities from the muddy morass of dejection and despair, into which he had fallen and sunk.

word in the stanza: *Atmavan – meaning* "be established in the Self". The persecutions of the pairs-of-opposites, the instinct to be impure, the desire to possess, and the anxiety to preserve, all of these belong to the ego-centre, which is born when the Self identifies with the body, the mind, and the intellect; and the consequent ego suffers the pangs of anxieties, pains and sorrows.

To detach ourselves from these by keeping a constant sense of awareness of our pure Divine Nature is the 'path' shown in the *Geeta*. When established in the Self, the individual ego that is ever pure and free from all anxieties finds itself beyond the experiences of the world. Necessarily, he will be trans-*gunas*. One who is beyond the *gunas* has no more use of the *Veda* textbooks. He is the Master thereafter, to amend the *Vedas* or to add to them. He is the Master who shall give the Divine sanction for these very *Vedic* declarations.

IF ALL THOSE ENDLESS PROFITS WHICH ARE SAID TO RESULT FROM THE *VEDIC* RITUALS ARE NOT TO BE SOUGHT AFTER, THEN TO WHAT END ARE THEY TO BE PERFORMED AND DEDICATED TO *ISWARA*? LISTEN TO WHAT FOLLOWS:

46. *To the BRAHMANA who has known the Self, all the VEDAS are of so much use, as is a reservoir of water in a place where there is flood everywhere.*

यावानर्थ उदपाने सर्वतः संप्लुतोदके ।
तावान्सर्वेषु वेदेषु ब्राह्मणस्य विजानतः ॥ ४६ ॥

yāvānartha udapāne sarvataḥ samplutodake
tāvānsarveṣu vedeṣu brāhmaṇasya vijānataḥ 46.

A wonderful simile is used here, that is fully applicable in the context in which it is used. So long as there is no flood, everyone from the vicinity will have to reach the well to collect drinking water. Although everywhere there is a vein of water running under our feet, it is separated from us by the crust of the earth. For the spiritual seeker, the *Veda* is the only source of True Knowledge, and every one must necessarily go to the sacred book for that knowledge. But when the area is flooded with water and the wells and the tanks have disappeared in the spread of the flood, at that time the reservoir of water which used to be of service becomes merged in the spread of water that lies all round.

Similarly, the *Vedas,* meaning here 'the ritualistic portion' which promises fulfilment of the various desires can be useful only so long as the individual is riddled with delusory desires for sensuous satisfactions. To a sincere student and seeker of spirituality (*Brahmana*) who has 'come to experience the Self' (*Vijanatah*), these ritualistic portions of the *Vedas* become useless inasmuch as the benefits that they can give are comprehended in the perfection that he has come to live.

The *Karma Kanda* prescribes only rituals for the satisfaction of desires whereby the individuals can gain some finite joy, may be here or in the hereafter. Thus upon discovering the Self within oneself, the seeker comes to experience the infinite Bliss of the Divine, and all the pleasures derived from the performance of work enjoined in the *Vedas* are comprehended in the Bliss, which the realised soul experiences as the very Essence of his own Self. Everyone must admit that all those limited 'satisfactions' are comprehended in the Infinite Bliss of the experience of the Self.

This does not mean that Vyasa is ignoring or ridiculing the *Karma Kanda* of the *Vedas* as such. The whip of the 'Cowherd Boy' is descending upon the bare backs of the unintelligent, who have mistaken the means for the goal, and who consider that through ritualism and its promised joys, the Supreme or the Infinite can be gained. *Karma* when undertaken with no anxiety for the results integrates the personality. When a heart is thus purified, a clearer discriminative power comes to play through it, and in its light, Truth becomes self-evident. After having once realised the Infinite-Self spreading out all around without any dimensions or frontiers, the limited satisfaction promised by ritualism has no more charm for the man-of-Knowledge who is now the Self-realised.

The Knowledge that the *Veda* indicates is comprehended in Pure Knowledge, which is the nature of the Self. So long as the ego exists, it craves for the blessings of the *Vedas*. When the ego has ended, the Self in Its Infinite Divinity is capable of blessing even the *Vedas*. A student of mathematics, upon having successfully passed his postgraduate course need not read the arithmetic tables, since his greater knowledge comprehends this elementary study.

AND AS FOR YOU:

47. *Thy right is to work only, but never to its fruits; let the fruit-of-action be not thy motive, nor let thy attachment be to inaction.*

कर्मण्येवाधिकारस्ते मा फलेषु कदाचन ।
मा कर्मफलहेतुर्भूर्मा तेसङ्गोऽस्त्वकर्मणि ॥ ४७ ॥

karmaṇyevādhikāraste mā phaleṣu kadācana|
mā karmaphalaheturbhumār te saṅago'stvakarmaṇi 47.

The traditional belief of Hinduism has not at all been shaken up in the *Geeta*-theory viz. that single-pointed, divine-dedicated *Karma* without desire for the fruits shall bring about inner purification, which is a condition precedent to spiritual awakening. The *Geeta* only gives an exhaustive exposition of this idea to incorporate in it ALL the activities in the social and personal life, while in the *Vedas, Karma* meant only the religious and the ritualistic activities.

Philosophy is not a subject that can be rightly understood by hasty students. The stanza that is now under review when not properly understood would seem to indicate an impossible method. At the best, it would look as if it was a religious sanction for the poor to continue to be poor and a sacred permission for the rich to continue tyrannising over the poor! To act in life WITHOUT ANY EXPECTATION OF RESULTS would seem to be almost impossible to the one who is only trying to understand the stanza mentally. But when the same individual after his studies walks out into the open fields of life and tries to practise it there, he shall discover that this alone is the very secret of all the real achievements.

Earlier on we have indicated how Krishna, through his *Karma Yoga,* was showing 'the art of living and acting' in a spirit of Divine inspiration. Here also we shall find as we tussle with this idea in our attempt to digest it, that Krishna is advising Arjuna on the secret-art of living an inspired life.

Wrong imaginations are the bane of life and all failures in life can be directly traced to have arisen from an impoverished mental equanimity that is generally created by unintelligent entertainment of fears regarding possible failures. Almost all of us refuse to undertake great activities while being afraid of failures. Even those who dare to undertake noble endeavours invariably become nervous before they finish them, again due to their inward dissipation. To avoid such wasteful expenditure of mental energy, and work with the best that is in us, while being dedicated to the noble cause of the work undertaken is the secret prescription for the noblest creative inspiration. Such work must always end in a brilliant success. This is the eternal law-of-activity in the world.

The future is always carved out in the present. Tomorrow's harvest depends upon today's ploughing and sowing. But in the fear of facing possible dangers to the crops if a farmer wastes his present chances of thoroughly ploughing and carefully sowing at the right time, it is guaranteed that he shall not have any harvest at all. The present moments are to be invested intelligently and well, so that we may reap a better time in the future. The past is dead; the future is not yet born. If one becomes unhealthy and inefficient in the present, certainly he has no reason to hope for a greater future.

This fundamental truth that is very well-known and easily comprehended by all, is in the language of the *Geeta* a simple statement: "If success you seek, then never strive with a mind dissipated with anxieties and fears about the fruits." In this connection it is very interesting to dissect carefully and discover exactly what the *shastra* means when it says; 'fruits-of-action'. In fact the reward of an action – when we understand it properly – is not anything different from the action itself. An action done in the PRESENT when is conditioned by a FUTURE-time appears as the fruit-of-action. In fact, the action ends or fulfils itself only in its reaction, and the reaction is not anything different from the action. An action performed in the present when defined in terms of a future moment is its reaction. Therefore, to worry over and get ourselves preoccupied with the anxieties for the rewards of actions is to escape from the dynamic PRESENT moment and live in a FUTURE moment that is not yet born! In short, the Lord's advice here is a call to man not to waste his present moment in fruitless dreams and fears, but to bring out his best, all of the best from within him, to the PRESENT moment, and vitally live every moment. The promise is that the future shall take care of itself, and shall provide the *Karma Yogin* with the achievements that are divine and accomplishments that are supreme.

In effect therefore, Arjuna is advised: "All that is given to you now is to act upon, and having known the cause of action to be a noble one, to bring into the activity all that is best in you and forget (immerse) yourself in the activity. Such an inspired action is sure to bear fruit, and again it has its own reward-spiritual."

The stanza gives the four injunctions while guiding us to be true workers. A real *Karma Yogin* is the one who understands that (a) his concern is with action alone; (b) he has no concern with results; (c) he should not entertain the motive of gaining a fixed (specific) fruit for a given action; and (d) these ideas do not mean that he should sit back courting inaction. In short, the advice is to make the worker release himself from all of his mental preoccupations, and thus through work make him live in the joy and ecstasy of inspired self-forgetfulness. The work itself is his reward; he gets himself drunk with the joy and satisfaction of a noble work done. The work is the means; the Higher Self-experience alone is the Goal-Divine.

By thus reacting readily to all external challenges, with his devoted attention upon Him, one can find peace easily. A bosom thus purged of its existing *vasana*-bondages is, to that extent considered to be better purified for the purposes of meditation and the final *Vedantic*-realisation of the Infinite glory of the Self.

IF A MAN SHOULD NOT PERFORM WORK PROMPTED BY DESIRES FOR THEIR RESULT, HOW THEN SHOULD HE PERFORM IT? THE REPLY IS AS FOLLOWS:

48. *Perform action O Dhananjaya, abandoning attachment, being steadfast in YOGA, and balanced in success and failure. Evenness of mind is called YOGA.*

From this stanza onwards we have an exhaustive discussion on the technique of *Karma Yoga* as conceived by Krishna in his Doctrine of Action, and expounded upon, in Vyasa's *Geeta*. A complete technique of how one can live the life as a truly inspired worker is explained here. To any careful student who understands all the implications of the terms, it must be clear that a complete effacement of the ego and its vanities is to be achieved to succeed on this path. This is gained by practising the equipoise that was mentioned in the previous stanzas.

In this stanza for the first time, the term *Yoga* has been used in the sense of the 'evenness of mind' through work. Before it concludes, we also get an exhaustive definition of the term *Yoga* as used in the stanza.

योगस्थ: कुरु कर्माणि सङ्गं त्यक्त्वा धनञ्जय ।
सिद्ध्यसिद्ध्यो: समो भूत्वा समत्वं योग उच्यते ॥ ४८ ॥
yogasthaḥ kuru karmāṇi saṅgaṁ tyaktvā dhanañjaya,
siddhyasiddhyoḥ samo bhūtvā samatvaṁ yoga ucyate 48.

'Evenness of mind', the tranquillity of mental composure in facing all pairs-of-opposites* is defined here as *Yoga*. Defined thus, the term *Yoga* indicates a special condition of the mind in which it comes to a neutral equilibrium, while in all the ebb and flow of life's tides. The instructions in the stanza advise us that desireless actions can be performed only when one gets completely established in *Yoga*. Here the terms precisely paint what Vyasa's definition means.

Not only is it sufficient that a true worker should act in the world being established in equipoise and equanimity, but that he should, amidst the changes of the world, also reinforce this poise, through renunciation of his 'attachment' (*sanga*) to the immediate fruits of his actions.

We shall try to enquire into the concept of 'attachment', as mentioned here, which a seeker should renounce, so that he may become more efficient in performing inspired activities. To all the sincere students who have so far followed the Lord's words, it should be clear that the term 'attachment' here means all factors against which Krishna has already warned us in the earlier stanzas, and has insisted that we must renounce them all, viz. wrong imaginations, false expectations, daydreams about the fruits-of-actions, anxieties for the results, and fears for future calamities that have not yet appeared to threaten our lives. When it is put thus, as a list of mistakes to be avoided, any true *Karma Yogin*, who is striving upon the path of *Yoga* will find it impossible to practise it. But when we analyse this further with our understanding of the *Upanishads*, we can easily solve the riddle.

* As indicated in Verse 38

All of the above mentioned nerve-racking mistakes belong to the delusory ego-centre. When we analyse closely the stuff of which the ego is made up, we can easily find that it is a bundle consisting of the MEMORIES OF THE PAST, AND HOPES AND EXPECTATIONS FOR THE FUTURE. The dead moments that are no more, constitute the past. The future is unborn, and does not yet belong to us. To live in the ego therefore, is to live either in the burial grounds of dead moments, or in the womb of time where the unborn future now rests. By indulging in all of these preoccupations, we lose the immediate moments given to us to act upon, to strive, to earn, and to achieve. It is this unintelligent squandering of the wealth of the present chances through our broodings and imaginations, that is hinted about here, by the genius of Vyasa when he says, "Act while established in equanimity, abandoning attachment".

Thus in complete self-forgetfulness to get intoxicated with the activities undertaken in the present is to live vitally, fully, and entirely with all the best that is in us. To dissolve ourselves thus – our past, our future, our hopes, our fears – into the fiery contents of the PRESENT is to work in inspiration. Inspired work ever promises the greatest returns.

An artist while at work, forgetting himself in the very ecstasy of his work, is an example. One need not for that matter be even a great artist. The one who is working interestedly with all his mind and intellect on any piece of work will not be aware immediately of any chance intruder. It will take time for the artist to come down from the realms of his joyous mood to the crystallisation of the ego in him to recognise the intruder, to understand his enquiry, and give him an intelligent answer. In all inspired activities, the worker forgets himself in the work that he is doing.

In all such activities, when the worker has gained almost a state of self-forgetfulness, he will not care for success or failure of his activity because, to worry for the results is to worry for the future, and to live in the future is not to live in the present. Inspiration is the joyous content of thrilled ecstasy of each immediate moment. It is said that this content of a moment in itself is 'the entire Infinite Bliss'.

"Established thus in equanimity, (upon) renouncing all of the egocentric attachments, forgetting to worry over the results of success or failure in the activities, act on", says in effect Krishna to Arjuna; and he adds that the great *Yoga* means to work thus with equipoise in all situations.

IN COMPARISON WITH ACTION THUS PERFORMED WITH EVENNESS OF MIND, KRISHNA DECLARES:

49. *Far lower than the YOGA-of-wisdom is action, O Dhananjaya. Seek thou refuge in wisdom; wretched are they whose motive is the 'fruit'.*

Work done with a mind undisturbed by anxieties for the results is indeed superior to the work done by a dissipated mind, ever worrying over the results. Here the term, '*Buddhi Yoga*' has tickled some commentators to discover in it a special *Yoga* as advised by the *Geeta*. I personally think that it is too

---

दूरेण ह्यवरं कर्म बुद्धियोगाद्धनञ्जय ।
बुद्धौ शरणमन्विच्छ कृपणाः फलहेतवः ॥ ४९ ॥

dñreãa hyavaraṣ karma buddhiyogṇddhanañjaya
buddhau řaraãamanviccha kṛpaãṇḶ phalahetavaḶ 49.

much of a laboured theory. *Buddhi* – as defined in the *Upanishads* – is the determining factor in the 'inner-equipment'; *Nishchyatmika* is 'intellect'; *Samshayatmika* is 'mind'. Thus when the thought flow is in a state of flux and agitated, it is called the 'mind'. When it is single-pointed, calm, and serene in its own determination, it is called the 'intellect'. Thus *Buddhi Yoga* means 'to be established in devotion to the intellect'. Being steady in your conviction, with your mind perfectly under the control of your discriminative intellect, to live thus as a master of your inner and outer world is called *Buddhi Yoga*. In *Buddhi Yoga* we pursue our duties without ever losing sight of our ultimate Goal in Life.

Upon analysing the meaning of the stanza in terms of what we have already seen regarding the split-personality and its cure through *vasana*-purgation*, we may interpret *Buddhi Yoga* as an individual's attempt to live and act from the zone of the intellect, which freely controls the mind's functions, and readily receives faithful obedience from the mind. The attempt of the mind to work in union with the intellect - the 'objective' mind working under the control and the order of the 'subjective' mind - is called *Buddhi Yoga*. By so doing, instead of incurring increasing liabilities of new *vasana*-bondages, the individual gains a release from the mental congestion created by the existing *vasanas*. Thus when an individual completely surrenders his ego, he is said to be 'Established in *Buddhi Yoga*'. Hence it is said, "SEEK REFUGE IN *BUDDHI*" meaning: "let your mind be perfectly under the control and direction of the intellect".

---

* See 'General Introduction' with Diagrams 'A' and 'B'.

There is a solid reason why we should live under the control of the intellect. Those who live in the mental zone being tossed about by the mind's tribulations get agitated by anxiety for the fruits-of-actions. Such people are termed here as 'wretched'. It is a powerful statement by which Vyasa condemns such thoughtless unintelligent people as WRETCHED ARE THEY WHO ACT FOR THE RESULTS. When understood properly, this is a wonderful guidance by following which we can totally eliminate all failures in life. Efficient activity in the present alone can order great results.

They are 'wretched' because they will be - in their desire-prompted activities - incurring new *vasanas* and thus will be thickening the veil of ignorance of their own glorious Divinity. Unselfish work performed in a spirit of dedication and egoless surrender is the secret method of exhausting our *vasana*-store. Such a mind alone when purged clean can reflect the Self clearly, and come to discover the Eternal God-hood.

NOW LEARN WHAT RESULTS HE GAINS WHO PERFORMS HIS DUTY WITH EVENNESS-OF-MIND:

50. *Endowed with the Wisdom of evenness-of-mind, one casts off in this life both good deeds and evil deeds; therefore, devote yourself to YOGA, Skill in action is YOGA. ?*

One who has an evenness of temper accomplished by his perfect withdrawal from the realm of sentiments and

---

बुद्धियुक्तो जहातीह उभे सुकृतदुष्कृते ।
तस्माद्योगाय युज्यस्व योगः कर्मसु कौशलम् ॥ ५० ॥

buddhiyukto jahātīha ubhe sukṛtaduṣkṛte
tasmādyogāya yujyasva yogaḥ karmasu kauśalam 50.

emotions, and who is established in his resolute intellect, gets himself transported from the arena of both the good and the bad, merit and demerit. The concept of good and bad is essentially of the mind, and the reactions of merit and demerit are left on the mental composition in the form of *vasanas* or *samskaras*. He, who is not identifying with the stormy sea of the mind, will not be thrown up or sunk down by the huge waves of *vasanas*. This idea is explained here by the term *Buddhi Yuktah;* the one whose actions are guided by the clear vision of his higher and diviner Goal.

The *Geeta* throughout this section is sincerely calling upon man not to live on the outskirts of his personality, which are constituted of the worlds of sense-objects, the physical body, and the mind; but to enter into the realm of the intellect and from there to assert his natural manliness. Man is the supreme creature in the kingdom of the living because of the rational capacities of his discriminative intellect. As long as man does not utilise this special equipment within him, he cannot claim his heritage as man.

Arjuna was asked by Krishna not to be a vain and hysterical person, but to be a he-man and therefore ever a master of all his external situations. The great hero, Arjuna, became so frail and weak because he started living in delusory identification with the sense of his own physical security, and with his various emotional attachments.

He, who lives constantly asserting his full evolutionary status as man becomes free from the chains and bondages of all his past impressions (*vasanas*) which he must have gathered in his pilgrimage through the different embodiments.

"Therefore, apply yourself" advises Krishna, "to the devotion of action-*Yoga*". In this context again, Vyasa is giving a definition of *Yoga* as he means it here. Earlier, he had already explained that "Evenness of mind is *Yoga*". Now he rewrites the same definition more comprehensively and says, "*Yoga* is dexterity in action".

In a science-book if the very same term is defined differently in every chapter, it would bring about confusion in its understanding. How is it then that in the science of Religion, we find different definitions of the same term? This riddle solves itself as soon as we carefully attempt an intimate understanding of the definition. The earlier definition is being incorporated in the latter one, because otherwise 'evenness of mind is *Yoga*' may be misunderstood as a mere 'evenness of mind' producing inaction and slothfulness. In this definition such a misunderstanding is completely removed and thus *Karma Yoga* as indicated in the all-comprehensive meaning implied herein indicates the art of working with perfect mental equilibrium in all the different conditions as indicated by the term 'pairs-of-opposites' (*Dwandwas*).

After dissecting this stanza thus, we come to understand what exactly the Lord's intention is. When *Yoga* i.e. 'the art of working without desire' is pursued, the *Karma Yogin* becomes detached from all of the existing *vasanas* within himself, both the good and the bad. The *vasana*-pressure in an individual causes restlessness within. The inner-equipment that has become peaceful and serene is called the pure *Antah-Karana*, which is an unavoidable prerequisite for consistent, discriminative self-application in meditation. Thus all actions when properly pursued become a means for the ultimate end of realising the Self through meditation, with a pure mind.

We have here yet another example of Vyaṣa using the frightening word *Yoga* in a tamer context, in order to make his society of that time feel at ease with it.

WHY SHOULD WE CULTIVATE* THIS EVENNESS OF MIND AND CONSEQUENTLY AN EXTRA DEXTERITY IN ACTION?

51. *The wise, possessed of knowledge, having abandoned the fruits of their actions, freed from the fetters of birth, go to the State which is beyond all evil.*

Being a man of action, extremely intelligent, and having not yet developed any blind faith in Lord Krishna's divine potentialities, Arjuna still questions mentally, And the Lord, anticipating his doubt, and explains here why a man of true devotion to work, should act, and with perfect evenness of mind strive to achieve. The wise - meaning those who know the art of true living - undertake all work, maintaining in themselves the full evenness of the mind, and thus abandon all anxieties for the fruits of their actions. These two conditions, under which the wise ones work, bring out fully the picture of an individual who acts upon renouncing both the ego and the ego-motivated desires.

कर्मजं बुद्धियुक्ता हि फलं त्यक्त्वा मनीषिण: ।
जन्मबन्धविनिर्मुक्ता: पदं गच्छन्त्यनामयम् ॥ ५१ ॥

karmajaṁ buddhiyuktā hi phalaṁ tyaktavā manīṣiṇaḥ
janmabandhavinirmuktāḥ padaṁ gacchantyanāmayan 51.

* Refer to Shloka *38, Chapter II.*

By identifying with the agitations of the mind, the ego is born. The ego so born gets riddled with desires as it gets anxious for the fruits-of-actions. When one works with neither the ego nor desires, one achieves *vasana*-purgation. This is possible only when one always has the Higher Goal in view.

52. *When your intellect crosses beyond the mire of delusion, then you shall attain to indifference as to what has been heard and what is yet to be heard.*

When the intellect crosses over the jumble of delusion and it sloughs off its delusions, (the stanza here assures Arjuna that) it will develop disgust "FOR ALL THAT IS ACTUALLY HEARD AND FOR THAT, WHAT IS YET TO BE HEARD". Here the term "WHAT IS YET TO BE HEARD" must be understood as a representative term that is standing for all "sense experiences that are yet to be experienced". Naturally so! When the intellect becomes purer it loses all its erstwhile charm for sense experiences – namely, what it had before, and what it may gain in the future.

Essentially Godly and Divine, the Spiritual Consciousness seems to fall under a self-delusion. When analysed, it becomes perfectly evident as to its effects. This cause of delusion is conceived of as the indescribable power called *Maya*. Like unmanifest electricity, *Maya* as such is not perceptible, except in its different manifestations. It is a phenomenon that can

---

यदा ते मोहकलिलं बुद्धिर्व्यतितरिष्यति ।
तदा गन्तासि निर्वेदं श्रोतव्यस्य श्रुतस्य च ॥ ५२ ॥
yadā te mohakalilaṁ buddhirvyatitariṣyati
tadā gantāsi nirvedaṁ śrotavyasya śrutasya ca 52.

be fully estimated and accounted for through its varied expressions.

Upon observing and analysing the effects of *Maya* within the constitution of all individualised and embodied souls, the *Vedantic* masters have beautifully concluded that it comes to play in two distinct modes of expression, at two different layers of the human personality. Thus at the intellectual level, it expresses itself as a film of doubt and hesitation in its understanding, or experiencing, of the Self in us. This expression *Maya* is coined by the Masters to mean the 'Veiling-Power' (*Avarana-Shakti*).

Due to this mist of ignorance that envelops the intellect, when it is unconscious of the Spiritual Reality behind it, the mind starts projecting the world of the not-Self and superimposes upon it two firm ideas that: (a) 'it is true' (*Satyattwa*), (b) 'I am nothing other than the projected world' (*Atmabuddhi*). This is *Maya*'s expression as the 'Projecting-Power' (*Vikshepa-Shakti*).

In this stanza it is said that once the intellect in us is purified through the art of steady-work called Devotion-through-work', it becomes possible for it to peep over the veil of ignorance that separates it from the splendour of the Spiritual Entity. When the intellect sloughs off its delusions, it goes beyond its attachment for the charms of the sensuous world. But before this happens, the intellect being ignorant of its spiritual destiny struggles to fulfill itself, and then surges forward, seeking satisfaction amongst the finite sense-objects of the world.

When the intellect discovers in itself a capacity to pierce through the dreary veil of ignorance, it comes to live its own

Real Nature of Bliss Infinite. Each fleeting joy in the sense-world only sharpens its appetite for the Infinite Bliss, which is Its Real Nature. To the extent that the clouds have moved and the sun has emerged, to that extent he who is warming himself up at the fireside moves away from that fireplace and walks into the openness, to bask in the all-enveloping warmth of the blazing sun. Similarly, to the extent that the illusion of ignorance melts away in an integrated intellect, to that extent its wanderings in the sensuous-world are curtailed.

The sense-world is beautifully indicated by two representative terms: 'what has been heard' (*Shrutam*) and 'what is yet to be heard' (*Shrotavyam*). We must include therein 'the seen and the unseen', 'the smelt and the unsmelt', 'the tasted and the not-tasted', and 'the touched and not-yet-touched'. The intellect of such a purified *Karma-Yogin* does not relive its memory of the sensuous joys that it had experienced in the past, and also it does not remember that it has to experience still more joys in the future through the sense organs, in the world of sense-objects.

If we take the word meaning of these terms literally, we get the usual interpretation of the commentators: "When a seeker's mind is not tossed about by the seemingly different and often opposing conclusions of philosophers, when they do not upset him any more, then he is established in inward purity."

SHANKARA CONNECTS THIS STANZA WITH THE FOLLOWING: "YOU MAY NOW ASK, WHEN SHALL I ATTAIN THE TRUE CONVICTION OF THE SELF? (WILL IT BE) AFTER CROSSING BEYOND THE VEIL OF IGNORANCE, AND OBTAIN WISDOM THROUGH THE

DISCRIMINATION OF THE SELF AND THE NOT-SELF?" LISTEN:

53. *When your intellect - though perplexed by what you have heard - shall stand immovable and steady in the Self, then you shall attain Self-realisation.*

When one's intellect comes to a steady equipoise, and is UNDISTURBED by any of the experiences that reach one through the five great archways of knowledge, then one is considered as having attained *Yoga*.

The mind gets agitated mainly due to the flooding-in of the ever-new rush of stimuli from the outer world. Sense-organs are the antennae through which the world's tickling signals creep in and disturb the mental-pool. One is considered as having attained *Yoga* only when one – even in the midst of enjoying sensuous pleasures, and while the sense organs are letting in a flood of stimuli - does not get at all disturbed within one's inner serenity and equipoise This idea is better developed and exhaustively dealt with later in the chapter, where Krishna enumerates the visible qualities and the perceptible signs of one established in Wisdom (*Sthita-Prajna*).

The discussion done so far makes Arjuna so interested that he is now no more under the influence of his hysteria. He has come to forget his dejection and sorrow, and is now taking an active interest in Krishna's exposition. He could

---

श्रुतिविप्रतिपन्ना ते यदा स्थास्यति निश्चला ।
समाधावचला बुद्धिस्तदा योगमवाप्स्यसि ॥ ५३ ॥

śrutivipratipannā te yadā sthāsyati niścalā,
samādhāvacalā buddhis tadā yogamavāpsyasi 53.

not control himself from expressing his sincere enquiry as to what exactly is the nature of such a perfected one, who is beyond the storms of sensuousness. The question evidently shows that though Arjuna's intellect had somehow come to appreciate Krishna's theory, something within him was not quite ready yet to accept it fully.

LINKING UP THIS STANZA WITH THE NEXT ONE, SANKARA SAYS: "ANXIOUS TO KNOW THE CHARACTERISTIC FEATURES OF THE ONE WHO'S INTELLECT HAS COME TO EQUIPOISE, HE ASKS THIS QUESTION AS SOON AS HE GETS A CHANCE TO INTERROGATE":

Arjuna said:

54. *What, O Keshava, is the description of him who has steady Wisdom and who is merged in the Superconscious state? How does one of steady Wisdom speak, how does he sit, how does he walk?*

In the last two stanzas the discussion naturally turned towards the Ultimate Goal which a *Karma-Yogin* reaches when he has, with evenness-of-mind, perfected the 'technique of work'.

The idea seems to be quite appealing and the theory indeed, logical. There is a ring of conviction in it, when the

---

अर्जुन उवाच
स्थितप्रज्ञस्य का भाषा समाधिस्थस्य केशव ।
स्थितधीः किं प्रभाषेत किमासीत व्रजेत किम्॥ ५४ ॥

arjuna uvāca
sthitaprajñasya kā bhāṣā samādhisthasya keśava
sthitadhīḥ kiṁ prabhāṣeta kimāsīta vrajeta kim 54.

theory comes from the mouth of Lord Krishna. Arjuna has such a mental constitution that *Karma Yoga* appeals to him the most.

The grief-stricken hero of the first chapter has forgotten his hysteria and has now come to take an active interest in the discussion. As a practical man he is afraid as to whether after gaining this great Goal of Life through *Buddhi Yoga*, he will be able to live so vigorously in the world outside.

Looking from the *Vedic* usage of the term, one is apt to misunderstand that the perfected *Yogin* who has come to rediscover the Self lives exclusively in a world of his own. The description of the *Upanishads* can give to a raw student the notion that a Perfected Sage is ill-fitted to live in the world. Arjuna as a child of the era of hatred and diplomacy was curious to know fully the condition of the Perfected Master, before he would actually accept the theory and try to live it.

His anxiety to know the entire Truth is clearly shown here in his very questions upon such non-essentials as: How does he speak, how will he sit, how will he walk etc. These questions must be considered quite appropriate and dramatic when they come from the one who had been till then a patient of hysteria. Again, the first-half of the stanza demands a description of a man of steady-Wisdom while established in *Samadhi*, that is, with regard to his inner life. The second half of the stanza is asking for a description of how such a Master will act in the world outside.

Arjuna is asking a forked question: (a) A description of the state of mind in a man-of-Realisation merged in the Self-experience, and (b) An explanation as to how that experience will influence his actions in the outer world, when he emerges from that Transcendental experience.

In this stanza and the following section, a man of steady-Wisdom (*Sthita-Prajna*) means one who has through direct realisation come to experience and live his Godly Self.

THE LORD NOW POINTS OUT THOSE CHARACTERISTIC ATTITUDES IN A REALISED SAINT, WHICH ARE ATTAINABLE BY ALL THROUGH RIGHT EFFORTS AND WHICH CONSTITUTE THE MEANS AS FOLLOWS:

The Blessed Lord said:

55. *When a man completely casts off O Partha, all the desires of the mind, and is satisfied in the Self by the Self, then he is said to be the one of steady-Wisdom.*

By narrating thus the inner and outer life of a Man of Self-Realisation, *Geeta* helps us to detect for ourselves the right type of Masters from the charlatans who – though wolves – wear a goatskin and enter the fold of the faithful ones. Apart from this, these passages have a direct appeal to all sincere *Sadhakas* inasmuch as this section gives to them an easy thumb-rule as to what types of values and mental attitudes they should develop during their practice, in order to realise the ever-effulgent Divinity within them i.e., the Pure Awareness.

श्रीभगवानुवाच
प्रजहाति यदा कामान्सर्वान्पार्थ मनोगतान् ।
आत्मन्येवात्मना तुष्टः स्थितप्रज्ञस्तदोच्यते ॥ ५५ ॥

śrībhagavānuvāca
prajñahāti yadā kāmānsavārnpārtha manogatān
ātmanyevātmanā tuṣṭaḥ sthitaprajñastadocyate 55.

The opening stanza in this section is a brilliant summary of all that we should know about the mental condition of a Perfect One. The words used in this stanza can be understood fully only when we remember the significant fragrance of these words as they stand dancing among the hosts of other blossoms in the Garden of the *Upanishads*. He is considered to be a man-of-Wisdom who has completely cast away ALL DESIRES from his mind. By reading this stanza in conjunction with what Krishna has so far said, we can truly come to enjoy the *Upanishadic* fragrance in these inspired words of Vyasa.

An intellect that is contaminated by ignorance becomes the breeding-ground of desires, and he who has relieved himself of this ignorance through Right-Knowledge gained in perception naturally becomes 'desireless'. By explaining here the absence of the EFFECT, the Lord is negating the existence of the CAUSE: Where desires are not, there 'Ignorance' has ended and 'Knowledge' has already come to shine forth.

If this alone was the distinguishing factor of the man of steady-Wisdom, any modern man would condemn the Hindu man-of-Wisdom as a rank lunatic. A Hindu wise-man would then become one who had not even the initiative to desire. Desire means a capacity of the mind to see ahead of itself a scheme or a pattern in which he who desires will probably be happier. "The wise-man seems to lose even this capacity, as he goes beyond his intellect and experiences the Self" – this is a criticism that is generally heard from the materialists.

This stanza cannot thus be condemned since it adds in its second line, that the Perfect-One is 'blissful' in his own experience of the Self. A Perfect man is defined here therefore, not only as one who has no desires, but also as one who has positively come to enjoy the Bliss of the Self!

When one is an infant, one has one's own playmates. As one grows from childhood to boyhood, one leaves one's toys and runs after a new set of things. Again, as the boy grows to youthfulness, he loses his desires for the fancy-things of his boyhood and craves for yet a newer set of things. Again in his old age, the same entity casts away all objects that were till then, great joys to him and comes to demand a totally different set of objects. This is an observed phenomenon. As we grow, our demands also grow. With reference to the new scheme of things demanded, the old sets of ideas come to be cast away.

In one's ignorance, when one conceives oneself as the ego, one has a burning desire for sense-objects, a binding attachment with emotions, and a jealous preference for one's pet ideas. But when the ego is transcended, when the ignorance like a mist has lifted itself, and when the finite ego stands face to face with the Divine Reality in him, it melts away to become one with the Infinite. In the Self, the man of Steady-Wisdom, SELF-SATISFIED IN THE SELF, can no more entertain any desire, or have any appetite for the paltry objects of the body, of the mind, or of the intellect. He becomes the very Source of all Bliss.

Such a one is defined here by Vyasa as the 'man of Steady-Wisdom'(*Sthita-Prajna*), and as the words come out from the mouth of Krishna, they gather the divine ring of an incontrovertible Truth.

MOREOVER:

56. *He whose mind is not shaken up by adversity, and who in prosperity does not hanker after pleasures, who is free from attachment, fear, and anger is called a Sage of Steady-Wisdom?*

In describing the attributes of a Perfect Sage, having explained that he is the one who has come to sacrifice all his petty desires in his self-discovered self-satisfaction in the Self, Krishna explains that another characteristic by which we can recognise a sage, is his EQUANIMITY IN PLEASURE AND PAIN. If in the last stanza Krishna considered man as an 'actor', herein he is considering him as an 'experiencer', A BEARER OF BODY-AFFLICTIONS.

The one who is a stable being, whose heart is undisturbed in sorrow or joy, who is unattached, fearless, and sans-anger (free of anger) is described here as a *Muni* -- a silent sage. About the emotions that must be absent in an individual who is a master in all situations, we are here pointedly told only these: (a) attachment (*Raga*), (b) fear (*Bhaya*) and (c) anger (*Krodha*).

In fact, when we read biographies of the perfected-ones in the entire history of mankind, we find in almost all of them an antithesis of an ordinary man. The hundred emotions common to ordinary man are not at all seen in a Perfect-one, and therefore, we feel surprised when the absence of only

---

दुःखेष्वनुद्विग्नमनाः सुखेषु विगतस्पृहः ।
वीतरागभयक्रोधः स्थितधीर्मुनिरुच्यते ॥ ५६ ॥

duḥkheṣvanudvignamanāḥ sukheṣu vigataspṛhaḥ
vītarāgabhayakrodhaḥ sthitadhīrmunirucyate 56.

these three qualities is asserted so emphatically here. Naturally, a careful student gets suspicious. Has Vyasa overlooked all of the other features? Can this be a complete statement? But on a closer study we shall discover that he has not committed 'the crime of inappropriate emphasis upon the non-essentials' as critics have been tempted to point out.

In the previous stanza we were told that "He is Perfect who has forsaken all cravings that bubble up in His mind", and this stanza asserts the mental stability of such a one. In the world outside, through our interaction with the sense-objects, we can very easily realise that our attachments with things create in us the pains of the perplexing fear-phobia. When an individual develops a desire that is strong enough to make a deep attachment, instinctively he starts entertaining a sense of fear for the non-winning of the object that is so deeply desired; and if it has been secured, then again he fears for the security of the same acquired object.

Similarly, when an object has charmed one to a point of deep attachment, and when fear itself has started coming up in waves to disturb the individual, then such an individual's attitude towards those that come between him and the object of his attachment is called ANGER. Anger is thus nothing but a feeling that arises within us because of our attachment to an object, towards an obstacle between ourselves and the object of our attachment; the anger thus arising in a bosom is directly proportional to the amount of fear one entertains on the score of the obstacle holding one back from winning one's object of love. Anger therefore, is only our *Raga* for an object expressed at an obstacle that has come between us and the object of our desire.

Shankara says that a man of Steady-Wisdom is not distressed by calamities such as: (a) Those that may arise from the disorders of the body (*Adhyatmika*) (b) Those arising from external objects such as tigers, etc. (*Adhibhautika*) (c) Those arising from unseen causes such as the cosmic forces causing rains, storms, etc. (*Adhidaivika*). Fire increases when fuel is added, but the 'fire of desire' in a Perfect One does not increase when more pleasures are attained. Such a person is called a man of Steady-Knowledge, a silent, serene sage.

MOREOVER:

57. *He who is everywhere without attachment, on meeting with anything good or bad, who neither rejoices nor hates, his Wisdom is fixed.*

An inspired artist while trying to express his idea on the canvas in the language of colour will, off and on stand back from his easel, and will again with growing tenderness and love approach the product of his art to place a few more strokes with his brush. Here Krishna being inspired by his own theme is again and again choosing the right words to add more light and shade to the picture of the Perfect, the one which he was painting upon the heart-slab of his listener – Arjuna.

He who, without attachment, squarely meets life with all equanimity and poise, is the one who is 'established in

---

यः सर्वत्रानभिस्नेहस्तत्तत्प्राप्य शुभाशुभम् ।
नाभिनन्दति न द्वेष्टि तस्य प्रज्ञा प्रतिष्ठिता ॥ ५७ ॥

yaḥ sarvatrānabhisnehastattatprāpya śubhāśubham
nābhinandati na dveṣṭi tasya prajñā pratiṣṭhitā 57.

Wisdom'. Here also we have to understand the entire stanza as a whole, or else there will be the danger of misinterpreting its true meaning. Mere detachment from the things of life is NOT the sign of perfection, or of the true discriminative understanding. But many unintelligent enthusiasts actually desert their duties in life and run away, hoping that since they have developed perfect detachment from the sensuous world, they will gain their 'goal' in the quietude of the jungle. Arjuna himself had earlier on stated that he would renounce the call of duty and the field of activity. By thus retiring into quietude, the Pandava-hero hoped to reach Perfection and Peace. To dissuade Arjuna from taking this calamitous step, Krishna started his discourse with a serious note in the second chapter.

Detachment from suicidal affections and unintelligent tenderness cannot by itself take man to the higher realms of Divinity. Detachment from the world outside must equally be accompanied by a growing balance in ourselves to face all the challenges in life i.e., the 'auspicious' (*shubha*) and the 'inauspicious' (*ashubha*) in perfect equipoise without either any uncontrolled rejoicing at the *shubha*, or any aversion for the *ashubha* experiences.

A mere detachment in itself is not the way of a perfect life, in as much as it is only a negative existence of constantly escaping from life. To live in ATTACHMENT is to live in slavery to the things of the world. But the Perfect-One is He who with divine freedom lives in the world, dexterously meeting both - the joys and the sorrows – which life may provide for Him. In winter to be out under the sun and lie basking in its rays is to enjoy its warmth and simultaneously suffer its glare. To complain of the glare is to bring sorrow into the very enjoyment of the warmth. One who is intelligent will either try to ignore the glare and enjoy the warmth fully or will shed off the glare and bask in the enjoyable warmth.

Similarly, life by its very nature is a mixture of both the good and the bad. To live ever adjusting ourselves - avoiding the bad and striving to linger in the experience of the good – is to live unintelligently. The Perfect-One experiences the best and the worst in life with equal detachment because He is ever established in THE TRUE AND THE ETERNAL, which is the very Self.

In his question Arjuna had enquired of Krishna as to how a Perfect Master would speak. This stanza may be considered as an answer to it. Since the Perfect man-of-Wisdom neither feels any aversion to the sorrows nor rejoices in the joys of life, he neither compliments anything in the world, nor does he condemn anything. To him everything is wonderful. He sees things AS THEY ARE, uncoloured by his mental moods. Such a Perfect One is beyond all the known principles of behaviourism of the Western psychology.

MOREOVER:

58. *When like the tortoise which withdraws its limbs from all sides, He withdraws His senses from the sense-objects then His Wisdom becomes steady.* **?**

यदा संहरते चायं कूर्मोऽङ्गानीव सर्वशः ।
इन्द्रियाणीन्द्रियार्थेभ्यस्तस्य प्रज्ञा प्रतिष्ठिता ॥ ५८ ॥

yadā saṁharate cāyaṁ kūrmo 'ngānīva sarvaśaḥ,
indriyāṇindriyārthebhyas tasya prajñā pratiṣṭhitā 58.

After explaining that a Perfect-One : (a) Is ever satisfied in the Self, (b) Lives in perfect equanimity in pleasure and pain, and (c) Has within Him a complete absence of attachment to rejoicing or any aversion, it is here mentioned that a man of Steady-Wisdom has the special knack for withdrawing his senses from all the disturbing 'fields-of-objects'. The simile used here is very appropriate. Just as a tortoise can, even at the most distant suggestions of danger, instinctively withdraw all its limbs into itself and feel safe within, a man-of-Perfection can consciously withdraw all his antennae that peep out through his five arches-of-knowledge called the sense-organs (organs-of-perception).

In the theory of perception[1] in *Vedanta*, the mind bearing the consciousness goes out through the sense-organs to the sense-objects, and there it takes as it were the shape of the sense-objects, and so comes to gain the 'knowledge' of the objects as perceived. This idea is figuratively put in the *Upanishad*[2] - the Light of Consciousness as it were beams out through the seven holes in the (skull), each special 'beam' of awareness illuminating only one specific type of 'object'. Thus the light that passes through the eyes is capable of illumining only the FORMS and COLOURS, while that which emerges through the ears illumines SOUNDS. In the material world we can take the example of the electric light that expresses through an ordinary bulb illuminating the objects in the room, while the electricity as light emerging from an X-ray tube penetrates through the form and illumines things that are ordinarily not visible to the naked eye.

1 Ref. Chapter II, *Shloka* 14

2 Ref. Swamiji's Discourses on *Kathopanishad*, Ch. II (Sec. IV) *Shloka* 1.

Thus, within each individual five distinct beams of the same Awareness protrude like antennae and give him complete 'knowledge' of the external world. These five avenues of knowledge bring to him the innumerable stimuli from the outer world, which upon reaching the mind provide all the disturbances that man feels in his life of contacts with the outer world. If I am blind the beauty that is passing by cannot disturb my mind; if I am deaf I cannot overhear criticism against myself and naturally it cannot reach me to agitate my bosom! The untasted, the unsmelt, or the unfelt sense-objects can never bring forth any pang of sorrow into the bosom. Here Krishna reassures Arjuna that a Man-of-Steady-Wisdom is He who has the ready capacity to fold back His senses from any, or all the fields of their activities.

This capacity within an individual to withdraw his senses at will from the fields-of-objects is called in *Yoga Shastra Pratyahara* which the *Yogin* accomplishes through control of breath (*Pranayama*). To a devotee this comes naturally, because he has the eyes and the ears only for the form and stories of his beloved Lord. To a *Vedantin*, again this (*Uparati*) comes from his well-developed and sharpened discriminative faculty, with which his intellect makes his mind understand the futility of licking the crumbs of joy and happiness in the wayside ditches of sensuousness, while he in his Real Nature is the Lord of the very store of Bliss Infinite.

THE SENSES OF A MAN WHO IS ILL AND CONSEQUENTLY UNABLE TO PARTAKE OF THE SENSUOUS OBJECTS ARE SEEMINGLY UNDER

CONTROL, BUT THE TASTE FOR THEM DOES NOT THEREBY, CEASE TO EXIST. HOW DOES EVEN THE TASTE FOR SENSE-OBJECTS FINALLY END? LISTEN:

59. *The objects of the senses turn away from the abstinent man leaving the longing (behind); but his longing also leaves him upon seeing the Supreme?*

Without *Pratyahara* (or *Uparati*), we can observe cases wherein an individual comes to maintain sense-withdrawal from the sense-objects due to some physical incapacity or due to some special mental mood of temporary sorrow or misery. In all these cases, though the sense-organs come to feel an aversion for the respective objects, their inclination for these objects merely remains dormant for the time being. Similarly, Arjuna doubts that even in a *Yogin* the capacity to withdraw from the temptations of the sense-world may be temporary, and that under favourable or sufficiently tempting circumstances, they may again raise their hoods to hiss and to poison. His doubt is answered here.

If you observe the flights of objects of sensuousness from shops to their customers, you can understand this point very clearly. They always reach only those who are courting them and are panting to possess them. The wine-cellars get emptied

---

विषया विनिवर्तन्ते निराहारस्य देहिनः ।
रसवर्जं रसोऽप्यस्य परं दृष्ट्वा निवर्तते ॥ ५९ ॥
viṣayā vinivartante nirāhārasya dehinaḥ,
rasa-varjaṁ raso 'pyasya paraṁ dṛṣṭvā nivartate 59.

when the bottles 'walkout' to replenish the sideboards of the drunkards! Ploughs made by a smithy are not purchased by artists, poets, doctors, and advocates; they must necessarily reach the homes of the farmers. Similarly, all sense-objects ultimately reach those who are courting them with burning desires. From the one who is completely abstinent sense-objects must necessarily get repelled.

But although the sense-objects may temporarily seem to turn away from him who is abstinent, the deep taste for them that is ingrained in his mind is very difficult to be erased completely. Here Krishna in his Supreme Wisdom assures the seeker that these mental impressions of sensuous lives that were lived in the past by the ego from the beginning of creation to date, will all be totally erased, or at least made ineffective, as roasted seeds, only when the seeker transcends the ego and comes to experience the Self.

This is not very difficult to understand, since we know that the objects of sorrow and occasions of tragedy within one plane of consciousness are not available in another. The kingship that I enjoy in my dream does not add even a bit to my dignity when I wake up to realise my insignificant existence. So too, my meager existence in the waking-state will not prohibit me from the full kingly glory in my dream-kingdom!

Similarly, the ego that exists now through the waking, dream and deep-sleep states, has gathered to itself a dung-heap of impressions, all purely sensuous. But these cannot be effective when the same ego upon transcending these three planes comes to experience the plane of God-Consciousness.

HE, WHO WOULD ACQUIRE STEADINESS OF RIGHT KNOWLEDGE (*PRAJNA*), SHOULD FIRST BRING HIS SENSES UNDER CONTROL. FOR, IF NOT CONTROLLED, THEY WILL DO HARM, SO THE LORD SAYS:

60. *The turbulent senses, O son of Kunti, do violently carry away the mind of a wise-man, though he (may) be striving (to control them).*

In his discourse so far, the Lord has emphasized that a perfect-Master is the one who has complete control over his sense-appetites. In India, a mere philosophical idea in itself is not considered to be anything more than a poetic ideology, and it is not accepted as a spiritual thesis unless it is followed by a complete technique by which the seeker can come to live it, in his own subjective experience. True to this traditional Aryan faith, in the *Geeta* too, the Lord indicates to Arjuna the practical method by which he should struggle hard, in order to reach the eminence of perfection as a man of steady-Wisdom.

The ignorance of the Spiritual Reality functions within any individual in three distinct aspects: 1. Unactivity(*sattva*), 2. Activity (*rajas*), and 3. Inactivity (*tamas*). When the *sattva* aspect in us is molested by the 'veiling of the intellect'

यततो ह्यपि कौन्तेय पुरुषस्य विपश्चितः ।
इन्द्रियाणि प्रमाथीनि हरन्ति प्रसभं मनः ॥ ६० ॥

yatato hyapi kaunteya puruṣasya vipaścitaḥ,
indriyāṇi pramāthīni haranti prasabhaṁ manaḥ 60.

(*avarana*), and the 'lack of tranquillity' of the mind (*vikshepa*), then we come to experience the sorrows that are caused by their endless roaming through the sense-organs. Unless well-controlled, they will drag the mind to the field of the sense-objects, and thus create a chaotic condition within, which is experienced as sorrow.

The fact that this happens even to a highly evolved seeker is here accepted by the statement of the Lord. With this assertion He is warning the seeker within Arjuna that he should not on any score let his 'objective-mind' take hold of, and enslave his 'subjective-intellect'. This warning is quite appropriate and timely within the scheme of thought in this chapter.

Invariably among those who are practising religion, the common cause by which very many true seekers fall away from the Path is the same all over the world. After a few years of practice, they no doubt, come to live in a certain inexplicable inward joy. Then being overconfident and often even vainful of their progress, they relax in their *tapas.* Once they come back to the field of the senses, 'the turbulent senses violently snatch the mind away' from the poise of perfect meditation!

61. *Having restrained them all, He should sit steadfast, intent on Me; His Wisdom is steady, whose senses are under control?*

तानि सर्वाणि संयम्य युक्त आसीत मत्परः ।
वशे हि यस्येन्द्रियाणि तस्य प्रज्ञा प्रतिष्ठिता ॥ ६१ ॥

tāni sarvāṇi saṁyamya yukta āsīta matparaḥ,
vaśe hi yasyendriyāṇi tasya prajñā pratiṣṭhitā 61.

Since the sense-organs are thus saboteurs in the Kingdom of the Spirit that bring the disastrous downfall of the Empire of the Soul, Arjuna is warned here that as a seeker of Self-Perfection, he should constantly struggle to control his sense-organs and their mad lustful wanderings in their respective fields. Modern psychology would certainly look down with a squint-eye upon this *Geeta* theory, because according to Freud and others, sensuousness is instinctive in man and to curb it would lead to an unnatural suppression.

According to the West, TO CONTROL is TO SUPPRESS. No science of mental life can accept that suppression is psychologically healthy. But the *Vedic* theory is not pointing to any mental suppression at all. It is only advising an inward blossoming, an inner growth and development by which one's earlier fields of enjoyments through the senses drop out to make room for the perception of a newer field of ampler joys and more satisfying Bliss.

This idea is very well brought out here, when Lord Krishna as though in the very same breath repeats both, the negative and the positive aspects of the technique of Self-development. He advises not only a withdrawal from the unhealthy gutters of sensuousness, but also gives the healthy method of doing so by explaining the positive technique of Self-Perfection. Through a constant attempt at focussing our attention ON ME – THE SUPREME, He advises the disciples to be steady.

In this simple-looking statement of half-a-verse, the *Geeta* explains the entire technique of Self-development. Immoral impulses and unethical instincts that bring a man down to the level of a mere brute, are the result of endless lives spent among sensuous objects during the infinite number of different manifestations, through which the embodied soul, the ego in each one of us, had previously passed. It is humanly impossible for an individual to erase and transcend in his lifetime the thick coating of mental impressions gathered along his journey from life to life, from embodiment to embodiment. Naturally this is the despair of all the promoters of ethics, the teachers of morality, and the masters of spirituality.

The *Rishis* of the old times in their lived experience discovered for themselves a technique by which, all these mental tendencies could be eradicated. To expose the mind to the quiet atmosphere of meditation upon the All-Perfect Being is to heal its ulcers. By this process the one who has come to gain a complete mastery over his sense-organs is considered as the one who is 'steadfast-in-Wisdom'.

The concealed suggestion in the stanza now becomes quite obvious as follows; No one who with an excessive force controls his *Indriyas* by sheer strength of will and a sense of abstinence has any chance of flowering into a full-blown spiritual beauty. He who has all of his sense-organs, of their own accord, lying tamely surrendered at his feet, and who has come to rediscover the Infinite Perfection in himself, is called a man-of-Perfection. Neither has he ruined his instruments-of-cognition, nor has he closed down the arches-of-knowledge in him. A Perfect One is he whose sway over the animal within is so complete that the inner Satan has become for the Sage in him a tame Caliban to run errands and serve faithfully.

NOW THE LORD PROCEEDS TO POINT OUT THE SOURCE OF ALL EVIL IN THE CASE OF THE UNSUCCESSFUL:

62. *When a man thinks of objects, 'attachment' for them arises; from attachment 'desire' is born; from desire arises 'anger'...*

63. *From anger comes 'delusion'; from delusion 'loss of memory'; from loss of memory the 'destruction of discrimination'; from destruction of discrimination, he 'perishes'.* ?

From this verse onwards, Lord Krishna explains in five noble stanzas the Hindu psychological theory of the fall of man from Godhood. This is done only to bring home to Arjuna that he, the mighty-armed, must try to conquer all of his *Indriyas* (senses) from all sides. Such a man, concludes Krishna, is a Man-of-Perfection as conceived in and contemplated upon, as explained in and glorified by the scriptural books of the Hindus.

This section also gives to us a clear pattern of the autobiography of all seekers who have after long periods of practice come to wreck themselves upon the rocks of failure and disappointment. To a true seeker, in *Vedanta* no fall is

---

ध्यायतो विषयान्पुंसः सङ्गस्तेषूपजायते ।
सङ्गात्संजायते कामः कामात्क्रोधोऽभिजायते ॥ ६२ ॥

dhyāyato viṣayān puṁsaḥ sangasteṣūpajāyate,
sangāt saṁjāyate kāmaḥ kāmāt krodho bhijāyate 62.

क्रोधाद्भवति सम्मोहः सम्मोहात्स्मृतिविभ्रमः।
स्मृतिभ्रंशाद् बुद्धिनाशो बुद्धिनाशात्प्रणश्यति ॥ ६३ ॥

krodhādbhavati saṁmohaḥ saṁmohāt smṛtivibhramaḥ,
smṛtibhraṁśādbuddhināśo buddhināśāt praṇaśyati 63.

ever possible. Instances of unsuccessful seekers are not few. In all of them, the mistake we notice is that they ultimately fell back to be victims of sense-entanglement; and in all those cases we also notice that the fallen ones drank the very dregs of it. There is no halfway house for such victims; a slip for them means their total destruction!!

The ladder-of-fall is very beautifully described here. The path of destruction for a seeker is so elaborately detailed in these stanzas that fallen as we are, we shall know how to get back to our pristine glory and inward perfection.

Like a tree which emerges from a seed, the source of all evil starts from our own wrong thinking or due to false imaginations. THOUGHT IS CREATIVE; IT CAN MAKE US, OR MAR US. If rightly harnessed, it can be used for constructive purposes; if misused, it can totally destroy us. When we constantly think about a sense-object, the CONSISTENCY OF THAT THOUGHT creates within us an ATTACHMENT for the object of our thought. When more and more thoughts flow towards that object of attachment, they crystallize to form a BURNING DESIRE for the possession and enjoyment of the object-of-attachment. The same force of the motion when directed towards the obstacles that threaten the non-fulfilment of our desires, is called anger (*Krodha*).

An intellect fumed with anger (*Krodha*) comes to experience DELUSION, and* the deluded intellect has no power of discrimination, because it loses all of the

* An angry man starts seeing things in his enemy which are really not there at all: hence 'delusion'.

MEMORIES OF THE PAST. Anyone who is filled with anger is capable of doing acts while totally forgetting himself and his relationship with all others. Sri Shankaracharya says in this connection that a deluded fool who is in this mental condition might even fight with his own teachers or parents, while forgetting his indebtedness to these revered persons.

Thus, when an individual through wrong channels of thinking becomes ATTACHED to an object, the attachment matures into a burning DESIRE to possess that object. When an obstruction to possess that object-of-desire shoots him up into a fit of ANGER, the mental disturbance caused by this emotion DELUDES the intellect and makes the individual FORGET his sense of proportion, and his sense of relationship with things and beings around him. When thus a deluded intellect forgets its dignity of culture, it loses its discriminative capacity, which is called, in common parlance, 'conscience' (*Buddhi*). Conscience is that knowledge to be enjoyed for differentiating the good from the evil, which often forms a standard within us, and whenever it can, warns the mind against its lustful sensuousness and animalism. Once this 'conscience' is dulled, the man becomes a two-legged animal with no sense of proportion, and no ears for any subtler call within him, than the howling urgent hungers of the flesh. Thereby, he is guaranteeing for himself a complete destruction inasmuch as such a bosom cannot come to perceive, or strive for the Higher, the Nobler, and the Diviner.

THE CONTEMPLATION OF SENSE-OBJECTS HAS BEEN DESCRIBED AS THE SOURCE OF ALL EVILS. NOW THE

MEANS OF DELIVERANCE (*MOKSHA*) IS DESCRIBED AS FOLLOWS:

64. *But the self-controlled man moving among objects, with his senses under restraint, and free from both attraction and repulsion, attains peace.*

He alone, who with perfect self-control, goes through life among the infinite number of sense-objects, each impinging upon him and trying to bind him with its charm, and approaches them with neither love nor hatred, comes to enjoy PEACE. By running away from the sense-objects nobody can assure for himself any inner peace, because the inner disturbance depends not upon the presence or the absence of the sense-objects in the outer-world, but essentially upon the mind's agitations for procuring the desirable objects, or for getting rid of the undesirable objects.

But a Master-of-Wisdom with perfect self-control moves among the objects of the world with neither any special love, nor any particular aversion for them. Wherever I go, my shadow must play all around me according to the position of the light; but the shadow can neither entangle me with love, nor destroy me with hatred! The outer world-of-objects is able to whip that man who lends the power to the objects to smother him!

रागद्वेषवियुक्तैस्तु विषयानिन्द्रियैश्चरन् ।
आत्मवश्यैर्विधेयात्मा प्रसादमधिगच्छति ॥ ६४ ॥

rāgadveṣavimuktaistu viṣayānindriyaiścaran,
ātmavaśyairvidheyātmā prasādamadhigacchati 64.

Supposing that there is a lunatic who is whipping himself up and weeping in pain; his sorrows can be ended only when he is persuaded not to take the whip in his hand. He could be advised, even if he kept the whip in his hand, not to swing his arms in the fashion in which he is doing! Similarly, here the mind woos the objects and gets beaten up. It is told as an advice that an individual who lives in self-control will no longer lend his own life's dynamism to an object to persecute him, through his own sentimental aversion to, or love for that object.

When the lunatic is taught not to wield the whip and strike himself, he is immediately saved from the sorrows of the whip. Similarly when a mind is trained in these two aspects to: (a) Live in self-control (b) Move among the sense-objects with neither an attachment for, nor an aversion to them, the disturbances and agitations in the mind caused by the sense-enchantments are all immediately brought under control. This condition of the mind is called tranquillity or peace (*Prasada*).

This is symbolically represented in the sweet's distribution after every *Puja service* in all religions, and is called among the Hindus as *Prasada* (or *Bhog*). The one who has, during the ritual practised perfect self-control and God-contemplation comes to enjoy as a result of his action tranquillity in the mind, which is termed as Spiritual Grace or Divine Peace (*Ishwara Prasada*).

Here, as far as a *Vedantin* is concerned, *Prasada* is a mental purification. Such a mind is considered as pure, which feels in itself the least sense-disturbances. The one who has learnt to live in self-control, and has trained himself to live among sense-objects in a spirit of least attachment to, or aversion for them, has the least disturbance, because of the ineffectiveness of the sense-objects upon him. Thereby, his mind automatically becomes increasingly calm and tranquil, and is considered as pure (*Prasada*) for the purposes of the spiritual life.

WHAT WILL HAPPEN WHEN PEACE IS ATTAINED? LISTEN:

65. *In that peace all pains are destroyed; for, the intellect of the tranquil-minded soon becomes steady.*

It is natural for an Arjuna-mentality of uncompromising intellectualism to ask Krishna: "Then what?" As an answer the Lord explains why he should develop and maintain tranquillity of the mind within himself. IN TRANQUILLITY ALL SORROWS ARE DESTROYED. This sentence is obviously commented upon as a definition of happiness. A peaceful mind is the significance of happiness. PEACE IS HAPPINESS; HAPPINESS IS PEACE. The least-agitated mind is a proof against all sorrows inasmuch as sorrow is nothing but a state of agitation in the mind.

This explanation does not satisfy us completely since Krishna's assertion is that 'sorrows will be destroyed' (*hanih*). In order to bring out clearly the meaning that is implied in the phrase 'destruction of sorrows', we will have to understand it as the 'elimination of *vasanas*'. Earlier on in the

---

प्रसादे सर्वदुःखानां हानिरस्योपजायते ।
प्रसन्नचेतसो ह्याशु बुद्धिः पर्यवतिष्ठते ॥ ६५ ॥
prasāde sarvaduḥkhānāṁ hānirasyopajāyate,
prasannacetaso hyāśu buddhiḥ paryavatiṣṭhate 65.

introduction, we have said that the *vasana* granulations upon giving a thick coating to the subjective mind are the cause for its delusion which creates all sorrows for the imperfect ones; while the Perfect One transcends the *vasanas* through the *Buddhi Yoga* as explained earlier.

It is very well known that all the *vasanas* existing within an individual, who is facing life constantly, cannot be fully eradicated by him. The secret of doing so has been explained here by the Lord. Keeping the mind exposed to an atmosphere of tranquillity (*Prasada*), consciously brought about through an intelligent life of self-control, is the secret whereby all the *vasanas* can get eliminated.

THIS TRANQUILLITY IS EXTOLLED HERE BY LORD KRISHNA:

66. *There is no knowledge (of the Self) to the unsteady; and to the unsteady no meditation; and to the unmeditative no peace; to the peaceless, how can there be happiness?*

Here is an explanation of why quietude of the mind is so often and so insistently emphasised in the literature explaining the Hindu-technique of Self-perfection. Unless the mind is quiet, the individual will have neither the intellectual leisure for cultural self-development, nor the inner energy for consistently living spiritual perfections that a truly developed man yearns for. Unless there is tranquillity, there cannot be

---

नास्ति बुद्धिरयुक्तस्य न चायुक्तस्य भावना ।
न चाभावयतः शान्तिरशान्तस्य कुतः सुखम् ॥ ६६ ॥

nāsti buddhirayuktasya na cāyuktasya bhāvanā,
na cābhāvayataḥ śantir aśāntasya kutaḥ sukham 66.

steadiness of intellectual application to the problems of life. Without this self-evaluation of life and true observation with a clear discriminative analysis, we cannot have within us the required amount of Devotion to Self-knowledge (*Bhavana*). Without such a glorious Goal before us constantly beckoning us unto itself like a pole star, our life shall be a lost ship in an ocean that is going nowhere, reaching nowhere, and ultimately floundering upon some treacherous rock.

The one who has no philosophical goal in life to strive and yearn for, will not know what the peace of mind is. To the one who is thus restless, where is happiness? To live in balance and sail safely on the uncertain waves of the ocean of life through both, its smiling weather and stormy days, we must have a constant perception of the Real. Without a drummer, the dancer's footwork cannot be rhythmic and cannot keep a perfect time.

WHY IS THERE NO KNOWLEDGE FOR THE UNSTEADY? LISTEN:

67. *For, the mind which follows in the wake of the wandering senses, carries away his discrimination, as the wind carries away a boat on the waters.*

Just as a ship with the sails up, and the helmsman dead would be completely at the mercy of the fitful storms and reckless waves, will not reach any definite harbour but gets

---

इन्द्रियाणां हि चरतां यन्मनोऽनुविधीयते ।
तदस्य हरति प्रज्ञां वायुर्नावमिवाम्भसि ॥ ६७ ॥

indriyāṇāṁ hi caratāṁ yanmano 'nuvidhīyate,
tadasya harati prajñāṁ vāyurnāvam ivāmbhasi 67.

destroyed by the very tossing of the waves, so too, life gets capsized and the individual is drowned, if his mind is unanchored and left to be carried hither and thither by the uncertain buffets of passionate sense-storms. Therefore, the senses are to be controlled if man is to live a better and more purposeful life designed and planned for enduring success.

AFTER HAVING EXPLAINED THE PROPOSITION ENUNCIATED EARLIER,* THE LORD NOW CONCLUDES BY RE-AFFIRMING HIS STATEMENT:

68. *Therefore, O Mighty-armed, his knowledge is steady whose senses are completely restrained from sense-objects.*

It is natural while in conversation, that we do not directly give our wise conclusions upon the, dos and dont's, of life without giving the logic of our thoughts that is leading to our conclusions. Without preparing our friend's mind to perceive the logic of these conclusions, we dare not declare to him any truth, however divinely acceptable the declarations are. Arjuna has been told earlier on about all the necessary arguments, and here in the stanza, Krishna reasserts the same proposition: "Life in self-control alone is life worth living, if we demand from it anything more enduring than tears, sobs, sighs, and groans".

तस्माद्यस्य महाबाहो निगृहीतानि सर्वशः ।
इन्द्रियाणीन्द्रियार्थेभ्यस्तस्य प्रज्ञा प्रतिष्ठिता ॥ ६८ ॥

tasmādyasya mahābāho nigṛhītāni sarvaśaḥ,
indriyāṇīndriyārthebhyas tasys prajñā pratiṣṭhitā 68.

*Chapter II, 61-62

He alone is a man-of-Wisdom, rooted in joy and bliss, who has completely restrained all his senses from their wild roaming among their sense-objects.

BY DESTROYING THE SENSE ORGANS (WHICH ARE) ROAMING IN THE SENSE-OBJECTS does not mean that a man of Self-development should destroy his capacities for perception of the world outside; nor does it mean that he is the one who has been rendered incapable of enjoying life. Sense-debility (incapacity) is not a sign of better knowledge. It is only meant here that the sense-objects filtering through the five archways of knowledge will not, in a Perfect man, flood his mind to bring chaos and destruction of his established inner peace and tranquillity.

The ordinary individual in his egocentric existence becomes victimized by the sense-organs, while he who has conquered the ego and has transcended his matter-identifications, comes to live in freedom and perfect control over the tyrannical sense organs.

IN ORDER TO MAKE THIS POINT CLEAR, THE LORD PROCEEDS:

69. *That which is night to all beings, in that the self-controlled man keeps awake; where all beings are awake, that is the night for the Sage (MUNI) who sees.*

In order to bring home to Arjuna the idea that the world as experienced by an individual through the goggles of the

---

या निशा सर्वभूतानां तस्यां जागर्ति संयमी ।
यस्यां जाग्रति भूतानि सा निशा पश्यतो मुनेः ॥ ६९ ॥

yā niśā sarvabhūtānāṁ tasyāṁ jāgarti saṁyami,
yasyāṁ jāgrati bhūtāni sā niśā paśyato muneḥ 69.

mind-intellect-body is different from what is perceived through the open windows of spirituality, this stanza is given. The metaphorical language of this verse is so complete in detail that the data-mongering modern intellect is not capable of entering into its poetic beauty. Of all the peoples of the world, the Aryans alone are capable of bringing about a combination of poetry and science. When the poet-philosopher Vyasa takes up his pen to pour out his art on to the ancient Palmyra-leaves to express the Bliss of Perfection in the ecstasy, he could not have used a better medium in the *Geeta,* than his poetry.

Here, two points of view namely, of the ignorant and of the wise are contrasted. The ignorant person never perceives the world as it is; he always throws his own mental colour on to the objects and understands the imperfections within his mind to be a part and parcel of the objects perceived. The world as viewed through a coloured glasspane must look coloured. When this colouring medium is removed, the world appears AS IT IS.

The Consciousness within us is today capable of recognizing the world only through the media of the body, the mind, and the intellect. Naturally, we see an imperfect world, not because the world is so, but because of the ugliness of the media through which we perceive it.

A Mastermind is he, who as rooted in his wisdom, opens up the windows of his perception and looks at the world through the eye-of-Wisdom.

When an electrical engineer comes to a city, and at dusk when the whole city smiles forth with its lights, he immediately enquires: "Is it AC or DC current?" While the same vision to an illiterate villager is a wondrous sight and he only exclaims: "I have seen lights that need no wick or oil!" From the standpoint of the villager, there is no electricity and no problem of AC or DC currents. The world that the engineer sees among the same lamps is not realised or known by the unperceiving intellect of the villager; nor is the engineer awake to the world of strange wonderment which the villager enjoys.

Here we are told that the egocentric, finite mortal is asleep to the world-of-Perception that is enjoyed and lived by the man of Steady-Wisdom; and that the Perfect One cannot see and feel the thrills, besides the sobs which the ego experiences in its selfish life of finite experience.

THE LORD PROCEEDS TO TEACH BY AN ILLUSTRATION THAT A WISE DEVOTEE ALONE, WHO HAS ABANDONED DESIRES AND WHOSE WISDOM IS STEADY, CAN ATTAIN *MOKSHA*, AND NOT HE WHO WITHOUT RENOUNCING CHERISHES DESIRES:

70. *He attains Peace into whom all desires enter, as waters enter the ocean, which filled from all sides, remains unmoved but not the 'desirer of desires'.*

आपूर्यमाणमचलप्रतिष्ठं
समुद्रमाप: प्रविशन्ति यद्वत् ।
तद्वत्कामा यं प्रविशन्ति सर्वे
स शान्तिमाप्नोति न कामकामी ॥ ७० ॥

āpūryamāṇamacalapratiṣṭhaṁ
samudramapaḥ praviśanti yadvat,
tadvatkāmā yaṁ praviśānti sarve
sa śāntim āpnoti na kāmakāmī 70.

It is very well known that although millions of gallons of water reach the ocean through the various rivers, the level of water in the ocean does not change even by a fraction. Similarly, even though an infinite number of sense-objects may pour in their stimuli and reach the mental zone of the Perfect Man through his five sense-channels, they do not create any commotion or flux within his bosom.

Such an individual who always finds his own level (of balance) in spite of the fact that he is living amidst the sense-objects, and with his sense-organs unavoidably ever in contact with the objects, is called a man-of-Perfection, a true Saint. Krishna asserts that such an individual alone can truly discover peace and happiness within himself. The Lord in the *Geeta* is not satisfied with this negative assertion, hence positively denies any true peace or joy to those who are 'desirers of desires'.

This idea is totally in opposition with the modern belief in the material world. The materialists believe that by fanning up their desires and satisfying as many of them as possible, one is helped to live a life of joy and happiness. Modern civilisation based upon industrialisation, large-scale production, and consumerism is attempting to whip up desires. This attempt has now succeeded to such an extent that the average man has a million times more desires today than his forefather ever entertained, a century ago. The financiers and the industrialists with the aid of modern scientific knowledge struggle hard to discover and satisfy new desires. To the extent that an individual has come to fulfil his newly created desires, he is taught by the day's civilisation that he is happier than ever before.

On the other hand, the great Indian thinkers of the past – perhaps through their experience, or through their more careful and exhaustive thinking – discovered that the joy created through satisfaction of desires can never be complete. They discovered that joy or happiness at any given time, is a quotient when the 'number of desires fulfilled' is divided by the 'total number of desires entertained' by the same individual at that time. This mathematical truth has been accepted by the modern preachers of secularism also but in their practical application, the old *Rishis* and the modern politicians seem to differ to a large extent.

In the modern world, the attempt is to increase the numerator which is represented by the 'number of the desires fulfilled'. The scriptural Masters of India were also living in a world peopled by a society of men. Their philosophical contemplations were upon man as a social being, and their aim too, was to bring about more happiness in their society. Unlike the present-day prophets of profit, these *Rishis* of Religion did not conceive that an attempt to increase the NUMERATOR without a corresponding attention upon the rate of increase of the DENOMINATOR could produce any palpable increase in joy. On the other hand, today we are struggling hard to increase the 'number of desires fulfilled', without at the same time, trying to control the 'number of desires entertained'. That, this state of affairs cannot produce any palpable increase in the QUOTIENT OF HAPPINESS is the scriptural verdict, which seems to be an easily understandable scientific truth.

Herein, the *Geeta* is only repeating what the *Upanishadic Rishis* never got tired of emphasising in the scriptures of India.

The 'desirer of desires' can never come to perfect peace (*shanti*). Only he, who has in a spirit of detachment gained a complete control over his mind so that the sense-objects of the outer world cannot create within him an infinite number of yearnings or desires, is the man-of-Peace and Joy. The objects in the outer world cannot tease a man by their existence, or by their non-existence. The outer world can borrow its capacity to ill-treat man only when he exposes himself unguarded, and gets wounded and crushed by his own attachments to a wrong valuation of the sense-objects.

In this stanza *Bhagawan* is only giving a more elaborate and complete commentary upon the opening line of this section[1] wherein He started the description of a man of Steady-Wisdom. Therein He explained that, "When a man completely casts off all the desires from within his mind, he is said to be the one of Steady-Knowledge".

BECAUSE IT IS SO, THEREFORE:

71. *That man attains peace who, abandoning all desires, moves about without longing, without the sense of 'I-ness' and 'My-ness'.*

There are commentators who believe that this and the following stanza explain the path-of-Renunciation, which is

---

विहाय कामान्यः सर्वान्पुमांश्चरति निःस्पृहः ।
निर्ममो निरहंकारः स शान्तिमधिगच्छति ॥ ७१ ॥

vihāya kāmānyaḥ sarvān pumāṁścarati niḥspṛhaḥ,
nirmamo nirahaṁkāraḥ sa śāntimadhigachati 71.

1 Ibid. Verse 55

in fact, not altogether ignored in the text of the *Geeta*. Since as we said earlier, the second chapter is almost a summary of the entire Divine Song, it has to indicate even this *Sannyasa Yoga*, which will be explained later on, at length and hinted at different places during the entire length of the *Geeta*.

This stanza seems to ring clearly the significant advice given earlier by Krishna, almost at the very opening of His philosophical discussions, in this chapter.[1] He had advised therein: "HAVING CONQUERED THE MENTAL AGITATIONS THAT WERE CREATED BY THE PAIRS-OF-OPPOSITES, FIGHT THE BATTLE OF LIFE". The same idea seems to be restated here at the close of the chapter.

The first line of the stanza explains the mental condition of the one who comes to discover Real Peace within himself. Such an individual, it says, renounces all desires and has no attachments or longings. The second line describes the condition of such an individual's intellect and it asserts that it is without any sense of 'I-ness' or 'My-ness'. The ego is the cause of the sense-attachments and longings. Where the ego is not perceptible - as in sleep, there are no longings or desires in the individual, or at least they are dormant. Thus, if the first line of the stanza is describing a negation of the effects of 'ignorance', the second line asserts the absence of the very cause from which desires and the agitations arise.

Earlier on, in the introduction we explained that the split in the personality of Arjuna was caused by the intervention of the sense of his ego and his egoistic desires, which broke up the subjective and objective aspects of his mind into two independent islands with a vast ocean of surging waves of desires between them. With a soft suggestion after explaining all the logic of thought, Krishna is carefully placing his finger upon the very ulcer in the Pandava's mind.

The stanza in its sum-total suggestions advises us that all of our sufferings in the world are caused by our own egocentric misconception and the consequent arrogance which is characterised by our ever-multiplying demands for wealth and our endless desires.

Sannyasa means sacrifice, and to live in a spirit of sacrifice after renouncing completely one's ego and its desires is true *Sannyasa*, wherein an individual comes to live in constant awareness of his fuller and ampler Divinity. The general misunderstanding that to run away from life is *Sannyasa*, or to colour the cloth is to become a true monk, has cast an irreparable slur on the philosophy of the *Upanishads*. Hinduism considers him alone to be a *Sannyasin* "who has learnt the art of living his life in constant inspiration, which is gained through an intelligent renunciation of his egocentric misconceptions".

Sankara beautifully explains this point of view in his commentary on the stanza. "THAT MAN OF RENUNCIATION, WHO AFTER ENTIRELY ABANDONING ALL DESIRES, GOES THROUGH LIFE BEING CONTENT WITH THE BARE NECESSITIES OF LIFE, WHO REGARDS NOT AS HIS, EVEN THOSE THINGS WHICH ARE NEEDED FOR MERE BODILY EXISTENCE, WHO IS NOT VAIN OF HIS KNOWLEDGE – SUCH A MAN OF STEADY KNOWLEDGE, WHO KNOWS *BRAHMAN*, ATTAINS PEACE (*NIRVANA*), THE END OF ALL THE MISERY OF MUNDANE EXISTENCE (*SAMSARA*). IN SHORT, HE BECOMES *BRAHMAN*.

THIS DEVOTION TO KNOWLEDGE IS EXTOLLED AS FOLLOWS:

72. *This is the BRAHMIC-state, O Son of Pritha. Attaining this, none is deluded. Being established therein, even at the end of life, one attains to oneness with BRAHMAN.*

To renounce all desires is to destroy completely the last vestures of one's ego. Renunciation of ego is not a state of dull, meaningless emptiness. Where the delusory ego has ended, the state of full-Knowledge or Selfhood has dawned. To realise the Self in one's own bosom is to realise at once the Self which is All-pervading and Eternal (*Brahman*).

When the ego has ended, the Consciousness is not known to be anything other than the Eternal, and as such the Knower of Truth in a brilliant experience of the Self becomes the Self, and therefore, this state is called Self-hood (*Brahmi-sthitih*).

A doubt may still arise that even after this realisation, we may again fall into the delusion of the ego and come to suffer the ego's world of imperfections and sorrows. To deny this tragedy, we have been told how having realised the Self once, no more can the individual fall back into his ancient delusions. This experience of the Self need not necessarily take place in the very youthful days of one's life. Even in old age, nay, even in the last moment of this embodiment, if a

---

एषा ब्राह्मी स्थितिः पार्थ नैनां प्राप्य विमुह्यति ।
स्थित्वास्यामन्तकालेऽपि ब्रह्मनिर्वाणमृच्छति ॥ ७२ ॥

eṣā brāhmī sthitiḥ pārtha naināṁ prāpya vimuhyati,
sthitvāsyām antakāle 'pi brahmanirvāṇamṛcchati 72.

seeker can come to experience, even for a moment this egoless state of tranquillity and poise, even a passing glimpse of the Selfhood, it is sufficient to gain this *Brahmic*-state as pointed out in the *Vedantic* literature.

"Negation of the false and assertion of the True" is the path that has been indicated in the *Upanishads*. The same path in its practical application is designated here in the *Geeta*, in Vyasa's original contribution as *Karma Yoga*. To work without attachment, desires, egoism and vanity, ever established in perfect equilibrium in both, success and failure, is to deny the ego its entire field of activity, and unconsciously to assert the greater Truth that is the Self. Thus, in technique, the *Geeta's Karma Yoga* is not at all different from the *Vedantic* technique of Meditation. But Arjuna got confused and perplexed because he took Krishna's words too literally, and therefore, in the following chapter, he expresses his mental confusion in the opening lines. The Lord, therefore, explains the *Karma Yoga* exhaustively in the next chapter.

Thus, in the UPANISHADS of the glorious Bhagawad Geeta, in the Science of the Eternal, in the Scripture of YOGA, in the dialogue between Sri Krishna and Arjuna, the second discourse ends entitled:

The *Yoga* of Knowledge

This chapter is named as '*Sankhya Yoga*' not in the sense that it is the *Sankhyan* philosophy that is here summarised or borrowed by Krishna. Here the word *Sankhya* is used only in its etymological sense as "the sequence of logic in any line of correct thinking and the logical enumeration of the arguments based upon which a certain intellectual conclusion has been arrived at". It is in this sense, that the highly philosophical

Chapter II of the *Geeta* is termed as *Sankhya Yoga* in its epilogue (*Sankalpa Vakya*).*

It is true that in the original Mahabharata, the *Geeta* chapters do not carry this *Sankalpa Vakya*. Commentators differ in attributing to any single individual, the authorship of this *Sankalpa Vakya*. However, it has been accepted that some scholar or scholars analysed the contents of each chapter and gave an appropriate title to each. To all the students of the *Geeta*, it is indeed a great help. Shankara however does not comment upon this portion at all.

Om Om Om Om Om

ॐ तत्सदिति श्रीमद् भगवद् गीतासूपनिषत्सु ब्रह्मविद्यायां
योगशास्त्रे श्रीकृष्णार्जुनसंवादे सांख्ययोगो नाम
द्वितीयोऽध्याय:

Oṁ tatsaditi śrīmadbhagavadgītāsū ūpaniṣatsu brahmavidyāyāṁ
yogaśāstre śrī kṛṣṇārjuna saṁvāde sāṅkhyayogo nāma
dvitīyo'dhyāyaḥ

*For commentary on it please refer to what has been said at the end of Chapter I.

III

The Karma Yoga
Introduction

SO far Sri Krishna vehemently argued against Arjuna's decision not to fight but to renounce the glory of success and retire to the quietude of the jungle to live there the life of a monk seeking the Divine. In his arguments, at one moment,* the Lord advised that Arjuna's duty was to work without getting himself preoccupied with its result. Krishna had also warned him, "LET NOT THY ATTACHMENT BE TOWARD INACTION". Later on, the chapter concluded (II-55 to 72) with the inspired advocacy of the path-of-Knowledge. Naturally, like any sincere student, Arjuna felt confused as to which of the paths he was to follow for his self-development.

The *Vedantic* philosophy of India is taught to the student during an intimate and free discussion between the teacher and the taught. In no other religion in the world, do we find so much freedom allowed to the disciple, to ask freely and openly, to contradict, and to argue with his teachers.

Vedanta being a complete and exhaustive science of Religion, the great *Rishis* never bypassed the intellect of their disciples by appealing to their blind faith or insisting upon their abject devotion. The masters of old encouraged doubts

*Refer to commentary on Verse II-47.

and invited discussions. It is during these discussions that the student wrestled with the teacher in the arena of the intellect, and in this exercise, he became spiritually stronger and perfectly agile in all the other layers of his personality. This *Upanishadic* style has been beautifully preserved and artistically employed by the great poet-Philosopher Vyasa, in his *Geeta*.

Any student, sincerely following up the second chapter with an irresistible appetite to live and enjoy the perfections pointed out, must necessarily entertain such a doubt, as Arjuna expresses at the opening of this chapter. In fact, the arguments raised by Krishna in his discourse create in us a grave doubt as to what exactly is that path which will take a seeker easily to the realization of the Absolute in Him. Is it: (a) Knowledge (b) Action or (c) both together practised in a synthesis, or lastly, (d) is it through a total renunciation of both? Such a doubt can come, as I have already said, only to a seeker who has the enthusiasm to live the life indicated earlier. According to Sankara, action and renunciation are advised in the *Vedas*, for a seeker to pursue SERIALLY. Ordinarily, no doubt, no living creature endowed with a mind and intellect can remain, even for a moment of his wakeful conscious existence, without doing some work or the other. Cessation of all activities is the signature of death upon insentient matter. Therefore, act we must, from birth to death.

Instinctively, in our inborn ignorance, we act, motivated by our ego and egocentric desires. An uncultivated man acts, thoughtlessly, propelled by his own wrong tendencies, ordering for himself ever a new lease of sorrowful existence. Entertaining these sensuous desires, he acts in the world seeking joy and earning for himself fleeting happiness, endless sorrows and inexhaustible mental impressions (*vasanas*). These *vasanas* invite new fields for exhaustion through their free expressions in action.

Naturally, the way out from this non-stop vicious circle of ego-motivated action which creates *vasanas* (and they demand more fields to exhaust themselves, wherein the individual again fattens his ego and comes to entertain fresh sets of desires) is the path of Right-Action. God-dedicated selfless actions performed in a spirit of devotion and self-surrender exhaust the existing *vasanas* and do not create, of their own accord, any more fresh tragic impressions, which in their turn would order fresh fields of activities.

In the limited concept of life in the *Vedic* period, work (*Karma*) meant only the ritualistic sacrifices. These activities, pursued for a sufficiently long period, purified the heart; meaning, integrated the personality and brought about a single-pointedness of mind in the individual. It is obvious that such a conditioned and steadied mind alone could successfully apply itself on the path of Self-enquiry, and come to rediscover the Self, the Divine Soul.

The *Geeta* was written as an answer to an urgent demand in the time of Vyasa. The old traditional thoughts became stereotyped and lifeless. Dead phrases and cliches cannot nourish a culture. Thus, through the *Geeta*, Krishna is made to give out a reinterpretation of the *Vedic* Truths in the context of His time, and in the language of the world in which He Himself happened to live. Arjuna, a warrior in the battlefield, is facing an army, which is championing a cause, at once immoral and foul. At this moment, for his spiritual evolution

– which no doubt has been fully accepted as the goal of existence – it is not possible for him to indulge in ritualism, unless he deserts his post of duty.

If ritualism alone was the 'Path', all people, at all times, would never be able to employ themselves for the highest Goal of life. In the *Geeta,* therefore, we have an expansion of the idea indicated in the *Vedas*. Krishna, in His Divine declaration, gives the sanction that ANY ACTION can be a glorious 'sacrifice', if only it is undertaken with the required purity of motive, with a spirit of surrender, and with the deep emotion of love.

Apart from the glory of the *Geeta*, as a book of original contribution inaugurating a development upon the *Vedic* technique, this chapter, with its opening query from Arjuna, vividly pictures his psychological confusion. We have noticed the psychosis into which Arjuna had sunk. Defining a patient of psychosis, modern psychology says; "The psychotic person loses his contact with reality. He may live in a dream world, perhaps unaware of his identity or surroundings, or he may be unable to control his behaviour. He may have fantastic ideas (delusions); he may misinterpret what he sees or hears (illusions); he may see, hear, feel, taste or smell things that are not there (hallucinations)".

Even though the patient, Arjuna, a victim of his own delusions, illusions and hallucinations, had completely surrendered to the Divine Wisdom of his friend, Lord Krishna, the words of his Charioteer were not fully appreciated by him, all at once. His mind was so much overwhelmed by sorrow that he could not decide upon the right line of action. He had, at first, resolved not to fight the mean fratricidal war and had vigorously marshalled a set of seemingly impressive arguments in support of his decision. Therefore, Arjuna is still and naturally too, partial to his own decision. All through the second chapter, Arjuna's intellect was trying to follow closely, the arguments of Krishna, mainly to find fault with them, if he could, or at least to seek in them some support for his own decisions.

Krishna's arguments seemed, to the preoccupied intellect of his friend, equivocal and vague. To Arjuna, in his consummate prejudice against everything that came as a challenge to his own decisions, Krishna's discourse was not clear. At one place, the Lord indicated that *Karma* was inferior to *Buddhi*; but in the same discourse in its conclusion, there was a vehement support of the path-of-Renunciation!

Arjuna was all the time seeking a confirmation that his cowardice was a noble emotion to be applauded and appreciated, commended and supported, by his friend and philosopher, Krishna. But unfortunately, he could not discover in the Lord's words any direct declaration supporting his own viewpoint. But, there was some indirect circumstantial evidence indicating that Arjuna's decision to desert his post of duty was noble and glorious! Did not the Lord elaborate upon the glory of the man of Steady-Wisdom? Arjuna means to say, "This is exactly what I wanted". But at the same time, in the same discourse, Arjuna had been pushed to the front, commissioning him to face the enemies, to take up arms and fight the bloody war. Under these circumstances, it is but natural that Arjuna should confront his Charioteer with this direct question as to why He confuses him with self-contradictory advice.

Arjuna said:

1. *If it be thought by you that 'knowledge' is superior to 'action', O Janardana, why then, do you, O Keshava, engage me in this terrible action?*

Arjuna still believes that, to fight against his cousins, teachers and grandfathers is a terrible (*ghora*) action. He seems to have forgotten, or not to have understood at all, Krishna's words in the last chapter. *Keshava* had therein explained and clearly indicated that the Mahabharata-war was not Arjuna's attempt to murder any of his cousins or teachers. Arjuna cannot have any individual personality in any army. It was a war. In a war, the two armies fight, and it represents the clash of two ideologies. The Pandavas were convinced of the moral purity, the spiritual worth, and the divine glory of their standpoint in the imminent test of strength. But unfortunately, Arjuna could not sink his egoism, and see himself totally identified with the army, championing the cause of the good. To the degree, he could not identify himself with the cause; to that extent, he nourished a self-centered egoistic vanity, and, therefore, his moral puritanism in fighting the war.

अर्जुन उवाच
ज्यायसी चेत्कर्मणस्ते मता बुद्धिर्जनार्दन ।
तत्किं कर्मणि घोरे मां नियोजयसि केशव ॥ १ ॥

arjuna uvāca
jyāyasī cetkarmaṇaste matā buddhirjanārdana
tatkiṁ karmaṇi ghore māṁ niyojayasi keśava 1.

Arjuna means to say that Krishna's arguments were supporting the path-of-Renunciation and yet they included an advice to Arjuna to undertake the great and terrible path-of-Action.

MOREOVER:

2. *With this apparently perplexing speech you confuse, as it were, my understanding; therefore, tell me that ONE way by which, I, for certain, may attain the Highest.*

Suffering from his own delusions as he was, Arjuna, intellectually an average man, had not in himself, that amount of subtle philosophical acumen to discriminate between the subtle arguments, and grasp for himself whether the path-of-Action or the way-of-Knowledge was the direct approach to the Infinite, the Eternal. His question concludes, therefore, with a humble request: "Tell me that ONE PATH by which, I, for certain, can attain the Highest".

As a child of that age, there was no doubt, even in Arjuna's mind, that life was not to be squandered away in merely producing, acquiring, hoarding and spending wealth. As a true child of Hinduism, he vaguely knew that he had to fulfil a great cultural mission in the world, and that material successes were only the means and not the end, or the goal. Partha's doubt was only on how best he could make use of

---

व्यामिश्रेणेव वाक्येन बुद्धिं मोहयसीव मे ।
तदेकं वद निश्चित्य येन श्रेयोऽहमाप्नुयाम् ॥ २ ॥

vyāmiśreṇeva vākyena buddhi mohayasīva me
tadekaṁ vada niścitya yena śreyo'hamāpnuyām 2.

the environments that presented themselves to him so that he might carve out for himself a greater cultural growth and a fuller spiritual unfoldment in himself.

THE BLESSED LORD GIVES THE FOLLOWING REPLY, WHICH IS IN CONFORMITY WITH THE QUESTION:

The Blessed Lord said;

3. *In this world there is a two-fold path, as I said before, O sinless one; the 'Path-of-Knowledge' of the SANKHYANS and the 'Path-of-Action' of the YOGINS.*

To consider the path-of-Action (*Karma Yoga*) and the path-of-Knowledge (*Jnana Yoga*) as competitive is to understand neither of them. They, being complementary, are to be practised SERIALLY one after the other. Selfless activity gives a chance to the mind to exhaust many of its existing mental impressions. Thus purified, the mind gains such a flight and ethereal poise that it can steadily soar into the subtlest realms of meditation, and finally come to gain the experience of the transcendental Absolute.

Men belonging to foreign cultures find it very difficult to understand Hinduism when they approach it with all their native enthusiasm. They feel overwhelmed when they read of such a variety of 'Paths' and seemingly contradictory

---

श्रीभगवानुवाच
लोकेऽस्मिन्द्विविधा निष्ठा पुरा प्रोक्ता मयानघ ।
ज्ञानयोगेन सांख्यानां कर्मयोगेन योगिनाम् ॥ ३ ॥

śrībhagavānuvāca
loke'smindvividhā niṣṭhā purā proktā mayānagha
jñānayogena sāṅkhyānāṁ karmayogena yoginā 3.

advices. But, to condemn Hinduism as unscientific because of this, would be a mistake, as colossal and as ludicrous as to say that medicine is no science at all, since, for each patient, the same doctor prescribes a different medicine, during a single afternoon!!

Religious men, men fit for spiritual discipline fall under two distinct categories: the active and the contemplative. Temperamentally, these two classes fall so widely apart, that to prescribe for both of them one and the same technique for individual development would be to discourage one section and ignore its progress. The *Geeta* is not merely a textbook of Hinduism but a Bible of humanity. As such, in its universal application, it has to show methods of self-development to suit the mental and intellectual temperaments of both these categories.

Therefore, Krishna clearly explains here that the twofold path of Self-development was prescribed for the world; the path-of-Knowledge to the MEDITATIVE, and the path-of-Action to the ACTIVE. It is added that this classification and careful prescription for the two different types of men has been in existence from the very beginning of creation.

For the first time, Lord Krishna is giving us here in this stanza, a glimpse of the identity of the man who is the author of the *Geeta*. If it were given out by the son of Devaki, a mere mortal who lived in that age, he would at best, have given us only an intellectual theory built entirely upon the observed data. Observed data always have a knack of changing, and when they change, the final conclusions also must necessarily change. We have now a hundred different political and economic philosophies, and numberless scientific theories that have all become outmoded when the social living conditions, the economic structure, or the collected and observed data have changed in their set up, or in their imperative messages. If the *Geeta* was the conclusion of a mere mortal Krishna's intellect, the values of life preached therein, would also have got outmoded and by now become fossilised!

Here, He clearly says that, at the very beginning of creation, these two 'Paths' were prescribed by 'Me'; thereby indicating that Krishna is talking here not as the Blue Boy of Vrindavana, not as the Beloved of the *gopis,* not as the great diplomat of His age, but as a man-of-Realization, a Prophet, and a Seer, who lived in that period of Indian history. It is neither as Arjuna's charioteer, nor as a friend, nor as a well-wisher of the Pandavas, that He is talking at this moment. Perfectly identifying with the spiritual dignity in Himself, experiencing His Absolute Nature, it is as the Eternal substratum for the entire PLURALISTIC world, as the Cause of all Creation, as the Might in all substances, that He is talking now. Transcending all time and causation, in a burning conviction of the lived Truth, He declares here "At the very beginning of creation, these two 'Paths' were given out by Me as the two possible methods by which the ACTIVE and the CONTEMPLATIVE could seek and rediscover the Eternal nature of their very Self".

THE PATH-OF-ACTION IS A MEANS TO AN END, NOT DIRECTLY, BUT ONLY AS A PREPARATION TO THE PATH-OF-KNOWLEDGE; WHEREAS THE LATTER, WHICH IS ATTAINED BY MEANS OF THE PATH-OF-ACTION, LEADS TO THE GOAL DIRECTLY WITHOUT EXTRANEOUS HELP. TO SHOW THIS THE LORD SAYS:

4. *Not by non-performance of actions does man reach 'actionlessness'; nor by mere renunciation does he attain 'Perfection'.*

Spiritually, as the Self, every one of us is all-full and Perfect. Due to our 'ignorance' of this spiritual experience, we entertain in our intellect unending desires, each of them being our own intellect's attempt to fulfill itself! It is very well known that we desire things that are not already with us in full, or in a satisfying quantity. As the desires in us, so are our thoughts; thoughts are the disturbances created in our mental zone by our desires. At every moment, the texture and quality of our thoughts are directly conditioned and controlled by our desires. Thoughts in an individual, expressed in the outer world-of-objects, become his actions; actions are nothing other than the actor's thoughts projected and expressed in the world. Thus, in this chain of ignorance, constituted of desires, thoughts and actions, each one of us is caught and bound.

If we observe them a little more closely, we find that these are not so many different factors, but are, in fact, different expressions of one and the same spiritual IGNORANCE. This ignorance (*Avidya*), when it functions in the intellect, expresses itself as DESIRES. When the desires, which are nothing other than the 'ignorance', function in the mental zone, they express themselves as THOUGHTS. These

---

न कर्मणामनारम्भान्नैष्कर्म्यं पुरुषोऽश्नुते ।
न च संन्यसनादेव सिद्धिं समधिगच्छति ॥ ४ ॥

na karmaṇamanārambhānnaiṣkarmyaṁ puruṣo'śnute
na ca sannyasanādeva siddhi samadhigacchati 4.

thoughts, when they express in the outer world, become ACTIONS. Naturally, therefore, if the Supreme can be defined as 'the experience beyond ignorance', it must necessarily be true that the Self is the state of DESIRELESSNESS or the condition of THOUGHTLESSNESS or the Life of ACTIONLESSNESS.

By mere renunciation-of-action (*sannyasa*) no one attains Perfection. Running away from life is not the way to reach the highest goal of evolution. Arjuna's intention, you may remember, was to run away from the warfront, and, therefore, this misguided Hindu was to be reeducated in the right understanding of the immortal culture of the *Vedas*. For this purpose was the Divine Song given out by Krishna.

Through action, to a purification of the inner instrument, applying which the seeker walks the path-of-Knowledge to reach ultimately the spiritual destination of self-development is indicated in this stanza. Hence it has been often quoted by all great writers on Hinduism.

FOR WHAT REASON, THEN, DOES A PERSON NOT ATTAIN PERFECTION THAT IS FREE FROM ACTIVITIES BY MERE RENUNCIATION, UNACCOMPANIED BY KNOWLEDGE? THE REASON THUS ASKED FOR IS GIVEN AS FOLLOWS:

5. *Verily, none can ever remain, even for a moment, without performing action; for, everyone is made to act helplessly, indeed, by the qualities born of PRAKRITI.*

न हि कश्चित्क्षणमपि जातु तिष्ठत्यकर्मकृत् ।
कार्यते ह्यवशः कर्म सर्वः प्रकृतिजैर्गुणैः ॥ ५ ॥

na hi kaścitkṣaṇamapi jātu tiṣṭhatyakarmakṛt
kāryate hyavaśaḥ karma sarvaḥ prakṛtijairguṇaiḥ 5.

Man is ever agitated under the influence of the triple tendencies of Unactivity (*sattva*), Activity (*rajas*) and Inactivity (*tamas*) inherent in him. Even for a single moment, he cannot remain totally inactive. Total inactivity is the character of utterly insentient matter. Even if we are physically at rest, mentally and intellectually we are active all the time, except during the state of deep-sleep. So long as we are under the influence of these three mental tendencies (*Gunas*), we are helplessly prompted to labour and to act.

Therefore, not to act at all is to disobey the laws of nature, which shall, as we all know, bring about a cultural deterioration in ourselves. If there is a creature that remains inactive physically, he will get dissipated in his thoughts. Therefore, the *Geeta* advises him to act vigorously with a right attitude of mind, so that he may avoid all internal waste of energy and learn to grow in himself.

NOW, FOR HIM WHO KNOWS NOT THE SELF, IT IS NOT RIGHT TO NEGLECT THE DUTY ENJOINED ON HIM. SO THE LORD SAYS:

6. *He who, restraining the organs-of-action, sits thinking in his mind of the sense-objects, he, of deluded understanding, is called a hypocrite.*

To sit back physically retired is not the way to reach anywhere, much less the final state-of-Perfection. If this

---

कर्मेन्द्रियाणि संयम्य य आस्ते मनसा स्मरन् ।
इन्द्रियार्थान्विमूढात्मा मिथ्याचारः स उच्यते ॥ ६ ॥

karmendriya saṁyamya ya āste manasā smaran
indriyāthārnvimūḍhātmā mithyācāraḥ sa ucyate 6.

physical retirement is not efficiently accompanied by an equal amount of mental and intellectual withdrawal from the sensuous fields, the spiritual future of such a misinformed seeker is surely very bleak and dreary.

The truth of this statement is very well supported by modern textbooks on psychology. To dissipate ourselves with immoral or criminal thoughts is more harmful than to physically indulge in them. The mind has a tendency to repeat its own thoughts. When a single thought is repeated off and on, it creates in the mind a deepening impression, and afterwards, all thoughts arising in the mind irresistibly flow in that prepared channel. Once the direction of the flow in the mind has become fixed, all external activities of that individual, become coloured by this characteristic tendency. A mind that constantly meditates on sensuous pleasures carves out for itself a deep sensuous tendency and ere long we discover that, the individual is helplessly egged on to act in the external world, as he had tragically planned for himself in his mind.

To give physically a show of morality and ethics, while mentally living a shameless life of low motives and foul sentiments, is the occupation of a man who is not a seeker of spiritual fulfilment, but as is termed here, a self-deluded hypocrite! Certainly, we all know that, even if we can physically discipline ourselves, it is not easy for an average man to control the sensuous tendencies at his mental level.

KRISHNA REALISES THAT AN ORDINARY MAN WOULD NOT KNOW HOW TO SAVE HIMSELF FROM THIS NATURAL INSTINCT AND, THEREFORE, HE PRESCRIBES THE FOLLOWING STANZA:

7. *But, whosoever, controlling the senses by the mind, O Arjuna, engages his organs-of-action in KARMA YOGA, without attachment, he excels.*

In these two innocent looking lines, we have the entire science of Right-Action and the complete technique of right living. The ECONOMICS OF THOUGHT is a science unknown to the modern world while the thought economists of yore carved out a *Rishi*-India and guided the country to the golden era of its spiritual culture.

The mind is fed and sustained, nurtured and nourished by the five organs-of-perception, with stimuli drawn from the outer world of sense-objects. The mind in us, as it were, flows out through the sense-organs, and when it comes in contact with their respective objects, the sense-organs perceive them. If the mind is not cooperating with the sense-organs, perception is impossible, even though the objects may be within the field of the organs. That is why sometimes, when we are deeply attentive and fully interested in reading a book, we do not hear even when somebody calls us at our elbow. Examples can be multiplied.

The prescription contained in this stanza asks a seeker to control the sense-organs by the mind. This can be effectively achieved only when the mind is given a brighter and diviner field to roam about in. To control the impetuosity of the mind with sheer will is like an attempt to dam a river while it is in

---

यस्त्विन्द्रियाणि मनसा नियम्यारभतेऽर्जुन ।
कर्मेन्द्रियैः कर्मयोगमसक्तः स विशिष्यते ॥ ७ ॥

yastvindriyāṇi manasā niyamyārabhate'rjuna
karmendriyaiḥ karmayogmasaktaḥ sa viśiṣyate 7.

flood. It is destined to be a futile attempt. Later on, the *Geeta* will explain the technique of this control.

This control of the sense-organs by the mind is only the negative aspect of the entire technique of right living. Ordinarily, we spend a lot of our life-energies in the fields of sense-objects. When the sense-organs are thus controlled, we are conserving a large quantity of energy, and unless this gathered energy is immediately given a more profitable field of activity it is sure to break the bounds and flood the inner world and, perhaps, sweep away the entire personality equilibrium. The second line of this stanza advises us what we should do with the energies, thus saved from their usual fields of dissipation.

The stanza says that these energies must be spent in directing the seeker's organs-of-action to the appropriate fields of activities. Even here, a very important precaution has been lovingly advised by Krishna. The *Karma-Yogin* has been warned to act with perfect detachment.

When a camera is loaded with a piece of plain white paper, however long we may keep the lenses open against any well-lit object, no impression of the object concerned can dirty the paper! On the other hand, if that very same sheet of paper is sensitized, then, even a slight exposure will leave the impressions of the object upon it. Similarly, a mind plastered with attachment soon gathers on to itself impressions (*vasanas*) during its contacts in the external fields of activity. The Lord advises us to act without attachment, so that, instead of gathering new impressions, we may make use of our activities for the exhaustion of the existing *vasana*-dirt in our mental equipment.

The logical and scientific exposition of this theory is so complete that, no student of the *Geeta* can discover in it any loopholes for hesitation or doubt.

By withdrawing the organs-of-perception from their unprofitable fields of activity, we save on the inner energy which is spent through the organs-of-activity on a chosen field of work; because of our inner attitude of non-attachment during the activity, no new rubbish is gathered by our mind, but, on the contrary, it gets itself burnished by the removal of its existing mental dirt. The very field of activity, which ordinarily becomes a snare to capture and imprison a soaring soul, itself becomes the exact art of self-liberation, when it is rightly employed by faithfully following the way-of-life advised in the *Geeta*.

WHEREFORE:

8. *You perform (your) bounden duty; for, action is superior to inaction. Even the maintenance of the body would not be possible for you by inaction.*

In our work-a-day world, we must understand this term 'bounden duty' (*Niyatam Karma*) in the text, to include all 'obligatory actions' of an individual in his home, in his office, and in the society as a national being. Thus, not to perform diligently all our duties in the home and in the world outside would be inaction. We are warned that even a healthy bodily

---

नियतं कुरु कर्म त्वं कर्म ज्यायो ह्यकर्मण: ।
शरीरयात्रापि च ते न प्रसिद्ध्येदकर्मण: ॥ ८ ॥

niyataṁ kuru karma tvaṁ karma jyāyo hyakarmaṇaḥ
śarīrayātrāpi ca te na prasiddhyedakarmaṇaḥ 8.

existence is not possible if we were to live in complete inertia and inactivity. Inactivity brings about the destruction of the nation, of the society, and of the home, and often the very individual himself becomes victimised by his own idleness and suffers physical debilities and intellectual deterioration.

IT IS ALSO WRONG TO SUPPOSE THAT ACTIONS LEAD TO BONDAGE AND THAT THEY SHOULD NOT, THEREFORE, BE PERFORMED – WHY?

9. *The world is bound by actions other than those performed 'for the sake of sacrifice'; do thou, therefore, O son of Kunti, perform action for that sake (for YAJNA) alone, free from all attachments.*

Every action does not bring about bondages upon the doer. It is only unintelligent activities that thicken the impressions in the mind, and thus successfully build a thick and impenetrable wall between the egocentre and the unlimited Divine spark-of-Life in us. Every action motivated by egocentric desires thickens the veil and permits not even a single ray of the essential Divinity to peep through it, to illumine the life in us. According to the traditional translation, all activities other than the *Yajna*-activities will bring about *vasana*-bondages, and the individual's ultimate development and growth will be arrested.

Yajna here means "any self-sacrificing work, undertaken in a spirit of self-dedication, for the blessing of all". Such an

---

यज्ञार्थात्कर्मणोऽन्यत्र लोकोऽयं कर्मबन्धनः ।
तदर्थं कर्म कौन्तेय मुक्तसङ्गः समाचर ॥ ९ ॥

yajñāthārtkarmaṇo'nyatra loko'yaṁ karmabandhanaḥ
tadarthaṁ karma kaunteya muktsaṅgaḥ samācara 9.

action cannot be self-degrading and, therefore, it is self-liberating. The following stanzas also will become more and more clear, and universally appropriate in their meaning, only when we understand *Yajna* as 'any social, communal, national, or personal activity into which the individual is ready to pour himself forth entirely in a spirit of service and dedication'.

Only when people come forward to act in a spirit of co-operation and self-dedication, can the community get itself freed from its shackles of poverty and sorrow. This is a fact endorsed by history. And such activities can be undertaken in a spirit of Divine loyalty, only when the worker has no attachment. Arjuna's defect was that he got too attached to the individuals in the opposing forces, and he developed, consequently, wrong relationships with them. Therefore, he came to feel that he must run away from the field of work that had presented itself before him.

FOR THE FOLLOWING REASONS ALSO, ACTION SHOULD BE DONE BY HIM, WHO IS QUALIFIED FOR IT:

10. *The PRAJAPATI (the Creator), having in the beginning (of creation) created mankind together with sacrifices, said, "by this shall you prosper; let this be the milch-cow of your desire–KAMADHUK" (the mythological cow which yields all desired objects).*

सहयज्ञाः प्रजाः सृष्ट्वा पुरोवाच प्रजापतिः ।
अनेन प्रसविष्यध्वमेष वोऽस्त्विष्टकामधुक् ॥ १० ॥

sahayajñāḥ prajāḥ sṛṣṭvā purovāca prajāpatiḥ
anena prasaviṣyadhvameṣa vo'stviṣṭakāmadhuk 10.

Even when the Creator, the Total-mind, puts up the show of the Universe of the Five Elements and brings forth the living organisms along with man, on this stage of life to work, to strive and to achieve, he creates also *Yajna* – the spirit of self-dedicated activities. The *Yajna*-spirit is seen everywhere; the Sun shines, the Moon appears, the Sea throbs, the Earth bears – all in a spirit of sacrifice and self-dedicated motherly love with never even a trace of attachment or any kind of self-arrogating motive.

The whole world of cosmic powers and nature's phenomena function instinctively in the service of all. Even before life could appear on the face of the earth, the elemental forces had prepared the field with their constant activities performed in the sacred spirit-of-dedication. Even when life developed and multiplied, at all levels, we can easily recognise different degrees of *Yajna*-activities, which keep up the harmonious growth of existence.

The above idea, when poetically put, becomes this pregnant stanza in the *Geeta*. The Creator created the world along with the spirit of service and the capacity for sacrifice. As it were, the Creator declared, "by this spirit of self-sacrifice shall you multiply; this shall be the milch-cow of your desires". *Kamadhenu* is a mythological cow, supposed to have belonged to Sage Vasishta, from which all our desires could be milked out. The term, therefore, means only that no achievement is impossible for man, if he knows how to act in the discipline of cooperation, and if he is ready to bring forth into his activities the required amount of non-attachment and spirit of sacrifice.

HOW CAN THIS BE ACHIEVED BY SACRIFICE?

11. *With this, you do nourish the gods and may those DEVAS nourish you; thus nourishing one another, you shall, attain the Highest Good.*

The whole *Vedic* concept of *Devas* is that of one Universal power, ever active in the world of phenomena, receiving appropriate names because of Its multiple functions. All *Vedic* gods are but functional names of the one Supreme Creative Power manifesting in myriad forms.

In understanding the stanza in its more universal application, we have to interpret the term *Deva* as the very 'presiding deity' in any field of activity, who blesses the worker in that field with his profit. The deity that blesses the worker in a field of activity can be nothing other than THE PRODUCTIVE POTENTIAL in that given field. When we apply in any situation our true and sincere work, the efforts and sacrifices so made, as it were, invoke the PRODUCTIVE POTENTIAL in that situation, which comes to manifest and bless the worker. This becomes obvious when we try to understand what we, in the modern world mean, when we say Mother India. In thus symbolising the might of a nation we mean the PRODUCTIVE POTENTIAL of that country in all her spheres of activities.

It is obvious that the productivity that is dormant in any situation can be invoked only by man's sincere efforts. This potential which generally lies dormant everywhere is the *Deva*

देवान्भावयतानेन ते देवा भावयन्तु वः ।
परस्परं भावयन्तः श्रेयः परमवाप्स्यथ ॥ ११ ॥
devān bhāvayatānena te devā bhāvayantu vaḥ
parasparaṁ bhāvayantaḥ śreyaḥ paramavāpsyatha 11.

to be cherished by the worker through the *Yajna* activities, and certainly the *Deva* will manifest itself to cherish, or to bless the worker. Thus cherishing one another, man shall gain the Highest Good, is the Divine intention in the mind of the creator, says Krishna in this stanza.

The law-of-*Seva* is faithfully followed by every sentient and insentient member of the cosmos instinctively. Man alone is given the freedom to act as he likes and to the extent, he disobeys this Universal law-of-Sacrifice, *Yajna*, to that extent he comes to suffer, because he, with his arrogant and egoistic actions, brings discord in the harmony of the existence around him.

MOREOVER:

12 *The DEVAS, nourished by the sacrifice, will give you the desired objects. Indeed, he who enjoys objects given by the DEVAS, without offering (in return) to them, is verily a thief.*

Here, Krishna repeats the unalterable ritualistic law 'that the *Devas*, cherished by *Yajna*, will provide us with the desired objects'. The truth of this statement becomes self-evident and clear when we reread this statement substituting our meaning for the terms *Deva* and *Yajna*. The productive potential (*Deva*), when cherished through 'self-dedicated work performed in a spirit of sacrifice' (*Yajna*), will provide the worker with the desired objects. This is the law of life.

इष्टान्भोगान्हि वो देवा दास्यन्ते यज्ञभाविताः ।
तैर्दत्तानप्रदायैभ्यो यो भुङ्क्ते स्तेन एव सः ॥ १२ ॥

iṣṭānbhogān hi vo devā dāsyante yajñabhāvitāḥ
tairdattānapradāyaibhyo yo bhuṅkte stena eva saḥ 12.

And when we thus earn a profit due to our sacrifices, we have every right to enjoy that profit SHARING AMONG OURSELVES. But no living creature should enjoy benefits of others' actions without contributing his own share to the total effort. In the capitalistic system of life, we notice the wrong tendency of self-aggrandisement of profits produced out of the collective efforts of millions of workers. This ultimately creates sad maladjustments in all spheres of activity, and national and international peace is threatened when we thus upset the law of harmony in life. When this idea, familiar in modern finance, "that a member of a society who consumes without producing is a liability to the nation", is reread in the language of the *Vedas*, it is spelt as the second line of this stanza.

HE WHO ENJOYS OBJECTS, GIVEN BY THE *DEVAS*, the productive potential tapped, without offering his own *Yajna*-efforts into it, is termed here by Krishna as a 'social thief'. Considering the moral and ethical idealism recognised and respected at the time of the *Geeta*, the term 'thief' used here is indeed a powerful word, fully implying the low depravity and disrespectful nature of such a social criminal who eats without producing.

ON THE OTHER HAND:

13. *The righteous, who eat the 'remnants of the sacrifices' are freed from all sins; but those sinful ones, who cook food (only) for their own sake, verily eat but sin.*

यज्ञशिष्टाशिनः सन्तो मुच्यन्ते सर्वकिल्बिषैः ।
भुञ्जते ते त्वघं पापा ये पचन्त्यात्मकारणात् ॥ १३ ॥

yajñaśiṣṭāśinaḥ santo mucyante sarvakilbiṣaiḥ,
bhuñjate te tvaghaṁ pāpā ye pacantyātmakāraṇāt 13.

As a contrast to such social criminals, feeding themselves upon the social wealth, in producing which they have not brought in any self-effort, in this stanza, we have the good, who receive for themselves their 'share', after sweating hard in sincere *Yajna*-activities. Such people, as explained here 'go beyond all sins'.

Sins of the past are the causes for the present pains, and the present sins would be the causes for the future sorrows. Thus, all causes for the sorrows in social life would, no doubt be removed, if the good and socially-conscious members of a community were to feel satisfied in enjoying the 'remnants' of their cooperative work performed in the true *Yajna*-spirit.

As a contrast to these, it has been declared that those who cook food for themselves alone 'eat but sin'. It seems that Krishna is perfectly against private property, not in the sense in which a communist would understand it. Krishna seems to be against the principle of arrogation of wealth, and of hoarding the same, motivated by lust of lucre, meant mainly for selfish enjoyment, utterly regardless of the privations and poverty of the unfortunate folks around in the community. It is said that such hoarders of wealth 'eat but sin'.

FOR THE FOLLOWING REASONS ALSO, ACTION SHOULD BE PERFORMED BY HIM WHO IS QUALIFIED FOR ACTION. FOR, IT IS ACTION THAT SETS THAT WHEEL OF THE UNIVERSE MOVING. HOW? THE ANSWER FOLLOWS:

14. *From food come forth beings; from rain food is produced; from sacrifice arises rain, and sacrifice is born of action.*

15. *Know you that action comes from BRAHMAJI (the Creator) and BRAHMAJI come from the Imperishable. Therefore, the all-pervading BRAHMAN (God-principle) ever rests in sacrifice.*

The cosmic wheel of cooperative-action is being narrated here in the familiar language of the *Vedas*. The living creatures are born out of food, and they are nourished by food. The mineral-wealth of the world becomes assimilable food - both as vegetarian and non-vegetarian - only by the action of rain upon it. But for rains the vegetables will not grow, and the lack of proper grazing-grounds is a danger to cattle-wealth. Rains come as a result of *Yajna*, and *Yajnas* are performed through human action.

This stanza may appear strange to those who are not ready to bring the full shaft of their intelligence for the purpose of understanding it. It is evident to any modern educated man that living creatures are born out of matter. Matter is rendered consumable and digestible, nutritive and assimilable,

---

अन्नाद्भवन्ति भूतानि पर्जन्यादन्नसम्भवः ।
यज्ञाद्भवति पर्जन्यो यज्ञः कर्मसमुद्भवः ॥ १४ ॥

annādbhavanti bhūtāni parjanyādannasambhavaḥ,
yajñādbhavati parjanyo yajñaḥ karmasamudbhavaḥ 14.

कर्म ब्रह्मोद्भवं विद्धि ब्रह्माक्षरसमुद्भवम् ।
तस्मात्सर्वगतं ब्रह्म नित्यं यज्ञे प्रतिष्ठितम् ॥ १५ ॥

karma brahmodbhavaṁ viddhi brahmākṣarasamudbhavam,
tasmātsarvagataṁ brahma nityaṁ yajñe pratiṣṭhitam 15.

only by the action of rains upon it. But the difficulty in understanding the stanza is when we come to the next assertion that 'the rains come as a result of *Yajnas*'.

But in Krishna's words here, we are not warranted in accepting that he is advising Arjuna to follow ritualism. In this stanza, as also elsewhere all along the *Geeta*, the familiar terms of the *Vedic* period has been charged with new meanings and significances. Rain is the essential condition for the conversion of the mineral raw material into enjoyable and nutritive food. Similarly, in all fields of activity there is an enjoyable profit which can be gathered only when the fields come under 'conditions favourable' for them to produce those profits. Self-dedicated activities (*Yajna*), when performed in any given field of endeavour, will be creating therein conditions necessary for the field to smile forth (rain) in a luxurious 'crop of profit' (*Annam*), enjoyable by the society.

For example, the wasteful waters of a river flowing idly can be dammed and made use of, if the waters are intelligently employed in irrigating the fertile lands now lying fallow on its banks. Through sacrifice and work alone can the dam be built and when it is built, it provides 'conditions helpful' for bringing the lands on either side under the plough. Again, for making use of irrigated land, man has yet to strive; ploughing, sowing, weeding, waiting, gathering – before he can come to enjoy the profit of his activities – the food.

We are shown how this wheel-of-Action (stanza-15), is connected with and includes the Supreme. The principle of right action, nay, even the power to act, has come out of the Creator himself and the Creator is none other than the Imperishable Supreme. Action IS in the newborn live-baby;

action is a gift from the Creator! Therefore, the All-pervading Supreme is ever centred in all undertakings pursued, by one or many people, in an honest spirit of Self-dedication, for the good of all.

HE, WHO LIVES IN UNISON WITH THIS WHEEL-OF-ACTION, IS CONTRIBUTING TO THE HARMONY OF LIFE. WHAT HAPPENS TO HIM WHO DISOBEYS?

16. *He who does not follow here the wheel thus set revolving, is of a sinful life, rejoicing in the senses. He lives in vain, O Son of Pritha.*

Every member in the entire kingdom of the minerals, the vegetables and the dumb-creatures, instinctively follows this principle of *Yajna* and contributes thereby to the smooth running of the Universal wheel-of-Action. Among living creatures, man alone has been allowed the FREEDOM OF ACTION to contribute to the harmony, or to bring about discord in the smooth running of this cosmic mechanism. So long as the majority of a generation manage to live abiding by the law of Harmony they shall grow from strength to strength, opening up fields of happiness for themselves. Such periods are called the golden eras of their social and cultural life.

But, this faithful obedience is not always possible, for all of them, at all times. At certain periods of history, man, as a

---

एवं प्रवर्तितं चक्रं नानुवर्तयतीह यः ।
अघायुरिन्द्रियारामो मोघं पार्थ स जीवति ॥ १६ ॥

evaṁ pravartitaṁ cakraṁ nānuvartayatīha yaḥ,
aghāyurindriyārāmo moghaṁ pārtha sa jīvati 16.

social being, comes to revolt against this Eternal Law, and then, life starts slipping away from its peaceful domain of constructive growth, and shatters itself in tearful ruin. Such ages are the dark ages of despair and restlessness, war and pestilence, flood and famine.

The question naturally arises as to why the bright day of the world slowly sets itself to bring in the dark night of chaos. The explanation is given here in the *Geeta.*

A community is made up of its individuals. However much we may glorify the achievements of the community as such, we cannot totally ignore the contributions made by the units constituting the community – the individuals. If the individuals are perfect, the community works smoothly. But, if the units are wrongly composed, then the entire healthy growth and strength of structure in the total collapses. The individuals' negative existence starts with their preoccupation with their senses. In their limited recognition that they are themselves nothing more than their body, they become preoccupied with its nourishment and fattening. As a body, they cannot perceive the Higher 'ways of life'; nor can they entertain any goal other than seeking satisfactions for their mere animal passions.

In such an era, nobody would come forward to work in the redeeming noble spirit of *Yajna*, without which, no 'favourable circumstances' (rain), could be created for the 'productive potentials' (*Devas*) to manifest themselves as nourishing joy. Seekers of sense (*Indriya-ramah*), they compete among themselves, each seeking with lustful greed, his own selfish happiness, and they, often unconsciously, bring about a discordant rhythm in the wheel-of-Action. Such people are considered by the *Geeta* as 'living in sin', and the Divine Song asserts, 'they live in vain'.

NOW THE LORD HIMSELF SUPPOSES ARJUNA TO ASK THE FOLLOWING QUESTIONS: "IS THE WHEEL-OF-ACTION, THUS SET IN MOTION, TO BE FOLLOWED BY ALL, OR BY HIM ONLY WHO HAS NOT YET ATTAINED FIRM FAITH IN THE PATH OF KNOWLEDGE?"

17. *But the man who rejoices only in the Self, who is satisfied with the Self, who is content in the Self alone, for Him verily there is nothing (more) to be done.*

The wheel-of-Action explained above is generally applicable to the majority of seekers, and actions in the world undertaken in a spirit of *Yajna* integrate their personality and make them more and more prepared for the highest vocation in life, meditation. Through selfless work, an individual gains an increasing amount of inner poise and when such a single-pointed mind is brought to function at the meditation seat, the meditator gains the experience of transcending his limited ego. To such a perfected one, work is not a training to purify himself but it is a fulfilment of his own God-realisation.

It is a fact that we are egged on to activity seeking and demanding a better SATISFACTION and a complete CONTENTMENT. Satisfaction and contentment are the two wheels of the life-chariot. In order to gain a better satisfaction

---

यस्त्वात्मरतिरेव स्यादात्मतृप्तश्च मानवः ।
आत्मन्येव च संतुष्टस्तस्य कार्यं न विद्यते ॥ १७ ॥

yastvātmaratireva syād ātmatṛptaśca mānavaḥ,
ātmanyeva ca santuṣṭastasya kāryaṁ na vidyate 17.

and to reach nearer the point of contentment we are goaded to act in the outer world, to earn and to save, to hoard and to spend. But the man-of-Perfection, who on transcending his limited identification with his matter-envelopments, when he gets himself ushered into the All-perfect Realm of the Spirit, he comes to feel so satisfied with the state of Self-hood which he thereby attains, that he experiences a complete sense of contentment in the very Divine Nature, and that provides eternal satisfaction for him.

Where satisfaction and contentment have arrived, there, in that bosom, desires cannot arise at all; and where the desires are not, there cannot be any action. Thus, the effects (*Karya*) are not possible in him; the effects of the spiritual ignorance, desires, thoughts and actions. Naturally, in such an individual there cannot be any 'obligatory duty'; all work has been at once fulfilled in him. Thereafter, he is free to act, or not to act, to serve, or not to serve, and lives as a God-man upon the earth.

MOREOVER:

18. *For him there is here no interest whatever in what is done, or what is not done; nor does he depend upon any being for any object.*

An ordinary man is whipped up to action either because of his anxiety to gain a profit or because of his fear that by

---

नैव तस्य कृतेनार्थो नाकृतेनेह कश्चन ।
न चास्य सर्वभूतेषु कश्चिदर्थव्यपाश्रय: ॥ १८ ॥

naiva tasya kṛtenārtho nākṛteneha kaścana,
na cāsya sarva-bhūteṣu kaścid-artha-vyapāśrayaḥ. 18

not doing work he will be incurring a loss. But an individual, who has the subjective experience of the spiritual stature in him, who has, therefore, discovered an Eternal satisfaction in his own Self, and who has reached perfect contentment therein, will have no more action to perform. He has nothing more to gain through activity, nor can he have any fear of losing anything in the world due to non-performance of any action. Such an individual, rooted in the experience of the Self, and depending upon nothing – neither any being nor any object – for his joy and bliss, has discovered the 'Subject'; the objects of the world are essentially nothing other than the 'Subject', being tossed on the waves of agitations in the mind.

"YOU HAVE NOT ATTAINED TO THE RIGHT KNOWLEDGE, ALL-PERVADING LIKE THE FLOOD WATERS, (II-46) WHEREFORE":

19. *Therefore, always perform actions which should be done, without attachment; for, by performing action without attachment, man attains the Supreme.*

We have already noticed that Krishna presupposes no knowledge in his friend, nor does he thrust upon Arjuna bare statements that are to be blindly believed and silently swallowed by him. Proselytisation is not the technique of *Vedanta*. Hindus are strangers to it. Every strong statement

---

तस्मादसक्तः सततं कार्यं कर्म समाचर ।
असक्तो ह्याचरन्कर्म परमाप्नोति पूरुषः ॥ १९ ॥

tasmādasaktaḥ satataṁ kāryaṁ karma samācara,
asakto hyācaran karma paramāpnoti pūruṣaḥ 19.

of fact is preceded by a line of logical thoughts explained at length. Till now Krishna was explaining the wheel-of-Action, and after exhausting the exposition of this entire theory, he, in this stanza, is crystallising his conclusions encouraging Arjuna to act.

Therefore, always perform actions, which are obligatory in your present social status, in your domestic situation, as a member of your community and the nation. Even here, Krishna is repeating his warning to Arjuna that he must be careful in all his activities, to keep his mind away from all dangerous attachments.[1] The Lord has already explained how 'attachments' directly help to form tendencies in the mind and deepen fresh *vasana*-impressions within.

FOR THE FOLLOWING REASONS ALSO YOU SHOULD PERFORM ACTION:

20. *Janaka and others attained Perfection verily through action alone; even with a view to protecting the masses you should perform action.*

Thus, the wise Kings of yore, such as Janaka and Ashwapati,[2] had tried to attain Perfection, (*Samsiddhi*), by the path-of-Action. They were men of right understanding as they tried to liberate themselves through right actions

---

कर्मणैव हि संसिद्धिमास्थिता जनकादय: ।
लोकसंग्रहमेवापि संपश्यन्कर्तुमर्हसि ॥ २० ॥

karmaṇaiva hi saṁsiddhim-āsthitā janak-ādayaḥ,
loka-saṁgrahamevāpi saṁpaśyan-kartum-arhasi. 20

1 *Chandogya Upanishad II-ii-4* and *Brihadaaranyaka Upanishad* VI-iii-1 to 3

2 Attachment = Ego+Egocentric desires; so without attachment means without Ego and Ego-prompted selfish desires.

performed in a spirit of detachment and self-dedication. They had set an example to the world by their achievement through an immaculate life of service.

Krishna means that Arjuna too, a prince by birth, and one who has taken upon himself the entire responsibility of mobilising and fighting the war, should respect his *Prarabdha* and act diligently without running away from the battlefield as he had earlier intended to do. This is the only method by which he can gain a complete *vasana*-exhaustion in himself. Born as a king, he had a greater responsibility towards the community, than any other member. Therefore, it was his duty that he should keep to his post and work diligently.

A creeper will never grow in a desert. It is nature's law that every living creature finds itself in the most conducive outer world conditions. Thus viewed, because of the very fact that he had manifested himself as a son of his father in the family of kings, nature had judged that the most conducive circumstance in life for Arjuna was the life of a prince, daring dangers, fighting enemies, and generally ordering peaceful and progressive growth for the society.

WHO SHOULD SECURE THE WELFARE OF THE WORLD? AND HOW? THE ANSWER FOLLOWS:

21. *Whatever a great man does, that other men also do (imitate); whatever he sets up as the standard, that the world (people) follows.*

यद्यदाचरति श्रेष्ठस्तत्तदेवेतरो जनः ।
स यत्प्रमाणं कुरुते लोकस्तदनुवर्तते ॥ २१ ॥

yadyadācarati śreṣṭhastattadevetaro janaḥ,
sa yatpramāṇaṁ kurute lokastadanuvartate 21.

Man is essentially an imitating animal. This is a psychological truth. The moral rejuvenation of a society in any period of history can take place only because of the example set up by the leaders of that nation. Students can be disciplined only when teachers are well behaved; the minor officials cannot be kind and honest when the rulers of the country are corrupt tyrants. Children's behaviour depends entirely upon, and is ever controlled by, the standard of purity and culture of their parents.

With this, Krishna raises his next argument on why Arjuna should act in the world. Unless he diligently acts, the chances are that the entire community will follow the low standard of retreat from action set up by him and thus they will ultimately invite a general decadence of culture in life.

Now, to emphasise the point and to make a lasting impression upon Arjuna of the teaching so far given (III-4 to 21), Lord Krishna indicates himself as an example. The Lord, though already a liberated soul (*Mukta*), is acting diligently, without attachment, as a model, for his generation to rise up above the slothfulness of the age into vigorous activity.

The very creed of Krishna is ACTIVE RESISTANCE TO EVIL. His non-violence is not the instinctive incapacity of the daydreaming coward who cannot stand up against injustice and fight for the accepted principles of national culture. There could not have been any doubt now left in the mind of Arjuna regarding the efficacy of the path-of-Action advised to him.

"IF YOU HAVE A DOUBT AS REGARDS THE NECESSITY FOR WORKING FOR THE PROTECTION OF THE MASSES, WHY DO YOU NOT OBSERVE ME? WHY DO YOU NOT FOLLOW MY EXAMPLE, AND TRY TO PREVENT THE MASSES FROM GOING ASTRAY, SETTING UP FOR THEM AN EXAMPLE IN YOURSELF?"

22 *There is nothing in the three worlds, O Partha, that has to be done by Me, nor is there anything unattained that should be attained by Me; yet, I engage Myself in action.*

Being a Perfect-Man, a true *Yogi*, Krishna had no more desire for achieving or gaining anything in the world. Had He wanted a kingdom all for Himself, He could have easily carved out one, but He was in the battlefront only with a sense of duty towards the noble and the righteous cause the Pandavas stood for.

The life of the Lord till the very moment of the Mahabharata war had been a perfect life of complete detachment and yet – even though there was nothing He had not gained, nor had He anything further to gain – He was spending Himself constantly in activity, as though work was to Him a rapturous game of enthusiasm and joy.

न मे पार्थास्ति कर्तव्यं त्रिषु लोकेषु किंचन ।
नानवाप्तमवाप्तव्यं वर्त एव च कर्मणि ॥ २२ ॥

na me pārthāsti kartavyaṁ triṣu lokeṣu kiñcana,
nānavāptam avāptavyaṁ varta eva ca karmaṇi 22.

CONTINUING THE SAME ARGUMENT, THE LORD SAYS:

23. *For, should I not ever engage Myself in action, without relaxation, men would in every way follow My Path, O son of Pritha.*

Why should the Lord work? What would be the loss to the generation if He were not to work at all? The masses always imitate their leaders and heroes in their dress, in their behaviour, in their moral values, in their actions, in all the branches of their activities. They fix their measure of perfection always by watching the standard of life of their leaders. If the Lord did not continue to work without relaxation, men also would follow in His wake and sink themselves into inactivity and so into an unproductive existence. In nature, everything acts constantly and sincerely. The entire Universe survives and sustains itself by activity.

In these stanzas, as everywhere, all along in the *Geeta*, the first person singular is used by Lord Krishna, not in the sense of the Blue Boy of Vrindavan, but as the *Atman*, or the Self-Realised man-of-Perfection. A liberated soul realises himself to be nothing other than the Spirit, upon which alone is the play of matter sustained, as the dream is sustained upon the waker. If this God-principle, though inactive in Itself, does not consistently serve the pluralistic phenomenal world as its permanent substratum, the world as it is now, cannot exist. The ocean never rises, in spite of

---

यदि ह्यहं न वर्तेयं जातु कर्मण्यतन्द्रितः ।
मम वर्त्मानुवर्तन्ते मनुष्याः पार्थ सर्वशः ॥ २३ ॥

yadi hyahaṁ na varteyaṁ jātu karmaṇyatandritaḥ,
mama vartmānuvartante manuṣyāḥ pārtha sarvaśaḥ 23.

the billows. Yet, it is a fact that without the ocean the waves cannot rise or dance. Similarly, if the Lord were not to keep on actively serving the world, the cultural life of the generation would stagnate.

"AND WHAT HARM IS THERE IF I DO NOT ACT?"... THE LORD SAYS:

24. *These worlds would perish if I did not perform action; I would be the author of confusion of 'castes', and would destroy these beings.*

If I do not perform action, it will not be conducive to the harmonious progress of the Universe, and the entire superstructure of our scientific laws and calculations will tumble down. The Universe is not a chaos; it is a cosmos. Lawlessness is not noticed anywhere in the working of the cosmic forces.

The phenomenal happenings, the movement of the planets, the rhythmic dance of the seasons, the music of creation, the law of colours are all happening in a harmony, implicitly obeying the law governing them all, and this Law is otherwise called the Mighty Power of Nature, or God. Lord Krishna, as an embodiment of Godhood, is declaring here; "If I do not perform work, the world would perish". Scientifically viewed, this declaration is not a superstitious absurdity, acceptable only to the blind believers, but it becomes a statement of fact, which even the microscope-gazers cannot honestly deny.

उत्सीदेयुरिमे लोका न कुर्यां कर्म चेदहम् ।
संकरस्य च कर्ता स्यामुपहन्यामिमा: प्रजा: ॥ २४ ॥

utsīdeyurime lokā na kuryāṁ karma cedaham,
saṁkarasya ca kartā syāmupahanyāmimāḥ prajāḥ 24.

The Lord represents not only the law governing the outer world of things and beings, but He is also the Law that governs the inner world of thoughts and emotions. The whole human society is divided into the four 'castes' (*Varna*), by the Hindu saints and sages, ON THE BASIS OF THE INDIVIDUALS' MENTAL TEMPERAMENTS. In case the law governing the inner psychological temperaments is not functioning strictly, there will be confusion in behaviour and instability in character. The general translation 'admixture of races' for *Varna-Sankara* contains a mischievous suggestion for the modern students inasmuch as they would directly understand it as a Divine sanction for the caste-tyrannies that are going on in the decadent Hindu society.*

"SUPPOSE, ON THE OTHER HAND, YOU, ARJUNA, THINK - OR FOR THAT MATTER, ANY OTHER MAN THINKS - THAT ONE WHO HAS ACHIEVED HIS GOAL OF SELF-REALISATION, EVEN HE SHOULD WORK FOR THE WELFARE OF THE OTHERS, ALTHOUGH FOR HIMSELF HE MAY HAVE NOTHING MORE TO ACHIEVE OR GAIN"...

25. *As the 'ignorant' men act from attachment to action, O Bharata, so should the 'wise' men act without attachment, wishing the welfare of the world.*

सक्ताः कर्मण्यविद्वांसो यथा कुर्वन्ति भारत ।
कुर्याद्विद्वांस्तथासक्तश्चिकीर्षुर्लोकसंग्रहम् ॥ २५ ॥

saktāḥ karmaṇyavidvāṁso yathā kurvanti bhārata,
kuryādvidvāṁstathāsaktaścikīrṣurlokasaṁgraham 25.

* For 'the confusion of caste' refer explanation under Chapter I-41.

It is very well known that all of us act in our own given fields of activities with all enthusiasm and deep interest, all day through, every day of the year and all through the years of our entire lifetime. An average member of society is seen to wear himself out in the strain of constant activity. Irrespective of his health, careless of the severity of seasons, through joy and sorrow, man constantly strives to earn and to hoard, to gain and to enjoy.

Here Krishna says that a Man of Self-Realisation also works in the world with as much diligence and sincerity, tireless enthusiasm and energizing joy, burning hopes and scalding fears, as any ordinary man striving in the competitions of the market place. The only difference between the two is that, while the ignorant acts and is motivated in his actions by his 'attachments and anxieties for the fruits', a man of Godly intentions or complete Perfection will work in the world, without attachment, only for the purpose of the redemption of the world.

This subtle difference between the activities of the 'wise' and the 'ignorant' may not strike the modern reader as very important unless his attention is directed towards its universal application. It is the anxious 'desire for the fruits' that dissipates the finer and nobler energies in the worker, and condemns his activity to utter failure. No doubt, even a man-of-God, when he acts, must bring into his field of activity his own mind and intellect.

The mind can function only when it is attached to something. It cannot remain alive, and yet, detached from every thing. 'Detachment of the mind' mentioned here is only its 'detachment from the FALSE irresistible fascination for objects' and this is gained through the process of 'attaching itself to the NOBLER'. Thus, when Lord Krishna says here, that the 'wise' man should work 'without attachments' he immediately indicates how this can be achieved. He advises Arjuna to act, 'Desirous of guiding the world'(*Loka-sangraha*).

Attachment becomes a clog or a painful chain on us only when it is extremely egocentric. To the extent, we work for larger schemes to bless a vaster section of humanity, to that extent the attachment loses its poison and comes to bless the age. Many poisons serve as medicines in their diluted form, while the same in a concentrated form can bring instantaneous death! The ego and egocentric desires bind and destroy man, but to the extent, he can lift his identifications to include and accommodate in it, larger sections of the living world, to that extent the attachment gathers an ethical halo, a divine glow, and becomes a cure for our subjective pains and imperfections.

Here, the practical method suggested is that Arjuna should work, unattached to his own egocentric, limited concept of himself and his relations, and he must enter into the battlefield as a champion fighting for a cause, noble and righteous, against the armies that have come up to question and challenge the deathless 'values of higher living' as propounded and upheld by the Hindu culture.

TO SUCH A MAN-OF-WISDOM WHO IS WORKING IN SOCIETY FOR THE SERVICE OF MAN, THE FOLLOWING ADVICE IS GIVEN:

26. *Let no wise man unsettle the minds of ignorant people, who are attached to action; he should engage them all in actions, himself fulfilling them with devotion.*

The chances are that when a man of equipoise and Self-discovery enters the field of activity, he will be tempted to advise his generation on pure ethics and abstract ideologies. The generation, misunderstanding the words and emphasis of such a Master, might come to a wrong conclusion that, to renounce activity was the direct path to Truth. The teachers are warned against such a hasty guidance, which might damp the enthusiasm of the generation to act.

Life is dynamic. Nobody can sit idle. Even the idler contributes to the general activity. In this ever-surging onward rush of life's full impetuosity, if there be a foolish guide who would plunge himself in the midstream and stand with upraised hands, howling to the generation to halt, he would certainly be pulverized by the ever-moving flood of life and its endless activities. Many a hasty Master has made this mistake and has had to pay for it. Krishna is declaring here only a Universal law for the guidance of the saints and sages of India that they should not go against the spirit of the times and be a mere revolt against life's own might and power.

न बुद्धिभेदं जनयेदज्ञानां कर्मसङ्गिनाम् ।
जोषयेत्सर्वकर्माणि विद्वान्युक्तः समाचरन् ॥ २६ ॥

na buddhibhedaṁ janayedajñānāṁ karmasaṅginām,
joṣayetsarvakarmāṇi vidvānyuktaḥ samācaran 26.

In this stanza is given out the art of guiding mankind, which can be used by every leader in all societies, be they social workers, or political masters, or cultural teachers. A society, that is functioning in a particular line of activity at any given period of history, should not be, all of a sudden, arrested in its flow, says Krishna. The leader should fall in line with the generation, and slowly and steadily guide it to act in the right direction, by his own example.

A traveller motoring with the idea of going to Hardwar may miss his way and speed down towards Saharanpur, but the way to guide him back to the main road is not to halt him; because, by halting, he will never reach his own destination, or any other goal. So long as the wheels are not revolving on the road, distances are not covered. Keeping the wheels on the move, he has to change the direction of his movements until he comes to his right path, heading towards Hardwar.

Similarly, man should act and even if he be acting in the WRONG DIRECTION, through action alone can he come to the RIGHT PATH of diviner activities, and gain the fulfilment of his Perfection. No wise man should unsettle his generation's firm faith in action. He must himself diligently perform the ordinary actions in a diviner and better fashion, and he must make himself an example to the world, so that the lesser folk may automatically imitate him and learn to follow his unfailing footsteps.

IN WHAT WAY IS AN IGNORANT MAN ATTACHED TO ACTION?

27. *All actions are performed, in all cases, merely by the Qualities-in-Nature (GUNAS). He whose mind is deluded by egoism, thinks "I am the doer".*

All along Krishna has been insisting that nobler actions are actions without attachment. This is easier said than done. Even if one intellectually accepts this idea, it is not at all easy for him to act up to it. To every one of us, the difficulty is that we know not how to get ourselves detached from our activities, and still act on in the field. The Lord gives here a method of discrimination by which we can easily develop the required amount of detachment.

We had explained earlier how spiritual IGNORANCE expresses itself at the intellectual level as DESIRES, which again, in the mental zone, manifests as THOUGHTS, and the very thoughts, coloured by our mental tendencies,* manifest themselves, in their fulfilment in the outer world-of-objects, as our ACTIONS. Thus, the tendencies of the mind (*vasanas)* express in the outer world as actions. Where there are noble thoughts, there, noble actions manifest. When the thoughts are agitated, the actions also are uncertain, faltering, and confused. And where the thoughts are dull and animalistic,

---

प्रकृतेः क्रियमाणानि गुणैः कर्माणि सर्वशः ।
अहंकारविमूढात्मा कर्ताहमिति मन्यते ॥ २७ ॥

prakṛteḥ kriyamāṇāni guṇaiḥ karmāṇi sarvaśaḥ,
ahaṅkāravimūḍhātmā kartāhamiti manyate 27.

* *Sattva, Rajas and Tamas*

the actions generated from them are correspondingly base, vicious, and cruel. Thus, the mind's projections in the outer world are, in fact, a kind of crystallisation of the mental *vasana* among the objects of the world and these constitute the 'actions'.

These actions are therefore, GENERATED by the mind, STRENGTHENED in the mind and ultimately PERFORMED with the mind. But the individual, due to his wrong identification with his own mind, gets the false notion that he himself is the 'actor' – the 'doer'. This action-arrogating ego naturally starts feeling an anxiety for its success and a burning attachment for the result of its actions.

In a dream, we create a world of our own and we identify ourselves with the world so made, and this IDENTIFIER is called the 'dreamer'. We all know that the sorrows of the dream all belong to the 'dreamer' and to no one else. The 'dreamer' is liberated from his pains when he ends his identification with the dream kingdom. Similarly, the actions in the world outside, which are nothing other than the *vasanas* existing in one's own mind, cannot of themselves, give one any attachment, but the attachment is felt by one who gets identified with one's own mental conditions. The moment one understands this simple fact, all one's attachments end, and therefore, one lives in perfect peace.

This identification with the mental condition creates the false sense of ego, which arrogates to itself the idea: "I am the doer". The 'doer' demands the FRUITS OF HIS ACTION. To get over this attachment is to end this misconception.

BUT AS REGARDS THE 'WISE' MAN:

28. *But he – who knows the Truth, O mighty-armed, about the divisions of the qualities and (their) functions, and he who knows that GUNAS-as-senses move amidst GUNAS-as-objects, is not attached.*

As a contrast to the point-of-view of the 'ignorant' man explained in the last stanza, Krishna explains here the attitude of the 'wise' man when he ploughs the field of activity. In him, attachment has no place, because of his constant, discriminating understanding that in all activities, it is his mind that projects out to form the action. When once the 'wise' man has realised that actions belong to the world of the mind, he is no more anxious for the fruits thereof. Success and failure thereafter, belong to the mind and not to him. Likes and dislikes thereafter, are of the mind and not his. Love and hatred are not his but of the mind. Thus, in complete inner freedom the God-man functions, as a true sportsman in his play-field, where the very enjoyment is in the sport and not in the score.

Here, Arjuna is addressed as the 'mighty-armed', and this is very significant in the mouth of Krishna at this moment. The very term reminds us of Arjuna's wondrous heroism as the greatest archer of his time. The implication is that a true hero is not one who can face an army and kill a few, but one

---

तत्त्ववित्तु महाबाहो गुणकर्मविभागयोः ।
गुणा गुणेषु वर्तन्त इति मत्वा न सज्जते ॥ २८ ॥

tattvavittu mahābāho guṇakarmavibhāgayoḥ,
guṇā guṇeṣu vartanta iti matvā na sajjate' 28.

who can save himself. A true warrior is only he who can tirelessly fight in the inner world, and gain a victory over his own mind and attachments. One who can act in the world's battlefield of actions, ever ruling over and never surrendering to the arrows of attachments that fly towards one from all directions, is the real Immortal Hero, who can thereafter sit unarmed on the chariots of mortal heroes, and without raising any weapon, can guide the destinies of many an army in every Kurukshetra! That Master Hero is called *Tattwavit* - one who 'knows' the Reality - the Self.

NOW:

29. *Those deluded by the qualities of nature, (GUNAS), are attached to the functions of the qualities. The man-of-Perfect-Knowledge should not unsettle the 'foolish', who are of imperfect knowledge.*

Although many know that all actions are the attempts of the mental impressions to fulfil themselves in the outer world, only the Perfect-one realises this Truth and generally becomes quiet and unattached in all his activities. The majority of us are in a state of complete delusion and are entirely victimised by our own mental temperaments. The flood of life, surging out through these existing *vasana*-channels, should not be blockaded in the activity. The advice given by Krishna in the

---

प्रकृतेर्गुणसंमूढाः सज्जन्ते गुणकर्मसु ।
तानकृत्स्नविदो मन्दान्कृत्स्नविन्न विचालयेत् ॥ २९ ॥

prakṛterguṇasaṁmūḍhāḥ sajjante guṇakarmasu,
tānakṛtsnavido mandān kṛtsanavinna vicālayet 29.

earlier stanza (26) is, again for the purpose of emphasis, repeated here in different words.

The dull-witted one, unconsciously victimised by his own mental impressions, acts in the world outside shackled by a thousand burning attachments. A sage or a saint should not come into the arena of life to decry such a man's activities all of a sudden. Krishna's suggestion is that, while feeding the fire of life, he should carefully guide its flow into the right channel wherein the flood of life can reach to water the gardens of cultural development in the individual as well as in the community.

"HOW THEN SHOULD ACTIONS BE PERFORMED BY THE 'IGNORANT' MAN WHO SEEKS LIBERATION FROM HIS OWN SENSE OF FINITUDE, WHEN HE IS QUALIFIED ONLY FOR ACTION?" THE ANSWER FOLLOWS:

30. *Renouncing all actions in Me, with the mind centered on the Self, free from hope and egoism (ownership), free from (mental) fever, (you) do fight!*

It has been clearly declared that the Divine opinion of the Lord is that Arjuna should fight. The Pandava prince is not, at present, fit for the higher contemplative life of pure meditation. Action has a tendency to create new impressions, which again procreate impulses to act more vigorously. In order to avoid creation of new *vasanas* even while acting for

---

मयि सर्वाणि कर्माणि संन्यस्याध्यात्मचेतसा ।
निराशीर्निर्ममो भूत्वा युध्यस्व विगतज्वरः ॥ ३० ॥

mayi sarvāṇi karmāṇi saṁnyasyādhyātmacetasā,
nirāśirnirmamo bhūtvā yudhyasva vigatajvaraḥ 30.

the purpose of *vasana*-exhaustion, Krishna had already advised the method of acting without the spirit of ego, or egocentric desires. The same theory is explained here while expounding a technique by which this consummation can actually be brought about.

RENOUNCE ALL ACTIONS IN ME—we have already noticed that by the first-person pronoun Krishna means the Supreme Self, the Divine, the Eternal. Renouncing all activities unto Him, with a mind soaked with devoted remembrances of the Self (*Adhyatma Chetasa*), the Lord advises Arjuna to act on. Renunciation of action does not mean an insipid life of inactivity. Actions performed through attachment and desires are renounced the moment we take away from action the egocentric and the selfish stink.

A serpent is dangerous only as long as its fangs are not removed. The moment these are taken out, even the most poisonous reptile becomes a tame creature incapable of harming anyone. Similarly, action gives rise to bondage only when it is performed with a heart laden with selfish-desires. Actions performed without desires are not actions at all, inasmuch as they are incapable of producing any painful reactions. Here, the renunciation of action only means the giving up of the wrong motives behind the actions.

The purification of the motives is possible only when the mind is made to sing constantly the Divine Songs praising the glories of the Self. In the song of Truth the heart begins to throb with the highest Divine impulses. Actions performed in the outer world by such an individual are no more the ordinary actions but they become expressions of the Supreme Will through that individual. When the limited ego is replaced by the constant feeling of the Lord – as "I am the Supreme" – such an individual becomes the most efficient instrument for the expression of the Divine Will.

Not only is it sufficient that we renounce thus all wrong actions, but we have also to make a few adjustments in our inner instruments in order to bring out an unobstructed flow of the Creator's Will through us. These are indicated here by the two terms 'without hope' and 'without ego'.

A superficial study of the stanza is sure to confuse the student and drive him to the dangerous conclusion that Hinduism preaches, not a dynamic conscious life, but an insentient existence through life in a spirit of cultivated hopelessness! But a closer study of the import of these two terms will make us understand clearly that, in this stanza, Krishna is hinting at a great psychological truth of life!

WITHOUT HOPE—Hope is 'the expectation of a happening that is yet to manifest and mature in a FUTURE PERIOD OF TIME'. Whatever be the hope, it belongs not to the present; it refers to a period not yet born.

WITHOUT EGO—our egocentric concept of ourselves is nothing but 'a bundle of happenings and achievements of ours, which took place, or were gained, in the past moments'. Ego is therefore 'the shadow of the past', and it has an existent reality only with reference to THE DEAD MOMENTS OF THE PAST.

If hope is thus the child of the unborn future, ego is the lingering memory of a dead past. To revel in ego and hope is an attempt on our part to live, either with the dead moments of the past, or with the unborn moments of the future. All the while, THE TRAGEDY IS THAT WE MISS THE

'PRESENT', THE ACTIVE DYNAMIC 'PRESENT', WHICH IS THE ONLY NOBLE CHANCE THAT IS GIVEN TO US TO CREATE, TO ADVANCE, TO ACHIEVE, AND TO ENJOY. Krishna advises Arjuna, therefore, to act renouncing both hope and ego; and this is indeed a primary instruction on how to pour the best that is in us into the 'present', blockading all unintelligent and thoughtless dissipation of our inner-personality-energies, in the 'past' and the 'future'.

The instruction is so exhaustive in vision, and complete in its minutest details, that the stanza under review should be a surprise even to the best of our modern psychologists. Even though the technique so far advised can, and does, avoid all wastage of energy among the funeral pyres of the dead moments and in the wombs of unborn Time, yet, there is a chance for the man of action wasting his potentialities in the very 'present'. This generally comes through our inborn nature to get ourselves unnecessarily over-anxious during our present activities. This FEVERISH ANXIETY is indicated here by the term 'fever' (*Jwara*). Krishna advises that Arjuna should renounce all actions unto the Lord and, getting rid of both hope and selfishness, must fight, free from all mental fever. How complete this technique is will be evident now to all students of the *Geeta*.

The term 'fight' is to be understood here 'as our individual fight with circumstances, in the silent battle of life'. Thus, the advice is not for Arjuna alone, but to all men who would like to live life fully and intelligently!

The advice contained in this stanza reads as though quite unorthodox for those who have read the *Vedas*, with a limited meaning for its term *Karma Yoga*.

IN ORDER TO HAMMER THIS NEW INTERPRETATION OF THE *VEDIC* TRUTH INTO THE ACCEPTANCE OF HIS GENERATION, THE LORD SAYS:

31. *Those men who constantly practise this teaching of Mine, full of faith and without cavilling, they too are freed from actions.*

It is clearly brought out here that the above technique can bless us not by a mere study of it, but only when it has been properly practised in life. The term religion (*matam*) in Sanskrit, means 'opinion'. This is Krishna's 'opinion' – Sri Krishna's m*atam*. The philosophy of spirituality is universal and, therefore, the same everywhere. But religions differ from prophet to prophet. For, there are many different OPINIONS entertained by these different Masters, regarding the best manner by which their particular generations could be guided towards the final experience of the Eternal-factor.

One ought not to live through life as a mere beast of burden doing its daily routine and sweating under the driver's whip. Work only hardens the muscles; it can smoothen out the ugly wrinkles in our character and add a glow of health and vitality to our inner personality only when we bring the inner equipments of our heart and head into the work, which our hands and legs perform in the outer world. This is accomplished by pursuing the *Karma Yoga* advised earlier, with full faith (s*hraddha*) and without cavilling (a*nasuyantah*).

ये मे मतमिदं नित्यमनुतिष्ठन्ति मानवाः ।
श्रद्धावन्तोऽनसूयन्तो मुच्यन्ते तेऽपि कर्मभिः ॥ ३१ ॥

ye me matamidaṁ nityamanutiṣṭhanti mānavāḥ,
śraddhāvanto'nasūyanto mucyante te'pi karmabhiḥ 31.

FAITH (*Shraddha*)—is a very pregnant word in Sanskrit which refuses to be defined fully by any single word in English.

But Sankara's explanation of *shraddha* has a purely intellectual import and it has no direct emotional appeal for the seeker. Faith in *Vedanta* means the ability to digest mentally, and comprehend intellectually, the full import of the advice of the saints and the declarations of the scriptures. In fact, without faith, no activity is ever possible; and 'faith' cannot grow where intellectual conviction has not come to play in full blaze.

WITHOUT CAVILLING (*anasuyantah*)—A mere intellectual theory cannot be understood and appreciated without our adverse criticisms of it. We criticise to know and understand more exhaustively a piece of knowledge. But here, Krishna is advising a technique of living which cannot fulfil itself in our life through mere criticism and questioning. Krishna is warning Arjuna that he will neither understand fully, nor come to gain the blessings of that way-of-Life, by deep study and noisy discussions. It can be understood and experienced ONLY by living it.

THEY TOO ARE FREED FROM WORK—Immature students of the *Geeta* have been seen to cool down in their enthusiasm when they meet with the use of such terms. All through the chapter Krishna was insisting that man should act – act diligently and rightly. All of a sudden He points to a strange-looking goal, WORKLESSNESS. Naturally, an intelligent reader immediately comes to feel a disgust at this ugly paradox. This is mainly because of our lack of appreciation of the term in its native scriptural import.

Earlier, we have explained how the IGNORANCE of our spiritual nature gives rise to DESIRES, which in their turn cause THOUGHT-AGITATIONS and, how WORK is nothing other than thoughts fulfilled among the sense-objects. Thus, the state-of-worklessness, is itself the state-of-thoughtlessness, which indicates the condition of Desirelessness. Absence of all desires can come only when we rediscover the All-full nature of the Self. In short, with the Knowledge of the Self, when spiritual 'ignorance' is terminated, desires can no more arise. Thus, the term 'FREED FROM WORK' indicates the state beyond 'ignorance', or the state of Selfhood.

This Supreme State, no doubt, can never be reached purely through work. Parliament Street is not the Parliament; but having reached Parliament Street, the Parliament cannot be very far away; one cannot miss reaching the Parliament there. Similarly, *Karma Yoga* is extolled here as the 'Path' that takes one ultimately to the Supreme, because through desireless activity one achieves *vasana*-purgation, thus making the mind purer and subtler for meditative purposes.

AS CONTRASTED WITH THE ABOVE, SHRI KRISHNA EXPLAINS WHAT HAPPENS TO THOSE WHO CARP AT THIS THEORY OF RIGHT ACTION:

32. *But those who carp at My teaching and do not practise it, deluded in all knowledge, and devoid of discrimination, know them to be doomed to destruction.*

ये त्वेतदभ्यसूयन्तो नानुतिष्ठन्ति मे मतम् ।
सर्वज्ञानविमूढांस्तान्विद्धि नष्टानचेतसः ॥ ३२ ॥

ye tvetadabhyasūyanto nānutiṣṭhanti me matam,
sarvajñānavimūḍhāṁstānviddhi naṣṭānacetasaḥ 32.

"Those who decry this great teaching of Mine and do not practise it" Krishna warns His students, "will become more and more deluded and will lose their discrimination".

Man is encouraged to follow a life-of-action, only when he comes to appreciate that way-of-Life completely in his understanding. When the very theory is decried, it is no longer conducive to the intellect to accept it. Thus, decrying a philosophy is a sign of one's intellectual rejection of it. Having once rejected intellectually, there is no chance of an individual ever striving to live that philosophy. *Karma Yoga* is a way-of-Life, and we have to live it if we want to come under its grace.

The path-of-Work lies through a process of elimination of the desires in us. When the ego and egocentric desires are eliminated, the work accomplished through such an individual is the true divine action, which is destined to having enduring achievements. To the extent, man is NOT practising this efficient way-of-work, he would grow necessarily unintelligent, and to that extent, his discriminative capacity will deteriorate and ultimately get destroyed.

The blessing, because of which man is considered superior to animals, is his Divine faculty of Discrimination. An intellect, strengthened by its own intrinsic capacity to distinguish between the Real and the unreal, the right and the wrong, is the mighty instrument of self-development in man. When this instrument is destroyed, man comes to behave in no better way than a biped animal; panting on the path of existence, bullied by its own lower instincts of miserable passions and low appetites. Naturally, he fails to make any true gain out of his life's chances, and finally destroys himself.

THEN WHY DO NOT MEN FOLLOW THIS DOCTRINE AND PERFORM THEIR DUTIES FULLY? WHY SHOULD THEY FOLLOW OTHERS, OR ACT ON THEIR OWN? IN DISOBEYING KRISHNA, WHY ARE THEY NOT AFRAID OF TRANSGRESSING THE LORD'S COMMANDS? THE LORD SAYS:

33. *Even a wise man acts in accordance with his own nature; beings will follow their own nature; what can restraint do?*

Even the man-of-Knowledge acts in conformity with his own nature, which is determined by the pattern of thoughts that arise in him. At any given instant of time, each one of us is determined by the thoughts that are in us at that moment; and the thoughts in us always get patternised by the channels of thinking, designed by the thoughts which we had entertained in the past. The nature of each individual is decided by the style of thinking which each is capable of.

The man-of-Knowledge mentioned here indicates one who has read and understood thoroughly the technique-of-Action as explained in this chapter. Even when he knows the technique, the Lord says that it is not easy for him to follow it, because his mind is designed to carry his thoughts through egocentric and selfish channels, ever panting to gain some desires. Because of these past impressions (*vasanas*), even an honest student finds it hard to practise this simple-looking technique in his life. The reason is quite universal: "BEINGS

सदृशं चेष्टते स्वस्याः प्रकृतेर्ज्ञानवानपि ।
प्रकृतिं यान्ति भूतानि निग्रहः किं करिष्यति ॥ ३३ ॥

sadṛśaṁ ceṣṭate svasyāḥ prakṛterjñānavānapi,
prakṛtiṁ yānti buūtāni nigrahaḥ kiṁ kariṣyati 33.

FOLLOW THEIR OWN NATURE". Naturally "WHAT CAN RESTRAINT DO" when nature is too powerful?

This last statement in the stanza "WHAT CAN RESTRAINT DO?" is not a cry of despair in Krishna's philosophy. It is the honest all-seeing vision of the philosopher in Krishna, who recognises that the higher ways of living are not meant for all. Men crowding on the lowest rung of the evolutionary ladder, overwhelmed by their own animal passions, find themselves incapable of renouncing them, and are, therefore, incapacitated to walk the path-of-Action. It is only a slightly evolved entity, full of enthusiasm, activity and a passion for progress (*Rajo-guna*), who can follow this sacred 'Path' and benefit himself. This honest confession shows the broad-mindedness and tolerance of Krishna, the Universal Teacher.

IF EVERY BEING ACTS ONLY ACCORDING TO HIS OWN NATURE – AND THERE IS NONE THAT HAS NOT A NATURE OF HIS OWN – THEN, THERE IS NO SCOPE FOR PERSONAL EXERTION AND THE TEACHING BECOMES PURPOSELESS. THE LORD EXPLAINS AS FOLLOWS:

34. *Attachment and aversion for the objects of the senses abide in the senses; let none come under their sway; for they are his foes.*

In the last stanza, it is said that, even a man, well read in the *shastras*, cannot easily follow the highly ethical life, which

---

इन्द्रियस्येन्द्रियस्यार्थे रागद्वेषौ व्यवस्थितौ ।
तयोर्न वशमागच्छेत्तौ ह्यस्य परिपन्थिनौ ॥ ३४ ॥

indriyasyendriyasyārthe rāgadveṣau vyavasthitau,
tayorna vaśamāgachet tau hyasya paripanthinau 34.

is demanded of a spiritual seeker, because his lower nature proves too strong for him. Prescribing a medicine, which is not available, is not the art of healing. It is the philosopher's duty, not only to indicate the weaknesses in our present life and the state-of-Perfection, but he must also show us ways and means by which we can transport ourselves from our weaknesses into this ideal state-of-Perfection. Then, and then alone, can the philosopher bless his generation.

Krishna indicates here the great robber in the 'within' of man, which loots away the true joys and thrills of 'right living'. Attachments and aversions of the sense-organs for their respective sense-objects are instinctive, and natural, in every one. The sense-objects, by themselves, are incapable of bringing any wave of sorrow or agitation into the 'within'. We get agitated and disturbed not at our sense-organs, but in our mind. The mind gets disturbed because, when the stimuli reach the mind, it accepts, in its inherent mischief, certain types of stimuli as GOOD, and their opposites as BAD. Thereafter, it gets attached to the stimuli it experiences as good and develops an aversion for the opposite type of stimuli. Now the mind is prepared to suffer the agonies of existence in the sorrowful plurality. Whenever it comes in contact with the infinite number of objects outside, it pants to court the things of its own attachment and labours to run away from the things of its own aversion. This excitement of the mind is truly 'its tragedy'.

Having stated this Truth, Krishna advises all seekers: "LET NONE COME UNDER THEIR SWAY".

The philosophy of *Geeta* does not suggest, even in its implications, any kind of running away from the world of sense-objects. Krishna's creed is to live HERE and NOW, in the midst of situations in life, in this very world, and to experience them through our sacred vehicles of the body, mind, and intellect. The only insistence is that on all occasions, a wise man should be a master of the vehicles and not a helpless victim of these matter-envelopments. And THE SECRET OF THIS MASTERY IN LIFE IS TO LIVE FREE FROM THE TYRANNIES OF ATTACHMENTS AND AVERSIONS.

In order to detach ourselves from both our likes and dislikes, we have to get rid of our false egocentric vanities. Likes and dislikes belong to the ego. Therefore, all egoless acts, as we have explained earlier,* accomplish a purgation of *vasanas*. *Vasanas* create the mind; where the mind is, there revels the ego. To the extent the *vasanas* have been reduced, to that extent the mind has become non-existent. Where the mind has ended, there the reflection of the Consciousness called the 'ego' has also ended.

THE METHODS BY WHICH WE CAN BRING ABOUT THE *VASANA*-PURGATION ARE EXPLAINED IN THE FOLLOWING:

35. *Better is one's own 'duty', though devoid of merit, than the 'duty' of another well discharged. Better is death in one's own 'duty'; the 'duty' of another is fraught with fear (is productive of positive danger).*

श्रेयान्स्वधर्मो विगुणः परधर्मात्स्वनुष्ठितात् ।
स्वधर्मे निधनं श्रेयः परधर्मो भयावहः ॥ ३५ ॥

śreyān svadharmo viguṇaḥ paradharmatsvanuṣṭhitāt,
svadharme nidhanaṁ śreyaḥ paradharmo bhayāvahaḥ 35.

*Please refer to the 'General introduction' to the *Geeta*.

The word *Dharma* in Sanskrit is the most elusive word for translation into English. It is used generally in more than one definite meaning. Terms like righteousness, good conduct, duty, noble quality, etc., are some of them. We have explained it earlier and found how *Dharma* essentially means the law-of-Being of anything in the world.

That which determines one man's personality as distinctly different from another's, it is very well known, is the texture of the thoughts entertained by him. This texture of his thoughts is, again, in its turn, determined by the pattern of thinking (*vasanas*), which his mind has gained from its own past. These predetermined 'channels-of-thinking' created by one's own earlier ways of thinking are called the *vasanas*.* Thus *Dharma* should be conceived here as the *vasanas* in our mind, for no other explanation will be correct since the very discussion now is upon mental control. The word 'duty', used by us in our translation, is, in this special sense, to be understood as *vasanas*.

Swadharma and *Para-dharma*—*Swadharma* is not the duty which accrues to an individual because of his 'caste', which is ever a sheer accident of birth. In its right import *swadharma* means the type of *vasanas* that one discovers in one's own mind. To act according to one's own taste, inborn and natural, is the only known method of living in peace and joy, in success and satisfaction. To act against the grain of one's own *vasanas* would be acting in terms of *Para-dharma* – and that this is fraught with danger is very well known.

---

* The compelling deep-urges in us, gathered in our past fields of action-that now determine our present emotional profile, are the '*Vasanas*'.

In the context of the *Geeta*, there is a direct message for Arjuna. Arjuna is born a prince, trained in the art of war and has exhibited in his life his insatiable thirst for heroism and adventure. Naturally, his *swadharma* is that of a prince and that can find fulfilment only in dangerous actions and endless exertions. Perhaps, as it was evident in the first chapter, Prince Arjuna had gathered during his early education, that the life of renunciation and meditation - the life of a *Brahmin* – was nobler than his own life. Therefore, he wanted to run away from the battlefield into the silent caves-of-meditation. In this stanza, Krishna reminds him that to act according to his own *vasanas*, even imperfectly, is the right path for his development. It is dangerous to suppress his own personality-expression and copy the activities of someone else, even if he be living a nobler and diviner life.

THOUGH THE SOURCE OF EVIL HAS BEEN POINTED OUT EARLIER (II-62 AND III-34), YET WITH A VIEW TO ELICITING A CONCISE AND CLEAR STATEMENT OF WHAT WAS BUT DESULTORILY AND VAGUELY EXPRESSED ARJUNA ASKS:

Arjuna said:

36. *But, impelled by what does man commit sin, though against his wishes, O Varshneya, constrained, as it were, by force?*

अर्जुन उवाच
अथ केन प्रयुक्तोऽयं पापं चरति पूरुषः ।
अनिच्छन्नपि वार्ष्णेय बलादिव नियोजितः ॥ ३६ ॥

arjuna uvāca
atha kena prayukto'yaṁ pāpaṁ carati pūruṣaḥ,
anicchannapi vārṣṇeya balādiva niyojitaḥ 36.

Following the tradition of the scriptures, the disciple now asks a definite question upon the very theme of the discussion. The very question shows that Arjuna has, to a large extent, got out of the hasty conclusions which he exhibited until the beginning of the second chapter. He has become introspective, and therefore, conscious of certain forces working within himself that were ruining and obstructing the play of his own higher impulses. The doubt is couched in such familiar words that it appears as though it is a doubt raised by some student of our own times.

There is no living man who has not in himself a sufficiently clear conception of the good and the meritorious. Every one understands intellectually what is RIGHT, but it is only when it comes to action that one invariably gets tempted to do the WRONG. This paradoxical confusion, between one's ideology and one's own actions, becomes quite a big problem to all those who try to introspect and review themselves. The Divine in us, with Its nobler aspirations, wants to fulfil Itself with Its higher impulses and subtler achievements, but the animal instinct in us tempts us away, and we walk the path of the baser joys of the flesh. This invariably happens even against our own wishes. Arjuna is enquiring of the Lord: "What is the exact nature of this satan in our bosom which thus systematically loots away the good in us?"

Varshneya is the name of Lord Krishna, meaning: "One born in the family of the *Vrishnis*".

THE LORD SAYS: "LISTEN. I SHALL TELL YOU WHO THAT ENEMY IS OF WHOM YOU ASK - WHO IS THE SOURCE OF ALL EVIL":

The Blessed Lord Said:

37. *It is desire, it is anger born of the 'active', all-devouring, all-sinful; know this as the foe here (in this world).*

IT IS DESIRE, IT IS WRATH—Desire is the inner SATAN in the individual's bosom. We have seen earlier that desire is nothing other than our own spiritual 'ignorance', expressing itself in our intellectual personality. This statement in the stanza is not to be understood as enumerating two different things. Desire itself, under certain circumstances, gains expression as anger. A constant agitation of the mind, expressing as an uncontrollable impatience to gain something, is called 'desire'. Desire is generally for something other than ourselves. In the clash of existence, beings and circumstances may come between ourselves and the 'object of our desire', and in such cases, our 'desire' – impulses, striking at the obstacle, gain the ugly look of 'wrath'.

Thus, whenever emotions for acquisition and possession of an object flow incessantly towards that object, the bundle of thoughts so flowing is called 'desire'; while the same emotions, when they get obstructed from reaching their desired objects, and get refracted at an intermediate obstacle, are called 'anger'. This 'desire-anger-emotion' is the very SATAN in us that compels us to compromise with our own intellectually known Higher values of existence, and tempts us to perpetrate

---

श्रीभगवानुवाच
काम एष क्रोध एष रजोगुणसमुद्भवः ।
महाशनो महापाप्मा विद्ध्येनमिह वैरिणम् ॥ ३७ ॥

śrī bhagavān uvāca
Kāma eṣa krodha eṣa rajoguṇa-samudbhavaḥ,
mahāśano mahāpāpmā viddhyenam-iha vairiṇam 37.

sins. Greater the desire, greater the power in the pull towards the sinful and the low. Once desire has come to manifest itself in our intellect, it enshrouds the wisdom in us.

Desire and anger, and their numberless children of sin and sorrow, must ever come to breed upon the marshy lands of our deluded intellect. To come under their sway is 'ignorance'. To come to rule over them is Wisdom.

THE LORD NOW ILLUSTRATES HOW DESIRE IS OUR FOE AND HOW IT VEILS OUR DISCRIMINATION:

38. *As fire is enveloped by smoke, as a mirror by dust, as an embryo by the womb, so this (wisdom) is enveloped by that (desire or anger).*

Three different examples have been given to illustrate how desires and the consequent anger delude our rational capacity and choke our discrimination. Repetition is an unpardonable crime against the 'scriptural-style', and the *Geeta* faithfully follows the immortal style common to all Bibles of the world. There is no redundancy, or wasteful repetition in the Divine Song. With this understanding, when we try to read the stanza we find that there are subtle implications in the three different illustrations used by the Lord. More is meant here than meets the eye.

The discrimination in man is screened off and obstructed in its exercise due to the attachment in his mind for the ever-changing worldly objects. We all know that our attachments

---

धूमेनाव्रियते वह्निर्यथादर्शो मलेन च ।
यथोल्बेनावृतो गर्भस्तथा तेनेदमावृतम् ॥ ३८ ॥

dhūmenāvriyate vahniryathādarśo malena ca,
yatholbenāvṛto garbhastathā tenedamāvṛtam 38.

to things can fall under three distinct categories. Our desires can either be low and vicious – mind for the craving-fleshy carnal pleasures – or our ambitions may be for an active exertion in order to achieve power and wealth, to gain strength and might, to win fame and glory. There can also be a burning aspiration to strive and to achieve a diviner perfection and a Godly Self-illumination. Thus, our desires can fall under three headings according to the quality of the attachment; inert (*tamasic*), or active (*rajasic*), or noble and divine (*sattvic*). The veilings that are created over our discrimination by these different types of qualities (*Gunas*) are indicated here by the three different examples.

AS FIRE BY SMOKE—A smoky fire-place, shrouded by dark curling smoke can sometimes, if not totally, at least partially, veil the brilliance of the light emitted by the flames. A wick without a chimney is less bright than with a chimney, proving the example under review. Even *sattvic* desires veil the infinite glory of the Spirit.

AS DUST ON A MIRROR—This illustrates the veiling caused by agitations that cover the purer intellect due to our thick desires for glory and power (*rajasic*). Compared with the former, this is indeed more complete, and the removal of it is, naturally, more difficult. The smoke rolls off even at a passing whiff of breeze, while the mirror cannot be cleaned even by a storm. It can be polished only by our own efforts at dusting it clean with the help of a clean, dry duster. Through the smoke, however thick it might be, the fire can be perceived; through the dust, if it be thick, no reflection at all can be seen in the mirror – if at all seen it will only be dim.

AS THE FOETUS IN THE WOMB—this is an illustration to show how completely the Diviner aspect in us is screened off by the low animal appetites and the vulgar desires for the sensuous. The foetus is covered by the womb until it matures, and there is no method of observing it as long as it is in the womb. The veiling is complete, and it can drop off only after a definite period. Similarly, the desires for the flesh-fleshy enjoyments build, as it were, a womb around the discriminative power in us, and such low mental preoccupations (t*amasic*) can drop off only after a longer period of evolutionary growth undergone by such a deluded mind and intellect.

In the true scriptural style, Krishna thus distinguishes between the different textures in the veils that come to cover the soul when the individual is entertaining different types of desires. In short, DESIRE IS THAT WHICH HIDES THE DIVINE IN US.

IN THIS STANZA IT IS NOT CLEARLY STATED, WHICH COVERS WHAT; THE LITERAL TRANSLATION OF THE WORDS AS THEY STAND IN THIS COUPLET ONLY SAYS, "SO IS THIS COVERED BY IT". THE TWO PRONOUNS, 'IT' AND 'THIS', ARE DEFINED IN THE FOLLOWING STANZA AND THEREIN WE FIND AN EXPLANATION OF BOTH:

39. *Enveloped, O Son of Kunti, is 'wisdom' by this constant enemy of the wise in the form of 'desire', which is difficult to appease.*

आवृतं ज्ञानमेतेन ज्ञानिनो नित्यवैरिणा ।
कामरूपेण कौन्तेय दुष्पूरेणानलेन च ॥ ३९ ॥

āvṛtaṁ jñānametena jñānino nityavairiṇā,
kāmarūpeṇa kaunteya duṣpūreṇānalena ca 39.

This stanza vividly explains to us that discrimination (*Jnana*) the capacity to distinguish the Real from the unreal, the permanent from the impermanent, the true from the false, which gives man his higher status in the scale of evolution -- is the divine faculty that gets screened off from us due to our own greedy and insatiable* desires. The pronouns in the previous stanza now stand clearly elucidated: the 'discriminative capacity' in us (it-*idam*) gets screened off by the insatiable 'desires' (by this-*tena*).

HE NOW TELLS US WHICH ARE THE SEATS OF 'DESIRE', WHICH, BY ENVELOPING WISDOM, FORMS THE ENEMY OF THE WHOLE WORLD. THE SEAT OF THE ENEMY BEING KNOWN, IT IS EASY TO KILL IT:

40. *The senses, the mind, and the intellect are said to be its seat; through these, it deludes the embodied, by veiling his wisdom.*

As a true soldier, Arjuna understands that there is an inner enemy called 'desire', which, like an efficient saboteur, undermines the wealth and security of his inner kingdom; and as a true prince, the royal demand of Arjuna is for immediate information as to the exact hideout of this

---

इन्द्रियाणि मनो बुद्धिरस्याधिष्ठानमुच्यते ।
एतैर्विमोहयत्येष ज्ञानमावृत्य देहिनम् ॥ ४० ॥

indriyāṇi mano buddhirasyādhiṣṭhānamucyate,
etairvimohayatyeṣa jñānamāvṛtya dehinam 40.

* In Mahabharata 'desire' is described as insatiable. Desires can never be satiated by the gratification of desires. The more they are enjoyed, the more they grow, as fire by the pouring of *ghee* (clarified butter) into it.

dangerous bandit. Krishna, as the Spiritual Teacher, has to indicate to his adventurous student where exactly the den of this devil is, from where he plans his nefarious activities. Indicating the secret fortresses of this inner enemy 'desire', the Lord says, "The senses, the mind, and the intellect are said to be its seats of action".

A true criminal, functioning as an efficient leader of a gang, operating in a large area, will generally have more places than one to function from. Three main offices, from where 'desire', in different forms, functions to destroy the peace and health of our inner life, have been indicated here very clearly.

The sense-organs, functioning without restraint in the world of sense-objects, are a very convenient theatre for 'desire' to function in. When the external stimuli reach the mind through the sense-organs, the mind also becomes a breeding centre of sorrows created by 'desire'. Lastly, the intellect, working and playing with the memories of the sense-enjoyments it had lived, and of the mental attachments it had entertained, becomes yet another safe den for 'desire' to function from.

The deluded ego, foolishly identifying with the body, desires sense-enjoyments. Thoughtlessly identifying with the mind, it thirsts to experience more and more emotional satisfactions. Lastly, identifying with the intellect, it plans to re-live the remembered experiences of sense-enjoyments and mental-joys.

TO HUNT FOR 'DESIRE' IN THESE THREE HIDEOUTS IS TO COME, AT LAST, FACE TO FACE WITH IT. HOW

FINALLY TO OVERCOME THIS INNER ENEMY IS DESCRIBED IN THE FOLLOWING STANZAS:

41. *Therefore, O best of the Bharatas, controlling first the senses, kill this sinful thing, the destroyer of knowledge and wisdom.*

As indicated earlier, Krishna declares a truth only when he has exhausted all the logical arguments leading to it. After giving all the arguments, he summarises here: "Therefore, restrain the senses first, so that you may finally throw overboard the inner enemy 'desire'."

Desire is called sinful, since, in its grosser manifestations, it tends to make us live and work satisfying our lower nature, and thus persuades us to live a lower devolutionary life. Even at its best (s*attvic*), like 'the smoke that covers the fire', 'desire' does not allow the full dawn of the Infinite, which is the Self in us. Thus, 'desire' in all its textures, contributes to the sins of man, and, therefore, it is styled here as THE SINFUL THING.

It is easy for a doctor to prescribe a medicine for my wound and promise me an immediate healing. It is indeed consoling to have the prescription in my hand. But, I am sure, I will never gain a cure if the prescription requires me to prepare an ointment out of 'sky-flowers'. Similarly, it is quite a dignified advice for a Spiritual Master to declare, "control the senses and cast off the 'desires', O man!". But, unless the teacher gives us a method by which we can get this

---

तस्मात्त्वमिन्द्रियाण्यादौ नियम्य भरतर्षभ ।
पाप्मानं प्रजहि ह्येनं ज्ञानविज्ञाननाशनम् ॥ ४१ ॥

tasmāttvamindriyāṇyādau niyamya bharatarṣabha,
pāpmānaṁ prajahi hyenaṁ jñānavijñānanāśanam 41.

prescription dispensed, it will be as useless as the 'sky-flower-treatment' for my painful wound.

WHERE SHOULD ONE TAKE ONE'S STAND, AND CAST OFF THE DESIRES?... THE ANSWER FOLLOWS:

42. *They say that the senses are superior (to the body); superior to the senses is the mind; superior to the mind is the intellect; one who is even superior to the intellect is He, (the Atman).*

This and the following stanza with which Vyasa concludes the third chapter of his incomparable *Geeta*, give every seeker a perfect technique by which he can bring about a successful hunting and capture his inner enemy, 'desire'.

Although we cannot expect in the *Bhagawad Geeta* – especially in one of the very opening chapters – an exhaustive treatment of the technique of meditation, yet we find that, in these stanzas, the Lord has etched out a complete outline of the scheme for Self-discovery. Compared with the objects of the world, we can easily understand that the sense-organs are more sacred and divine. Of the instruments that constitute our physical structure, certainly the sense-organs are subtler than the organs-of-action. Every one of us can easily experience that our mind controls and orders our sense-organs, and, therefore, we know that the mind is subtler than the *Indriyas*.

No doubt, the mind has a vast kingdom to roam about in, but even so, it has its own limitations and fixed frontiers.

इन्द्रियाणि पराण्याहुरिन्द्रियेभ्यः परं मनः ।
मनसस्तु परा बुद्धिर्यो बुद्धेः परतस्तु सः ॥ ४२ ॥

indriyāṇi parāṇyāhurindriyebhyaḥ paraṁ manaḥ,
manasastu parā buddhiryo buddheḥ paratastu saḥ 42.

From knowledge to knowledge, we extend the frontiers of our mind and all along this aggressive march of new conquests, it is the intellect that first crosses the existing frontiers of the mind, and wins for it the neighbouring kingdoms of 'fresh knowledge'. In this sense, the intellect has a greater pervasiveness than the mind, and, therefore, it is conceived of as being subtler than the mind. That which lies beyond the intellect is called the Supreme, the *Atman*.

The Consciousness in man, which lights up the very intellectual ideas in him, must necessarily be subtler than the intellect itself. In the *Upanishads* it has been finally declared that there is nothing subtler than the Self, the *Atman*. The technique of meditation* lies in the conscious withdrawal of all our identifications with our body, mind and intellect. All efforts end when we have thus gathered our entire awareness from its delusory preoccupations and made it live in Itself as Itself -- as Objectless Awareness.

THE GOAL GAINED BY PURSUING THIS ART OF MEDITATION IS EXPLAINED IN THE FOLLOWING:

43. *Thus knowing Him, who is superior to intellect, and restraining the self by the Self, slay you, O mighty-armed, the enemy in the form of 'desire', no doubt, hard indeed to conquer.*

एवं बुद्धेः परं बुद्ध्वा संस्तभ्यात्मानमात्मना ।
जहि शत्रुं महाबाहो कामरूपं दुरासदम् ॥ ४३ ॥

evaṁ buddheḥ paraṁ buddhvā saṁstabhyātmānamātmanā,
jahi śatruṁ mahābāho kāma-rūpaṁ durāsadam 43.

* Read Swamiji's 'Meditation and Life', where he has indicated a complete set of exercises by which the seekers can gain a certain amount of dexterity in the art-of-Meditation.

With this stanza, not only does the chapter conclude, but the special advice demanded by Arjuna has also been finally given. Through 'knowledge' alone is 'ignorance' ended; through a lived experience of the Self alone, can we end our ignorance of the Self. This spiritual 'ignorance', we have already found, creates 'desires'. The Lord has indicated earlier that 'desire' functions and thrives in the fields of the sense-organs, the mind, and the intellect. Through the processes of meditation, when we withdraw from our false identifications with the objects, the body and the mind, the 'desire'-faculty, that was till now roaming about and functioning in the outer fields, is gathered and established in the intellect.

As long as we maintain in ourselves the limiting adjuncts of the matter-envelopments, so long we cannot realise our divine potentialities. Instead, in our delusion, we will understand ourselves to be nothing more than the little ego; limited, bound, finite and ever-sobbing. After the rediscovery of our own diviner existence, we will be able to live 'restraining the self by the Self'. In a perfect, 'Buddha's life, his ego functions completely under the control of the diviner in him. No more then can the 'desire'-impulses, if at all they arise in the mind, play their mischiefs and bring about any devastation in his inner life.

It is very interesting to note that the philosophy of the *Geeta* preaches a constructive reorganisation of life and not the destruction or rejection of life's possibilities. 'Desire', being a painful leprous oozing wound, we are lovingly advised about a balm to cure this malady, and to live thereafter, in all efficiency, as a master of circumstances and a lord of our own emotions. A seeker who has accomplished this in himself is called a God-man, a Sage, a Prophet!

Thus in the UPANISHADS of the glorious Bhagawad Geeta, in the Science of the Eternal, in the Scripture of YOGA, in the dialogue between Sri Krishna and Arjuna, the third discourse ends entitled:

The *Karma Yoga*

This chapter is called *Karma Yoga*. The term *Yoga* means the act of connecting the lower with the higher, through a technique consisting of one's own self-evolution. Any method by which the lower in us is educated and trained to live a Higher way-of-life – wherein we gain a more effective control upon both our life without and life within – is called *Yoga*.

Here is a method of self-development pointed out to the Arjuna-type of men, who, fully armed and standing on the battle-field of life, facing an array of opposing forces, more powerful, better organised, and well-supplied with equipments, are ready to fight and destroy them. In fact, every honest man in life is to a large extent – be he a fool, be he a saint – an Arjuna facing his problems with hesitations... wanting to run away, and yet, not daring to do so! The training of *Karma Yoga* prepares us for the greater fights on life's battlefields.

Om Om Om Om Om

ॐ तत्सदिति श्रीमद् भगवद् गीतासूपनिषत्सु ब्रह्मविद्यायां
योगशास्त्रे श्रीकृष्णार्जुनसंवादे कर्मयोगो नाम
तृतीयोध्याय:

Oṁ tatsaditi śrīmad bhagavadgītāsū ūpaniṣatsu brahmavidyāyāṁ yogaśāstre śrī kṛṣṇārjuna saṁvāde 'Karmayogo' nāma tṛtīyo'dhyāyaḥ.

IV

Ending action in knowledge

Introduction

FOR the Aryan mind, novelty in the spiritual kingdom has no charm. Any new idea, however logical and intellectual it might be, is not readily accepted by the children of the Aryan culture as a part of their *Brahma-Vidya*, unless the interpreter of the new idea can show that his technique has already been envisaged in the existing scriptures of this culture. In this way, we can say that we are *Veda*-bound as a cultural unit.

In the last chapter, Krishna propounded a revolutionary idea in the form of *Karma Yoga*, which sounded as though it was a novel intellectual theory cooked in Krishna's own brain. Arjuna, as a true student of the Hindu culture, would not willingly accept it unless his teacher gave an endorsement that, what he had lectured upon was nothing other than an intelligent reinterpretation of the ancient sacred *Vedic* Science. In this chapter, an all-out effort is made by Krishna to bring home to Arjuna that the Lord Himself, the author of the *Vedas*, had been asserting the same old *Vedic* Truth and nothing new.

Again, whenever a teacher, in his inspiration, emphasises a particular stage of self-development, chances are that the dull-witted seekers may misunderstand the import of the words and conclude that the partial path explained is the entire route to the Infinite. In order to remove this misunderstanding, the fourth chapter indicates the greater path of *Jnana Yoga*, the path-of-Knowledge, which is the only main archway through which all pilgrims must pass in order to reach the temple of the Self. Up to this archway, seekers living in different psychological and intellectual domains may walk their own 'paths', but the main gate is *Jnana Yoga* through which all must pass to have *Darshana* at the glorious altar. According to Shankara, this *Yoga* alone forms the subject of the Lord's teachings throughout the *Geeta*.

A secular science can be successfully taught and ingrained on the grey-matter of the student by any teacher. It is not at all necessary that the student must have any love for, or faith in, or reverence towards, the teacher who, in such a case, is nothing more than an 'instrument of instruction'. Thus, today a professor in a modern college is only a 'talking instrument', with as much importance as the blackboard, or the desk, or the platform! But, on the other hand, if a cultural flavour, a moral dignity, and an ethical glow are to be imparted to the personality of the student, it is essential that the student must approach his teacher in a spirit of reverence and love, devotion and friendliness. These are the emotional requirements, which alone can bring about the necessary conditions in us, so that, when the teacher drops his divine apparel, it may fall upon our shoulders.

To Arjuna, Lord Krishna was only a friend, the cowherd boy of Vrindavana. Familiarity, if it does not breed contempt, is at least sure to pull down the familiar in our estimation of its importance and sanctity. This chapter is also intended to invoke in Arjuna's mind the necessary amount of reverence and respect towards his Charioteer. In short, Krishna is here divesting himself of his work-a-day clothes and is putting on, for the first time, his full Divine apparel of Omnipotence and Omniscience, and the Aura of God, descended upon the earth.

Through an earlier training in *Karma Yoga*, when an individual has integrated his mind and intellect, he becomes fit for the absorption and assimilation of the greater Truth, through the process of contemplation and meditation. Therefore, there is a strong recommendation of the path-of-Knowledge in this chapter.

The Blessed Lord said:

1. *I taught this Imperishable YOGA to Vivasvan; Vivasvan taught it to Manu; Manu taught it to Ikshvaku.*

As we said in our introduction to this chapter, the Lord is making an open statement, that what He had been saying so far was nothing other than an intelligent reiteration of what is the content of the immortal *Vedas*. Inspired by a Divine remembrance, the Lord declares that He Himself, at the very beginning of creation, imparted the Knowledge of the *Vedas* to the Sun, and later on, the Sun-god conveyed it to his son, Manu, the ancient law-giver of India. Manu, in his turn,

---

श्रीभगवानुवाच
इमं विवस्वते योगं प्रोक्तवानहमव्ययम् ।
विवस्वान्मनवे प्राह मनुरिक्ष्वाकवेऽब्रवीत् ॥ १ ॥

śrī bhagavānuvāca
imaṁ vivasvate yogaṁ proktavānahamavyayam
vivasvānmanave prāha manurikṣvākave'bravīt 1.

declared it to Ikshvaku, the ancestor of the Solar-dynasty who ruled over Ayodhya for a long period of time.

The word *'Veda'* is derived from the root *Vid,* 'to know'; *Veda,* therefore, means 'Knowledge'. The 'Knowledge' of divinity lurking in man and the technique by which it can be brought out to full manifestation are the theme of the *Veda* textbooks and the Truth of this theme is eternal.

Just as we can say that electricity is eternal, as there was electricity even before the first scientist discovered it, and electrical energy will not be exhausted because of our forgetfulness of its existence, so too, the divine nature of man will never be destroyed because of our non-assertion of it. The knowledge of the divine content and its possibilities in man are indeed eternal.

The creation of the universe, it is accepted even by modern science, must have started with the Sun. As the source of all energy, the Sun was the first of the created objects, and with its very creation, this Great Knowledge of the Self was given out to the world.

The theme of *Vedic* literature being the subjective divinity, language fails to express it completely. No deep experience can be exhaustively expressed in words. Therefore, a study of the scriptures by one's own self is apt to create misunderstanding in the mind of the student, rather than a right appreciation of it. Thus, it is a time-honoured tradition in India that spiritual lessons are directly heard from a true Master, who has vivid inner experiences in the realm of the Spirit. It has been handed down from Master to disciple and we have been given here the identity of the earliest students of *Brahma-Vidya.*

2. *This knowledge, handed down thus in regular succession, the royal sages knew. This YOGA, by long lapse of time, has been lost here, O Parantapa (burner of the foes).*

This *Yoga*, the *Yoga* in which the *Vedic* teachings regarding activity (*Pravritti*) and retirement (*Nivritti*) are comprehended, thus handed down in regular succession among the 'Royal sages', has its own destinies. At certain periods of history, this Knowledge seems to be readily available for the service of mankind, but at certain other periods of history it falls into disuse and becomes, as it were defunct. The golden era of spirituality dies down to inaugurate the dark ages of undivine life. At such periods of monstrous materialism, the generation is not left in neglect to suffer and groan under its own negative values. For, at that time, some great master appears on the horizon to inspire, to encourage and to lead the generation away from the ruts of sorrow onto the highroads of cultural revival.

Krishna rightly evaluates the period of the Mahabharata and declares "THIS *YOGA*, BY LONG LAPSE OF TIME, HAS BEEN LOST HERE".

SEEING THAT THE '*YOGA*' HAD BEEN LOST BY FALLING INTO THE HANDS OF THE WEAK, WHO COULD NOT CONTROL THEIR SENSES, AND SEEING THAT THE GENERATION HAD NOT BEEN ABLE TO

एवं परम्पराप्राप्तमिमं राजर्षयो विदुः ।
स कालेनेह महता योगो नष्टः परंतप ॥ २ ॥

evaṁ paramparāprāptamimaṁ rājarṣayo viduḥ
sa kāleneha mahatā yogo naṣṭaḥ parantapa 2.

ATTAIN THE OBJECT OF LIFE, THE LORD ADDS THE FOLLOWING:

3. *That same ancient 'YOGA' has been today taught to you by Me, for you are My devotee and My friend. This is a Supreme Secret.*

With a direct statement in the style of an open confession, Krishna is here removing all possible misgivings of the orthodox, by insisting that the Truth he has declared in the last chapter... *Karma Yoga*... is nothing other than the same ancient *Yoga*.

A Master can feel really inspired and instruct efficiently, only when he establishes a certain type of affectionate rapport with the students. Krishna finds that his friend Arjuna is fully devoted to Him, and that he will certainly follow the 'Path' indicated by Him. The relationship between teacher and taught should not be a mere commercial arrangement of 'you-pay' and 'I-teach'. Mind and intellect blossom forth only in a warmer climate of love and freedom, friendship and mutual understanding. These qualities required for a healthy transference of the subjective knowledge were found in full measure in Arjuna and therefore, Krishna says "I taught you" this *Yoga* in the earlier chapter.

The secrecy mentioned here only indicates that a man, however wise he might be, may not come to suspect the existence of the *Atman* in himself without being so advised

---

स एवायं मया तेऽद्य योगः प्रोक्तः पुरातनः ।
भक्तोऽसि मे सखा चेति रहस्यं ह्येतदुत्तमम् ॥ ३ ॥

sa evāyaṁ mayā te'dya yogaḥ proktaḥ purātanaḥ
bhakto'si me sakhā ceti rahasya hyetaduttamam 3.

by a man of Experience. The Self being that which is beyond the intellect, (III-41) the reasoning capacity in a man cannot come to suspect the existence of an Eternal, Changeless, Conscious Principle, subtler than the intellect, ever illumining the thoughts rising in the very intellect. Hence, this Science of Truth is called here as the Supreme Secret.

IN ORDER NOT TO LEAVE IN ANYBODY'S MIND AN IMPRESSION THAT ANY INCONSISTENT STATEMENT HAS BEEN MADE BY THE LORD, ARJUNA ASKS, AS THOUGH RAISING AN OBJECTION:

Arjuna said:

4. *Later was Your birth, and prior was the birth of Vivasvan (Sun); how am I to understand that You taught this YOGA in the beginning?*

There is a palpable anachronism in the opening stanza of this chapter. Krishna says that he taught this Eternal Truth to Lord Sun in the beginning of creation. It was quite natural for Arjuna to think of Krishna as the son of Devaki, the Flute-bearer of Gokula. To Arjuna, his charioteer Krishna had a definite date of birth, and was only his own contemporary. Therefore, Krishna Himself could not have advised the Sun, who, by all calculations, is the one who manifested in nature much earlier than all the planetary worlds.

अर्जुन उवाच
अपरं भवतो जन्म परं जन्म विवस्वतः ।
कथमेतद्विजानीयां त्वमादौ प्रोक्तवानिति ॥ ४ ॥

arjuna uvāca
aparaṁ bhavato janma paraṁ janma vivasvataḥ
kathametadvijānīyāṁ tvamādau proktavāniti 4.

TO REMOVE FROM THE MINDS OF THE HASTY READERS THE POSSIBLE MISUNDERSTANDING THAT KRISHNA, THE SON OF DEVAKI, IS THE SPEAKER OF THE GEETA, VYASA MAKES THE BLESSED LORD DECLARE THE FOLLOWING:

The Blessed Lord said:

5. *Many births of Mine have passed as well as yours, O Arjuna; I know them all but you know them not, O Parantapa (scorcher of foes).*

The scriptural masters of the Hindus exhibit an infinite amount of patience and understanding, which almost amounts to an intellectual daring, and they readily come out to satisfy all possible doubts of all the students. Here we find Krishna trying to explain how He was the very Infinite in His Real Nature and that He had Himself, in the very beginning of creation, given out *Brahma-Vidya* to Lord Sun.

In this section, we find an exhaustive discussion of the Theory of incarnation (*Avatara*), as propounded in the *Pauranic* literature. To many foreigners, this portion of the Hindu philosophy and belief has been very confusing, and many of

---

श्रीभगवानुवाच
बहूनि मे व्यतीतानि जन्मानि तव चार्जुन ।
तान्यहं वेद सर्वाणि न त्वं वेत्थ परंतप ॥ ५ ॥

śrī bhagavānuvāca
bahūni me vyatītāni janmāni tava cārjuna
tānyahaṁ veda savārṇi na tvaṁ vettha parantapa 5.

them have expressed such opinions about it; and, perhaps, none has put it so vehemently as Max Mueller.[1]

But, when we try to understand it with a sufficient background of the *Vedantic* concept of creation, it is not very difficult for us to follow the idea. We have elsewhere[2] explained in the fall-of-Man'[3] how, when the Infinite Reality functions through 'unactivity' (s*attva*), we have the concept of the God-Principle. Later on in this section, Krishna Himself explains how He, in all freedom, takes upon Himself the matter-envelopments and plays the game of the Immortal among the mortals - but all the time Himself being ever conscious of His own complete Divine Nature.

Not a single mortal embodiment can be the result of sheer accident. Every man comes to the field of the world only as a result of his evolutionary progress, even according to the Darwinian theory. Each embodied life indicates a long autobiography of that ego, and it is only after a long chain of existence in different forms that it has at last reached its present destination. In each life, as soon as the ego expresses itself in its given field of activity, fortunately, forgets the entire past, and carries with it only a distinct flavour (*vasana*) thereof. But a Mastermind like Lord Krishna, in His Divine Omniscience, understands that both He and Arjuna had been through many vicissitudes of existence, and that "I KNOW THEM ALL WHILE YOU KNOW THEM NOT".

---

1 He criticised the theory of Reincarnation as 'Metaphysical twaddle, and scholastic hair-splitting'.

2 Refer 'Kindle Life' by Swamiji

3 Refer 'Kenopanishad ' by Swamiji.

"HOW THEN CAN YOU, THE ETERNAL LORD, HAVE A BIRTH IN THE ABSENCE OF *DHARMA* AND *ADHARMA*?" LISTEN:

6. *Though I am unborn and am of imperishable nature, and though I am the Lord of all beings, yet, ruling over My own Nature, I take birth by My own MAYA.*

Here is the most daring and original thought of Vyasa, we may say, throughout the entire *Geeta*. The Supreme, on account of His unquestioned freedom, by His own perfectly free will, takes upon Himself the conditioning of matter, and manifests Himself in a particular embodiment in the world, for serving the deluded generation of that time. To the Lord, His 'ignorance' is but a pose assumed, not a fact lived. A mortal becomes victimised by his *Avidya*, while the Lord is Master of His *Maya*. A driver is bound by his duty to the vehicle, while the owner of the vehicle is Lord of it. He uses the vehicle for his purposes, and whenever he reaches his immediate destination, he leaves the vehicle with all freedom, and enjoys his own independent activities. But, the poor driver, bound to the vehicle, will have to guard it against intruders and serve the vehicle as its servant. The Lord uses the matter-envelopments and their limitations as a convenience and as a set of necessary tools in His game of protecting the creation.

अजोऽपि सन्नव्ययात्मा भूतानामीश्वरोऽपि सन् ।
प्रकृतिं स्वामधिष्ठाय संभवाम्यात्ममायया ॥ ६ ॥

ajo'pi sannavyayātmā bhūtānāmīśvaro'pi san
prakṛtiṁ svāmadhiṣṭhāya sambhavāmyātmamāyayā 6.

Thus, though the Lord is Unborn and Changeless in His Nature, and ever a Lord of matter, yet, keeping His *Maya* perfectly under His own control, He comes into the world, through His own free will. All the time He is fully conscious of His own Divine status and unchallenged prerogative. He does not come into being as others do, compelled by His past *Karma*, to live here in the world under the thraldom of Nature. He is not bound by His mental temperaments but He is ever free from the mischiefs of His own *Maya*.

You ask your servant to take your heavy motorcycle to the nearby garage for refilling it. If you watch him doing it you will have some idea of what the Lord is trying to express here. To that poor man, the unwieldy machine is a calamity, a suffering. To push it across the road is a risky adventure for him, because the machine, by its own weight, guides him, he being powerless to assert his mastery over it. On the other hand, if you yourself were to ride, or push, the motorcycle, you can joyously, and easily, do so. The vehicle remaining the same, in your hands it becomes a slave to carry you, while the poor servant was being dragged by the clumsy weight of the heavy machine!

To an ordinary man who is ignorant of the working of his vehicle, it becomes a painful agony and a difficult responsibility to make use of these instruments. To the Lord, the world is no problem, and His personal equipments and their appetites are always perfectly under His own control. He comes to lord over every situation.

This perfect freedom of a God-man could not have been more beautifully brought out in so few words as in these incomparable lines.

WHEN AND FOR WHAT PURPOSE IS THE INFINITE SO BOUND? THE ANSWER FOLLOWS:

7. *Whenever there is a decay of righteousness, O Bharata, and a rise of unrighteousness, then I manifest Myself.*

"Whenever there is a decline of *Dharma*, I create for Myself a body". The term *Dharma*[*] has already been exhaustively explained. *Dharma*, The law-of-Being is a sacred Truth, and when the majority of the members of a community do not obey this great Truth, there is a conquest of the world by a herd of biped-animals, and not a cooperative happily-living family of men, pursuing life in their full dignity as intelligent social beings. In all such dark periods of history, some great Master comes to present himself as the leader of men to revive the standard-of-life and its moral values. This is generally done, not only by giving a fillip to the existing nobler values, but also by a corresponding policy of total elimination of the wicked.

It is for this purpose that the Infinite, from time to time, wears the 'matter-apparel' and appears on the scene of activity, like the owner of an estate, who now and then puts on his gumboots to inspect and reorganise his estate. Even while he is on the work-spot, in the burning sun, among his workers, he is conscious of his lordship over, and ownership of the entire estate. Similarly, the Supreme, which is the substratum for

---

यदा यदा हि धर्मस्य ग्लानिर्भवति भारत ।
अभ्युत्थानमधर्मस्य तदात्मानं सृजाम्यहम् ॥ ७ ॥

yadā yadā hi dharmasya glānirbhavati bhārata
abhyutthānamadharmasya tadātmānaṁ sṛjāmyaham 7.

[*] Refer the closing paras of the introduction to Chapter I.

the pluralistic world, puts on the body-gown and, as it were, walks into the dusky atmosphere of the immoral life of mankind, for the purpose of reorganising and conducting a thorough spring-cleaning of the bosom of man.

In the descent of God explained here, it is very clearly said that the Lord takes upon Himself, a body projected for the purpose by Himself, and that He reserves for Himself the Divine freedom to be IN it, and yet not OF it: "THEN I BODY MYSELF FORTH".

FOR WHAT PURPOSE?

8. *For the protection of the good, for the destruction of the wicked and for the establishment of righteousness, I am born in every age.*

It is quite evident that the Infinite cannot project Itself forth unless there is some 'desire'. The state-of-Desirelessness is but the state-of-Actionlessness. Without some equipment or the other, electricity cannot, of its own accord, manifest itself. Similarly, the Supreme cannot, and need not project out into a Divine, or an undivine form – as an Immortal Omniscient God or as a mortal foolish ego – unless there is some desire, or the other, to precipitate the manifestation A super-saturated solution, if left alone, undisturbed, can carry its extra quantity of crystals in itself; but the moment a minutest particle of the same substance is thrown into that beaker, immediately, all

---

परित्राणाय साधूनां विनाशाय च दुष्कृताम् ।
धर्मसंस्थापनार्थाय संभवामि युगे युगे ॥ ८ ॥

paritrāṇāya sādhūnāṁ vināśāya ca duṣkṛtām
dharmasaṁsthāpanārthaya sambhavāmi yuge yuge 8.

the extra crystals get thrown out in crystal-form. Similarly, the Dynamic Supreme, the Womb of Infinite potentialities, cannot bring forth any form, or forms, unless there is an intention – it may be Divine, it may be good, it may be bad.

The DESIRE that made the Supreme assume the Divine form of Krishna - the Enchanting Cowboy, the Blue Lover-of-All-is here explained in Vyasa's own words. In the stanza, Vyasa makes Krishna confess His initial 'desire', that caused His manifestation.

The divinest of all 'desires' is, indeed, a selfless thirst to serve the world; but all the same it is a DESIRE. In order to PROTECT THE GOOD, when the Absolute starts IT's Godly career, it is the very necessity of *Maya* that He, the very Lord of Delusion, has to take upon Himself one more added mission. "THE DESTRUCTION OF THE WICKED".

Here DESTRUCTION is not annihilation of the individuals as much as the REMOVAL OF THE WRONG TENDENCIES in the individuals. It is a process of refitting the wardrobe wherein some old clothes are irredeemably spoiled, and have to be eliminated in order to make more space for newly made and other refitted items. Similarly, Prophets, when they come, they encourage the good; sometimes they rejuvenate the bad, and often eliminate the poisonous specimens from the garden-of-life.

This much Lord Krishna was compelled to explain about Himself because it was perfectly evident that Arjuna was blissfully unaware of the true Divine nature of Krishna. The line of arguments adopted by Arjuna in the opening chapter* to justify his conduct in his friend's eyes would be meaningless if Arjuna

---

* Refer the closing paras of the introduction to Chapter I.

did not, in fact, believe that he was addressing a human being. It would, in such a case, suggest that Arjuna was an utter atheist who would not rely for his victory upon his Divine companion. All the same, when Krishna comments upon Arjuna, characterising him as a non-caviller, a friend and a devotee, deserving His assistance, Arjuna appeals to Krishna, with a childlike simplicity: "DO TEACH ME, I AM THY DISCIPLE". This was undeniably an attitude of profound respect but no indication that Arjuna treated Krishna as God-Almighty, Himself.

WHY IS THE LORD GIVING THIS BIT OF HIS AUTOBIOGRAPHY?

9. *He who thus knows, in true light, My divine birth and action, having abandoned the body, he is not born again; he comes to Me, O Arjuna.*

After explaining the how and the why of incarnations in general, Krishna declares that those who, by constant contemplation upon this fact, understand the Divine birth and activities of the Lord end their limitations and reach Godhood. That it is not a mere understanding or knowing that is indicated here is clear from the very words, IN TRUE LIGHT (t*attwatah*), that is, we have to experience subjectively how and when the Supreme *Atman* takes Its *Avatara* in us. Today, no doubt, individually, we live as limited mortal brutes, but, at certain moments, when we are entertaining

---

जन्म कर्म च मे दिव्यमेवं यो वेत्ति तत्त्वत: ।
त्यक्त्त्वा देहं पुनर्जन्म नैति मामेति सोऽर्जुन ॥ ९ ॥

janma karma ca me divyamevaṁ yo vetti tattvataḥ
tyaktavā dehaṁ punarjanma naiti māmeti so'rjuna 9.

pure selfless 'desires', the very same spark-of-Life in us comes to manifest a divine potency and a celestial dash.

The stanza also subtly indicates that for one's spiritual development, the practice of *Upasana* of the blissful form of the Lord is as efficient a method as meditation upon the formless-Self. There are some professional *Vedantins* who cannot accept the concept of the Lord having an embodiment. They are merely barking at a shadow. To one who is practising sincerely and whole-heatedly, the goal is equally available whether it is through the *Upasana* of the Truth with a form (*Saguna*), or without any form (*Nirguna*).

Krishna is indicating here the Supreme state-of-Perfection, the state-of-Existence from where ONE IS NOT BORN AGAIN. In the earlier *Vedic* literature the state-of-Godhood is described as the state-of-Deathlessness (a*maratva*), while in the later *Vedic* literature we find a slow change-over, and the Eternal is explained as the state from which ONE IS NOT BORN AGAIN (a*jah*). The evolution of this concept clearly indicates the intellectual development in this country at that time. When a society is immature, its members are afraid of death; but as they grow and evolve, it is not death that frightens them so much as the possibility of a new birth, for, it starts a new lease of agonising existence in imperfect environments.

It is evident that the state-of-Deathlessness is itself the state-of-Birthlessness, because death can come only to that which is born. And yet, the change in expression declares the maturity that was gained by the *Vedic* students of that period.

THIS PATH OF SALVATION IS NOT ONE MERELY REASONED OUT BY KRISHNA TO SUIT HIS PRESENT

PURPOSE, BUT IT WAS WALKED EVEN IN ANCIENT TIMES:

10. *Freed from attachment, fear and anger, absorbed in Me, taking refuge in Me, purified by the Fire-of-Knowledge, many have attained My Being.*

The entire path of Self-development and the final Goal that is to be reached has been indicated in this stanza. Without renouncing attachment and its by-products, which always disturb one's mental equipoise, no progress is ever possible for a seeker. Once this mental discipline is gained, absorbed in the idea of self-perfection, the seeker comes to take total refuge in this great victory. Thereafter, the mission of self-perfection becomes a passion with him to thrill his life. When an individual has thus gained this stage of self-development, he becomes fit for the study and practice of the great scriptures – the *Upanishads*.

(a) The study of the scriptures at the feet of a Master, followed by (b) independent analysis of *Vedantic* Truths by oneself in an attempt to understand their real import, and lastly, (c) the seeker's slow and steady attempt at balancing himself in single-pointed meditation – all these three together constitute the technique of self-development as visualised in Hinduism. A study of the theory of *Vedanta* and all our attempts to live the life of tranquillity and love indicated therein, together constitute *Jnana Tapas*.

वीतरागभयक्रोधा मन्मया मामुपाश्रिताः ।
बहवो ज्ञानतपसा पूता मद्भावमागताः ॥ १० ॥

vītarāgabhayakrodhā manmayā māmupāśritāḥ
bahavo jñānatapasā pūtā madbhāvamāgataḥ 10.

There are some commentators who read into the stanza a synthesis of all the three paths. The path-of-Action is indicated in the first-half of the first line, because, unless one trains oneself in the field of activity, DETACHMENT FROM DESIRES, FEAR, AND ANGER cannot be gained. The second-half, "ABSORBED IN ME AND TAKING REFUGE IN ME" indicates the path-of-Love, wherein the devotee, binding himself with love to the Lord of his heart lives his life, taking refuge in nothing other than the Lord. The path-of-Knowledge is indicated by the discriminative analysis and the constant and continued attempts at identification with the Self (*Jnana tapas*). The import is, that seekers walking all the seemingly different paths reach but the same Goal, the Supreme, 'Me'.

In fact, these three paths, are but three different techniques to perfect our mind; all spiritual paths are but attempts to purify the mind, meaning, to make it steady and single-pointed. Some of us identify ourselves more with our bodies than with anything else. Others are, by temperament, living more in their mental zones. And there are some again who live more in their rational personalities. To all these three types of seekers, if one and the same 'Path' is indicated, the chances are that the technique prescribed will not be universal in its acceptance and application.

But whatever be the 'Path' pursued, and whatever be the type to which the seekers belong, the ultimate experience of spiritual Perfection gained by every one of them at the moment of illumination, is one and the same. This is an incontrovertible fact, for the mystical literature of the world reads as though every saint has borrowed and copied from all the earlier Masters across the world!

THEN LORD KRISHNA MUST BE CHERISHING FEELINGS OF AFFECTION AND AVERSION, SINCE HE LIBERATES SOME, AND NOT ALL. THE ANSWER FOLLOWS:

11. *In whatever way men approach Me, even so do I reward them; My path do men tread in all ways, O son of Pritha.*

Attachment and aversion are not the weaknesses of the Lord. He is a mass of Dynamism, the source of all activities and achievements. We are given the equipment through which we can, as we like, invoke this Infinite Mind. If we rightly invoke and carefully use the equipments, as a reward for our intelligent self-application, we can reach the Goal of our activities. If we misuse them, the very same Divine Force can be the cause of our utter disaster.

The fuel-strength in the petrol can be converted into horse-power through the mechanism under the bonnet. We can invoke the horsepower to reach our destination, or we can easily dump ourselves into a mass of twisted wreckage on the wayside and become a bundle of broken bones. These accidents are caused by the carelessness of the driver, although the strength and power with which the car dashes down the embankment of the road is, no doubt, supplied by the same petrol. But the strength in the petrol had no attachment for those whom it guided home safe. Nor can we say that it had a hatred for those whom it wrecked. With neither attachment

---

ये यथा मां प्रपद्यन्ते तांस्तथैव भजाम्यहम् ।
मम वर्त्मानुवर्तन्ते मनुष्याः पार्थ सर्वशः ॥ ११ ॥

ye yathā māṁ prapadyante tāṁstathaiva bhajāmyaham
mamavatmārnuvartante manuṣyāḥ pārtha sarvaśaḥ 11.

nor hatred, the petrol gives its power when invoked through the mechanism of the engine, and how to make use of the power depends upon us and our wisdom in employing it.

Similarly, here the Lord says, "I, AS LIFE, LEND MY POWER TO ALL WITHOUT ANY PARTIALITY; IN WHATEVER FORM THEY INVOKE ME, IN THAT FORM I SERVE THEM". An electric plug in the house can be made use of to hear a song over the radio, to cool ourselves with the breeze of a fan, to boil water, to cook or to warm the room with a heater; it all depends upon what instrument we plug into it. It is never possible that electricity flowing through the fan, of its own accord, can start emitting fire or light. Similarly, the unmanifest Eternal Force of Life can be invoked, and It shall fulfil all DESIRES through us according to the type of our invocations.

IF GOD BE THUS FREE FROM ALL ATTACHMENTS AND OTHER EVIL PASSIONS, HE, THE LORD, MUST BE GRACIOUS TO ALL CREATURES ALIKE AND MUST BE ABLE TO GRANT THEM ALL THEIR DESIRES. THEN WHY IS IT THAT ORDINARILY MEN DO NOT DESIRE TO SEEK THE LORD AND GAIN THE INFINITE? – LISTEN WHY IT IS SO;

12. *They who long for satisfaction from actions in this world, make sacrifices to the gods; because satisfaction is quickly obtained from actions in the world-of-objects.*

काङ्क्षन्तः कर्मणां सिद्धिं यजन्त इह देवताः ।
क्षिप्रं हि मानुषे लोके सिद्धिर्भवति कर्मजा ॥ १२ ॥

kāṅkṣantaḥ karmaṇāṁ siddhiṁ yajanta iha devatāḥ
kṣipraṁ hi mānuṣe loke siddhirbhavati karmajā 12.

If the *Atmic*-force guides us on both, the path-of-good and on the path-of-evil, then how is it that in this world of ours we see but a rare few who are honestly trying to travel the path-of-righteousness, while the majority are pursuing the road-of-evil? This question must necessarily come to the mind of all intelligent students, and Lord Krishna is answering this possible query. He says, whether the mind wants to pursue an extrovert life, or live the introvert joys, it can do so only by borrowing its capacity and capability from the Omnipotency of the *Atman*; but the mind ever chooses an extrovert career, in stinking sensuality, because it is easy to gain cheap pleasures by satisfying the sensuous tickling of nerve-tips.

This is the cause for sensuality in the world, and Krishna explains why a majority of us, in spite of our best efforts, live a life of animal passions: "BECAUSE SUCCESS RESULTING FROM ACTION IS QUICKLY ATTAINED IN THE HUMAN WORLD".

On this globe of ours, the quickest results are gained when our sense-organs come in contact with their desired objects as the result of deliberate actions. Since a sensuous life is a life of least resistance, though of cheap pleasures, the ordinary man, in his keen appetite for joy and peace, wastes his spiritual strength in hunting after, procuring, and enjoying the fleeting sense-objects. The truth of the statement is well within the experience of every one of us.

The passage should not be understood only to say that worldly success is easily gained, but that, as men, we can intelligently plan our actions in such a way that we can, out of our actions, create or compel nature to yield a greater dose of happiness than the members of the vegetable and animal kingdoms.

MEN WHO ARE SEEKING THE LOWER OR THE HIGHER WAYS OF LIFE THROUGH THE EMPLOYMENT OF THEIR SPIRITUAL STRENGTH CAN BE DIVIDED, UPON THE BROAD BASIS OF THEIR INTROVERT AND EXTROVERT NATURES; AND THE EXTROVERT MEN CAN AGAIN BE DIVIDED INTO FOUR TYPES, ON THE BASIS OF THEIR FINER DISTINCTIONS OF THE TEXTURES OF THEIR THOUGHT AND ACTION.

13. *The fourfold-caste has been created by Me according to the differentiation of GUNA and KARMA; though I am the author thereof know Me as non-doer and immutable.*

This is a stanza that has been much misused in recent times by the upholders of the social crime styled as the caste system in India. *Varna,* meaning different shades of texture, or colour, is employed here in the *Yogic*-sense. In the *Yoga Shastra,* they attribute some definite colours to the triple *gunas,* which mean, as we have said earlier, 'the mental temperaments'. Thus, *sattva* is considered as white, *rajas* as red, and *tamas* as black. Man is essentially the thoughts that he entertains. From individual to individual, even when the thoughts are superficially the same, there are clear distinctions recognizable from their temperaments.

On the basis of these temperamental distinctions, the entire mankind has been, for the purpose of spiritual study, classified into four 'castes' of *Varnas*. Just as, in a metropolis, on the basis

---

चातुर्वर्ण्यं मया सृष्टं गुणकर्मविभागशः ।
तस्य कर्तारमपि मां विद्धयकर्तारमव्ययम् ॥ १३ ॥

cāturvraṇyaṁ mayā sṛṣṭaṁ guṇakarmavibhāgaśaḥ
tasya katārramapi māṁ viddhyakatārramavyayam 13.

of trade or professions, we divide the people as doctors, advocates, professors, traders, politicians, *tongawalas*,* etc., so too, on the basis of the different textures of thoughts entertained by the intelligent creatures, the four 'castes' had been labelled in the past. From the standpoint of the State, a doctor and a *tongawala* are as much important as an advocate and a mechanic. So too, for the perfectly healthy life of a society, all 'castes' should not be competitive but co-operative units, each being complementary to the others, never competing among themselves.

However, later on, in the power politics of the early middle-ages in India, this communal feeling cropped up in its present ugliness, and in the general ignorance among the ordinary people at that time, the cheap *pandits* could parade their assumed knowledge by quoting, IN BITS, stanzas like this one.

The decadent Hindu-*Brahmin* found it very convenient to quote the first quarter of the stanza, and repeat, "I CREATED THE FOUR *VARNAS*" and give this tragic social vivisection a divine look having a godly sanction. They, who did this, were in fact, the greatest blasphemers that Hinduism ever had to reckon with. For Vyasa, in the very same line of the couplet, as though in the very same breath, describes the basis on which this classification was made, when he says, "BY THE DIFFERENTIATION OF THE MENTAL QUALITY AND PHYSICAL ACTION (OF THE PEOPLE)".

This complete definition of the *Varna* not only removes our present misunderstanding but also provides us with some data to understand its true significance. Not by birth is man a *Brahmana* (*Brahmin*); by cultivating good intentions and noble thoughts alone can we ever aspire to *Brahmana*-hood; nor can we pose as

---

* Those who run horse-driven coaches... Ed.

Brahmana merely because of our external physical marks, or bodily actions in the outer world. The definition insists that he alone is a *Brahmana*, whose thoughts are as much *sattvic*, as his actions are. A *Kshatriya* is one who is *rajasic* in his thoughts and actions. A *Shudra* is not only one whose thoughts are *tamasic*, but also he who lives a life of low endeavours, for satisfying his base animal passions and flesh-appetites. The scientific attitude, in which this definition has been declared, is clear from the exhaustive implications of the statement: "ACCORDING TO THE DIFFERENTIATION OF *GUNA* AND *KARMA*".

We had tried to explain how the Self, functioning through Its own self-forgetfulness (*Maya*) as it were, came to project forth temperamentally in three distinct conditions of mental and intellectual life: Unactivity, Activity and Inactivity. Through these triple channels flow the expressions of Life manifesting the different ideas, agitations and actions of the embodied-Life. None of the vagaries of existence would have been possible if the equipments were not tickled by the touch-of-Life.

Krishna, as the very Source-of-Life, emphatically asserts here, that He is the author of it all, in the sense that the ocean could say that it is the author of all the waves, ripples, foam, bubbles, etc., and gold can assert that it is the very creator and sustainer of all gold-ornaments in the world, inasmuch as no gold-ornament can exist when the gold element is removed from it.

But, at the same time the Infinite, being All-Pervading, as we have already explained, cannot participate in any action and therefore, the Lord, in one and the same breath, declares that though "HE IS THE AUTHOR OF IT", in His own Real Nature, "HE IS AT THE SAME TIME A NON-DOER".

Such contradictions in *Vedanta* become confusing to the students, as long as they are not initiated into the SECRETS OF ITS STUDY. In our conversation, we generally hear people say "that they reached their destination ten miles away by sitting in a bus"; "I caught a train and reached here". Since we understand their meaning in our usual routine conversation, we do not try to dissect such statements to discover the contradictions they contain. Sitting you cannot travel. By catching a train, none can cover distances. And yet it is so true. When we travel in a bus or a train, we do not move; we only sit and hang on to our seats! But still we cover the distance because the vehicle, in which we sit, moves on. In other words, the motion of the vehicle is attributed to us. Similarly, the creation of the temperaments, which should be attributed to the mind and intellect, is attributed to the Lord. In fact, the Lord, in His Essential Nature, being Changeless and All-Pervading, is neither the Doer nor the Creator.

"SINCE I AM NOT IN REALITY THE AUTHOR OF THOSE ACTIONS OF WHICH YOU THINK ME TO BE AN AUTHOR"

14. *Actions do not taint Me, nor have I any desire for the fruits-of-actions. He who knows Me thus is not bound by his actions.*

The Ever-pure and the All-full cannot be tainted, nor can It have any sense-of-imperfection which can germinate any 'desire'. The Lord, the Self, declares here "ACTIONS DO NOT TAINT ME NOR HAVE I ANY ANXIETY FOR THE FRUITS

न मां कर्माणि लिम्पन्ति न मे कर्मफले स्पृहा ।
इति मां योऽभिजानाति कर्मभिर्न स बध्यते ॥ १४ ॥
na māṁ kamārṇi limpanti na me karmaphale spṛhā
iti māṁ yo'bhijānāti karmabhirna sa badhyate 14.

OF ACTIONS". Taint or 'desire' can come only to an ego, which is 'the Self, functioning through a given mind and intellect'. When the subtle-body is tainted by 'desires' and agitations then the ego in it seems to be played upon by these two. This is better understood by the following analogy.

The sun, reflected in a bowl of water, is entirely dependent upon the condition of the water. The reflected-Sun is shaken when the water in the bowl is disturbed and it appears to be dim when the water is muddy. Neither the dimness nor the agitations of the reflection have caused any change at all in the original object – the sun in the Infinite Heavens. Similarly, the ego suffers the evil tendencies and such other taints of the mind and also gets disturbed, due to the desires for the FRUITS OF ITS ACTIONS. The Self, in Its Pure Conscious-nature, is not at all affected by these delusory disturbances of Its own reflection in the mental pool.

THIS SEEMS TO BE A NOVEL INTERPRETATION OF THE USUAL *VEDIC* TECHNIQUE OF SELF-PERFECTION. IS THERE ANY PRECEDENT? ... LISTEN:

15. *Having known this, the ancient seekers-after-freedom also performed action; therefore, you too perform action, as did the ancients in the olden times.*

After knowing Me that "I AM NON-AGENT AND I HAVE NO LONGING FOR THE FRUITS OF ACTIONS", and realising the All-full Self-hood, there shall no more be any 'desire' or

---

एवं ज्ञात्वा कृतं कर्म पूर्वैरपि मुमुक्षुभिः ।
कुरु कर्मैव तस्मात्त्वं पूर्वैः पूर्वतरं कृतम् ॥ १५ ॥

evaṁ jñātvā kṛtaṁ karma pūvarirapi mumukṣubhiḥ
kuru kamariva tasmāttvaṁ pūvariḥ pūrvataraṁ kṛtam 15.

'egoistic vanities'. The technique of *Karma Yoga*, as enunciated and propounded in the last chapter, was practised, says Krishna, even in olden times by many an intelligent seeker. In short, there is nothing new in the path-of-Action and all seekers trying to realise the Self had been following the same technique.

"IF *KARMA YOGA* IS TO BE PERFORMED, I CAN DO IT BECAUSE OF YOUR ADVICE. BUT WHY SHOULD YOU ADD THAT THE ANCIENTS DID THE SAME?" IN REPLY TO THIS, THE LORD SAYS "LISTEN, THERE IS GREAT DIFFICULTY IN UNDERSTANDING WHAT CONSTITUTES RIGHT ACTION" ... HOW?

16. *What is action? What is inaction? As to this even the 'wise' are deluded. Therefore, I shall teach you 'action' (the nature of action and inaction), knowing which, you shall be liberated from the evil (of SAMSARA – the wheel of birth and death).*

All of us understand that ACTION means movement of the limbs with relation to things in the outer world, and INACTION means a state of existence wherein there is a total cessation of such vigorous and conscious movements. This is the popular definition of 'action' and 'inaction' which, no doubt, is quite acceptable as far as the everyday activities of life are concerned. But from the philosophical standpoint, the concept and features of both 'action' and 'inaction' change.

For purposes of self-development, when we consider 'action', it is not to be valued merely by observing its manifested qualities

---

किं कर्म किमकर्मेति कवयोऽप्यत्र मोहिताः ।
तत्ते कर्म प्रवक्ष्यामि यज्ज्ञात्वा मोक्ष्यसेऽशुभात् ॥ १६ ॥

kiṁ karma kimakarmeti kavayo'pyatra mohitāḥ
tatte karma pravazyāmi yajjñātvā mokṣyase'śubhāt 16.

but we must also take into consideration the unmanifested but subtly working motives behind the very same action. An action, in itself, cannot be considered either as good or bad. It is the MOTIVE BEHIND IT, which determines the quality of the action. Just as the beauty of a fruit is not the last word for its edibility, but it depends upon its contents, so too, a beautiful action in itself could be a poisonous act of criminality, if the motive behind it is low and vicious.

Therefore, it is said that, in discriminating between what is 'action' and what is 'inaction', EVEN THE POET-SEERS OF OLD ARE CONFUSED. The word *'Kavi'*, now-a-days mainly used for the poets, was the name for the *Rishis*, the Seers of *Upanishadic* declarations. Any inspired man, recognising and expressing a truth that was noble and immortal, was called a *Kavi*.

After stating this difficult problem of discriminating between 'action' and 'inaction', Krishna promises here that He will teach Arjuna what exactly constitutes right action, by knowing which, naturally, one can save one's self from all evil.

IT IS FAMILIAR TO ALL THAT ACTION MEANS MOVEMENT AND INACTION MEANS ABSENCE OF IT: TO SIT QUIET. WHAT IS THERE TO LEARN ABOUT THEM?

17. *For verily (the true nature) of 'right action' should be known; also (that) of 'forbidden (or unlawful) action' and of 'inaction'; imponderable is the nature (path) of action.*

कर्मणो ह्यपि बोद्धव्यं बोद्धव्यं च विकर्मण: ।
अकर्मणश्च बोद्धव्यं गहना कर्मणो गति: ॥ १७ ॥

karmaṇo hyapi boddhavyaṁ boddhavyaṁ ca vikarmaṇaḥ
akarmaṇśca boddhavyaṁ gahanā karmaṇo gatiḥ 17.

Life means activity. Where activity has ended, death has entered. In active life alone, can we progress or deteriorate. A stagnant pool of water decays and soon gets putrefied; while the flowing water of a river ever keeps itself fresh, pure and clean.

Life being dynamic, it cannot, even for a moment, cease to function. Complete cessation from activities is impossible so long as life exists.

Activity, therefore, is the very corner stone of life. Since man must always actively exist all his lifetime, the entire possibilities of activities have been taken into consideration by the great Seers of old in evaluating life. The accompanying chart will vividly explain their classifications.

LIFE

- Activity
  - *Karma* (Actions to be done)
    - *Nitya* (daily duties)
    - *Naimittika* (duties on special occasions)
    - *Kamya* (desire-prompted duties)
  - *Vi-Karma* (Actions to be avoided)
- Inactivity

Life is constituted of moments of activity and moments of inactivity. Through inactivity, neither progress nor deterioration is ever possible. Deep-sleep or periods of complete cessation in existence are intervals of total holidaying from life, and they can neither make nor mar the individual's progress in his evolution.

Periods of activity create man. This creative-period depends upon what type of activity we venture upon.

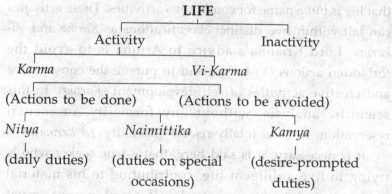

According to the ancient Seers, activities can be of two types, constructive or destructive. Constructive activities which contribute towards the evolution of the individual are termed here as *Karma*.

Destructive activities are those that are totally condemned by the *shastras*, because they tend to devolve the individual, and those are termed in our textbooks as *Vi-karma*. The constructive activities (*Karma*) can be of three kinds: *Nitya*- constant duties, *Naimittika* - special duties on special occasions, and *Kamya* - work purposeful and self-determined for winning a desirable result or reward.

Built upon the ancient *Vedic* doctrine, Krishna here expounds an elaborate theory of self-development. He says that life is but a name for continuous activities. These activities can fall within two distinct classifications as *Karma* and *Vi-karma*. Lord Krishna's advice to Arjuna is to avoid the forbidden actions (*Vi-karma*) and to pursue the constructive and creative activities of self-development (*Karma*). In this scientific analysis, without any formality, or mental reservation, Krishna totally rejects 'inactivity' (*A-karma*).*

It is necessary, it is said here, that a true seeker who is trying to live a diligent life, contributing to his material progress and to his spiritual self-development, must necessarily know this triple classification of life, considered as a bundle of activities.

---

* There are commentators who had considered *Akarma* as the state-of-Actionlessness – the Self-hood. It was already said that the Lord is a NON-DOER. This interpretation seems to be more acceptable in the light of how the *Akarma* term is employed in the next verse (IV-18). We consider *Akarma* to mean 'unactivity' – the state of *sattvic* peace and joy.

Even after so beautifully defining the three clear and distinct classifications, Krishna admits that, for an ordinary man it is not easy to distinguish the one from the other, and to readily and successfully classify all his activities under these three headings, because, Krishna says, "THE NATURE OF *KARMA* IS IMPONDERABLE".

In this statement lies the secret suggestion that an action is to be evaluated not merely on its face value but after a sincere consideration of the motive working behind it. If the motive, or desire, or intention of one is pure and constructive, then the action too is noble and meritorious for that particular individual. Since in this evaluation of actions the individual factor is so very predominant, one must agree with Krishna over the imponderability of the nature of *Karma*.

WHAT IS THERE TO LEARN ABOUT ACTION AND INACTION? THE ANSWER FOLLOWS:

18. *He who recognises inaction in action and action in inaction is wise among men; he is a YOGI and a true performer of all actions.*

By thus following the rules of right-living (*Karma*), as indicated in *Vedanta*, when an individual has lived a sufficiently long period of time, the doubt arises as to when exactly we can say that he has completely reached the state-of-Perfection. This question should necessarily throb in

---

कर्मण्यकर्म यः पश्येदकर्मणि च कर्म यः ।
स बुद्धिमान्मनुष्येषु स युक्तः कृत्स्नकर्मकृत् ॥ १८ ॥

karmaṇyakarma yaḥ paśyedakarmaṇi ca karma yaḥ
sa buddhimānmanuṣyeṣu sa yuktaḥ kṛtsnakarmakṛt 18.

the intellect of all sincere students, and Krishna, is trying to indicate this noble goal of fulfilment of all *Karmas* in this stanza.

Action, as we have already seen, is a gross expression in the outer world of some known, or unknown, deep 'desire' in the intellect. A complete state of ACTIONLESSNESS would be necessarily the state of DESIRELESSNESS or the state of INFINITE GOD-HEAD. But the goal indicated here is not this state of INFINITE PERFECTION, but only a wayside station on the pilgrimage. A true and diligent man can discover and recognise in himself that even in physical inaction there can be an intense mental and intellectual activity, and he can also recognise that he, even in the most intense activities, himself as an observer of it, is revelling in 'unactivity' (*Akarma*). This is the maximum s*attvic* state.

Such an individual has thereby reached a state of Great Equanimity, which is almost unavoidable in living a successful life of meditation. It is not said here, as it is usually believed, that right action itself will take us to the Infinite. This is impossible. As action itself is a child of 'desire', through action alone we can create things; and created 'results' are, in their very nature, finite. Thus, a God-head reached through activity can only be a Sunday-God-head which must depart from us the following Monday morning!

Shankara and other great *Acharyas* have all been tirelessly repeating that, right action, undertaken with a sense of devotion and dedication creates in the bosom of the student a sense of complete detachment, as though he himself is a disinterested observer of all that is happening within and without him. When thus an individual detaches himself and observes his own activities as part and parcel of the world of activities around, he gains in himself an indescribable poise which is essential for the practice of meditation.

Merely because an individual is keeping quiet, we cannot ever conclude that he is inactive. Physical inactivity is no criterion to call one an idler. On the other hand, it is a fact well-known to all of us that, when we are intensely thinking – whenever we are in a state of creative thinking - we are invariably quiet and inactive, physically. Therefore, in the physical inactivity of one, which is labelled as idleness by the hectic footpath-walkers in life, we can detect intense activity in his deep 'within'. A Buddha under the fig-tree, an artist at his easel, a musician at his instrument, a writer at his desk – all of them punctuate their activities with 'still moments of intense inactivity' – called unactivity - and they bend forward to pour out their artistic and literary creations. All these physical moments of cessation are not mere inactivity but they are the necessary quietude and silence when the mind and intellect function with the highest velocity. Thus, he who has a capacity to introspect can easily detect perfect action in complete inaction.

As I am writing these words, a certain part in me can stand apart and visualise how my fingers, constituted of mere minerals, can hold the pen at the right slant and carry it along the paper so that the words may be spelt properly thereon. So, in all activities, this capacity to visualise discriminatingly our own activity - this capacity to observe ourselves functioning in a given field with or without the other members of the community - is not very rare and those who can do it can realise how, inspite of all our activities, the observer in us which OBSERVES the activities is most INACTIVE.

The train runs, but not the steam. The fan moves, but not the electricity. The fuel burns, but not the fire. The body, mind and intellect function and act, but not the Self, the Life in them!

Such an individual who can thus stand constantly apart from himself and observe THE ACTIVITY IN INACTIVITY and COMPLETE INACTIVITY EVEN IN THE HIGHEST ACTIVITY – called UNACTIVITY – is termed here, we must carefully note, not a man-of-Realisation (*Jnani*), but an intelligent, full-grown human creature (*Buddhiman*). "He is the intelligent one among men", and he is certainly one who is very near to the Self (*Atma Yuktah*).

In short, desireless activities, when undertaken and performed in a spirit of dedication, purify us, and the intellect thereby gains a new keenness. Out of such a purified head, a new faculty, as it were, arises. The capacity to observe oneself as an actor on the stage of life is a capacity divine and noble, inasmuch as it immediately redeems us from our selfish preoccupations with life's ever-changing incidents and accidents.

REALISATION OF 'INACTION IN ACTION' AND 'ACTION IN INACTION' IS EXTOLLED AS FOLLOWS:

19. *Whose undertakings are all devoid of desires and purposes, and whose actions have been burnt by the Fire-of-Knowledge, him the 'wise' call a Sage.*

यस्य सर्वे समारम्भाः कामसंकल्पवर्जिताः ।
ज्ञानाग्निदग्धकर्माणं तमाहुः पण्डितं बुधाः ॥ १९ ॥

yasya sarve samārambhāḥ kāmasaṅkalpavarjitāḥ
jñānāgnidagdhakārṇaṁ tamāhuḥ paṇḍitaṁ budhāḥ 19.

He is called a Saint, a man-of-Perfection, whose undertakings are all devoid of plan and desire-for-result. Planning is a shackle upon the freedom of one's activities. In all planning, we are forcing the circumstances into a desired mould, a wished-for pattern. In thus driving the situations to mould themselves into a planned pattern, we are exhausting ourselves and vainly fighting against terrible odds. This method of activity drains away all inspiration and joy from the worker.

We have already discussed how the desire for results during any activity dissipates our energies. The fruits of an action can only mature in a future period of time and therefore, to court the results is to escape from the present and live in the unborn periods of time. It is a law that the effects depend entirely upon the causes, and so to be sincere and complete in our activities is the greatest guarantee for all successful achievements.

One who is a perfect Sage, says Krishna, is one who will undertake to act WITHOUT PLANNING and WITHOUT ANY DESIRE FOR FRUITS. In this context, these two qualifications of a perfect act are to be understood with kindness and sympathy. A literal meaning of these two terms should not be used here, as in that case the statement would become absurd.

The instruction to act WITHOUT PLANNING AND DESIRE does not mean that a man of equilibrium, in his inspired activity, should not make use of his better intelligence and plan his activities to gain a desired result. It only means that, WHILE HE IS AT WORK, he should not allow his abilities and capacities to run to waste, with his mental preoccupations and sentimental fears regarding the results of his work. *Vedanta* does not in any way ignore man's intellect. The way-of-life as advised in the *Geeta* provides only a more efficient means to act and achieve, to live and to enjoy, cultivating and applying our own potentialities more intelligently.

An individual, who has thus come to live intelligently and act diligently, becomes fully wedded to the piece of work in hand and gets so entirely drunk with the joy of his own inspiration, that the action cannot leave upon him even a trace of its reaction. Our mind and intellect will venture forth to worry over the unknown possibilities and dangers, unless they can find a more secure hold upon something nobler and diviner. A perfect Sage is one whose mind is ever hitched on to the cognition of the Divine, so that, even when he functions in the world outside, he is revelling in his own Consciousness within.

By thus painting the psychology of a Sage at work, Lord Krishna is indicating with what mental attitude and intellectual composure, Arjuna, a seeker, should enter his fields of activity. These instructions, given by Vyasa through the mouth of Krishna, are meant for all generations of seekers and, therefore, words addressed to Arjuna are also words addressed to you and to me.

When my son wants to become a doctor, I would certainly explain to him the story of the struggle of some known doctors, so that my son may understand how best he himself can become a true doctor. So too here, by the description of a perfect Sage-at-work, Arjuna is being initiated into the path of Self-development, which he is to follow faithfully, if he is to reach the goal of life.

DEVOID OF ALL DESIRE-PROMPTED ACTIONS, AND ATTACHMENTS TO THEIR RESULTS, AND THEREFORE, HAVING NO SELFISH END IN VIEW, WHEN A SAGE

PERFORMS KINDLY ACTS IN THE COMMUNITY, HE REALLY DOES NO ACTION; HIS ACTION IS EQUIVALENT TO 'INACTION', SINCE ALL HIS ACTIONS ARE CONSUMED IN THE FIRE OF KNOWLEDGE. TO TEACH THIS 'UNACTIVITY, THE LORD SAYS :

20. *Having abandoned attachment to the fruits-of-action, ever content, depending on nothing, he does not do anything, though engaged in actions.*

We are not asked here to renounce the fruits of actions as such nor to ignore them, but we are only warned to renounce our MENTAL SLAVERY and INTELLECTUAL CLINGING to the 'expected fruits'. Only when we get preoccupied with the expected fruits of our actions do we come to exhaust ourselves, and thus become inefficient in our activities. Forsaking (*tyaktwa*) our clinging (*sanga*) to the fruits of action (*Karma-phala*), we are advised to strive for and to achieve the welfare of the society.

A true painter never willingly sells his masterpiece! To him, that piece of canvas upon which he has lavished long periods of effort, is now by itself a complete reward, even if he be starving!! As compared to the satisfaction and joy that it gives to the painter, he feels that even all the wealth in the world would but be too little a payment for it. If a mere finite piece of art could thus give to an ignorant man of agitations and desires, such an

---

त्यक्त्वा कर्मफलासङ्गं नित्यतृप्तो निराश्रय: ।
कर्मण्यभिप्रवृत्तोऽपि नैव किंचित्करोति स: ॥ २० ॥

tyaktavā karmaphalāsaṅgaṁ nityatṛpto nirāśrayaḥ
karmaṇyabhipravṛtto'pi naiva kiñcitkaroti saḥ 20.

invaluable joy, how much more intense must be the diviner joys of a perfect saint working in the world of names and forms? Indeed, the Self-realised Ones, after their experience of the Infinite Reality as their own Self, become perfectly independent of everything else.

Again, the anxiety for the fruits-of-action, the sense of discontentment and the feeling of dependency upon the things and beings of the world - all belong to the misconceived notion of the ego-centre. The ego in us is the sufferer of all the above-mentioned incapacities and inabilities. When the seeker after Truth rediscovers his ego to be the Infinite Truth, the limited ego ends its career of sorrow, and naturally, the agony and the incapacities of the imperfect ego also end. The reflection of the sun in a cup of water can be broken up when the water in the cup is shaken. But when the water is poured out, the reflection also ends, and no more can the sun in the sky be shaken by any known method.

Such an individual, who has rediscovered the Self, THOUGH SEEMINGLY ENGAGED IN ACTIVITY, does not do anything.

The body, mind and intellect act in the world-of-objects, but not the All-pervading Self – the Life – in us. Without LIFE, the body cannot function; but when the body functions, LIFE as such cannot be said to function. Therefore, one who is established in the Self, though he engaged himself in action, cannot be said to do any action. The train may move but it would be incorrect to say that the steam is moving.

There is generally a doubt with the students that, even if all the reactions of the past actions have ended at the time of Self-rediscovery, when such a prophetic Master undertakes activity in the world, he would, perhaps, be initiating new actions of sins and merits for the enjoyment of which he may again have to take up births. This false idea has been completely eradicated in this stanza. After the God-experience, when the saint functions in the world outside, THOUGH ENGAGED IN ACTION HE DOES NOT DO ANYTHING.

EVERY ACTION HAS A REACTION. NATURALLY, EVEN THE BODILY ACTIONS OF A SAINT SHOULD HAVE SOME REACTION. THIS IS THE ORDINARY ARGUMENT. TO NEGATE THIS ASSUMPTION THE LORD SAYS:

21. *Without hope, with the mind and Self controlled, having abandoned all possessions, doing mere bodily action, he incurs no sin.*

Mere bodily activity is not action that will merit a reaction. It has already been seen that the reactions of actions take place in the mental and in the intellectual zones. An action can leave a mark on our subtle-body only when we act with an egocentric consciousness that we are the actors, and these marks can be effective only when our actions are motivated by powerful and strong egocentric 'desires'.

Ego is created only when the Self, in its assumed delusion, identifies itself with the body, mind and intellect and their respective fields of objects. This ego draws its sustenance from

---

निराशीर्यतचित्तात्मा त्यक्तसर्वपरिग्रहः ।
शारीरं केवलं कर्म कुर्वन्नाप्नोति किल्बिषम् ॥ २१ ॥

nirāśīryatacittātmā tyaktasarvaparigrahaḥ
śārīraṁ kevalaṁ karma kurvannapnoti kilbiṣam 21.

the 'hopes of the future', and also from the 'satisfaction of the present' possessions.

Therefore, the stanza declares that an individual (a) when he has completely renounced hope, (b) when he has brought his body and mind under perfect control, and (c) when he has relinquished all possessions, can no longer sustain the illusory concept of the ego in him. When the ego has ended, the actions performed by that individual's body become incapable of leaving any permanent mark upon his mental constitution, or on his intellectual character.

In sleep if I become naked I am not charged of any indecent behaviour; if, in my sleep, my body kicks my own son, I am not accused of cruelty to my child. For, in both the above cases we know that 'for the actions of my body I am not responsible, since I was absent in that body during those activities'. This clearly shows that the egocentric identity with the body is the actor and the sufferer, and where the ego is not; there the mere bodily actions cannot bring about any consequences.

A Self-Realised Saint's activities do not touch him at all since he is not the actor; the actions only flow through him. Such a truly Great One becomes not a doer of actions, but serves as a glorious instrument for the Lord's will to express itself.

If the music coming from a violin is not good, the audience does not attack the violin, although the violinist cannot be very safe! The violin, of its own accord, does not make music but it allows music to emanate from it at the touch of the flying bow and the tickling fingers of the performer. Its duties end when its supple chords have bent under the touch of the musician's dancing fingers. An egoless man-of-Perfection is the 'wonder instrument' through which the Divine orchestra plays, singing the song of the Lord's own Will, faithfully. Any activity undertaken by a Perfect Master does not and cannot bring about any consequences, good or evil, upon him; he is only a Divine-instrument.

THOUGH A SELF-REALISED MAN RENOUNCES ALL ACTIONS, HE HAS, OF NECESSITY, TO BARELY MAINTAIN HIS BODY; SUCH A MAN STEADY ON THE PATH-OF-KNOWLEDGE IS EVER LIBERATED. TO TEACH THIS THE LORD SAYS:

22. *Content with what comes to him without effort, free from the pairs-of-opposites and envy, even-minded in success and failure, though acting he is not bound.*

Such an individual, who has gone beyond his own ego, can thereafter, commence no desire-prompted activity with any definite fruit-motive. Naturally, he will feel quite contented and happy in whatever gain spontaneously rises out of his actions. The state of egolessness indicates a condition of perfect conquest over the mind and intellect. Naturally therefore, the pairs-of-opposites; heat and cold, success and failure, good and bad, joy and sorrow, etc. – cannot affect him, they being always the interpretations of the world-of-objects by the mind.

Where the mind has ended, the intellect too can no more bring its own affections and prejudices, or its spirit of competitions and jealousies. We generally get agitated due

---

यदृच्छालाभसंतुष्टो द्वन्द्वातीतो विमत्सरः ।
समः सिद्धावसिद्धौ च कृत्वापि न निबध्यते ॥ २२ ॥

yudṛcchālābhasantuṣṭo dvandvātīto vimatsaraḥ
samaḥ siddhāvasiddhau ca kṛtvāpi na nibadhyate 22.

to the pulls of success and failure. On the rising tide of success, our ego dances in a vain joy, while in the hollows of failures it feels miserable and crushed. But when the ego is completely divinised, the individual will, thereafter, automatically remain equanimous in both success and failure. Such an individual who has thus conquered his egocentric misconceptions about himself, THOUGH ACTING, IS NOT FETTERED by the natural consequences of the actions performed (*Karma-phala*).

When such a Perfect master of Realisation lives amidst us he is generally seen to act in no way different from an ordinary sensible man, and yet, all the same, his activities show an extra dynamic capacity to carve out a more complete and enduring success. According to the Lord's words, the activities of a man-of-Knowledge do not, in any sense of the term, affect him. Naturally, it becomes a little difficult for an ordinary man to know readily how this is accomplished by the Sage.

TO EXPLAIN THE DIVINE MOTIVE AND ATTITUDE WITH WHICH MEN-OF-PERFECTION ACT IN THE WORLD, THE FOLLOWING NINE STANZAS ARE DECLARED BY THE LORD:

23. *Of one who is devoid of attachment, who is liberated, whose mind is established in knowledge, who acts for the sake of sacrifice, all his actions are dissolved.*

गतसङ्गस्य मुक्तस्य ज्ञानावस्थितचेतसः ।
यज्ञायाचरतः कर्म समग्रं प्रविलीयते ॥ २३ ॥

gatasaṅgasya muktasya jñānāvasthitacetasaḥ
yajñāyācarataḥ karma samagraṁ pravilīyate 23.

A man-of-Wisdom has been fully comprehended in the first line of this stanza. The qualifications are beautifully enumerated serially and they themselves explain the path-to-Perfection. Economy of words is the very essence of the style in all scriptural books. Even so, they are particularly careful to use the most suggestive terms for their purpose and take an artistic joy in ordering the very sequence of the words used; here is a brilliant example of it.

DEVOID OF ATTACHMENT (*Gatasangah*)—the divinity attained by the *Rishis* is not a new status strangely acquired by them from some unknown and secret quarters. It is only a rediscovery of the Perfection that is already in each one. We are self-exiled from ourselves due to our attachments with the finite world-of-objects. Thus, a 'wise' man is he, from whom all his attachments with the finite things of the world have dropped away.

LIBERATED (*Muktah*)—the majority of seekers have only a vague idea of what this 'liberation' means. The bondages are created upon our personality and life by none other than ourselves. These bondages, infinite in their number, are produced by the subtle chords of our own attachments with things. The deluded ego feels fulfilled only through the world-of-objects. Thus, as a body, it gets attached to the world of its sense-objects; as a mind it lives enslaved to the world of emotions; and as an intellect, it gets bound with its own ideas.

WITH MIND CENTRED IN KNOWLEDGE (*Jnana-avasthita-chetah*)—the above phenomenon of perfect detachment, which produces a sense of complete liberation, can be accomplished only when the mind of the seeker gets centred in right discriminative knowledge and develops for itself a capacity to distinguish between the permanent and the impermanent, the fleeting and the lasting.

A Perfect Sage, who has thus cut himself free from all attachments, with his mind well balanced under the light of his own wisdom, becomes completely liberated from the chains of all moral debilities, ethical imperfections, and sensuous appetites. Such a Sage too performs work for the rest of his life in his perfected manifestations. Krishna says that all such activities undertaken and performed by him are ever done in a spirit of 'dedicated activity' (*Yajna*).* When a Sage thus functions in a spirit of *Yajna*, that action itself does not and cannot produce any reaction, or forging of thicker bondages with newly formed *vasanas*.

The term '*Yajna*' borrowed from our scriptures, is employed here by Krishna to yield a more elaborate sense implying a wider and a more universal application. In the *Geeta*, the *Vedic Yajna* has become a self-dedicated activity performed in a spirit of service to the many. All actions, performed without ego, and not motivated by one's egocentric desires, fall under the category of *Yajna*.

All through the NEXT SIX STANZAS, we get an enumeration of something like twelve different *Yajnas* which can be practised by everybody, on all occasions, in every field, under all conditions.

When a sage of the description given in the stanza, performs actions in a spirit of *Yajna*, they dissolve away without leaving any impression upon his mind, just as the

* An action undertaken in a spirit of Divine dedication is called a *Yajna* – Sacrifice.

rainbow that disappears when the thin shower falling against the sunlight ends.

IF THIS BE SO, THE QUESTION ARISES - "FOR WHAT REASON THEN DO ALL ACTIONS WHICH HE PERFORMS ENTIRELY DISSOLVE, WITHOUT PRODUCING THEIR NATURAL RESULTS?" LISTEN WHY IT IS SO:

24. *BRAHMAN is the oblation; BRAHMAN is the clarified butter, etc., constituting the offerings; by BRAHMAN is the oblation poured into the fire of BRAHMAN; BRAHMAN verily shall be reached by him who always sees BRAHMAN in all actions.*

This is a famous stanza, which is chanted throughout India as a prayer at the table before the Hindus eat their meals, although, today, ninety per cent of those who chant this stanza before their meals do not understand or care to follow its meaning. All the same it contains infinite suggestions and almost summarises the entire philosophic content of *Vedanta*.

The Infinite Reality, which is the changeless substratum behind and beneath the changing panorama of the world, is indicated by the *Vedic* term *Brahman*, and this is contrasted with that aspect of Truth which functions in and through the body as the *Atman*. But though the Eternal Truth has been thus indicated by two different terms, *Vedanta* roars that "The *Atman* is *Brahman*".

ब्रह्मार्पणं ब्रह्म हविर्ब्रह्माग्नौ ब्रह्मणा हुतम् ।
ब्रह्मैव तेन गन्तव्यं ब्रह्मकर्मसमाधिना ॥ २४ ॥

brahmārpaṇaṁ brahma havirbrahmāgnau brahmaṇā hutam
brahmaiva tena gantavyaṁ brahmakarmasamādhinā 24.

The metaphor is borrowed from the very well known divine ritualism of the *Vedas*, the *Yajnas*. In every *Yajna* there are four essential factors (1) the deity invoked to whom the oblations are offered, (2) the fire in which the offerings are poured, (3) the material things that constitute the offerings and (4) the individual who is performing the *Yajna*.

Here the stanza explains the mental attitude and the experience of the Perfect-Sage when he performs the *Yajna*. To him Truth alone exists and not the delusory plurality which his erstwhile ignorance had conjured up for him in his mind. Therefore, to him, all *Yajnas* arise from *Brahman*; (III-14, 15) in which *Brahman*, the Truth, is the performer; offering *Brahman*, the material to the sacred fire, which is also nothing other than *Brahman*; invoking but *Brahman*. When one wave jumps over another and breaks itself to embrace and become one with its comrade, we, who know that all waves are nothing but the ocean, can certainly understand that in this act of union between two waves nothing has happened except that the ocean rising over the ocean, broke itself to become one with the ocean.

If an individual can thus see the substratum, or the essential nature, in and through, all names and forms, actions and behaviours, to him, irrespective of all conditions and circumstances, all beings and things are but a remembrance of the Infinite Blissful Truth. If actions are performed by a Saint, invoking no deity other than *Brahman*, ALL HIS ACTIONS DISSOLVE AWAY because he is invoking but the One Truth through all his actions.

The significance of the stanza as a prayer to be said before food is amply self-evident. To live we must eat. Food is necessary for existence. Whatever be the type of food, when one is hungry one will enjoy one's meals. The suggestion is that even at this moment of natural enjoyment, we are not to forget the great Truth that it is *Brahman* eating *Brahman*, and that during our meals we are offering to *Brahman*, the food that is *Brahman*, invoking nothing but the grace of *Brahman*. To keep this idea constantly in the mind is to get perfectly detached from the enjoyment and raise ourselves to a greater and endless beatitude, which is the reward of Super-manhood.

AFTER REPRESENTING THE VERY SPIRIT IN ALL *'YAJNAS'*, THE LORD IS TRYING TO SHOW ARJUNA HOW ALL THROUGH LIFE, ALL OUR ACTIONS CAN BE CONVERTED TO BECOME A *'YAJNA'*. RIGHT KNOWLEDGE (*BHAVANA*) MAKES EVERY ACT A *'YAJNA'*. LISTEN:

25. *Some YOGIS perform sacrifice to DEVAS alone (DEVA-YAJNA); while others offer 'sacrifice' as sacrifice by the Self, in the Fire of BRAHMAN (BRAHMA-YAJNA).*

In the following few stanzas, Lord Krishna is explaining the mental attitude of a Saint at work. One doubt is generally raised by every intelligent student at all times. The spiritual experience, no doubt, can be had when the seeker in

---

दैवमेवापरे यज्ञं योगिन: पर्युपासते ।
ब्रह्माग्नावपरे यज्ञं यज्ञेनैवोपजुह्वति ॥ २५ ॥

daivamevāpare yajñaṁ yoginaḥ paryupāsate
brahmāgnāvapare yajñaṁ yajñenaivopajuhavati 25.

meditation transcends even his intellect. But then, this transcendental experience is bound to remain only for a limited time. The Realised-Saint is found working in the world, sometimes, in an elaborate fashion, like a Buddha or a Christ; in some cases, he works in a limited fashion, like a Ramana Maharshi, and at certain moments he may not undertake any activity at all, but merely continue living among the world-of-objects. Now the doubt is "what would be the mental attitude of such a Perfect-Master when he comes in contact with the world and functions in it?"

A *Yogi* is one who is always trying, through all the means that are in him, to raise himself from his state of physical, mental and intellectual imperfections to a more perfect state of existence. In this sense of the term, it would be unjust to read into the stanza merely the obvious meaning.

The word *'Deva'* comes from a root, meaning 'illumination'. Subjectively viewed, the greatest *'Devas'* are the five sense organs: eyes illumining forms and colours, ears illumining sounds, the nose illumining smells and the tongue and the skin illumining tastes and touches. Seekers and Perfected Masters (*Yogis*) too, when they move in the world, no doubt, perceive sense-objects through sense stimuli. But in their understanding and experience, perception is but "a world of sense-objects continuously offering themselves into the fires of his perception in order to invoke the *Devas* (sense-perceptions)". Such seekers and masters walk out into life, and when they come across the sense world, they only recognise and experience that the world-of-objects is paying a devoted tribute to the powers of sense perceptions!

When this mental attitude is entertained constantly by a seeker he comes to feel completely detached from the sense experiences and, irrespective of the quality of experience, he is able to maintain a constant sense of inward equanimity.

As contrasted with this method (*Deva-Yajna*) there are others who perform *Brahma-Yajna*, says Krishna, wherein they come to OFFER THE SELF AS A SACRIFICE BY THE SELF IN THE FIRE OF THE SELF. This statement becomes perfectly clear when subjectively analysed and understood. As long as we exist in the body manifestation, we have to come across the world of sense-objects. The outer world can yield to us its joy or sorrow not by itself but only as a result of our healthy or unhealthy attitude towards it. The objects in themselves are impotent to give us either joy or sorrow.

The Perfect Masters understand that the sense-organs are only INSTRUMENTS of perception and that they can work only when in contact with the Supreme, the *Atman*. All Masters live in this true understanding allowing the sense-organs to sacrifice themselves in the Knowledge-of-*Brahman*. By this statement, seekers are also advised as to how they too, can gain a certain amount of freedom from their senses by dedicating their sense-life in the service of the world. When an individual's sense organs of perception and action are to function and act, not for his own egocentric, selfish satisfactions but for the sake of serving the society or the world, then, even if such an individual lives in the world-of-objects he will not be enslaved by his attachments to his possessions.

AFTER THUS ENUMERATING THE *'DEVA-YAJNA'* AND THE *'BRAHMA-YAJNA'*, LORD KRISHNA EXPOUNDS TWO MORE METHODS IN THE FOLLOWING:

26. *Some again, offer hearing and other senses as sacrifice in the fires-of-restraint; others offer sound and other objects of sense as sacrifice in the fires of the senses.*

SOME OTHER GREAT MASTERS OFFER HEARING AND OTHER SENSES IN THE FIRES OF RESTRAINT—in all these *Yajnas* described, the metaphor is taken from the most familiar ritualism known at the time to Arjuna. Oblations were offered, in *Vedic* ritualism, into the sacred-fire in order to invoke the blessings of the deity. In these examples, we are shown how, when some materials are offered into a sacred-fire, not only the oblations get burnt up and consumed by the fire, but also, as a result, a great blessing accrues. Here, it is said that some Masters live on, in life constantly offering their senses into the fire of self-control, so that the senses, of their own accord get burnt up, contributing a greater freedom and joy in the inner life of the man. It is also a fact very well experienced by all of us, that the more we try to satisfy the sense-organs the more riotous they become and loot away our inner joy. By self-control alone can the sense-organs be fully controlled and mastered. This is yet another method

---

श्रोत्रादीनीन्द्रियाण्यन्ये संयमाग्निषु जुह्वति ।
शब्दादीन्विषयानन्य इन्द्रियाग्निषु जुह्वति ॥ २६ ॥

śrotrādīnīndriyāṇyanye saṁyamāgniṣu juhavati
śabdādīnvisyānanya indriyāgniṣu juhavati 26.

shown to the seekers by which they can come to experience and live a more intense life of deeper meditation.

If in this method the path of 'sense-control' is indicated, in the second line the path of 'mind control' is suggested. The mind is sustained and fed by the stimuli that reach it from the outer world. The sense-objects perceived by the organs create and maintain the mind. The mind can never function in a field which cannot be interpreted in terms of the five types of sense-objects. Therefore, to make the mind non-receptive to the perceptions of the *Indriyas* is a method by which one can gain a better poise in life for purposes of meditation. Such an individual who has controlled the mind completely and has withdrawn it totally from the sense-centres is indicated here when the Lord says: "OTHERS OFFER SOUND AND OTHER OBJECTS IN THE FIRES OF THE SENSES".

If the former method is a technique of controlling the stimuli at the very gateway of the senses, the latter is a different technique of controlling the same from the inner, and therefore, more subtle level of perception, called the mind.

AFTER THUS EXPLAINING THESE FOUR METHODS, YET ANOTHER TECHNIQUE HAS BEEN PROPOUNDED BY THE LORD IN THE FOLLOWING STANZA:

27. *Others, again, sacrifice all the functions of the senses and the functions of the breath (vital energy) in the fire of the YOGA of self-restraint, kindled by knowledge.*

सर्वाणीन्द्रियकर्माणि प्राणकर्माणि चापरे ।
आत्मसंयमयोगाग्नौ जुह्वति ज्ञानदीपिते ॥ २७ ॥

savārṇīndriyakamārṇi prāṇakamārṇi cāpare
ātmasaṁyamayogāgnau juhavati jñānadīpite 27.

ALL THE ACTIVITIES OF THE SENSE-ORGANS (*JNANA-INDRIYAS*), AND THE ORGANS OF ACTION (*PRANA-INDIRYAS*) ARE OFFERED INTO THE KNOWLEDGE-KINDLED FIRE OF RIGHT UNDERSTANDING – Control of the ego by the better understanding of the Divine Reality is called here as the *'Yoga* of Self restraint' (*Atma-Samyama-Yoga*).

The path-of-Discrimination (*Vichara*) lies through a constant attempt at distinguishing between the limited lot of the ego and the divine destinies of the Spirit. Having discriminated thus, to live more and more as the Self, and not as the ego, is to RESTRAIN THE SELF BY THE SELF (*Atma-Samyama*).* By this process, it is evident how the mad ramblings of the organs of perceptions and actions can be completely restrained and entirely conquered.

EXHAUSTING THE ABOVE-MENTIONED FIVE DIFFERENT TECHNIQUES, AS THOUGH TO BRING TO THE UNDERSTANDING OF ARJUNA, THAT A HUNDRED OTHER METHODS CAN BE INDICATED, KRISHNA ENUMERATES IN HASTE FIVE MORE DIFFERENT METHODS IN THE FOLLOWING STANZA :

28. *Others again offer wealth, austerity and YOGA as sacrifice, while the ascetics of self-restraint and rigid vows offer study of scriptures and knowledge as sacrifice.*

द्रव्ययज्ञास्तपोयज्ञा योगयज्ञास्तथापरे ।
स्वाध्यायज्ञानयज्ञाश्च यतयः संशितव्रताः ॥ २८ ॥

dravyayajñāstapoyajñā yogayajñāstathāpare
svādhyāyajñānayajñāśca yatayaḥ saṁśitavratāḥ 28.

* Controlling of the sense-organs of both perceptions and knowledge is not possible until the Seeker's mind is turned fully upon the "Contemplation of the Self"; hence this is called as the restraint of the self (individual personality) by the Self.

Dravya-Yajna (Offering of Wealth)—Sacrifice of wealth is to be understood in its largest connotation. Charity and distribution of honestly acquired wealth, in a sincere spirit of devotion to and in the service of the community, or of the individual who is the recipient of the benevolence, is called *Dravya-Yajna*. This includes more than a mere offering of money or food.

The term *Dravya* includes everything that we possess, not only in the world outside but also in our worlds of emotions and ideas. To pursue thus a life of charity, serving the world as best as we can, with all that we possess physically, mentally and intellectually is the noble sacrifice called 'wealth sacrifice'.

In order to perform this, it is not at all necessary that the devotee should be materially rich. Even if we are poor and physically debilitated, from our bed of pain and penury, we can still be charitable, because our inner treasurers of love, kindness, sympathy and affection, do not at all depend either upon our material circumstances nor on our physical condition. Sometimes, a word of sincere sympathy, a look of love, a smile of true affection, or a word registering true friendship, can give to the receiver more than a heartless cheque, even if it be for a very fat sum.

Tapo-yajna—Some live, offering unto their Lord, a life of austerity. There is no religion in the world, which does not prescribe, by some method or the other, periods of austere living. These austerities (*vratas*) are invariably undertaken in the name of the Lord. It is very well known that the Lord of Compassion, who feeds and sustains even the lowest of the low, can gain no special joy because of a devotee's self-denial.

But it is generally done in a spirit of dedication, so that the seeker might achieve some self-control. This activity, in some extreme cases very painful indeed, is undertaken in orde r that the devotee may learn to control himself in his sense-life.

Yoga-yajna—an earnest attempt of the lesser in us to grow into a better standard of diviner living, is called *Yoga*. In this attempt, devoted worship of the Lord of the heart, called *Upasana*, is a primary method. This worship and love, offered to the Lord of the heart, when performed without any desire or motive, is also called *Yoga*, since it directly hastens the seeker's self-development.

Swadhyaya-yajna—the daily deep study of the scriptures is called *swadhyaya*. Without a complete study of the scriptures we will not be in a position to know the logic of what we are doing in the name of spiritual practice, and without this knowledge our practices cannot gain the edge and the depth that are essential for sure progress. Thus, in all religions, the daily study of the scriptures is insisted upon, as an essential training during the seeker's early days. Even after Self-realisation, we find that the Sages spend all their spare-time reading and contemplating upon the inexhaustible wealth of details and suggestions in the scriptures.

In its subjective implications, *swadhyaya* means 'self-study including the art of introspection pursued for understanding our own inner weaknesses'. If, in the case of a seeker, it is a technique of estimating his own spiritual progress, in the case of a Seer, it will be for revelling in his own Self.

Jnana-yajna—the sacrifice-of-Knowledge: this word has very often been used in the *Geeta* and it constitutes one of the many original terms coined out by Vyasa to beautify the Lord's declarations. The sacrifice-of-Knowledge is the term given to that activity in man by which he renounces all his ignorance into the fire-of-knowledge kindled BY him and IN him. This is constituted of two aspects; negation of the false, and assertion of the Real Nature of the Self. These two activities are effectively undertaken during the seeker's meditation.

All these five methods of Self-development -- sacrifice of wealth, austerity, *Yoga*, study and knowledge -- can be practised with profit only by those who are men of rigid determination and who can find in themselves an inexhaustible enthusiasm to apply themselves consistently to reach this great goal. It is not sufficient that we know these paths, or that we decide to gain these developments. Progress in spirituality can come only to one who is sincere and consistent in his practices (*Yatayah*).

IN THE FOLLOWING VERSE KRISHNA EXPLAINS *PRANAYAMA* AS YET ANOTHER METHOD, THE ELEVENTH IN THE SERIES:

29. *Others offer as sacrifice the out-going breath in the in-coming, and the in-coming in the out-going, restraining the courses of the out-going and in-coming breaths, solely absorbed in the restraint of breath.*

In this verse, we have a description of the technique of breath-control regularly practised by some seekers, in order

---

अपाने जुह्वति प्राणं प्राणेऽपानं तथापरे ।
प्राणापानगती रुद्ध्वा प्राणायामपरायणाः ॥ २९ ॥

apāne juhavati prāṇaṁ prāṇe'pānaṁ tathāpare
prāṇāpānagatī ruddhvā prāṇāyāmaparāyaṇāḥ 29.

to keep themselves under perfect self-control, when they move amidst the sense-objects in the work-a-day world.

As a sacrifice, some offer THE OUTGOING BREATH INTO THE INCOMING BREATH AND OTHERS OFFER THE INCOMING INTO THE OUTGOING. The latter is, in the technique of *Pranayama,* called the *Puraka,* meaning the process of filling in; while, the former is the process of blowing out, technically called the *Rechaka*. These two processes are alternated with an interval, wherein the breath is held for sometime, within and without, which is called the *Kumbhaka*. This process of *Puraka-Kumbhaka-Rechaka-Kumbhaka,* when practised in a prescribed ratio, becomes the technique of breath-control (*Pranayama*). This technique is again explained here as a *Yajna* by which the practitioner, in the long run, learns to offer all the subsidiary *Pranas* into the main *Prana*.

Prana is not the breath; this is a general misunderstanding. Through breath-control, we come to gain a perfect mastery over the activities of the *Pranas* in us. When very closely observed, we find that the term *Prana* used in the Hindu Scriptures indicates the various manifested activities of life in a living body. They generally enumerate five different kinds of *Pranas,* which, when understood correctly, are found to be nothing but the five different physiological functions in every living body.

They are: (1) the function of perception, (2) the function of excretion, (3) the function of digestion and assimilation, (4) the circulatory system, which distributes the food to all parts of the body, and lastly (5) the capacity in a living-creature to improve himself in his mental outlook and intellectual life.

These activities of life within, about which an ordinary man is quite unconscious, are brought under the perfect control of the individual through the process of *Pranayama*, so that a seeker can, by this path, come to gain a complete capacity to withdraw all his perceptions. This is indeed a great help to a meditator.

IN THIS SERIES OF TECHNIQUES ENUMERATED BY KRISHNA, AS A LAST METHOD, WE HAVE IN THE FOLLOWING STANZA THE TWELFTH METHOD DETAILED:

30. *Others, with well-regulated diet, offer vital-airs in the Vital-Air. All these are knowers of sacrifice, whose sins are destroyed by sacrifice.*

There are some who, through systematic regulation of their diet, come to gain a complete mastery over themselves and their appetites and passions. Dieting is not at all a new technique in India. The ancient *Rishis* not only knew the vitamin-contents and the calorie-values of the various food materials, but also prescribed very scientific combinations of the available vegetables and cereals to suit the temperament, function, and duties of persons belonging to different levels of society. Not only this; they so well perfected their knowledge that they even showed how, through regulated dieting, a man's character and behaviour, and ultimately his very cultural quality, can be purified and raised.

अपरे नियताहाराः प्राणान्प्राणेषु जुह्वति ।
सर्वेऽप्येते यज्ञविदो यज्ञक्षपितकल्मषाः ॥ ३० ॥

apare niyatāhārāḥ prāṇānprāṇeṣu juhavati
sarve'pyete yajñavido yajñakṣapitakalmaṣāḥ 30.

The verse adds that all these KNOWERS OF *YAJNA*, meaning all those who know the art of living these techniques, when they practise them in a spirit of self-dedication and selfless enthusiasm, can fully come to profit by them. These methods and techniques do not promise that they will, of themselves, guide us or lead us to the Supreme. It is promised that all those who practise all, or a few, or even one of them for a sufficiently long period, can become PURIFIED OF THEIR SINS.

Sin, we have already discussed, is but a wrong pattern of thought-channels that is etched in a mind by devolutionary thoughts, entertained by a deluded ego in its extreme misunderstanding and its consequent attachment with the body and sense-objects. It is these sinful *vasanas* that make the ego act like an animal and force it to commit low and vicious criminalities. The above-mentioned practices not only wipe clean the existing wrong-*vasanas* but cut out in their place new channels of thoughts, more constructive and evolutionary in their very nature.

Thus, it must be carefully noted that all practices, physical, mental, or intellectual, that are generally known as divine and religious, are, without exception, only techniques by which the mind-and-intellect equipment gets adjusted for greater and more effective self-application in meditation. Meditation is the 'path' in which the ego learns to withdraw its false evaluations of itself in particular, and of life in general, and comes to the final experience of its own divine nature. We often find sincere seekers getting so extremely attached to their own 'path' of practice that they constantly argue about it among themselves. Therefore, Arjuna has been instructed here that all 'paths', however noble and great they may be, are all but means, and not an end in themselves.

IN ALL THE ABOVE-ENUMERATED TWELVE DIFFERENT *YAJNA*-TECHNIQUES, SELF-EFFORT IS A COMMON FACTOR, AND THEREFORE, THE LORD SAYS:

31. *The eaters of the nectar - remnant of the sacrifice - go to the Eternal BRAHMAN. Even this world is not for the non-performer of sacrifice; how then the other (world), O best of the Kurus?*

EATING THE SACRED REMNANT OF THE *YAJNA*— In the ancient ritualism of fire-sacrifices, things that were 'left over' in the pot from which the offerings were made, were called the 'sacred remains', and they were considered by the devotees as divinely potent-remnants from the Lord's own plates. This was generally eaten by the devotees with great reverence, and it was considered that, thereby their minds would get purified.

In the metaphor used here, when we try to find its corresponding implication in the subjective world, we must understand 'the remnant that is left over' to mean 'the result of the above-mentioned twelve types of *Yajnas*'. The result of any one of the above *Yajnas* is, as we know, a greater amount of self-control and the consequent inner integration of the individual personality. Those who have gained this have prepared themselves for the greatest vocation in life called 'intense meditation'.

यज्ञशिष्टामृतभुजो यान्ति ब्रह्म सनातनम् ।
नायं लोकोऽस्त्ययज्ञस्य कुतोऽन्य: कुरुसत्तम ॥ ३१ ॥
yajñaśiṣṭāmṛtabhujo yānti brahma sanātanam
nāyaṁ loko'styayajñasya kuto'nyaḥ kurusattama 31.

Such an integrated man can gain a greater inner poise in his meditation through which he can easily come to experience the Infinite and the Eternal, indicated by the term *Brahman*. The second line of the verse contains a beautiful generalisation which clinches the main idea, that self-development and inner growth cannot be had without investing continuous and sincere self-effort. Inaction can never bring about any profit even in this world, in any field whatsoever. Without self-dedicated and selfless activity, no great and enduring profit can be achieved in this world, and therefore, Krishna exclaims: "How could a seeker hope to achieve the Highest without any conscious effort at gaining it?"

Two doubts can arise in the minds of ruthlessly intelligent students. It may be doubted: "Can all these different 'Paths' lead us to one and the same goal, or do they lead to different goals?" It may also be doubted: "Are these not mere intellectual theories propounded by Krishna himself as an original contribution to Hindu thought?"

THE FOLLOWING EXPLAINS THESE TWO DOUBTS:

32. *Thus innumerable sacrifices lie spread out before BRAHMAN – (literally at the mouth or face of BRAHMAN) – Know them all as born of action, and thus knowing, you shall be liberated.*

In the world, no two different activities produce the same set of results. The twelve different *Yajnas* described so far,

---

एवं बहुविधा यज्ञा वितता ब्रह्मणो मुखे ।
कर्मजान्विद्धि तान्सर्वानेवं ज्ञात्वा विमोक्ष्यसे ॥ ३२ ॥

evaṁ bahuvidhā yajñā vitatā brahmaṇo mukhe
karmajānviddhi tānsavārnevaṁ jñātvā vimokṣyase 32.

are all conspicuously different from one another, and so they must all be producing not an identical result but a series of different effects. In order to show that though the 'Paths' are different, all of them ultimately lead to the same goal, it is said here: "Various *Yajnas* lie open, leading to the gate of *Brahman*, the ETERNAL". Just as all roads lead to Rome, all the above-mentioned techniques of *Yajna* also ultimately lead to one and the same goal.

KNOW THEM ALL TO BE BORN OF ACTION—This timely reminder of the Lord has more than one direct suggestion: (a) these paths prescribed in the *Vedas* are all to be pursued through self-effort, and therefore, Arjuna is reminded of the inevitability of right action, if he wants to move ahead in his cultural self-development; and (b) it also suggests that all these paths are only the means and not the end. Action is born of desires, and, therefore, as long as there is action there is no redemption from 'desires'. The state of Desirelessness is the state-of-Perfection, and therefore, in the context of our understanding, these pregnant words of the verse ring a note of warning that we should not misunderstand these *Yajnas* as the very goal of life.

UNDERSTANDING THUS, YOU SHALL BE FREE—Here the word 'understanding' is not a mere intellectual apprehension but a complete spiritual comprehension, in a vivid subjective experience of Reality.

Right-Knowledge was represented as a Knowledge-Sacrifice (IV-24). Then, several sacrifices have been mentioned. Knowledge is now being extolled, as compared with these latter kinds of sacrifices, which are all means of attaining the *Purushartha* - the inner integration.

33. *Superior is 'knowledge-sacrifice' to 'sacrifice-with-objects', O Parantapa. All actions in their entirety, O Partha, culminate in Knowledge.*

Krishna compares the *Dravya-Yajna*, the sacrifice of material oblations, with *Jnana-Yajna*,* and declares that, for cultural self-development, *Jnana-Yajna* is any day, nobler and diviner than mere formalistic ritualism with material offerings (*Dravya-Yajna*).

In the second line of the verse the Lord explains how and why He considers the sacrifice of 'ignorance' in Knowledge (*Jnana-Yajna*) as greater and nobler than the sacrifice of food and other materials in the sacred fire (*Dravya-Yajna*). Ritualistic *Karmas* produce results to enjoy which the individual ego has to take up new manifestations, wherein again, he has yet to undertake and perform more and more activities. *Karma* never ends *Karma*, and therefore, action cannot be a complete fulfilment in itself.

On the other hand, Right-Knowledge (*Jnana*) ends all *Karmas*, once and for all, inasmuch as the deluded-ego destroys itself in the light of Self-Knowledge. We have already seen that ignorance causes desires, and desires are the seeds from which all actions arise. When this ignorance, the primary source of all activities, ends at the dawn of Knowledge, all actions naturally get fulfilled. Therefore, "ALL ACTION IN

श्रेयान्द्रव्यमयाद्यज्ञाज्ज्ञानयज्ञ: परंतप ।
सर्वं कर्माखिलं पार्थ ज्ञाने परिसमाप्यते ॥ ३३ ॥

śreyāndravyamayādyajñājjñānayajñaḥ parantapa
sarva kamārkhilaṁ pārtha jñāne parisamāpyate 33.

* 'Knowledge-Sacrifice' – refer Ibid. Verse 28, 2nd line.

ITS ENTIRETY, O PARTHA, ATTAINS ITS CONSUMMATION IN KNOWLEDGE".

IF THUS, BY KNOWLEDGE ALONE WE CAN REALLY GAIN THE FULLEST SATISFACTION, THEN HOW ARE WE TO GAIN THIS KNOWLEDGE BY WHICH ALL ACTIONS CAN AT ONCE BE BURNT UP AND EXHAUSTED?

34. *Know that by long prostration, by question, and service, the 'wise' who have realised the Truth will instruct you in (that) 'Knowledge'.*

The verse explains the qualities that are necessary in a teacher, who alone can instruct us on the path-of-Knowledge and guide us to the great consummation in all life. It also explains the mental attitude and the intellectual approach, which a successful student must adopt, so that his contact with the *Guru* may be fruitful.

PROSTRATING YOURSELF—all that is meant here is that the student must have an intellectual attitude of surrender and meekness, respect and obedience, when he approaches the teacher who has to instruct him upon the secret of life. Regarding the world within and the methods of its control, ordinarily, the students are completely ignorant, and therefore, they must approach the teacher with a readiness to understand, grasp and follow his instructions.

तद्विद्धि प्रणिपातेन परिप्रश्नेन सेवया ।
उपदेक्ष्यन्ति ते ज्ञानं ज्ञानिनस्तत्त्वदर्शिनः ॥ ३४ ॥

tadviddhi praṇipātena paripraśnena sevayā
upadekṣyanti te jñānaṁ jñāninastattvadarśinaḥ 34.

Just as water flows always from a higher to a lower level, so too, 'Knowledge' can flow only to a lower level. It is, therefore, necessary that the student must have a spirit of prostration in him so that he may be able to get himself surcharged with the 'Knowledge' that flows from the teacher. Thus the prostration, as used here, essentially defines more, the required mental and intellectual attitude of the student, than his physical readiness to fall-flat on the ground at the feet of his Master.

BY QUESTIONS—by raising doubts to the teacher we are opening up the cistern of 'Knowledge' locked up in the Master's bosom. A perfect *Guru* immediately detects from the questions, the false line of thinking in the student, and while removing the very doubt, he imperceptibly orders and reorganises the right way of thinking in the inner thought-life of the student. When this intellectual wrestling has been practised for a long time, the fragrance of perfection in the teacher, as it were, gets transferred to the student's life!

Therefore, it has been an immortal tradition among the Hindus to have open discussions between the teacher and the taught, called *satsanga*. This privilege is not available in all religions of the world. In fact, *Vedanta* alone thus dares to proclaim a perfect freedom for the intellect. It never trades upon the blind faith of the seekers. In all other religions, faith is a great power and force, and therefore, many of the intellectual imperfections in their scriptures cannot be completely answered; and the priests therein must necessarily check the full freedom of the seekers to question their sacred texts.

BY SERVICE—the offering of flowers and sweetmeats is

not what constitutes *seva*. These have been understood as the service of the teacher only as a by-product of institutionalism and *ashrama* organisation. A true service of the teacher lies in the attempt of the student to attune himself to the principles of life advocated and advised to him by the Master. To live the life indicated by the *Rishis* is the greatest *seva* that an imperfect mortal can offer to the man-of-Perfection.

The two main qualifications essential for a fully useful teacher on the spiritual path are: (a) a perfect knowledge of scriptural literature and (b) a complete subjective experience of the Infinite Reality. These two factors are indicated here. Each, without the other, is totally useless in guiding a seeker. Mere knowledge of the scriptures can make only a learned *Pandita* and not a Perfect-Master. A man of intimate experience of Truth will, in himself, become completely silent, because he will find it impossible to explain and express his own transcendental experience to other seekers.

BY THIS THE LORD MEANS TO SAY THAT, THAT KNOWLEDGE ALONE, WHICH IS IMPARTED BY THOSE WHO HAVE REALISED THE TRUTH – THAT KNOWLEDGE ALONE AND NO OTHER 'KNOWLEDGE' – CAN PROVE EFFECTIVE. THEN THE FOLLOWING STATEMENT HOLDS GOOD:

35. *Knowing that, you shall not, O Pandava, again get deluded like this; and by that, you shall see all beings in your Self, and also in Me.*

यज्ज्ञात्वा न पुनर्मोहमेवं यास्यसि पाण्डव ।
येन भूतान्यशेषेण द्रक्ष्यस्यात्मन्यथो मयि ॥ ३५ ॥

yajjñātvā na punarmohamevaṁ yāsyasi pāṇḍava
yena bhūtānyaśeṣeṇa drakṣyasyātmanyatho mayi 35.

After all these painful troubles, it may chance that we may get 'Knowledge' but after one's death one may again fall back to ignorance and come to repeat the same process. Even in our own lifetime there have been many things learnt and experienced which we do not now remember. Similarly, this 'Knowledge' also may be lost to us in which case it will be indeed a great loss.

This doubt is fully cleared here by an assertive, confident declaration that after regaining this 'Knowledge' "YOU SHALL NOT, O PANDAVA, AGAIN GET DELUDED LIKE THIS". This declaration, rather fanatical in style, has to be, for the time being, accepted by all seekers. All teachers unanimously declare this idea and since they have no particular reason to deceive their generation, it is but intelligent that we should accept the truth of this declaration in good faith - until we come to confirm it in our own personal experience.

No doubt, an immature child can never understand the physical thrills of the nuptial chamber, and thereby it cannot be said that the newly-weds are always telling lies!! The little child has not matured enough even to feel sympathetically the thrills explained. Similarly, we, living in delusion, cannot UNDERSTAND the thrills of the transcendental, or EXPERIENCE its Eternal Nature – however vividly the teachers may explain, until we also grow to the required inner maturity.

By this rediscovery of the Self, Krishna promises that the Pandava Prince will thereafter, be able to recognise the entire creation - constituted of the world of objects, emotions, and ideas – as nothing other than the Self, which is his own real

Nature; which again is nothing other than 'Me', Lord Krishna, the *Paramatman*. Having for once realised the ocean, all the waves are recognised by the intelligent-eye as nothing but the ocean.

In this stanza, thus, tests of having realised 'that Knowledge' – discussed in the previous stanzas, are given. It also indicates how long we must hold on to the apron of a true *Guru*. As long as we have not realised that the whole creation is nothing but our own Self, which is as divine and omnipotent as the Lord of Dwaraka Himself, so long we cannot afford to leave our intimate relationship and complete dependence upon the Preceptor and Guide, the *Guru*.

MOREOVER, SEE HOW EXCELLENT 'KNOWLEDGE' IS:

36. *Even if you are the most sinful of all sinners, yet you shall verily cross all sins by the raft of 'Knowledge.'*

While Arjuna was promised such a glorious transcendental experience, too divine for him to believe, he felt a certain amount of lack of confidence in himself, which was, perhaps, reflected, on his face. He had a feeling that he was not fit for such a great inner experience. Such a feeling can come to anyone of us, because there is none among the intelligent who is not painfully conscious of his own shortcomings.

अपि चेदसि पापेभ्य: सर्वेभ्य: पाप *कृत्तम:* ।
सर्वं ज्ञानप्लवेनैव वृजिनं संतरिष्यसि ॥ ३६ ॥

api cedasi pāpebhyaḥ sarvebhya pāpakṛttamaḥ
sarvaṁ jñānaplavenaiva vṛjinaṁ santariṣyasi 36.

Vedanta is not a philosophy that heartlessly keeps the sinners out of its halls of wisdom. It does not believe that there is any lost soul who will ever wander among the heathens, and who can be redeemed ONLY IF he enters the portals of the Church of *Vedanta*. Tolerant to a fault, *Vedanta* declares the Truth and nothing but the Truth. The All-pervading Divine manifests everywhere and therefore, there is no sinner who cannot, through his endeavour, come to claim his own heritage of Absolute Perfection.

The *Geeta* is a scripture of life written for man, and its universality is unmistakably seen in the statement here. It assures man that "EVEN IF HE BE THE MOST SINFUL AMONG THE SINFUL", he too, can cross over his painful destinies of the present and reach the shores that lie beyond finitude and imperfections. Such a clear charter of man's right to the Divine has never so far been written in any other existing scripture of the world!!

To rediscover that, in reality, the ego is nothing other than the Self in us, and to live thereafter as the Self of all, is called true Wisdom (*Jnana*). Having thus awakened to our Real Nature, the dreamy cravings of the flesh can no more enchant us away from our pristine glory and make us run down the channels of sensuousness, to wreck ourselves on the stony bed of sin and sorrow. This is indicated by a beautiful metaphor: "BY THE RAFT OF KNOWLEDGE ALONE SHALL YOU GO ACROSS ALL SINS".

IN WHAT MANNER DOES THIS WISDOM DESTROY SIN? ... HERE IS AN EXAMPLE:

37. *As the blazing fire reduces fuel to ashes, O Arjuna, so does the Fire-of-Knowledge reduce all actions to ashes.*

JUST AS FIRE REDUCES FUEL TO ASHES—this example has been given by the Lord in His sheer fatherly love for Arjuna. These words, familiar in all *Yajnashalas*,* when used apart from their word meaning, are capable of creating, in their association, brilliant suggestions of a serene atmosphere and a thrilled sense of divinity.

Besides, the example is very striking. Whatever be the quality, shape, condition, colour, etc., of the fuel pieces, when all of them are taken to the fireplace and digested by the fire, they become one homogeneous mass of ash! In the samples of ash left in the hearth, we cannot recognise the ash of a particular twig as different from that of another. Similarly, all *Karmas*, it is said, good, bad, or indifferent, get burnt up in the Fire-of-Knowledge and will become something altogether different from what they were in their cause-and-effect condition. Solid fuel having girth, weight, smell, etc., becomes almost weightless, with no specific colour except a light-grayness, when it comes to the final state of ash.

Actions leave reactions. The reactions mature at different periods of time depending upon the quality and intensity of the

---

यथैधांसि समिद्धोऽग्निर्भस्मसात्कुरुतेऽर्जुन ।
ज्ञानाग्नि: सर्वकर्माणि भस्मसात्कुरुते तथा ॥ ३७ ॥

yathaidhāṁsi samiddho'gnirbhasmasātkurute'rjuna
jñanāgniḥ sarvakamārṇi bhasmasātkurute tathā 37.

* The sacred canopy under which the Fire-Altar and devotees are all sheltered during the *Vedic*-ritual, *Yajna*, is called the *Yajnashala*.

actions. From beginningless time, in our different manifestations, we have been, at every moment, acting in our egocentric vanity and individuality. All those actions must have left their residual impressions and they have to be lived through.

This entire *Karma* has been scientifically considered as falling under three classifications. They are called 'not yet operative' (*sanchita*), 'operative' (*prarabdha*), and 'to be operative in future' (*agami*). When, in the *Geeta*, it is said that all *Karmas* are burnt down, the Lord means the entire *sanchita* and *agami*.

WHEREFORE:

38. *Certainly, there is no purifier in this world like 'Knowledge'. He who is himself perfected in YOGA finds it in the Self in time.*

So glorious is the result of Self-Realisation that Lord Krishna explodes in enthusiasm and cries "VERILY THERE EXISTS NOTHING IN THIS WORLD MORE NOBLE AND SACRED THAN SELF-KNOWLEDGE". Just as to a drowning man, there is nothing more precious than a life belt, so too, to the deluded ego there cannot be a greater possession and a nobler endeavour than the acquisition of 'Knowledge' of its own Real Nature.

The Knowledge of the Self can be attained in one's own bosom when one has gained in oneself a full MASTERY IN *YOGA* – when one has sincerely and diligently practised the

---

न हि ज्ञानेन सदृशं पवित्रमिह विद्यते ।
तत्स्वयं योगसंसिद्धः कालेनात्मनि विन्दति ॥ ३८ ॥

na hi jñānena sadṛśaṁ pavitramiha vidyate
tatsvayaṁ yogasaṁsiddhiḥ kalenātmani vindati 38.

above-mentioned twelve *Yajnas* and gained a complete self-mastery through them. This mastery of the Self over the flesh is not given by any teacher. The traditional story of a teacher spiritualising a student by his touch is a myth; it is impossible. Had it been so, in the presence of such a perfect Prophet like Krishna, Arjuna could have attained - especially when the Lord felt such a great friendliness and love towards him - in a wink, all the spirituality needed to become a God-man.

Many devotees have, from time to time, wasted their chances and brought dishonour to their noble teachers, because they expected their *Gurus* to impart their acquired Wisdom to them, their *Chelas* (disciples), for the physical services rendered or the intellectual support given. Many of the existing seekers are, today, thoughtlessly squandering away their noble opportunities by vainly waiting for this cheap and ready method of purchasing God-hood! Let them be warned that, in spite of such glorifications of some *Gurus* available in the market and sold at some *Ashramas* in this country, it has no scriptural support. Here, Krishna, in all love, plainly tells the truth to Arjuna that he has to purify himself (*swayam*) and then he himself will realise the Truth 'in good time' (*kalena*).

No definite time schedule is promised for Perfection to manifest. It is only said that he who is practising sincerely and devotedly, all the twelve different subjective-*Yajnas* that are described earlier, will attain the necessary growth within, and will IN GOOD TIME come to experience the Self, the Beatitude of Perfection, the state-of-Godhood.

IN GOOD TIME (*Kalena*)—This does not mean either immediately, nor does it promise us the Supreme only after trillions of impossible years. The same idea has been more beautifully described in the following stanza by a more self-explanatory term 'ere long' (*achirena*). It gives a direct suggestion of hope and guidance to all seekers of all times that they need not become impatient. In fact, it would be far better for them constantly to apply themselves on the right path in the full confidence that they shall 'ere long' reach their goal.

THE SUREST MEANS OF ACQUIRING WISDOM IS DECLARED AS FOLLOWS:

39. *The man who is full of faith, who is devoted to It, and who has subdued the senses, obtains (this) 'Knowledge'; and having obtained 'Knowledge,' ere long he goes to the Supreme Peace.*

The qualities that are necessary for an individual to be assured of the Knowledge-Divine are being enumerated here as vividly as from the leaf of a science textbook. Three great qualities have been indicated and to understand them is to understand why the so-called seekers, in spite of their claims to sincere self-application, do not actually reach anywhere near the ladder of development. Faith, devotion, and self-control are the three imperative necessities to be acquired ere we can hope to evolve to the diviner stature from our present mortal encumbrances. But these three words are more often misunderstood than rightly evaluated.

श्रद्धावाँल्लभते ज्ञानं तत्परः संयतेन्द्रियः ।
ज्ञानं लब्ध्वा परां शान्तिमचिरेणाधिगच्छति ॥ ३९ ॥
śraddhāvāṁllabhate jñānaṁ tatparaḥ saṁyatendriyaḥ
jñānaṁ labdhvā parāṁ śantimacireṇādhigacchati 39.

FAITH (*Shraddha*)—Exploiters of religions have been making capital out of repeating this word as their safest excuse for all spiritual problems, to clear which devotees may approach these men who pose themselves as guides in religion. Invariably, we find that the ordinary devotees are completely rendered, sometimes fanatical and often poorer, in their intellectual and mental growth, because of the unintelligent insistence of *shraddha* translated as 'blind faith and unquestioned acceptance of any declaration said to be divine'.

Sankara tolls the death-knell of this misunderstanding when he explains *shraddha* as "that by which an individual readily understands the exact import of the scriptural text as well as the pregnant words of advice of the preceptor".

DEVOTED TO IT (*Tatparah*)—Whatever be the path of divine self-development that he may be following, it is an unavoidable necessity that the seeker must give his undivided attention to it, and must, on all occasions, maintain in his mind a continuous consciousness of the Divine. A mere intellectual study of the scriptures will not help us in purifying and shaping our 'within' to the glorious Beauty of the Divine. It is necessary that we must pour out our mind and intellect into the scheme of living that the *Upanishads* advise.

WHO HAS SUBDUED THE SENSES—The *shraddha* and *Jnana* explained above will not sustain themselves, and no seeker can consistently hope to entertain them unless he is constantly striving his best to live in a spirit of self-control. It is the sense organs that seduce us away into the life of excessive sensuousness, and when one has entered into the troubled waters of a sensuous life, one has no chances of maintaining oneself quietly in the higher values of life. To walk the Path-Divine is to get out of the gutters of sensuousness. Excessive sense-life and Absolute God-life are antitheses to each other; where the one is, the other cannot be. Where the light of inward serenity and deeper peace have come, the darkness created by sense passions and animal appetites must depart. It is imperative, therefore, that a seeker should learn to live in steady and constant sense-control.

Why should we live renouncing sense enjoyments, and employing our mind in remembering constantly the Divine goal of life, with faith both in ourselves and in the science of religion? Ordinarily, an intellect can enquire only as to the cause-and-effect of things. The ego is ever employed in its own motive hunting. A seeker in the initial stages of his self-development remains constantly in his intellect. Naturally, he will enquire what the result of such a conspicuous sacrifice would be. To convince him, the second line is given.

That a seeker who lives the above-mentioned triple-programme of Divine life, reaches the state-of-Knowledge is the promise and guarantee of the *Rishis*, who are the authors of the immortal scriptures. A doubt again arises as to why we should, after all, acquire the Knowledge-Divine. Krishna explains here that, having gained the right-knowledge, the individual SOON REACHES THE SUPREME PEACE. The promise of reaching the great Goal of life is not guaranteed to take effect in a definite period of time. Just as, in the previous stanza, it was said, 'In good time' (*kalena*), so too, here it is said, 'Ere long' (*achirena*). In short, after gaining this 'Knowledge', one would 'soon' reach the Goal of Life.

SUPREME PEACE (*Param Shantim*)—The Goal of Life is labelled here as the GREAT PEACE that knows no diminution. In these days of peace-mongers getting ready for war in the name of peace, one is apt to become honestly skeptical about the goal indicated in this stanza. The term 'peace' here is not that undefined vague concept that is often repeated in politics, whenever it is convenient for a set of politicians to do so, but the term *'shanti'* has a wealth of psychological suggestiveness.

It is very well known that every living creature is, at all moments, trying to gain a better happiness, through all its activities in life. From breathing and eating, to the organised endeavour in capturing the world-market through war and destruction, all activities are attempts by the frail individuals to discover a greater and a better joy or happiness. This is true not only in man but in the animal kingdom, and even in the vegetable world. In short, no action is possible unless the actor is motivated by an inner urge in him to seek a greater sense of fulfilment or joy unto himself.

If thus, the whole world is striving to win the highest joy that it possibly can, and having gained it, to invest all energy and intelligence to retain the same, then the goal of life should be ABSOLUTE HAPPINESS, where all strife ends, all desires are fulfilled, all thoughts and agitations are finally exhausted. Desires for joy give rise to thought disturbances, which, trying to fulfil themselves in the outer world, become the visible actions in everyday life. The restlessness of the mind and the weary fatigue of the body shall both end, when Absolute Joy is attained. Therefore, Absolute Joy is Absolute Peace.

Here, in this stanza the Goal of Life is indicated as the Supreme Peace, which may be, in other words, explained as the Supreme Joy.

"THOU SHALT NOT DOUBT THIS, FOR DOUBT IS MOST SINFUL." HOW? ... LISTEN:

40. *The ignorant, the faithless, the doubting-self goes to destruction; there is neither this world, nor the other, nor happiness for the doubter.*

In the previous verse, it was said that those who had faith and knowledge would soon reach the Supreme Peace. In order to hammer this very same Truth in, Krishna is here emphasising through a negative declaration that they, who have NOT these qualities cultivated, gained and developed in them, will get themselves ultimately destroyed and completely ruined. He who has neither the Knowledge of the Self - if not a spiritual realisation, at least a clear intellectual understanding - nor 'the intellectual readiness to grapple with and fully understand the true import of the scriptural declarations and the words of the Masters' (*shraddha*), Krishna asserts, will certainly get ruined, if he be also a 'doubting Thomas' (*samshaya-atma*).

In the next line, Krishna, with all emphasis, condemns such men of endless doubts, and points out their tragedy in

---

अज्ञश्चाश्रद्दधानश्च संशयात्मा विनश्यति ।
नायं लोकोऽस्ति न परो न सुखं संशयात्मन: ॥ ४० ॥
ajaścāddadhānaśca saṁśayātmā vinaśyati
nāyaṁ loko'sti na paro na sukhaṁ saṁśayātmanaḥ 40.

life. The Lord says that such men who DOUBT THE SELF will not find any joy or happiness ANYWHERE – NEITHER HERE NOR IN THE HEREAFTER. In explaining thus, the *Geeta* seems to express that there may be a small chance perhaps, for one who is devoid of knowledge and faith to discover some kind of a happiness in this world, here and now, but that those who are constant doubters can enjoy neither here nor there. Such men are psychologically incapable of enjoying any situation, because the doubting tendency in them will poison all their experiences. He whose teeth have become septic must constantly poison the food that he is taking; so too, those who have this tendency of doubting everything, will never be able to accommodate themselves to any situation, however perfect and just it might be. The line contains a spot of satire, almost vitriolic in its pungency, when it is directed against the intelligent skeptic.

WHEREFORE -- FOR THIS REASON ONLY:

41. *He who has renounced actions by YOGA, whose doubts are rent asunder by 'Knowledge', who is self-possessed, actions do not bind him, O Dhananjaya.*

This being the penultimate verse in the chapter, it is a beautiful summary of all the main secrets of Life explained

---

योगसंन्यस्तकर्माणं ज्ञानसंछिन्नसंशयम् ।
आत्मवन्तं न कर्माणि निबध्नन्ति धनञ्जय ॥ ४१ ॥

yogasannyastakarmaṇaṁ jñānasañchinnasaṁśayam
ātmavantaṁ na kamārṇi nibadhnanti dhanañjaya 41.

in it at length in it. When, through the practice of *Karma Yoga*, we have learnt to renounce our attachments to the fruits of action, and yet to work on in perfect detachment when every doubt in us regarding the Goal of Life has been completely removed in our own inner experiences of the nobler and the diviner in us - as a result of the above two, the ego comes to rediscover itself to be nothing other than the *Atman*. Then the individual ego comes to live POISED IN THE SELF AS THE SELF. When such an individual works, his actions can never bind him.

It is only egoistic activities motivated by our egocentric desires that leave gross impressions on our inner personality, and thus painfully bind us to reap their reactions. With a sense of detachment and in right-knowledge, as indicated in the above scheme, when an individual has destroyed his ego-sense, his actions cannot bind him at all. As a dreamer, I might commit a murder in my dream upon my dream-wife. But when I awake from my dream, I shall not be punished for the crime that I seem to have committed in my dream. For, the dreamer has also ended along with the dream. The dreamer committed the murder and deserves punishment; but in the waker, the dreamer is absent. Similarly, the egocentric actions can bind and throttle only the ego, but when the ego has become *Atmavantah*, meaning POISED IN THE SELF – just like the dreamer when he gets poised in the waker – the activities of the ego can no more bind the Self. The ego POISED IN THE SELF , is the experience of the Real Self; the dreamer poised in the waker, is the waker.

THIS BEING THE WONDROUS RESULT AND THE SUPREME PROFIT THAT 'TRUE-KNOWLEDGE' CAN GIVE TO THE DELUDED, KRISHNA ADVISES ARJUNA :

42. *Therefore with the sword-of-Knowledge, cut asunder the doubt-of-the-Self, born of 'ignorance', residing in your heart, and take refuge in 'YOGA'. Arise, O Bharata.*

In this concluding stanza the Lord's advice is precise and it is given with a loving insistence. The stanza rings with a spirit of paternal urgency felt by the Lord towards the Pandava Prince.

In the language of war, Krishna advises his warrior-friend on the battlefield, how best to live the life of dedication and perfection as advised by the Hindu *Rishis* from the quiet and peaceful Himalayan valleys. With the sword of KNOWLEDGE, Arjuna is encouraged to cut off the bonds of ignorance and CLEAVE ASUNDER THIS DOUBT OF THE SELF LYING IN THE HEART.

The spiritual doubt is explained here as working from the heart. This may read rather strange to a modern man: doubt must come from the intellect; it cannot come from the heart.

It is the traditional belief in *Vedanta* that 'the intellect is seated in the heart', wherein the term HEART does not mean the fleshy pumping-instrument in the human bosom. The

---

तस्मादज्ञानसंभूतं हृत्स्थं ज्ञानासिनात्मन: ।
छित्त्वैनं संशयं योगमातिष्ठोत्तिष्ठ भारत ॥ ४२ ॥
tasmādajñānasambhūtaṁ hṛtsthaṁ jñānāsinātmanaḥ
chittvainaṁ saṁśayaṁ yogamātiṣṭottiṣṭa bhārata 42.

term HEART is used here not in its physiological meaning but in its literacy usage, where HEART means 'the source of all love and sympathy – of all noble human emotions'. An intellect functioning from and through an atmosphere of sympathetic love, kindly charity and such other noble qualities alone can be considered in the science of philosophy as the human reason. Therefore, when the *Upanishads* talk of the doubts lying crystallised in the heart, the *Rishis* mean the intellectual perversions in some of the seekers that make them incompetent to feel and appreciate the vision of the Soul.

These doubts can be completely annihilated only when the individual gains an intimate, subjective experience of the Self in him.

This can be achieved only by *Yoga* - NOT a strange mystical process, secretly advised to a few, by mysteriously rare groups of *Gurus*, to be practised in the unknown dark caves of the Himalayas, living altogether a frightful life of unnatural privations. In the *Geeta*, the word *Yoga* has been forever tamed and domesticated to be with all of us, serving us faithfully at all times in our life. By the term *Yoga*, in this last stanza, Krishna means the 'twelve techniques' which He has explained as the subjective-*Yajnas*.

The chapter concludes with a spirited call to Arjuna: "ARISE, O BHARATA". In the context of the *Geeta*, though the word may be rightly said to mean only a call to Arjuna, it is a call to every seeker, especially to this country as a whole, to get up and act well in the spirit of *Yajna*, and thereby, to gain more and more inner purity, so that through true meditation everyone of us can come to experience and gain the Supreme Peace which is the final fulfilment of evolution.

Thus, in the UPANISHADS of the glorious Bhagawad Geeta, in the Science of the Eternal, in the scripture of YOGA, in the dialogue between Sri Krishna and Arjuna, the fourth discourse ends entitled:

The *Yoga* of Renunciation of Action In Knowledge

Om Om Om Om Om

ॐ तत्सदिति श्रीमद् भगवद् गीतासूपनिषत्सु ब्रह्मविद्यायां
योगशास्त्रे श्रीकृष्णार्जुनसंवादे ज्ञानकर्मसंन्यासयोगो नाम
चतुर्थोऽध्याय:

Oṁ tatsaditi śrīmadbhagavadgītāsū ūpaniṣatsu brahmavidyāyāṁ yogaśāstre śrī kṛṣṇārjuna saṁvāde jñānakarmasannyāsayogo nāma caturtho'dhyāyaḥ

V

True Renunciation
Introduction

THIS chapter opens with a doubt raised by Arjuna. It is almost similar to, but not the same as, the one he raised in the beginning of the third chapter. At the end of Krishna's discourses in Chapter II, the disturbed mind of Arjuna could not definitely come to a decision whether action had any place at all in the life of spiritual-seeking. Here, in this chapter, the Pandava Prince only asks which of the two – 'renunciation of action' or 'participation in action', is the nobler and the greater. The very construction of the question indicates how far Arjuna has been persuaded rightly by Krishna's advocacy of 'right-action and conscious resistance to all positive evil'. The great *Acharya* had, to a large extent, hauled Arjuna out of his inward psychological disaster. He had regained a certain amount of equilibrium and had understood and accepted that action, intelligently pursued, was the right way for progress and self-development.

To Arjuna, *Karma* meant *Vedic* ritualism such as *Yajnas, Yagas* and *Homas*, etc., and *Sannyasa* meant renunciation of everything and total retirement to a quiet Himalayan jungle, living there in constant inactivity, a strange life of self-denial and, perhaps, conscious self-persecution. When this was the type of misunderstanding in the mind of an educated, intelligent member of royalty of those times, we can easily imagine how much more pathetic must have been the general condition of desperate ignorance into which the Hindus of that age had sunk!

Krishna's attempt is to revitalise these dead terms in our scriptural tradition and bring about rehabilitation in the understanding of the Hindus (II-61). We have already found, in the previous chapter, how the elaborate ritualisms called *Yajnas*, have been brought out from their glass-houses of secrecy and cellars of artificial sanctity into the broad daylight of everyday activity. The secret wealth of the *Vedas*, which was enjoyed by only a choice few, was 'nationalised' to become a free heritage to be enjoyed by all seekers among mankind. With this subtle missionary work, Krishna brought Hinduism and its scientific methods within the life of every man living in the world.

After thus describing *Karma Yoga* (Chapters III and IV), Krishna had to describe how one should intelligently renounce *Karma* and enter a nobler spiritual technique for completing the pilgrimage to Perfection. To whip man out of his sleepy inertia, vigorous activity is advised here as the first step. Activities are, at this stage, necessarily motivated by the individual's egocentric desires. Inertia (t*amas*) is thus invigorated into the 'agitations of dynamic activity' (r*ajas*). This state is again to be transcended through the process of 'non-egocentric Divine activities undertaken in a spirit of goodwill and love for all' especially termed in the *Geeta* as *Yajna*. Thus sublimated, the individual reaches a certain amount of tranquillity and peace, purity and joy (s*attva*). In this mental composure alone, can one meditate properly to reach the frontiers of the finite and experience the state of the Infinite.

This theory of self-development in three definite stages, of desire-prompted activities, of desireless activities, and finally, of pure meditation, is not an original contribution of the philosopher-poet Vyasa, the author of the Mahabharata and the *Geeta*. Even here, we find that it is only an intelligent reinterpretation of the technique already indicated in the *Vedas*. In *Vedic* literature too, we find a systematic development of the technique of Self-Perfection. The '*Mantra*' portion of the *Vedas* expresses an all-absorbing sense of wonderment of the deluded at the sight of Nature's vastness in strength and beauty. The '*Brahmana*' portion prescribes ways and means by which ritualistic activities can be undertaken for the satisfaction of one's material desires. After the '*Brahmana*' portion, there is, in all the textbooks of *Vedas*, a clear section called the '*Aranyakas*' which prescribes varieties of worship-methods called the *Upasanas*, which are to be undertaken by pure minds uncontaminated by any desire. These desireless activities (*Yajna*s) make fine adjustments in the mind-and-intellect equipments of the seekers and provide them with a pair of wings with which they can fly across the finite straight into the realms of the Infinite.

This same technique is confirmed by the *Geeta*, with slight adjustments, here and there, in the word-meaning. In fact, the technique remaining the same, only the garb of language has been remodelled to appeal to the available fashions of thought at the time of the Mahabharata. This change has often been characterised by enthusiastic critics as a total revolution, which has mischievous suggestions. Revolution is a term that is generally used when the old scheme of things is totally destroyed and is replaced by an entirely new set-up. For example, the Industrial Revolution completely replaced the patriarchal scheme of social living that the West had before their windmills started revolving. No such destructive revolution has taken place with the introduction of the *Geeta* by Vyasa, or by the acceptance of it as a scriptural textbook by the *Acharyas*.

And yet, the *Geeta* represents a revolution. When a flower matures into a fruit, certainly, it is a destruction of the flower as such, but in the fruit, the essence of the flower, namely, its fertilised ovum, has found fulfilment. Those who do not know the science of plant life may mourn the destruction of the flower when they see the fruit standing where the flower stood before. But a botanist clearly understands that only the unnecessary aspects in the flower have withered away and that the essential in the flower has grown to its fulfilment in the fruit.

Similarly, the elaborate ritualism, its show and mystery, its detailed preparations and arrangements, which constitute the bulk of *Vedic* books, have all withered away. The essential technique, which lies almost imperceptible in the *Vedic* volumes, has found a perfect fulfilment, inasmuch as it has been brought out as a complete and self-evident science in the *Geeta*.

Lord Krishna, after indicating the Supreme Goal of Perfection,* exhausts Himself in the following two chapters enunciating the methods of true activity. Activity in life, intelligently undertaken, is a means to reach the highest spiritual consummation. Primary education is as unavoidable as higher secondary education for a student to fulfil his ambition to become a doctor or an advocate, an engineer or an economist. Just as a student, after his primary lessons, must

* Through his inimitable description of a man-of-Equipoise in Ch.II, 55-72.

enter the higher secondary classes, after the fulfilment of which, he must again strive hard to pass the early college lessons before he can hope to enter any of the specialised branches of education, so too, from desireless activities undertaken with a *Yajna* Spirit, a seeker must change over to the path-of-Meditation.

Chapters III and IV have described the *Yajna* and Chapter VI will explain the path-of-Meditation. Therefore, this chapter has been rightly named the "*Yoga* of Renunciation-of-Action". What is the spirit of renunciation, how the "*Yoga* of Renunciation-of-Action" can be practised, what would be the result of practising this way of activity in this special mental attitude, and how far that could contribute to the inward development and growth of the human personality – all these are discussed in this chapter. In fact, Chapter V stands as a bridge between *Karma Yoga* and Pure Meditation. In the *Vedas* this subtle point in the chain of discussions is almost missing. Chapter V of the *Geeta* rediscovers for us this 'missing link' in the *Vedic* thought. I have said, 'rediscovers' and not 'deliberately creates' or 'originally supplies'.

As Shankara puts it,* in many places the Lord has spoken of the renunciation of all actions and at the close of the chapter, Krishna has advised Arjuna to engage in *Yoga* in the 'performance of actions'. When thus viewed, there is, in the last chapter, a perceptible inconsistency according to Arjuna. Hence the doubt with which he opens his discussion with Lord Krishna in this chapter.

---

* Refer the *Sankalpa-Vakya* discussed at the end of Chapters I, II and III.

Arjuna said:

1. *Renunciation-of-actions, O Krishna, You praise and, again YOGA – performance of actions. Tell me conclusively that which is the better of the two.*

It is evident that Arjuna has unconsciously walked out of the neurotic confusions in his mind and has started taking a lively intellectual interest in following the arguments of his friend and beloved comrade. Action being in line with his own nature, Arjuna very joyously and almost instinctively accepts the path-of-Action indicated by Lord Krishna in the two previous chapters. Arjuna, however, has not yet grown to be at complete rest with himself. To him, there seems to be a repeatedly jarring note in Krishna's discourse, inasmuch as there is a constant undertone, often very clear, in which Krishna insists that renunciation of action is nobler and diviner than all *Yajna*-actions. Hence this enquiry.

Moreover, a patient of hysteria, even when he comes out of it, cannot immediately discover in himself a complete self-confidence. This is generally experienced by everybody. When the dreamer wakes up after a horrible dream, it takes some time for him to compose himself again to sleep. In the same manner, Arjuna, after the shattering experience of his emotional neurosis expressed in the opening stanzas of Chapter II, has not yet found his own balance to develop

---

अर्जुन उवाच
संन्यासं कर्मणां कृष्ण पुनर्योगं च शंससि ।
यच्छ्रेय एतयोरेकं तन्मे ब्रूहि सुनिश्चितम् ॥ १ ॥

arjuna uvāca
sannyāsaṁ karmaṇāṁ kṛṣṇa punaryogaṁ ca śaṁsasi
yacchreya etayorekaṁ tanme bruhi suniścitam 1.

complete self-confidence and feel capable of discriminating and understanding rightly the learned discourses of the Divine Charioteer. The Pandava Prince concludes that Krishna is giving him a free choice between two independent ways of living; selfless-Action and renunciation-of-Action. He, therefore, requests Krishna to indicate to him decisively one definite path of self-perfection by which he can positively achieve his spiritual fulfilment. This chapter indicates to the children of the *Vedas* that these two are not two identical factors to be chosen from, nor are they a complementary pair of equal yoke-fellows.

Renunciation of action and full participation in action are two different exercises to be practised serially and not simultaneously. This theme is elaborated in this chapter.

The Blessed Lord said:

2. *Renunciation-of-action and YOGA-of-action both lead to the highest bliss; but of the two, YOGA-of-action is superior to the renunciation-of-action.*

From the very type of the question with which Arjuna approached Krishna in the opening verse of this chapter, the Lord understood the abject state of ignorance that Arjuna was in. According to Arjuna, *Karma Yoga* and *Karma-Sannyasa-Yoga* were two distinct paths, which would lead the practitioner to two different goals in life.

श्रीभगवानुवाच
संन्यासः कर्मयोगश्च निःश्रेयसकरावुभौ ।
तयोस्तु कर्मसंन्यासात्कर्मयोगो विशिष्यते ॥ २ ॥

śrībhagavānuvāca
sannyāsaḥ karmayogśca niḥśreyasakarāvubhau
tayostu karmasannyāsātkarmayogo viśiṣyate 2.

Man is essentially prone to be inert. If left to themselves, the majority of men would demand in life only food to eat, with the least amount of exertion and plenty of idle hours. From this unproductive inertia, the first stage of man's growth is his being awakened to activity, and this is most easily and efficiently done when the individual's desires are whipped up. Thus, in the first stage of his evolution, desire-prompted activity takes man out of his mental and intellectual inertia to vigorous activity.

In the second stage of his growth, he becomes tired of the desire-motivated activities, and feels energetic when advised to spend at least a few hours in a noble field, with a spirit of dedication and service. Such activities are generally undertaken in the service of others, where the individual works with the least ego. The secret of working in this spirit of self-dedication has been already described in an earlier chapter. When an individual in this second stage of self-development works with his ego subdued, in a spirit of devotion and dedication, he comes to exhaust his *vasanas*. Thus unloaded, his mind and intellect develop the wings of meditation and become capable of taking longer flights into the subtle realms of joy and peace.

The third stage of development is accomplished through meditation, which will be discussed in Chapter VI. To summarise, we may say that the spiritual processes of self-evolution fall into three stages: (a) desire-prompted activity, (b) selfless dedicated activity and (c) quiet meditation. Of these, the first has already been described in the earlier two chapters. The technique of meditation will be described in the following chapter. Naturally therefore, in this chapter, we are having a discussion on how we can renounce the ego-motivated activities and learn to take to selfless, dedicated activities.

In this stanza Krishna explains that both activity and the renunciation of activity can take the individual to the highest goal. But he warns his disciple that of the two, participation in action (*Karma*) is any day, superior to the renunciation of action (*Karma-sannyasa*). Here, we must understand that Krishna is not, in any sense of the term, decrying renunciation as inferior to vigilant and vigorous activity. To say so would be parading our ignorance, or at least, a lack of understanding of what the Lord has said so far, or the spirit in which he is continuing his discourses hereafter. The *Geeta* is given out in the form of a conversation between Krishna, the Immortal Teacher, and Arjuna, a particular student facing a given problem and having some definitely known mental weaknesses and intellectual debilities. Essentially, here the Pandava warrior is full of *vasanas* and for their exhaustion he has to act in the battlefield. To those of us who are psychologically in the state of Arjuna – and almost all of us are in that condition, suffering from the Arjuna-disease - the treatment is activity with the least conscious selfishness. The advice given here that the performance-of-action is nobler than the renunciation-of-action is therefore to be very carefully understood.

WHY SO? ... IT IS SAID:

3. *He should be known as a perpetual SANNYASI who neither hates nor desires; for, free from the pairs-of-opposites, O Mighty-armed, he is easily set free from bondage.*

ज्ञेयः स नित्यसंन्यासी यो न द्वेष्टि न काङ्क्षति ।
निर्द्वन्द्वो हि महाबाहो सुखं बन्धात्प्रमुच्यते ॥ ३ ॥

jñeyaḥ sa nityasannyāsī yo na dveṣṭi na kāṅkṣati
nirdvando hi mahābāho sukhaṁ bandhātpramucyate 3.

Why participation in work is said to be easier for a beginner than renunciation-of-action is explained here. While defining a *sannyasi*, Krishna's revolutionary statement cleanses the idea of renunciation from all its external embellishments. He gives more importance to the internal mental condition than to the external uniform. According to the Lord, he is a *sannyasi* who 'neither likes nor dislikes'.

Likes and dislikes, success and failure, joy and sorrow and such other pairs-of-opposites are the wheels on which the mind rolls forward earning the experiences of life. Our intellect can register a situation or a condition only with reference to the comparative estimate of its opposite. Thus, I can understand light only with reference to my knowledge of darkness. Comparison is the only way of understanding given to man. If there is no contrast for a thing, we cannot gain knowledge of that thing.

If comparison and contrast are the methods of 'knowing' for the mind-and-intellect instrument, then, to renounce them is to renounce the vehicle. A car is a vehicle that moves on the earth. It cannot be used in water. Thus, if I am sailing on the ocean, I am certainly not moving in the car, but I am using a boat, which floats on water. In the field of plurality where comparison and contrast are possible, I can use the vehicle of the intellect-and-mind. The stanza here states that he is a true *sannyasi*, who has gone beyond the perception of contrast, which necessarily means that he is one who has transcended the inner instrument of mind-and-intellect.

This is no easy task; to free oneself from the pairs-of-opposites is to be free from all the limitations of mortal existence among finite objects. By thus defining a *sannyasi*, Krishna is not trying to paint a dreary picture of hopelessness for the seekers. He has in mind the growth and development of Arjuna. The Pandava Prince was then having, in his intellect, thick *vasana*-coatings of heroic instincts and kingly impulses for action. This stanza is given in order to persuade him to keep away from a hasty dash into *sannyasa*.

4. *Children, not the wise, speak of SANKHYA (Knowledge) and YOGA (YOGA-of-action) as distinct; he who is truly established even in one, obtains the fruits of both.*

Two methods aere indicated for turning an ordinary act into a divine action of dedication and worship. It can either be done by the renunciation of the concept of agency in every action or by a consistent refusal to get dissipated by our unintelligent preoccupation with our anxieties for the fruits of our action. The former is called the *Sankhya* method and the latter is called simple *Karma Yoga*.

The *Sankhya* technique is not available to everyone, since the renunciation of agency is not easy unless the practitioner is highly intellectual and has, in himself, a capacity to see the collective universe in action. Only when we see the total logic of things, can we really come to feel the insignificance of our individual ego in all our achievements and in our successes.

Here, the Lord insists that only undeveloped, childish minds can find contradiction between these two methods, while wise men who have lived either of the paths will vouchsafe for the equal effectiveness of both of them. Whether we practise the

---

सांख्ययोगौ पृथग्बालाः प्रवदन्ति न पण्डिताः ।
एकमप्यास्थितः सम्यगुभयोर्विन्दते फलम् ॥ ४ ॥
sāṅkhyayogau pṛthagbālāḥ pravadanti na paṇḍitāḥ
ekamapyāsthitaḥ samyagubhayorvindate phalam 4.

renunciation of our agency-idea or live a life of detachment from the fruits of our actions, if, we as seekers, are consistently persevering in our chosen path, we shall come to the Goal, which is the same whether we follow one or the other of the paths.

HOW CAN A MAN OBTAIN THE RESULTS OF BOTH, BY THE RIGHT OBSERVANCE OF ONLY ONE? ... THE ANSWER FOLLOWS:

5. That place which is reached by the SANKHYAS (JNANIS) is also reached by the YOGINS (KARMA-YOGINS). He 'sees' who 'sees' SANKHYA and YOGA as one.

Categorically, Lord Krishna insists herein that the goal reached by the *Sankhya*-method is also readily reached by the *Karma*-technique. He, who experiences this common Goal of both paths, is the one who really understands the Truth of the *Vedas*.

Here the word 'seeing' (*pashyati*) is used in the scriptural meaning of the term, and so does not indicate a mere physical act of perception. In the *Advaita* philosophy, *Atman* is not seen as anything other than the seer, but it is the experience of the Seer himself BY the Seer himself. The term 'seeing' is used here only to confirm that the experience of Reality could be as intimate and beyond all doubts, as it would be, when we see any object with our own eyes from very near.

In thus synthesising both *Sankhya* and *Karma*, it is not meant that they together form an alloy; they both must be

---

यत्सांख्यैः प्राप्यते स्थानं तद्योगैरपि गम्यते।
एकं सांख्यं च योगं च यः पश्यति स पश्यति ॥ ५ ॥

yatsāṅkhyaiḥ prāpyate sthānaṁ tadyogairpi gamayate
ekaṁ sāṅkhyaṁ ca yogaṁ yaḥ paśyati sa paśyati 5.

practised serially. We can consider them as one and the same inasmuch as *Karma Yoga* purifies the Intellect and gives a greater poise for meditation (*Sankhya*) through which alone is the final experience achieved. Thus, a combination of these two is possible serially and not simultaneously. This is to be very carefully noted by all sincere students.

HOW IS IT THAT THE AIM OF *KARMA YOGA* IS *SANNYASA*? - LISTEN:

6. *But renunciation, O mighty-armed, is hard to attain without YOGA; the YOGA-harmonised man of (steady) contemplation quickly goes to BRAHMAN.*

The Lord, with all the emphasis at his command, is declaring, once and for all, the final conclusions that were arrived at by the Immortal Sages of yore regarding the place of right action in Self-rediscovery. Without performance of action, the renunciation of action is impossible; without having a thing we cannot renounce it; to renounce life and the world, because one has sadly been thwarted in one's hopes and ambitions, is not renunciation.

In this sense, the polishing of the mind is a process very similar to that by which we clean metalware by using metal-polish. The item that is darkened by time is purified by applying some polishing chemical on its surface. The polish is the solvent of the oxide that is covering the brilliance of the vessel. After a

---

संन्यासस्तु महाबाहो दुःखमाप्तुमयोगतः ।
योगयुक्तो मुनिर्ब्रह्म नचिरेणाधिगच्छति ॥ ६ ॥

sannyāsastu mahābāho duḥkhamāptumayogataḥ
yogayukto munirbrahma nacireṇādhigacchati 6.

time, when we remove the coating of the 'polish', we find that not only is the chemical-polish removed but the black oxide also is removed, thereby leaving the vessel bright and attractive.

Similarly, the mind can be purified only by the process of treating it with right action. When thus treated, the mind gets purified from its *vasana*-blemishes and with such a purified mind alone can we, during the deeper meditation hours, come to renounce all activities. Before this preparation, if we try to renounce activities, we may remain physically inactive, but mentally very active. Extrovertedness of the mind is not conducive to the inner polishing. In fact, extrovertedness is the very mud that sullies the Godly-beauty and strength of the mind.

This is the greatest discovery that Hindu Masters made in the ancient days, in the technique of Self-development and Self-growth.

While mental purity and meditative power cannot be gained without performance of right action with the right mental attitude, Sri Krishna gives a positive assurance here that such a conducive mental quality can be created by right actions undertaken by the seekers.

Yoga Yuktah - one who is well established in the path of selfless and unattached activities, soon develops the qualities of poise and single-pointedness of mind. *Karma* fulfils itself in making the *Yogi* fit for continuous and fruitful meditation. When such an individual who has practised the path of *Karma* diligently -- either through the renunciation of his sense of agency or through detachment from all his over-anxious preoccupations with the fruits of his actions – such a meditator (*muni*) soon attains the Supreme experience of the Self in himself.

No definite time limit can be fixed for declaring when exactly the Supreme experience will come to a meditator.

The indecision regarding the time-element in this promise of certainty is very well brought out by the term used, '*Na-chirena*' - not long afterwards, meaning 'ere-long'.

With this knowledge in mind, when we read the stanza, it becomes very clear why earlier (V-2) the Lord, in his opening verse in this discourse, insisted that for Arjuna performance of action is superior to the renunciation of action.

WHEN THE DEVOTEE RESORTS TO *KARMA YOGA* AS A MEANS OF ATTAINING RIGHT KNOWLEDGE:

7. *He who is devoted to the Path-of-action, whose mind is quite pure, who has conquered the self, who has subdued his senses, who realises his Self as the Self in all beings, though acting, is not tainted.*

In the previous verse, it was said in a sweeping generalisation, that he who pursues *Karma Yoga* along with meditation, would ere-long reach the state-of-Perfection in his own personal experience. Here, in this verse, Krishna is trying to give us the logic of the state of inward revolution that will take place when we make the pilgrimage to the Infinite in us, from our own present state of finitude and bondage.

With scientific thoroughness and logical precision, all the different stages of development and change that take place in an individual through *Karma Yoga* are enumerated here.

योगयुक्तो विशुद्धात्मा विजितात्मा जितेन्द्रियः ।
सर्वभूतात्मभूतात्मा कुर्वन्नपि न लिप्यते ॥ ७ ॥
yogayukto viśuddhātmā vijitātmā jitendriyaḥ
sarvabhūtātmabhūtātmā kurvannapi na lipyate 7.

He who is well established in *Karma Yoga*, accomplishes purification of his intellect. Any purification in the subtle body means a better state of quietude within. The lesser the agitations caused in us by our desires or emotions, the purer we are considered by *Vedanta*. Through action, which is selfless and without anxiety for the fruits, the practitioner exhausts his existing *vasanas*. When the inner equipment is swept clean of its desire-waves, it must, necessarily, become more and more quiet and peaceful. When once the intellect is purified, meaning, rendered immune to desire-disturbances, the mind, which reflects the condition of the intellect, cannot have any disturbances. The sentimental and emotional life of one, who has controlled the floodgates of desires, automatically becomes tame and equanimous.

When, through *Karma Yoga*, a man has gained inward peace, both at his mental and at his intellectual levels, it becomes a child's play for him to deny and to restrain, to control and to guide his sense-organs and their never ending appetites. A seeker (*Yogi*), who has thus controlled his body, mind and intellect, is best fitted for the highest meditation. In fact, all obstacles in meditation are nothing other than the milestones of sensuous appetites, emotional agitations and desire-problems. Once these chains are snapped, he comes to the natural condition of deep meditation, wherein the rediscovery of the Self must be instantaneous and complete.

This realisation of the Self cannot be partial; it is not realisation, if the meditator understands only himself to be Divine. To the realised, Divinity or the Self is Infinite and All-pervading. From the innermost sanctum of the Spirit when he looks out, he realises nothing but Divinity – everywhere, in everyone, at all times. Therefore, the Lord says, such a person "realises his own Self as the Self in all beings".

When a wave has realised its true nature to be the ocean, in its true ocean-vision, there cannot ever be any other wave which is other than the ocean-essence.

When an individual, who has thus, through a total inner revolution, come to realise his essential Infinite Divinity, acts thereafter in his *Atmic*-Consciousness, his actions cannot leave any reactions upon him. Reactions of actions can be claimed and arrogated only by the ego, and since, after God-realisation there is no sense of ego left in the God-man's bosom, his actions can thereafter leave no impression upon him. Like a signature upon running waters, nothing can ever stay in him to leave behind a *vasana*.

On the whole, the theory of *Karma Yoga* propounded by Krishna* has been consistently kept up by the Lord in all His declarations; and often it is conceived beautifully in the suggestive fragrance of his words. In the stanza under discussion also, it has been amply brought out that egocentric activities, motivated by desires, alone can create *vasana*-granulations upon the intellect, and consequently dim its discriminative awareness to know, to feel and to experience the Eternal Divinity, which is the essential nature of man as a spiritual being.

IN THIS CONSCIOUSNESS OF UNIVERSALITY AND SUPREME SENSE OF DIVINITY, WHEN A SAGE ACTS, WHAT EXACTLY WILL BE HIS ATTITUDE IN LIFE?

---

* Read 'General Introduction' to *Geeta* amplified by the two figurative representations A and B.

8. *"I do nothing at all", thus would the harmonised knower of Truth think seeing, hearing, touching, smelling, eating, going, sleeping, breathing,*

9. *Speaking, letting go, seizing, opening and closing the eyes; convinced that the senses move among the sense-objects.*

Such a perfect one is found to live, not sitting like a stone-statue, but acting diligently, like any one else in the world. A list of these common and natural activities is indicated in these two stanzas: "seeing, hearing, touching, smelling, eating, going, sleeping, breathing, speaking, dropping, holding, winking" etc. In all these unavoidable activities of life, it is explained here, a Sage or a prophet, living in the world, will not have any egoistic vanity.

In deep-sleep, we breathe, but we are not conscious of it at all, since at that time, the ego in us is not functioning. Similarly, when the ego has ended, all these activities take place instinctively. Even while carrying on these activities, the Seer has a constant awareness that "I DO NOTHING AT ALL". This does not mean that a Perfect Master is an irredeemable sleepwalker! The essential difference between the two is that the sleepwalker is unconscious, while a Sage is ever conscious, of the Consciousness.

नैव किंचित्करोमीति युक्तो मन्येत तत्त्ववित् ।
पश्यञ्शृण्वन्स्पृशञ्जिघ्रन्नश्नन्गच्छन्स्वपञ्श्वसन् ॥ ८ ॥
naiva kiñcitkaromīti yukto manyeta tattvavit
paśyañśṛṇvanspṛśañjighrannaśnanācchansvapañśvasan 8.
प्रलपन्विसृजन्गृह्णन्नुन्मिषन्निमिषन्नपि ।
इन्द्रियाणीन्द्रियार्थेषु वर्तन्त इति धारयन् ॥ ९ ॥
pralapanvisṛjangṛhaṇannunmiṣnnapi
indriyāṇīndriyārtthesu vartanta iti dhārayana 9.

That this attitude of total surrender of the sense of agency can come only to a Perfect Master is very clearly indicated here by the two terms 'centered' and 'steadfast', *Yuktah* meaning, 'centered in the Self'. This Self-centeredness can be in two grades of intensity: one, indicating the self-centeredness of a seeker who, through study, reflection and meditation, tries to remain intellectually centered in the Self; and another, the self-absorption of one who, after the final realisation of the Self in himself, comes to live vitally, at every moment, the experience of the Self (*Atmavit*).

In order that we may come to withdraw ourselves from the wrong conceptions of our own agency, we must have a substitute 'Knowledge-bit' in ourselves, which will help us in living the new experience. When I am ignorant of my waking state-personality, I become victimised by my own dream identity. This dream-identification ends only when I rediscover my real waking-state-personality and come to live in the unbroken awareness of "I am the waker". Similarly, in order to maintain in myself the attitude, "I am not the actor", it is necessary that I must have another positive assumption to replace this negative false belief. This is indicated in the last line of the stanza that a man of perfection, living in unison with the Truth, is ever an observer of the varieties of his own actions that are executed by the various layers of matter in him, among the world-of-objects.

Just as the ocean, were it conscious, could watch and observe its own waves rising and setting upon its own surface, declaring its own glory, so too, from the infinite depths of his own personality, the Master watches the actions performed by the various layers of matter in him.

As I am typing these lines, I can watch my own fingers typing and the more detached I grow, the more entertaining becomes the play of the fingers on the keyboard. Similarly, a Sage can, once having entered the innermost sanctum of his Self, ever afterwards watch the inert matter entities in him getting thrilled with activity in a thousand channels of independent preoccupations. He is unconcerned; he is unperturbed; from the bottomless depths of His own Being He watches on, in perfect detachment born of His realised knowledge, and He is ever confident that "I DO NOTHING AT ALL".

BUT, WHAT SHOULD BE THE ATTITUDE OF A MAN WHO IS NOT A TRUTH-KNOWER AND IS ENGAGED IN ACTION?

10. *He who does actions, offering them to BRAHMAN, abandoning attachment, is not tainted by sin, just as a lotus leaf remains unaffected by the water on it.*

What has been said in the previous stanza may be true for those rare few who have realised the Truth and are revelling in God-consciousness. But the strange life-of-detachment by which we can renounce completely the sense of agency, is not available for all of us. We are but aspirants and seekers of this Perfection. The way in which we can train ourselves to renounce the

---

ब्रह्मण्याधाय कर्माणि सङ्गं त्यक्त्वा करोति यः ।
लिप्यते न स पापेन पद्मपत्रमिवाम्भसा ॥ १० ॥

brahmaṇyādhāya kamārṇi saṅgaṁ tyaktavā karoti yaḥ
lipyate na sa pāpena padmapatramivāmbhasā 10.

sense of agency will be the problem of all true students of the *Geeta* who want to LIVE the *Geeta* rather than talk about its ideas. In this stanza we have a prescription by which every one of us can come to live the life of intelligent detachment in life.

RESIGNING TO *BRAHMAN*—Total detachment is impossible for the human mind and that is exactly what spiritual seekers often fail to understand. As long as there is a mind, it has to attach itself to something. Therefore, detachment from the false can be successful only when we attach ourselves to the Real. This psychological fact is scientifically enunciated in this stanza, wherein Lord Krishna advises the seeker to surrender all his attachments to *Brahman* and continue striving. To remember constantly an ideal, is to become more and more attuned to the perfections of the ideal. In order that we may surrender all our sense of agency in our actions to *Brahman*, we have to remember this concept of Truth as often as we now remember our limited ego. When the frequency of our thoughts upon the Lord becomes as high as the frequency with which we now remember the ego-idea, we shall come to realise the *Brahman*-ideal as intimately as we now know our own ego.

In short, today we are EGO-REALISED SOULS; the *Geeta*'s call to man is to become SOUL-REALISED EGOS.

Once our Real Nature is realised, the actions of the body, mind and intellect can no more leave any impression upon the Self. Merits and demerits belong to the ego and never to the *Atman*. The imperfections of my reflections in a mirror cannot be my imperfections, but can only be because of the distortions in the reflecting surface. The reflection may look shortened or lengthened according to the type of the mirror into which I am looking. Similarly, the ego comes to suffer the perfect and the imperfect reactions of its own actions.

Having thus realised the Self, to remain in the matter-envelopments and their world of objects, is to remain ever perfectly detached 'as the lotus leaf in the water'. Though the lotus leaf exists ONLY in water, draws its nourishment from the very water and dies away in the same water, yet, during its life as a leaf, it does not allow itself to be moistened by water. Similarly, a saint in the world, as a matter-entity, draws the nourishment for his individual existence from the world of objects but ever remains perfectly detached from his own merits and demerits, from his own concepts of beauty and ugliness, from his own likes and dislikes in the outside world.

Of the two methods by which ordinary *Karma* can be transformed into *Karma Yoga*, we have here the technique of renouncing one's sense of agency in one's actions exhaustively described. This is no strange theory; nor is it a unique doctrine. At every moment, all around the world, we see this enacted in a thousand ways. A doctor's attachment to his wife makes him incapacitated to perform an operation on her, although the same doctor, on the same day, may perform the same operation upon another patient, towards whom he has no self-deluding attachment.

If man were to act as a representative of the Infinite and the Eternal, he would discover in himself mightier possibilities and greater effectiveness, which are all wasted and squandered to-day by his misconception of the finite-ego as himself.

BECAUSE OF THIS:

11. *YOGIS, having abandoned attachment, perform actions merely by the body, mind, intellect and senses, for the purification of the self (ego).*

A *Karma-Yogi's* attempt is to keep himself within himself - as a detached but interested observer of all that is happening around and within himself. When he thus observes himself, from within himself, as a worker in any given field, it becomes easy for him to see that all actions belong to the above-mentioned instruments-of-action and not to the detached OBSERVER in him. Here, however, he must realise that the OBSERVER in himself is not the Truth, but this OBSERVER is 'Truth standing on the open balcony of the intellect'. Even while thus observing ourselves in action, we are ever conscious of the very OBSERVER in ourselves. "The Consciousness that illumines the very OBSERVER, is the Spiritual-centre, the Self" is the declaration of all *Upanishads*.

If thus, the spiritual-centre itself is something beyond the 'observer' why should a *Karma-Yogi* practise this technique of self-observation called in our *shastras* the 'witness-attitude' (*sakshibhava*)? This is answered at the end of the verse when *Bhagawan* says, 'for the purification of the ego'.

By such a practice, the seeker will be entering into the field of activity and pursuing the work without the self-

---

कायेन मनसा बुद्ध्या केवलैरिन्द्रियैरपि ।
योगिनः कर्म कुर्वन्ति सङ्गं त्यक्त्वात्मशुद्धये ॥ ११ ॥
kāyena manasā buddhayā kevalairindriyairapi
yoginaḥ karma kurvanti saṅgaṁ tyaktavātmaśuddhaye 11.

arrogating ego, thereby rendering himself available for an easy and effective purgation of the existing *vasana*-impurities. To the degree, these are removed; to that degree the inner equipments become clearer and steadier, rendering the reflection of the Divine-Consciousness in them more and more vivid.

ALSO BECAUSE OF THE FOLLOWING FACT, THE *KARMA*-YOGINS PRACTISE WORK WITH DETACHMENT:

12. *The united one (the well-poised or the harmonised), having abandoned the fruit of action, attains Eternal Peace; the non-united (the unsteady or the unbalanced), impelled by desire and attached to the fruit, is bound.*

Through right actions, undertaken without any self-dissipating anxiety for the fruits of those actions, a *Karma-Yogin* can reach an indescribable peace, arising out of the sense of steadfastness within him. Peace is not a product manufactured by any economic condition or cooked up by any political set-up. It cannot be ordered by constitution-making bodies or international assemblies. It is the mental condition in the bosom of an individual when his inner world is not agitated by any mad storms of disturbing thoughts. Peace is an unbroken sense of joy and it is the fragrance of an integrated personality. That, this can be brought about through selfless actions undertaken in a spirit

---

युक्तः कर्मफलं त्यक्त्वा शान्तिमाप्नोति नैष्ठिकीम् ।
अयुक्तः कामकारेण फले सक्तो निबध्यते ॥ १२ ॥
yuktaḥ karmaphalaṁ tyaktavā śāntimāpnoti naiṣṭhikīma
ayuktaḥ kāmakāreṇa phale sakto nibadhyate 12.

of *Yajna*, is the revolutionising theory given here. When the worker is ESTABLISHED IN HIS RENUNCIATION OF THE EGOISTIC SENSE OF AGENCY and when he has RENOUNCED HIS EGOCENTRIC DESIRES FOR THE FRUITS OF HIS ACTIONS, he soon becomes integrated and comes to experience the peace of steadfastness.

Not satisfied by this positive assertion, the Lord is re-emphasising this very same philosophical truth in the language of negation. He says that when one is not ESTABLISHED (a*yuktah*) in the renunciation of 'agency' and because of his desires, gets himself tied down to some expected results of his actions; he gets bound and persecuted by the reactions of his own actions. Some medicines, which, in small doses can give a complete cure, can also spell death in larger doses - for example, the sleeping tablets. An instrument by which we can defend ourselves can itself be the instrument for our own suicide.

In the same way, when we work in the outer field unintelligently, instead of gaining a greater glow of satisfaction and joy within, we will get ourselves more and more bound, and hurled down into bottomless darkness. The cause for this has been beautifully explained by Sri Krishna. Due to desires for specific fruits, we are mentally attached to those wished for patterns to be fulfilled in future. This is compelling life to pattern itself to our will at a future moment. If a frog were to imitate a bull and grow to the bull's size, it would end in a tragedy. A mortal finite mind ordering a pattern for a future period of time is in no way better equipped than the frog that tries to expand to the size of a bull.

BUT AS TO THE MAN WHO SEES THE SUPREME BEING:

13. *Mentally renouncing all actions and fully self-controlled, the 'embodied' one rests happily in the nine-gate city, neither acting nor causing others (body and senses) to act.*

Sannyasa is not a mere physical escapism but a mental withdrawal from things that are unintelligent and thoughtless. It is a mental attitude and not an external symbol. Therefore, he who is a self-controlled individual and who has brought all his sense-appetites under perfect control, and renounced all his egocentric and desire-prompted actions, comes to experience and live in a nameless joy, contentment and peace which well up from the very depths within him. He thus remains contented and happy, in the 'city of nine gates'.

This is a famous metaphor used in the *Upanishads*, to indicate the physical body of the seeker. The body is considered a fortress city, having nine main gates, which are the nine apertures in the physical structure, seven of them on the face (two eyes, two nostrils, two ears and one mouth) and the two apertures on the trunk, the genital organ and the excretory organ. Without these nine holes or at least a majority of them, life within the body is impossible. A King, remaining in the fortress, rules over his kingdom through his ministers, giving them the encouragement, strength and sanction by his mere presence. So too, the *Atman*, within the physical structure, though Itself doing nothing, by Its mere presence, vitalises the various instruments

---

सर्वकर्माणि मनसा संन्यस्यास्ते सुखं वशी ।
नवद्वारे पुरे देही नैव कुर्वन्नकारयन् ॥ १३ ॥

sarvamārṇi manasā sannyasyāste sukhaṁ vaśī
navadvāre pure dehī naiva kurvanna kārayan 13.

of cognition and action, within and without and governs the LIFE in them all.

This famous metaphor is used here by Sri Krishna, and He says that a self-controlled man lives within the physical body, a nameless joy of pure Divine life, ever watching over the activities of the matter-envelopments around him!! Such an individual, ever identifying with the Self, continues to observe, unaffected, unattached and without agitations, all the thrilled activities in the layers of matter, but 'neither does he act nor does he cause others to act'.

MOREOVER:

14. *Neither agency nor actions does the Lord create for the world, nor union with the fruits of actions. But it is Nature that acts.*

In the ritualistic portion of the *Vedas*, God is the Supreme Intelligence, ever dynamic and potent, who observes and watches over all our actions, and who, with perfect justice dispenses to each his reward for all his actions. Here, however, the Lord, the Creator, is described not so much as what HE IS as what HIS RELATIONSHIP with the Universe is.

The Supreme Self neither creates any sense of agency nor does It sanction any action. The Supreme has no such function as marrying every action to its correct fruits. In this very assertion, we can find how far the ordinary commentators, who jump to the conclusion that this passage is a description

---

न कर्तृत्वं न कर्माणि लोकस्य सृजति प्रभुः ।
न कर्मफलसंयोगं स्वभावस्तु प्रवर्तते ॥ १४ ॥

na kartṛtvaṁ na kamārṇi lokasya sṛjati prabhuḥ
na karmaphalasaṁyogaṁ svabhāvastu pravartate 14.

of the *Vedic* God-principle (*Karma-phala-data*), are in the wrong. Any close student of the *Geeta* can clearly see that there is an attempt on the part of Krishna to indicate to Arjuna the function and nature of the Self and Its relationship with the three bodies: the physical, the mental and the causal.

If the Reality, the Self, has nothing to do with the above-mentioned agency or their fruits, our life, which is nothing without them, must have no relationship at all with the Self. And yet, where the Self is not, existence and activities are not possible. Therefore, there must be some relationship between the Self and the non-Self and here this strange CONTACTLESS-CONTACT is being explained.

It is very well known that my nose is a permanent fixture on my face. It has neither a voluntary nor an involuntary movement. And yet, the other day, when I was looking into a basin of water, I saw my nose and ears moving rhythmically sideways as though upon well-oiled-hinges! Even when I saw it, I knew that my nose was not moving; but, all the same, I saw what I saw. Because my reflection in the water depended entirely upon the reflecting surface, it gathered unto itself its abnormalities from the vagaries of the reflecting medium. The Self or the *Atman* has neither activities nor an agency, and yet when in this life I function through the equipments that are natural to me, the conditioned Self, the ego, gathers unto itself these peculiarities of agency, actions and anxieties for their fruits.

Electricity in itself is static energy. But when it is generated, stored and sent through the distribution system, and reaches the terminals in my room, and when I plug on to it the various equipments, the same energy becomes dynamic. When the Self, pregnant with all potentialities, functions through the matter-conditionings, It assumes to Itself the egocentric attitudes of agency, action, fruits, etc.

The ENJOYER of the fruits and the PERFORMER of actions in us are the ego and not the *Atman*. I do not shake or shiver but my reflection can be shaken when the reflecting medium is disturbed. The *Atman* becomes the performer, etc., only when It gets conditioned by *Swabhava* - Nature, or *Maya* THE DIVINE *MAYA* MADE UP OF THE THREE *GUNAS*, as the Lord Himself calls it.

IN REALITY HOWEVER, THE LORD IN HIS ABSOLUTE NATURE IS EVER UNINVOLVED:

15. *The Lord takes neither the demerit nor even the merit of any; knowledge is enveloped by ignorance, thereby beings are deluded.*

The Supreme, who is All-pervading (*Vibhuh*), contrary to all our *Pauranic* concepts of stocktaking gods and deities, is declared here as not taking any note of the merit or the demerit of the living creatures. It is such passages that shock the story-reading devotee-class, and therefore, they generally ignore the *Geeta* and read instead the glories of Krishna. The concept that God sits just over the clouds, peeping down and observing every sin and merit of all the people all over the world, and that He keeps a perfect account of all these so that on the Day-of-Judgment, each one will approach the Father who will pass the judgement - is a concept which can

---

नादत्ते कस्यचित्पापं न चैव सुकृतं विभुः ।
अज्ञानेनावृतं ज्ञानं तेन मुह्यन्ति जन्तवः ॥ १५ ॥

nādatte kasyacitpāpaṁ na caiva sukṛtaṁ vibhuḥ
ajñānenāvṛtaṁ jñānaṁ tena muhyanti jantavaḥ 15.

appeal only to simple folk in whom the intellect is the least developed faculty!

The Eternal-Principle underlying life's activities cannot be conceived of as taking any active note or interest in the created or in the finite. From the Infinite standpoint, the finite exists not. It is only when the Supreme functions through Self-forgetfulness that It comes to see Itself split up into the concepts of agent, action, fruit, etc. Sunlight passing through a plane glass, in spite of the medium through which it has passed, emerges in its pure nature, if the glass be clean, flawless and colourless. If, on the other hand, a pencil of light were to pass through a glass prism, we all know that it would emerge in its seven component colours, constituting the spectrum. Similarly, the Self passing through Knowledge (*Jnana*) emerges as Self, which is the One-without-a-second, All-pervading, All-perfect. But the same Self, when It passes through ignorance - meaning, the body, mind and intellect – It splits up into the endless world of plurality.

The relationship between Knowledge and Ignorance is very beautifully explained here. Ignorance cannot be Knowledge, nor can Knowledge be a part of Ignorance. Where Ignorance is, there Knowledge cannot be. Where Knowledge has come, Ignorance must depart. But here, we are told KNOWLEDGE IS ENVELOPED BY IGNORANCE, just as a solitary light in a dark jungle, seen from a distance can be described as a light encaged in darkness. This relationship and the method of stripping Knowledge naked, is more elaborately indicated in the following stanza.

THE UNVEILING OF TRUTH IS A PROCESS OF THE REMOVAL OF IGNORANCE AND NOT A CREATION OF KNOWLEDGE. THEREFORE, IT IS ONLY AN ACT OF REDISCOVERY AND NOT A CREATIVE ACHIEVEMENT.

THIS IS AMPLY BROUGHT OUT BY VYASA'S WORDS IN THE FOLLOWING:

16. *But to those whose ignorance is destroyed by the Knowledge of the Self, like the sun, to them Knowledge reveals the Supreme (BRAHMAN).*

In the case of finite mortals, sighing and sobbing in ignorance, the Self is screened off from them by lifeless walls of nescience (*Avidya*). The man-of-Realisation is one in whom Knowledge has lifted this veil of ignorance. Darkness is removed by light not by degrees but instantaneously - however old the darkness may be and however thick its density. Similarly, in one who has Knowledge (*Jnana*) of the Self, the beginningless ignorance is lifted and within a lightning flash, his ignorance ends. Ignorance creates the egocentric concept and the ego thrives in the body, mind and intellect. With the end of ignorance, the ego too ends.

At this stage of *Veda*ntic discussion, the dualists (*Dwaitins*) generally feel like collapsing in sheer despair. They fail to understand how the Self can be experienced when the experiencer, the ego and the instruments of experiencing, which are familiar to them in perception, feeling and thinking, have all ended. Any intelligent student must surely entertain this doubt. Foreseeing this possibility, Krishna is here trying to explain how, when the ego has ended, Knowledge becomes self-evident.

ज्ञानेन तु तदज्ञानं येषां नाशितमात्मनः ।
तेषामादित्यवज्ज्ञानं प्रकाशयति तत्परम् ॥ १६ ॥

jñānena tu tadajñānaṁ yeṣāṁ nāśitamātmanaḥ
teṣāmādityavajjñānaṁ prakāśayati tatparam 16.

This explanation cannot be brought so easily within the comprehension of a thinking intellect but by the example, which the Lord gives in the second line: 'LIKE THE SUN'. It is the experience of all of us that, during the monsoon, we do not see the sun for days together, and we, in our hasty conclusions, cry out, the sun has been covered by clouds.

When we reconsider this statement, it is not very difficult for us to understand that the sun cannot be covered by a tiny bit of a cloud. Also, the region of the cloud is far removed from the centre of the Universe where the sun, in its infinite glory, revels as the one-without-a-second. The minute humans observing from the surface of the globe with their tiny eyes, experience that the glorious orb of the sun is being veiled because of a wisp of cloud. Even a mighty mountain can be veiled from our vision if we put our tiny little finger very near our eyes!

Similarly, the ego (*Jiva*) looking up to the *Atman* finds that ignorance is enveloping the Infinite. This ignorance is not in Truth, just as the clouds are never in the sun. The finite ignorance is certainly a limited factor compared with the infinitude of Reality. And yet, the mist of Self-forgetfulness that hangs in the chambers of the heart gives the ego the false notion that the Spiritual Reality is enveloped by ignorance. When this ignorance is removed, the Self becomes manifest, just as when the cloud has moved away, the sun becomes manifest.

To see the sun, we need no other light; to experience the Self we need no other experience. The Self is Awareness. It is Consciousness. To become conscious of Consciousness, we need no separate consciousness; to know knowledge we need no knowledge other than Knowledge; Knowledge is the very faculty of knowing. Similarly, when the ego rediscovers the Self, it becomes the Self.

When a dreamer has ended his dream-career along with his dream, he rediscovers himself to be the waker. The waker is never known or understood or recognised as an object by the dreamer. The dreamer himself transcends the dream-world and enters the realm of waking, wherein he knows himself to be the waker. In the same fashion, the deluded ego, when it walks out of ignorance and enters the realm of Pure Consciousness, it BECOMES the Consciousness which is the *Atman*. This relationship between the ego and the *Atman*, and the technique of rediscovery of the *Atman* by the ego, are beautifully described by this metaphor which is full of deep significance - for those who know how to chew upon it in independent thinking. THE SAGE, WHOSE INTELLECT IS ABSORBED IN TRUTH, WILL HAVE NO MORE BIRTHS.

17. *Intellect absorbed in That, their Self being That, established in That, with That for their Supreme Goal, they go whence there is no return, their sins dispelled by Knowledge.*

With a deep study of the Reality, the seeker in all his various personal identities thereafter comes to live in unison with that understanding of the Divinity. His intellect gets, as it were, absorbed in That Knowledge and his mind cannot but sing the song of Godliness through every one of its

---

तद्बुद्धयस्तदात्मानस्तन्निष्ठास्तत्परायणाः ।
गच्छन्त्यपुनरावृत्तिं ज्ञाननिर्धूतकल्मषाः ॥ १७ ॥

tadbuddhayastadātmānastanniṣṭhāstatparāyaṇāḥ
gacchantyapunarāvṛttiṁ jñānanidhirūtakalmaṣāḥ 17.

emotions. He becomes ever intent upon the Infinite Bliss which he has come to recognise as the essence in him. To such an individual the very Goal is nothing but the Self, which he has understood as illimitable and unlimited.

An individual, who has thus educated himself upon the world-of-Truth within himself, shall thereafter, have no reason or chance to get caught up again in this world of likes and dislikes. This is the result of full PARTICIPATION in the studies. The next stage is to live up to what is understood from the studies; the active INVOLVEMENT in spiritual life. Then comes complete COMMITMENT.

How can we say that the ego will not rise again in such a man's bosom? The reason is indicated here, when Krishna qualifies such men as THOSE WHO'S IMPURITIES HAVE BEEN SHAKEN OFF BY KNOWLEDGE. The impurities mentioned here are the *vasanas* which are the very materials with which the ego is conjured up. These *vasanas* together constitute what we philosophically call, 'the ignorance of Spiritual Divinity'. The antidote for ignorance is Knowledge. Thus, when, with the rise of the Knowledge of Spiritual Bliss, the dreary darkness of ignorance ends, the ego too comes to a total extinction from which it cannot restart its career. Without a cause, no effect is ever possible. In short, in this stanza, we are meeting the most optimistic philosophy in the world, declaring courageously that, Self-Realisation is the final experience in the pilgrimage of evolution, and that, in it; the evolver in us shall come to fulfil himself. God-realisation is the last stage of growth, and thereafter, to be the Supreme is the goal of all evolutionary struggles, to achieve which, the ego had, in its self-evolution, roamed about so long in the field of its own self-created world of finitude and imperfections!

HOW DO THOSE WISE MEN, WHOSE IGNORANCE OF THE SELF HAVE BEEN REMOVED BY KNOWLEDGE, SEE TRUTH? – IT IS SAID:

18. *Sages look with an equal eye upon a BRAHMANA endowed with learning and humility, on a cow, on an elephant, and even on a dog and an outcaste.*

The wise cannot but see and recognise the same presence of Divinity everywhere. The ocean has no difference in feeling for different waves. Gold cannot recognise itself as different in different pieces of ornaments. From the standpoint of mud, all mud pots are the same. Similarly, an egoless man, having recognised himself to be God, can find in no way, any distinction in the outer world of names and forms. The distinctions generally recognised, are all the distinctions of the containers. Man to man, there may be differences in form, shape and colour of the body, or the nature of the mind or the subtlety of the intellect. But as far as Life is concerned, It is the same everywhere, at all times.

Therefore, it is said in this stanza, that the Self-realised cast an equal eye on a *Brahmana* endowed with scholarship coupled with humility, on a cow, on an elephant, on a dog or on a pariah. Everywhere he realises the presence of the same Truth, whatever be the container.

Equal vision is the hallmark of Realisation. The perfected cannot make distinctions based upon likes and dislikes. In and through all forms and situations, he sees the expressions

---

विद्याविनयसम्पन्ने ब्राह्मणे गवि हस्तिनि ।
शुनि चैव श्वपाके च पण्डिताः समदर्शिनः ॥ १८ ॥
vidyāvinayasampanne brāhmaṇe gavi hastini
śuni caiva śvapāke ca paṇḍitāḥ samadarśinaḥ 18.

of the same dynamic Truth which he experiences as his own Self.

Shankara, in his commentary on this stanza, quotes *Goutama-Smriti* which says that it is not only sinful if we do not respect those whom we must respect, but it is equally sinful if we respect those whom we should not respect. Thus, from the standpoint of this *Smriti's* declaration, to respect a dog as much as a *Brahmana* or to respect a *Brahmana* only as much as we generally respect a dog, would both be sin indeed. In order to show that it is not so, the following stanza is given.

THESE ARE NOT SINFUL, FOR:

19. *Even here (in this world), birth (everything) is overcome by those whose minds rest in equality; BRAHMAN is spotless indeed and equal; therefore they are established in BRAHMAN.*

In this stanza, almost a whole scripture is indicated. In the context of the development of the theme, Lord Krishna had to show, first of all, that the Perfection, described in the previous few stanzas, is not a Godly idealism to be experienced after death, in a specialised world beyond the clouds, called the Heavens. *Pauranic* Hinduism and all Semitic religions promise a Heaven as the glorious goal of existence and spiritual effort. However, to an intelligent man; this promise is nothing more than a charming hallucination, and not a positive gain. Such a vague goal cannot be sufficiently encouraging to coax out of an intelligent man all his enthusiasm and sincerity.

इहैव तैर्जितः सर्गो येषां साम्ये स्थितं मनः ।
निर्दोषं हि समं ब्रह्म तस्माद्ब्रह्मणि ते स्थिताः ॥ १९ ॥
ihaiva tairjitaḥ sargo yeṣāṁ sāmye sthilaṁ manaḥ
nirdoṣa hi samaṁ brahma tasmād brahmaṇi te sthitāḥ 19.

Contrary to this vague hope, here in *Vedanta*, the naked truth is declared when Krishna repeats what the *Rishis* had earlier asserted a thousand times. It is expressly mentioned that the relative existence as a limited egocentre can be ended, and the imperfect individual can realize himself to be the Infinite Godhead. This goal can be reached not only at a post-mortem stage, but also in this very same life, here in this very body, among these very same worldly objects. One can live in the Consciousness of God, evolving oneself from the immaturities of the deluded ego-sense.

Who is capable of gaining this ascendancy in himself? What is the secret method by which this consummate self-redemption can be effectively fulfilled? The assertion that man can reach this goal in this very life is made in the first line by a detailed description of how it can be executed and practically lived. It is said that the one, WHOSE MIND RESTS IN EVENNESS, gains the Divine tranquillity of a God-man.

Patanjali *Yoga-Sutra* also explains the same fact in different words.[1] Where the thought-flow, which creates unequal and spasmodic mental fluctuations, is arrested, there the mind ends. Where the mind ends, it being the equipment through which Life expresses as a limited ego, this sense of separative existence also ends. When the ego has ended, the egocentric thraldom of *samsara* also ends. The ego, thus undressed of its *samsaric* sorrows, rediscovers itself to be nothing other than the Self Itself. Unless one comes to this mental equipoise, one is not capable of experiencing the *samatwam* of the *samadarshin* described in the above stanza.[2]

---

1 *'Yogah Chitta Vritti Nirodhah'* – Pantanjali *Yoga-Sutras* - 2

2 Refer *'Samatwam Yoga uchyate'* – *Geeta* II-48

Such an individual who has conquered his mind and has come to live in perfect equanimity, in all conditions of life, in all its relationships, Krishna vehemently asserts, "HE INDEED RESTS IN *BRAHMAN*". This may look rather illogical at the first reading, and therefore, as an explanation in a parenthetical clause, Krishna gives his reasons for such a daring assertion; he says, "SINCE *BRAHMAN* IS EVEN AND EVER-PERFECT".

Brahman is homogeneous and All pervading. Everything happens IN IT, and yet, nothing happens TO IT. Thus, the Truth remains changeless and ever the same, just as the riverbed remains ever motionless, although the units of water flowing in it are ever-changing. It is a quality of the substratum to remain changeless; all manifestations and super-impositions, by their very nature, must change. An individual, in his identifications with his body, etc., becomes a changing factor, a victim of every passing disturbance; but the substratum, the Self, ever remains the same.

An individual, who has discovered for himself a sufficient amount of tranquillity in which nothing dares disturb him anymore, is certainly one who has plumbed the depths and touched the bottom. A reed on the waves will be tossed up and down by the waves, but a lighthouse built upon firm rocks always remains upright and changeless, allowing even the stormy waves to exhaust their anger at its feet. Krishna's argument is thus logically sound when he declares that a mortal among us, who can maintain his equanimity under all conditions as explained in the foregoing stanzas, is indeed one who has contacted the Divine and the Eternal in Himself, "HE INDEED RESTS IN *BRAHMAN*".

BECAUSE *BRAHMAN*, THE SELF, IS HOMOGENEOUS AND WITHOUT BLEMISHES, THEREFORE:

20. *Resting in BRAHMAN, with steady intellect and undeluded, the knower of BRAHMAN neither rejoices on obtaining what is pleasant, nor grieves on obtaining what is unpleasant.*

Just as an excellent artist working at his masterpiece on his canvas would again and again approach his piece of art to add more details with finer strokes to his picture, and would again and again retreat from the canvas to gaze at his art from a distance, so too here, the Lord is creating with his chosen words the picture of the mental life of a man of equipoise and perfection upon the canvas of man's heart. He dedicates many stanzas in order that the picture may clearly and vividly come into the recognition and appreciation of even the ordinary, casual student. Here is yet another stanza offered with a burning enthusiasm and almost missionary zeal, so that Arjuna, the confused, may come to gain a vivid picture of the man-of-Perfection, who is not a mere impotent stone idol on the Ganges-banks, but a veritable dynamic factor that moulds and influences his generation of fellow beings.

Ordinarily, man gets excited or becomes despondent, not because of the happenings in the outer world, but because of his individual contact with them. If any man dies in the city, it is not tragedy to me, but when my father dies, it is my calamity. This clearly proves that the death of a man, in itself,

---

न प्रहृष्येत्प्रियं प्राप्य नोद्विजेत्प्राप्य चाप्रियम् ।
स्थिरबुद्धिरसंमूढो ब्रह्मविद्ब्रह्मणि स्थितः ॥ २० ॥
na prahṛṣyetpriyaṁ prāpya nodvijetprāpya cāpriyam
sthirabuddhirasammūḍho brahmavid brahmaṇi sthitaḥ 20.

cannot bring any disturbance to my mind, unless my mind had already projected itself on its relationship to the individual who has died. The man-of-Perfection who has won over his mind and has come to experience the Infinite Self, can no more, therefore, FEEL ANY JOY ON RECEIVING WHAT IS PLEASANT, NOR GRIEVE ON RECEIVING WHAT IS UNPLEASANT. It does not mean that a man-of-Perfection is a wooden doll or an iron statue, incapable of reacting to the external things whether they are pleasant or unpleasant. It only means that a man of true inward culture discovers in himself, in his own wisdom, a balance and an equipoise, which cannot be shattered very easily.

When a man of such superhuman mental steadfastness is analysed, we can easily discover that no condition or circumstances in the outer world can ever gain an entry into the inner precincts of his personality. His intellect becomes steady, since it is not poisoned with the usual egocentric misconceptions. It is, in fact, very interesting to note how the ideas arranged in this stanza, in their very sequence, explain a wondrous truth. One who is unaffected by the presence of things, good or bad, is the one whose INTELLECT IS STEADY, and the one whose INTELLECT IS STEADY is the ONE IN WHOM ALL DELUSIONS HAVE ENDED. A steady intellect from which all delusions have dropped becomes the instrument for KNOWING *BRAHMAN* - and the 'one who knows *Brahman* becomes *Brahman*', and therefore, comes to live 'ESTABLISHED IN THE *BRAHMIC* CONSCIOUSNESS OF INFINITE BEATITUDE', a living God-man walking upon the earth that is Olympus to him.

MOREOVER, RESTING IN *BRAHMAN*:

21. *With the self unattached to external contacts, he finds happiness in the Self; with the self engaged in the editation of BRAHMAN, he attains endless happiness.*

The foregoing stanza might give to an unprepared student, the idea that spiritual life is a static existence where a baked, stony heart, vainly comes in contact with the heart-throbs in the world of objects, and feels for itself nothing but a monotonous equanimity. In that case, a majority of us, without much discussion, can take our hats off and say 'goodbye' to all spirituality immediately. For, who can deny the fact that the world, as it is constituted to-day, in spite of its imperfections, when it comes in contact with our own inner world, however, maladjusted the inner world may be, can and does give minute flashes of joy? Why should I deny myself the brilliant flashes of momentary joys in exchange for a steady stone-like, impregnable monotony, call it equilibrium or equanimity, peace or God-hood? By changing the name, the thing itself is never changed!

This doubt is not a mere exaggeration. This is often heard in the halls of *Vedanta* from the lips of all sincere seekers. Any sensible seeker entering the halls of spiritual study with his intellect bright and clear, should come to doubt its efficacy and utility. No teacher can afford to ignore answering these questions and reassuring the students. Krishna, as a professional Teacher, is doing the same in this stanza.

बाह्यस्पर्शेष्वसक्तात्मा विन्दत्यात्मनि यत्सुखम् ।
स ब्रह्मयोगयुक्तात्मा सुखमक्षयमश्नुते ॥ २१ ॥

bāhyasparśeṣvasaktātmā vindatyātmani yatsukham
sa brahmayogayuktātmā sukhamakṣayamaśnute 21.

THE ONE, WHO HAS GAINED COMPLETE DETACHMENT FROM THE EXTERNAL OBJECTS, REALISES THE BLISS THAT IS THE NATURE OF THE SELF. Though the process of self-development is essentially a process of detachment, this technique of negation does not take us to an empty and purposeless zero, but when we have negated all that is false, we come to experience and live a total positivity. When the dreamer has renounced all his contacts with the dream world and thrown away his dream personality, he does not become a nonentity, but he rediscovers himself to be the more vital, the more effective personality, and the waker.

Similarly, whenever contacts with the external world through the media of the body, the mind and the intellect are clipped off clean, we are awakened in the meadows of God-Consciousness and come to live the joy that is the eternal nature of the Self. A seeker having thus redeemed his own mind and intellect from their preoccupations with the external world, at least during his meditation, when he comes to keep his HEART DEVOTED TO THE MEDITATION OF *BRAHMAN*, attains imperishable happiness. Here the term 'heart' is to be understood as a collective name for the inner instruments of knowing and experiencing.

FOR THE FOLLOWING REASONS ALSO HE SHOULD WITHDRAW THE SENSES FROM THE EXTERNAL WORLD- OF-OBJECTS:

22. *The enjoyments that are born of contacts are only generators of pain, for they have a beginning and an end. O son of Kunti, the wise do not rejoice in them.*

ये हि संस्पर्शजा भोगा दु:खयोनय एव ते ।
आद्यन्तवन्त: कौन्तेय न तेषु रमते बुध: ॥ २२ ॥

ye hi saṁsparśajā bhogā duḥkhayonaya eva te
ādyantavantaḥ kaunteya na teṣu ramate budhaḥ 22.

We, as seekers, try to detach ourselves from the external contacts in order to enjoy the Infinite Bliss, which is the nature of the Self. Even an average intelligent man, if he cares to investigate his own experiences with the outer world, will discover, all by himself, that joy hunting among the finite objects is no profitable preoccupation. The law of diminishing utility works in all our experiences and the very thing that gave a certain unit of joy in the beginning, itself soon becomes a stinking putrefying pit of sorrow. The experiences with the first *laddu** and the twenty-fifth *laddu* when you are not hungry are a practical demonstration of this fundamental truth, that sensuous joys are doomed to pain from the very beginning.

A sense-object can only be as beautiful and joyous as a leprous whore, painted, powdered and dressed up to smile at strangers in the dark alleys of a dilapidated commercial town. Lord Krishna beautifully brings out this idea, when he points out to Arjuna, how sense-objects and their joys, being finite in nature, do not enchant a wise man.

Man, if he is wise, is satisfied only with the Infinite. Finite things can only torture us with hopes of getting a more satisfactory joy, and whip us along the path of sensuousness making us pant in sheer exhaustion, hunting for a complete satisfaction; from ditch to ditch, from gutter to gutter. The chaster, the fuller, the Diviner joy, is gained only when we come to experience the Self as explained in the previous stanza.

AND THERE IS ALSO A WICKED THING, AN ENEMY ON THE PATH OF BLISS, A MOST DIFFICULT THING TO DEAL WITH, THE SOURCE OF ALL EVIL, VERY

* An Indian sweetmeat.

DIFFICULT TO WARD OFF. MIGHTY EFFORTS SHOULD BE MADE, SAYS THE LORD, TO REPEL THIS ENEMY:

23. *He who is able, while still here (in this world) to withstand, before the liberation from the body (death), the impulse born out of desire and anger, he is a YOGI, he is a happy man.*

Krishna Himself feels that his over-enthusiastic description of the Perfect-man and his mental life may give to any reader a despairing sense of impossibility or futility. No one living the present life of agitations can ever dare to hope that such a perfect happiness is ever possible for a mortal living upon this ever-spinning globe. If a philosophy is only an idealism which has no contact with the practical world, that philosophy is merely Utopian poetry fit for entertaining a pleasant idea, but never capable of making man a nobler being.

In order to remove that misunderstanding, Krishna, in this stanza, gives the assurance that man is capable of living that perfect joy in this VERY WORLD, if only he makes the necessary adjustments in himself.

My great-grandfather was a great violinist. His violin was preserved and worshipped in my house until now. I too have now gained a preliminary nodding acquaintance with music. Suddenly an idea struck me "Why not take my great-grandfather's instrument and play upon it and thus become a great musician overnight?" If I play directly upon that ancient and faithful instrument, I will be forced to break it

---

शक्नोतीहैव यः सोढुं प्राक्शरीरविमोक्षणात् ।
कामक्रोधोद्भवं वेगं स युक्तः स सुखी नरः ॥ २३ ॥

śaknotīhaiva yaḥ soḍhuṁ prākśarīravimokṣaṇāt
kāmakrodhodbhavam vegaṁ sa yuktaḥ sa sukhī naraḥ 23.

into pieces. That violin, in that condition, cannot give me perfect music. It needs general cleaning and dusting; perhaps, restringing and a lot of tuning up. When these adjustments are made, then only can it faithfully give out all the notes, implicitly obeying the strokes of my bow and the tickling of my finger. In the same fashion, today, our mind and intellect, the instruments of singing the song of Perfection, neglected from beginningless time, need a lot of readjustments before they can gurgle out their contents of laughter and joy.

The technique of readjusting the inner-instruments is beautifully summarised here by Lord Krishna. The very brevity and simplicity of this verse are the obstacles to our understanding its full import. The advice has a deceptive look of simplicity. "WITHSTAND THE IMPULSE OF DESIRE AND ANGER", then he is a *Yogi*, even while here, before his death, the happy man. To a modern student of Freud and others, soaked with the ideas of behaviorism and such other modern superficialities of psychology, this may look rather an unscientific expression of a crude enthusiast. But when we analyse and try to grapple with its full import and implication, we shall see that it contains volumes of suggestions.

'Desire' is the avalanche of thoughts sweeping down from the pinnacles of our intellect, along the valleys of our heart, towards an object-of-desire in the outer world. When this avalanche of thought is barricaded in its sweep by a substantial obstacle ere it reaches its destination, the blast with which it shatters itself on that obstacle is called 'anger'. It is these two types of thoughts that generally agitate our bosom. The greater the desire with which we ponder over an object, the greater shall be the anger against any obstacle that comes between our object-of-desire and us.

To one who has won over joy and grief, and who has gained a certain amount of detachment from external objects, desire for obtaining the pleasant or avoiding the unpleasant is no emotion at all. Where there is no desire, hatred is an unknown alien factor there. He who has gained mastery over these two impulses, powerful and almost irresistible as they are, is he who can afford to live in this world of multiplicity and imperfections as an independent solitary man of true and steady happiness.

Thus Krishna assures Arjuna - and through Arjuna all others like us who will read and try to understand this immortal Scripture - that man can live perfectly happily even while in this form, among these very objects, in this very world, during this very life, if only he, in his spiritual evolution, learns to renounce his impulses of desire and hatred.

WHAT SORT OF A MAN RESTING IN *BRAHMAN* ATTAINS *BRAHMAN*? ... THE LORD SAYS:

24. *He who is happy within, who rejoices within, who is illuminated within, that YOGI attains Absolute Freedom or MOKSHA, himself becoming BRAHMAN.*

From the above three stanzas it becomes clear that, according to Krishna, none of the usual fields of joy and happiness are visited by the man of perfection. Neither the warmth of the flesh, nor the thrills of emotions nor the

---

योऽन्तःसुखोऽन्तरारामस्तथान्तर्ज्योतिरेव यः ।
स योगी ब्रह्मनिर्वाणं ब्रह्मभूतोऽधिगच्छति ॥ २४ ॥

yo'ntaḥsukho'ntarārāmastathāntarjyotireva yaḥ
sa yogī brahmanivārṇaṁ brahmabhūto'dhigacchati 24.

ecstasies of thinking are available for him. Renouncing them all and conquering both love and hatred, the *Yogi*, in sheer transcendence, attains a realm of bliss, and Krishna declares that such a man alone can be said to be really happy.

It becomes very difficult to believe that a man in that condition would feel any happiness at all. All instruments of happiness have been rejected by him. There is no more any field for him to gain joy or satisfaction. Renouncing all food one cannot have any joy of eating.

Again, it is against the very logic and rhythm of life to say that man will be satisfied by a mere emptiness, a dark cave of total negation. Every living creature roams about in all its available fields of activity seeking to gain and achieve a greater fulfilment of joy. Even the state of complete absence of pain - though it is a platform of relief – is not the summit where an individual will feel contented and fully satisfied.

Under the above circumstances, it will be mere exaggeration to believe Krishna's assertion in the previous three stanzas. To avoid such a serious misunderstanding among the students, the Lord is here trying to find out for us the positive glow of assured Divinity when the ego rediscovers itself to be the Self as it renounces all its delusory preoccupations with the false and the fleeting. The substantial and definite experience of solid bliss enjoyed and lived by the Self, in the Self, as the Self, is indicated here in this stanza.

The seeker, in his detachment, not only withdraws himself from the world-of-objects outside, but also discovers in himself an ampler sense of bliss and security. This inward joy is not a rare flickering flash, but a constantly experienced factor. Such a well-developed seeker striving constantly on the path comes to discover a field of fruitful 'entertainment' and engaging 'recreation' in the brilliant light of joyous satisfaction within himself.

To him his entire 'within' is flooded with the Light of Pure Consciousness. His heart is thereafter alit with the Glow Divine.

Such an individual, who has withdrawn himself completely within, where he has learnt to enter at will and court and live in It, is the one who has come to KNOW *Brahman*. In his realization of the Infinite, he has come to experience the Bliss of *Brahman*, the smokeless shrine of Truth.

MOREOVER:

25. *Those RISHIS obtain Absolute Freedom or MOKSHA — whose sins have been destroyed, whose dualities are torn asunder, who are self-controlled and intent on the welfare of all beings.*

When a man-of-Meditation, striving diligently, with his senses well under his control, comes to wash off all his sinful mental impressions (which had been creating in him the veiling of the Self behind an unending array of doubts regarding the Reality), he gains the joy of the Self. When his

---

लभन्ते ब्रह्मनिर्वाणमृषयः क्षीणकल्मषाः ।
छिन्नद्वैधा यतात्मानः सर्वभूतहिते रताः ॥ २५ ॥
labhante brahmnivārṇamṛṣayaḥ kṣīṇakalpaṣāḥ
chinnadvaidhā yatātmānaḥ sarvabhūtahite ratāḥ 25.

ignorance, which is nothing other than agitations of the mind (*vikshepa*) and the consequent veiling of the Truth (*avarana*), has been removed, Knowledge of his Real Nature dawns in his bosom and he rediscovers himself as the Self!

Having thus rediscovered the Self, having thus gained the goal of all evolution, what would be the duties of such an individual in this existence, till finally, with a cheerful farewell, he drops his mortal coil down, to merge himself with what he knows to be his own Self ? The general impression is that he will move about in the world like a mad, walking, stone-statue - that eats at least once a day, a threat to society, a moving bundle of contagion and a screaming pillar of despondency and despair. Such a living death is not the goal indicated by the *Vedas* nor did the Hindu *Rishis* ever try to carve out of a man, a walking corpse!

Self-realisation is not a melancholy parade, crawling to a pre-destined tomb, but it is a joyous ride to the palace-of-Truth, from which man has wandered away in his own ignorance and confusion. A true prophet is one who lives, consumed in an ever-reviving fire of love. He ceaselessly strives to bring out the Self from the non-Self that is veiling It, in all other forms around and about him. This is indicated by the term 'engaged in the good of all-beings'.

This *lokaseva* becomes his recreation, his self-appointed engagement. His body, mind and intellect are offered as oblations into the sacred fires of activity and while remaining at rest within himself, the Saint lives on, in an unbroken Consciousness of the Divine, the Eternal.

MOREOVER:

26. *Absolute Freedom (or BRAHMIC Bliss) exists on all sides for those self-controlled ascetics, who are free from desire and anger, who have controlled their thoughts and who have realised the Self.*

By the work of serving mankind - the duties of reinstating Godly life in the bosom of the *satanic* Age, the love in the heart that tries to redeem the prostitute or to cure the leper, the joyful enthusiasm to light and guide where darkness and blindness revel - the Master is not bartering away his chances to live as a God of gods even in this world, here and now. Just as a doctor working among the unhealthy and the suffering is not himself contaminated by the diseases or the sorrows, so too a mastermind working amongst the wretched and the lustful, the passionate and the sensuous, the false and the low, is not in any sense of the term touched, even by a passing breeze of the stink around him.

How this immunity is maintained and preserved by a man of equipoise even amongst the temptations of the vicious atmosphere is indicated here in this stanza. When a sincere seeker has, through his own intelligent self-effort and divine self-application, redeemed himself from the secret charms of the ever murmuring hosts of sense-appetites in himself -

---

कामक्रोधवियुक्तानां यतीनां यतचेतसाम् ।
अभितो ब्रह्मनिर्वाणं वर्तते विदितात्मनाम् ॥ २६ ॥

kāmakrodhaviyuktānāṁ yatīnāṁ yatacetasām
abhito brahmanivārṇaṁ vartate viditātmanām 26.

when he has conquered the instincts of lust and anger in him - when he has thus completely mastered all threats arising from within him and those that come to him from without, such a sincere pursuer of the Life Divine, when he has known the Self, gains the Bliss of Perfection BOTH HERE AND HEREAFTER.

AND NOW, TO ENUNCIATE THE *DHYANA YOGA*, THE NEAREST AND THE MOST EFFICIENT MEANS TO RIGHT KNOWLEDGE, THE LORD TEACHES THE PATH OF MEDITATION IN THE FOLLOWING FEW APHORISTIC VERSES:

27. *Shutting out (all) external contacts and fixing the gaze (as though) between the eyebrows, equalising the outgoing and incoming breath moving within the nostrils,*

28. *With senses, mind and intellect (ever) controlled, having liberation as his Supreme Goal, free from desire, fear and anger -- the sage is verily liberated for ever.*

In these two aphoristic stanzas, the Lord has hinted at the summary of the entire following chapter. This is the traditional style in Sanskrit textbooks on *Brahma-Vidya*, wherein each section is closed, often indicating the following section.

स्पर्शान्कृत्वा बहिर्बाह्यांश्चक्षुश्चैवान्तरे भ्रुवोः ।
प्राणापानौ समौ कृत्वा नासाभ्यन्तरचारिणौ ॥ २७ ॥

spaśārnkṛtvā bahibārhyāṁścakṣuścaivāntare bhruvoḥ
prāṇāpānau samau kṛtvā nāsābhyantaracāriṇau 27.

यतेन्द्रियमनोबुद्धिर्मुनिर्मोक्षपरायणः ।
विगतेच्छाभयक्रोधो यः सदा मुक्त एव सः ॥ २८ ॥

yatendriyamanobuddhirmrumokṣaparāyaṇaḥ
vigatecchābhayakrodho yaḥ sadā muktā eva saḥ 28.

The above verses give us a complete picture of the man-of-Perfection and his purposeful life at all levels of his existence. Students of *Vedanta* are ever anxious to live the Perfection. They are not dreamers, content with flirting with Utopian idealisms, but they are the most utilitarian, practical men of the world, who want to live a more purposeful, efficient and effective life in this world. Therefore, they are not enamoured of mere ideas, however noble they may be, unless those ideas can actually be lived in life.

How to achieve the perfect mental equipoise, which has been indicated in the previous stanzas, should be the question that must agitate the minds of all true seekers. Here, as a summary, with lots of dots and dashes, Krishna is giving the scheme of practice, by which every diligent pursuer can gain a complete integration. These two stanzas become rough notes to be enlarged upon and exhausted with details and descriptions in the next chapter.

The external world-of-objects, it has already been said, cannot by itself bring any disturbance to any one of us. It is only when we are in contact with the world-of-objects that we suffer the agitations in life. So long as we are standing on the bank of a river or on the seashore, the waves in the water cannot buffet us. It is only when we are in contact with them that we will be tossed hither and thither. Forms, sounds, tastes, smells and touches constantly bring their objects to agitate the mind, but we shall get agitated by them only when we are identifying ourselves with our mental conditions. If we, therefore, shut out the external object, not by physical methods such as plugging the ears, but by a discreet intellectual detachment from our mental reactions to the external world-of-objects, we shall discover in ourselves, the necessary tranquillity to start meditation.

It is a great mistake that seekers often take the foregoing instruction too literally. They converge their eyeballs and gaze towards the space between the eyebrows for the purpose of meditation. This is an exaggeration, though it faithfully follows the instructions laid down here. It is to be understood, as Sankara says, 'TO GAZE AS IT WERE' towards the point between the two eyebrows. It is psychologically very true that when we are looking 'as it were towards the brow' our gaze would be turned upward at about forty-five degrees to the vertical backbone. In that attitude of upward gaze, the human mind is held uplifted and it becomes the right vehicle for higher contemplation.

There is an intimate relationship between the rhythm of the flow of breath in us and our own mental thought-conditions. The more agitated the mind is, the more spasmodic and uncertain becomes the rhythm of our breathing. Therefore, the instructions here, which advise us to control our breath-flow to make it EVEN WITHIN THE NOSTRILS becomes a conducive physical practice for coaxing the mind to a relatively quieter existence.

These instructions are all mainly physical adjustments for creating a conducive mental atmosphere. In the following stanza, the necessary adjustments to control the mental and the intellectual sheaths are hinted at. The tireless seeker is asked to control his sense appetites, mental oscillations and intellectual storms by dedicating all his outer and inner activities to the one great eternal goal of reaching Perfection; realizing the Self. As far as the taming of the intellect is concerned, the advice given by Krishna is that the seeker should RENOUNCE DESIRES, FEARS AND ANGER.

In enumerating these three qualities, psychologically speaking, Krishna has expounded an exhaustive theory of self-development and inner growth. There is an intimate relationship between these three: DESIRE, FEAR AND ANGER. Desire, we had found earlier, is that pattern of thought in which the mind runs constantly towards a given object with an anxious expectation of procuring and possessing it. Where there is desire, there we come to experience fear. And it is very well known that when we desire a thing so much as to live ever in the fear of losing it, maddening anger can exhibit itself at any moment against any threat of an obstacle between ourselves and our object-of-desire. When these three emotions - desire, fear and anger - are controlled, we have controlled almost all the mad impulses of our intellect.

He who has thus freed himself from desire, fear and anger, who has controlled his senses, mind and intellect, in his all-consuming ambition for liberation, and who has quietened the flow of his breath, such an individual could remain in the contemplation of Truth, without contact with the external world, his eyes fixed steadily and held in an upward gaze. Krishna says, "such a man-of-Meditation is verily free for ever".

This assertion that such an individual IS VERILY FREE FOR EVER is an anticipatory truth and not an accomplished fact. In ordinary conversation, we use the phrase 'baking of bread', which, in its literal meaning is false, since bread need not be baked; we bake only dough. But in such usages, what we mean is that the goal is not too far away from the particular act we are doing. Even while boiling water, we say that we are making tea; the idea is that tea making cannot be far away when the water has already been boiled. Similarly, here also, when we have made all the above-mentioned adjustments, at all levels of our existence, and when we sit in contemplation of the Self, we become released from all our misunderstandings and come to experience the freedom of Godhood ... ere long (*achirena*).

WHAT HAS HE, WHOSE MIND IS THUS STEADILY BALANCED, TO KNOW AND MEDITATE UPON, IN THE *DHYANA YOGA*?

29. *Knowing Me as Enjoyer of sacrifices and austerities, the Great Lord of all worlds, the friend of all beings, he attains Peace.*

HE ATTAINS PEACE ON KNOWING ME—It is never to be forgotten that, in the *Geeta* whenever Lord Krishna uses the first person singular, he does not mean the mortal framework of the son of Devaki, but indicates the Self in the individual – the Eternal Principle, Sri Krishna *Paramatman*. The Self is the real vitality behind the ego (*Jiva*) which functions in identification with the matter-envelopments and feels that it is the doer and enjoyer. The term *'Yajna'* has been already explained earlier. In its *Geeta* implication, *Yajna* is the self-dedicated work, which one performs in any field of activity. *Tapas* means all self-denial and practices of self-control which the ego undertakes in order to integrate and revive its own capacities to seek its real identity with the Eternal.

The Self is certainly the *Maheshwara* – the Lord of all lords, the God of all gods. Here the *Ishwara* is to be understood as the controller of all fields of activities: activities of perception and expression. Each one of them is considered as presided over by various faculties, and they are termed as *devas*, meaning 'illuminators'. The faculty of seeing illumines the field of the eyes and thus gives the knowledge of forms and colours; the faculty of hearing illumines the field of the ears and thus provides the knowledge of sound, and so on. The Self is in fact the Lord of all these individual lords governing, controlling and ruling over the various fields. Therefore, Lord

---

भोक्तारं यज्ञतपसां सर्वलोकमहेश्वरम् ।
सुहृदं सर्वभूतानां ज्ञात्वा मां शान्तिमृच्छति ॥ २९ ॥
bhoktāram yajñatapasāṁ sarvalokamaheśvaram
suhṛdaṁ sarvabhūtānāṁ jñātvā māṁ śāntimṛcchati 29.

Krishna as the Self confers upon Himself the title of *Sarva-Loka-Maheshwara*.

In our ordinary experiences in the world, a man who has kingly powers is very difficult to approach, and the King of kings, a personality striking awe and reverence in the heart of the ordinary man, becomes almost unapproachable to the ordinary people. Therefore, the Lord has to qualify his title of *Sarva Loka Maheshwara* with the epithet that he is at the same time A FRIEND OF ALL LIVING CREATURES.

The term 'knowing' is not objectively knowing Krishna, in the sense in which we come to know a flower or a fruit, but here the term 'knowing' is to be understood as 'realising'. Spiritual experience is the realisation of the Self to be the one great ruler within, who presides over all the activities within the body politic. He who is the One, at whose altar the perfection-seeking ego surrenders all its spiritual activities, and as a tribute to whom, the seeker brings all his self-denial and asceticism.

KNOWING HIM TO BE NONE OTHER THAN KRISHNA, THE INDIVIDUAL REACHES THE GOAL OF PEACE, THE ETERNAL SANCTUM OF PERFECTION.

Thus in the UPANISHAD of the glorious Bhagawad Geeta, in the Science of the Eternal, in the Scripture of YOGA, in the dialogue between Sri Krishna and Arjuna the fifth discourse ends entitled:

Yoga of True Renunciation

Om Om Om Om Om

ॐ तत्सदिति श्रीमद् भगवद् गीतासूपनिषत्सु ब्रह्मविद्यायां
योगशास्त्रे श्रीकृष्णार्जुनसंवादे कर्मसंन्यासयोगो नाम
पञ्चमोऽध्यायः

Oṁ tatsaditi śrīmadbhagavadgītāsū ūpaniṣatsu brahmavidyāyāṁ yogaśāstre śrī kṛṣṇārjuna saṁvāde karmasannyāsayogo nāma pañcamo'dhyāyaḥ

VI

Meditation

Introduction

WITH this chapter we are coming to the close of a definit section in the scheme of thought in the *Geeta*. This is the opinion of some of the well-known critics and students of the Lord's Song. According to them, the eighteen chapters of the *Geeta* fall into three definite sections, each of six chapters, and they group themselves to expound the implications and significances of the sacred *Vedic mantra "Tat Twam Asi"* – "THAT THOU ART". The first six chapters together constitute an explanation of the philosophical significance indicated by the word 'Thou' (*Twam*). In the general scheme of thought developed in that section, the contents of the sixth chapter constitute a fitting conclusion.

In Chapter II, in a language almost foreign to Arjuna, in quick strokes, Lord Krishna painted the philosophical perfection, which is the theme of all the *Upanishads*. He concluded that chapter with a vivid and expressive picture of a saint-of-Perfection and mental equipoise. Naturally, the interest of a seeker is excited and he seeks to find means and methods by which he too, can grow within himself and reach those diviner heights of self-control and equipoise.

The *Geeta* is personally and specifically addressed to Arjuna, a confused average man, at a moment when he felt completely confounded by the problem that was facing him. Naturally, the highest methods of subtle meditation, the mental drill by which one can renounce all one's preoccupations, etc., are not easy methods that can be practised with confidence. At the same time, it will not be true to say that *Vedantic* methods are meant only for a few. If they are immediately useful only to a few, there must be, in *Vedanta,* preliminary techniques by which everyone can steadily grow to become fit to enter the hall-of-Perfection.

That there are graded lessons for one's spiritual unfoldment is not really understood by the modern lip-*Vedantins.* It is this general ignorance that has brought about the misconception in Hinduism that the study of the *Vedas* is the guarded preserve of some rare ones. And, *Vedanta* would have been an incomplete science if it did not contain *Upasana* methods for purifying the students' inner equipment.

Krishna, as a true teacher, understood Arjuna's mental debilities and intellectual incompetence at that particular moment. Hence, He did not start right away upon the arduous lines of pure meditation and clear detached thinking. In order to bring him to the level of perfection, various lower methods of self-integration had to be prescribed. Thus in Chapter III we found an exhaustively scientific treatment of the *Karma Yoga;* the path-of-Action.

Activities in the outer world, however noble they may be in their motive, cannot but leave deep ulcerations and painful restlessness in the bosom of the worker. To mitigate the 'reactions' of action (*Karma Phala*) and as a balm to soothe the bleeding mental wounds, new methods of maintaining the mind in quietude and ease have been expounded in Chapter IV under the title 'Renunciation-of-Action In Knowledge'. It is the theory of Krishna that, constantly maintaining in the mind the awareness of the Greater Principle that presides over all human endeavours, the worker can, even in the thick of activities, maintain a healthy and well-ventilated inner life.

Naturally, the limited intellect of Arjuna got extremely confused, since the teacher argued in the beginning for 'action' and at the conclusion, for the Renunciation-of-Action. In Chapter V, therefore, the way-of-Renunciation is explained and the technique of guaranteeing immunity to our mind from reactions, even while it is engaged in activity, is explained. The *Yajna* spirit - the spirit of dedicated activity for the benefit of the larger majority and not for any self-arrogating profit – is the antiseptic that Krishna prescribes for a mind and intellect that are to work in the world. In Chapter IV is prescribed an unavoidable treatment for curing the mind of its own pox of painful impressions of the past (*vasanas*).

In Chapter V, the way-of-Renunciation is explained under two different categories, which show the two methods of achieving the same goal; renunciation of (a) our sense of agency in activities; and (b) our unintelligent anxieties arising out of our thoughtless preoccupations with the fruits of our actions. The chapter exhausts these two techniques and explains how, by the renunciation of agency or by the renunciation of our attachment to the fruits-of-actions, we can come to gain a release from the *vasana*-bondages which generally shackle our personality during our activities.

One, who could faithfully follow the technique so far unravelled by the Lord, should have thereby come to a condition wherein the insentient and inert mind has been stirred into a field of intense activity. A mind developed through this training, is now taught to come under the intelligent will of its determined trainer, the seeker himself. The mind thus gathered and trained, is certainly a better-equipped instrument for the higher purposes of Self-contemplation and Self-unfoldment.

How this is done through the famous technique-of-Meditation is, in a nutshell, the theme of the sixth chapter. During our discussions, we shall not stand in sheer surprise and wonderment and swallow down the ideas in the verses without dissecting, discovering, analysing and understanding every facet of each of those ideas. This chapter promises to give us all the means by which we can give up our known weaknesses and grow positively into a healthier and more potent life of virtue and strength. This technique is called Meditation, which in one form or another, is the common method advocated and advised in all religions, by all prophets, at all times, in the history of man.

The Blessed Lord said :

1. *He who performs his bounden duty without depending on the fruits-of-actions – he is a SANNYASIN and a YOGI; not he who (has renounced) is without fire and without action.*

Arjuna's plan, in his own words in the first chapter, was to escape from the battlefield in order to live the *Sannyasa*-life. He did not know that a truly selfless worker is the greatest *Sannyasi*, for, without renunciation, his action would become, at best, only a mischievous meddling with the harmony of the Universe.

To escape from the buzz of life in our present state of unpreparedness into the quiet atmosphere of the banks of the Ganges, is only the fall of an average good man to the level of the insentient stone in the very Ganges. At the close of this verse, Krishna laughs at Arjuna's sad misconceptions.

श्रीभगवानुवाच
अनाश्रित: कर्मफलं कार्यं कर्म करोति य: ।
स संन्यासी च योगी च न निरग्निर्न चाक्रिय: ॥ १ ॥

śrī bhagavānuvāca
anāśritaḥ karmaphalaṁ kārya karoti yaḥ
sa sannyāsī ca yogī ca na cākriyaḥ 1.

There is no bitterness in the irony of the Lord. Soon we shall find that Arjuna also comes to laugh at his own misunderstandings.

The whole chapter is fully and entirely dedicated to expounding the technique of cultivation, direction and application of the inner forces of thoughts and feelings. Hence, it is very appropriate for Krishna to indicate the greater importance of revolutionising our inner motives and mental attitudes before we enter the path of spirituality.

AS AN ELUCIDATING ANNOTATION FOR THE QUIBBLE, WHICH THE LORD HAS DECLARED IN THE STANZA, WE HAVE HIS ADDED EXPLANATIONS IN THE FOLLOWING, WHICH SHOW HOW, *SANNYASA* ITSELF IS *YOGA*:

2. *O Pandava, please know YOGA to be that which they call renunciation; no one verily becomes a YOGI who has not renounced thoughts.*

Krishna is repeating the same idea, lest Arjuna should overlook the fact that what they call *Sannyasa*, the renunciation of agency, is itself *Yoga*, the renunciation of the fruits-of-action. *Sannyasa* is the state reached through *Yoga*, the practice; and the spiritual practice of *Yoga* cannot even be thought of without the spirit of *Sannyasa* in the bosom. The two are the obverse and the reverse of the same coin of spiritual perfection!

It is but natural that the intellectually independent thinker in Arjuna should, at this juncture, with raised brows ask the question 'Why?' Seeing this, the Charioteer implicitly gives the logical reasons behind his seemingly outrageous and daring conclusion. The Lord explains that, never can one

---

यं संन्यासमिति प्राहुर्योगं तं विद्धि पाण्डव ।
न ह्यसंन्यस्तसंकल्पो योगी भवति कश्चन ॥ २ ॥

yaṁ sannyāsamiti prāhuryogaṁ taṁ viddhi pāṇḍava
na hysannyastasaṅ kalpo yogī bhavati kaścana 2.

become established in the practices for one's own cultural-rehabilitation unless one has learnt the art of renouncing all *sankalpas*.

Man cannot ordinarily remain without imagining and constantly creating, in his exuberant fancy. In his imagination, he invariably tries to pull down the beautiful veil thrown over the face of the future. Ripping open this veil over the unknown, every one of us, on all occasions, in our imagination, fixes for ourselves a goal to be fulfilled by us in the near future. Having fixed up the temporary goal, our mind plans and creates a method of achieving that hazy goal. But ere we execute our plans and enter into the field of effort to carve out a success for ourselves, the never-tiring, ever-active power of imagination in us would already have wiped clean the goal fixed earlier, and have rewritten a modified destination to be gained in the future.

By the time we prepare ourselves mentally and start executing our ideas in life, our mischievous fancy would again have wiped the distant goal clean. Thus, each time the goal remains only so long as we have not started our pilgrimage to it; the moment we start the pilgrimage, the goal fades away from our vision!

In short, when we have a goal we have not yet started acting, and the moment we start the strife, we seem to have no goal to reach. The subtle force in our inner composition which unconsciously creates this lunatic temperament in us is called the unbridled *Sankalpa Shakti*.

We need no help from any great commentators to understand that no achievement, either without or within us, can be gained so long as we have not pursued, arrested, and finally destroyed this dangerous inner saboteur called *Sankalpa*.

To show that there is no compromise in this, *Bhagawan* is using a very positive term that none (*kashchana*) can ever reach any progress on the path of self-redemption without acquiring a capacity to renounce this self-poisoning *Sankalpa*-disturbance.

KARMA YOGA, PRACTISED WITHOUT REGARD TO THE FRUIT-OF-ACTION FORMS AN EXTERNAL AID (*BAHIRANGA SADHANA*) TO *DHYANA YOGA*. THE LORD NOW PROCEEDS TO SHOW HOW *KARMA YOGA* IS A MEANS TO BETTER AND GREATER MEDITATION.

3. *For a MUNI or sage who 'wishes to attune to YOGA', action is said to be the means; for the same sage who has 'attuned to YOGA', inaction (quiescence) is said to be the means.*

To one who is DESIRING TO SCALE OVER THE PRACTICE OF MENTAL CONCENTRATION AND SELF-IMPROVEMENT, WORK IS SAID TO BE THE MEANS. By working in the world with neither the egocentric concept of agency nor the egocentric desires for the fruits of those actions, we are causing *vasanas* to play out without creating any new precipitate of fresh impressions.*

The metaphor used here is borrowed from horse riding, and it is very powerful in its suggestions. When a wild horse is being broken in, for some time, it will ride the rider before the rider can ride it. If one desires to bring a steed under perfect control, there is a period when, with one leg in the stirrup, the individual has to hang on to the saddle and with

---

आरुरुक्षोर्मुनेर्योगं कर्म कारणमुच्यते ।
योगारूढस्य तस्यैव शमः कारणमुच्यते ॥ ३ ॥

ārurukṣormruyogaṁ karma keeraṇamucyate
yogārūḍhasya tasyaiva śamaḥ kāraṇamucyate 3.

* Refer 'General Introduction'

the other leg on the ground, must learn to kick himself off from the ground and spring up and throw his legs over the back of the animal, until he sits with the steed completely between his own legs. Having mounted, it is easy to control the animal but, till then, the rider, in his attempt to mount the horse, must pass through a stage when he is totally neither on the horse nor on the ground.

In the beginning, we are merely workers in the world; desire-prompted and ego-driven, we sweat and toil, weep and sob. When an individual gets tired of such activities, he comes to desire to mount the steed of the mind. Such an individual, desiring to bring the mind under his control and ride over it (*Arurukshuh*) takes upon himself the same work as before, but without the ego and egocentric desires. Such desireless activities undertaken in the *Yajna*-spirit explained earlier, (IV-18,19 20, 21, and 25 to 30.) cleanse the mind of its past impressions and integrate the entire inner equipment. When thus the required amount of concentration has been gained by the individual as a result of the *vasana*-purgation effected, he is to stop his activities slowly and apply himself more and more to live in deeper meditation. When once his mind has been conquered, and his agitations have become well controlled, the seeker in that state of mental growth and development, is termed as 'having mounted the steed of the mind' (*Yoga-Arudhah*). To such an individual, in that state of mental equipoise and self-application, 'quiescence' (*shama*) is the means for gaining higher perfection and self-growth.

By thus prescribing two methods at the two distinct stages of the individual's growth, it is meant that they are not contradictory. Selfless activity is good at one stage but afterwards it becomes a positive agitation which brings the mind down from its serener flights, and frequently bumps it on the ground with a shattering shock. Specially prepared milk powder, diluted with hot water, is the full diet for an infant. But the same feeding bottle will not satisfy the growing demands of a boy vigorously working and mischievously knocking about all day. The more solid bread and butter are his diet. We need not be great intellectuals to understand that buttered toast will choke and kill an infant.

Similarly here, work without selfishness is healthy for the beginner, but a developed seeker needs more and more quietude and self-withdrawal for growing in the steady contemplation of life within. Earlier, 'work-without-self' is the means; afterwards 'work-on-self' is the means. This process is continued until, working or not working, through meditation, it is realised that the Self alone is the essence in the ego which, till then, was recognised as the only reality.

In this sense of the term, we clearly know how ritualism has a definite place in the scheme of things as mapped out by the *Vedantin* Seers of unimpeachable intellectual eminence.

WHEN IS A MAN SAID TO BE A *YOGARUDHAH* - TO HAVE ATTUNED TO *YOGA*? ... THE ANSWER FOLLOWS:

4. *When a man is not attached to sense-objects or to actions, having renounced all thoughts, then he is said to have attuned to YOGA.*

It is the experience of everyone, and therefore, it is not very difficult for a young seeker to know the state of an aspirant (*Arurukshuh*). It has been said by the Lord that so long as we are in the state of seeking, the path of Self-

---

यदा हि नेन्द्रियार्थेषु न कर्मस्वनुषज्जते ।
सर्वसंकल्पसंन्यासी योगारूढस्तदोच्यते ॥ ४ ॥

yadā hi nendriyārtheṣu na karmasvanuṣajjate
sarvasaṅ kaloasanyāsī yogarūḍhastadocyate 4.

Perfection lies through the highroad of selfless activity. Withdrawal from activity is to be undertaken only when you have reached the state of mental mastery (*Yogarudhah*). To renounce activity at an earlier stage, would be as unhealthy as to continue disturbing the mind with activities after having reached the second stage, where, we are told, quiescence is the means for gathering speed in our flight through meditation. Naturally, it is necessary for the seeker to know when exactly he reaches the second stage, indicated here by the term *Yogarudhah*.

In this stanza, Krishna is pointing out the physical and mental conditions of one who has broken in the steed of his mind and ridden it. He says that when one is feeling no mental attachments, either to the sense-objects or to the actions in the outer world, it is one of the symptoms of perfect mastery over the mind. This should not be over-stressed to a dreary literal meaning, making it a grotesque caricature of Truth. It only means that the mind of a seeker in the meditation seat is so perfectly withdrawn from the external world of sense-objects and activities, that it is perfect in its equipoise at the time of self-application. The sense organs can run into the channels of sense-objects only when the mind is flowing out of the organs. If the mind is kept engaged in the contemplation of a great Truth, providing a larger quota of an ampler joy in the inner bosom, it will no more go hunting for bits of joy in the gutters of sensuality. A well-fed pet dog will not seek the public dustbins for its food.

When thus the mind is not gushing out either through the sense-channels nor through the fields of its egocentric activities, it becomes completely engaged in the contemplation of the greater truth - the Self. Here the term used to indicate complete non-attachment, is to be noted very carefully. The Sanskrit word *anu-shajjate* is a word-symbol created by prefixing an indeclinable *anu* to the verb *saj*, meaning 'attached'. The prefix *anu* indicates 'not a bit'. Therefore, the term used here forbids even traces of attachment either to the sense-objects or to the fields of activity.

When the mind has been withdrawn from the sense-organs and completely detached from all its external physical activities, it is possible that it is still tossed and agitated by the gurglings of its own inner instincts of willing and wishing, desiring and earning. This power of *sankalpa* can bring more storms into the bosom of a man than the disturbances his mind could ever receive from the external world. Krishna indicates here that he who has gained a complete mastery over his mind is one who has not only withdrawn himself from all sense-contacts and activities in the outer world, but has also dried up all the *sankalpa*-disturbances* in his own mind. Such an individual is, at the moment of meditation, in that inward state which is described here as *Yogarudhah*. It is clear that, to such an individual, meditation can be intensified only by quietude (*shama*).

WHEN A MAN HAS ATTAINED *YOGA*, THEN THE SELF IS RAISED BY THE SELF, FROM THE NUMEROUS EVILS OF FINITE EXISTENCE THEREFORE :

5. *Let a man lift himself by his own Self alone, and let him not lower himself; for, this Self alone is the friend of oneself, and this Self is the enemy of oneself.*

उद्धरेदात्मनात्मानं नात्मानमवसादयेत् ।
आत्मैव ह्यात्मनो बन्धुरात्मैव रिपुरात्मनः ॥ ५ ॥

uddharedātmanātmānaṁ nātmānamavasādayet
ātmaiva hyātmano bandhurātmaiva ripurātmanaḥ 5.

* Oh Desire, I know where your roots lie. You are born of *Sankalpa*. I shall not think of you and you will cease to exist along with your roots. – *Mahabharata, Shanti Parva: 177-25*

As a complete *shastra*, the *Geeta* has to be faithful to Truth and Truth alone, irrespective of what the tradition of the country, at a given period, might have made the faithful ones believe. It is not very unhealthy to believe that Grace from an external source is constantly helping a true seeker striving on his path - but this is really healthy only when this thought is correspondingly complemented with sufficiently intense self-effort. MAN SHOULD UPLIFT HIMSELF BY HIMSELF is an open statement declared by no less a person than Lord Krishna Himself. It is not cooed in a playful mood in the company of the *gopis* on the Jamuna-banks at a hilarious hour of laughter and play, but roared to Arjuna on the battlefield at a serious moment of His life's fulfilment as an *Avatara*. Man, if he wants to exalt himself into the greater cultural and spiritual possibilities now lying dormant in him, has to raise the lower in himself to the greater perfection that is the true and eternal core in himself.

Everyone has in himself a picture of the ideal. This intellectual conception of ourselves is always very vivid in each one of us. But unfortunately, this ideal remains only in the realm of thought and is not lived in the world of activity. Intellectually we may have a clear and vivid picture of what we should be, but mentally and physically, we behave as though we were the opposites of our own ideal concepts. The gulf between the IDEAL-ME and the ACTUAL-ME is the measure of man's fall from his perfection.

Most of us are generally unconscious of this duality in ourselves. We mistake ourselves to be the ideal and are generally blind to our own ACTUAL imperfections. Thus, we find a notoriously selfish man in society warmly and sincerely criticising the slightest trace of selfishness in his neighbour. In a world of no mirrors, it is possible that a squint-eyed man may laugh at another squint-eyed person because the one who laughs knows not the angle at which his own eyeballs are facing each other!!

Within ourselves, if we, carefully watch, we can discover that intellectually we have a clear concept of a morally strong, ethically perfect, physically loving and socially disciplined man that 'we should be'; but in the mental zones of our emotions and feelings, however, we are tantalised by our own attachments, likes and dislikes, loves and hatreds, appetites and passions. Hence we behave like curs fed by the wayside gutters and ever quarrelling with others of the same ilk over dry and marrowless bones!!

As long as the individual has not realised the existence of this dual personality in himself, there cannot be any religion for him. If an individual has discovered that there is 'enough in him to be divided into two portions', and when he wants to keep the lower as brilliant and chaste as the higher, the technique that he will have to employ to fulfil this aspiration is called RELIGION.

Mind is the saboteur that enchants us away from perfection, to be a slave to the flesh and the external objects of brittle satisfaction. Mind is the conditioning that distorts the ideal and creates the lower satanic, sensuous self in us, which is to be brought into unison with the intellect, the equipment for the higher Self to manifest. In short, when the rational and discriminative capacities of a limited intellect are brought to bear their authority upon the wavering and wandering, sense-mongering mind, the lower is brought under discipline and made to attune with the nobler and the diviner in us. The processes by which the lower is brought under the direct management and discipline of the higher are all together called the spiritual techniques.

This process of self-rehabilitation and self-redemption of

the Satan in us cannot be executed by inviting tenders and giving the contract to the lowest bidder! Each will have to do it all by himself: "ALONE TO THE ALONE ALL ALONE" IS THE WAY. No *Guru* can take the responsibility; no scripture can promise this redemption; no altar can, with its divine blessings, make the lower the higher. The lower must necessarily be trained slowly and steadily to accept and come under the influence of the discipline of the higher. In this process, the teacher, the scripture, and the houses-of-God, all have their proper appointed duties and limited influences. But the actual happening depends upon how far we ourselves learn to haul ourselves out from the gutters of misunderstanding in ourselves.

So far *Bhagawan* has indicated an exhaustive treatment which may be, in many of its aspects, considered as equivalent to the modern psychological process called introspection. Realising our own weaknesses, rejecting the false, asserting the better, and trying to live, generally, as best as we can, the higher way-of-life, is the process of introspection. But this is only half of the entire process and not the whole of it.

The other half also is insisted upon, here, by Krishna. It is not sufficient that we look within, come to note our weaknesses, erase them, substitute the opposite good qualities, and develop in ourselves the better. We must also see to it, that, whatever little conquests we might have made out of Satan's province are not again handed back to Satan's dominion. Krishna warns, almost in the same breath, "DO NOT ALLOW THE SELF THEREAFTER TO FALL DOWN AND BE DRAGGED AGAIN" to the old level of the cheaper way of existence.

The second line of the stanza contains a glorious idea shaped into a beauty of expression which almost immortalises Vyasa. We are considered as both our own friend and our own enemy. Any intelligent man observing and analysing life will vouchsafe for the truth of the statement, but here, more is meant philosophically, than meets the eye. Generally, we do not fully understand the import when we say THE SELF IS THE FRIEND OF THE SELF.

The lower in us can raise itself to the attunement of the Higher, but the Higher can influence only when the lower is available for Its influence. To the extent the lesser in us surrenders itself to the influence of the Higher, to that extent; It can serve the lower as a great friend. But if the lower refuses to come under the influence of the Diviner in us, the Divine Presence is accused as an enemy of ourselves. This is so because the dynamism of life provides us Its energy both for our life of higher aspirations and the life of low temptations.

Ultimately, it is for the aspirant himself to accept the responsibility for blessing or damning himself. The potentiality for improvement, the chances for self-growth, the strength to haul ourselves out from our own misconceptions, are ever open for employment. But it all depends upon how we make use of them.

NOW IT MAY BE ASKED: "WHAT SORT OF A MAN IS THE FRIEND OF HIMSELF AND WHAT SORT OF A MAN IS THE ENEMY OF HIMSELF?" THE ANSWER FOLLOWS:

6. *The Self is the friend of the self for him who has conquered himself by the Self, but to the unconquered self, the Self stands in the position of an enemy like the (external) foe.*

The Divine in us becomes a friend when, under its influence, the Satan in us gets converted. To the extent, the

---

बन्धुरात्मात्मनस्तस्य येनात्मैवात्मना जितः ।
अनात्मनस्तु शत्रुत्वे वर्तेतात्मैव शत्रुवत् ॥ ६ ॥

bandhurātmātmanastasya yenātmaivātmanā jitaḥ
anātmanastu śatrutve vartetātmaiva śatruvat 6.

lower ego withdraws itself from its identifications with the body and the sense organs, feelings and ideas relating to the extrovert life, to that extent that given ego has come under the salutory influence of the nobler and the Diviner. To such an ego, available for corrective proselytisation, the Self is a friend. But where the little self remains a constant rebel against the Higher, to that unconquered-self, the Diviner Self is as if inimical in Its attitude.

In short, the higher Self becomes a friend to the lower which is available for and which allows itself to be conquered by the higher influence; and the Diviner becomes inimical to the undivine when the lower limited ego remains unconquered by the higher aspirations in us. This stanza is an elucidating annotation on the previous one.

EARLIER,* THE STATE OF MENTAL EQUIPOISE, CALLED *YOGARUDHAH*, WAS EXPLAINED. WHAT EXACTLY IS THE FULFILMENT OF SUCH A STATE IN *YOGA* IS BEING EXPLAINED NOW:

7. *The Supreme Self of him who is self-controlled and peaceful, is balanced in cold and heat, pleasure and pain, as also in honour and dishonour.*

When a seeker has come in his inner life to the state explained as *Yogarudhah*, and when in that state of equipoise, the mind is held steadfast in contemplation of the Supreme, the self-controlled one, in all serenity, is capable of

---

जितात्मनः प्रशान्तस्य परमात्मा समाहितः ।
शीतोष्णसुखदुःखेषु तथा मानापमानयोः ॥ ७ ॥

jitātmanaḥ praśāntasya paramātmā samāhitaḥ
śītoṣṇasukhaduḥkheṣu tathā mānāpamānayoḥ 7.

* Ibid., 3 and 4

maintaining his consistency of meditation in all circumstances, favourable and adverse, at all levels of his personality. In the second line of the stanza, it is clearly indicated that no excuse in the world is sufficiently strong to justify a seeker's inability to continue keeping the awareness of his Eternal Nature in himself.

Three pairs-of-opposites are indicated here as: (i) heat and cold; (ii) joy and sorrow; (iii) honour and dishonour. In enumerations of these three pairs of conditions, Krishna is exhausting, through the mention of the types, all possible threats to his equipoise and tranquillity that an individual may get from the outer world.

HEAT AND COLD—these are stimuli that are felt and experienced by the body, at the body level. Whether in heat or in cold, thoughts, we know, do not expand or shrink, and the ideas cannot shiver or perspire. All these reactions can be only in the body, and therefore, Krishna is indicating by this pair all the vicissitudes that may visit the body, such as health and disease, youth and old age, etc.

PLEASURE AND PAIN—by the second pair-of-opposites, the Lord is symbolically indicating all the destinies suffered in the mental zone. Pleasure and pain are experienced not by the body but always by the mind. It includes all the tyrannies of our different emotions which might threaten the mental arena, at one time or another in a man's life. Hatred and love, affection and jealousy, kindness and cruelty... a thousand varieties of emotions may storm the 'within'; but none of them is an excuse, according to Krishna, for the diligent and the sincere to lose hold of himself from the steadfastness in his contemplation.

HONOUR AND DISHONOUR—the last pair-of-opposites shows how no threat of any storm in the intellectual zone is a sufficient plea to sympathise with an individual who has fallen away from the state-of-Perfection. Honour and dishonour are evaluated and reacted to only by the intellect.

Thus, by these three representative pairs-of-opposites from the three worlds of the body, the mind, and the intellect, Krishna is trying to exhaust all possibilities of obstacles in man's life. Then he adds that in all such conditions, the Supreme Self is to be the object of constant realisation for one who is perfectly self-controlled and serene. He ever remains unruffled in all circumstances, favourable or unfavourable; in all environments - good or bad; in all company - wise or foolish.

WHAT IS THE GLORY OF SUCH AN INDIVIDUAL? WHAT DOES HE BECOME BY SUCH A PROCESS? WHY SHOULD HE GO THROUGH SUCH A LABORIOUS INWARD TRAINING AND SELF-DISCIPLINE?

8. *The YOGI who is satisfied with knowledge and wisdom, who remains unshaken, who has conquered the senses, to whom a lump of earth, a stone and gold are the same, is said to be harmonised (i.e., is said to have attained NIRVIKALPA SAMADHI).*

Such an individual, self-controlled and serene, whohas constantly come to contemplate upon the nature of the Self as understood from the *shastras*, through all his circumstances in life, soon becomes, says Krishna, filled with a divine satisfaction and becomes an unshakable *Yogi*. Here, the satisfaction is not merely the joy that an intelligent man comes to enjoy when he carefully studies and masters *Vedanta*. According to Krishna, the satisfied contentment which a true

---

ज्ञानविज्ञानतृप्तात्मा कूटस्थो विजितेन्द्रियः ।
युक्त इत्युच्यते योगी समलोष्टाश्मकाञ्चनः ॥ ८ ॥
jñānavijñānatṛptātmā kūṭastho vijitendriyaḥ
yukta ityucyate yogī samaloṣṭāśmakāñcanaḥ 8.

Yogi comes to experience is much superior to the thrilled joys experienced in all intense studies.

The knowledge gained through study is indicated here by the term *Jnana*, and the first-hand experience gained by the seeker of the Self in himself is called the Knowledge of direct perception, which is termed here, in the *Geeta*-vocabulary, as *Vijnana*.*

UNCHANGING, IMMUTABLE (*Kootasthah*)—This is the term used for the Eternal Self. Its expressiveness becomes apparent when we understand that the term *'koota'* in Sanskrit, means the 'anvil'. The anvil is that upon which the blacksmith places his red-hot iron-bits and hammers them into the required shapes. In spite of the hammerings, nothing happens to the anvil. The anvil resists all modifications and change, but allows all other things to get changed upon it. Thus, the term *'kootasthah'* means that which 'remains anvil-like' and though itself suffers no change, it makes others change.

He is a saint and has the full-blown fragrance of perfection, who has sought and discovered a perfect contentment which arises out of this subjective experience of what the *shastra* says, and has come in contact with the Self that changes not. And such a saint becomes tranquil and a master of equal-vision in all conditions of life. To him, a clod of mud, a precious stone and costly gold are all the same. This equanimity of mind in profit and loss, at the acquisition of precious things or at the presentation of mere filth, is the very test to show that the individual has spiritually evolved and that to him, no gain can bring any extra joy, or any loss – any sorrow!!

---

* It is Shankara's interpretation and the *Acharya* distinguishes between *Jnana* and *Vijnana*, inasmuch as, according to this father of modern *Vedanta*, *Jnana* is 'book knowledge' and *Vijnana* is 'wisdom gained through direct realization' of the things so learnt.

In my dream, I earned a lot of wealth, but ere I enjoyed it fully, I woke up to my waking-state, poverty. In my destitution, when I am suffering the pangs of hunger, I will not feel, in any sense of the term, consoled by the thought that I was rich in my dream and that in my dream-bank I had my dream-riches in its dream-vaults! Similarly, to a master who has gained perfection and transcended the world of the mind and intellect, and achieved the true awakening of the Soul, thereafter, a lump of earth, a piece of gold or a precious stone of this world are all equally futile things.

They cannot add even a jot of extra joy or pain unto him. He has become the sole proprietor of Bliss Absolute. To *Kubera*, the treasurer of the heavens, a kingdom on the globe is no profit and has no power to make him dance in ecstasy!!

MOREOVER:

9. *He who is of the same mind to the good-hearted, friends, relatives, enemies, the indifferent, the neutral, the hateful, the righteous and the unrighteous, excels.*

In the previous stanza it was indicated that the man-of-perfection develops equal-vision as far as things of the world are concerned. The universe is not made of things alone, but is constituted of beings also. Now the doubt arises, as to what will be the relationship of a perfect man of equipoise with the living kingdom of beings around him? Will he negate the whole lot as unreal? In his preoccupations with the experience of the Eternal and the Immortal, which is the substratum for the entire world of changing phenomenal beings, will he

---

सुहृन्मित्रार्युदासीनमध्यस्थद्वेष्यबन्धुषु ।
साधुष्वपि च पापेषु समबुद्धिर्विशिष्यते ॥ ९ ॥

suhṛnmitrāryudāsīnamadhyasthadveṣyabandhuṣu
sādhuṣvapi ca pāpeṣu samabuddhirviśiṣyate 9.

ignore to serve the world and help the living generation? This idea is taken up here for discussion.

Such a man of excellence, says Krishna, regards all relationships with an equal love and consideration, be they FRIENDS OR FOES, OR INDIFFERENT OR NEUTRAL, OR HATEFUL, OR NEAREST RELATIONS. In his equal-vision, all of them are equally important and he embraces, in his Infinitude, all of them with the same warmth and ardour. His love knows no distinction between the righteous and the unrighteous, the good and the bad. To him a sinner is but an ego living in its misunderstandings, since sin is only a mistake of the soul and not a positive blasphemy against Itself. Rama Tirtha beautifully expresses it when he says that 'we are punished BY the sin and not FOR it'.

In the right understanding of his own self and the resulting realisation of his own Self, he becomes the Self everywhere. He discovers a unity in the perceived diversity and a subtle rhythm in the obvious discord in the world outside. To him, who has realised himself to be the Self which is all-pervading, the entire universe becomes his own Self, and therefore, his relationship with every other part of the universe is equal and same. Whether I get wounded in the hand or the leg, on the back or in the front, on the head or on the shoulder, it is the same to me, since I am identifying equally with my head, my trunk, and my legs, as myself.

THROUGH WHAT METHODS CAN ONE ATTAIN THIS HIGHEST GOAL AND ASSURE FOR HIMSELF THE SUREST RESULT? IT IS EXPLAINED:

10. *Let the YOGI try constantly to keep the mind steady, remaining in solitude, alone, with the mind and body controlled, free from hope and greed.*

In the Mahabharata, Krishna is conceived as a voluntary manifestation of the Supreme and hence He is addressed as Shri Krishna *Paramatman*. He is giving here an advice to His most intimate friend and life's companion, Arjuna, on the methods of self-development and the techniques of self-perfection. Even then, it is not said that the Lord will give him a secret method by which he will not have to make any struggle at all and that the entire responsibility will be borne by the Creator of the Universe. The very opening words of the stanza weed out any such false hopes in the minds of the seekers. "O MAN OF SELF-CONTROL (*YOGI*), YOU SHOULD CONSTANTLY PRACTISE CONCENTRATION." It is only through the practice of meditation that a mortal can grow out of his weaknesses and flower forth culturally into the greater perfection-possibilities within himself.

Details of how the meditation is to be conducted are given in the rest of the stanza. SITTING IN SOLITUDE, one should practise meditation. This word has been, unnecessarily, so overstretched in recent times in India that the term 'meditation' brings a sense of horror and fear into the minds of the early seekers. It does not mean that meditation can be practised only in the jungles and in the solitude of caves. It only means that the seeker should try to withdraw himself from his mental and physical

---

योगी युञ्जीत सततमात्मानं रहसि स्थित: ।
एकाकी यतचित्तात्मा निराशीरपरिग्रह: ॥ १० ॥

yogī yañjīta satatamātmānaṁ rahasi sthitaḥ
ekākī yatacittātmā nirāśīraparigrahaḥ 10.

preoccupations and should retire to a corner in his house, for the purpose of early meditation.

Solitude can be gained only when there is a mental withdrawal from the world outside. One, who is full of desires and constantly meditating upon the sense-objects, cannot hope to gain any solitude even in a virgin forest. Again, the word solitude (*Rahasi*) suggests a meaning of secretiveness, indicating that religion should not be a broadcast of self-advertisement, but must be a set of true values of life, secretly practised within the heart, ordering our way of thinking and encouraging our pursuit of the nobler values in life.

PHYSICALLY ALONE (*Ekaki*)—for the purpose of meditation, when one strives, his success in inward quietude will be directly proportional to the amount of self-control he is practising in his daily life. Self-control is not possible unless we know how to free ourselves from the 'eagerness to possess' and the 'anxiety to hoard'. To renounce our preoccupations with our endless plans for possessing more is indicated here by the term 'free from hope' (*Nirashih*). And the term 'free from possessions' (*Aparigraha*) indicates all our anxieties in saving, hoarding and protecting what we possess.

When one, well established in these necessary physical self-controls and essential mental and intellectual habits, sits meditating upon the Truth in all secrecy, he is a true seeker striving on the right path to achieve and acquire the highest that is possible in life.

NOW, IN THE SEQUEL, THE LORD PROCEEDS TO PRESCRIBE FOR THE *YOGA*-PRACTITIONER PARTICULAR MODES OF SITTING, EATING, RECREATION AND THE LIKE, THAT ARE AIDS TO *YOGA*. FIRST OF ALL, HE EXPLAINS THE MODE OF SITTING AS FOLLOWS:

11. *Having, in a clean spot, established a firm seat of his own, neither too high nor too low, made of a cloth, a skin and KUSHA-grass, one over the other...*

If meditation is the path by which one can gain tranquillity and equal-vision within oneself, it is necessary that, in this textbook on self-perfection, Lord Krishna should give a complete and exhaustive explanation of the technique of meditation. In order to fulfil this demand, hereunder we get a few verses explaining the position, the means and the ends of a meditator at work.

In these words is a description of the seat and the place for perfect meditation.

IN A CLEAN PLACE—this is important inasmuch as the external conditions have a direct bearing upon the human mind. In a clean place there is more chance for the seeker to maintain a cleaner mental condition. Apart from this, commentators explain that the place should be rid of mosquitoes, houseflies, bugs, ants and such other creatures that may disturb the beginner's mental concentration which he is trying to turn inward.

In his seat, the meditator is asked to sit steady (*Sthiram*). Without moving the physical body at short intervals and without swinging the body either forward and backward or sideways, the seeker is asked to get firmly established on his seat, because physical movement contributes immensely to the shattering of mental concentration and inner equipoise.

शुचौ देशे प्रतिष्ठाप्य स्थिरमासनमात्मनः ।
नात्युच्छ्रितं नातिनीचं चैलाजिनकुशोत्तरम् ॥ ११ ॥

śucau deśe pratiṣṭhāpya sthiramāsanamātmanaḥ
nātyucchritaṁ nātinīcaṁ cailājinakuśottaram 11.

* Refer Swamiji's 'Meditation and Life'.

This is very well realised by all of us, if we only remember our attitude when we are sincerely and seriously thinking over something. In order to get established in a firm posture it would be advisable to sit in any 'comfortable seat' (*Asana*), with the vertebral column erect, fingers interlocked and hands thrown in front.*

Adding more details, Krishna says that the seat of meditation 'should not be too high or too low'. If it is too high there will be a sense of insecurity in the meditator, created as a result of the instinct of self-preservation. He will find it difficult to extricate himself from his outer-world-consciousness and plunge himself into the inner. Again, we are told that the seat should not be too low; this is to avoid the mistake of meditating in any damp underground cellar, where perchance, the seeker may develop rheumatic pains in his body. During meditation the heart-action becomes slightly low, and, to the extent we are withdrawn into ourselves, even the blood pressure falls. At such a time of low resistance, if the place be damp, there is a great chance of a seeker developing pains in his joints. To avoid such troubles, the warning is given here.

When the *Geeta* is out to give details, She leaves nothing to the imagination of the student. The exhaustive details regarding the ideal seat for meditation is an example. It is said here that a mattress of *Kusha*-grass on the ground, with a deerskin covered with a piece of cloth on top of it, is the perfect seat for long meditations. Dampness is avoided by the *Kusha*-grass which keeps the seat warm during winter. In summer the skin becomes too hot and also some seekers are allergic to the animal skin, especially when their skin has become slightly moist with perspiration. This contingency is being avoided by spreading over the skin a piece of clean cloth. Having thus established himself firmly on the meditation seat, prepared as above, what exactly he is to do mentally and intellectually, is now explained.

WHAT SHOULD BE DONE AFTER ESTABLISHING ONESELF UPON THE PREPARED SEAT?

12. *There, having made the mind one-pointed, with the actions of the mind and the senses controlled, let him, seated on the seat, practise YOGA, for the purification of the self.*

However scientifically prepared it might be, to sit in an appropriate *Asana* (seat) is not, in itself, *Yoga*. The appropriate physical condition is conducive to generating the right mental attitude for the spiritual practices, but a mere physical posture cannot in itself, guarantee any spiritual self-development.

In this verse, Krishna is giving what the seeker should practise in his seat of meditation. Having made the body steadfast in posture, how one should employ his mind and intellect in the process of divine contemplation and meditation is the theme being discussed here. The first instruction given is that "YOU SHOULD MAKE THE MIND SINGLE-POINTED". This instruction cannot be worked out by a seeker unless he knows how he can bring about this necessary inward condition in himself. It is very cheap and easy for a *Rishi* to advise the members of the confused generation to make their minds integrated.

Such an advice, when not sufficiently supported by practical details, becomes a mere high-sounding philosophy and not a useful guidance for the seekers. The *Geeta*, being a

---

तत्रैकाग्रं मनः कृत्वा यतचित्तेन्द्रियक्रियः ।
उपविश्यासने युञ्ज्याद्योगमात्मविशुद्धये ॥ १२ ॥

tatraikāgnaṁ manaḥ kṛtvā yatacittendriyakriyaḥ
upaviśyāsane yuñjyādyogamātmaviśuddhaye 12.

textbook which translates philosophy into life in its typical spirit, here the stanza immediately explains how we can bring the mind to an ideal single-pointedness.

SUBDUING THE FACULTY OF IMAGINATION AND THE ACTIVITIES OF THE SENSE ORGANS—this is the instruction given by Krishna. Single-pointedness is the very potent nature of the mind. The mind gets stunned by its own silence, or confused and even mad when it gets dynamised by either the inner forces of its own surging imaginations or the outward pull exerted by the hallucinations of the sense organs. If these two venues of dissipation are blocked, instantaneously the mind becomes, by its own nature, single-pointed.

Thus, seated on the prepared meditation-seat, and making the mind single-pointed through the process of subduing mental imaginations and controlling the wild activities of the sense organs, the seeker is encouraged to practise *Yoga*. To keep the single-pointed mind constantly in the steady contemplation of the Ultimate Self is the inner *Yoga* that has been mentioned here.

Naturally, every seeker would desire to know why he should meditate thus. In order to remove all misunderstandings of the meditators whether they would thereby directly come face to face with the *Atman*, Krishna here appends to the verse the effects of such meditation. Through steady and regular meditation, the *shastra* promises only inner purification. Agitations in the mind are its impurities. A purified mind is that which has no agitations and when the mind has thus become pure and steady, the Consciousness, looking at the steady reflection of Itself, comes to rediscover Its own Real Nature. This process is similar to the techniques by which we understand ourselves while consulting our own reflections in a mirror.

THE EXTERNAL SEAT HAS BEEN DESCRIBED. NOW, WHAT SHOULD BE THE POSTURE OF THE BODY? LISTEN:

13. *Let him firmly hold his body, head and neck erect and still, gazing at the tip of his nose, without looking around.*

After describing in detail the arrangement of the seat of meditation and how to sit there properly, Lord Krishna had thereafter explained what the meditator should do with his mind and intellect. He has also said that the mind should be made single-pointed by subduing all the activities of the sense-organs and the imagination. Adding more details to the technique of meditation, it is now said that the meditator should firmly hold his body in such a fashion that his vertebral column is completely erect. The head and the neck should be erect in this posture, which is geometrically perpendicular to the horizontal seat upon which the *Yogi* is firmly settling himself; it is pointedly indicated that he should hold his body 'firmly'.

This term should not be misunderstood as holding the body in tension. 'Firmly' here means that the body should not be held stiff but relaxed, it must be held in such a manner that there should not be any tendency to swing forward and backward or sideways from right to left.

The seeker, having thus made himself ready for meditation, should 'GAZE AT THE TIP OF THE NOSE'. This does not mean that an individual should, with half-opened eyes, deliberately turn his eyeballs towards the 'tip of his own nose'. There are many seekers who have come to suffer physical discomforts, such as headaches, giddiness, exhaustion, tensions, etc., because they have tried to follow this instruction too literally. Sankara, in his commentary, has definitely given us the right direction. He says that the term

---

समं कायशिरोग्रीवं धारयन्नचलं स्थिरः ।
संप्रेक्ष्य नासिकाग्रं स्वं दिशश्चानवलोकयन् ॥ १३ ॥

samaṁ kāyaśirogrīvaṁ dhārayannacalaṁ sthiraḥ
samprekṣya nāsikāgram svaṁ diśaścānavalokayan 13.

here means only that the meditator, while meditating, should have his attention 'AS THOUGH TURNED TOWARDS THE TIP OF HIS OWN NOSE'. That this interpretation is not a laboured and artificial intellectualism of the *Acharya* is clearly borne out by the next phrase in the second line.

NOT LOOKING AROUND—this instruction clearly shows what was in the mind of Krishna when he gave the instruction that the meditator should direct his entire attention towards the tip of his own nose - so that his concentration may not be dissipated and his mind may not wander all around. Where the eyes go, there the mind faithfully follows; this is the law. That is why, when an individual is confused, we find that his gaze is not steady. Many a time, we judge another individual as behaving funny or suspiciously, and in all such cases, our only evidence is nothing other than the unsteadiness in his gaze. Watch anyone who is indecisive and who is unsteady in his determination and you can immediately observe that the individual's look is definitely unsteady and confusedly wandering.

MOREOVER:

14. *Serene-minded, fearless, firm in the vow of BRAHMACHARYA, having controlled the mind, thinking on Me and balanced, let him sit, having Me as the Supreme Goal.*

When the meditator has thus practised meditation for a certain period of time, as a result of his practice, he comes to experience a larger share of quietude and peace in his mind.

प्रशान्तात्मा विगतभीर्ब्रह्मचारिव्रते स्थितः ।
मनः संयम्य मच्चित्तो युक्त आसीत मत्परः ॥ १४ ॥

praśāntātmā vigatabhīrbrahmcārivrate sthitaḥ
manaḥ saṁyamya maccitto yukta āsīta matparaḥ 14.

This extremely subtle form of inward peace is indicated here by the term '*Prashanta*'. This inward silence, a revelling in an atmosphere of extreme joy and contentment - is the exact situation in which the individual can be trained to express the nobler and the diviner qualities, which are inherent in the Divine Self.

A meditator invariably finds it difficult to scale the higher realms of experience due to sheer psychological fear-complex. As the *Yogi* slowly and steadily gets unwound from his sensuous *vasanas*, he gets released, as it were, from the cruel embrace of his own mental octopus. At this moment of transcendence, the unprepared seeker feels mortally afraid of the thought that he is getting himself dissolved into NOTHINGNESS. The ego, because of its long habit of living in close proximity to its own limitations, finds it hard even to believe that there is an Existence Supreme, Divine and Infinite. One is reminded of the story of the stranded fisher-women who complained that they could not get any sleep at all when they had to spend a night in a flower-shop, till they put their baskets very near their noses. Away from our pains, we dread to enter the Infinite Bliss!

This sense of fear is the death-knell of all spiritual progress. Even if progress were to reach the bosom of such an individual, he would be compelled to reject it, because of the rising storm of his subjective fear.

Even though the mind has become extremely peaceful and joyous, and has renounced all its sense of fear through the study of the scriptures and continuous practice of regular meditation, progress is not assured. The possibility of failure shall ever hang over the head of the seeker, unless he struggles hard to get established in perfect *Brahmacharya*.

THE ASCETICISM OF *BRAHMACHARYA*—Here the

phrase implies not only its *Upanishadic* implications, but definitely something more original, especially when it comes from Lord Krishna's mouth and that too, in the context of the *Geeta*. *Brahmacharya*, generally translated as 'celibacy', has a particular meaning, but the term has also a wider and a more general implication. *Brahmacharya* is not ONLY the control of the sex-impulses but is also the practice of self-control in all avenues of sense-impulses and sense-satisfactions. Unless the seeker has built up a perfect cage of intelligent self-control, the entire world-of-objects will flood his bosom, to bring therein a state of unending chaos. A mind thus agitated by the inflow of sense stimuli, is a mind that is completely dissipated and ruined.

Apart from this meaning, which is essentially indicative of the goal, or rather, a state of complete detachment from the mind's courting of the external world-of-objects, there is a deeper implication to this significant and famous term. *Brahmacharya*, as such, is a term that can be dissolved in Sanskrit to mean 'wandering in *Brahma-Vichara*'. To engage our mind in the contemplation of the Self, the Supreme Reality, is the saving factor that can really help us in withdrawing the mind from external objects.

The human mind must have one field or another to engage itself in. Unless it is given some inner field to meditate upon, it will not be in a position to retire from its extrovert preoccupations. This is the secret behind all success in 'total celibacy'. The successful *Yogi* need not be gazed at as a rare phenomenon in nature. His success can be the success of all, only if we know how to establish ourselves in this inward self-control. It is because people are ignorant of the positive methods to be practised for a continuous and successful negation and complete rejection of the charms of the sense organs that they invariably fail in their endeavour.

Naturally, it becomes easy for the individual who has gained in himself all the three above-mentioned qualities to control and direct the newfound energies in himself. The inward peace, an attribute of the intellect, comes only when the discriminative faculty is relatively quiet. Fearlessness brings about a great control over the exhausting thought commotions in the mental zone. *Brahmacharya,* in its aspect of sense-withdrawal, lends a larger share of physical quietude. Therefore, when, by the above process, the intellect, mind and body are all controlled and brought to the maximum amount of peace and quietude, the way-of-life pursued by the seeker provides for him a large saving of mental energy which would otherwise have been spent away in sheer dissipation.

This newly discovered and fully availed-of strength makes the mind stronger and stronger, so that the seeker experiences in himself a growing capacity to withdraw his wandering mind unto himself and to fix his entire thoughts 'in the contemplation of Me, the Self'.

The concluding instruction in this most significant verse in the chapter is: "LET HIM SIT IN *YOGA* HAVING ME AS HIS SUPREME GOAL". It has been already said in an earlier chapter that the meditator should continue meditation and ere long *(achirena)*, he will have the fulfilment of his meditation. The same idea is suggested here. Having made the mind tame, and keeping it away from its own endless dissipations, we are instructed to keep the single-pointed mind in contemplation of the Divine Self and His Eternal Nature. Immediately following this instruction is the order that we should remain in this attitude of meditation, seeking nothing else but "ME AS THE SUPREME GOAL". Ere long, in the silence and quietude within, the withering mind and other equipments will exhaust themselves, and the seeker will wake up to realise his own Infinite, Eternal, Blissful and quiet Nature, the Self.

15. *Thus, always keeping the mind balanced, the YOGI, with his mind controlled, attains the Peace abiding in Me, which culminates in total liberation (NIRVANA or MOKSHA).*

After thus describing the physical pose, the mental stability and the consequent intellectual self-application, the Lord now describes the last lap in the technique of meditation to His beloved friend, the Pandava Prince. When all the above details are worked out by anyone, that individual becomes a man steadfast both in his physical and in his subtler life, and thereby, he comes to release from himself a large quantity of his psychic vitality. In this stanza it is said that, when a meditator controls his mind and 'constantly' (*sada*) keeps his mind away from its agitations, he can easily and surely reach the Supreme.

The term 'always' (*sada*) should not be misunderstood as suggesting that the practitioner should live, criminally neglecting all his duties towards his home and the world around himself. Here the term 'always' only connotes 'a duration of constant and consistent inner silence' during one's meditation. At the peak of meditation, the practitioner comes to a point of perfect 'halt'.*

The individual comes to experience infinite peace, which is 'the peace that resides in him'. The Self is Peace Absolute (*shantam*), inasmuch as the processes of physical excitements, mental agitations and intellectual disturbances are not in the Self, It being beyond these matter-envelopments. Here it may

---

युञ्जन्नेवं सदात्मानं योगी नियतमानसः ।
शान्तिं निर्वाणपरमां मत्संस्थामधिगच्छति ॥ १५ ॥

yuñjannevaṁ sadātmānaṁ yogī niyatamānasaḥ
śāntiṁ nivārṇaparamāṁ matsaṁsthāmadhigacchati 15.

*Refer Swamiji's 'Meditation and Life'.

look as though Krishna is advocating the dualistic school of philosophy, since it is said: "The meditator reaches the peace that is My own nature". To conceive of a Truth having qualities, is to reduce the Eternal to the finite status of a substance (*dravya*). Again, if the meditator experiences "THE PEACE THAT RESIDES IN ME", then the goal gained becomes an 'object' apart from the meditator.

The subtle philosopher, Sri Krishna, recognises this unavoidable imperfection of the spoken language, and therefore, he tries to neutralize the fallacy in his expressions by the significant terms 'the Peace, that ultimately culminates in the Supreme liberation' (*Nirvana-paramam*).

In short, when the meditator has come to the moment of perfect silence within, he comes to experience, at first, a peace that is unknown in the world without. Soon, as it were, the experiencer gets slowly acted upon and digested into the very substance of the Truth. Peace is the fragrance of the Truth, which the dying ego of the meditator seems to experience at the gateway of its own Real Divine Nature. In fact in the last stage of fulfilment in meditation, the meditator 'awakens' to his status of Self-hood. This *Advaita* experience is the one fact that has been repeated and emphasised all through Krishna's Song Divine.

FOLLOWING ARE THE REGULATIONS, AS REGARDS THE MEDITATOR'S FOOD, ETC:

16. *Verily, YOGA is not possible for him who eats too much, nor for him who does not eat at all; nor for him who sleeps too much, nor for him who is (always) awake, O Arjuna.*

नात्यश्नतस्तु योगोऽस्ति न चैकान्तमनश्नतः ।
न चातिस्वप्नशीलस्य जाग्रतो नैव चार्जुन ॥ १६ ॥

nātyaśnatastu yogo'sti na caikāntamanaśnataḥ
na cātisvapnaśīlasya jāgrato naiva cārjuna 16.

When the above technique and goal are so clearly given out, one is apt to wonder at one's own incapacity to reach anywhere near the indicated goal, in spite of the fact that one has been sincerely and constantly meditating upon it for a number of years. What exactly is the behaviour that unconsciously takes a seeker away from the grand road to success? No scientific theory is complete unless it enumerates the various precautions that are to be taken for achieving complete success. The next few stanzas warn us of all the possible pitfalls on the path of the *Dhyana Yoga*.

Moderation in indulgence and activities at all levels of one's personality is an imperative requisite, which alone can assure true success in meditation. Intemperance would bring discordant and riotous agitations in the various matter layers of the personality, shattering the harmonious melody of integration. Therefore, strict moderation in food, sleep and recreation is enjoined: everything should be well measured and completely defined.

YOGA IS NOT POSSIBLE FOR HIM WHO EATS TOO MUCH NOR FOR HIM WHO DOES NOT EAT AT ALL— Here, the term 'eat' should be understood in its comprehensive meaning as including all sense enjoyments, mental feelings, and intellectual perceptions. It is not only the process of consuming things through the mouth; it includes the enjoyments gained through all the avenues of sense perceptions and inward experiences.

Drawing our conclusions from these standards, we may understand the rule to be, "Eat whatever comes to us handy, without creating unnecessary destruction to the living kingdom just for our personal existence, and intelligently consume a quantity which does not load the stomach". This is the golden rule of diet for a successful meditator.

It is rightly said that neither 'too much sleep' - which unnecessarily dulls our faculties and renders the individual more and more gross – nor 'no sleep at all' is the right policy for a student in spiritual life. Intelligent moderation is the law.

THIS STANZA MIGHT CONFUSE THE DULL-WITTED, AND THEREFORE, THE FOLLOWING VERSE ANSWERS THE QUESTION: "HOW THEN CAN *YOGA* BE ACHIEVED?"

17. *YOGA becomes the destroyer of pain for him who is moderate in eating and recreation, who is moderate in his exertion during his actions, who is moderate in sleep and wakefulness.*

This stanza plans the life, living which; *Yoga* can be more successfully cultivated. Moderation in eating and recreation, in sleep and activities, is the prescription that has been insisted upon for *Yoga* by the Lord.

In indicating the blessed life of temperance and self-control, Krishna has used such a selected vocabulary that the words have the fragrance of an ampler suggestiveness. An ordinary seeker takes to some sacred work in a misguided belief that 'selfless work' will create in him more worthiness for his spiritual life. Many seekers have I met, who have, in the long run, fallen a prey to their own activities because of this false notion. In this stanza, we have a clear direction as to how to avoid the victimization of ourselves by the work that we undertake.

Not only must we be temperate – discriminately careful in choosing the right field of activity - but we must also see

---

युक्ताहारविहारस्य युक्तचेष्टस्य कर्मसु ।
युक्तस्वप्नावबोधस्य योगो भवति दुःखहा ॥ १७ ॥

yuktāhāravihārasya yuktaceṣṭasya karmasu
yuktasvapnāvabodhasya yogo bhavati duḥkhahā 17.

that the EFFORTS that we put into that activity are moderate (*cheshtasya*). Having selected a divine work, if we get bound and enslaved in its programme of effort, the chances are that the work, instead of redeeming us from our existing *vasanas*, will create in us more and more new tendencies, and in the exhaustion created by the work, we will slowly sink into agitations and, perhaps, even into animalism.

When Krishna wants to indicate the Absolute necessity for moderation regarding sleep and wakefulness, the phrases, which he uses, are very significant. '*Swapna*' is the term used for indicating that total conscious life of the ego's active experience in the world. Elsewhere, in the *Upanishads* also, the entire life's experiences have been classified under the 'state of sleep' (the non-apprehension of Reality) and the 'state of dream', (the misapprehension of Reality) wherein the waking state is also included.

The term *Avabodha*, used here, echoes the scriptural goal explained as Absolute Knowledge. To all intelligent and serious students of the *Upanishads*, the term, as used here, carries a secret message; that the meditator should not over-indulge either in the life of mis-apprehensions nor in those deep silent moments of pure meditation – the moments of *avabodha*. Krishna indicates that *sadhakas*, during their early practices, should not over-indulge in the world of their perceptions nor try to practise meditation for too long and weary hours and force inner silence.

In the same stanza, by two insignificant-looking words, Krishna has conveyed to all generations of *Geeta* students, an indication why *Yoga* is to be practised at all. "IT IS CAPABLE OF DESTROYING ALL MISERIES."

WHEN DOES ONE BECOME A SAINT PERFECTLY STEADFAST (*YUKTAH*) ?

18. *When the perfectly controlled mind rests in the Self only, free from longing for all (objects of) desire, then it is said: "he is united" (YUKTAH).*

This and the following five stanzas are a dissertation on the fruits of *Yoga* and they explain what a perfect meditator can gain in life, and what his experiences are while living in this world during and after his spiritual realisation.

Throughout the *Geeta*, so far, Krishna has been stressing the necessity of one quality, steadfastness (*yuktah*). A complete and exhaustive definition has not so far been given to explain this crucial term, although sufficient hints have been thrown in here and there, to indicate the nature of the man who is steadfast in devotion and *Yoga*; here we have almost a complete definition of it.

When the mind is completely under control, the stanza claims, it RESTS SERENELY IN THE SELF ALONE. A little reflection can bring the truth of the statement into our easy comprehension. An uncontrolled mind is one which frantically gallops on, seeking satisfaction among the sense-objects. We have already been told that the mind can be withdrawn from its preoccupations with its usual sense-objects, only when it is firmly tied down to the contemplation of the Self, which is the Eternal Substratum, the Conscious Principle that illumines all perceptions and experiences. Naturally, therefore, a mind that is fully controlled is a mind, which has lost itself, as it were, in the steady and continuous contemplation upon the Self.

The above explanation is endorsed by the second line of the stanza, which gives us inkling as to the means by which

---

यदा विनियतं चित्तमात्मन्येवावतिष्ठते ।
निःस्पृहः सर्वकामेभ्यो युक्त इत्युच्यते तदा ॥ १८ ॥

yadā viniyatam̐ cittamātmanyevāvatiṣṭhate
niḥspṛhaḥ sarvakāmebhyo yukta ityucyate tadā 18.

we can fix our mind on the Supreme. 'FREE FROM LONGING AFTER ALL DESIRES' – is the means that has been suggested repeatedly throughout the Lord's Song. It is unfortunate that hasty commentators have unconsciously, come to over-emphasize the 'renunciation of all desires' as the cardinal virtue in Hinduism. There is an ocean of difference between the DESIRES and the LONGING AFTER DESIRES. Desires in themselves are not unhealthy, nor can they actually bring about any sorrow unto us. But the disproportionate amount of our clinging to our desires is the cancer of the mind that brings about all the mortal agonies into life.

For example, desire for wealth is healthy, inasmuch as it encourages the mind to act and to accomplish, to acquire and to keep, to earn and to save. But when desire POSSESSES an individual in such a way that he becomes almost hysterical with over-anxiety, it makes him incompetent to put forth any substantial creative effort and accomplish glories worthy of the dignity of man.

A desire in itself cannot and does not bring about storms in the mind, as does our longing after those very same desires. The *Geeta* advises us to renounce only our YEARNINGS for all objects of desires.

Through discrimination and proper intellectual evaluation of the sense objects, when an individual has withdrawn his mind from its usual sense-gutters, the mind comes to take hold of the subtler and the diviner theme of the Self for its contemplation. The limited and the finite sense objects agitate the mind, while the Unlimited and the Infinite Self brings peace and joy to it. This condition of sense-withdrawal and the entry of the mind into the Self is called its condition of steadfastness (*yuktah*). Such an individual has a fully integrated (*yuktah*) personality.

SUCH A *YOGI'S* INTEGRATED MIND IS DESCRIBED BELOW:

19. *"As a lamp placed in a windless place does not flicker" -- is a simile used to describe the YOGI of controlled-mind, practising YOGA of the Self (or absorbed in the YOGA-of-the-Self).*

As an efficient complement to the previous verse, this stanza explains the mind of the *Yogi* of collected thoughts, who is absorbed in *Yoga*. This explanation is given through the help of a famous simile: "as a lamp in a spot sheltered from the wind does not flicker". The example is quite appropriate inasmuch as the mind is fickle and unsteady as the tip of a flame. Thoughts appear in the mind every second, in a continuous stream, and these constant thought disturbances – each dying, yielding its place to a new one - give us the apprehension of a solid factor called the mind. Similarly, the tip of a flame also, (it can be experimentally proved) is never steady, but the flickering is so fast, that it gives us an illusion of a definite shape and solidity.

When this flame is well protected from the fickle breeze, it becomes steady in its upward flight. In the same fashion the flame of the mind, flickering at the whims and fancies of the passing sensuous desires, when arrested in meditation, becomes steadily brilliant although its thoughts are employed in the contemplation of the Self by a constant flow of *Brahmakara Vritti*. In short, repeated and constant thoughts of *Brahman* - Vast and Infinite, Eternal and Blissful, the substratum for the entire Universe - is the *Yoga* of the Self (*Yogam atmanah*).

यथा दीपो निवातस्थो नेङ्गते सोपमा स्मृता ।
योगिनो यतचित्तस्य युञ्जतो योगमात्मनः ॥ १९ ॥

yathā dīpo nivātastho neṅgate sopamā smṛtā
yogino yatacittasya yuñjato yogamātmanaḥ 19.

HAVING THUS, THROUGH MEDITATION, BECOME SINGLE-POINTED, WHAT WOULD BE THE STAGES OF PROGRESS ACCOMPLISHED? THIS IS DESCRIBED IN THE FOLLOWING FOUR STANZAS:

20. *When the mind, restrained by the practice of YOGA, attains quietude and when seeing the Self by the self, he is satisfied in his own Self;*

21. *When he (the YOGI) feels that Infinite Bliss – which can be grasped by the (pure) intellect and which transcends the senses – wherein established he never moves from the Reality;*

22. *Which, having obtained, he thinks there is no other gain superior to it; wherein established, he is not moved even by heavy sorrow.*

23. *Let it be known: the severance from the union-with-pain is YOGA. This YOGA should be practised with determination and with a mind steady and undespairing.*

यत्रोपरमते चित्तं निरुद्धं योगसेवया ।
यत्र चैवात्मनात्मानं पश्यन्नात्मनि तुष्यति ॥ २० ॥
yatroparamate cittaṁ niruddhaṁ yogasevayā
yatra caivātmanātmānaṁ paśyannātmani tuṣyati 20.

सुखमात्यन्तिकं यत्तद्बुद्धिग्राह्यमतीन्द्रियम् ।
वेत्ति यत्र न चैवायं स्थितश्चलति तत्त्वत: ॥ २१ ॥
sukhamātyantikaṁ yattadbuddhigrāhymatīndriyam
vetti yatra na caivāyaṁ sthitaścalati tattvataḥ 21.

यं लब्ध्वा चापरं लाभं मन्यते नाधिकं तत: ।
यस्मिन्स्थितो न दु:खेन गुरुणापि विचाल्यते ॥ २२ ॥
yaṁ labdhbā cāparaṁ lābhaṁ manyate nādhikaṁ tataḥ
yasminsthito na duḥkhena guruṇāpi vicālyate 22.

तं विद्याद् दु:खसंयोगवियोगं योगसंज्ञितम् ।
स निश्चयेन योक्तव्यो योगोऽनिर्विण्णचेतसा ॥ २३ ॥
taṁ vidyād duḥkhayaṁyogaviyogaṁ yogamañjñitam
sa niścayena yoktavyo yogo'nirviṇṇacetasā 23.

These four verses together give a complete picture of the state of *Yoga* and Krishna ends with a very powerful call to man that everyone should practise this *Yoga* of Meditation and self-development. In order to encourage man and make him walk this noble path of self-development and self-mastery, *Bhagawan* explains the goal which is gained by the meditator. When the mind is completely restrained, as explained in the above four stanzas, it attains a serene quietude and in that silence gains the experience of the Self, not as anything separate from itself, but as its own true nature.

This self-rediscovery of the mind is in fact nothing other than the Divine Conscious Principle; is the state of Infinite Bliss. This awakening to the cognition of the Self can take place only when the individual ego has smashed its limiting adjuncts and has thereby transcended its identifications with the body, mind and intellect.

That this bliss is not an objective experience such as is gained among the pleasures of the world, is evident by the qualification that it 'transcends the senses' (*ati-indriyah*). Ordinarily we gain our experiences in the world outside through our sense-organs. When the spiritual masters promise that Self-Realisation is a state of Bliss, we are tempted to accept it as an objective goal, but when they say that it is beyond the senses, the seekers start feeling that the promises of religion are mere bluff. The stanza, therefore, has to clearly insist that this Bliss of Self-recognition is perceivable only through the pure intellect.*

---

*Intellect that is purified of its *Rajoguna* and *Tamoguna* is called in *Vedanta* the 'Pure intellect'. *Tamas* and *Rajas* respectively create in man the 'veiling of Truth' (*Avarana*) and the consequent agitations (*Vikshepa*). When both of them are to a degree removed, to that degree the percentage of *Sattva* increases in the intellect. When an intellect comes under the influence of pure *Sattva*, it ends in an experience of Infinite tranquillity, and the Self is thus experienced on transcending the intellect.

A doubt may now arise that when, as a result of these almost superhuman efforts, an individual has at last, come to experience this Transcendental Bliss, it may provide only a flashy moment of intense living, which may then disappear, demanding, all over again, similar superhuman efforts to regain one more similar moment of Bliss-experience. To remove this possible misunderstanding, the stanza insists: "ESTABLISHED WHEREIN, HE NEVER DEPARTS FROM HIS REAL STATE". The *Geeta* repeatedly endorses that the experience of the Self is an enduring state from which there is no return.

Even supposing one has gained this Infinite Bliss, will he not again come to all the sorrows that are natural to every worldly being? Will he not thereafter feel as great an urge as anyone else to strive and struggle, to earn and hoard, the thirst to love and be loved, etc.? All these excitements which are carbuncles upon the shoulders of an imperfect man are denied to a perfect one, as the following stanza (VI-22) explains the Supreme Truth as "HAVING COME TO WHICH NO ONE CAN CONSIDER ANY OTHER GAIN AS EQUAL TO IT, MUCH LESS EVER ANYTHING GREATER".

Even after these explanations, the Lord Himself raises the question which a man of doubts may entertain. It will be quite natural for a student, who is striving to understand *Vedanta* purely through his intellect, to doubt as to whether the experience of Divinity can be maintained, even during moments of stress and sorrow and in periods of misery and mourning. In other words, is not religion a mere luxury of the rich and the powerful, a superstitious satisfaction for the weak, a make-believe dream-heaven for the escapist? Can religion and its promised perfection stand unperturbed in all our challenges of life: bereavements, losses, illness, penury, starvation? This doubt - which is quite common in our times too - has been unequivocally answered here with a daring statement that "WHEREIN BEING ESTABLISHED ONE IS NOT MOVED EVEN BY THE HEAVIEST SORROW".

To summarise: when by the quietude of the mind, gained through concentration, one comes to rediscover one's own Self, his is the Bliss Absolute. This cannot be perceived[1] through the senses and yet, can be lived, through a 'pure intellect'.[2] Having reached it there is no more any return; having gained which there is no greater gain to strive for; and which is not shaken even by the lashings of the greatest tragedies of our existence. This is the wondrous Truth that has been indicated as the Self by the *Geeta,* the goal of all men of discrimination and spiritual aspirations.

This Self is to be known. The means of knowing this goal, as well as the state of its experience, is called *Yoga* in the *Geeta*. (VI-23). Here we have one of the noblest, if revolutionary, definitions of *Yoga*.

We have explained earlier* how the *Geeta* is an incomparable restatement of the declaration of the *Upanishads,* in the context of the Hindu-world available at the time of the Mahabharata. The old idea that *Yoga* is a strange phenomenon, too difficult for the ordinary man to practise or to come to experience, has been remodelled here to a more tolerant and all-comprehensive definition. *Yoga,* which was till then a technique of religious self-perfection available only for a reserved few, has now been made a public park into which everyone can enter at his free will and entertain himself as best as he can. In this sense of the term, the *Geeta* has been rightly called a revolutionary Bible of the Hindu Renaissance.

---

1 And therefore, not gross

2 Meaning when the intellect has been transcended; since pure *Sattva*-intellect cannot maintain itself as a time-space-causality-instrument.

* Please refer 'General Introduction'.

Apart from the divine prerogative of one who is an incarnation, we find a brilliant dash of revolutionary zeal in Krishna's Godly personality in both His emotions and His actions. When such a divine revolutionary enters the fields of culture and spirituality, He could not have given a more spectacular definition of *Yoga* than that which He has given us here: "*Yoga* - a state of disunion from every union-with-pain". This reinterpretation of *Yoga* not only provides us with a striking definition but at the same time, it is couched in such a clapping language of contradiction that it arrests the attention of every student and makes him think for himself.

The term '*Yoga*' means 'contact'. To-day, man in his imperfection has contacts with only the world of finite objects and therefore, he ekes out of life only finite joys. These objects of the world are contacted through the instruments of man's body, mind and intellect. Joy ended is the birth of sorrow. Therefore, life through the matter vestures is the life of pain-*Yoga* (*dukha samyoga*).

Detachment from this pain—*Yoga* is naturally a process in which we disconnect (*viyoga*) ourselves from the fields of objects and their experiences. A total or even a partial divorce from the perceptions of the world of objects is not possible, as long as we are using the mechanism of perception, the organ of feeling, and the instrument of thinking. To get detached from the mechanism of perceptions, feelings and thoughts would naturally be the total detachment from the pain-*Yoga* (*Dukha-Samyoga-Viyoga*).

Existence of the mind is possible only through its attachment; the mind can never live without attaching itself to some object or other. Detachment from one object is possible for the mind only when it has attached itself to another. For the mind, detachment from pain caused by the unreal is possible only when it gets attached to the Bliss, that is the Nature of the Real. In this sense, the true *Yoga* – which is the seeking and establishing an enduring attachment with the Real – is gained only when the seeker cries a halt in his onward march towards pain, and deliberately takes a 'right-about-turn' to proceed towards the Real and the Permanent in himself. This wonderful idea has been most expressively brought out in the phrase which *Bhagawan* employs here, as a definition of *Yoga* (*Dukha-Samyoga-Viyoga*).

A little scrutiny will enable us to realise that in defining *Yoga* thus, Sri Krishna has not introduced any new ideology into the stock of knowledge that was the traditional wealth of the Hindu Scriptures. Till then, *Yoga* was emphasized from the standpoint of its goal, rather than from the exploration of its means. This over-emphasis of the goal had frightened away the faithful followers from its salutory blessings. And the technique of *Yoga* had sunk to become a mysterious and a very secret practice meant only for a few.

This *Yoga* is to be practised, insists Krishna, with AN EAGER AND DECISIVE MIND. To practise with firm resolve and an undespairing heart is the simple secret for the highest success in the practice of meditation. The '*Yoga* with the True' is gained through a total successful '*Viyoga* from the false'.

If we feel uncomfortably warm by being very near the fireplace we have only to move away from it to reach the cool and comforting atmosphere. Similarly, if, to live among the finite objects and live its limited joys are sorrow, then to get away from them is to enter into the Realm of Bliss which is the Self. This is *Yoga*.

FURTHER INSTRUCTIONS REGARDING *YOGA* ARE NOW CONTINUED AFTER THE ABOVE SHORT DIGRESSION. MOREOVER:

24. *Abandoning without reserve all desires born of SANKALPA, and completely restraining the whole group of senses by the mind from all sides.*

25. *Little by little, let him attain quietude by his intellect, held firm; having made the mind established in the Self, let him not think of anything.*

In the previous section, the entire goal of *Yoga* was indicated as that state WHEREIN THE MIND, THROUGH THE PRACTICE OF CONCENTRATION, COMES TO GET ITSELF ABSOLUTELY RESTRAINED. Later on, we have been given a glorious word-picture of the state of enjoyment and perfection that one will get introduced to, in this state of meditation. This theoretical exposition has no practical value unless exhaustive instructions are given, as to how a diligent seeker can bring about this total mental poise, consciously, in a deliberate spiritual act of perfect self-control.

In these two brilliant stanzas, the subtle art of meditation has been explained. The secrets of how to bring the mind to single-pointedness, and what to do thereafter with that mind in concentration and how to approach the Truth and ultimately realise It in an act of deliberate and conscious becoming - are all exhaustively indicated in these two significant stanzas.

Renouncing all (*sarvan*) desires fully (*asheshatah*) by the

---

संकल्पप्रभवान्कामांस्त्यक्त्वा सर्वानशेषतः ।
मनसैवेन्द्रियग्रामं विनियम्य समन्ततः ॥ २४ ॥
saṅkalpaprabhavānkāmāṁstyaktavā savārnaśeṣataḥ
manasaivendriyagrāmaṁ viniyamya samantataḥ 24.
शनैः शनैरुपरमेद्बुद्ध्या धृतिगृहीतया ।
आत्मसंस्थं मनः कृत्वा न किंचिदपि चिन्तयेत् ॥ २५ ॥
śanaiḥ śanairuparamedbuddhyā dhṛtigṛhītayā
ātmasaṁsthaṁ manaḥ kṛtvā kiñcidapi cintayet 25.

mind control all the sense-organs from their entire world of sense-objects. Herein, every word demands a commentary, since every phrase leaves a hint, which is so important in ultimately assuring the seeker a complete success. It is not only sufficient that ALL desires are renounced, but each desire must be TOTALLY eradicated. By these two terms (*sarvan* and *asheshatah*), no trace of doubt is left in the mind of the seekers, as to the condition of their mental equipoise, during moments of higher meditation. The term *asheshatah* means that even the desire for this perfection in *Yoga* is to be, in the end, totally renounced!

Renunciation of desires is advised here as a very necessary and important qualification. Unfortunately, the unintelligent ignored this significant qualification, and perverted our sacred religion by acting and behaving as though it recommended a life of indolence with neither any ambition to achieve, nor any desire to accomplish. The term 'BORN OF *SANKALPA*' is a very significant term qualifying the desires that are to be renounced totally and fully. The term '*sankalpa*' has already been explained earlier (VI-2) – so here the term used mean that it is the renunciation of all agitation-breeding desires.

When once this renunciation of disturbing desires has been accomplished, the individual's mind gains strength and stamina to assert itself, at first to make the wild horses of the sense-organs tame so that they run under greater control and then to restrain all the sense-organs from all sense objects from all sides.

It is scientifically very true that our mind is not able to control our sense organs, for it has been rendered weak and thoroughly impotent due to the permanent agitations caused by its own false desires. Once the mind gets strong, as a result of its conquest over desires, it discovers in itself all the strength and capacity to control the *indriyas* from all sides.

This process of quietening the mind can never be accomplished by any hasty action or by any imagination, or by any strange and mysterious method. It is clearly indicated by the very insistence that the *Geeta* makes in this stanza, that the seeker should ATTAIN QUIETUDE AS A RESULT OF HIS WITHDRAWAL FROM THE WORLD OF SENSE-OBJECTS, BY DEGREES. Slowly, slowly (*shanaih-shanaih*), the mind gains more and more quietude.

No doubt, when the sense-organs have stopped their mad onrush to their respective sense-objects, a certain amount of mental quietude is gained. The methods of intensifying this inner peace have been indicated in this stanza.

PATIENTLY, WITH THE INTELLECT THE MIND IS TO BE CONTROLLED, AND RESTED IN THE CONTEMPLATION OF THE SELF. This advice is extremely important to every seeker as it gives the next item of the programme for a meditator, when he has accomplished, through the exertion of the mind during his meditation, a total withdrawal of himself from the sense-world. A total rejection of the sense-world is possible only during meditation.

The mind that is thus brought to a relative quietude is next to be controlled by the still subtler personality layer in the meditator, which is his intellect. Just as the sense organs are controlled and restrained by the mind, the mind is now treated by the discriminating intellect and brought under complete restraint. The mind cannot be restrained except by fixing its entire attention on one idea to the total exclusion of all other ideas. The mind is THOUGHT-FLOW and as such, the constant thought of the Nature of the Self, is to be the exercise by which the mind should be restrained by the intellect. A mind that has merged in the steady contemplation of the Self becomes still, and a divine quietude comes to pervade its very substance. This is the last lap of the journey to which deliberate and conscious action (*purushartha*) can take any seeker.

Krishna's exhaustive theory, which can be practised by any sincere devotee, concludes in these two stanzas with a warning as to what the seeker should avoid at his moment of inward silence and peace; the Lord does not instruct the seeker here on what he should positively do. The Divine Flute-player says, "LET HIM NOT THINK OF ANYTHING" when he has once reached this state of peace within.

After the 'halt-moment'* there is nothing more for the seeker to act and achieve. All that he has to do is to avoid starting any new line of imagination. "UNDISTURBED BY ANY NEW THOUGHT WAVE, LET HIM MAINTAIN HIS INNER SILENCE AND COME TO LIVE IT MORE AND MORE DEEPLY" is all the instruction that the technique of meditation gives to the meditator. "Knock and thou shalt enter" is the promise; you have 'knocked', and into the Supreme Presence, thou shalt enter ... ere long (*achirena*).

No two simple looking stanzas, anywhere in the spiritual literature of the world, including the sacred books in Hinduism, can claim to have given such an exhaustive wealth of useful instructions to a seeker, as these two stanzas in the *Geeta*. Even in the entire bulk of the Divine Song–*Geeta* itself, there is no other similar couple of stanzas, which can, in their pregnant import, stand a favourable comparison with this perfect pair.

AS AN INSTRUCTION TO THOSE WHO HAVE A FICKLE, UNSTEADY MIND, THE FOLLOWING IS ADDED:

---

* Refer Swamiji's 'Meditation and Life'.

26. *From whatever cause the restless and the unsteady mind wanders away, from that let him restrain it, and bring it back under the control of the Self alone.*

Every student who tries to understand the above two verses and tries to put them into practice will despair at his own incapacity to control the mind and fix it constantly in the contemplation of the Self. In utter despair, every seeker will realise that the mind irresistibly wanders away from its point-of-concentration because the mind is, by its very nature, 'restless' (*chanchala*) and 'unsteady' (*asthira*). It can neither constantly think of one object nor consistently think of different objects. By these two terms qualifying the mind – restlessness and unsteadiness – Krishna has brought out a vivid and a very realistic picture of the mind, as it is experienced by all true seekers striving on the path of Meditation. These two phrases are so impressive that later on Arjuna himself, while crystallising his doubts into language, uses them quite naturally.

Thus, during practice, even though the seeker has brought his sense organs to a large extent under his control, still the mind, disturbed by the memories of its past experiences, will shoot out in search of sense-objects. These are the moments of dejection and despair for the seekers. These wanderings of the mind may be due to very many reasons: the memory of the past, the vicinity of some tempting objects, the association of ideas, some attachment or aversion, or maybe, even the very spiritual aspiration of the seeker. Lord Krishna's instruction here is very categorical and all-embracing. He says

---

यतो यतो निश्चरति मनश्चञ्चलमस्थिरम् ।
ततस्ततो नियम्यैतदात्मन्येव वशं नयेत् ॥ २६ ॥

yato yato niścarati manaścañcalamasthiram
tatstato niyacyaitadatmanyeva vaśṁ nayet 26.

"WHATEVER BE THE REASON BECAUSE OF WHICH THE RESTLESS AND THE UNSTEADY MIND WANDERS AWAY" the seeker is not to despair, but should understand that it is the nature of the mind to wander, and that the very process of meditation is only a technique to stop this wandering.

LET HIM BRING IT BACK—the seeker is advised to bring back the mind that has rushed out into dissimilar channels of thinking. This withdrawal of the mind by sheer will power may be successful to a degree, but as soon as it is brought back, it will, and it should, rush out again into another fanciful line of thinking. Very rarely do the *sadhakas* realise that the mind means the 'flow-of-thought'. A steady, motionless mind is no mind at all! Therefore, in the technique of meditation, when the mind is withdrawn from the sense-objects, this very process of withdrawal is to be completed by a conscious effort on the part of the meditator, in applying the same mind, at once, in the contemplation of the Self. This idea has been remarkably well brought out when the Lord complements his instruction by the term "BRINGING IT UNDER THE SWAY OF THE SELF ALONE".

THE FOLLOWING FEW STANZAS EXPLAIN THE EFFECT OF THE *'YOGA'* OF MEDITATION UPON ITS TRUE PRACTITIONERS:

27. *Supreme Bliss verily comes to this YOGI, whose mind is quite peaceful, whose passion is quietened, who is free from sin, and who has become BRAHMAN.*

प्रशान्तमनसं ह्येनं योगिनं सुखमुत्तमम् ।
उपैति शान्तरजसं ब्रह्मभूतमकल्मषम् ॥ २७ ॥

praśāntamanasaṁ hyenaṁ yoginaṁ sukhamuttamam
upaiti śāntarajasaṁ brahmabhūtamakalṣam 27.

As we have just indicated in the previous stanza, when an individual's mind has been arrested from its agitated roamings in the world-of-objects, and fixed consistently upon the Self, by degrees the mind gathers more and more quietude and ultimately, when the flow of thoughts ceases, the mind also ends. Where the mind has ended, there the individual is awakened to the experience of the Infinite Nature of the Self. Naturally, the Meditator (*Yogi*) COMES TO THE SUPREME BLISS.

An intelligent enquirer has every right to question this assertion; for, in a true science, the scientist has no right to assert his own opinion and to expect the students to swallow it. In the second line of the verse, the reasons are given to show how and why the quietened mind becomes an open-window through which the prospect of the Self comes to our view. A mind, thus held steadily in the inner atmosphere of thrilled silence, comes to drop off all its previous *vasanas*; the mind gets FREED FROM TAINT (*akalmasham*).

In *Vedanta*, technically the impurities of the mind are called *mala*, and it is considered as constituted of SPIRITUAL NON-APPREHENSION and the consequent MENTAL AGITATIONS. The 'veiling power' (*avarana*) generated by the inertia of the intellect (*tamas*), creates in its wake the disturbing 'agitations' (*vikshepa*) in the mental zone. The agitation-nuisance in the mind is most prominent when it is under the influence of *rajoguna*. This *Vedantic* theory, explaining the fall-of-man into sorrow, is fully echoed in the words of the Lord here: (a) 'passions quietened' (*shanta-rajasam*) and (b) 'freed from taint' (*akalmasham*).

An individual in whom all agitations have ceased, and consequently, who has become perfectly freed from his ignorance of the Reality, should naturally be considered as one who has regained his Knowledge of the Self. As long as there is agitation, so long there is the mind; and the Self identified with the mind, is the ego - the seeker who started meditating. When, as it has been explained, the meditator has exposed his mind to the atmosphere of inner peace and quietude, he comes to end completely all his mental agitations, and therefore, the ego rediscovers itself to be nothing other than the Self. This non-dual Truth has been openly declared by the Lord through His brilliant phrase '*Brahman*-become' (*Brahma-bhootam*) in describing the man of Self-realisation.

HAVING THUS EXPLAINED THE ACHIEVEMENTS OF A TRUE MEDITATOR THE LORD EXPLAINS HOW THIS EXPERIENCE OF THE SELF CAN BE, THEREAFTER, THE CONSTANT LIFE OF THE PERFECT ONE:

28. *The YOGI engaging the mind thus (in the practice of YOGA), freed from sins, easily enjoys the Infinite Bliss of "BRAHMAN-contact".*

Engaging himself thus in the battle for evolution and inward mastery, a meditator steadily grows out of the shadowy regions of his own spiritual ignorance and imperfections, to smile forth in luxurious extravagance into the sparkling sunshine of Knowledge. When the meditator keeps his mind undisturbed in the roaring silence within, in the white heat of meditation, his mind gets purified, like a piece of iron in the smithy furnace. In short, as we said earlier,

---

युञ्जन्नेवं सदात्मानं योगी विगतकल्मषः ।
सुखेन ब्रह्मसंस्पर्शमत्यन्तं सुखमश्नुते ॥ २८ ॥

yuñjannevaṁ sadātmānaṁ yogī vigatakalmaṣaḥ
sukhena brahmasaṁsparśamatyantaṁ sukhamaśnute 28.

* Refer Swamiji's 'Meditation and Life'.

and elsewhere,* the 'halt-moment' is the frontier-line upto which human-effort can raise the mind.

There it ends itself just as a balloon, as it goes higher and higher, blasts itself in the rarified atmosphere of higher altitudes, and drops down, merging the balloon-space with the space outside. Similarly, the mind too, at the pinnacle of meditation, shatters itself, drops the ego down and merges with the Supreme. Just as the space in the balloon automatically merges with the space outside when it has exploded, so too, when the finite mind is ended, WITH EASE IT ATTAINS "THE INFINITE BLISS ARISING OUT OF ITS CONTACT-WITH-*BRAHMAN*".

Krishna is here trying to make an agitated, restless, inquisitive intellect understand that positive and dynamic Reality, which can and shall be gained when the mind and intellect are transcended. Had he said "THE SEEKER WILL BECOME HAPPINESS", Arjuna would have hesitated to accept it, believing that in the Self there is no positive joy. To make his unprepared intellect perceive the experienceable joy of the Infinite, the Divine Cowherd has to borrow a vivid phrase from ordinary life and so he says that the meditator "ATTAINS THE INFINITE BLISS THROUGH THE *BRAHMAN*-CONTACT". This phrase '*Brahman*-contact' should be understood as 'Self-contact' – in contrast to the finite joys, which we ordinarily gain in life through the 'not-Self-contact'.

IN THE FOLLOWING STANZAS, WE GET A DESCRIPTION OF THE EFFECTS OF *YOGA* AND THE CONSEQUENT PERCEPTION OF ONENESS IN THE PLURALISTIC WORLD:

29. *With the mind harmonised by YOGA he sees the Self abiding in all beings, and all beings in the Self; he sees the same everywhere.*

All religions in the world are great, but indeed, none of them is as perfect as the religion of *Vedanta*, if by religion we mean the science of Self-Perfection. In this stanza, the author of the Geeta says, in unequivocal terms, that the perfect man of Self-knowledge or God-realisation is not merely one who has realised his own divinity, but is also one who has equally understood and has come to live in an intimate knowledge and experience of the divinity inherent in all creatures, without any distinction whatsoever. The Awareness in us is the Awareness everywhere in all names and forms and this Divine Awareness is the very essence in the entire world of perceptions and experience. To contact the Infinite in us is to contact the Eternal everywhere.

To a true man-of-realisation, in Hinduism, there is no more a world to be addressed, even be it in divine compassion, by the disgusting phrase: "O! Ye Children of Sin!" Rama Tirtha, a Hindu saint of Perfection, could not but address the entire living kingdom as "O! Children of Light!" This idea of the consummate revelation of "God-I AM" gained by the meditator is the peak-of-Perfection endorsed and aimed at by the Hindu Seers. This idea has been most effectively brought out in this stanza.

That this pluralistic phenomenon is a manifestation of and a projection upon the Immortal Truth is very well brought out in almost all the *Geeta* chapters. The essence in all names and forms, thus, is the same transcendental Self. Just as the

---

सर्वभूतस्थमात्मानं सर्वभूतानि चात्मनि ।
ईक्षते योगयुक्तात्मा सर्वत्र समदर्शनः ॥ २९ ॥

sarvabhūtasthamātmānaṁ sarvabhūtāni cātmani
īkṣate yogayuktātmā sarvatra samadaśarnaḥ 29.

mud in all mud-pots, the gold in all gold ornaments, the ocean in all waves, the electricity in all bulbs, the Self is the Essence in and the substratum for the entire world of objects.

Through the physical body, we perceive the physical world, and from our emotional level, we perceive the emotions in others. So too, from our intellectual level alone, can we intelligently contact the ideas in other intellects. As asserted in the previous chapter, when an individual transcends his intellect, he rediscovers his own Divine Nature. From that spiritual centre, when he looks out, he finds the Self pervading everywhere. The meditator, on transcending his intellect, becomes the Self; and to the Self there is nothing but the Self everywhere. To the mud, there are no pots; to the gold, there are no ornaments separate from itself.

With this understanding in our mind, the stanza becomes quite clear when it says: "HE BEHOLDS THE SELF IN ALL BEINGS AND EQUALLY BEHOLDS ALL BEINGS IN THE SELF". Such a Perfect One, who has realised the Unity in the world of diversity, alone can afford to entertain the equality of vision in all circumstances and conditions; on a noble *Brahmana*, a cow, an elephant, a dog and a *Pariah* (V-18).

NOW WILL BE DESCRIBED THE EFFECT OF THIS PERCEPTION OF UNITY OF THE SELF:

30. *He who sees Me everywhere, and sees everything in Me, he never gets separated from Me, nor do I get separated from him.*

योो मां पश्यति सर्वत्र सर्वं च मयि पश्यति ।
तस्याहं न प्रणश्यामि स च मे न प्रणश्यति ॥ ३० ॥

yo māṁ paśyati sarvatra sarvaṁ ca mathi paśyati
tasyāhaṁ na praṇaśyāmi sa ca me na praṇaśyati 30.

Earlier we were told that on reaching his goal, the meditator ATTAINS INFINITE BLISS OF THE *'BRAHMAN'*-CONTACT (V-28). We explained that the term 'contact' indicates only the non-dual Reality, which is the theme of all the *Upanishads*. Here, in this stanza, we have Krishna's own commentary upon that term. Once having awakened to the Self, the Perfect Master thereafter recognises everywhere nothing but the Self.

HE WHO SEES ME IN ALL THINGS AND SEES ALL THINGS IN ME—In this stanza, as everywhere else, the first person singular 'I' and 'Me' are to be understood as the Self. To one who is rereading the stanza in the light of this annotation, this and the previous stanza together express more fully the pregnant meaning of the most famous *Upanishadic* declarations found in the *Ishavasya*-4.*

HE NEVER BECOMES SEPARATED FROM ME—On transcending the intellect, the experience of the ego is not that it sees or perceives or cognises the Eternal but that it discovers itself in essence to be nothing but the Self (*Shivoham*). The dreamer, on awakening, himself becomes the waker; a dreamer can never see or recognise the waker as separate from himself.

NOR DO I BECOME SEPARATE FROM HIM—the dualists are rather hesitant to accept that Infinite Divinity is their Real Nature, for they are, as ego-centres, conscious of their own bodily vanities and sins. In no clearer terms can we more exhaustively describe the unadulterated Truth of the Essential Divinity in man. Lord Krishna here is in no way trying to conceal His meaning that a meditator, when he has fulfilled the process of detachment from the not-Self, himself BECOMES the Eternal and the Infinite. It may be a staggering truth, but all the same, it is The Truth. Those who are

---

* The second line of this *Geeta*-verse is almost a commentary upon the last word in the *Upanishad Mantra* referred above: (*Na-vijugupsate*).

hesitating and wavering may well continue to disbelieve their own divine potentialities. But the intimate experience of the long hierarchy of *Gurus* in India and the mystic saints all over the world has endorsed this unbelievable, yet plain Truth that, "the Self in an individual is the same Self everywhere".

At present, we are divorced from ourselves; the ego is a rebel who has exiled himself from his native kingdom, the Self. On rediscovery of the Self, the ego BECOMES the Self in such a happy blending that thereafter there is no distinction between the ego and the Self. On awakening, the dreamer becomes the waker; not only does the dreamer become the waker, but the waker can never remain separate from the dreamer. In ordinary divorces, either party can divorce the other, and yet maintain an emotional relationship with each other. Here the Lord says that not only does the seeker come to feel the Self-hood, but I, the Self, become homogeneously one with him.

In fact, once we understand that 'misguided God is a man', it becomes amply clear that, rightly guided, a man rediscovers himself to be nothing other than the Supreme. An actor playing the part of a beggar is not really a beggar; the moment he drops the part he is playing, he becomes what in fact he is. In fact, even while he was playing his role, he was not a beggar. This daring declaration of *Vedanta* is not at all difficult to understand, but the deluded are aghast at this revelation, and in their imperfections, refuse to believe this Truth. They have not the guts to take the responsibilities of living a Godly life. Krishna's courageous statement in this stanza leaves not even a pinhole of a doubt on this sacred conclusion of all the Scriptures of the world, especially that of the immortal *Upanishads*.

EMPHASISING THE IDEA THAT THE MAN OF PERFECT SELF-CONTROL AND MEDITATION, ON REALISING THE SELF, BECOMES THE SELF, THE FOLLOWING IS ADDED:

31. *He who, being established in unity, worships Me, dwelling in all beings, that YOGI abides in Me, whatever be his mode of living.*

The meditator who has integrated himself in a single-pointedness, steadily contemplates (*bhajati*) upon Me, the Self, which is the essential spark-of-Life in all forms in the world. Such an individual, whatever be his activities in the external world, ever lives in 'Me' through a conscious awareness of the Self. This stanza is given here mainly to indicate that the man-of-Realisation need not necessarily retire to some secret cave in some forgotten valley of the Himalayas, but can maintain his Divine Consciousness in all states of existence, in all conditions of life, and under all happy or unhappy circumstances. When a man is ill, he has to withdraw himself from the fields of activities, strains, and exhausting recreations, and go to a sanatorium to recuperate. Having regained his natural health, he need not thereafter live forever in the sanatorium. On the other hand, he should come back to his old fields of work and live, perhaps a more active life than ever before.

Similarly, a disintegrated man of unhealthy temperament is, in spiritual life, treated through meditation, and when he regains his Godly strength and vitality, he can certainly re-enter the fields of his earlier activity, and yet maintain in himself the cultural perfection and spiritual knowledge that

---

सर्वभूतस्थितं यो मां भजत्येकत्वमास्थितः ।
सर्वथा वर्तमानोऽपि स योगी मयि वर्तते ॥ ३१ ॥

sarvabhūtasthitaṁ yo māṁ bhajatyekatvamāsthitaḥ
sarvathā vartamāno'pi sa yogī mayi vartate 31.

he has gained during his spiritual treatment.

Work, in fact, can be performed and really enduring fruits be gained, only when the worker is established in the Self. The message of the *Geeta* is that dedicated work is a means of self-development.

There is a deeper significance in the fact that Krishna, the Perfect, is exposing Himself, perhaps, more to the dangers of the battle than Prince Arjuna himself. A charioteer meets the arrows earlier than the warrior who stands behind him! Entering the battlefield, armed with nothing but His irresistible smile, He, in effect, almost becomes the Lord of the battlefield, wherein the entire war, as it were, comes to revolve round Him, the central personality. This means that a man-of-Realisation will in all conditions be able to enter into any activity, and still maintain in himself the unbroken Awareness of the Divine that he is.

While reading this commentary, some students might feel that we are, in our over-enthusiasm, reading a bit too much into the stanza. We can only request them to ponder over the comprehensiveness of the words used in the daring statement: "Whatever his mode of life be (*sarvatha-vartamanopi*) the meditator (*Yogi*) abides in Me".

32. *He who, through the likeness (sameness) of the Self, O Arjuna, sees equality everywhere, be it pleasure or pain, he is regarded as the highest YOGI.*

True meditators, well established in their intellectual understanding and spiritual experience, intuitively recognise the Divine Presence immanent in everything. Such Men-of-

---

आत्मौपम्येन सर्वत्र समं पश्यति योऽर्जुन।
सुखं वा यदि वा दुःखं स योगी परमो मतः ॥ ३२ ॥

ātmaupamyena sarvatra samaṁ paśyati yo'rjuna
sukhaṁ vā yadi vā duḥkham sa yogī paramo mataḥ 32.

Perfection see in all activities the glory of the Self and understand their own bodily functions as nothing but the Grace of the Self. For them, there is no experience but of the Divine. Everything experienced in the gross world outside, and in the subtle realm within, is nothing but an emanation from the Eternal Self.

The highest *Yogi*, according to the *Geeta*, is one who feels the pains and joys of others as intimately as if they were his own. The famous ethical rule: "Do unto others as you would have them do unto you" is a most unpleasant instruction to the average man, because, in his selfishness, he is easily tempted to ask why he should consider others as himself. The uninitiated, in his instinctive selfishness, would naturally be tempted to follow the unethical ways of life.

The previous few stanzas explained why one should love one's neighbors. The *Yogi*, after his experience of the Self, comes to recognise the whole world as nothing but himself. As all the limbs and parts of one's body are equally dear to an individual, one can easily experience one's intimate identity with all the different parts of the body. If your tongue were to be accidentally bitten by your own teeth, you would never think of punishing the teeth for the crime they had done, for, you pervade equally both IN the tongue and IN the teeth. Having realised the Self, when I come to feel everywhere the presence of Me as the Self everywhere the whole Universe of names and forms becomes for Me the one integrated form, in which at all places and at all times, "I alone AM".

Such an individual, who has in his realisation come to feel the entire universe as his own form, is called a true *Yogi* by the Singer of this Celestial Song. In short, a Seer of Self-Realisation instinctively becomes a divinely compassionate man, producing in society more than what he consumes, and creating in the community much more than what he destroys during his lifetime. Love is his very breath, kindness his very sustenance.

In thus concluding the description of a perfect *Yogi*, with a word-picture of the perfect man's attitude to life, and his relationship with the world outside, Krishna would fascinate any eagerly listening student. Yet Arjuna, a practical man of the world, immediately discovers his incapacity to attain the goal pointed out here, and raises his own doubts, in the form of a question.

SEEING THAT THE *YOGA* DESCRIBED – THE *YOGA* OF RIGHT KNOWLEDGE – IS VERY DIFFICULT TO ATTAIN, ARJUNA WISHES TO KNOW THE SUREST MEANS OF GAINING THIS *YOGA*.

Arjuna said:

33. *This YOGA of Equanimity, taught by Thee, O slayer of Madhu,*
I see not its enduring continuity, because of the restlessness
(of the mind).

The most practical-minded Aryan that he was, Arjuna, the man-of-action, could not at all be moved merely by the poetic beauty of an ideology. He was thirsty to live, and therefore, the philosophy of meditation and successful victory over the cravings of the flesh could not charm him away to any idle intellectual pursuit. He shot some very relevant

---

अर्जुन उवाच
योऽयं योगस्त्वया प्रोक्तः साम्येन मधुसूदन ।
एतस्याहं न पश्यामि चञ्चलत्वात्स्थितिं स्थिराम् ॥ ३३ ॥
arjuna uvāca
yo'yaṁ yogastvayā proktaḥ sāmyena madhusūdana
etasyāhaṁ na paśyāmi cañcalatvātsthitiṁ sthirām 33.

questions to explode the seemingly impractical philosophy that has been explained in this chapter.

DETACHMENT FROM PAIN-ATTACHMENTS (*Duhkha-samyoga-viyoga*) was the definition of *Yoga* that Krishna provided in this chapter. The process of achieving success in this 'detachment-*Yoga*' has been explained herein as the technique of withdrawing the mind from the objects by lifting it to the planes of higher contemplation. The theory is that the mind, when it comes to a single-pointed devotion in the contemplation of the Self, becomes stilled and redeems itself by ending its egocentric pilgrimage through the ignorance of Truth, and the consequent misjudgment of the world.

The goal pointed out – perfect equanimity in all conditions, challenges, and circumstances of life – is an admirable gain, but to Arjuna the technique seems to be sheer poetic fantasy, with no roots in the soil of the actualities of life. The acute intellect of Arjuna, systematically approaching the science of Self-Realisation, discovers as it were, a dangerous missing link in the chain of arguments. Mercilessly, the man-of-war is hammering at this weak point, with the absolute confidence that he will expose immediately the hollowness of Krishna's philosophy.

Thus, Arjuna tauntingly points out: "THIS *YOGA* WHICH YOU HAVE BEEN TEACHING ME, WITH SUCH MENTAL TRANQUILLITY, IS NOT AT ALL PRACTICABLE". The argument given out by Arjuna and the daring with which he directly faces his teacher, show the characteristic spirit of a true student of *Vedanta*. Blind faith can gain no entry into the fields of pure spirituality. The teachers are to answer and clear all the doubts of the seekers. But, in questioning the philosophy expounded by a teacher, the student must indicate the logical arguments by which he had come to feel the particular weakness in that philosophy. Here, Arjuna gives all his arguments, to show why the state of evenness of mind would remain only a dream, as long as the human mind was, by its very nature, 'restless' in its own agitations.

In contradicting the Krishna-philosophy, Arjuna is extremely careful. He does not say that mental equanimity cannot be gained through meditation at all, but his doubt is that it cannot be an experience of LONG ENDURANCE. The implication is that, even if after years of practice the mind were to be won over, the experience of the Self can only be momentary. Although a full 'experience' of the Infinite can be had in that split-moment, that direct realisation could not be maintained by the man-of-Knowledge for any length of time, the mind, being by its very nature, ever restless.

AS IF MAKING HIMSELF MORE CLEAR TO HIS TEACHER, ARJUNA ADDS THE FOLLOWING STANZA WHICH, IN FACT, TAKES THE EDGE OFF FROM THE SPEARHEAD OF HIS LOGIC IN THE PREVIOUS STANZA :

34. *The mind verily is, O Krishna, restless, turbulent, strong and unyielding; I deem it quite as difficult to control as the wind.*

There is an ocean of difference between a modern man condemning the sacred scriptures of our land, and a true seeker questioning the same philosophy, in his honest attempt to understand the full import, and the wealth of suggestiveness contained therein. In his acute awareness, Arjuna realises, deep within himself, his own subjective

---

चञ्चलं हि मनः कृष्ण प्रमाथि बलवद्दृढम् ।
तस्याहं निग्रहं मन्ये वायोरिव सुदुष्करम् ॥ ३४ ॥
cañcalaṁ hi manaḥ kṛṣṇa pramāthi balavad dṛḍham
tasyāhaṁ nigrahaṁ manye vāyoriva suduṣkarm 34.

experience that a mind cannot be stilled; "as it is ever TURBULENT, STRONG and UNYIELDING".

These three terms are quite pregnant in their own import. Turbulence shows not only the speed in the flow of thoughts but also their restlessness and agitations, causing undulating waves rising on the surface. Not only does the flood of thoughts flow fast and rough, but having reached its destination at some sense-object or the other, it gets so powerfully attached to it, that it becomes strong in its new roots. Mind in turbulence is, no doubt, difficult to arrest; when it gets strongly rivetted, it is difficult to pluck it away from its attachments. And the third characteristic feature of the mind is that, when it has flown into any new channel of its own choice, for the moment, it is 'unyielding'. Hence, it is impossible for the individual to pull it back from its flight and persuade it to stay at any chosen point-of-concentration. It is to be remembered that this was the technique advised by Krishna for the practice of meditation earlier in this chapter (VI-26).

The strength and vigour, the vivacity and treachery, the penetrativeness and all-pervasiveness of the mind, cannot be better expressed than by the simile given here 'AS THE WIND'. In raising this question, Arjuna is asking Krishna for some practical tips by which he can gain perfect control over the stormy nature of 'the unyielding, strong, turbulent and restless mind'. Herein, unlike the previous stanza,* the Lord is addressed by His most familiar name 'Krishna'; a word that comes from the root Krisha – 'to scrape'. The term 'Krishna' is applicable to the Self because, on realisation of the Truth, the threats of the delusory mind and the consequent dreamy *vasanas* will all be scraped away from our cognition.

The bloody hands of the dreamer get automatically cleaned and all the moral stigma attached to the murder

* Wherein He was addressed by Arjuna as 'the destroyer of the demon, Madhu'.

immediately gets cleared, when the dreamer wakes up. Similarly, the mind and its onslaughts, its *vasanas* and their tyranny, the intellect and its quest, the physical body and its appetites ... all end with the rediscovery of the true nature of the Self. Therefore the poet-philosopher Vyasa, in his immortal classic, Mahabharata, paints the inner Self as Lord Krishna, the Flute-player of Vrindavana. In Sanskrit, this is a special art, unknown to any other language in the world: the coining of a proper noun for a person to indicate a particular quality that is to be suggested in the context of the narration.

ACCEPTING THE ARGUMENTS OF ARJUNA, THE LORD ANSWERS THAT THERE IS A METHOD BY WHICH THE INVINCIBLE MIND CAN BE BROUGHT UNDER CONTROL:

The Blessed Lord said:

35. *Undoubtedly, O mighty-armed one, the mind is difficult to control and is restless; but, by practice, O Son of Kunti, and by dispassion, it is restrained.*

Krishna knew his Arjuna; the warrior, the man of action, the daring adventurer, the ruthless realist. When such a tumultuous personality spurs himself on with a drawn dagger, as it were, either to agree with or to condemn the noble philosophy of a true missionary, the teacher must have the balance of mind to approach the rebel-intellect with divine understanding and extreme tact. At this juncture in the *Geeta*, the situation, in a nutshell, is this: the Lord propounds the theory that MIND STILLED IS SELF GAINED, and Arjuna

---

श्रीभगवानुवाच
असंशयं महाबाहो मनो दुर्निग्रहं चलम् ।
अभ्यासेन तु कौन्तेय वैराग्येण च गृह्यते ॥ ३५ ॥

śrībhagavānuvāca
asaṁśayaṁ mahābāho mano durnigrahaṁ calam
abhyāsena tu kaunteya vairāgyeṇa ca gṛhyate 35.

argues that mind cannot be stilled and so Self cannot be gained.

When an impetuous man like Arjuna gets hold of an idea in all enthusiasm, the best technique is to yield to him to start with. 'Stooping to conquer' is the secret of success in philosophical discussions, especially in such cases of prejudice natural to the ignorant. Thus, the great psychologist Krishna, with the very first word in His reply, quietly disarms his mighty adversary, and tickles his vanity with the term, 'NO DOUBT, O MIGHTY-ARMED'. Krishna admits that the mind is turbulent, strong, unyielding and restless and that it is very difficult to control, and therefore, the goal of perfect and enduring tranquillity, cannot EASILY be achieved.

By this admission Arjuna is flattered. By reminding him that he is a mighty-armed soldier in life, he is mentally brought to a restful peace. The taunting implication in it is obvious. To achieve the impossible and the difficult is the job of the mighty-armed: it is no glory for a warrior to claim that he has plucked half-a-dozen flowers from a bush in his own courtyard! The mind is, no doubt, a great enemy – but, the greater the enemy, the nobler the victory.

In the second line of this stanza, the eternal missionary in Krishna, very carefully weighs his words and uses the most appropriate terms to soothe the mind of Arjuna. "O SON OF KUNTI, IT CAN BE BROUGHT UNDER CONTROL" is an assertion which comes only at the very end of the stanza. Through practice and renunciation, the mind can be brought under control in the beginning, and ultimately to a perfect 'halt' - this is the confident, reassuring declaration of the Lord in the *Geeta*.

Renunciation has been already described earlier in the *Geeta* as *sannyasa*, which was defined as renunciation of (a) all clinging attachments to the objects of the world, (b) lingering expectations for the fruits-of-action. These two are the main causes for the agitation of thoughts, which further thicken the flood of the thought-flow, and make the mind uncontrollable. As Sankara declares, 'practice' (*abhyasa*) is 'constant repetition of an idea regarding one and the same object-of-thought'.* This consistency of thought during steady meditation generally gets dissipated because of the frequent explosive eruptions of desires. Whipped up by the new desires that are rising at every moment, the thoughts wander into dissimilar channels of activities, upsetting the inner equilibrium, and thereby shattering the true vitality of the inner personality.

Thus viewed, practice (*abhyasa*) strengthens renunciation (*sannyasa*), which generates detachment (*vairagya*), and which in its turn deepens meditation (*abhyasa*). Hand in hand, each strengthens the other. Thus, the total progress is steadily maintained.

In scriptural textbooks, the arrangement of words is to be carefully noted, for, in all cases, the words are arranged in a descending order of importance. To every seeker the question comes at one time or the other, whether he should wait for the spirit of detachment arriving in his mind of its own accord, or he should start his practice. The majority wait in vain for the accidental arrival of the moment of *vairagya* before they start their *abhyasa*. The *Geeta*, in this stanza, by putting the word 'practice' (*abhyasa*) before the word 'detachment' (*vairagya*) clearly declares that such an expectation is as ridiculous as waiting for the harvest of the crops that we have never sowed!

Let us analyse life, question its experiences, argue with ourselves and note carefully how much we put into life and how much, as a return, we gain from life. When we become aware of the deficit balance, each time, we, out of necessity, shall start enquiring how our life could be more profitably

---

* Refer Swamiji's 'Meditation and Life'.

reorganised, so that our coffers of joy and happiness could be replenished to their brim. Soon, the study of the *shastras* will follow, which will give us a peep into the wonders of a moral life, the wisdom of ethical values, the joys of self-control, the thrills of growth, and the consequent suffocation of the egocentric little life.

From the moment we start trying to become aware of our own lives, we are in the realm of 'practice' (*abhyasa*). As a result of this, the detachment that comes automatically to us is the true and enduring 'detachment' (*airagya*). All else is a sham show of stupid self-denial, which cramps a human being and distorts and perverts his intelligence into an ugliness riddled with hysterical ravings and bleeding with psychological ulcers. *Vairagya* born out of *abhyasa* alone is the charter for free spiritual growth. Of your own accord, never renounce anything. Let your attachment with things drop off, of its own accord, as a result of your intellectual growth into the higher planes of better understanding and truer estimation of things and beings, happenings and behaviours, occurrences and incidents in life. When through right 'practice' enduring 'detachment' has come into our inner lives, then, the mind comes under our control. Now it has no more any world of pluralistic objects to roam into, and the only world which it now knows is the world of equanimity and sameness. (V-19; VI-32).

WHAT THEN WILL BE THE LOT OF THOSE WHO HAVE NO SELF-CONTROL?

36. *YOGA, I think is hard to be attained by one of uncontrolled self; but the self-controlled, striving, can obtain it by (proper) means.*

असंयतात्मना योगो दुष्प्राप इति मे मतिः ।
वश्यात्मना तु यतता शक्योऽवाप्तुमुपायतः ॥ ३६ ॥

asaṁyatātmanā yogo duṣprāpa iti matiḥ
vaśyātmanā tu yatatā śakyo'vāptumupāyataḥ 36.

In the previous stanza, extreme emphasis was placed on practice. But what constitutes the spiritual practice (*abhyasa*) was not indicated, even indirectly, in that verse. A scientific book that leaves missing links, either in its arguments, or in its logic, is no textbook at all. In the stanza under review, Krishna is giving a direct clue to what He means by the term 'practice' (*abhyasa*).

He declares that the uncontrolled, and therefore, the totally dissipated person, cannot bring into the field of religion the necessary amount of dynamic vigour and vitality to sustain himself till he reaches the peak of his Self-rediscovery. It is therefore said: "*YOGA* IS HARD TO BE ATTAINED BY ONE OF UNCONTROLLED SELF".

An individual who barters himself away to slave among the sense-objects according to the mad dictates of his flesh - or he who dances to the death-tunes sung by his sensuous mind - or he who roams about endlessly to fulfil the tyrannical demands of a drunken intellect – such a one has neither peace of mind nor the strength of sustained aspiration to goad him on towards the temple-of-Truth within himself.

As long as the sense organs are not properly controlled, 'the agitations of the mind' cannot be pacified. An agitated mind is no instrument, either for listening or for reflection or for meditation - and without these three; the 'veiling power' cannot be rolled up. The agitations (*vikshepa*) and veiling (*avarana*) are caused by 'activity' (*rajas*) and 'inactivity' (*tamas*). We have already found that, without controlling these two temperaments, the 'unactivity' (*sattva*) cannot come to predominate in the seeker.

It is natural, in a discussion that you have to present your own arguments against a team of opposite arguments so that the discriminative intellect of the listener may see the contrast and judge the acceptability and logic of your viewpoint. Krishna uses here this commonplace technique of every drawing room, when He, in the second line, explains as a contrast, how "HE SELF-CONTROLLED, STRIVING HARD, BY RIGHT MEANS, CAN OBTAIN IT". Self-control, achieved through the process of total withdrawal of the sense-organs from their respective objects, is the beginning of spiritual life... and this is never possible until we learn to turn our minds to the Higher Truth.

Even in ordinary life, when he wants to achieve something solid, a man of the world will have to live to a large extent in self-denial. The life of a candidate during election time, that of a student before examinations, or of an actor or a dancer before his first performance... are all examples wherein we find that the individuals deny themselves all their idle preoccupations in their anxiety for success in their respective chosen fields. If, for material gains and flimsy ephemeral glories, we have to deny ourselves, how much more should we deny ourselves the joys of the world outside in order to win the glories of the Eternal and the Permanent, the Infinite and the Absolute Bliss of the Self!

It is not that the seeker should deny himself all sense-objects. This seems to be the general misunderstanding among almost all seekers in India today. In the name of religion or spiritual practice, many seekers, at least for some years, live seemingly in self-denial and self-punishment, shamelessly insulting themselves and carelessly persecuting their own physical urges and even biological needs. This sort of a devilish and suicidal self-condemning tyranny to oneself always ends in an outburst of *satanic* forces from within the very seeker.

Lest the student of the *Geeta* should also fall a prey to

such a misunderstood and misconceived spirituality, *Bhagawan* indicates here, that the self-controlled seeker can, STRIVING RIGHTLY, OBTAIN IT. Not going to a cinema and not visiting the playgrounds are not, in themselves, assurances that the students will pass their examinations. The time wasted in such merry-making must be properly utilised in intelligent study, which alone can vouchsafe for them a success in their examinations. Here too, if a student appearing for an examination in mathematics were to read geography textbooks all night, he cannot hope for any glorious success; he must STRIVE RIGHTLY in order to gain true success.

Similarly, when through self-control, a seeker has conserved in himself energies which would otherwise have got dissipated in the gutters of sensuality, he must know how to direct those energies into the right channels, whereby he can get himself detached from his misconceived self-projections and ultimately realise for himself his own Self-hood. That such an intelligent seeker CAN OBTAIN IT is the optimistic philosophy of this ever-smiling God of the Hindus, Lord Krishna.

With these two verses, Krishna exhaustively answers the question raised by Arjuna, and what follows clearly indicates that the Pandava Prince has been convinced by the Lord's reply.

THE QUESTION YET REMAINS OF WHAT WOULD BE THE LOT OF ONE, 'SELF-CONTROLLED, AND STRIVING' HARD THROUGH RIGHT MEANS; WHO COULD NOT YET FULFIL HIMSELF AND REACH THE GOAL:

Arjuna said:

37. *When a man, though possessed of faith, is unable to control himself, and his mind wanders away from YOGA, to what end does he, having failed to attain perfection in YOGA go, O Krishna?*

In this and the following two verses Veda Vyasa makes Arjuna raise a pertinent question, so that Krishna may get yet another chance to bring the supremely optimistic philosophy of *Vedanta* right in the footlights. None, striving on the Path Divine, can ever be destroyed; and whatever he accomplishes will be faithfully carried over, as a legacy, by the individualised-self in its pursuit here and in the hereafter. Each today is an added link in the endless chain of the dead-and-gone yesterdays. The chain continues growing, by adding to itself link after link, all the yesterdays. Death is only one of the incidents in a human existence and the tomorrow has no accidental or arbitrary beginning. It is only a perfect continuation of yesterday MODIFIED by the thoughts and actions of today.

Carefully voicing his vague doubt, Arjuna asks as to what will happen to one, who strives with deep faith (*shraddha*), but fails to accomplish complete self-control during his lifetime, or due to lack of sufficient self-control falls from *Yoga*. The doubt is that such an individual may thereby come to lose both the little joys of the sense-objects and the Absolute Bliss in the hereafter. The *Vedantins*, even while they condemn

---

अर्जुन उवाच
अयतिः श्रद्धयोपेतो योगाच्चलितमानसः ।
अप्राप्य योगसंसिद्धिं कां गतिं कृष्ण गच्छति ॥ ३७ ॥
arjuna uvāca
ayatiḥ śraddhayopeto yogāccalitamānasaḥ
aprāpya yogasaṁsiddhiṁ kāṁ gatiṁ kṛṣṇa gacchati 37.

a mere life of sense-joys, do not for a moment deny the fact that there ARE traces of joy in the sense life also. According to them, daring thinkers that they are, the joys of the sense-objects (*vishaya-ananda*) are, in their essence, nothing other than glimpses of the Spiritual Bliss (*Brahmananda*). The secret import of the question is that those who faithfully follow Krishna's theory may come to lose both the chances of experiencing the finite and the Infinite joy.

Such a seeker, striving all his life to live in self-control, will be a conscious escapist – avoiding all the finite joy-temptations in the gross world here. But, if the uncertain factor – death – were to creep in to clip the thread of his life with the scissors of time, he would lose his chances of gaining the Absolute Beatitude, which is the goal that Krishna seems to point out in his Divine Song. Again, suppose that a seeker, due to a lack of self-control, falls from *Yoga*. To win in *Yoga*, no doubt, is a great victory, a GAIN PAR-EXCELLENCE. But if, in the race, one were to get knocked down by the stealthy club of sensuousness, one would stand to lose both here and hereafter. Naturally, Arjuna wants some guidance from Krishna as to what will happen to such an individual.

In this verse also, we must note very carefully, that the term *shraddha* is not some maddening superstition which encourages a blind faith. According to Sankara, *shraddha* is the right intellectual apprehension of the deeper import and the fuller significance of what the teachers teach and the Scriptures declare. The inspired devotion that springs up in a bosom, from among its solid intellectual convictions, gained through a true appreciation, is the mighty power called faith that can move mountains and can bring the very heavens on the earth.

TO THROW MORE COLOUR ON TO THE PICTURE OF THE SPIRITUALLY DESPERATE SEEKER, WHOM ARJUNA

HAS ATTEMPTED TO PAINT IN THE PREVIOUS STANZA, THE FOLLOWING IS ADDED:

38. *Fallen from both, does he not, O mighty-armed, perish like a rent cloud, supportless and deluded in the path of BRAHMAN?*

A sincere wayfarer, faithfully treading the path of self-control to rediscover the Self, may get lost, if death were to rob him on his way, or for want of complete self-control he were to fall from *Yoga*. The striking example, with which this idea is brought out by Arjuna, is one of the most brilliant poetic strokes in the entire *Geeta*. This is often quoted in literary circles, whenever an attempt is made to evaluate Vyasa, the poet, in Sanskrit literature.

In summer, mushroom-shaped floating castles of clouds arise from behind the mountains to peep into the valleys below. At the touch of some strong current of wind, the mass takes to flight, leaving along its trail, small bits of fleecy cloudlets. Those little ones, torn away from the parental bulk, get knocked about and are at the mercy of every puff of breeze. Such summer cloudlets, aimlessly kicked about according to the whims and fancies of the winds, can never fulfil the expectations of the farmers, or the clamour of the thirsty. Unfulfilling themselves, they get tossed hither and thither without any haven for themselves. LIKE THE RENT CLOUD, Arjuna asks, 'will not the aspiring self in the seeker be forced to roam about and ultimately get lost in the vast amphitheatre of the Universe?'

कच्चिन्नोभयविभ्रष्टश्छिन्नाभ्रमिव नश्यति ।
अप्रतिष्ठो महाबाहो विमूढो ब्रह्मणः पथि ॥ ३८ ॥

kaccinnobhayavibhraṣṭaśchinnābhramiva naśyati
apratiṣṭho mahābāho vimūḍho brahmaṇaḥ pathi 38.

WHY DOES ARJUNA ASK THIS QUESTION?

39. *This doubt of mine, O Krishna, please dispel completely; because it is not possible for any one but You to dispel this doubt.*

In this concluding verse of this section, Arjuna frankly asks: "THIS DOUBT OF MINE, O KRISHNA, YOU SHOULD COMPLETELY DISPEL".

'The Eternal Scraper', Lord Krishna, alone has the Pure Wisdom that can rub out this doubt and quieten the agitations caused by it, in the bosom of Arjuna. With this question, it becomes amply clear that his previous doubt has been totally dispelled. The earlier doubt was that: Self-Realisation is impossible, since the mind which is ever turbulent can never be stilled. The reply of the Lord had smoothened out this knotty kink in Arjuna's mind.

Every true seeker, if he be diligent enough, must come to discover a couple of new doubts, when a previously existing doubt has been cleared. The process of slowly eliminating all these doubts is the process of *vichara* that is practised both consciously and unconsciously, during all *satsangas.*

THE GLORIOUS LIFE OF THE HEREAFTER ASSURED TO EVERY EVOLVER IS CLASSIFIED HEREUNDER, ON THE BASIS OF THE INTENSITY OF THE MENTAL ATTITUDE AND THE SPIRITUAL APTITUDE IN EACH OF THEM.

IN THE FOLLOWING FIVE STANZAS, *BHAGAWAN* TRIES TO EXPLAIN THE PATH OF PROGRESS OF A SEEKER WHOSE SPIRITUAL ENDEAVOURS HAVE BEEN EITHER

एतन्मे संशयं कृष्ण छेत्तुमर्हस्यशेषतः ।
त्वदन्यः संशयस्यास्य छेत्ता न ह्युपपद्यते ॥ ३९ ॥

etanme saṁśayaṁ kṛṣṇa chettumarhasyaśeṣataḥ
tvadanyaḥ saṁśayasyāsa chettā na hyupapadyate 39.

CLIPPED BY AN UNTIMELY DEATH, OR ARRESTED BY THE INTERVENTION OF SOME SENSUOUS TEMPTATION.

The Blessed Lord said:

40. *O Partha, neither in this world, nor in the next world is there destruction for him; none, verily, who strives to be good, O My son, ever comes to grief.*

At the very opening of this section, Krishna assures, with all emphasis at his command, that "NEITHER HERE NOR IN THE HEREAFTER, IS THERE ANY DESTRUCTION FOR HIM, WHO PERFORMS RIGHT ACTION".

This statement is not a mere emotional assurance built upon some blind faith, or a Godly declaration that is to be swallowed by the faithful, because of its being sacred words that have come out of the lips of a Prophet. The Hindus do not accept any divine prerogative, even for their gods, by which they can bypass the individual intellect and the rules of logic. Religion is a SCIENCE-OF-LIFE and it must completely explain the WHY and the WHEREFORE of its practices.

True to this incomparable trait in our culture, Krishna supports his statement with the philosophical truth: "NEVER FOR THE DOER OF GOOD, DEAR SON, A WOEFUL END". One, who acts rightly in the present, can come to no grief in the future, because the future is but a product of the past and the present.

श्रीभगवानुवाच
पार्थ नैवेह नामुत्र विनाशस्तस्य विद्यते ।
न हि कल्याणकृत्कश्चिद्दुर्गतिं तात गच्छति ॥ ४० ॥

śrībhagavānuvāca
pārtha naiveha nāmutra vināśastasya vidyate
na hi kalyāṇakṛtkaściddurgatim tāta gacchati 40.

The fear of Arjuna that the unsuccessful *Yogi* – a seeker obstructed and held up on the path – will get lost as a rent cloud, here and in the hereafter, has risen from his failure to appreciate the logical continuity and the perfect sequence that is ever found in life. To consider that death is the end of an existence, which started with the accident of birth, is a philosophy too rudimentary to be considered complete and exhaustive. In fact, it is only with a stretch of imagination that we can consider such a theory as a philosophy.

Daring intellects, bravely pushing ahead in the quest to understand and comprehend the laws of life and the meaning and purpose of the Universe, cannot but accept that the existence of an individual in its present embodiment is but a single pearl in the necklace of Infinite Beauty adorning the bosom of Truth. The present is the product of the past, and thought by thought, action by action, knowledge by knowledge, we are creating for ourselves in the present the blueprint of our future. Therefore, the Hindus believe in previous lives as well as in future births for all embodied souls; this is otherwise called the theory of reincarnation.

Based upon this principle, Krishna insists that no seeker is ever lost, although he may slip and fall, or even end his present manifestation; tomorrow is but today modified, but directly continued.

In addressing Arjuna as 'O MY SON!' Krishna has here not only followed the traditional practice of the *Upanishads*, but there is also a deeper significance. However deceitful, cunning and cruel a brute one might be to everyone else in the world, one cannot ever come to advise a false philosophy to his own son. With fatherly love, the man-of-Wisdom in Krishna is assuring Arjuna that one who is striving in the direction of evolution shall never come to suffer any REAL fall. On the ladder of cultural growth, each step that is placed forward is an ascent towards the Absolute Perfection.

WHAT EXACTLY WOULD BE THE DESTINY OF A MAN WHO COULD NOT COMPLETE HIS PILGRIMAGE IN YOGA? WHAT HAPPENS TO HIM THEN?

41. *Having attained to the worlds of the righteous, and having dwelt there for everlasting (long) years, he who had fallen from YOGA is born again in the house of the pure and the wealthy.*

The hereafter is ordered by the actions performed and the motives entertained here. Actions in life can be mainly classified as good and evil; and the pursuers of evil can only slip down the path of evolution. Those who are doing good work alone can start their climb to the higher points on the tower of their spiritual progress. Even here, our textbooks make a careful distinction and classify all good activities under two main headings: (a) actions performed with desires, and (b) those that are performed in a spirit of dedicated love and in a sense of divine worship. Since reactions to actions depend entirely upon the motives that propel those actions, the results accruing from selfish and selfless activities must necessarily differ from one another. Naturally, there must be different routes of progress to the same pinnacle of Perfection. All of them are being indicated here in this section.

Those who are employing themselves in the worship of the Lord with desire for heavenly enjoyments will, after their death, reach those planes of consciousness, which are conducive for

---

प्राप्य पुण्यकृतां लोकानुषित्वा शाश्वतीः समाः ।
शुचीनां श्रीमतां गेहे योगभ्रष्टोऽभिजायते ॥ ४१ ॥

prāpya puṇyakṛtāṁ lokānuṣitvā śāśvatī samāḥ
śucīnāṁ śrīmatāṁ gehe yogabhraṣṭo'bhijāyate 41.

exhausting all such desires. Having exhausted these desires therein, they will then take their birth again, here in the world, in the houses of the pure and the prosperous. In short, all burning desires of every human will be fulfilled at one time or another, if the desires are strong enough and are accompanied by intense activities appropriate for their fulfilment.

BUT WHAT HAPPENS TO THOSE WHO ARE PURSUING THE GOOD, IN A SPIRIT OF SELFLESS DEDICATION?

42. *Or, he is even born in the family of the wise YOGIS; verily, a birth like this is very difficult to obtain in this world.*

The other type, which makes a direct and immediate manifestation, in which the continuity of the past is clearly noticeable, is the theme of this stanza. Those who are pursuing selfless *Upasanas*, thereby gain more and more inner integration and as a result of it, they become dynamic minds capable of the highest meditation. The more integrated a personality, the more spiritual he becomes, and therefore, he must be given a chance to fulfil himself, not in heaven, which is a plane for enjoyment, but he must arrive right here to strive more diligently and achieve the highest. Such an ego-centre (*Jeeva*), as soon as it leaves one embodiment immediately comes to manifest itself in a conducive atmosphere, where it can continue its pilgrimage without any obstruction. It being an aspiring heart, it should necessarily come to be born only in a family of wise men of meditation.

अथवा योगिनामेव कुले भवति धीमताम् ।
एतद्धि दुर्लभतरं लोके जन्म यदीदृशम् ॥ ४२ ॥

athavā yogināmeva kule bhavati dhīmatām
etaddhi durlabhataraṁ loke janma yadīdṛśam 42.

This theory gives a lot of insight into the present-day fallacy which gives such an exaggerated importance to one's unhealthy environments and makes everyone protest against one's surroundings. No doubt, in some ways man is a creature of his environments; but the same statement, when viewed through the glasses of philosophy, gives also an insight into the fact that the individuals, in their own freedom, had themselves ordered in the past their own present environments. By merely changing his environments, the individual concerned cannot progress; a habitual drunkard may still continue drinking on the sly, even if he were to be brought into a dry city to live among teetotallers.

Examples like Sankara, Christ, Buddha, and other great masters can be considered as supporting this philosophical theory. Such men of brilliant genius, who, from their very early youth, exhibit superhuman knowledge and Godly wisdom, are no doubt, rare. Krishna Himself accepts here that such persons are VERY RARE TO OBTAIN IN THIS WORLD. If the previous stanza explained the rebirth of an ego (*Jeeva*) after an interval of existence in the heavens, this stanza explains the lives of the few, who, after departing from one embodiment, immediately arrive in this world to continue their pilgrimage to Perfection.

AFTER REACHING SUCH CONDUCIVE AND HELPFUL ENVIRONMENTS, WILL THE FALLEN *YOGI* OF THE LAST LIFE CONTINUE HIS SPIRITUAL LIFE? LISTEN:

43. *There he comes to be united with the knowledge acquired in his former body and strives more than before for Perfection, O son of the Kurus.*

तत्र तं बुद्धिसंयोगं लभते पौर्वदेहिकम् ।
यतते च ततो भूयः संसिद्धौ कुरुनन्दन ॥ ४३ ॥

tatra taṁ buddhisaṁyogaṁ labhate paurvadehikam
yatate ca tato bhūyaḥ saṁsiddhau kurunandana 43.

It may be feared, that an individual who is thus born again, will have to start his studies and practices all over again. To remove any such doubt, Krishna explains here that such an individual, in his new life, under the conducive circumstances, gets naturally united with the intelligence acquired in his former body. Such a born-*Yogi* completes his education much more easily than others, since, to him, it is not an education that is needed, but only a revision, or a recapitulation. In a very short time, he discovers that all knowledge is bubbling up from within himself, and to him study is but a rediscovery of a digested knowledge which was already lying dormant in him.

Not only does he discover in himself the knowledge that he had acquired in the past, but he easily finds in himself the required enthusiasm and energy for a consistent self-application and vigorous pursuit. Knowledge without practice is a dull, dreary load upon the shoulders of a seeker. Krishna asserts here that one 'fallen from *Yoga*' in the past, when he is reborn in the right atmosphere, not only regains all knowledge easily, but he comes to "STRIVE MORE THAN BEFORE, FOR PERFECTION, O SON OF THE KURUS".

HOW CAN ONE GET UNITED WITH THE INTELLIGENCE ACQUIRED IN HIS FORMER EMBODIMENT? LISTEN:

44. *By that very former practice he is borne on inspite of himself. Even he who merely wishes to know YOGA goes beyond the SHABDA BRAHMAN.*

पूर्वाभ्यासेन तेनैव ह्रियते ह्यवशोऽपि सः ।
जिज्ञासुरपि योगस्य शब्दब्रह्मातिवर्तते ॥ ४४ ॥

pūvārbhyāsena tenaiva hniyate hyavaśo'pi sah
jijñāmurapi yogasya śabdabrahmātivartate 44.

At any given moment, our bank balance is the balance to our credit shown in our 'statement of account'. No banker can give us more, nor can he cheat us with a smaller amount. Almost in the same fashion, in the cultural growth of a given mind and intellect, no God can either take away any or give some more, but can only hand over to each one of us his own exact 'balance'. Each birth has a logical continuity with its own past, as strictly as we experience in day-to-day life. Today is but an extension of yesterday. With the full understanding of this law of life in our mind, if we are to re-read the stanza, its suggestions become quite clear automatically, without any strain.

An individual who has been in *Yoga* in his past life, will be, BY THAT VERY FORMER PRACTICE, BORNE ON IN SPITE OF HIMSELF. This is true even in our life here. An educated man will, IN SPITE OF HIMSELF, be carried away in his behaviour and conversation to exhibit his cultivated mental and disciplined physical habits. No cultured man can successfully imitate an idiot for a long time; so too, no rascal can act the part of a noble-born for any length of time. Both will, sooner or later, be compelled, IN SPITE OF THEMSELVES, to exhibit unconsciously their true nature through their words, ideas, and actions.

Similarly, a man who had in the past lived the life of self-control, study, and practice gathers unto himself those cultural traits. He, in this life, IN SPITE OF HIMSELF and in spite of all his adverse circumstances, environments and conditions of life, cannot but instinctively come to exhibit – in his attitudes to life, and in his behaviour towards the things and beings in the world – a tranquillity and a balance, which are a surprise even to himself.

This is not a mere theory. The truth of the statement is amply evident everywhere in any society, in all strata of its life, in all its professions and in all departments of its activities. Each one of us has an instinctive bent of mind, and we are irresistibly drawn towards it, IN SPITE OF OURSELVES. This pull is most powerful when arising from our essential evolutionary tendencies. Even a bandit chieftain can, overnight, turn himself to be a determined seeker and, ere long, become a great poet of the land, as Valmiki did in the past. Hundreds of such examples could be noted from our recent history and even amidst us today. In all those cases, the only satisfactory explanation will be that the individual mind-and-intellect was expressing through its given physical structure its own characteristic tendencies, which it had acquired by itself in its past incarnations, through its own willful actions and deliberate motives.

When an individual, who was a fallen *Yogi* in the past, is reborn, IN SPITE OF HIMSELF he is drawn towards a life of meditation and quietude, of seeking and striving, of self-control and discipline. Let him be put on the throne of a kingdom, or in the bustle of a market place, or in the ignominy of the gutters, he cannot but express his nobility of heart and the philosophical bent of his mind. All the wealth in the world brought under his command, unquestioned might and power gained, love and respect given ... yet he cannot be dissuaded from his Path Divine. If the whole world stands surprised at his peculiar tendencies, he himself is one of those who is gazing on with the wildest surprise, with the utmost amazement!! "BY THAT PREVIOUS PRACTICE ALONE IS HE BORNE ON IN SPITE OF HIMSELF."

After observing this philosophical truth, Lord Krishna is naturally tempted to express the glory of meditation (*Yoga*). He says, "ONE WHO HAS EVEN THE WISH TO KNOW CONTROL (*YOGA*), HE PASSES BEYOND THE *VEDIC* RITUAL". According to Shankara, the term *Shabda-brahman* used here denotes the words in the *Veda*, wherein the term *Veda* indicates only the 'ritualistic portion'. Therefore, the *Acharya*, commenting upon this portion, says that such an individual goes beyond all the charms for the promised fruits of the *Vedic* rituals. This may rightly be considered as too laboured a commentary, although its implications are only too true. One, who has aligned his mind to the practice of self-control, study, and meditation in the past, could not have any more fascination for the material wealth or the sensuous life, however celestial they might be. Even if this interpretation fits in with the context, we must admit that it has been laboriously stretched by the teacher of the *Advaita*-philosophy.

HOW IS THE PATH OF MEDITATION NOBLER THAN ALL OTHERS? LISTEN:

45. *But the YOGI, who strives with assiduity, purified from sins and perfected (gradually) through many births, he then attains the highest Goal.*

As already noticed, the mind-intellect equipment of an individual functions through his body in the world outside as per the traits chalked out upon it by the actions performed in its earlier lives. These channels of thinking cut across the fields of the mind and determine the direction of its thoughts and the texture of its actions in the present. These lacerations on the subtle body are called in *Vedanta* as SINS, or as the DIRT OF THE WITHIN. These impurities are removed and the existing ulcers healed through selfless action.*

प्रयत्नाद्यतमानस्तु योगी संशुद्धकिल्बिषः ।
अनेकजन्मसंसिद्धस्ततो याति परां गतिम् ॥ ४५ ॥

prayatnādyatamānastu yogī saṁśuddhakilbiṣaḥ
anekajanmasaṁsiddhastato yāti parāṁ gatim 45.

* Refer 'General Introduction'.

But even while rejecting the wrong negative tendencies of the mind, the individual will have to plough the fields of his mind with new patterns representing the constructive divine tendencies. These meritorious *vasanas* (*punya*) can also provide a severe obstruction for a man of meditation. After having purified his mind of its unethical and sensuous tendencies, the aspirant should practise meditation. During the still moments of peace in the depth of his depths, when he exposes his mind to the thrilled atmosphere of its vibrant silence, the noble traits also get completely wiped off. A state of mind which is thus rendered completely impressionless (*vasana*-less) is the end of the mind, since mind is nothing but a bundle of *vasanas*. Where the mind has ended, there the ego has also ended having THEN REACHED THE HIGHEST GOAL, or gained Self-rediscovery.

The explanation of this theory would not perhaps occupy more than half a page, but in actually carving it our into our individual life, it may be a programme for very many lives' consistent practice. 'Through many births' is a phrase used in the *Upanishads* by the honest scientists of Life, the *Rishis*. They are perfectly right. Evolution, as we all know, is not a drama played out during an afternoon, but it is the slow revelation of the history of progress through endless aeons.

To one who has the proper temperament to seek Life, the anxiety to realise the Perfection, the capacity to understand the hollowness of sense-life, the daring to follow the narrow foot-prints of the Seers of the world, the appetite for Infinite peace and tranquillity, the courage to live the moral and the ethical values, the heroism to barter one's all to achieve the highest... such a one is not a 'mineral-man', nor a 'vegetable-specimen', nor an 'animal-man'. He is the noblest creation under the Sun, a perfect 'man-man', standing right in front of the Doors of Truth, demanding as a God-man his admission into the SANCTUM SANCTORUM!

Right now, this very life IS OUR LAST BIRTH, if we have a taste to meditate, an urge to seek, a daring to live the Life Divine!

There is nothing which may sound original in this interpretation to all diligent students of the *Geeta*. A sacred textbook that has been roaring, time and again, in an irrepressible spirit of optimism, the message of hope and cheer, with no threats of hell and brimstone anywhere in it, cannot be considered to have changed its music all of a sudden, to declare that man has hopes of salvation only after 'many births' and not 'here and now'. Even though this misinterpretation may perhaps be helpful to the saboteurs of our religion, no intelligent student of the *Geeta* can, even for a moment, be hoodwinked by such false notes.

THEREFORE:

46. *The YOGI is thought to be superior to the ascetics, and even superior to Men-of-Knowledge (mere scholars); he is also superior to Men-of-Action; therefore (you strive to) be a YOGI, O Arjuna.*

In order to bring out the importance of meditation among the various practices in the science of Spiritual development, Lord Krishna is providing here a tabulated list of the various types of seekers, indicating the greatest of the whole lot. Compared with those who practise thoughtless and dull-witted physical self-denial (*tapaswins*), the meditator is certainly nobler.

Nobler than those who vigorously read the scriptures and try to learn and remember their declarations (*Jnanis*), is the *Yogi* (Meditator).

तपस्विभ्योऽधिको योगी ज्ञानिभ्योऽपि मतोऽधिकः ।
कर्मिभ्यश्चाधिको योगी तस्माद्योगी भवार्जुन ॥ ४६ ॥

tapasvibhyo'dhiko yogī jñānibhyo'pi mato'dhikaḥ
karmibhyaścādhiko yogī tasmādyogī bhavārjuna 46.

There are others who strive towards the same bright peak-of-Perfection, treading along the path of selfless work (*Karmis*), undertaken in the world outside in a spirit of *Yajna*, (IV-24-30) and those who perform worship (*Upasana*) in a spirit of divine dedication. These ritualists, both in the secular and in the sacred fields of activities, believe that they can reach the Infinite Bliss through these very activities.

Krishna concludes here that a silent and quiet meditator, who struggles hard to withdraw himself from his own false identifications with his body, mind and intellect, through constant and consistent contemplation upon the nature of the Self, is ever the best.

Thus, comparing a meditator with: (a) a man of utter self-denial, (b) deep students of the scriptures and (c) ritualists, Krishna concludes His observations that a meditator alone is the best among the whole lot, standing nearest to Truth and "THEREFORE, YOU BE A *YOGI* (MEDITATOR), O ARJUNA".

THERE ARE DIFFERENT TYPES OF MEDITATORS, EACH MEDITATING UPON A DIFFERENT POINT OF CONTEMPLATION. WHO AMONG THEM IS THEN THE BEST AND THE GREATEST MEDITATOR? LISTEN:

47. *And among all YOGIS, he who, full of faith, with his inner-self merged in Me, worships Me, is, according to Me, the most devout.*

Whereas the previous stanza gives us a relative estimate of the different paths in spirituality, and finally declares that

---

योगिनामपि सर्वेषां मद्गतेनान्तरात्मना ।
श्रद्धावान्भजते यो मां स मे युक्ततमो मतः ॥ ४७ ॥

yogināmapi sarveṣāṁ madgatenāntarātmanā
śraddhāvān bhajate māṁ sa me yuktatamo mataḥ 47.

meditation is the best among the lot, the stanza now under review explains who exactly is the best among all the meditators. Meditation is, in the beginning at least, a deliberate act by which the seeker strives to keep his thoughts channelised into one predetermined divine line of thinking; and this is maintained by disallowing the mind to run into dissimilar thought-channels. Meditation, therefore, must of necessity start with an effort on the part of the meditator to fix his mind upon some object of contemplation.* The art-of-Meditation can be classified under different types, according to the nature of the object of contemplation chosen and according to the nature of the persuasions adopted in curtailing the mind from its mad roamings.

Thus, we have, in the tradition of our practices, meditations prescribed upon a symbol, on the God-principle with a form, on the teacher, on the *Kundalini*, on any of the great elements, or on a chosen scriptural text. Accordingly, the practitioners may be considered as followers of different kinds of meditation. The Singer of the *Geeta* is trying to indicate here, who exactly is to be considered as the best and the most successful meditator among the types mentioned above.

In this concluding stanza of the chapter, the Lord insists that of all the meditators, he who "WITH HIS INNER-SELF (MIND-AND-INTELLECT) MERGED IN THE SELF, AND WITH '*SHRADDHA*' DEVOTES HIMSELF TO THE SELF, IS THE MOST FIRM AND STEADFAST MEDITATOR". The pregnant suggestions contained in this stanza can fill volumes, inasmuch as it is a summary of the entire *Yoga Shastra*. Naturally therefore, Lord Krishna dedicates the entire length of the next chapter as an annotation to this *mantra*-like stanza.

---

* Refer Swamiji's 'Meditation and Life'.

For the purpose of our understanding this chapter, it is sufficient for the time-being if we gather from this stanza that the essence of meditation is not so much in our attempt at integrating the mind as in the ultimate merging of the inner equipment (*antahkarana*), and getting it completely sublimated in the final experience of the Self. That, this can be done only by one who does proper *Bhajan* upon the Self with all *shraddha*, is the truth-declaration made here with a loving insistence by the Eternal Lover of the *gopis*.

The term *Bhajan* has come to gather to itself such a lot of adventitious superstitions that, as it is understood today, it means elaborate rituals, which, almost always, mean nothing to the priest, nor to the devotees who are mere onlookers of the priestly performances. Sometimes it means a lot of loud singing with noisy accompaniments, and an entire crowd roaring away on their march towards an emotional ecstasy, each session often ending in hysteria and exhaustion. Very rarely do they gain even a vague experience of the spiritual thrill. In the *Vedantic* textbooks, *Bhajan* is 'the attempt of the ego to pour itself out' in an act of devoted dedication towards the principle-of-Reality, whereby the devoted personality successfully invokes the experience that lies beyond the noisy shores of the mind-intellect equipment. One who does this invocation (*Bhajan*) of the Self, and naturally gets himself merged in that awakening, is declared here by the teacher of the *Geeta*, as belonging to the highest type of meditators.

It is quite evident to every student of *Vedanta* that such a meditator comes to transcend all his identifications with the false matter-envelopments, and becomes, through the experience of his Real Nature, the very Self. Yet, the mouthpiece of renascent Hinduism, Lord Krishna, in His modesty and reverence for the tradition in our culture, attributes this statement in the stanza as His own personal opinion.

Thus, in the UPANISHADS of the glorious Bhagawad-Geeta, in the Science of the Eternal, in the Scripture of YOGA, in the dialogue between Sri Krishna and Arjuna, the sixth discourse ends entitled:

The *Yoga* of Meditation

Nowhere else in the entire extent of the voluminous spiritual literature that we have in the *Upanishads*, the *Brahmasutra* and the *Geeta* (*Prasthana Traya*), can we find such a wealth of details, explaining not only the technique of meditation but also the possible pitfalls and how to avoid them successfully, as we have them so clearly and vividly explained here. No scripture fails to hint at the path-of-Meditation, as the way to reach the highest possibilities in life, and yet, nowhere have we, among our reported and compiled heritage of sacred books, such a vivid discussion of the entire path. To a true seeker, indeed, a thorough study of the Sixth Chapter is ample direction and guidance to reach the highest through Meditation. It is therefore, but proper that this chapter is titled: "The *Yoga* of Meditation".

Om Om Om Om Om

ॐ तत्सदिति श्रीमद् भगवद् गीतासूपनिषत्सु ब्रह्मविद्यायां
योगशास्त्रे श्रीकृष्णार्जुनसंवादे आत्मसंयमयोगो नाम
षष्ठोऽध्याय:

Oṁ tatsaditi śrīmadbhagavadgītāsū ūpaniṣatsu brahmavidyāyāṁ
yogaśāstre śrī kṛṣṇārjuna saṁvāde ātmasaṁyamayogo nāma
ṣaṣṭho'dhyāyaḥ

VII

Knowledge And Wisdom

Introduction

THE Eighteen Chapters of the *Geeta*, in the arrangement of their ideas, fall into three sets of six chapters each. This is the conclusion arrived at by many *Geeta*-students. According to them, the *Geeta*, being a book which reinterprets the very essence of the *Vedic* lore in the entire scheme of its discussions, the Divine Song expresses the Truth of the *Mahavakya*: "THAT THOU ART".

The *Mahavakyas* are four* in number - one taken from each of the four *Vedas*, and they form four definite pointers, all indicating the one and the same sacred Truth, which the *Vedas* unanimously declare. Of these "THAT THOU ART" (*Tat Tvam Asi*) is called the 'instructional message' (*Upadesha Vakya*). This crisp sentence summarises the entire *Vedic* lore and its philosophy, and therefore, voluminous commentaries are necessary to elucidate the true significance of each of these three short words.

According to some reviewers of the *Geeta*, the first section of the Divine Song, comprising the opening six chapters, explains the significance of the term 'Thou' (*Tvam*), in this *Mahavakya*. The second section, opening with the seventh chapter and concluding with the twelfth, explains the term 'That' in the same declaration. From this chapter onwards, therefore, we will be gaining a true glimpse of the 'goal of the spiritual science' as indicated in the Hindu cultural

* The four *Mahavakyas* are: 1. "Consciousness is *Brahman*" (*Prajnanam Brahma*); 2."That Thou art" (*Tat-Tvam-Asi*); 3. "This *Atman* is *Brahman*"

tradition. The last six chapters naturally express the meaning of the term 'Art' (*Asi*) and explain the identity between 'That-essence' and 'Thou-significance'.

The previous chapter not only gave us the technique of Self-realisation through the methods of concentration and meditation, but also concluded with Krishna's own personal opinion upon, who exactly was the noblest among the different seekers pursuing the different paths. According to the Lord of *Vrindavana*, a meditator who tries to concentrate his mind upon the Self is superior to those who strive to deny all sense enjoyment to this body (*Tapaswins*), or to those who make deep and learned investigations into the scriptural literature (*Jnanis*), or to those who have dedicated themselves to selfless service of the society (*Karmis*). The Flute-bearer has again tried to express his opinion as to who, among the meditators, is the most noble. It was declared in the concluding stanza of the previous chapter that, of all the meditators, the one who has successfully merged his mind in the nature of the Pure Consciousness, through the path of single-pointed meditation, is the highest seeker, and the dearest to the Lord.

Naturally, there would be a possible doubt, in the mind of Arjuna, as to how a limited and mortal mind-and-intellect of a finite creature could ever embrace and comprehend the entire limitless Infinite. In order to remove this doubt, Krishna opens this particular chapter, with a promise that he would explain to Arjuna the entire science, both in its theoretical and speculative aspects, and clear all his possible doubts on the subject. Indeed, for exhaustiveness in treatment and thoroughness in exposition there is, perhaps, no other religious textbook that can stand a favourable comparison with the *Geeta*. In this sense of the term, we should appreciate the *Geeta*, not only as a textbook of our philosophy, but also as a literary masterpiece of beauty and erudition in the world's literature.

The Blessed Lord said:

1. *With the mind intent on Me, Partha, practising YOGA and taking refuge in Me, how thou shalt, without doubt, know Me fully, that do thou hear.*

It would be, naturally, the doubt of all seekers, especially before they enter the seat of meditation, as to how it is possible for a limited mind to understand or embrace the unlimited. This doubt can come to such seekers, who try only for intellectual appreciation of the philosophy of *Vedanta*; but all seekers could only be, in the beginning, mere scholarly students of the *Vedantic* literature. This is an unavoidable state in the path-of-Knowledge. The science of *Vedanta* exhaustively deals with this problem and tries to explain how the mind, when made to meditate upon the Infinite, comes to transcend its own limitations and comes to experience the Infinite.

Here Krishna, introducing the theme to be dealt with, in the next six chapters, assures Arjuna that He would explain the entire science and technique, which will clearly show how a meditator, by fixing his integrated mind upon the contemplation of the NATURE of the Self, can come to experience the Divine. From this chapter onwards the term 'mind' is to be understood, not as a debilitated and disintegrated mind, but as an integrated

---

श्रीभगवानुवाच
मय्यासक्तमनाः पार्थ योगं युञ्जन्मदाश्रयः ।
असंशयं समग्रं मां यथा ज्ञास्यसि तच्छृणु ॥ १ ॥

śrībhagavānuvāca
mayyāsaktamanāḥ pārtha yogaṁ yuñjanmadāśrayaḥ
asaṁśayaṁ samagraṁ māṁ yathā jñāsyasi tacchṛṇu 1.

mind properly tutored to walk, implicitly obeying the will of the discriminative intellect. When such a mind is firmly established in full concentration upon the divine nature of its Godly potentialities, the seeker evolves double quick. The logic of this inward development, it is promised, will be the theme of this section.

"NOW LISTEN TO WHAT I AM GOING TO SAY AS TO HOW YOU ALSO, THUS ACTING, WILL, WITHOUT DOUBT, KNOW ME IN FULL, POSSESSED OF INFINITE GREATNESS, STRENGTH, GRACE AND OTHER APPARENT ATTRIBUTES."

2. *I shall declare to thee in full this knowledge combined with realisation, which being known, nothing more here remains to be known.*

According to Sankara, speculative knowledge is *Jnana*, and actual experience of the perfection is *Vijnana*. Here Krishna is promising that he would not only deliver to Arjuna the theoretical explanation of the Art of Divine Life, but also, during the very discourse, take him to the highest peak of Self-rediscovery. This may look rather unbelievable but unlike *Yoga* and other types of philosophies in India, *Vedanta* is not an indirect process, inasmuch as, after the study of this *shastra*, it is not necessary for A FIT STUDENT to retire into the jungles to practise and bring the experience of perfection into his cognition.

During the very discourse, if the student is mentally fit to walk along with the teacher step by step and follow carefully

---

ज्ञानं तेऽहं सविज्ञानमिदं वक्ष्याम्यशेषत: ।
यज्ज्ञात्वा नेह भूयोऽन्यज्ज्ञातव्यमवशिष्यते ॥ २ ॥

jñānaṁ te'haṁ savijñānamidaṁ bakṣyāmśeṣataḥ
yajjñātvā neha bhūyo'nyajjñātavyamavaśiṣyate 2.

the logic and significance of his explanations, he can gain glimpses of realisation during the very hours of his study. It is because of this that *Vedanta* is taught only to a student who has been made fit for this flight to the beyond. If an individual student is perfectly integrated inwardly and if he can continuously maintain his adventurous thirst to experience the Reality, then he, in his attempt to identify himself with the thought and the spirit of his teacher's discourses, can ultimately come to revel in the experience of the very goal that is indicated by *Vedanta*. Self-realisation is instantaneous, during the study and understanding of scriptures, gained through the teacher-taught discussions.

IF *VEDANTA* IS THUS A COMPLETE SCIENCE, AND THE EXPERIENCE OF THE DIVINITY OF THE SELF CAN BE HAD EVEN DURING THE VERY TEACHER-TAUGHT DISCUSSIONS, HOW IS IT THAT SELF-REALISED MASTERS ARE SO RARE IN THE WORLD? LISTEN:

3. *Among thousands of men, one perchance strives for perfection; even among those successful strivers, only one perchance knows Me in essence.*

The idea that *Vedantic* realisation and knowledge can come into the experience of only a rare few has been repeatedly emphasised in different portions of spiritual literature in India, by different Masters, in different expressions. We were told previously (II-29) how the very theoretical side of *Vedanta* is

---

मनुष्याणां सहस्रेषु कश्चिद्यतति सिद्धये ।
यततामपि सिद्धानां कश्चिन्मां वेत्ति तत्त्वत: ॥ ३ ॥

manuṣyāṇāṁ sahasreṣu kaścidyatati siddhaye
yatatāmapi siddhānāṁ kaścinmāṁ vetti tattvataḥ 3.

* Please refer Swamiji's discourses on *'Kathopanishad'* I-(ii)-7.

heard and understood as a marvel. In the *Upanishads* also, the same idea has been very clearly expressed by the *Rishis*.*

Here, however, Krishna shifts the entire responsibility for not realising the Self upon the individual seeker himself and attributes it entirely to the *sadhaka's* lack of self-application. *Vedanta* being a subjective science, it is not sufficient that we know how to eradicate our weaknesses and cultivate our inward strength, but we must also live up to those ideals and try to bring about the necessary readjustments in ourselves. Very few can discover in themselves this necessary urge to evolve.

Of the thousands that hear intelligently, and perhaps understand all the theory and text of *Vedanta*, only a few sincerely apply themselves to live fully the *Vedantic* way-of-Life. Even among a thousand such sincere seekers, only a rare-few "COME TO KNOW ME AND MY REAL NATURE".

The chances are that when this *Vedantic* way of life is perfectly explained by a *Sad-Guru* to a student, who is seemingly attending with all enthusiasm, with sincerity and concentration, he may raise himself up to, perhaps, the very gates of Truth, but there, he himself may come to bar his own entry into the sanctum 'within'. There, some imperceptible vanity, or unsuspected desire, is sufficient to exile him from himself. In this sense, there is a wealth of meaning in Lord Christ's declaration that a camel can pass through the eye of a needle more easily then a 'rich' man through the gates of heaven - the RICHES here are not the 'worldly wealth', but the individual's mental *vasana*-wealth. Unless the mind is perfectly naked, it has no entry into the Bliss of Truth.

Viewing the stanza in the light of the Krishna-spirit, it only means that rare indeed are people who come to study sincerely and get a true glimpse of the *Vedanta*-literature, and only a low percentage of these again can discover in themselves the necessary mental stamina, the intellectual vision and the physical forbearance to live that life of truth and purity in the world. Since Arjuna and all the students of the *Geeta* are such rare souls, they represent the community of evolvers. To them Krishna promises that He can, through His Divine Song, not only deliver the speculative part of the philosophy of *Vedanta* but also practically hand over chances to live subjectively the vital moments of vivid inner experience of the Self.

HAVING PREPARED THE LISTENER FOR THE TEACHING, BY INDUCING IN HIM A TASTE FOR IT, THE LORD PROCEEDS THUS:

4. *Earth, water, fire, air, ether, mind, intellect, egoism - these are My eightfold PRAKRITI.*

In an attempt to explain the world outside as a marriage between matter and spirit, great thinkers of the *Vedic* period had exercised their philosophical acumen and had given us the *Sankhyan* Philosophy. According to them, the Spiritual Factor (*Purusha*) presiding over a given matter envelopment, dynamises the inert matter and makes the insentient mineral assembly to act, as though it is intelligent and vital. This idea becomes clear to us when we take an example from the modern world.

With steel and iron, the manufacturer completes a steam-engine and when the cold engine is harnessed to steam, at high pressure, it does work. Steam by itself can never express its

---

भूमिरापोऽनलो वायुः खं मनो बुद्धिरेव च ।
अहंकार इतीयं मे भिन्ना प्रकृतिरष्टधा ॥ ४ ॥
bhūmirāpo'nalo vāyuḥ khaṁ mano buddhireva ca
ahaṅkāra itīyaṁ me bhinnā prakṛtiraṣṭadhā 4.

dynamic capacity and strength; on the other hand, when it is made to work through a given equipment, it is capable of adding motion and performance to the inert iron assemblage.

Thus, one of the schools of philosophy in India tries to explain scientifically, how the Eternal and the Perfect Self comes to express Itself as the world of plurality, in the embrace of matter. This also explains the relationship between Spirit and matter. The technical terms used in the philosophy for those two items are: *Prakriti*, for the 'matter-envelopments', and *Purusha* for the 'Spirit-factor'.

Krishna explains in this and the following stanza, all the items that together constitute the matter and those that constitute the Spiritual Entity within a living man. Once the individual comes to understand clearly the distinction between matter and Spirit he will indeed come to understand that the Spirit identifying with matter, is the cause for all Its sufferings and when It is detached from Its identifications, it rediscovers for itself its own essential nature as Perfection and Bliss Absolute. The spirit identifying with matter, and sharing the destinies of the inert equipment, is called the 'ego' (*Jeeva*). It is the 'ego' that comes to rediscover itself to be nothing other than the Spirit that presides over matter.

In order to make Arjuna realise how exactly one is to understand the true nature of the Self, in all Its divine might and glory, Lord Krishna tries to enumerate the matter-aspect, as distinct from the Spiritual-Truth in each individual.

The five great elements, mind, intellect and ego constitute, according to the *Geeta*, the eight-fold *Prakriti* that has come to be superimposed upon the Truth through ignorance. The five great cosmic elements are represented in the microcosm by the five sense-organs by which the individual comes to experience and live in the world of sense-objects. Thus, the list making up *Prakriti* is nothing other than the subtle body and its vehicles of expression that are constituted of the sense-organs. The sense-organs are the channels through which the world of stimuli reaches within, and the inner point of focus of the five sense-organs is called the 'mind'. The impulses received by the mind are rationally classified and systematised into the knowledge of their perception by the intellect. At all these three levels of sense perception, mental reception, and intellectual assimilation, there is a continuous sense of 'I'-ness, which is called the 'ego'. These constitute the equipments through which, at the touch of Life, man functions as the intelligent being that he is.

WHAT THEN IS YOUR HIGHER NATURE? LISTEN:

5. *This is the 'lower' PRAKRITI; different from it, know thou, O mighty-armed, My 'Higher' PRAKRITI, the very Life-element, by which this world is upheld.*

After enumerating in the above stanza the 'lower' nature of the Self, Krishna says that this is not all. The Self possesses, besides these equipments, a Higher-Nature which is constituted of Pure Consciousness, or Awareness. It is this Spiritual Entity that makes it possible for the body, mind and intellect, made up of mere inert minerals, to act as if they were in themselves so vitally sentient and intelligent.

The Spiritual Factor is the entity by whose contact the

अपरेयमितस्त्वन्यां प्रकृतिं विद्धि मे पराम् ।
जीवभूतां महाबाहो ययेदं धार्यते जगत् ॥ ५ ॥
apareyamitasvanyāṁ prakṛtiṁ viddhi me parām
jīvabhūtāṁ mahābāho yayedaṁ dhāryate jagat 5.

equipments function, and without which the equipments become dull and insentient. If Consciousness were not in us, we would not be able to experience either the world outside or the world within us. It is the Consciousness that maintains, nourishes, and sustains all the possibilities in us. Without this Spiritual Spark functioning in us, we would be no more intelligent or divine than the 'stone-world'.

Even by a more material consideration, we can logically come to accept the conclusions declared in this stanza. I am standing on the floor of my house; the house is supported by my piece of land; the land is protected by the city corporation; the city is supported by the country; and the country is supported by the world; the world is supported by water, the waters of the ocean; water is held in position by the atmosphere, and the atmosphere is a part of the planetary system! The universe stays in space, and this space rests upon the 'concept of space' that is in our mind! The mind gets its support from the judgement of the intellect. Since the decision of the intellect is known and realised by the Consciousness in us, this Spiritual Entity is, indeed, the ultimate support for the entire world-of-change (*Jagat*)!!!

In philosophy, the term *Jagat* means not only the world-of-objects perceived by us through our sense-organs, but it includes in its concept the world experienced through and interpreted by the mind and intellect also. Thus the world-of-objects, the world-of-feelings, and the world-of-ideas that we experience, together, in their totality, constitute the *Jagat*. This is supported by the Conscious Principle with Its grace showering upon them all. In this sense also, Krishna's declarations are scientifically true, when He says that the Higher *Prakriti*, the principle-of-Consciousness, is that BY

WHICH THIS ENTIRE WORLD OF EXPERIENCES IS SUSTAINED.

HOW IS THE SELF THE CREATOR, SUSTAINER AND THE DESTROYER OF THE WORLD? LISTEN:

6. *Know that these (two PRAKRITIS), are the womb of all beings.*
So I am the source and dissolution of the whole universe.

The above-mentioned Higher and lower-nature, each functioning in the embrace of the other, cause all the manifestations of the world of plurality. If matter were not there, the latent dynamism in the Spirit will not find a field for Its expression. Matter, by itself, in its inertness, will not be able to express the similitude of Consciousness unless the Spirit were there to dynamise it. Electricity, expressing itself through the filament in the bulb, manifests as light. Without the bulb, the light in the electricity cannot manifest itself, nor can the bulb shine forth in light without the electrical current flowing through it. The bulb is the equipment, functioning through which, electricity expresses itself as light. Similarly, the Spirit, when it comes to function through the five layers of matter,* discovers for Itself a field to express Its own potentialities.

Keeping this idea in mind, Lord Krishna declares here: "THESE TWO ARE THE WOMB OF ALL BEINGS". It is not very difficult for an intelligent student to understand what it actually means. Not only does the pluralistic world of objects, feelings, and ideas rise from, and stay in the Spirit, but it dissolves into It, again to become the Higher-Nature. Thus, the lower-nature is, in its essential constitution, nothing other than the

---

एतद्योनीनि भूतानि सर्वाणीत्युपधारय ।
अहं कृत्स्नस्य जगतः प्रभवः प्रलयस्तथा ॥ ६ ॥
etadyonīni bhūtāni savārṇītyupadhāraya
ahaṁ kṛtsnasya jagataḥ prabhavaḥ pralayastathā 6.

* Refer Swamiji's 'Meditation and Life'.

Higher. The Higher, forgetting Its own divinity, identifies Itself with the lower and comes to the egocentric sorrows and imperfections. The Higher seemingly suffers, at present, in Its own delusions, the sorrows of the lower. Its own rediscovery of Its native divine glory is the redemption of matter. The idea that the lower has arisen from the Higher is likened to the way in which pots of different shapes and colours have all arisen from the mud. Just as the mud is the truth in all the pots, the Higher is the essential Reality in all the objects of the sense organs, mind and intellect which the lower procreates.

THEREFORE:

7. *There is nothing whatsoever higher than Me, O Dhananjaya.*
All this is strung in Me, as clusters of gems on a string.

There are two possible points of view of life, if the above-mentioned theory is accepted. There is a point of view from the lower and distinctly different from it, there is a point of view from the Higher also. Just as in mud there are none of the different shapes and colours of the pots, so too, in the Pure Consciousness there are none of the worlds-of-objects, or feelings or ideas. "BESIDES ME THERE IS NAUGHT".

After waking up, to the waker, there is nothing of the dream-world for his recognition. In the endless waves that rise in the ocean there is nothing other than the ocean itself. None of the waves can rise, nor stay, nor ultimately reach anywhere but the ocean itself. In short, nothing can remain ever totally divorced from its own essential-nature.

The first line indicates that each one of us has a 'lower-

मत्तः परतरं नान्यत्किंचिदस्ति धनञ्जय ।
मयि सर्वमिदं प्रोतं सूत्रे मणिगणा इव ॥ ७ ॥

mattaḥ parataraṁ nānyatkiñcidasti dhanañjaya
mayi sarvamida protaṁ sūtre maṇigaṇā iva 7.

nature' which is married to our own Self, but still, the doubt might come into the minds of the students of the *Geeta*, "that the Self in me is different from the Self in all others". This logic of thinking may, as a result, take us to the conclusion that there are as many different selves as there are different bodies in the world.

To show that the Self is one and the same in all forms, it has been said here that the Lord is the common factor in all forms in the universe. He holds them all intact as the string holds all the pearls in a necklace. These words have deep significance. Not only is it beautiful in its poetic suggestion, but it has also a very exhaustive philosophical implication. The pearls in the necklace are necessarily uniform and homogeneous, and its thread, which is generally unseen, passes through the central core of every pearl, and holds them all, the big and the small, into a harmonious ornament of beauty.

Again, the substance of which the pearls are made is totally different from the constituents that go to make the thread. Similarly, the world is constituted of an infinite variety of names and forms, which are all held together by the Spiritual Truth into a complete whole. Even in an individual, the mind, the intellect, the body, each different from the others, can harmoniously work and unitedly give the music of life for him because the same Conscious Principle works through all those different and varying matter-envelopments.

Here is an instance wherein we see Shri Veda Vyasa typically expressing himself as the poet-philosopher of the world. This example is not only poetical but also deeply philosophical.

FURTHER:

8. *I am the sapidity in water, O son of Kunti, I am the light in the moon and the sun; I am the syllable OM in all the VEDAS, sound in ether, and virility in men;*

9. *I am the sweet fragrance in earth and the brilliance in fire, the life in all beings, and I am austerity in the austere.*

How the Supreme Self can be the 'thread' upon which the 'pearls' consisting of individual elements of plurality are strung together to become the 'necklace' of the harmonious universe, is described in these two verses. It has already been said, "MY HIGHER *PRAKRITI*, THE PRINCIPLE OF CONSCIOUSNESS" is the womb of all beings, and that "BEYOND ME THERE IS NAUGHT". What can be this Eternal Factor, which is common in every one – and yet not readily perceptible to all – is the doubt that has been cleared here.

That which remains in a substance from the beginning to the end, constantly, and without which the thing cannot ever maintain its identity, is called its *Dharma* – which is its law-of-Being. The examples of sapidity in water, radiance in the sun

---

रसोऽहमप्सु कौन्तेय प्रभास्मि शशिसूर्ययोः ।
प्रणवः सर्ववेदेषु शब्दः खे पौरुषं नृषु ॥ ८ ॥
raso'hamapsu kaunteya prabhāsmi śaśisūryayoḥ
praṇavaḥ sarvavedeṣu śabdaḥ khe pauruṣaṁ nṛṣu   8.

पुण्यो गन्धः पृथिव्यां च तेजश्चास्मि विभावसौ ।
जीवनं सर्वभूतेषु तपश्चास्मि तपस्विषु ॥ ९ ॥
puṇyo gandhaḥ pṛthivyāṁ ca tejaścāsmi vibhāvasau
jīvanaṁ sarvabhūteṣu tapaścāsmi tapasviṣu   9.

and the moon, OM in all *Vedas*, sound in *Akasa*, sweet smell in earth, luminosity in fire, manhood in man, and austerity in the austere – all clearly indicate that the Self is that which gives each individual phenomenon its own existence. In short, as the stanza declares, the Self is the LIFE IN ALL BEINGS.

AS A MORE VIVID EXAMPLE, FOR THE READY GRASP OF GROSSER INTELLECTS, THE LORD GIVES THE FOLLOWING SET OF EXAMPLES:

10. *Know Me, O Partha, as the eternal seed of all beings; I am the intelligence of the intelligent. The splendour of the splendid (things and beings), am I.*

Not satisfied with the above enumeration, which can truly indicate its full significances only to those who have a fairly well developed subtle intellect, the Lord is compelled to indicate the same Truth through a set of more obvious examples. He says in the stanza, "I AM THE ANCIENT SEED OF ALL BEINGS". Not satisfied with this statement, as an artist would mix more colours afresh and paint, again and again, to bring out his theme more vividly to the perception of the onlookers, *Bhagawan* gives here two more beautiful instances by which we can get an insight into the relationship between the gross perceivable matter and the subtle imperceptible Spirit.

I AM THE INTELLIGENCE OF THE INTELLIGENT—the intelligent man constantly expresses a greater amount of divinity in his thoughts and ideas. In that intelligent man, the Self is the intelligence, that subtle-power, because of which the individual

---

बीजं मां सर्वभूतानां विद्धि पार्थ सनातनम् ।
बुद्धिर्बुद्धिमतामस्मि तेजस्तेजस्विनामहम् ॥ १० ॥

bījaṁ māṁ sarvabhūtānāṁ viddhi pārtha sanātanam
buddhirbuddhimatāmasmi tejastesvināmaham 10.

is capable of manifesting such brilliant comprehension. Similarly, it is also said that the Self is that which beams out through the beautiful and the energetic.

In other words, through the instrument of our intellect, it is the Consciousness in us that expresses itself as an intelligent individual. As a parallel we can say that electricity is the 'light in the bulb', is the 'heat in the heater', is the 'music in the radio'.

YET ANOTHER EXAMPLE IS GIVEN IN THE FOLLOWING VERSE:

> 11. *Of the strong, I am the strength - devoid of desire and attachment, and in (all) beings, I am the desire - unopposed to DHARMA, O best among the Bharatas.*

Having thus served with different samples the seekers of the average intelligence[1] and the dullest[2] in this stanza the Lord is trying to indicate the Eternal Self to the most intelligent students, who have the capacity to do subtle reflection upon such philosophical ideologies.

I AM THE STRENGTH IN THE STRONG—This statement is evidently as easy of comprehension as the example given in the previous stanza. But the statement outshines the above set of examples when here, Krishna gives the phrase qualifying *'Balam'*. Generally, an individual expresses his might and strength only when he is goaded by his desires or attachments.

Without these two inner urges it is impossible for us to

बलं बलवतां चाहं कामरागविवर्जितम् ।
धर्माविरुद्धो भूतेषु कामोऽस्मि भरतर्षभ ॥ ११ ॥

balaṁ balavatāṁ cāhaṁ kāmarāgavivarjitam
dharmaviruddho bhūteṣu kāmo'smi bharatarṣabha 11.

[1] Ibid., 9

[2] Ibid., 10

see any expression of might or strength. Desire (*Kama*) and attachment (*Raga*) are generally considered by students of *Vedic* literature as almost synonyms; but Shankara, in his commentary, has very thoughtfully given us the distinction between these two powerful impulses. He says *Kama* is 'desire for what is absent' at present in the scheme of our life, and *Raga* is 'affection for what one already has'. These are the two emotions, lashed by which, individuals or communities, or societies or nations, generally express their might and strength (*Balam*). Riots and agitations, battles and wars, are all ever motivated by these two dangerous urges. In the subtle definition of the Self, the Lord brings a new life of thought here for the contemplation of the seeker. He says, the Self is not merely the strength in the strong but "I AM THE STRENGTH DEVOID OF DESIRE AND ATTACHMENT".

As though not satisfied with his own definition, the Lord gives yet another example. "I AM DESIRE IN BEINGS, UNOPPOSED TO *DHARMA*." We have already explained the term *Dharma* as the law-of-Being. The essential factor in man is the Divine Consciousness. All actions, thoughts and ideas entertained by him which are not opposed to his essential Divine Nature constitute his *Dharma*. All actions and thoughts that hasten the evolution of man to rediscover his essential Divine Nature are considered righteous action (*Dharma*), while all activities of the mind and intellect that take him away from his true Divine Nature and make him behave like an animal and degrade him in his evolutionary status, are called unrighteous behaviour (*A-dharma*).

With this understanding of the term *Dharma*, the second line of the stanza becomes very clear. "ALL DESIRES THAT ARE NOT UNRIGHTEOUS FOR THE BEINGS" therefore, means the glorious urge in the EVOLVERS to meet their own inner weaknesses courageously and bring out a complete consummation of their evolutionary urge to seek and to discover the goal of Self-perfection. This is the subtle power that is indicated here. The Lord says: "I am not the *Sadhaka*, but I am the burning aspiration in him, to discover and become one with the Immutable Self".

BY THE ABOVE EXAMPLES, DOES IT MEAN THAT THE SPIRIT HAS BEEN REALLY CAPTURED AND JAILED IN BY MATTER? HOW CAN THE LIMITED LIMIT THE UNLIMITED? LISTEN:

12. *Whatever beings (and objects) that are pure, active and inert, know them to proceed from Me; yet, I am not in them, they are in Me.*

In this stanza, the Lord concludes the topic of His discussion, which He undertook while commenting upon. His own statement, "ALL THIS IS STRUNG IN ME AS A ROW OF PEARLS ON A STRING".

The term *Maya*, as used in *Vedantic* literature, is nothing other than the different impulses under which the mind and intellect of the living kingdom act. The infinite varieties of thoughts and ideas that rise in the heart of the living kingdom have been observed and classified under the three main moods, governed by which alone do the instruments of feeling, thinking and action come to play their parts everywhere. These three characteristics, the eternal moods of the 'subtle-body', are called 'unactivity' (*Sattva*), 'activity' (*Rajas*), and 'inactivity' (*Tamas*).

With this knowledge of the three *gunas*, as they are called,

---

ये चैव सात्त्विका भावा राजसास्तामसाश्च ये ।
मत्त एवेति तान्विद्धि न त्वहं तेषु ते मयि ॥ १२ ॥

ye caiva sāttvikā bhāvā rājasāstāmasāśca ye
matta eveti tānviddhi na tvahaṁ teṣu te mayi 12.

when we try to understand the stanza, it becomes a very easy reading. "Whatever states pertain to these three natural temperaments of the heart and the head, they all rise from the Self." This is a statement which is only a re-interpretation, in philosophical terminology, of what has already been explained. The Infinite Consciousness is the Supreme Reality, the Spirit, upon which matter, constituting Its lower-nature, is but an APPARENT experience. They all rise from the Truth, inasmuch as all the waves rise from the ocean, all mud-pots rise from the mud, all ornaments made of gold come from gold.

This verse concludes with a beautiful statement which reads like a conundrum. The use of such arresting statements is an art deliberately indulged in by Hindu philosophical writers. It has the charm that invites an independent, intellectual investigation by the student, all by himself, upon the declaration, in order that he may find the sweet secret of its true import and significance. "STILL, I AM NOT IN THEM, THEY ARE IN ME".

Such a statement would necessarily be false in any situation because, if A is not B, the latter cannot be in the former – if "I am not in them, they CANNOT be in me". This sweet paradoxical statement clearly indicates that the relationship between Spirit and matter is not in terms of cause and its effect, but it is only as a super-imposition of matter upon the Spirit. Addressing the deluded, the post can only explain, "the ghost of your vision had risen from me alone, inasmuch as, I alone lend to it its existence; but I, the post, am not in the ghost". So, too, shall the ocean cry, "the waves rise, stay and dissolve away in me; but I am not in the waves".

As Shankara would have it, the Self declares here that

even though matter depends entirely for its existence upon the Conscious Principle, yet the Divine Spark is in no way under the thraldom of matter. Matter ekes out its existence from the Spirit; but, the Spirit is – in no way at no time, howsoever little – controlled, contaminated, or shackled by the sad lot of the finite, imperfect matter.

IN THE FOLLOWING STANZA, LORD KRISHNA REGRETS THAT THE WORLD DOES NOT UNDERSTAND HIM IN HIS TRUE NATURE. WHAT IS THIS IGNORANCE ON THE PART OF THE WORLD DUE TO? LISTEN:

13. *Deluded by these natures (states or things) composed of the three GUNAS (of PRAKRITI) all the world knows Me not as Immutable and distinct from them.*

If there be such a Divine Factor, beyond the usual cognition of the ordinary mortals, how is it that they are not in a position to understand, at least the presence, if not a complete realisation of this great Truth? This question is answered here in this verse.

DELUDED BY THE MODIFICATIONS OF THE THREE *gunas*, the worlds of living creatures become blind to the divine possibilities in themselves, and live totally a life of mere identification with the matter-envelopments. The post is covered by the ghost-vision for the deluded. It is a fact that as long as the ghost is viewed, not even a portion of the post will be available for the perception of the deluded!

Similarly, identifying with the *Maya*-products, the Self

त्रिभिर्गुणमयैर्भावैरेभिः सर्वमिदं जगत् ।
मोहितं नाभिजानाति मामेभ्यः परमव्ययम् ॥ १३ ॥

tribhirguṇamayaibhārvairebhiḥ sarvamidaṁ jagat
mohitaṁ nabhijānāti momebhyaḥ paramavyayam 13.

comes to play the tragic role of the ego, and the ego, in its preoccupations with the outer-world and with its idle imaginations, finds itself incapable of knowing its own true nature. This play of hide and seek - ourselves with ourselves in ourselves - is the strange and mysterious play of the ego, creating the universal sorrow and the endless mental squalor therein.

THIS 'POWER OF VEILING' IN EVERY ONE OF US IS DEFINED AND DESCRIBED IN THE FOLLOWING STANZA:

14. *Verily, this divine illusion of Mine, made up of GUNAS (caused by the qualities) is difficult to cross over; those who take refuge in Me, they alone cross over this illusion.*

Lord Krishna himself admits that it is not easy for any egocentric individual to transcend this delusion in himself which is caused by 'My *Maya*'. If a doctor were to come and diagnose a disease and declare that there was no cure for it, nobody will have the faith to follow that doctor's prescription and advice carefully and cheerfully. Similarly here, if Krishna's diagnosis of the world's sorrows and problems is to be defined by the term *Maya*, and if the Doctor of the Universe declares that this *Maya*-disease is difficult to cure, nobody would faithfully follow such a sad pessimistic philosophy.

Krishna realises these defects and therefore, immediately removes any such misconception from the minds of the students of the *Geeta*. Sometimes a doctor will have to use

---

दैवी ह्येषा गुणमयी मम माया दुरत्यया ।
मामेव ये प्रपद्यन्ते मायामेतां तरन्ति ते ॥ १४ ॥

daivī hyeṣā guṇamayī mama māyā duratyayā
māmeva ye prapadyante māyāmetāṁ taranti te 14.

strong words in describing the illness to the patient in order to bring home to the sufferer the seriousness of his malady; so too, Krishna is here only bringing home to us, by a direct merciless thrust, the seriousness of the mental tragedy into which the Supreme has seemingly fallen, to become the finite mortal ego! After declaring the seriousness of the disease and after giving the prescription, He hastens to guarantee a complete cure for this painful malady of man.

THOSE WHO DEVOTE THEMSELVES TO ME ALONE shall cross over their subjective delusion, which has created for man the objective worlds of sorrows and imperfections. How to do this has been already explained while discussing the technique of meditation, in the last chapter. With single-pointed mind, to contemplate upon the Self is the direct path; and in order to walk this narrow-way, the mind is to be made steady and concentrated, through the processes that have already been discussed. (in Chapter VI-14).

THEN WHY ALL THOSE WHO MEDITATE UPON THEE ARE NOT EXPERIENCING THE GLORY?

15 *The evil-doers, the deluded, the lowest of men, do not seek Me; they, whose discrimination has been destroyed by their own delusions, follow the ways of the demons.*

The last stanza talked of those that can transcend their own subjective delusion, and here, naturally, Krishna is trying to talk about the negative nature in those who cannot overcome this delusion to realise the Divine in themselves. Unless the contrast of ideas is given, the student will not be in a position

---

न मां दुष्कृतिनो मूढाः प्रपद्यन्ते नराधमाः ।
माययापहृतज्ञाना आसुरं भावमाश्रिताः ॥ १५ ॥

na māṁ duṣkṛtino mūḍhāḥ prapadyante narādhamāḥ
māyayāpahṛtajñānā āsuraṁ bhāvamāśritāḥ 15.

to understand properly what exactly are the mind's tendencies and appetites that are the true symptoms of delusion.

LOW MEN, DELUDED AND INDULGING THEMSELVES IN EVIL ACTIONS FOLLOW THE PATH OF THE DEVIL (*ASURA*) AND GET DEPRIVED OF THEIR DISCRIMINATION—We all know that the insignia of the higher evolution in man is his rational intellect, which can discriminate between the good and the bad, the high and the low, the moral and the immoral. This discriminative awareness is the subtle instrument by which individuals are rendered capable of awakening from the dream of their imperfections to their own Essential Nature of Absolute Divinity.

This faculty can function effectively only in a bosom that is unagitated by sense-impulses. The more an individual misunderstands himself to be only a mere mass of flesh, and continuously pants for self-gratification through sense indulgences, the more is he considered a sinner. Sin, in this sense, is but a devolutionary action which is not appropriate to the dignity and status of the highest evolutionary glory in man. Sin can be perpetrated only by those who have deluded themselves, believing that they are masses of flesh, with minds hungry for emotional satisfactions and intellects trying to assert and express their own ideas. Such people are here called by the *Geeta*, as deluded (*Moodhah*). The way-of-life, in such 'deluded men' (*Asura bhava*) has been exhaustively described to us by indicating the opposite good qualities of the 'perfect one' (*Daivi bhava*), later in the *Geeta* (XVI-3).

PEOPLE REACH ME THROUGH FOUR DIFFERENT APPROACHES; LISTEN:

16. *Four kinds of virtuous men worship Me, O Arjuna, the dissatisfied, the seeker of (systematised) knowledge, the seeker of wealth, and the wise, O best among the Bharatas.*

Since the Self is the source of all existence and energy, all other apparent activities that are seen at the level of matter, must come from the same great, grand motive force. Every part of a railway engine is made up of cold iron, and if the engine can run forward carrying along with it a trainload of passengers and goods, there must be something other than iron that is giving it the power to move. Similarly, when egocentric deluded men, considering themselves to be their body or mind or intellect, act in the world outside, they express a kind of seeming dynamism through their matter vestures. When those who are living in the matter-outskirts of the Palace of Truth, struggle hard to eke out satisfaction and happiness, fulfilling their desires, they too act invoking all their energies from the Spirit.

Even when the deluded egocentres want to live in their realm of ignorance and sorrows, they must necessarily invoke the required energy and sentiency from the Pure Consciousness, the Self. Whether they seek consolation in moments of distress, or whether they are mere seekers of satisfaction for the demands of the body, for the urges of the mind, for the questions of the intellect, or whether they be mere men of desires, striving hard to fulfil their desires or to satisfy their emotions - they all need the energy to function, the capacity to feel and the ability to act. This dynamic motive

---

चतुर्विधा भजन्ते मां जना: सुकृतिनोऽर्जुन ।
आर्तो जिज्ञासुरर्थार्थी ज्ञानी च भरतर्षभ ॥ १६ ॥

caturvidhā bhajante māṁ janāḥ sukṛtino'rjuna
ārto jijñāsurathārrthī jñānī ca bharatarṣabha 16.

power can reach the inert matter and vitalise it, only when the Spirit is invoked and contacted.

This invocation of the required type of energy to flow into a particular channel and act therein is called prayer (*Bhajana*). In all true prayers the ego surrenders itself to the Spirit with a demand to its Lord to manifest and function in any given scheme of activity. As an analogy we may take the example of how we make use of an electric plug on the wall. The various equipments such as the fan, or the heater, or the toaster, or the refrigerator – all are in themselves mere iron and steel gadgets which have no capacity of their own to perform any work. Only when the electric current is flowing through them, can these machines serve society.

If I plug a fan into the wall-socket, it is an act where the fan is, as it were, invoking the dynamic 'current' to flow through it. If the right instrument is contacted with the 'current', I will be served by the required manifestation. But supposing, in winter, I switch the fan on, I have no right then to complain that the electricity is cruel to me. If, unintelligently, I invoke the Truth to play through my mind which is maladjusted with wrong tendencies, the Spirit flowing through such an instrument can bring about nothing but sorrows for myself and disturbances to others.

With this scriptural idea that the Self has the total monopoly of all sentience and life, Krishna says here that everyone, be he a sinner or a saint, foolish or wise, dull or energetic, cowardly or courageous, must 'invoke Me' (*Bhajana*) and "I express Myself through the individual mental composition as the one who has the above qualities". "Each individual must approach Me", be it consciously or unconsciously, ere he can express himself at the intellectual, mental, or physical level of his personality.

If everyone must thus invoke the Self in expressing himself, or in fulfilling his ideas and emotions, then everyone is 'sacred' and 'virtuous' for, all of us, without an exception, are devotees at the temple of the Spirit. Lord Krishna, the Self, now expounds how the numberless persons that reach him with endless prayers can all be classified under four distinct groups:-

(a) Men who are dissatisfied with even the best in life (*Artah*) approach this Life Energy in themselves, for fighting against and for gaining a total relief from the spiritual distress that is threatening them in their within. They turn to Me, the Lord.

(b) Seekers of knowledge and understanding, *Jignasu* from a mere idle curiosity to study and come to know My Nature, ever invoke the grace of the Spirit.

(c) All men, throughout their lifetime, spend themselves irresistibly in some field of activity or the other, under the whip of their desires. Fulfilment of desires for wealth, position, name and fame (*Artharthi*) is the urge under which every member of the living kingdom acts restlessly, all through his lifetime. The inert materials of the body and intellect cannot act unless the Spirit is invoked to play through them.

(d) We have yet a rare few, who approach the sanctum sanctorum of the Temple of the Spirit, demanding nothing, expecting nothing, carrying with them only themselves as their offerings. They offer themselves as an oblation in a pure spirit of love-inspired total self-surrender. The only cry in their heart is that the Spirit should end their sense of separation and accept them back into the embrace of the Lord, to be made one with Him. These *Jnanis* constitute the last type who tries to invoke the Spirit.

OF THESE FOUR TYPES WHICH IS THE BEST?

17. *Of them the wise, ever steadfast and devoted to the One, excels; for, I am exceedingly dear to the wise, and he is dear to Me.*

Comparing and contrasting these four above-mentioned groups among themselves, the Lord declares here that the *Jnani*, who with a steadfast mind, surrenders himself to the Self, with an integrated heart of total devotion, which is not dissipated by other parallel aspirations, represents the best. Single-pointedness of mind can be gained only when the goal of the meditator is fixed and steady. The unbroken and all-out aspiration of the seeker to reach his own Real Nature, the Self, is called single-pointed-devotion (*Eka bhaktih*).

This is possible only when one withdraws oneself totally from all other extrovert demands of the lower nature in him. In the case of a *Jnani*, therefore, the Spirit is invoked not for the acquisition of anything, but for the annihilation of all the self-destructive channels through which his spiritual dynamism gushes out day-to-day, only to get wasted on the dry rocks of the world of hallucination. Naturally, therefore, the Self, as a personification in Krishna, declares in the *Geeta* that the *Jnanis* are the highest and the best among the living kingdom who reach the PORTALS OF TRUTH with their individual demands and aspirations, to experience their final merger in the Self.

To the truly wise "SUPREMELY DEAR AM I". Love is measured by the amount of identification the lover has gained with the beloved. Self-surrender is the tune in which the song of love is truly sung. Selfessness is the key in which the duet of

---

तेषां ज्ञानी नित्ययुक्त एकभक्तिर्विशिष्यते ।
प्रियो हि ज्ञानिनोऽत्यर्थमहं स च मम प्रियः ॥ १७ ॥
teṣāṁ jñānī nityayukta ekabhaktirviśiṣyate
priyo hi jñānino'yyarthamanaṁ sa ca mama priyaḥ 17.

love is played. Love demands 'giving without expecting any return' at all times, in all circumstances. With this understanding of the nature of true love, when one tries to understand the attitude of the *Jnani* towards the Self, it is true that a *Jnani* alone knows how to love wholly, completely.

One-sided love never culminates in any consummation. Man may approach the Spiritual Centre in himself in an attitude of discrimination and surrender – with all his aspiration and love - but if it is not reciprocated by the Spirit, it might become as tragic as the case of the Greek boy who fell in love with his own reflection. Here, when Krishna declares, "AND HE IS DEAR TO ME", a great psychological truth has been expounded. It is the Eternal Law that love, with no strings attached to it, can not only order its own fulfilment, but can also convert even the base into the noble by its silent persuasions and mysterious charms.

Scientifically viewed, it is an observable fact that if a mind is powerfully charged with a certain emotion - be it sorrows, hatred, jealousy, love or kindness - it can bring about sympathetic vibrations of similar emotions in the chambers of the hearts that come near it. When one full of hatred approaches us, he can influence and fill our hearts to the full with hatred. So too, if we can give the required dose of pure and sincere love, unmotivated by any desire or selfishness, it is a law that even the bitterest enemies, with their hearts full of hatred, can be forced to reflect nothing but love towards us. This psychological truth, in all its implications, has been brought out vividly when the *Geeta* states that even the Infinite and Eternal Truth has, helplessly, to come under the charm of pure and selfless courting of the meditator with *Eka-bhaktih*.

THEN, ARE NOT THE THREE OTHERS, THE DISSATISFIED AND THE REST, DEAR TO VASUDEVA? NOT SO. THEN HOW IS IT?

18. *Noble indeed are all these, but the wise man, I deem, as My very Self; for, steadfast in mind he is established in Me alone as the Supreme Goal.*

With the large-heartedness of a mastermind, Lord Krishna declares here that all creatures living the life of intelligent seeking and industrious efforts are blessed, inasmuch as they all are, in their own way, approaching the same fountain of the Infinite for tapping out their required energies. Although some are invoking the Eternal Spiritual Strength for the purposes of reducing their distress, or for fulfilling their desires, they all are, for one reason or the other, approaching the Self, and therefore, relatively, diviner than the insentient 'mineral world'. However, comparing and contrasting them with the *Jnanis*, the Lord says: "BUT, THE MAN OF KNOWLEDGE, I REGARD AS MY OWNSELF".

It is very well known that there is a lot of difference between maintaining one's friendship with the minister, and oneself becoming a minister. No doubt, to be a friend of a minister is to gain some amount of influence and power in society; but the entire might and glory come to the man when he himself becomes the minister. Similarly, to be capable of invoking and directing the spiritual strength is certainly divine; but a man of Knowledge is one who, courting Truth in a spirit of total identification with It, successfully attains the total transcendence of his individual mind-and-intellect, whereby his ego rediscovers itself to be nothing other than

---

उदाराः सर्व एवैते ज्ञानी त्वात्मैव मे मतम् ।
आस्थितः स हि युक्तात्मा मामेवानुत्तमां गतिम् ॥ १८ ॥

udārāḥ sarva evaite jñānī tvātmaiva me matam
āsthitaḥ sa hi yuktātmā māmevānuttamāṁ gatim 18.

the Self. He becomes one with It.

Such a *Jnani*, thereafter, ever remains in the divine sense of identification with the Self. This emphasis of extra preference to the status of a man-of-Wisdom, is according to Krishna, his personal opinion (*Matam*).

19. *At the end of many births the wise man comes to Me, realising that all this is Vasudeva (the innermost Self); such a great soul (MAHATMA) is very hard to find.*

That such pure men-of-Wisdom are necessarily few in the history of the world, is the declaration here, which, in decadent Hinduism, we have learnt to consider as an extremely pessimistic assertion (VI-45). A little thought should clearly make the fallacy of this wild conclusion quite evident to us. The entire human kingdom is, indeed, a very negligible and small proportion of the total sentient creatures in the world. In the community of man, not all have a fully developed instrument of rational thinking and divine emotion.

Even among those who have fully developed mental and intellectual capacities, it is a rare few that seriously take up the study of the scriptures. All those who STUDY scriptures do not LIVE the scriptures, but they come to feel fulfilled in a mere understanding of its contents. Therefore, it becomes evident that only a rare few can ever reach the goal of evolution and come to discover their true Divine Nature of Perfection.

बहूनां जन्मनामन्ते ज्ञानवान्मां प्रपद्यते ।
वासुदेव: सर्वमिति स महात्मा सुदुर्लभ: ॥ १९ ॥

bahūnāṁ janmanāmante jñānavānmāṁ prapadyate
vāsudevaḥ sarvamiti sa mahātmā sudurlabhaḥ 19.

Like Darwin in our own days, the ancient *Rishis* also had observed in their times, that this development can take place only when, in the flood of time, the different circumstances have rubbed down and polished the imperfect into the shape and beauty of the perfect. It takes trillions of years for an organism to evolve from one given form of existence into a higher form of life. Naturally, it becomes quite clear that for a rational being of subtlest potentialities, it should take an indefinitely large number of lives in different manifestations to scrape off all his ignorance, and thereby, ultimately reach the perfect realm of all Knowledge.

This does not mean that none among us, now striving so hard, has any chance of reaching the goal of life in this very birth. It is not in any pessimistic hopelessness and total despair, that this statement is made by the Lord in the *Geeta*. On the other hand, it is solely for bringing into the recognition of the student the urgency of his faithful pursuit of the higher life. The very fact that a seeker has come to feel a disappointment with his present state of existence, and the fact that he has discovered enough intellectual capacity to appreciate and comprehend the subtle thoughts of the *Upanishadic* lore, clearly shows that he has reached the very archway to the temple of the Self. A little more sincere and steady self-application can take him to the highest state of his evolution.

NOW IT WILL BE SHOWN WHY THE PEOPLE ARE NOT GENERALLY AWARE THAT THE SELF, OR VASUDEVA, ALONE IS THE ALL:

20. *Those whose wisdom has been looted away by this or that desire go to other gods, following this or that rite, led by their own nature.*

Desire for the sense-objects of the world and the urge for sense-gratification are the great factors which cloud the discriminative potentialities in the human intellect. It is impossible that an individual is not made conscious of his own Self, in the light of a powerful and strong discrimination.

Earlier, we were told that the deity for whose propitiation we performed the *Yajna* was none other than 'the productive potential in any given field of activity'. Reading the stanza in the light of this interpretation we may say that the deity mentioned here denotes nothing other than the various joys contained in the different sensuous fields which are courted by us, when we get lashed by desires, in order that we may gain a complete and exhaustive satisfaction from them.

Desires are the springs from which thoughts continuously gurgle up to flood the mental zone, and disturb the glorious reflection of Truth in it. When the mind is thus disturbed, the discriminative capacity in the intellect is rendered dull, then naturally, that individual becomes incapable of distinguishing in his understanding, the Real from the unreal. When the brilliance of the human intellect has been clouded with the vapours of desire, the owls of negativity and

---

कामैस्तैस्तैर्हृतज्ञाना: प्रपद्यन्तेऽन्यदेवता: ।
तं तं नियममास्थाय प्रकृत्या नियता: स्वया ॥ २० ॥
kāmaistaistairhṛtajñānāḥ prapadyānte'nyadevatāḥ
taṁ taṁ nuyamamāsthāya prakṛtyā niyatāḥ svayā 20.

delusory attachments start hooting in the jungles of that mind.

It is not the mere appearance of desires in the mind that causes the fall of man. No individual can resist the compelling charm of the desires rising in his bosom. But when he comes to identify himself with them, the thoughts rising in him are directly governed by his desires. When once a given desire has been identified with, the desirer himself, unconsciously, comes to lend an uncontrollable amount of dynamism to the upsurge of the flood of thoughts.

Thoughts themselves are inert matter, inasmuch as they are the by-product of food, being constituted of the subtlest aspect of the food consumed. These inert thought-waves gather a momentum and force by borrowing their strength and vigour from the Self, through the individual's enthusiastic identification with those desires. The urge of thoughts determines the action. The actor in the field, for the time being, is rendered incapable of discriminating whether the action undertaken can, or cannot, ultimately bring to him a permanent and an enduring satisfaction. Drunk with the idea that he will be at least temporarily appeased, the individual struggles hard and strives intensively to invoke and propitiate THE PRODUCTIVE POTENTIAL OF ANY GIVEN FIELD OF HIS ACTIVITY (*DEVATA*).

In thus invoking the *Devata* of a given field, the individual has to strive in a proper and fitting fashion. The methods of assembling the required instruments, the techniques of their application, the time intervals necessary for maturing the results, and the type of gains accrued from the different kinds of application... all these differ from field to field in the world. Therefore, each one will have to follow this or that rite, according to the type of his desires.

The reason why different persons thus struggle hard so differently, leaving aside all sincere struggles to realise the Self, as 'VASUDEVA IS ALL THIS' is explained here in the second line. Each individual helplessly functions in the different fields of his temporary fascinations, according to the mental impressions, gathered in his earlier moments of activity and thought. To conceive that the Creator is putting ideas into each one of us, because of which one is good and another vile, is a philosophy of the defeatist, of the impotent, of the sluggard. True men of action, with the daring of a well-developed intellect, can very easily see through men and their behaviours and come to this bold conclusion that each man acts as per the schedule, maintained and ordered by himself, during his own past actions.

In short, a deluded person strives hard, running after the mirage of sensuality, vainly hoping to gain therein a satisfaction that is at once infinite and immortal, while another is found to have the subtle discrimination to discover for himself the hollowness and futility of sense-pursuit. This latter type withdraws from all these ultimately unprofitable fields, and with avidity seeks the path to the Real.

WHAT THEN IS THE FUNCTION OF THE *ATMAN*, THE GUARDIAN ANGEL IN EACH ONE OF US?

21. *Whatsoever form any devotee desires to worship with faith --that (same) faith of his I make (firm and) unflinching.*

In the very opening of this chapter (VII-7), discriminating

यो यो यां यां तनुं भक्तः श्रद्धयार्चितुमिच्छति ।
तस्य तस्याचलां श्रद्धां तामेव विदधाम्यहम् ॥ २१ ॥

yo yo yāṁ yāṁ tanuṁ bhaktaḥ śraddhayārcitumicchati
tasya tasyācalāṁ śraddhā tāmevā vidadhāmyaham 21.

the Self from the not-Self, it was shown how Krishna is the Spiritual Principle, the Common Truth that holds together the multiple universe of names and forms. It was also said (VII-14) that the three-fold mental temperaments (*gunas*), that work up the 'divine illusion' hoodwink the individual from right cognition of the Divine Self within him. But for the Conscious Principle thrilling the inert matter walls that seemingly encircle the spirit, neither our physical, nor mental, nor intellectual personalities can ever come to function, as they do now. It is very well known that all men do not worship at the same altar. Each one approaches the same Truth by worshipping the idol of his own heart. Krishna here declares the sacred truth that in all Churches, Mosques, and Temples, in public places, or in private institutions, in the open, or on the sly, in the quiet huts, and in the silent caves - wherever and in whatsoever form, any devotee seeks to worship with *Shraddha*, "HIS FAITH DO I MAKE UNWAVERING". A faithful follower of the *Geeta* can never be contaminated by sectarianism or intolerance. At the foot of every altar, it is Krishna, the Self, that constantly supplies more and more faith to water the expanding fields of devotion in the sincere devotees.

Applying this general statement to the subjective worship in the human bosom, we can very easily understand the greater import of this stanza.

In the world outside, it is very well known that the greater the consistency with which an idea or an attachment is maintained by an individual, the greater does he become fixed in that temperament or relationship. The more often a particular type of thought is entertained in the mind, the deeper becomes that thought channel, strengthening that very mental impression. These deep-cut patterns of thought, ploughed along the valleys of the mind, indicate the pattern of desires which the individual had entertained. In the law that governs this psychological rule, we can spy and detect the Spiritual Reality and Its infinite and glorious might.

In short, the Lord says that "as we think so we become" and the more we become, the more we think in the same given pattern. Applying this principle of psychology, it becomes clear, beyond all doubts, why everyone of us is bound by our own habits, and how we get chained by our own peculiar type of thinking. The sensuous are not to be condemned, and equally so, the divine need not be congratulated! Both of them are the exact products of their individual types of thinking. Thought belongs to the realm of nature (*Prakriti*); thoughts create the world and the all-pervading Self is the Essential Substratum (*Purusha*) that provides the world-drama with its stage and scenario.

WITH THIS EVER-GROWING FAITH, HOW DOES THE MAN-OF-THE-WORLD GAIN HIS PARTICULAR DESIRE?

22. *Endowed with that faith, he engages in the worship of that 'DEVATA' and from it he obtains his desire-fulfilments; all these being ordained, indeed, by Me (alone).*

Imbued with this faith he invokes the *Devata* of his choice and gains the fulfilment of his desires. And, Lord Krishna

---

स तया श्रद्धया युक्तस्तस्याराधनमीहते ।
लभते च ततः कामान्मयैव विहितान्हि तान् ॥ २२ ॥

sa tayā śraddhayā yuktastasyā rādhanamīhate
labhate ca tataḥ kāmānmayaiva vihitānhi tān 22.

adds that in all cases these desires are "BEING VERILY DISPENSED BY ME ALONE". The Self is the source of all activities, gains, fulfilments and despairs. The sense of joy or sorrow, of success or failure, is but a mental thought-wave; but for the Conscious principle illumining it, we would not have any such experience.

Faithful activity in any given field of action brings about complete success, but the very existence of the field, the capacity to act, the fervour of faith that supplies consistency to all efforts -- all these are possible only in the medium of the Changeless, the Actionless, the Attributeless, Eternal Self. And Krishna, identifying Himself with this Spiritual Centre of the Universe, rightly declares here, that He alone is the One that supplies an ever-growing faith in all activities, and ultimately, when the laws of action are fulfilled to the last bit, both in their intensity and application, it is He alone who dispenses the exact result of each action.

When a well-adjusted radio is plugged onto the current, the electric current says that it alone is the 'dispenser' of the programme available at the station for the listeners!

SINCE THE DELUDED ONES DESIRE THE FINITE SENSE OBJECTS, THEY DO NOT COME TO THE ALL-SATISFYING PEACE; AND HENCE, IT IS SAID:

23. *Verily the 'fruit' that accrues to those men of little intelligence is finite. The worshippers of the DEVAS go to the DEVAS but My devotees come to Me.*

The fruits accruing to "THESE MEN OF LITTLE

अन्तवत्तु फलं तेषां तद्भवत्यल्पमेधसाम् ।
देवान्देवयजो यान्ति मद्भक्ता यान्ति मामपि ॥ २३ ॥

antavattu phalaṁ teṣāṁ tadbhavatyalpamedhasam
devāndevayajo yānti madbhaktā yānti māmapi 23.

UNDERSTANDING ARE LIMITED". Fleeting desires for finite objects, even when fulfilled through the impermanent activities, must surely prove to be ephemeral. Out of gold whatever ornament is made, it also must be gold alone; when chocolate is made out of sweet things, the resultant stuff cannot be bitter. The effects entirely depend, for their nature and quality, upon those of the causes.

Finite actions undertaken in finite fields, employing finite instruments, cannot but produce - whether joy or sorrow - finite 'fruits'. Joy arrested or ended is sorrow; and therefore, in each instance of a sensuous desire satisfied, though there is a joy and a fulfilment, the sense of satisfaction soon putrefies to provide the sourness of dissatisfaction, or more often, the bitterness of sorrow.

This statement of the Lord is supported by the following general rule that, 'THE WORSHIPPERS OF THE *DEVAS* REACH THE *DEVAS*'. Those who are invoking a desired 'profit potential' in any given field of activity, can, even when completely successful, gain only THAT profit.

The above statement is declared as a contrast to a pure philosophical truth, when the Lord, says: "THOSE WHO DEVOTE THEMSELVES TO ME, COME TO ME". Seekers of happiness in the world of sense-objects, as a result of their strife and struggle, can gain their insignificant success in the field of sense-enjoyments. If the same effort is applied by them in the right life of constructive living, they can come to discover their identity with the Eternal Absolute, the Self. Due to the extrovertedness of the deluded ego, it comes to identify itself with its finite matter-envolopments, and revels in a world of its endless number of objects, called in Sanskrit as the *Jagat*.

Discriminative and careful seekers, understanding the utter uselessness of the pursuit of finite pleasures, detach themselves from their false egocentric lives, and through the process of meditation upon the Self, as advised in the previous chapter, come to rediscover their own Real Nature in the sunny fields of Bliss that lie unrolled beyond the thorny by-lanes of all physical, psychological and intellectual quests.

In the language of the *Geeta,* the first person singular stands always, at all places, for the Infinite Reality which is the substratum for the individual as well as for the whole. Therefore, "MY DEVOTEES COME TO ME" is not the assertion of a limited historical figure as the son of Devaki, but the Singer of the *Geeta,* in His divine inspiration, entirely identifies Himself with the Principle of Consciousness that is the core of the pluralistic dream of the mind-intellect equipment. Thus, to understand the above statement, without its seeming limitations, is to understand the *Geeta,* the Scripture of Man, as declaring that the seekers of the Self discover themselves and become the Self.

THEN WHY DO PEOPLE IN GENERAL FAIL TO REACH THE SELF? LISTEN:

24. *The foolish think of Me, the Unmanifest, as having come to manifestation, not knowing My higher, immutable and peerless nature.*

Men, who lack discrimination and the capacity to perceive

अव्यक्तं व्यक्तिमापन्नं मन्यन्ते मामबुद्धयः ।
परं भावमजानन्तो ममाव्ययमनुत्तमम् ॥ २४ ॥

avyaktaṁ vyaktimāpannaṁ manyante māmabuddhayaḥ
param bhāvamajānanto mamāvyamanuttamam 24.

* Ibid., 7

the subtle Truth that shines in and through the vast disturbances of the endless plurality, fail to realise the immutable and the peerless Self. In their extreme preoccupation with the ever-changing glory of the perceivable, the *Prakriti*, (VII-4 and 6) they do not understand that "ALL THIS IS STRUNG IN ME AS A ROW OF PEARLS ON A STRING".*

This fundamental Reality, that is the beam of brilliance in which like dust particles the Universes dance about, is termed as the 'Unmanifest'. This term is to be understood in all its philosophical implications. That which is called the MANIFEST is available either for the perceptions of the sense-organs, or for the feelings of the mind, or for the understanding of the intellect. That which is not available for any one of these instruments of cognition, feeling or understanding is considered as the UNMANIFEST.

The Self, indeed, should then be considered as the UNMANIFEST, for it is the VITALITY behind the sense-organs, the FEELER – potential in the mind and the very LIGHT that illumines the intellect.

The distorted intellects of the extroverts, in their miscalculations, come to the false judgement that the physical glory of the Prophet, or of the incarnation, is all that is the Eternal Truth. The point of concentration (*Upasya*) is to be considered, no doubt, as the symbol of the Truth which the devotee is seeking, but it cannot IN ITSELF be the Truth. If it were the Truth, then after carving out an idol, or after approaching a *Guru*, the devotee has nothing more to do, since he has gained the Truth! Idol worship is only a convenience for gathering true concentration, for getting an initial momentum for the final flight into themselves, to reach the Self and discover therein their own oneness with It.

This stanza gives us a clear insight into the futility of mistaking the bottle for the medicine, the physical form for the *Guru*, the idol for the God! All whitewood is not the fragrant sandalwood. Any bright light high up in the sky, however resplendent it might be, is not a star. Some men of incomparable foolishness may come to declare that the light from a tower is the Sun, but no wise man of the town will accept it. The idea of Divine Incarnation is accepted in Hinduism, and according to its theory, EVERYONE IS AN INCARNATION TO A DEGREE! The same Truth pervades all, and is in each. It expresses through the enveloping layers of the mind-and-intellect. The clearer the mind and the purer the intellect, the greater is the effulgence of the Divine that beams out through them.

When the Self in anyone beams out through the steadied and purified mind and intellect completely sublimating his lower nature (*Prakriti*), he becomes a Prophet, a Sage. Krishna, Rama, Christ, Mohammed, Buddha, Mahavira are some of the examples. These men-of-Realisation, discovering their Self, understood and lived every moment of their lives in the Self, as the Self of all. To mistake their physical structure, or the lingering traces of their mind, or the film of their intellectual personality, for the very Essence of Truth, which these God-men were, is to make as miserable a mistake as taking the waves to be the ocean!

Naturally, therefore, Krishna uses here a severe term, to indicate such deluded men of superstitious false understanding, as UNINTELLIGENT FOOLS (*A-Buddhayah*).

WHAT CAUSES THIS PREVALENT IGNORANCE OF THE TRUE NATURE IS EXPLAINED IN THE FOLLOWING:

25. *I am not manifest to all (in My Real Nature) veiled by Divine-'MAYA'. This deluded world knows not Me, the Unborn, the Imperishable.*

If there be such a glorious Essential Truth, which is the core of everything, why is it that it is not freely known and experienced by everyone at all times? In short, "what stands between me and my Self?" Why is it that we behave as though we are but limited egocentric entities, incapacitated as we are, to comprehend that in essence we are the Infinite, the Immortal? These questions are unavoidable to an intelligent seeker, when he, in his aspirations, comes face to face with the staggering revelations contained in *Vedanta*.

"THIS DELUDED WORLD KNOWS ME NOT, THE UNBORN AND THE IMMORTAL because their own ILLUSION, BORN OUT OF THE THREE *gunas*, VEILS ME". *Maya* is the most difficult theme of all for elementary students of *Vedanta*, when they try merely to understand this science of Life objectively. The moment a student tries to experiment with this 'Knowledge' upon himself subjectively, the explanations contained in the theory become evident. *Maya* is the conditioning through which, when the Non-dual Truth expresses Itself, the One Reality seems to fan out as the spectrum of the multiple universe.

The principle of *Maya* functioning in the individual is termed ignorance (*Avidya*). This subjective malady, which provides in its wake, the dreamy hallucinations of a sorrowful

---

नाहं प्रकाशः सर्वस्य योगमायासमावृतः ।
मूढोऽयं नाभिजानाति लोको मामजमव्ययम् ॥ २५ ॥

nāhaṁ prakāśaḥ sarvasya yogamāyāsamāvṛtaḥ
mūḍho'yaṁ nābhijānāti loko māmajamavyayam 25.

world of change and imperfections, has been very closely observed, and the *Rishis* of old have declared that it is caused by three types of 'moods' in man's inner personality. These three temperaments (*gunas*), called *Sattva*, *Rajas* and *Tamas*, provide a prism, viewed through which, the kaleidoscopic world seems to dance, flashing its infinite patterns. *Rajas* creates mental agitations (*Vikshepa*), and *tamas* creates the intellectual veiling (*Avarana*).

To him who becomes confused and confounded by the play of these triple temperaments, the Self is not available for direct experience. Special instructions from teachers and diligent practice on the part of students are both necessary in order to make one realise one's own Real Nature. To an ignorant man of the jungle, electricity is unmanifest in the bulb and in its incandescent filament. In order to perceive the electrical current that flows through the equipment, theoretical knowledge and experimental confirmation are essential. After having gained the knowledge of the electrical energy and its properties, when the student happens to see the very same bulb, he comes to cognise through the perceived bulb the imperceptible, the unmanifest electrical energy!

Similarly, when through self-control, listening, reflection, and meditation, the agitations of the mind are quietened, and when the veiling has been pulled down, the seeker rediscovers "ME THE UNBORN, THE IMMUTABLE". As long as the agitations of the mind veil the intellect from its awareness of the Self, so long the limited ego (*Jeeva*) pants to fulfil itself and to gain the Infinite among the gutters of its sensual cravings!

Such frenzied hearts reeking with desires and lacerated with disappointments, crushed by dissatisfactions and smothered by the fear of their own annihilation – can never have the integrated equipoise to live even a moment of still-awareness to experience the Pure Consciousness. "THE DELUDED WORLD KNOWS ME NOT" as it is steeped in "THE ILLUSION BORN OUT OF THE THREEFOLD *GUNAS*". Screened off by this universe of names and forms, which is but an apparent projection on the Self, the sense-organs, mind or intellect fail to perceive It. The ghost veils the post! The mirage-waters clothe the desert!! The waves screen off the ocean!!!

THE PRESENT CONDITION OF IGNORANCE AND CONFUSION IN THE LIMITED FINITE EGO IS BROUGHT OUT VERY VIVIDLY IN THE FOLLOWING, BY CONTRASTING IT AGAINST THE BACKGROUND OF THE SELF, WHICH IS OF THE NATURE OF ALL KNOWLEDGE:

26. *I know, O Arjuna, the beings of the past, and present and the future, but no one knows Me.*

The idea that God is Omniscient is common to all religions of the world, but a satisfactory explanation of this concept is given only in *Vedanta*. In the *Geeta* too, as a Bible of the Hindu religion, as a handbook of easy reference for the students of the *Upanishads*, we find a wider hint as to what we mean by the Omniscience of the Self.

The Self, as the Pure Consciousness, is the illuminating principle that brings the entire field of the mind and intellect under the beam of Its clear awareness. Even the world-of-objects is brought within our understanding only when it enters, through the sense-organ-doors, and reaches the mental lake, and makes therein its characteristic thought-waves; the thought-waves make the intellect function in

---

वेदाहं समतीतानि वर्तमानानि चार्जुन ।
भविष्याणि च भूतानि मां तु वेद न कश्चन ॥ २६॥

vedāham samatītāni vartamānāni cārjuna
bhaviṣyāṇi ca bhūtāni māṁ tu veda na kaścana 26.

classifying and determining them. Both these mental and intellectual disturbances are illumined for us by the ever-wakeful Consciousness, the Self in us.

Sunlight illuminates all the objects of the world. When my eyes or ears illumine a given form or sound, I say that I see or hear that particular form or sound. In short, to be aware of a thing is to know that thing; and to know is to illumine. Just as the Sun can be considered as the 'eye of the world', inasmuch as without the Sun all organs-of-vision will be blind apertures, so too, the Self can be considered as the knower of everything, in everyone, at all times, and in all places. This Omniscience of the Supreme is vividly hinted at here, when Krishna declares, "I KNOW THE BEINGS OF THE PAST, OF THE PRESENT, AND OF THE FUTURE".

It must be noted that the Eternal Self is not only the Awareness that lights up all bosoms at this present moment, but it was the awareness that illumined the objects, feelings and thoughts in all bosoms from the beginningless beginning of creation and it shall be the same Principle behind every knower that knows anything in all the future generations till the endless end of time!

Electricity revolves the fan; but the fan can never fan the electricity! The gazer surveys the heavens through a telescope, but the telescope can never survey the gazer! The Conscious Principle vitalises the food-made mind and intellect and makes them capable of feeling and thinking. Without the Self dynamising them, they are incapable of sense-perceptions; but neither the mind, nor the intellect, can perceive, feel, or comprehend the Subjective Principle, the Self. The Lord declares here that, though he knows everything, at all times,

* The congress of the three *gunas* wherein *Sattva* predominates over the other two. "*Sattvaguna-pradhana mayopahita Brahma, Ishwarah*" is Lord, the *Ishwara*.

in all places, He is known by none at any place or at any time – "BUT ME NONE KNOWS".

According to the strictest *Vedantic* philosophy, the Self is not a 'knower', just as in the strictest logic of thought it would not be correct to say that the Sun 'illumines' the world. From our standpoint, contrasting with the hours of night when things are not illumined, we may rightly attribute the function of illuminating things during the day to the 'principle of light' called the Sun. However, from the standpoint of the Sun, which is ever brilliant, there is no moment when he is not blessing the objects with his shining touch. Therefore, it is as meaningless to say that the Sun 'illumines' the objects, as to say that "I am too busy now-a-days breathing!"

'Knowerhood' is a status gained by Self when It functions through the equipment of *Maya*; and the Self, that functions in and through delusory *Maya*,* is called the God-principle, termed in the *Vedantic* literature as *Ishwara*. Here Krishna is pictured by Vyasa as the divine embodiment of Truth, and an Incarnation of the Self, and therefore, it is perfectly right if He arrogates to Himself the nature of Omniscience and declares Himself as "THE KNOWER OF EVERYTHING IN ALL THE THREE PERIODS OF TIME".

But unfortunately, an egocentric mortal viewing the universe through the pinhole of his congested, constricted and limited mind-and-intellect, fails to see the harmonious rhythm in the macrocosm. He who can rip open his own self-made bondages of ignorance and rise to attune himself with the macrocosm, can certainly come to experience the Krishna viewpoint. Anyone who successfully comes to live thus in unison with the cosmic mind, is the Krishna of that age and forever thereafter.

IF THE SELF IS THE ETERNAL KNOWER OF ALL

CONDITIONED-KNOWLEDGE, THEN, WHAT VEILS THIS ESSENTIAL NATURE FROM OUR REALISATION? LISTEN:

27. *By the delusion of the pairs-of-opposites arising from desire and aversion, O Bharata, all beings are subject to delusion at birth, O Parantapa (scorcher of foes).*

A highly scientific and extremely subtle philosophical truth has been suggested in this stanza. In His attempt to explain why and how the egocentric personality in man fails to cognise His all-full nature, the Lord touches, by implication, the very fundamentals discovered and discussed by modern biologists in explaining the evolution of organisms. The instinct of self-preservation is the most powerful urge under which the individualised ego tries to live its life of continuous change. This instinct of preservation expresses itself in the intellectual zone as binding desires for things that contribute to the continuous welfare and well-being of the individual's mundane existence.

When the impulse of desire, flowing from a bosom towards an object of attachment, gets halfway bumped upon an object or a being that stands between the bosom that craves and the object-of-craving, the refracted desire-thoughts express themselves as aversion (II-52,53). In the tug of war between these two forces of desire and aversion, the hapless ego gets torn asunder and comes to suffer the agonising pain of lynching tensions within. Naturally, its mind-and-intellect becomes fully preoccupied with its pursuits of the things of its desire, and with its efforts at running away from the objects

---

इच्छाद्वेषसमुत्थेन द्वन्द्वमोहेन भारत ।
सर्वभूतानि संमोहं सर्गे यान्ति परंतप ॥ २७ ॥

icchādveṣasamutthena dvandvamohena bhārata
sarvabhūtāni sammohaṁ sarge yānti parantapa 27.

of its aversion. Soon the egocentric personality becomes endlessly preoccupied, totally confused and completely exhausted. The hosts of thought-disturbances that are thereby created in the mental, and in the intellectual zones, breed among themselves and add day by day to the chaos within. The 'agitation' (*Vikshepa*) is that which veils (*Avarana*) the Truth from the direct cognition of the individual.

Therefore, the only way by which we can come to rediscover our equipoise and tranquillity as the Eternal Self, is to arrest, control and win over the agitations of the mind. All spiritual practices in all religions of the world are techniques - either emotional, or intellectual or physical - that aim at bringing about at least one solitary moment of perfect mental poise. Such a moment of poise is the moment of perfect mental illumination, the auspicious hour of Self-rediscovery and fulfilment of the reunion.

But unfortunately, adds the Lord in a divinely pathetic note, "ALL BEINGS FALL INTO THIS DELUSION AT THEIR VERY BIRTH". This is not a pessimistic submission as to the sorrowful destiny of a man, to escape from which he is incapacitated from birth. Unlike the Christ-religion, our Krishna-religion does not conceive a man as 'a child of sin'. The Master-optimist, the Teacher of Hope, the Joyous Dancer of the Jamuna banks, is expressing here only a philosophical truth, that the very birth of an individual into a given embodiment, with its available environment, is the tragedy that he himself had planned out elaborately for the fulfilment of his own deep cravings and secret desires.

To get out of these delusions and gain the right knowledge constitutes the sacred goal of life, and the *Geeta* is the Song of the Self that enchants the erring souls away from their confusions to the inviting fields of the joyous Perfection.

TO SHOW THEN WHAT THE QUALIFICATIONS OF THOSE WHO SEEK THE TRUTH ARE, THE FOLLOWING IS GIVEN:

28. *But those men of virtuous deeds whose sins have come to an end, who are freed from the delusion of the pairs-of-opposites and steadfast in vows, worship Me.*

"MEN OF VIRTUOUS DEEDS" as a result of their actions, "COME TO CLEANSE THEIR SINFUL NATURE" -- is a declaration that needs to be correctly understood. Sin is not the nature of man; according to *Vedanta*, it is only the tarnish that has come to dim the brilliance of the Self, due to an error of judgement in the individual. The craving of the mind-and-intellect, to live in subservience to the calls and appetites of the grosser outer world, is the root-cause for the negative values entertained by us, which ultimately result in 'sins'. He is called a sinful-person in whom his body makes the heaviest calls on his time and attention. In such a person, the body becomes the dominant partner, and it 'enslaves' the Self. An extrovert life - a life spent in pursuing the satisfaction of his sensuous desires, to comfort and console every one of his paltry emotions - is the way of the sinful.

Such a passionate animal-life leaves gross impressions upon the mind and intellect. Impressions (*Vasanas*) decide the future flow of thoughts. "As the thoughts, so the actions" and the actions deepen the *Vasanas*.

To break this '*vasana*-thought-action' chain which is now digging the grave of the individual's peace and tranquillity,

---

येषां त्वन्तगतं पापं जनानां पुण्यकर्मणाम् ।
ते द्वन्द्वमोहनिर्मुक्ता भजन्ते मां दृढव्रताः ॥ २८ ॥

yeṣāṁ tvantagataṁ pāpaṁ janānāṁ puṇyakarmaṇām
te dvendvemohanimuktā bhajante māṁ dṛḍhavratāḥ 28.

it is advised that he start a new life of meritorious actions. Merit (*punya*) is a contrast to sin (*papa*) and therefore, it is constituted of actions, feelings and thoughts, dedicated to the godly and the divine. All introvert actions undertaken in the cognition of "THE SELF I AM" would create in their wake new impressions. In the long run, the patterns of sin that existed in the bosom are wiped out and new divine designs are created therein.

Such a prepared mind-intellect, from which almost all its negativities have been rubbed off, is "FREE FROM THE DELUSION OF THE PAIRS-OF-OPPOSITES". It then becomes an instrument that can, with a single-pointed steadfastness and firm resolve, meditate upon the Self.

WHAT WOULD BE THE MOTIVE IN THE HEART OF THOSE WHO ARE THUS MEDITATING UPON THE SELF AFTER THEIR MINDS HAVE BEEN READJUSTED BY LIVING THE LIFE-DIVINE? LISTEN:

29. *Those who strive for liberation from old age and death, taking refuge in Me – They realise in full that BRAHMAN, the whole knowledge of the Self and all action.*

Those who thus strive diligently to cleanse their hearts of their wrong tendencies and bring their minds so purified for higher contemplation upon the Self, do so in order to gain freedom from old age and death. But the modern world is also striving to discover methods of arresting death and avoiding old age. However, this physical continuity of existence in the world is not the goal that has been hinted at

---

जरामरणमोक्षाय मामाश्रित्य यतन्ति ये ।
ते ब्रह्म तद्विदुः कृत्स्नमध्यात्मं कर्म चाखिलम् ॥ २९ ॥

jarāmaraṇamokṣāya māmāśritya yatanti ye
te brahma tadviduḥ kṛtsnamadhyātmaṁ karma cākhilam 29.

here in the science of spiritual evolution.

Birth, growth, disease, decay and death are the natural modifications that come to every man, or being, living in a given manifestation to the ripe old age of its full existence. Such modifications as experiences of change are the agonising sources of all pains in life. But for this change, a complete and unbroken happiness could be our lot. The attempt of a spiritual seeker, in his meditation upon the Self, is to get over all his identifications with the realm of change, and the entire province of change is indicated by these two familiar terms 'OLD AGE AND DEATH'.

Such a true meditator, meditating upon the Self, comes to realise his identity with the Conscious Principle in him, the Self. The Self in the individual (*Atman*) is the Eternal Truth, which is the substratum for the whole universe (*Brahman*). To realise the Self is to become *Brahman*, since the Self in the individual is the One Self everywhere. This non-duality of the Truth is implied here in this stanza when it declares that "THOSE WHO MEDITATE UPON ME, THE SELF, COME TO KNOW *BRAHMAN*".

That the man-of-Realisation is not therefore an impotent fool in worldly transactions, has been clearly brought out here, when Krishna says that the Perfected One not only realises the All-pervading Self, but at once comprehends "THE WORKING OF THE PSYCHOLOGICAL FORCES (*Adhyatma*) IN HIM AND BECOMES PROFICIENT IN ALL ACTIVITIES (*Karma*)". It is very well realised by all men of experience, that he alone can serve the world who has a full and complete knowledge of the psychology of the world, and also has a perfect control over his own mind. A man of harmonious perfection is the fittest instrument to sing the Song-of-Truth, and such an individual must be the best integrated personality, smart and efficient in all activities.

CONTINUING THE SAME IDEA AND EXPRESSING HOW A MAN OF WISDOM IS A MAN OF ALL KNOWLEDGE AND ALL EFFICIENCY, KRISHNA DECLARES:

30. *Those who know Me with the ADHIBHUTA (pertaining to elements; the world-of-objects), ADHIDAIVA (pertaining to the gods; the sense-organs) and the ADHIYAJNA (pertaining to the sacrifice; all perceptions), even at the time of death, steadfast in mind, know Me.*

Not only that the man-of-Realisation understands all the vagaries of the mind and the nature of all activities, but he also gains a perfect knowledge of the world-of-objects (*Adhibhuta*), the secrets behind the workings of the sense-organs, mind, and intellect (*Adhidaiva*), and the conditions under which all perceptions – physical, mental and intellectual (*Adhiyajna*) can best take place.

The common idea that a man-of-God is an impractical man, inefficient to live a successful life in the world, may be true as far as a dedicated devotee of a particular god-form, or a prophet, is concerned. The *Upasaka* is one who is so fully engrossed with his emotions and thoughts, dedicated to the

---

साधिभूताधिदैवं मां साधियज्ञं च ये विदुः ।
प्रयाणकालेऽपि च मां ते विदुर्युक्तचेतसः ॥ ३० ॥

sādhibhūtādhidaivaṁ māṁ sādhiyajñaṁ ca ye viduḥ
prayāṇakāle'pi ca māṁ te viduryaktacetasaḥ 30.

Lord of his heart, that he has neither the interest nor the capacity to know the ways of the world. But the man-of-Perfection, as conceived by the science of *Vedanta*, is not only a man of experience in the realm of Spirit, but he is also, at all times, on all occasions, under all situations, a master of himself, and a dynamic force to be reckoned with.

He essentially becomes the leader of the world, as he is a master of his own mind, as well as the minds of the entire living kingdom. To him, thereafter, everything becomes clear, and such a man-of-Perfection lives in the world as God in his Knowledge of the worlds, both within and without.

In short, the chapter closes with a total assertion that "HE WHO KNOWS ME KNOWS EVERYTHING"; he is the man who will guide the destinies of the world, not only in his own times, but also in the days to come, as Lord Krishna Himself did.

These two closing stanzas of this chapter do not of themselves explain all the terms used in them. They represent a summary of the following chapter. In a *shastra* this is one of the traditional methods in the art of connecting two consecutive chapters together. In the form of *Mantras*, these two stanzas indicate the contents and the theme of the following chapter.

Thus, in the UPANISHADS of the glorious Bhagawad Geeta, in the Science of the Eternal, in the Scripture of YOGA, in the dialogue between Shri Krishna and Arjuna, the seventh discourse ends entitled:

The *Yoga* of Knowledge and Wisdom

Vedantic ideologies, preached in the *Upanishads* had become, by the time of Vyasa, mere speculative narrations of poetic perfection, divorced from the actualities of life. The Hindus, thus estranged from the essential glory and strength of their culture, were to be resurrected by showing them the particular beauty and fire that lie concealed in the philosophical speculations. In this chapter, Krishna has emphasized and indicated beyond all doubt, how *Vedantic* perfection can be achieved and lived to the glory of the successful seeker and to the blessing of the generation in which he lives. It is most appropriate, therefore, that the chapter is entitled "THE *YOGA* OF KNOWLEDGE AND WISDOM".

Mere knowledge is of no particular use. Wisdom is the glow that knowledge imparts to the individual. The fulfilment of knowledge in an individual is possible only when he becomes a man-of-Wisdom. Knowledge can be imparted, but wisdom cannot be given. The philosophical portion of all religions provides the knowledge, the instructional section of all religions provides techniques by which knowledge can be assimilated and digested into the very texture of the devotees' inner lives, and thereby every religion seeks to create men-of-Wisdom, who have fulfilled their lives, justified their religion, and blessed their generation.

Om Om Om Om Om

ॐ तत्सदिति श्रीमद् भगवद् गीतासूपनिषत्सु ब्रह्मविद्यायां
योगशास्त्रे श्रीकृष्णार्जुनसंवादे ज्ञानविज्ञानयोगो नाम
सप्तमोध्याय:

Oṁ tatsaditi śrīmadbhagavadgītāsū upaniṣatsu brahmavidyāyāṁ yogaśāstre śrī kṛṣṇārjuna saṁvāde jñānavijñānayogo nāma saptamo'dhyāyaḥ.

VIII

Imperishable Brahman
Introduction

TO discriminate between the higher and the lower nature of the Eternal Self, and identifying with the Higher, to play at will with all freedom and joy in the fields of its lower manifestations, is to be the perfect man-of-Wisdom; a God upon the earth, ever-liberated from the threats and sorrows of the finite. The aim of *Vedanta* is to carve out of ordinary folk such blissful men-of-Wisdom. In the earlier chapter, therefore, a vivid description of both knowledge and wisdom was elaborately given.

Continuing the idea contained in the previous chapter, Krishna starts with the glorification of the man-of-Wisdom and declares that he is perfect not only because of his special knowledge and experience of the Self, but also because he becomes thereby a well-integrated personality at all levels of his existence and contacts with the world. He easily proves himself to be a man of godly efficiency and balance, in all situations and conditions, at all places and times.

In the preceding chapter, a mere mention was made that there is a practical aspect of *Vedanta*, apart from its theoretical literature, but no definite technique for carving out the *Vedantic* ideals in practice was given there. Here, however, the technique has been completely and fully explained, and the relationship between the Eternal Spirit and the delusory realm of names and forms, the lower *Prakriti*, has been clearly indicated. Exemplary definitions indicating the Inexpressible, the Absolute Truth, are found in this chapter. Only a dull simpleton, vainly labouring to follow the path of pure reason and discrimination, cannot feel thrilled or uplifted to a divine height of inspiration by this chapter.

The last chapter concluded with a statement that the man-of-Wisdom not only realises the Absolute Essence that sustains the world, but that he also, at once, comes to master the world-of-objects, the organs of perception and action, and the instruments of comprehension, so that he proves himself to be a dynamic 'doer' ever carving out enduring successes all along, everywhere. Herein, this idea has been made more and more clear by Lord Krishna, with His explanations; when once we know the ocean, the waves, wavelets, the foam, and the lather are all known by us. Similarly, the Self is the Reality upon which all actions, the instruments-of-action, and the world-of-perceptions are superimposed, and therefore, by knowing the Self everything is known.

Arjuna said:

1. *What is that BRAHMAN? What is the ADHYATMA? What is 'action'? O best among men, what is declared to be the ADHIBHUTA? And what is ADHIDAIVA said to be?*

अर्जुन उवाच
किं तद्ब्रह्म किमध्यात्मं किं कर्म पुरुषोत्तम ।
अधिभूतं च किं प्रोक्तमधिदैवं किमुच्यते ॥ १ ॥

ajurana uvāca
kiṁ tadbrahma kimadhyātmaṁ kiṁ karma puruṣottama
adhibhūtaṁ ca kiṁ proktamadhidaivaṁ kimucyate 1.

2. *Who, and how, is ADHIYAJNA here in this body, O destroyer of Madhu? And how, at the time of death, are you to be known by the self-controlled?*

The new technical terms, used all of a sudden in the last two stanzas of the previous chapter (the Essential Being, the Essential Deity, the Essential Sacrifice etc.), which are to be known* so that such men-of-Wisdom "CONTINUE TO KNOW ME EVEN AT THE TIME OF DEATH STEADFAST IN MIND" (VII-30) confuse Arjuna.

The chapter opens with the seeker questioning his teacher with a view to get an exact definition for each new term used in His learned discourse. Not only does Arjuna ask for an explanation of the terms used, but he is also anxious to know how exactly one can realise the Self at the time of death, when one gains perfect self-control as a result of one's constant spiritual practices in life.

THE LORD EXPLAINS EACH TERM EXHAUSTIVELY IN THE FOLLOWING STANZAS:

अधियज्ञ: कथं कोऽत्र देहेऽस्मिन्मधुसूदन ।
प्रयाणकाले च कथं ज्ञेयोऽसि नियतात्मभि: ॥ २ ॥

adhiyajñaḥ kathaṁ ko'tra dehe'sminmadhusūdana
prayāṇakāle ca kathaṁ jñeyo'si jñeyo'si niyatātmabhi 2.

* Some commentators attempt to assign various kinds and degrees of knowledge to the various types of votaries. This is rather artificial and sectarian, and the Sanskrit text under review surely cannot bear the strain of such an interpretation.

The Blessed Lord said:

3. *BRAHMAN is Imperishable, the Supreme; His essential nature is called Self-knowledge, the creative force that causes beings to spring forth into manifestation is called 'work'.*

4. *ADHIBHUTA (or elements) constitutes My perishable nature, and the Indweller (or the essence) is the ADHIDAIVATA; I alone am the ADHIYAJNA here, in this body, O best of the embodied.*

IMPERISHABLE IS THE SUPREME *BRAHMAN*—The term *Brahman* indicates the one changeless and imperishable subjective Essence behind the phenomenal world. It becomes the Self, the Conscious Principle which illumines the body, mind and intellect, during all their pilgrimages from birth to death through the infinite varieties of their vicissitudes.

ITS PRESENCE IN EACH INDIVIDUAL BODY IS CALLED *ADHYATMA*—Though the Self is formless and subtle, and therefore, all-pervading, Its glory and might,

---

श्रीभगवानुवाच
अक्षरं ब्रह्म परमं स्वभावोऽध्यात्ममुच्यते ।
भूतभावोद्भवकरो विसर्गः कर्मसंज्ञितः ॥ ३ ॥

śrībhagavānuvāca
akṣaraṁ brhma paramaṁ svabhāvo'dhyātmamucyate
bhūtabhāvodbhavakaro visargaḥ karmasañjñitaḥ 3.

अधिभूतं क्षरो भावः पुरुषश्चाधिदैवतम् ।
अधियज्ञोऽहमेवात्र देहे देहभृतां वर ॥ ४ ॥

adhibhūtaṁ kṣaro bhāvaḥ puruṣaścādhidaivatam
adhiyajño'hamevātra dehe dehabhṛtāṁ vara 4.

* *Swabhava* is called *Adhyatma*.

power and grace, are felt, experienced and lived by each physical structure; and this Self, expressing Itself through a given embodiment, as though conditioned by it, is called the *Adhyatma*. Sankara brings it out very clearly when he explains the term as, "THE PRINCIPLE THAT GRACES ALL BODIES AS THEIR ESSENTIAL SELF".*

Work is not only the turnover; the turnover can be ordered and brought about by sheer labour. The term 'work' connotes something deeper, subtler, diviner. The creative urge that is behind every active intellect, which ultimately fulfils itself in the creation of things and beings, that subtle spiritual strength is called *'karma'*; all else is mere sweat and toil, dust and blood, heaving and sobbing, smiling and singing, hoarding and wasting.

THE *ADHIBHUTA* IS THE PERISHABLE EXISTENCE — as a contrast to the Imperishable (*Akshara*) is the perishable-equipment (*Kshara*), the world of *Prakriti*, through which the potential dynamism, vigour and glory of the Infinite Self express themselves. Between the *Kshara* and *Akshara*, there is as much difference as between a steam engine and the steam, a running car and the horsepower in the petrol, a singing radio and the electric current that makes it possible for the radio to sing. In short, by the term 'perishable' (*Kshara*) the whole world of phenomena of the Universe is indicated. Subjectively, the equipments of cognition, feeling, and perception constitute, in the main, the destructible or the perishable factors in us.

ADHIDAIVA IS THE INDWELLER—the term Indweller (*Adhidaiva*) is used to indicate the special faculty that presides over each apparatus of knowledge and activity in the living creatures (the *Purushah*). The presiding deities of the sense organs, of the mind, and of the intellect, are called the *Devatas*, which are nothing other than the faculty of vision in the eyes, the faculty of audition in the ears, the power of smelling in the nose, and so on.

ADHIYAJNA, HERE IN THIS BODY, I ALONE AM—we have already seen that the *Yajna* here means the 'act of perception, feeling, or thought'. As in the *Yajna*, here also oblations, the sense-objects; are poured into the *Yajna*-altar, the sense-organs; when the *Devata*, the particular faculty in it; gets propitiated and invoked, and as a blessing from it we gain the 'fruit' thereof, viz., the knowledge of the perception. In this *Adhiyajna*, in the subjective *Yajna*-act of perception, it is quite evident that the One vital factor that dominates the entire activity is the Self, the Principle-of-Life.

By giving these definitions, the Lord is on the whole suggesting with a subtle undercurrent of the implications, that the Eternal Self alone is the Real, and that all else are delusory superimpositions upon it. Therefore, to know the Self is to know everything and having known the Eternal as one's own Real Nature, one is free to act or not to act, and to play or not to play, in any of the fields of the not-Self.

An individual who lives in the Awareness of this Knowledge, ever-conscious of the play of the Self at all levels of his personality – physical, mental and intellectual – such an individual, naturally, comes to experience himself as a Divine Witness, observing the very process of death that clips off layer by layer his self-chosen connections with the not-Self!

WHAT HAPPENS TO ONE WHO LEAVES THE BODY IN THE AWARENESS OF THE SELF? LISTEN:

5. *And whosoever, leaving the body, goes forth remembering Me alone, at the time of his death, he attains My being; there is no doubt about this.*

Vyasa is never tired of emphasizing the cardinal philosophical idea in *Vedanta* that an individualised ego continues identifying with a given physical body only so long as it needs that particular instrument for eking out its desired quota of experiences. Once it is over, it 'kicks the bucket' as it were, and walks off – forgetting all its duties, its relationships and its vanities in that particular existence.

At this moment of divorce from a given body it is logical to believe that its thoughts would be about the most predominant desire or aspiration in it – either gathered in its past embodiments, or acquired in its present life. The techniques of meditation and devotion constitute the art of tutoring the mind to keep in it an unflickering flame of aspiration, so carefully trimmed and fed that such a seeker, "AT THE TIME OF DEATH, MEDITATING ON ME ALONE, GOES FORTH LEAVING THE BODY".

This last powerful willing, determined by the last thought, decides its destinies in the future. An ego that lived all its life, in its egocentric vanities, identifying Itself with merely the flesh and ever catering to its appetities, will be hoarding such sensuous *vasanas* that it must necessarily take a form, lower in the evolutionary scale, in order that its acquired animal instincts may thereby be fulfilled to the maximum.

अन्तकाले च मामेव स्मरन्मुक्त्वा कलेवरम् ।
यः प्रयाति स मद्भावं याति नास्त्यत्र संशयः ॥ ५ ॥

antakāle ca māmeva smaranmuktavā kalevaram
yaḥ prayāti sa madbhāvaṁ yāti nāstyatra saṁśayaḥ 5.

On the other hand, when an individual, in his discrimination, comes to recognise the futility of a lascivious life, and, therefore, aspires to release himself from the thraldom of the flesh, he surely moves higher up on the ladder of evolution when he retires from his present embodiment. Faithfully following this theory which is at once logical and reasonable, the science of Life, as enunciated in *Vedanta*, declares that the last thoughts of a dying man order his future embodiments and their environments.

Therefore, Krishna insists here that one who leaves the physical structure with his mind completely turned towards the Self-will; naturally, reach the Eternal and the Immortal, "THE SUPREME ABODE, reaching which there is no return" (VIII-21).

BUT THEN, ARE THERE NO ARGUMENTS THAT CAN CONCLUSIVELY PROVE THE STATEMENT? LISTEN:

6. *Whosoever, at the end, leaves the body, thinking of any being, to that being only he goes, O Kaunteya (O son of Kunti), because of his constant thought of that being.*

Declaring this well thoughtout conclusion of the *Rishis*, the Self-dedicated thinkers of India, the Lord says "WHATEVER OBJECT ONE REMEMBERS WHILE LEAVING THE BODY, THAT ALONE IS REACHED BY HIM" – be it a dog or a god.

यं यं वापि स्मरन्भावं त्यजत्यन्ते कलेवरम् ।
तं तमेवैति कौन्तेय सदा तद्भावभावित: ॥ ६ ॥

yaṁ yaṁ vāpi smaranbhāvaṁ tyajatyante kalevaram
taṁ tamevaiti kaunteya sadā tadbhāvabhāvitaḥ 6.

"As you think so you become" is a theory which is obvious to every intelligent man even without an explanation from any philosopher. Thoughts guide all actions, and at any given moment the run of thoughts in an individual is governed and ordered by the channel of thinking, which he himself has ploughed in his bosom with his conscious and wilful thoughts and actions in the past. Naturally, therefore, a mental equipment that has been struggling during its existence in an embodiment to detach from all its identifications with that embodiment, and to fix itself in the contemplation of the Real and the Eternal, would be creating new channels of divine aspirations (*Adhyatma Samskaras*). The time of death, when the occupant of the body has packed up to quit, is not the moment to decide or to plan the travel. At such a moment, instinctively, its thoughts would run through its habitual channels, and the flight of thoughts at that moment would determine the direction of the ego's pilgrimage.

THEREFORE:

7. *Therefore, at all times, remember Me, and fight, with mind and intellect fixed (or absorbed) in Me; you shall doubtless come to Me alone.*

No religion can continuously serve the society unless it gives its faithful followers specific instructions and guidance on how best to live their day-to-day life. Here is an instruction

---

तस्मात्सर्वेषु कालेषु मामनुस्मर युध्य च ।
मय्यर्पितमनोबुद्धिर्मामेवैष्यस्यसंशयम् ॥ ७ ॥
tasmātsarveṣu kāleṣu māmanusmara yudhya ca
mayyarpitamanobuddhimārmevaiṣyasyasaṁśayam 7.

which is at once applicable in the secular fields of living and in the divine realms of life. Here is a simple instruction by which not only the STANDARD OF LIVING could be raised but also the STANDARD OF LIFE could be divinised.

There are many who suspect that this method of splitting the mind between religion and life is detrimental to true success in either of them. This, in fact, is a thoughtless argument. Hardly ever is man's mind totally invested where his hands function. Ordinarily, a major portion of the mind, all the time, wanders into the jungles of dreadful fears, or into the caves of jealousies or into the deserts of imaginary possibilities of failures. Instead of thus, wasting the total mental energy and dynamism, Krishna advises us that a truly successful man, striving to achieve the highest, both in the outer world of plurality, and in the realms within, should rest his mind at the gracious and peaceful feet of Truth. He can then pour out the entire wealth of his capacities into the work in his hand, and thereby assure for himself the highest laurels both here and in the hereafter.

In Hinduism, religion is not divorced from life. If they are separated, both of them will die away. They are as intimately connected as the head and the trunk; separated from the other neither can live. Even while living through the turmoils of existence, a true seeker must learn to keep his mind continuously upon the awareness of his Real Nature and the substratum of the world in one vast embrace of blissful homogeneity. This is not difficult, nor is it impracticable.

An actor, playing the part of a king in a drama, can never completely forget that he has a wife and a child in his own house on the outskirts of the city. If he forgets his personal identity and acts as the king even outside the stage, he will immediately be segregated, and moved to a lunatic asylum for the safety of the society! He is efficient as the actor because he constantly remembers his own real identity. Similarly, even with continuous cognition of our Divine Nature, we can act in the world without any hindrance, and thereby add a glow to our achievements, and soften the reactions of any disappointments that we might meet within life's pilgrimage.

A truly educated man never forgets his education; it becomes part and parcel of his very nature and in every thought, word and action of his, he brings out the fragrance of his education. So, too, the man of constant Awareness will act in the world as a mastermind – all his actions soaked in selflessness, all his thoughts flavoured with love, and all his feelings matured in kindness. This is the secret with which the *Vedic* civilisation enchanted the world of its time and compelled the adoration of all later generations.

Krishna is here quite clear when He says that, in the case of an individual who lives a life of battle to win righteous profits, and constantly remembers the Lord while doing so, his "MIND AND INTELLECT GET ABSORBED IN ME". Following the above (VIII-5, 6) theory of "as you think so you become" "YOU SHALL COME TO ME" when once the mental equipment gets absorbed in the Self, through the process of constant contemplation on the Self with single-pointed devotion.

FURTHER:

8. *With the mind not moving towards any other thing, made steadfast by the method of habitual meditation, and constantly meditating on the Supreme PURUSHA, the Resplendent, O Partha, he goes (to Him).*

The term 'death' mentioned here does not mean only the irrevocable physical death, but also the 'death of the ego' which is to be brought about through the steady practice of meditation. This stanza is added to the discourse to show that after the sublimation of the limited ego, one can live in full Godly Awareness as a liberated God-man, even here, while living this very life!

One who is practising the above method of living in the world AS A SOJOURNER THEREIN, AND NOT AS A NATIVE OF IT, and who is training the mind constantly to rest upon the contemplation of the Self, becomes single-pointed in his concentration. This, in fact, is a revolutionary interpretation of the techniques of prayer and concentration (*Upasana*) as explained in the *Vedas* and also the methods of devotion and surrender championed in the *Puranas*, while what is advised in the preceding stanza is religion lived in the marketplace, the everyday-*Sannyasa* for the man-of-action, in the very fields of his own activities.

By this practice the devotee develops single-pointedness of the mind which helps to integrate his intellect. With such well-tuned up and nobly adjusted instruments of perception and comprehension, and intuitive realisation of the Divine, the Self

---

अभ्यासयोगयुक्तेन चेतसा नान्यगामिना ।
परमं पुरुषं दिव्यं याति पार्थानुचिन्तयन् ॥ ८ ॥

abhyāyayogayuktena cetasā nānyagāminā
paramaṁ puruṣaṁ divyaṁ yāti pāthārnucintayan 8.

becomes an easy experience: "DWELLING ON THE SUPREME, RESPLENDENT *PURUSHA*, O SON OF PRITHA, ONE GOES TO HIM". With integrated mind, whatever the individual meditates upon intensively, he must come to gain it soon enough. Thus, the stanza indicates an ampler significance than what has been so far declared. "This realisation of the Self, and thereby gaining one's identity with It, can actually take place in this very same life, if, with prepared mind and intellect one can, with steadfastness, meditate upon Me, THE SUPREME RESPLENDENT *PURUSHA*".

The term that has been used to indicate the one who meditates upon the Self (*Anuchintayan*) is very significant. Thoughts of the same species, made to run towards one fixed ideal or goal, in an unbroken flow, are called 'meditation'. The prefix *'Anu'* in *'Anuchintayan'* provides this significant meaning of the 'continuity' of the flow-of-thought, in one determined channel of contemplation.

WHAT ARE THE SPECIFIC QUALITIES OF THIS GREAT *PURUSHA* UPON WHOM WE ARE CONSTANTLY TO MEDITATE?

9. *Whosoever, meditates upon the Omniscient, the Ancient, the Ruler (of the whole world), minuter than the atom, the Supporter of all, of Form inconceivable, Effulgent like the Sun and beyond the darkness (of ignorance) ...*

कविं पुराणमनुशासितारम्
अणोरणीयांसमनुस्मरेद्यः ।
सर्वस्य धातारमचिन्त्यरूपम्
आदित्यवर्णं तमसः परस्तात् ॥ ९ ॥

kaviṁ purāṇamanuśāsitāram
aṇoraṇīyāṁsamanusmaredyaḥ
sarvasya dhātāramacintyarūpam
ādityavarṇaṁ tamasaḥ parastāt 9.

By holding the mind constantly in the contemplation of the Self, the devotee was promised that he could develop in himself such a powerful and divine trait that at the time of his departure he can easily come to entertain the thoughts of the Divine. By a very subtle implication, it was also suggested in two previous stanzas (VIII-5, 6), that even while continuing to live in the present embodiment, the seeker can reach a point where the egocentric life is ended. Such a total annihilation of ignorance-created misconceptions, and the consequent vanities, can be successfully accomplished by the seekers only when their minds get totally withdrawn from their attachments to the false matter-envelopments through the process of continued contemplation upon the Self.

In the preceding stanza, it was also vaguely hinted that the contemplation of the Self must be as 'THE SUPREME RESPLENDENT *PURUSHA*'. If I am advised by somebody to meditate upon or think out the possibilities of 'OXYGENELITEEN' it will be impossible for me, however wise a man I might be, unless I know what that is. Merely upon a name, no consistent contemplation is possible. 'OXYGENELITEEN' is merely a word constituted of letters -it means nothing; it is only a sound represented by a few letters of the alphabet. Similarly, to be advised by a *shastra,* to meditate upon the SUPREME RESPLENDENT SELF, could only be as futile as to be asked to think over the possibilities of 'OXYGENELITEEN'.

In a practical textbook of instruction as to how *Vedanta* can be lived, Krishna has to provide Arjuna with sufficient material indicating the line of contemplation to be undertaken by the meditator. The two stanzas now under review, give an exhaustive design for the students to make themselves successfully and profitably disciplined.

These qualifying terms are as many different indications of the Truth (though none defines It), which is the thrilling core that gives a similitude of life and reality to inert, unreal matter. No single term here, therefore, is to be understood as complete in itself. Geometrically, a point can be defined and indicated only with reference to two different sets of data. So too, here the inexpressible Reality has been almost accurately explained with these different qualifying terms.

Contemplation upon the Reality, through an attempt at exhaustively comprehending all the secret suggestions in the above stanza, is to prepare a mental condition in which, if a mind lives well-integrated and turned inward, it can come to pause in an atmosphere of Infinite Experience.

The Conscious Principle, serving as the Soul in an embodiment, is that which illumines all the thought waves that rise in that particular mind, functioning in that given embodiment. The Infinite Self being One everywhere, it is the same Principle that illumines all the different embodiments, all the thought-experiences, at all times. Just as the Sun is said to be SEEING EVERYTHING, because it illuminates all the objects on the globe, so too, is the Divine Principle-of-Awareness - the factor without which no knowledge is ever possible. Thus, the Self is considered, in terms of the world of conditioned-knowledge which we experience today, as the Supreme Knower who knows everything, Omniscient (*Kavih*), and without whom no knowledge is ever possible.

ANCIENT (*Puranah*)—The Self is considered as the most ancient because the Eternal Truth is that which was before all creation, which remains the same all through the ages of

---

* Chapter II-24 (*Sanatanah*)

existence, and which shall ever remain the same even after the projections of plurality have ended. To indicate that the One Self ever remains the same everywhere, providing a substratum even for the concept of time, It is indicated here as the ancient.*

THE OVER-RULER (*Anushasita*)—It is not in any way indicated here that the Self is a *Sultan*, tyrannically ruling over the world. Here the term 'Over-ruler' is only to indicate that if the Principle of Awareness were not presiding over the multiple faculties of perception, feeling, and comprehension in us, our physical, mental and intellectual experiences could not have been harmonised into the meaningful existence of our lifetime.

The Over-lordship, mentioned here, only indicates that the Knowing Principle of Consciousness is the very essence but for which life - defined as a continuous series of experiences - in any form is never possible. Without mud the mud-pots cannot exist; in all pots the mud is the OVER-RULER. Just as gold in all gold ornaments, the ocean in all waves, sweetness in all candy, so too is the Self in the Universe of names and forms. It is in this sense that the term 'Over-ruler' is to be understood. To conceive of God as a mighty policeman standing with two keys, one made of gold to open the gates of heaven, and the other of iron to open the doors of hell, is a barbarous concept of Godhood that has nothing sacred in it to attract the intellectually awakened generations!

MINUTER THAN AN ATOM (*Anoraniyan*)—the simplest and the smallest physically divisible particle of any element which still maintains the specific properties of that element is called its atom. Thus, it is indicated here that the Self is the subtlest of the subtle. The subtler a thing, the greater is its pervasiveness. Water is considered subtler than a block of ice, and the steam ensuing when water is boiled is considered subtler than the water itself. In all these stages, pervasiveness is the measuring rod of their comparative subtleties. In the *Upanishadic* lore, it is usual to consider the Self as 'the subtlest of the subtle' which only indicates that It pervades all, and nothing pervades It.

THE NOURISHER OF ALL (*Sarvasya Dhatarah*)—the nourisher here means the support that sustains everything. In a cinema theatre, the changeless white-screen can be considered as the nourisher of the entertainment, inasmuch as, without it the ever changing flow of pictures could not have given us the impression of a continuous story. However glorious might be the message that a master-painter has brought out with his brush, it is the consistent strength of the canvas behind, that nourishes and sustains the integrity and beauty of the picture. Similarly, if the One Consciousness were not constantly illumining the ever-changing flux of things and happenings around and within us from birth to death, through all conditions and states of our existence, the homogeneous oneness of life would never have been ours to react to and feel fulfilled with.

OF FORM INCONCEIVABLE (*Achintya-roopah*)—If there be a factor that is omniscient, ancient, over-ruler, subtlest of the subtle, and nourisher of all, and if we are advised to meditate upon It, then it is possible that we immediately get a false notion that the Self can be thought of and comprehended, as any other finite object or idea, by our limited faculties of the head or the heart. To remove this wrong idea and to emphasize that the Infinite cannot be comprehended by the finite instruments of perception, feeling and understanding – but can only be apprehended when these equipments are transcended - the Lord is particularly anxious to tell His students that the Self is of THE FORM IN-CONCEIVABLE. Though it is thus, in fact, inconceivable, yet, on transcending the equipment of experiences, the individual, in a process of Divine Awakening, can subjectively apprehend It to be his own Essential Nature.

LUMINOUS LIKE THE SUN (*Aditya-varnah*)—if the implication of the above term (*Achintya-roopah*) be true, no intelligent seeker can arrest his temptation to doubt as to how the Self can ever be realised. As seekers, we live and strive within the limitations of our own mind and intellect. Every moment of our existence, we gather a harvest of experiences only through the use of the different equipments given to us. Living as we are, rooted in our false identifications with these equipments in the early days of our spiritual efforts, the seeker in us should necessarily despair at the impossible conception and the mad mission of 'knowing the UN-KNOWABLE'; conceiving the IN-CONCEIVABLE understanding the UN-UNDERSTANDABLE or experiencing the IN-EXPERIENCABLE !!!

The Self is defined as the UN-UNDERSTANDABLE, or the IN-CONCEIVABLE, or IN-EXPERIENCABLE, etc. only to indicate that the instruments of cognition, experience and apprehension are not available for functioning in the Self. The dream-gun, with which the dreamer had shot the enemies of his dream-world, cannot be any longer handled by him, when once he has awakened. Even the bloody hands of a dreamer, after a dream-murder, become automatically clean, without either soap or water, the moment he wakes up! As long as man is identifying with his limiting adjuncts, he lives in the external world of his self-projected delusory multiplicity, wherein the Self is IN-CONCEIVABLE, and IN-EXPERIENCABLE. But the moment these adjuncts are transcended through a process of steadfast contemplation on the Self, he gets awakened to his own nature of Pure Being.

Once having understood this much of the fundamental concepts of *Vedanta*, it becomes easy to appreciate the matchless beauty of the example of the Sun. In order to see the Sun, no other light is necessary, as the Sun is the SOURCE of all light, the one illuminator that illuminates everything else. Just as, in the physical world, the Sun, in its self-effulgence, is self-evident, so too, in the spiritual realm, to know the Knowledge Absolute, no other knowing-principle is needed. The dreamer can never KNOW the waker, for, while knowing the waking-state the dreamer himself ends to BECOME the waker; to awaken oneself from the dream is to know the waker; to KNOW the waker is to BECOME the waker. So too, on ending the egocentric existence, in the flash of the spiritual awakening, the misguided, panting ego ends itself in the rediscovery that it has been nothing but the Self, at all times. This vast suggestion is cramped into a mystic word-picture: LUMINOUS LIKE THE SUN.

BEYOND ALL DARKNESS (*Tamasah-Parastat*)—the limited and the finite example of the Sun calls into the heart of a student some dangerous misgivings. The Sun in the heavens is, no doubt, resplendent, but only during the day; and even during the daytime there are various degrees of intensity of the sunlight experienced by the living kingdom. If the Self is LUMINOUS LIKE THE SUN, then the industrious student may gather that the Self also varies in Its intensity, and that there are periods of time when It is not at all available! To remove these two fallacious ideas - that the Self is variable in nature and sometimes totally absent, this qualifying term is used here. The very limitation of the Sun, meaning the darkness of the night, is negated when Krishna says that the

Self is BEYOND THE DARKNESS of ignorance, or *Maya*.

He who meditates upon the Self thus, as omniscient, ancient, over-ruler, subtlest of the subtle, nourisher of all, of Inconceivable Form, Self-illuminating as the Sun, and beyond all traces of ignorance, is the one who 'goes to Him'.

10. *At the time of death, with an unshaken mind full of devotion, by the power of 'YOGA' fixing the whole 'PRANA' (breath) between the two eyebrows, he (the seeker) reaches the Supreme Resplendent 'PURUSHA'.*

Following the word meaning only, this stanza has been indeed, very often, sadly misunderstood and badly interpreted.

This section in the *Geeta* is describing single-pointed meditation upon the Highest. Therefore the expression AT THE TIME OF DEATH is to be understood as AT THE MOMENT OF THE DEATH OF THE EGO. When all identifications with the body-mind-intellect are consciously withdrawn through the process of meditation, at the HALT-MOMENT of perfect inner silence and tranquillity, WITH THE MIND UNMOVING, the meditator can follow the instructions contained in this stanza.

The term *'Bhakti'* is not to be understood in its cheap connotation, which it has come to gather in its direct

---

प्रयाणकाले मनसाचलेन
भक्त्या युक्तो योगबलेन चैव ।
भ्रुवोर्मध्ये प्राणमावेश्य सम्यक्
स तं परं पुरुषमुपैति दिव्यम् ॥ १० ॥

prayāṇakāle manasācalena
bhaktayā yukto yogabalena caiva
bhruvormadhye prāṇamāveśya samyak
sa taṁ paraṁ puruṣamupaiti divyam 10.

translation as 'devotion'. Selfless love, seeking a fulfilment in itself, when directed towards the divine with firm faith and an all-out belief, is called *Bhakti*. Love itself means identifying with the object of love in such a way that the joys and sorrows of the beloved become equally poignant joys and sorrows of the lover. In short, the lovers become one with their beloveds, both in their physical and emotional lives. Therefore, Shankara describes *Bhakti* as 'the identification of the ego with its Real Nature'.

In the context of the stanza here, the important suggestion given to the meditator is that his meditation should be accompanied by a readiness to identify himself intensely with the Principle of Awareness, which has been exhaustively indicated in the previous stanza. He must come to live the Self, within himself, at that still moment of Inward Silence, which rings the death-knell of the deluded-ego.

BY THE POWER OF *YOGA* (*Yoga-balena*)—Here we are not talking of some secret and mysterious strength -- the Serpent Power -- which is the highly guarded secret of a rare few, which should not be spilt to everyone even among those who profess to be the devotees of the Lord. The strength acquired by a meditator, when he meditates upon the Supreme regularly for a long period of time, is the strength – the POWER OF *YOGA* – that is indicated here. This is nothing other than the inward strength, the inward fire, that grows when the mind is withdrawn from its endless agitations and the intellect is peacefully rested in its contemplations upon the infinite qualities of the Absolute.

The meditator, in a relatively short time, discovers in himself a wealth of mental equipoise and an indescribable efficiency, ready to bring his entire mental equipment into the contemplation of the Self in him. When an individual is thus engaged in meditation, all his *pranas* are concentrated at the point of his meditation - maybe between the eyebrows, as it represents the frontal-brain, the seat of steady thought.

Prana is the term used in the science of *Vedanta* to indicate all the different expressions of life's vitality, through the various instruments and organs of the body. Life expressing itself as the various functions in a living physical body is called the *Prana*, which, according to its varied manifestations is classified under five main headings as: *Prana*: the faculty of sense perception; *Apana*: the excretory system; *Vyana*: the digestive system; *Samana*: the circulatory system; and *Udana*: the capacity in us to see beyond our present world of knowledge into the field of some greater concept and live it. All these different activities are channels of dissipation through which the vital attention in us is getting exhausted. When an individual gets lost in the silence within at the moment of his merger with the Self, all these faculties are temporarily arrested. For a seeker walking the path-of-Meditation no other violent physical practices at all are needed.

Such an individual – in whom, during the deepest moments of concentration, the mind becomes perfectly silent and tranquil; in whom, through the strength of his steadfast meditation, all manifestations of life's presence through his physical body become controlled and arrested and when he, in his enthusiasm, totally identifies with the point of his contemplation, the Self – "HE GOES TO THAT SUPREME RESPLENDENT SELF (*PURUSHA*)".

AS AN INTRODUCTION TO THE MEDITATION UPON *OM*, THE FOLLOWING IS GIVEN:

11. *That which is declared Imperishable by the VEDA-knowers; That into which, the self-controlled and desire-freed enter; That desiring for which BRAHMCHARYA is practised – That Goal I will declare to thee in brief.*

This stanza, which is reminiscent of a famous *Upanishadic* declaration,* while glorifying the goal, is promising that Krishna will, in the following verses, explain the Supreme destination of Perfection and the means of achieving it.

Worship (*Upasana*) of the syllable *OM* is frequently advised in almost all the *Upanishads* as a sure method of making the final adjustments in the mind-intellect-equipment of the meditator, so that complete success in meditation may be assured to him. From the *Pauranic* era onwards, meditation with faith and devotion, regularly, upon any of the recognised incarnations, has also been found to serve the same purpose with the same efficiency.

Here, very many necessary precautions and warnings are given to the seeker, so that his spiritual pilgrimage may be comparatively easy and pleasant. The obstacles about which meditators generally complain arise from their own lack of

---

यदक्षरं वेदविदो वदन्ति
विशन्ति यद्यतयो वीतरागा: ।
यदिच्छन्तो ब्रह्मचर्यं चरन्ति
तत्ते पदं संग्रहेण प्रवक्ष्ये ॥ ११ ॥

yadakṣaraṁ dedavido vadanti
viśanti yadyatayo vītarāgāḥ
yadicchanto brahmacarya caranti
tatte padaṁ saṅgraheṇa pravakṣye 11.

* Refer Swamiji's Discourses on *Kathopanishad* – II-15

self-withdrawal from the finite matter-envelopments. It is necessary that, as a science of Self-Perfection, *Vedanta* should not only give the techniques of meditation, but also indicate for the seekers the possible pitfalls on the path and equip them, sufficiently early, with all instructions as to how they can get out, in case they fall into any of these jamming ruts. This verse indicates how one can be assured of an easy path while moving ahead on the track of meditation – carefully avoiding all extrovert desires that cater to one's sensuous appetites, and by practising severe and consistent self-control.

In the opening of this chapter, (stanza-3) the Supreme was defined as the Imperishable. Quoting Himself, Krishna emphasises here that the very same Imperishable Truth can be realised - they come to 'enter into the Imperishable' – when they, the men of self-control, who are unagitated by desires, withdraw successfully from the changeable and the perishable in themselves.

FREED FROM ATTACHMENT (*Veeta-ragah*)—The entire *Geeta* is a Song of renunciation; not a dull-witted and uncreative renunciation, but a healthy detachment through right knowledge, which is the harbinger of all progress and development everywhere. The renunciation of desires is not a psychological suppression of the existing appetites, but that which takes place as a result of a natural blossoming of the intellect. The newly opened buds, after a time, renounce their soft, beautiful skirts and stand naked, expressing a renunciation of the gorgeous; but in nature, this happens only when the flowers are pollinated and the fruits are well in the making. The shedding of the petals may be a sacrifice or renunciation from the standpoint of a casual flower-gazer, but to the farmer who knows, it is a sacrifice or renunciation of the flowers in their newly gained maturity that has automatically made the beautiful petals fall off.

Similarly, in the Spiritual Science of India, no doubt, there is an emphasis on the necessity of renunciation, but it is not a sad and melancholy self-denial or self-punishment, which some other religions do preach and practise. A renunciation that has sprung up from the fertile lands of efficient discrimination is that which is insisted upon by the intellectual giants of the *Upanishads*. The term 'ONE FREED FROM ATTACHMENT' is therefore, to be understood as one who has grown out of his passionate attachments to the finite, that constitute the insignificant parade of the world, in his more mature and steady understanding of the nature and the goal of his life.

Also, it is true that the more the number of desires entertained, the greater is the mental tossing, and the consequent agitation. The greater the disturbance in the mind, the lesser is the mental potentiality expressed. A meditator's success depends upon his mental dynamism, and the only wealth that can ease the rigours of the journey is his own mental equipoise and inward peace. Therefore, as a policy, it is advised that men of least desire have the maximum chance for the greatest success in the path-of-Knowledge.

IN ORDER TO INDICATE WHAT THE EARLY STAGES OF '*UPASANA*' AND THEIR RESULTS ARE, THE FOLLOWING IS ADDED:

12. *Having closed all the gates, having confined the mind in the heart, having fixed the life-breath in the 'head', engaged in the practice of concentration,*

13. *Uttering the one-syllabled 'OM' – the (symbol of) BRAHMAN - and remembering Me, he who departs, leaving the body, attains the Supreme Goal.*

The practice of concentration can most effectively be undertaken and efficiently continued only when three necessary conditions are fulfilled by the meditator. These are narrated here in the verses in the sequence they have to be practised.

CONTROLLING ALL THE SENSES—each sense organ is an aperture in the physical body. The porous skin, the ear, the nose, the eyes, and the taste buds are the five main gates through which the external stimuli reach the mental zone to agitate it. To shut these five doors through discrimination and detachment is the first process, before the meditator can ever hope to enter the field of meditation. These are the five inlets through which not only the external world storms in and agitates the mind, but our mind also runs out to wander among its sensuous ditches. When once these tunnels-of-

---

सर्वद्वाराणि संयम्य मनो हृदि निरुध्य च ।
मूर्ध्न्याधायात्मनः प्राणमास्थितो योगधारणाम् ॥ १२ ॥
sarvadvārāṇi saṁyamya mano hṛdi virudhya ca
mūdhnyārdhāyātmanaḥ prāṇamāsthilo yogadhāraṇāma 12.

ओमित्येकाक्षरं ब्रह्म व्याहरन्मामनुस्मरन् ।
यः प्रयाति त्यजन्देहं स याति परमां गतिम् ॥ १३ ॥
omityekākṣaraṁ brahma vyāharanmāmanusmaran
yaḥ prayāti tyajandehaṁ sa yāti paramāṁ gatim 13.

disturbance are blockaded, the new flow of disturbances is shut out.

CONFINING THE MIND IN THE HEART—Even though the mind is not now directly open for any onslaught by fresh contingents of sense stimuli, it is capable of getting disturbed due to the previous impressions that it might have gathered in its past experiences in the finite world of change and pleasure. Therefore the mind, the instrument of emotion and feeling, it is advised, is to be confined in the 'heart'.

The term 'heart' in *Vedanta* is not the pumping-organ that maintains the circulatory system in a physical structure. In the field of literature and philosophy, heart is a conceptual centre in the mind from where all positive and noble thoughts of love and tenderness, kindness and charity, devotion and surrender, constantly spring up. When once the gross stimuli are held back from entering the mind, the seeker is advised not to choke his faculty of emotion and feeling but to DIVINISE IT. Let the mind function only in the dignity and status of the heart. It has already been discussed how positive thinking brings into the mind the least amount of disturbance. Negative thoughts are those that bring into the mind stormy conditions of agitation and restlessness.

WITHDRAWING ALL THE *PRANAS*, THE VITAL MANIFESTATIONS OF LIFE THROUGH THE DIFFERENT EQUIPMENTS, INTO THE INTELLECT means the total withdrawal of the intellect from all its identifications with the lower, gained by dissociating ourselves from all our perceptions, etc. This is accomplished through a process of totally engaging the mind-intellect in the contemplation of the Self. When the meditator's mind, drawn away from the sense-disturbances, is purified in the realm of the diviner thoughts, and when such a mind is perfectly controlled and held steady by an intellect gushing out towards the contemplation of the Self, as explained earlier, (Ibid.-9, 10) the existing mental condition is said to be occupied in the practice of concentration (*Yoga-dharanam*).

Every meditator who can make an attempt at forgetting his immediate sensual surroundings, and, surcharged with joy and contentment, can bring his mind under total control of his discriminative intellect, can mentally chant *OM* with ease and enthusiasm, and observe the rising *OM*-waves in this otherwise silenced mind ... is the student fit for the worship of *OM*. The following line in its amplitude of significance clearly brings out the same viewpoint.

HE WHO DEPARTS, LEAVING THE BODY—while chanting and contemplating upon the significance of *OM*, the seeker becomes so detached from all his delusory identifications with the false matter-envelopments that the ego is sublimated; this is the true death LEAVING THE BODY. In his single-pointed, all-out, self-forgetting contemplation upon the significance of *OM* – as the substratum on which is played the drama of life and death, projected by the mischievous mind – the seeker, in Krishna's own words, ATTAINS THE SUPREME GOAL.

IS SELF REDISCOVERY SO DIFFICULT EQUALLY FOR ALL PEOPLE WHO ARE WALKING THE PATH OF MEDITATION?

14. *I am easily attainable by that ever-steadfast YOGI who constantly remembers Me daily, not thinking of anything else, O Partha.*

To the one who is ever steadfast in the Life Divine and 'REMEMBERS ME', THE SELF, ALWAYS AND DAILY, with a mind unshattered, to him the Self is easily attainable. The statements in the previous stanzas are all again summarised here in a more emphatic and direct language.

PRAYER IS NO INSECTICIDE TO BE SPRAYED NOW AND THEN; NOR SHOULD THE DIVINE ALTAR BE CONSIDERED AS A BATHROOM, WHERE ONE ENTERS DIRTY AND WALKS OUT CLEAN! Here Krishna is very careful to insist, with all the strength and emphasis that He can command, that the Divine Consciousness must be maintained by the seeker constantly and continuously ALL THROUGH THE DAY, DAILY.

To such an individual, "I AM EASILY ATTAINABLE, O ARJUNA". This positive assertion has a very important significance inasmuch as it indicates that the negation of these conditions will not be conducive even to hope for success in meditation.

WHY SHOULD ONE STRUGGLE SO HARD TO REALISE THE SELF? LISTEN:

अनन्यचेताः सततं यो मां स्मरति नित्यशः ।
तस्याहं सुलभः पार्थ नित्ययुक्तस्य योगिनः ॥ १४ ॥

ananyacetāḥ satataṁ yo māṁ smarati nityaśaḥ
tasyāhaṁ sulabhaḥ pārtha nityayuktasya yoginaḥ 14.

15. *Having attained Me, these MAHATMAS (great souls) do not again take birth, which is the house of pain and is non-eternal, they having reached the Highest Perfection, MOKSHA.*

Estimating the benefit enjoyed by a man-of-Perfection, through the realisation of the Self, it is said that "HAVING ATTAINED ME, THE HIGH-SOULED ONES ARE NO MORE SUBJECT TO RE-BIRTH". To the philosophically thoughtful, rebirth is the starting point of all pains and imperfections. Krishna also says in the verse that rebirth is a HOUSE OF PAIN AND IS EPHEMERAL.

In the history of thought in the *Upanishads*, it is quite interesting to note how the goal of life, which was considered in the beginning as 'the state of deathlessness' (*Amritatwa*), came to be reckoned, later on, as the 'the absence of rebirth' (*Na-punar-janma*). In the beginning, the anxiety of the seeker was to end the unavoidable and the most horrid of all experiences called 'death'. As knowledge increased through the right evaluation of the happenings in life, it soon became clear to the subjective research-scholars, the *Rishis*, that death had really no sting at all for those who had understood that it is nothing but one of the different experiences in life. Death can in no way clip off the continuity of existence. Those relentless thinkers had, in the logic of their thoughts, come to the conclusion that birth was the beginning of all pains, and therefore, the goal of life, if at all it was possible to achieve, should be THE STATE OF NO MORE REBIRTH.

मामुपेत्य पुनर्जन्म दुःखालयमशाश्वतम् ।
नाप्नुवन्ति महात्मानः संसिद्धिं परमां गताः ॥ १५ ॥
māmupetya punarjanma duḥkhālayamaśāśvatam
nāpnuvanti mahātmānaḥ saṁsiddhiṁ paramāṁ gatāḥ 15.

The dream of rebirth and its destinies belongs to the delusory ego, which is nothing but the Unborn Self identifying with its delusory matter-envelopments. Electricity conditioned by the bulb is the light; when the bulb gets broken, the light which is an effect merges with its cause, the current, one-without-a-second, everywhere the same, illumining all the bulbs in the world. Similarly, the Self conditioned by a given mind and intellect is the ego (*Jeeva*), which suffers the rebirth, the agonies of imperfections, the disease, the decay and the death. The ego comes to rediscover that it is nothing other than the Self, once the mind-intellect equipment has been stilled.

He who thus experiences the Self as his own Real Nature realises that he has never any relationship at all with the equipments of feeling and understanding. Just as an awakened man has no more relationship with his own dream-wife and children, the ego ends its march through the thorny path of pain and finitude, when it awakens to the spiritual cognition of the Self. Such great souls will no more have any need to manifest in the plane of plurality to be presented with the repeated lashes of sorrow and misery.

He who has, through the process of CONSTANT CONTEMPLATION OF THE SELF (VIII-14) during his lifetime, learnt to control all the senses, to regulate the mind and the heart, to control and to arrest all *pranas* in the intellect -- he directly comes to identify himself with the Infinite and the Eternal, and shall no more come back into a limited embodiment to continue his futile search for infinite satisfaction among the finite world-of-objects.

BUT ARE THERE ANY WHO COME BACK NOT REACHING THE HIGHEST? LISTEN:

16. *Worlds upto the 'world-of-BRAHMAJI' are subject to rebirth, O Arjuna; but he who reaches Me, O Kaunteya, has no birth.*

It is a characteristic technique, often employed by the teacher in the *Geeta*, to bring home his ideas, by expressing them, for purposes of emphasis, against the background of their opposites. Thus, we find here in the verse two contradictory factors put in opposition to each other so that, each, as a contrast to the other, may shine out the best in the mental horizon of the students. 'UP TO THE REALM OF *BRAHMAJI* ALL ARE SUBJECT TO REBIRTH'. This idea is contrasted with the result of realising directly and totally the Self, the Eternal: 'BUT, AFTER ATTAINING ME THERE IS NO REBIRTH'.

The theory of gradual liberation (*Karma Mukti*), accepted in *Vedanta*, says that ritualism (*Karma*), accompanied by meditation (*Upasana*), takes the ego to the realm-of-the-Creator (*Brahma-loka*) where, at the end of the *Kalpa* (the cycle of creation and dissolution), it merges with the Supreme. Even in *Brahma-loka* it is necessary that the ego must, through self-effort, live strictly all the spiritual directions of the Creator, and through constant contemplation upon the Self (*Atma-Vichara*) come to deserve the total liberation, by ending all its connections with 'ignorance'. Those who have not reached the realm of the Creator, may not come to enjoy the Supreme-merger. They will, at the end of the *Kalpa*, have to come back and take their manifestation in embodiments, ordered by

---

आब्रह्मभुवनाल्लोकाः पुनरावर्तिनोऽर्जुन ।
मामुपेत्य तु कौन्तेय पुनर्जन्म न विद्यते ॥ १६ ॥

ābrahmabhuvanāllokāḥ punaravartino'jurana
māmupetya tu kaunteya punarjanma na vidyate 16.

their remaining *vasanas*. This principle is kept in mind when Krishna says that rebirth is for everyone, even to those who have attained any high plane up to *Brahma-loka*; having once reached *Brahma-loka*, there is no return, but from there the meditator rises to merge in the Self.

But to those who have awakened to the rediscovery of their essential, Eternal Nature and realised themselves to be the One, All-pervading Self – AFTER ATTAINING ME – to them, thereafter, there is no return to the plane of limited-existence. To the waker there is no readmission into the realm where he was when he was dreaming; to awake is to miss forever the joys and sorrows of that dream which he had dreamt. After attaining the wakerhood (Me) there is no return (rebirth) into the dreamland (*Samsara*).

17. *Those people who know (the length of) the day-of-BRAHMA which ends in a thousand YUGAS (aeons), and the night which (also) ends in a thousand YUGAS (aeons), they know day-and-night.*

Einstein's 'Theory of Relativity' has pricked the bubble and it has been accepted even in the West that the concepts of time and space depend upon individual factors governing their measurements. Time hangs heavily and moves at a snail's pace when one is in agitation, as when one is anxiously waiting for something; while, to the same individual, time flies when

सहस्रयुगपर्यन्तमहर्यद्ब्रह्मणो विदु: ।
रात्रिं युगसहस्रान्तां तेऽहोरात्रविदो जना: ॥ १७ ॥

sahasrayugaparyantamaharyad brahmaṇo viduḥ
rātriṁ yugasasrāntām te'horātravido janāḥ 17.

* The *Satya Yuga* consists of 1,728,000 years; the *Treta Yuga* consists of 1,285,000 years; the *Dwapara Yuga* has 854,000 years and the *Kali Yuga* has 482,000 years; together the four *Yugas* constitute the length of a 'cycle'.

he is quite at ease with himself, under circumstances happy, pleasant, and entertaining. One playing cards, knows not when the night was spent and he is surprised when he notices the early dawn peeping through the windows. The same person will complain that each moment has lengthened itself to become hours, when he is at some unpleasant work, or is suffering some pain. He, who is enjoying the homogeneous experience of sleep, has no concept of time at all while he is sleeping.

From the above, it has been logically concluded in the philosophy of the Hindus, that time is truly the measure of the interval between two different experiences. The greater the number of experiences that flood the mind to agitate it, the slower will the time move; while the longer the same experience continues, the faster moves the time. In a single given experience there is no perception of time just as there is no concept of distance when there is only one point; distances can be measured only between two or more points. Basing their calculations upon this theory, the *Pauranic*-poets rightly conceived that their gods had a larger dial for their divine clocks! In the *Upanishads* also, we find a scale of relative intensity of Bliss-experience, from a mortal, healthy, young man, living in conducive environments, upto the very Creator Himself. This ascending scale of joy, experienced in different realms of Consciousness, is showing the relative mental equipoise and tranquillity at those different levels of existence.

It is said here that a thousand 'cycles' constitute the daytime of the Creator; and an equally long thousand 'cycles' constitute the night-time of the Creator. This declaration of those, WHO KNOW THE TRUE MEASURE OF THE DAY AND THE NIGHT, calculated in terms of 'cycles' has been translated in terms of our 365-day years. Each 'cycle' consists of aeons (*Yugas*).* Four aeons (*Yugas*) together constitute one 'cycle' and a thousand 'cycles' are conceived of as constituting the daytime of the Creator!

As the individual units, so is the sum total of the assembly. The individual mind projects, creates and sustains what its fancies dictate, and without any regret scraps the whole lot, only to create afresh. This constant function does take place in each individual only during the daytime, as representing the waking state. In the same fashion the Total Mind - the Cosmic Creator - also is conceived as creating the gross world of dense objects and intelligent beings only during His waking hours.

18. *From the unmanifested all the manifested proceed at the coming of the 'day'; at the coming of 'night' they dissolve verily in that alone which is called the unmanifest.*

19. *This same multiple of beings are being born again and again, and are dissolved (into the unmanifest); helplessly, O Partha, at the coming of 'night,' and they come forth again at the coming of 'day'.*

In these two stanzas an explanation is given on how the Creator employs Himself, during his day, which is a thousand aeons long, and during his night, which also is an equally long interval. It is also added here, that the Creator creates during the day, and the entire created world, at the approach of His night, merges into 'the unmanifest' (*Avyakta*).

अव्यक्ताद्व्यक्तय: सर्वा: प्रभवन्त्यहरागमे ।
रात्र्यागमे प्रलीयन्ते तत्रैवाव्यक्तसंज्ञके ॥ १८ ॥

avyaktādvyaktayaḥ savār prabhavantyaharāgame
rātryāgame pralīyante tatraivāvyaktasañjñake 18.

भूतग्राम: स एवायं भूत्वा भूत्वा प्रलीयते ।
रात्र्यागमेऽवश: पार्थ प्रभवत्यहरागमे ॥ १९ ॥

bhūtagrāmaḥ sa evāyaṁ bhūtvā bhūtvā pralīyate
rātryāgame'vaśaḥ pārtha prabhavatyaharāgame 19.

In the worldly sense of the term, 'creation' is generally understood as the production of something new. Philosophically viewed, 'creation' has a subtler significance and a more intimate meaning. A pot-maker can 'create' pots out of mud, but he cannot 'create' *Laddus* (a popular Indian sweetmeat) out of the same mud! The act of 'creation' is only the production of a name and form, with some specific qualities, out of a raw material in which the same name, form, and qualities already exist in an unmanifest condition. The 'POT-NESS' was in the mud, while the '*Laddu*-ness' is not therein, and therefore, a pot can be 'created' from a given sample of mud, not so even a tiny bit of *Laddu*. Hence, it is concluded by the thinkers of *Vedanta* that CREATION IS BUT A CRYSTALLISATION OF THE UNMANIFEST DORMANT NAMES, FORMS, AND QUALITIES, INTO THEIR MANIFEST FORMS OF EXISTENCE.

Anyone, living as he does on any given day, is but the product of the numerous yesterdays that he has lived in his intellectual thoughts, his emotional feelings and his physical actions. The actions of the past, supported by the thoughts entertained and the valuations accepted by him, leave a distinct flavour upon his mind and intellect, and the future thoughts and their flow are controlled and directed by the previously made thought-channels.

Just as there is consistency of species in procreation, so also, there is a consistency noticeable in the multiplication of thoughts. Just as frogs breed frogs, and men breed men, or mango seeds germinate and grow to put forth mangoes, so too, good thoughts creating good thought-currents can multiply only into a flood of good thoughts. These thought-impressions in the mind (*vasanas*), that lie unmanifest to our sense organs and often to our own mental and intellectual perceptions, become manifested as gross actions, thoughts and words, making our path of life either smooth or rough, according to the texture and quality of the thoughts manifested.

Suppose a doctor, an advocate, a devotee and dacoit are all sleeping in a rest house. While sleeping, all of them look the same - masses of flesh and bones, warm and breathing. The advocate is in no way different from the dacoit, nor is the doctor different from the devotee. The specific qualities in each bosom, at this moment, though totally absent from observation are not non-existent but they remain in a condition of dormancy.

These unmanifested temperaments, capacities, inclinations and tendencies come to project forth and manifest when they wake up, and once they leave the rest house, each will be pursuing his own particular thought-tendencies. In the rest house, the doctor, the advocate, the devotee and the dacoit, were all in their 'unmanifest-state' (*Pralaya*) while they were asleep; but at dawn, when they wake up, these four different specimens are projected forth into manifestation. This, in the language of religion and philosophy, is called 'creation'.

With this correct understanding of the process of 'creation' it would be certainly easy for us to understand the cosmic processes of creation and dissolution. The Creator, or the Total-mind, during His waking hours of thousand aeons, projects out the already existing *vasanas*, and AT THE APPROACH OF NIGHT, THEY MERGE VERILY INTO THAT ALONE, WHICH IS CALLED THE 'UNMANIFEST'.

It is insisted here by Lord Krishna, that THE VERY SAME MULTITUDE OF BEINGS ARE BORN AGAIN AND AGAIN, AND MERGE IN SPITE OF THEMSELVES. Subjectively, this declaration provides us with a clearer understanding of how man becomes enslaved by his own thoughts and emotions. It is never possible that an animal-man, pursuing consistently the life of sensuality, perpetrating unkind cruelties in order to satisfy his passions can wake up overnight, to be a gracious man of all perfections - however great his teacher, however divine the occasion, and whatever the sanctity of the place or the time may be.

No teacher can, or shall ever, teach his disciple and thereby transform him, instantaneously, into a divine person, unless, of course, the student has the divine tendencies lying dormant and ready for manifestation in him! The moment anybody argues that, as a rare instance, one great soul had been so transformed in the past, by one unique teacher, then there must have been some equally unique instance of some magician producing a *Laddu* out of mud! In the latter case, we know that it was only magic and that the *Laddu* was NOT produced from the mud. Similarly, intelligent people, with some understanding of the science of Life, and with at least a little share of respect for and devotion to the Prophet of the *Geeta*, will hoot down such a fantastic story. Such a story can be accepted only in a mood of poetic exaggeration indulged in by the disciples, in praise of their teacher.

THE VERY SAME MULTITUDE OF BEINGS, meaning the very same bundles of thought-impressions – an individual being nothing other than the thoughts that he entertains – arrive at different fields of activity and states of Consciousness in order to exhaust themselves. 'IN SPITE OF THEMSELVES' (*Avashah*), is a powerful expression indicating the incapacity of an individual to disinherit himself from his past. The past always faithfully follows us like our shadow – darkening our path when we turn our back to the light of knowledge, and accompanying us submissively at our heels like a guardian angel when we turn towards the effulgent Self and wend our way towards It.

On leaving a physical embodiment, a particular mind-intellect-equipment continues its existence in just the same way as an actor who drops down the apparel of the king at the close of the play and continues to exist in his individual capacity as the father of his children, the husband of his wife, etc. The taking up of a physical structure and singing the song of one's mental *vasanas*, in the form of actions, is called 'creation' and when that physical structure is given up, the thoughts and ideas, having no equipment to express themselves, become the unmanifest. A violinist playing on his violin makes the music in him manifest; and, when the violin is kept away in its box, the music in the individual becomes unmanifest.

This realm of the unmanifest in each bosom undergoes constant change, whenever it comes in contact with the world of manifestation and reacts to it. We already know that change cannot take place unless it is upon a changeless substratum.

UPON WHAT PERMANENT PLATFORM DOES THE UNMANIFEST COME TO PLAY ITS DRAMA OF LIFE?

20. *But verily there exists, higher than that unmanifest (AVYAKTA), another Unmanifested, which is Eternal, which is not destroyed when all beings are destroyed.*

The same blackboard is approached by different teachers to explain different subjects, during a single day in a classroom. The mathematics teacher's geometrical figures and calculations are wiped clean by the geography teacher to design his maps of the world and to trace the path of rivers, the location of lakes and the position of mountains. When the chemistry teacher arrives, he erases the entire world of mountains, rivers and oceans represented on the blackboard, and he, in his turn, writes on it the laws of chemical reactions among the various elements and their compounds. The

---

परस्तस्मात्तु भावोऽन्योऽव्यक्तोऽव्यक्तात्सनातनः ।
यः स सर्वेषु भूतेषु नश्यत्सु न विनश्यति ॥ २० ॥

parastasmāttu bhāvo'nyo'vyakto'vyaktātsanātanaḥ
yaḥ sa sarveṣu bhūteṣu naśyatsu na vinaśyati 20.

history teacher makes the blackboard clean again, to scribble on it the ancestral trees of dynasties destroyed and families forgotten. Each teacher comes and writes on the blackboard different words and symbols which represent the design of knowledge that he has in his bosom. But all designs were chalked out and executed upon the same blackboard, which illumined the mathematical calculations, the geographical data, the chemical formulae, and the historical facts, in turn.

Similarly, the changing world of the unmanifest must have one Changeless substratum, "THAT WHICH IS NOT DESTROYED BY THE DESTRUCTION OF ALL BEINGS (*bhutas*)". When, in the evening, the students and teachers have all left the classroom, the blackboard still remains. The principle of Pure Consciousness, Itself Unmanifest - inasmuch as It is not perceivable by the sense organs or comprehensible by the mind and intellect - is indicated here as the changeless substratum of all, when the Lord declares, "BEYOND THIS UNMANIFEST, THERE IS THE OTHER ETERNAL EXISTENCE, THE UNMANIFESTED".

The unmanifest (*vasanas*) are the seeds of the manifest and they constitute, what *Vedanta* indicates by its very familiar term, 'Ignorance' (*Avidya*). Ignorance can be only of an existent something; I cannot be ignorant of my tail, since I do not have a tail. This proves the existence of some positive factor called the Truth, the Self – the blackboard upon which all other conditional knowledges are scribbled – serving as the Permanent and Changeless substratum. The ignorance of the Real Nature of this Eternal Factor, is called *Avidya*, which, in its turn projects the manifested ever-changing world of names and forms. The Ultimate Reality, the Self, is being indicated here as something that lies beyond the hazy frontiers of the delusory experiences of creation, dissolution, and re-creation, over and over again.

IS THIS UNMANIFEST THEN THE SUPREME? OR, IS THERE YET ANOTHER FACTOR WHICH ALONE IS FIT

TO BE THE GOAL OF LIFE?

21. *That which is called the Unmanifest and the Imperishable, that, they say is the Highest Goal (path). They who reach It never again return. That is My highest abode (state).*

What has been indicated in the previous stanza as THE OTHER UNMANIFEST, WHICH IS THE ETERNAL EXISTENCE, WHICH KNOWS NO DESTRUCTION, is explained here as the Imperishable mentioned earlier in this chapter. The Imperishable was defined as the *Brahman*, the substratum for the entire universe, and we were also advised that we must meditate upon *OM* as the symbol of this Imperishable. The Self which is of the nature of Pure Awareness is that which lends existence and dynamism to the unmanifested *vasanas*, and makes them capable of projecting out to form the manifested world of activities and behaviours. This Eternal Unmanifested Factor, the Imperishable Self, is the highest goal for man to achieve.

In all other states of existence, there is again and again the experience of return* Just as sleep is not the end of life, but only a refreshing pause between two spans of activity, so too death is not an end, but often, only a restful pause in the unmanifested condition, that comes between two successive manifested existences in different embodiments. It was already indicated that even from higher levels of Consciousness, the egocentres will have to return to exhaust

अव्यक्तोऽक्षर इत्युक्तस्तमाहुः परमां गतिम् ।
यं प्राप्य न निवर्तन्ते तद्धाम परमं मम ॥ २१ ॥

avyakto'kṣara ityuktastamāhuḥ paramā gatim
yaṁ prāpya na nivartante taddhāma paramaṁ mama 21.

* *Samsarati iti samsarah*: the whirl of birth-and-death. The shuttle between the unmanifested and the manifested is 'life' as we know it now.

their unmanifested cravings, the *vasanas*. Birth, we have already been told, is A HOUSE OF PAIN AND FINITUDE, and therefore, complete satisfaction can be reached only when there is no rebirth - no return.

Often, educated students of the present generation ask: "Why, after realising the Self, should there be no-return?" The question, though natural, cannot stand even a moment's scrutiny. Generally, cause hunting is for things that happen and not for things that do not happen! Nobody anxiously enquires why I am not in a hospital but an intelligent enquirer has every right to enquire why I have gone to the hospital. We may enquire why the Infinite has become the finite; but the question does not arise at all why the Infinite should not fall again into the finite. This question is as absurd as my enquiring as to why you are not yet in jail. For not going to jail, no cause hunting is necessary. And if you have actually gone to jail, there is certainly a justification to ask and enquire what is the exact crime for which you have been sent to jail.

We can never explain to a little girl and make that child understand what are the physical and emotional thrills of married life; in her childhood she has not the vehicle for comprehending the biological thrills of sex-life. But, as the same girl grows in her maturity, she develops in herself the biological antennae to feel and mentally comprehend the very same thrills which were to her but empty suggestions in early childhood -- when all she wanted was that her mother should marry her! In the same fashion, a seeker who lies burrowed in the dung-heap of his mind and intellect, cannot, in its filthy atmosphere, know the vast embrace of the horizon and the glorious fragrance of the fresh breeze. As he detaches himself from his false identifications, through the process of meditation advised, (VIII-12, 13 and 14) he, as it were, hatches out of his limiting adjuncts, and enters the vaster fields of subtler experiences. On waking up alone can one realise the falsehood of one's dreams; the dreamer can never, so long as he dreams, realise the delusion from which he is suffering. Having awakened from a dream, the waker cannot be persecuted by his dream sorrows and his dream-happenings.

The Self, or Pure Consciousness, is poetically described here by Vyasa as the dwelling place of Krishna, "THAT IS MY HIGHEST DWELLING-PLACE". In the *Geeta,* the Singer of the Song Divine, is THE Self, and as such the Highest Goal is to reach the State of Pure Consciousness, the Imperishable, which is available for the experiencer of the Self. This was described at length while the teacher was indicating the nature of Knowledge gained by one who attains the state of the Divine *Purusha*.

THE DIRECT PATH BY WHICH THIS CONSUMMATE GOAL CAN BE REACHED IS EXPLAINED IN THE FOLLOWING:

22. *That Highest 'PURUSHA', O Partha, is attainable by unswerving devotion to Him alone, within whom all beings dwell, by whom all this is pervaded.*

Here Krishna, the Prophet of the Hindus, vividly chalks out the technique and the path by which WHAT HAS BEEN CALLED THE UNMANIFEST, THE IMPERISHABLE -THAT SUPREME *PURUSHA* IS ATTAINABLE. Single-pointed devotion is the way and the means. Devotion - total selfless identification with the Supreme *Purusha* can be achieved only when the devotee has learnt to dissociate himself from all

---

पुरुषः स परः पार्थ भक्त्या लभ्यस्त्वनन्यया ।
यस्यान्तःस्थानि भूतानि येन सर्वमिदं ततम् ॥ २२ ॥

puruṣaḥ sa paraḥ pārtha bhaktayā labhyasvananyayā
yasyāntaḥsthāni bhūtāni yena sarvamidaṁ tatam 22.

his preoccupations with his world of body, mind, and intellect. This detachment from the false is gained in a growing attachment with the Real, the Permanent. An act of inspired seeking, of identifying oneself totally with the experience of "SELF I AM" is the WHOLE-SOULED DEVOTION TO HIM ALONE, that is mentioned in this verse.

The Self, thus identified by the seeker in his meditation as himself, should not be conceived of as merely the Divine Spark that presides over his own individual matter-envelopments. Though the seeking is subjective, in identifying with the Self, in the final experience, It is to be realised as the very substratum of the entire universe. Implying this oneness of the Self with the Truth behind the entire world of phenomena, *Bhagawan* says, as an indication of the nature of the *Purusha*, "IN WHOM ALL BEINGS ABIDE AND BY WHOM ALL THIS IS PERVADED".

All mud-pots exist in the mud, and the mud pervades all mud-pots irrespective of their shape, size, or colour. Whether it be a breaker, or a wave, or a wavelet, all are nothing but the ocean, and the ocean pervades all of them. Within and without, the substance of all pots is the substance with which they are made; the Essential Nature of all the waves, big, small, or tiny is nothing other than the ocean from which they are born.

Pure Awareness is the Eternal Truth in which the unmanifest comes to be projected forth as the manifest. But for the cotton, the weaver's unmanifested conception of beauty and proportion cannot be projected and spread out through his creative art of weaving a design on the cloth he is making. At all points in that design of cloth, the one factor without which the design cannot stand is the substance of the threads in the cloth - the cotton.

Pure Awareness, poured into the molds of *vasanas*, when frozen with 'ignorance' becomes the multiple world of names and forms – recognised, craved for, and fought over to acquire and to possess – everywhere by everyone. Therefore, one who has identified oneself with the Self, in that vivid experience, comes to understand the very Essence out of which the confusing multiplicity has risen up into manifestation, to confound the stupid ego and to torment it with the delusory dream of its *samsara*!

After enumerating the two distinct ways of procedure to go back from the manifest to the unmanifest, in the following, Krishna devotes an entire section to explain the different routes taken by seekers to reach the two different destinations. Some reach a destination from where there is a return and others attain a level of experience from which there is no return.

WHAT ARE THE TWO PATHS?

23. *Now at what time (path) departing, YOGIS go, never to return, as also to return, that time (path), I will tell you, O Chief of Bharatas.*

The Lord has already explained that there are two goals in life which men seek: the extrovert life of satisfying the ego and gaining its flickering joys among the sense-objects -- each experience of which soon sours itself to become sorrow; and the Divine Mission of seeking the Imperishable by ending the ego in a rediscovery of its own real Nature as nothing other than the Eternal Consciousness, the Changeless substratum of the whole universe.

These two goals, it has been indicated, differ from each other inasmuch as the former ensures a return again to a

---

यत्र काले त्वनावृत्तिमावृत्तिं चैव योगिनः ।
प्रयाता यान्ति तं कालं वक्ष्यामि भरतर्षभ ॥ २३ ॥

yatra kāle tvanāvṛttimāvṛttiṁ caiva yoginaḥ
prayātā yānti taṁ kālaṁ vakṣyāmi bharatarṣabha 23.

finite embodiment, to live the consequent egocentric life of limitations, and the latter promises a goal, having reached which, there is no return. The Realised One comes to experience and enjoy the Infinite Beatitude of the Bliss Absolute as his own Real Self.

If thus, there are two goals to be gained, there must necessarily be two different paths guiding the two types of seekers to their respective destinations. In the stanza under review, the Lord promises that he will explain to the Chief of the Bharata family, both the path-of-return and the path of no-return.

There is a pun on the word *'Kale'* used here; it shows both the TIME of departure and the PATH pursued by the different types of seekers at the end of their present manifestations.

THE PATH PURSUED BY THOSE WHO HAVE NO RETURN IS AS FOLLOWS:

24. *Fire, light, daytime, the bright fortnight, the six months of the northern solstice; following this path, men who know BRAHMAN go to BRAHMAN.*

Here, in the stanza, the path of gradual liberation (*Krama-mukti*) is explained. According to the *Upanishadic* tradition, "he who lived a life of rituals (*Karmas*) and worship (*Upasana*), to enjoy the result so accrued, will walk the path of the gods (*Devayana*) and entering through the Sun, will go beyond it to *Brahma-loka*". There he enjoys the super-sensuous Bliss till the end of the 'cycle' when, along with the Creator, he gets total

---

अग्निर्ज्योतिरहः शुक्लः षण्मासा उत्तरायणम् ।
तत्र प्रयाता गच्छन्ति ब्रह्म ब्रह्मविदो जनाः ॥ २४ ॥
agnirjyotarahaḥ śuklaḥ ṣaṇmāsā uttarāyaṇam
tatra prayātā gacchanti brahma brahmavido janāḥ 24.

liberation. This path of the gods, is indicated here by the terms borrowed from the *Upanishads* which have a wealth of suggestiveness to all students of the *Rishi*-declarations.*

FIRE, FLAME, DAYTIME, THE BRIGHT FORTNIGHT, THE SIX MONTHS OF THE NORTHERN SOLSTICE OF THE SUN—These indicate the path of the gods presided over by the Sun. In the *Prashnopanishad* this has been vividly brought out when the *Upanishad* supplies the students with a theory of the creation of multiplicity from the one Great Truth. It is explained that *Prajapati*, the Creator, Himself became the Sun and the Moon, and these two phenomenal objects are mentioned as representing energy and matter respectively.

Identifying with the Dynamic Centre in himself, a seeker tries to live the life. Such an *Upasaka* of Truth, at the time of his departure from his present manifestation in the world, comes to think of the object of contemplation of his whole lifetime, and naturally, he goes to the world of his thoughts - "as you think so you become". By entertaining evolutionary thoughts in one's mind all through one's life, one must, after leaving the present embodiment, walk the ascending path of evolution, the path of the-gods, indicated here as THE PATH-OF-LIGHT AND FIRE, OF DAYTIME, OF THE BRIGHT FORTNIGHT, OF THE NORTHERN SOLSTICE OF THE SUN. Thus, in the mystic language of the *Upanishads*, the path pursued by those who are great devotees of *Brahman*, the Eternal, is described as stretching towards the North. These implications are all epitomised and the *Upanishadic Rishis*

---

* There is a description of these two paths mentioned here, in the *Brahma-sutras* formulated by the author of the *Geeta*, as well as in the *Chandogya, Brihadaranyaka, Prashna* and *Katha Upanishads*. In *Brahma-sutra* read IV-ii, 17 and 20.

often use the term 'Northern Route' to indicate the path of the 'Gradual Liberation'.

AS CONTRASTED WITH THIS PATH OF NO-RETURN THERE IS THE PATH OF SURE-RETURN WHICH IS EXPLAINED IN THE FOLLOWING:

25. *Smoke, nighttime, the dark fortnight, also six months of the southern solstice, attaining by these to the Moon, the lunar light, the 'YOGI' returns.*

The path-of-Return is called the 'path of the ancestor' (*Pitryana*), and is considered as presided over by the Moon, which represents the world-of-matter. Those who leave the world after spending their lifetime in doing good and performing rituals (*karmas*), unaccompanied by any worship (*upasana*), are those who go to the world-of-ancestors (*Pitrus*), otherwise popularly known as Heaven. These denizens of Heaven, on having exhausted their merits, gained by them through their divine actions, will have to return into deserved embodiments, ordered by their individual *vasana*-balance that is ardently pressing for expression and fulfilment.

SMOKE, NIGHTTIME, THE DARK FORTNIGHT, THE SIX MONTHS OF THE SOUTHERN SOLSTICE—these indications chalk out 'the Path through the Moon' (*Pitryana*) to the world of the ancestors. The moon, as we said, represents the world-of-matter and is the presiding deity of the sense enjoyments. Such people do return after having

---

धूमो रात्रिस्तथा कृष्ण: षण्मासा दक्षिणायनम् ।
तत्र चान्द्रमसं ज्योतिर्योगी प्राप्य निवर्तते ॥ २५ ॥

dhūmo rātristathā kṛṣṇaḥ ṣaṇmāsā dakṣiṇāyanam
tatra cāndramasaṁ jyotiryogī prāpya vivartate 25.

attained through the grace of the Moon the Heavenly enjoyments for a period.

In short, these two stanzas indicate that, in his lifetime, a seeker struggling to raise himself above the various matter-envelopments and his identifications with them reaches the higher spiritual realms from where, in the stream of his spiritual progress, he reaches the Ultimate. But in case he be a courtier of pleasures, ever singing at the temple of sensuality, then he falls on the path of realising those developed instincts, and comes back again into the field of action here, wherein he can again make or unmake himself.

IN CONCLUSION KRISHNA ADDS:

26. *The 'Path-of-Light' and the 'Path-of-Darkness' available for the world are verily thought to be both eternal; by the one, the 'Path-of-Light', a man goes to return not; by the other, the 'Path-of-Darkness', he returns again.*

The two paths so vividly described above, are renamed here as the path-of-Light and the path-of-Darkness, according to the goal to which each 'Path' leads the pilgrims. One takes the travellers to the brilliant heights of evolutionary success; the other into the dark abyss of devolutionary sorrow. These two 'Paths' described here, in their general implications, can be considered as showing the path-of-*Moksha* and the path-of-*Samsara*.

The ways of life in any given generation always fall under two categories; the secular and the sacred. The former, the

---

शुक्लकृष्णे गती ह्येते जगतः शाश्वते मते ।
एकया यात्यनावृत्तिमन्ययावर्तते पुनः ॥ २६ ॥
śuklakṛṣṇs gatī hyete jagataḥ śāśvate mate
ekayā yātyanāvṛttimanyayāvartate punaḥ 26.

secular, is pursued by those who feel that food, clothing and shelter are the absolutes and the fulfilment of life lies in the satisfaction of the largest number of physical and emotional sense-ticklers, and whose intellects are cold and satisfied, feeling no urge to seek anything nobler and diviner. The latter, the sacred, however, is pursued by those who can feel no encouragement in their bosom, when the sense-objects giggle and dance in front of their sense-organs, and whose intellects are ever on fire with a great seeking of something beyond, something deeper than the mere surface existence in life.

These two paths - which mean not only the two impulses of the sacred and the secular, but also all those who follow these two paths - the seekers of materialism and the seekers of spirituality ARE TO BE CONSIDERED AS TRULY ETERNAL. In the largest sense of the term, these two impulses together constitute the entire *Samsara*, and since the world of finitude and change is eternal, these two contrary impulses are also eternal. But it is the *Vedantic* theory, approved and upheld by the lived experiences of the Seers and Sages, that *Samsara* for the individual can be ended.

Subjectively considered, this stanza may perhaps have a secret suggestion to make to true *Yogis,* meaning, the sincere meditators. Even in an elderly *sadhaka*, who has been on the 'path' for years, the existing *vasanas* in him may now and then come up to insist upon his extroversion. At such moments of inner revolt in us, we, as seekers and meditators, need not at all get flabbergasted because, as the Lord explains, the aspirations for the higher-life and the temptations for the lower-existence are the two opposing forces that are eternally at tug-of-war with each other.

WHAT EXACTLY IS THE GAIN IN KNOWING THESE TWO PATHS, AND THEIR ETERNAL NATURE?

27. *Knowing these paths, O Partha, no YOGIN is deluded; therefore, at all times be steadfast in YOGA, O Arjuna.*

After knowing that the path-of-Light and the path- of-Darkness are the two opposing forces that function in our mental life eternally, a true seeker will not fall into any sense of despair, when he watches a revolt rising in his bosom. "No *YOGI* IS DELUDED, KNOWING THESE PATHS."

The entire line of argument pursued by Krishna, is to reveal slowly and steadily the path of Return and the path of No-Return and now, in this, the penultimate stanza of this chapter, the Lord summarises the thesis and purpose, and says, "THEREFORE, ARJUNA, YOU BE A *YOGI* AT ALL TIMES". Here, he who has withdrawn himself from his false identifications and has come to fix his single-pointed mind in the contemplation of the Self, is a *Yogi*.

In short, the entire chapter is a divinely powerful plea recommending that Arjuna should, even while acting in the world, continuously strive to be one living in the awareness of the Divine, through a process of selfless identification with the Eternal, Imperishable *Purusha*.

BY MERE MEDITATION HOW WILL WE GAIN THE SPECIFIC MERITS THAT ARE PROMISED BY THE *SHRUTI*

नैते सृती पार्थ जानन्योगी मुह्यति कश्चन ।
तस्मात्सर्वेषु कालेषु योगयुक्तो भवार्जुन ॥ २७ ॥
naite sṛtī pārtha jānānyogī muhyati kaścana
tasmātsarveṣu kāleṣu yogayukto bhavārjuna 27.

AND THE *SMRITI* WHEN WE FOLLOW CERTAIN NOBLE ACTIONS IN LIFE?

28. *Whether the fruit of merit is declared (in the scriptures) as springing up from study of the VEDAS, from performance of sacrifices, from practice of austerities, and from charity— beyond all these goes the YOGIN, who having known this (the two 'paths') attains to the Supreme, Primeval (Essence).*

Here Krishna is emphasizing that meditation can be undertaken by anyone who is even slightly capable of it, because, the Lord explains, WHATEVER MERITORIOUS RESULTS ARE PROMISED IN THE SCRIPTURES TO ACCRUE FROM THE STUDY OF THE *Vedas*, PERFORMANCE OF *YAJNAS*, PRACTICE OF AUSTERITIES, AND SELFLESS CHARITY, a true *Yogi*, meaning, a sincere meditator, gains them all. Besides, the Lord is emphatic when He says, "THE *YOGI* EVER RISES OVER ALL THESE". Attempts at meditation can integrate the personality a million times more easily and quickly than by the slower processes described above - it being understood that the devoted meditator has developed in himself the necessary amount of dispassion, and discriminative thinking. Even these can grow

---

वेदेषु यज्ञेषु तपःसु चैव
दानेषु यत्पुण्यफलं प्रदिष्टम् ।
अत्येति तत्सर्वमिदं विदित्वा
योगी परं स्थानमुपैति चाद्यम् ॥ २८ ॥

vedeṣu yajñeṣu tapaḥsu caiva
dāneṣu yatpuṇyaphalaṁ pradiṣṭam
atyeti tatsarvamidaṁ viditvā
yogī paraṁ sthānmupaiti cādyam 28.

when meditation is pursued regularly and sincerely.

When thus, a meditator who has, through meditation, gained the results of selfless *Karma* and *Upasanas*, continued his practices, he learns to soar higher and higher, until at last he comes to realise 'THIS' – the Imperishable *Purusha*, and ATTAINS TO THE PRIMEVAL, SUPREME ABODE – having attained which, MY HIGHEST STATE, there is no return.

Thus, in the UPANISHADS of the glorious Bhagawad-Geeta, in the Science of the Eternal, in the scripture of YOGA, in the dialogue between Sri Krishna and Arjuna, the eighth discourse ends entitled:

The *Yoga* of Imperishable *Brahman*

Here the term '*YOGA* OF THE IMPERISHABLE *BRAHMAN*' is to be understood as 'THE WAY TO THE IMPERISHABLE *BRAHMAN*'. After answering in this chapter the questions raised by Arjuna, the Lord was borne away on the high tides of His Divine inspiration, to explain how those who can remember the Infinite at the time of their departure from the body will reach the Infinite. Therefore, He advised Arjuna to remember the Infinite always and face his life diligently.

Naturally, Krishna has to explain what is the nature of that Infinite upon which the seeker is to fix his single-pointed mind. We had thus, in stanzas 9 and 10, a set of brilliant phrases, which, in their suggestiveness, explain the Inexplicable. Having described the Imperishable *Brahman*, Krishna explains the path-of-Light and the path-of-Darkness, the former leading to the Imperishable, and the latter abducting the ego away from its divine home into the house of pain and finitude. Rightly, indeed, has the chapter been captioned as "THE WAY TO THE IMPERISHABLE *BRAHMAN*".

Om Om Om Om Om

ॐ तत्सदिति श्रीमद् भगवद् गीतासूपनिषत्सु ब्रह्मविद्यायां
योगशास्त्रे श्रीकृष्णार्जुनसंवादे अक्षरब्रह्मयोगो नाम
अष्टमोऽध्याय:

Oṁ tatsaditi śrīmadbhagavadgītāsū ūpaniṣatsu brahmavidyāyāṁ
yogaśāstre śrī kṛṣṇārjuna saṁvāde akṣarabrahmayogo nāma
aṣṭamo'dhyāyaḥ

IX

The Royal Secret
Introduction

SRIMAD BHAGAWAD GEETA, as a textbook of Hindu renaissance, has necessarily to carry within it the seeds of a complete reformation, almost revolutionary in its dynamic onslaught. The fundamental principles remaining the same, a religion that keeps pace with life has to readjust itself to accommodate current social problems and political conditions. Religion was not extinct in the era of the Mahabharata. But the *Vedic* principles needed a readjustment and a reaffirmation in the context of the life available in that era.

When the fundamentals forming the foundation are to be kept sacredly the same, the only adjustment that is possible for the expansion of the Science of Life, is to discover a more liberal means for its application, and to annotate the same in the language of the conflict and struggle available in that period. Blind faith can have a compelling charm only in the early history of a people, and, when they grow and become stalwart in their reason and muscular in their movements, the impetuosity of the generation can no more be tamed and kept within bounds by the sandy beaches of barren faith. It demands and expects walls of unshakable logic and reason to support the stream of assertions in the philosophy of the thinkers. To a large extent, an interpreter of a philosophy – not the philosopher himself – will have to dance to the rhythm of the inundations and the direction of the current of thought and life in his age.

This new interpretation, at once intelligent and meaningful, has, no doubt, injected a new vigour and brought fresh blood into the senile values of life and their ineffectual application in society. Such repeated transfusions of youthfulness and vitality into the dilapidated body of religion has sustained the ageless tradition of the Hindus through its chequered career down the aisles of Time. One of the most powerful rejuvenation treatments that the immortal lore received in recent times was from the hands of Vyasa, and the *Bhagawad Geeta* reports that operation divine.

In Chapter Seven, we find how the Champion of the Revolt throws His gloves down, in a challenge, when He says: "I shall tell you about KNOWLEDGE, both speculative and practical". Thereafter, Krishna has been pursuing the theme of spiritual practices, like a mathematician solving his problem, stage by stage, for the benefit of his students. Nowhere has He insisted upon any blind faith in what He said. On the other hand, at every stage, He has been scrupulously careful to supply the necessary data and the rational arguments for the why and the wherefore of the *Vedantic* beliefs and the ways of self-perfection advocated by *Vedanta*.

The same tempo of ruthless intellectual estimation is being continued in Chapter Nine also and its very opening stanza promises that the Lord will be giving, during His discourse, not only the theory of self-perfection but also the logic behind it all. It is very clear, if sympathetically considered, that the kind teacher in Krishna is carefully avoiding the usage of vague and mystic technical terms then in use in the *Vedantic* literature, except for the most elementary ones.

Ideas have been simplified here, so that they can be easily grasped by Arjuna, the representative of the ordinary, educated men of his time. However, the same principles will be found to have been explained again in a later chapter (XIII) under the orthodox terminology of *Vedanta* as *Kshetra*, *Kshetrajna*, *Jnana*, *Jneya*, *Purusha*, *Prakriti*, etc.

Dividing the subject of enquiry into its main divisions; analytical explanation of the divisions; categorical treatment of the subject under each division; discussion of the relation between the various parts and setting down the conclusions drawn therefrom – these would in our days be considered as the proper scientific method for the treatment of a subject. In this sense of the term, the *Geeta* is not at all scientific. But, at the same time, the conversational style of the *Geeta* has its own characteristic clarity and *shastraic* precision. Krishna Himself calls it 'the most Secret (profound) Science'. To every careful student of the *Geeta*, it will be clear that in its scientific outlook and systematic explanations the discourses leave nothing to be desired.

The Blessed Lord said:

1. *To you who do not cavil, I shall now declare this, the greatest secret, the most profound knowledge combined with experience (or realisation); which having known, you shall be free from the sorrows of life.*

श्रीभगवानुवाच
इदं तु ते गुह्यतमं प्रवक्ष्याम्यनसूयवे ।
ज्ञानं विज्ञानहितं यज्ज्ञात्वा मोक्ष्यसेऽशुभात् ॥ १ ॥

śrībhagavānuvāca
idaṁ tu te guhyatamaṁ pravakṣyāmyanasūyave
jñāna vijñānasahitaṁ yajjñātvā mokṣyase'śubhāt 1.

Lord Krishna has found, in Arjuna, one who is really anxious to evolve. Only, he wanted help from some quarter, to develop in himself an intellectual conviction for the way-of-life he was to pursue. The Lord says that He will declare the philosophy to Arjuna, 'WHO DOES NOT CARP OR CAVIL' and the benefit of this knowledge and its practical application has also been indicated in this stanza; "HAVING KNOWN WHICH, YOU SHALL BE FREE FROM ALL LIMITATIONS OF FINITE EXISTENCE".

An individual becomes incapable of facing the challenges of life and meeting its rising demands, because, in his false estimation of things and beings, he comes to play out of tune with the whole orchestra of life. To understand ourselves and the world outside is to know the secret of keeping a healthy and happy relationship with the world outside. He, who is capable of tuning himself up thus with the whole, is the one who is marked out for sure success and complete victory in life.

Because of his internal maladjustments, we found Arjuna, the hero of his age, behaving as a shattered personality. Such an individual, split in himself, comes to feel the problems of life too heavy, the duties of life too irksome, and life itself too much to bear. All those, who thus allow the engine of life to run over them and crush them down, are termed as *Samsarins*. Those who know the art of self-development can easily learn how to steer the engine of existence from its driver's seat, safely around every impediment, and they are the men-of-Realisation, the Saints, and the Sages. This status is the heritage of man, of every intelligent person, who has the enthusiasm and the courage to master life and live like a God upon earth ruling over the circumstances, and smiling at the adversities.

TO GENERATE AN ALL-OUT ENTHUSIASM IN THE ART OF LIVING, WHICH EACH STUDENT HAS TO BRING ABOUT IN HIS OWN LIFE, THE ART OF SELF-PERFECTION IS PRAISED IN THE FOLLOWING:

2. *Royal Science, Royal Secret, the Supreme purifier is this, realisable by direct intuitive knowledge, according to the DHARMA, very easy to perform, imperishable.*

Vedanta is no religion in the ordinary concept of the term, which implies the formalistic observance of some physical and mental discipline, in some House of God, during a specific day of the week, for a prescribed length of time. If we consider religion as an Art of Right Action, then *Vedanta* is indeed the noblest of religions, because it provides a scientific explanation for the entire way of right living. Krishna here glorifies it: "THIS IS THE ROYAL SCIENCE, THE ROYAL MYSTERY, PURE AND VERY HIGH".

Even if there be a science, royal in its import, deep in its profundity, and 'supreme in its purifying effect', unless it be available for our comprehension, it is almost useless. Here, Krishna promises that it is CLEARLY COMPREHENSIBLE, since it can be apprehended directly by an immediate experience of the Self.

Also it is a science pertaining to *Dharma* (*Dharmyam*). The term *Dharma* has already been explained.* Man is nothing but

---

राजविद्या राजगुह्यं पवित्रमिदमुत्तमम् ।
प्रत्यक्षावगमं धर्म्यं सुसुखं कर्तुमव्ययम् ॥ २ ॥

rājavidyā rājaguhyaṁ pavitramidamuttamam
pratyakṣāvagamaṁ dharmyaṁ susukhaṁ kartumavyayam 2.

* As the Law-of-Being : Refer General Introduction.

IX/2

ninerals in their gross and subtle states, if the rinciple were not blessing them with awareness. eness, called the Self, is then the *Dharma* of man, iple-of-Life in him. The Spiritual Science, that the *Vrindavana* promises to enunciate in this chapter, is the physical science of the biology of the objects of orld, nor the science of psychology that explains the of emotions and thoughts - but the science of the Self, deepest essence in each individual.

VERY EASY TO PERFORM—Religion is a subjective technique to be pursued and accomplished by each in himself. If this great science, into which Lord Krishna is proposing to initiate Arjuna, is an extremely difficult proposition in life, then, naturally, it is a futile philosophy. The poverty of a country is not removed by the declaration of its scientists that there are inexhaustible quantities of unclaimed gold, awaiting free transportation, on Mars! In order to remove this vague fear, it has been fully confirmed that the technique of self-integration and the ultimate gaining of complete mastery over oneself is an art easy to master for the sincere and the diligent.

Even if it be easy, no intelligent man can pursue the path, if the gain acquired thereby is perishable and temporary. It is endorsed here that the gains acquired through a faithful pursuit of this Royal Science of self-development and self-mastery are OF AN IMPERISHABLE NATURE. To realise the Self is to become the Self, the Eternal, and the Infinite Reality behind the phenomenal world of appearances.

AS A CONTRAST TO THOSE WHO ARE SEEKING, THE DESTINY OF THOSE WHO ARE NOT SEEKING THE IMPERISHABLE IS DECLARED TO BE THE DISTURBED LIFE OF *SAMSARA*:

3. *Persons without faith in this DHARMA (the Di... O Parantapa, without attaining Me, return to the ...elf), rebirth, fraught with death?*

Those who live in complete disregard of the ... necessarily RETURN WITHOUT ATTAINING ME. Me... extroversion, meditating upon the sense objects and bartering away their intellectual capacities, emotional powers, and physical strength for seeking, acquiring and possessing the implements to work out their sensual satisfaction, must necessarily return to THE PATH OF REBIRTH, FRAUGHT WITH DEATH.

The more an individual meditates upon the finite, strives to gain the changeable, and gets choked by the sorrows of the perishable, the more he comes to worship and court the lower nature of the Self, the *Prakriti*. However big the ocean may be, a drop of it, taken from anywhere in its infinite expanse, should taste saline. In the same way, whatever be the motive behind the courting, once we allow ourselves to be courtiers of the world-of-objects; we are doomed to taste the saline tears of sorrow, because of the very ephemeral nature of the 'objects of our love'.

The world of names and forms is finite and ever-changing. At every moment, every object is living through a process of change, and each change is death to the previous state of existence of the object. Thus, the term 'death' used here by

---

अश्रद्दधानाः पुरुषा धर्मस्यास्य परंतप ।
अप्राप्य मां निवर्तन्ते मृत्युसंसारवर्त्मनि ॥३॥

aśraddadhānāḥ puruṣā dharmasyāsya parantapa
aprāpya māṁ nivartante mṛtyusaṁsāravartmani 3.

· Faith is the bird, That feels the light, And sings when, The dawn is still dark. – Tagore

Krishna in his phrase FRAUGHT WITH DEATH is to be understood in this liberal meaning of the term. In short, courtiers of the finite reach the tragic realms of constant death.

In the perfect Science of *Vedanta*, though *shraddha* also implies 'faith' in the Tagorean sense of the term,* it is not built upon the misty vapours of emotionalism, but upon the solid beams of intellectual understanding and perfect awareness of the logic of thought behind the theory. Sankara defines *Shraddha* as the molding of the life and living, on the basis of right intellectual comprehension of what the scripture indicates and the teachers explain. It is the enduring faith that lifts us to realms beyond the reach of the mind and intellect, and helps to carve out of the mortal and the finite, the Immortal and the Infinite.

Something without which a substance cannot be that very substance is called its *Dharma* or essence; e.g., heat in fire, cold in ice. Those who have no faith in the Divine Essence, which is the Self in them, get easily abducted by the cooing of their emotions, or the barking of their intellect, or the whisperings of their flesh. They slip into devolution and come to live as biped animals, when they lose their faith in the Divine core which is the Essential Being. A mad king, who has forgotten his own kingship, throws his kingly dignity to the winds and runs about naked on the streets, behaving as though he were a homeless vagabond. Similarly, an individual, in his forgetfulness of the dignity of his essential Self-hood, comes to live in the open streets of sense pleasures, hunting for his satisfactions, as though he were nothing better than a crawling worm in some wayside ditch.

Simple looking though it be, this stanza is pregnant with untold suggestiveness. By contrasting thus the path-of-Knowledge with the path-of-Ignorance in the most vivid terms, Krishna brings to the comprehension of Arjuna the advisability of the blessed path of Higher seeking, the realisation of the Imperishable.

IN THE FOLLOWING, KNOWLEDGE IS THEREFORE GLORIFIED, WHEN KRISHNA EXPLAINS THAT *DHARMA*, WHICH IS TO BE FOLLOWED, IS:

4. *All this world is pervaded by Me in My Unmanifest form (aspect); all beings exist in Me, but I do not dwell in them.*

ALL THIS WORLD IS PERVADED BY ME IN MY UNMANIFESTED FORM—the subtlety of a thing is measured in terms of its pervasiveness and therefore, the subtlest must necessarily be the All-pervasive. As all limited things must have forms, the All-pervasive alone can be Eternal and Infinite. All forms are perishable substances (*Dravya*). Thus the Self, in its essential Unmanifest nature, must be pervading everything, as the mud pervades all forms and shapes in all mud-pots.

If thus, the Infinite pervades the finite, what exactly is the relationship between them? Is it that the finite rose from the Infinite? Or is it that the Infinite PRODUCED the finite? Has the Infinite Itself become the finite, as a modification of Itself, or do they both, among themselves, keep a father-son, or a master-servant relationship? Various religions of the world abound in such questions. The dualists can afford to indulge in such a fancied picture of some relation or other between the finite and the Infinite. But the *Advaitins* (non-

---

मया ततमिदं सर्वं जगदव्यक्तमूर्तिना।
मत्स्थानि सर्वभूतानि न चाहं तेष्ववस्थितः॥ ४॥
mayā tatamidaṁ sarvaṁ jagadavyaktamūrtinā
matsthāni sarvabhūtāni na cāhaṁ teṣvavasthitaḥ 4.

dualists) cannot accept this idea, since to them the Eternal Self alone is the ONE and the ONLY REALITY.

The second line of this stanza is a classical description of this 'relationless-relationship' between the Real and unreal. "All beings exist in Me but I dwell not in them". To a hasty reader this would strike as an incomprehensible paradox expressed in a jumble of empty words. But to one who has understood well the theory of superimposition, this is very simple. The ghost-vision can come only upon the post. And what exactly is the relationship between the ghost and the post from the standpoint of the post? The innocent post, in infinite love for the deluded fool, can only make a similar statement as the Lord has made here. "The ghost", the post would say, "is no doubt in me, but I am not in the ghost; and therefore, I have never frightened any deluded traveller at any time". In the same fashion the Lord says here, "I, IN MY UNMANIFEST NATURE, AM THE SUBSTRATUM FOR ALL THE MANIFESTED chaos of names and forms, but neither in their joys nor in their sorrows, neither in their births nor in their deaths, AM I SHARING THEIR DESTINIES, BECAUSE I DO NOT DWELL IN THEM".

This line sounds a faithful echo of the same idea, perhaps more crisply expressed earlier (VII-12), where it was said "I AM NOT IN THEM, THEY ARE IN ME". In short, it is indicated here that the Self which, through Its identification with the matter-envelopments, has come to DWELL IN THEM is the pain-ridden mortal, while the same Self which has successfully withdrawn all Its false arrogations with the matter layers and has come to realise that, "I DO NOT DWELL IN THEM" is the Self, Immortal and Unmanifest.

THEN THERE MUST BE SOME SORT OF AN EXISTENCE FOR THE FINITE IN THE INFINITE:

5. *Nor do beings exist (in reality) in Me – behold My Divine YOGA supporting all beings, but not dwelling in them, I am My Self, the 'efficient-cause' of all beings.*

Continuing the strain of His arguments in the previous stanza here He says, "NOR DO THINGS EXIST IN ME" although "I DWELL NOT IN THEM". Now here he says that in the Infinite, never has the finite ever risen! Continuing our example of the post and the ghost this is equivalent to the post declaring that, 'in me, the electric post, never has a ghost existed'. In Pure Awareness, in Its Infinite Nature of sheer Knowledge, there never was, never is and can never be any world of pluralistic embodiment, just as, for the waker, the pleasures of the dream world ARE NEVER AVAILABLE. In short, at the time of the direct subjective experience of the Self there is no cognition of the pluralistic world, which is born out of the forgetfulness of the Infinite.

The Self brings forth and supports all beings just as the ocean gives birth to, supports and nourishes all the waves in it. "AND YET", says Krishna, "I, MYSELF NEVER DWELL IN THEM". Just in the same way the ocean can cry that "I am never the waves". The mud is the womb of all pots, the sustainer of their shapes, the nourisher of their forms, and yet, none of the pots, nor all the pots put together, can ever define or give a total knowledge of the mud. Pure Consciousness, Divine and Eternal, is the substratum that sustains and illumines the entire panorama of the ever-changing plurality.

न च मत्स्थानि भूतानि पश्य मे योगमैश्वरम् ।
भुतभृन्न च भूतस्थो ममात्मा भूतभावनः ॥५॥

na ca matsthāni bhūtāni paśya me yogmaiśvaram
bhutabhṛnna ca bhūtastho mamātmā bhūtabhāvanaḥ 5.

The objects of the world conveying their stimuli through the doors of the sense organs create mental waves which are illuminated by the Conscious Principle residing in all forms. If the Awareness is not there, the external world must necessarily fail in giving the mind-and-intellect the concept of its life as a series of unbroken experiences. Just as the cotton is in the cloth, or the gold in all ornaments, or the heat in the fire, so too, the Imperishable is in the perishable. The dreamer can function only in the waker; the waker pervades the dream-experiences, and at the same time, the waker is not in the dream nor in fact, when awakened fully, does the dream ever exist in the waker.

KRISHNA FEELS THAT THE LANGUAGE OF PARADOX IS PROVING TOO MUCH OF A RIDDLE TO THE GROSS INTELLECT OF THE AVERAGE MAN IN ARJUNA, AND THEREFORE, IN HIS DIVINE KINDNESS, THE LORD PROVIDES FOR HIS DISCIPLE AN EXAMPLE:

6. *As the mighty wind, moving everywhere, rests always in space (the AKASHA), even so, know you, all beings rest in Me.*

The confused Prince, trying to solve the riddle, is helped here by the Kingly Teacher in Krishna who gives him a vivid example. To imagine a substance that exists everywhere, allowing everything to exist in it, but at the same time, it in itself not getting conditioned by the things that exist in it, is very difficult, and the ordinary intellect cannot easily soar to comprehend those heights of understanding and appreciation. As a prop for the ordinary intellect, to raise itself up so that

---

यथाकाशस्थितो नित्यं वायुः सर्वत्रगो महान्।
तथा सर्वाणि भूतानि मत्स्थानीत्युपधारय ॥ ६ ॥

yathākāśsthito nityaṁ vāyuḥ sarvatrago mahān
tathā savārṇi bhūtāni matsthānītyupadhāraya 6.

it may peep over its own limitations and gain a vision of the unravelling expanse of the Infinite, here is a brilliant example.

The gross can never condition the subtle. As the poet sings, "Stonewalls do not a prison make" for, even though we may imprison the body of the prisoner, his thoughts are ever free to reach his kith and kin at their hearth. The gross stonewalls cannot limit the flight of the subtle thoughts. If once this principle is well understood the example becomes very expressive exhibiting all its secret suggestions.

KNOW YOU ARJUNA, that the winds curl, swirl and whirl around everywhere in space; the space supports and envelopes them everywhere, and yet, they do not ever limit the space. This beautiful example, when meditated upon by any seeker, if he has at least an average amount of intellectual comprehension, will enable him to define, in his own mind, the right relationship that exists between the Self and the non-Self. The Real supports the unreal; the unreal seemingly lives... through its history of misery and sorrows, fleeting joys and passing pleasures ... in the Real and yet, the unreal can never condition the Real. When the wind is moving, the space need never move. None of the qualities of the wind is the quality of the space (*Akasha*). Compared with the outstretching Infinite space, in which the universes keep on revolving at a speed measured in light years, the atmospheric disturbances are only upto the height of a few miles off the surface of the globe. In the infinite vastness of the Real, the arena of disturbances caused by Its flirtations with Its own assumed self-ignorance is only a negligible area ... and even there, the relationship between the false and the Real is the relationship between the fickle breeze and the Infinite space.

These two are stanzas not merely to be explained away by words, however true the commentator may be; they are to be meditated upon by the students, individually.

THEN WHAT ABOUT YOUR WONDERFUL THEORY OF A SYSTEMATIC LAW OF REBIRTH -- THE STORY OF A CREATOR CREATING THE WORLD DURING HIS DAY-TIME -- AND DISSOLVING THE ENTIRE LOT DURING HIS NIGHT-TIME, ETC..? ... LISTEN:

7. *All beings, O Kaunteya (O Son of Kunti), go into My PRAKRITI (nature) at the end of a KALPA; I send them forth again at the beginning of (the next) KALPA.*

8. *Animating My PRAKRITI, I, again and again send forth all this helpless multitude of beings, by the force of nature (PRAKRITI).*

The Eternal *Brahman* functioning through the equipment of the total mind is the God-principle, the Creator, and the same Absolute *Brahman* functioning through the limited individual mind-and-intellect is the individualised Self, the mortal ego (*Samsarin*). The same Sun gets reflected in the clear still waters of a vast lake and in the disturbed muddy pool on the roadside; the difference between the two distinctive reflections, in the different equipments, will explain the difference between the individual-ego and the God Principle. Just as the Sun in the sky can rightly say: "I am the cause for the brilliant reflection in the lake and the broken, dull reflection in the wayside puddle" so

---

सर्वभूतानि कौन्तेय प्रकृतिं यान्ति मामिकाम् ।
कल्पक्षये पुनस्तानि कल्पादौ विसृजाम्यहम् ॥ ७ ॥

sarvabhūtāni kaunteya prakṛtiṁ yānti māmikām
kalpakṣaye punastāni kalpādau visṛjāmyaham 7.

प्रकृतिं स्वामवष्टभ्य विसृजामि पुनः पुनः ।
भूतग्राममिमं कृत्स्नमवशं प्रकृतेर्वशात् ॥ ८ ॥

prakṛtiṁ svāmavaṣṭabhya visṛjāti punaḥ punaḥ
bhūtagrāmamimaṁ kṛtsnamavaśaṁ prakṛtervaśāt 8.

too, Krishna, the Self declares: "I am the vital animating Reality behind the Creator, and also behind the created".

The Adjunct of the God Principle, the total body-mind-intellect equipment, constitutes the lower nature of the Self, called the *Prakriti*. At the beginning of a cycle the existing *vasanas* in the lower nature get projected and at the end of the *Kalpa* all beings go to My *Prakriti*.

The act of invigorating or fertilising the *Prakriti* to grow up again into the tree-of-*samsara*, is an act of grace from *Brahman*. If the Supreme Consciousness were not to identify with *Prakriti*, (*Maya*), she, being inert in herself, cannot project forth any life at all. The entire multitude of *vasanas*, "I project again and again". When the Self animates *Prakriti*, the *vasanas* have no freedom at all to refuse expression because; THEY ARE HELPLESS UNDER THE SWAY OF *PRAKRITI*.

In philosophy, the *Rishis* often explain the Universe from the standpoint of the macrocosm (*Samashti*) which has a knack of confusing the students, unless each student strives hard to understand its implications subjectively in himself, as microcosm (*Vyashti*). Viewed thus, in the individual subjective inner-life-story, the statement proves to be indeed true, since without the life in us – the Self – identifying with the lower nature in us, the mind and intellect equipment cannot create the characteristic ego, which comes to suffer its limited existence.

We have already found that the greatest scoundrel and the noblest saint are both the same when neither of them is identifying with his mind and intellect, in the state of deep sleep. On waking up, the scoundrel-mind projects a scoundrel, and the saintly-mind projects the saint; and the vitality behind both is the same spark-of-Life, Consciousness Absolute. Thus, the scoundrel is incapable of not behaving as a scoundrel, as much as the saint cannot, by any chance, play the scoundrel, even for a moment. The scoundrel is as helpless as the saint, both being HELPLESSLY UNDER THE SWAY OF *PRAKRITI* in each. And the entire drama of the dissolution of *vasana*-expressions and the projection of the *vasana*-dances is performed upon the Changeless Imperishable Eternal platform of the Self; "I PROJECT AGAIN".

THE LAW OF *KARMA* IS INCONTROVERTIBLE. AS THE ACTION SO THE REACTION. IF THE SELF ADMINISTERS THE DISSOLUTION AND SUPERVISES THE PROJECTION OF THE PLURALISTIC WORLD, HOW FAR DOES THE LAW OF *KARMA* SHACKLE THE INFINITE? ... LISTEN:

9. *Sitting like one indifferent, and unattached to these acts, Dhananjaya, these acts do not bind Me.*

In the case of the limited ego, its egocentric actions leave their impressions behind, which ultimately persecute the little ego with their reactions. All egocentric actions, which are always motivated by selfish desires, leave their ugly footprints upon the shores of the mind (*vasanas*), while actions which are not ego-motivated leave no trail (*vasanas*), as birds leave no footprints as they move along in the sky. We can compare an ungrateful son kicking his own father, with an innocent child in a playful mood kicking his own father with both its legs. A philosopher's subtle vision is not necessary to understand the difference in texture between these two persons performing the same action, kicking the father. Wherever and whenever an egocentric action, whipped by

---

न च मां तानि कर्माणि निबध्नन्ति धनंजय ।
उदासीनवदासीनमसक्तं तेषु कर्मसु ॥ ९ ॥

na ca māṁ tāni kamārṇi nibadhnanti dhanañjaya
udāsīnavadāsīnamasaktaṁ teṣu karmasu 9.

selfish desires, is undertaken, gross and painful reactions (*vasanas*) must necessarily ensue.

In the case of Eternal animating Its *Prakriti*, and projecting out AGAIN AND AGAIN THE MULTITUDE OF BEINGS, there is neither any attachment (*Raga*) nor any aversion (*Dvesha*), and therefore, by this mere happening on the Eternal, the Supreme is not affected: "THESE ACTS DO NOT BIND ME". It is neither egocentric nor desire-motivated.

However tragic and murderous the play may be, however tearful and sad the story be, however rainy and stormy the scene be, the white screen in the cinema hall at the end of the play carries neither the marks of the blood spilt, nor the stains of the tears shed, nor the wear and tear of the storm that raged. At the same time, we all know that but for the changeless screen, the story could never have been unravelled through the medium of light and shade. In the same fashion, the ever-pure Infinite, as the Self, becomes the enduring platform for the drama of sorrow that is expressed in the language of plurality, ceaselessly enacted by the infinite number of egos, helplessly repeating the parts ordered by their *vasanas*, gathered by them in the past.

The steam in the engine is not punished for the disaster of derailment, nor is the steam complimented when the train reaches its destination in time! Again, neither the disaster nor the successful accomplishment of the journey could ever take place without the steam. The engine without the steam is inert iron assembled in a particular shape, dull and heavy; it is the steam that dynamises and renders it capable of its actions of cruel destruction, or kindly construction, as the case may be. Since the steam in the engine has neither an anxiety to move the train, nor an aversion to move it, the steam is ignored in the achievements of the train, whether good or bad. It is the motive behind the action that determines its reaction.

The Self is the source of all dynamism. It dynamises the mind. Each mind is a bundle of *vasanas*. Good *vasanas* make the mind sing the song of joy and harmony. Bad *vasanas* in the mind make it groan with sobs and tears.

The needle in the gramophone is not responsible for the song that the record sings. As the record, so the music. Similarly, the Self is Eternal. It is unmindful of what type of world is projected forth. Nor is It anxious in any sense of the term, to create a better world. Sunlight illumines whatever happens to be there in its light, be it a murder, or be it martyrdom. Neither the glory of the martyr, nor the crime of the murderer can reach the Sun. The Self, as Pure Consciousness, illumines the *vasanas* and lends them the capacity to project out, be it for the damnation of themselves or for their own glorification. SITTING LIKE ONE INDIFFERENT AND UNATTACHED TO THESE ACTS the Self revels in the realm of Its lower nature (*Prakriti*).

WHAT EXACTLY IS THIS STRANGE RELATIONSHIP BETWEEN THE INFINITE AND THE FINITE? THE FINITE ACTS BECAUSE OF THE INFINITE, AND YET THE INFINITE IS SAID TO BE NEUTRAL ... HOW?

10. *Under Me as her Supervisor, PRAKRITI (nature) produces the moving and the unmoving; because of this, O Kaunteya, the world revolves.* ?

In *Vedanta*, this relationship between the actionless Self and the active non-Self has been brought out by a bunch of

---

मयाध्यक्षेण प्रकृतिः सूयते सचराचरम्।
हेतुनानेन कौन्तेय जगद्विपरिवर्तते ॥ १० ॥

bhayādhyakṣeṇa prakṛtiḥ sūyate sacarācāram
hetunānena kaunteya jagadviparivartate 10.

analogies, each one trying to throw much light upon this sacred tie of 'relationless-relationship'.

The rays of the Sun warm up the objects upon which they fall, without warming the intervening medium through which they pass. Similarly, the Self remains in Its own Infinite glory, and the non-Self gets dynamised to act, as *Prakriti*, in the mere 'presence' of the Self.

The king gets a fancy that he should visit a given pilgrim centre on the full-moon day of the following month, and having expressed this intention to his minister, the king forgets all about it. But on the day prior to the following full moon, the minister approaches the king to remind him that it is time for the royal procession. The next day, when the king comes out, he finds that the entire route is thronged with his subjects. Welcoming arches are raised at different places. All detailed arrangements are planned out and colourfully executed for his royal visit and return. All the officers and subjects have poured out all their capacities and endeavour to make the royal trip to the temple a great success.

In all these feverish activities, everyone gained his authority and power only because of the king, and yet, the king himself was nowhere in the picture. The minister had his sanction from the king, and therefore, his orders were faithfully executed by all others. Had the minister tried to organise such a show as an ordinary citizen, he would never have succeeded. Similarly, in the mere presence of the Self, *Prakriti* borrows her sanction to plan and to execute, to act and to achieve.

Subjectively, this becomes more clear. The *Atman*, merely by Its 'presence' illumines the mind and intellect and creates for the expression of their *vasanas* an entire field of world-objects and the required instruments of experience, constituted of the organs-of-perception and the organs-of-action. "NATURE, WHILE I PRESIDE, GIVES BIRTH TO THE WORLD OF THINGS AND BEINGS" - 'Nature' here means "The Unmanifest, that gets projected forth as the manifest".

The continued dance of the world-of-plurality to the rhythm of change and death is maintained in the 'presence' of the Self; THE WORLD WHIRLS ROUND AND ROUND BECAUSE OF THIS. In the final analysis, the Self does nothing. It is the *Prakriti* that projects and executes; the *Prakriti* that gets animated in the proximity of the Self. It is the Light of the Self that vitalises the *Prakriti* and makes her exist and act. That is all the relationship between the Self, the *Purusha* and the non-Self, the *Prakriti*.

This will become more clear if the student tries to understand this relationship exactly as the relationship that can exist between the wayside post and the ghost that is superimposed upon it by the deluded.

IF THE SELF BE THUS THE ESSENTIAL REALITY IN EVERY FORM AND IF IT BE EVER FREE FROM THE SORROWS AND TRIBULATIONS OF THE FINITE, WHY IS IT THAT ALL BEINGS ARE NOT ABLE TO IDENTIFY THEMSELVES WITH IT AND EXIST AS THE SELF? LISTEN:

11. *Fools* disregard Me when I dwell in human form; they know not My Higher being as the Great Lord of all beings.*

अवजानन्ति मां मूढा मानुषीं तनुमाश्रितम्।
परं भावमजानन्तो मम भूतमहेश्वरम्॥ ११॥

avajānanti māṁ mūḍhā mānuṣīṁ tanumāśritam|
paraṁ bhāvamajānanto mama bhūtamaheśvaram 11.

* This also suggests that they are fools who are not able to recognise Me in all human forms; My devotees shall respect and revere one another as though the other is I, expressing through him.

In the seventh chapter, while giving a discourse upon the 'Higher' and 'Lower' natures of the Eternal, Krishna declared that the FOOLISH, in their ignorance of the Supreme state of the Higher Self, as Immutable and Transcendental, regard the 'Unmanifest' as having come into manifestation. In this chapter while claiming to be the Self in all, Krishna uses the same strong word, 'fools', to condemn those who cling to the form and lose the essence. 'UNAWARE OF MY HIGHER NATURE, FOOLS REGARD ME' as dwelling in a particular form only!

To mistake the idol for God, or the form of the *Guru* for the Infinite, is to mistake the container for the contents. An idol is only a symbol (*Pratika*) for an imperceptible and subtle Truth. To play with the milk-bottle is not to feel refreshed when one is hungry or thirsty; playing with a spoon and fork over an empty plate is no satisfaction when one is really hungry. To mistake the idol to be itself the goal is to mistake the means for the end. And such a misunderstanding alone breeds fanatics, who sow seeds of rivalry and jealousy, to reap, in time, a harvest of death and disaster, all in the name of their stone-deities, wooden-symbols, or brass-gods! Three tiny bits of coloured khadi-cloth may make the national flag, but that is not my motherland; but when I bow my head as my country's flag goes up, I adore my nation; the flag is the sacred symbol of my country's culture and its aspirations.

With this idea in mind, if we read the stanza it becomes very vivid and clear. The Lord says: "ordinary devotees are unaware of My real status AS THE GREAT LORD OF ALL BEINGS" and adds that these deluded "FOOLS SCORN ME WHEN I DWELL IN HUMAN FORM" meaning, when they consider Him, the Self, as merely a human-form, which He

* The same idea has been described with equal clarity in Chapter VII-15

may take for Himself, to bless a particular generation.

WHY ARE THE FOOLS RENDERED INCAPABLE OF RIGHT UNDERSTANDING AND CORRECT JUDGMENT REGARDING THE TRUE NATURE OF THE SELF?

12. *Of vain hopes, of vain actions, of vain knowledge, and senseless, they verily are possessed of the delusive nature of RAKSHASAS and ASURAS.*

13. *But the MAHATMAS (great-souls) O Partha, partaking of My divine nature, worship Me with a single mind (with a mind devoted to nothing else), knowing Me as the Imperishable Source of all beings.*

In order to drive home an argument, it is the style in Krishna's discourses that He always brings the contrasting factors together so that each may come to shine all the more against the background supplied by the other. Here is a pair of stanzas in which, if the former explains the low men deluded to pursue their baser nature (*Rakshasas* and *Asuras*), the latter paints the picture of the great souls (*Mahatmas*), possessed of all the divine qualities.

Deluded by false desires and wearied with false activities to fulfil those wrong desires, some become confused in intellect and totally confounded in their reasoning. Such

---

मोघाशा मोघकर्माणो मोघज्ञाना विचेतसः ।
राक्षसीमासुरीं चैव प्रकृतिं मोहिनीं श्रिताः ॥ १२ ॥

moghāśā moghakamārṇo moghajñānā vicetasaḥ
rākṣasīmāsurīṁ caiva prakṛtiṁ mohinīṁ śritāḥ 12.

महात्मानस्तु मां पार्थ दैवीं प्रकृतिमाश्रिताः ।
भजन्त्यनन्यमनसो ज्ञात्वा भूतादिमव्ययम् ॥ १३ ॥

mahātmānastu māṁ pārtha daivīṁ prakṛtimaśritāḥ
bhajantyananyamanaso jñātvā bhūtādimavyayam 13.

people lose all divine perspective and become monstrous in their activities, expressing nothing but their demoniac sensuous nature at all times. Such men are called here as *Rakshasas* and *Asuras*, belonging to the tradition of *Ravana*.*

The actions undertaken in the present leave their impressions on the mind, and order the future desires and thoughts in the individual. Out of vain actions, only negative *vasanas* can arise, and they can only thicken the dull-witted stupidities of the intellect. When an individual has lived in this ditch of falsehood and impurity, he cannot become any nobler than a monster, in the eyes of the wise.

As a contrast to this *Rakshasa*-culture, we are shown how men-of-Wisdom feel and act. This dissection of man's bosom reveals to the seekers of self-development, the right attitude they must adopt and the correct perspective with which they must look at the things of the world.

THE GREAT-SOULS POSSESSED OF THE DIVINE NATURE of the Self, and desiring this Infinite, seeks the Immortal by realising the Self, THROUGH SINGLE-POINTED SELF-APPLICATION. They know Me to be the Origin of all beings; and those who know the mud to be the origin of all mud-pots, cannot fail to see the mud in all pots. So too, the true children of the Hindu culture, who understand the Divine Principle as the Source-of-all-beings, cannot but respect every other member of the society as they would respect themselves. There is no greater and more effective socialism ever preached in the world. If the present generation is not able to understand and appreciate this spiritual socialism, which is the only panacea for the ills of the world, the reason for it has been already given in the preceding stanza – it is because of the predominance of the *Asuric* forces in it.

THE GREAT-SOULS "WORSHIP ME WITH THE SINGLE-POINTED MIND" ... HOW?

14. *Always glorifying Me, striving, firm in vows, prostrating before Me, and always steadfast, they worship Me with devotion.*

Even though in the previous stanza, while describing the high-souls, (a) the path-of-Knowledge was indicated,* here the other two main paths of self-integration and self-development are hinted at, viz., (b) single-pointed devotion and (c) selfless activity undertaken in the true *Yajna*-spirit.

GLORIFYING ME ALWAYS—the grossest type of glorification is done usually by a noisy crowd singing the Lord's glories with the accompaniment of equally noisy and crude instruments! But the implication of *Kirtana* is much more sacred. Indeed, to adore an ideal with reverence and devotion, and to sing His glories, at all times, continuously, is the silent act of a mind that has fully opened up to appreciate the ideal that one has learnt to glorify.

The silent adoration of society by the social workers, or the steady flow of love that beams out from a man-of-Knowledge for the entire kingdom of the living, constitute a greater and a more potent type of *Kirtana*, than the type indulged in by the noisy crowds that assemble from their different fields of dubious activities, for a short period each day, only to return to the same dens of vices, after the *Bhajana*.

STRIVING WITH FIRM RESOLVE—these are simple logical facts that are generally overlooked by the seekers and

---

सततं कीर्तयन्तो मां यतन्तश्च दृढव्रताः ।
नमस्यन्तश्च मां भक्त्या नित्ययुक्ता उपासते ॥ १४ ॥

satataṁ kīrtayanto māṁ yatantaśca dṛḍhavratāḥ
namasyantaścamaṁ bhaktayā nityayuktā upāsate 14.

* "Knowing Me to be the origin of beings, and Immutable".

they dig the graves for their own success in spiritual practices. The majority of people believe that some specific routine acts of devotional flavour pursued physically for a short period of time on particular days of the week, is all their part of the game. The rest is for their imaginary Gods to cook and bring in front of them, dressed to taste! This absurd, superstitious idea has nothing to do with the science of Self-perfection, of which religion constitutes its technical aspect.

Constant and conscious effort is unavoidable if an individual is to get himself hauled out from his present ruts of wrong thinking and false evaluations of life and living. The disharmony he experiences in life, and the wrong notes that are sung by the situations in life upon the harp of his heart are all due to the maladjustments in his instruments-of-experience. Their readjustment calls for continuous vigilance, non-stop self-application, and sincere pursuit.

Of course, while thus striving for self-redemption, vacillations caused by instinctive biological temptations would often reach the seeker to whisper in his ears and make him eat the forbidden fruit. But at such moments of strong temptations, he must make a firm resolve (*Dhridha-Vratah*) to reject the false and to walk steadily the path-of-the-Real.

True devotion is unalloyed love. Love is measured in terms of the lover's identification with the beloved. "Devotion to ME, THE ORIGIN OF BEINGS, AND THE IMMUTABLE" is the way for the deluded ego to identify itself with the Self. And this is brought to a successful culmination only by the process of detaching itself from its non-Self conditionings. This negative aspect of self-withdrawal from the layers of the non-Self is indicated by the BOWING DOWN TO ME. The positive side of the art of Self-realisation is pursued, when, with a steady single-pointed mind, the seeker comes to meditate till, ultimately, he re-discovers for himself his total identification with the Self. This positive aspect is indicated by the phrase 'IN DEVOTION'. The withdrawal of ourselves from our misconceived identities and the final rediscovery of our infinite potentialities, through our constant devotion to the Self, can be achieved only by those among us who ARE STEADFAST AND WORSHIP ME.

The path-of-Knowledge knows no flower-throwing or *chandana*-sprinkling methods of ritualistic worship. To keep in the mind an alert and vigilant flow of thoughts in our adoration for the nature of the Self as the substratum of the entire Universe and the Essence in all beings is the truest worship that can open up the buds of our egocentric lives into blossoms of God-men, wafting their fragrance of perfection around.

> 15. *Others also, offering the 'Wisdom-sacrifice' worship Me, regarding Me as One, as distinct, as manifold - Me, who in all forms, faces everywhere.*

Jnana Yajna has no ritualism. It is a constant attempt on the part of the performer to see, in and through the experienced names and forms, the expression and vitality of the One Conscious Principle, the Self. The seeker here, practising *Jnana Yajna* has understood the significance of the *Vedantic* assertion that the Immutable Self pervades all, penetrating everything, and in Its homogeneous web of existence, It holds together the phenomenal multiplicity and their variegated interactions.

Chocolates made by different firms, irrespective of their

ज्ञानयज्ञेन चाप्यन्ये यजन्तो मामुपासते
एकत्वेन पृथक्त्वेन बहुधा विश्वतोमुखम् ॥ १५ ॥

jñānayajñena capyanye yajanto mamupāsate
ekatvena pṛthaktavena bahudha viśvatomukham 15.

shapes and colours, flavours and prices, are all chocolates and, therefore, their essential nature of sweetness is common to all of them; and the child who is seeking the sweetness of the chocolates will enjoy them, whatever be their shape, size or packing.

Similarly, a seeker of the Self watches for, observes and detects the expression of the Self in all forms and names, in all situations and conditions. Whatever be the setting in which diamonds are held together, to a diamond merchant all of them are so many points of brilliance and light, and he evaluates them according to the light-content in each one of them and not the design or beauty of the ornament.

A man-of-Realisation moves about the world, seeing his own Self, expressed through every movement and action, word and thought that clusters round him at all times. Just as one light in the midst of a thousand mirrors comes to provide crores of reflections everywhere, so too, the one centred in the Self, when he walks out into the world, sees everywhere his own Self dancing, shooting glances at him from all around at once, thrilling him always with the homogeneous ecstasy of perfection and bliss.

In the sparkle of the eyes, in the smile of a friend, in the grin of an enemy, in the harsh words of jealousy and in the soft tones of love, in heat and in cold, in success and in failure -- among men, among animals, amidst the trees and in the company of the inert, everywhere, he successfully gains the auspicious vision of the Supreme, either as EXISTENCE PURE or as KNOWLEDGE ABSOLUTE or as BLISS INFINITE!! This is the meaning of *Ishwara Darshana* or the *Atma Darshana* which is sung so gloriously in all the scriptures of the world. To watch for and discover the smile of the Divine through the trellis of names and forms is to live in the constant spirit of *Jnana Yajna*.

To adore Him in all visions, to recognise Him in all situations, to feel Him with each thought, is to live in a constant remembrance of the Self, and therefore, such people worship the Self through the wisdom-sacrifice (*Jnana Yajna*).

In the beginning, this attempt of seeing the Self is a conscious act, not without its unpleasant strain. But as the seeker develops in his own spiritual cognition of the Self, the Awareness Divine within him, it becomes easy for him to recognise the One Self splashing Itself upon the myriad forms of Its own effulgent glory: 'ME, WHO IN ALL FORMS FACES EVERYWHERE'.

The man-of-Realisation not only experiences the Pure Self, uncontaminated by the pluralistic equipments, but, also recognises the same Self as playing through the endless variety of conditionings available in the universe. Having known the one Sun in the sky, even if we see a thousand reflections of the same in different equipments, in all of them, we see and recognise only the one Sun.

According to *Vedanta*, Self-realisation is not at all complete if the realised one can keep his composure and equanimity only in solitude and silence; if he recognises and experiences the Divine only at some rare moments of his transcendental experiences, then he is not the man-of-Wisdom glorified by the *Rishis* of the *Upanishads*. This is not the way of the *Yogis*. A man of True Knowledge is he to whom the Self alone is the Truth within, without, and everywhere. "The One pervades all and nothing pervades It." To him a market place of the busiest tensions is as much a conducive place for cognising the Self as the quiet Himalayan valleys and their deep caves of roaring silence. With his eyes shut, he, from the balcony of the Infinite in himself, gazes out to experience nothing but his own Self everywhere.

In my legs as well as in my hands, I pervade equally at all moments. I know I am there. To say that this knowledge makes my hands and legs disappear, as mist disappears at sunrise, is sheer lunacy and not the assertion of a true science. Just as I permeate, exist, enjoy, and experience in and through every little portion of my body, all through my waking hours, at one and the same time, so too, the man-of-Realisation realises that at all times, his own Self permeates the entire universe, in His Infinite domain -- AS ONE, AS DISTINCT, AS MANIFOLD.

Vedanta preaches the recognition of Divinity and the experience of the Infinite in and through life. It is not a passing experience lived through an accidental movement. It is not an occasion to celebrate by distributing *laddus** and then to retire forever from that experience. Just as the knowledge acquired by an individual through his education keeps him constant company, at all times and in all conditions - even in his dream - even so, nay, much more powerfully, much more intimately, much more irredeemably, the Knower-of-the-Self becomes the Self; there is no doubt about it. The truth of the *Vedantic* declaration is upheld by the assertion in the second line: "ME, THE ALL-FORMED, THEY WORSHIP, AS ONE, AS DISTINCT AND AS FACING EVERYWHERE, IN EACH FORM".

All that we have so far said is being endorsed here. No doubt, through meditation, when the mind is stilled, the Pure Self, the One-without-a-second, is realised. The knower of the mud can easily recognise the mud in all pots; the shape, size and colour of the pot do not destroy the mud. Similarly, the apparent and delusory names and forms, superimposed upon the Truth, cannot and do not veil the Truth from the 'vision' of the man-of-Truth. Not only does the Seer recognise the Self in each individual separately, but Krishna, the upholder of *Vedanta* thunders that the Truth is recognised IN

* An Indian sweetmeat traditionally distributed on celebrations.

EACH FORM, AS FACING EVERYWHERE. It is absurd to say that one discovers the essential nature of the pot only on the right-hand bottom of the mud-pot! The mud is in the pot, facing everywhere, at all times; where the mud is not, there the pot is non-existent. When the Self is not, there, the perception of the multiple existence is never possible.

IF, IN A VARIETY OF FORMS, DIFFERENT TYPES OF WORSHIP ARE PERFORMED, HOW DO THEY ALL BECOME THE WORSHIP OF THE ONE SELF?

16. *I am the KRATU; I am the sacrifice; I am the offering (food) to PITRIS (or ancestors); I am the medicinal herb, and all plants; I am the MANTRA I am also the clarified butter; I am the fire; I am the oblation.*

Repeating the idea already expressed earlier in a famous stanza in the *Geeta,* (IV-24) this verse expresses how the Self is the existence everywhere, in all actions and factors constituting actions. Ritualistic actions constitute worship. At the time of the Mahabharata, divine worship was always undertaken in *Vedic* ritualism (*Kratu*), by ritualistic adoration of the deity as prescribed in the *Smriti* (*Yajna*), or by food-offerings for the ancestors (*Swadha*). Arjuna is here taught that all these methods of worship are, in a sense, nothing but the worship of the Self.

Not only are the different ritualistic prescriptions all presided over by the Self, but the medicinal herbs (*Oushadha*) used in the sacrifice, the *ghee* (*Ajya* - clarified butter) poured into the altar-of-fire the oblations (*Hutam*) offered, the fire (*Agni*) that is invoked, the *mantras* chanted - all of them are

---

अहं क्रतुरहं यज्ञः स्वधाहमहमौषधम् ।
मन्त्रोऽहमहमेवाज्यमहमग्निरहं हुतम् ॥ १६ ॥

ahaṁ kraturahaṁ yajñaḥ svadhahamahamauṣadham
mantro'hamahamevājyamahamagniraham hutam 16.

nothing but the Self alone expressed through different equipments in different fields. When a variety of ornaments is made from a mass of gold, the gold can certainly say that "I am the pendant, I am the ring, I am the chain, I am its shine, I am its hook; I alone am its shape and its glory". Similarly, the Self, being the essence of all happenings and circumstances in which the devotee attempts to adore the Eternal, this assertion here is perfectly acceptable to all philosophic-minded readers.

AGAIN:

17. *I am the Father of this world, the Mother, the supporter and the grandsire; the (one) Thing to be known, the Purifier, (the syllable) OM, and also the RIK, the SAMA and the YAJUH also?*

The Self is not a vague imperceptible Spirit of Existence in all fields of divine activities, sans-emotion, sans-relationship, sans-qualities. In order to show that there is an ardour of love that permeates the very essence of the Self everywhere, the finite relationships of the world are mentioned to indicate the mass of love that the Self is. "I AM THE FATHER, THE MOTHER, THE SUSTAINER, THE GRANDSIRE, THE PURIFIER OF THE WORLDS."

The verse insists, "I AM THE ONE THING TO BE KNOWN" - and this is the repeated assertion in all the scriptures. The Self is "That, having known which, everything else becomes known". To know the Self is to destroy the consciousness of imperfection, the existence finite, and the sorrows poignant. To live in the ego, as a mere embodied self, is to live self-exiled from all the Divine potentialities

---

पिताहमस्य जगतो माता धाता पितामहः।
वेद्यं पवित्रमोंकार ऋक्साम यजुरेव च॥ १७॥

pitāhamasya jagato mātā dhātā pitāmahaḥ
vedyaṁ pavitramoṅkāra ṛksāma yajureva ca 17.

that one is heir to. To rediscover this infinite Beatitude is the only satisfying end and goal of life, where alone an awakened intellect can discover a heaven of peace and an enduring existence in perfect tranquillity.

The Self, the substratum of the entire universe, is symbolised by the *Vedic mantra* called *Omkara*. Life is conceived of as "the flow during our waking, dreaming and deep-sleep states". The substratum for these three states and their experiences must be something other than these three, inasmuch as the rider is always different from the ridden, the container is different from the contents. The substratum is different from the superimposition upon it.

This fourth state, supporting and embracing the three ordinary states of consciousness in every one of us, is termed as *Turiya* by the *Upanishad* Seers. The one symbol representing all these four states is called *Omkara*, and naturally, therefore, the Ultimate indicated by *OM*, is the Self, conceived of, for the purpose of worship, as Krishna in *Shrimad Bhagavata*.

The Self is the Essence indicated by OM, and this Absolute Reality is the One theme, tacitly expressed, or indirectly implied, in all the *Vedas*, and therefore, it is said "I AM ALSO THE *RIK*, *SAMA* AND *YAJUH*".

FURTHER:

18. *I am the Goal, the Supporter, the Lord, the Witness, the Abode, the Shelter, the Friend, the Origin, the Dissolution, the Foundation, the Treasure-house and the Seed Imperishable.*

गतिर्भर्ता प्रभुः साक्षी निवासः शरणं सुहृत्।
प्रभवः प्रलयः स्थानं निधानं बीजमव्ययम्॥ १८॥

gatirbhatār prabhuḥ sākṣī nivāsaḥ śaraṇaṁ suhṛt
prabhavaḥ pralayḥ sthānaṁ nidhānaṁ bījamavyayam 18.

Continuing the theme of the status of the Self as the very essence behind the seeming plurality of the world – recognised in our ignorance, is in fact, nothing but a dreamy superimposition gathering its existence from the Reality behind it – the Lord describes Himself with a host of suggestive words strung together to form this exquisite verse, pregnant and full, for all students of meditation.

I AM THE GOAL (*Gati*)—all our seeking ends when all imperfections vanish in the total experience of the Perfect. To one frightened by the vision of a delusory serpent in a piece of rope, consolation and satisfaction can come only when his delusion has ended by the discovery of the rope. The Self is the substratum of the sorrow-ridden universe of multiplicity; to realise the Self is to transcend all the choking sense of limitations. The Knowledge-Absolute by gaining which all becomes known, is shown here as the Self.

I AM THE SUPPORTER (*Bharta*)—Just as the desert supports the illusory pool of water, which the thirsty traveller sees in his delusion, so too, the Self is the supporter of everything. As Absolute-Existence It lends a semblance of reality to the perceptions of the sense organs, and thus holds together the flood-of-change into a consistent pattern, called life.

I AM THE LORD (*Prabhu*)—Even though the Self thus lends Its grace to the realm of imperfections sustained and maintained by the agitations of the mind, as the Pure Awareness, It is ever beyond the sorrows and joys of the apparent and illusory universe. Through different equipments, electricity may pass; manifesting different expressions of its own glory, but in none of them does electricity lose itself, if we consider the current as pure energy.

In all this panorama of expressions, the Self, though It lends Existence to them, Itself remains as a mere Witness. "I am the

Witness" (*Sakshi*) - He is considered a true witness of an incident, who is not in the incident, but who happened to witness it, not from too far, with neither attachment nor aversion. When things happen of their own accord in one's presence then one becomes the witness of that happening. The Infinite is but a witness of the finite inasmuch as the Self is an uninterested illuminator of what is happening in the harem of the intellect, in the arena of the mind, in the courtyard of the body, and in the wide expanse of the world without.

I AM THE ABODE (*Nivasah*)—Truth is the House of all, of every being and thing. On an innocent wayside post, it is reported that some travellers saw a grinning ghost, others a smiling ghost, and yet others, a ghost with a bleeding mouth and sparkling eyes, naked and horrid, and some an innocent ghost, dressed in white, invitingly smiling and lovingly guiding them onto the right track. All of them saw delusory projections of their individual minds upon the same wayside post. Naturally, the post is the 'Abode' of the smiling, of the grinning, of the bleeding, of the horrid, and of the tender ghost, that different minds, on different occasions, projected upon the same post. Similarly, wherever our equipments of experiences gain the apprehension of the pluralistic phenomena, for all of them the Self, the Awareness, is the ABODE, the place of existence and security.

I AM THE REFUGE (*Sharanam*)—Delusion breeds sorrows, Knowledge produces joy. The universe is pain-ridden because it is delusion-projected. Naturally, the harbour of tranquillity, projecting a confused ego from the mountainous breakers of the stormy ocean-of-*samsara* is the rediscovery of the substratum, the Essence of the Self. When once the Self gets individualised, when it walks out to identify with the play, through the equipments of the intellect, mind and body, it is wandering away from the safety of the shore into the stormy, high seas of adventure. When the frail boat of the ego is thus threatened from all sides – the darkening clouds above, the bumping sea below, and the screaming storms all round - the sailor's only refuge is to come back to the tranquil harbour, the Self!

The above descriptions put together, add up to give the conception of the Reality as a heartless noumenon, a dignified deity, an unapproachable realm of Perfection. To wipe off this idea from the tender heart of emotional seekers – and Arjuna was one - the Eternal, in the form of the beloved friend of man, Krishna, is using here more humane terms in defining Himself.

I AM THE FRIEND (*Suhrit*)—The Infinite is a friend of the finite, not a nodding acquaintance from whom you can borrow a matchbox, but a friend, whose only anxiety is for the security and the well-being of the befriended.

I AM THE ORIGIN AND DISSOLUTION, THE SUBSTRATUM, THE STOREHOUSE—As gold in all ornaments and mud in all pots, the Self is in the whole universe, and therefore, all things can come to manifest from and dissolve into the unmanifest, the substratum, which can hence be considered as the the storehouse of all names, forms and qualities that constitute the multiple world.

I AM THE IMMUTABLE SEED (*Beejam Avyayam*)—There is a contrast here with all other seeds, which perish when they germinate and produce trees. The Self is no doubt the origin of the tree-of-*Samsara*, but in the production of this tree, the Self is not transformed, It being ever Immutable. The idea of the Eternal Principle, modifying itself to become the created world is a disgrace to the logic of human thinking, and *Vedanta* discards such a philosophically fallacious notion. The dualists, however, are compelled to take it up, or else, the very edifice of their arguments will crumble down like a castle of clouds, built upon an autumnal sky.

This, as we have already indicated, is a verse replete with simple terms, each an avenue for the meditator to reflect upon, and in a pleasant stroll reach the gateway of Truth.

FURTHER:

19. *(As Sun) I give heat; I withhold and send forth the rain; I am Immortality and also death, both Existence and Non-existence, O Arjuna. ?*

I GIVE HEAT—The electricity can rightly say that it gives heat in the heater, light in the bulb, cold in the refrigerator, because electricity conditioned through those equipments expresses itself as the above-mentioned – heat, light and cold. Similarly, the Self, the one Existence, identifying with the phenomenon called the Sun becomes the source of all heat for the entire universe.

I WITHHOLD AND SEND FORTH RAIN—Not only do the modern meteorologists understand the influence which the Sun has upon the climatic conditions of the world, but the *Rishis* of old too had a perfect knowledge of the ways and behaviour of nature, and had well understood that the position, condition and nature of the Sun determines the climate that comes to bless, or curse, the world. The influence of the Sun controls the fields of experience of every living creature on the globe, since it controls the climatic conditions. If the Sun were to send out a few more degrees of heat the entire flora and fauna of the world would change. So too, will be the transformation, complete and total, of the entire look of the world, if the Sun were to withhold even a few

तपाम्यहमहं वर्षं निगृह्णाम्युत्सृजामि च ।
अमृतं चैव मृत्युश्च सदसच्चाहमर्जुन ॥ १९ ॥

tapāmyahamahaṁ varṣaṁ nigṛhaṇāmyutsṛjāmi ca
amṛtaṁ caiva mṛtyuśca sadasaccāhamarjuna 19.

calories of the heat that it is radiating now. Immediately, there would be a march from the north pole and the south pole towards the equator, driving men and beings towards the central belt of the globe, causing more intense sorrows of over-population and lack of sufficient food!

I AM IMMORTALITY AND ALSO DEATH—If life, the Consciousness, were not illumining experiences, it would become meaningless and purposeless, and the Self, being the spark-of-life, is the essential stuff that gives a realistic experience of existence to the very phenomenon of death. To realise the Self as the Immutable and the Eternal, is to reach the state of Immortality. Change is death, and therefore, the phrase is to be understood as saying that "the Self is the illuminator of change, Itself ever the Changeless".

I AM EXISTENCE AND NON-EXISTENCE—To perceive and experience 'Existence' and 'Non-existence', a positive illuminator of both is necessary, and the illuminating Consciousness must be able to embrace both *Sat* and *Asat* in its all-comprehending Knowledge. It is impossible to know and gain an experience of the total Non-existence; wherever we experience Non-existence, we experience it as 'the Non-existence that exists'.

Apart from this highly subtle philosophical interpretation there is a simpler significance for the phrase. *Sat* and *Asat* are terms used in *Vedanta* to indicate the 'cause' and 'effect': the UNMANIFEST and the MANIFEST. The Self being that Illuminating Factor - without which we can experience neither the unmanifest (THOUGHTS) nor the manifest (OBJECTS) - the Self Eternal is conceived of as the Essence in both the manifest and the unmanifest. Without the mud, no pot is possible; with mud all pots can exist; and therefore, the mud can claim: "I am the pots of all sizes, shapes and colours".

This stanza can provide a lifetime inspiration to the meditators at their seat of contemplation, while 'barrelling their thoughts' before shooting forth into the voiceless and Nameless.

THOSE WHO DEVOTE THEMSELVES IN THE WORSHIP OF THE ETERNAL WITH DESIRES, WILL COME TO THEIR FULFILMENT... HOW?

20. *The Knowers of the three VEDAS, the drinkers of SOMA, purified from sin, worshipping Me by sacrifices, pray for the way to heaven; they reach the holy world of the Lord-of-the-gods and enjoy in heaven the Divine pleasures of the gods.*

21. *They, having enjoyed the vast heaven-world, when their merits are exhausted, enter the world-of-the-mortals; thus abiding by the injunctions of the three (VEDAS), desiring (objects of) desires, they attain to the state of 'going-and-returning' (SAMSARA).*

त्रैविद्या मां सोमपाः पूतपापा
यज्ञैरिष्ट्वा स्वर्गतिं प्रार्थयन्ते ।
ते पुण्यमासाद्य सुरेन्द्रलोक-
मश्नन्ति दिव्यान्दिवि देवभोगान् ॥ २० ॥

traividyā māṁ somapāḥ pūtapāpā
yajñairiṣṭvā svargatiṁ prārthayante
te puṇyamāsādya surendraloka-
maśnanti divyāndivi devabhogān 20.

ते तं भुक्त्वा स्वर्गलोकं विशालं
क्षीणे पुण्ये मर्त्यलोकं विशन्ति ।
एवं त्रयीधर्ममनुप्रपन्ना
गतागतं कामकामा लभन्ते ॥ २१ ॥

te taṁ bhuktavā svargalokam viśālaṁ
kṣīṇe puṇye martyalokaṁ viśanti
evaṁ trayīdharmanuprapannā
gatāgataṁ kāmakāmā labhante 21.

When those who are well-read in the three *Vedas* and who know the prescriptions laid down for the rituals, perform those sacred acts of devotion and sacrifice with a desire to enjoy the celestial bliss, "THEY COME TO ENJOY, IN HEAVEN, THE DIVINE PLEASURES OF THE *DEVAS*".

The *Soma* drink is the milky juice of a creeper-plant[1] which is used in the rituals and taken in very small quantities at the end of the function. Thus, the phrase 'DRINKING THE *SOMA*-JUICE' is to be understood as 'when the performance of the ritual has concluded.'[2] These desire-prompted ritualisms yield finite results and Krishna indicates that these ego-centres, after having enjoyed in the celestial realms, "ENTER THE MORTAL WORLD ON EXHAUSTION OF THEIR MERITS".

The disgust which the Lord feels for such men and their unintelligent seeking for the finite, is clearly expressed when He concludes how these ritualists, "ABIDING BY THE INJUNCTIONS OF THE THREE *VEDAS*, DESIRING DESIRES. THEY REPEATEDLY COME AND GO".

WHAT ABOUT THOSE MEN WHO WORSHIP THE ETERNAL WITH DESIRELESS LOVE, AS THE SUBSTRATUM FOR THE ENTIRE UNIVERSE?

---

1 Perhaps, belonging to the group of ephdira or periploca.

2 Something equivalent to what we mean, in modern times, when we say, 'when they finish their small coffee'. We mean 'when the dinner party has come to a close'.

22. *To those men who worship Me alone, thinking of no other, to those ever self-controlled, I secure for them that which is not already possessed (YOGA) by them, and preserve for them what they already possess (KSHEMA).*

Here is a stanza which, with equal emphasis, discloses a secret by which glorious success can be assured for the spiritual as well as the material seekers. It is significant that this stanza is almost in the centre of the *Geeta*.* We shall try to follow the implications, both spiritual as well as secular, of this stanza, one by one.

Those who, with a single-pointed mind, thus meditate upon Him as the One and the Only Reality behind the entire universe, Krishna promises here that "TO THEM EVER SELF-CONTROLLED, I BRING *YOGA* AND *KSHEMA*" meaning more and more spiritual vigour (*Yoga*) and the final experience of Beatitude (*KSHEMA*) which is liberation resulting from the fulfilled *Yoga*.

Now, considering it as a tip for the men in the marketplace, sweating and toiling in the world, the very same stanza yields a code of secret instructions by which they can assure for themselves complete success in their worldly life. In any undertaking, if a man is capable of pouring out his self-willed thought (*Sankalpa*) constantly and with a singleness-of-purpose, he is sure to succeed. But unfortunately, the ordinary man is

---

अनन्याश्चिन्तयन्तो मां ये जनाः पर्युपासते ।
तेषां नित्याभियुक्तानां योगक्षेमं वहाम्यहम् ॥ २२ ॥

ananyāścintayanto māṁ ye janah paryupāsate
teṣāṁ nityābhiyuktānāṁ yogakṣemaṁ vahāmyaham 22.

* The general belief that the verse is in the mathematical centre is evidently incorrect, as it is the 360th stanza out of the total 701 stanzas in the *Geeta*. However, this traditional belief has crept among us and we hear it repeated from all platforms, from all vocal commentators of the *Geeta*.

not capable of successfully keeping his thoughts in one channel of thinking. Therefore, his goal seems to be ever receding and flickering. His determination to achieve a particular goal ever changes, since his goal itself seem to be ever changing. To such a man of haphazard determination, no progress is ever possible in any line of undertaking.

The greatest tragedy of the age seems to be that we ignore the obvious fact that thoughts alone create. Activities gain a potency from the thought-power that feeds them. When the feeder behind is choked and dissipated, the execution-power in the external activities becomes feeble in strength and efficiency. Thoughts, from a single-pointed mind, must flow steadily in full inspiration, enthusiasm and vigour towards the determined goal which the individual has chosen for himself in life.

Mere thinking, in itself, is not sufficient. No doubt, actions are necessary. Many of the present-day youths, though capable of consistently maintaining a goal-of-life in their intellect, are not ready to get into the field and act as best as they can for its achievement. The term '*Upasana*' means 'worship'. Through worship we invoke the deity, meaning 'the profit potential in any given field'* and the prefix '*Pari*' to this familiar term '*Upasana*' indicates a total-effort in which no stone is left unturned for carving out one's victories in one's field of endeavour.

So far, two main secret factors without which success in life will not be assured are revealed – (a) CONSISTENCY OF WILLING AND THINKING, and (b) POURING OUT OURSELVES WITH A SINGLENESS OF PURPOSE in meeting the situation in its entirety. The third main factor that is essential in the constitution of one who is marked out for spectacular success and brilliant gains in life is (c) SELF-CONTROL.

* The *Yajna* spirit in which the actions are to be undertaken as explained in Chapter IV.

As an aspiring individual, consistently maintaining his ambition in mind, walks out into his fields of activity to battle with the immediate problems, he will meet with many a tempting channel of more fascinating plans, through which he can dissipate himself and get exhausted, rendering himself incapable of conquering the highest success in his own field. To keep oneself SELF-CONTROLLED, so that one may not thus get derailed as one shoots forward to reach the temple of success, is the third great factor that is to be kept in mind and lived fully, in order that success in life be assured.

The terms *'Yoga'* and *'Kshema'* defined as the power to gain (*Yoga*), and the power to guard (*Kshema*) respectively, by Shankara in his commentary,* are quite applicable in the context of our discussion. In life, all conflict and contests, all struggles and sorrows, whatever be the form in which they may appear, are always different from individual to individual, from place to place, and from time to time, and all of them distinctly fall into two groups, as (a) the struggles to gain, and (b) the efforts to guard what might have been gained. These two tensions tear into bits the joy and tranquillity of life. He who is without these two preoccupations is the luckiest, in the sense that he has gained all that is to be gained; and when these two factors are totally blotted out from one's life, one is dead to the world of sorrows – and one awakens to the world of joy imperishable.

It is promised here by the Lord that to the one who is capable of maintaining the three factors described above, and pursuing them diligently, there need be NO ANXIETY TO GAIN, NOR WORRY TO GUARD, because these two responsibilities will be voluntarily undertaken by the Lord Himself. Here the term Lord may be understood as the Law

---

* "*Yogah apraaptasyaprapanam, Kshemah tadrakshanam*"– Sankara. *'Yoga'* means procuring what is not procured, and *'Kshema'* means protecting what is already procured.

behind the world-of-plurality and all the happenings therein. When water is let out from a height for purposes of irrigating the lower planes, we have only to allow it to flow in the right direction, to reach the required area - and nature itself will carry it down, for, it is the law-of-nature that water always flows from a higher to a lower level. Similarly here, to one who is working, fulfilling the three great laws pertaining to the physical, mental and intellectual disciplines, success SHALL dog the heels of such a careful ruler of circumstances.

OPENING UP A NEW SECTION, TO DISCUSS THE MISGUIDED WORSHIPPERS, WHO ADORE AT THE ALTARS OF THE DEITIES THAT PRESIDE OVER FINITE, MATERIAL GAINS, THE FOLLOWING IS SAID:

23. *Even those devotees, who, endowed with faith worship other gods, worship Me alone, O son of Kunti, (but) by the wrong method?*

All the people in the world do not worship at the same altar. Not only is this physically impossible, but it is psychologically absurd, since tastes differ from person to person.

The devotees, during their respective worship at the different altars, adore the same Vitality that is the substratum for the created world of change. Even when they worship different deities, if their devotion is sufficiently reinforced with perfect faith, they are invoking nothing but the one Eternal Truth expressed through the form of their adoration. When once we accept the Infinite Reality as 'One-without-a-

---

येऽप्यन्यदेवता भक्ता यजन्ते श्रद्धयान्विताः ।
तेऽपि मामेव कौन्तेय यजन्त्यविधिपूर्वकम् ॥ २३ ॥

ye'pyanyadevatā bhaktā yajante śraddhayānvitāḥ
te'pi māmeva kaunteya yajantyavidhipūrvakam 23.

second' remaining the same in the past, present, and future, it is evident that the Self, as Consciousness – that expresses through the equipments of all Saints and Sages, Prophets and Incarnations of the past, is one and the same.

Toleration is the very breath of the Hindu creed, and we have already discussed earlier, how non-dualists, accepting the Absolute as Infinite, cannot but be tolerant. Intolerance is the creed of those who accept a single Prophet as God. Even among Hindus, all those who worship as members of a particular creed or sect, are generally found to be unrelenting fanatics. Some crude examples are even noticed where a devotee of one deity believes that, to utter blasphemies against the deities of others is adoration of his own beloved Lord! These are mere perversions, obnoxious and vulgar, which have no sanction in the Bible of the Hindus or anywhere in the cultural tradition initiated by the *Rishis*.

The large-heartedness and endless love in the heart of Krishna makes him declare here that "THEY TOO, WORSHIP ME ALONE, EVEN THOUGH BY WRONG METHODS".

The stanza, viewed as an instruction for the external life in the work-a-day-world, suggests that, instead of seeking the infinite profit of the Bliss of Self-hood, those devotees who are trying to invoke other limited gains in the different fields of human activity, are also invoking the Grace of the Self - only BY THE WRONG METHOD.

Even the most sensuous, when he is planning to earn, to save and to spend so that he may procure, possess and enjoy the sensuous objects, are invoking the dormant capacities that lie in the Self in him. Sans Self none will be able to act either negatively or positively. Even in the case of suicide, a person is invoking Life, inasmuch as, even in the act of raising a weapon against himself, he is misusing the Grace of the manifested Life in him.

In this context the phrase 'BY THE WRONG METHOD' only indicates that ultimately, it leads the seekers to the wells of dejection and sorrow that lie in the darkness of the not-Self, instead of leading to the Bliss-of-Perfection which is the nature of the Self.

WHY DO WE CALL THEIR METHODS AS AGAINST WHAT THE LAW ORDAINS?

24. *(For) I alone am the enjoyer in and the Lord of all sacrifices; but they do not know Me in Essence, and hence they fall (return to this mortal world).*

In all ritualistic sacrifices, the Self alone is THE ENJOYER AND THE LORD. It is the Self, in one form or another, expressing some special power that goes to form the different deities, for the invocation of whom the various sacrifices are performed by the seekers of their grace. Here the Lord says "I am the Immutable Reality that is behind all the deities that are invoked during every sacrifice with faith and devotion, be it in a Temple or a Church, in a Mosque or a Synagogue. But because they invoke 'limited potentials in Me' (*Devatas*) they do not come to realise 'My Infinite Glory revelling as their Self' and therefore, jumping from one worship to another, they slip down to fall into delusory confusions and endless entanglements".

Applying it to life, in all fields of activity wherein men strive (*Yajna*), they are invoking some finite profit or the other (deity), and do not strive to improve spiritually so as to come

---

अहं हि सर्वयज्ञानां भोक्ता च प्रभुरेव च।
न तु मामभिजानन्ति तत्त्वेनातश्च्यवन्ति ते॥ २४॥

ahaṁ hi sarvayajñānāṁ bhoktā ca prabhureva ca
na tu māmbhijānanti tattvenātaścyavanti te 24.

to rediscover the Self as their own essential nature. Treading on the slippery slopes of sensuality, they fall to the levels of brutal animalism and prove themselves a disgrace to the dignity and status of man.

Complete happiness and satisfaction, perfect contentment and peace; lie only in the innermost precincts of the bosom and not in the extrovert fields of profit and success, glory and fame. Unmindful of this enduring profit that lies within themselves, men, bitten by a thousand scorpions of desire, run amuck - bringing about chaos and sorrows not only to themselves but also to others walking the same road. Necessarily, therefore, when a generation of such deluded people come to live, freely encouraging their own mental weaknesses, and never caring to pause and estimate their own actions, the history of that period can be written only upon the face of a blasted world with the very blood of the killed and the maimed - diluted with the tears of the bereaved mothers and widows! Indeed, they return to the sorrows of the mortals (*Chyavanti te*).

HOW CAN WE SAY THAT EVEN THOSE WHO ARE INVOKING THE ETERNAL BY METHODS WHICH THE LAW DOES NOT ORDAIN, COME TO ENJOY THEIR CERTAIN FRUITS? ... LISTEN:

25. *The worshippers of the DEVAS or gods go to the DEVAS; to the PITRIS or ancestors go the ancestor-worshippers; to the BHUTAS or the elements go worshippers of the BHUTAS; but My worshippers come unto Me.*

यान्ति देवव्रता देवान् पितॄन्यान्ति पितृव्रताः ।
भूतानि यान्ति भूतेज्या यान्ति मद्याजिनोऽपि माम् ॥ २५ ॥

yānti devavratā devān pitṛvratāḥ
bhūtāni yānti bhūtejyā yānti madyājino'pi mām 25.

It is the law-of-life that as you think so you become. The thoughts entertained at a given moment get crystallised to form a blueprint for the individual's character formation in days to come. This is a fact, very well realisable by everyone in his own life. Applying this natural law of psychology in the field of spiritual self-development, Lord Krishna says: "VOTARIES OF THE *DEVAS* GO TO THE *DEVAS*" etc. The worshippers of the *Devas*, ancestors (*Pitris*), and the elements (*Bhutas*), as a result of their worship and adoration with single-pointed mind for a sufficiently long time, come to attain the desires of their constant meditation.

Devas, we have seen, represent the various sense-organs, through which we experience the world. To indicate the work done, by the term denoting the instrument with which the work is executed, is quite common in life. To axe, to scissor, to knife, to hammer, to steer, to pen, etc., are examples wherein the name of the instrument is employed to indicate the work done with it. Similarly, here also, the plural noun '*Devas*' may be taken to mean the entire field of all physical experiences. Those who are courting the external world of joys and successes consistently and with the required amount of devotion, come to gain that field of demanded experiences.

Accepting the term '*Pitri*' as denoting the ancestors, votaries of ancestors, would mean 'persons who are enthusiastically alive to the cultural purity and tradition of their ancients, and who are striving to live up to those ideals'. An individual, who is constantly endeavouring to live up to the ancient cultural tradition of spiritual India, as a result of his constant self-application, comes to gain the beauty and the shine of the exquisite life of purity and perfection.

The ancient Seers of our land did not overlook the fact that, apart from the spiritual aims, in any society, there would also be active scientific enquiries and repeated discoveries that were possible among the folds of Mother Nature's own garments. The active quest in the field of objective-sciences is a part of man's hunt for knowledge, and therefore, the worshippers of the *Bhutas,* are the secular scientists who try to observe, codify and systematize the observed knowledge of physical nature and behaviour of things and beings as it is now done under such classifications as Physics, Chemistry, Biology, Zoology, Botany, Engineering, Agriculture, Politics, Sociology, Geography, History, Geology, and so on - an endless array of specialised lines of investigation, adopted, pursued and accepted by the modern world. A large portion of the *Atharvana Veda* gave us the accepted theories of nature and its behaviour, as finally conceived of by the *Rishis* of that time. The psychological theory, which Krishna is observing here, is applicable to all branches of human endeavour - that is, if one were to pursue diligently even in the secular field, success would be assured in direct proportion to the amount of self-application put forth by the seeker.

Thus, if consistency of meditation upon the *Devas* yields the *Devas;* if constant meditation upon the 'ancestors' takes us to our ancestral heritage; and if diligent self-application in the fields of intellectual enquiry (*Bhutas*) can ultimately assure us a positive success in ripping open the secret vaults of nature - then, according to the same principle, we are assured that, MY VOTARIES COME UNTO ME. By constant meditation, with a single-pointed mind, upon the nature of the Self, the meditator can, in the long run, successfully discover his total identity with the Self, Eternal and Immutable. In our elementary textbooks on *Vedanta,* this technique of the ego's constant meditation on the Self and its ultimate transformation into the Divine Self has been indicated by comparing it with the manner in which a worm is transformed into a wasp.*

The attempt of the *Geeta* is to give, not only the *Jnana* but also to supply the *Vijnana*. In order to convince the student that this elementary technique can take the seeker to the highest achievements, this stanza is given. Just as consistent pursuit with all dedicated self-application brings, in the end, sure success in all fields of activity of art or science, so too, in the realm of the 'within' and ultimately in the field of spiritual achievement, constant meditation will definitely pay. The logic behind this assurance is given here by the Lord.

CAN MERE WORSHIP WITH DEVOTED THOUGHTS, HOWEVER SINCERE, BRING ABOUT SUCH AN ABSOLUTE SUCCESS? IS IT NOT NECESSARY THAT WE SHOULD PURSUE ALL THE ELABORATE RITUALS THAT THE *VEDAS* PRESCRIBE, AND OFTEN SEEM TO INSIST UPON? ... LISTEN:

26. *Whoever offers Me with devotion a leaf, a flower, a fruit, water, that I accept, offered by the pure-minded with devotion.*

There is no religion in the world which does not recognise and encourage offerings by the devotees. The modern educated man is rather surprised as to why the Infinite Lord, in all religions, needs insignificant things like a spoonful of oil for His lamp, or a candle, or even an edifice to house Himself - be it a church, a mosque, or a temple. Dreary intellects, poisoned with their own misunderstanding, have even come shamelessly to insist that these Houses-of-God should be converted into hospitals and schools, lunatic asylums and maternity homes!*

पत्रं पुष्पं फलं तोयं यो मे भक्त्या प्रयच्छति ।
तदहं भक्त्युपहृतमश्नामि प्रयतात्मनः ॥ २६ ॥

patraṁ puṣpaṁ phalaṁ toyaṁ yo me bhaktayā praycchati
tadahaṁ bhaktayupahṛtamaśnāmi prayatātmanaḥ 26.

* *Bhramara-keeta-nyaya.*

But I believe that I am talking to a world which has not reached this nadir of depravity. Not yet. In a society where there is still the play of healthy hearts and virulent intellects, there is certainly a need for temples and worship. And in these Houses-of-God, it is not the intricacies of their design, elaborateness of the ritual, nor the splendour of gold and wealth exhibited, nor even the number of devotees attending, that contribute to their essential success.

The very language and diction of the stanza clearly sound the note that the material objects that one might offer are of no value to the Lord of the Universe, but it is the devotion and love that prompt the offerings that are accepted by the Deity. Be it a leaf, a flower, a fruit, or water, it is but an insignificant thing that you offer; be it a golden temple, or be it a dry leaf, WHOSOEVER OFFERS WITH DEVOTION, whatever be the offering, the Lord of *Vrindavana* assures "THAT I ACCEPT". For, when lovingly given, it becomes A DEVOUT GIFT and when it is offered by a sincere PURE-MINDED student, the Lord has to accept it.

There are several carefully coined words in the stanza which explain the theory of sacrifice insisted upon in all religions. No doubt, the Absolute requires no offering at all from the finite mortals to complete Its Perfection, or to maintain Its Infinite Glory. The limited individuals try to offer at the Altar of their Lord something that they have MISAPPROPRIATED from the Lord's own garden, the world.

---

* I for one, rather sympathise with them, and will certainly declare that their wishes are perfectly justifiable in a society where there are more sick persons than healthy ones, more breeding than even our wildest imagination could ever believe possible, more misguided education than illiteracy, and more mad ones than sane men are. A society of mad men, wherein the illiterates are miseducated, suffering from all possible physical, mental and intellectual ulcers, when they come to live thickly in lust and passion, breeding enormously... in such an era of brutes, worsens than animals, no more temples are needed. Certainly they need more hospitals, asylums, maternity homes and elementary schools!!!

In a public park, a lover often pinches a flower from the nearby bush and offers it to his beloved. Similarly, a devotee steals something from the Lord's own palace, and offers the same unto Him. In fact, when thus we analyse carefully, we know the hollowness of the vanity of offering something unto the Lord.

And yet, this is insisted upon as an important ritual in all forms of worship. In offering a flower, or a fruit unto the Lord, if the devotee feels that he is making a sacrifice of the very thing that he offers, he is misusing the very act. The flower, here, serves only the purpose of a spoon in conveying something unto the Lord. While taking soup, one, no doubt, lifts the spoon many times to the mouth but at the end of the dinner the spoon remains the same as before, having finished its work. The flowers and fruits in the garden or in the temple remain the same, but when the devotee gathers and carries them to the Altar, and offers them, they become the conveyors of his love and dedication unto the Lord of his heart.

This idea has been brought out in this stanza, when the Lord says: "THAT I ACCEPT ... THE DEVOUT GIFT OF THE PURE-MINDED".

Therefore, on the whole, it is clear that an offering can be efficient, only when it is accompanied by the two required conditions; (a) offered with devotion and (b) by the pure-minded. To the extent these features are absent; all offerings are mere economic waste and superstition-breeding false-beliefs. If properly done, it can serve as a good vehicle to tread the spiritual path of self-development.

THEREFORE:

27. *Whatever you do, whatever you eat, whatever you offer in sacrifice, whatever you give in charity, whatever you practise as austerity, O Kaunteya, do it as an offering to Me.*

Through all activities of life one can constantly live in the spirit of 'devout offering' unto the Supreme. Throughout the *Geeta* it has been, time without number, insisted upon that the mental attitude is of supreme importance, rather than the mere physical act. And, this is a fact which ordinarily the seekers forget.

All acts of perception and our reactions to the perceived be they on the physical, mental, or intellectual levels, make them all a DEVOUT OFFERING UNTO HIM. In fact, this is not an unnecessary make-belief or a mere fancied exaggeration. Nor is it in any way, very difficult for an individual to practise. The one Self revels everywhere; in the teacher, in the devotee and in the Lord. In all our life's transactions, we behave, act and deal with other names and forms, and all of them, we know, require the Existence of the Self to uphold them. To remember the Self during all transactions of life is to remember the substratum. In a cloth shop where there are cotton clothes of different colours and sizes, textures and prices, the shopkeeper is advised always to remember that he is dealing with cotton clothings. This cannot be very difficult for any sane shopkeeper, and it will be safe and profitable for him to remember this fact, for it would prevent him from entertaining misconceptions and thereby either charging the exorbitant prices of woollens, or selling off his goods as cheap as gunny bags! If a goldsmith is

---

यत्करोषि यदश्नासि यज्जुहोषि ददासि यत्।
यत्तपस्यसि कौन्तेय तत्कुरुष्व मदर्पणम्॥ २७॥

yatkaroṣi yadaśnāsi yajjuhoṣi dadāsi yat
yattapasyasi kaunteya tatkuruṣva madarpaṇam 27.

asked to remember that he is working on gold, it is only for his own benefit.

Just as cotton is in all cloth, gold in all ornaments, the Self is the Essential-stuff in all names and forms. A devotee, who can constantly remember the Divine in all his contacts in life, is alone the one who can give to life the respect and reverence that it deserves. It is a law in life that as you give unto life, so shall life give unto you. Smile at life and life smiles; frown at life and life frowns at you; approach life with due reverence and respect, born out of the cognition of the Divine essence in it, and life shall respect and revere you.

When all activities are performed in the spirit-of-offering, not only our love for the Supreme increases but also our entire life becomes sanctified with a noble purpose and a divine aim. In the context of the *Geeta's* insistence on single-pointedness of mind, and devoted contemplation of the Self, so far described, we can easily see how this stanza provides us again with an efficient and secret method by which the seekers are unconsciously made to remember the Supreme constantly - not in the deep jungles, nor in the secret caves, but right in the field of life's contentions.

WHAT WOULD BE THE EFFECT OF SUCH A MANNER OF LIVING LIFE IN THE PURE SPIRIT OF DEDICATED OFFERING? ... LISTEN:

28. *Thus shall you be freed from the bonds-of-actions yielding good and evil 'fruits'; with the mind steadfast in the YOGA of renunciation, and liberated, you shall come unto Me.*

शुभाशुभफलैरेवं मोक्ष्यसे कर्मबन्धनैः ।
संन्यासयोगयुक्तात्मा विमुक्तो मामुपैष्यसि ॥ २८ ॥

śubhāśubhaphalairevaṁ mokṣyase karmabandhanaiḥ
sannyāsayogayuktātmā vimukto māmupaiṣyasi 28.

This spiritual goal remaining the same, the Divine-paths are different; and when the different paths are explained, though they look very different from each other, they all have the same scientific basis that justifies each one of them. At many places in the *Geeta*, this fundamental basis has been directly brought to the recognition of the students, while in a few instances it is slightly veiled; yet, careful students can always come to recognise it. In this section, we are in the midst of a discussion on how, by living life in a spirit-of-offering, the individual can come to claim and finally enjoy the Highest Perfection which meditation promises and the *Yajna*-spirit guarantees.

When actions are undertaken without ego, the reactions of those actions (*vasanas*), whether good or bad, cannot reach us, since he who is to suffer or enjoy the reactions would be out-of-station from the given bosom. The ego acts, and it is the ego that receives the reactions.

Hence *Bhagawan* says, "YOU SHALL BE FREE FROM THE BONDAGES OF ACTIONS, GOOD OR EVIL". Since the reactions (*vasanas*) arising from fresh actions do not add their impressions on to the mind, and since the existing impressions (*vasanas*) get wiped out during the mind's activities in the world outside, slowly and steadily, the mind gets almost a total purgation of all its existing *vasanas*. In short the mind becomes more and more PURIFIED – the term being used in its scriptural sense.* A purified mind has more concentration and single-pointedness.

The next stage of evolution is that such a purified mind, discovering in itself more and more discrimination, learns to live a life of *Sannyasa* and *Yoga*. Both these terms are to be understood in the *Geeta*-way. Earlier these terms have been

---

* Less *vasanas*, less agitations, and a mind with least thought-agitations in it is called a purified mind - it has more single-pointed steadiness in meditation.

very elaborately discussed. *Sannyasa* or renunciation is not the physical rejection of the world, but in the language of the *Geeta, Sannyasa* is the renunciation of: (a) all egocentric activities and (b) all anxieties or cravings for the fruits-of-actions. These two effects would be natural in one who is striving diligently in the world, as an expression of his love for the Lord, only to dedicate, in the end, all the results unto the Lord as his humble, simple, 'offering'.

To the one who has come to live the *Geeta-Sannyasa* and has developed, by discrimination, a mind full to the brim with purity, *Yoga* is natural; especially so, because all through the hours of his activity he is constantly remembering the SELF, the INFINITE.

Naturally, such a seeker discovers that his earlier identifications with the false and the consequent sense of limitations and pains of mortality fall off from him and he discovers for himself his Divine Nature: "BY PRACTICE AND RENUNCIATION YOU SHALL FIND RELEASE AND COME TO ME".

THE SEEKER IS PROMISED THAT HE WILL GO TO THE SUPREME. WHAT THEN IS THE NATURE OF THE SELF?

29. *The same am I to all beings, to Me there is none hateful nor dear; but those who worship Me with devotion, are in Me and I am also in them.*

The Self is ONE in all beings; the same Conscious Principle illumines the emotions and thoughts in all bosoms of all living

---

समोऽहं सर्वभूतेषु न मे द्वेष्योऽस्ति न प्रियः।
ये भजन्ति तु मां भक्त्या मयि ते तेषु चाप्यहम्॥ २९॥

samo'haṁ sarvabhūteṣu na me dveṣyo'sti na priyaḥ
ye bhajanti tu māṁ bhaktayā mayi te teṣu cāpyaham 29.

creatures. "I AM IN ALL BEINGS". The same Sun illumines all objects of the world and its rays get reflected on all surfaces – whether the dull, rough surface of a rock, or the bright polished facet of a jewel.

TO ME THERE IS NONE HATEFUL NOR DEAR—If the same Self revels in Krishna and Buddha, Shankara and Christ, in a lunatic and in a murderer, in the good and in the bad, why is it that some are able to recognise the divine status of the Self and others live like worms? In the emotional literature, expounding the *Bhakti*-cult, there is always the sentimental explanation that it is because, under the Lord's direct grace, some come to manifest a greater amount of divinity. This theory may be satisfactory to the few, who do not bring their reasoning capacity into the field of religious discussion. But to the intelligent ones, this explanation should appear absurd, inasmuch as the Supreme would have to be considered as exhibiting partiality to some in the world. To negate this imperfect explanation, and to express the purely scientific theory, Krishna declares here that the Self is the same everywhere, always, and that to the Self there is no distinction between the good and the bad; the Self entertains neither a particular love nor any special hatred for any of the living beings.

This should not be understood as meaning that the Self is an impotent factor, inert, and emotionless, with no capacity in Itself to bless or to help. Employing the analogy of the sunlight which we have already examined, the idea implied here can be better understood. Even though the same sunlight reflects upon the different types of objects in the world, it is true that the quality and the nature of the reflecting surface will determine the clarity and the intensity of the light reflected. On a dull piece of rough stone there will be the least amount of light reflected, while in a bright clean and polished mirror there will be, perhaps, the maximum reflection.

Because of this difference, sunlight cannot be accused of having special love for the mirror, or a disgust for the rough stone. Applying the analogy to the subjective life, it becomes clear that if the spiritual strength and beauty get reflected more from the golden-hearts of the rare few and not at all from the iron-hearts of the many, it is not because the Self entertains in Itself any preference for, or any prejudice against, anyone, but it is only a natural phenomenon, happening in perfect obedience to the law of the universe.

Though in the first line there is a total negation of any relationship whatsoever between the Self and the not-Self, in the following line, there is a striking idea expressed, which as it were smothers the readers with its vivid contradiction. "BUT THOSE WHO WORSHIP ME WITH DEVOTION ARE IN ME, AND I TOO AM IN THEM". Even though the Self has neither any favour for, nor any prejudice against the not-Self, to the extent the not-Self "WORSHIP ME WITH DEVOTION" they are "IN ME AND I TOO AM IN THEM". We can say that the ghost is in the post and the post is in the ghost, meaning thereby the non-dual nature of the essence and the super-impositions upon It. Those who worship the Self with devotion come to rediscover that the worshippers themselves are none other than the Self that is worshipped by them.

Even while recognising the GHOST the deluded one is looking at the POST only; for the POST is the permanent 'reality' upon which the projection of the 'non-real' GHOST has been made by the deluded observer.

THOSE WHO WORSHIP ME WITH DEVOTION—this phrase can be initially understood as a mere ritualistic injunction, and it calls for a closer and deeper study to realise its spiritual implications. Worship is a technique by which, in essence, the entire 'thought-forces' in the worshipper are mobilised and turned to flow towards a diviner point-of-contemplation, ever seeking a total identity with the Truth so meditated upon. When this is done in a spirit of devotion or love,* the worshipper comes to realise his total oneness with his object-of-worship.

With this implied meaning well in mind, when we re-read the stanza, what Krishna means in this philosophical statement becomes amply clear. Even though Truth has neither a preference for, nor a prejudice against anyone, some noble souls come to experience, and later on exhibit in themselves the effulgence of divinity, because, as the Lord says, they, through their devoted worship, have sought and discovered their oneness with the Divine Principle, the Self. Theirs becomes the elegance of the Divine.

A mind, which is preoccupied with its own egocentric attachments with the not-Self, cannot come to live the Bliss-of-Perfection, while, the same mind, when it has detached itself from its extrovert preoccupations, becomes a ready instrument to seek and to discover its true identity with the Self. The condition of the mind declares whether the individual is confused or clear, bound or redeemed. A mind that is turned outward, rushing out and panting to gain its satisfactions in the world-of-objects, gets bound to the finite, and comes to groan with pain and disappointment; while the same mind when turned inward, away from the objects, seeking the Self, comes to rediscover its own identity with the spiritual centre.

In winter, inside a room one suffers from cold, while outside there is plenty of sunshine. He who walks out of the room into the sunshine comes to be blessed by the warmth of the Sun while they who bury themselves in their rooms

---

* We have already explained how love is nothing but the lover's own identity with the beloved one.

suffer the discomforts of the cold. The Sun has neither a preference for those who are basking under its rays, nor has it any prejudice against those who do not come out under its shine and warmth. In the language of this stanza, we may call those who have walked out to the sunny courtyard as 'blessed' by the Sun, while those who stay indoors as 'not blessed' by that luminous energiser in the sky?

Never does the *Geeta*, at any point, encourage man's surrender to circumstances, or to his own debilities and incompetencies. As a scripture of activity and optimistic endeavour, the *Geeta* unmistakably emphasizes the ultimate supremacy of man over his weaknesses and even over his circumstances.

IS THIS PATH OF SELF-DISCOVERY AVAILABLE ONLY FOR THE GOOD? ... LISTEN:

30. *Even if the most sinful worships Me, with devotion to none else, (or with single-pointedness), he too should indeed be regarded as 'righteous' for he has rightly resolved.* ?

The practice of devotion, understood in the special meaning in which it is used in the *Geeta*, is glorified here by indicating its effects upon each individual practitioner. In the *Geeta*, *Bhakti* is selfless contemplation with a single-pointed mind upon the non-dual *Brahman* considered as nothing other than the very Essence in the devotee. When this *Bhakti* is practised for a sufficiently long time, with the required intensity and sincerity, the evolution in the individual is mapped out here showing the various stages in its efflorescence.

अपि चेत्सुदुराचारो भजते मामनन्यभाक् ।
साधुरेव स मन्तव्यः सम्यग्व्यवसितो हि सः ॥ ३० ॥

api cetsudurācāro bhajate māmananyabhāk
sādhureva sa mantavyaḥ samyagvyavasito hi saḥ 30.

Ordinarily, there is a vague belief that a vicious sinner or a desperate criminal is an outcaste, who can never dare to enter the courtyard of heaven. This condemnation of the immoral sinner is an unhappy misreading of the spirit of *Vedic* literature. THE *VEDAS* CONDEMN THE SIN, NOT THE SINNER. The evil ways of the sinner are but expressions of the evil thoughts in his mind, and so, if the texture of the thoughts flowing in his mind could be changed, the texture of his behaviour would also be transformed. He who has come to keep consistently in his mind, thoughts of the Lord, accomplishes, in the warmth of his growing devotion, so total a rehabilitation of the mental life that he cannot thereafter carry on his career in sin.

EVEN IF A WICKED PERSON WORSHIPS ME—Not only does the *Geeta* throw its gates open to the sinners, but the Singer of the Divine Song also seems to have great missionary zeal to redeem all sinners, and bless them. Even those who are given to evil ways are not debarred from entering the field of spirituality because of their undivine actions and the impurity of their lives. The only insistence is that the worship of the Self must be performed by the devotee with 'undivided devotion'. Here the term 'undivided' (*Ananya*) can be applied both to the 'mind of the meditator' and to the 'goal meditated upon'. On the whole, the phrase implies that devotion can pay its promised dividend only when the devotee, with a single-pointed mind, contemplates upon a goal that is non-dual and permanent. The non-dual Self is not to be considered as different from the very Essence in the devotee himself (*Ananya*).

HE SHOULD BE REGARDED AS GOOD—Even though he has been, till this day, a man of evil ways, wicked and cruel, living the life of the senses, uncontrolled and passionate, even then, from the moment he has taken to the path of contemplation upon the Supreme, with devotion, he is to be considered, says Krishna, as SAINTLY AND GOOD. Such usage of words is common to every language, when we want to emphatically assert a state or condition to be fulfilled in the immediate future. In all such cases, we claim it as a state accomplished, even in the present baking the bread, making the tea, are all examples when, even while kneading the flour or boiling the water, we refer to these acts with a term indicating anticipatory fulfilment. Similarly here, one who has taken to the Path Divine is called, from that very moment, as GOOD AND SAINTLY because he will soon (*Acirat*) grow out of himself to thrive and flourish in the vaster atmosphere of spiritual glory; it is an anticipatory statement.

Such an individual is to be considered good and divine, FOR, as Krishna puts it, "HE HAS RIGHTLY RESOLVED". In the Life Divine, right resolution is more important than mere routine. The majority of seekers only plod on their 'paths' - a melancholy brood, like famished cattle, treading their way to the meat-market! Such a melancholy procession can reach nowhere but the butcher's block where Time hacks them into pieces! He who steadily walks the path with an iron-heart of resolution, open-eyed and enthusiastic, cheerful and heroic, alone is noted for sure success and therefore, the Flute-bearer emphatically asserts that the rightly resolved man of evil ways is to be considered, from the moment of his noble decision, as one especially marked out to be soon a successful man-of-Perfection.

HOW DO WE KNOW THAT WHAT YOU ARE TALKING IS NOT A BLUFF? WHAT EXACTLY IS THE EFFECT OF SUCH A SINGLE-POINTED DEVOTION?

31. *Soon he becomes righteous and attains Eternal Peace, O Kaunteya, know for certain that My devotee is never destroyed.*

The logical thoughts that lie behind the daring assertion* of Krishna are being indicated in this stanza. When a man of evil ways takes to a life of single-pointed devotion propelled by his ardent resolve, that man SOON BECOMES RIGHTEOUS. The term *Dharma* was already explained as the Law-of-Being. Just as heat is the specific quality (*Dharma*) of fire, without which fire cannot exist, the *Dharma* of man is the Divine *Atman* in his heart, without which none of his personality layers can ever come to express themselves. Therefore, the term '*Dharmatma*' in the stanza, is not fully expressed when it is translated as 'a man of righteousness'.

Single-pointed devotion and self-application develop concentration, and therefore, enhance the subtlety of perception of the mind, and such a mind finds its balance even in the highest altitudes of meditative flights. 'IN GOOD TIME' meaning, ere long, he gains glimpses of the Infinite experience and thus, comes to live more and more as a dynamic saint, wafting the fragrance of divinity through his motives, thoughts, and actions.

This substantial edifice of peace which strengthens and fortifies the existence in us, is the tranquillity divine, which we come to live as our essential being when the mind stops

---

क्षिप्रं भवति धर्मात्मा शश्वच्छान्तिं निगच्छति ।
कौन्तेय प्रतिजानीहि न मे भक्तः प्रणश्यति ॥ ३१ ॥

kṣipraṁ bhavati dhamārtmā śaśvacchantiṁ nigacchati
kaunteya pratijānīhi na me bhaktaḥ praṇaśyati 31.

* Made in the previous stanza, in its anticipatory fulfilment that even a wicked person, when rightly resolved, must be, from that moment, considered as good and saintly.

its mad revelry among its agitations and excitements. There is no religion in the world which does not point to this goal, which can be experienced when the mind is at rest. A still mind is an open window through which man peeps out to see himself reflected in the mirror of Truth. The term guaranteeing here that "a true devotee soon REACHES the Supreme Peace" is to be rightly understood not as a destination that lies far away from us, but only as a REDISCOVERY IN OURSELVES OF OUR OWN REAL NATURE.

The perfection indicated in religion lies only as far away from us as our waking state is from our dream. It is a question of rightly adjusting the focus; if a camera is out of focus the photograph will give only a blurred representation of a fairyland, while the same scene photographed by the same camera, well-focussed and adjusted, gives us the photograph in all its gorgeous beauty, and wealth of detail. A mind and intellect, maladjusted and incessantly getting shunted among the ever-rising waves of desires and passions, are not the right instruments to cognise and discover the Truth that lies within itself.

The second line of the stanza brings out the incomparable missionary in Krishna, who bursts out into an assertion, in his own rising fire and enthusiasm. After declaring the truth that even a man of dire evil ways can start his pilgrimage on the very day he takes unto himself the firm resolve to re-educate his mind, and after indicating the stages of his growth, till he reaches the Supreme Peace, Krishna, as it were, pats Arjuna on the back and declares "MY DEVOTEE IS NEVER DESTROYED".

Toeing the line of the *Rishis*, Krishna says that Arjuna should declare from house-tops the one unchallengeable truth that the seeker of the nobler values shall know no failure if his resolve is firm and if he be sincere in his self-application.

The special phrase, employed here to declare Krishna's advice to Arjuna, *Prati janeehi*, has, in Sanskrit, its own special powers of assertion, and it can express a sort of imperative urgency. Those who are students of the Sanskrit language can easily perceive it; those who are not, may make a note of the same.

In short, this and the previous stanza together express that he who has come to entertain constantly, at least in one corner of his mind, a continuous awareness of the Divine Principle and allows it to influence the rest of his mental field, is the one marked out for progress and growth, both in his life within and in his life without. Just as a blue street light adds a blue tinge to the colour of the dresses of all those who pass under it, irrespective of the actual colour of their various dresses, so too, in the blaze of Divine Awareness, even criminal thoughts rising in that mind would gather the golden hues of godly perfections. Just as mothballs kept in a wardrobe protect all the clothes kept therein and keep away all the worms, so too, the constant *Smarana* of the Divine Nature of the Self protects the human personality from the destructive worms of its inner negativeness.

FURTHER:

32. *For, taking refuge in Me, they also, who O Partha, may be of a 'sinful birth' – women, VAISHYAS as well as SHUDRAS - even they attain the Supreme Goal.*

As an annotation and an explanatory appendix to the immediately preceding pair of stanzas, it is added that it is

---

मां हि पार्थ व्यपाश्रित्य येऽपि स्युः पापयोनयः ।
स्त्रियो वैश्यास्तथा शूद्रास्तेऽपि यान्ति परां गतिम् ॥ ३२ ॥

mām hi pātha vyapāśritya ye'pi syuḥ pāpayonayaḥ
striyo vaiśyāstathā śūdrā ste'pi yānti parām gatim 32.

not only those who are placed under wrong influences and unfavourable external conditions who are redeemed by the constant remembrance of the Divine, but those who are victims of congenital maladjustments, both in their mental make-up and in their intellectual constitution, also can get their equipments readjusted and tuned up properly by the same process of constant remembrance of the Truth Eternal.

No doubt, there are expressions in the *Vedas*, in the *Puranas*, and in the *Smritis*, which seemingly fall in line with the language of this stanza. To condemn women, traders (*Vaishyas*) and workers (*Shudras*) as individuals of inferior births is equivalent to accepting that religion has an effective influence ONLY upon a mere handful of members of our society. This would be a denial of what Krishna had been hammering upon from the opening stanza onward. Therefore, we have to understand the true implications of His words as He uses them here.

Religion is not a technique for developing the physical body, nor is it an art to be fulfilled through the play of the physical body. The condition and status of the physical body have nothing to do with the evolutionary progress which religion aims at through all its preachings. The spiritual practices contribute to the integration of the mind and intellect and to their progressive unfoldment, until, in their ripeness, they shed themselves, leaving the Spirit naked in all its divine glory. Thus, these terms, as used in this stanza, are to be understood as indicating some special qualities of the human mind-and-intellect, manifested in varying degrees in different individuals, at different times.

The 'feminine-minds' (*Striyah*) are those that have a larger share of deep affections and binding attachments. So too, there are people, who have a commercial attitude in all their thoughts and actions and who live in their mental life as traders (*Vaishyas*), ever calculating the profits that would accrue from all their psychological investments. Such a calculating mind, ever looking to the profits that could be raised, is not fit for easily evolving through the path-of-Meditation. To surrender all fruits of actions is the secret of holding the mind still, and of making it live vitally, the Infinite, that is the content of a single present-moment. Thus, when the science of Spirit-development condemns the traders, it is only a denunciation of the particular commercial tendency of the mind. Those who fall under the group of traders PSYCHOLOGICALLY cannot hope to progress on the Path Divine.

Lastly, mental attitudes of slumber and slothfulness are indicated by the term '*Shudra*' here.

When we have understood that these terms, familiar in that age, are borrowed by Krishna to indicate special types of mind-intellect-equipments, we have understood the stanza rightly, without pulling down the entire *Geeta* from its well-merited pedestal of dignity as a scripture of Man.

The verse promises that, through constant remembrance of the Lord, not only are all men of evil ways redeemed, but even those who are not able to walk the Path Divine, because of some psychological and intellectual debilities in them, will be cured and steadily strengthened to walk the 'Path' efficiently, if they too, with single-pointed mind and sincere devotion, learn to remember continuously, and meditate daily upon the Divine Self.

BORN OUT OF THE WOMB OF SIN—Sin, according to *Vedanta*, is a wrong tendency in the mind created out of the past unhealthy thought and negative living. These wrong channels of thought (*vasanas*), irresistibly drive man to live false values and bring about confusion and chaos into his life, as well as into the lives of others. It is these wrong tendencies, ploughed on the mental fields, that are the sources of the feminine nature of the mind (*Stritvam*), or the commercial attitude of the intellect (*Vaishyatwam*), or the general dullness and somnolent morbidity in one's inner life (*Shudratwam*). A dull-witted *pundita* alone will have the audacity to commit the folly of interpreting this stanza, adhering faithfully to the literal meaning, conveniently forgetting Sri Krishna's own definition of *Varnashrama Dharma* given previously in his discourses.*

In short, when these wrong tendencies are in the mind, the *Rishis* have declared, in sheer kindness, that it is useless for that mind to undertake a study of the *Vedas*. Therefore, such minds were debarred from doing so. To attain the necessary qualification for a successful study of the sacred lore, the prescription is *Sadhana*. Of all the spiritual practices (*Sadhana*), the most efficient is the constant remembrance of the Lord with a heart overflowing with love and devotion (*Upasana*). It is the *Vedantic* declaration that through *Upasana* the mind gets purified - purified of its debilities which are classified and indicated by the terms, WOMEN, TRADERS AND WORKERS.

When once these negative qualities have been removed from a mind, it gains in its powers of achieving concentration, single-pointedness and balance for its flight to the very horizons of thought. When once the equipment is ready and rigged for the pilgrimage, the destination will soon be reached; and therefore, Krishna promises "EVEN THEY ATTAIN THE SUPREME GOAL".

KRISHNA GOADS ARJUNA TO WALK THE PATH OF SELF-REALISATION.

---

* *Chaturvarnyam maya srishtam gunakarmavibhagasah.* - Chp.IV-13

33. *How much more (easily) then the holy BRAHMINS, and devoted Royal saints (attain the goal). Having reached (obtained) this impermanent and joyless world, do worship Me devoutly.*

If the above-mentioned mental types are highly handicapped in the race for the divine, Krishna, by a self-answering question, very emphatically points out here, how easy and almost natural Self-realisation and godly life must be to those who have the mental purity of a *brahmin*, or the large heart and the clear head of a *Rajarshi*. A king who, having enjoyed intelligently his power and wealth, in his complete satiation arising out of his growing inner discrimination, comes to experience the inward peace of true contemplation upon the Self, is called a *Rajarshi*.

After describing all possible types of 'heads-and-hearts' and after prescribing treatment for all of them to rediscover their own Divine Nature, the Lord, concluding the section, makes a general statement in the second line. "HAVING ATTAINED THIS TRANSIENT AND JOYLESS WORLD, WORSHIP ME DEVOUTLY". This instruction to Arjuna is an instruction for all, since, in the *Geeta* if Lord Krishna represents the Self, Arjuna represents the confused man standing impotent against the challenges of life.

Life is lived in a field always constituted of objects, instruments, and mental moods. These three are ever in a state of change. Naturally, the flickering joys that come to us in life prove to be transient. And the intervals between any two experiences of joy are only FULL OF PAIN.

किं पुनर्ब्राह्मणाः पुण्या भक्ता राजर्षयस्तथा ।
अनित्यमसुखं लोकमिमं प्राप्य भजस्व माम् ॥३३॥

kiṁ punabrārhmaṇāḥ puṇyā bhaktā rājarṣayastathā
anityamasukhaṁ lokamimaṁ prāpya bhajasva mām 33.

In tune with the positive and energising philosophy of optimism which the *Geeta* preaches, here Krishna declares the world to be a mere pit of sorrows, or a ditch of despair, or a mire of disappointments, or a field of joylessness (*Asukham*).

HAVING REACHED THIS WORLD, IMPERMANENT AND JOYLESS, Krishna advises Arjuna, that he must occupy himself in the worship of the Self. In this spiritual activity, Arjuna has been well encouraged by the Lord with his statements that to a heart that has not the weakness natural to the lower evolutes* but has a wealth of poise and understanding which are the hall-marks of a higher evolutes (*Brahmins* and *Rajarshis*), success is easy and sure. Therefore "WORSHIP ME DEVOUTLY".

HOW THEN AM I TO WORSHIP YOU, MY LORD, WHEN I AM TO FACE MY ENEMIES AND FIGHT MY BATTLE?

34. *Fix your mind on Me; be devoted to Me, sacrifice to Me, bow down to Me; having thus united your (whole) Self with Me, taking me as the Supreme Goal, you shall come to Me.*

This stanza is a beautiful summary of the entire chapter for it throws a flood of light upon many of the other stanzas. We may say that this stanza especially serves as a commentary to more than one verse in the chapter (Verses 14 and 27).

In all textbooks of *Vedanta* (*Brahma-Vidya*), the technique of self-development and self-perfection through the paths of

---

मन्मना भव मद्भक्तो मद्याजी मां नमस्कुरु ।
मामेवैष्यसि युक्त्वैवमात्मानं मत्परायणः ॥ ३४ ॥

manmanā bhava madbhakto madyājī māṁ namaskuru
māmevaiṣyasi yuktavaimātmānaṁ matparāyaṇaḥ 34.

* Indicated by the terms, Women, *Vaishyas* and *Shudras*, as applied to the mental condition.

right Knowledge and Meditation, has been defined as, "Contemplation on That, talks on That, mutual discussion on That - and thus, to live ever mentally drowned in the Bliss-concept of the spiritual Reality, is called by the knowers of It, as the pursuit of *Brahman*".* Keeping this classical definition in mind, Vyasa steadily delineates his aesthetic path-of-Devotion in this stanza. The same idea has already been brought out earlier in the chapter on more than one occasion.

With "THE MIND EVER FILLED WITH ME, MY DEVOTEE MAKES ALL SACRIFICES, ALL SALUTATIONS TO ME" at all times, whatever be the type of work that engages him. In brief, the evolution of the mind is the very essence of all spiritual reformation in life. Neither the conditions in which we are, our circumstances and habits, nor the available ways of life, nor our past, nor our present, none of these is a bar for evolving spiritually.

Constant awareness, maintained diligently, is the secret of success.

When thus "YOU TAKE ME AS THE SUPREME GOAL" Krishna promises Arjuna, "YOU SHALL COME TO ME". We are what we are because of our thoughts. If the thoughts are noble and divine, we become noble and divine.

Thus, in the UPANISHADS of the glorious Bhagawad Geeta, in the Science of the Eternal, in the scripture of YOGA, in the dialogue between Sri Krishna and Arjuna, the ninth discourse ends entitled:

---

* *Tat cintanam, tat kathanam,*
Anyonyam tat prabodhanam,
Etadekaparatwam ca,
Brahmabhyasam vidurbudhah – *Panchadashi* – VI-106, XIII-83

The *Yoga* of Royal Knowledge and Royal Secret

This chapter has been rightly entitled as the chapter discussing the Royal Knowledge and the Royal Secret. These two terms have been already discussed at length. Earlier in the chapter (Verse 2) we find that, since Pure Consciousness is the Knowledge, in whose light all conditioned-knowledges are made possible, this science, dealing with the Absolute, has been rightly called as the Royal-Knowledge. Elsewhere in the *Upanishads*, it has been termed as the "Knowledge of all Knowledges"* because, "having known which there is nothing more to be known", declares *Mundakopanishad*.

Om Om Om Om Om

ॐ तत्सदिति श्रीमद्‌ भगवद्‌ गीतासूपनिषत्सु ब्रह्मविद्यायां
योगशास्त्रे श्रीकृष्णार्जुनसंवादे राजविद्याराजगुह्ययोगो नाम
नवमोऽध्यायः

om tatsaditi śrīmad bhagavad gītāsu upaniṣatsu brahmavidyāyāṁ
yogaśastre śrīkṛṣṇārjuna saṁvāde rājavidyārājaguhyayogo nāma
navamo'dhyāyaḥ.

---

* *"Sarva Vidyanam Vidya" – Para-Vidya – Raja-Vidya.*

X

The Divine Glories
Introduction

IN any textbook of a systematic exposition of thought, later chapters will have their roots in earlier ones, and the continuity of narration in, and the consistency of development of the themes are both unavoidable. Although these chapters are named separately, and therefore look almost completely independent of one another, there is an imperceptible matrix of ideas holding them all together. Viewed thus, this chapter may be traced back to some dozen different verses in different earlier chapters. Of them, the most predominant and striking source is the stanza in the seventh chapter (VII-6) wherein, after describing the Higher and the Lower Nature of the Eternal, the Lord concludes "I AM THE ORIGIN AND THE DISSOLUTION OF THE WHOLE UNIVERSE"; and therefore, he adds, "BEYOND ME THERE IS NAUGHT. ALL THIS IS STRUNG IN ME, AS A ROW OF JEWELS IN A THREAD". (VII-6, 7)

Similarly, although Krishna, as the Self, Eternal and All-Pervading, is the Source of all names and forms, He has to indicate to Arjuna His exact place and worth in the comity of things and beings in the Universe.

This chapter is called the *Vibhuti Yoga* inasmuch as it describes (a) the Power or Lordship, and (b) the Pervasiveness, or Immanence of the Self. The Self is the Essence in the world of plurality as described in this chapter; therefore, we find

Krishna indicating Himself both as (1) the most prominent and Chief Factor in all classes of beings, and (2) as that Supreme Factor without which specimens belonging to each class cannot maintain themselves as existent beings. We shall notice these as we dissect the stanzas one by one to discover their individual contents.

In this chapter, we discover that Arjuna feels extremely inspired when he gets re-educated in his knowledge of the *Vedas*, through the sparkling words of Lord Krishna. The teacher in Krishna confesses that He Himself feels encouraged by Arjuna's happiness, and therefore, this chapter is added.

In this chapter, Arjuna enquires of Krishna as to how one can constantly keep in touch with the Eternal aspect of Truth, even while one is perceiving the pluralistic world and transacting with its objects (X-17). As an answer to this particular question, the rest of the chapter is packed with indications of the joyous Infinite among the joyless finite objects.

However, the chapter concludes with a cry of despair on the part of Krishna which drives home to Arjuna, the impossibility of a teacher ever exhausting the analysis of all the things and beings in the world, and indicating in each the glorious spirit, both as separate and yet not separate from matter. No electrical engineer can ever hope to exhaust all the bulbs and fans and other electrical equipments in the world, one by one, to indicate to a student of electrical engineering what exactly constitutes, in each, the equipment as separate from the electrical current. The chapter concludes: "OF WHAT AVAIL IS IT TO YOU TO KNOW ALL THESE DIVERSITIES? I EXIST SUPPORTING THE ENTIRE UNIVERSE BY A PORTION OF MYSELF".

In *Vedanta*, the Self, seemingly conditioned by, or reflected in, or functioning through, the individual mind-and-intellect is the ego (*Jiva*), limited and thwarted by its own imperfections. While, the same Eternal Self, conditioned by, reflected in, or functioning through, THE TOTAL MIND-AND-INTELLECT is the God-principle (*Ishwara*), unlimited and ever a Master of its own Perfection. If once this idea of the Self, as seen through the individual-mind and the cosmic-mind, is understood properly, both the Chapters X and XI become amply self-evident and self-explanatory.

In the tradition of democracy, the concept of a Government or the idea of a nation should give us a healthy analogy with which we can vaguely comprehend to a certain extent, the entire suggestiveness underlying this ancient *Vedantic* concept of the God-principle. In a democracy with adult franchise, every grown-up member of society has his vote to express his will and he alone can come up to govern the country who represents, in himself, the will of the majority. Such an individual may be considered as one who has identified himself with the will of the largest number of the people in that nation during that particular period of its history. One, who has been thus elected to govern, will have to rule the nation according to the demands of the people. The Government is thus created out of the powers and rights surrendered to a central pool by each individual; yet, once a Government is formed, it is very well known, how the Governors become mightier than those governed!

I, the Self, identifying with my limited intellect and mind, become the mortal ego, bound and conditioned on all sides; while I, the Self identifying with the Total-Mind-and-Intellect become the Mighty and Powerful, the Omnipotent and Omniscient God-principle, constituting in Myself the Creator (Brahma), the Sustainer (Vishnu), and the Annihilator (Maheshwara).

It is a matter of common experience that our world gets coloured by the condition of our minds. When we are happy, the world, to us, is a dance hall of light and laughter, mirth and happiness; while the same world becomes a miserable dungeon of agony and tears when our mental conditions change. Also, in each one of us, our world of success and joy or of misery and sorrow becomes completely and totally extinct whenever we are in the state of deep-sleep ; meaning, whenever our mind-intellect-equipment does not function. Classifying all these observations, it can be enunciated that "as the mind, so is the world, and where there is no mind, there is no world".

Thus, I create my world with my mind; you create your world with your mind; and he creates his world with his mind. No doubt, into the pool of my world, certain aspects and portions of the world of others creep in to overlap, for varying periods of time. Philosophically viewed, therefore, the total world of forms and beings is created, sustained, and destroyed by the number of minds totally available to cognise and to experience this whole Universe. This Total-mind includes, in itself, even the rudimentary perceptions of a 'mind' in the plant kingdom, the relatively better-developed minds and intellects of the animal kingdom, and also the well-developed mind of man. When the theory of the God-principle, as propounded by *Vedanta*, is understood completely, it appeals to the faculty of reasoning in all intelligent creatures.

The implications of this theory are vast. It not only proves and explains the omniscience and the omnipotence of God but it also lends a comprehensible import to the term generally employed in describing the Supreme as The Lord of the Universe (*Sarva loka maheshwarah*).

While listening to this discourse, Arjuna seems to have

lost himself in an experience bordering upon the transcendental. This preparation, given to Arjuna, provides a necessary mental elevation in cosmic self-expansion, without which the special power of cognition to experience the concept of the Cosmic-Man as described in the following chapter, would never have been possible.

The Blessed Lord said:

1. *Again, O mighty-armed, listen to My Supreme word; which I, wishing your welfare, will declare to you, who delight in hearing me.*

The trembling man of indecision, whom we met in Arjuna in the first chapter of the *Geeta*, has by now developed an almost incomparable inward equipoise. This inward peace that comes from an intelligent study of the Hindu philosophy is vividly brought out in the opening stanza of this chapter when Lord Krishna himself describes his disciple Arjuna, as one 'who is delighted' with what he has heard so far.

No teacher can feel sufficiently inspired to continue his discourses unless his students nourish his enthusiasm with interested 'listening'. As one understands more and more the implications of the philosophy of *Vedanta*, one cannot but come to feel an inward glow of peace and satisfaction. The Lord of the *Geeta* gets encouraged to expound his philosophy more exhaustively with a revived appetite. "AGAIN HEAR MY SUPREME WORD, WHICH I WILL DECLARE,

---

श्रीभगवानुवाच
भूय एव महाबाहो श्रृणु मे परमं वचः ।
यत्तेऽहं प्रीयमाणाय वक्ष्यामि हितकाम्यया ॥ १ ॥

śrībhagavānuvāca
bhūya eva mahābāho śṛṇu me paramaṁ vacaḥ
yatte'haṁ prīyamāṇāya vakṣyāmi hitakāmyayā 1.

BECAUSE I DESIRE YOUR WELFARE".

Here Arjuna is addressed as 'Mighty-armed' which is a reminder to the Pandava that he should be a hero in his inner life to carve out of his present, a kingdom of divine joy, which is his real heritage! It is evident that the Lord's discourse is not upon any secular subject, but it is upon the greater possibilities in man, and on how man can rediscover them in himself; for, it is said that Arjuna should listen "TO MY SUPREME WORD, WHICH I, WISHING YOUR (SPIRITUAL) WELFARE (*HITAM*) WILL NOW DECLARE".

WHY THE LORD HAS DECIDED TO CONTINUE HIS DISCOURSES IS NOW EXPLAINED:

2. *Neither the hosts of heaven, nor great RISHIS know My origin; for, in every way, I am the source of all the DEVAS and the RISHIS.*

Whenever we cannot gather knowledge from direct experience, we gather it from those who are supposed to know about it. Even this indirect method of self-education is not available in *Brahma-Vidya*, because, as the Lord says "NEITHER THE HOSTS OF HEAVEN NOR THE SEERS KNOW MY ORIGIN".

Later on (Ibid. X-5) we will have occasion to understand what actually the Lord means by the term the great Seers. It is not the men-of-Wisdom, explained in our mythology,[1] the Seven great *Rishis* starting with Bhrigu and ending with Vasishtha.

न मे विदुः सुरगणाः प्रभवं न महर्षयः ।
अहमादिर्हि देवानां महर्षीणां च सर्वशः ॥ २ ॥

na me viduḥ suragaṇāḥ prabhavaṁ na maharṣayaḥ
ahamādiri devānāṁ maharṣīṇaṁ sarvaśaḥ 2.

[1] *Sapta Rishis* – the immortal Seven Seers.

The following is a philosophical explanation of the 'Seven Seers'.

When the Infinite is seemingly identified with the Total-intellect, or Cosmic-intellect (*Mahat*), and develops thereby an egocentric personality of Its own (*Ahamkara*), It projects Itself, for Its own joy-transactions, as a world of sense objects. These sense-objects are called the five '*Tanmatras*'.[2] The '*Mahat*', the '*Ahamkara*' and the five '*Tanmatras*' together constitute the Seven *Rishis* personified in the *Puranas* under different names. These Seven *Rishis* together represent the intellectual and the mental life of man, the EFFICIENT and MATERIAL causes for all creation.

Devas do not literally mean the hosts of heaven; the word *Deva* rises from its root, meaning, 'to illumine'. The *Devas*, therefore, are the 'sense-organs' which illumine for us the world-of-objects for our innumerable experiences.

It is, therefore, clear that the Self, the Pure Consciousness, is the source of all the *DEVAS* and the great *RISHIS*, meaning that the Conscious Principle is the substratum for both the physical and mind-intellect life in each one of us. Even though they are thus sustaining themselves in Truth, they cannot 'KNOW MY ORIGIN'.

So the Consciousness, being the very SUBJECTIVE-Truth in us, can never become an OBJECT-of-perception for the sense-organs, or an OBJECT-of-feeling for the mind, or an OBJECT-of-knowing for the intellect.

IS IT THEN TRUE THAT NOBODY CAN COME TO KNOW AND REALISE THE SELF, WHICH IS THE ORIGIN

---

[2] The rudiments that constitute among themselves the five Great Elements. They are nothing but the qualities that predominate in each of the five elements; in Ether - the Sound, in Air - the Touch, in Fire - the Form, in Water - the Taste and in Earth - the Smell. Thus, the *Tanmatras* are the very 'sense-objects' themselves.

FOR OUR PHYSICAL, MENTAL AND INTELLECTUAL LIFE? TO DISPEL THIS FEAR IT IS SAID:

3. *He who amongst the mortals, knows Me as unborn and beginningless, as the great Lord of the worlds, is undeluded and is liberated from all sins.*

HE WHO KNOWS ME—not merely knowing in an emotional sweep, or even an intellectual comprehension, but it is a true and full spiritual apprehension, which comes to one during moments of one's intimate identification with the Self. The Self is to be realised as UNBORN, BEGINNINGLESS, THE GREAT LORD OF ALL THE WORLDS. These three terms, each pregnant with suggestions to those who know a little of the ancient traditions in the Hindu philosophical thought, are generally meaningless to the uninitiated. The world-of- matter is the realm of finitude, where, each being, or thing, or experience, has a beginning and an end, a birth and a death.

The Infinite cannot ever be born, inasmuch as It never expresses as Itself in any of the finite manifestations. The ghost is born, and therefore, it must also die; but it cannot be said either that the post has given birth to the ghost, or that the post has come to be born out of the ghost. The post was, is, and shall ever be. The Self is Eternal, and therefore, It is birthless; everything else is born in the Self, exists in the Self, and when all things are totally destroyed, they end in the Self. The waves are born out of the ocean but the ocean is

---

यो मामजमनादिं च वेत्ति लोकमहेश्वरम् ।
असंमूढः स मर्त्येषु सर्वपापैः प्रमुच्यते ॥ ३ ॥

yo māmajamanādiṁ ca vetti lokamaheśvaram
asammūḍhaḥ sa martyeṣu sarvapāpaiḥ pramucyate 3.

birthless. Every wave, every manifestation, has a beginning, an existence, and an end. But the essence cannot have a beginning; and therefore, in this stanza here, the Self is qualified as BEGINNINGLESS.

THE LORD OF ALL THE WORLDS (*Sarva-loka maheshwarah*)—The term 'loka' is one of the Sanskrit words which has a vast range of implications which are ignored generally by the translators who render it as the 'world'. '*Loka*' comes from a root meaning 'to experience', and therefore, the world should, in its full import, mean 'a field for experiencing'. In this sense, we make use of the word '*loka*' even in ordinary, everyday usage: 'the world of the rich', 'the world of the under-dog', 'the world of the poets', etc. In its ampler meaning, the Universe, indicated by the word '*loka*' is not only the physical world experienced by our physical equipments, but it also includes the world of feelings and the world of ideas recognised, reacted upon and experienced by all of us in our lives.

Thus, my '*loka*' is the 'field of experiences' that I revel in at all levels of my body, my mind and my intellect - and it is evident that these experiences can never be mine unless I am constantly aware of them. This Essential Factor, pure Awareness or Consciousness, without which I am dead to the world, with which I perceive the world and live in it actively, should necessarily be the Presiding Chieftain that rules with His Grace, my '*loka*'.

The Self being the same everywhere, the *Atman* that rules my world is the *Atman* that rules the worlds of all individuals. The entire universe is the sum total of the worlds of experience of each individual, and evidently, the 'ruler' that governs the entire Universe must necessarily be the Absolute Self Itself. The term 'the Lord of the worlds' is to be rightly understood thus. The Lord is not a 'tyrant over life' or a '*Sultan* of the skies', or an 'Autocrat who rules over our world'. The Self is the Lord of our experiences, just as the Sun, in the same fashion, is the Lord of our daytime world.

HE WHO KNOWS ME AS BIRTHLESS, BEGINNINGLESS AND AS THE GREAT LORD OF THE WORLDS, ends his delusion. In and through the grinning ghost that frightened me, I gain a glimpse of the wayside lamp-post, and forthwith, I go beyond my delusion and find myself released from every fear. In Hinduism, the concept of sin is not a frightening picture of some horrid inevitability. Man is not punished FOR his sins but he is punished BY his sins. Sin is a self-insulting act arising out of a misunderstanding in the sinner as to his own identity.

When one wanders away from one's own Real Nature as the Self, identifies oneself with the happenings of the world and behaves as a mass of repulsive flesh, or a bundle of throbbing emotions, or a pack of ideas, one is, in a manner, dishonouring one's Godly dignity and divine status, the One-without-a-second. Such acts and thoughts chain a person down to a pursuit of the low pleasures only, never allowing him to rise above and climb the higher peaks of real Perfection.

On rediscovering the nature of the Self and gaining thereby a perfect and complete identification with the Self, he can no longer perpetrate any more of his past 'sins'. The 'sins' in us are the carbuncles from which we suffer the pains of our limitations and the sorrows of our bondage. The moment we understand and live in the realisation that the Self is unborn and beginningless, and that It is not concerned with decaying and perishable matter, we have gained all that has to be gained, and known all that has to be known. Such an individual of True Realisation becomes himself the Lord of the worlds.

HOW IS THE SELF, THE LORD OF THE WORLD?

4. *Intellect, wisdom, non-delusion, forgiveness, truth, self-restraint, calmness, happiness, pain, birth or death, fear and also fearlessness,*

5. *Non-injury, equanimity, contentment, austerity, beneficence, fame, infamy – all these different kinds of 'qualities-of-beings' arise from Me alone.*

Continuing the general idea that the Lord is the MATERIAL cause as well as the EFFICIENT cause of the world-of-plurality within and without an individual, Krishna is enumerating in these two stanzas the various qualities expressed by the mind-and-intellect of man.

Ordinarily, when we talk of Creation, we are apt to mean only the world of physical forms. All the said qualities indicate a larger comprehensiveness of the term 'Creation' and clearly indicate that it means also our mental and our intellectual lives.

Again, men and beings are usually classified under these qualities, and each individual is bound up with his own mental qualities. As the mind, so the man. It is to be noted that here only the POSITIVE qualities are enumerated. Following the traditional style of Sanskrit commentators, we can interpret the second conjunction, the indeclinable *'cha'* as denoting the

---

बुद्धिर्ज्ञानमसंमोहः क्षमा सत्यं दमः शमः ।
सुखं दुःखं भवोऽभावो भयं चाभयमेव च ॥ ४ ॥

buddhijñārnamasammohaḥ kṣamā satyaṁ damaḥ śamaḥ
sukhaṁ duḥkhaṁ bhavo'bhāvo bhayaṁ cābhayameva ca 4.

अहिंसा समता तुष्टिस्तपो दानं यशोऽयशः ।
भवन्ति भावा भूतानां मत्त एव पृथग्विधाः ॥ ५ ॥

ahiṁsā samatā tuṣṭistapo dānaṁ yaśo'yaśaḥ
bhavanti bhāvā bhūtānāmmatta sva pṛthagvidhāḥ 5.

opposite of these qualities also. However, the Lord is directly mentioning only the positive qualities inasmuch as, in a man who has these noble qualities, his essential divinity will be more available for perception.

These different types of emotions and thoughts, which provide for each individual different patterns of life, and whip him forward to act and live in the external world accordingly - all arise from 'ME ALONE'. Whether the ghost be pleasantly smiling, or angrily grinning, or vengefully threatening, its smiles, grins and threats are all qualities that have no substratum other than the post. If the Pure Awareness were not there to illumine all the qualities in the bosom, they would have no existence for us.

These qualities are almost a complete classification of the entire world-of-beings and their fields of experiences, and therefore, as Shankara observes, we can consider these two stanzas as an exhaustive commentary upon the Self's status as the Lord of the worlds (*Sarva-loka-maheshwarah*).

6. *The seven great RISHIS, the ancient four and also the MANUS, possessed of powers like Me, were born of (My) mind; from them are these creatures in the world (originated and sustained).*

The idea which was hinted at in the second stanza is being taken up here to prove how the Seven Seers, the four *Kumaras*, and the fourteen *Manus*, are all born out of the Lord's own mind, and they together constitute the MATERIAL and the EFFICIENT causes of the world, since it is stated here FROM THEM ARE THESE CREATURES IN THE WORLD born.

महर्षय: सप्त पूर्वे चत्वारो मनवस्तथा |
मद्भावा मानसा जाता येषां लोक इमा: प्रजा: || ६ ||

maharṣayaḥ sapla pūrve catvāro manavastathā
madbhāvā mānasā jātā yeṣāṁ loke imāḥ prajāḥ 6.

THE SEVEN *RISHIS*—The personified representation of the Seven Seers, as found in the *Puranas*, when understood subjectively, are nothing but one's intellect, ego and the five sense stimuli, which, together, constitute the world experienced by each one of us (X-2).

Subjectively analysed, it is very easy for us to perceive the implication of this allegory provided by the Seven-*Rishis* picture. We know that when thoughts rise in us, they, in their individual manifestations, are incapable of disturbing us. At a certain moment, some desire in us gets concentrated, and, identifying with it, we maintain it in a steady stream of dynamic thoughts. Thus dynamised, the initial thought becomes mighty and powerful enough to destroy our peace and tranquillity, and projecting itself, creates the perceptions of, and our reactions to the world of the five sense objects. The thought-stream and its projections together supply us with both the MATERIAL and the EFFICIENT causes for our own tiny world of joys and sorrows, victories and failures, yearning and fulfilments.

THE FOUR ANCIENTS AND THE *MANUS*—*Sri* Shankara, in his commentary, reads the stanza as THE ANCIENTS, AND THE FOUR *MANUS*,* in the context of a subjective analysis, which is recommended and ably supported by the next line, wherein the Lord says that all of them are children of MY MIND.

It is described in the *Puranas*, the Brahmaji, the Creator, at the very beginning of Creation, produced out of his own mind four eternal boys (*Kumaras*), Sanatkumara, Sanaka, Sanatana, and Sanandana. The Creator in us is the life in us functioning through an 'urge-to-create' in any field. Whenever the creative urge expresses itself immediately the factors constituting the subtle-body (*Antahkarana*) express themselves and function in full

---

* And explains that the four *Savarna Manus*, out of the total of fourteen, are indicated here. These *Manus* formulated the laws of behaviour, private and public, for every one of us to be a decent person - as a member of the family, of the community, of the nation, and of the world.

vigour. When the Creator of the whole Universe comes under the 'urge-to-express', he has to maintain a constant *sankalpa*, which immediately produces a channel of 'constant thoughts' create the stuff for the 'inner-instruments'. This 'bundle of thoughts', flowing constantly, functions as the mind, intellect, ego, and *chit*. These four factors, comprising the total inner-instrument, are represented by the Eternal Boys of Wisdom, born out of the mind of the Creator, at the very beginning of his creative activity.

Thus, in one and the same stanza, the macrocosmic (*Samashti*) and the microcosmic (*Vyashti*) causes of Creation have been indicated. Macrocosmically, the Total-intellect (*Mahat*), ego (*ahamkara*), and the five rudimentary sense objects (*tanmatras*) supply the causes for the projection of the world and its sustenance, while microcosmically the 'creative-urge' in us gets fulfilled through the intervention and play of our inner equipment constituted of the intellect, mind, ego and *chit*.

The Seven Seers and the Four Ancients together indicate, thus, both the efficient and the material causes of the macrocosmic and microcosmic worlds created.

WHY SHOULD ONE UNDERSTAND THESE IMPLICATIONS OF CREATION FROM THE STANDPOINT OF THE INDIVIDUAL AND THE COSMIC MINDS? ... LISTEN:

7. *He, who in truth knows these manifold manifestations of My being (Macrocosm), and (this) YOGA-power of Mine (Microcosm), becomes established in the 'tremorless-YOGA'; there is no doubt about it.*

"He, who in reality knows these two, My *Vibhuti* and My *Yoga* gets established in the realisation of the Supreme". We find that the terms *Vibhuti* and *Yoga*, which appear in this stanza, are invariably translated as Manifold manifestation of beings (*Vibhuti*) and My power (*Yoga*).

In effect, although these translations are true, they are not efficient enough to convey the subtle and the brilliant connection between the statement and what has been indicated in the previous stanza. Macrocosmic projection of a created Universe, through the intervention of the Seven Seers, is the Absolute's own *Vibhuti*, while the microcosmic experience of a limited world, through the intervention of the mind-born 'Four Ancient *Kumaras*' is the Divine *Yoga* of the Self in each one of us. Since the Self, presiding over the destinies of the individual is Itself the Absolute that forms the substratum for the entire Universe, he who realises both the *Vibhuti* and the *Yoga* as divine expressions of the Eternal, realises the Infinite.

That this understanding of the macrocosm and its influence upon the play-of-life in the field of plurality should not be merely a professor's book-knowledge, is indicated here, when Krishna insists that the seeker must know it 'in reality' (*tattwatah*). This means that the above-mentioned knowledge is to be realised in a subjective experience, and intuitively lived, as "I am the Self".

एतां विभूतिं योगं च मम यो वेत्ति तत्त्वतः ।
सोऽविकम्पेन योगेन युज्यते नात्र संशयः ॥ ७ ॥

etāṁ vibhūtiṁ yogaṁ ca mama yo vetti tattvataḥ
so'vikampena yogena yujyate nātra saṁśayaḥ 7.

"When I play through the Seven Seers I paint the Universe, and when I play through the Four Ancients I LIVE the tearful life of an individual." It is not then very difficult for us to feel the appropriateness of the statement in the last stanza that the *Rishis*, Ancients and the Manus, all WERE BORN OF MIND. When the Self, therefore, detaches Itself from both the INDIVIDUAL-mind and the COSMIC-mind, It comes to revel in all Its Absolute glory. Identifying Itself with the COSMIC-mind It becomes the Creator (*Ishwara*) CREATING THE UNIVERSE, and identifying with the individual-mind It becomes the limited ego (*Jiva*), suffering the limited world. To know this implication and to live up to this is the tremorless-*Yoga* -- wherein a permanent and steady establishment in the experience of the Self is assured. As at many points earlier, Vyasa is making his Divine mouthpiece use the sacred word *Yoga* in a familiar and a daringly novel context, so that the awe and dread which had gathered round this blessed term may disappear. The tremorless-*Yoga* is as novel as the various definitions of *Yoga* given earlier in different verses* of the *Geeta* - the one, single, irreplaceable Bible-of-revolt in all Hindu renaissance movements.

WHAT EXACTLY IS THE TECHNIQUE BY WHICH WE CAN GET OURSELVES ESTABLISHED STEADILY AND PERMANENTLY IN THE UNBROKEN EXPERIENCE OF THE INFINITE AS OUR OWN REAL NATURE? ... LISTEN:

8. *I am the Source of All; from Me everything evolves; understanding thus, the 'wise' endowed with 'loving consciousness' worship Me.*

The difference between the microcosm and the macrocosm is the difference in the equipments through which the same Truth, the Eternal and the All-perfect, expresses.

When life surges through the Cosmic-mind, It (*Ishwara*) comes to project out the entire Universe-of-plurality; and when the same Infinite expresses through an individual-mind, it (*Jiva*) projects out the individual-world. In both these manifestations - the God-principle (*Ishwara*) and the individual ego (*Jiva*) - the Essence is one and the same, just as, for the manifestation of light-in-the-bulb and heat-in-the-heater, the energy is one and the same, i.e., electricity. In electricity, considered as pure energy, there is neither light nor heat. In the same way, in the Pure Self, in its Essential Nature, there is neither the God nor the ego. He who realises this IN REALITY, we are told, will become established in the Supreme Awareness through the tremorless-*YOGA*.*

We prepare a ball of mud of the required plasticity from a sample of mud after kneading it properly with water. The ball of mud is next put on the potter's wheel and roughly

---

अहं सर्वस्य प्रभवो मत्तः सर्वं प्रवर्तते ।
इति मत्वा भजन्ते मां बुधा भावसमन्विताः ॥ ८ ॥

ahaṁ sarvasya prabhavo mattaḥ sarvaṁ pravartate
iti matvā bhajante māṁ budhā bhāvasamanvitāḥ 8.

* i) *Samatwam Yoga Uchyate* – II-48
ii) *Yogah Karmasu Kaushalam* – II-50
iii) *Dukha-samyoga-viyogam Yogasamjnitam* – VI-23
Please read the discourses upon all the above three verses.

* More familiarly known in our scriputres as the '*Samadhi Yoga*'.

shaped. In the third stage, the pot is finished, dried and polished. And in the fourth stage, the pots so made are baked and painted. The mud can certainly insist that it is the 'origin and essence' of the pot, and that it is only in the mud that the four stages of the pot's evolution had taken place and are never divorced from it. This is true for all mud-pots at all times; none of them has any existence, growth, or development, without the mud which is the sustaining material in all of them. So too, the same Principle in its different manifestations becomes *Ishwara* and *Jiva*.

An individual, whose intellect is soaked with discriminative awareness – of the subtle difference between the cosmic and the individual – is alone capable of turning his mind away from the created world-of-objects, and towards the one and the same Subjective Reality, both in the Creator and in himself. The attitude of a mind successfully employing itself in this inward quest is being indicated here by the pregnant term 'with loving consciousness' (*Bhaava samanvitah*).

Love, or devotion, is measured by the capacity of the lover to identify himself with the beloved. In short, love is fulfilled when identification is complete, and when the devotee is capable of experiencing in himself that he is none other than the Infinite Self which, functioning through the Cosmic-mind, plays the part of the *Ishwara*, the Creator, and, which, when functioning through an individual-mind-intellect equipment, behaves as though It is the *Jiva*, the limited ego.

What has been asserted courageously in the previous stanza has been systematically developed here into a technique by which the above-mentioned experience can be brought within the intimate personal comprehension of every student.

9. *With their minds wholly resting in Me, with their senses absorbed in Me, enlightening one another, and ever speaking of Me, they are satisfied and delighted.*

WITH A MIND WHOLLY TURNED TO ME (*Mat-chittah*)—only with a mind completely integrated into steady single-pointedness can the seeker meditate efficiently upon the Supreme. Single-pointedness is lost if the mind is entertaining more than one idea. To remember electricity in all the bulbs, fans and heaters involves no deliberate effort; it is the very nature of our knowledge about it. To remember that all mud-pots are made of mud, we need not strain ourselves. Similarly, once the intellect is soaked with a convincing realisation that the Essence behind the God-principle (*Ishwara*) and the individual ego (*Jiva*) is one and the same, whatever feelings may arise in the mind or whatever thoughts may arise in the intellect, it is not very difficult for the Truth-seeker to remain constantly aware of the Conscious Principle behind them all and this constant 'awareness of the Self' is indicated here by the term '*Mat-chittah*'.

WITH THEIR SENSES ABSORBED IN ME (*Mat-gata-pranah*)—The term *Prana* is not to be translated merely as 'Vital-air'; it constitutes the five different manifestations of life* available for recognition in any living body. Here, however, the term *Prana* is used mainly to indicate the five sense-organs. These organs-of-perception are the only peep-

मच्चित्ता मद्गतप्राणा बोधयन्तः परस्परम् ।
कथयन्तश्च मां नित्यं तुष्यन्ति च रमन्ति च ॥ ९ ॥

maccittā madgataprāṇā bodhayantaḥ parasparam
kathayantaśya māṁ nityaṁ tuṣyanti ca ramanti ca 9.

* Five in number, each presiding over a definite physiological function within the living body.

windows through which the mind wanders out and the world-of-objects enters the mind on its return to the bosom. *Vedanta* never asks the seekers to retire, or to run away as fugitives, from the fields of sense objects - which can never be possible as long as we are alive. The path of intellectual pursuit is the path of discrimination, a process through which we can so regulate and train our thoughts that, at the impact of any object of the world, it is immediately reminded of the Eternal Consciousness, without which the object would not have been illumined for the mind's experience.

DISCUSSING WITH ONE ANOTHER—When students with a common intellectual interest come together and discuss among themselves their pet subject, they not only crystallise their knowledge, but often achieve a reassuring degree of confident knowledge in place of what was till then some stray information gathered from silent books. This technique of common discussion has been tirelessly emphasised in *Vedanta* in its very definition of *Brahma-Vidya** where it upholds it as one of its most important limbs of *Sadhana*.

A true seeker is he who maintains in himself a constant remembrance of the Conscious Principle in him; whatever be the activities of the mind, or of the sense organs. He maintains this channel of thinking steadily through mutual discussions on, and a constant seeking of, the *Atman*. Such seekers ultimately experience a scintillating joy lubricating life's wheels as they roll along their stony path. In the *Upanishads* the same idea has been beautifully put by using a similar pair of words, 'sports' (*kreedami*) and 'revels' (*ramanti*). Here, however, the former word is replaced by an equally efficient term to indicate the meaning (*tushyanti*).

Even while walking the path-of-perfection, Lord Krishna asserts that the seekers on the path-of-discrimination will

* Read footnote to stanza IX-34 the verse quoted from *Panchadashi*.

come to experience and live a sense of CONTENTMENT AND DELIGHT. These two provide the healthy mental attitude, generating the required inward atmosphere in which spiritual progress can be guaranteed. The discontented, ever-mourning seekers, painting a miserable picture of mental stagnation and intellectual destitution, are not the blessed ones who will gain easy entry into the portals of joyless joy and silent laughter, the Eternal Goal to be realised.

HAVING REACHED THIS STAGE OF PROGRESS IN THEIR MARCH, FROM WHERE DO THE SEEKERS GET GUIDANCE AND STRENGTH TO FULFIL THEIR PILGRIMAGE? ... LISTEN:

10. *To the ever-steadfast, worshipping Me with love, I give the BUDDHI-YOGA, by which they come to Me.*

Withdrawal of one's identifications with the perceived world-of-objects, or the world-of-thoughts, or the world-of-ideas, can be successful only when one has discovered in oneself some other all-consuming thought to serve as an efficient substitute, yielding a satisfactory quota of absorbing happiness. The Bliss-Absolute-Self has enough captivating charm to engage the human attention entirely, and therefore, to the extent an individual gets attached to the Truth; to that extent he gains detachment from the painful embrace of the false. This *Vedantic* Truth is indicated, when Lord Krishna, as though in one and the same breath, states AND SERVING ME WITH AFFECTION, INVOKING ME WITH

तेषां सततयुक्तानां भजतां प्रीतिपूर्वकम् ।
ददामि बुद्धियोगं तं येन मामुपयान्ति ते ॥ १० ॥

teṣāṁ satatayuktānāṁ bhajatāṁ prītipūrvakam
dadāmi buddhiyogaṁ taṁ yena māmupayānti te 10.

AFFECTIONATE DEVOTION.

We have already indicated that love means identification. To the extent the ego identifies with the Self, to that extent is one a devotee of the Truth, and when one becomes steadfast in It, one comes really to invoke (*Bhaja*) the divinity that is now dormant in the bosom.

To those individuals, who are steadily contemplating upon the Self in an atmosphere of love, delight and contentment, identifying themselves with the Infinite – to them the Lord promises, "I give that *Buddhi Yoga* BY WHICH THEY CAN COME UNTO ME".

This term *Buddhi Yoga* already mentioned earlier (II-39) has been described as 'the right knowledge gained through meditation upon the Infinite Nature of the Self'. In the context of its use here, we may say that a devotee striving diligently, as explained above, will be blessed with an intellectual contact with, or comprehension of Reality. No doubt, we do not mean that the intellect can comprehend the Infinite. We are merely borrowing a familiar phrase from the realm of finite experiences. As long as what we have comprehended intellectually is not contradicted by any other different comprehension, we are capable of experiencing what we have comprehended, beyond all traces of doubt. Similarly, the power of an intuitive awareness of Reality comes only to such seekers in whom the maturity of a steady and continued contemplation upon the Self has come about.

When, through the above process of bringing the mind to quietude, a meditator has succeeded in arresting the mind's agitations (*Vikshepa*), and has consequently lifted the veiling (*Avarana*) from his intellect, he comes to the State of Transcendental Experience (*Samadhi*), which is the fulfilment of *Buddhi Yoga*.

THROUGH THIS *'BUDDHI YOGA'* WHAT EXACTLY DOES THE LORD PROVIDE FOR THE SEEKER? ... LISTEN:

11. *Out of mere compassion for them, I, dwelling within their hearts, destroy the darkness born of ignorance by the luminous Lamp-of-Knowledge* ?

A thing existing in the outside world may sometimes be veiled from our perception because; we need certain favourable conditions for its full perception. In order to hear a sound, the sound produced must have the necessary frequency and the sound waves must also reach the eardrum of the listener. Similarly, it is not sufficient that an object be in front of the eyes to give us the perception of it; it must be bathed in a beam of light, and only then can the eyes recognise it.

If I am groping in the darkness for a key that is on my table, and somebody switches the light on, I can say that he, with his kindly act, has brought me to the key. It is absurd to assume that the light has created the key.

Following this analogy, the Self that already exists in us, now ducking, as it were, behind conditions not favourable for its cognition, gets unveiled when these unfavourable conditions are removed. This negative atmosphere in our bosom that screens the Self is indicated here by the term THE DARKNESS BORN OF IGNORANCE. Even in the darkness of ignorance, remember, the Self is abiding; only it is not available for our intimate subjective experience. When the seekers, who have established themselves in the above-

---

तेषामेवानुकम्पार्थमहमज्ञानजं तमः ।
नाशयाम्यात्मभावस्थो ज्ञानदीपेन भास्वता ॥ ११ ॥

teṣāmevānukampārthamahamajñānajaṁ tamaḥ
nāśayāmyātmabhāvastho jñānadīpena bhāsvatā 11.

mentioned 'constant awareness of the Supreme', master the *Buddhi Yoga*, they become fit for the final experience of their real identity with the Self.

Earlier, we mentioned that *Buddhi Yoga* amounts to the *samadhi*-experience, even though there is yet a thin film of egocentric experience-of-Bliss. In this stanza, we have a description of how, from the *Savikalpa*, the seeker is transported, unaware, as though by the intervention of some Divine Grace, into the consummate *Nirvikalpa* experience of the Infinite. In fact, upto the *Savikalpa* alone is the realm of conscious self-effort, and even the *Buddhi Yoga* comes 'from above' - meaning, it comes not as a result of any deliberate action, but is a spontaneous 'partial revelation' when the density of the mist between the ego and the Self is thinned. The final phase experienced when the mist of ignorance is completely lifted is Self-revelation which comes in Its own Light.

A radium-dialled watch is kept on the table in a dark room. In the enveloping darkness I am searching for the watch. As I remove the various papers and books that have accumulated on the table, suddenly I come to recognise, by its own light, the watch so earnestly sought. The self-effulgent Truth, when hidden behind the fumes of ignorance, may, for the time being, appear as though non-existent. When the enveloping ignorance is removed, Its own Self-effulgence is sufficient to illumine it.

When the darkness of ignorance is destroyed by the luminous lamp-of knowledge, the Self stands revealed in its own glory as the One-without-a-second, All-pervading, and All-full. This act of Self-revelation is undertaken and performed by the Lord, the Self, who ever abides in the heart of his very devotees. This kindly act of revealing the Self is undertaken 'in a spirit of compassion', in fact, towards Itself. When I am tired of walking, I sit on the roadside in my pilgrimage, out of compassion for myself.

This compassion cannot be directly invoked unless the seeker pays the price for it. In day-time, when I open the windows of my room, the sunlight, 'out of compassion', illumines the room for me; and, we know that the sunlight has neither the freedom to withdraw this compassion so long as the windows are open, nor has it the capacity to show its compassion before the windows are opened. In short, the sunlight is invoked the moment, the object which obstructs the sunlight is removed.

Similarly, when a seeker, through the above-mentioned processes, comes to deserve *Buddhi Yoga*, and practises it diligently, he succeeds in removing from himself all the veils of ignorance which are nothing but his own mental agitations caused by the cloudiness of his intellect. The self-effulgent Self then spontaneously reveals Itself, in Its own light. Lightning needs no other light to illumine it when it passes from one mass of clouds to the neighbouring clouds.

The instruction-portion for the highest vocation in life, viz., self-development and Self-realisation, concludes here, and yet, Arjuna is not satisfied, and is raising his doubt here requesting the Lord to help him gain a confirmation through actual experience.

HAVING HEARD THUS BOTH THE *VIBHUTI* AND *YOGA* OF THE LORD, DESCRIBED SO ELABORATELY IN THE FOUR-RUNNING VERSES, ARJUNA ASKS:

Arjuna said:

12. *You are the Supreme BRAHMAN, the Supreme Abode, the Supreme Purifier, Eternal, Divine PURUSHA, the God of all gods, Unborn, Omnipresent.*

13. *All the RISHIS have thus declared You, as also the DEVA-RISHI Narada, so also Asita, Devala and Vyasa; and now the same You Yourself say to me.*

Arjuna confesses that he had already been taught, through the *Vedic* passages, that the great seers of old had indicated the INFINITE, the ETERNAL, through suggestive phraseologies, such as "THE SUPREME *BRAHMAN*, THE SUPREME ABODE, THE SUPREME PURIFIER, THE ETERNAL *BRAHMAN*, THE SELF-LUMINOUS *PURUSHA*, THE FIRST *DEVA*, THE BIRTHLESS AND THE ALL-PERVADING". In all these cases he had heard them only as attributes of the Truth. So when he heard in his own presence, the same phrases used by Krishna, in the first person singular, he, the son of Kunti, feels lost, not knowing how to comprehend that Krishna, his charioteer, is the Source of the Whole Universe!

अर्जुन उवाच
परं ब्रह्म परं धाम पवित्रं परमं भवान् ।
पुरुषं शाश्वतं दिव्यमादिदेवमजं विभुम् ॥ १२ ॥

arjuna uvāca
paraṁ brahma paraṁ dhāma pavitraṁ paramaṁ bhavān
puruṣaṁ śāśvataṁ divyamādidemajaṁ vibhum 12.

आहुस्त्वामृषयः सर्वे देवर्षिर्नारदस्तथा ।
असितो देवलो व्यासः स्वयं चैव ब्रवीषि मे ॥ १३ ॥

āhustvāmṛṣayaḥ sarve devarṣinārradastathā
asito devalo vyāsaḥ svayaṁ caiva bravīṣi me 13.

A practical man-of-the-world as Arjuna was, he needed more data, and we shall discover that in order to satisfy this demand, Krishna supplies enough information in this very same chapter. But, instead of satisfying Arjuna, it only sharpens his curiosity and compels him to demand from Krishna an experimental demonstration, which also is provided by Krishna in the following chapter (Chapter XI).

The ancient Seers mentioned here, Narada, Asita, Devala, and Vyasa, cannot be very familiar to the students of the *Upanishads*. Vyasa, perhaps, deliberately quotes these *Rishis* mentioned in his *Puranas*.

Arjuna acknowledged and recognised these phrases, indicating the attributes of the Lord, only as empty and purposeless words, though they had come from accepted great teachers. His actual surprise was clearly expressed in his words 'SO ALSO YOU YOURSELF REPEAT TO ME'. Here the occasion for Arjuna's staggering confusion was, how his own contemporary, Lord Krishna – a living creature standing right in front of him, whom he knew all these years, and was even related to – could Himself be the Infinite, the Supreme, the Birthless, and the All-pervading.

Arjuna looks at Krishna with his physical eyes and he sees only Krishna's physical structure. Krishna has been declaring Himself as the pure Self throughout the *Geeta* and not as a living member of the society. '*Sri* Krishna *Paramatman*' is the teacher in the *Geeta* and not the son of Vasudeva, or the lover of the *gopis*. Arjuna could not comprehend Krishna-the-Spirit, in his preoccupation with Krishna-the-friend, Krishna-the-lover, Krishna-the-dependable man of intellect and diplomacy. Hence the Pandava prince's wonderment and confusion.

THE FOLLOWING IS GIVEN TO BRING OUT CLEARLY THE ATTITUDE OF THE SEEKER IN ARJUNA WHEN HE ASKS THIS QUESTION:

14. *I believe all this that You say to me as true, O Keshava; verily, O Blessed Lord, neither the DEVAS nor the DANAVAS know Your manifestation (identity).*

Here Arjuna exposes himself and expresses his unfaltering faith in his teacher and confesses "I REGARD ALL THAT YOU SAY TO ME AS TRUTH". *'Keshava'* is one who removes all sorrows of those who have surrendered to him . Even though he accepts as truth all that Krishna says, he cannot comprehend the significance of the Lord's declarations. In short, Arjuna admits here that his heart is satisfied and is overflowing with faith and belief but his intellect is starved and thirsty.

The thirst to know, under which the famished personality of Arjuna groans, is echoed in the second half of the second line, when he admits that NEITHER THE DEVAS NOR THE *DANAVAS* KNOW YOUR PERSONALITY. The *'Danavas'* are the sons of *Danu*, and frequently challenge the heaven, obstruct the sacrifices, and lead generally an undivine life. *'Devas'* are highly sensitive denizens of the heaven who are described in the *Puranas* as persons who have subtler perceptions, stronger emotions and mightier intellectual comprehensions than the mortals have.

Subjectively, *'Devas'* stand for the nobler and the higher comprehensions in us, and the *'Danavas'* for the hosts of negative urges. Arjuna, the son of Kunti, is expressing his

---

सर्वमेतदृतं मन्ये यन्मां वदसि केशव ।
न हि ते भगवन्व्यक्तिं विदुर्देवा न दानवा: ॥ १४ ॥
sarvametadṛtaṁ manye yanmāṁ vadasi keśava
na hi te bhagavanvyaktiṁ vidurdevā na dānavāḥ 14.

despair that the IDENTITY of the Self can be fixed up neither by the subtlest and the noblest of our perceptions, nor can we apprehend this Self through our *Danava*-like challenge to possess, to acquire, to investigate and to know. Neither the good in us can embrace the Truth, nor can the bad in us challenge and bring up the Truth as an opposing force right in front of us. There are only two methods of meeting another being or thing; either as a friend or as a foe, either as something that we like or as something that we abhor. In neither way can we come to apprehend the individuality, the total personality (*Vyakti*) of the Self – It being the subject, both in Its expression as an individual (*Yoga*) and in Its expansion as the cosmic (*Vibhuti*).

IF NONE CAN KNOW THE TRUTH, WHY IS ARJUNA ASKING KRISHNA TO EXPLAIN? WHAT EXACTLY IS THE SPECIAL QUALITY THAT ENABLES HIM TO EXPLAIN THAT WHICH NONE ELSE CAN EVEN KNOW?

15. *Verily, You Yourself know Yourself by Yourself, O PURUSHOTTAMA (Supreme PURUSHA), O Source of beings, O Lord of beings, O God of gods, O Ruler of the world.*

This stanza indicates how Krishna is capable of explaining the Supreme which is not known by the denizens of the heaven or the hoards of the other kingdom. The Self is, of course, not known as an 'object' through the intervention of our instruments of knowing, nor can It be apprehended as the 'subject' – through either the best, or the worst in us. But, at

---

स्वयमेवात्मनात्मानं वेत्थ त्वं पुरुषोत्तम ।
भूतभावन भूतेश देवदेव जगत्पते ॥ १५ ॥
svāyamevātmanātmānaṁ vettha tvaṁ puruṣottama
bhūtabhāvana bhūteśa devadeva jagatpate 15.

the same time, the Self being Awareness, It in Itself is Knowledge – and to 'know' Knowledge, no other knowledge is needed. Therefore, it is said by Arjuna "YOU YOURSELF KNOW YOURSELF BY YOURSELF".

In the *Sankhyan* philosophy, the Spark-of-Life in each individual is called the *Purusha*, in whose presence, the matter-envelopments constituting *Prakriti*, become vitalised. Here Krishna is addressed as *Purushottama* meaning the Self of all selves, the One-without-a-second. In the *Geeta*, the term *Purushottama* is sometimes used as the 'most glorious of men' and sometimes in the purely technical usage as the Supreme Self.

Lord Krishna is now being recognised and glorified by Arjuna as the Pure *Brahman*, when he addresses Him as 'THE SOURCE OF BEINGS, THE LORD OF BEINGS, THE *DEVA* OF *DEVAS*, AND THE RULER OF THE WORLD'. The essential stuff in any object is the ruler and maintainer of its qualities. The quality of gold rules over all the qualities of various gold ornaments whatever their shape, design, polish, etc. More than this is the controlling and the ruling power of the Consciousness in our lives, inasmuch as, without Consciousness, we know nothing, can do nothing. An awareness or knowledge of a thing or an event is possible only when the mental and intellectual disturbances caused by it are illumined by the Pure Consciousness.

AFTER THE ABOVE INTRODUCTORY WORDS, EXPRESSING HIS SENSE OF WONDER, REVERENCE, AND DEVOTION, ARJUNA IS NOW EXPRESSING DIRECTLY HIS INTELLECTUAL DEMAND TO THE LORD:

16. *You should indeed, without reserve, tell me of Your Divine glories by which You exist pervading all these worlds.*

The Prince is convinced that the Lord is the Essence without which the multiple worlds cannot exist. At the same time, when he looks out into the world through his familiar instruments of the intellect, mind and body, he recognises nothing but ideas, feelings and objects; and they are anything but divine.

When a building is illuminated on a ceremonial occasion, we see many points of light emanating from the innumerable coloured bulbs of varying intensity, but, when we are told that all of them are sustained and fed by the same electricity, it would be quite natural for the ignorant to demand that he be shown the electricity in each of its manifestations! As the Cosmic-man (*Ishwara*), the Lord is both Transcendental (*Vibhuti*), and Immanent (*Yoga*), in all names and forms that constitute *Saṃsara*. This can be felt by a heart of faith but cannot be comprehended by the intellect, even if it be sharp. Naturally, Arjuna asked Krishna for an exhaustive discourse upon YOUR COSMIC-GLORY, *VIBHUTI*, BY WHICH, FILLING ALL THESE WORLDS, YOU EXIST. Arjuna, being a man-of-action and supremely practical-minded, wanted to gather sufficient data for his intellect to ponder over, classify and understand It.

IS IT MERELY INTELLECTUAL CURIOSITY IN ARJUNA THAT MADE HIM ASK THIS QUESTION? ... LISTEN:

वक्तुमर्हस्यशेषेण दिव्या ह्यात्मविभूतयः ।
याभिर्विभूतिभिर्लोकानिमांस्त्वं व्याप्य तिष्ठसि ॥ १६ ॥

vaktumarhasyaśeṣeṇa divyā hyātmavibhūtayaḥ
yābhirvibhūtibhirlokānimāṁstvaṁ vyāpya tiṣṭhasi 16.

17. *How shall I, ever-meditating, know You, O YOGIN? In what aspects or things, O Blessed Lord, are You to be thought of by me?*

HOW AM I TO MEDITATE UPON THEE, SO THAT I MAY COME?—The goal of a seeker is to KNOW the Truth in his own personal experience, while he is in an intimate identification with It. The *Geeta* was advocating, so far, not a life of retirement, for purposes of quiet meditation, in solitary caves, on the banks of some river, all alone! Krishna's call to man was a call to duty, the call of work, the call of living the God-experience in and through life. *Geeta,* the scripture, we should not forget, was declared in the Mahabharata battlefield at a moment when the world of that time was facing the greatest known historical crisis, both secular and sacred.

Arjuna has been completely converted into accepting the *Geeta* as Religion of Right-Action. This is indicated especially when Arjuna addresses Krishna in this stanza as 'O *Yogin'*- the greatest *Karma Yogin* that ever freely lived in the thickest of life, yet, never let himself down from the Consciousness of the Divine Essence.

Moreover, he makes it very clear why he has requested Krishna to explain 'without reserve', His Cosmic-Stature. Arjuna asks: 'IN WHAT FORMS ARE YOU TO BE THOUGHT OF BY ME?' Even while living life and meeting its problems, if one were to remember constantly the Divine Presence everywhere, one must know exactly where to see It, among the individual objects of the world, among the combinations of things and in the community of beings.

कथं विद्यामहं योगिंस्त्वां सदा परिचिन्तयन्।
केषु केषु च भावेषु चिन्त्योऽसि भगवन्मया ॥ १७ ॥

kathaṁ vidyāmahaṁ yogiṁstvāṁ sadā paricintayan
keṣu keṣu ca bhāveṣu cintyo'si bhagavanmayā 17.

STATING AGAIN PRECISELY WHAT HE WANTS KRISHNA TO EXPLAIN, ARJUNA MAKES IT CLEAR THAT EVEN IF THE ANSWERS BE RATHER LENGTHY, HE WILL NOT FEEL TIRED OF LISTENING TO THEM AND UNDERSTANDING THEM ALL:

18. *Tell me again, in detail, O Janardana, of your YOGA-power and Immanent glory; for I do not feel satisfied by hearing your (life-giving and so) nectar-like speech.*

A student of philosophy – and for that matter, a true student of any knowledge – should have, first of all, an insatiable thirst to understand, to know, and to appreciate. Without this appetite, no knowledge can be digested by the student with profit. This is especially so in the SUBJECTIVE SCIENCE of self-development. For, here, as nowhere else, the knowledge gained is not only to be digested and assimilated, but lived intensively. Therefore, anxiety to listen (*Jijnasa*) has been recognised as one of the noblest qualities, unavoidable for a fit student in *Vedanta*, if he is TO BE ASSURED OF ANY PROGRESS on the path-of-Knowledge.

Arjuna, the Pandava Prince, had this noble trait to a large extent, for he confesses, 'I AM NEVER SATISFIED WITH LISTENING TO THE NECTARINE WORDS OF YOUR DISCOURSES'. No doubt, it is true; *satsanga* has a chastening effect upon all intelligent and interested listeners. This intoxication, vicariously experienced by the students when a true teacher discourses upon the Truth, is only a temporary

---

विस्तरेणात्मनो योगं विभूतिं च जनार्दन ।
भूयः कथय तृप्तिर्हि श्रृण्वतो नास्ति मेऽमृतम् ॥ १८ ॥

vistareṇātmano yogaṁ vibhūtiṁ ca janārdana
bhūyaḥ kathaya tṛptirhi śṛṇvato nāsti me'mṛtam 18.

exhilaration, a passing mood of false peace, which cannot stand in good stead when the student is left all alone by himself.

And yet, however volatile it may be, it can enchant the new initiates, and some, like Arjuna, may become addicted to it. This state of fascination for hearing more and more spiritual discourses is amply indicated here. Though this is not the end, this is a good beginning, no doubt, and those who feel a fulfilment in the study of philosophy are certainly much nobler than the thousands who cannot even stand a philosophical discourse, discussing the Nature of the Divine!!

THE TIRELESS MISSIONARY IN KRISHNA, WITH MOTHERLY PATIENCE, ANSWERS ARJUNA:

The Blessed Lord said:

19. *Alas! Now I will declare to you My Divine glories, immanent, in their prominence; O best of the Kurus, there is no end to the details of My extent.*

The elaborate and exhaustive reply of Krishna, which forms the bulk of this chapter, explains the exact identity of the Self in individual beings and things and in the combination of things and beings. It must be carefully noted that in the following stanzas, while he explains his Immanence (*Yoga*) and Transcendence (*Vibhuti*), he is very careful to indicate

---

श्रीभगवानुवाच
हन्त ते कथयिष्यामि दिव्या ह्यात्मविभूतयः ।
प्राधान्यतः कुरुश्रेष्ठ नास्त्यन्तो विस्तरस्य मे ॥ १९ ॥

śrībhagavānuvāca
hanta te kathayiṣyāmi divyā hyātmavibhūtayaḥ
prādhānyataḥ kuruśreṣṭha nāstyanto vistarasya me 19.

two factors at one and the same time: (1) His Supreme importance in individual things, and (2) the fact that without Him none of the constituent members of an assemblage, or of a community, will have any synchronised existence or organised life.

The word 'alas' (*hanta*) with which the section opens, expresses the Divine Master's loving sympathy and anxious consideration for Arjuna's seeming incapacity to realise in himself THAT which is ever the nearest to him. The usual translation 'O *Kurushreshtha*' (*hanta Kurushreshtha*) cannot be accepted without the sacrifice of a volume of significance inherent in that exclamation – *hanta* meaning 'alas'.

Even though there is no end to the infinite variety of the Self's manifestations in plurality – where all the time It gets projected out, either through the Total-mind (*Ishwara*), or through the individual-mind (*Jiva*) – the All-merciful One undertakes the impossible, out of His infinite kindness for His disciple, Arjuna, who has totally surrendered unto Him. He admits that 'there is no bound to my extent', and yet, He undertakes to explain to Arjuna His All-pervading Power-Divine, only those glories that are most important.

In the physical world also it is true that sunlight gets reflected from all objects equally, be it a dull stone, or a mirror; but in the mirror, the reflection is more clear, and effectively brilliant. Similarly, the Lord promises that He will indicate through very carefully chosen examples, the vital spots and instances at which the Divinity manifests itself the clearest.

BEFORE WE ENTER INTO THIS DISCUSSION, YOU HAD BETTER LISTEN TO THE FUNDAMENTAL TRUTH, SAYS THE LORD, AND PROCEEDS:

20. *I am the Self, O Gudakesha, seated in the hearts of all beings;*
I am the Beginning, the Middle and also the End of all beings.

I AM THE SELF THAT EXISTS IN THE HEART OF ALL BEINGS—This is a general statement with which Krishna opens his entire discourse. A real master of research who is trained well to be a scientific thinker starts a discussion upon his pet subject of study and experience by summarising his entire talk in a general statement. Later on, he will work at the warp and the woof of his descriptions, and at the logical reasoning for the elaboration of his theme, and will, of necessity, come back to the same statement at the conclusion of his talks. Here also we find, in the last stanza of this chapter, how Krishna concludes with the same thought, more powerfully expressed, "I EXIST SUPPORTING THIS WHOLE BY A PORTION OF MYSELF".

If, in the first half of the verse it is declared that Krishna, as the Self in all, is the essence in the world of multiplicity, the same idea is expressed in other words, in the second line of the verse, "I AM THE BEGINNING, THE MIDDLE, AND ALSO THE END OF ALL BEINGS". The world of things and beings is essentially a projection of the mind; the world outside is only the Infinite, misinterpreted by the finite mind. Therefore, this idea can be understood subjectively, as referring to the world-of-thoughts also. Every thought rises from the Consciousness, and when it dies away, it merges back to leave behind nothing but Consciousness. There can be no thought where there is no Consciousness. Later on also

---

अहमात्मा गुडाकेश सर्वभूताशयस्थित: ।
अहमादिश्च मध्यं च भूतानामन्त एव च ॥ २० ॥
ahamātmā guḍākeśa sarvabhūtāśayasthitaḥ
ahamādiśca madhyaṁ ca bhūtānāmanta eva ca 20.

we shall find the same idea forcefully repeated (X-32) and Krishna never seems to tire of repeating this great Truth.

THE FOLLOWING ARE THE METHODS OF MEDITATING UPON THE SELF WHILE LIVING AMONG THE ENDLESS VARIETIES OF OBJECTS AND BEINGS THAT CONSTITUTE THE WORLD OF PERCEPTIONS:

21. *Among the (twelve) ADITYAS I am Vishnu; among luminaries, the radiant Sun; I am Marichi among the MARUTS; among asterisms, the Moon am I.*

OF *ADITYAS* I AM VISHNU—In the *Vedic* tradition, *Adityas*, described in some places as five, and in other places as six, are the children born of Aditi. Later on, the traditional belief considered twelve *Adityas*, each representing one of the twelve months of the year. In the Vishnu-*Purana*, however, we read that Vishnu is one of these twelve *Adityas*, and He is described therein, as the most important amongst the whole lot.

OF THE LUMINARIES I AM THE RADIANT SUN—Modern physics admits that the Sun is the source of all energy. Naturally, the phrase stands amply self-explained. The Self is the source of all energy wherever it is seen manifested.

OF THE WINDS I AM MARICHI—In *Vedic* verses, *Maruts* are the sons of *Rudra* and the *Rig Veda* mentions *Marichi* as the chief among them. In *Vedic* lore, the *Maruts* represent the presiding deity of the storms, wind and breeze – in short, air-in-motion.

आदित्यानामहं विष्णुर्ज्योतिषां रविरंशुमान् ।
मरीचिर्मरुतामस्मि नक्षत्राणामहं शशी ॥ २१ ॥

ādityānāmahaṁ viṣṇurjtotiṣāṁ raviraṁśumān
marīcirmarutāmasmi nakṣatrāṇāmahaṁ śaśī 21.

OF THE ASTERISMS I AM THE MOON—the Sanskrit term *'Nakshatras'*, as used in Indian astronomy, indicates the asterisms strewn on the Moon's path. Conceiving exclusively thus the route of the Moon in the Universe, the line may be interpreted as expressing the Lord's glory, inasmuch as, among the asterisms the Moon is the controller, the regulator; and in splendour, the most wondrous of all of them.

But we could as well accept the word *'Nakshatras'*, in its common understanding, as the endless twinkling little stars that we see studded in the night-sky. There are commentators, who go a step further, and consider the word as representing all 'lights of the night'. This also is an acceptable interpretation, which can convey to us a wealth of suggestions to ponder over and meditate upon. The Self is as incomparably glorious, soothing and pleasant as the moon is in the entire world-of-lights that illumines the night, from the modest hut to the Parliament House.

It is to be remembered that in this series of twenty-two stanzas, Lord Krishna is trying to supply the seekers with seventy-five items of thought for helping those who are on the path-of-Knowledge, to meditate upon and intensify their integration and sharpen their single-pointedness. These are seventy-five independent exercises in meditation.

22. *Among the VEDAS, I am the Sama-VEDA; I am Vasava among the gods; among the senses I am the mind; and I am the intelligence among living beings.*

वेदानां सामवेदोऽस्मि देवानामस्मि वासवः ।
इन्द्रियाणां मनश्चास्मि भूतानामस्मि चेतना ॥ २२ ॥
vedānāṁ sāmavedo'smi devānāmasmi vāsavaḥ
indriyāṇā manaścāsmi bhūtānāmasmi cetanā 22.

OF ALL THE *VEDAS* I AM THE *SAMA-VEDA*—The bulk of the *Sama-Veda* is nothing but the essence of the *Rig-Veda* and the latter is considered as the most important of all the four *Vedas*. In *Chandogya Upanishad*, the *Sama-Veda* has been beautifully glorified. Again, in *Sama-Veda*, there is the added joy of music, inasmuch as, the *Samans* are to be sung in complicated tunes, the melody and rhythm of which are evidences revealing a mighty art that has been exquisitely developed by our ancients. Through the beauty of the comparison, we may read that Krishna is (I am) the Infinite Essence tuned to music, as *Rig-Veda Mantras* are in the *Samans*.

OF THE *DEVAS* I AM *VASAVA*—Among the denizens of heaven, *Vasava* is King Indra. It is interesting to note that according to the Hindu concept, there is the highest standard of living imaginable in heaven, but even among its denizens there are the 'haves' and the 'have-nots'. Individuals who perform meritorious acts reach heaven to enjoy the wealth of goodness so acquired, and therefore, one who has acquired a larger wealth of merits while living HERE, should necessarily come to enjoy THERE a subtler joy and a life of greater satisfaction. Of such lives, the most powerful and mighty, the most splendid and luxurious life will necessarily be of Indra. The Self is as Indra among the Gods, ruling over the others, controlling and directing them and organising their lives so that they may enjoy the highest standard of living.

OF THE SENSE-ORGANS I AM THE MIND—The above phrase that the Self is INDRA among the GODS itself contains the subjective idea to all those who are well fed upon the *Upanishadic* lore, that It is the mind among the *Indriyas*. The term 'Indra',* in Sanskrit can also be dissolved as the King of the sense-organs. We have earlier mentioned that *Devas*, since the word means 'to illumine', are the sense-organs, and, among them, naturally, the mind is the patron and the controller without which the sense-organs will not have their play in any intelligent field of activity.

Of all things created in the world, the most magnificent and wondrous item is the mysterious power, called the 'intelligence', which has not yet been brought within the understanding of modern scientists beyond certain vague and fanciful theories.

23. *And among the RUDRAS I am Sankara; among the YAKSHAS and RAKSHASAS I am the Lord of Wealth (KUBERA); among the VASUS I am Pavaka (AGNI); and among the mountains I am the MERU.*

OF *RUDRAS* I AM SHANKARA—The concept of *Rudra*, as the deity of destruction, is to be recognised by every student of life because destruction is a necessary precedent to every subsequent construction. The flower must die to yield its place to the fruit. The fruit must perish for the seeds to come out. The seeds must rot to bring forth the seedling. Thus, in every progress there is a continuous stream of constructive destruction. This is recognised by the subtlest thinkers that were ever born among men, the *Rishis*, and in their full understanding they fearlessly respected and adored the blessed deity of creative destruction -- Sankara.*

रुद्राणां शंकरश्चास्मि वित्तेशो यक्षरक्षसाम् ।
वसूनां पावकश्चास्मि मेरुः शिखरिणामहम् ॥ २३ ॥

rudrāṇāṁ śaṅkaraścāsmi vitteśo yakṣarakṣasām
vasūnām pāvakaścāsmi meruḥ śikhariṇāmaham 23.

* *'Indriyanam raja-Indrah'*

* *'Sham Karoti iti Shamkarah'*: He who does *kalyana* (*sham*) is Shankara.

I AM THE TREASURER OF WEALTH (KUBERA) AMONG THE *YAKSHAS* AND *RAKSHASAS*—The Chancellor of the Exchequer in heaven is described in the *Puranas* as Kubera, a monstrous, ugly creature, three-footed, fat and short, with a spreading belly, a small head and eight protruding teeth. The divine cashier is helped by *Yakshas* and *Rakshasas* - an equally ugly, materialistic, heartless brood - in protecting his treasures. It is interesting to note how the Indian *Rishis* were typically against capitalism and how they cartooned the master-of-wealth in such a grotesque caricature, so ugly that it cannot bring about even an indulgent smile to our lips.

OF THE *VASUS*, I AM PAVAKA—There are eight *VASUS* and they are *Vedic* deities presiding over the seasons. In *Chandogya Upanishad* it is described that the mouth of these *Vasus* is fire; there, the word 'mouth' may be conceived of as the instrument of enjoyment and experience. Therefore, it means that the Self is the very source from which we gain all our experiences of all seasons.

The six seasons which the world outside gives us, and the two seasons which the mind supplies us with, viz., joy and sorrow, together constitute the eight seasons mentioned here. Even the spring-time flowers will shed tears for us, if, at that time, we are in tragic bereavement, while even the naked trees of the autumn season will be quivering with joy for us, if, in that season, we have the joy of success, full and complete --thereby the two internal seasons. All of them are experienced by us only when we are under the grace of our own Consciousness within.

---

* Which had been often desrcibed in the *Shastras* as Ganga, Jnana-Ganga, Akasha-Ganga, Mother-Ganga, etc.

OF ALL THE PEAKS I AM MERU—A mythological mountain, believed to be the centre of the Universe, according to ancient Hindu Geography, is Meru. On top of it lives the Divine, and below it, lie scattered the Seven Islands that constitute the world. Meru is conceived as having an altitude of seven to eight thousand miles and it is described that from its top, the Ganges flows in all directions. This statement has made many believe that it may be the Himalayas – which is not, of course, very unsatisfactory. But we would rather believe it to be a mystical phraseology – representing some special field of influence, having its base in *Jambu-dweepa* and its extent rising up to the peak described above, from where Spiritual Knowledge* flows out on all the four sides to bless all of the islands.

CONTINUING TO INDICATE THE STATUS OF THE SELF AMONG THE THINGS OF THE KNOWN WORLD:

24. *And among the household priests, O Partha, know Me to be the chief, Brihaspati; among generals, I am Skanda; among lakes, I am the ocean.*

OF THE HOUSEHOLD PRIESTS KNOW ME TO BE THE CHIEF, BRIHASPATI—The lord of the planet Jupiter, Brihaspati, is mentioned in the Rig *Veda* as Brahmanaspati, which is self-explanatory of his status, among the hosts of heaven. He is considered as the spiritual teacher of the celestials. Similarly, the Lord indicates, "I AM SKANDA" – the son of Shiva, the peacock-rider, and the wielder-of-the-spear – "AMONG THE GENERALS".

पुरोधसां च मुख्यं मां विद्धि पार्थ बृहस्पतिम् ।
सेनानीनामहं स्कन्दः सरसामस्मि सागरः ॥ २४ ॥

purodhasāṁ ca mukhyaṁ māṁ viddhi pārtha bṛhaspatim
senānīnāmahaṁ skandaḥ sarasāmasmi sāgaraḥ 24.

OF WATER, I AM THE OCEAN—In all these examples, it is quite clear that the Lord is indicating Himself to be not only transcendent, but also immanent. Especially, the last analogy of the series in the stanza proves itself to be a typical example. No doubt, the waters of Ganga seem to have no relationship with the waters of the ocean. Yamuna, Godavari, Saraswati, Narmada, Sindhu or Kaveri, Tigris or Nile, Thames or Amazon - the water of the various lakes of the world, of the ponds of the villages, in all irrigation canals, individually, is independent and has nothing to do with the ocean that embraces the world. And yet, it is a fact that but for the waters of the ocean, all these rivers and water-pools would have long ago dried up. Similarly, in the sentient and the insentient beings, and things of the world, though individually they might look as if they have no direct relationship with the Infinite Ocean of Truth, the Lord indicates here that, but for It, the phenomenal world would have ended its existence long ago.

STILL ELABORATING THE SAME IDEA:

25. *Among the great RISHIS I am Bhrigu; among words I am the one-syllabled 'OM'; among sacrifices I am the sacrifice of silent repetition (JAPA-YAJNA); among immovable things, the Himalayas.*

OF THE GREAT *RISHIS* I AM BHRIGU—*BHRIGU* is the chief of the Seven-*Rishis* mentioned earlier in this very chapter

---

महर्षीणां भृगुरहं गिरामस्म्येकमक्षरम् ।
यज्ञानां जपयज्ञोऽस्मि स्थावरणां हिमालयः ॥ २५ ॥

maharṣīṇāṁ bhṛguraham girāmasmyekamakṣarama
yajñānāṁ japayajño'smi sthāvaraṇāṁ himālayaḥ 25.

(Ibid., Verses 2 and 5). Bhrigu is the one who recites the *Manava Dharmashastra*, wherein he is recognised as Manu's son.

OF WORDS, I AM THE ONE-SYLLABLED *'OM'**—Words are symbols of sounds to express one's thoughts. A speaker, with his words, tries to rise in the bosom of his listeners, a pattern of thought-experiences which the speaker feels in himself. Thus, the word 'tomato' is the sound symbol which creates in the mind of all those who know the 'tomato' the same form-experience. To bless those who do not react to this word, but stand confused, the speaker will necessarily try to use a series of words arranged into sentences, and the sentences will be properly marshalled to give a full picture of what a 'tomato' is. To the extent the describer can mould the form, colour, taste and qualities of the 'tomato' in the thought-world of the listener, to that extent the listener also can experience mentally what the speaker is speaking about. Thus, ordinarily, language is full of such sound-symbols to indicate experiences and to communicate thoughts.

If ordinary word-symbol indicates only the finite, the *Rishis* thought that they must conceive a word-symbol to indicate the Eternal. Thus, they discovered the one-syllabled word *'OM'**, which is the greatest *mantra* in all the *Vedas* and traditionally, upto recent times, this has been, in the spiritual world, the one sound idol used as a prop (*alambanam*) for all early meditators.

---

* For an exhaustive description of this word constituted of the three, sounds A U M - how each sound indicates the 'waking', the 'dream' and the 'deep-sleep', how its last lengthening 'M' indicates the fourth state, *'Turiya'*; and how, in the silence between two successive OMs, is the Infinite and the Eternal indicated – please refer Sri Swamiji's discourses on Mandukya-Karika. Chapter-I

* *'Nitya nirantara anavachcchinna Brahmaatmeti smaranam: tadeva atmasakshatkarah'*

OF SACRIFICES I AM THE *JAPA*—This universal spiritual exercise, *Japa*, is a technique by which the '*Japist*' tries to maintain a constant stream of the same divine thoughts in his mind. All other sacrifices - be they on the path-of-Devotion or on the path-of-Action, or on the path-of-Knowledge - are ritualistic, or meditative attempts, for a given period of time, to restrain the mind in one channel of deliberate thought. As such, in one form or the other, 'thought repetition' of the same species is the attempt in all *Sadhanas*. No doubt, *Japa* is a path in itself, having an independent existence of its own; but, at the same time in one form or the other, it is the core of all the 'paths'.

Thus, *Japa Yajna* is glorified here, not only because it is the essential core of all the other *Yajnas* but also because it transcends them all as an independent 'Path' in itself. Unbroken remembrance of the Self * is the very experience of Perfection and the moment of perfect intellectual tranquillity - *Samadhi*.

OF THINGS MOTIONLESS, I AM THE HIMALAYAS—The motionless is conceived as the inert, the insentient. Mud and rocks, trees and plants, birds and animals intermixed with the splendour of the phenomenal might, such as whistling storms, tearing thunders, roaring rivers cascading through silent valleys, still pools of eternal lakes, faithfully reflecting the blue sky and duplicating mountain peaks in their love-lorn hearts -all these together constitute the picture of all mountains. But, OF THEM, the Lord says, "I AM THE HIMALAYAS". Certainly He gives to the Himalayan ranges a more glorious and divine status because of their special significance. Unlike anywhere else in the world, in India, the Himalayas have the secret peaks where man sat to rocket his thoughts even beyond the frontiers of his intellect and did it successfully as was never before done by any living creature from the beginningless history of the world.

NOT SATISFIED YET, THE LORD IS VIGOROUSLY TRYING THROUGH FINER EXAMPLES AND WORDS TO CONVEY HIS INFINITE GLORY TO THE DATA-MONGERING AND WORLDLY INTELLECT OF HIS WARRIOR-FRIEND, ARJUNA;

26. *Among all trees (I am) the ASHWATTHA-tree; among Divine RISHIS, Narada; among GANDHARVAS, Chitraratha; among Perfected ones, the MUNI Kapila.*

OF ALL THE TREES I AM THE *ASHWATTHA*-TREE—Both in its magnitude and life-span, the *Ashwattha* tree (*Pipal*) can be considered as the 'all-pervading' and the 'Immortal', inasmuch as it lives generally for centuries.

The Hindu has learnt to worship it, and there is a sentiment of divinity attached to it. It is also a fact that the *Ashwattha* brings up in our mind fresh memories of the *Upanishadic** comparison of it with *samsara*. Later, in the *Geeta* itself (XV-I) we have a mention of the *peepal* tree as representing the pluralistic phenomenal world that has shot up to spread itself like mushrooms of false sorrows over what is dreamy nothingness.

OF THE *DEVARISHIS* I AM NARADA—Of the heavenly Seers, Krishna describes Himself as Narada, a favourite figure in our legends. In our *Puranas*, Narada is described as a great devotee of *Hari;* he is not only a great Seer among the celestials, but he often comes down to the world to play the deliberate fool and ultimately guide the deluded mortals to

---

अश्वत्थः सर्ववृक्षाणां देवर्षीणां च नारदः।
गन्धर्वाणां चित्ररथः सिद्धानां कपिलो मुनिः॥ २६॥

aśvatthaḥ sarvavṛkṣāṇāṁ devarṣīṇāṁ ca nāradaḥ
gandhavārṇāṁ citrarathaḥ siddhānāṁ kapilo muniḥ 26.

* *Kathopanishad*: II-iii-I

the parlour of heaven. Perhaps Krishna, himself being a great missionary, entertains a great respect for Narada, because of his missionary zeal and enthusiasm. Many are the converts whom Narada has won for heaven as described in our *Puranas*. A missionary cannot but feel a comradeship with another working in the same field and nothing can create a greater tie of identification than the similarity of aspiration in two individuals.

'*Gandharvas*' are the mythological concept of subtle entities who constitute the celestial choir, who entertain the denizens of heaven with their art and music. They are the 'stars' of entertainment in heaven. Among them, Chitraratha is the most brilliant.

OF THE *SIDDHAS*, I AM THE *MUNI* KAPILA—These *Siddhas* are not magic-mongers. The term *Siddha* in Sanskrit indicates one who has achieved the Goal (*Sadhya*) and therefore, it means the Perfected One. Among men-of-Realisation, therefore, Krishna says, 'I am *Muni* Kapila'. The term *Muni* need not bring into our mind the traditional picture supplied by illiterate painters of an aged, silver-haired, almost naked *fakir*, generally roaming about where others will not dare to enter, eating a strange diet, a strange creature of the forests, rather than a decent normal man of the town. *Muni* is a term in Sanskrit derived from the word *Manana* which is the 'art of reflection'.* The term *Muni*, therefore, only means a thinker; 'OF THE THINKERS I AM KAPILA'.

Kapila, the author of the *Sankhya* philosophy has been here particularly singled out for this great status as the best among all thinkers, because the *Geeta* mainly follows the *Sankhyan*-philosophical thoughts.

The Lord uses the framework of thoughts in the *Sankhya* philosophy to paint His concept of the One Truth, Absolute and Eternal, and therefore, Kapila, the promoter of the *Sankhyan* school of thought, has been given the special glory of being compared with the Lord Himself.

FEELING THAT HE HAS NOT DELIVERED THE GOODS YET, THE LORD CONTINUES:

27. *Know Me among horses as 'UCHAISHRAVAS', born of AMRITA; among lordly elephants, the 'AIRAVATA' and among men, the King.*

The *Pauranic*-story of the churning of the Milky-Ocean by both the gods and the demons for the purpose of getting out of it the Nectar* is very famous. Two of the products that came up during the churning process were the winged-horse, mighty and powerful, called the *Uchaishravas*, and the white-elephant, *Airavata*. Both of them were presented to the King of the gods, Indra. Altogether, it is described that thirteen such tempting objects of might and glory presented themselves during the churning.

28. *Among weapons, I am the 'thunderbolt'; among cows I am 'KAMADHUK'; I am 'KANDARPA', the cause for offspring; among serpents I am 'VASUKI'.*

उच्चैःश्रवसमश्वानां विद्धि माममृतोद्भवम् ।
ऐरावतं गजेन्द्राणां नराणां च नराधिपम् ॥ २७ ॥

uccaiḥśravasamaśvānāṁ viddhi māmamṛtodbhavam
airāvataṁ gajendrāṇāṁ narāṇāṁ ca narādhipam 27.

**Manana-sheelavan-munih*. A *Muni* is one capable of penetrating reflections upon the deep significances in the scriptural declarations.

आयुधानामहं वज्रं धेनूनामस्मि कामधुक् ।
प्रजनश्चास्मि कन्दर्पः सर्पाणामस्मि वासुकिः ॥२८ ॥

āyudhānāmahaṁ vajraṁ dhenūnāmasmi kāmadhuk
prajanaścāsmi kandarpaḥ sapārṇāmasmi vāsukiḥ 28.

* *Ambrosia - Amrita*

* Subjectively, it seems that it is nothing other than the *Sankalpa-Shakti* that automatically rises in an individual as he increases the powers of his concentration, and gains progress in his inward integration.

OF WEAPONS, I AM THE THUNDERBOLT—The weapon called *'Vajra'* is an item in the divine artillery which can never be shattered. The *Vedic* legend explains how a great seer, Dadheechi, offered his own rib-bone for the construction of this secret weapon to annihilate a demon who was threatening to shatter the peace of the heavens.

OF COWS I AM *KAMADHUK*—This strange animal called *Kamadhuk,* from which we can milk all our desires, whatever they be, is also one of the early by-products that rose up during the churning of the Milky-Ocean.*

OF ALL THE CAUSES OF OFFSPRING, I AM *KANDARPA*—Cupid, the god of love of the Indian concept, is conceived of as a mischievous boy, chubby and lively, ever carrying with himself his bow-of-smile, with five flower-tipped arrows, each meant to smother one sense-organ!! The suggestion is a biological truth. Procreation is not merely an animal act of insemination, or a vegetable-act of cross-pollination, but it is, according to the science of Sex (*Kama-shastra*) in India, a fulfilment of all passionate urges that express themselves through all the sense organs. A philosopher is a perfect scientist and as such he has none of the false shyness, which is generally expressed by immoral people when they pose themselves as sandal-coated puritans. *Vedantins* and teachers, when they talk of sex-life, are as much brutally open as the professors are in a medical college.

Of all the causes of offspring, the Lord declares, 'I AM CUPID', who in himself, as the Lord of love, represents, in the field of sensuality, the total satisfaction of the physical, mental and intellectual sheaths in man.

OF SNAKES, I AM *VASUKI*—The serpent *'Vasuki'*, is described in our mythology as ever living on Shiva's ring-

* Refer Swamiji's discourses on *Kathopanishad,* I-ii-20

finger, as an adornment. Though small enough to become a ring on the finger of the Lord, it was the *'Vasuki'*. Serpent, who volunteered to serve as a rope in the churning process of the 'milky-ocean'. This naturally reminds one of the *Upanishadic* declarations,* that the Truth is at once the 'minutest of the minute', and 'the greatest of the great'. Naturally, it is very apt that the Lord declares Himself to be *'Vasuki'* among the snakes. The term *'Sarpa'* is to be rightly understood, in contrast with the *Nagas*, mentioned in the next stanza. *Sarpas* are single-hooded; while *Nagas* are multi-hooded.

CONTINUING IN THE TUNE, THE SINGER-DIVINE SINGS OF HIS OWN SONGFUL GLORY:

29. *I am 'Ananta' among NAGAS; I am 'Varuna' among water deities; I am 'Aryama' among the ancestors; and I am 'Yama' among controllers.*

OF THE *NAGAS* I AM ANANTA—*'Naga'* means the many-hooded serpents. Of them, the thousand-hooded *Sesha Naga* is the one that has been described as forming the 'bed' for Lord Vishnu to recline in His *'Yoga*-sleep'. Here Krishna only means that, among the many-hooded serpents, He is the mightiest and the most divine, because He is the very substratum upon which Vishnu, the Sustainer, and Brahmaji, the Creator of the multiple world, recline and function.

OF THE WATER DEITIES I AM *VARUNA*—*'Varuna'* is a *Vedic* conception of the Spirit governing the waters, the third

---

अनन्तश्चास्मि नागानां वरुणो यादसामहम्।
पितॄणामर्यमा चास्मि यमः संयमतामहम्॥ २९॥

anantaścāsmi nāgānāṁ varuṇo yādasāmaham
pitṝṇāmaryamā cāsmi yamaḥ saṁyamatāmaham 29.

of the five great elements. Deifying the elemental forces in the phenomenal world was the method of adoration and worship in the early *Vedic* period. It was only later, that we started the *Pauranic*-tradition of humanising gods and got into the muddy pool of religious differences, sectarian prejudices, and credal warfare, between colonies of ignorant folks, gathered round a Jerusalem Master or a Vrindavana Boy, or a Mecca Messenger. *Varuna* is conceived of as a being, half-fish and half-man, almost something like Arnold's Merman! He is the Ruler of the Oceans and the Lord of the Waters.

OF THE *PITRIS*, I AM *ARYAMA*—In Hinduism, death is one of the experiences in life when the subtle-body* chooses to leave permanently its present residence within a given physical structure. The mind-intellect-equipment, maintaining a separate egocentric concept in itself, continues its existence and it is commonly called 'departed soul' or 'ancestor'.

These 'departed souls' live together in a world of their own, called the world-of-the manes (*Pitriloka*). We have already discussed the *Vedic* concept of the six children of the twelve *Adityas*, each presiding over a month of the year. Of these, *Aryama* is the ruler of the world of the ancestors.

OF THE CONTROLLERS, I AM YAMA—*'Yama'* is the mythical Lord-of-Death, the Chief Messenger of the Annihilator. In India, we worship the terrible, the sad, and the tragic also, because, to us God is the substratum for both the good and the bad, for the pleasant and the unpleasant. We are not satisfied by any theory of compromise by which we reject, in God, any association with what we do not like.

---

* 'Subtle-body' is a term used in *Vedanta* to denote mainly the mind-intellect-equipment in each one of us.

Whether we like it or not, the Principle-of-Death is the governing factor that controls and regulates life, and, at every moment, prepares a progressive field for creative developments everywhere. The childhood must die before youth can express itself. I must leave my high school in order to enter college. Step by step, I must die in order to be born into the next step. Progress in itself is a partial picture of life; it is only a squint-eyed vision of life's total dynamism. Every development is preceded by prior destruction. Annihilation, thus contributing to positive progress, is called 'Death's own creative art.

No new thing can be created unless correspondingly we also destroy that which existed before. We arrive at this assertive but logical conclusion when we sufficiently digest the observed physical law of the world that no two things can ever remain at one and the same period of time occupying one and the same space. When a painter paints a flower, he not only pours his colour on to the canvas to paint his subject, but his creative art is a constant destruction of the surface coating that was earlier given to the canvas!

Thus, when life is viewed in its totality, there is as much importance for the Principle-of-Death as for the very Principle-of-Creation.

But for Death functioning intelligently at almost the same speed as the rate of Creation, there would have been an inordinate flood of things in life; and life itself would have been choked by its own magnitude and number. If Death were not there, the great-great-great-grandfather of our great-great-great-grandfather might still be living, even now, in our own present two-roomed apartment! Even when there is a slight rise in population, the entire balance and political peace in the world get shattered. What will not happen, if Death were not as sincerely serving us as the Creator? Indeed, of all the Controllers, Death alone is the Chief and the analogy given here is irreplaceable and supremely apt.

IN A SPELL OF PLEASANT ENTHUSIASM THE LORD CONTINUES:

30. *I am 'Prahlada' among DAITYAS, 'Time' among reckoners, the 'Lord-of-beasts' (Lion) among animals, and 'Vainateya' (Garuda) among birds.*

I AM 'PRAHLADA' AMONG THE *DAITYAS*—The story of 'Prahlada', very famous among the Hindus, is the story of a boy-devotee who, with adamantine faith and firm devotion, challenged his father Hiranyakashipu in defence of his own faith in *Hari*, and stood many a trial and persecution from his father.

AMONG RECKONERS I AM 'TIME'—the logicians form among themselves a staunch group of Hindu philosophers, and they not only support the concept of pluralism, but also challenge the very existence of the God-Principle. They have, through their purely intellectual deductions, arrived at the final conclusion that Time is the Eternal Factor, and the individual mind-and-intellect are instrumental causes to split It up and see in It the play of the past, the present, and the future. According to them, it is this 'play of the mind' that bombards Time and makes It look as though It were finite and momentary. Perhaps Vyasa had this concept in his mind when he tried to bring this analogy to express the Infinite Substratum supporting the finite multiplicity.

प्रह्लादश्चास्मि दैत्यानां कालः कलयतामहम् ।
मृगाणां च मृगेन्द्रोऽहं वैनतेयश्च पक्षिणाम् ॥ ३० ॥

prahyalādaścasmi daityānāṁ kālaḥ kalayatāmaham
mṛgāṇāṁ ca mṛgendro'haṁ vainateyaśca pakṣiṇām 30.

* The white-necked-eagle (*Garuda*) is the vehicle of Hari, the Protector.

There are some commentators who rather accept this analogy as a simple-looking direct statement; and, according to them, Time, which is beginningless and endless, is the ultimate measure of all things in the relative field.

AMONG BEASTS, I AM THE LORD OF BEASTS AND, AMONG BIRDS, I AM THE SON OF VINATA—The majesty and grandeur, the dignity and 'manliness' of the lion among animals, make him the Royal Lion. Its flight, its powers of perception, and the altitudes, to which it can climb, make Garuda - the King of birds.*

31. *Among purifiers, I am the 'wind'; among warriors, I am 'Rama', among fishes, I am the 'shark'; among rivers, I am the 'Ganges'.*

OF CLEANSING AGENTS, I AM THE 'WIND'—No antiseptic or sanitary equipment is as efficient to clean a place as the Sun and the wind. If the wind alone is indicated here it is because of Vyasa's perfect knowledge that wind can rise only when the Sun is hot. Where there is constant wind, there the Sun also must be available; in a cave there can be neither sunlight, nor movement of air.

OF THOSE WHO ARE WIELDERS OF WEAPONS, I AM 'RAMA'—The hero of Ramayana, Sri Ramachandra was delineated by Valmiki, the first poet in India to use metrical compositions and write out a full-fledged *Kavya*, very elaborately, of a 'perfect man' in all aspects of his existence: perfect as a son, as a husband, as a brother, as a friend, as a fighter, as a teacher, as a ruler, and even as a father. Such an

---

पवनः पवतामस्मि रामः शस्त्रभृतामहम्।
झषाणां मकरश्चास्मि स्त्रोतसामस्मि जाह्नवी ॥ ३१ ॥

pavanaḥ pavatāmasmi rāmaḥ śastrabhṛtāmaham
jhaṣāṇāṁ makaraścāsmi strotasāmasmi jāhnavī 31.

all-round perfect one - his perfections shining out all the more against the background of seeming imperfections and extremely irritating and confusing circumstances - should necessarily be the noblest hand that ever wielded an honest bow to shoot out the most effective arrows!

OF THE FISHES I AM THE 'SHARK' AND OF THE RIVERS I AM *JAHNAVI*—The story goes that Saint Jahnu drank the Ganges dry, and later, for the redemption of man, let her out to flow through his ears! The concept of the Ganges, we have indicated earlier, is a symbolism, freely used by the Hindus, to represent the 'spiritual culture' of India. The wealth of the *Rishi*-knowledge, as it reaches a seeker, at the seat of his meditation, at first makes him swallow and dry it up. 'Drinking at the fountain of Knowledge', to satiate the thirst for knowledge, etc., are usual expressions in almost all languages of the world that have some slavery to the mother of all languages, Sanskrit.

Here the stream of knowledge is described as having flown out through Jahnu's ears; it is indeed a brilliant poetic concept to connect the term *Shruti* (heard), which means the contents of the *Upanishads*, comprising what the Masters declared to the world and what the disciples 'heard' from them. In India, teachers come from time to time to reinterpret the Ancient Wisdom in the context of their own age, only after having gained their own personal experiences of *Vedic* Truth-declarations. Without the stamp of realisation, no teacher worth the name will dare come into the world to propagate the old Truth in a new language.

Of the many names by which the sacred river Ganges is known in India, this particular name has been chosen here in order to emphasize the above-mentioned special implications.

AMONG FISHES I AM THE 'SHARK'—the shark is the most dangerous fish in the ocean. So among fishes, *Bhagawan* declares Himself to be the 'shark'.

AND ALSO:

32. *Among creations, I am the beginning, the middle and also the end, O Arjuna; among sciences I am the Science of the Self and I am the logic in all arguments.*

OF CREATIONS, I AM THE BEGINNING, AND THE END, AND THE MIDDLE TOO—Here there is an echo of the general statement with which the Lord started His discourse earlier in the chapter (X-20), for enumerating His infinite glories. However, therein He had explained how He was the Essential Stuff in all individual beings; and here it is a more universal statement by which He indicates how He is the Essence in all Creation.

No substance can ever remain divorced from the essential stuff of which it is made. No gold ornament can be made without the metal, gold. No wave from the ocean can be packed separately for the Himalayas. No mud-pot can exist, divorced from the mud. The material-cause is the unavoidable essence in all the names and forms, and nothing can ever remain divorced from its own essential-essence. By the above statement, the Lord is indicating that He, as the Self-in-all, is "the beginning, the end and the middle too" of all things in the Universe. The names and forms have arisen from Him, are supported by Him, and they can only merge back into Him when they are destroyed.

सर्गाणामादिरन्तश्च मध्यं चैवाहमर्जुन ।
अध्यात्मविद्या विद्यानां वादः प्रवदतामहम् ॥ ३२ ॥

sagārṇāmādirantaśca madhyaṁ caivāhamarjana
adhyātmavidyā vidyānāṁ vādaḥ pravadatāmaham 32.

The science that explains that Knowledge-Principle, without which no other 'knowledge of things' is ever possible, and which, playing upon the field-of-things, accomplishes our knowledge of them, should necessarily be the science of all sciences, the best knowledge. In sunlight, all objects are illumined. Sunlight reflected upon the non-luminous objects of the world makes them perceptible. Naturally, the Sun is the 'eye of all eyes', the source of all perceptions. Similarly, the science of Spirituality' is explained as the science of all sciences.

OF ARGUMENTS I AM '*VAADA*'—The term *Pravadatam* used here, should be understood by us, according to Sankara, as the various forms of arguments.* Three types of approaches are often used in all discussions, in all walks of life. In *Jalpa*, the attempt is to smother the opposition and its arguments by vehement criticism and bitter rejoinders, spoken with an overbearing arrogance in assertions. In the case of *Vitanda*, the champion of discussion mercilessly criticises the arguments of the opposition, exposing by means, fair or foul, both the real and the imaginary fallacies in their line of arguments; the aim being to destroy the edifice, built by the other. The third, *Vaada*, is the technique of discussion by which the one arguing is trying to read the letter and the verse as directly as possible, with the object of coming directly to truth, without indulging in any hair-splitting arguments.

It is evident, therefore, that both the former techniques (*Jalpa* and *Vitanda*) are only strategies to weaken the enemies, while the actual thrust into the enemy lines and the ultimate real conquest is only through *Vaada*.

FURTHER:

33. *Among letters I am the letter 'A'; among all compounds I am the dual (co-ordinates); I am verily, the inexhaustible, or the everlasting time; I am the (All-faced) dispenser (of fruits-of-actions) having faces in all directions.*

OF THE ALPHABET I AM THE LETTER 'A'—It is very well-known that, without the help of vowels, words cannot be pronounced. Of all languages, Sanskrit is particularly sweet because of the preponderance of the 'A' sound in it. In fact, every letter in its combination is to be pronounced in Sanskrit with the sound of 'A' added to it to lengthen it to its full sweetness. This, as it were, lubricates the words, and consequently the language has no backfiring disturbances of rattling nuisance or disgusting hoarseness. Because of this smooth run of the 'A' sound in every letter, there is a melody even between words and a lingering echo between sentences. In fact, after a long chanting of a Sanskrit text in a hall, there is, for the sensitive, a perceptible atmosphere of soothening music in the air that can lull all the agitations of the human mind.

The sound 'A' is not only the essence in each letter of a word – not only does it transcend, or overflow the sentences and flood the very atmosphere – but it has itself the first

---

अक्षराणामकारोऽस्मि द्वन्द्वः सामासिकस्य च ।
अहमेवाक्षयः कालो धाताहं विश्वतोमुखः ॥३३॥

akṣarāṇāmakāro'smi dvandvaḥ samāsikasya ca
ahamevākṣayaḥ kālo dhātāhaṁ viśvatomukhaḥ 33.

*Either the arrogant rejoinders (*Jalpa*), or the tiresome destructive criticisms (*Vitanda*), or logical arguments (*Vaada*).

1 *'Akaro Vai Sarva Vak.'*

2 Rama and Lakshmana are expressed as 'Ramalakshmanau'.

place among the alphabets in all the languages. Realising these implications, the *Upanishads* declare that the 'A' sound is the essence in all speech.[1]

OF ALL COMPOUND WORDS, I AM THE PAIR—One of the Sanskrit forms of compounds is the 'pair' (*dwandwa*) in which the essential components co-ordinate with each other in the newly formed compound word.[2] According to Sridhara, perhaps the only commentator who tried to give us the why of this analogy, the *dwandwa*-method of combining words is very important among all the other types, because of this easy and direct coordination of its components. In the context of the usage here, the Self and the non-Self are as though mixed up together and they constitute the world-of-perceptions experienced by us; but, to the discriminate, the component parts are as distinct as the dissolution of a *dwandwa* compound is to an educated man.

I ALONE AM THE INFINITE TIME—Earlier (X-30) also there was a mention that OF RECKONERS I AM TIME. There the finite time was mentioned, while here, as a contrast, the Infinite and the Absolute Time is indicated. In short, both these statements put together mean that the Self is the substratum for both the Absolute Concept of pure-Time, and the finite experiences of each moment. But for the awareness of each fraction of time, the total concept of Time is impossible. Here "I am IMMANENT in each individual unit-of-time, and I am TRANSCENDENT, to serve as a substratum for the total-Time".

I AM THE SUSTAINER—*Acharya* Shankara comments upon this term and concludes that the Self is the sustainer of

---

1 *'Karma-phalasya Vidhata'.*

mental impressions,[3] and therefore, of the particular trait in a given individual which determines how he will react to the world outside.

FACING ALL QUARTERS AT ONCE—This term has been exhaustively described earlier by us (IX-16) where it was described that the Self is not only 'ONE IN ALL, BUT IS ALSO DIFFERENT FROM ALL, AND, IN EACH, IT FACES EVERYWHERE'. The entire implication of that stanza is to be read into this simple-looking phrase, 'Facing everywhere' (*Vishvato-mukhah*). In all perceptions, whether physical, mental or intellectual, there is the grace of the Consciousness which is the Self, and therefore, the phrase is quite self-expressive.

CONTINUING, THE LORD SAYS:

34. *And I am all-devouring Death, and the prosperity of those who are to be prosperous; among the feminine qualities (I am) fame, prosperity, speech, memory, intelligence, firmness and forgiveness.*

I AM THE ALL-CONSUMING DEATH—Death, the leveller, brings even the sceptre and the crown to the level of the begging bowl and the staff. Every existing thing maintains its separateness from all others only during its lifetime, due to its individual relationship with things and beings other than itself. After death, the wise and the fool, the good and the bad, the strong and the weak, the ruler and the ruled –

मृत्युः सर्वहरश्चाहमुद्भवश्च भविष्यताम् ।
कीर्तिः श्रीर्वाक्च नारीणां स्मृतिर्मेधा धृतिः क्षमा ॥३४॥

mṛtyuḥ sarvaharaścāhamudbhavaśca bhaviṣyatām
kīrti śrīvārkca nārīṇāṁ smṛtirmedhā dhṛtiḥ kṣamā 34.

all come to dust, levelled into a uniformity that recognises no distinction within itself.

I AM THE SOURCE OF ALL THAT IS TO BE—The Supreme is not merely the destroyer of all, reducing them into a lifeless commonality but, He is, certainly, the source of all new creations that are to come in the future. To conceive destruction, without taking into consideration its unavoidable accompaniment, i.e., the new construction is but to insist upon a partial viewpoint. In a total and complete vision-of-life, taken as a whole, we find that the so-called destruction is only a transformation, or modification, of the existing form of an object, or scheme of things, into something dissimilar and varying. Destruction leaves no total blank anywhere. When we view a wave separately, we may say that, after playing for a moment on the bosom of the ocean, it has destroyed itself, but if we view it from the standpoint of the ocean, for each wave which appears to have been destroyed, there are innumerable new waves that rise up, unnoticed by our limited powers of observation.

We find that Krishna is gathering these ideas against the contrast contained in his immediately prior statement, altogether, the line stresses that the Infinite playing Itself, ceaselessly, and in repeated succession, the game of both destruction and construction, is, in fact, what we call as the finite-Universe.

FAME, FORTUNE, SPEECH, MEMORY, INTELLIGENCE, STEADFASTNESS, AND PATIENCE, AM I, OF THE FEMININE QUALITIES—The Sanskrit terms conveying these abstract nouns are all feminine in gender. Maybe the Lord means that if ever we find these qualities in women, we can perceive a clearer flicker of divinity than anywhere else. Again, the philosophical content of the line is perfect, and beyond all criticism. It is not said that the person having these qualities is divine. Whoever be the person, and whatever be his past, when on occasions he expresses these qualities, we can perceive a clearer vision of Life's glory THROUGH HIM.

In short, these are the qualities which, when manifest, create such adjustments in the inner equipments in man, that we can perceive, through him, more clearly the awesome vitality of Life's surge. As a transferred epithet, Lord the Self declares that among the feminine qualities, "I am any one of these, or all of them put together".

THE LORD AGAIN GIVES FOUR MORE INDICATIONS TO MAKE THE SELF-INTRODUCTION CLEAR TO ARJUNA:

35. *Among hymns also I am the 'BRIHAT-SAMAN'; among metres 'GAYATRI' am I; among months I am parts of December-January (MARGA-SHIRSHA); among seasons I am the 'flowery-spring'.*

OF THE *SAMANS* I AM THE *BRIHAT-SAMAN*—The songs of the *Sama-Veda* are called the *Samans*. These hymns are all in different metres, and they are to be sung in different tunes. It is no easy task, and the students who can sing the *Samans* well had to spend years of practice at the feet of their Master. Of all the metres that are met with in the volume of the *Sama-Veda*, the most difficult and complicated is the metre called *'Brihati'*; and the *Samans* composed in; the *Brihati*-metre are called the *'Brihat-sama'*.

बृहत्साम तथा साम्नां गायत्री छन्दसामहम्।
मासानां मार्गशीर्षोऽहमृतूनां कुसुमाकरः ॥३५॥

bṛhatsāma tathā sāmnāṁ gāyatrī chandasāmaham
māsānāṁ mārgaśīrṣo'hamṛtūnāṁ kusumākaraḥ 35.

X/35

OF ALL ... RES I AM *GAYATRI*—Talking of metres Bhagawan ... to have all of a sudden remembered that there ... nt varieties of metres and, of them; *Gayatri* is c... s the most divine and extremely powerful. ...tre composed of three lines, each fulfilled in ... This metre is held in India in great esteem, ... sense of divinity, because the most famous ...ving the Sun (*Savitru*), chanted by all *Brahmins*, ...ning and evening ablutions, is composed in this ...

...he metres none has been so uniformly glorified ...e as '*Gayatri*', and no *mantra* has had so far the ...of being chanted by so many devotees, continuously for su...h a long number of years, in any other religion in the world.

OF THE MONTHS I AM THE *MARGA-SHIRSHA*—this corresponds to parts of the English calender months of December and January which are the months in India, each year, when people do not think of the fatiguing summer which is to arrive soon and they have stopped complaining about the wet monsoon.

OF THE SEASONS I AM THE FLOWER-BEARING SPRING—spring, with its colourful message and fragrant songs, gives a thrill to all prospects wherever one may turn in India. Flower-valleys clothe the hills. Crops cover the field. Tanks and pools get strewn with lotuses and lilies. The meadows roll out green carpets of grass. There is an air of celebration and festivity in the hearts of all, and in order to crown the joyous spirit in the world, the moon seems to dress herself in more glory than usual.

NOT ONLY AM I TO BE RECOGNISED AMONG THE MAJESTIC AND THE DIVINE, AMONG THE BEAUTIFUL AND THE CHARMING, BUT ALSO AMONG THE LOWEST OF THE LOW: I AM WHAT I AM: FOR, LISTEN:

X/36

36. *I am the gambling of the fraudulent; I am the s*
splendid; I am victory; I am the industry (in t
determined); I am the goodness in the good.

OF ALL THE DECEPTIVE GAMES I AM T PLAY—The *Geeta* contains the discourses given (the royal warrior, a Prince of that time) by K great missionary spirit, to help the Prince to rediscov vitality of his own religion - Hinduism. The attempt o *Geeta* is, therefore, to reorient the Hindus about Hinduism missionary cannot bring about this reorientation successfull unless the spirit of our scriptures is explained to the common folk in their own language. To Arjuna, the example given here is the most striking. For, his entire life had been a series of tragedies which he had to suffer because of his elder brother's irresistible weakness to play the dice. No other example would have delivered the goods to Arjuna as efficiently as this one.

To modern students, this may not strike as very effective since dice is not a game very popular with us just now. But the substitutes are very easily recognised.*

SPLENDOUR IN THE SPLENDID AM I—At the same time, a seeker, who is ready to make use of this portion for meditation as it should be, will easily understand that the *shastra* has said almost nothing. The splendour in a splendid object has not the qualities of the object from which the shine

---

द्यूतं छलयतामस्मि तेजस्तेजस्विनामहम् ।
जयोऽस्मि व्यवसायोऽस्मि सत्त्वं सत्त्ववतामहम् ॥३६॥

dyūtaṁ chalayatāmasmi tejastejasvināmaham
jayo'smi vyavasāyo'smi sattvaṁ sattvavatāmaham 36.

* Of all card-games I am 'Cut-throat'; of all gambling I am the 'crossword'; of the weapons I am the 'atom-bomb'; of the social crimes, I am 'forgery', etc. These examples should, perhaps, speak to us more eloquently and directly.

comes out. The splendour, in itself, has no qualities even - it is merely AN EXPERIENCE. To facilitate that 'experience', the mind borrows the light to illumine the magnitude and the glory of the object, but the splendour itself has nothing to do with the ingredients or constituents that together give rise to the experience of the splendour in our bosom. In short, as Sri Ramakrishna Paramahamsa once said, "Truth, no doubt, is Light, but it is 'Light' without its properties".

I AM VICTORY; I AM EFFORT, I AM THE GOODNESS IN THE GOOD—As explained above, here also it is these qualities, nay, the 'experiences' lived in the presence of these qualities, that gives us an occasion to live the Self. These qualities connote a certain mental condition created by the very special type of its thought-vibrations. When these are sustained for a long period, the bosom becomes quiet and still. The reflected glory of Awareness becomes, in such a bosom, almost as glorious as the Reality and, therefore, as we said earlier, here too, by employing a transferred-epithet, The very qualities are declared as the self.

We should not forget that these FIFTY-FOUR items of analogy, given in this chapter to indicate THE ONE IN THE MANY are all meant to be as many items of contemplation, to be meditated upon by all sincere seekers. This is not an OBJECTIVE narration and, as such, no true student of the *Geeta* can ever expect his education to be complete unless he understands the true meaning of these stanzas in his SUBJECTIVE experience.

STILL IF YOU NEED ELABORATION, ARJUNA, YOU MAY HAVE SOME MORE. LISTEN:

37. *Among the VRISHNIS I am 'Vaasudeva'; among the PANDAVAS, (I am) 'Dhananjaya'; also among the MUNIS I am 'Vyasa'; and among the poets I am 'Ushana', the great Seer.*

OF THE *VRISHNIS*, I AM *VAASUDEVA*—Among the *Yadavas*, the ancestor Yadu had a son *Vrishni*. All the descendants of *Vrishni* together constitute the tribe called the '*Vrishnis*'. In this tribe was born Vasudeva as the great-great-grandson of *Vrishni*. Vasudeva married Devaki, the sister of the Mathura-tyrant, Kamsa, and to her was born Krishna. As the son of Vasudeva, the Lord is called 'Vaasudeva'.

OF THE *PANDAVAS*, I AM *DHANANJAYA*—Just as Krishna was the mighty one that had given pride and glory to both the *Yadavakula* and the *Vrishni*-clan, because of which they have a glorious existence in the memory of man, so too among the *Pandavas*, He again was the soul-giving factor, but for whom, the five brothers would perhaps have achieved nothing. The term *Dhananjaya* literally means 'the winner of wealth'. Generally, this term is considered as a title of Arjuna, and therefore, this portion is usually translated as 'I AM ARJUNA, AMONG THE *PANDAVAS*'.

OF ALL THE SAINTS I AM *VYASA*—this is not an unfair passage of self-advertisement thrown in by Vyasa himself, the author of the *Geeta*. Vyasa was a pen-name which came to

---

वृष्णीनां वासुदेवोऽस्मि पाण्डवानां धनंजयः ।
मुनीनामप्यहं व्यासः कवीनामुशना कविः ॥३७॥

vṛṣṇīnāṁ vāsudevo'smi pāṇḍavānāṁ dhanañjayaḥ
munīnāmapyanahaṁ vyāsaḥ kavīnāmuśanā kaviḥ 37.

* *Vyasanaat Vyasah – Vyasa* is one who elaborates every point of discussion – whose style is rather verbal – who repeats AD NAUSEAM.

symbolise the new style of literature that was discovered and introduced into the realm of philosophical and religious writings of that age. The style was revolutionary, for, till then, philosophical literature was in *mantra*-form – thoughts packed into small language-capsules. With the *Puranas*, a new style was initiated and developed, where elaboration was the motive and repeated over-emphasis of the fundamentals was the general technique. This was innovated by Krishna Dwaipayana under a suggestive pen-name, Vyasa, explaining in itself his own literary art of elaboration.*

Thus OF ALL THE *MUNIS*, I AM *VYASA* should suggest that of all the men of reflection, the Lord is He, who is behind the stupendous work that stands today under the title *'Puranas'*.

OF THE SEERS, I AM *USHANA*—nowhere do we find any mention of this seer in the available popular books. But Anandagiri somehow identifies *Ushana* with *Shukra*, though he too does not explain how he identifies these two together. The planet Venus, also called *Shukra*, was the son of Bhrigu, and the preceptor of the *Daityas*. *Shukra* is called *Kavi* in the *Rig-Veda*.

In the *Upanishads, Kavi* means a seer of the *Vedic mantras*. Men of inspiration, declaring their experiences, without egocentric awareness, were called *Kavis*; later on the term deteriorated to mean writers of poetry, who too, at the sight of the spectacular Universe got themselves lifted from themselves and seemed to enter into a realm of their own brilliant notions, from the caves of which they sang their harmonious rhythm of poetic cadence. Here, however, it is used in the original meaning as a seer.

FURTHER, IF I MAY ELABORATE, I AM, SAYS THE LORD:

38. *Among punishers I am the 'Sceptre'; among those who seek victory, I am 'Statesmanship'; and also among secrets, I am 'Silence'; and I am the 'Knowledge' among knowers.*

OF THE CHASTISERS, I AM THE SCEPTRE—the ruler and the ruled must both prevail in the State, if they desire progressively to push ahead the standard of living in the various communities. The lawgiver must see that he governs by enforcing the laws. In the function of the government, the governor will, of necessity, become the punisher of the unsocial members of the community, who are tempted, in their selfishness, to disobey the existing laws in the community. The ruled, in their loyalty and reverence to the existing laws, generally succumb to the punishments meted out to them by their rulers. But, in fact, who is that who really gives the powers, to the King or the President, to punish the misbehaving individuals? After all, in modern states, individuals have no right to take the law into their own hands.

The King wields the sceptre, which is the symbol of his power to punish. To the President in a democratic institution, the sanction to punish is given by the public will of the people. In the policeman at the street-corner, the power to arrest is attached to his uniform. A King devoid of his sceptre, a President who has been thrown out, or a dismissed policeman – none of them has any longer the power to chastise the wicked. Naturally, therefore, 'OF ALL THOSE WHO PUNISH', the Lord says,' I AM THE SCEPTRE'. Without the symbol of the social sanction, no individual in the community

---

दण्डो दमयतामस्मि नीतिरस्मि जिगीषताम्।
मौनं चैवास्मि गुह्यानां ज्ञानं ज्ञानवतामहम्॥३८॥

daṇḍo damayatāmasmi nītirasmi jigīṣatām
maunaṁ caivāsmi guhyānāṁ jñānaṁ jñānavatāmaham 38.

has any right over the others. After all, be he a King or a President, be he a policeman or a judge, all of them are in themselves only members of the community, but they play the part of guarding the security of the community, because of the special privileges they possess due to the status of their office.

OF CONQUERERS, I AM STATE-CRAFT—that a mere physical conquest is no victory at all, is the repeated declaration of all history textbooks. No nation, community, society, or individual can, in fact, be considered as having conquered merely because of the force that has smothered their enemy, or because of the might that is standing guard over them. The conquest of a community can be complete only when the conqueror has, through intelligent administrative policies, brought the conquered to identify their culture and thought-patterns with his own. If the conquerors are not capable of converting the conquered, or getting themselves converted to the cultural values of the conquered, the conquest is never complete. This is an open secret to every student of history. After the military conquest, through statesmanship alone, can real baptism come, and this alone can bring the conquered permanently under the will of the conqueror. "I AM STATE-CRAFT" by which all conquerors are really conquerors.

OF THINGS SECRET, I AM SILENCE—Secrecy is maintained in and nourished by silence. When a secret is ventilated in open discussions, it is no longer a secret. Thus the very essence of a secret lies in silence. So too, it may be noted that the Knowledge of the Self is described in our textbooks as 'the secret of secrets', because it is not generally known. This great secret is also experienced, and the divine experience is maintained and enjoyed, sustained and nourished, as well as fed and grown, only upon the deep inner silence. Of all secret things, the Lord is the deep and unbroken Silence!

THE KNOWLEDGE OF THE KNOWER AM I—The wisdom of the wise is not the wise themselves, and yet, it is not anything different from them. The Self is not the body, and yet, we cannot say that the body is anything different from the Self, which is All-pervading. The envelopments of matter and their worlds of experiences are all the aura of glory that shines out around the Self. The knowledge in the knower or the wisdom in the wise is the expression of the Glory Divine, because of a certain pattern maintained among the inner personalities in the individuals concerned.

SUMMING UP ALL THAT HE HAD SAID SO FAR IN A BEAUTIFUL PERORATION, THE LORD SAYS:

39. *And whatsoever is the seed of all beings, that also am I, O Arjuna; there is no being, whether moving, or unmoving, that can exist without Me.*

I AM THAT WHICH IS THE SEED OF ALL—In all the above descriptive phrases, indicating through analogies, the nature, place and function of the Self in the scheme of the perceptible world of forms, thoughts and ideas, it was constantly suggested that the Self is the 'Source of all creation'. In order to hammer this idea into the dull-witted so that no student of the *Geeta* might overlook and ignore this wonderful idea which is the essence of all Knowledge-spiritual, Vyasa, again and again, makes Krishna repeat this essential truth, in a hundred different suggestive expressions.

यच्चापि सर्वभूतानां बीजं तदहमर्जुन ।
न तदस्ति विना यत्स्यान्मया भूतं चराचरम् ॥३९॥

yaccāpi sarvabhūtānāṁ bījaṁ tadahamarjuna
na tadasti vinā yatsyānmayā bhūtaṁ carācaram 39.

The analogy of the seed and the tree is an inexhaustible theme for the meditators to contemplate upon. Under favourable conditions, the dormant life-content in the seed can manifest itself, and, ere long, the germinated seed can grow out to inconceivable heights and may thereafter look as though it has no relationship to the very seed from which it has sprung up. One who is viewing only the finite world of plurality – and mourning under the sledge-hammer of change and constant death – may not find in *samsara* anything to remind him of the Divine, Infinite and Blissful, as the Source from which the finite and sorrowful *samsara* has burst forth into expression.

The 'seed-condition of the Universe' is equivalent to the dormant condition of the tree before its manifestation among the two lobes of the dicotyledonous seed. Under favourable conditions, of course, the primary-shoot and the root-system will emerge, one ascending upwards to be the tree and the other burrowing down into the soil, to be the roots. The entire Universe of names and forms, in its condition of dormancy, remaining in seed-form, is the 'state-of-*pralaya*', conceived by and accepted in our *Upanishads*. This cosmic dissolution becomes more intelligible to us when we notice it happening in ourselves. In the state-of-sleep, our individual temperament, character, capability, education, culture, decency, etiquette, etc., all are in a condition of dormancy. In short, in sleep our personality-peculiarities remain in a seed-condition. When these *vasanas*, after an interval of restful poise, get impatient to express themselves, they emerge, and when the conditions are favourable, each of them manifests itself fully.

The restful state of the TOTAL-mind-intellect, and therefore, of all the *vasanas* in all of us in their condition of rest, would be the TOTAL-*pralaya* and, at that time the whole

Universe merges back to become the 'seed'. This is an illuminating example of the poetic way of expression used by all our ancient seers. This pregnant condition of the potential energy, which, after a time and under suitable circumstances, will emerge to express itself, is termed by the brilliant seers of *Upanishads* as the state-of-*Hiranyagarbha*. To translate this marvellous term as the 'Golden Egg' is one of the blasphemies unconsciously committed by the Western translators who have thereby outraged the beauty of our scriptures. The womb of all things and beings, is all that is indicated by the term, *Hiranyagarbha*.

The Lord is here identifying himself with the Total-causal-bodies of the world, meaning the total-*vasana* in all the creatures, and therefore, as *Ishwara*, He declares that the Self is the One-great-seed from which the tree-of-*samsara* has emerged and will, in future, emerge for an infinite number of times.

By the statement "I AM THE SEED OF THE UNIVERSE", the students of the *Geeta* might, during their reflection, come to a wrong conclusion altogether, inasmuch as in the outer world the seed itself dies to become the tree. Similarly, the Lord, while creating the world, might have destroyed Himself! To remove this misconception, Krishna says here, "NONE CAN EXIST WITHOUT ME, NEITHER THE MOVING, NOR THE UNMOVING".

Not only is the Lord the Seed of the Universe, but even after its germination and growth, the 'tree' is also sustained by the Self. The ocean is the 'seed', no doubt, of all waves that arise on the sea's surface. And yet, when all the waves germinate as it were, and grow up, none of them can stand apart from the Source, from which they arose. Where there is no ocean, no waves can stand, and wherever there are waves, they cannot sustain themselves except upon the grace of the ocean.

The cosmos rises up from the PRINCIPLE OF IGNORANCE that seemingly veils the Truth. This *avidya* (ignorance) also exists, drawing its potencies, however delusory they may be, from the total-source of all projections. This IGNORANCE of the Self, we know, is the 'seed' from which all the experienced worlds of the Universe have risen up. If the Awareness in us, Absolute and Eternal, were not to illumine the very IGNORANCE for us, the ignorance-produced sighs and sorrows, and the perceptions of plurality will not at all be available for us; we would not have been aware of them.

Thus, just as water is the cause for starting the germination in the seed and again, it is water alone that can nourish and sustain the tree, even after the tree has expanded itself to its greater dimensions, so too, the Divine Self, which, by its magic-touch, thrills the seed of *samsara* to germinate and thrive, is Itself the nourisher and the sustainer of its dimensions at all times.

When we are told that ten sample-pieces of ornaments have all emerged from one mass of gold, and when this statement is reinforced by a pertinent codicil that, without gold, none of these sample pieces can ever exist by itself even for a moment, it becomes evident that all of them are nothing but gold. Drawing a parallel, the Lord tells us that He is the very seed from which the entire multiple Universe has risen; and this partial statement of truth is complete when it is amended by the statement in the second line that "NONE CAN EXIST WITHOUT ME". Lord Cotton can say, "all the samples of cloth that are manufactured and used in the world have come from Me"; then it will be only true if Lord Cotton completes his statement by saying, "No sample of cloth can ever exist without Me, the Cotton-Essence".

DRAWING TOGETHER THE VARIOUS LINES OF ARGUMENTS MADE SO FAR, KRISHNA NOW WINDS UP THIS SECTION OF HIS DISCOURSE IN THE FOLLOWING THREE VERSES:

40. *There is no end to My Divine Glories, O Parantapa; but, this is but a brief statement by Me of the particulars of My Divine Glories.*

THERE IS NO END TO MY GLORIES—these enumerations of the transcendental glories of the Eternal were actually started in this chapter, in a cry of intelligent despair at the magnitude of the task and at the frailty of language to express them all. And yet, out of sheer love for the disciple, the Eternal Master in Krishna took the job in hand and tried to make the best of a bad job. No pot-maker can ever indicate to an enquirer, the 'mud essence' distinctly in each of the existing pots and congratulate himself in the end that he has exhausted all the pots that were, are, and shall ever be. It will be foolish vanity to hope to succeed in such a hopeless endeavour. And, in fact, it is not necessary also. If, in ten or twenty specimens, the Knower of the Essence indicates to the seeker, the 'Essential Stuff' in each distinctly, as separate from their names and forms and other attributes,

---

नान्तोऽस्ति मम दिव्यानां विभूतीनां परंतप।
एष तूद्देशतः प्रोक्तो विभूतेर्विस्तरो मया॥ ४०॥

nānto'sti mama divyānāṁ vibhūtīnāṁ parantapa
eṣa tūddeśataḥ prokto vibhūtervistaro mayā 40.

it should be possible for the seeker to recognise for himself the Essence when he meets the next specimen.

In this chapter, the Lord has given to Arjuna and over his shoulders to the entire generations of *Geeta*-students who may listen to Him in the world, the above FIFTY-FOUR instances, wherein the play of the Infinite, as recognised through the apparent veils of matter, has been shown. By now, any student who has meditated sufficiently upon those instances must have educated his mind fully to discover for himself the One Infinite behind the finite multiplicity.

In utter despair at not being able to exhaust the infinite varieties of the pluralistic phenomenal world, Krishna declares that "There is no end to the rays of My glory when I, being resplendent in My Absolute Perfection, shine out in my Self-effulgence".

If this knowledge was already with the Lord, why did He, as a spiritual teacher, bluff His disciples all along in a futile attempt to reveal Himself through the finite forms? Why this deception by the Divine? Why disappoint the students after straining them so long? Is this the general trait of all the religious teachers, prophets, seers and masters?

The answer to such accusations against the technique of religion is that - 'there is no other way'! A medical college student is asked to do a series of operations, upon a dead body, that has become cold last week-end!! This is no bluff; but, it is true, for all the careful and efficient surgery, the 'patient' dead as he is, will not start his life again. Such training on the dumb objects is necessary to give the student the required experience before he can start his independent activities in the profession. Similarly, here too, the Lord provides Arjuna with some specific examples in order to teach him the ART OF SEEING THE UNSEEN THROUGH THE SEEN.

This intention in his heart is clear in his own confession in the second line: "BUT, BY BRIEF EXAMPLES ONLY HAVE I DECLARED MY DIVINE GLORY". The Lord has not exhausted Himself; but He chooses a few effective examples to educate the mind of His listeners. Those who have ardently meditated upon these examples will learn to recognise the Infinite in all its unending resplendence enthroned in the bosom of every finite form.

IN SHORT, THE LORD SUMMARISES ALL THAT HE HAS SAID SO FAR:

41. *Whatever it is that is glorious, prosperous or powerful in any being, know that to be a manifestation of a part of My splendour.*

The above examples have made a frail attempt to indicate the glories of the Lord, but in no sense can those descriptions be considered as having defined the Truth. However, we have been given an idea that the Divine, the Imperishable, can be detected in the realm of the undivine and the perishable, if we look for it with discriminative judgement. From the above examples it becomes clear that the Lord is present in all names and forms, revealing Himself as the glorious, or the great, or the mighty aspect in all things and beings.

यद्यद्विभूतिमत्सत्त्वं श्रीमदूर्जितमेव वा ।
तत्तदेवावगच्छ त्वं मम तेजोंऽशसम्भवम् ॥ ४१ ॥

yadyadvibhūtimatsattvaṁ śrīmadūjintameva vā
tattadevāvagaccha tvaṁ mama tejoṁ'śasambhavam 41.

Here, Krishna directly summarises what exactly constitutes the Divine Presence in the world of plurality, and provides Arjuna with an acid test in knowing it. Whatever is great, or glorious, or mighty is nothing but the expression of a ray of the Lord's own Infinite Splendour. This is no doubt, a wonderful summary of the above mentioned fifty-four assorted items. Each one of these examples is a clear-cut instance, indicating the Lord, either as the Great one in the whole species, or as the noblest and the most glorious thing, or happening, or as the most mighty among all that is powerful.

This indication was given expressly to facilitate Arjuna's recognition of the IMMANENT glory of the Lord in the things of the world. It can be equally useful for us, students of the *Geeta*, in seeking and perceiving the play of the Infinite among the finite and the changing phenomena of names and forms.

IN THE END, PANTINGLY CONCLUDING THE ENUMERATIONS, THE LORD SAYS:

42. *But, of what avail to thee is the knowledge of all these details, O Arjuna? I exist, supporting this whole world by one part of Myself.*

In an inspired surge of friendliness and love, though Krishna, in all haste, promised that He would explain 'His expression in the individual' (*Yoga*) apart from the description of His glory as the Cosmic man (*Vibhuti*).

अथवा बहुनैतेन किं ज्ञातेन तवार्जुन।
विष्टभ्याहमिदं कृत्स्नमेकांशेन स्थितो जगत्॥ ४२॥

athavā bahunaitena kiṁ jñātena tavārjuna
viṣṭabhyāhamidaṁ kṛtsnamekāṁśena sthito jagat 42.

He Himself realised, whilst trying to indicate Himself object by object, the impossibility of exhausting the treatment. Infinite are the total number of things and beings in the Universe, and it is never possible to exhaust all of them one by one. With a cry of despair, and yet in an attitude of extreme love for his disciple, Lord Krishna brilliantly summarises this chapter in this closing stanza.

WHAT WILL IT AVAIL THEE TO KNOW ALL THESE DIVERSITIES—In fact it is useless to explain the presence of the Infinite in every finite form. It is impossible for a pot-maker to show the mud in all the existing pots in the world; nor can any one indicate the ocean-aspect in every wave in the sea. All that we can do is explaining to the student the art of recognising the mud aspect in a few pots so that the student can independently come to recognise mud in all existing pots. It is never possible for a mathematics teacher to exhaust all the examples, but the student is taught the art of solving problems through a limited number of typical examples, and thereafter, the student, all by himself, gains the capacity to solve any similar problem independently.

I, WITH ONE PART OF MYSELF, SUPPORT THIS WHOLE UNIVERSE—In philosophical usage, the term *Jagat* means 'all the fields of experiences which man has, as a physical body, as a psychological being and as an intellectual entity.' This would mean that the *Jagat* is the sum-total of the world perceived by my senses, plus the world of my emotions and sentiments, plus the world of my ideas and ideologies. The entire field* that is comprehended by the sense-organs, the mind and the intellect, is to be understood in its totality as *Jagat*. In short, this term conveniently embraces, in its meaning and import, the entire realm of objects.

---

* *Jagati-iti-Jagat*: that which is ever changing is *Jagat*. So it embraces the entire universe of things and beings conditioned by time and space.

The declaration here in the last line, therefore means that the total world-of-objects is supported, tended and nourished by a quarter of–meaning, a portion of the Subject, the Self. Krishna, as the Self, naturally declares here that the whole *Jagat* is supported by a portion of His glory. The statement has yet another philosophical implication, inasmuch as it declares that there are in the Truth vast portions which are uncontaminated by the disturbances which we call *Jagat*. No doubt, in the homogeneous Truth, there cannot be distinctly separate portions of different features; however, this is a kindly method of indicating a transcendental idea with the terrestrial words of finite language.

Thus, in the UPANISHADS of the glorious Bhagawad-Geeta, in the Science of the Eternal, in the scripture of YOGA, in the dialogue between Sri Krishna and Arjuna, the tenth discourse ends entitled.

The *Yoga* of Divine Glories

We have already explained the term *'Vibhuti'* during our discussions in this chapter. This becomes a *Yoga* inasmuch as students, earnestly following the path, would try to attune their mental perception and intellectual comprehensions so as to recognise the greatness, or the glory, or the might in the things and situations, and recognise them as a pencil of the Divine ray in themselves emerging from the glorious effulgence of the Self, to peep through the manifold finite embodiments.

Om Om Om Om Om

ॐ तत्सदिति श्रीमद् भगवद् गीतासूपनिषत्सु ब्रह्मविद्यायां
योगशास्त्रे श्रीकृष्णार्जुन संवादे विभूतियोगो नाम
दशमोऽध्यायः

Oṁ tatsaditi śrīmadbhagavadgītāsū ūpaniṣatsu brahmavidyāyāṁ
yogaśāstre śrī kṛṣṇārjuna saṁvāde vibhūtiyogo nāma
daśamo'dhyāyaḥ

XI

The Cosmic-Form Divine
Introduction

IN the general scheme of developing the theme, Lord Krishna had already explained His immanence in all objects of the world (*Vibhuti*). This expansion of Himself in all objects and beings, as a perceptible Divine Presence, is exhaustively explained in the previous chapter entitled *'Vibhuti Yoga'* – the Divine Glories.

Studying this chapter, keeping in view this scheme of development in the *Geeta*, we detect here that a perfectly modern and scientific method of investigation is employed. An intellectual enquiry seeks, first of all, to gather enough data to support a theory, and thereafter, it demands an experimental demonstration of the same, without which, the theory cannot be established. If in the previous chapter, therefore, the *Geeta* has supplied us with enough data to prove that the Self is the substratum for the multiple worlds, in this chapter, the attempt is to supply Arjuna with a practical demonstration that everything does exist only in the Self.

The declaration that the mud is the essence of all pots, is established only when we prove, not only that all pots have mud in them, but also that the mud always potentially contains all pots of all shapes and dimensions. To see the mud in every pot, one has only to train one's eyes to detect the mud as separate from the pot-shapes, but to see all pots in the mud, no doubt, the observer needs a special 'eye'. He needs a sufficient sense of detachment and a scholarly amount of imagination without which it is impossible for him to detect the world-of-pots in any sample of mud.

Similarly, as was described in the last chapter, to see the Self peeping through the windows of finite objects is relatively an easy task; but it is hard, indeed, for a mortal to cognise at once the entire Universe in one Reality, the Self. And yet, this is possible with the 'eye' of knowledge, which knows so well the art of discrimination, and which has developed in itself a sufficient sense of detachment, so that the observer can forget, for the moment, all his attachments, and view on, in a spirit of hushed expectancy and thrilled wonderment.

What exactly makes the things of the world exist separately from one another? My physical structure is certainly separated from the form and substance of the book that I am reading, or the chair in which I sit, or the table that is in front of me. I am separated from all others, and every one of them is separate from everything else. Scientifically viewed, the factor that determines the physical existence of all things in the world is the same. And yet, we do not feel the oneness – they, being separated from each other, exist as individualised entities. What exactly are the factors that divide body from body, that separate object from object?

On a careful analysis, it will be quite clear to the thinker that it is the concept of space that divides the physical structures into independent islands. That which separates me from you, or me from my book, is the intervening space. Within my forearm, from the elbow to the wrist, there is certainly a sense of oneness, because, there is no intervening space present within the homogeneity of its entire length, while my fingers are separate, each being interleaved with space. If the concept of space is totally blotted out, it will be clear that all objects will immediately come together into a happy embrace, and will represent themselves as one congenial, homogeneous whole. And, in this mass of things, there must be all the shapes and forms of all the things of this world at one and the same place and time. This is the concept of the Cosmic-Man; the vision of the world, when viewed by a mind in which the concept of time and space has been dried up! Though, not totally.

Supposing a toy-maker makes out of wax hundreds of forms of animals, birds, and creatures and stocks them in a cupboard. Viewed through its glass panes, no doubt, the monkey-doll is different from the cow-doll and both of them are separate from the baby-doll. But suppose the doll-maker changes his mind and he decides to destroy the whole lot and to make out of the stuff something more profitable. On the shelf of the cupboard, the same toys are separated from each other by the intervening space. Suppose the toy maker decides to squeeze them into one ball of wax. In this act, the maker of the dolls has eliminated the spaces that were there, between the dolls, and in thus bringing them together he created a huge ball of wax on the surface of which we could see the traces of almost all the dolls that were brought together; perhaps, the tail of the monkey, the face of the cow, the smile of the child, and the head of the dog!

Similarly, if Krishna could dry up 'the concept of space' in the mind of Arjuna, the Prince would be able to see the whole Universe as though on his own palm. However, here we find that Arjuna's mind was given enough freedom to move above within the space-limit of Krishna's divine structure. Naturally, he sees in the Krishna-form the entire Universe compressed and packed.

This concept of the Cosmic-Man, and the actual vision of it in the *Geeta,* satisfies the demand for demonstration in any age of intellectual self-assertion. Having seen the form Arjuna gets completely converted both in his faith and in his understanding.

In this chapter, we find how the exquisite dramatist in Vyasa has squeezed the Sanskrit language dry to feed the beauty of his literary masterpiece. Apart from the chosen words and the mellifluous phrases, every metrical dexterity is being employed here, as an effective strategy to heighten the dramatic situation and to paint clearly the emotions of wonderment, amazement, fear, reverence, devotion, etc., in Arjuna. Altogether, in the dignity of concept, in the beauty of diction, in the artistry of its depiction and in its inner stream of drama, this chapter has been rightly upheld by all as one of the highest philosophical poems in the world's treasure house of sacred books.

Arjuna Said:

1. *By this word of the highest secret concerning the Self, which You have spoken out of compassion towards me, my delusion is gone.*

In this opening stanza, Arjuna expresses his complete satisfaction at the details regarding the glories of the Lord which were described in the previous chapter, Arjuna appreciated that so much labour was spent by Krishna only to bless his disciple and bring him out of delusion. To realise the unity in the diversity is to get an inoculation against the sorrows of plurality. The deft pen of Vyasa beautifully

---

अर्जुन उवाच
मदनुग्रहाय परमं गुह्यमध्यात्मसंज्ञितम् ।
यत्त्वयोक्तं वचस्तेन मोहोऽयं विगतो मम ॥ १ ॥

arjuna uvāca
madanugrahāya paramaṁ guhyamadhyātmasañjñitam
yattvayoktaṁ vacastena moho'yaṁ vigato mama 1.

registers the effectiveness of the last chapter upon a sincere student when he makes Arjuna confess, "THIS, MY DELUSION, IS GONE".

Removal of a delusion or a misunderstanding is not in itself the acquisition of knowledge of the Real. Removal of delusion is one aspect of the process of knowing the Truth. Arjuna must be rightly feeling that his delusion -- his firm faith in the separativeness of names and forms -- can no longer hold its grounds when his intellect has been educated to look forward to, and detect the 'presence' of the Divine in the very world of his perceptions. But at the same time, he has not gained any visible experience of the Unity in the diversity; he has no personal experience of the oneness of things and beings, although theoretically at least, his intellect has come to accept this inherent Oneness.

The Pandava Prince, Arjuna, realises that Krishna has so elaborately explained the theme in the previous chapter only 'out of compassion towards me' (*mad-anugrahaya*). This reminds us of Krishna using almost the same term (X-2) when He explains how He, abiding in the hearts of his devotees, destroys all their inner darkness born out of ignorance.

OUT OF COMPASSION FOR ARJUNA, WHAT WERE THE SUPREMELY PROFOUND WORDS THAT WERE GIVEN OUT BY THE LORD? LISTEN:

2. *The origin and destruction of beings verily, have been heard by me in detail from You, O Lotus-eyed Krishna, and also Your inexhaustible greatness.*

भवाप्ययौ हि भूतानां श्रुतौ विस्तरशो मया ।
त्वत्तः कमलपत्राक्ष माहात्म्यमपि चाव्ययम् ॥ २ ॥

bhavāpyayau hi bhūtānāṁ śrutau vistaraśo mayā
tvattaḥ kamalapatrākṣa māhātmyamapi cāvyayam 2.

It is natural, in a discussion between the teacher and the taught, that at the end of a difficult lesson, on approaching the teacher with his doubts, the student should first of all prove to him that he has sufficiently understood the theme of the discussion. This entitles the student to ask the teacher his doubts and get them cleared. Following this traditional method, Arjuna is trying to show Krishna that he has completely understood the main theme of the last chapter. He has listened to Krishna and understood the 'ORIGIN AND DISSOLUTION OF BEINGS, AND THE GREATNESS AND THE INEXHAUSTIBLE GLORY OF THE LORD'.

And yet, a doubt remains which can be removed only when his intellect is convinced by a confident knowledge arising out of an actually observed demonstration. The stanza is preparing to meet such a demand. When a student, who has proved to have understood the logic of discussion already carried out, asks a legitimate question, or enquires after the remedy for a possible obstacle, a true teacher must help him out of his troubles by all possible means. We shall observe here in this chapter that the great *Yogeshwara* (Krishna), out of sheer kindness, even condescends to show Arjuna the form of the Cosmic-Man because the disciple has demanded that he must see it.

THE DEMAND OF THE DISCIPLE IS DESCRIBED IN THE FOLLOWING VERSE:

3. *(Now) O Supreme Lord! As you have thus described Yourself, I wish to see (actually) Your Form Divine, O PURUSHOTTAMA.*

एवमेतद्यथात्थ त्वमात्मानं परमेश्वर ।
द्रष्टुमिच्छामि ते रूपमैश्वरं पुरुषोत्तम ॥ ३ ॥

evametadyathāttha tvamātmānaṁ parameśvara
draṣṭumicchāmi te rūpamaiśvaraṁ puruṣottama 3.

Indicating by a familiar idiom in Sanskrit, "So be it" (*evam-etat*), Arjuna accepts the technical thesis that has been declared by the Lord. Intellectually, it has been satisfactorily proved that the Lord is immanent in all names and forms. Still the intellect awaits the baptism of a demonstration. Therefore, Arjuna says, "I DESIRE TO SEE YOUR *ISHWARA*-FORM". He is *Ishwara* who in Himself, expresses Omnipotence, Infinite Wisdom, Strength, Virtue and Splendour; these are the six qualities that are described in our *shastras* as forming the characteristic features of the God-principle.

This was the occasion on which Krishna decided to show to Arjuna that the LORD IS NOT ONLY IMMANENT in all forms, but He is also the vehicle or receptacle in which all names and forms have their existence and play – HE IS ALSO TRANSCENDENT.

Though, with the enthusiasm of a fanatic believer in intellectualism, Arjuna demands a demonstration, he immediately realises that his audacity has, perhaps, crossed the frontiers of decency.

HE IS TRYING TO SMOOTHEN HIS WORDS OUT IN THE FOLLOWING STANZA:

4. *If you, O Lord, think it possible for me to see It, if You please, then, O Lord of YOGAS, show me Your Imperishable Self-form.*

मन्यसे यदि तच्छक्यं मया द्रष्टुमिति प्रभो ।
योगेश्वर ततो मे त्वं दर्शयात्मानमव्ययम् ॥ ४ ॥

manyase yadi tacchakyaṁ mayā draṣṭumiti prabho
yogeśvara tato me tvaṁ darśayātmānamavyayam 4.

The demand in the previous stanza has been repeated here, with a dignified humility and pure reverence. In our ordinary life, in all our respectful appeals and humble petitions we use such phrases as, "If I may be permitted to say", "I shall be much obliged if", "I have the honour to submit", "If I may have the leave to say so", etc. The Pandava Prince, as a result of a second thought, as it were, smoothens his soldier-like abrupt language used in the previous stanza and says that the Lord's IMMUTABLE Universal Form may be shown to him – "IF YOU THINK I AM CAPABLE OF SEEING IT".

The modesty and reverence shown here are not expressions of a faked emotion for cheap fulfilment of desires. This is evident from the term he is using in addressing the Lord in the verse. In the first line we find Krishna being addressed as 'O Lord' (*Prabho*), and in the following line He is again addressed as 'the Lord of *Yogas*' (*Yogeshwara*). These clearly indicate that Arjuna has come to feel that Krishna is not a mere mortal teacher, capable of giving only some intellectual ventilations and spiritual discourses, but that "He is Himself Divine and a Master-of-*Yoga*" and therefore, he is capable of fulfilling the request, if the 'teacher' in Krishna is satisfied that the 'student' in Arjuna will be benefited by such a demonstration.

THE HUMBLE REQUEST OF AN EARNEST STUDENT NEVER FALLS ON DEAF EARS, IF IT IS MADE TO A TRUE TEACHER:

The Blessed Lord said:

5. Behold, O Partha, forms of Me, by hundreds and thousands, of different sorts Divine, of various colours and shapes.

If gold is the essential stuff in all the ornaments, every ornament in the world must be available in the total gold. To see the gold in the ornaments is relatively easy, it being a physical perception. But to detect the presence of all ornaments of different shapes and colours in the total gold is comparatively difficult, inasmuch as it is the vision of the intellect.

Keeping this idea in mind, when you read the opening lines of the Lord's words, it becomes strikingly significant. "BEHOLD, BY HUNDREDS AND THOUSANDS, MY DIFFERENT FORMS CELESTIAL, VARIED IN COLOURS AND SHAPES." It was not necessary for Krishna to change His form to that of the Cosmic-Man; all that Arjuna had to do was to BEHOLD THE FORM right in front of him. But, unfortunately, the instrument-of-perception was not tuned up for the object of his investigation, and therefore, Arjuna could not perceive that which was already in Krishna.

That which is lying beyond the focal length of a telescope, cannot be viewed by the observer even though the object may be present in line with the axis of the instrument. In order to bring the farther object within the span of vision, the observer will have to make the required adjustments in

---

श्रीभगवानुवाच
पश्य मे पार्थ रूपाणि शतशोऽथ सहस्रशः ।
नानाविधानि दिव्यानि नानावर्णाकृतीनि च ॥ ५ ॥

śrībhagavānuvāca
paśya me pārtha rūpāṇi śataśo'tha sahasraśaḥ
nānāvidhāni divyāni nānāvaṇārkṛtīni ca 5.

the telescope. Similarly, Krishna did not TRANSFORM Himself into His Cosmic-Form, but He only helped Arjuna to make the necessary inward adjustments so that he could perceive what was there evidently in Krishna. Naturally, the Lord says, 'BEHOLD'. The total world of perceivable beings of all shapes and colours is indicated in the enumeration made by the Lord in the stanza.

WHAT ARE THOSE?

6. *Behold the ADITYAS, the VASUS, the RUDRAS, the (two) ASHWINS and also the MARUTS; behold many wonders never seen before, O Bharata.*

In enumerating the items that are to be seen in Krishna's Cosmic-Form, the Lord hints at the most important and striking of them. This is generally done when we try to describe a crowd of people or things by using a short representative term. Mention is made on all such occasions of the most important items or personalities – the few who represent the whole crowd.

With a note of despair ringing through his words, the Lord concludes "BEHOLD MANY MORE SUCH WONDERS AS NEVER SEEN BEFORE". The various items enumerated have all been already explained in the previous chapter* of them the only new term used here is the *Ashwini Kumaras*, the Horsemen-Twins. It is not very clear in literature as to what exactly is the identity of these twins with heads of horses.

पश्यादित्यान्वसून्रुद्रानश्विनौ मरुतस्तथा ।
बहून्यदृष्टपूर्वाणि पश्याश्चर्याणि भारत ॥ ६ ॥

paśyādityānvasūnrudrānaśvinau marutastathā
bahūnyadṛṣṭapūvārṇi paśyāścyārṇi bhārata 6.

*

It is not very easy to decide what they represent. In some places they are described as the Dawn and the Dusk, and in other places there are sufficient evidences to make us suspect that they represent the Morning-Star and the Evening-Star. Anyway, they are Angels that go to serve their devotees in times of utter need and despair.

BY GIVING A COMPREHENSIVE SUMMARY OF THE THINGS TO BE EXPECTED IN THE COSMIC-VISION, KRISHNA HAS INCREASED THE INTELLECTUAL CURIOSITY OF HIS DISCIPLE. WHERE EXACTLY IS HE TO LOOK FOR THESE THINGS? ... LISTEN:

7. *Now behold, O Gudakesha, in this Body, that the whole universe centres in One – including, the moving and the unmoving—and whatever else you desire to see.*

The enthusiastic seeker's adventurous mind having been sufficiently educated so far to develop an unending wealth of 'eagerness to know', Krishna further educates, sharpening in the student, the 'anxiety to know' in his mind, with sufficient details on what he may expect in the Divine Vision that is to follow. This secret technique then makes the student ardently converge all this attention towards one given Form Divine. This is achieved by this verse. If we follow the technique, developed through the expressed words, we shall find that Vyasa has here explained the entire science-of-Love

---

इहैकस्थं जगत्कृत्स्नं पश्याद्य सचराचरम् ।
मम देहे गुडाकेश यच्चान्यद्द्रष्टुमिच्छसि ॥ ७ ॥

ihaikastham jagatkṛtsnam paśyādya sacarācaram
mama dehe guḍākeśa yaccānyad draṣṭumicchasi 7.

* Chapter XI-Introduction

as enumerated in the cult of *Bhakti*, or 'Devotion to the Supreme'.

The entire Universe, constituted both of the moving and the unmoving - of the sentient and the insentient – is being shown by Krishna on his own physical structure as described by the effective intimate term, 'Here, concentrated' (*Iha-ekastham*). And this term has been annotated in the same stanza as 'In this, My Body' (*mama dehe*). The entire Universe of gross forms, both movable and immovable, is to be compressed within the framework of Krishna's girth and height. As we explained earlier* the concept of space has not been completely sponged out of Arjuna's mind but a total space-concept equivalent to Krishna's own mortal dimensions is left in him. With this mind, when Arjuna looks out, he must necessarily see framed in Krishna all at once, the entire Universe compressed and miniatured with all its multiple details intact.

Even though 'the entire Universe, including both the moving and the unmoving' is a term sufficiently elastic so as not to leave anything outside its implications, Krishna again sharpens the enthusiasm of Arjuna by stating that the Pandava could see anything ELSE THAT YOU DESIRE TO SEE. As a typical mortal, Arjuna is preoccupied with the particular problem of life and his anxiety naturally grows to peep into the future and discover its solution rather than to realise the underlying oneness that embraces even the forms in the outer world-of-matter.

'THE ONE IN THE MANY' HAS BEEN DESCRIBED IN THE LAST CHAPTER, AND HERE WE ARE ABOUT TO SEE 'THE MANY IN THE ONE'.

8. *But You are not able to behold Me with these Your own eyes;*
I give You the divine-eye; behold My Lordly YOGA.

We have already explained how it is relatively easy to see the essential stuff as the core of individual names and forms, but the reverse of it – to discover the many in the one – is the work of a subtle intellect functioning through right philosophical understanding. TO READ a poem, only knowledge of the alphabet is necessary; but TO UNDERSTAND its subtler beauties and to classify it in a comparative study with other similar poems, it needs a masterly mind that has been well soaked with the masterpieces in poetry. Similarly, to see 'THE ONE IN THE MANY' is the work of a 'heart' soaked with faith; but to perceive 'THE MANY IN THE ONE', we need, besides the 'heart', an educated 'intellect' that has learnt to see for itself the logic of the philosophers. This peculiar capacity of an educated intellect to see the extraordinary is the vision of the intellect, which is gained when we develop the faculty to perceive and to know.

This obvious fact is explained by the Lord in this stanza, "YOU CANNOT SEE ME WITH THESE EYES OF YOURS; I GIVE THEE THE VISION DIVINE". There are very many critics who try to explain this 'Divine-eye' through fantastic suppositions and ridiculous theories.

Such commentators are certainly men, not much educated in the style of the Hindu scriptures, the *Upanishads*. Expressly

---

न तु मां शक्यसे द्रष्टुमनेनैव स्वचक्षुषा ।
दिव्यं ददामि ते चक्षुः पश्य मे योगमैश्वरम् ॥ ८ ॥

na tu mā ṁśakyasedraṣṭunenaiva svacakṣuṣā
divyaṁ dadāmi te cakṣuḥ paśya me yogamaiśvaram 8.

and tacitly, all through the *Upanishads*, it is repeatedly explained that the subtler cannot be brought within the scope and compass of the instruments of perception given to man. The external sense organs can play freely only in the outer world-of-objects. Even when we ordinarily 'see an idea' it is not done with our outer pair of eyes. The intellectual comprehension is meant here by the term 'seeing' and the capacity of the intellect to comprehend is the 'Divine-eye'.

This 'special-vision' is given to the Pandava Prince so that he may see MY SUPREME *YOGA*-POWER by which the whole Universe of multiplicity is being supported by the Lord's own form. Earlier, this particular *Yoga*-Power of the Lord, has been already described at two different places, (VII-12 and IX-4) almost in identical terms.

THE SCENE SHIFTS TO HASTINAPURA, IN THE PALACE OF DHRITARASHTRA:

Sanjaya said:

9. *Having thus spoken, O King, the great Lord of YOGA, Hari, showed to Partha His Supreme Form, as the Lord (of the Universe).*

The versatile genius of Vyasa has never left anything that he has touched without raising it to the most sublime heights of perfection. With unimaginable capacities for composing

---

सञ्जय उवाच
एवमुक्त्वा ततो राजन्महायोगेश्वरो हरिः ।
दर्शयामास पार्थाय परमं रूपमैश्वरम् ॥ ९ ॥

sañjaya uvāca
evamuktavā tato rājanmahāyogeśvaro hariḥ
darśayāmāsa pātharya paramaṁ rūpamaiśvaram 9.

incomparable poetry, unique prose-diction, chaste descriptions, artistic, literary designs, original innovations both in thought and form – a brilliant philosopher, a man of consummate wisdom, a genius in worldly knowledge, at one time in the palace, at another time in the battle-field, at still another time in Badrinath, and again, among the silent snow peaks – strode the colossus, Sri Vyasa, as an embodiment of what is best in the Hindu tradition and in the Aryan culture. Such an all-round genius has not yet been reported ever to have been born, lived or achieved so much in the history of this globe, at any other time!

After Lord Krishna gave Arjuna a hint as to what he should expect and where he would gain the vision of the Cosmic-Man, etc., Vyasa introduces a small section in which Sanjaya reports to Dhritarashtra, the blind father of the wicked Kauravas.

The literary purpose served by this stanza is only to show to the readers that Krishna, according to his promise, had actually revealed his Cosmic-Form to Arjuna. But along with that, the deft mastery of the ancient writer of Mahabharata tries to paint for us the mental attitude and the inward sympathies of Sanjaya. We have stated earlier that Sanjaya is our own special correspondent. His sympathies are clearly with the Pandavas, the friends of the Lord. This tendency in Sanjaya is unquestionably revealed when he addressed his own master merely as 'O King' (*Rajan*) while he uses the terms, (a) *Mahayogeshwara* ... 'the Great Lord of *Yoga*' and (b) *Harih* ... 'the one who maintains the champions of Truth by destroying the powers of falsehood', to indicate Lord Krishna. The implied suggestions of these words point at a bloodless murder of the blind old King!

With Sanjaya's words, the crowd of listeners and students of *Geeta* are shifted from the field of the battle to the palace of the battle-monger. This is perhaps necessary to remind the readers that the philosophy of the *Geeta* has an intimate practical application to life. Sanjaya informs Dhritarashtra that the Great Lord of *Yoga* showed to Arjuna his Supreme *Ishwara*-form. Sanjaya entertains a thin hope that, at least on hearing that the Lord of the Universe is on the side of his nephews, the blind King will foresee the sure defeat of his sons and, in his discrimination, will cry a halt to the impending disastrous war.

IN A ROUGH OUTLINE SANJAYA DESCRIBES THE LIST OF THINGS THAT WERE VISIBLE WITHIN THE FRAMEWORK OF THE DIVINE CHARIOTEER:

10. *With numerous mouths and eyes, with numerous wonderful sights, with numerous divine ornaments, with numerous divine weapons uplifted (such a form He showed).*

11. *Wearing divine garlands (necklaces) and apparel, anointed with divine unguents, the All-wonderful, Resplendent, Endless, facing all sides.*

अनेकवक्त्रनयनमनेकाद्भुतदर्शनम् ।
अनेकदिव्याभरणं दिव्यानेकोद्यतायुधम् ॥ १० ॥

anekavaktranayanamanekādbhutadarśanam
avekadivyābharaṇaṁ divyānekodyatāyudham 10.

दिव्यमाल्याम्बरधरं दिव्यगन्धानुलेपनम् ।
सर्वाश्चर्यमयं देवमनन्तं विश्वतोमुखम् ॥ ११ ॥

divyamālyābaradharaṁ divyagandhānulenam
savārścaryamayaṁ devamanantaṁ viśvatomukham 11.

When a painter at his easel tries to express his artistic ideas through the medium of colour he invariably begins by outlining his theme roughly on the canvas. Later on, inch by inch, he adds more and more details to make the canvas sing the song of his message. Similarly in the word-picture of the literary artist, Vyasa, this stanza containing Sanjaya's words, represents the rough outline of the Universal Form of the Lord.

The Vision appearing before Sanjaya is no vision for a mortal intellect to live comfortably by. An ordinary man must feel dazed with wonderment and fear at this august and mighty Vision. The total Cosmos is no easy subject-matter for the mind to conceive of or for the intellect to comprehend, and therefore, when it comes as it does in the *Geeta,* in the stark realism of the Vision, Sanjaya stammers these phrases.

"DIVINE HIS GARLANDS AND ROBES" – "DIVINE THE PERFUME OF HIS ANOINTMENT" – "ALL MARVELLOUS, THE LORD, BOUNDLESS AND FACING EVERY SIDE" – these represent the remaining strokes which, when added to the previous set of lines, bring out the picture of the Cosmic-Man roughly in its full outline.

CONTINUING IN HIS LANGUAGE OF DOTS AND DASHES, SANJAYA DESCRIBES:

12. *If the splendour of a thousand Suns was to blaze all at once (simultaneously) in the sky, that would be like the splendour of that Mighty Being (great soul).*

दिवि सूर्यसहस्रस्य भवेद्युगपदुत्थिता ।
यदि भा: सदृशी सा स्याद्भासस्तस्य महात्मन: ॥ १२ ॥

divi sūryasahasrasya bhavedyaupadutthitā
yadi bhāḥ sadṛśī sāa syādbhāsastasya mahātmanaḥ 12.

After giving this hasty sketch of the Total-Form to the blind King, Dhritarashtra, Sanjaya explains to him the glory of the Mighty One. The Lord, in His Universal-aspect, was dazzling in His own brilliance, and the divine glory of it was almost blinding; and this may be another reason why more intimate details are not given by Sanjaya in the previous two verses. In order to convey this idea, Sanjaya is using this strange, but powerful, simile.

The glorious shine of that Mighty Being is almost; it is said, as luminous as that of a thousand Suns if they were to rise up all at once in the sky. In the *Upanishadic* lore also, we have the description of the *Atman* almost in the same language. But somehow or other, it must be admitted that in the mouth of Sanjaya, especially when he is describing the Divine-Form of Krishna, it gathers a new glamour and glory.

BEAUTIFYING THE PICTURE WITH SOME MORE DETAILS, SANJAYA ADDS:

13. *There, in the body of the God of gods, the Pandava (Son of Pandu) then saw the whole Universe resting in one, with all its infinite parts.*

In that Divine Form of the Lord, Arjuna perceived how the entire world of manifold varieties had been brought together and packed to rest at one and the same place. We have already noticed that the concept of the Cosmic-Man is

---

तत्रैकस्थं जगत्कृत्स्नं प्रविभक्तमनेकधा ।
अपश्यद्देवदेवस्य शरीरे पाण्डवस्तदा ॥ १३ ॥

tatraikasthaṁ jagatkṛtsnaṁ pravibhaktamanekadhā
apaśyar devadevasya śarīre pāṇḍavastadā 13.

the vision of the Universe through a mind which has ceased to act with the concept of time or space. This vision of 'the many in one' is not so much a physical perception as an intellectual comprehension. It is not that the Universe has shrunk into the size of Krishna. It is quite sufficient if Arjuna has the required sense of oneness in the world of matter and if he looks at the Universe through his understanding so that, intellectually, he can come to estimate the oneness of the Universe.

To quote a parallel in modern science, we may consider the attempt of Chemistry to classify all the existing substances. When so many things in the world are brought on the laboratory tables, it is found that they are constituted of the elements, in all about one hundred and three in number. This understanding of the elements soon yields place when the atom-contents in them are discovered to be nothing other than the electrons, protons and neutrons. If a scientist, who knows these three, were to look through his knowledge, at the manifold substances, it would be very easy for him to see that all things of the world are in the three factors, which are the contents of each atom. In fact now there are only three elements in the world, the triple factors in the Atom. Similarly here, when Arjuna gained his special knowledge through the grace of Krishna, he comes to recognise the whole Universe in the very body of the God-principle, the Total-intellect.

ARJUNA'S PSYCHOLOGICAL AND PHYSICAL REACTIONS ON SEEING THIS FORM, ARE BEING VERY CAREFULLY NOTED AND REPORTED BY SANJAYA:

14. *Then, Dhananjaya, filled with wonder, with his hair standing on end, bowed down his head to the God and spoke with joined palms.*

On seeing this transcendental vision, emotions of wonderment and consequent horripilations are noticed in Arjuna. Though Sanjaya is far away, he not only seems to see minute physical details of each soldier upon the battle-field but also seems to have a power to peep over the body into the mind-and-intellect equipment of each individual. The inner wonder-emotion in Arjuna's mind is as much evident to Sanjaya, as was his hair standing on his body. Arjuna, with folded palms, bending his head low, now opens his mouth for the first time to talk. That Arjuna did not speak so long is in itself a positive indication of the choking emotion that he must have felt at the sight of this sweetly unnerving Divine-Form.

WHAT WERE THE ACTUAL WORDS OF WONDERMENT THAT BURST OUT FROM ARJUNA? ... LISTEN:

ततः स विस्मयाविष्टो हृष्टरोमा धनञ्जयः ।
प्रणम्य शिरसा देवं कृताञ्जलिरभाषत ॥ १४ ॥

tataḥ sa vismayāviṣṭo hṛṣṭromā dhanañjayaḥ
praṇamya śirasā devaṁ kṛtāñjalirabhāṣata 14.

Arjuna said:

15. *I see all the gods, O God, in Your body, and (also) hosts of various classes of beings. BRAHMA, the Lord of Creation, seated on the Lotus, all the RISHIS and celestial serpents.*

When the Prince addressed Krishna as the Resplendent (*Deva*), he is endorsing the comparison of the Lord to the light of thousand-Suns which was used earlier by Sanjaya. Enumerating the features recognised by him on the body of Krishna, Arjuna says, 'IN THY BODY I SEE ALL THE *DEVAS* AND HOSTS OF ALL GRADES OF BEINGS'.

This was already indicated by Sanjaya when he described the Universal Form as 'WEARING NUMEROUS ROBES', 'ADORNING ITSELF WITH DIFFERENT TYPES OF DIVINE ORNAMENTS', 'WEARING GARLANDS OF CELESTIAL BEAUTY', and bearing 'AN ARSENAL OF WEAPONS IN ITS INNUMERABLE HANDS'.

These descriptions show that in Krishna one could recognise not only the things of the world, but in the *Virata*-form of the Lord even the *Devas* are represented. The same *adhidaiva*-idea is very directly insisted upon by Arjuna in this stanza when he describes among the things that he saw in Krishna, the Creator, Brahmaji (*Brahmaanam*), the Annihilator,

---

अर्जुन उवाच
पश्यामि देवांस्तव देव देहे
सर्वांस्तथा भूतविशेषसंघान् ।
ब्रह्माणमीशं कमलासनस्थम्
ऋषींश्च सर्वानुरगांश्च दिव्यान् ॥ १५ ॥

arjuna uvāca
paśyāmi devāṁstava deva dehe
savārṁstathā bhūtaviśeṣasaghān
brahmaṇamīśaṁ kamalāsanastham
ṛṣīṁśca savārnuragāṁśca divyān 15.

Shiva (*Isham*), and the Sustainer, Vishnu (*Kamal-asana-stham*); along with a host of ancient Seers!

AND CELESTIAL SERPENTS—In poetry, it is a technique, often very effective, employed by great poets wherein they suddenly step down from the sublime to the ridiculous or the grotesque, only to shock the readers and thereby tap out of them the degree of special attention which the theme demands. It is indicated here that from Brahmaji in the heavens, to the serpents in the holes of the earth, all are represented in the Lord's Cosmic-Form. The microcosm (*Vyashti*) is in the macrocosm (*Samashti*). And this is explained and realised by all great thinkers of the world.

But nobody has ever before tried to express this philosophical idea in the form of a vivid objective representation. Vyasa was the pioneer in this art and none has yet dared to follow him in this arduous task.

THE GRIPPING DETAILS THAT CAN UNNERVE EVEN THE MOST COURAGEOUS ARE GIVEN OUT NOW BY ARJUNA:

16. *I see Thee of boundless form on every side, with manifold arms, stomachs, mouths and eyes; neither the end, nor the middle, nor also the beginning do I see; O, Lord of the Universe, O, Cosmic-Form.*

अनेकबाहूदरवक्त्रनेत्रं
पश्यामि त्वां सर्वतोऽनन्तरूपम् ।
नान्तं न मध्यं न पुनस्तवादिं
पश्यामि विश्वेश्वर विश्वरूप ॥ १६ ॥

anekabāhūdaravaktranetraṁ
paśyāmi tvāṁ sarvato'nantarūpam
nāntaṁ na madhyaṁ na punastavādiṁ
paśyāmi viśveśvara viśvarūpa 16.

A limited human intellect is not the instrument with which one can perceive in one sweep the Infinite majesty of the Universal-Form. It must necessarily stand staggered at the vastness of the concept and the significances of Its sheer dimensions. That the Lord is the ONE dynamic Truth behind every organ of activity and in every existent thing is indicated here when Arjuna says "I SEE THEE OF BOUNDLESS FORM ON EVERY SIDE, WITH MANIFOLD ARMS, STOMACHS, MOUTHS AND EYES". This is not to be construed as a caricature of Truth. This warning is necessary for all hasty artists, who, inspired by the theme, generally rush to this field of thought, to represent this Cosmic Form with their brushes and colours. And they all but fail miserably!

The Universal Oneness is not an object of perception; it is only a fact to be realised or apprehended. This is endorsed by the very words of Arjuna that immediately follow in the stanza, "NEITHER THE END, NOR THE BEGINNING, NOR THE MIDDLE OF THEE DO I SEE". The description of the Truth -- from which all names and forms arise, in which they exist, and into which they all merge back at the end of their temporary play -- cannot be better done in any other way and those who, with sympathetic understanding, get at the real import of these stanzas can appreciate their rich beauties and luxurious warmth.

The above stanzas express the oneness that threads through the mortal beings and finite things of the world, making a single garland of them all!

IT MAY BE DOUBTED WHETHER THE DEIFIED DENIZENS OF THE DIVINE HIERARCHY ARE ALSO REPRESENTED UPON THIS WONDER-FORM, THIS IS ANSWERED IN THE FOLLOWING:

17. *I see Thee with Crown, Club, and Discus; a mass of radiance shining everywhere, very hard to look at, all round blazing like burning fire and Sun, and incomprehensible.*

Continuing his description of the Cosmic-Form, the Pandava Prince gives more and more details of what he comprehends in that incomprehensible Divine extravaganza. He sees therein the Crown, the Club, and the Discus. These are the insignia which Lord Vishnu is said to carry, in all mythological descriptions.

Hindu gods are represented as having certain divine symbols, and they all have their own respective special significances – of Kingship and Lordliness over the world of finite things and happenings. He alone is the Lord who is a Master of circumstances and a Ruler of impulses. A slave to life and its enchantments is a weakling, on whose head a crown rests only temporarily like the gilted-cardboard-crown of an actor playing on a stage. No authority or effectiveness in life is possible unless the man in power has self-control and self-mastery. No man can live a happy and mighty life unless he has conquered his passions and crowned himself with kingship over himself. He is Vishnu and He alone then deserves the crown!

किरीटिनं गदिनं चक्रिणं च
तेजोराशिं सर्वतो दीप्तिमन्तम् ।
पश्यामि त्वां दुर्निरीक्ष्यं समन्तात्
दीप्तानलार्कद्युतिमप्रमेयम् ॥ १७ ॥

kirīṭinaṁ gadinaṁ cakriṇaṁ ca
tejoraśiṁ sarvato diptimantam
paśyāmi tvaṁ durnirīkṣyaṁ samantād
dīptānalārkadyutimaprayam 17.

The four-armed Vishnu carries in his hands the Conch, the Discus, the Club, and the Lotus. This is extremely symbolical. In India the Lotus represents 'peace and joy, auspiciousness and happiness'. The Conch blows and calls man to duty; and if there be a generation of men who listen not to the Higher-call in themselves, restlessness, war, pestilence, famine, storms, and chaotic social and communal disturbances visit them – the Club descends to hammer the generation to shape and discipline. Even after this punishment, if there be a generation so totally dissipated that it cannot improve, then comes the Discus – the sharp-toothed wheel, ever revolving, the Whirling of Time (*Kaala-chakra*) to annihilate the irredeemable generation.

When we find these in Arjuna's description as part of the Universal Form, it becomes evident that the same Truth is the Substratum, not only of the lowest of low worms, but even of the Divine Trinity. The Eternal Truth is one and the same, everywhere, at all times; only Its manifestations are varied, and the degree of Divinity sparkling from each differs according to the grossness or subtlety of the equipment through which the same Infinite Reality expresses Itself.

AS A MASS OF RADIANCE SHINING EVERYWHERE, ALL ROUND GLOWING LIKE THE BLAZING SUN AND FIRE, HARD TO GAZE ON—One of the most expressive lines in this description, this brings home to us the glory of Pure Awareness. This is not 'light' in the physical sense of the term; but all the same we have to use the word, borrowed from ordinary language, though it is applied here with a special significance. Consciousness is the 'Light' in which we so clearly 'SEE' our own thoughts and emotions. It is the same light which, beaming out through the eyes, throws 'Light' upon the world and illumines for us the FORMS AND SHAPES. The same Consciousness, beaming out through the ears, with its special 'Light', illumines SOUND, and so on. Naturally, therefore, the Universal-Form of Krishna, representing in Himself the Infinite Awareness, had to be described, in the faltering language of Arjuna, as a mass of resplendent light, blinding all faculties of perception, feeling and understanding.

INCOMPREHENSIBLE (*Aprameya*)—So far, though Arjuna described, as best as he could, the Form, and the feelings It had engendered in him, there is a streak of despair running in these stanzas. Arjuna feels that he has not captured the theme fully in the web of his language. Language expresses that which is perceived, or felt, or understood. Here is a form which Arjuna experiences. He beholds. He feels. And he comprehends it in himself. Yet, strangely enough, here is an experience that volatilises and eludes all attempts at being bottled in language! He seems to be not satisfied by the objective description which he gave in the language of his eyes, ears, etc., and he feels equally unhappy with the language of his emotion, as felt by his mind.

True to himself, the wonder-struck mortal is trying to sing the glory of what he lives, in the language of his intellect. But even here he can only cry in despair, "OH LORD THOU ART EVER INCOMPREHENSIBLE". Though the universal Form is painted here by the author, in the language of an 'objective experience', he makes us understand that the Truth is the SUBJECT and not an object of even the intellect. The Self is the KNOWER, THE FEELER, the PERCEIVER; It is not the perceived, the felt, or the known.

FROM THIS VISION OF THE POWER OF *YOGA*, I INFER:

18. *You are the Imperishable, the Supreme Being worthy to be known. You are the great treasure-house of this Universe. You are the imperishable Protector of the Eternal DHARMA. In my opinion, You are the Ancient PURUSHA.*

From every experience, all intelligent men try to gather their own conclusions, which alone, in fact, constitute true knowledge. Arjuna had a great experience, too subtle for words to express, or for his intellect to comprehend, in its entire entirety. But from what he saw, he tries to draw certain conclusions. Crystallised into his understanding, the conclusions are that the Power behind this Cosmic Form is that which is the Imperishable Supreme Truth.

When we see all the waves playing on the surface of the ocean, manifesting and disappearing after a temporary existence into the very waters from which they rose, we generally conclude that the ocean is the source of all waves. It becomes at once the rest-house for the waves, or the treasure-house for all the disturbances. Similarly, Arjuna comes to the intelligent conclusion that Krishna, as the Cosmic-Form, is the very substratum from which the pluralistic world of phenomena arises, exists in, and merges into. The Universe (*Vishwa*) mentioned here, is not merely

---

त्वमक्षरं परमं वेदितव्यं
त्वमस्य विश्वस्य परं निधानम् ।
त्वमव्ययः शाश्वतधर्मगोप्ता
सनातनस्त्वं पुरुषो मतो मे ॥ १८ ॥

tvamakṣaraṁ paramaṁ veditavyaṁ
tvamasya viśvasya paraṁ nidhānam
tvamavyayaḥ śāśvatadharmagoptā
sanātastvaṁ puruṣo mato me 18.

the astronomers' universe of physical things, but, in *Vedanta*, *Vishwa* is the sum-total experience of everyone, gained through the individual instruments of perception, feeling and understanding. The Lord is the foundation (*Nidhaanam*) for the entire universe of disturbances, experienced by us at our physical, mental and intellectual levels.

Things that change can continue to do so only on a changeless substratum. The world-of-change plays ever to the tune of Time and Space. But, in order that we may feel a continuity of the happenings and thereby gain a comprehensive experience of the total, there must be one constant and changeless 'Knowing-principle' that registers the happenings, without itself in the least being involved in the change. That truth is the Self, and the Self alone is that which could take upon itself the stupendous Universal-Form (*Vishwaroopa*). Keeping these ideas in mind, Arjuna declares that He who has transformed Himself into this Wonder-Form is the One Changeless Truth, that permeates the entire realm of changes and modifications.

In India, to the Hindus, the protector of their *Dharma* is not a mortal king, or a priest class. The Supreme alone is its guardian, for the Hindus are not the followers of any accidental prophet, who has a fleeting historical reality and a limited mission of serving his immediate generation with the best he had. To the Hindu, THE ETERNAL TRUTH IS HIS GOAL, HIS MASTER AND HIS WAY. We demand no mortal power with its poison-gas and atom-bomb to protect our *Dharma*.

THAT YOU ARE THE ANCIENT *PURUSHA*, IS MY OPINION—In *Vedanta*, the very physical structure is considered as a Capital-city with nine gates, each controlled and guarded by its presiding deity. That which dwells in the city, here meaning the body, is in Sanskrit '*Purusha*'. In the context of the stanza, it only means that the solution for the riddle of life, which is the source, or substratum of the whole universe, is to be sought, not among the world-of-objects but within the very layers of personalities in us, until we discover it as the *Purusha*, the Eternal. The Conscious Principle, which is the Spark of life in everyone, is here indicated to be the very Eternal Truth which alone can take up the Form-Universal, as it stands now in front of Arjuna's bewildered gaze.

MOREOVER:

19. *I see You without beginning, middle, or end, infinite in power, of endless arms, the sun and moon being Your eyes, the burning fire Your mouth, heating the whole universe with Your radiance.*

Continuing the description of the Infinite as comprehended by the subtle perception of Arjuna and interpreted by his intellect in terms of the Universe of things and names, it is explained, "I SEE THEE WITHOUT BEGINNING, MIDDLE AND END, INFINITE IN POWER, OF INFINITE ARMS". This pen-picture, drawn by Vyasa with his eloquent poetry, gives a false impression that the theme is an object, and many are the artists who have tried to capture this form on the canvas. The folly is clear to every intelligent

---

अनादिमध्यान्तमनन्तवीर्यम्
अनन्तबाहुं शशिसूर्यनेत्रम् ।
पश्यामि त्वां दीप्तहुताशवक्त्रम्
स्वतेजसा विश्वमिदं तपन्तम् ॥ १९ ॥

anādimadhyāntamanantavīryam
anantabāhu śaśisūryanetram
paśyāmi dīptahutāśavaktraṁ
svatejasā viśvamidaṁ tapantam 19.

student of *Vedanta*. That which is Infinite, without beginning or end, cannot be brought within the area of a limited canvas-piece. But, at the same time, the phrase 'OF INFINITE ARMS' tickles the painter to express it through his own art. In fact, the Universal-form, standing out so clearly in relief work in this transcendental apprehension of the author, can be comprehended only by students of deep understanding and developed intuition.

Here, by the term 'OF INFINITE ARMS' it only means that the Supreme Self, as the dynamic life, is the one essential strength behind every hand that acts and achieves.

The 'principle of light' is the very 'principle' in the eye. If the eyes were not there, light itself would have no meaning. At the same time, if the 'principle of light' were not blessing the objects of form, the instruments of cognition – the eyes – could not have functioned at all. We have here the description of the totality. The 'principle of vision', i.e., all the eyes in the whole universe, is described as the pair of eyes, in the Universal-form of the Lord. Therefore, in the technical language of *Vedanta*, it has been aptly described here that "THE SUN AND THE MOON ARE YOUR EYES".

BURNING FIRE OF YOUR MOUTH—here fire has been considered as the principle behind speech and the principle governing taste. Warm food tastes better; frozen-food has no taste. The presiding deity of speech can FIRE the generation. HEATED discussions always take place; cold discussion is a painful monotony. Speeches that freeze the audience are only lullabies. And the mouth being the seat for both the instruments of speech and taste, the mouth of the *Vishwaroopa* is explained here as 'Fire'.

HEATING THE WHOLE UNIVERSE WITH YOUR RADIANCE – The Self cannot but be luminous, because Consciousness illumines all experiences, at all times, in all living organisms. This light of Consciousness not only illumines, but also imparts the Warmth of life to the entire Universe. From the very statement it is evident that the ancient Hindu had turned his gaze inward only when he had exhausted his observations and study of the world outside. It seems that he knew well that at a certain degree of temperature alone life could continue on this globe; below the required minimum and above the maximum temperature, life would be extinct.

The light that is emanating from Truth is Its own light, and not something which It has derived from any other source. It is by 'Your own Radiance' (*swa-tejasa*) that the life is sustained in the world of names and forms.

20. *This space between earth and the heavens and all the quarters is filled by You alone; having seen this, Your wonderful and terrible form, the three worlds are trembling with fear, O great-souled Being.*

Truth, as apprehended by Arjuna, pervades the entire world-of-objects and even the concepts of time and space are not independent of this Truth. The theme that has been

---

द्यावापृथिव्योरिदमन्तरं हि
व्याप्तं त्वयैकेन दिशश्च सर्वाः ।
दृष्ट्वाद्भुतं रूपमुग्रं तवेदम्
लोकत्रयं प्रव्यथितं महात्मन् ॥ २० ॥

dyāvāpṛthivyoridamantaraṁ hi
vyāptaṁ tvayaikena diśaśca sarvāḥ
dṛṣṭvādbhutaṁ rūpamugraṁ tavedaṁ
lokatrayaṁ pravyathitaṁ mahātman 20.

described here, we should not forget, is the Infinite, the Eternal. Naturally, it is said here, "BY YOU ALONE, THE SPACE BETWEEN HEAVEN AND EARTH AND ALL THE QUARTERS OF THE SKY, IS PERVADED".

The concept of universal oneness cannot be easily grasped. The more one realises it, the more one gets staggered at the immensity of it all. A limited intellect cannot but shudder at the manifestation of such a vast and majestic Truth.

SEEING THE MARVELLOUS AND THE AWFUL FORM, ARJUNA SAYS, "THE WORLDS ARE TREMBLING". It is psychologically true that each man sees the world as he himself is. We look at the world through the windows of our mind; as our mind is, so is the world to us. Arjuna felt staggered and trembling in himself when he looked at the world in that mental condition and he could not but see that the whole world was equally wonder-struck and trembling as he himself was. Even while he is preoccupied with the great theme in hand, Vyasa does not forget the fundamental behaviour in man. These fine touches add a glow of realism to this mystic picture of imcomparable beauty and immeasurable depth.

ARJUNA HAD A DOUBT REGARDING THE POSSIBILITIES OF SUCCESS IN THE WAR.* IN ORDER TO REMOVE THIS, LORD KRISHNA NOW GIVES ARJUNA A PEEP INTO THE FUTURE THAT IS IN STORE FOR THE WORLD:

21. *Verily, into You enter these hosts of DEVAS; some extol You in fear with joined palms; "May it be well" thus saying, bands of great RISHIS and SIDDHAS praise You with hymns sublime.*

The running commentary given out so long by Arjuna was the description of a stagnant Cosmic-Form, at once 'marvellous and awful'. Here we find Arjuna describing the movements and actions that he observes in that Cosmic-Form of the Lord. 'These hosts of deities' enter into and disappear in the Universal-form. Shankara, commenting upon the expression 'hosts of deities', interprets it to mean the Duryodhana-fold. Though this interpretation is not inconsistent with what is yet to follow, it is true that this meaning is not the natural interpretation of the terms used in the text.

If some, who are thus irredeemably drawn towards the Lord's form, disappear therein, others who are waiting and watching the process are necessarily getting panicky with fear. When man is threatened with a sure mishap, and when he knows of no remedy or defence against it, he, in his despair, always turns to prayer. This psychological truth is beautifully brought out here, when it explains how "SOME IN FEAR EXTOL THEE WITH JOINED PALMS".

अमी हि त्वां सुरसंघा विशन्ति
केचिद्भीताः प्राञ्जलयो गृणन्ति ।
स्वस्तीत्युक्त्वा महर्षिसिद्धसंघाः
स्तुवन्ति त्वां स्तुतिभिः पुष्कलाभिः ॥ २१ ॥

amī hi tvāṁ surasaṅghā viśanti
kecidbhītāḥ prāñjalayo gṛṇnti
svastītyuktavā maharṣisiddhasaṅghā
stuvanti tvāṁ stutibhiḥ puṣkalābhiḥ 21.

* *'Yadva jayema, Yadi va no jayeyuh'* – II-6

And this is not all. Bands of great *Rishis* and perfected-men (*Siddhas*)[1] who are not at all perturbed by the vision of the totality, because of their superhuman tranquillity and inward peace arising from their own wisdom, merely sing sublime[2] hymns of glory to the mighty appearance of the total phenomenal world of multiplicity. They do so wishing 'MAY PEACE BE' to all, always. They realise in their 'wisdom' that the face of the cosmos assumes such a terrible ferocity only when it has launched a wholesale reconstruction scheme. The men-of-Wisdom also know that nothing is lost in such a programme of 'construction through destruction'. Therefore, they hail this process and wish the world a brilliant golden era, which is sure to follow immediately after such a total upheaval.

In this stanza, the entire world of phenomena has been beautifully brought under three heads; the 'Sub-normal', the 'Normal', and the 'Super-normal'. The 'Sub-normal' unconsciously die away. They are the victims of the process of death and they are so miserably unaware of the very process that they do not at all revolt against it. The 'Normal' dread when they intelligently observe and become aware of the process of decay and death. They become apprehensive of their own fate; and failing to realise that nothing is lost by death, they, in their ignorance, shudder at the inescapable lot of all living names and forms.

There is yet another set constituted of 'Super-normal' men,

---

1 It is believed that there are about 18,000 such Perfect-Masters who are goldly in their wisdom and are ever serving the cause of life Divine and subtly guiding each seeker towards his consummate goal.

2 Shankara interprets '*Pushkalabhih*' as meaning 'complete'. Both meanings are possible.

who have sufficient apprehension of the Totality and Its behaviour, and who are not at all perturbed even if what is happening in the Universe everyday, were to visit them also one day. When bubbles are broken, there is no occasion to regret for those who know what they are and how they are born. Similarly, when these *Siddhas* see the upheaval that precedes a dying culture's reorientation, they recognise therein the mighty Power of Truth and wish only good luck and peace to the world so reconstructed by the very hands of the Lord.

In whichever light we may observe this work, we must come to realise how great a psychologist Vyasa himself must have been and also how beautifully the knowledge of the mental behaviour has been harnessed for quickening the evolution of man to reach the fulfilment of all his struggles.

HOW THEN DID THE GODS OF THE HEAVENS REACT TO THIS SPECTACULAR VISION OF THE COSMIC-MAN IN ACTION?

22. *THE RUDRAS, ADITYAS, VASUS, SADHYAS, VISHWE-DEVAS, THE TWO ASHWINS, MARUTS, USHMAPAS AND HOSTS OF GANDHARVAS, YAKSHAS, ASURAS AND SIDDHAS – they are all looking at you, all quite astonished.*

रुद्रादित्या वसवो ये च साध्या
विश्वेऽश्विनौ मरुतश्चोष्मपाश्च ।
गन्धर्वयक्षासुरसिद्धसंघा
वीक्षन्ते त्वां विस्मिताश्चैव सर्वे ॥ २२ ॥

rudrādityā vasavo ye ca sādhyā
viśve'śvinau marutaścoṣmapāśca
gandharvayakṣāsurasiddhasaṅghā
vīkṣante tvāṁ vismitāścaiva sarve 22.

Continuing the description, Arjuna says that among the hosts of beings who gaze on at the mysterious form, there are Deities who are all the Lords of the phenomena, worshipped and revered by the generations of the *Vedic* period. Even they, looking at the Universal form, stand struck with wonder and astonishment.

The terms used here have all been described during our discourses on the previous chapters. The Spirits of Destruction (*Rudras*), the Sun (*Adityas*), the Lord of the Seasons (*Vasus*), the Spirits of the Sky (*Sadhyas*),[1] the Lesser Lords (*Vishwe-devas*),[2] the Horsemen Twins (*Ashwins*), the Storm-Lords (*Maruts*), the Heat-drinkers (*Ushmapas*),[*] the hosts of Heavenly Musicians (*Gandharvas*), *Yakshas*, *Asuras* and *Siddhas* -- these constitute the crowd that gaze at the terrible form of the Lord, 'ALL QUITE ASTOUNDED'.

This stanza may not be quite appealing to us who are today strangers to the conceptions which these terms represent. But Arjuna was a student of the *Vedas*, and was the child of the age; he was naturally well versed in these *Vedic* thoughts and therefore the vocabulary of Arjuna could not have been otherwise. We have only to watch for, and understand, the general effect produced upon the Pandava warrior by the vision

---

1 Refer *Rig Veda* – X-90:15. They are personifications of sacrificial rites and prayers: they are, as it were, the divine 'middle men' who convey the devotees' prayers to that Lord to whom they were raised and ultimately bring about the fruition of the desires entertained by the devotees.

2 This is a collective name for a set of inferior *Deities* mentioned in the *Rig Veda*. In the *Puranas*, we find mention of these *Deities*, where it is considered that they are altogether ten in number. They include abstract qualities like *Satya*, *Dhriti*, etc.

* This is a term used to indicate the dead ancestors – *Pitris* – who are supposed to be 'heat-drinkers' in as much as it is believed that they come during functions dedicated to them and enjoy the offerings made to them only so long as it is hot. The idea, perhaps, must be that they absorb the aroma that rolls up from the steaming food offered.

of the totality and the different reactions created in different types of minds. Each, according to its own intrinsic capacity, comprehended and appreciated the vision of the entire Universe, so crystallised into the definite shapeless shape.

GIVING MORE AND MORE SURE STROKES, ARJUNA IS BRINGING OUT HIS EXPERIENCES TO A PRECISE CONCEPTION UPON THE CANVAS OF HIS LISTENER'S MIND:

23. *Having seen Your immeasurable Form, with many mouths and eyes, O Mighty-armed, with many arms, thighs, and feet, with many stomachs and fearsome with many tusks, the worlds are terrified and so too am I.*

24. *On seeing you, with Your Form touching the sky, flaming in many colours, with mouths wide open, with large fiery eyes, I am terrified at heart, and I find neither courage, nor peace, O Vishnu!*

रूपं महत्ते बहुवक्त्रनेत्रं
महाबाहो बहुबाहूरुपादम् ।
बहूदरं बहुदंष्ट्राकरालं
दृष्ट्वा लोकाः प्रव्यथितास्तथाहम् ॥ २३ ॥

rūpaṁ mahatte bahuvaktranetraṁ
mahābāho bahubāhūrupādam
bahūdaraṁ bahudaṁṣṭrākarālaṁ
dṛṣṭvā lokāḥ pravyathitāstathāham 23.

नभःस्पृशं दीप्तमनेकवर्णं
व्यात्ताननं दीप्तविशालनेत्रम् ।
दृष्ट्वा हि त्वां प्रव्यथितान्तरात्मा
धृतिं न विन्दामि शमं च विष्णो ॥ २४ ॥

nabhaḥspṛśaṁ dīptamanekavarṇṇaṁ
vyāttānanaṁ dīptaviśālanetram
dṛṣṭvā hi tvāṁ pravayathitāntarātmā
dhṛtiṁ na vindāmi śamaṁ ca viṣṇo 24.

The uncommon vision, MARVELLOUS AND AWFUL, experienced by Arjuna, was not a localised form on a six-footed Lord Krishna. It was, in fact, a manifestation, wide and varied, extending almost to the frontiers of the All-pervading. And yet, the Pandava Prince realised it all in his inward vision as a limited form, having a definite shape. In the intellectual understanding of all shapeless qualities (like freedom, love, nationality, etc.), one gives them each a substantiality, a form, well-defined and precisely outlined for one's own intellect, although never for one's own sense-organs. Similarly, Arjuna too, feels that, the experience of the Universal-form, though All-pervading, has for him a definite shape. But when he tries to define the form-Universal, so well realised by him, his very expressions belie his own feelings and defeat his own purpose.

Arjuna finds that the entire world is terrified by the Great Grand Form representing in itself MANY MOUTHS AND EYES, MANY ARMS AND THIGHS, WITH MANY STOMACHS, AND FEARSOME WITH MANY TUSKS. He also adds, "SO AM I". Psychologically, when an individual is in a crowd of excited people or in the company of good men of peaceful contemplation, he vicariously gathers unto himself the mental qualities of the crowd in which he finds himself. 'THE WORLD IS TERRIFIED', and, Arjuna confesses, "I TOO, AM".

At the same time, the Pandava Prince feels it insulting and cowardly for his royal heart to feel any fear. Therefore, justifying his own fear, he describes the Terrible-form to be in fact formless, and says that it absorbs into itself everything. The Universal-form touches the very skies above. It glows with a variety of colours. Its fiery-eyes glow. Its open mouths consume everything. Altogether, the vision is capable of unnerving even the gods. Seeing that VISION Arjuna confesses, "MY HEART QUAKES, AND I LOSE MY COURAGE AND MY PEACE". It is very significant that it is in this condition of benumbing fear that the great hero addresses the cosmic-vision, 'O, Vishnu'.*

As I said in the beginning, the conception-form so clearly defined in the intuitive understanding of Arjuna, is in fact the Infinite described in terms of Its own endless manifestations as the names and forms in the Universe. We, the students of the *Geeta,* should never forget these subtle undercurrents of thought that Vyasa has so secretly kept for the profit of all diligent and sincere seekers of Truth.

ELABORATING HIS OWN SELF-EXPLANATIONS ON WHY HEROIC HEARTS SHOULD TREMBLE IN FEAR, THE PANDAVA PRINCE CONTINUES:

25. *Having seen your mouths fearsome with tusks (blazing) like PRALAYA fires, I know not the four quarters, nor do I find peace; be gracious, O Lord of the DEVAS, O Abode of the Universe.*

SEEING THE UNIVERSAL-MOUTH TERRIBLE WITH TUSKS, THREATENING AS THE FIRE-OF-DELUGE,

---

दंष्ट्राकरालानि च ते मुखानि
दृष्ट्वैव कालानलसन्निभानि ।
दिशो न जाने न लभे च शर्म
प्रसीद देवेश जगन्निवास ॥ २५ ॥

daṁṣṭrākarālāni ca te mukhāni
dṛṣṭvaiva kālānalasannibhāni
diśo na jāne na labhe ca śarma
prasīda deveśa jagannivāsa 25.

CONFESSES ARJUNA, "I HAVE LOST MY SENSE OF DIRECTION AND I FEEL NO PEACE". This is the picture of Time – Time, the leveller of everything, and the consumer of all forms. When the intellect comes to comprehend such a vast field, and that too all of a sudden, the very magnitude of it smothers all powers of discrimination and benumbs the individual for a moment. This chaotic condition of confusion is expressed here, "I KNOW NOT THE FOUR QUARTERS". And this is not all. "I FIND NO PEACE" either.

In such a condition of extreme wonderment, the astounded mortal comes to realise that his physical might, his mental capacities and his intellectual subtleties are all, both individually and in their aggregate, unimportant vehicles indeed. The little ego drops down its veil of vanity and its armour of false strength, and stands naked meekly surrendering itself to the influence of the Cosmic-Power. Prayer is the only resort of the individual, who has thus fully realised the emptiness of his own hollow vanities, in the presence of the Mighty-Total and the Supreme-Divine.

In concluding the stanza with the humble prayer, "BE GRACIOUS, O LORD, THOU ART THE HOME OF THE UNIVERSE", Vyasa has rightly indicated that true prayers can never rise up from a heart that is swollen with pride and entertains an exaggerated sense of self-importance. Only when man understands his own individual insignificance, in the context of the total Universe, then true prayer can rise up from him almost involuntarily.

---

* The term Vishnu appears in *Vedic*-literature, where it is used in its etymological meaning as 'one having long strides.' The measures between the two feet, when one walks, is called the 'stride' (or reach). The stride of a child is short, when compared with the stride of a man. The all-pervading Infinite, if it were to take its longest stride, would be from the 'beginningless' to the 'endless'. Thus the term Vishnu has the implication 'the All-pervading the All-reaching'.

THIS PARTICULAR SECTION (starting from XI-21) IS MAINLY FOR REASSURING ARJUNA OF THE SUCCESS THAT IS YET TO COME IN THE FUTURE FOR HIMSELF AND HIS ARMY. THEREFORE, THE LORD DIRECTLY SHOWS THE FORCES ENTER THE INESCAPABLE 'MOUTH OF TIME' AND DISAPPEAR:

26. *All the sons of Dhritarashtra with hosts of kings of the earth, Bhishma, Drona and the son of a charioteer, Karna, with the warrior chieftains of ours;*

27. *Into Your mouths, with terrible teeth, and fearful to behold, they precipitately enter. Some are found sticking in the gaps between the teeth with their heads crushed into pulp.*

A philosophy that comprehends the totality without fear or favour and is even true to its mission of seeking Truth,

---

अमी च त्वां धृतराष्ट्रस्य पुत्राः
सर्वे सहैवावनिपालसंघैः ।
भीष्मो द्रोणः सूतपुत्रस्तथासौ
सहास्मदीयैरपि योधमुख्यैः ॥ २६ ॥

amīṁ ca tvāṁ dhṛtarāṣṭrasya putrāḥ
sarve sahaivāvanipālasaṅghaiḥ
bhīṣmo droṇaḥ sūtaputrastathāsau
sahāsmadīyairapi yodhamukhyaiḥ 26.

वक्त्राणि ते त्वरमाणा विशन्ति
दंष्ट्राकरालानि भयानकानि ।
केचिद्विलग्ना दशनान्तरेषु
संदृश्यन्ते चूर्णितैरुत्तमाङ्गैः ॥ २७ ॥

vaktrāṇi te tvaramāṇā viśanti
daṁṣṭrākarālāni bhayānakāni
kecidvilagnā daśanāntareṣu
sandṛśyante cūrṇitairuttamāṅgaiḥ 27.

cannot afford to ignore the destructive-aspect in nature. No creation is possible without being preceded by the process of destruction of its own existence as the raw material from which the created is produced. On the face of the Universe also, wherever there is 'existence' it is nothing but a repetition of constant change, and change can be interpreted either in terms of constant creation with regard to the products made, or as a process of constant destruction with regard to the raw-material that changed.

Thus, we see that in Hinduism, the daring Masters of the Aryan fold, while extolling the beauty of the Reality, indulged themselves in viewing It not only as the Omniscient-Creator, or as the Omnipotent-Sustainer, but also as the All-powerful-Devourer of all names and forms. This may look dreadful to those creeds that have not yet come to watch and analyse life in its totality.

Arjuna's words are significant. He does not see the Universal-form itself devouring the names and forms. On the other hand, he observed that all names and forms "ENTER IN HASTE INTO THY MOUTH". When we watch an ocean, we do not find the ocean ever rising up to absorb the waves, but the waves which have risen from the ocean, after a momentary play upon the surface, rush back to disappear into the very ocean. The multiplicity that has risen from the totality, after its play upon the surface of Truth, must necessarily rush back in all hurry into the very 'whole' from which they had arisen.

Arjuna watches "all the sons of Dhritarashtra, the hosts of kings, Bhishma, Drona, Karna-the son of a charioteer, along with the warrior chieftains of ours" entering precipitately into the yawning mouth of the Principle of Destruction in nature.

This not only frightens Arjuna and unnerves him, but also gives him a confidence to look ahead – in spite of the fact that in numerical strength, in supplies, and in technicians, his own army was much inferior to the mighty forces of the Kurus. The Vision which he saw was in fact a peep into the future. In the *Vishwaroopa*, when the Lord expresses Himself as the entire world of phenomena, a conception of oneness arises in which not only space shrinks, but even Time becomes an object of observation.

It is no wonder, therefore, that Arjuna saw in that picture THE PAST MERGING WITH THE PRESENT AND MOVING FORWARD TO MINGLE WITH THE ENTIRE FUTURE. When I have the entire *Geeta*-book before me, I can either read the preceding two pages or can skip over them and read the third page ahead or, according to my will and desire, continue reading this very same page. Similarly, when the whole Universe is brought at once within the compass of Arjuna's vision, he could see herein at one gaze "ALL THE HERE AND THE THERE, AND THE EVERYWHERE" – so too, THE PAST, THE PRESENT AND THE FUTURE. The modern scientists also have now come to realise and accept that Time and Space are one and the same, and they are each expressed in terms of the other.*

The seekers of Truth, themselves truthful, were not at all afraid if their enquiry took them to the aspect of the terrible in the Truth. The world is a combination of the beautiful and the ugly, the good and the bad, the soft and the hard, the sweet and the bitter. God, the Lord, has Himself become all

* It is not very rare that we say, 'in the space of an hour'.

these, and therefore, no adoration of the Lord, or estimate of the Reality, will be complete, if, according to our taste, we recognise only the beautiful, the good, the soft, and the sweet aspects of Him. An unprejudiced and detached mind will have to recognise Him as the ugly and the bad, the hard and the bitter also. That philosophy alone is complete which points out that the Supreme is, in fact, in Its Absolute Nature, beyond all these qualities.

In a purely scientific approach, therefore, Arjuna is made to express all the details, even if they be blood-curdling and gruesome. No doubt, the *Geeta* has its own sense of realism. The mouth of death is described here with all faithfulness as "TERRIBLE WITH TUSKS, FEARFUL TO BEHOLD".

HOW DO THEY ENTER THY MOUTH? ARJUNA SAYS:

28. *Verily, as many torrents of rivers flow towards the ocean, so these heroes in the world of men enter Your flaming mouths.*

In this stanza, the analogy of the torrential rivers, gushing ahead to reach the ocean and become one with it, is used. Each river has, no doubt, its own distinct personality, gathered from the nature and condition of the very terrain through which it has flowed. At no point does any river pause or

---

यथा नदीनां बहवोऽम्बुवेगा:
समुद्रमेवाभिमुखा द्रवन्ति।
तथा तवामी नरलोकवीरा
विशन्ति वक्त्राण्यभिविज्वलन्ति ॥ २८ ॥

yathā nadīnāṁ bahavo'mbuvegāḥ
samudramevābhimukhā dravanti
tathā tavāmī naralokavīrā
viśanti vaktrāṇyabhivijvalanti 28.

hesitate to gush forward. An observer of limited powers of understanding may say that each drop of water in its flow in the river is moving towards a known point down on its way; but, to a true observer, all rivers flow towards the ocean and they cannot, and will not, stop until they reach the ocean, having reached which, all distinctions end.

Each drop of water in the river came from the ocean, in the form of a cloud it reached the mountains, and there in the form of rain it manifested; watering the lands on the banks and supplying life and nourishment to the fields, they gushed down in their torrential haste to the very basin from which they took off on this 'MERCY FLIGHT'. Similarly, from the Totality, the individuals have come to serve the race, to nourish the culture, to contribute to the beauty of the world...and yet, on their pilgrimage none of them can pause even for a moment en route. All must rush towards the Source from which they arose. The river loses nothing by reaching the ocean. Even though it gathers enroute certain special qualities, and therefore, a special name, and has, for itself, a separate tangible form, it is all a temporary phase, a convenience taken up by 'the waters of the ocean' to make the dry land smile in plenty.

The more the thought given to it, the more can this stanza yield its secret joys and expose its innate beauty.

WHY AND HOW DO THEY ENTER?

Arjuna says:

29. *As moths rush hurriedly into a blazing fire for their own destruction, so also these creatures hastily rush into Your mouths of destruction.*

The essential oneness between the MANIFEST that has come out of the UNMANIFEST, and the very UNMANIFEST which is the womb of manifestation, has been beautifully brought out by the picture of the river, which has risen from the ocean and is, in all haste, rushing down only to lose its very name and form, and become one with the ocean.

No analogy can be complete in itself. The picture of the river does not show any intrinsic conscious effort on the part of the river to reach the ocean. The living kingdom, with its own free discrimination, it may be doubted, may not act as the inert waters of the river. To show that even the sentient beings are irresistibly drawn towards the mouth of their own destruction, by the whipping hand of instinct, the example of 'the moths precipitately rushing into the blazing fire to perish' is given. To Vyasa, the entire nature seems to be an open book of scripture, explaining everywhere in all its happenings, the fundamental facts that the projection of the unmanifest to the manifest-condition is the 'process of creation' and that 'the manifest merging back to its own heaven of the unmanifest is DESTRUCTION or DEATH. That terrible looking monstrous

---

यथा प्रदीप्तं ज्वलनं पतङ्गा
विशन्ति नाशाय समृद्धवेगा: ।
तथैव नाशाय विशन्ति लोका
स्तवापि वक्त्राणि समृद्धवेगा:॥ २९ ॥

yathā pradīptaṁ jvalanaṁ pataṅgā
viśanti nāśāya samṛddhavegāḥ
tathaiva nāśāya iśanti lokā
stavāpi vaktrāṇi samṛddhavegāḥ 29.

happening called 'death', when approached in a correct perspective and with true understanding, unmasks itself to reveal a gladdening face, ever cheerful and gay.

Arjuna's mental tension was mainly created by his hasty evaluation of the enormous destruction he would be causing in the battlefield of Kurukshetra. Krishna has to cure him, by lifting him to heights from which he could witness and realise, in one sweeping gaze, the unavoidable phenomenon of death. A close and full understanding of any happening removes the fangs from its threatening hood! It is only when the discriminating intellect of man becomes doped with 'ignorance', that the happenings around him can threaten to smother him down. As the river hastens to the ocean, and the moths into the fire, so too, all names and forms must, and most irresistibly do, rush towards the unmanifest. With this realisation, anyone can thereafter face life, fearless of death, since life itself becomes to him a process of continuous change.

THEREFORE DEATH, AS A PLAY-OF-TIME, BECOMES A STINGLESS PHENOMENON. THIS IS GLORIFIED IN ALL ITS FEROCIOUS BEAUTY IN THE FOLLOWING VERSES:

30. *Devouring all worlds on every side with Your flaming mouths, You are licking (in enjoyment). Your fierce rays, filling the whole world with radiance, are burning, O Vishnu.*

लेलिह्यसे ग्रसमान: समन्तात्
लोकान्समग्रान्वदनैर्ज्वलद्भि: ।
तेजोभिरापूर्य जगत्समग्रं
भासस्तवोग्रा: प्रतपन्ति विष्णो ॥ ३० ॥

lelihyase grasamānaḥ samantā-
llokānsamagrānvadanairjvaladbhiḥ
tejobhirapūrya jagatsamagraṁ
bhāsastavogrāḥ pratapanti viṣṇo 30.

After composing some surging poetry, Vyasa faithfully comes back to the line of thought he was developing earlier. Hosts of men and things of the world reach the 'mouth' to perish therein. The hungry 'mouth' is never tired, for, the principle of destruction has a never-ending appetite, and after 'swallowing all the world all around, you are licking your lips', exclaims Arjuna.

In fact, the stanza clearly brings forth the implication underlying the concept of the Trinity. The Creator, the Sustainer, and the Destroyer are three distinct entities in concept, but in their actual workings, they constitute a simultaneous process. Creation is continued in a chain of destruction, and the process of destruction is not a total annihilation but only a change from one form to another thereby ending in a new Creation. 'Constructive destruction' is the secret philosophy behind the continuity of existence observed everywhere.

In a cinema show, the various poses on the film are made to run on in front of the arclight, and each picture that has passed away from the arclight may be considered as dead, and those reaching the arclight as those that are born. The continuity in these two series of happenings of births and deaths, or constructions and destructions, gives us the hallucination of a logical sequence in the theme revealed on the screen. Conditioned by 'place and time', things and beings, happenings and circumstances, come and go in the plane of our experiences and their continuity is what we experience as 'existence'.

The above idea can be repeated in the language of our traditional belief in the Trinity. Brahmaji, the Creator, cannot create unless Shiva, the Destroyer, is functioning simultaneously on the same anvil. And Vishnu, the Sustainer, will never come to play unless the Creator and the Destroyer work feverishly and consistently. The whole world of multiplicity is thus an expression of Vishnu, the Sustainer, which is nothing other than the product of the game played by both the Creator and the Destroyer!

When, with such depth of understanding, Arjuna looks at the mighty resplendence of the Totality-Form, he feels almost blindfolded by 'the fiery radiance of its fierce rays'.

YOU ARE FEARSOME; THEREFORE:

31. *Tell me, who You are, so fierce in form? Salutations to You, O God Supreme; have mercy. I desire to know You, the Original Being, I know not indeed Your purpose.*

Arjuna realises suddenly the sanctity and the divinity of the Lord's Power, and so, in an inspired rush of veneration, he bows down to Him whom till now he took to be but a cowherd boy of Vrindavana. Intellectual though he may be, here is an experience too big for him to observe fully, analyse carefully, and digest completely. The only thing he can do is to surrender himself at the very feet of the Lord, requesting Him, "TELL ME WHO YOU ARE."

आख्याहि मे को भवानुग्ररूपो
नमोऽस्तु ते देववर प्रसीद ।
विज्ञातुमिच्छामि भवन्तमाद्यं
न हि प्रजानामि तव प्रवृत्तिम् ॥ ३१ ॥

ākhyāhi me ko bhavānugrarūpo
namo'stu te devavara prasīda
vijñātumicchāmi bhavantamādyaṁ
na hi prajānāmi tava pravṛttima 31.

To reinforce the solidity of the query, Arjuna indicates that his question deserves an answer, for, "I DESIRE TO KNOW THEE, O PRIMEVAL ONE." It is very well known in the textbooks of spirituality, that 'a burning aspiration to know' is the motive force behind every seeker's mind and intellect. But here Arjuna is preoccupied with the problem of a challenge that is facing him, and therefore, he is not, in fact, directly seeking the Divine Truth behind the Vision. His enquiry is highly coloured by the emotion of fear in him and his anxiety to know what would be the outcome of the war. This is clear from the last line wherein he himself explains: Indeed I know not your purpose. The enquiry made here is "What is the mission of the Lord in taking such a terrible form, and in presenting Himself in front of Arjuna, exhibiting how the Kaurava forces are marching in all hurry towards the burning mouth of Death?" When he intensely longs for a thing to happen and when sure signs, forecasting his success, present themselves, he needs a confirmation from others. Here Arjuna is witnessing what he exactly wishes should happen. But the Prince wants to get a confirmation of the same from Krishna Himself. Hence this question.

INTRODUCING HIMSELF AS THE MANIFESTATION OF TRUTH IN ITS ASPECT OF DESTRUCTION, THE LORD IN THE UNIVERSAL FROM DECLARES:

The Blessed Lord said:

32. *I am the mighty world-destroying Time, now engaged in destroying the worlds. Even without You, none of the warriors arrayed in hostile armies shall live.*

No construction of a thing is possible without a corresponding destruction of its own previous condition. The world is created by a continuous process of destruction. Today has arisen from the graves of yesterday. Childhood dies before youth appears. And when youth passes away, old age takes its birth. The power visibly playing behind constructive destruction is the fundamental Power that rules over and governs the life of beings. Krishna introduces Himself here as "I AM THE MIGHTY WORLD-DESTROYING TIME" who has manifested to wipe out the generation that has suffered decay in its own false sense of values and wrong assumptions about life and its purpose.

The world-destroying attitude of the Lord is not at all against His all-merciful concept. Sometimes there is mercy in destruction. A broken bridge, a dilapidated dam, and an ancient building are instances in point. To pull them down is

---

श्रीभगवानुवाच
कालोऽस्मि लोकक्षयकृत्प्रवृद्धो
लोकान्समाहर्तुमिह प्रवृत्तः ।
ऋतेऽपि त्वां न भविष्यन्ति सर्वे
येऽवस्थिताः प्रत्यनीकेषु योधाः ॥ ३२ ॥

śrībhagavānuvāca
kālo'smi lokakṣayakṛtpravṛddho
lokānsamāhartumiha pravṛttaḥ
ṛte'pi tvāṁ na bhaviṣyanti sarve
ye'vasthitāḥ pratyanīkeṣu yodhāḥ 32.

the most merciful act of charity that any considerate government can do to the community; so too here.

By declaring that the very purpose behind this manifestation is to destroy totally the negative forces that strangle the cultural life of the country, Krishna is confirming Arjuna's vague hope that there is yet a chance of victory for his army. Reassuring the very same idea, the Universal-form here declares that in the great mission of reconstruction, the Lord is not depending upon any individual or individuals. It is Time that is going to bring the renaissance and achieve the revival. In such a colossal movement of universal rehabilitation, individuals are but mere creatures of destiny. In spite of them, and with or without their cooperation, Time's plans will be worked out. The country needs the revival; the world demands man's rehabilitation. Krishna clearly says, EVEN WITHOUT YOU none of the warriors manning the secular folly of sheer materialism shall survive the war of the imminent cultural upheaval.

In the context of the Mahabharata story, it almost amounts to saying that the Kaurava forces have all been killed already by Time, and that Arjuna, by cooperating and servicing the Army of Renaissance, is only backing the sure success.

THEREFORE, AS A REPRESENTATIVE MAN OF ALL TIMES, ARJUNA IS ADVISED TO PERFORM FEARLESS ACTION IN LIFE:

33. *Therefore, stand up, and obtain fame. Conquer the enemies and enjoy the flourishing kingdom. Verily by Myself they have already been slain; be you a mere instrument, O left-handed archer.*

34. *Drona, Bhishma, Jayadratha, Karna, and other brave warriors—those have already been slain by Me; you do kill; be not distressed with fear; fight and you shall conquer your enemies in battle.*

Here Lord Krishna is very directly consoling Arjuna that he should stand up and catch the Time and claim success and glory. Whatever be the might and strength of the negative forces, the all-consuming might of Change has already destroyed them all, and Arjuna has only to come forward, act the part of a hero and claim the crown of victory all to himself: "I HAVE ALREADY SLAIN THEM, BE MERELY AN APPARENT CAUSE, YOU, O LEFT-HANDED ARCHER".

तस्मात्त्वमुत्तिष्ठ यशो लभस्व
जित्वा शत्रून्भुङ्क्ष्व राज्यं समृद्धम् ।
मयैवैते निहताः पूर्वमेव
निमित्तमात्रं भव सव्यसाचिन् ॥ ३३ ॥

tasmāttvamuttiṣṭha yaśo labhasva
jitvā śatrun bhuṅkṣva rājyaṁ samṛddham
mayaivaite nihatāḥ pūrvameva
nimittamatrāṁ bhava savyasāacin 33.

द्रोणं च भीष्मं च जयद्रथं च
कर्णं तथान्यानपि योधवीरान् ।
मया हतांस्त्वं जहि मा व्यथिष्ठा
युध्यस्व जेतासि रणे सपत्नान् ॥ ३४॥

droṇaṁ ca bhīṣmaṁ ca jayadrathaṁ ca
karṇaṁ tathānyānapi yodhavīrān
mayā hatāṁstvaṁ jahi mā vyathiṣṭhā
yudhyasva jetāsi raṇe sapatnān 34.

In fact, to every thinking man, the truth is obvious that in life, he is at best only an instrument in His hands. We are not generally ready to accept this proposition, because, the self-arrogating ego-sense in us will not easily retire so as to allow the Divine in us to play out in all its omnipotence. Everywhere, in all our activities, when we analyse each one of our actions, we find that our actual contribution in them all is a meagre share, compared to what nature has applied, and what the unseen hand has achieved for us. At best, we can only combine things that already exist, and coax out of their own natural qualities and properties, a certain result, and then claim vainly that we have created something new.

The radio, the aeroplane, the roaring engines, the subtle machinery, the wonder-drugs, in short, the entire 'Brave New World', and all its achievements in progress -- are all nothing but the play of children in the lap of the Lord who, in fact, is the One who has ordered and allowed us to have electricity, iron, ether, air, etc., with their special properties. Without these, no achievement is ever possible; and achievements are nothing but intelligent acts of the assembling and reassembling of these very God-given things.

The concept of self-surrender and the theory of serving the world in constant awareness of the Lord are not idle dreams prescribed for escaping the gross realities of the world. It is essential for man to raise his calibre and temper so as to work efficiently and achieve success in the world. It is the technique of keeping oneself constantly in a mood of tireless enthusiasm and joyous inspiration.

The world is too much with the ego. To the extent the ego is surrendered in the awareness of the greater and the nobler, to that extent, the entire world and achievements therein become a game of simple and sure success everywhere. Earlier in the *Geeta,* it was, at many points, strictly pointed out that through the technique of self-surrender, the greater possibilities can be milked out of us. The same idea is again repeated here. The entire army has been invited here only to play the part of the Hero – serve as His Instruments and let them claim for themselves the crown and the glory as their wages.

Arjuna had certain reasons why he should be particularly afraid of some of the top men in the Kaurava forces. They are taken up one by one and the Lord indicates how even they have already been killed by the All-consuming Time-Spirit.

Drona was Arjuna's teacher who taught him the art of archery. The *Acharya* had with him some special weapons and he was particularly revered and respected by Arjuna. The grandsire Bhishma had his death at his command, and he too, had very powerful celestial weapons. Once in the past Bhishma had made Parashurama lick the ground. Jayadratha was invincible; for, his father who was engaged in *tapas*, had firmly resolved that 'whoever causes my son's head to drop down on earth, his head too shall fall'. Karna also had a powerful missile given to him by Indra. It becomes clear now why these four names are particularly enumerated by the Lord in the list of personalities that Time had already devastated. Even these great warriors have been eliminated by the Principle of Destruction, and thereby, it has been brought home to Arjuna that the field is clear for him to play his part and advance towards the throne and crown, and claim the entire glory as his own.

IT IS NATURAL THAT, WHEN A BURNING DESIRE IN AN INDIVIDUAL IS FULFILLED, HE SUDDENLY BURSTS INTO AN IRRESISTIBLE GLORIFICATION OF HIS KINDLY PATRON:

Sanjaya said:

35. *Having heard that speech of Keshava (Krishna), the crowned-one (Arjuna), with joined palms, trembling and prostrating himself, again addressed Krishna, in a choked voice, bowing down, overwhelmed with fear.*

The dramatist in Vyasa, with his innate craftsmanship, lifts the scene from the battle front to the quiet and silent chambers of the palace, where the blind Dhritarashtra is listening to 'the running commentary' given by Sanjaya. In thus lifting the reader more than once* away from the awe-inspiring atmosphere of Kurukshetra, Vyasa is not only adding dynamic movement to the picture but also giving a necessary psychological rest for the reader's mind from such a subtle theme of awful beauty.

It is not to be forgotten at all that Sanjaya in the *Geeta* is OUR OWN SPECIAL CORRESPONDENT, who is fully sympathetic with the righteous cause of the Pandavas. Naturally, therefore, as soon as he reports the Lord's own

सञ्जय उवाच
एतच्छ्रुत्वा वचनं केशवस्य
कृताञ्जलिर्वेपमानः किरीटी ।
नमस्कृत्वा भूय एवाह कृष्णं
सगद्गदं भीतभीतः प्रणम्य ॥ ३५ ॥

sañjaya uvāca
etacchrutvā vacanaṁ keśavasya
kṛtāñjalirvepamānaḥ kirīṭī
namaskṛtvā bhūya evāh kṛṣṇaṁ
sagadgadaṁ bhītabhītaḥ praṇamya 35.

* In this very chapter, we have been taken thrice to the palace and back again to the battlefield.

words, that all the mighty men of the times, who are the top-ranking men in position in the Kaurava forces, have already been annihilated, he wants to bring to the blind old man's awareness, the magnitude of the impending disaster. As we have noticed earlier, the only one who could call the war off, even at this moment, is Dhritarashtra himself. And Sanjaya is very anxious to see that the war is not fought. Thus, we see here, in the stanza, in the very language used, the motive of the reporter.

Having heard the words of Keshava, Arjuna, the crowned-one, with folded palms and trembling with fear, addressed again – The very language used and the picture drawn, reflect the mind of the reporter. Suddenly, Arjuna is called here as 'the crowned-one', perhaps, as a bold forecast, by which Sanjaya expects Dhritarashtra to see the folly of the disastrous war. But a blind man can never see things, and much less if he is intellectually blind with delusion.

If the good sense of the blind king cannot be invoked because of his extremely deluded love for his children, Sanjaya expects to give a psychological treatment to the royal father. A lengthy description of how others are getting frightened is a sure method of spreading panic even among moderately courageous listeners. If Arjuna, the warrior, the bosom friend of Krishna is trembling and addressing the lord in a choked voice, overwhelmed with fear, Sanjaya expects every sensible man to realise the horrors of the war that is imminent, and the dire consequences that are in store for the vanquished. Even these words of Sanjaya have no effect upon Dhritarashtra who is blind to everything except his mad affection for his own children.

ARJUNA APOSTROPHIZES THE UNIVERSAL-FORM:

Arjuna said:

36. *It is but meet, O Hrishikesha (Krishna), that the world delights and rejoices in Thy praise; RAKSHASAS fly in fear to all quarters, and all hosts of SIDDHAS bow to Thee.*

Again from the luxurious chambers of riches and splendour, the students of the *Geeta* are lifted, on the lyrical charm of the poem, to the humming ground of the battlefield and to the Wonder-Form of the Lord. The picture of Arjuna addressing the Lord with his hands folded, trembling with fear, singing songs of adoration, with a throat choked with fear and wonderment is effectively drawn. This passage, containing the following eleven stanzas, represents one of the most beautiful prayers that we have in Hinduism. In fact, the words and the ideas expressed hereunder are so general in their import and significance that we can almost say that no better Universal Prayer can ever be conceived of, either in its concept, beauty, or cadence, or in the depth of the message in its words.

अर्जुन उवाच
स्थाने हृषीकेश तव प्रकीर्त्या
जगत्प्रहृष्यत्यनुरज्यते च ।
रक्षांसि भीतानि दिशो द्रवन्ति
सर्वे नमस्यन्ति च सिद्धसंघा: ॥ ३६ ॥

arjuna uvāca
sthane hṛṣīkeśa tava prakītyār
jagatprahṛṣyatyanurajyate ca
rakṣāṁsi bhītāni diśo dravanti
sarve namasyanti ca siddhasaṅghāḥ 36.

In these passages, the cognising power in Arjuna is steadily realising the diviner Truth behind the details of that Total-Form. When one watches and sees one's own reflection in a mirror, it is rarely that the observer sees the mirror-surface. When one watches the surface of the mirror, the reflection is either not at all available or, at best is only dimly recognised. So long as Arjuna is preoccupied with the details of the Universal-Form, he does not realise, or recognise, the Infinite which is the very core of the *Vishwaroopa*. In these passages, it is evident that Arjuna has started sensing the deeper meaning that lies behind the cosmic wonder represented to him in his vision Divine.

37. *And why should they not, O Great-souled One, bow to Thee, greater (than all else), the Primal Cause even of Brahma, O Infinite Being, O Lord of Lords, O Abode of the Universe, You are the Imperishable, that which is beyond both the Manifest and the Unmanifest.*

WHY SHOULD THEY NOT BOW DOWN TO THE GREAT ONE—Because the Lord as the Primal Cause of even the Creator, who creates the entire universe of multiplicity, is like the mud in all mud-pots, or the gold in all gold ornaments. The ornaments or the pots have no existence at all apart from the

---

कस्मच्चा ते न नमेरन्महात्मन्
गरीयसे ब्रह्मणोऽप्यादिकर्त्रे ।
अनन्त देवेश जगन्निवास
त्वमक्षरं सदसत्तत्परं यत् ॥ ३७ ॥

kasmācca te na namernmahātman
garīyase brahmaṇo'pyādikartre
ananta deveśa jagannivāsa
tvamakṣaraṁ sadasattatparaṁ yat 37.

gold-essence or the mud-essence in them. Thus, the Primal Cause is that which pervades everything and is that which holds together all names and forms. Infinite in nature, the Lord is not only the Universe, but he is the Lord of all Lords, inasmuch as even the denizens of the heavens and the great phenomenal powers -- all derive their individual might from the Source of all Powers, this Infinite Truth.

The entire world of things-and-beings that exist can fall under two categories: the Manifest (*sat*) and the Unmanifest (*asat*). The manifest is that which can become objects of experience for the organs-of-perception, for the instrument-of-feeling and the equipment-of-thought. The Unmanifest is that which causes the perceptions, feelings, and thoughts. These subtle causes that order the individuals to live in the world outside are called *vasanas* and these constitute the Unmanifest. Arjuna's beautiful definition of the Lord accepts that the Lord is not only the Manifest (*sat*), but the Unmanifest (*asat*) as well. And He is also that which transcends them both.

AND THAT WHICH IS BEYOND THEM—In the theatre we can enjoy both tragedy and comedy, but the light that illumines the stage is that which transcends them both. The wedding ring is, no doubt, made of gold; the wedding-necklace is also, no doubt, made of gold. But gold cannot be defined as the necklace or the ring. We will have to say that gold is not only the ring or the necklace but also that which transcends them both. In this sense, the Lord, being the essential Truth in all names and forms, is both the Manifest and the Unmanifest, and He also has a status that transcends both these conditions. In fact, that which makes both the Manifest and the Unmanifest

---

* *Shashanka* (the moon) literally it means the 'hare-marked' indicating the rabbit-like-form that is seen as a patch on the moon's face.

possible is the Light-of-Awareness, the Pure Consciousness, and the Universal Lord, whom Arjuna is invoking here.

THESE FEW STANZAS* REPRESENT THE MOST UNIVERSAL PRAYER THAT WE HAVE IN ALL THE RELIGIOUS LITERATURE OF THE WORLD. THERE CANNOT BE ANY CREED OR CASTE WHICH HAS ANY OBJECTION TO THESE, INASMUCH AS THEY SUMMARISE THE ENTIRE GALAXY OF PHILOSOPHIC THOUGHTS REGARDING THE ETERNAL, AND EXPAND WITH THEM THE DEVOTEE'S HEART WHICH CAN REACH DIMENSIONS ALMOST UNKNOWABLE, YET WITHIN A DEVOTEE'S EXPERIENCE.

ARJUNA EXTOLS THE LORD THUS:

38. *You are the Primal God, the Ancient PURUSHA; You are the Supreme Refuge of this universe. You are the knower, the knowable, and the Abode-Supreme. By Thee is the universe pervaded, O Being of Infinite forms.*

YOU ARE THE PRIMAL GOD—The Self is the Supreme Creator. The Pure Consciousness is the womb from which even the Creator has risen. The Self, conditioned by Its own creative urge, plays the part of the Creator.

त्वमादिदेवः पुरुषः पुराणः
त्वमस्य विश्वस्य परं निधानम् ।
वेत्तासि वेद्यं च परं च धाम
त्वया ततं विश्वमनन्तरूप ॥ ३८ ॥

tvamādidevaḥ puruṣaḥ purāṇa-
stvamasya viśvasya paraṁ nidhānam
vettāsi vedyaṁ ca paraṁ ca dhāma
tvayā tataṁ viśvamanantarūpa 38.

* From to, in this Chapter.

YOU ARE THE SUPREME ABODE OF THE UNIVERSE— The entire *Vishwa* is housed in the Lord, and therefore, it is said that the Lord is the Abode for the Universe. Here, the term *Vishwa* is to be correctly understood. When this is translated as the Universe, we are apt to confuse it with the astronomers' universe or the scientists' universe. The Sanskrit term *Vishwa* includes these and even more. It includes the entire world of perceptions and the whole field of emotions and the total realm of thought that we, as intelligent individuals, experience in all our lives. This totality of the world of experience through the body, mind and intellect together is indicated by the term *Vishwa*.

With this understanding of the term *Vishwa*, it should not be very difficult for the students of *Vedanta* to understand the full meaning of this life. We are all now experiencing our world through the matter equipments of our body, mind and intellect. These, being products of inert matter, have no Consciousness of their own except that which they borrow from the Infinite, the Self.

These matter envelopments, we have already indicated, are not produced from the Self, as the Self is changeless. The world of matter cannot be said to arise from any other independent source, since the Self is All-pervading and is the One-without-a-second. Therefore, it is explained that the *Vishwa* is but a superimposition upon the Truth, as the ghost-vision gained on a post. In all such hallucinations, the post is the abode of the ghost, of the emotions which it creates, and of the thoughts it generates. There is no truth in the ghost apart from the post from which it borrows its ghost-form.

Thus, it is the Self that is indicated here by Arjuna when he so beautifully sings that the Lord is the 'Supreme Abode' of the entire *Vishwa*.

THOU ART THE KNOWER AND THE KNOWABLE—The Awareness in us is the Factor that completes all our experiences as realities. If the Light of Awareness were not to illumine the inert world-of-matter, no knowledge would have been possible, and therefore, the Principle of Consciousness, represented here as Lord Krishna, the Charioteer – is described here as the Knower. All the techniques of Self-realisation are methods of gathering our Consciousness from all its channels of dissipation, so that, in the still moments of thoughtless Awareness, the Self is automatically recognised. It is thus said 'the Knowable', or the realisable.

YOU PERVADE THE ENTIRE UNIVERSE OF FORMS—Just as sweetness pervades all chocolates, as the ocean pervades all waves, the Lord, being the essence, pervades everything. It was said just a little before, that the super-impositions cannot exist apart from the Substratum upon which they are being perceived. The Self is the Substratum on which the multitude of the world-of-plurality is visualised, and therefore, it is rightly said that 'HE PERVADES ALL'. This is only a repetition of the great *Upanishadic* Truth that 'the Infinite pervades all, and nothing pervades It'. You are VAYU, YAMA, AGNI, VARUNA, the Moon, PRAJAPATI, and the great-grandfather of all. Salutations! Salutations unto You a thousand times, and again salutations unto You!

39. *So far Arjuna was chanting the glories of the God in His transcendental form. A devotee (Upasaka) may wonder what exactly the relationship of the Supreme with his particular Lord-of-the-heart (Upasya) is. The forms and names of Deities conceived of, and fervently prayed to in ancient times, are generally representations of the manifested phenomenal powers.*

In the *Vedic* period, *Vayu* (the wind), *Yama* (the destroyer), *Agni* (the fire), *Varuna* (the sea-god), *Shashanka* (the moon)* and *Prajapati* (The Creator) were considered as deities for reverence and devotion, concentration and growth of the seeker's inner personality. These gods were invoked in those days through chantings and worship, through rituals and sacrifices, and therefore, they were the only popular concepts of God even in the minds of the educated. Oftentimes and everywhere, 'means' have a tendency to get misunderstood as the very 'goal'. Arjuna, here in his true understanding, indicates the Infinite, the Source of all potentialities, the Lord, as nothing other than Krishna, the Infinite.

That the Supreme Lord, in fact, expressing through various functions, Himself plays the part of these *Deities*, is an acceptable view from the standpoint of *Vedanta*. In our own times it is usual for the devotees to invoke the Lord and assert that 'the

---

वायुर्यमोऽग्निर्वरुणः शशाङ्कः
प्रजापतिस्त्वं प्रपितामहश्च।
नमो नमस्तेऽस्तु सहस्रकृत्वः
पुनश्च भूयोऽपि नमो नमस्ते ॥ ३९ ॥

vāyuryamo'gnirvaruṇaḥ śaśāṅkaḥ
prajāpatisvaṁ prapitāmahaśca
namo namaste'stu sahasrakṛtvaḥ
punaśca bhūyo'pi namo namaste 39.

Lord of their heart' is the Lord of all Lords. To this Lord of all Lords, Arjuna prostrates.

40. *Salutations to You, before and behind! Salutations to You on every side! O All! You, Infinite in Power, and Infinite in Prowess, pervade all; wherefore You are the All.*

The Supreme dwells everywhere within, without, above, below and around, and there is no place where He is not. This is not an original idea at all. This has been the constant state of actual experience of all the great *Rishis* of the *Upanishads*.

The Lord, to whom Arjuna thus mentally prostrates from all sides, is not only the All-pervading Essence like space in the Universe, but is also the 'womb' from which all power and daring flow out. Wherever there is an incentive to act, or a capacity to achieve, it is all a ray of His infinite potentiality. The Supreme as Pure Existence dwells everywhere, in everything and in all beings. Since nothing can exist without Existence, He, as Pure Existence, penetrates all, and in fact He alone is the All. Ocean alone is all the waves; mud alone is all the mud-pots.

I HAVE BEEN A SINNER DUE TO LACK OF 'RIGHT KNOWLEDGE' OF THY GREATNESS, AND SO VERY MUCH LIVED FOOLISHLY IN THE PAST. THEREFORE:

नमः पुरस्तादथ पृष्ठतस्ते
नमोऽस्तु ते सर्वत एव सर्व ।
अनन्तवीर्यामितविक्रमस्त्वं
सर्वं समाप्नोषि ततोऽसि सर्वः ॥ ४० ॥

namaḥ purastādatha pṛṣṭhataste
namo'stu te sarvata eva sarva
anantavīyārmitavikramastvaṁ
sarvaṁ smāpnoṣi tato'si sarvaḥ 40.

41. *Whatever I have rashly said from carelessness or love, addressing You as "O Krishna, O Yadava, O friend" and regarding You merely as a friend, unknowing of this greatness of Yours ....*

42. *In whatever way I may have insulted You for the sake of fun, while at play, reposing or sitting, or at meals, when alone (with You), O Achyuta, or in company – that, O Immeasurable One, I implore You to forgive.*

Here are two beautiful stanzas that bring to the forefront with dramatic precision, the exact type of emotions that will naturally be generated in any ordinary man, when he suddenly realises the Glory of the Divine. Till now, Arjuna had thought Lord Krishna to be nothing more than an intelligent cowherd boy, whom he had graciously patronised so long with his royal friendship. And with the realisation and recognition of Krishna

---

सखेति मत्वा प्रसभं यदुक्तं
हे कृष्ण हे यादव हे सखेति ।
अजानता महिमानं तवेदं
मया प्रमादात्प्रणयेन वापि ॥ ४१ ॥

sakheti matvā prasabhaṁ yaduktaṁ
he kṛṣṇa he yādava he sakheti
ajānatā mahimānantavedaṁ
mayā pramādātpraṇayena vāpi 41.

यच्चावहासार्थमसत्कृतोऽसि
विहारशय्यासनभोजनेषु ।
एकोऽथवाप्यच्युत तत्समक्षं
तत्क्षामये त्वामहमप्रमेयम् ॥ ४२ ॥

yaccāvahāsārthamasatkṛto'si
vihāraśayyāsanabhojaneṣu
eko'thavāpyacyuta tatsamakṣaṁ
tatkṣāmaye tvāmahamaprameyam 42.

the Infinite, the mortal in Arjuna prostrates in all loyalty and adoration and pleads for His Divine mercy and forgiveness.

There is a very intimate personal touch in these two stanzas wherein the philosophical discussions are tempered with the emotional touch of deep intimacy. The very effect of the *Geeta* is to bring the sonorous truths of the *Vedas* and the *Upanishads* to the happy tune of the work-a-day world. Great and thought-provoking *Vedantic* truths have been suddenly brought down to the easy familiarity of a drawing-room-chat by such frequent psychological touches given by Vyasa's masterly pen. As an intimate friend, Arjuna must have, in rashness, not knowing Krishna's real Divine Nature, called Him familiarly by His pet names.

FOR:

43. *You are the Father of this world, moving and unmoving. You are to be adored by this world. You are the greatest GURU, (for) there exists none who is equal to You; how can there be then another, superior to You in the three worlds, O Being of unequalled power?*

Here we find that Arjuna, bursting under the pressure of his voiceless emotion and his great regard for the Lord, addresses

---

पितासि लोकस्य चराचरस्य
त्वमस्य पूज्यश्च गुरुर्गरीयान् ।
न त्वत्समोऽस्त्यभ्यधिकः कुतोऽन्यो
लोकत्रयेऽप्यप्रतिमप्रभाव ॥ ४३ ॥

pitāsi lokasya carācarasya
tvamasya pūjyaśca gururgarīyān
na tvatsamo'styabhyadhikaḥ kuto'nyo
lokatrayepyapratimaprabhāva 43.

him: "THOU ART THE FATHER OF THE WHOLE WORLD CONSTITUTED OF THE MOVING AND THE UNMOVING". No doubt, the three worlds – consisting of our experiences in waking, dream, and deep-sleep states – are the interpretations of the same Eternal from the levels of the gross, the subtle and the causal bodies, and the Truth that illumines those experiences is everywhere one and the same.

NATURALLY, THE LORD IS, AS ARJUNA SAYS, 'OF UNEQUALLED GREATNESS', AND THERE IS NONE "SUPERIOR TO THEE IN THE THREE WORLDS". BECAUSE IT IS SO:

44. *Therefore, bowing down, prostrating my body, I crave your forgiveness, adorable Lord. As a father forgiveth his son, a friend his friend, a lover his beloved, even so should You forgive me, O* DEVA.

Arjuna seems to discover in himself a greater eloquence and a subtler ability to argue logically, with the realisation that he is in the presence of the Almighty, the Blessed. Prostration,

---

तस्मात्प्रणम्य प्रणिधाय कायं
प्रसादये त्वामहमीशमीड्यम् ।
पितेव पुत्रस्य सखेव सख्युः
प्रियः प्रियायार्हसि देव सोढुम् ॥ ४४ ॥

tasmātpraṇamya praṇidhāya kārya
prasādaye tvāmahamīśamīḍyam
piteva putrasya sakheva sakheva sakhyuḥ
priya priyāyārhasi deva soḍhum 44.

* Mind, intellect, thought-stuff (*chitta*), and the ego-sense – *Mano-Buddhi-Chitta-Ahamkara*.

in Hinduism, though generally practised as a physical act of 'touching the feet' of the revered, is a significant act that is to be actually accomplished in our heart as a special inward attitude. Surrendering ourselves, so that we may rise above ourselves into the spiritual fields, is true prostration. The ego and egocentric vagaries arising out of our false identifications with matter vestures have robbed us of our experience of the Divinity which is already in us. To the extent the misconceptions are annihilated, we, without these over-growths, are sure to realise the serener beauty of the Divine, which in reality, we are. In surrendering the ego unto the Lord, in fact, we have to bring to His feet nothing but a dirty bundle of animal *Vasanas*, putrified in our own stupidity and lust! Naturally, a devotee, reaching the feet of the Lord in a spirit of surrender and love, has to apologise for the filth that has been offered, as the only tribute of his love, at His Divine feet.

Arjuna is pleading here with the Lord to bear with him as 'a father would with his son', as 'a friend with his friend', as 'a lover with his beloved'. These three examples bring within their embrace all the types of immodest crimes that man, in his ignorance, can perpetrate against his Lord, the Creator.

ARJUNA NOW PRAYS TO THE LORD TO RESUME HIS USUAL FORM AND GIVE UP THE TERRIFYING ASPECTS OF THE TRANSCENDENTAL AND THE UNIVERSAL:

45. *I am delighted, having seen what was never seen before; and (yet) my mind is distressed with fear. Show me your previous form only, O God; have mercy, O God of gods, O Abode of the Universe.*

Every devotee falls in love with the Lord of his devotion and thus when, from the FORM he gets transcended to the Infinite and Full nature of the FORMLESS, that was represented so long by the FORM, he experiences, no doubt, an Infinite Joy, but at that very moment he is overtaken by the emotion of 'fear'. This is the experience of every seeker during the days of his early attempts at getting over the evil of spiritual 'ignorance'. The new realm of joy lived within is, no doubt, absolutely blissful, but a sudden sense of fear exiles him back to body-consciousness and the consequent mental agitation.

At the dawn of his experience Divine, the limited ego, escaping all its limitations, enters into a world unknown to it so far, and it experiences with all joy the vastness of its own dynamism. Arjuna expresses his idea when he says, 'I AM DELIGHTED, HAVING SEEN WHAT UNSEEN WAS BEFORE'. But in the earlier attempts, a seeker is not fit to

---

अदृष्टपूर्वं हृषितोऽस्मि दृष्ट्वा
भयेन च प्रव्यथितं मनो मे ।
तदेव मे दर्शय देव रूपं
प्रसीद देवेश जगन्निवास ॥ ४५ ॥

adṛṣṭapūrvaṁ hṛṣito'smi dṛṣṭvā
bhyena ca pravyathitaṁ mano me
tadeva me sarśaya deva rūpaṁ
prasīda deveśa jagannivāsa 45.

maintain for long his equilibrium in that Divine Realm, and his mind seemingly dissolved to enter the STILL MOMENT-OF-MEDITATION, revives again to flutter into activity, and we find, almost always, that it is the emotion of 'fear' that the mind first experiences, when, with a dreadful shudder it crystallizes itself to sink into the welter of the body and its demands. At this time, a devotee identifies himself with his own emotions of love and devotion and implores the "Lord of his heart" to manifest His own sportive form of smiles and softness, of musical words and loving looks.

WHAT EXACTLY IS THE FORM IN WHICH ARJUNA WANTED THE LORD TO APPEAR BEFORE HIM, IS DESCRIBED IN THE FOLLOWING:

46. *I desire to see You as before, crowned, bearing a mace, with a discus in hand, in Your Former Form only, having four arms, O Thousand-armed, O Universal Form.*

Arjuna makes an open confession here of what he actually wishes. "I WISH TO SEE YOU AS BEFORE". He is afraid of the Universal-form into which the Lord has expanded to express His oneness with the essence in the entire gross-world of matter.

किरीटिनं गदिनं चक्रहस्तम्
इच्छामि त्वां द्रष्टुमहं तथैव ।
तेनैव रूपेण चतुर्भुजेन
सहस्रबाहो भव विश्वमूर्ते ॥ ४६ ॥

kirīṭinaṁ gadinaṁ cakrahastam
icchāmi tvāṁ draṣṭumahaṁ tathaiva
tenaiva rūpeṇa caturbhujena
sahasrabāho bhava viśvamūrte 46.

When the *Vedantic* concept of Truth is thus experienced or expressed in its universal majesty and grandeur, few have the required intellectual stamina to conceive of the Totality and adore It. Even at moments when the intellect can handle such an idea, the heart of the devotee will often fail to tune up its emotion to live the Absolute-experience for long. From the mental zone, Truth can be conceived of and enjoyed only through its symbols and not directly in Its Total-grandeur.

Defining the form of Vasudeva in his milder-manifestation, Arjuna explains in this stanza the traditional form of Vishnu, the Lord of the *Bhagavata*. The concept of God as represented in the phenomena, has been described in all *Puranas*, as having four hands. This may look like a biological freak to students of physiology. We are apt to forget that they are figurative representations symbolising the concept of Truth.

The four hands of the God-form represent the four facets of the 'inner-instrument' in man.*

The Lord Himself, the Self who wields these four hands is represented everywhere as BLUE in colour, and clothed in YELLOW. The significant hue of BLUE is the colour of the Infinite, and the measureless always appears as BLUE, just as the summer-sky or the deep-ocean. YELLOW is the colour of the earth. Thus the Infinite, clothed in the finite, playing the game of life through the four 'inner-instruments' is the symbolism behind Lord Vishnu.

It is also interesting to note that the concept of God in every religion is the same inasmuch as He is the Supreme-most with every power and all knowledge. Man achieves things by the strength of His hands, and the Lord, who is all-powerful, can therefore be symbolised only by showing that He has four hands. The four symbolical instruments which the Lord is represented to carry in His four hands are the club, the discus, the conch and the lotus. The call of the Divine comes to everyone's bosom, when He blows His conch, and if man were not to listen to the call of the Higher dictates in himself, the club follows to punch him, and in spite of that, if man continues his own mistakes, the discus chops him down. In case the roar of the 'conch' is obeyed implicitly, then he gains the lotus, a flower that represents, in Hinduism, what the white-dove and the poppy-flower stand for in Western tradition. Peace and prosperity are the significance of 'lotus' in India. Lotus signifies PERFECTION SPIRITUAL.

Arjuna, in short, wants the Lord to appear in his serener-form and quieter-attitude. For all early seekers and new initiates in *Vedanta*, it naturally becomes difficult to keep, in themselves, the same tempo for their philosophical pursuits. At such moments of dissipation and drowsiness of the intellect, the aspiring heart must discover some reposeful resting-place wherein it can revive itself. This bed of peace and tranquility, upon which the inner personality of man can revive and grow into its fuller stature, is the glorious form of the Lord.

SEEING ARJUNA AFRAID, THE LORD WITHDREW HIS UNIVERSAL FORM; AND CONSOLING ARJUNA WITH HIS SWEET WORDS, HE SAID:

---

1 *'Tat Tvam Asi'*, 'That Thou Art'; or *'Aham Brahma Asmi'*, *'Brahman* I Am'; or *'Ayam Atma Brahma'*, This Self is *Brahman.*

2 *Tadeva Me Roopam-Idam* – That very same My Form.

The Blessed Lord said:

47. *Graciously by Me, O Arjuna, this Supreme-Form has been shown to you by My own YOGA-power – Full of splendour, Primeval, Infinite, this Universal-Form of Mine has never been seen by any other than yourself.*

Here we have the confession that it is not the privilege of all devotees to come to perceive this 'Form-tremendous' and that Arjuna is enjoying It as a special favour due to His Infinite Grace. He also asserts that, "THIS SPLENDID, PRIMEVAL, INFINITE, UNIVERSAL-FORM OF MINE" has not been seen by anyone else.

It does not mean that Vyasa, the author of the *Geeta,* is propounding a new theory, and is making the Lord of his own creation testify to the veracity of it. It only means that this intellectual realisation of the Universal-Oneness has not been gained by anyone placed in the same circumstances as those of Arjuna in the war-front. Mentally shattered, physically worn-out, emotionally upset -- the miserable condition of Arjuna and this Arjuna-state of utter despondency are, in fact, far removed from the favourable conditions for a single-pointed intellectual quest, without which the underlying

---

श्रीभगवानुवाच
मया प्रसन्नेन तवार्जुनेदं
रूपं परं दर्शितमात्मयोगात् ।
तेजोमयं विश्वमनन्तमाद्यं
यन्मे त्वदन्येन न दृष्टपूर्वम् ॥ ४७ ॥

śrībhagavānuvāca
mayā prasannena tavārjunedaṁ
rūpaṁ paraṁ darśitamātmayogāt
tejomayaṁ viśvamanantamādyaṁ
yanme tvadanyena na dṛṣṭapūrvam 47.

Principle of Oneness in the multiplicity of the gross world, cannot easily be comprehended. But Krishna had, due to his tremendous powers, given the required 'eye-of-wisdom' to Arjuna and made him realise, in a chance moment of mental pause, the vision of the Cosmic Form.

WHAT WAS AT THE BACK OF THE MIND OF THE LORD, WHEN HE EXPRESSED THIS STANZA, IS CLEAR FROM THE FOLLOWING:

48. *Neither by the study of the VEDAS and sacrifices, nor by gifts nor by rituals, nor by severe austerities, can I be seen in this form in the world of men by any other than yourself, O great hero among the Kurus.*

Explaining why Arjuna deserves a special congratulation for having gained this extraordinary experience, the Lord says that none can 'SEE' this Universal-form merely because of one's study of the *Vedas,* or on the strength of one's sacrifices. Nor can one gain it by the merits gained through the distribution of gifts, or through performing rituals, or even through constant practice of severe austerities. These are, no doubt, necessary and always helpful in preparing the seeker to realise the essential unity beneath the perceived plurality, but neither a mere book-study,

---

न वेदयज्ञाध्ययनैर्न दानै:
न च क्रियाभिर्न तपोभिरुग्रै: ।
एवंरूप: शक्य अहं नृलोके
द्रष्टुं त्वदन्येन कुरुप्रवीर ॥ ४८ ॥

na vedayajñādhyayanairna dānaiḥ
na ca kriyābhirna topobhirugraiḥ
evaṁrūpaḥ tvadanyena kurupravīra
draṣṭuṁḥ tvadanyena kurupravīra 48.

nor empty ritualism, nor physical *tapas* in themselves will, as an effect of them, bring about this understanding and the final experience. It can come only when the mind is steady. This 'Vision' can be illumined only in the clear light of an integrated 'in-turned intellect'.

In thus making light of the study of the *Vedas*, performance of sacrifices, distribution of gifts, practice of rituals and a life of grim penance, Lord Krishna should not be misunderstood as ridiculing these great prescriptions of the *Vedas*. He merely means to say that although these are means, preparatory to the final end, they are not to be confused with the goal. Cooking, in itself, cannot appease hunger, but that does not mean that cooking is unnecessary; after cooking there is, and must be, the eating. It is in this sense that we must understand the stanza, criticising ponderous study and futile efforts of misguided enthusiasts.

FOR, NONE OF THE KNOWN METHODS OF SELF-DEVELOPMENT IS CAPABLE OF PRODUCING THIS GLORIOUS ACHIEVEMENT. IT IS SAID:

49. *Be not afraid, nor bewildered on seeing such a terrible-Form of Mine as this; with your fear dispelled and with gladdened heart, now behold again this Form of Mine.*

मा ते व्यथा मा च विमूढभावो
दृष्ट्वा रूपं घोरमीदृङ्ममेदम् ।
व्यपेतभी: प्रीतमना: पुनस्त्वं
तदेव मे रूपमिदं प्रपश्य ॥ ४९ ॥

mā te vyathā mā ca vimūḍhabhāvo
dṛṣṭvā rūpaṁ ghoramīdṛṅmamedam
vyapetabhīḥ prītamanāḥ punastvaṁ
tadeva me rūpamidaṁ prapaśya 49.

Vyasa's dramatic genius will not fail to seek its fulfilment whenever an occasion arises. Here is an artistic example of such fine brush-work, accomplished by Vyasa with words, on the canvas of the *Geeta.* Arjuna's emotional agitations are dramatically indicated here when the Lord says, "BE NOT AFRAID, NOR BEWILDERED, HAVING SEEN THIS FORM OF MINE, SO TERRIBLE".

Krishna consoles his friend Arjuna by words and actions and helps him to be in a state of reassuring joys. The Lord comes back to His original form and announces His entry into it with the words; "NOW SEE AGAIN THIS, MY FORMER-FORM".

This passage, which announces the return of the Lord into His 'gentler attitude' and 'loving form', should remind all *Vedantic* students of at least one of the great *Mahavakyas*.[1] The identity between the Universal-form, the Terrible-Totality and the gentle form-of-Krishna, the Divine-individual, is beautifully brought about by the term "THIS MY FORMER-FORM".[2] In fact, the microcosmic representation of Truth smiling temporarily from an assumed mortal-form of Krishna, is Itself the macrocosmic Universal-Form, wherein He expresses Himself as the Essence in all forms and names. The wave is in essence, the ocean; and if the ocean is mighty and fierce, terrible and gigantic, the wave itself is tame and bashful, lovable and attractive.

THE SCENE AGAIN SHIFTS FROM KURUKSHETRA AND THE WAR-FRONT TO THE QUIET CHAMBERS OF THE LUXURIOUS PALACE IN HASTINAPURA, WHERE THE BLIND OLD DHRITARASHTRA IS LISTENING TO THE RUNNING COMMENTARY GIVEN BY HIS MINISTER, SANJAYA:

Sanjaya said:

50. *Having thus spoken to Arjuna, Vaasudeva again showed His own Form, and, the Great-souled One, assuming His gentle Form, consoled him who was so terrified.*

Sanjaya confirms here to the blind old king that the terrible Universal-form, after announcing Its intentions of coming back again to its original sweet form had actually accomplished that promise. What form Krishna reentered is evident: "THE VERY FORM IN WHICH HE WAS BORN IN THE HOUSE OF VASUDEVA".* He assumed the pleasant shape of Lord Krishna, the familiar friend of Arjuna, the Blue-Boy of the *Gopikas*, and thus consoled the mighty warrior, who was aghast with wonder, and trembling with 'fear'.

In these words of Sanjaya, we also can notice the minister's anxiety that Emperor Dhritarashtra should see the suggestion that the Lord of the Universe is Krishna, and that Krishna is on the side of the Pandavas. But how ... how will a blind man ever see?

THE SCENE AGAIN SHIFTS TO THE WAR-FRONT WHEN SANJAYA REPORTS THE WORDS OF ARJUNA IN THE FOLLOWING STANZA:

सञ्जय उवाच
इत्यर्जुनं वासुदेवस्तथोक्त्वा
स्वकं रूपं दर्शयामास भूय: ।
आश्वासयामास च भीतमेनं
भूत्वा पुन: सौम्यवपुर्महात्मा ॥ ५० ॥

sañjaya uvāca
ityarjunaṁ vāsudevastatthoktavā
svakaṁ rupa darśayāmāsa bhūyaḥ
āśvasayāmāsa ca bhītamenaṁ
bhūtvā punaḥ saumyavapurmahātmā 50.

* *'Vasudeva grihe jatam roopam'* – Shankaracharya in his commentary.

Arjuna said:

51. *Having seen this, Thy gentle human-Form, O Janardana, I am now composed and restored to my own nature.*

Arjuna admits here that, when he sees the normal and the gentle-form of Lord Krishna, he feels relieved from his inner tensions and agitations. When an unprepared student like Arjuna is suddenly pushed forward on the spiritual ladder and made to experience truths that are transcendental, and too vast for his intellectual comprehension, it is natural that even in that Realm-of-Bliss, he feels giddy confusions and heaving sobs. Arjuna admits; "I have now become collected in mind and am restored to my normal nature, having seen the milder aspect of Krishna's gracious human form."

TRUE DEVOTION TO THE UNIVERSAL FORM IS EXPLAINED HEREUNDER:

अर्जुन उवाच
दृष्ट्वेदं मानुषं रूपं तव सौम्यं जनार्दन ।
इदानीमस्मि संवृत्तः सचेताः प्रकृतिं गतः ॥ ५१ ॥

arjuna uvāc
dṛṣṭvedaṁ mānuṣaṁ rūpaṁ tava saumyaṁ janārdana
idānīmasmi saṁvṛttaḥ sacetāḥ prakṛtiṁ gataḥ 51.

The Blessed Lord said:

52. *Very hard, indeed, it is to see this Form of Mine which you have seen. Even the gods are ever longing to behold this Form.*

53. *Neither by the VEDAS, nor by austerity, nor by gift, nor by sacrifices can I be seen in this Form as you have seen Me (in your present mental condition).*

The Universal-form of the Lord is no easy experience for anyone, and it can be gained neither by study of the *Vedas*, nor by austerities, nor by gifts, nor by a sacrifice. Even the gods, the denizens of heaven, with their ampler intellects, longer lives, and harder endeavours, are unable to behold this Universal-form, and they keep on longing for this experience.

And yet, Krishna has shown this Form, mighty and wondrous, to His friend through His Grace, as He Himself admitted earlier.*

श्रीभगवानुवाच
सुदुर्दर्शमिदं रूपं दृष्टवानसि यन्मम ।
देवा अप्यस्य रूपस्य नित्यं दर्शनकाङ्क्षिणः ॥ ५२ ॥
śrībhagavānuvāca
sudurdraśamidaṁ rūpaṁ dṛṣṭavānasi yanmama
devā apyasya rūpasya nityaṁ darśanakāṁkṣiṇaḥ 52.

नाहं वेदैर्न तपसा न दानेन न चेज्यया ।
शक्य एवंविधो द्रष्टुं दृष्टवानसि मां यथा ॥ ५३ ॥
nāhaṁ vedairna tapasā na dānena na cejyayā
śakya evaṁvidho draṣṭuṁ dṛṣṭavānasi māṁ yathā 53.

* XI-47: "Through My Grace this Form has been shown to you".

We may wonder what makes the Lord shower His grace upon one, and not upon another. It cannot be a haphazard distribution of an Omnipotent, who does things as He likes, arbitrarily, without any rhyme or reason! For, in that case the Lord will be accused of partiality and arbitrariness.

HERE, IN THE FOLLOWING STANZA, WE GET THE SCIENTIFIC EXPLANATION OF WHAT COMPELS THE LORD TO SHOWER HIS SPECIAL FAVOURS UPON SOMEONE SOMETIMES AND NOT UPON ALL AT ALL TIMES:

54. *But, by single-minded devotion, can I, of this Form, be 'known' and 'seen' in reality, and also 'entered' into, O Parantapa (O scorcher of your foes)!*

Regarding devotion Sankara says: "No doubt, of the means available for liberating ourselves, the most substantial hardware is *Bhakti*; and identifying ourselves with the Self is called *Bhakti*".

Identification is the truest measure of Love. The devotee, forgetting his own individual existence and, in his love, identifying to become one with his beloved Lord, is the culmination of Divine Love. The *Vedantic* student, who is the seeker of the Self, is spiritually obliged to renounce all his abject identification with his matter vestures and to discover his true nature to be the Self.

भक्त्या त्वनन्यया शक्य अहमेवंविधोऽर्जुन ।
ज्ञातुं द्रष्टुं च तत्त्वेन प्रवेष्टुं च परंतप ॥ ५४ ॥

bhaktayā tvananyayā śakya ahamevaṁvidho'rjuna
jñātuṁ draṣṭuṁ ca tattvena praveṣṭuṁ ca parantapa 54.

Only those who are thus capable of identifying themselves with the One unifying Truth that holds together, in its web-of-love, the plurality, can experience, "ME IN THIS FASHION" – in my Cosmic form.

The three stages in which realisation of Truth comes to man are indicated here when the Lord says, "TO KNOW, TO SEE, AND TO ENTER". A definite intellectual knowledge of the goal and the path is the beginning of a seeker's pilgrimage – TO KNOW. Next comes the seeker's attempt to masticate the ideas intellectually understood through his own personal reflections upon the information which he has already gathered – TO SEE. Having thus KNOWN and SEEN the goal, thereafter, the seeker, through a process of detachment from the false and attachment to the Real, comes to experience the Truth as no object other than himself – TO ENTER. By the term 'entering', it is also indicated that the fulfilled seeker becomes the very essence of the sought. The dreamer, suffering from the sorrows of the dream, ends it all, when he no more sees, but 'enters' the waking-state, himself to become the waker.

HOW? ... I SHALL EXPLAIN, SAYS THE LORD AND ADDS:

55. *He who does actions for Me, who looks upon Me as the Supreme, who is devoted to Me, who is free from attachment, who bears enmity towards none, he comes to Me, O Pandava.*

When he heard that anyone can, through undivided devotion, not only recognise the cosmic might of the Lord but also experience that glory in himself, the Pandava Prince's face must have reflected an anxiety to acquire this status. As an answer to this unasked question from Arjuna, Krishna explains here how one can grow towards this great fulfilment in life.

The Krishna-plan, for finite man to gain the stature and strength of the Cosmic, seems to consist of five distinct schemes. This is clear from the conditions required of a seeker as given in this verse. They are: (1) whose work is all dedicated to the Lord, (2) whose goal is the Lord, (3) who is a devotee of the Lord, (4) who is free from all attachments, and (5) who is devoid of all sense of enmity towards everyone.

In these five schemes, we find the entire line of self-discipline summarised. Detachment from all activities, whether physical, mental or intellectual, can take place only when one is constantly thinking of the Self. Enmity is possible only when one considers the other as separate from oneself. There cannot be enmity between my own right hand and my left hand. The awareness of the Oneness should be

---

मत्कर्मकृन्मत्परमो मद्भक्तः सङ्गवर्जितः ।
निर्वैरः सर्वभूतेषु यः स मामेति पाण्डव ॥ ५५ ॥

matkarmakṛnmatparamo madbhaktaḥ saṅgavarjitaḥ
nivariraḥ sarvabhūteṣu yaḥ māmeti pāṇḍava 55.

experienced through the vision of the same Self everywhere and then alone can the total avoidance of enmity with any creature be fully accomplished.

Total detachment is impossibility at the mind-and-intellect level. The mind and intellect cannot live without attaching themselves to some thing or being. Therefore, the seeker, through God-dedicated activity, learns first to withdraw all his attachments from other things, and then to turn his mind with the fervour of devoted attachment to the Lord. In accomplishing this, all the schemes explained earlier are, indeed, very helpful.

Thus, when the whole scheme is reevaluated, we can find in it logic quite acceptable and perfectly psychological. Each subsequent item in the scheme is beautifully supported and nourished by the previous one. From the stanza, it is evident that the spiritual seeker's great pilgrimage starts with God-dedicated activities. Soon, that God-principle Itself becomes his very goal in life. He will develop, in himself, a consummate liking for this glorious goal. Naturally, all his other finite attachments with the world-of-objects will end, and at last, he will come to contact the Self. Having become the Self, he recognises himself everywhere, in everything, and so, in him there cannot be any sense of enmity at all.

LOVE FOR ALL AND HATRED FOR NONE can be considered the *Geeta* 'touch-stone' to know the quality of realisation and intensity of experience a seeker has gained through his *sadhana*.

Thus, in the UPANISHADS of the glorious Bhagawad-Geeta, in the Science of the Eternal, in the scripture of YOGA, in the dialogue between Sri Krishna and Arjuna, the eleventh discourse ends entitled:

The *Yoga* of the Vision of the Universal Form

The Chapter is rightly named as the Vision of the Universal-form. In Sanskrit scriptural terminology, it is pointed out that the term *Vishwa Roopa* used here is actually the *Virata Roopa*. The Self, identifying itself with an 'individual physical body', experiences the waking-state happenings, and in this condition the Self is called in *Vedanta* as *Vishwa*. When the same Self identifies Itself with the total physical gross-bodies of the Universe, in that condition the Self is called the Cosmic-*Virata*. Here the Lord showed His Cosmic-form but the Chapter is titled as *Vishwa-Roopa*.

Om Om Om Om Om

ॐ तत्सदिति श्रीमद् भगवद् गीतासूपनिषत्सु ब्रह्मविद्यायां
योगशास्त्रे श्रीकृष्णार्जुनसंवादे विश्वरूपदर्शनयोगो नाम
एकादशोऽध्याय:

Oṁ tatsaditi śrīmadbhagavadgītāsū ūpaniṣatsu brahmavidyāyāṁ yogaśāstre śrī kṛṣṇārjuna saṁvāde viśvarūpadarśanayogo nāma ekādaśo'dhyāyaḥ.

XII

Path of Devotion
Introduction

KNOWING full well the essential temperament of Arjuna, the royal hero, Krishna had tickled his kingly ambition at the closing of the last chapter (XI-54). To a true king, the challenge of a greater glory is too strong to resist. Wherever a vaster field, a greater profit, a more glowing resplendency is recognised, he cannot resist the temptation to fight for it, to conquer it and bring it within his ruling hand, and thereby spread his unquestioned sway over the conquered domain. Expecting this reaction in his royal friend of endless heroism, Krishna had not only exhibited the divine glory of the Lord and His cosmic-form, but also declared to Arjuna that 'through single-minded devotion can this cosmic-form be known and seen and entered into by anyone'. On hearing that this Infinite glory can be his through devotion, the Pandava Prince optimistically determines to make an attempt to conquer and bring to himself this spiritual glory.

Psychologically, Arjuna was already prepared to feel this heroic urge and he had the divine inspiration to make any sacrifice necessary and to put forth all the efforts needed for the conquest of the spiritual goal. We have found in the last two chapters how Arjuna, as an intelligent man, was hesitant to accept his charioteer as Divine. The Prince demanded an analytical explanation for the Lord's philosophical exposition. "I am not in them, they are in Me". This was given out earlier (IX-4) but the scepticism in the intelligent Arjuna was still too deep to be totally annihilated by a mere verbal declaration of the glory of the Divine.

Naturally, the Prince demanded a physical demonstration of the same and the Lord showed the total Cosmic-Form. Once fully convinced by the double process of analysis and synthesis – discussion and a demonstration of the same – Arjuna's intellect surrenders totally with an aspiration to realise and become the Spirit.

Every individual wants to become and live what he is convinced of; 'as the thoughts, so the man'. And, one who is convinced is a greater seeker than a man of blind faith jogging along the thorny path of timeworn habits.

It is a fact that the subtler personality can come to assert itself only when the grosser one is completely satisfied. As long as one is hungry, one's emotional nature goes on choking one's heart. When the stomach is full, the heart has the freedom to demand its emotional satisfaction of love and affection. The intellect can come to its full play only when the physical and the emotional aspects are at rest – or, temporarily at least, satisfied. If there is an imperfection or incompleteness, either in the physical or in the emotional personality of man, he is not capable of invoking and directing the efficient play of his emotional and intellectual abilities.

In the same way, the spiritual urge for intuitive experience in a seeker expresses itself only when all earlier and outer demands are fully satisfied. This truth is beautifully brought out to us in the discussions contained in the chapter on the Path- of-Devotion. When Arjuna is intellectually convinced and emotionally satisfied that the cowherd-boy is the Infinite's own playful manifestation, his scepticism as a soldier ends and he feels an urge to seek, to discover, to conquer, to possess and to rule over the kingdom of the Spirit.

In the 'Form-Terrible', Arjuna had observed the endless thralldom of the PAST, passing through the avenues of the PRESENT, to reach the courtyard of the FUTURE and meet the Lord of Time, Krishna Himself there. Similarly, in the Lord, the Infinite, he saw 'here' and 'there' mingling with each other, and the farthest horizons nestling in the lap of the 'here'! Naturally, Arjuna raised the question as to whether he should seek, love, and meditate upon the infinite form of the Formless, or upon the manifest divinity in the Cosmic-Form of Krishna.

The previous two chapters had completely satisfied the sceptic in Arjuna through discussion (Ch.-X) and actual demonstration (Ch.-XI) of the Lord's Cosmic-Form. The newly converted Royal-Prince now feels an irresistible urge to conquer the Kingdom Divine within himself. The secret strategy for the sure conqueror was also indicated in the concluding stanza of the last chapter; devotion and consistency of self-application, free from all egocentric attachment to the world-of-objects is the way charted out in the *Geeta,* and it is assured that thereby, "you shall enter into Me, O PANDAVA" (XI-55).

As a practical man-of-action, Arjuna is no idle philosopher, seeking a vain satisfaction in mere bookish erudition and profitless scholarship. He was not at all charmed by the theory as such. The warrior was impatient to enter the field of strife and bring under his sway the realm of glory demonstrated by his Charioteer. Therefore, the chapter starts rightly with a question that means business.

As a student of the *Vedas*, from his childhood, Arjuna was taught that the Absolute is Formless and Nameless and beyond the perceptions of the sense organs, feelings of the mind, and comprehensions of the intellect. But the Prince had a vivid first-hand experience of Krishna and His Cosmic-Form. Naturally, the doubt is raised by him as to whether it is more profitable to meditate upon the Truth as unmanifest or as manifest – like the one shown by Sri Krishna.

The question raises a very moot point in religion. From time to time, Prophets and Masters had appeared to support, or to condemn, the worship of the God-Principle in and through a Divine-Form. Can the ocean be fully realised through the knowledge of the waves, or will the knowledge of the waves obstruct our comprehension of the ocean? In short, is idol-worship justified? Can it provide a helpful prop for the meditative mind to swing on and dive into the Infinite? If it can, what exactly is the technique? The entire chapter is dedicated to answer this question.

For its scientific thoroughness and for its wealth of details, the *Geeta* can always stand a good comparison with any of the modern textbooks on secular sciences. Lord Krishna is ever conscious that He is talking to a man-of-action, Arjuna, a brainy sceptic.

Arjuna said:

1. *Those devotees who, eversteadfast, thus worship you, and also those who worship the imperishable, the unmanifested - - which of them are better versed in YOGA?*

अर्जुन उवाच
एवं सततयुक्ता ये भक्तास्त्वां पर्युपासते ।
ये चाप्यक्षरमव्यक्तं तेषां के योगवित्तमाः ॥ १ ॥

arjuna uvāca
evaṁ satatayuktā ye bhaktāstvāṁ paryupāsate
ye cāpyakṣaramavyaktaṁ teṣāṁ ke yogavittamāḥ 1.

The philosophical discourses contained in the Divine Song, though written in a conversational style, never overlook the systematic development of its thoughts, not only within the chapter but also from chapter to chapter. The last chapter ended with an assurance from the Lord that any seeker can realise the glory of the Cosmic-Form, if only he can entertain an unwavering devotion. As a prince of royal blood, Arjuna must have felt tickled by this great challenge thrown at him. As a practical man of the world, he enquires here as to the form on which he should meditate.

The question is very intelligently put. It is quite well known that in the world there are two types of seekers, seeking one and the same goal. Some meditate upon the manifested-form of the Infinite and others contemplate upon the unmanifested-Supreme. Both of them are sincere; both progress onwards. But the question is as to which, out of these two types of seekers, is better versed in *Yoga*?

In philosophy, the unmanifest (*avyakta*) is that which is not directly perceptible to the sense-organs (*indriya-agocaram*). The objects that can be brought within the perceptible powers of our sense-organs are called the manifested (*vyakta*). Arjuna was taught in his early studies of the *Vedas* that the Supreme was unmanifest and all-pervading. But he had, in the previous chapter, a personal experience of the Divine Cosmic-Form. Naturally, the determined prince, seeking to understand the right path of spiritual evolution, asks here a pertinent question as to who is the better seeker – is it the one who devotes himself in love to the Lord-manifest, or he who, with complete detachment from all external stimuli, meditates with ease and poise upon the unmanifested-Infinite?

The question expresses the great controversy that exists even today in the world. Can the Lord be meditated upon and realised ultimately through idol worship? Can any symbol represent HIM? Can a wave represent the ocean?

EXPLAINING THE PATH-OF-MEDITATION ON A FORM REPRESENTATIVE OF THE DIVINE, KRISHNA THE INFINITE, STARTS HIS DISCOURSE.

The Blessed Lord said:

2. *Those who, fixing their mind on Me, worship Me, ever steadfast and endowed with supreme faith, these, in my opinion, are the best in YOGA.*

In this very opening stanza, Krishna points out three conditions that are absolutely necessary in order that devotion unto the Lord may yield its promised dividend. Generally, there is a feeling that the path-of-Devotion is very easy. It is equally true to say that no chosen 'Path' is difficult for the seeker who has chosen it. 'Paths' are different only because of the vehicles employed; in a boat we can never travel through the Grand-Trunk road, nor can we sail over the waves in a plane, nor on a cycle dash at 60-miles an hour! There are limitations to each vehicle. But progress is assured to the intelligent and the careful even with any such vehicle. Similarly, for self-development, each type of seeker, according to the vehicle available, chooses either the path-of-Devotion or the path-of-Action or the path-of-Knowledge. To each one of them, his 'Path' is the easiest.

श्रीभगवानुवाच
मय्यावेश्य मनो ये मां नित्ययुक्ता उपासते ।
श्रद्धया परयोपेतास्ते मे युक्ततमा मताः ॥ २ ॥

śrībhagavānuvāca
mayyāveśya mano ye māṁ nityayuktā upāsate
śraddhayā parayopetāste me yuktatamā matāḥ 2.

Fixing their thoughts on me—Thought is the content of our subtle body. Both the mind and intellect are nothing but thoughts. It is not sufficient if they leisurely wander around the concept of the Lord, but they have actually to penetrate, delve into, merge, and ultimately dissolve themselves to become the very ideal perfection which the Lord represents. The word that is being used here in the stanza (*aveshya*) indicates not merely a 'thought contact' but an actual 'thought penetration'. In fact, human thought takes the form of, gathers the fragrance of, and even puts on the glow of the qualities in the objects of its contemplation. Thus, when a devotee's thoughts gush forward in sincerity, in a newly found urge of irrepressible love towards the Lord, the devotee, as a personality, ends for the time being, and himself acquires the glow and beauty of the Lord of his heart.

Ever self-controlled, worship Me—The second condition necessary for a devotee to accomplish his evolution through the path-of-Devotion is that he must have sufficient balance in himself to exercise regular self-control while worshipping the Lord. The mind, by its very nature, will always try to run wild from its objects of contemplation, and the art of keeping the thoughts balanced at its point-of-concentration is called self-control. The Sanskrit term *Upasana* though it can be translated as 'worship', should not be misunderstood by the superficial suggestion that automatically comes to us when we hear the word 'worship'. True *Upasana* is an inward act of attunement with the Higher Principle so as to get ourselves completely merged with It.

With SUPREME faith—Faith is generally understood as 'blind belief'... blind belief is not *Shraddha*. *Shraddha* is "my belief in something I do not know, so that I may come to know what I believe in". Without this faculty developed in him, a devotee may not succeed sufficiently in bringing about a self-divinisation in himself even after years of practice.

Thus, three main conditions are enumerated in this stanza as essential and unavoidable for one to become a true devotee, viz., (1) Perfect faith, (2) Ever steadfast in worship and (3) One's mind totally merged with the concept of the Lord. If these are accomplished in anyone, he is considered as the most steadfast devotee by the Lord.

THEN, ARE NOT THE OTHERS *YOGIS*? "WAIT, HEAR NOW WHAT I HAVE TO SAY REGARDING THEM":

3. *Those who worship the imperishable, the indefinable, the unmanifest, the omnipresent, the unthinkable. the unchangeable, the immovable and the eternal, ...*

4. *Having restrained all the senses, even-minded everywhere, rejoicing ever in the welfare of all beings – verily they also come unto Me.*

In the previous stanza, the essential conditions under which alone a devotee can practice contemplation upon a Manifest-Form of the Lord to become a steadfast *Yogi* were described. In these two stanzas, Lord Krishna is trying to describe those who meditate upon the Unmanifest-Form of the Lord.

ये त्वक्षरमनिर्देश्यमव्यक्तं पर्युपासते ।
सर्वत्रगमचिन्त्यं च कूटस्थमचलं ध्रुवम् ॥ ३ ॥

ye tvakṣaramanirdeśyamavyaktaṁ paryupāsate
sarvatragamacintyaṁ ca kūṭasthamacalaṁ dhruvam 3.

संनियम्येन्द्रियग्रामं सर्वत्र समबुद्धयः ।
ते प्राप्नुवन्ति मामेव सर्वभूतहिते रताः ॥ ४ ॥

sanniyamyendriyagrāmaṁ sarvatra samabuddhayaḥ
te prāpnuvanti māmeva sarvabhūtahite ratāḥ 4.

IMPERISHABLE (*Akshara*)—All those that have forms and qualities are substances and all substances are perishable. The Imperishable is, therefore, that which has no qualities. Qualities alone can be perceived, and it implies that it is impossible for the sense-organs to perceive the Imperishable.

INDEFINABLE (*Anirdeshyam*)—Definitions are always in terms of perceived experiences and when a thing is imperceptible, naturally, it cannot be defined and distinguished from other things.

ALL-PERVADING (*Sarvatra-gam*)—The Infinite that has no qualities, that is not manifest, that which is, therefore, Indefinable, should necessarily be All-pervading and existing everywhere. If the Supreme can be indicated as not existing in any place, then the Supreme will have a particular shape. And that which has a shape will perish.

UNTHINKABLE (*Achintyam*)—That which can be conceived of by a human mind will immediately become the object of feelings and thoughts and since all objects are perishable, the Imperishable must necessarily be Inconceivable, Incomprehensible, and Unthinkable.

UNCHANGING (*Kootasthah*)—The Self, the Consciousness, remains unchanged even though it is the substratum on which all changes constantly take place. '*Koota*' in Sanskrit, is an 'anvil'. Just as the iron block in a smithy's workshop, without itself undergoing any change, allows other pieces of iron to be beaten out on it, and changed into any shape; so too, the Consciousness allows our personalities to grow well or ill in contact with It.

IMMOVABLE (*Achalam*)—Motion is change in the time-space system. A thing can never move in itself; it can do so only to a point in space and time where it is not already. Here, now, I remain in my chair. I can move to another place to occupy it in the coming minute. But here and now in my own chair, I cannot move in myself, since I pervade the whole of me. The Infinite is all-pervading and there is no point in space or time where It is not, and therefore, the Infinite cannot move. It is here, there, everywhere; It has the past, the present and the future IN it.

ETERNAL (*Dhruvam*)—that which can change is a thing that is conditioned by time and space. But the Supreme, the substratum of all, at all times and in all places, is the One that supports the very play of time and space, and therefore, these two factors cannot condition the Infinite. Consciousness, which is the Infinite Self in us, is the same everywhere and at all times – in our childhood, youth and old age, in all places and at all times – and in all conditions of joy and sorrow or success and failure. It is only when we come down to the levels of our intellect, mind, and body that we step into Einstein's world with its Relativity Theory in the play of time and space. The Supreme is unconditioned by time; It is the ruler of time. It is Eternal.

We must note that all these terms used here are expressions borrowed from our *Upanishads* to indicate that which provides the Eternal substratum for the ever-changing universe of names and forms, behaviours and happenings, perceptions and feelings, thoughts and experiences. Meditation upon the Lord, symbolized in the form, demands three unavoidable conditions.

HAVING RESTRAINED ALL THE SENSES—to dissipate our energies through the sense organs is the vulgar hobby of the thoughtless mortal. A seeker, who is aspiring to reach the summit of Perfection and rule over the state of deathless joy, must necessarily curtail such dissipations and redirect the energies so conserved for the higher flight. The sense organs are the real gateways through which the disturbing world of plurality steals in, to storm our inner bosom and plunge us into destruction. It is again through the organs-of-action that the mind gushes out into the world-of-objects. These two transactions break up our harmonious equipoise and steady balance. Krishna rightly emphasizes here that, if a meditator is to succeed in the path-of-Meditation he must cultivate a habit of living with his senses in control.

ALWAYS EQUANIMOUS—the second of the conditions that has been prescribed here by the Lord for a successful meditator is his intellectual equanimity in all conditions and experiences. It is very foolish indeed for a thinker to hope for a condition in life, wherein no disturbance from the outer world can reach him to distract his meditation. Such a perfect condition is impossible. The things of the world in themselves and in their patterns keep on changing. In such a kaleidoscopic design of existence, it is indeed unintelligent to expect any desirable system to remain continuously for the benefit of a seeker's steady practice. Such a thing is impossible. In the world of change, therefore, a seeker must discover his own balance and equipoise, by controlling his intellectual evaluations, mental attachments and physical contacts with the world outside.

The intelligent relationship maintained by a seeker towards the world outside, whereby he experiences a uniform steadiness in himself, in spite of the mad revelry of things and beings around him, is called the condition of equanimity. He, who has developed the right sense of discrimination, can easily watch for and see the golden chord of beauty that holds together all that is enchanting and grotesque constituting the outer world. This capacity is called *Sama-buddhi*.

My child may be dirty at one moment, mischievous at another; screaming in the morning, laughing in the noon; bullying in the evening and wild at night! Yet, through all such conditions, the father in me sees but one and the same son, therefore, I give my love equally in all these different manifestations of my own son. This is a loving father's *sama-buddhi*. In the same way, a true seeker learns to recognise the Lord of his heart in grim tragedies, in the pleasant comedies, in the tremendous successes, in the sighing sorrows and in the disappointing failures in his own day-to-day life. Therefore, he becomes equanimous intellectually.

INTENT ON THE WELFARE OF ALL BEINGS— Enumerating the third of the qualifications necessary for a successful meditator, the Lord says that he should ever be self-dedicated in serving at his best, all beings. It is impossible for anyone, as long as he is in the embodiment, to give all his mind and intellect, at all times, towards the higher contemplation. He must necessarily come in contact with the world and react to it. In all such activities, a seeker should be, by the very nature of his philosophy, one who is ever devoted in tirelessly serving the entire living kingdom. Love for all beings becomes his creed.

Thus, if the meditators, fixing their mind upon the Imperishable, the Unmanifest, are able to control their sense-organs, keep themselves equanimous and make it their nature to serve others, they too, "reach Me alone". Krishna declares that they too reach the same goal, the Supreme Self.

The question as raised by Arjuna is rather of a controversial nature, while Krishna's answer to it is a declaration of an incontrovertible truth. Here, the great divine philosopher points out how both the Paths take the practitioner to one and the same goal and the same general rules of conduct in their dealing with the world are here clearly prescribed for both of them. Whether the devotee is seeking his spiritual unfoldment through meditation upon a personal, or an impersonal God, the result achieved, it is shown, remains the same, if the disciplines required of him are all fully and faithfully followed.

BUT, GENERALLY SPEAKING TO THE MAJORITY, THE LORD ADDS:

5. *Greater is their trouble whose minds are set on the 'Unmanifest'; for the goal, the 'Unmanifest', is very hard for the embodied to reach.*

After explaining how the goal reached by all meditators is one and the same Supreme Perfection, Lord Krishna tries to compare the two incomparable 'Paths', both of equal efficacy and merit. He says "Greater is the toil of those whose thoughts are fixed on the Unmanifest". This declaration, when read as such and in itself, is not only an advocacy of the path-of-Devotion to a personal god, but almost amounts to a positive condemnation of meditation upon the Formless. Such an erroneous and misleading interpretation will render the *Geeta* a scripture that contradicts the 'eternal wisdom' of the *Upanishads*. And yet, there are vocal champions of devotion (*Bhakti*), who quote this half stanza to beguile the faithful!

The first line is commented upon and elucidated by the following line in the stanza. Lord Krishna explains why it is hard ordinarily for seekers to contemplate upon the Formless. "The Unmanifest is very hard indeed for the embodied to reach". The crucial word in the stanza is *'embodied'*. It is often very directly understood to mean 'all those who have a physical structure'. The absurdity of such an understanding would become evident if we follow the natural corollary of such an interpretation.

क्लेशोऽधिकतरस्तेषामव्यक्तासक्तचेतसाम् ।
अव्यक्ता हि गतिर्दुःखं देहवद्भिरवाप्यते ॥ ५ ॥

kleśo'dhikatarasteṣāmavyaktācetasām
avyaktā hi gatirduḥkham dehavadbhiravāpyate 5.

If all those who are having a physical body can meditate only upon the form of the Lord, then it follows that pure meditation upon the Formless is to be undertaken only after the body is dropped and the seeker is dead.

Shri Shankaracharya, therefore, clearly explains that the 'embodied' means 'those who are attached to their bodies'. Sunk in flesh, if one personality lives only a life of sensuality and satisfaction of one's body-cravings, one will find it too difficult to take to steady and continuous meditation upon the subtle theme of the Infinite, Formless and All-pervading. An old man whose vision is lost and whose hands are shaky, may find it very difficult to thread a needle; so too, a mind and intellect agitated, panting and restless, suffering from desire-plays, are not vehicles that can successfully fly beyond the frontiers of names and forms to the endless spiritual glory.

In short, to the majority of us, meditation upon the Lord, as expressed in the universe, is easier and more profitable. Man can worship the myriad forms through service undertaken in a spirit of worship and divine dedication. By doing so, the body-attachments and sense-appetites get purged from his inner make-up and his mind becomes subtle enough to conceive and contemplate upon the Formless and the Imperishable Unmanifest.

EVEN THOUGH, LATER ON, WE SHALL MEET WITHIN THIS CHAPTER, THE WAY OF LIFE PRESCRIBED FOR MEN CONTEMPLATING UPON THE 'UNMANIFEST', HEREUNDER WE SHALL FIND THE DISCIPLINES IN LIFE FOR A STUDENT WHO IS TRYING TO STEADY THE MIND THROUGH HIS DEVOTION FOR THE 'MANIFEST-LORD':

6. *But those who worship Me, renouncing all actions in Me, regarding Me as the Supreme Goal, meditating on Me with single-minded devotion (YOGA)...*

7. *For them, whose minds are set on Me, verily I become, ere-long, O Partha, the Saviour, (to save them) out of the ocean of finite experiences; the SAMSARA.*

Here Krishna prescribes certain definite conditions to be faithfully followed by all meditators upon the Form of the Lord, and concludes that those who are following His instructions fully will be saved from their mortal limitations, by the Lord Himself, on whose Form they are contemplating. A careful study of these conditions will show us how the devotee grows mentally to a stature so divine and high that, thereafter he needs no help from anyone at all. But, in the beginning, a seeker needs some assurances from his teacher in order to instil in him the required self-confidence to start his practices.

THOSE WHO WORSHIP ME, RENOUNCING ALL ACTIONS IN ME—to renounce all our actions to an INSTITUTION, to an IDEA or to a POWER, is to end our individual limitations and identify ourselves with that for which we renounce. Thus, an ordinary man, as ambassador of his country, becomes a mighty personality in the foreign

---

ये तु सर्वाणि कर्माणि मयि संन्यस्य मत्पराः ।
अनन्येनैव योगेन मां ध्यायन्त उपासते ॥ ६ ॥

ye tu savārṇi kamārṇi mayi sannyasya matparāḥ
ananyenaiva yogena māṁ dhyāyanta upāsate 6.

तेषामहं समुद्धर्ता मृत्युसंसारसागरात् ।
भवामि नचिरात्पार्थ मय्यावेशितचेतसाम् ॥ ७ ॥

teṣāmahaṁ samuddhatār mṛtyusaṁsārasāgarāt
bhavāmi nacirātpārtha mayyāveśitacetasām 7.

courts, because he talks, acts, thinks and expresses the will of an entire people. Similarly, when a devotee of the Infinite Lord surrenders himself totally at His feet and acts as a messenger, or as a representative of the Will of the Lord, he becomes, not only divinely 'dynamic', but in and through his own activities, aware of the presence and grace of the Universal Spirit.

REGARDING ME AS THE SUPREME GOAL—a dancer never forgets the rhythm of the drum which accompanies her steps. A musician is ever conscious of the background hum. Similarly, a devotee is advised not to take up religion as a part-time entertainment, or as a temporary escapism, but to consider the Lord as the Supreme Goal to be achieved in and through life. In short, we are advised that in order to ascend to the Higher summits of cultural perfection, it is necessary that we direct all our contacts, transactions, and experiences in our life, towards the achievement of this cumulative goal of Self-Perfection, as symbolised in the Lord of our heart.

WITH UNSWERVING *YOGA*—all attempts with which we develop our mental attunement with any chosen state-of-Perfection constitute *Yoga*. To lift our minds from its present agitations and wasteful tendencies towards a greater goal of ampler joy and fuller wisdom is *Yoga*. This faculty of *Yoga* is in every one of us. At all times we are practising it. But the results of *Yoga* will depend upon the goal towards which we are heaving forward; unfortunately, ours is not generally a Divine Goal; to strive for the sense-enjoyments is called *Bhoga*.

Ordinarily, our goal keeps on changing and we reach nowhere even though our struggle is consistent. If a holidaymaker has two spots in view, and he cannot come to a decision as to which place he wants to visit, then he can reach neither of them. He will be in a helpless state of confusion, travelling up and down the road, reaching nowhere, and wasting his time and energy. *'Anya'* means 'other'; *'Ananya'* means 'without otherness'. Krishna is advising here *Ananya Yoga*, meaning a *Yoga* in which the goal is ever steady and our mind has no sense of 'otherness' about it.

It may be noted here that mental disintegration can come both because of the 'otherness' in our goal, and because of the mind wandering into other channels of preoccupations.

Thus "those (a) who have renounced all actions in Me (b) who regard Me as the Supreme Goal and (c) who, with a single-pointed mind and goal strive, are the best of My devotees, when their striving is constituted of meditation (*Dhyana*) and worship (*Upasana*)". We have already indicated that *Upasana* is not merely meditation upon a goal, but becoming, in an active way, one with the Goal contemplated upon. At-one-ment with the goal is the meditator's aim and fulfilment.

Enumerating the conditions necessary for a devotee at his seat of meditation, Krishna assures him that he need not wonder how he will go beyond the shores of sorrows, agitations, and imperfections, which are the lot of all mortals. "I shall be their saviour" is a divine assurance and an infinite guarantee. It is possible that seekers may become rather impatient when even after months and years of practice, they do not come anywhere near any spiritual experience.

The Lord's assurance also indicates the time limit; He says that He will save the seeker from his own imperfection 'ere-long' (*nachirat*).

TO THOSE WHOSE MIND IS SET ON ME—The mind generally takes the form of the object it contemplates upon. When an integrated mind-intellect-equipment of a devotee, through constant practice, gains the capacity of engaging itself entirely on the concept of the Lord, to the exclusion of all agitations and undivine thoughts, the entire mind assumes the stature of the Infinite. It is the mind that gives us the hallucination of our egocentric limitations, and again, it is the mind that rediscovers the Infinitude. Bondage and liberation are both for the mind. The Self is ever free; ever liberated; never bound.

8. *Fix your mind on Me only, place your intellect in Me; then, (thereafter) you shall, no doubt, live in Me alone.*

Meditation is not a physical act but it is a subtle art developed by the inner personality in man. Every seeker must be experiencing that what his intellect accepts, his heart does not appreciate; and what his heart craves for, the intellect laughs at. To bring both the head and the heart to the same Enchanting Form of thrilled satisfaction, would be the secret of harnessing the entire inner man to the spiritual effort. The technique of this art is beautifully explained in this stanza.

FIX THY MIND ON ME ALONE—The mind cannot contemplate on any theme that cannot be conditioned by the senses. Therefore, by meditation upon the enchanting form of the Immortal Flute-player, the human mind can readily be made to rest entirely at the feet of the form. The Lord, being all-pervading, is at once the Divine Grace behind all names and forms. The mind of a devotee cannot wander to any place where he is not reminded of the smile of the Crowned Cowherd-boy!

Merely to ruminate over a decorated marble symbol of the Eternal Child is not in itself sufficient food for the inner personality of man. The intellectual aspect in us is starved, although the heart nestles in satisfaction at the soft feet of

---

मय्येव मन आधत्स्व मयि बुद्धिं निवेशय ।
निवसिष्यसि मय्येव अत ऊर्ध्वं न संशयः ॥ ८ ॥

mayyeva mana ādhatsva mayi buddhiṁ niveśaya
nivasiṣyasi mayyeva ata ūrdhvaṁ na saṁśayaḥ 8.

the Lord. Any over-development will bring about an ugly situation; perfection is harmony and uniform growth. Therefore, technically, the *Geeta* rightly advises that the devotee must bring his discriminating intellect to pierce through the stony idol and contact the pulsating Truth it represents.

PLACE THE INTELLECT IN ME—To contact thereby the cosmic total-intellect which is the Lord's equipment.

Every one of us, at any given moment, is the sum-total of what we think and what we feel. If our minds are resting on the Lord and our intellects have dived into the very depths of the Infinite, our individualities end and we merge to become one with the Infinite, the all-pervading. Therefore, the Lord says, "Thereafter you shall live in Me".

This statement may look as an exaggeration for the finite mortal, who is standing agitated and shy at the gateway of the Temple-of-Truth. In his habitual concept that he is a finite mortal entity – pressed under a thousand limitations, suffering from a host of imperfections, and persecuted by an army of despairs – he fails to accept that he can rediscover himself to be Himself, the ever-Divine. Therefore, as a kindly teacher, Lord Krishna reassures him by affirming directly, 'no doubt' (*nasamshayah*).

A TYPICAL MAN OF THE WORLD, ARJUNA, LOOKS UP TO THE LORD, DECLARING HIS ABJECT HELPLESSNESS TO ACCOMPLISH THESE TWO SEEMINGLY SIMPLE, BUT PRACTICALLY IMPOSSIBLE CONDITIONS OF MEDITATION. AS AN ALTERNATIVE, THE LORD SAYS:

9. *If you are unable to fix your mind steadily upon Me, then by the YOGA of constant practice, seek to reach Me, O Dhananjaya.*

अथ चित्तं समाधातुं न शक्नोषि मयि स्थिरम् ।
अभ्यासयोगेन ततो मामिच्छाप्तुं धनञ्जय ॥ ९ ॥

atha cittaṁ samādhātuṁ na śaknoṣi mayi sthiram
abhyāsayogena tato māmicchāptuṁ dhanañjaya 9.

The technique of self-unfoldment was irrevocably declared by the Lord in the previous verse. The seeker has to fix his mind totally at the feet of the Lord and bring his intellect to play upon and rip open the significance of the Form-Divine. This double act needs an extremely subtle intellect and single-pointedness of the mind. Perhaps Arjuna felt, as any average man would, that this 'Path' was almost impossible for him to pursue successfully. The kindly teacher in Krishna, reading this despair from the face of his disciple, tries to give him an alternative method of Self-unfoldment.

IF YOU ARE UNABLE TO FIX YOUR THOUGHTS STEADILY ON ME—Then the only practical method would be to pursue the *Yoga* of constant practice (*Abhyasa-Yoga*). This *Yoga*-of-practice was earlier described (in VI-26) as; "wherever the mind wanders, restless; from there, let him subdue it and bring it under the sway of the Self alone." In short, whenever a meditator tries to meditate by fixing his mind upon a chosen point-of-concentration, the fickle mind will always try to run wild into dissimilar thought-channels. The advice here is to gather all the rays of the mind, whenever they wander away from their main point of concentration, and focus them all again and again on the Divine Form.

Every meditator must admit that the mind steadily fails to balance on, for any length of time, totally engaging itself with the theme of its contemplation. That the mind runs away into a wild wool-gathering is not in itself such a tragedy as that when the meditator himself gets abducted by the mind and unconsciously follows it into the fields of ready distractions. The *Yogeshwara* (Krishna) is only advising us not to get enticed away by the mind from our divine pursuit.

In order to gather the dissipated and riotous mental rays and to focus them at the point of concentration, the meditator must develop a capacity to stand by himself, and in himself, apart from his wandering mind. If we identify ourselves with the mind, wherever the mind takes us, we also must go. Therefore, in order to control the mind, the meditator must stand apart from his mind, identifying himself with that power in him which possesses the ability to rule over and direct his mental energies. This direct controller and ruler of the mind is the higher faculty in man called the intellect.

With our discriminating capacity alone can we rule over the lesser faculties of the mind in ourselves.

This alternative method suggested by the Lord is to help those who are not able to accomplish the most direct 'Path' indicated in the previous stanza. By striving hard in *Abhyasa-Yoga* for a length of time, our mind gets so well disciplined that we will be able to practise the immediate method of self-unfoldment advised in the earlier couplet.

IF THIS ALSO IS NOT POSSIBLE, THEN:

10. *If you are unable even to practise Abhyasa-Yoga, be you intent on performing actions for My sake; even by doing actions for My sake, you shall attain perfection.*

The thoroughness of the Hindu scriptures consists in suggesting varying and exhaustive techniques of self-development. Psychologically, the technique is so analytical that the more one studies it, the more one is convinced of the 'Path'. There is no 'do it or else to hell' sort of threat ever seen anywhere in our great *shastras*. Any young man, open to intellectual conviction and scientific appraisal, can get totally

---

अभ्यासेऽप्यसमर्थोऽसि मत्कर्मपरमो भव ।
मदर्थमपि कर्माणि कुर्वन्सिद्धिमवाप्स्यसि ॥ १० ॥

abhyāse'pyasamartho'si matkarmaparamo bhava
madarthamapi karmāṇi kurvansiddhimavāpsyasi 10.

convinced of the Hindu way of life.

If a meditator is agitated and wild in his mental personality he will be incapacitated even to perform the *Yoga*-of-practice (*Abhyasa-Yoga*). Here, Krishna advises him not to struggle hard and thereby bring about avoidable and unnecessary mental repressions and psychological suppressions. The inner personality is a million times more delicate than an unopened flower-bud and to hasten its unfoldment is to ruin for ever its beauty and fragrance. Meditation is only an attempt on our part to create the necessary conditions, most favourable for an early blossoming of the greater man in us. Naturally, therefore, one who is incapable of performing one kind of practice must be given an alternative method of self-development.

An individual will find it easy to gather his mind from its chosen fields of dissipation only when the mind is gliding now and then into unworthy channels along the impression-routes created by his own past actions. But if a seeker is too full of such impressions and is so extremely extrovert in nature as to make the practice of concentration futile, then he is advised to surrender all his actions unto the Lord in a spirit of dedication. In doing so, even the most extrovert man will remember the Lord all through his day's activities.

This is the method unconsciously adopted and silently pursued by all fathers towards their newborn child. Every son is born to his father as a stranger. But, in a couple of months, the father's love for the child increases, and as years roll by, it gathers itself into a magnitude wherein the father lives literally in the son. This happens because, after the birth of the son, all actions and experiences of the father are influenced by background memory of the son, i.e., an unconscious spirit of dedication towards him.

Krishna, the Lord of *Yoga*, is most practical in showing

here the 'Path' to an ordinary average man. It gives a hope even to the most extrovert among us. It is indeed a royal 'Path' to the majority of us. Just as a firm's representative, while talking, always associates himself with his firm and says 'we shall try to supply'; 'we are producing'; 'we are not responsible', etc., and he identifies himself with the great manufacturers, as if he is one of the directors of the firm, although, in fact, he is only a low-paid local agent. Similarly, if anyone of us were really to entertain in our mind the firm idea that we are the agents of the Divine, executing His will in all our external activities, then, not only will our mind thereby be made to contemplate on the Lord continuously, but we shall be drawing from ourselves miraculous powers of efficiency, organisational dexterity, and confident courage in all our undertakings, big or small.

To a student of the ancient *Vedic* lore, as Arjuna was, this statement, seemingly so simple, may bring along with it a doubt as to its real potency. The orthodox are always suspicious of an unorthodox declaration, even if it be made by the greatest living man of the era, or even by a Divine manifestation. Therefore, Krishna assures his readers of the efficacy of the 'Path' advocated in the second line: "even by doing actions for My sake you shall attain perfection".

Even while boiling some water, we are apt to call it as 'making tea'. Though factually it is a lie, it is the whole truth, for; once the water is boiled it does not take much time, nor great labour to make tea. And therefore, whenever water is boiled with the intention of making tea, we generally name the initial act itself by the final goal. Similarly, by the art of dedicating ourselves totally unto the Lord, in and through all our daily activities and contacts with the outer world, we will be developing, in ourselves, the divine *vasanas*, and during our actions we will be exhausting the existing impressions.

Such a prepared mind gets properly tuned up for the *Yoga-*of-practice and soon it gains sufficient balance and equipoise to contemplate steadily upon the Truth and get itself merged therein.

AND SUPPOSING THERE BE ONE TO WHOM EVEN THIS IS NOT POSSIBLE?

11. *If you are unable to do even this, then taking refuge in Me, self-controlled, renounce the fruits of all actions.*

In the previous stanza, we were advised to act in the world outside, renouncing totally our ego, or the sense of a separate, individualised existence. To the strongly egoistic and self-opinionated one, this is not an easy task. Such a man is extremely agitated (*rajasic*), with the force of low impulses (*tamas*) poisoning his personality-structure. Even to such seekers, belonging to the lowest conceivable type, the *Geeta* has a 'Path' to advice. Ordinarily, such persons would have been despair to all religions. Even such chronic cases are taken up by the *Geeta*, treated considerately, with simple methods, and finally elevated to the highest personality-lustre and efficiency.

If self-dedication unto the Lord, in all activities, is impossible, such individuals are advised here an equally powerful alternative, viz., at least to "ABANDON THE FRUITS-OF-ACTIONS, AND, TAKING REFUGE IN ME, BE SELF-CONTROLLED" in all actions.

Lord Krishna seems to hate all those who are mere wage-earners. This is not the *Bourgeois*-contempt for the labourer, or the higher-class vanity that makes some look down upon

---

अथैतदप्यशक्तोऽसि कर्तुं मद्योगमाश्रितः ।
सर्वकर्मफलत्यागं ततः कुरु यतात्मवान् ॥ ११ ॥
athaitadapyaśakto'si kartuṁ madyogamāśritaḥ
sarvakarmaphalatyāgaṁ tataḥ kuruḥ yatātmavān 11.

the sweating wage-earners. In a socialistic pattern of society, especially in an era of the welfare State, any educated man must entertain this Krishna-impatience with every worker in the nation who works only for his wage or profit. In such a socialistic scheme of national life, a worker, who works only for 'higher wages, with less hours of work, and with maximum inefficiency' is a criminal who deserves to be punished, in any society. It is this modern attitude, which we see reflected in Krishna's condemnation of all those who work in the world merely for the fruit – meaning pay or wages.

The fruit of an action is the action of the *present*-moment maturing itself in a *future*-period of time. Today, if I plough and sow the seeds, the profit in my harvest will come only after a couple of months. And supposing a farmer broods over the amount of profit that he is to get out of the cultivation and thus wastes his time and energy in dreaming over the possibilities of a success or a failure of the crops, he will surely be an utter failure. Even though this fact is very well known, the majority of us waste our PRESENT chances, opportunities and time in brooding over the FUTURE. All our energies get wasted in our anxieties and fears of a horrid future which has not yet come – and which may not at all materialise! Krishna urges us here only to curb these wasteful imaginations and to live vitally, sincerely, fully and dynamically in the PRESENT, shutting off all negative imaginations regarding the FUTURE. Even this act can integrate our personality and make it single-pointed and strong.

The above three verses give us three alternatives which are in fact only three different types of mental medicines to cure the mind of its various distractions. All of us are, to a certain extent, extrovert. We differ from each other only in the thickness of the *vasana*-layers that we entertain in our inner-equipment. When a brass vessel is slightly dim, an ash-treatment is sufficient to polish it; if it is with a thicker layer of oxide, some acid-dipping will be needed. Similarly, here, if the mind is thinly coated with *vasanas*, the slight distractions created by them can be controlled by the *Yoga*-of-practice. But if the layer of *vasanas* is thick, then it can be treated with the *Yoga*-of action performed in a spirit of Divine dedication. If the mind is shackled with still thicker layers of *vasanas*, then the seeker is advised to curb his imagination and act in the world (*Karma-phala-tyaga*). As I said earlier, nowhere in the world's spiritual literature do we see such an exhaustive treatment of the different 'Paths' for self-development, as in the *Geeta*.

BUT THEY MUST BE PERFORMED SERIALLY, TO INDICATE THAT THESE ARE NOT TO BE PURSUED TOGETHER. NOW THE LORD EXTOLS THE ABANDONING OF THE FRUITS OF ALL ACTIONS:

12. *'Knowledge' is indeed better than 'practice'; 'meditation' is better than 'knowledge'; 'renunciation of the fruits-of-actions' is better than 'meditation'; peace immediately follows 'renunciation'.*

When a divine philosopher gives a discourse for the benefit of a disciple who is confused and broken-down, it is not sufficient if he merely enumerates the dry philosophical truths; he must so beautifully arrange his ideas that the very scheme of the discourse must help the student to gather all the ideas together in a bunch. The stanza, now under review, gives us one of the typical examples in Krishna's discourse wherein

---

श्रेयो हि ज्ञानमभ्यासाज्ज्ञानाद्ध्यानं विशिष्यते ।
ध्यानात्कर्मफलत्यागस्त्यागाच्छान्तिरनन्तरम् ॥ १२ ॥

śreyo hi jñānamabhyājjñānāddhyānaṁ viśiṣyate
dhyānātkarmaphalatyāgastyāgācchāntiranantaram 12.

he directly makes an attempt to systematise his theoretical disquisitions into a well-arranged pattern of thought.

Here we find a sequence of ideas, arranged in a descending order of importance. When once this ladder-of-ideas is brought completely within a seeker's comprehension and when he learns the art of moving up and down this ladder, he will master almost all the salient points so far expounded in this chapter.

BETTER INDEED IS KNOWLEDGE THAN PRACTICE— Spiritual practices are not mere physical acts but are disciplines that should ultimately tune up our mental and intellectual levels. The inner personality cannot be persuaded to toe the line with the physical acts of devotion unless the practitioner has a correct grasp of what he is doing. An intellectual conversion is a prerequisite to force the mind to act in the right spirit and to gain a perfect attunement with the physical act. A correct and exhaustive knowledge of what we are doing, and why we are doing it, is an unavoidable precondition for making our *Yoga* fruitful. Therefore, it is said here that knowledge of the psychological, intellectual and spiritual implications of our practices is greater in importance than the very external *Yogic* acts, or devotional performances.

MEDITATION IS SUPERIOR TO KNOWLEDGE—more important than mere KNOWLEDGE is meditation upon the very 'knowledge' so gathered. The technical explanation – of the why and the wherefore of religious practices – can be more easily learnt than understood. To convert our learning into our understanding, there must be necessarily a process of intellectual assimilation and absorption. This cannot be accomplished by a mere factual learning of the word-meanings. The students will have to understand, in a hearty enthusiasm, the very meaning of the *shastra*, and this is possible only through long, subjective, independent ponderings over the significant terms in the *shastra*-declarations. The process of inward assimilation of knowledge can take place only through meditation. Hence, in the hierarchy of importance, 'meditation' has been given a greater place than the 'Knowledge of the technique'.

BETTER THAN MEDITATION IS THE ABANDONMENT OF FRUITS-OF-ACTION—Meditation is an attempt of the intellect to fly from the fields of its present knowledge to a yonder destination of a better understanding. In this flight to a vaster field, the intellect must have the necessary energy and equipoise. Meditation can never be possible for an individual in whom all energies and steadiness of mind are shattered by the agitations created by his own ruinous imaginations of the future. In our discourses upon the previous stanza, we have already shown how our anxiety for the future generally depletes our vitality to face the present. All fruits-of-actions definitely belong to the FUTURE, and to be over-anxious about them is to invite a lot of idle agitations into our bosom. Stormed by these agitations, we lose all our equipoise and such an individual has no ability to meditate upon and thereby assimilate the silent significance of the great *shastras*. Therefore, Krishna here gives a greater place of importance in his ladder of ideas to "The renunciation of the fruits-of-action".

As a footnote to his own declaration, he adds how renunciation of our anxiety for the future immediately brings about a healthy condition within ourselves. "Peace immediately follows renunciation". In fact, in Hinduism, renunciation (*sannyasa*) is nothing other than giving up all our clinging attachments to the pleasures arising out of our contact with the external sense objects.

As a result of this renunciation, therefore, a dynamic quietude comes to pervade the bosom in which the intellect can meditate upon the knowledge of the *shastras*, and thereby understand the ways of self-development as explained therein. And when, with this knowledge, one uses one's seat of meditation, one is assured of definite success and steady progress.

WITH REFERENCE TO THOSE WHO ARE MEDITATING UPON THE IMPERISHABLE, THE INFINITE, THE LORD PRESCRIBES A CERTAIN MENTAL AND INTELLECTUAL CONDUCT WHICH FORMS THE DIRECT MEANS TO PERFECTION:

13. *He who hates no creature, who is friendly and compassionate to all, who is free from attachment and egoism, balanced in pleasure and pain, and forgiving...*

14. *Ever content, steady in meditation, self-controlled, possessed of firm conviction, with mind and intellect dedicated to Me, he, My devotee, is dear to me.*

In the following seven stanzas (XII-13 to 19), in six different sections, Lord Krishna enumerates the characteristic features of a man-of-Perfection, and thereby prescribes the correct mode of conduct and the way-of-life for all seekers. In these stanzas, the *Yogeshwara* has very well succeeded in painting the picture of a true devotee for Arjuna's understanding. As a true painter would again and again step back from his canvas to judge his own production and then

---

अद्वेष्टा सर्वभूतानां मैत्रः करुण एव च।
निर्ममो निरहंकारः समदुःखसुखः क्षमी ॥ १३ ॥

adveṣṭā sarvabhūtānāṁ maitraḥ karuṇa eva ca
nirmamo nirahaṅkāraḥ samaduḥkhasukhaḥ kṣamī 13.

संतुष्टः सततं योगी यतात्मा दृढनिश्चयः।
मय्यर्पितमनोबुद्धिर्यो मद्भक्तः स मे प्रियः ॥ १४ ॥

santuṣṭaḥ satataṁ yogī yatātmā dṛḍhaniścayaḥ
mayyarpitamanobuddhiryo madbhaktaḥ sa me priyaḥ 14.

go forward to it to lay a few more strokes to bring out his theme into a more effective relief on his canvas, so too Krishna is trying in these seven stanzas to paint the mental beauty and the intellectual equipoise of a true devotee, along with his relationship with the world around him. No other part in the whole *Geeta* can be compared with the beauty of expression that we have in these stanzas, except perhaps, the description of the man of Steady-Wisdom (II-55 to 68) that we read in the second chapter.

Moral rules and ethical codes of behaviour are in Hinduism not arbitrary commandments thrust upon its followers by a son of God, or by a Messiah. These rules of conduct are copied from the behaviour of God-men who had attained the spiritual perfection and had actually lived among us. Seekers are those who are striving hard to attain the spiritual experience of those Saints and Seers. A devotee who is trying to attune himself with these Masters of *Yoga* should necessarily start at least copying their external behaviour and mental beauties, which constitute the moral and ethical rules prescribed in our religion.

Eleven noble qualities are indicated in the above two stanzas which constitute the opening section. Every one of them declares a moral phase in the character of man-of-Perfection. One who has realised that the Spirit everywhere is one and the same, and that the Spirit in All alone is his own Self, cannot, thereafter, afford to hate anyone, because, from his vision of understanding, there is no one who is other than Him! No living man can afford to hate his own right hand because he is in it too. Nobody hates himself!

His attitude to all living creatures will be friendly, and he is ever compassionate to all. He offers security of life to all beings. He cannot regard anything as his and he is completely free from the notion of egoism. Even-minded in pain and pleasure, he remains supremely unaffected even when beaten or abused. Always content, he discovers a *flawless* infinite joy in himself whether he obtains even the means of his bodily sustenance or not. Steadfast in his meditation, self-controlled and firm in his resolve, he lives on joyously, his mind and intellect 'ever centered in Me'. "Such a perfect, devoted *Yogi*" the Lord says, "Is dear to me".

The truth expressed in the stanza earlier, "I am very dear to the man-of-Wisdom and he is dear to Me" (VII-17), is being more elaborately elucidated in all these seven verses of this chapter.

MOREOVER:

15. *He by whom the world is not agitated (affected), and who cannot be agitated by the world, who is freed from joy, envy, fear and anxiety -he is dear to me.*

This stanza constitutes the second section in which again Lord Krishna enumerates three more characteristic features of a real devotee.

HE BY WHOM THE WORLD IS NOT AGITATED—A man-of-Perfection is one who will not create any agitations in the world around him. Where the Sun is, there cannot be any darkness, where the peaceful Master of Equanimity and Perfection dwells, he, by the intrinsic divinity in him, creates, as it were, an atmosphere of serene joy and endless peace around him; and even those, who are agitated in the world, will suffer no more from such agitations when they approach such a mastermind, and enjoy a peace in themselves. In fact,

---

यस्मान्नोद्विजते लोको लोकान्नोद्विजते च यः ।
हर्षामर्षभयोद्वेगैर्मुक्तो यः स च मे प्रियः ॥ १५ ॥

yasmānnodvijate loko lokānnodvijate ca yaḥ
harṣāmarṣabhayodvegairmukto yaḥ sa ca me priyaḥ 15.

the world irresistibly rushes to such a saint to bask in his brilliance and comes to experience the joy which he wafts all around him!

WHO CANNOT BE AGITATED BY THE WORLD—Not only does a man-of-Perfection quieten the very world around him, into a dynamic peace, but also the world, however chaotic, revolting, boisterous, and vengeful it may be, cannot create any agitations in him. The world-of-objects will almost always be in a state of flux, and its maddening death-dance cannot bring even a whiff of its storms to disturb the calm serenity of the saint. He is made of stronger mettle and his life is built upon surer foundations.

The floating reeds dance on the surface of the sea but the lighthouse that is built on the rocks beneath stands erect and motionless, watching the smooth sea turning rough with the rise of the tidal waves. The personality of a perfect-man is rooted in his realisation of the deeper substratum of life; and, since he is not attached to the superficial conditions of matter and its playful magic, any amount of wild agitations outside cannot bring any disturbance to his inner equipoise. In and through the battling circumstances, he perceives the changeless ground - he hears the harmony that runs through the various discordant notes in life around.

HE IS COMPLETELY FREED FROM all the usual causes for inward agitations such as JOY, ENVY, FEAR AND ANXIETY.* A devotee of this type, ever peaceful with himself and the world, who rules over the circumstances and never yields to be victimised by them, who has crossed over the usual weaknesses of the mortal heart—such a devotee Is dear to me".

---

* When a desired object is gained, JOY comes; if not gained, ENVY at those who have; when satisfied, GREED for more; when we possess what we desire, FEAR of losing it – when the desired object is missing ANXIETY over its destiny – all these are NOT in one who has no desire for objects.

CONTINUING THE SAME TOPIC THE LORD DECLARES:

16. *He who is free from wants, pure, alert, unconcerned, untroubled, renouncing all undertakings (or commencements) -- he who is (thus) devoted to Me, is dear to Me.*

This stanza represents the third section, which throws more light upon the picture of the perfect-devotee as conceived by the Lord Himself. Already in the above two sections, fourteen indications were given and to that total picture are added in this section six subtler items.

FREE FROM DEPENDENCE (*Anapekshah*)—a true devotee no more depends upon either the objects of the world outside, or their pattern, or their relationships with himself. An ordinary man discovers his peace and joy only in the world-of-objects available for him, their conditions, and their arrangements around him. When the right type of object is in the right pattern courting him favourably, a man of the world feels temporarily thrilled and joyous. But a real devotee is completely independent of the world outside and he draws his inspiration, equanimity and joyous ecstasy from a source, deep within himself.

WHO IS PURE (*Shuchih*)—Dirt has no place anywhere within or without a true devotee. One who is aspiring to reach perfection will necessarily be so well-disciplined physically that he will be clean not only in his relationship with others but even in the very condition and arrangement of his belongings around him. It is very well known that the condition of a man's table or shelf, and the cleanliness of his apparel, can

---

अनपेक्षः शुचिर्दक्ष उदासीनो गतव्यथः |
सर्वारम्भपरित्यागी यो मद्भक्तः स मे प्रियः || १६ ||

anapekṣaḥ śucirdakṣa udāsīno gatavyathaḥ
sarvārambhaparityāgī yo madbhaktaḥ sa me priyaḥ 16.

give a great insight into the mental nature, discipline and culture of that man. Great emphasis has been laid in India on this physical purity, not only in the person of the man but also of his contacts in the world. Without external purity, internal purification will be but a vague dream, an idle hope, and a despairing vision.

ALERT (*Dakshah*)—to be alert always becomes the second nature of an integrated person. Enthusiasm is the key to success in any undertaking. A dynamic person is not one who slips in his behaviour or action. He is mentally agile and intellectually vigorous. Since there is no dissipation in him, he is ever on his toes to spring forward to activity, once he determines to shoulder any endeavour. If we observe the degree of idleness, carelessness, and ugliness in execution of any work, from which all religious persons are suffering, we can understand how far Hinduism has wandered away from its pristine glory!

UNCONCERNED (*Udaseenah*)—it is not difficult for one to observe many devotees in this land who have resigned themselves to a state of unexpressed sorrow, because they have been cheated by others, ill-treated by society, and persecuted by the community. The foolish devotees think that they will be unconcerned about these outrages practised on them and then their own devotion for the Lord must prove to themselves a wretched liability, rather than a positive gain! Philosophy misunderstood can easily end in the suicide of the community.

The 'unconcerned attitude' is only meant here to economise our mental energies. In human life, small difficulties, simple illnesses, discomforts, wants etc., are but natural. To exaggerate their importance and strive to escape from them all is to enter into a lifelong struggle of adjustments. In all such instances, the student is warned not to squander away his mental energies but to conserve them by overlooking these little pinpricks of life in an attitude of utter indifference towards them.

FREE FROM TREMBLING—the inward tremors are experienced only when any burning desire has conquered us completely. Once victimised by a desire or fascination for an object, the individual personality becomes tremulous in fear that its desire may not be fulfilled. A true seeker is one, who never allows the inner person in him to enter into any such fears or agitations.

RENOUNCING EVERY UNDERTAKING—In Sanskrit '*Aarambha*' means beginning. 'To end all beginnings', does not mean not to undertake anything. This literal translation has made the majority of Hindus incompetent idlers and our religion has been criticized as glorifying idleness as a divine ideal! The deeper suggestions are overlooked. To perceive any definite beginning in an undertaking, the individual actor must have a solid and gross egoistic claim that he has begun it himself. He must have the strong feeling that he is beginning an activity, for the purpose of gaining a definite goal, whereby he will be fulfilling a specific desire of his, or will thereby be gaining a positive profit. One who is a seeker of the Divine, striving to reach the higher cultural perfections, must renounce this egoistic sense of self-importance and work on in the world.

No undertaking in our life, in fact, is a new act that has an independent beginning or end. All actions in the world are in an eternal pattern of the total world-movements. If correctly analysed, our undertakings are controlled, regulated, governed and ordered by the available world-of-things and situations. Apart from them all, no independent action is undertaken, or can be fulfilled by anyone. A devotee of Truth is ever conscious of this oneness of the Universe, and therefore, he will always work in the world only as an instrument of the Lord and not as an independent agent in the undertaking.

"Such a devotee who possesses all the six qualifications enumerated above IS DEAR TO ME".

ADDING A FEW STROKES, KRISHNA PAINTS THE PICTURE INTO A MORE REALISTIC VIVIDNESS:

17. *He who neither rejoices, nor hates, nor grieves, nor desires, renouncing good and evil, full of devotion, is dear to Me.*

A perfect devotee is one who has lifted himself from the world of his mind-intellect and has awakened to his inner Spiritual Nature. As such, the ordinary experiences of joy and sorrow, of pain and pleasure, which generally give the restlessness of life, do not affect him.

HE WHO NEITHER REJOICES—'Rejoicing' is the feeling of satisfaction and fulfilment that comes to us on attaining a desired object, which is extremely desirable, and extremely difficult to realise.

NOR HATES—the sense of revulsion that comes to us towards undesirable things and circumstances, when they crowd around us, is generally the sense of hatred. In short, these two terms indicate that there are no objects which he would ardently like to acquire, nor is there any occasion to fret about on coming in contact with things or situations that are undesirable from his standpoint.

NEITHER GRIEVES, NOR DESIRES—Grief is generally experienced while parting with a beloved object, and desires are entertained when one yearns to have and to possess something unattained at present. A man-of-Perfection is one whose beloved object, the Self, can never be apart from him. And he has no sense of attachment with any other object.

यो न हृष्यति न द्वेष्टि न शोचति न काङ्क्षति ।
शुभाशुभपरित्यागी भक्तिमान्य: स मे प्रिय: ॥ १७ ॥

yo na hṛṣyati na dveṣṭi na śocati na kāṅkṣati
śubhāśubhaparityāgī bhaktimānyaḥ sa me priyaḥ 17.

Having attained the Self, the inhabitant of his heart, he has such a complete sense of fulfilment that he has no more any desire for attaining anything that he has not attained. The Self being the All, he has attained everything.

RENOUNCING GOOD AND EVIL—the happenings in the world around us can fall under these two categories, according to whether they arouse in us a feeling of joy or sorrow. To any person who is living away from the realm of the dualistic experiences, and who has learnt the art of drawing inspiration from something beyond, none of the happenings, here at the level of the mind and the intellect, can be of any serious consequences.

The above terms used in the stanza, for painting a perfect-man, have a secret import. If we consider only the literal meaning, we will think that such a perfect-man is a dead corpse, 'NEITHER REJOICES, NOR HATES; NOR DESIRES; RENOUNCING GOOD AND EVIL' – he lies dead! This is a very striking example of how the literal meanings are not at all what is to be understood in scriptural declarations.

Similarly, when a true devotee, being awakened to the God-Consciousness, evaluates life from his new height of experience, he cannot rejoice or hate, grieve for or desire anything in this world and he comes to renounce totally the very concepts of good and evil. The Divine Charioteer (Krishna) declares: "HE WHO IS SUCH A DEVOTEE IS DEAR TO ME".

The stanza represents the fourth section in which again the Lord has enumerated six more qualities that make up a perfect devotee. So far we have been told of twenty-six subtle traits which are the 'intrinsic qualities of a Perfect *Yogi*'.

IN A LAST WAVE OF ENTHUSIASM KRISHNA ENUMERATES:

18. *He who is the same to foe and friend, and also in honour and dishonour, who is the same in cold and heat and in pleasure and pain, who is free from attachment...*

19. *To whom censure and praise are equal, who is silent, content with anything, homeless, steady-minded, full of devotion – that man is dear to Me.*

EQUAL TO FOE AND FRIEND—the estimation of our relationship with another as foe or friend is generally our own psychological reaction towards another. It belongs essentially to the heart. It is experienced by the PSYCHOLOGICAL *being* in us. A man-of-Perfection is one who is not identifying himself with his mental estimation of things, and therefore, he is equanimous and maintains a uniformity of attitude towards his friends and foes.

AND SO TOO, IN HONOUR AND DISHONOUR—A situation is judged by the intellect as honourable or dishonourable with reference to its own existing values and cultivated habits of thinking. That which is ordinarily considered dishonourable can Itself come to be estimated by the same person as honourable in a new pattern of circumstances ordered by a change in time and place. On the whole, these are all different tides in the intellect; and those

---

समः शत्रौ च मित्रे च तथा मानापमानयोः ।
शीतोष्णसुखदुःखेषु समः सङ्गविवर्जितः ॥ १८ ॥

samaḥ śatrau ca mitre ca tathā mānāpamānayoḥ
śītoṣṇasukhaduḥkheṣu samaḥ saṅgavivarjitaḥ 18.

तुल्यनिन्दास्तुतिर्मौनी संतुष्टो येन केनचित् ।
अनिकेतः स्थिरमतिर्भक्तिमान्मे प्रियो नरः ॥ १९ ॥

tulyanindāstutirmaunī santuṣṭo yena kenacit
aniketaḥ sthiramatirbhaktimānme priyo naraḥ 19.

who are living in that realm are affected by them.

WHO IS THE SAME IN HEAT AND COLD—Heat and cold are only the experiences of the *body*. By remembering the preparation process of nitric acid, my 'thoughts' cannot get corroded; by feeling the smouldering beauty of the burning embers in the fire-place, my 'mind' cannot get blisters. My knowledge or my capacity to love cannot freeze at the North Pole; nor get evaporated in the Sahara desert. Heat and cold affect only the body. And this idiom in Sanskrit, whenever it is used in the context of philosophy, represents all types of experiences to which the physical equipment is the heir.

The above three terms thus comprehend the entire possibility of experiences in life: physical, mental, and intellectual. In all of them, a true devotee is unagitated because he IS FREE FROM ATTACHMENT. Attachment to and identification with the matter equipments – body, mind and intellect – is the cause by which we are helplessly made to dance to the mad tunes which the chance happenings dictate. One who is detached from these equipments is the one who is a master of them all.

TO WHOM CENSURE AND PRAISE ARE EQUAL—not that he is immune to insults, nor is it because he is not intelligent enough to understand them. To a great devotee, living as he is in a realm of his own, full of transcendental and blissful experiences of the Divine, the worldly censure or even praise has no significance or importance at all. He realises that one who has been praised today will be censured by society tomorrow, and that yesterday's censured man becomes the praiseworthy leader of today!! Praise and censure are in themselves nothing more than the passing fancy of those who express them!

HE IS SILENT—a true seeker of wisdom becomes a man

of few words – not only physically but also even mentally. Silence within is real silence (*Mouna*). Keeping physical silence but letting the mind loose to talk in itself, generally results in a serious type of repression which ultimately drives many to the porch of a mental hospital. Be silent and understand how really silent silence can be!

CONTENT WITH ANYTHING—Contented with anything that might reach him accidentally, unasked and unexpected, is the motto of all serious seekers of inward growth. To entertain the demands in life and to strive forth to satisfy them would be an unending game, as the mind has a knack of breeding its own demands very fast. The policy of contentment is the only intelligent attitude to be taken up by all sincere seekers or else there will be no time to seek, to strive for and to achieve the diviner goal of life. Self-integration is a reward promised for faithful pursuits and all-out attention. It is said in the Mahabharata* "he who is clad with anything, who is fed on any FOOD, who lies down ANYWHERE, HIM THE GODS CALL A *BRAHMANA*".

HOMELESS—Home is generally that which provides shelter from the external inclemencies of weather, for the resident who is dwelling under its roof. The man of spiritual realisation is one who is trying to pull down all his conditionings and striving to free himself from all sense of possession and material shackles.

Living under a roof, in itself, does not make the place a home. To spend a night on a railway station, or in the retiring room at an aerodrome, does not make the place the traveller's own home. It is only along with a sense of possession, reinforced with a sense of happiness and comfort, that the place under a roof becomes a home. A true devotee has for himself a

---

* *Shanti Parva, 'Moksha Dharma'* 246-12

satisfactory shelter only at the feet of the All-Pervading, and therefore, his mental condition is indicated here by the simple pertinent word 'homeless'.

Steadfast in his intellectual understanding of the goal, and ever striving to attain his Divine ideal, that the *Bhakta* dwells on - THAT MAN IS DEAR TO ME. There is almost a suggestion, even though by implication, that one who is at least striving to live these values is a full-grown man (*Nara*) to the *Geeta Acharya*.

These two verses represent the FIFTH SECTION which enumerates ten more different qualities. In short, in thirty-six artistic strokes, Lord Krishna has brought about a complete picture of the seeker-of-Perfection – his relationship with the world outside, his psychological life and his intellectual evaluation of the world of beings and happenings.

THE ENUMERATION OF THE VARIOUS MORAL, ETHICAL AND SPIRITUAL QUALITIES OF A TRUE DEVOTEE IS CONCLUDED WITH THESE:

20. *They indeed, who follow this 'Immortal DHARMA' (Law of Life) as described above, endowed with faith, regarding Me as their Supreme Goal -- such devotees are exceedingly dear to Me.*

THIS IMMORTAL LAW PRESCRIBED ABOVE—the *Sanatana Dharma* is summarised in the above lines. To realise the Self and live in that wisdom at all our personality levels – physical, mental and intellectual – is the fulfilment of the life of a Hindu. It is not sufficient that a Hindu understands this, or reads regularly his scriptures, or even explains them intelligently. He must be able to digest them properly,

---

ये तु धर्म्यामृतमिदं यथोक्तं पर्युपासते ।
श्रद्दधाना मत्परमा भक्तास्तेऽतीव मे प्रियाः ॥ २० ॥

ye tu dhamyārmṛtamidṁ yathoktaṁ paryupāsate
śraddadhānā matparamā bhaktāste'tīva me priyāḥ 20.

assimilate them fully, and become Perfect. Therefore, *Bhagavan* says that he must be 'endowed with faith' here the term 'faith' means 'the necessary capacity to assimilate spiritual ideas into ourselves through subjective personal experience'.

SUCH DEVOTEES ARE SUPREMELY DEAR TO ME— this concluding stanza of the chapter constitutes the SIXTH SECTION adding no definite trait to the list of THIRTY-SIX qualities already explained. But it forms a commandment, a divine reassurance to all spiritual seekers that when they accomplish these qualities in themselves they will gain the Supreme Love of the Lord.

Thus, in the UPANISHADS of the glorious Bhagawad-Geeta, in the Science of the Eternal, in the scripture of YOGA, in the dialogue between Sri Krishna and Arjuna, the twelfth discourse ends entitled:

The *Yoga* of Devotion

Though this chapter is styled as *Bhakti Yoga,* to read and assimilate it is to cherish true love for the Lord and cure ourselves of the various misconceptions that we have today in our practice of Devotion. The path-of-Devotion is not a mere sentimental explosion, or an excessive emotional display. It is not a mere frivolous hysteria. It is the blossoming of the human personality through the surrender of our limitations and by acquiring new vitality during the inspired moments of deep contemplation.

Om Om Om Om Om

ॐ तत्सदिति श्रीमद् भगवद् गीतासूपनिषत्सु ब्रह्मविद्यायां
योगशास्त्रे श्रीकृष्णार्जुनसंवादे भक्तियोगो नाम
द्वादशोऽध्याय:

Oṁ tatsaditi śrīmadbhagavadgītāsū ūpaniṣatsu brahmavidyāyāṁ
yogaśāstre śrī kṛṣṇārjuna saṁvāde bhaktiyogo nāma
dvādaśo'dhyāyaḥ.

XIII

The Field and Its Knower
Introduction

THIS is one of the most famous chapters in the *Geeta* which gives the student a very direct explanation for, and almost a personal experience of, the Subject in him, the Self, free from his material equipments and their misinterpretations, the world-of-objects. Here we have an exhaustive exposition of how to meditate directly upon the Imperishable Formless Spirit.

The *Geeta*, being a philosophical poem – however much it may try to hide its austere beauty behind an enchanting veil of its own lyricism, fragrant with the human touches provided by the Krishna-love and the Arjuna-weaknesses – is a thunderous pronouncement of the wisdom of the *Rishis*. As such, the theme developed in this philosophical poem is unrelentingly logical and uncompromisingly scientific. And it has an unyielding framework in the very continuity of its systematic thought-development.

This chapter has its direct theme-parentage in the ideas discussed already in Chapter-VII entitled "Knowledge and Experience", and in Chapter-VIII entitled the "Imperishable *Brahman*". The intervening four chapters (IX, X, XI and XII) were occasioned due to Arjuna's intellectual hesitations and mental doubts. But the philosopher in Krishna never forgets the main theme that he has developed upon the "Imperishable *Brahman*". And when once he has consoled his disciple, and temporarily removed his doubts, he serenely goes back to take up the melody of his discussion.

The eighteen chapters of the *Geeta* fall into three distinct groups, each of six chapters* according to some reviewers of the Lord's Song. These three sections explain, according to them, the three sacred words in one of the great *Vedantic maxims* (*Mahavakyas*): 'THAT THOU ART'. The first section consisting of the first six chapters, explained the term 'THOU'; the second section constituted of the next six chapters, explained the term 'THAT'; and the last set of six chapters will explain the correlative verb 'ART' in the sacred commandment, and so in this section we have an explanation of the term 'ART'.

Spirit functioning through matter-envelopments is the living organism. 'THAT' dressed up in matter is the vainful 'THOU'. Therefore, man undressed of matter, is the Eternal and the Infinite Spirit.

To undress, and thereby to get rid of matter, we must have a precise knowledge of all that constitutes matter in us. This discrimination between the inert matter-equipments and the vibrant spark-of-Life, the Spirit, is presented to us in this chapter which is rightly called the 'Field' and the 'Knower-of-the-Field'; *Kshetra-Kshetrajna Yoga*.

The process of undressing is the process of meditation. The pose, the attitude and the other technical secrets of meditation were all exhaustively explained earlier (in chapter V and VI). But having sat in meditation, what exactly has our integrated mind-and-intellect to do now? Can we draw ourselves from ourselves and seek our identity with the Infinite? These are exhaustively explained in this chapter.

The matter-equipments and their perceived world-of-objects together constitute the 'FIELD'; and the Supreme

* Refer 'General Introduction'.

Consciousness, illumining them, and therefore, seemingly functioning within the field, gather to itself as a consequence, the status of the 'Knower-of-the-field'. One is a knower only as long as one is in the field-of-knowables.

A driver is one who is driving; a rider is one who is riding a horse; a swimmer is one who is swimming at the moment. Off the steering-wheel, off the saddle, away from the waters, the driver, the rider and the swimmer are but three individuals. While functioning in a given field, the subject gathers to itself a certain special status depending upon the nature of the field and the type of functions performed by him therein.

The Pure Consciousness, perceiving the world-of-plurality through Its own conditionings, becomes the 'Knower-of-the-field', and this knower thereby comes to experience joys and sorrows, successes and failures, peace and agitation, jealousies, fears and a million other wrecking storms and upheavals. The sorrows of *samsara* are thus entirely the private wealth of the 'Knower-of-the-field' – the *Jiva*.

If, through discrimination, the 'Field' and its 'Knower' are known separately, through meditation the student can detach himself from the matter-equipments, and therefore, get away from the 'Field' of these sorrow-ridden experiences. Thereby the 'Knower-of-the-field', who was the 'experiencer' of the sorrows, transforms himself to be the experiencer of Absolute Knowledge.

Mathematically, Knowledge in a field of known things and happenings becomes the 'Knower' which suffers the imperfections of the known. The 'Knower' minus the 'field-of-the-known' becomes Pure Knowledge, Itself ever perfect and joyous. A careful study of the chapter will open up enough secret windows on to the vast amphitheatre of spiritual insight within ourselves.

Arjuna said:

1. *Prakriti (Matter) and Purusha (Spirit), also the Kshetra (the Field) and Kshetrajna (the Knower-of-the-Field), Knowledge and that which ought to be known - these, I wish to learn, O Keshava.*

In several manuscripts, this stanza is not found. But in some others, it is met with as a doubt expressed by Arjuna.

PRAKRITI AND PURUSHA—In the *Sankhyan* Philosophy in India, the *Acharyas* have used these two technical terms to indicate the inert-equipments (*Prakriti*) and the vital sentient-Truth (*Purusha*) that sets the entire assemblage of matter in action. In short, *Prakriti* is matter and *Purusha* is the Spirit. The Spirit, in Itself, has no expression except when It plays through matter. When *Purusha* weds *Prakriti*, the experiences of good and bad are in legion born. Electricity, in itself, cannot manifest as light. But when it weds the bulb, it is manifested as light.

THE FIELD AND THE KNOWER-OF-THE-FIELD—we have already explained these two terms in our introduction to this chapter. The Knower-of-the-field is the status of the Knowing-Principle when It is functioning in the Field-of-the-known. Bereft of the field-of-objects, the 'Knower' himself becomes nothing but 'Pure Knowledge', without the functions of knowing attached to It.

THE MECHANISM AND THE OBJECTS OF KNOWLEDGE—Conditioned knowledge-bits, meaning, knowledge-of-things, are the constant experiences of all living

---

अर्जुन उवाच
प्रकृतिं पुरुषं चैव क्षेत्रं क्षेत्रज्ञमेव च ।
एतद्वेदितुमिच्छामि ज्ञानं ज्ञेयं च केशव ॥ १ ॥

arjuna uvāca
prakṛtiṁ puruṣaṁ caiva kṣetraṁ kṣetrajñameva ca
etat veditumicchāmi jñānaṁ jñayañca keśava 1.

creatures in life. Naturally, an investigation into the 'mechanism of knowing' and its manipulations and the 'true object to be known' will be helpful to all seekers.

LISTEN, HOW THE LORD ANSWERS ALL THESE QUESTIONS CATEGORICALLY:

The Blessed Lord said:

2. *This body, O Kaunteya is called Kshetra (the Field) and he who knows it is called Kshetrajna (the Knower-of-the-Field) by those who know them (Kshetra and Kshetrajna) i.e., by the sages.*

The experience of Perfection is subjective. The *Vedantic* seers of Hindu Scriptures are unanimous in their conclusion that a subjective quest is the 'Path' to rediscover and ultimately realise the Self. In this chapter, we find a beautiful philosophical dissection of the subjective structure of man, exposing the matter envelopments that condition the Spirit. A discriminative knowledge of the matter layers, as distinct from the 'Spiritual-Core', will show the seeker the way to rediscover his identity with the Spirit, and realise the actual non-existence of matter, when viewed from the realm of the Spirit.

A 'waker' in a certain mental framework, himself becomes a 'dreamer', and, to the 'dreamer' the dream is real as long as the dream continues. But on awakening, the 'dreamer' realises that the dream was only a misinterpretation of the waking, rendered by the 'dreamer's own mind. Similarly, the pluralistic world is perceived when the Spirit views through its own

---

श्रीभगवानुवाच
इदं शरीरं कौन्तेय क्षेत्रमित्यभिधीयते ।
एतद्यो वेत्ति तं प्राहुः क्षेत्रज्ञ इति तद्विदः ॥ २ ॥

śrī bhagavānuvāca
idaṁ śarīraṁ kaunteya kṣetramityabhidhīyate
etadyo vetti taṁ prāhuḥ kṣetrajñā iti tadvidaḥ 2.

imaginary world of matter, and on awakening to Its own spiritual status it rediscovers Its own Absolute Reality in which the 'phantom' of matter has no existence at all.

Thus, in a living man, philosophically viewed, there are two aspects: the inert and insentient matter-layers, and the sentient and vital Consciousness. These two aspects are defined in this stanza.

THIS BODY O! SON OF KUNTI, IS CALLED THE FIELD—In this mechanical age, it is very easy to understand that there must be a 'Field' for energy to play in, and that, then alone it can manifest as work done and serve man. Steam-energy cannot be resolved into locomotion unless it is made to pass through a steam-engine. Electricity cannot give us breeze unless it passes through the machine of a fan. The equipments (or assembly of matter layers), through which Life passes when an individuality is expressed, are defined here by Krishna as the 'Field'.

HE WHO KNOWS IT IS CALLED THE 'KNOWER-OF-THE-FIELD'—this field is made up of lifeless matter, the minerals. And yet, as long as it lives and functions, it KNOWS. This 'principle-of-knowing', functioning in the 'field' is the 'enjoyer-of-the-field'; the 'knower', the EGO.

As long as life exists in any living organism, it expresses an urge to know. The degree of this urge may vary from individual to individual in the Universe. But the urge to know, expressed through equipment, is what we recognise as its life. The capacity of an organism to receive stimuli and send forth responses is the transaction of life, and when this 'knower', the individuality, has departed from the equipment, we consider it as dead. This is the 'Knower-of-the-Field' (*Kshetrajna*).

BY THOSE WHO KNOW THEM—Here, Lord Krishna has assured his listeners that the definitions given by him to the terms 'Body' and the 'Knower-of-the-body' are not arbitrary declarations or hypothetical suppositions, but are in keeping with the actual experiences of all the great Masters of yore. In short, here we have a definition of matter (*Kshetra*) and the Spirit functioning through it (*Kshetrajna*). The entire world-of-objects constitutes the kingdom of matter; and the vital knower of the world-of-matter, constituted of the equipments and their array of perceptions, feelings and thoughts, is the Spirit.

IS THIS ALL THE KNOWLEDGE THAT ONE HAS TO ACQUIRE ABOUT THEM? NO! LISTEN:

3. *Know Me as the 'Knower-of-the-Field' in all 'Fields', O Bharata; Knowledge of the 'Field' as also of the 'Knower-of-the-Field' is considered by Me to be My Knowledge.*

After indicating, in the previous stanza, the world-of-matter and the thrilling Spirit-of-Truth that presides over it, here is a staggering announcement, "I AM THE KNOWER-OF-THE-FIELD IN ALL FIELDS". If, in all 'Fields' the 'Knower' is one, then the plurality is only in the matter-envelopments, and the Life that presides over them is one everywhere. This Universal One, the Transcendental Truth is indicated here by the first person singular 'I AM' because every seeker has to rediscover in himself, "That I am" (*Soham*).

We had already indicated earlier that Lord Krishna is expounding the *Geeta* in a rare moment of *Yogic* integration (*Yogarudha* state).* He is identifying himself with the Self that

---

क्षेत्रज्ञं चापि मां विद्धि सर्वक्षेत्रेषु भारत ।
क्षेत्रक्षेत्रज्ञयोर्ज्ञानं यत्तज्ज्ञानं मतं मम ॥ ३ ॥

kṣetrajñaṁ cāpi māṁ viddhi sarvakṣetreṣu bhārata
kṣetrakṣetrajñayorjñānaṁ yattajjñānaṁ mataṁ mama 3.

* Later in Mahabharata, when Arjuna had returned to Hastinapura, one day he requested Krishna to repeat the *Geeta* and the Lord admitted that he could not do so with the same efficiency as he did in the battlefield. 'Because', He said, "I was then in a full state-of-*Yoga*".

is everywhere. This is something like electricity declaring; "I am the one energy that gives the glow in all filaments all over the world".

After indicating the One Spirit behind the entire world-of-matter, wherever it may be, Krishna declares that, according to Him, a correct knowledge (vitally experienced and lived) of what constitutes in each one of us the perishable, changeable, finite, inert matter, and of the nature of the Infinite, Imperishable and Sentient Spirit is the Supreme Knowledge. *Kshetra* is the 'field-of-matter' which is constituted of the various equipments of perception and the vast fields of the perceived. *Kshetrajna* is the subject that enjoys the activities of the instruments of perception and the world perceived by them. To distinguish the world-of-the-subject from the world-of-objects is the salutary Knowledge, which can redeem us from the confusions and sorrows from which we suffer today as individualised egos.

SINCE A PRECISE KNOWLEDGE OF THE WORLD OF SUBJECT AND OF THE OBJECTS IS UNAVOIDABLE TO A TRUE SEEKER WALKING THE PATH OF KNOWLEDGE, WE WILL HAVE TO MAKE AN EXHAUSTIVE STUDY OF THEM. THEREFORE:

4. *What that Field is; of what nature it is; what are its modifications; whence it is; and also who He is; and what His powers are --these hear from Me in brief.*

OF WHAT NATURE—Not only are we going to have a discussion of what constitutes the 'Field', the *Kshetra*, but also

---

तत्क्षेत्रं यच्च यादृक्च यद्विकारि यतश्च यत् ।
स च यो यत्प्रभावश्च तत्समासेन मे शृणु ॥ ४ ॥
tatkṣetraṁ yacca yādṛkca yadvikāri yataśca yat
sa ca yo yatprabhāvaśca tatsamāsena me śṛṇu 4.

of what it is in itself. 'Of what nature', meaning, what are its properties. 'And whence is what' meaning, what effects arise from what causes i.e. what are the by-products when it changes its form? What is its origin? Who is He, the Knowing Principle in the field? What are His powers of perception, feeling and thought? All these 'hear, briefly from Me'.

A mere repetition of the qualities of the Infinite Self is, in itself, of no profit at all to a true seeker. Nor can any evolution actually take place by an over-emphasis of the qualities of the Spirit. To close our eyes to the causes that create our present problems is not to solve the problems. The world-of-matter that has been projected by ourselves around us and the process by which we work through it to perceive the infinite varieties of objects, feelings and thoughts – all these are to be brought under our close observation and study. To ignore them is to cheat ourselves so much about the 'essential knowledge'.

At least a working knowledge of the enemy's strategy is essential in planning our anti-strategic movements. To know the nature of all matter envelopments – their play and how they behave under given sets of different circumstances - is to know the 'Field' where we have to battle for release and win our victory.

Thus physiology, biology, psychology and all the natural sciences have a real quota of help to give us. The spiritual path, especially the path-of-Knowledge, is the culmination and the fulfilment of the secular sciences. This is very well brought out by the fact that, when Lord Krishna, even in the midst of the battlefront, is trying to explain the secrets of the Spirit to the warrior Arjuna, He does not fail to emphasise the importance of a close study of the 'Field' provided by the world-of-matter.

IN ORDER TO CREATE A LIVELY ENTHUSIASM IN THE STUDENTS TO OBSERVE, STUDY AND

UNDERSTAND THE 'WORLD-OF-MATTER' AROUND THE SPIRIT, KRISHNA IS GLORIFYING THE VERY THEME OF THIS CHAPTER. LISTEN:

5. *Rishis have sung (about the 'Field' and the 'Knower-of-the-Field') in many ways, in various distinctive chants and also in the suggestive words indicative of Brahman, full of reason and decision.*

The explanations that are to follow are not idle talk, or clever intellectual manifestations, springing from the fertile imagination of Sri Krishna. In the entire discourse, (in Chapter XIII itself) Krishna assures us that what He explains is only a healthy restatement of what 'HAS BEEN SUNG BY THE *RISHIS* IN MANY WAYS, IN DIFFERENT HYMNS, SEVERALLY'. In short, the subject-matter dealt with here is the very theme which the *Upanishads* have indicated in their secret verses, especially so in its passages about *Brahman*.

Why should we so readily accept these statements of the *Rishis* in the *Upanishads* except in a stunned admiration nurtured by our blind belief in them? Krishna points out that even if we had no great respect or reverence for the *Rishis* as such, we will have to accept their declarations because they are not intellectual dictations, or divine commandments, thrust upon the helpless laity by some winged angels assuming divine prerogative and claiming special sources of secret knowledge. This is the general attitude that poisons the scriptures of almost all other religions. As a contrast to them,

---

ऋषिभिर्बहुधा गीतं छन्दोभिर्विविधैः पृथक् ।
ब्रह्मसूत्रपदैश्चैव हेतुमद्भिर्विनिश्चितैः ॥ ५ ॥
ṛṣibhirbahudhā gītaṁ chandobhirvividhaiḥ pṛthak
brahmasūtrapadaiścaiva hetumadbhirviniścitaiḥ 5.

our *Upanisadic* declarations are FULL OF REASONING AND SO CONVINCING.

When a truth is declared, along with logical reasoning, the conclusions arrived at are acceptable to any intelligent student by the sheer force of its appeal.

WHEN ARJUNA IS THUS PREPARED TO LISTEN ATTENTIVELY TO THE DISCOURSE OF THE 'FIELD' AND ITS 'KNOWER', THE LORD SAYS:

6. *The great elements, egoism, intellect, and also the unmanifested (moola-Prakriti), the ten senses and the one (the mind) and the five objects-of-the-senses...*

7. *Desire, hatred, pleasure, pain, aggregate (body), intelligence, fortitude -- this Kshetra has been thus briefly described with its modifications.*

From here onwards, the promised themes for discussion are taken up one by one by the teacher and upon each of them He gives an exhaustive exposition. These two verses, enumerate the various items together constituting the 'Field' (*Kshetra*), which was indicated in a previous stanza (Ibid., verse 2.) as 'this body' (*Idam shariram*).

THE GREAT ELEMENTS (*MAHABHUTAS*)—They are five in number; space, air, fire, water and earth. They are the

---

महाभूतान्यहंकारो बुद्धिरव्यक्तमेव च ।
इन्द्रियाणि दशैकं च पञ्च चेन्द्रियगोचराः ॥ ६ ॥
mahābhūtanyahaṅkāro buddhiravyaktameva ca
indriyāṇi daśaikaṁ ca pañca cendriyagocarāḥ 6.

इच्छा द्वेषः सुखं दुःखं संघातश्चेतना धृतिः ।
एतत्क्षेत्रं समासेन सविकारमुदाहृतम् ॥ ७ ॥
icchā dveṣaḥ sukhaṁ duḥkhaṁ saṅghātaścetanā dhutiḥ
etatkṣetraṁ samāsena savikāramudāhṛtam 7.

rudimentary elements (*tanmatras*) out of the combinations of which the grosser elements; indicated here in the stanza by the term 'Perceptible' (*Indriya-gocharaah*) Great Elements, are formed.

THE EGOISM (*AHAMKARA*)—This is the sense of 'I'-ness and 'My'-ness that arises in us in our identification with the world-of-objects. It is this that is the 'perceiver' and 'enjoyer' of this world, and that enjoys and suffers the joys and sorrows of its own world of likes and dislikes, loves and hatreds, and ever weeps in its innumerable attachments in the world outside. The individuality arising out of our relationships with the world-of-matter is called the 'Ego'.

INTELLECT (*BUDDHI*)—The 'determining-faculty' which rationally thinks and comes to its own conclusions and judges good and bad in every experience of a living man is called the intellect.

UNMANIFESTED (*AVYAKTA*)—that which rules the functions of a given mind and intellect, and determines their activities in the world-outside, is the unmanifested factor called the *vasanas*. The impressions, left over in the mental equipment as a result of our conscious enjoyment of the world-outside, determine the direction and the pattern of all our subsequent perceptions and feelings.

Mental capacities and intellectual decisions are determined in each individual, and his aptitudes are ordered by the type of impressions (*vasanas*) left over in his subtle-body as a result of his previous egocentric existence amidst the world-of-objects. This source of all individual activities is the residual *vasanas* in the individual. Naturally, therefore, in its macrocosmic aspect, the total universe of men and things, and their behaviours, must spring from the total *vasanas* called in Sanskrit as the *Moola-Prakrit* by the *Sankhyans*, or as *Maya* by the *Vedantins*. The Supreme functioning through *Maya* (*Moola-Prakriti*) is the Creator of the total Universe; and the same Supreme, functioning through the *vasana*-layers in the individual (*Avidya*), is the creator, sustainer and destroyer of the individual life, the 'Ego'.

From this, it is so evident that the Unmanifested is but the unseen cause, total *vasanas*, which has manifested as the 'seen'—the world-of-objects.

THE TEN SENSES—the five sense organs-of-perception and the five sense-organs-of-action are the vehicles by which each individual perceives the stimuli and responds to them.

THE ONE (*Ekam*)—in the context here, this stands for the mind. Even though the sense organs are many, the faculty in us that receives all the stimuli, from all the five avenues of perception, is one and the same, the mind. Not only does the mind receive the stimuli but it also executes the judgement of the intellect and sends forth responses to the outer-world. It is again the only outlet for the individual personality to express through. The 'one' here, therefore, represents the mind.

THE FIVE OBJECTS OF THE SENSES—each sense-organ has only one definite field of sense-objects to perceive. The eyes can perceive only forms; the ears can listen to sounds; the nose can smell; the tongue can taste; and the skin can perceive the touches. No one of the sense-organs can perceive the objects of the other sense-organs. Thus, there are five distinct types of sense-objects. And, in fact, the entire gross world perceived is nothing other than a play of all these five types of sense-objects.

The twenty-four factors so far enumerated* are the famous 24 principles (*tattwas*) of the *Sankhyan* Philosophy.

* The unmanifested (7+1), the sense-organs (8+10), mind (18+1) and the five sense-objects (19+5)=24

Lord Krishna, in enumerating the items constituting the 'Field', does not stop with these gross 'equipments-of-matter'; but includes even their modifications such as desire, hatred, pleasure, pain, the assemblage of the body (*samghata*), intelligence, steadfastness, etc. In short not only do the gross body, mind and intellect constitute the entire world-of-objects, but even the perceptions experienced through them, the world-of-objects, the emotions and thoughts are also included in the all-comprehensive term; the 'Field' (*Kshetra*) - 'this body' (*Idam shariram*).

Anything other than the subject belongs to the world-of-objects, and can be perceived as an object. Mental, emotional, and intellectual ideas are also the objects of our knowledge, and therefore, with reference to the Subject all that is seen, felt, or known are but objects. This entire world-of-objects is indicated in the *Geeta* in this chapter by the phrase 'this body-the Field'.

In a word, the entire world of 'knowable' together in a bunch can be labelled as the Field (*Kshetra*). And the Knowing-Principle, seemingly functioning as the 'Knower' (*Kshetrajna*), is the Subject. To distinguish the Subject from the world-of-objects, an exhaustive understanding of what constitutes the object is necessary. Hence this elaborates enumeration. The entire world-of-matter in the cosmos has been directly, as well as by implication, embraced in these two stanzas.

The following section, constituted of five consecutive verses, together lists twenty qualities, which in their totality indicate the 'Knower' (*Kshetrajna*). In fact, the Knower-of-the-Field is directly described (in XIII-12) but, in the following couplets, (in XIII-8 to 12) certain mental and emotional attributes, moral attitudes and ethical principles are prescribed since they are essential prerequisites for the seeker who is anxious to apprehend and experience the Infinite Self.

THEY ARE ENUMERATED AS FOLLOWS:

8. *Humility, unpretentiousness, non-injury, forgiveness, uprightness, service to the teacher, purity, steadfastness, self-control...*

From this stanza onwards, we get a description of the elements of 'Knowledge' and they include moral qualities and ascetic practices which are conducive to spiritual awakening.

HUMILITY—meaning, absence of self-pride; MODESTY - the virtue of not proclaiming one's own greatness; NON-INJURY to any living being mainly by our own vicious intentions and feelings; FORGIVENESS (PATIENCE) – capacity to suffer long without being upset; UPRIGHTNESS – comes to him who harmonises thoughts, words and deeds, and who is intent on right conduct; SERVICE TO THE TEACHER - not merely physical, for real service to the teacher is an attempt on the part of the student to seek a mental and intellectual identity with the teacher's pure heart and intellect; PURITY – not merely the cleanliness of the seeker's thoughts and physical structure, but also of his dress and other belongings and of the environments in which he is living. It also comprehends the inner purity of

---

अमानित्वमदम्भित्वमहिंसा क्षान्तिरार्जवम् ।
आचार्योपासनं शौचं स्थैर्यमात्मविनिग्रहः ॥ ८ ॥
amānitvamadambhitvamahiṁsā kṣāntirārjavam
ācāryopāsanaṁ śaucaṁ sthairyamātmavinigrahaḥ 8.

thoughts and emotions, intentions and motives, passions and urges; STEADFASTNESS – consistency of purpose and concentration of all efforts towards achieving the cultural and the spiritual goal striven for; SELF-CONTROL - self-restraint practised at all the personality-layers, both in their collective and several contacts with the world outside...

MOREOVER:

9. *Indifference to the objects of the senses, and also absence of egoism, perception of (or reflection upon) evils in birth, death, old age, sickness and pain....*

ABSENCE OF ATTACHMENT FOR OBJECTS—this does not mean running away from the objects of the world. Living in the midst of these objects, to switch off our mental preoccupations with them; living amidst the objects detachedly and not getting shackled by them – this is meant here by the term *Vairagya*. To run away from the objects and to indulge in them mentally amounts to suppressions, and such a suppressed individual is labelled (in III-6) as a hypocrite (*Mithyachara*) by the Lord Himself.

ABANDONMENT OF THE THOUGHT OF 'I'—the individuality-sense comes only when we identify ourselves with the equipments and their perceptions. To reduce this delusory misconception of ourselves is an essential prerequisite for asserting and living our own real divine nature. This is equivalent to the weeding that must precede planting in any field of cultivation.

इन्द्रियार्थेषु वैराग्यमनहंकार एव च ।
जन्ममृत्युजराव्याधिदुःखदोषानुदर्शनम् ॥ ९ ॥

indriyārtheṣu vairāgyamanahaṅkāra eva ca
janmamṛtyujarāvyādhiduḥkhadoṣānudarśanam 9.

PERCEPTION OF THE EVIL OF PAIN—Feeling of discontentment with the available situation alone can goad us to discover a new state of existence. Whether it be a nation, a community or a society, as long as they are not aware of the fact that their present conditions are despicable and tragic, they will adapt themselves to living in that condition oblivious of their sorrows. Every political or social worker first makes the people understand their present state of degradation and destitution. When such realisation comes to them, they are ready with all enthusiasm, to seek fresh fields of greater joys and a fuller life.

The same technique is applicable in the cultural field. Unless a seeker is fully conscious of the inward personality-shackles in himself, he will live on in his own ditch of sorrows, never striving to get out of it. Both the human mind and body have a tremendous amount of adaptability. They can adapt themselves to any condition and even come to enjoy them.

Unless a seeker is constantly conscious of the evil of the pain in his present stage of existence, he will not discover the necessary spiritual urge, intellectual dynamism, emotional enthusiasm or physical courage to seek, to fight for, to win, and to possess the Divine Fields of Perfection.

IN BIRTH, DEATH, OLD AGE, AND SICKNESS—every physical body in the world, goes through these modifications; and each one of them is an inlet for fresh sources of sorrow. Birth, growth, decay, disease and death are the tragic destinies of all living equipments. In all these stages of our metamorphosis, to constantly recognize pain is to feel impatience with it. This sense of revolt against pain is the fuel that drives the seekers faster and faster to seek the Peaks of Perfection.

MOREOVER:

10. *Non-attachment; non-identification of Self with son, wife, home and the rest; and constant even-mindedness on the attainment of the desirable and the undesirable...*

NON-ATTACHMENT—the mind's sticking on to the various objects of the world with extreme liking for them is called attachment. It is the mental contacts with the world-outside that bring agitations into the mind. It dances a number to the tune of death to which the finite objects of the world most often dance. Fire in itself cannot burn, but a child gets its fingers burnt, not because of the fire but because its fingers, propelled by a force called desire, come in actual CONTACT with fire.

ABSENCE OF EXCESSIVE LOVE FOR CHILD, WIFE, HOME AND THE LIKE—Excessive love, or affection, is an intense form of attachment to another. It consists in our total identification with the object of our affection. The lover loses his personal identity in his identification with the beloved to such an extent, that he is happy or sorrowful when she lives in joy or suffers from pain. Such an intimate relationship is generally met with in the attachment of a mother to its child.

To build a wall of discrimination around our inner personality and to keep such disturbances away is to discover the equipoise in ourselves – without which no progress or growth is ever possible.

With a little practice, this evenness of mind can be maintained unbroken in all situations of life - DESIRABLE

असक्तिरनभिष्वङ्गः पुत्रदारगृहादिषु ।
नित्यं च समचित्तत्वमिष्टानिष्टोपपत्तिषु ॥ १० ॥

asaktiranabhiṣvaṅgaḥ putradāragṛhādiṣu
nityaṁ ca samacittatvamiṣṭāniṣṭoopapattiṣu 10.

AND UNDESIRABLE. A human mind, relieved from its preoccupations with its own present attachments and affections, unintelligent though they be, will discover in itself a tremendous amount of surplus energy conserved, which might flow into dangerous channels unless rightly directed.

THE RIGHT CHANNELLING OF THIS NEWLY DISCOVERED ENERGY IS INDICATED BELOW:

11. *Unswerving devotion unto Me by the YOGA of non-separation, resorting to solitary places, distaste for the society of men...*

Perhaps compelled by the nature of Arjuna, a man of action, or perhaps forced by the very spirit of the reformer in the *Yogeshwara*, the Divine Song, as it comes to us, is the most practical textbook on Self-rediscovery. The moment the *Geeta-Acharya* advises his disciple to develop any given mental or intellectual beauty; he always suggests a practical method by which this can actually be accomplished.

If a seeker tries to develop in himself the virtues described in the previous three stanzas - not only in his inward life but also in all his contacts with the world around him, it is certain that he, an ordinary man of the world, will thereby conserve in himself a lot of energy. This stanza describes the right application of this conserved energy in proper channels so as to profit thereby and gain a better Self-unfoldment.

UNFLINCHING DEVOTION TO ME—Concentration is the focussing of the mind upon a particular point to the exclusion of all mental excitements and agitations. This

---

मयि चानन्ययोगेन भक्तिरव्यभिचारिणी ।
विविक्तदेशसेवित्वमरतिर्जनसंसदि ॥ ११ ॥

mayi cānanyayogena bhaktiravyabhicāriṇī
viviktadeśasevitvamaratirjana saṁsadi 11.

steadiness in contemplation may be destroyed by causes arising at two different points - either in the individual's own mind or in the object contemplated upon. Unless both are steady, concentration cannot be successful. If our devotion wavers from idol to idol, then our practice of concentration will get unsteady, because the point of attention becomes ever-changing. Therefore, it is said that unflinching devotion towards Me, the Self, is one of the conditions necessary for steady progress and growth in *Yoga*.

BY THE YOGA OF NON-SEPARATION—Undivided attention and enthusiasm in the mind of the devotee is another condition that will accomplish better concentration. Otherwise the mind may revolt against its own devoted self-application, and will, either partially or wholly, wander away into its own delusory enchantments. A certain amount of steadiness of purpose is to be maintained by the mind. Wild imaginations and futile daydreaming are the preoccupations of only a disintegrated mind.

The typical expression used here by Shri Krishna to indicate the abject and despicable vacillations of the human mind at the seat of *Yoga* clearly shows the force with which he wants to condemn such vacillations. He says, the mind should be 'unprostituting' with its point-of-contemplation. Prostitution denotes an attitude of selling away one's own capabilities and beauties for the sake of some paltry profit heedless of the higher bonds of faithfulness and chastity. A mind, wedded to the Lord, is a mind at faithful contemplation. The warning 'not to prostitute' is indeed very powerful to express that the point-of-concentration should not be at a crowd of deities or a host of ideas, but must faithfully serve some chosen single ideal.

Similarly, the other powerful expression used in the stanza is the *Yoga* of non-otherness (*Ananya-Yoga*). Inspired as He is, the *Yogeshwara* coins a new and powerful phrase on the spur of the moment to bring a new fire into his reinterpretation of the ancient Hindu way of life and techniques of self-culture.

Such an integrated life of stable mind and steady contemplation upon a firm ideal is impossible, unless the practitioner works in a conducive environment. This is prescribed in the two indirect advices (a) to resort to solitary places and (b) to develop distaste for the crowded society life. The more integrated the personality grows and the more maddening becomes its enthusiasm for the quest of that which is dear to its heart, the more it automatically lives alone in itself away from the noisy crowd. This is true of every thinker – be he a poet, be he a scientific research-scholar or be he a man with an acute problem. Whenever the mind is fascinated by an enchanting ideal, it loses all its contact with other preoccupations and becomes wedded faithfully to its own all-absorbing theme of interest.

Thereafter – just as poet lives in his own world, just as the scientist is a solitary man even in the market-place -- the devotee also enters a cave of his own experiences and he walks alone in the world. He hates other thoughts entering his mind, and so lives alone in himself. These two terms should not be misunderstood as physical escapism into a tomb-like solitude, or as a physical aversion to the society of men.

MOREOVER:

12. *Constancy in Self-knowledge, perception of the end of true knowledge – this is declared to be 'knowledge', and what is opposed to it is 'ignorance'.*

अध्यात्मज्ञाननित्यत्वं तत्त्वज्ञानार्थदर्शनम् ।
एतज्ज्ञानमिति प्रोक्तमज्ञानं यदतोऽन्यथा ॥ १२ ॥

adhyātmajñānanityatvaṁ tattvajñānārthadarśanam
etajjñānamiti proktamajñānaṁ yadato'nyathā 12.

In this concluding stanza of this section, explaining the various essential qualifications in a seeker, the Lord adds to the aforesaid list eighteen qualifications, two more items, viz., constancy in Self-Knowledge and understanding the end of True Knowledge.

CONSTANCY IN SELF-KNOWLEDGE—The Knowledge of the Self is to be lived and not to be merely learnt. If the Self is one everywhere and the Self alone is real, the seeker should try to live as the Self at all levels of his personality. The constancy of living the Spiritual-knowledge at all levels of one's contacts with the world-outside is one of the unavoidable practices a seeker should always keep up.

UNDERSTANDING THE END OF TRUE KNOWLEDGE—To remember constantly the goal of our endeavour is to add more enthusiasm to our activities. Sincerity of purpose in, and undying devotion to, any endeavour can be had only if the seeker is thrilled by the vision of the goal that he has to reach. Thus, the end should be kept in view. Liberation (*Moksha*) from all our imperfections and limitations is the 'end' striven for by all spiritual seekers. The attributes* are declared to be 'Knowledge' because they are conducive to the final Realisation of the Self.

A train in full steam waiting for the signal at a platform is generally described as 'Madras is ready to leave now'. In the language of the Railway Station, it is usual to say - 'Delhi is expected', 'Calcutta is late', 'Bombay has left', etc. In each of these cases only the train leaving for, or coming from, these various cities is meant. Similarly here, the very qualities are called the 'Knowledge' (*Jnana*) because, once these qualities have been fully developed, the mind so cultivated becomes

---

* From 'Humility' in stanza 7 to 'Perception of the Goal' in stanza 12.

the ready vehicle to go forward and it is easier to reach the goal, the Pure Knowledge of the Self.

WHAT IS THAT WHICH HAS TO BE KNOWN BY THE KNOWLEDGE? IN ANSWER TO THIS QUESTION IT IS SAID:

13. *I will declare that which has to be 'known' knowing which one attains to Immortality -- the beginningless Supreme Brahman, called neither being nor non-being.*

After explaining, in the previous section of five verses, the various secondary or auxiliary steps-in-aid for 'Knowledge', the Lord promises that He will explain 'What is to be known'. There are critics who allege that though Krishna, the teacher, promises that He will explain 'What is to be known', He does not directly do so, but merely gives an elaborate description of what is the RESULT of gaining such a 'Knowledge'. This criticism is unfair. The glorification of the result of 'Knowledge' can create in the hearer a greater desire to realise it.

KNOWING WHICH, ONE ATTAINS THE IMMORTAL—Mortality is the destiny of matter. Identifying with the finite, the Immortal Spirit Itself is conditioned by matter and suffers the delusory sense of finitude and mortality. To rediscover the Spiritual Nature in itself and to live that glory is to end the fearful concept and experience of death, and to enter into a field of joyous Spiritual Nature. This is the goal, for accomplishing which, our inner-

---

ज्ञेयं यत्तत्प्रवक्ष्यामि यज्ज्ञात्वामृतमश्नुते ।
अनादिमत्परं ब्रह्म न सत्तन्नासदुच्यते ॥ १३ ॥

jñeya yattatpravakṣyāmi yajjñātvāmṛtamaśnute
anādimatparaṁ brahma na sattannāsaducyate 13.

equipments of meditation are to be properly tuned up by the disciplines already described.

WITHOUT BEGINNING, THE HIGHEST *BRAHMAN* (*Anaadimat-param*)—A beginning can be conceived and calculated only with reference to what is the substratum of all, which substratum must be existent even before Time. Thus, the Supreme is always considered as 'beginningless'. From the Supreme even Time is born.

THE SUPREME CONSCIOUSNESS, which is the 'illuminator' of all experiences and which exists, transcending all realms of experiences, cannot be caught within the web of our perceptions—It being the very Perceiving-Principle in all equipments. With reference to It, everything else is an 'object'. It is the one Subject, and since it cannot be perceived, felt or thought of, It is not said to be existent (*Sat*).

Nor can Truth be defined as non-existent, such as the sky-flower or man's tail, for It manifests as the world. Therefore, Truth can be defined only as 'neither *sat* nor *asat*'. The Supreme *Brahman* cannot be characterised either positively or negatively.*

Sankara says that '*Brahman* cannot be existent (*Sat*) as it belong to no GENUS, nor possesses any qualities, but at the same time It shows Itself to be not '*asat*' by manifesting Itself through living bodies.'

In fact, these concepts of '*Sat*' and '*Asat*' are judgements of the human mind and intellect. The Consciousness that illumines these judgements is the Self. The illuminator and the illumined cannot be one and the same. Therefore, the one Subject, the *Brahman*, as opposed to all 'objects', cannot be either Existent or non-Existent, because '*Sat*' and '*Asat*'

* Refer '*Shvetaashvatara Upanishad*' VI-19 and also Swamiji's discourses on

are two types of thought-waves, and the Self illumines them both. That *Brahman* is 'NEITHER BEING, NOR NON-BEING' is all that the scriptures can declare.

DESCRIBING THE ALL-PERVADING SELF CONSCIOUS PRINCIPLE, WE HAVE THE FOLLOWING STANZAS:

14. *With hands and feet everywhere, with eyes, heads and mouths everywhere, with ears everywhere, He exists in the world, enveloping all.*

WITH HANDS AND FEET EVERYWHERE—It is easier to describe an unmanifest power for the comprehension of students of lesser calibre, when the unknown principle is defined in terms of the known. Though the hands and legs of the living creatures are made up of inert matter, they seem to be quite conscious and vital in their movements. This Principle of Consciousness, functioning behind them all, everywhere, is one and the same Self, the Supreme *Brahman*, indicated by the expression 'POSSESSING HANDS AND FEET EVERYWHERE'.

Every eye, head and mouth functions in the world because of the Life that pulsates through it. Life is one everywhere. Therefore, that Life Principle is described here as 'EVERYWHERE POSSESSING EYES AND EARS AND MOUTHS'. All activities of perception, feeling and thinking are successively pursued only as long as Life presides over

---

सर्वतः पाणिपादं तत्सर्वतोऽक्षिशिरोमुखम् ।
सर्वतः श्रुतिमल्लोके सर्वमावृत्य तिष्ठति ॥ १४ ॥

sarvataḥ pāṇipādaṁ tatsarvato'kṣiśiromukham
sarvataḥ śrutimalloke sarvamāvṛtya tiṣṭhati 14.

* *Shvetaashvetara Upanishad* III-3 and 16

the body, and therefore, the One Life is defined here as 'EVERYWHERE POSSESSING EYES, ETC'.

THAT EXISTS PERVADING ALL—If this Principle of Consciousness is defined as functioning through known physical equipments, the student may doubt that Life, like stars studding the sky, expresses itself only wherever equipments function. To remove this fallacious idea, it is rightly said that the Truth, the Principle of Consciousness, 'EXISTS PERVADING ALL'. This is reminiscent of the famous hymn to the Cosmic-man (*Purusha Sooktam*) in the *Rig Veda*.*

CONTINUING THE DESCRIPTION OF THE ETERNAL TRUTH THE LORD SAYS:

15. *Shining by the functions of all the senses, yet without the senses; unattached, yet supporting all; devoid of qualities, yet their experiencer...*

One of the ways of defining the indefinable Supreme, the subject in the seeker himself, is to indicate It in a language of contradiction, which, without confusing the intellect, tickles it to a special kind of activity, thereby facilitating the realisation of the Eternal. The language of contradiction is the characteristic feature of all scriptural textbooks. Hasty readers of the scriptures quote these lines to justify their scepticism, or atheistic tendencies. This stanza is met with in the *Upanishads* also.*

सर्वेन्द्रियगुणाभासं सर्वेन्द्रियविवर्जितम् ।
असक्तं सर्वभृच्चैव निर्गुणं गुणभोक्तृ च ॥ १५ ॥

sarvendriyaguṇābhāsaṁ sarvendriyavivarjitam
asaktaṁ sarvebhṛccaiva nirguṇaṁ guṇabhoktṛ ca 15.

* *Shvetaashvetara Up*. III-17 and 19.

SEEMING TO POSSESS THE FUNCTIONS OF ALL SENSES YET DEVOID OF ALL SENSES—The Self in us, while functioning through the equipment, the sense organs, and conditioned by them, looks as though It has all the sense organs. But when we analyse, we have to admit that the sense-organs are material and that they decay and perish, while the Consciousness—functioning in and through them and providing each of them with its own individual faculty, is Itself Eternal, and Changeless. The Truth, while functioning through the sense organs, looks AS THOUGH It possesses them. But in fact, It has Itself none of these faculties.

Electricity is not the light in the bulb, nor the heat in the heater; yet while functioning through the bulb, or the heater, and conditioned by them, the same Electricity looks AS THOUGH it is light or fire.

DETACHED, YET UPHOLDING ALL—This relationship of 'detached support' is not too easy for the initiate to understand.[1] But it is generally brought within our comprehension by the great teachers of our country through analogies. No wave is all the ocean; all the waves put together are also not the entire ocean. We cannot say the ocean is attached to the waves since the ocean is the very nature of the waves and, though detached, all the waves are always supported by none other than the ocean itself. Cotton is in all cloth; cloth is not cotton. And yet, it is the cotton in the cloth that 'supports' the cloth.

Similarly, the world of plurality is not Consciousness. Yet Consciousness supports it. Between the ghost and the post, no attachment is ever possible and yet, the post alone is the

---

[1] Unseen seer, unheard hearer... etc., *Brihadaaranyaka Up*.IV-iii-7, *Kaivalya Up*.121, *Shvetaashvatara Upanishad*, III-19

[2] *Sattva* (Unactivity), *Rajas* (activity) and *Tamas* (inactivity).

'support' of the ghost – as the waking mind alone can support the 'dreams'.

WITHOUT *GUNAS*, YET ENJOYING ALL *GUNAS*—The moods in which, and influences under which, human minds come to play and experience themselves are called *'gunas'*.[2] These are influences that govern the mind and yet they are the objects of realisation or perception for the Conscious Self. A live mind alone can experience these influences. Consciousness conditioned by the mind is the Ego (*Jiva*), and is the experiencer (*Bhoktr*) of the *guna*. Unconditioned by the mind, in Its own nature, It is the Absolute.

Thus, in the stanza, the Self, as the Absolute, is described as beyond the sense organs, mind and intellect and detached from everything and without any relation to the various *gunas*.

But the same Self, conditioned by the sense organs, looks AS THOUGH possessing them all, and proves AS THOUGH It is the sustainer of them all, and expresses Itself AS THOUGH It is the experiencer of all the *gunas*.

NOT ONLY THIS, BUT THE SELF, FUNCTIONING IN AN INDIVIDUAL, IS THE ONE SELF IN ALL:

16. *Without and within (all) beings, the 'unmoving' and also the 'moving'; because of its subtlety unknowable; and near and far away – is That.*

The all-pervasiveness of the Principle of Consciousness is indicated here in the inimitable style borrowed from the *Upanishads*.

बहिरन्तश्च भूतानामचरं चरमेव च ।
सूक्ष्मत्वात्तदविज्ञेयं दूरस्थं चान्तिके च तत् ॥ १६ ॥
bahirantaśca bhūtānāmacaraṁ carameva ca
sūkṣmatvātttdavijñeyaṁ dūrasthaṁ cāntike ca tat 16.

WITHOUT AND WITHIN ALL THINGS—The Conscious Principle that bursts Itself into activity through the various individualised equipments is all-pervading and is, therefore, in an unmanifest condition. It is present even where no special equipment is available. Even though we can listen to our national radio broadcasts only through available receiving sets, we cannot say that there are no electrical sound waves in places where there are no receiving sets. Where there is a body, mind and intellect ready to function, there, no doubt, is the expression of Consciousness. But Consciousness is All-pervading not only within the equipment but even outside it.

The phrase quoted can also be interpreted as 'WITHOUT THE BEINGS AND YET WITHIN THEM ALSO'. Something like this: the ocean is without the waves and is something other than the waves and, yet, the very mass of each wave is nothing but the ocean itself.

MOVING AND UNMOVING—All that moves of its own volition is 'alive' and that which has no motion falls under the category of the 'inert'. This phrase is sometimes explained as 'UNMOVING AND YET MOVING', wherein the Truth, in Its Absolute nature is motionless—there is no place where It can move since It is All – yet, conditioned by the things moving, IT LOOKS AS THOUGH it has movement. SITTING in a bus you can TRAVEL a long distance; yourself only sitting! Thus the bus travels, and therefore, in yourself though there is no motion, yet you, conditioned by (meaning, carried by) the bus, are the traveller.

Thus there is an Eternal, All-perfect Principle, revelling as the very core in our personality, which is not only within but which is everywhere – without which no activity is ever possible, and so, which is in every activity. It is manifested everywhere. Then how is it that we are not able to perceive

It, or feel It, or intellectually comprehend It? – 'BECAUSE OF ITS INCOMPREHENSIBLE SUBTLETY'.

The grosser the thing, the more perceptible it is. Earth can be smelt, can be tasted, can be seen, and can be heard. Water cannot be smelt. Fire cannot be tasted. Air cannot be seen. Space has only sound as its property.

Cause is always subtler than effect. Space itself being a gross product, it must have a cause. That which is the cause for *Akasha* is the Eternal Substratum, from which all the *Elements* have arisen. Consciousness being thus the 'subtlest of the subtle', pervading even *Akasha*, It is incomprehensible to the gross equipments of thought, feeling and perception.

IT IS FAR AND NEAR—limited and conditioned things can be defined by their location in space as 'here' or 'there'. And with reference to their distance from the observer, we can say they are *'near'* or *'far'*. But that which is All-pervading must be at once 'here' and 'there'. And therefore, it is 'NEAR' and 'FAR'. This phrase also has been sometimes interpreted as 'FAR AND YET NEAR'. 'FAR'; in its Transcendental Absolute nature the Truth is 'FAR AWAY' from all the hallucinations of names and forms, which, in their aggregate, constitute the Universe, but at the same time as Existence, Truth exists in every name and form: 'NEAR'.

In short, this verse, in its staggering beauty arising out of its deliberate language of contradiction, shakes the reader from his intellectual complacency and whips him up to reflect and to realise that the Absolute Reality is at once transcendent and immanent.

THIS *BRAHMAN*, WHICH CAN BE REALISED WITHIN OURSELVES AS SELF, IS ONE AND THE SAME IN ALL, AND REVELS AS THE SELF IN ALL. THIS IS EXPLAINED BELOW:

17. *And undivided, yet He exists as if divided in beings; That is to be known as the Supporter of Beings; He devours and He generates.*

UNDIVIDED, AND YET, IN BEINGS, IT EXISTS AS IF DIVIDED—Electricity is All-pervading, and yet, conditioned by the bulb it manifests as effulgence at the filament. So too, though the *Paramatman* is All-pervading, It individualises itself as special manifestations only at points where equipments are available. Though space is one, it can manifest as room-space, pot-space etc., only when seemingly conditioned by the four walls of the room, or the pot.

It is the supporter of all, devouring as well as generating them—The post is the supporter of the ghost. It 'creates' the ghost vision and 'devours' it. The earth is the supporter of all plants. It creates and it devours them all. The ocean is the supporter of all waves, waves are born from the ocean, and they are devoured by the same ocean. Similarly, Truth is that solid Omnipotent Substratum upon which is projected the world-of-plurality by the deluded mind and intellect; and when the mind and intellect are transcended, the vision of *samsara* gets devoured in the very experience of the Tranquil, just as, on waking, the dream merges into the essence of the waker's mind.

IT IS TO BE KNOWN—the theme of all the discussions in the previous stanzas (Stanza 13 onwards) was 'THAT WHICH IS THE KNOWABLE'. This is to be 'known' by a mind that

---

अविभक्तं च भूतेषु विभक्तमिव च स्थितम् ।
भूतभर्तृ च तज्ज्ञेयं ग्रसिष्णु प्रभविष्णु च ॥ १७ ॥

avibhaktaṁ ca bhūteṣu vibhaktamiva ca sthitam
bhūtabhartṛ ca tajjñeyaṁ grasiṣṇu prabhaviṣṇu ca 17.

has been prepared for it through the disciplines advocated in the earlier section.

IF THERE BE THUS AN ALL-PERVADING TRUTH, EVER PRESENT IN US, AND IF WE CANNOT PERCEIVE OR EXPERIENCE THIS SELF, IT MUST BE SURELY A PRINCIPLE OF DARKNESS. THIS IS NOT SO. LISTEN:

18. *That (BRAHMAN), the Light-of-all-lights, is said to be beyond darkness; (It is) Knowledge, the Object-of-Knowledge, seated in the hearts of all, to be reached by Knowledge.*

Brahman, the illuminator in all, is the One Consciousness by which everything is known intellectually, realised intuitively, and experienced spiritually. Since the Consciousness in us brings our various experiences within our understanding and knowledge, it is generally compared with light. To see an object, it is not only sufficient that the object is in line with a healthy pair of eyes, but the object must also be bathed in light. Taking this experience in the outer world of cognition as an illustrative analogy, within us too we must have some 'Light' to illumine, since we can see and have the knowledge of the different types of emotions and thoughts that arise and exist in our bosom. This Light-of-Wisdom, by which we become aware of our own mental and intellectual conditions at any given moment, is called the Light of the Soul, or the Self, the Consciousness.

By the Light-of-Consciousness, every thought is brilliantly lit in the awareness of our life. Thus, it has become a spiritual tradition to call Consciousness as 'Light'.

ज्योतिषामपि तज्ज्योतिस्तमसः परमुच्यते ।
ज्ञानं ज्ञेयं ज्ञानगम्यं हृदि सर्वस्य विष्ठितम् ॥ १८ ॥
jyotiṣāmapi tajjyotistamasaḥ paramucyate
jñānaṁ jñayaṁ jñānagamyaṁ hṛdi sarvasya viṣṭhitam 18.

The moment the student comes across such an expression, he is apt to misunderstand it as the 'LIGHT' he has experienced in the world. The brilliance of the light experienced in the outer world belongs to the realm-of-objects, and it cannot be the subject that is conscious of it. Therefore, it is necessary that the teacher should indicate, in some way, what exactly is meant by such familiar terms as 'the Illumination of the Soul', 'the Effulgence of the Self', 'the Incandescence of the Consciousness'.

LIGHT OF ALL LIGHTS—to indicate the Subject, we have to negate the entire field-of-objects. Sources of light such as the Sun, moon, stars, lightning or even fire, are described as having no illumination at all in the blinding luminosity of the Self.* Therefore, Krishna indicates that the Self, in each, is the 'Light' which illumines all other perceptible lights! Even the Sun, though it has light of its own, is immaterial to the living world of beings, if the Consciousness in them does not illumine it. If I am not aware, but I am told by some wise-looking sage, that I have a pair of horns, it does not matter to me, because they are not available for my enjoyment, nor are they useful in my life, as long as I am not aware of them. My world can give me my quota of cherished joys and pains only when I am conscious of it. Light, as a principle manifested, can serve my world only when it comes into my awareness. Thus, all sources of light are illumined by my Consciousness. Therefore, the Self is indicated as the Subject that experiences the entire world of objectified light.

THAT IS SAID TO BE BEYOND DARKNESS—Even after the indication that the Self is Consciousness that illumines all other Lights of the world, the impression of Light, as an object of our experience is so powerful in our finite intellect that the average student can still retain only his 'relative concept' of

* *'Na Tatra Sooryo Bhaati ..'* *Kathopanishad* II-v-15

light. In the world outside, light, in its empirical sense, is that which we comprehend as a contrast to darkness. If there were no light, there would have been no days; in the Sun there is no meaning for the word light, since the Sun knows no darkness! Thus, to indicate the Absolute nature of the Infinite 'Light' of the Soul, it is stated that it is beyond the concept of darkness; it is Absolute Light, the Consciousness.

Even to say that THERE is darkness, we must be conscious of it. The 'Light' of awareness is so subtle and Absolute, that It illumines not only the various sources of light in the world, but also the experience of darkness itself! That which illumines both light and darkness must be a factor that transcends both these experiences. Thus, the Spirit is indicated as that which transcends even darkness.

The second line indicates that the Spirit is (a) Knowledge (*Jnanam*), (b) that which is to be known (*Jneyam*), and (c) that which is to be reached by Knowledge (*Jnana-gamyam*). In short, this is the final experience that is to be gained for which we have prepared ourselves through moral perfections such as 'humility', etc., (XIII-5 to 11) and have tried to concentrate upon the 'Knowledge' (XIII-12 to 17). This is the point-of-concentration for the head and the heart that have been already disciplined for the final flight in meditation. The Consciousness that transcends our experiences and illumines our life is the very goal in all spiritual endeavours, at all times, and everywhere.

DWELLING IN THE HEART OF ALL—If there is an Infinite Light of Knowledge to be known -- without which life is impossible, in the presence of which alone all experiences can have a meaning and existence -- then this Infinite Goal is certainly to be acquired and possessed. Where am I to seek it? What pilgrimage must I undertake? Am I capable of making an expedition? Probably, I am not in possession of it today as it must be something to be experienced yonder in some unknown time and place. To negate all such misconceptions, it is boldly declared here that this Infinite dwells in the hearts of all.

Philosophically, 'heart' means the area in the mental zone from where noble and pious thoughts spring forth. In an atmosphere of goodness, when the intellect steadily contemplates upon the 'Light' that lies beyond darkness -- the Absolute Non-dual Self that exists, transcending all -- but also immanent in its subtle all-pervading nature – It can be contacted and realised, and therefore, the 'heart' is considered as the dwelling place of the Self.

The Consciousness functioning in the seekers' mind and intellect, if lived and experienced by Itself, must give the experience of the Infinite, just as by knowing the composition of a minute particle of salt, the world of sodium-chloride is understood.

SEEK THE 'LIGHT' THROUGH DEVOTION: HERE FOLLOWS A CONCLUDING REMARK FOR THE THEME DISCUSSED SO FAR:

19. *Thus the Field, as well as the knowledge and the knowable have been briefly stated. Knowing this, My devotee enters into My Being.*

What has been described in this chapter so far is the whole doctrine, the doctrine of the *Vedas*, taught in brief as the doctrine of the *Geeta.* The FIELD described above (XIII-6 & 7)

इति क्षेत्रं तथा ज्ञानं ज्ञेयं चोक्तं समासतः ।
मद्भक्त एतद्विज्ञाय मद्भावायोपपद्यते ॥ १९ ॥

iti kṣetraṁ tathā jñānaṁ jñeyaṁ coktaṁ samāsataḥ
madbhakta etadvijñāya madbhāvāyopapadyate 19.

beginning with the 'Great Elements' and ending with 'Fortitude'; KNOWLEDGE comprising the moral and ethical rules ordering our right relationship with the world, (XIII-8 to 12), starting with 'humility' and ending with 'the perception of the end of knowledge' and the KNOWABLE described just now, (XIII-2 & 7), these have been briefly dealt with.

Now the question is: Who among the seekers is really fit for this great 'Knowledge'? It is prescribed by the Lord that "HIS DEVOTEES ALONE ARE FIT FOR MY STATE". Devotion here is not merely an emotional surrender in love unto the Lord, but an intellectual appreciation of the Truth, through a correct discrimination between the 'Field' and the 'Knower-of-the-Field'. One who is able to recognise the one Vaasudeva, who is the vitalising Conscious-Principle in all Fields-of-matter-envelopments (VII-5), is the true devotee "WHO IS FIT FOR MY STATE" (*Mat Bhava*).

THE 'FIELD' AND THE 'KNOWER-OF-THE-FIELD' TOGETHER IN THEIR COMBINATION PROVIDE US WITH ONE WORD FOR THE ENTIRE UNIVERSE...

20. *Know you that Matter (PRAKRITI) and Spirit (PURUSHA) are both beginningless; and know you also that all modifications and qualities are born of Prakriti.*

Earlier Krishna had described the world-of-matter (*Prakriti*) as falling under two groups, the Higher and the Lower. Both these are explained in this chapter as the 'KNOWER' and the 'FIELD'. During the discussion of the Higher and the Lower *Prakritis*, it was said that they together

---

प्रकृतिं पुरुषं चैव विद्ध्यनादी उभावपि ।
विकारांश्च गुणांश्चैव विद्धि प्रकृतिसंभवान् ॥ २० ॥
prakṛtiṁ puruṣaṁ caiva viddhayanādī ubhāvapi
vikārāṁśca guṇāṁścaiva viddhi prakṛtisambhavāna 20.

constitute the source of Creation. Continuing the same thought in this chapter, in a fresh phraseology as the 'Field' and its 'Knower', it is repeated that they together constitute the womb of all beings.

Matter (*Prakriti*) and Spirit (*Purusha*) are both beginningless. Matter and Spirit are the two aspects of *Ishwara*, the Lord. As the Lord is Eternal, it is but natural that His nature -- Matter and Spirit – should also be Eternal, meaning beginningless. It is these two, in their inter-play, that project Creation, continue to preserve it, and dissolve the Universe created by them. Thus, the play of Matter and Spirit is the cause of *samsara* and the substratum for both of them is the Lord, the Light of lights.

Subjectively, when the creative power in me, ordered by my *vasanas* (*avidya*), comes to play in the field of its expression, dynamised by its 'Knower', it projects a world of experience, which I maintain and destroy according to the nature, the condition and qualities governing the Matter-Spirit factors in me.

All forms and qualities are born of Matter. All forms and emanations (*vikaras*) which have been explained (XIII-6 and 7) already and all qualities (*gunas*) such as those which express themselves as pleasure, pain, delusion and such other mental states,* spring from Matter (*Prakriti*). In short, 'Matter' is that out of which all forms and qualities come into existence. All changes and modifications belong to the realm-of-Matter and the *Atman* is the Changeless substratum (*Kutasthah*), in the presence of which, all these changes take place.

WHAT THEN ARE THESE FORMS AND QUALITIES WHICH ARE DESCRIBED HERE AS BORN OF P*RAKRITI*?

21. *In the production of the effect and the cause, PRAKRITI is said to be the cause; in the experience of pleasure and pain, PURUSHA is said to be the cause.*

IN THE PRODUCTION OF CAUSE AND EFFECT—The 'effects' mentioned here are thirteen in number and are constituted of the five great elements, the five senses, mind, intellect and *ahamkara*. The macrocosmic gross elements in their *gunas* are themselves represented in the microcosm as the five *indriyas*. We had discussed this in the description of the Cosmic-Form of the Lord (Chapter XI). These sense-organs cannot bring their stimuli of the outer world to the individual personality unless there is the converging point of all the *indriyas*, called the mind.

In order to respond properly to the stimuli, there must be a coordinating and understanding, discriminating and reasoning principle that governs the mind; and that principle is the intellect. In the world-of-objects, constituted of the elements, in the realm of the mind and in the responses sent out by the intellect, there must be a constant sense of I-ness, born out of the individual's identification with all that is mentioned above. This is called the 'Ego'. All these thirteen items, together in their aggregate, represent the 'effect' (*karya*), mentioned in the stanza.

PRAKRITI IS SAID TO BE THE CAUSE—All the above-mentioned together constitute the world-of-matter. The five

---

कार्यकरणकर्तृत्वे हेतुः प्रकृतिरुच्यते ।
पुरुषः सुखदुःखानां भोक्तृत्वे हेतुरुच्यते ॥ २१ ॥
kāryakaraṇakartṛtve hetuḥ prakṛtirucyate
puruṣaḥ sukhaduḥkhānāṁ bhoktṛtve heturucyate 21.

* To be discussed later on elsewhere in Chapter XIV of the *Geeta*.

elements in their combination become the entire world-of-objects including the body, the senses, sensation and the instrument-of-judgement. From the five great elements down to the ego, all items enumerated together form the world-of-objects – since all of them can be perceived.

AS EXPERIENCING PLEASURE AND PAIN—That which perceives the entire world-of-objects and their reactions upon the ego which is the individual's direct reaction to the world, is the Self. The Light of Consciousness is that which illumines the world-of-objects outside and the instruments of perception, feeling and thought within.

PURUSHA IS SAID TO BE THE CAUSE—Pleasure and pain are the reactions in our intellect. When desirable objects in a conducive pattern reach our life, the experience is called 'pleasure'. And the opposite sensation, produced by undesirable objects, is called 'pain'. Every experience, in its final analysis, is adjudged either as pain or as pleasure. The Awareness in us illumines these. It would be impossible to be conscious of the flow of experiences without the Grace of the Consciousness. Therefore, the Spirit (*Purusha*) is explained here as the cause for the experiences in life. In short, *Purusha** is the cause for *samsara*. The Spirit, functioning in a field as the 'Knower' of it, suffers the sorrows of *samsara*. He who stands in the sun suffers the heat; if he retires into the shade, he enjoys its coolness.

THUS, IT IS SAID IN THE ABOVE THAT THE 'KNOWER-OF-THE-FIELD' (*PURUSHA*) IS THE ENJOYER OF THE PLEASURE AND PAIN – *SAMSARA*. WHAT IS THIS *SAMSARA* DUE TO? – THE LORD SAYS:

22. *The Purusha, seated in Prakriti, experiences the qualities born of Prakriti; attachment to the qualities is the cause of his birth in good and evil wombs.*

PURUSHA RESTS SEATED IN *PRAKRITI*—the *Purusha* (Spirit) has no *samsara*. But the 'Knower-of-the-Field', *Purusha*, when It identifies Itself with the 'Field' (*Prakriti*), becomes the experiencer. He identifies with the body and the senses which are the effects of *Prakriti*.

HE EXPERIENCES THE QUALITIES BORN OF *PRAKRITI*—the sensations arising out of the matter-envelopments (*Prakriti*) such as pleasure and pain, heat and cold, success and failure etc., constitute the painful shackles on the 'Knower-of-the-Field'. The destinies of Matter become the tragic experiences of the Spirit, not because they are in the Spirit, but because the Spirit unnecessarily makes an unhealthy contact, through its own identification, with the realm of sorrow.

He not only experiences the joys and sorrows in life but also develops a blind attachment to them and this is 'THE CAUSE FOR ITS BIRTH IN GOOD OR EVIL WOMBS'. "As its desire, so is its will" is a scriptural declaration of an eternal truth. While living in the world, the 'Knower-of-the-Field' experiences the pleasures and joys interpreted by the world-of-Matter and gets attached to them, and thereby develops

---

पुरुष: प्रकृतिस्थो हि भुङ्क्ते प्रकृतिजान्गुणान् ।
कारणं गुणसङ्गोऽस्य सदसद्योनिजन्मसु ॥ २२ ॥

puruṣaḥ prakṛtistho hi prakṛtijānguṇān
kāraṇaṁ guṇasaṅgo'sya sadasadyonijanmasu 22.

* "*Purusha, Jiva, Kshetrajna, Bhoktri* are all synonymous terms" – Sankara. *Anandagiri*, in his footnotes on this statement of Shankara adds: "The three last terms (*Jiva, Kshetrajna, Bhoktri*) are respectively hinted at to show that the *Purusha*, here referred to is not the *Paramatman* or the Inner Self, but it is the intelligent Principle (*Chetana*) in a conditioned being."

residual impressions (*vasanas*), and takes to conductive fields where it can eke out its cherished satisfaction through vivid experiences.

When the Spirit, eternally joyous and infinitely all-full, orders a 'Field' and identifies Itself with it, It becomes the 'Knower-of-the-Field' (*Purusha*). The Spirit, as *Purusha*, suffers its own delusory *samsara*, because, having entered the field in its pre-occupation with the world-of-objects, and in its clinging attachment to the 'Field', it looks, *as though* it has forgotten its own nature divine. Thus, 'ignorance' (*avidya*), and attachment to the 'Field', are the two causes because of which the *Satchidananda* seems to have become the miserable, bemoaning, tearful, *samsarin*. The rediscovery of the Self and the awakening to our spiritual nature would, therefore, be through the path of (a) detachment from the 'Field' and (b) experience of the Real-Knowledge; *vairagya* and *viveka* are the means for regaining the God in ourselves.

THE LORD CONTINUES TO TEACH US DIRECTLY WHAT THAT 'SAVING KNOWLEDGE' IS:

23. *The supreme PURUSHA in this body is also called the Spectator, the Permitter, the Supporter, the Enjoyer, the great Lord and the Supreme Self.*

As a contrast to this deluded sorrowful 'Knower-of-the-Field', *Purusha*, there is the Pure Spirit uncontaminated by the 'Field'. The moon in the bucket is the reflected moon and for every reflection that dances with the conditionings of the reflecting surface, there must be a real object. The reflection

---

उपद्रष्टानुमन्ता च भर्ता भोक्ता महेश्वरः ।
परमात्मेति चाप्युक्तो देहेऽस्मिन्पुरुषः परः ॥ २३ ॥

upadraṣṭānumantā ca bhartā bhoktā maheśvaraḥ
paramātmeti cāpyykto dehe'sminpuraṣaḥ paraḥ 23.

is always conditioned by the reflecting medium while the object reflected is never contaminated by the changes in the reflecting surface. It is completely independent of all conditions.

The 'Knower-of-the-Field' is 'Knowledge' or Consciousness conditioned by the 'Field'. Naturally, therefore, there must be 'Knowledge', in fact totally unconditioned, which appears conditioned, when it plays in the realm of its conditionings.

Thus, in this stanza, Krishna mentions for the purpose of his scientific analysis and investigation, two *Purushas*; the LOWER, which has already been described and indicated as the 'Knower-of-the-Field', and the HIGHER, which is the Pure Consciousness unconditioned by *Prakriti*. Both of them function in this body.

This Supreme Self is indicated in terms of what it looks like in Its silent manifestations when the matter equipments (*Prakriti*) are weaving their different patterns. When an individual is completely deluded and totally unconscious of the Self, in and through him the Infinite Divine expresses Himself as though He is only an 'onlooker' (*Upadrashtaa*); that is to say when a person murders an innocent victim, the Infinite All-powerful Lord expresses through that criminal's vehicle only as a silent spectator of it all (*Upadrashtaa*). When proper actions are undertaken, the mind is in a quiet mood. When the individual actor is not totally forgetful of the Self, in such a being, the Supreme expresses Himself as a 'Permitter' (*Anumantaa*).

When proper actions are done with full consciousness of the Self and in a spirit of total surrender to the Lord, the Lord is the 'fulfiller' (*Bhartaa*). Such actions are filled with success by His grace. He aids, as it were, the fulfilment of all such activities.

When, with entire dedication unto Him the individual is completely a *Yoga-Yuktah*, in his Eternal Conscious nature (*Nitya Chaitanya Swaroopa*), It seems to be the very 'enjoyer' (*Bhoktaa*). The stanza concludes by saying that the great Ishwara, the Lord of Lords (*Maheshwara*) is the Higher Self in this very same body.

HOW DOES THE ONE WHO KNOWS THE HIGHER SELF, UNCONDITIONED BY THE 'FIELD', REACT IN LIFE?

24. *He who thus knows the PURUSHA and PRAKRITI together with the qualities, in whatsoever condition he may be, he is not born again.*

In the previous stanza, it was said that the identification of the *Purusha* with the 'Field' is the cause for Its participation in the tragic destinies of matter. If there were no contact, indeed, the *Purusha* would have been a mere observer of the world-of-matter without undergoing any suffering or sorrow. But the Infinite plays the part of the miserable mortal because of Its delusory imagination that It is directly conditioned by the mental and intellectual reactions.

These vivid experiences in the world outside leave impressions, to fulfill which the *Purusha* is born again and again either in the higher wombs of enjoyment or to suffer among the lower manifestations.

य एवं वेत्ति पुरुषं प्रकृतिं च गुणैः सह ।
सर्वथा वर्तमानोऽपि न स भूयोऽभिजायते ॥ २४ ॥
ya evaṁ vetti puruṣaṁ prakṛtiṁ ca guṇaiḥ saha
sarvathā vartamāno'pi na sa bhūyo'bhijāyate 24.

But he who has realised in himself: (a) that which is the Matter; (b) that which is the Spirit; (c) how the Spirit, deluded by its own preoccupations, gets identified with Matter and behaves as 'Knower-of-the-Field' and also (d) the mysteries of the *gunas*, under the influences of which, the equipments function -- he becomes a man-of-Wisdom.

To know a thing we must stand apart from it, whereas, if we are ourselves involved in any situation, we cannot understand it fully. To realise at once the world-of-objects, the instruments of contact and their behaviour and qualities, is to stand apart from them all – and in that state, the Spirit, the Substratum, is realised. Thus, to recognise our own nature to be the absolute, infinite, Pure Consciousness, is to end all misconceptions (*avidya*). To one who has thus ended all *avidya*, there is no more any reason to get completely identified thereafter with the 'Field-of-Matter'. Therefore, it is said, such an individual thereafter: 'WHATEVER BE HIS CONDUCT, HE IS NOT BORN AGAIN' – that is to say, no new *vasanas* can be created in him and the old *vasanas* functioning in the mind and intellect have dropped away from him, since, in him there is no more any false egocentric contact with the world outside.

It is the *Jiva* that creates more and more *vasanas* in the mind, and through the mind, according to the *vasanas*, it projects different equipments and different worlds of experiences in order to eke out its desired quota of joy and pain. That, in such an individual of Self-realisation no *vasanas* are left over, that he will be in the embodiment only so long as this body exists, that the Knower of *Brahman* himself becomes the Infinite, and that all the accumulated reactions of his actions perish at the moment of Self-realisation – are all truths declared by the *Upanishads*.

NOW THERE ARE SEVERAL 'PATHS' TO SELF KNOWLEDGE AND THEY ARE MENTIONED HERE AS FOLLOWS:

> 25. *Some, by meditation, behold the Self in the Self by the Self; others by the 'YOGA-OF-KNOWLEDGE' (by SANKHYA YOGA); and others by KARMA YOGA.*

This realisation of the Self in its pure nature, undressed of all its matter envelopments, is the final goal of spiritual seeking and there are more 'paths' than one, prescribed for this Divine Achievement. Integration of a human personality must start from the point where an individual finds himself to be at present. No education can be successful unless the students are given graded lessons.

A totally disintegrated individual must also be given a 'path' which he can easily follow with his restless equipment. Spiritual unfoldment cannot take place merely because of an intellectual appreciation of the theory of Perfection. Evolution actually takes place only when a corresponding change in the very subjective life is accomplished. Therefore, an active, intelligent and enthusiastic participation of the seeker in controlling, directing, and re-educating his thought-life is necessary -- hence the difficulty in accomplishing inward spiritual unfoldment in every individual.

The great spiritual scientists of the past, discovering ways of evolving the entire mankind, consisting of different types,

---

ध्यानेनात्मनि पश्यन्ति केचिदात्मानमात्मना ।
अन्ये सांख्येन योगेन कर्मयोगेन चापरे ॥ २५ ॥

dhyānenetmani paśyanti kecidātmānmātmanee
anye sāṅkhyena yogena karmayogena cāpare 25.

evolved various 'roads' – all converging at the same goal. Each 'path' is the fittest for the one who is walking it. No 'path' can be said to be nobler than the other. In a pharmacy there are different medicines; each one serves a definite type of patient and the medicine prescribed for a given disease is the fittest medicine for that patient as long as his ailment continues.

The difference between the various seekers is the difference in their mental equanimity and intellectual equipoise. The lesser 'paths' are mainly meant for purifying the inner equipments, and when the mind becomes steady and concentrated, when the intellect is redeemed from its wasteful habits of wrong imaginations, then the equipments are ready for Higher flights through the path-of-Meditation.

BY MEDITATION SOME BEHOLD THE SELF – MEDITATION* CONSISTS IN 'WITHDRAWING, BY CONCENTRATION, ALL THE SENSE-ORGANS AWAY FROM THEIR RESPECTIVE SENSE-OBJECTS INTO THE MIND, AND THEN WITHDRAWING THE MIND INTO THE INNER INTELLIGENCE, AND THEN CONTEMPLATING UPON THE HIGHEST'. It is a continuous and unbroken thought-flow, like a stream of flowing oil. In order to pursue this path, naturally, the individual must have a dynamic head and heart -- both least disturbed by their own subjective defects.

To 'behold' does not mean to see the Self as an object, which would then mean something against the very assertion of the scriptures. The Self is the 'SUBJECT'; therefore, the term 'behold' is used to mean only 'an inward experience of a total subjective rediscovery.' The experience is so vivid that it is comparable to our unshakable knowledge of anything after we have once objectively SEEN it ourselves.

* According to Shri Shankara Bhagawatpada.

BY THE SELF IN THE SELF—The subjective experience of the very core of our personality is accomplished by the head in the pure heart. Sankara explains the portion: "By meditation, the *Yogins* behold the Self, the Pure consciousness, in the Self (*Buddhi*), by the Self -- by their own intelligence, that is, by the *Antahkarana*, refined by *Dhyana*". All sincere attempts at meditation with steady mind-and-intellect, and the steady mental-pool of thought, with its passions and *vasanas* subsided, and to an extent, even eliminated, provide a clear reflected surface in which the glory of the Self is seen reflected, and this is recognised intuitively.

One may wonder why the same term is used to indicate the instrument of recognition (*Atmani*), the subject recognising it (*Atmana*) and object recognised (*Atmanam*). The reason is, in the final realisation, it is experienced that the intellect, the mind, the seeker and the sought are all in fact nothing other than the One Self. The waves, the ripples, the foam are all nothing but the ocean. The dreamer, the dreamt, and the dream are all nothing but the waker's own mind. In this sense, in our scriptural lore, we often find the term '*Atman*' used to indicate even our outer personalities brought about by our identifications with the matter-envelopments in us.

This 'path' of quietening the mind, steadying the intellect and with an integrated mind-and-intellect, contemplating steadily upon the transcendental Self, is not a 'path' that is available to all, as it calls for certain mental and intellectual perfections which are not commonly seen in everyone. Those who have these qualifications are considered as the highest type of aspirants. The seekers of the best type – who have developed in themselves a sufficient detachment (*vairagya*) from the sense objects, and a ready discrimination (*viveka*) to distinguish the permanent from the impermanent – alone can steadily walk this Highest 'path'.

OTHERS BY THE 'PATH' OF *SANKHYA YOGA*—In the case of those who have not the required amount of steadiness in mind and intellect -- not because of any lack of aspiration but for want of right understanding of the Goal (*viveka*) – their sense of detachment (*vairagya*) waxes and wanes. Naturally, sometimes they are good at meditation, and at other times, they experience a tremendous amount of restlessness and agitation. For such seekers, the only remedy is a more intelligent and enthusiastic study of the *shastras*. The term '*Sankhya*' means 'the sequence of logical thought through which we reach a definite philosophical conclusion, unassailable by any doubts any more'.

This deep study and reflection (*vichara*), since it provides the seeker with a better understanding of the text, and therefore, a deeper conviction of the goal, will discover for him a very healthy and steady self-application and a divine equipoise in his meditation. Since *vichara* can safely take us to the *Yoga*-of-Meditation, and help us to establish ourselves therein, the very study of the *shastra* and reflections upon it (*Sankhya*) is here called as *Yoga*. That which ultimately takes one to *Yoga* is called *Yoga*, just as a vehicle is often named by the destination to which it is proceeding. '9.30 is Delhi departure time' does not mean that at that time the capital-city is packing off from our country and going to the Nicobar Islands! It only shows that a train will be leaving for Delhi at that scheduled time. The seekers, who are not fit for steadily following the 'path' of deep meditation, are advised to steam themselves up by the *Sankhya Yoga*: by the 'path' of deep study and reflection.

OTHERS AGAIN BY *KARMA YOGA*—there is still another type of seekers for whom even study of the *shastra* and effective reflections upon it becomes almost impossible because their inward personality is so much poisoned by the existing hosts of sensuous *vasanas*. They are in a state of mental agitation in which no dynamic and effective meditation is possible. The instrument is not fit for it, and therefore, the selfless activity in a spirit of *Yajna* is prescribed for them. When the path-of-Action is pursued for a time, as contemplated in the *Geeta* (III-30), the existing *vasanas* exhaust themselves and more and more quietude and tranquillity are experienced by the seeker. A mind, thus steadied, is fit for delving into the deeper significances of the *mantras*, and when the conviction of the goal is intensified in the individual, as a result of these reflections, his meditation gathers a momentum and a dash which can take him to the Highest Peaks.

In short, seekers with the noblest *Sattvic* qualities need only practice meditation; seekers of a slight *Sattvic* temperament with a large share of agitations, must develop the 'creative stillness' in themselves through the path-of-Perfection; those who are suffering from the worst mental oscillations, created by the *vasana*-disturbances, must through *Karma Yoga*, develop *Sattvic* traits, nurture and nourish them through reflection, and thus gain enough *Sattvic* dynamism and steady meditation.

IN THAT CASE, WHAT 'PATH' IS PRESCRIBED FOR THOSE WHO ARE COMPLETELY STEEPED IN '*TAMAS*' -- MENTAL AND INTELLECTUAL INERTIA? THEY TOO ARE SERVED. LISTEN:

26. *Others also, not knowing this, worship, having heard of it from others; they too, cross beyond death, if they would regard what they have heard as their Supreme Refuge.*

अन्ये त्वेवमजानन्तः श्रुत्वान्येभ्य उपासते ।
तेऽपि चातितरन्त्येव मृत्युं श्रुतिपरायणाः ॥ २६ ॥

anye tvevamajānantaḥ śrutvānyebhya upāsate
te'pi cātitarantyeva mṛtyuṁ śrutiparāyaṇāḥ 26.

The previous verse defines the 'path' that is conducive to the best type of students (*uttama adhikarins*), and to the mediocres and weaklings (*madhyama adhikarins*). To the low class of aspirants too, the *Geeta-Acharya* prescribes a 'path'.

HAVING HEARD FROM OTHERS—there are some who are not capable of meditation. They have neither the intellectual capacity to follow the logical thoughts in any philosophy, nor the necessary inward equipoise to follow the path-of-Action. Even such people can evolve, though they are ignorant of the 'paths', if only they worship the Principle of Truth on the strength of what they have heard from others.

THEY TOO GO BEYOND DEATH—If such people are capable of constantly worshipping the Lord as they have been instructed by other devotees, they too can transcend the finite life of plurality and experience the Changeless. The term 'DEATH' here, should not be understood as meaning only the phenomenon of death that happens to a personality expressed in a body. The term is used in its all-embracing significance, indicating in its expanse of meaning, the total principle-of-change as experienced by any given human mind-and-intellect. As long as we identify with the body – gross, subtle or causal -- the experiences can only be of the finite. To experience the Infinite, is to enter the status of Immortality, beyond the thralldom of death.

This verse, while explaining the efficacy of prayer and worship, even when unscientifically performed, is not recommending that all the methods are equally efficient, but it is only emphasizing the idea that, in the practice of worship, correct knowledge shall surely provide a better guarantee of success. If seekers can progress upon the authority of others' instructions, when they are themselves ignorant, Sankara exclaims: 'How much more so then can they progress, who can independently appreciate the *shastra* texts and discriminate?'

THROUGH THESE VARIOUS 'PATHS' AVAILABLE, WHAT EXACTLY IS THE ULTIMATE GOAL TO BE REALISED? LISTEN:

27. *Wherever any being is born, the unmoving or the moving, know you, O best of the Bharatas, that it is from the union between the 'Field' and the 'Knower-of-the-Field'.*

All things in the world that are born -- both the world of inert matter (unmoving) and the world of conscious beings (moving) -- arise neither from the 'Field' (*Prakriti*) nor from the 'Knower-of-the-Field' (*Purusha*). The source is from the marriage of *Prakriti* and *Purusha*. This combination of Matter and Spirit is not an accomplished union but is only a mutual super-imposition.

In every super-imposition, a delusion is recognised upon a substratum: the ghost in the post. Not only the form and all attributes of the ghost come to be projected upon the post, but the post also lends its existence to the non-existent ghost. As a result of their mutual exchange, we find that the non-existent ghost comes to exist in our experience, while the existing post becomes a non-existent ghost with illusions of physical limbs and ghastly behaviour. This process, which is a trick of the human mind, is called mutual super-imposition. In the Pure Consciousness there is no Field-of-Matter. The Field-of-Matter has neither existence, nor sentiency. But the spirit plays in the 'Field' (*Prakriti*), and becomes the 'Knower-of-the-Field' (*Purusha*), and when this *Purusha* works in *Prakriti* the combination breeds the entire phenomenal Universe constituted of the moving and the unmoving.

यावत्संजायते किंचित्सत्त्वं स्थावरजङ्गमम् ।
क्षेत्रक्षेत्रज्ञसंयोगात्तद्विद्धि भरतर्षभ ॥ २७ ॥

yāvatsañjāyate kiñcitsattvaṁ sthāvarajaṅgamam
kṣetrakṣetrajñasaṁyogāttadviddhi bharatarṣabha 27.

When, through careful discrimination, we successfully discover this play in ourselves, the vision of plurality recedes and we understand that the ultimate Truth is the substratum on which both *Prakriti* and *Purusha* play.

Ordinarily, I am a quiet man. But sometimes my heart's passion is endless. When I identify myself with the passion in my heart, I play in the world as the passionate man and perform deeds for which I myself might later on regret! Now in this example, the regret, and the regretting person, the passion and passionate entity—all of them revel in me. They all belong to me but I am not they! Yet, when I identify myself with them, I become the perpetrator of the regrettable actions and the passionate actor in me comes to brood over what has happened, and so it suffers. Similarly, the Self contains matter possibilities – the Self being *Paripoorna*. To project matter and to identify with it, is to become the *Purusha*, and the *Purusha*, maintaining Itself in the Field-of-Matter so projected, becomes the source of the entire *samsara*. To analyse closely with discrimination, to detach courageously with vitality, to carefully and heroically live as an observer of all that is happening within, not allowing ourselves to be misled by our own imaginations – is the method of realising the Perfection in ourselves.

THIS SELF, WHICH IS THE SUBSTRATUM OF A GIVEN *'PURUSHA'* AND *'PRAKRITI'*, IS ITSELF THE ONE SELF EVERYWHERE AS INDICATED BELOW:

28. *He sees, who sees the Supreme Lord existing equally in all beings, the unperishing within the perishing.*

समं सर्वेषु भूतेषु तिष्ठन्तं परमेश्वरम् ।
विनश्यत्स्वविनश्यन्तं यः पश्यति स पश्यति ॥ २८ ॥

samaṁ sarveṣū bhuteṣu tiṣṭhantaṁ parameśvaram
vinaśyatsvavinaśyantam yaḥ paśyati sa paśyati 28.

HE SEES, WHO SEES THE SUPREME LORD—The Supreme Lord (*Parameshwara*), on whom the 'Field' and the 'Knower-of-the-Field' play the game of delusory identification and consequently suffer the endless sorrows of *samsara*, is the Eternal Principle of Pure Existence. The one factor that binds all the waves of the ocean together, that EXISTS in all waves and SUPPORTS the entire self-destroying and mutually procreating play of the waves, is the ocean. Similarly, the Substratum that supports all is the Supreme Lord 'remaining the same in all beings'.

THE UNDYING IN THE DYING—to a superficial observer, the world is a field of perpetual change, a constant death. Nothing remains the same even for a moment. Things change themselves and naturally, their relationships with each other also change. This welter of change is what we observe in the world of perceptions, in the realm of feelings and in the field of thoughts. In terms of this world-of-plurality, and its ever-changing nature, the Absolute Truth is indicated as the Changeless Platform upon which these changes are staged.

Everything in the phenomenal world is subject to modifications such as birth, growth, disease, decay and death. The entire chain of modifications starts with birth; that which is born alone can grow, and ultimately passing through the various changes, reach the final change in 'death'. When the Supreme Lord is indicated here as the 'Deathless', all other modifications are also denied in Him. This Changeless Consciousness, that supports all changes, is the undying Principle that illumines the ever-dying world-of-plurality. The gold in the ornaments is the only constant factor; out of the same bar of gold various types of ornaments are made and destroyed to make other types of ornaments. The shape and the size of the ornaments change, but the changeless factor in them all, is pure gold.

He who is capable of recognising the Supreme Lord (*Parameshwara*), who revels everywhere as the Pure Spirit, in all names and forms, who changes not, while the outer equipments change; he alone is the one who sees what is really to be seen. In this stanza, the term 'seeing' is a phrase borrowed from our ordinary world-of-perception, but used in the sense of 'spiritual Self-realisation'.

The physical world is recognised and perceived through our physical equipments. Emotions in the world around us are felt and recognised by our minds. The world of ideas is comprehended by our intellect. The Spiritual substratum in the Universe of beings and things can be apprehended only from the spiritual centre in ourselves. Just as the EYES cannot see THOUGHTS, so too the equipments of perceptions, feelings and thoughts cannot recognise the Spirit that is subtler than them, and It lies transcending all of them.

HE ALONE SEES WHO SEES THIS—this is a very powerful and direct assertion. Everybody sees, but not the Real. Wrong perceptions indicate maladjustments in the instruments of perception. Hallucinations and illusions, false imaginations and delusory projections of the mind veil the reality of the thing observed. Therefore, here the *Yogeshwara* asserts that he who recognises this harmony of the one Truth, this thread of Reality, which holds all experiences together, which is one in all beings, experiences the Truth to be realised in the world. Others see, and yet do not see; he alone sees who realises this Supreme Lord, which is the Imperishable.

TO EULOGISE THE RIGHT KNOWLEDGE BY INDICATING THE RESULT OF ITS POSSESSION, THE LORD CONTINUES:

29. *Indeed, he who sees the same Lord everywhere equally dwelling, destroys not the Self by the Self; therefore, he goes to the Highest Goal.*

Vedanta preaches not so much the negation of the world, as the reevaluation of things, beings and happenings constituting the world. Generally we perceive our own pet ideas and emotions, coloured by our unsteady understanding and changing emotions. To see the world, not through these equipments, but with the clear eye of wisdom, is to recognise perfection and bliss, divinity and sanctity in the very drab and dreary world of today, amidst its very sorrows and ugliness. Erroneous perception of the Reality, through maladjusted equipments, is the perception of the world, which, in its turn is throttling the individual perceiving it.

When the Pure Consciousness looks upon Itself through the refracting medium of matter envelopments, It perceives, as it were, a world-of-plurality, and the pluralistic world grins and dances, whistles, shrieks and howls – ever ugly, stinking and sweating – according to the maddening changes that take place in the very equipments (FIELD) through which the ego (KNOWER-OF-THE-FIELD) happens to gaze. To rediscover the spiritual Reality, the Supreme Lord, in and through this horrid welter of change and sorrow is to end all our agitations and unprofitable aims and exertions, 'FOR HE SEES THE LORD DWELLING IN EVERY PLACE ALIKE'. Such an individual, in his own experienced wisdom, no more suffers from sorrow or fear. When the post is realised, the dread created by the ghost is ended.

समं पश्यन्हि सर्वत्र समवस्थितमीश्वरम् ।
न हिनस्त्यात्मनात्मानं ततो याति परां गतिम् ॥ २९ ॥

samaṁ paśyahi sarvatra samavasthitamīśvaram
na hinastyātmanātmānaṁ tato yāti parāṁ gatim 29.

HE DESTROYS NOT THE SELF BY THE SELF—Earlier the Lord has explained when exactly the self becomes the enemy of the Self (VI-5 & 6). Whenever the lower egocentric individuality is not available for sure guidance by the Higher Principle of Wisdom in ourselves, the lower becomes our enemy. When a vehicle is no more under our control, it will cease to be of any service to us and becomes, as it were, an engine of destruction. Similarly, when the lower in us is not available for the guidance of the Higher, the former turns out to be an enemy of the latter. And in an individual who recognises and experiences the one *Parameshwara* that revels everywhere, the lower cannot fight against or shadow any longer the glory of the Higher.

THEREFORE HE GOES TO THE HIGHEST GOAL—The true nature of the Self remains undiscovered due to the non-apprehension of Reality (*ajnana*), or due to the mis-apprehension (*mithya jnana*) arising out of the non-apprehension. The non-apprehension of the one *Parameshwara* everywhere, makes an individual act in the world in a way which renders him incapable of appreciating the glory of the Self in all other living beings. Thus, he becomes a source of sorrow to the community of living beings around him. The nonapprehension (*ajnana*) creates a veil because of which, not only do we not recognise the one Eternal Divine everywhere, but we also identify ourselves with the body and the mind, and behave as though they alone are real; in consequence, sensuality, materialistic pursuits, and selfish satisfactions become the only worthwhile objects or pursuits in our life, which we destroy for ourselves and others. The state an individual gains when both these, non-apprehension (*ajnana*) and mis-apprehension (*mithya-jnana*) are ended, is that

Absolute experience, the experience of the Highest Goal, and therefore, 'he goes to the highest'.

INDIVIDUALS ACT DIFFERENTLY, AND THEREFORE, THE *PARAMESHWARA*, PLAYING BEHIND EACH INDIVIDUAL MUST BE A SEPARATE SELF. TO CONTRADICT THIS CONCEPT OF PLURALITY IN THE SELF, IT IS SAID:

30. *He sees, who sees that all actions are performed by PRAKRITI alone, and that the Self is actionless.*

If a caravan of motor vehicles, manufactured by different companies, with different horsepowers, at different periods of history, is put on the road, the performance of each vehicle will be unique. We cannot conclude therefrom that the petrol in each vehicle is of different typical potencies. The same electrical energy illumines different electric bulbs, manifesting different intensities of incandescence at different points. The electricity is one; the petrol is one; and yet the performance of the cars and the light manifested in the bulbs are different from equipment to equipment because of the very quality of the equipments. This analogy can explain the wonderful idea expressed in this stanza.

PRAKRITI ALONE PERFORMS ALL ACTIONS—Matter is the equipment that orders the types of action that should manifest. If the mind is bad, the life expressed through it will also be bad. All actions are according to the types of desires entertained by the intellect. Thus, in the presence of Spirit, the 'equipments' (*Prakriti*) function, and the Self (*Atman*), functioning in the 'Field', called the 'Knower-of-the-

---

प्रकृत्यैव च कर्माणि क्रियमाणानि सर्वशः ।
यः पश्यति तथात्मानमकर्तारं स पश्यति ॥ ३० ॥
prakṛtyaiva ca karmāṇi kriyamāṇāni sarvaśaḥ
yaḥ paśyati tathātmānamartāraṁ sa paśyati 30.

Field' (*Purusha*), acts in the world outside. When the 'Knower-of-the-Field' leaves the 'Field', there is no more any activity in the 'Field', nor is there any activity for the Self Itself.

THE SELF IS ACTIONLESS (NOT ACTING)—The Self is all-pervading, perfect and, as such, there is no desire in It. And where desires have ended, actions are impossible. In the Infinite, there is no action, and the very many reasons as to why there is no action in the Self, will be described presently (XIII-32).

He who is capable of recognising how his own vehicles function and realising that the Self in him is ever actionless, is alone the right perceiver, who is recognising and experiencing the 'IMPERISHABLE AMIDST THE PERISHABLE'. 'HE SEES WHO SEES'.* The manifestations of individuals are different from person to person because of the differences in the composition and make-up of the various equipments (*upadhis*), and, when they are destroyed, all differences merge to express the one Infinite experience, the Supreme Lord.

WHILE EXPLAINING THE SELF, AS THE SOURCE-OF-ALL-BEINGS, THE LORD INDICATES THE STATE OF A MAN WHO CAN DECLARE THAT HE HAS HAD FULL EXPERIENCE OF THE INFINITE ONE:

31. *When he (man) sees the whole variety-of-beings, as resting in the One, and spreading forth from That (One) alone, he then becomes BRAHMAN.*

यदा भूतपृथग्भावमेकस्थमनुपश्यति ।
तत एव च विस्तारं ब्रह्म संपद्यते तदा ॥ ३१ ॥

yadā bhūtapṛthagbhāvamekasthamanupaśyati
tata eva ca vistāraṁ brahma sampadyate tadā 31.

* "Let him know that *Maya* is *Prakriti* and that the great Lord is the possessor of *Maya*" *Shwetaashwatara Upanishad* – IV-10

A scientific investigation is complete only when the phenomenon intellectually analysed, is applied physically and brought within the limits of our observation.

When one has understood that the atoms are the physical units of matter, one must also realise at once that these atoms in different combinations of numbers and patterns create the world of infinite forms and qualities. Similarly, to know that the Self is the Ultimate Truth behind the names and forms, is, in itself, only a partial knowledge. The complete understanding of Life can arise only when we, at once, understand how from the Self the endless multiplicity of names and forms rise up and spread to become the Universe.

Just as in our understanding we can comprehend all the waves as inherent in the ocean, so too, a man of right understanding can recognise 'THE SEPARATE EXISTENCE OF ALL BEINGS IN THE ONE'. Once having understood the ocean, we do realise how the numberless waves rise from that one ocean; so too a man of right understanding also realises 'THE EXPANSION OF PLURALITY FROM THAT ONE ALONE'. Such moments of complete understanding, wherein the man-of-Wisdom experiences the One Self within and without –enveloping and embracing, penetrating and nourishing not only the depthless and the measureless Infinite, but also the superficial world of pluralistic names and forms -- are the sacred moments when he has 'BECOME *BRAHMAN*'.

The Self alone can recognise the Self. He who is recognising the one homogeneous Self, he who is experiencing that the Consciousness in him is one with the homogeneous-mass, Consciousness everywhere, and he who also understands how on his coming into the body awareness, the world-of-plurality throws the mantle of its magic upon the fair face of the Infinite and makes It look ugly with all its perishable names and forms -- such a person is of 'True Wisdom' and 'Right Perception'. At that moment, he has himself transcended his own equipments and has come to identify himself with the One-Consciousness-everywhere.

IF THE ONE SELF BE THE SELF IN ALL BODIES, THEN IT MUST BE NECESSARILY ACTING AND EARNING THE REACTIONS - *VASANAS*. TO PROVE THE FALLACY OF SUCH A CONCLUSION IT IS SAID:

32. *Being without beginning, and being devoid of qualities, the Supreme Self, the Imperishable, though dwelling in the body, O Kaunteya, neither acts, nor is tainted.*

Even though by Its touch It thrills the matter equipments into various activities, the fact that the Spirit is actionless is emphasised by the scriptures, and this is not an idea so easy for early students of *Vedanta* to understand. Therefore, the *Upanishads* have taken great pains to make us understand that the All-full Infinite, being One-without-a-second in its All-pervasiveness, has nothing to accomplish for Itself. Earlier we have discussed in the *Geeta*: 'it is Nature that acts' (V-14). This Spirit, identifying Itself with 'Field' (*Prakriti*), becomes the 'Knower-of-the-Field' (*Purusha*) and it is this 'individualised ego' that acts and accomplishes.

Here we are given some logical reasons why the Infinite Consciousness, 'THOUGH DWELLING IN THE BODY, NEITHER ACTS, NOR IS TAINTED'. When the local Judge, Shri Gopal Rao, condemns a murderer to be hanged, the Judge is not considered as having committed a murder; the

---

अनादित्वान्निर्गुणत्वात्परमात्मायमव्ययः ।
शरीरस्थोऽपि कौन्तेय न करोति न लिप्यते ॥ ३२ ॥

anāditvānnirguṇatvātparamātmāyamavyayaḥ
śarīrastho'pi kaunteya na karoti na lipyate 32.

individuality in the Judge can gain no taint. Shri Gopal Rao in the chair acts as the Sessions Judge and it is the Judge who has passed the death sentence.

HAVING NO BEGINNING—that which has a cause alone has a beginning. 'No beginning', means 'no cause'. Truth being 'that from which everything comes', it is the Uncaused Cause for all that has been created. That which owes its existence to a CAUSE becomes itself an EFFECT, and every EFFECT is nothing other than its CAUSE 'which has undergone a change'. All effects are thus changeable and things that are subject to change must necessarily perish.

HAVING NO QUALITY—That which has no change cannot have any quality since that which has qualities is a substance and all substances are perishable. The Imperishable Infinite, THE CAUSE for everything, Itself caused by nothing, must, therefore, be without any quality.

THIS SUPREME SELF, IMPERISHABLE—The Uncaused Cause for the entire world of phenomena, the *Paramatman*, which is devoid of qualities, must necessarily be, by its own logic, 'Imperishable'. The process-of-change, happening in the properties and to the qualities of a thing, is the phenomenon of its decay. That which is Changeless cannot perish. And that which has no quality cannot change!

Therefore, the Beginningless, the Qualityless, the Imperishable Supreme Self, though living in the physical structure, and thrilling the inner matter-field around each embodied creature into the play of life, does not, in Itself, and by Itself, act.

This is one of the subtle concepts in *Vedanta* which lesser intellects must find rather difficult to grasp. This is a well-recognised difficult portion in the *Vedantic* literature. But a little effort at reflection can clear the confusions and remove all the difficulties.

HERE THE LORD GIVES SOME PARALLEL EXAMPLES TO ILLUSTRATE THE ACTIONLESSNESS OF THE SELF AND ALSO THE QUALITYLESSNESS OF THE SPIRIT IN ESSENCE, IN SPITE OF THE DISCORDANT AND DEVILISH ACTIVITIES OF MATTER AROUND IT:

33. *As the all-pervading ether is not tainted, because of its subtlety, so too the Self, seated everywhere in the body, is not tainted.*

AS THE ALL-PERVADING *AKASHA* (SPACE) IS NEVER SOILED—Space is an example we can take to indicate the relationship of Spirit with Matter. *Akasha* means 'that which gives accommodation to things'. In short, it is the concept of pure Space. It is the subtlest of all gross elements, and since greater subtlety implies greater pervasiveness, Space pervades everything that is grosser than it. A subtler thing cannot be conditioned by a grosser factor – the stonewalls do not a prison make, nor iron bars a cage, for the thoughts of the captive, being subtler than the stone walls and iron bars, can penetrate them – *Akasha* is the subtlest of all.

Space, being subtle, it allows everything to remain in it, yet, nothing that it contains can contaminate it. The Supreme Self, which is the very cause for the *Akasha* itself, and therefore, subtler than it, 'IT PERVADES ALL: NOTHING PERVADES IT'... It cannot be contaminated by anything that exists or happens in the world-of-plurality.

यथा सर्वगतं सौक्ष्म्यादाकाशं नोपलिप्यते ।
सर्वत्रावस्थितो देहे तथात्मा नोपलिप्यते ॥ ३३ ॥
yathā sarvagataṁ saukṣmyādākāśaṁ nopalipyate
sarvatrāvasthito dehe tathātmā noplipyate 33.

Murders committed in the dream cannot soil the hands of the waker! The bloody garb of the ghost cannot leave its marks on the post. The mirage waters cannot wet even a grain of sand in the desert. These are examples of hallucinations, or delusory super-impositions. The world of plurality being nothing but misapprehensions of Reality arising out of the non-apprehension of the Real, the realm-of-matter (*Prakriti*) and its activities cannot contaminate and soil the Perfect and the Eternal.

THE SELF, THOUGH IT PERMEATES AND PERVADES THE WHOLE BODY, IS NOT SOILED, JUST AS SPACE CANNOT BE DIRTIED BY ALL THE AMOUNT OF FILTH THAT IT MAY ACCOMODATE IN ITSELF. THEN WHAT EXACTLY IS THE SPIRIT'S FUNCTION IN THE BODY? LISTEN:

34. *Just as the one Sun illumines the whole world, so also the Lord-of-the-Field (Param-Atman) illumines the whole 'Field', O Bharata.*

Here is one of the most striking examples in our scriptural literature, given to us by the Divine Charioteer. It conveys to our intellectual comprehension the exact relationship of the Consciousness, the Eternal Principle-of-Life, with reference to the various worlds-of-matter and their expressions. Just as the one Sun illumines the entire Universe from afar and at all times, so too the Consciousness merely illumines the world-of- objects, the body, the mind, and the intellect.

यथा प्रकाशयत्येक: कृत्स्नं लोकमिमं रवि: ।
क्षेत्रं क्षेत्री तथा कृत्स्नं प्रकाशयति भारत ॥ ३४ ॥

yathā prakāśayatyekaḥ kṛtsnaṁ lokamimaṁ raviḥ
kṣetraṁ kṣatrī tathā prakāśayati bhārata 34.

Though generally in our everyday talks we attribute the ACTIVITY of lighting up the world to the Sun, we find on close examination that we cannot attribute any such ACTIVITY to the Sun. An action is that which has a beginning and an end and it is generally undertaken to fulfil a deep desire, or a silent purpose. The Sun does not illumine the world in this sense of the term. On the other hand, 'light' itself is the nature of the Sun, and in its presence everything gets illumined. Similarly, Consciousness is of the nature of awareness and in Its presence, everything becomes known – illumined.

In the world there is only one Sun and it illumines everything, good and bad, the vicious and the virtuous, the ugly and the beautiful. And yet the Sun is not sullied by the ugly, the vicious and the bad, nor is it blessed by the good, the virtuous or the beautiful. So too, in our inner life, the Ever-perfect and Joyous Consciousness functions through the equipments and illumines them, but It never gets contaminated by the sins of the mind, by the perversions of the intellect, or by the crimes of the physical body. It only illumines. This illumination of the Self, playing upon our thoughts and emotions, gets splashed to form the ever-changing patterns of the multiple individuals, with their ever-changing behaviours.

THIS DOCTRINE OF THE 'FIELD' AND THE 'KNOWER-OF-THE-FIELD', BOTH PLAYING IN THE SUPREME, DISCUSSED IN THIS CHAPTER IS CONCLUDED IN THE FOLLOWING STANZA:

35. *They who, with their eye-of-wisdom come to know the distinction between the 'Field' and the 'Knower-of-the-Field', and of the liberation from the 'PRAKRITI of the being', go to the Supreme.*

After explaining that the Spirit is the Illuminator, and that, being the Illuminator, It cannot be tainted by the qualities of the illumined, here Lord Krishna directly advocates that man's life is fulfilled only when he, in his subtle discrimination, successfully meditates upon and realises the constitution, behaviour and relationship among the 'Field', the 'Knower-of-the-Field', and the 'Supreme Self' in himself. This can be done only with a well-integrated instrument, a combination of a fully developed head-and-heart, which alone can apprehend the Invisible, Imperishable One. The faculty that comes to experience this divine infinitude is often termed as 'intuition', and in the language of the Hindu *shastras*, it is called the 'Eye-of-Wisdom'.

They who realise and perceive the nature and the essential distinction between the 'Field', the 'Knower-of-the-Field' and the 'Supreme', and thus come to experience the non-existence of the 'Field' (*Prakriti* or *Avidya* or *Avyakta*), and, therefore, the 'Knower-of-the-Field' (the individuality, the ego, the *samsarin*, the limited), theirs is the Knowledge Absolute. The 'Field' is the material-cause, which has no existence apart from mere imaginations and hallucinations. Non-apprehension of Reality gives rise to misapprehensions of It. To realise the non-existence of the very material-cause is to live the Infinite Nature of the Supreme Self in ourselves, as ourselves.

क्षेत्रक्षेत्रज्ञयोरेवमन्तरं ज्ञानचक्षुषा ।
भूतप्रकृतिमोक्षं च ये विदुर्यान्ति ते परम् ॥ ३५ ॥

kṣetrakṣetrajñayorevamantaraṁ jñānacakṣuṣā
bhūtaprakṛtimokṣaṁ ca ye viduryānti te param 35.

Thus, in the UPANISHAD of the glorious Bhagawad Geeta, in the Science of the Eternal, in the scripture of YOGA, in the dialogue between Sri Krishna and Arjuna, the thirteenth discourse ends entitled:

The Field and the Knower-of-the-Field

This is one of the most brilliant chapters in the *Geeta* which gives us a direct subjective method of meditating upon and realising the Imperishable and the Eternal in ourselves. To wake up from our dream is to end all the sorrows that we might have suffered in the dream state of Consciousness. There is no traffic between the frontiers that clearly mark out the worlds of waking, dreaming and the deep-sleep. In the same way, the Knower-of-the-Field suffers the sorrows and the imperfections of the 'Field' but when through analysis the 'Knower-of-the-Field' understands its own real nature apart from the 'Field', it rediscovers its own Divine Nature and, in this awakening, the dream that it saw as the 'Knower-of-the-Field', ends.

The plurality and the sorrows are all the tearful details in the dream-plot. To rediscover Pure Awareness and to realise that it is the Self, which, dressed up in the 'Field', becomes the agitated 'Knower-of-the-Field' – is to know all that is to be known. In the entire *Geeta*, we fail to come across a clearer and more direct indication of Reality.

Om Om Om Om Om

ॐ तत्सदिति श्रीमद् भगवद् गीतासूपनिषत्सु ब्रह्मविद्यायां
योगशास्त्रे श्रीकृष्णार्जुनसंवादे क्षेत्रक्षेत्रज्ञविभागयोगो नाम
त्रयोदशोऽध्यायः

Oṁ tatsaditi śrīmadbhagavadgītāsū ūpaniṣatsu brahmavidyāyāṁ yogaśāstre śrī kṛṣṇārjuna saṁvāde kṣetrakṣetrajñavibhāgyogo nāma trayodaśo'dhyāyaḥ.

XIV

The Gunas – (The Three Moods)
Introduction

WE have been told so far that the Spirit, functioning through Matter, brings forth the expression of an individual who lives his experiences in the world. It is very well known to students of science that the world-of-Matter is the same everywhere. The minerals, the liquids and the gases -- each true to its own properties, is the same everywhere. The spiritual teachers of all times have uniformly declared that the vitalising principle in Matter is the Spirit, and this Spirit is universally the same everywhere. It is all-pervading and eternally dynamic. In short, we are told that when the One Truth expresses through a world-of-Matter, which is also homogeneously the same – the varieties that constitute the Universe arise – obviously, this contains in itself an uncompromising paradox.

The above idea, expounded exhaustively in the previous chapter, does not provide us with any explanation for the innumerable varieties that we meet with in the world. There are evident distinctions in nature between the kingdom of plant and that of animal, and the world of man. Even within each species we observe a variety of specimens; no two species express the same features, either physical or mental. There is no explanation for the endless varieties, if we accept the idea that the One Spirit, enveloped in the same Matter, could produce such a heterogeneous multiplicity.

The explanation for the observed variety of experiences in life has been indicated in haste in the earlier chapter. (XIII-22). "The *Purusha,* seated in Matter, experiences the *gunas* born of Matter." This, no doubt, gives us a truly scientific explanation as to why the same Spirit, when expressed through Matter, manifests Itself differently from expression to expression.

When the same Ganges water is poured into a hundred different bottles, each one will look different from the other, not because the waters are different but because of the shape and colour of each bottle. They are but qualities of the bottles, belonging to the glass-material of the bottles, and when the same sacred water is seen through the coloured bottles, the properties of the bottles get superimposed upon the contents; the blue-water, the yellow-water, the red-water, the green-water etc. Similarly, the One Eternal Principle expresses Itself in the various matter equipments as different individuals, even though the elements that constitute Matter are one and the same everywhere – due to the '*gunas* born of *Prakriti*'.

The term *guna,* used in the dialectics of the *Geeta,* indicates not the 'properties' of a material but the 'attitude' with which the mind functions. The psychological being in every one of us comes under the influence of three different 'climatic conditions' prevalent in our bosom. These three are called the *gunas:* Unactivity (*sattva*), Activity (*rajas*) and Inactivity (*tamas*).

These three, in different proportions, influence the mental and the intellectual calibre of every individual and these influences provide the distinct flavour in each personality. All three are always present in every bosom, but from man to man their proportion slightly differs; hence the distinct aroma in the character, conduct and behaviour of each individual.

The *Geeta,* being a discourse upon the science of Self-perfection, has to be extremely logical in the development of the theme. We have been watching how, from chapter to chapter, the theme has been evolving, very systematically.

Ideas hinted at in a previous chapter are taken up one by one in the following chapters for a thorough treatment and an exhaustive investigation. Dozens of fresh, regulated ideas are supplied at the right time to facilitate perfect digestion and right assimilation for the student's understanding. In the context of the theme-development in *Geeta*, this is the most appropriate occasion when the seeker must know precisely what are the nature and behaviour of these *gunas*. In the exhaustive discussions in this chapter we are introduced to each one of these *gunas*.

The three *gunas* function within each one of us, and therefore, each seeker must know the art of subjectively diagnosing them in himself. Diagnosis is generally accomplished through the observation of symptoms manifest in the patient. Symptomatic treatment is one of the methods of medical treatment. In this chapter, certain symptoms are enumerated by the *Geetacharya* and they indicate the preponderance of one or the other of the *gunas* in an individual.

Thus, a careful study of the chapter provides us with the secret capacity of detecting within ourselves the most powerful tendency that rises up to rule our mental life at any given moment. A seeker, who is sensitive enough to recognise the various influences under which he is forced to function from time to time in the world outside, will be able to discard all wrong impulses, immoral tendencies, unethical urges and animal passions, and keep himself safely balanced in righteous living, in self-control and in serene purity.

This chapter is an exhaustive handbook of instructions explaining the working of the subtle body and providing us with some tips as to how we can readjust ourselves when the inner mechanism gets choked up and starts misfiring. If a man, totally ignorant of the behaviour and nature of the machine under the bonnet, were to drive a car wishing to make a long pilgrimage, he may not have a very pleasant journey if and when the engine starts misbehaving. On the other hand, if he be an experienced driver, knowing the nature and behaviour of the engine, he can immediately stop the car, open the bonnet, readjust the machine, and drive on towards the goal.

Many a seeker ends his brilliant and promising spiritual career because, on his way to self-perfection, he develops 'engine trouble', and, not knowing why his mind behaves in the peculiar fashion, he gets victimised by lust or passion and suffers from the sorrows of his spiritual fall. Knowledge of this chapter assures us of a steady progress on our path, as it introduces us to the secret methods of the mind on all occasions. This chapter is very important for all seekers.

The Blessed Lord said:

1. *I will again declare (to you) that Supreme Knowledge, the best of all knowledges, having known which, all the sages have attained Supreme Perfection after this life.*

Even a very intelligent man will need repeated consolation when he is extremely agitated by any dire emotion. He who identifies himself with his outward personality and behaves as a finite mortal, cannot, in his life of agitations and sorrows, easily comprehend and appreciate that in his essential nature, he is the Infinite, the Divine. Spiritual truths are to be constantly repeated, again and again, by the teacher, until the student's rebellious intellect apprehends them sufficiently. A mother feeding a little baby in an Indian home is a typical

---

श्रीभगवानुवाच
परं भूयः प्रवक्ष्यामि ज्ञानानां ज्ञानमुत्तमम् ।
यज्ज्ञात्वा मुनयः सर्वे परां सिद्धिमितो गताः ॥ १ ॥

śrībhagavānuvāca
paraṁ bhūyaḥ pravakṣyāmi jñānānāṁ jñānmuttamam
yajjñātvā munayaḥ sarve parāṁ siddhimito gatāḥ 1.

example; the mother will have to coax the child repeatedly until sufficient food goes into its stomach. Similarly, spiritual ideas will have to be repeated many times by the teachers until they develop into strong inward personal convictions in the student.

Therefore, the chapter opens with a declaration by the Lord, "AGAIN WILL I TELL THEE". Not that the Supreme theme has not yet been declared, but, for the purposes of elucidation and correct appreciation, repetition is unavoidable.

The theme of this chapter declared here is, "THAT SUPREME KNOWLEDGE WHICH IS BETTER THAN ALL OTHER KNOWLEDGES". This should not be taken too literally. The subject-matter of the chapter deals with the behaviour of man and the different influences that play on his subtle body in life. This cannot be the Supreme theme in philosophy. But it is declared here as the 'highest Knowledge', inasmuch as, without a correct understanding of this theme, and without self-detection and timely self-correction of the mental mechanism, it will be impossible for a seeker to walk safely the path divine.

HAVING KNOWN WHICH, ALL THE *MUNIS* HAVE ATTAINED TO THE HIGHEST PERFECTION—A precise knowledge of the *gunas*, it is claimed here, will make the pilgrimage easier for all seekers. A true and exhaustive knowledge of the 'path', the possible dangers en-route, the difficulties that might arise – these should pre-warn a pilgrim and he can undertake his journey well equipped to meet all these possible dangers. An understanding of the possible mischiefs of the mind is a healthy warning to a diligent student of spirituality, so that he can easily avoid the usual dangers, and meet his subjective problems efficiently whenever they arise in him.

Muni does not mean an old man with a beard, living in a jungle, eating roots and berries, but it means, "A man of reflection and contemplation" (*Manana Sheelavan*). Thus, an understanding of the *gunas*, their nature and their tyranny, when and how they rise up in revolt against our peaceful progress, are all preliminary information useful for all men-of-Reflection, who constantly digest and assimilate their experiences in life and thereby gain wisdom.

AFTER THIS LIFE—the attainment of Perfection is promised here, as in many *Upanishads*, AFTER THIS LIFE. Some thinkers take this declaration too literally and say that Perfection cannot be gained in this life while living here. Very efficiently and logically, Shri Shankaracharya and others break up this argument and assert, again and again, that Perfection can be gained, here and now, by any diligent seeker. According to these *Acharyas*, 'AFTER THIS LIFE' means 'at the end of our egocentric misconceptions of life'.

Even in our life, we find that the bachelor must die to become the married man; the virgin must die before she becomes a mother. In the above cases, the person is not dead but bachelorhood and virginity have ended, so that they may acquire husbandhood and motherhood. Thus, the individuals remaining the same, their status changes. Through right reflection and true understanding, our false values-of-life can end, and in the newly found 'wisdom', a life of better illumination and greater equanimity can be lived. This hatching of the 'perfect', out of its shell-like imperfections around, is achieved in the inward warmth of constant contemplation. The mind of an individual, who lives diligently with intellectual dynamism, may come under the destructive influences of any of these *gunas*, and thereby lose its serene equilibrium in contemplation. Avoid it and cent-percent success is assured. Thus knowledge of the three *gunas* and their behaviour helps indirectly every enthusiastic seeker.

THE LORD NOW PROCEEDS TO DECLARE THAT THIS 'KNOWLEDGE' DEFINITELY LEADS TO SUPREME

PERFECTION:

2. *They who, having refuge in this "Knowledge" have attained to My Being, are neither born at the time of Creation, nor are they disturbed at the time of dissolution.*

The greatness of the 'knowledge' contained in the chapter is not so much in its philosophical implications as in the benefit which is available to a seeker who diligently makes use of it. He who has realised correctly the deep significances in this chapter, can reach the state-of-Perfection; he shall "ATTAIN TO MY BEING" says the Lord.

Whenever Krishna uses the first person singular 'I' in the *Geeta* he indicates the state of spiritual Perfection. The theme of the chapter, as we have already indicated, is a thorough study of the play of the *gunas* that bind us down to the lower plane of matter identifications, and therefore, to the ego-sense. When once we get away from the *gunas* and totally stop their play in our mental life, we get redeemed from our limited sense of individuality, and instantaneously, we shall experience our Absolute Universal Nature.

The sorrows of the dream – though very true to the dreamer while he dreams – cannot affect him the moment he wakes up. The joys and sorrows belonging to one plane-of-Consciousness cannot stretch their arms to throttle us in another plane-of-Consciousness. A seeker who has, through meditation, mastered his mind and has transcended it, and therefore, has reached beyond the ordinary realms of Consciousness, cannot thereafter have any sense of finitude and the consequent material sorrows, as in his earlier days of Matter identifications. He rediscovers himself to be the

---

इदं ज्ञानमुपाश्रित्य मम साधर्म्यमागताः।
सर्गेऽपि नोपजायन्ते प्रलये न व्यथन्ति च ॥ २ ॥

idaṁ jñānamupāśritya mama sādhamrmamāgatāḥ
sarge'pi nopajāyante pralaye na vyathanti ca 2.

Omnipresent Reality, which knows neither Creation nor dissolution, in Its Absolute State.

This is indicated here; "NEITHER ARE THEY BORN AT THE TIME OF CREATION" – Creation is a trick of the mind and when we are no more expressing through the mind, and therefore, no longer conditioned by it, we cannot have the experience of any Creation. When anger conquers my mind, I experience and behave as an angry man; but when anger has receded and my mind is calmed, I can no longer continue to behave as a bad-tempered man. The tricks of the mind consist in projecting a world-of-Creation, thought by thought, and in feeling oneself irredeemably conditioned by one's own imaginations. As long as one is drowned in the mind, the storms of the bosom must necessarily toss one about. On transcending the mind, we realise the Self and its Infinite Nature, and therefore, there is no Creation; nor shall we feel ourselves as having been born.

NOR ARE THEY DISTURBED AT THE TIME OF DISSOLUTION—the sorrows of destruction are the pangs of death. While dreaming one can go through the sorrows of a dream-death, and yet, if at that time one wakes up, one will at that very moment, laugh at one's sorrows at the delusory death-pangs suffered in the dream. Having realised the Absolute Nature, thereafter in that State of Infinite Existence, one can no longer experience either the sorrows of death or the troubles of finitude.

But in order to conquer the mind, a seeker must know very clearly the tricks by which the mind generally hoodwinks him. Knowledge of the strategy of our enemies is an essential prerequisite to plan out our attacks successfully. The stanza is, therefore, right when it declares that a thorough knowledge of the *gunas* will be helpful to everyone trying to master his own mind and reach the freedom from all its moral agitations and ethical imperfections.

The following two stanzas explain how the universe is evolved by the union between spirit and matter – Spirit enveloped in Matter is the pluralistic expression of *Existence** in the world. From the inert stone to the greatest Prophet-of-Wisdom, every *existence* is but the Spirit expressing through Matter-vestures. In an earlier chapter, we have already seen very clearly how the Knower-of-the-Field working in the 'Field' and identifying himself with it, becomes the individualised 'Ego', extremely sensitive to the sorrows and tragedies, joys and successes of its environments.

THE LORD NOW PROCEEDS TO EXPLAIN, IN WHAT WAY THE MARRIAGE BETWEEN THE 'KNOWER-OF-THE-FIELD' AND THE 'FIELD' TAKES PLACE, AND HOW THE UNION COMES TO BREED OUR ENDLESS SORROWS:

3. *My womb is the great BRAHMAN (MULA PRAKRITI); in that I place the germ; from which, O Bharata, is the birth of all beings.*

MY WOMB IS THE GREAT *BRAHMAN* (*MULA PRAKRITI*)—Krishna, the Pure Consciousness, is trying to explain the 'One-Womb' from which the entire Universe has arisen. On many occasions, in our discourses, we had stopped to explain how the One-Consciousness, identifying with various layers of Matter, manifests Itself as different entities, with different potentialities. A Prime Minister is also a voter – just a single voter under the constitution of the country. But a Prime Minister's powers are a million times more than any average voter can ever hope to have. This omnipotency is

---

मम योनिर्महद्ब्रह्म तस्मिन्गर्भं दधाम्यहम् ।
संभवः सर्वभूतानां ततो भवति भारत ॥ ३ ॥

mama yonirmahadbrahma tasmingarbhaṁ dadhāmyaham
sambhavaḥ sarvabhūtānāṁ tato bhavati bhārata 3.

* Aspirations, hopes, plans, ambitions, views etc. of the average voters.

gained by his OFFICE, because the voter in him has been successful in identifying himself with the 'heart'* of the majority of voters.

The Supreme, identifying Itself with the subtle *vasanas* in an individual, becomes an individualised 'Ego'. If any one of us (as a single voter) can renounce his limited tendencies and identify himself with the total thought-life of the Universe (the total aspirations of the *Janata*), the Consciousness that identified Itself with 'total mind' (the individual who identifies himself with the majority of voters) becomes the *Ishwara* (Prime Minister).

In the stanza, in the language of *Vedanta*, it is said that the total-*vasanas* of the world, meaning the 'total-causal-body', is the 'Womb', which gets impregnated by the Lord. When life functions as the 'total-causal-body', it becomes dynamic and expresses itself as the 'total-mind-intellect' (*Hiranya-garbha*).

It has already been explained that the Light-of-Consciousness conditioned by the mind and intellect-reflected in the mental pool of thought – is the sense of ego, the individuality, manifest in each of us. The total potential factor, from which the world-of-Matter emerges, is termed as Nature - *Prakriti*. The *Prakriti* then is called the 'Great Cause' because it embraces the entire Universe which is but its effect. Again, from Nature, the entire Universe has arisen and the Universe of names and forms is nourished and fattened by the very source which has given birth to it. Therefore, the total nature is termed here, as elsewhere in *Vedanta*, as the Great (*Mahat*)-*Brahma*, the total-mind-intellect-equipments.

IN THAT, I PLACE THE GERM—this total potential Nature is the virgin 'Womb', in which, when the shaft of Consciousness penetrates, the Light-of-Awareness that consequently plays in it, is Its act of impregnation.

Thus vitalised by Life, the inert *Prakriti* becomes dynamised, grows, and manifests itself as the spectacular

Universe. Hence it is said, "FROM WHICH IS THE BIRTH OF ALL BEINGS".

Every creative action owes its origin and progress to a tendency for it in the artist. When this tendency in him becomes vibrant with a part of the life in him, it becomes potential, struggles to express itself in terms of ideas and feelings, and later on gets expressed in the particular medium of art chosen by the artist. He may express it through colours, as in painting; through songs, as in music; through stones, as in sculpture; or through words, as in literature. But a dead artist can no more express anything – even in terms of artistic ideas or thoughts. The total Universe of ideas and tendencies (*vasanas*), when graced by Life, becomes vigorous and expresses as the Universe created.

The world of *vasanas*, of ideas, of thoughts, and of actions, together constituting the total Nature, is ever controlled and directed by the *gunas*, and therefore, the three *gunas* are together called in *Vedanta* as *Maya*, the 'cause of the Universe'. *Maya*, expressed in the individual bosom, is called 'ignorance' (*avidya*). The 'ignorance' is, therefore, the microcosmic expression of *Maya*, and the total 'ignorance', in its macrocosmic expression, is *Maya*. An individualised EGO is under the control of *avidya*, while *Maya* is under the control of *Ishwara*.

We are only to remember that we have been told already in the previous chapter, viz., that the 'Field' and the Knower-of-the-Field are the two aspects of Nature (*Prakriti*), and both of them function on the same substratum, the Absolute Eternal Truth, the Lord Krishna Himself. The Supreme, functioning in the 'Field', becomes the Enjoyer-of-the-Field, and therefore, the Knower-of-the-Field, detaching from the 'Field', rediscovers himself to be the Pure-Absolute-Consciousness.

CONTINUING TO ELABORATE THIS SUBTLE RELATIONSHIP BETWEEN MATTER AND SPIRIT, AND

EXPLAINING HOW THE ABSOLUTE IS THE UNCONTAMINATED AND EVER-VITALISING PRINCIPLE IN BOTH THE 'FIELD' AND IN THE 'KNOWER-OF-THE-FIELD':

4. *Whatever forms are produced, O Kaunteya, in all the wombs whatsoever, the great BRAHMA (MULA PRAKRITI) is their womb, and I the seed-giving Father.*

IN ALL WOMBS—in the living world, infinite varieties of beings are born and continue to live, and they are replaced at every moment by millions of new births. If the whole Universe is looked at in one gaze, we find therein, seething activities of new births. Everywhere, the birth of an organism is nothing but an expression of Spirit through a given matter-envelopment. Thus viewed, every Matter particle is the 'womb', which, when dynamised by the Light-of-Consciousness," becomes a potential living being. Every expression of life is Matter containing within its bosom a tiny spark of the Spirit.

Lord Krishna, as the Supreme Consciousness, Absolute and Infinite, declares here figuratively: "I AM THE FATHER OF THE UNIVERSE", who places the sperm-of-life in the womb-of-Nature (*Prakriti*). A 'Field', in itself, has no existence without the Knower-of-the-Field vitalising it. A steam engine, minus steam, is only so much iron in that particular shape! But when steam passes through it, the engine expresses its motive force and strength, and its particular ability, locomotion. Similarly, the body-mind-intellect are only so much minerals unless Consciousness expresses Itself, through it. No doubt, a bachelor, in himself, can have no child to claim

---

सर्वयोनिषु कौन्तेय मूर्तयः संभवन्ति याः ।
तासां ब्रह्म महद्योनिरहं बीजप्रदः पिता ॥ ४ ॥

sarvayoniṣu kaunteya mūrtayaḥ sambhavanti yāḥ
tāsāṁ brahma mahadyonirahaṁ bījapradaḥ pitā 4.

as his own, however potent he may be. He has to get married and his seed is to be placed in the womb. The Spirit cannot express Itself without the Matter. These ideas are summarised in this stanza when Lord Krishna says that He is the Eternal Father, who impregnates the entire world-of-Matter and arranges the play of life on the stage of the world.

The *Geeta* happened to be declared and written long before Christ, and therefore, the Bible cannot claim, as some of us have been coaxed to believe, that the great Fatherhood of God is a fact recognised ONLY by the Christian faith. At best, we can say that it is an idea borrowed from earlier religions. The Hindus did not over-emphasise this Fatherhood of God, because, even though the idea is quite poetic, philosophically, if cannot hold much water. But as later religions found such ideas more easily digestible for the not-so-intelligent masses, they seem to have borrowed them liberally.

TAKING UP THE MAIN THEME OF THE CHAPTER, LORD KRISHNA EXPLAINS WHAT THE *'GUNAS'* ARE, AND HOW THEY BIND THE SPIRIT WITHIN MATTER TO CREATE THE INDIVIDUALISED EGO-SENSE IN US:

5. *Purity, passion, and inertia -- these qualities (GUNAS), O! Mighty-armed, born of "PRAKRITI" bind, the Indestructible, Embodied one, fast in the body.*

GUNAS BORN OF PRAKRITI—it is indeed difficult to find an adequate rendering for the word *'guna'* in English. The tradition of thought in the West has nothing equivalent to these terms, as the science of psychology in the West is even

---

सत्त्वं रजस्तम इति गुणाः प्रकृतिसंभवाः ।
निबध्नन्ति महाबाहो देहे देहिनमव्ययम् ॥ ५ ॥

sattvaṁ rajastama iti guṇāḥ prakṛtisambhavāḥ
nibadhnanti mahābāho dehe dehinamavyayam 5.

today passing through its very early childhood. The influences (*gunas*) under which the thoughts function in each bosom, will be considered by it only when analytical and experimental psychology has exhausted its observations and study.

The concept of *sattva* is rather that of perfect purity and luminosity, the opposite of 'foul-darkness' called *tamas*, and distinctly different from the 'dusky-colour' of *rajas*. We find in our literature that these *gunas* are associated with light (*sattva*), red-colour (*rajas*) and darkness (*tamas*).

The term *guna* also means 'rope', by which, the spiritual beauty of life in us is tied down to the inert and insentient Matter-vestures. In short, *gunas* are the three different influences under which every human mind has to play in such an endless variety at different moments of its changing environments.

These *gunas* are born of Matter. Produced by Nature, the 'Field', they generate a feeling of attachment, and successfully delude the indwelling Self and chain It AS IT WERE, to the cycle of birth-and-death, in a stream of constant change and pain. The *gunas* have no separate existence as attributes inherent in a substance. All that we can say is that they are as many different mental climates in which the minds behave so differently from each other, according to their given moods, governed by the predominating *gunas* at any particular moment of observation.

These *gunas*, like chords, AS IT WERE, bind the Spirit to Matter and create, in the Infinite Spirit, the painful sense of limitations and sorrows. The Infinite and All-pervading Spirit can never be contaminated by the dreamy projections of a delusory world-of-Matter. The *ghost* that emerges from a *post* cannot leave its marks on the *post*. Even after murdering a dozen people in my dream, my hands, that were dripping with blood, cannot, when I wake up, carry any bloodstains. While dreaming, no doubt, the 'dream world' of my own imaginations was real to the dreamer in me. But, on waking, the waker in me cannot have any marks left over on him from the dream. Similarly, the Eternal Life, functioning in Matter, gets, AS IT WERE, bound to the limitations and finitude of Matter and this delusory experience is continued as long as the *gunas* bind It to and entangle It in Matter.

Now it becomes evident how a clear understanding of what constitutes the *gunas* and how they bind us to Matter will provide us surely with a charter of freedom, a scheme for getting ourselves freed from the tentacles of our own imaginations.

The embodied-self, though Indestructible and Infinite, in Its identifications and attachments with the body, feels the changes in the body as Its own changes. This delusion is maintained, in each one of us, by the play of the three *gunas* in us. In the following stanzas, we have a clear enumeration of the behaviour of the mind when it comes under the influence of each of these *gunas* separately.

OF THESE THREE *GUNAS*, *"SATTVA"* IS THUS DEFINED:

6. *Of these, "SATTVA" which because of its stainlessness, is luminous and healthy, (unobstructive). It binds by (creating) attachment to 'happiness' and attachment to 'knowledge,' O sinless one.*

Nothing can be defined as such – this is an accepted fact in all sciences. No disease can be defined by itself; nor can any emotion be described as such – without explaining its symptoms and expressions. So too, no *gunas* can be defined directly. In the following stanzas we find descriptions of a mind under the

---

तत्र सत्त्वं निर्मलत्वात्प्रकाशकमनामयम् ।
सुखसङ्गेन बध्नाति ज्ञानसङ्गेन चानघ ॥ ६ ॥

tatra sattvaṁ nirmalatvātprakāśakamanāmayam
sukhasaṅgena badhnāti jñānasaṅgena cānagha 6.

influence of each of these *gunas*, by enumerating the type of emotions that are aroused in it, and its peculiar and distinct behaviours. This symptomatic description is, no doubt, more helpful to us, the seekers, because each of us can observe and analyse the types of emotions and thoughts arising in our mind-intellect equipments and determine what type of *guna* is governing us at any given time.

BECAUSE OF ITS STAINLESSNESS, SATTVA IS LUMINOUS—when *sattva* comes to dominate as the most important influence in our thought-life, because of its purity, it is ever luminous – it has neither the dull-colour of *rajas*, nor the dark impurities of *tamas*. Under the *sattva*-influence, the mind is steady, reflecting ever faithfully, the Consciousness, the Self.

FREE FROM EVIL i.e. HEALTHY—Evil tendencies must rise in the mind long before the action expressing the same is committed in the world outside; as the thought, so the actions. Thus the evil starts germinating in the mental life. We call that an evil whereby we try to satisfy the appetites of the flesh, the selfish agitations of the mind and the egocentric desires of our head. Egocentric self-gratification is the womb from which all evils are born. Such low impulses and confusions can arise only when the mind is under the influence of *rajas* and *tamas*. Therefore, what is meant here is, *sattva* is free from all evils, as it is relatively free from *rajasic* agitations or *tamasic* darkness. Though *sattva* is thus the most divine mental attitude, still it binds us and acts as a limitation on our divine nature.

SATTVA BINDS BY ATTACHMENT TO 'HAPPINESS' AND 'KNOWLEDGE'—When the mind is purified from all its agitations (*rajas*) and the intellect is cleansed of its low passions and criminal lusts (*tamas*), no doubt, the personality becomes purified, experiencing a greater share of inward peace and happiness and enjoys a greater share of subtle understanding and intellectual comprehension. But even these can create bondage on the freedom of the Absolute Self. A gold-chain, if sufficiently strong can also bind as any iron-chain. 'Goodness', though it gives us freedom from all vulgarities, can also shackle us within its own limitation! A perfect one, absolutely free, is bound neither by goodness, nor by evil.

Consciousness, the All-pervading Principle of Awareness, expressed as the Self, in each one of us, does not directly comprehend any object or idea in the world outside. What we generally understand as intelligence is the Eternal Light of Consciousness, reflected in our mind-intellect equipment. Naturally therefore, the capacity to perceive the world intelligently differs from person to person because in no two of us the inner equipments can be the same.

The reflection in a reflecting medium will depend entirely upon the cleanliness and steadiness of the medium. If the mind is clean and the intellect steady, a more efficient intelligence is manifest. Thus, whenever a given mind is in an inspiring and creative mood, it is actually intelligent and it is capable of taking longest flights into the realms of wisdom. On all such occasions of vast knowing and deep understanding, the inner equipment is under the influence of *sattva*, wherein the agitations, created by *rajas*, and the murkiness, created by *tamas*, do not express themselves.

Sattva also binds the Infinite to Matter through the attachment to 'knowledge' and 'happiness'. When once one has experienced the thrilling joys of creative thinking and the inspiring life of goodness and wisdom one gets so attached to them that one will thereafter sacrifice anything around in order to live constantly that subtle joy. A true scientist, working self-dedicatedly in his laboratory; a painter working at his canvas in his shabby studio, pale with hunger and weak with disease; a poet hunted out from society, living in public parks, seeking his own joys in his own visions and words; martyrs facing cruel persecutions; politicians suffering long years of exile; mountaineers embracing death – are all examples of how, having known the subtler thrills of a higher joy, when the bosom is inspired with *sattva*, the individual becomes as much bound with attachment to them as others are to their own material joys and possessions.

NOW THE DIAGNOSIS OF *'RAJAS'*, WHEN IT COMES TO PLAY ITS HAVOC IN THE HUMAN BOSOM:

7. *Know thou 'RAJAS' (to be) of the nature of passion, the source of thirst and attachment; it binds fast, O Kaunteya, the embodied one, by attachment to action.*

A seeker, who is striving to conquer his own mind must know all its subtle inclinations by which, again and again, his thoughts run amuck only to return and increasingly sabotage his inner personality.

KNOW *'RAJAS'* TO BE OF THE NATURE OF PASSION— where there is an onslaught of *Rajoguna* influences in the bosom, man's mind is wrecked with a hundred painful passions. Passions are the main symptoms of the working of *Rajoguna* in the psychological field. Passion expresses itself in a million different urges, desires, emotions, and feelings. Yet, all of them can fall only under two distinct categories: desires and attachments. Thus, in the *Geeta*, Lord Krishna mentions these two as the very sources from which all passions arise.

GIVES RISE TO THIRST AND ATTACHMENT—the term used in Sanskrit for 'desire' is 'thirst'. When an individual is thirsty, nothing, for the time being, is of as much importance as water, which alone can satisfy his thirst. Just as a thirsty man would struggle and suffer, wanting nothing but water to relieve his pangs, so too, a human personality thirsts for

---

रजो रागात्मकं विद्धि तृष्णासङ्गसमुद्भवम् ।
तन्निबध्नाति कौन्तेय कर्मसङ्गेन देहिनम् ॥ ७ ॥

rajo rāgātmakaṁ viddhi tṛṣṇāsaṅgasamudbhavam
tannibadhnāti kaunteya karmasaṅgena dehinam 7.

the satisfaction of every desire that burns him down. Once the desire is fulfilled, a sense of attachment comes like a vicious passion to smother down all the peace and joy of the mind. DESIRE is our mental relationship towards 'objects' which have not yet been acquired by us and ATTACHMENT is the mental slavishness binding us to the objects so acquired.

These two – DESIRE for the acquisition of things and the creation of situations which are expected to yield a certain quota of personal happiness, and the sense of clinging ATTACHMENT to things already so acquired – are the volcanoes that constantly throw up their molten lava to scorch and raze the smiling fields of life. The burning lava, that is emitted by these fiery mountains, comprising the various passions that man expresses in his sensual life, make up the strifes and struggles to acquire, to possess and to guard what is already gained.

IT BINDS FAST THE EMBODIED ONE BY ATTACHMENT TO ACTION—When once an individual has come under the influence of *rajas*, he expresses innumerable desires, and bound in his own attachments, he lives on in the world manifesting a variety of passions. Such a passionate being-goaded by his desires for things not yet acquired, and crushed under the weight and responsibility of his attachments to things that he possesses – can never keep quiet but must necessarily act on endlessly earning and spending, and yet thirsting for more and more. Anxious to have more, fearing to lose, he becomes entangled in the joys of his successes, involved in the pangs of his failures, and lives as an 'embodied-one', chained by his own actions.

Actions are born of passions. Passions arise from desires and attachments. And all these are the symptoms of the presence of the *Rajoguna*-influences upon our mind. Thus, if *sattva-guna* binds us with its own anxieties for happiness and peace, wisdom and knowledge, as has been said in the previous stanza, *Rajoguna* also seemingly binds the Infinite Self to Matter-vestures and makes It play the part of a limited being through an endless array of inexhaustible actions. Though the Self is not an agent (ACTOR), *rajas* makes It act with the idea "I AM THE DOER".

TAMAS ALSO HELPS TO BIND THE DIVINE TO THE MORTAL FLESH. HOW?

8. *But, know thou TAMAS is born of ignorance, deluding all embodied beings, it binds fast, O Bharata, by heedlessness, indolence and sleep.*

TAMAS IS BORN OF 'IGNORANCE'—under the influence of *tamas* man's intellectual capacity to discriminate between the right and wrong gets veiled and he starts acting as if under some hallucination or stupefaction. Lord Krishna says that *tamas,* in the human personality, binds it to its lower nature by providing it with endless misconceptions and miscomprehensions of the true divine purpose of life, which, naturally, forces one in that condition to live in indolence, heedless of the higher purposes. One thereafter lives ever asleep to the nobler and the diviner aspirations of life. There is no consistency of purpose, brilliance of thought, tenderness of emotion, or nobility of action in an individual who comes under the contamination of the *Tamoguna*-influences.

So far, the Lord has been systematically mentioning the symptoms which are observed in our mental life when these *gunas* pollute our inner tranquillity. These three *gunas** not only bring about different amounts of divine brilliance in a given individual but also limit the Eternal Self, in all Its

तमस्त्वज्ञानजं विद्धि मोहनं सर्वदेहिनाम् ।
प्रमादालस्यनिद्राभिस्तन्निबध्नाति भारत ॥ ८ ॥

tamastvajñānajaṁ viddhi mohana sarvadehinām
pramādālasyanidrābhistannibadhnāti bhārata 8.

* *Gunas* in Sanskrita also means 'ropes', as mentioned before.

perfection, to feel and act as though It is limited and conditioned by the matter-envelopments.

AGAIN, THE ACTIONS OF THE *'GUNAS'* IN OUR INNER WORLD ARE BRIEFLY INDICATED:

9. *SATTVA attaches to happiness, RAJAS to action, O Bharata, while TAMAS, verily, shrouding knowledge, attaches to heedlessness.*

These are the ideas that have already been described in the three stanzas; but, the *Geeta* is given out as a conversation between two individuals; a Divine man-of-Wisdom, anxious to help the other, who is an ordinary man of average intelligence.

SATTVA ATTACHES ITSELF TO HAPPINESS—An individual, who has experienced the thrills of the creative moments in life – a scientist, an artist, a poet, or for that matter any independent thinker – will not ever like to come down to the passionate world of *rajas*, or into the dark sorrows of *tamas*. *Sattva* makes us attached to the inward happiness, arising from life fully lived.

RAJAS TO ACTION—If, on the other hand, one is under the influence of *rajas*, it makes one naturally passionate with hundreds of thirsty 'desires' and deep 'attachments', and in the course of their fulfilment, one is made to sweat and toil in the fields of endless activities.

TAMAS, SHROUDING KNOWLEDGE ATTACHES ONE TO HEEDLESSNESS—when *tamas* comes to play, by its very nature, it veils right judgement, and in the resultant

---

सत्त्वं सुखे संजयति रजः कर्मणि भारत ।
ज्ञानमावृत्य तु तमः प्रमादे संजयत्युत ॥ ९ ॥

sattvaṁ sukhe sañjayati rajaḥ karmaṇi bhārata
jñānamāvṛtya tu tamaḥ pramāde sañjayatyuta 9.

indiscrimination, we get attached to wrong comprehensions. We become heedless to the calls of the Higher in us.

WHEN DO THE '*GUNAS*' PRODUCE THE EFFECTS DESCRIBED ABOVE?

10. Now SATTVA rises (prevails), O Bharata, having over-powered RAJAS and inertia (TAMAS); now RAJAS, having over-powered SATTVA and inertia; and inertia (TAMAS), having over-powered SATTVA and RAJAS.

At this level of our discussion, any intelligent student should wonder whether these *gunas* produce their effects, or act, at different times, each by turn. If they act, all at one time, do they act in perfect concord, or in mutual discord? Naturally, the Lord, in His Divine Song, anticipates this doubt, and answers it in this stanza. He explains how these *gunas* act at different times – each one of them becoming prominent and powerful for the time being.

SATTVA RISES—the stanza clearly shows that at any given moment, a human personality, if analysed, can be found to work under the influence of one predominating *guna*, wherein the other two *gunas* are not totally absent, but are only of secondary importance. When we say that one is under the influence of *sattva*, it means that *rajas* and *tamas* in him are, at that given moment, not quite prominent to contribute enough of their particular nature.

Thus, when *sattva* predominates over *rjas* and *tamas*, it produces, in that bosom, at that time, its own nature of happiness and knowledge.

रजस्तमश्चाभिभूय सत्त्वं भवति भारत ।
रजः सत्त्वं तमश्चैव तमः सत्त्वं रजस्तथा ॥ १० ॥

rajastamaścābhibhūya sattvaṁ bhavati bhārata
rajaḥ sattvaṁ tamaścaiva tamaḥ sattvaṁ rajastathā . 10

When *rajas* predominates over *sattva* and *tamas*, it expresses its own nature of passions and desires, attachments and actions.

When *tamas* predominates over *sattva* and *rajas*, it produces its own effects of shrouding knowledge and making the personality heedless of its nobler duties.

BUT HOW ARE WE TO KNOW WHEN A PARTICULAR *'GUNA'* IS PREDOMINATING OVER THE OTHER *'GUNAS'*?

11. *When, through every gate (sense) in this body, the light-of-intelligence shines, then it may be known that 'SATTVA' is predominant.*

Here follows a discussion of three stanzas, each giving us a more subjective insight into the symptoms produced by the *guna* concerned, from which we can understand, under the influence of which *guna* the personality is working at any given moment.

WHEN THROUGH EVERY GATE (SENSE) IN THIS BODY, THE LIGHT OF INTELLIGENCE SHINES—the apertures of the physical structure, through which the perceived world-of-objects enters us, are the windows-of-knowledge, the sense-organs. Through these holes, the Light-of-Awareness goes out, AS IT WERE, to illumine the various objects of the world. The Knowledge in me pouring out through the eyes becomes the power of vision and illumines for me all the forms and colours of the world. The same Eternal Awareness, through the ears, which cannot illumine form, brings within my comprehension the world of sound

---

सर्वद्वारेषु देहेऽस्मिन्प्रकाश उपजायते ।
ज्ञानं यदा तदा विद्याद्विवृद्धं सत्त्वमित्युत ॥ ११ ॥

sarvadvāreṣu dehe'sminprakāśa upajāyate
jñānaṁ yadā tadā vidyādvivṛddhaṁ sattvamityuta 11.

around me. So too, the Divine Light of Cognition beaming out through the tongue illumines the taste.

Thus, 'seven tongues of flame' shoot out from the same Fire-of-Knowledge, the Self, in us. Each beam of light, as it emerges from each window in the body, illumines one aspect of the world outside. It must be the experience of all that, while we perceive something, and efficiently illumining it, we are really in a state of *sattva*, at this moment. If there be at the time *rajas* and *tamas* in us, our perception is hampered.

If the mind is agitated by *rajas* and the intellect is veiled by *tamas*, even ordinary, efficient perceptions become almost impossible. Thus, the more often and more completely we go beyond *rajas* and *tamas*, and thereby make our bosom full of *sattva*, the more grows our capacity to observe, to analyse, to understand and to become aware of the world outside and judge it correctly.

It has already been explained that the mechanism of knowing the world outside is the intellect; and, the Consciousness, reflected in the intellect, is the Light-of-intelligence by which we illumine the world of ideas, feelings, and objects available in our life. The sunlight outside never comes directly to a room to illumine the things in the room. It is always the light of the Sun reflected on the walls that illumines a cosy room. Similarly the Light-of-Consciousness, reflected in the intellect, is the beam of light that illumines the world-of-objects. The *gunas* are the influences under which the mind and intellect live.

It is very well known that a clean and steady reflecting medium will reflect more efficiently than an unsteady, unclean surface. *Rajas* creates agitations and makes the intellect unsteady; *tamas* creates veilings and makes the intellect unclean. Naturally, the greater the proportion of *rajas* and *tamas* in a bosom, the lesser will be its quota of intelligence.

Therefore, it is highly scientific to say that, 'at the moment of knowing and comprehending the world' one's bosom is surely in its pure *sattvic*-mood.

THE CHARACTERISTIC MARKS THAT INDICATE THE PREDOMINANCE OF 'RAJAS' ARE DESCRIBED IN THE FOLLOWING:

12. *Greed, activity, undertaking of actions, restlessness longing --these arise when RAJAS is predominant, O best in the Bharata family.*

GREED, ACTIVITY, ENTERPRISE, (UNDERTAKING OF ACTIONS) UNREST (RESTLESSNESS), LONGING — Enumerating the type of thoughts and motives that rise up in a mind in which *rajas* predominates, Lord Krishna lists the following as the most important. GREED is the inexhaustible desire to appropriate the property of another, an appetite which has the tendency of growing more in volume as we satisfy it. By ACTIVITY is meant here, officially engaging oneself in matters which are not one's own. The term 'ENTERPRISE' is here used to indicate all activities motivated by extreme egoism, undertaken with the intention to fulfil and satisfy the egocentric, and therefore, the selfish desires. RESTLESSNESS is another type of experience that is lived through by a *rajasic* personality. Because of restlessness, the individual fails to enjoy quietude. The term 'UNREST' is oscillation of the mind which is defined by Shri Shankaracharya as 'Giving vent to joy, attachment', etc.

लोभ: प्रवृत्तिरारम्भ: कर्मणामशम: स्पृहा ।
रजस्येतानि जायन्ते विवृद्धे भरतर्षभ ॥ १२ ॥

lobhaḥ pravṛttirārambhaḥ karmaṇāmaśamaḥ spṛhā
rajasyetāni jāyante vivṛddhe bharatarṣabha 12.

To a large extent these three are interconnected, and each successive one can be seen to have risen from the previous tendency. Greed must make the greedy very active indeed, and, when an activity motivated by greed is undertaken, it expresses in selfish enterprises, and once a man enters such a field of selfish activities – in his anxiety for the results, in his mental agitations – he creates a set of unhealthy circumstances around him and gets dragged towards their centre, where he is led to perpetrate more and more bitter cruelties, base immoralities and bloody crimes; and his inward quietude gets completely shattered. He experiences extreme unrest. Naturally, one who is in this condition of mind, sweating and labouring in the outer fields, with a heart poisoned by *rajas,* must come under the sway of endless longings – for things not-yet-accomplished, for objects not-yet-acquired, for profits not-yet-gained.

In short, under the contagion of *rajas,* the psychological being in us gets extremely persecuted by its own restlessness which gets expressed in its endless plans, exhausting actions, agonising desires, painful longings, maddening greed and oppressive restlessness. When such an individual works in society, his sorrows do not rest with himself – they spread, like contagion, to many thousands around him.

SIMILARLY, WHEN *'TAMAS'* PRE-DOMINATES, WHAT EXACTLY ARE THE SYMPTOMS? LISTEN:

13. *Darkness, inertness, heedlessness and delusion—these arise when TAMAS is predominant, O descendant-of-Kuru.*

अप्रकाशोऽप्रवृत्तिश्च प्रमादो मोह एव च।
तमस्येतानि जायन्ते विवृद्धे कुरुनन्दन ॥ १३ ॥

aprakāśo'pravṛttiśca pramādo moha eva ca
tamasyetāni jāyante vivṛddhe kurunandana 13.

DULLNESS, INERTNESS, HEEDLESSNESS AND DELUSION—When these symptoms are recognised by an individual in himself, according to the *Geeta*, the seeker can take it that he is suffering from *tamas*. Dullness (*aprakashah*) is that condition of the intellect where it is incapable of arriving at any decision, a state when a sort of drowsiness veils the potentialities of one's intelligence and makes it impossible for one to discriminate between the right and the wrong. This condition is experienced everyday by every one of us, as sleep conquers our nature at night.

INACTION (*Apravritti*), IDLENESS—the tendency to escape all responsibilities, the sense of incapacity to undertake any endeavour and the lack of enthusiasm to strive for and achieve anything in the world – is the state of inaction explained herein. When *tamas* predominates, all ambitions are sapped. Energy is dormant; capacity is gone, and thereafter, eating and sleeping alone become the individual's main occupations in life.

The natural effect on the personality of a man who is living such a life is that, as an individual, he becomes heedless to the higher calls within himself. Nor can one be, in fact, a Ravana-like destructive criminal. Even to be bad, it needs a good amount of enthusiasm and an endless spirit of activity.

He not only becomes incapable of responding to the good or the bad in him, but also slowly sinks into delusions. He miscalculates the world around him, misinterprets his own possibilities, and always makes mistakes in determining his relationship with the world around. When thus an individual fails to understand rightly himself, the world outside, and his own right relationship with the world around him, the life becomes an error – his very existence, a sad mistake.

After thus indicating how the mind and intellect would react under the three distinct influences of s*attva*, *rajas* and *tamas*, the *Geetacharya* wants us to understand that, not only are these *gunas* effective while we live the present embodiment, but the tendencies of the mind, cultivated and developed, pursued and strengthened while living, will determine the life and condition of the individual even after death.

Life after death is a topic that does not seem to have been fully thought out in any other school of philosophy except in the exhaustive Science of Life, Hinduism. All other creeds have their own different explanations but none of them actually believes that there is no life after death. The other creeds have only dogmatic declarations regarding life after death, but they have no logical thought development regarding this topic which can be crystallised into a complete philosophy.

Earlier in the *Geeta*, we had exhaustively dealt with this topic of reincarnation. We had indicated that death is the total divorce of the subtle-body from its physical-structure. Therefore, death is the destiny of the body in me and not a tragedy of my ever-existing personality. I, as my subtle-body, move out of the present physical-structure, when I have exhausted my purpose with the present body. The subtle-body is constituted of my mind-and-intellect which is nothing but a bundle of thoughts. Even while I am living in this body, my thoughts determine my movements, both physical and subtle. Therefore, the Hindu philosophers are logical when they indicate that after death, one would still be pursuing the resultant of one's thoughts, which one had in life while acting through the body.

When I am transferred from my present station of office to another area, I can call at my bank and expect to get from them not the total amount of money I had DEPOSITED in the past, but only the BALANCE that stands to my credit. So too, the resultant of the positive and negative thoughts entertained, actions done, motives and intentions encouraged, should determine the type and texture of the thoughts in us at the moment of our leaving the physical-structure.

That the quality of our thoughts is influenced by the type of *guna* that influences our inner make up is a truth that is already known. Therefore, it is logical that the predominant *guna*, cultivated by each one of us through the life of activities and thoughts, should determine the direction and the range of the disembodied, in its flight to the beyond after its release from the body. These possibilities are explained in this section of the *Geeta*.

WHATEVER LIFE IS OBTAINED AFTER DEATH IS CAUSED BY THE QUALITY AND QUANTITY OF DESIRES AND ATTACHMENTS, AND THE NATURE AND NUMBER OF DESIRES AND ATTACHMENTS ARE DETERMINED BY THE '*GUNAS*'. THIS IS TAUGHT HERE:

14. *If the embodied one meets with death when SATTVA is predominant, then he attains to the spotless worlds of the "Knowers of the Highest".*

IF THE EMBODIED ONE MEETS WITH DEATH WHEN '*SATTVA*' IS PREDOMINANT—In the scheme of the thought-development in *Geeta*, Krishna now gives us an idea as to the direction in which the mental-equipment of a dead one will move after death. This can be, to a large extent, scientifically determined by a close and intelligent observation of his mental behaviour even during life. A doctor cannot, all of a sudden, one fine morning, start thinking of and solving a subtle architectural problem nor can an engineer overnight

---

यदा सत्त्वे प्रवृद्धे तु प्रलयं याति देहभृत् ।
तदोत्तमविदां लोकानमलान्प्रतिपद्यते ॥ १४ ॥

yadā sattve pravṛddhe tu pralayaṁ yāti dehabhṛt
tadottamavidāṁ lokānamalānpratipadyate 14.

feel inspired to write out a prescription for cancer. The doctor has trained his mind for thinking on medicines and disease and the engineer has trained himself to solve the problems of constructive destruction! At any given moment, the mind of a doctor will be thinking of medicines alone, in conformity with his education and the type of thoughts his mind is trained to entertain.

Thus, there is a continuity of thought-life in this embodiment; this year's thoughts have a continuity with our last year's thoughts; this month's thoughts are determined by the last month's thoughts; this week's thoughts are an extension of last week's thoughts; today's thoughts are continued tomorrow. And every moment is an extension of the previous moment's thoughts. If, thus, there is a continuous development and growth observable in the thought-life, in its unbroken continuity connecting the past, the present, and the future into one unbroken flow, then, there is no reason why, at the time of death, this continuity should suddenly end. Death is only another experience; it will certainly colour the thoughts that follow it – but then all experiences have been colouring all our past thoughts, and our future thoughts are being coloured by our present experiences. Therefore, the type of thoughts entertained during our lifetime should determine the type of thoughts we will entertain soon after our departure from this physical structure.

If the embodied one leaves the present physical structure –and therefore, his present environments and relationship – he should continue his thought-life. The direction in which it will make its flight is determined by the type of training it had acquired during its sojourn in its embodied state here.

If *sattva* predominates, then, HE ATTAINS TO THE

SPOTLESS REGIONS OF THE 'KNOWERS OF THE HIGHEST' – It is a concept in our Scriptures (*Agamas*) that the highest realm of abundant joy, unaffected by any excessive *Rajas* or *tamas*, is the realm of the Creator, *Brahmaloka* – supremely happy and extremely creative.

WHILE IN '*RAJAS*', IF ONE DEPARTS:

15. *Meeting death in RAJAS, he is born among those attached to action; and dying in TAMAS, he is born in the womb of the senseless.*

MEETING DEATH IN *RAJAS*, HE IS BORN AMONG THOSE ATTACHED TO ACTION—If, at the time it leaves the body, the mind is under the influence of *rajas*, it takes, according to its tendencies and desires, to fulfil them, an embodiment among those who are extremely attached to action. It means that the mind will seek and successfully discover a field where it can completely exhaust its existing tendencies.

On the other hand, if one dies, when one's mind is drowned in extreme '*tamas*', one reaches the lower realms of irrational beings such as the animal and the vegetable kingdoms.

It is a consoling philosophy, no doubt, to believe that once having come up the ladder of evolution to become man, never shall we go into the lower strata of evolution. But it is against the truth of what we observe around us. We find, in fact, that even after having been given the best set of circumstances and environments, the members of the human community are not all equally ready to make use of them and evolve in

---

रजसि प्रलयं गत्वा कर्मसङ्गिषु जायते ।
तथा प्रलीनस्तमसि मूढयोनिषु जायते ॥ १५ ॥

rajasi pralayaṁ gatvā karmasaṅgiṣu jāyate
tathā pralīnastamasi mūḍhayoniṣu jāyate 15.

their cultural status. A rich man's son, having average intelligence and a good start in life, is not always ready to make use of those conducive circumstances, but invariably, he lives a careless unhealthy life and destroys himself later on.

Having been born as rational beings, how many of us behave with discrimination? A few in society even look up to the cattle and declare that they have a nobler life and a happier existence! That is to say, to a minority of bipeds the life of the quadrupeds is of higher evolution!! And, when such an idea is entertained in the mind of an individual, the life of the cattle is no devolution to him, but is only an acquisition of something which he is thirsting for. To a teetotaller, a drinking booth is nothing but a den of sorrow and death; but, to the drunkard the same is his haven of joy and harbour of happiness.

To the *tamasic*, to be born in the animal kingdom is a wonderful chance to exhaust their appetites and to express fully their nature. Thus, philosophically viewed, we have to accept without any reservation that the *tamasic* must mentally find a complete fulfilment in animal embodiment. So they are born there to fulfil their own elected purpose.

HERE FOLLOWS A SUMMARY OF WHAT HAS BEEN TAUGHT IN THE PRECEDING FEW VERSES:

16. *The fruit of good action, they say, is SATTVIC and pure; verily, the fruit of RAJAS is pain, and the fruit of TAMAS is ignorance.*

In this stanza, Krishna, the great conversationalist, is summarizing again what he has already mentioned in the

---

कर्मण: सुकृतस्याहु: सात्त्विकं निर्मलं फलम् ।
रजसस्तु फलं दु:खमज्ञानं तमस: फलम् ॥ १६ ॥

karmaṇaḥ sukṛtasyāhuḥ sāttvikaṁ nirmalaṁ phalam
rajasastu phalaṁ duḥkhamajñānaṁ tamasaḥ phalam 16.

previous stanzas. Herein, he is indicating in brief the results gained when a psychological being lives the three *gunas* severally.

THE FRUIT OF GOOD ACTIONS, THEY SAY, IS *'SATTVIC'* AND PURE—if we carefully analyse, we shall find that thought is the father of all action. Thoughts are the seeds sown, and actions the harvest gathered. Seeds of weeds cannot but produce weeds; bad thoughts can manifest only as bad actions. And the negative actions in the outside world fatten the wrong tendencies of the mind and thus multiply the inward agitations.

It is, therefore, true in the logic of our philosophy – and extremely true in the logic of our worldly experiences too –that if one is to live a quiet, contented and cheerful life of service and devotion, of love and kindness, of mercy and compassion, and live thus a good life, certainly such a life indicates the *sattvic* nature of one's mind. And such an individual, living such a noble life, must necessarily grow in his inward purity.

It may be asked how one can start becoming good when one is already so bad at present. If actions are the expressions of thoughts, and if the existing mental nature is negative, how can we expect such an individual to bring about a change in the climatic conditions within his bosom? All religions, the world over, answer this question in their injunction and insistence that seekers of truth, devotees of the Lord, and votaries of culture-all must strive to live ethically a pure, moral, and noble life.

No doubt, disciplining the mind and changing the quality of thoughts are not easy jobs; but to change the type of actions and to discipline our external movements is relatively easy. Therefore, to practise goodness, to discipline our behaviour, to act the good Samaritan, are all the beginnings of this great scheme of self-revival. When noble action is undertaken soon it becomes a habit and this external habit of discipline tends to discipline the mind.

Hence, the insistence, in all cultures, that from childhood, elders must be respected, authority should be obeyed, lies must not be uttered, scriptures are to be read, education must be undertaken, cleanliness must be practised etc. When these are enforced upon the child, it, perhaps, takes them all as varieties of tyranny under which it is compelled to live. In the long run, however, these rules bring about unconsciously a discipline in the minds of the children.

A thrilling joy of mental serenity, a state of minimum agitation, a capacity to direct this mental strength of such a dynamic mind towards any single-pointed self-application – these are all indicated as the fruits of good actions, when the mind grows in *Sattvaguna* and purity. Passions and agitations are the impurities in the mind; bad actions increase them; good actions, by their very nature, quieten the mind and sap its passions.

THE FRUIT OF *'RAJAS'* IS PAIN—this phrase only supports our commentary on the previous one. It has already been said that *rajas* is of the nature of passion, giving rise to insatiable desires and extreme attachment, and in our attempts to fulfil them, we get drowned in a multiplicity of actions. (Stanzas 7, 12). Thus, one with a mind under the influence of *rajas*, entertains desires, and in order to pacify the stormy conditions, one is forced to act in the world outside striving to acquire, to possess, to keep, to spend, to enjoy, to save, and to preserve what has been saved. Slowly, the individual is dragged into an entombing morass of suffocating death, in a stinking pit of pain and agony. VERILY THE FRUIT OF *RAJAS* IS PAIN.

IGNORANCE IS THE FRUIT OF *'TAMAS'*—that dullness in action, heedlessness and illusion are the symptoms of *tamas* in our subtle-body, has already been indicated. Here it is said that *tamas* veils our discriminating capacity and foils our attempts at understanding and rightly judging the world of things and beings and the world of happenings around us.

Rajas breeds agitations in the mind. And *sattva* is that condition within us when the mind has least thought agitations and the intellect is clear and bright in its rational and discriminative powers. In short, *sattva* is the 'condition of dynamic quietude' which is the creative moment in man's inward nature.

AND WHAT ARISES FROM THE *'GUNAS'*?

17. *Knowledge arises from SATTVA, greed from RAJAS, heedlessness, delusion and also ignorance arise from TAMAS.*

The functions of the *gunas*, while they appear on the stage of the mind-intellect, are explained here.

FROM *SATTVA* ARISES WISDOM—It has already been explained how Pure Consciousness, of Its own accord, has nothing to illumine or understand. In the Pure, Homogeneous Self, there is nothing other than Itself for It to understand, It being the Undivided and Indivisible One Eternal Truth. Consciousness reflected in the subtle-body is the 'intelligence' by which we gain knowledge of the world outside. The knower is the Spirit conditioned by the mind-intellect. Naturally, when the mind is pure and serene, when there is the least agitation in it, the light emerging through it is steady and properly focussed. Therefore, the result of the predominant *sattva* in our mind is ultimately the rediscovery of the Self, the experience of PURE WISDOM.

GREED, FROM *'RAJAS'*—When the mind is seething with a constant eruption of desires it will be continuously in a state of agitation, and, in its natural anxiety to pacify itself, it has

---

सत्त्वात्संजायते ज्ञानं रजसो लोभ एव च ।
प्रमादमोहौ तमसो भवतोऽज्ञानमेव च ॥ १७ ॥
stvātsañjāyate jñānaṁ rajaso lobha eva ca
pramādamohau tamaso bhavato'jñānameva ca 17.

to rush out into the world to procure and fulfil its endless demands; and in doing so it expresses its greed.

HEEDLESSNESS, DELUSION AND IGNORANCE ARISE FROM *'TAMAS'*—Inertia or indolence, *tamas*, veils the intellect. The capacity to discriminate between the right and the wrong, and the ability to reject the wrong and accept the right, are the privileges of man and not the impulses of an animal. True manhood comes to manifest only when one's intellect is clean and free from all shackles of false prejudices and wrong tendencies. *Tamas* veils the capacity to perceive rightly the world outside, and it also destroys our powers of right judgement.

When anything is not properly understood it is but natural that we will misunderstand it. This misunderstanding of the world outside compels us to expect joys, which are impossible to arise from the miserable state of our imperfections. Can there be even a single cup of sweet-water in the entire expanse of the saline-waters of the ocean? In a world of change and pain, how can there be constant joy, or even one instance of perfect happiness?

And yet, he who is under the deluding effects of *tamas* in himself, miscalculates the world and expects from it these experiences, which are impossible, and in the delusion, curses the world for its imperfections!

MOREOVER:

18. *Those who are abiding in SATTVA go upwards; the RAJASIC dwell in the middle; and the TAMASIC, abiding in the function of the lowest GUNA, go downwards.*

ऊर्ध्वं गच्छन्ति सत्त्वस्था मध्ये तिष्ठन्ति राजसाः ।
जघन्यगुणवृत्तिस्था अधो गच्छन्ति तामसाः ॥ १८ ॥

ūrdhvaṁ gacchanti sattvasthā madhye tiṣṭhanti rājasāḥ
jaghanyaguṇavṛṇavṛttisthā adho gacchanti 18.

In the ladder of evolution, we can conceive of these stages of development. The lowest state of development is seen in the vegetable and the animal kingdoms. The middle stage of evolution is seen in man who has intelligence, health, and brightness. And a higher state of existence is seen in the disembodied heavenly beings. Here evolution means: 'a greater awareness of experience, a lesser amount of agitations and a sharper power of intelligence'. The yardstick used here to measure evolution is the quantity of joy or happiness, peace or bliss, experienced by the being.

No doubt, in this measurement, the stone-life is of zero evolution, inasmuch as it has no awareness at all of the world. The plant-life comes next, wherein Consciousness has dimly started expressing Itself. In the animal kingdom, this Awareness has become clearer and more vivid. Of the animals, man is, no doubt, the greatest being with the fullest Consciousness and the sharpest intellect. But, man also has his own limitations, and functions only within a limited field of time and space. The ample possibilities reached when once these limitations of man are broken down are indicated as the greatest state of existence enjoyed by beings of a still higher evolution, and they are called the 'Denizens of Heaven'.

Every double-storeyed house must also have its staircase. Invariably, after climbing a few steps, there is a landing from which we turn and climb up the rest of the stairs to reach the rooms on the first floor. Those who are standing on the lower flight of steps are considered of a lower evolution. Those who are standing on the landing are of the middle type and those who are standing on the top-flights are of the highest evolution. The vegetable and the animal kingdoms stand on the lower rungs. Man stands on the landing and the Higher Beings on the upper flights of steps.

Remember, none of them has reached upstairs to enjoy the comforts of its halls and rooms. Those who are standing on the landing have the freedom either to go up or to go down. If this picture has come into our mind, we have, to a large extent, understood the concept of evolution as conceived by Hindu-Philosophy, wherein 'the evolution of a specimen is always measured by the degree of Consciousness unveiled through Matter in the given subject under observation'.

THE *SATTVA*-ABIDING GO UPWARDS—Those who are living a pure life of discrimination, clear thinking, right judgement and self-discipline, cultivate more and more *sattva* in themselves. When the mind is thus kept in quietude, at once creative and dynamic, it evolves upwards.

THE *RAJASIC* DWELL IN THE MIDDLE—Those who are of *rajasic* nature, with all their desires and agitations, ambitions and achievements, again and again manifest as men until they acquire the required purity.

THE *TAMASIC* GO DOWNWARDS—Those who are revelling in misconceptions, heedless of the higher calls in themselves, deluded by their own lust and passion, existing in a state of drowsiness and inertness, devolve themselves into the lower natures.

The stanza is only summarising the ideas expressed earlier, when Krishna discussed the effects of the *gunas* even in the continuity of existence after death. But where then is the release? That even *sattva* binds us with our attachment to knowledge and happiness has been already explained. Then when can I be free? All these three, *sattva, rajas* and *tamas*, are *gunas* meaning 'ropes', that bind us down to the flesh and its sorrows, the world and its imperfections, the mind and its agitations, the intellect and its throbbings. When is man free to enjoy the Godhood, as a being totally released from all his contacts with the pluralistic world and from all his subtle attachments to it?

So far we were told at length of the nature of the *gunas*, of the symptoms from which the most predominating *guna* in us can be diagnosed, of their reactions in our life, and of how they affect our future, etc. We were told that the predominant *gunas* in us is the heritage which we gather from our past and the present is coloured by it and the future again is determined by the play of these *gunas*. All these are but explanations of the causes of bondage – a sense of bondage rooted in illusion, arising from the fact that the Self in us gets identified with the Matter-vestures around it.

The experience of the finite world, the misery of the jerks, the sorrows of its imperfections, the tragedies of its disappointments – all together constitute the *samsara* of the EGO which is nothing other than the Infinite Self (*Purusha*), expressing through Matter (*Prakriti*), and identifying with it. Release can be had only when we transcend all the *gunas*.

A patient is suffering from high temperature, excruciating headache and back pain. All three are symptoms of his illness. When the fever is down the patient is still suffering. We can say the patient has fully recovered, not when these three symptoms have ended, but only when the patient has also regained his old health and energy. Similarly, the three *gunas* may be present in each of us, in different proportions, but the true release comes not only when all chains have been snapped – meaning all the *gunas* are transcended – but when we are also established in the Spiritual Experience.

This process of escaping from the subjective shackles on our psychological and intellectual nature is called liberation or *Moksha*. Bound by their own limitations, the greater possibilities in us are now idling away in our own bosoms. To redeem them from their prison-houses of confusions and pains, agitations and sorrows, passions and lust, are all that spirituality seeks.

TO DESCRIBE THE PATH OF LIBERATION AND EXPLAIN *'MOKSHA'* GAINED, FROM A RIGHT JUDGEMENT OF THE WORLD OUTSIDE, THE LORD SAYS:

19. *When the Seer beholds no agent other than the GUNAS and knows him who is higher than the GUNAS, he attains to My Being.*

The thought that was developed so far has indeed painted a miserable picture of the Spirit inescapably entangled in the three *gunas*. A student of the *Geeta* would, at this stage, perhaps, feel despaired at a false idea that there may be no escape at all for him. One who is standing in a running train is himself constantly on the move even though he is standing motionless! As long as he is travelling on the train, the movement of the train is also his movement. But the moment he alights and stands on the platform the train alone moves, and not he. So too, the Spirit identifying Itself with, and therefore, riding on the mind-intellect equipment, dances to the moods of the mind determined by the three *gunas*. To stand apart from the mind by ending all our identifications with it, is to get complete freedom from the thraldom of our thought entanglements.

WHEN THE SEER BEHOLDS—This art of disentangling ourselves from our own thought-processes within, is the very art of meditation. A meditator, who is capable of doing so, will BEHOLD, EXPERIENCE SUBJECTIVELY, the state of Pure

---

नान्यं गुणेभ्यः कर्तारं यदा द्रष्टानुपश्यति ।
गुणेभ्यश्च परं वेत्ति मद्भावं सोऽधिगच्छति ॥ १९ ॥

nānyaṁ guṇebhyaḥ kartāraṁ yadā draṣṭānupaśyati
guṇebhyaśca paraṁ vetti madbhāvaṁ so'dhigacchati 19.

Knowledge, uncontaminated by the dance of the thoughts. It is called 'seeing', not in the sense one is seeing a table or a chair; God cannot be seen; He is not an OBJECT of our perception, or feeling, or thought. He is the SUBJECT, that PERCEIVES through us, that FEELS in us and that THINKS with us. But here the word 'behold' is used only to indicate that the subjective experience shall be so total, so complete and so convincing, as when we have actually SEEN an object – that afterwards there can be no more any speculations about such an experience! Having seen a thing, no man can ever have any doubt regarding the appearance of the thing he has seen.

NO AGENT OTHER THAN THE *GUNAS*—The experiencer of the Self not only realises himself to be the Infinite but also understands that his ego, which was previously claiming to be the agent in all his activities, was none other than these *gunas* themselves. *Gunas* govern and direct the entire thought-life at all times in every one of us and, therefore, *gunas*, here means the very SUBTLE-BODY. When we say 'a crowded assembly of intelligence' we mean intelligent men. Similarly, please note carefully, *gunas* here means the MINDS of individuals of distinct and differing temperaments.

AND KNOWS HIM WHO IS HIGHER THAN THE *GUNAS*—The mind cannot function of its own accord, nor can it perceive by itself its feelings, it being a by-product of inert matter. Consciousness which functions in and through the mind, making it brilliant and dynamic must be a principle that is other than the mind. If a bucket of water looks like molten silver, it must have borrowed the brilliance from the Sun or the moon, for it to shine forth. Water in itself has no brilliance. Now, if the reflection dances or breaks up, it must be because of the nature of the water in the bucket and not because the Sun itself is dancing in the sky! The Consciousness reflecting in the mind is the 'agent', the individualised ego (*jiva*) in us, who suffers the sense of self-shattering.

He who has understood that he is not 'the reflection in his own mind' but that which is reflected therein – something other than the mind and therefore something higher than the *gunas* –he is the one who has escaped forever the shackles of all limitations, the tears of all sorrows and the sighs of all disappointments.

HE ATTAINS TO MY BEING—An individual who has thus transcended his own mind and intellect and has positively rediscovered himself to be that which was lending to his own mind the capacity to delude himself, that Man-of-Wisdom becomes the Self. Lord Krishna is not to be confused with Shri Krishna, the son of Devaki, or the Divine Flute-player of Vrindavana. He is talking here as the Life in every one of us and each student of the *Geeta* must understand that his own life is talking to the confused ego within himself.

A WAKER creates sorrowful situations in himself and comes to fear and weep, lose and gain, mourn and smile in his dream. All his joys and sorrows belong to the 'dreamer' in himself. When awake, the dream and the dream-sorrows end, and the 'dreamer' himself becomes the 'waker'. If, to the 'dreamer' in his sorrows, the waking-consciousness were to manifest and advise, it would have repeated this stanza to the 'dreamer': "When you, the dreamer, behold no agent other than the dreaming mind and know in yourself THAT which is higher than the dreaming mind, you shall attain to My being – the waking consciousness."

Similarly here, Krishna, the manifested God-Consciousness is explaining to man that his egocentric life and activities, its sorrows and joys, achievements and despairs -- all belong to the waker-dreamer-sleeper-personality and on transcending them all, he shall really AWAKE to the Truth, and there BECOME one with It. A dreamer, on waking, cannot still remain a 'dreamer' but must himself become the 'waker'. Similarly,

Spirit entangled in Matter is man and, man disentangled from its Matter identifications not only rediscovers but also becomes the Spirit; ATTAINS TO MY BEING.

NOW THE LORD PROCEEDS TO TEACH HOW ONE CAN ATTAIN THIS GREAT GOAL:

20. *The embodied-one having crossed beyond these three GUNAS out of which the body is evolved, is freed from birth, death, decay, and pain, and attains to Immortality.*

So long as you stand near the open oven in the kitchen, you must necessarily feel the heat of the fire and the smoke in the atmosphere. To walk out of the kitchen is to escape both these inconveniences because heat and smoke are the properties of fire in the oven and not the qualities of the atmosphere. In burning summer, out in your courtyard, there is both heat and glare, to escape which, you have only to walk into the shelter of your room. So too, identifying ourselves with the *gunas* and thus playing in the mental and intellectual zones, we suffer the imperfections and sorrows of an ordinary life. But when these are transcended we shall no more be under the tyranny of these sorrows. Finitude and agitations, mortality and pangs, change and sorrow are not in the Perfect, Immortal, and Changeless Self.

HAVING CROSSED THE THREE *'GUNAS'* OUT OF WHICH THE BODY IS EVOLVED—The three *gunas* are the expressions of 'ignorance' or NESCIENCE, which constitutes

---

गुणानेतानतीत्य त्रीन्देही देहसमुद्भवान् ।
जन्ममृत्युजरादुःखैर्विमुक्तोऽमृतमश्नुते ॥ २० ॥

guṇānetānatītya trīndehī dehasamudbhavān
janmamṛtyujarāduḥkhairvimukto'mṛtamaśnute 20.

the very causal-body. We are experiencing the pure causal-body in our deep-sleep, and this is nothing other than the *gunas*. They emerge from the causal-body to express themselves first as the subtle-body, expressing as qualities of our thoughts and feelings, and again as the gross-body to express themselves into good, bad, or indifferent actions.

If the art in me is to be expressed in colours, I need the canvas and the brushes. If I am a musician, I need musical instruments and accompaniments to express my art. Each artist employs appropriate instruments to express himself. A violin in the hands of a painter, and a brush with colour and canvas in the hands of a musician are both useless because they are not the media of expression for them. If my thoughts are dull and animalistic, it would be sorrow for me to bear the physical body of man. Thus, each body-plant, animal or man – is the exact instrument given for the full expression of its subtle-body. And the nature and quality of the subtle-body are determined by the texture of the causal-body, consisting of the *gunas*.

It is, therefore, evident that, those who have gone beyond the *gunas*, are no more under the tragedies of the subtle and the causal bodies.

THE EMBODIED ONE IS FREED FROM BIRTH, DEATH, DECAY AND PAIN—As we said earlier, the heat and smoke are the qualities of the fire in the oven and as long as we are near the oven, we suffer from these hardships. Matter changes forever and these changes have been systematised into definite stages. They are common to all bodies everywhere. These stages are birth, growth, decay, disease, and death. These five stages are common to all. Each one is a packet of pain; birth is painful, growth is agonizing, decay is disturbing, disease is tyrannical and death is terrible indeed!

But all these sorrows are only the sorrows of Matter and not of the Consciousness that illumines them. One, who has realised himself to be the Awareness, transcends all these sorrows. The Sun may illumine floods, famine, war, pestilence, funerals, marriages and a million varieties of happenings, and yet, none of them is IN the Sun. Similarly, the Consciousness in us illumines the various changes in our matter-envelopments, but they do not appertain to the Spirit. Therefore, he who has realised himself to be the Spirit, goes beyond all these struggles.

AND ATTAINS TO IMMORTALITY—Not only does the man of realisation experience the absence of sorrow but he also lives the positive joy of perfection. This is indicated by this phrase. In deep-sleep, a man in his sick bed forgets his pain; the disappointed one escapes his disappointment; the hungry no more feels his hunger; and the sad is no longer sorrowful. But, thereby, the illness is not cured, the disappointment is not removed, the hunger is not satisfied, the sorrow is not mitigated. Sleep is a temporary truce with the existing world of sorrows within. On waking, the sorrows too return; but the State of Bliss experienced at the moment of realisation of the Self is not a mere temporary cessation of sorrows of life, but it is a vivid experience of the Changeless, Infinite Nature. Hence it is said here that one experiences the State of Immortality even while living in this very same embodiment.

It is, indeed, a rare experience to be a God-man upon the earth. What then are the marks of such a liberated soul, so that we may understand him and also recognise this State in ourselves? How will he conduct himself in society and what exactly will be the relationship of such a Master living the God-experience, with the world outside?

ARJUNA GETS AN OCCASION FOR ASKING THESE QUESTIONS REGARDING THE NATURE AND BEHAVIOUR OF SUCH A GOD-MAN:

Arjuna said:

21. *What are the marks of him who has crossed over the three GUNAS, O Lord? What is his conduct, and how does he go beyond these three GUNAS?*

The *Geeta* is written in a conversational style, to remove the tedium unavoidable in the early studies of any philosophy, and to make it more entertaining. In this conversation between the Lord of Perfect Knowledge and the mortal of extreme delusion, Vyasa, the poet, has evidently not forgotten the human element in his philosophical preoccupation. In any Hall-of-Knowledge, the questions of Arjuna sound like some childish inquisitiveness, the play of some intellectual pranks. The patience with which the Lord answers all the questions of the lesser types of intellect, clearly indicates the duties of a true *Brahmana* in answering exhaustively all the questions raised by the sceptic, nay even by the non-believers.

Even though we are blessed by such a healthy tradition

अर्जुन उवाच
कैर्लिङ्गैस्त्रीन्गुणानेतानतीतो भवति प्रभो ।
किमाचारः कथं चैतांस्त्रीन्गुणानतिवर्तते ॥ २१ ॥

arjuna uvāca
kairliṅgaistrīnguṇānetānatīto bhavati prabho
kimācāraḥ kathaṁ caitāṁstrīnguṇānativartate 21.

in our literature, somehow, a cruel spirit of secrecy has come to rob this healthy spirit from our glorious culture. Philosophical ideas putrefy when they are not properly ventilated. Every disciple has the full freedom to seek, first of all, to understand properly the logic of the philosophy. Understanding alone can give rise to a true appreciation, and unless we appreciate an idea, we will never be able to live it in our day-to-day life. The Hindu philosophy is a way-of-life, and therefore, it is essentially to be lived.

Arjuna asks here three definite questions: (1) What are the marks by which a man who has gone beyond the influences of these three *gunas* can be recognised? (2) what would be, in that state-of-Perfection, his relationship with the world outside and how is his behaviour among us who are still under the persecutions of the three *gunas*? And lastly, (3) how does such a man-of-Perfection conquer his inner confusions and entanglements and attain spiritual glory?

THE LORD PROCEEDS TO ANSWER ALL THESE QUESTIONS IN THE FOLLOWING STANZAS. FIRST, HE ENUMERATES THE CHARACTERISTIC MARKS BY WHICH WE CAN RECOGNISE ONE WHO HAS CROSSED THE

THREE *GUNAS*:

The Blessed Lord said:

22. *Light, activity, and delusion, when present, O Pandava, he hates not, nor longs for them when absent.*

In answering the first question of Arjuna, the Lord tries to explain how the man of right understanding does not hate the effects of the three *gunas* when they are clearly present in his inner life; nor does he long for them when they have disappeared. Equanimity is the essence of perfection and a man-of-Knowledge is ever in perfect balance. He craves for nothing, nor does he strive to acquire anything new. To have and not to have – both are equal to him, because he is beyond both, living a life of inward peace which is totally independent of all environments.

LIGHT, ACTIVITY AND DELUSION, WHEN PRESENT, HE HATES NOT—The three terms LIGHT, ACTIVITY and DELUSION are the effects of their respective causes, the predominance of *'sattva'*, of *'rajas'* and of *'tamas'*. The three *gunas* are indicated here by their effects. Their presence within him, does not create in him either any special attachment nor any particular aversion. Whether his mind and intellect are under the influence of *rajas* or *tamas*, even when he feels agitated or deluded, he is not in the least affected by them, and therefore, he hates them not. It is only in the absence of Self-Knowledge, that one hates them.

He, who has risen above the *gunas*, is unaffected when

श्रीभगवानुवाच
प्रकाशं च प्रवृत्तिं च मोहमेव च पाण्डव ।
न द्वेष्टि संप्रवृत्तानि न निवृत्तानि काङ्क्षति ॥ २२ ॥

śrībhagavānuvāca
prakāśaṁ ca prakṛttiṁ ca mohameva ca pāṇaṛava
na dveṣṭi sampravṛttāni na nivṛttāni kāṅkṣati 22.

they appear in his mind. No doubt, a man who is *sattvic* develops an attachment for its essential peace and serenity, its thrills and joys, and he hates when this inward joy is disturbed by agitations (*rajas*) or by dullness (*tamas*).

NOR LONGS FOR THEM WHEN ABSENT—Not only has he no particular attachment for them, but also, he is not at all worried by their absence, because he has risen much above these three *gunas*, and they, together or severally, have nothing to offer him which he has not already gained! To a millionaire, it is immaterial whether or not he gets, by chance, a 25-paise coin on the roadside. He may stoop down and pick it up but he would never congratulate himself for it as much as a poor man would do under the same circumstances.

Thus, he who has extricated himself from the entanglements of the *gunas*, has transcended fully the equipments of the mind and intellect and lives the infinite joys of the Self. To him, the ordinary vehicles of joys and sorrows can no more supply any special quota of experiences. Ever steady and balanced, he lives beyond all storms and clouds in a realm of unbroken peace and brilliance. He conquers the world of Pure Awareness – attains the state of Godhood.

NOW FOLLOWS AN EXHAUSTIVE ANALYSIS AND VIVID DESCRIPTION OF THE CONDUCT OF HIM WHO HAS RISEN ABOVE THE '*GUNAS*':

23. *He who, seated like one unconcerned, is not moved by the 'GUNAS,' who, knowing that the 'GUNAS' operate, is self-centred and swerves not ...*

In this section, constituted of the following three verses,

उदासीनवदासीनो गुणैर्यो न विचाल्यते ।
गुणा वर्तन्त इत्येव योऽवतिष्ठति नेङ्गते ॥ २३ ॥

udāsīnavadāsīno guṇairyo na vicālyate
guṇā vartanta yo'vatiṣṭhati neṅgate 23.

we have an exhaustive picture of the relationship that a man-of-Perfection maintains with the things and beings of the world. A man's culture may be a false mask. Many of us can act the part of God as long as the situations around us are not too tempting. A man may not be a tyrant as long as he has no power; he may live a quiet life, as long as he is poor; he may be above corruption, as long as he has no seducing chances. Thus, many good qualities which we attribute to many people around are all a falsely painted, superficial beauty, concealing behind its artifice a weak and unhealthy personality.

Potential devils stalk about in the world in the borrowed garbs of artificial raiment. Therefore, the real test of a Perfect One is not in the jungle or in a cave, but in the market-place where he is teased by the mischiefs of the world. Christ was never so great as when he was nailed to the cross! The true nature in us will come out only when we are crushed; the fragrance of *Chandana* (Sandal-wood) emerges only when rubbed; *Tulasi* (Ocimum) leaves leave their fragrance on the very fingers that crush them.

HE WHO, SEATED LIKE ONE UNCONCERNED, IS NOT MOVED BY THE *GUNAS*—In all his experiences in the world, good, bad or indifferent, he is unconcerned, since he knows that it is the play of the mind and intellect. In a cinema hall, the tragedies and comedies on the screen need not affect us, since we know that it is a show put up for our entertainment. This does not mean that the Seer is totally unconcerned with the happenings of the world. Vyasa is very careful in his choice of expression. He says that the man-of-Perfection looks LIKE ONE UNCONCERNED. That is to say, he is not in the least agitated; nor does he become hysterical by anything that is happening around him in life.

WHO, KNOWING THAT THE '*GUNAS*' OPERATE—He understands that the changes in his own inward personality are all nothing but the kaleidoscopic changes of the *gunas* and that the world outside changes according to one's mental conditions. A man of true Wisdom lives, ever fully aware of the technique behind the changes in himself and in the world around him.

IS SELF-CENTERED AND SWERVES NOT—In order to watch the play of the three *gunas* in himself, he should be an observer from beyond the *gunas*. Thus, established in his Pure Spiritual Nature, he is able to observe detachedly and enjoy the play of the *gunas* in himself and in the world around him. An observer of a street fight, looking down from his balcony, is not affected by what he observes; so too, the man-of-Wisdom, awakened to the Spiritual Consciousness, swerves not from his consummate equilibrium, when he witnesses the play of the *gunas* in himself and ever remains established in his own Divine Nature (*ava-tishthati*).

CONTINUING TO ELUCIDATE THE THOUGHT SUGGESTED IN THE PREVIOUS STANZA, THE LORD SAYS:

24. *Alike in pleasure and pain; who dwells in the Self; to whom a clod of earth, a precious stone, and gold are alike; to whom the dear and the not-dear are the same; firm; the same in censure and self-praise. ...*

The equanimity and balance of personality which are observed in a Perfect Man, in the midst of the changing vicissitudes of life, are brought out in this stanza. One who has gone beyond the tyrannies of the three *gunas* lives in a kingdom of his own, wherein neither the thrills of *sattva*, nor the noisy clamours of *rajas*, nor the weariness of *tamas* have any admission at all. Serenely self-composed, he dwells in

---

समदुःखसुखः स्वस्थः समलोष्टाश्मकाञ्चनः ।
तुल्यप्रियाप्रियो धीरस्तुल्यनिन्दात्मसंस्तुतिः ॥ २४ ॥

samaduḥkhasukhaḥ svasthaḥ samaloṣṭośmakāñcanaḥ
tulyapriyāpriyo dhīrastulyanindātmasaṁstutiḥ 24.

the Self, far away from the sweat and agitations of base appetites, low impulses, and selfish passions.

To the average man, this state of equipoise may look like complete death. And, no doubt, it is so; it is the death of the limited, finite life of relative experiences, lived by the baser ego. Spirit, conditioned by Matter, behaves like a reed upon the tumultuous surface of an ever-agitated mind. Always disturbed by the constant storms of love and hate, likes and dislikes, this unhappy sense of individuality suffers its shattering agitations and endless sorrows.

To withdraw, therefore, from this chaotic field of desires and attachments into the shelter of the Self, is to release the diviner possibilities in ourselves. The dreamer dies to be reborn as the waker; the individual sense of the ego dies to release the infinite glories of the Self.

Having awakened from the dream, what would be the waker's relationship with his dream-world is the question that Arjuna asks Krishna! One, who has gone beyond the shackles of the three *gunas*, has awakened from all the misconceptions of the world, fed by one's 'I'-ness and 'my'-ness. In that state of godly awakening, there cannot be any deep and sincere relationship with the experiences of the lower world, whether it be joy or sorrow, things dear or not-dear, blame or praise. In all the experiences, he is a balanced, unattached witness.

WHO DWELLS IN THE SELF (*Svasthah*)—One who has transcended the *gunas* that rule the tendencies of the mind, becomes the Self, just as one who has crossed the frontiers of a dream, discovers himself to be the 'waker'. What would be the relationship of one who dwells in the Self, with the things around him, and what would be his attitude to things happening around him, is being answered here? Established as he is in Supreme Wisdom, the world that is contacted from the levels of the body, the mind and the intellect does not touch him. He lives in a world of his own, far above the plane of Matter.

ALIKE IN PLEASURE AND IN PAIN—To come in contact with the outside world through sense-perceptions, to evaluate them in terms of similar experiences in the past, and to experience pleasure or pain, is a trick of our individual personality. The worlds of stimuli march into us and we respond to them and these intelligent responses can fall under two categories: pleasure and pain. That which is pleasurable to one is bound to be painful to another. If the things of the world were in their own nature either pleasurable or painful, they would have certainly caused the same uniform reactions in all of us.

It is the nature of the Sun to be hot, and therefore, the heat of the Sun is common to us all. But the things of the world do not produce reactions in everyone in the same way, and therefore, it is an interpretation of our mind and intellect, which is coloured by our own past experiences. He who is not looking at the world through these coloured goggles of the mind and intellect will be alike in pleasure and pain.

REGARDING A CLOD OF EARTH, A PRECIOUS STONE AND GOLD ALIKE—Possession of things is another appetite which the majority of living creatures have. People like to possess and hoard precious stones or gold, but do not care for a clod of mud. But to an awakened man-of-Wisdom, all these possessions are one and the same and from his estimation none of them has any real value.

Children collect peacock feathers, shells, marbles, broken glass-bangles, old stamps, shapely stones, etc., from the roadside or from waste-paper baskets, and with extreme possessiveness, they keep them as their precious possessions. But as they grow, without regret, they throw them away and the younger ones in the family accept them with gratitude as a precious inheritance from their elders. Similarly, a man living his egocentric life of desires for possessions, may value gold and precious stones; but to the Awakened Soul, in his sense of Infinitude, these limited possessions, hugged on to by lesser minds, have no charm at all.

THE SAME TOWARDS THINGS DEAR AND THINGS NOT-DEAR—In our relationship with others, where there is an agreeable nature, we come to love it dearly, while, wherever there is a disagreeable nature, we hate it. Love and hate, dear and not-dear, are all our reactions to the agreeable and disagreeable nature of things or situations. These reactions are, no doubt, from the levels of the mind. One who is standing on windy shores wearing a thick coat will not feel the cold that another must feel, when, in his nakedness; he is dipping in the sea. The cold waters come in contact with the skin of the naked man and he experiences the discomforts, while the man on the shore, comfortably warm in his coat, knows no cold.

The average man plunged in identification with his own mind and intellect, suffers the world and interprets it as agreeable or disagreeable, and brings down upon himself a lot of confusions and problems. The man of steady-Wisdom is he, whose equilibrium is not disturbed by the onslaught of things and circumstances of the world, whether they be dear or not dear.

SAME IN CENSURE AND IN PRAISE—A man-of-Perfection is the same in censure and praise. The experience of a dream cannot contribute either joy or sorrow to one who has 'awakened', he might have been a beggar insulted by the entire society in the dream-world or might have been an adored *Raja* ruling a vast empire in his dream. But when he wakes up, neither the PRAISE he received as a *Raja*, nor the CENSURE he suffered as a beggar can leave any reactions upon him. Awakened from the dream, the man-of-Wisdom evaluates the blame and praise of the world outside and finds them both utterly insignificant.

In the above four beautiful, chosen phrases, Vyasa has indicated some of the main conditions of life in which the ordinary man comes to eke out his joys and sorrows. Pleasure and pain, good and bad possessions, agreeable and disagreeable experiences, joys, and sorrows provided by praise and censure, are some of the conditions of life by which we get entangled in a web of agitations and sorrows.

MOREOVER:

25. *The same in honour and dishonour; the same to friend and foe; abandoning all undertakings -- he is said to have crossed beyond the GUNAS.*

If the above has drawn a flat picture of the man-of-Perfection, herein we have added strokes that shade the outlines and give them a rounded beauty to depict them vividly for our keener observation and closer vision.

THE SAME IN HONOUR AND DISHONOUR—The sense of equanimity in honour and dishonour is described here as one of the definite signs of perfection attained. Rooted in his own lived experiences of divinity, a man of Vision is not afraid of life and its rewards, because, such a Perfect One looks at things and happenings from his own special angle. The egoistic evaluation of life tends to respect honour and shun dishonour.

Even in ordinary life, we have found martyrs courting what others consider as dishonour. They energetically love and serve their generation in spite of the insults and disgrace piled upon them by ignorant people. For Archimedes, running along the streets naked from his bathtub crying 'Eureka', 'Eureka', might have been a dishonour on any other day

---

मानापमानयोस्तुल्यस्तुल्यो मित्रारिपक्षयो: ।
सर्वारम्भपरित्यागी गुणातीत: स उच्यते ॥ २५ ॥

mānāapamānayostulyastulyo mitrāripakṣayoḥ
sarvārambhaparityāgī guṇātītaḥ sa ucyate 25.

except on that day of his discovery! Honour and dishonour are the evaluations of the intellect that change from time to time, from place to place. To one who has transcended the ordinary planes of egoism and vanity, both are the same; a crown of thorns is as welcome as a crown of roses!!

THE SAME TO FRIEND AND FOE—To one who treads the path-of-Wisdom and has risen above the *gunas*, there is no foe in the world; nor is he attached to anyone in earthy friendships. My right hand is never a foe to me; nor is it merely a friend; it is myself. Another, other than myself, alone can claim enmity or friendship with me. When I have realised the ONENESS of my spiritual nature, Infinite and All-pervading, as the Spirit, I have no relationship with the world outside; I live my vivid personal experience: 'THEY ARE I'.

ABANDONING ALL UNDERTAKINGS—The man of tranquillity, living in God-consciousness, has no more ego in him, nor is he pestered by the endless egocentric desires which are the sorrows of life. Desire-motivated activities, undertaken with an anxiety to earn and to acquire, to possess and to hoard, to aggrandise and to claim ownership are indicated by the term 'undertaking'. All these are possible only when the ego is there. When the limited ego-sense has volatilised in the realisation of the Infinite, all ego-motivated activities also end. Thereafter, he, the God-inspired, works in the world as a God-man.

HE IS SAID TO HAVE GONE BEYOND THE *GUNAS*—The above three stanzas together paint the complete picture of one who has transcended the *gunas*. These three stanzas answer Arjuna's second question.

Sankara recognises in these three stanzas A RULE OF CONDUCT LAID DOWN FOR THE *SANNYASIN* WHO SEEKS *MOKSHA*. These qualities are to be cultivated by every SEEKER who is trying to live the Hindu-culture. Once the seeker has gained inner freedom, these become the characteristic features of his nature. They form the essential marks that indicate one who has risen above the *gunas.*

THE LORD PROCEEDS NEXT TO ANSWER THE QUESTION "HOW DOES ONE TRANSCEND THE *GUNAS*?"

26. *And he, serving Me with unswerving devotion, and crossing beyond the GUNAS, is fit to become BRAHMAN.*

Being a practical textbook of religion, the *Geeta* is never satisfied by giving mere philosophical discourses. Every discourse, after explaining a definite aspect of our philosophy, prescribes immediately a way of training by which the imperfect can aspire to be and ultimately achieve Perfection.

HE WHO SERVES ME WITH UNSWERVING DEVOTION—Love for God is called devotion. Our minds revel readily and with pleasure wherever there is love. Our entire nature is fed by our thoughts, and, as the thoughts, so the mind. To contemplate steadily upon the Infinite Nature of the Self is, ultimately, to become the Self, and thus end our limited, mortal ego.

Contemplation upon the nature of the Lord in all sincerity and intensity cannot be maintained effectively at all times. As we are today, we are not capable of maintaining the mind in a state of meditation all the time. Therefore, Krishna, knowing this weakness of man, advises a practical method of maintaining this thought for a longer period of time through the process of dedicated service (*seva*). That all work, if intelligently undertaken in a spirit of dedication and service,

---

मां च योऽव्यभिचारेण भक्तियोगेन सेवते ।
स गुणान्समतीत्यैतान्ब्रह्मभूयाय कल्पते ॥ २६ ॥
mām ca yo'vyabhicāreṇa bhaktiyogena sevate
sa guṇānsamatītyaitānbrahmabhūyāya kalpate 26.

can be readily converted into worship, has already been explained in Chapter-III. This clearly and evidently shows that mere devotion to the Lord is not enough. The *Geeta-Acharya* expects his devotees to bring religion from the *Pooja*-rooms and temples to the fields of their every-day-life of activities and in all their contacts with others around.

Such a practice of constant God-awareness and dedicated service removes the agitations of the mind and tunes up the inner instrument for a more efficient flight through meditation. *Tamas* and *rajas* get more and more reduced, and thereby the proportion of *sattva* in the seeker's subtle constitution increases. And such a seeker IS FIT TO BECOME *BRAHMAN*. Such an individual who has gained a wealth of *sattva* in his inward composition will discover in himself a greater ability and poise during his meditation. The reawakening to the consciousness of the Self cannot then be very far off.

Here, it is said that the seeker is fit for becoming *Brahman*. To realise *Brahman* is to become *Brahman*, to realise the waker is to become the waker.

HOW CAN THE SAGE HIMSELF BE *BRAHMAN*? LISTEN:

27. *For I am the Abode of BRAHMAN, the Immortal and the Immutable, of everlasting DHARMA and of Absolute Bliss.*

In describing the *Yoga*-of-Devotion and its ultimate goal, the *Geeta* has already indicated: (XII-8) "YOU SHALL NO DOUBT LIVE IN ME THEREAFTER"; and the devotee, under the inspiration of his love, will forget himself as a separate individual, and his mind will merge with his point-of-

---

ब्रह्मणो हि प्रतिष्ठाहममृतस्याव्ययस्य च ।
शाश्वतस्य च धर्मस्य सुखस्यैकान्तिकस्य च ॥ २७ ॥

brahmaṇo hi pratiṣṭhāhamamṛsyāvyayasya ca
śāśvatasya ca dharmasya sukhsyaikāntikasya ca 27.

contemplation, the Lord. In the previous stanza, we were told, "HE WHO SERVES ME WITH UNSWERVING *YOGA*-OF-DEVOTION" will steadily transcend his identification with his Matter-envelopments. To the extent the ego dies, to that extent the experience of the Divine can manifest. To retire from waking is to enter the hall-of-sleep; and while one is dozing, one is walking further and further away from the realm-of-wakefulness and proportionately entering the peaceful abode-of-sleep.

To leave completely one plane-of-Consciousness, is to enter entirely into another plane-of-Consciousness. The WAKER himself totally becomes the DREAMER and the DREAMER knows no waking-state. The DREAMER ends his dream when he either wakes up to the world or slides into the joys of peaceful slumber. There is no transaction across the frontiers of these distinct planes-of-Consciousness.

FOR, I AM THE ABODE OF *BRAHMAN*—The Self that vitalises the seeker's bosom is the Pure Consciousness, that is the same everywhere, IMMORTAL and IMMUTABLE, ETERNAL and BLISSFUL. To realise the Self within, is to realise the Infinite Self. To taste a piece of cake is to taste all cakes of all times and for all times, because the KNOWLEDGE of the taste of cake is ever the same. In the realm of experience, if a meditator apprehends the Self in him, he at once experiences the Omnipresence of the Self. As long as a pot exists, the pot-space is seen distinct from the space around. Once the pot is broken, the pot-space itself becomes the unbounded space in the Universe; similarly, when life's false identifications with the body, mind and intellect are broken down – in short, when the ego is dead, the Awareness of the Infinitude rises up to flood the bosom with THE ETERNAL *DHARMA* AND THE UNFAILING BLISS.

Shri Sankara, in his extremely rational and analytical commentary, gives for this stanza three alternative interpretations, each one not contrary to the others, but each one elucidating more and more the philosophical contents of this verse. Sankara says "*BRAHMAN* IS *PARAMATMAN*, IMMORTAL AND INDESTRUCTIBLE. HE ABIDES IN ME WHO AM THE SELF (*PRATYAG-ATMAN*). THAT BEING THE SELF, ONE RECOGNISES, BY RIGHT KNOWLEDGE, THE IDENTITY OF THE SELF IN ONESELF AND THE SELF EVERYWHERE."

Sankara gives an alternative meaning to the verse: IT IS THROUGH THE POWER (*MAYA*) INHERENT IN *BRAHMAN*, AS *ISHWARA*, THAT HE SHOWS GRACE TO HIS DEVOTEES. "I AM THAT POWER IN MANIFESTATION, AND THEREFORE, BRAHMAN AM I".

Again, as another alternative interpretation, he suggests a third meaning which, as we said earlier, is not contrary to the former two suggestions, but, in fact, paints in greater detail, the beauty of the stanza and its contents. BY *BRAHMAN* IS MEANT HERE THE 'CONDITIONED-*BRAHMAN*'; WHO ALONE CAN BE SPOKEN OF BY SUCH WORD AS '*BRAHMAN*'... 'CONDITIONED-*BRAHMAN*' ALONE CAN BE CONCEIVED OF IN THE FINITE INTELLECT, PERCEIVED BY THE MIND AND EXPRESSED THROUGH LANGUAGE AS A CONTRAST TO MATTER. Here the term *Brahman* only means Spirit as opposed in nature to inert Matter. Thus, Matter and Spirit, both factors conceived by the limited intellect, are limited and so finite objects of knowledge. But both are known by the Consciousness, the Supreme. Therefore "I, THE UNCONDITIONED AND THE UNUTTERABLE, AM THE ABODE OF THE CONDITIONED-*BRAHMAN*, WHO IS IMMORTAL AND INDESTRUCTIBLE".

The Illuminator is always different from the illumined. The 'SUBJECT' is the knower, and the 'OBJECT' is the known. Krishna, the Infinite, represents the Eternal Subject, and therefore, He is the Abode of all OBJECTS, including the concept of the Self which is the Spirit that vitalises and gives a similitude of sentiency and appearance of activity to all the Matter-envelopments. The conditioned *Brahman* (*sa-upadhika*) rests upon the Consciousness that is aware of it, which is the Unconditioned (*nir-upadhika*) *Brahman*.

In the following chapter (15, 16, 17 and 18) it will be explained as the three *Atmans*, *Anatman*, *Jivatman* and *Paramatman*.

Thus, in the UPANISHADS of the glorious Bhagawad Geeta, in the Science of the Eternal, in the scripture of YOGA, in the dialogue between Sri Krishna and Arjuna, the fourteenth discourse ends entitled:

The *Yoga* of *Gunas*

Om Om Om Om Om

ॐ तत्सदिति श्रीमद् भगवद् गीतासूपनिषत्सु ब्रह्मविद्यायां
योगशास्त्रे श्रीकृष्णार्जुनसंवादे गुणत्रयविभागयोगो नाम
चतुर्दशोऽध्याय:

Oṁ tatsaditi śrīmadbhagavadgītāsū ūpaniṣatsu brahmavidyāyāṁ yogaśāstre śrī kṛṣṇārjuna saṁvāde guṇatrayavibhāgayogo nāma caturdaśo'dhyāyaḥ.

XV

The Supreme Spirit
Introduction

IN this section consisting of the concluding six chapters of the *Geeta,* there is, as all through the *Geeta,* a systematic development of ideas and a logical building up of the theory that the ever-changing, finite world of multiplicity is but a PROJECTION on the Infinite, and that the endless painful experiences are all caused by our own MISAPPREHENSION OF REALITY. In the Thirteenth Chapter, the world-of-Matter and the realm-of-Spirit were beautifully described and brought within our intellectual comprehension. The Field-of-Experience (*Kshetra*), and the Knower-of-the-Field (*Kshetrajna*) were clearly pictured and it was shown that the Knower-of-the-Field minus the Field-of-Experience is the Pure Awareness, at once Infinite and Permanent.

In this chapter, the *Geetacharya* discusses the nature of the Spirit in all its implications. In terms of the known alone can the unknown be indicated. The world of the known is the manifested objects of perception, emotions and thoughts. No effect can be without a cause, and all effects sustain themselves in their own material cause.* Basing his arguments upon this logical fact, the Divine Charioteer helps us lift our minds from the known phenomena to the unknown Noumenon.

With reference to the perishable, finite world of constant change, the spirit is defined, in this chapter, as the

* Without cotton (cause) no cloth (effect) can exist and wherever there is cloth (effect) it is sustained by cotton (cause) which is its material cause.

Imperishable, Infinite, Changeless Factor, which is at once the substratum and the nourishment for the imperfect world-of-plurality. The Infinite is thus defined as the Imperishable (*Akshara*) with reference to the perishable (*Kshara*) equipment-of-Matter. After thus indicating the antithesis of change as changelessness, He will explain how the Experiencer of the changes, which are infinite in variety, is even something other than that which we know as the CHANGELESS. This Unconditional Eternal Factor is called by the *Geeta* as the *Purushottama*.

In the concluding lines, Lord Krishna assures Arjuna that He has given out this greatest secret: "HE WHO WITHOUT CONFUSIONS, KNOWS ME THUS AS THE PERSON SUPREME, KNOWS ALL; AND WITH HIS WHOLE BEING DEVOTEDLY WORSHIPS ME". In short, this chapter is one of the rarest pieces of literature available in the world, that so directly indicates the Infinite. For the beauty and brevity of the stanzas in this chapter, no other portion even in the *Geeta* can stand a favourable comparison. In India, from the ancient days onwards, this chapter has been recited before taking food as a prayer by the *Brahmins*.

The Blessed Lord said:

1. *They (wise people) speak of the indestructible ASHWATTHA tree* as having its roots above and branches below, whose leaves are the VEDAS; he who knows it, is alone a Veda-knower.*

श्रीभगवानुवाच
ऊर्ध्वमूलमधः शाखमश्वत्थं प्राहुरव्ययम् ।
छन्दांसि यस्य पर्णानि यस्तं वेद स वेदवित् ॥ १ ॥

śrībhagavānuvāca
ūrdhvamūlamadhaḥ śākhmaśvatthaṁ prāhuravyayam
chandāṁsi yasya parṇāni yastaṁ veda sa vedavit 1.

* *Peepal* Tree (Ficus Religiosa).

Reminiscent of the casual picture of the '*Peepal*-tree' brought up in the *Kathopanishad* (VI-1), here Vyasa exhaustively paints the tree-of-life and shows its relationship with the Infinite. If the Spirit be one-without-a-second, out of this one Consciousness how did the world-of-matter; constituted of the body and its perceptions, the mind and its feelings, the intellect and its thoughts arise? Even if it has so risen up, what nourishes it and sustains it? What exactly is the relationship between God, the CREATOR; and the world, the CREATED – the Infinite and the finite? These are some of the questions that generally rise up in any human intellect, once it is set to contemplate upon life.

The picture of the '*Peepal*-tree' unveiled in these three stanzas serves as a beautiful allegory of the entire spiritual concept expounded in this chapter.

Ashwattha is botanically known as *Ficus Religiosa*, popularly called the '*Peepal*-tree', which, according to some, has gathered its name because horses used to stand under its shade (*Ashwattha*). According to Shankara, this tree has been chosen to represent the entire cosmos because of its derivative meaning - '*Shwa*' means tomorrow; '*Stha*' means that which remains; therefore, '*Ashwattha*' *means* that which will NOT remain the same till tomorrow. In short, the word indicates the ephemeral, the ever-changing, world of the phenomena.

It is described here that the *Ashwattha*-tree has its roots 'up' (*Urdhwa*). Accepting directly the literal meaning, we have got some spiritually absurd, religiously mischievous, and aesthetically ugly pictures of this tree-of-*Samsara*, painted by some illiterate artists, and made easily available in the Indian markets. It is an insult to the mighty majesty of this scriptural picture.

According to Anandagiri,* *Samsara* is represented as a tree (*Vriksha*) because of the etymological meaning of the Sanskrit term, *Vriksha,* 'that which can be cut down'. The experiences of change and sorrow which the world-of-plurality gives us can be totally ended through detachment. The tree-of-multiplicity that has seemingly sprung forth from the Infinite Consciousness Divine, can be cut down by shifting our attention from the tree to the Divine.

Luckily, we who are educated in modern universities, have a similar use of the term 'tree' in our history textbooks. The 'family trees' of kings and dynasties are, without any exception, shown as branching down from their ancestral source. Similarly, the tree-of-*Samsara* has its roots UP in the Divine Consciousness. A tree holds itself up and gets nourished by its roots; similarly, the experiences of change, and the experiencer of them, are all established in the Infinite and draw their sustenance from It alone.

Even then, many of our friends doubt, why is the word 'UP' (*Urdhwa*) used? It is used here in the same connotation as we use the term 'UP' in our everyday expressions, like 'HIGH-command', 'HIGHER-officials', 'TOP-men', 'UPPER-class', 'HIGH-class jewellery' etc. In all these cases, by the term HIGH or UP or TOP, no geometrical elevation is indicated, but it indicates a superiority, a greater nobility, or value. Psychologically, it is natural for man to concede, for the subtler and the diviner, a HIGHER place of reverence and to consider the grosser and the devilish as belonging to a LOWER status. The Perfect is the Highest Consciousness, illumined and vitalised by which alone can the body-mind-intellect equipment experience its world of perception-emotion-thought. Naturally, therefore, the world-of-plurality

---

* Anandagiri wrote 'notes' on Shri Shankara's commentary.

is allegorically pictured here as the fig-tree; arising from and sustained by the Higher Consciousness, the Reality.

This world-of-change (*Ashwattha*) is considered here as eternal (*Avyaya*), only in a relative sense. Any '*Peepal*-tree' in any village must have observed many generations playing and growing up under its shade, and thus, with reference to man's average age, the fig-tree can be considered as RELATIVELY eternal. Similarly, with reference to the generations that grow, conceive, plan, strive, achieve and die away, the world itself can be considered as RELATIVELY immortal.

For this tree-of-life THE *VEDAS* THEMSELVES ARE THE LEAVES—*Veda* means 'knowledge'. Knowledge does bring forth a greater spurt of dynamism of life into the world. In comparison with the modern world – with its colossal endeavours, mighty achievements, and superhuman aspirations – the ancient generations were, relatively speaking, not even alive. More the knowledge a generation acquires, clearer becomes its vision of a greater future and diviner possibilities, and therefore, more is the amount of effort put forth by it to achieve the perceived goal. Now, to compare *Veda* - 'knowledge' to the leaves of the 'tree' is not quite inappropriate. Leaves are areas from which the water contents get evaporated in all trees, and this, in its turn, creates the 'osmotic-pressure' in the roots and facilitates the roots to draw more quantity of nourishment from the earth. Cut down the leaves of a tree and its growth is immediately stunted; the larger the number of branches and leaves, the greater is the tree's dimension and growth. Where there is greater knowledge, there we are sure to find a greater flare of manifest-life.

HE WHO KNOWS IT, IS A KNOWER OF THE *VEDA* —He alone, who has realised not only the *Ashwattha*-tree, but also the Higher, from which it derives its existence, is the one who has fulfilled his knowledge of the *Vedas*. The *Vedas* indicate the One Eternal Principle from which all the realms of experience have sprung. Neither pure science, nor mere devotion, can achieve the truth of perfect knowledge, is the conclusion of the *Geeta*. Knowledge is perfect only when we know of the here and the hereafter, of the finite and the Infinite, of the created and the Creator. All the rest of the pursuits of knowledge, however spectacular they might be, are, at best, only one-sided views of the whole Truth. The man of Perfect Wisdom, as conceived by the *Vedas*, is the knower of both the PERISHABLE and the IMPERISHABLE; and such a man alone is recognised by Krishna as the *Vedavit* - knower of the *Vedas*.

NOW FOLLOWS ANOTHER FIGURATIVE REPRESENTATION OF THE MEMBERS OF THIS TREE OF *SAMSARA*:

2. *Below and above are spread its branches, nourished by the GUNAS; sense-objects are its buds; and below, in the world of men, stretch forth the roots, originating in action.*

Continuing to paint the picture of the tree-of-*Samsara*, we have here the etching in more details. Such mystical representations should not be taken too literally, whether in literature or in art. The very style of the *Vedas* is couched in mysticism. Taking any convenient object of the world and

---

अधश्चोर्ध्वं प्रसृतास्तस्य शाखा
गुणप्रवृद्धा विषयप्रवालाः ।
अधश्च मूलान्यनुसंततानि
कर्मानुबन्धीनि मनुष्यलोके ॥ २ ॥

adhaścordhvaṁ prasṛtāstasya śākhā
guṇapravṛddha vhṣyapravālāḥ
adhaśca mūlānyanusantatāni
karmānubandhīni manuṣyaloke 2.

describing it in such a poetic style so as to express some of the subtler philosophical truths and thereby to convey some deeper religious message is called mysticism.

Describing the tree-of-life and adding more details to it, Vyasa says: 'UPWARDS AND DOWNWARDS ITS BRANCHES SPREAD' – the flow of life in the individual, as well as in the world, is sometimes towards the higher evolutionary purposes, but more often it tends to cater to the lower animal nature. These two tendencies are significant here when it is said that the branches of the tree-of-life grow both 'upwards and downwards'.

FATTERNED BY THE *GUNAS*—These urges for living the higher and the lower values are maintained and nourished by the particular type of psychological tendencies – *gunas* available in the individual. In an earlier chapter (XIV) the play of the *gunas* (moods of the mind) has been exhaustively discussed.

In any tree there are nodular buds which are potential branches that have not yet developed, but are waiting for a chance to burst forth. Corresponding to them, Krishna says, in the *Ashwattha*-tree, are the sense-objects, the 'buds'. It is a fact that in the presence of an 'object' our tendencies revolt against all our higher concepts and ideals, and run amuck to gain their gratification – a new 'branch'.

DOWNWARD THE ROOTS EXTEND—If the main root of the tree-of-*Samsara* is lost in the Absolute Reality, High above, the 'secondary roots' which spring from it are spread all around, and grow even downward, IN THE WORLD OF MAN, INITIATING ALL ACTIONS. Here, secondary roots are thought-channels (*vasanas*), which are created in us, and which propel each one of us towards his own typical actions and reactions in the world. They are the very causes that promote man's evil as well as meritorious activities in the world. Just as the main tap-root, while spreading its secondary roots, claws the earth through them and gets the plant well-rooted, so too, these *Samskaras*, actions and their reactions, both good and evil, bind the individuals fast to the earthly plane of likes and dislikes, of profits and losses, of earning and spending.

THE FOLLOWING TWO STANZAS INDICATE HOW WE CAN ANNIHILATE THE TREE AND THEREBY COME TO EXPERIENCE THE PURE SOURCE OF ALL LIFE'S MANIFESTATIONS, THE INFINITE LIFE:

3. *Its form is not perceived here as such, neither its end, nor its origin, nor its foundation, nor its resting-place; having cut asunder this firm-rooted ASHWATTHA-tree with the strong axe of non-attachment...*

4. *Then that Goal should be sought after, where having gone, none returns again. I seek refuge in that 'primeval PURUSHA from which streamed forth, from time immemorial, all activity (or energy).*

न रूपमस्येह तथोपलभ्यते
नान्तो न चादिर्न च संप्रतिष्ठा ।
अश्वत्थमेनं सुविरूढमूलम्
असङ्गशस्त्रेण दृढेन छित्त्वा ॥ ३ ॥

na rūpamasyeha tathopalabhyate
nānto na cādirna ca sampratiṣṭhā
aśvatthamenaṁ suvirūḍhamūlam
asaṅgaśastreṇa dṛḍhena chittvā 3.

ततः पदं तत्परिमार्गितव्यं
यस्मिन्गता न निवर्तन्ति भूयः ।
तमेव चाद्यं पुरुषं प्रपद्ये
यतः प्रवृत्तिः प्रसृता पुराणी ॥ ४ ॥

tataḥ padaṁ tatparimārgitavyaṁ
yasmingatā na nivartanti bhūyaḥ
tameva cādyaṁ puruṣaṁ prapadye
yataḥ pravṛttiḥ prasṛtā purāṇī 4.

SEEK REFUGE IN THAT PRIMEVAL *PURUSHA* WHENCE STREAMED FORTH THE ANCIENT CURRENT".

The stanza indicates that when our personality has, to a maximum degree, retired from its extrovert pursuits, the intellect is to be consciously turned, in an attitude of love and surrender, to the goal – the goal from which the stream of Consciousness flows to the matter-vehicles facilitating them to play their parts. In short, HALT the manifestations of life, and seek the Eternal Life, the Source of all expressions of life. What this primeval *Purusha* is, and how one is to conceive It, is the theme of the entire chapter.

WHAT SORT OF SEEKERS REACH THE GOAL? LISTEN:

5. *Free from pride and delusion, victorious over the evil of attachment, dwelling constantly in the Self, their desires having completely retired, freed from the pairs-of-opposites -- such as pleasure and pain -- the undeluded reach that Goal Eternal.*

Philosophy, in India, is something to live and to practise. Ultimately, it is fulfilled only when we come to experience its goal. It is natural, therefore, that in our scriptures and spiritual textbooks, we find a wealth of instructions and elaborate discussions on the theories of Perfection. This stanza is a typical example of the detailed instructions supplied to guide the adventurous seekers trying to follow the 'path'.

निर्मानमोहा जितसङ्गदोषा
अध्यात्मनित्या विनिवृत्तकामा: ।
द्वन्द्वैर्विमुक्ता: सुखदु:खसंज्ञै:
गच्छन्त्यमूढा: पदमव्ययं तत् ॥ ५ ॥

nirmānamohā jitasaṅgadoṣā
adhyātmanityā vinivṛttakāmāḥ
dvandvairvimuktāḥ sukhaduḥkhasañjñai
garcchantyamūḍhāḥ padamavyayaṁ tat 5.

Five conditions are explained herein which are nothing but certain disciplines, adjustments and reeducation of the vehicles of life; and Krishna concludes that those who have accomplished these shall reach the Divine experience and live a life enjoying a sense of supreme fulfilment.

FREE FROM PRIDE AND DELUSION—Both these qualities of pride and delusion indicate a false, exaggerated estimate of oneself and of others. Erroneous estimate of one's own importance is called pride and it brings about an enormous amount of heavy responsibilities upon oneself to maintain it. There is no time thereafter to cultivate oneself, or to seek knowledge, or to get truly educated. Similarly, error in judgement regarding things and beings, happenings and situations, in the world outside, is called DELUSION. It makes us live in a false world of our own imagination without actually facing the immediate problems around us, as they really are.

WITH THE EVIL OF ATTACHMENT CONQUERED—To live in the flesh, seeking our life's fulfilment only in the joy derived from our contact with the sense-objects in the world around us, is to live in the outer layer, cheating ourselves entirely of life's deeper possibilities. Such an ignorant fool gets extremely attached to the objects of the world, and once this attachment has grown, all his attention in life will be irresistibly turned towards those objects. Shackled by them, ever dancing to their rhythm of change and destruction, he comes to lay waste his powers, without ever realising the nobler purpose of the Life-Divine.

EVER DWELLING IN THE SELF—Detachment from the world-of-objects is never possible without attaching ourselves to something nobler and diviner. The human mind-intellect-equipment can exist only in the positive contemplation of some object. It cannot remain in a void of not contemplating anything. For example, from tomorrow onwards, let us determine NOT to think of a bald-headed man, let us say, as soon as we wake up; it is absolutely certain that the following morning, the very first thing which we will remember will be a bald-head. But supposing we give the mind a positive point to contemplate upon, '*Narayana-Narayana*', we shall find that the mind has totally avoided the thought. In the same way, in order that the mind may not have the evil attachment in it, it should live in a spirit of contemplation upon the Self.

THEIR DESIRES COMPLETELY AT REST—Desire is the function of the intellect. When the intellect desires, the mind starts contemplating upon the desired objects; as the desire, so the thoughts. Therefore, the intellect should be disciplined not to desire the finite joys arising out of the ephemeral sense-objects of the world. When the desires have ended, the mind becomes still.

RELEASED FROM THE PAIRS-OF-OPPOSITES, LIKE PLEASURE AND PAIN—When the body comes in contact with a sense-object, it is the mind that comes to experience, as it were, the final result of the contact as pleasure or pain. Once the mind starts recognising this pair, then it is natural for it to revolt against 'pain' and instinctively seek 'pleasure'. Unfortunately, in this mad onrush of seeking pleasure and avoiding pain, there is no stability, for the very things that constituted joys yesterday, prove to be sources of sorrow today. To cater to the whims and fancies of such an unsteady entity is to barter away our chances to bring about any cultural unfoldment in ourselves.

And the stanza concludes by a positive and optimistic declaration, having in its force and style, the vehemence of a commandment, when it says, 'THE UNDELUDED REACH THAT GOAL-ETERNAL'. Consciousness expressed through

Matter-vehicles is the miserable man, torn by his own stresses and strains; and the same Consciousness, gathered from these vehicles and experienced as such, is the Divine moment of Infinite Realisation.

THE GOAL IS AGAIN CLEARLY SPECIFIED THUS:

6. *Neither does the Sun shine there, nor the moon, nor fire; to which having gone they return not; that is My Supreme Abode.*

Consecutively, in the two previous stanzas, it was repeatedly asserted that the goal sought in spiritual life is one, 'HAVING ATTAINED WHICH THERE IS NO RETURN EVER'. The very same idea, that Perfection gained is an irrevocable fact and that there is no more any fear of return to the natural stupidities of a limited egocentric life, is being emphasised in this stanza also. Repetition is a method of emphasis in all scriptural literature. No doubt, this method is not used everywhere. Wherever logic is available, ideas are nailed in by logical reasonings. but there are realms, into which the teacher alone has admission in the beginning and not the student-class, and therefore, the *Rishis* had no other go but to repeatedly assert for our acceptance, the nature and condition of the unknown experience of the Infinite.

This glorious state-of-Perfection is the Goal which almost all stanzas in the *Geeta* consistently indicate and though it is an Absolute State, here an honest attempt is being made to describe It in terms of finite phenomena.

न तद्भासयते सूर्यो न शशाङ्को न पावकः ।
यद्गत्वा न निवर्तन्ते तद्धाम परमं मम ॥ ६ ॥
na tadbhāsayate sūryo na śaśāṅko na pāvakaḥ
yadgatvā na nivartante taddhāma paramaṁ mama 6.

NEITHER SUN, NOR MOON, NOR FIRE ILLUMINES THAT—Herein are enumerated almost all the sources-of-light, blessed by which the physical eyes experience vision. To see a thing is to know it; and in order that the organ-of-vision might use its power of seeing, it is not only sufficient that objects are in front of the sense-organs, but they must also be bathed in light. In the medium of light alone can the eyes see forms and colours. Again, not only do the eyes perceive; but also the ears pick up sounds, the nose the smell, the tongue the tastes, and the skin the touch. Each instrument perceives its objects. Even this is not all. We can perceive our feelings and also our ideas. The 'light', in which we thus perceive all our sense-objects, all our emotions, and all our thoughts, is the light-of-Consciousness by which alone we become AWARE of all our experiences.

This light-of-Consciousness cannot be illumined by the gross sources of light available in the world outside, such as the Sun, the Moon or the Fire.* In fact the very light of the Sun, or the Moon, or the Fire is an 'object' of our Consciousness; we are constantly conscious of it. An OBJECT of perception cannot illumine the SUBJECT that perceives it – the SUBJECT and the OBJECT cannot be at any time one and the same. The AWARENESS by which we come to experience all our life's joys and sorrows is the Eternal Self, and that Consciousness is indicated as the Supreme Goal by the *Geeta*.

THAT IS MY SUPREME ABODE—This state-of-Consciousness into which we can rise on transcending the agitations of the mind and intellect* is described here as the Abode of the Divine, the Dwelling Place Supreme, wherein

---

* For further details, refer discourses on *Kathopanishad*, II-v-15.

* On accomplishing the spiritual conditions laid down in stanza 5 above, in this very chapter.

we can confidently make an appointment with Truth and meet the Infinite!

Utilitarian as we are, certainly all seekers will doubt whether the experience of Truth is worth having after such a tremendous effort. Is there not a risk of our falling back into our present confusions and getting deluded by a finite pain-ridden world of plurality? This fear is allayed and the seekers are assured, for the third time continuously in this stanza, when Krishna qualifies, "MY SUPREME ABODE" as one "TO WHICH HAVING GONE NONE RETURNS".

It is an experienced fact that when one has mastered a knowledge, it is almost impossible for one to make any more mistakes in it; to a great musician, to sing deliberately out of tune, in disharmonious notes, is as difficult as it is for a beginner to sing correctly. Having known a language, to talk ungrammatically is as difficult as it is for the illiterate to talk correctly. If, in the imperfect world of imperfect knowledge, a cultured man, educated and artistic, cannot easily fall back to the levels of the uncivilised and the illiterate, how much more must it be an impossible act for the Perfect to come back and fall into the earlier confusions which are created by 'ignorance'!

This is one of the rarest stanzas in the religious literature of the world which, in so simple a style, has indicated, so exhaustively, the Unconditioned-Pure-Self, the Infinite-Reality. In Hinduism, it has always been emphasised that there is a continuity of existence after death and an individual continues his biography in a new embodiment under a new set of environments. The individuality, thus undergoing experiences of birth and death repeatedly, is called the *Jiva*, or the embodied-self. This *Jiva* is the Eternal Light of Consciousness, playing upon, and seemingly conditioned by, the subtle-body, constituted of the mind-intellect-equipment.

In short, death is only a phenomenon, wherein a given subtle-body changes its physical-equipment, seeking fresh fields and pastures new for its expression and expansion. This process is not the reaching of the Infinite, for, "MY ABODE IS THAT WHEREIN HAVING GONE THERE IS NO RETURN".

TO CLEAR THIS POSSIBLE DOUBT, THE STRUCTURE AND THE NATURE OF THE EGO (*JIVA*) IS EXPLAINED IN THE FOLLOWING STANZAS:

7. *An eternal portion of Myself, having become a living souls in the world of life, abiding in PRAKRITI, draws (to itself) the (five) senses, with mind for the sixth.*

A RAY OF MYSELF—The Infinite has no parts. It can suffer to the four walls of my room I consider the 'room-space' as different from the 'outer-space', so too, with reference to a given mind-intellect vehicle, the Infinite Light of Consciousness playing upon it is considered, by the ignorant, as limited by its vehicles. The moon in the bucket, trembles at the touch of a passing breeze. Even if a million such reflected moons were to be broken and shattered, the immortal moon in the heavens will not suffer any destruction. Similarly, the egocentric personality (*Jiva*), born out of the Consciousness playing upon a given subtle-body, suffers not any sense of limitations. Even though the ego changes with its joys and sorrows, with its knowledge and ignorance, with its peace and agitations, the essential nature of the Infinite Consciousness that sparkles in our heart is External indeed,

---

ममैवांशो जीवलोके जीवभूत: सनातन: ।
मन:षष्ठानीन्द्रियाणि प्रकृतिस्थानि कर्षति ॥ ७ ॥

mamaivaṁśo jīvaloke jīvabhūtaḥ sanātanaḥ
manaḥ ṣaṣṭhānīndriyāṇī prakṛtisthāni karṣati 7.

and hence the stanza qualifies the Self-in-man as: THE ETERNAL *JIVA* IN THE WORLD OF *JIVAS*.

ATTRACTS THE SENSES—This spark of Consciousness vibrates the entire body with life, renders existence possible for a living creature, and maintains, by its mere presence, the sense-faculties and the mental capacities around Itself. No doubt these are faculties that belong to matter, but at the same time, these powers of seeing, hearing, etc. and also of feeling, thinking, etc., are not the powers of the sense-organs, or even of the inner organs (*Antah-karana*). They are the expressions of the Spirit when It functions through matter, and hence, it is said that along with the mind and the five sense, 'ABIDING IN THE *PRAKRITI*', (Chapter XIII) it functions. That this conditioned-Self is experienced as the limited ego, the mortal, because of our ignorance or error of judgement that It is only a portion, as it were, an imaginary portion of the indivisible whole, etc.; have all been proved in the *Geeta*.*

WHEN DOES THE INFINITE DRAW THESE FACULTIES AROUND IT?

8. *When the Lord obtains a body, and when He leaves it, He takes these and goes (with them) as the wind takes the scents from their seats (the flowers).*

When the Lord acquires a body, meaning, when the Infinite deludes Itself that It is conditioned by the mind-

---

शरीरं यदवाप्नोति यच्चाप्युत्क्रामतीश्वरः ।
गृहीत्वैतानि संयाति वायुर्गन्धानिवाशयात् ॥ ८ ॥

śarīraṁ yadavāpnoti yaccāpyutkrāmatīśvaraḥ
gṛhītvaitāni saṁyāti vāyurgandhānivāśayāt 8.

* i.e., these faculties have their respective seats-of-expression in the world of Matter, the body.

intellect, It becomes the *Jiva*; and the *Jiva* takes to itself various bodies from time to time and incarnates in different environments, which are ordered by its own burning desires and aspirations, and which are most suited for exhausting and fulfilling all its demands. From the moment the *Jiva* enters a body till it leaves it, it keeps these sense faculties and mental impressions at all times with itself. In fact, the 'subtle-body' includes all these faculties.

At death, the 'subtle-body' permanently departs from the 'gross-body' which is left inert. The dead-body, though found to maintain the shape of the very individual, has no more, any sense-faculty or mental-ability or intellectual capacity that it had expressed before. These expressions, physical, mental and intellectual, were those which gave the body an individual personality-stature. All these constitute the subtle-body, and the gross-body, bereft of its subtle essence, is called as the dead-body.

At the time of death, the subtle-body, as it is described here, moves off gathering unto itself all faculties, "EVEN AS THE WIND TAKES SCENTS FROM THEIR RESTING PLACES", a passing breeze is not at any time separate from atmospheric air that is everywhere, and yet, when the breeze passes over a flower, or some sandal-paste, or a scent-bottle -- which are all seats of fragrance – it carries with it the respective aroma. Similarly, the subtle-body, when it moves out, carries along with it the senses, mind and intellect, not in any gross form, but as a mere 'fragrance' of what all they had lived through, felt in, and thought of. Thus viewed, the mind is nothing but a bundle of *vasanas*. These *vasanas* can exist only in the Infinite Consciousness, and the Light of Awareness illumining the *vasanas* is called the 'individual personality' -- *Jiva*.

In this stanza the *Jiva* is called the Lord (*Ishwara*) only because the individual personality is the Lord of the body, that orders, commands, and regulates all its actions, feelings and thoughts. Just as an officer, on receiving his transfer orders from the government, packs up his belongings and moves out of his residence for the time being, and having reached the new seat of appointment unpacks and spreads out his furniture for his comforts, so too, at the time of departing from the body, the subtle-body gathers itself from the gross dwelling place,* and on reaching the new physical structure, it spreads itself out again to use its faculties through that new 'house-of- experience'. These stanzas are really a summary of the *Upanishadic* declarations.

THIS SUBTLE-BODY, DESCRIBED IN THE PREVIOUS STANZAS ROUGHLY AS "THE FIVE SENSES AND THE MIND AS THE SIXTH" IS BEING EXPLAINED FURTHER IN THE FOLLOWING STANZAS:

9. *Presiding over the ear, the eye, the touch, the taste and the smell, so also the mind. He enjoys the sense-objects.*

The *Jiva* through the equipment of the mind enjoys the world-of-objects available in the new environment, through the sense-organs of hearing, seeing, touching, tasting, and smelling, which are expressed through their respective organs of the ear, the eye, the skin, the tongue, and the nose.

श्रोत्रं चक्षुः स्पर्शनं च रसनं घ्राणमेव च ।
अधिष्ठाय मनश्चायं विषयानुपसेवते ॥ ९ ॥

śrotraṁ cakṣuḥ sparśanaṁ ca rasanaṁ ghrāṇameva ca
adhiṣṭhāya manaścāyaṁ viṣayānupasevate 9.

* *Bhogaayatanam: Atmabodha*, V-11 describes gross-body as the 'hut of pleasure' – the 'house of experiences'.

The pure light-of-Consciousness never illumines any object, because in the Pure Light of the Infinite, there are no objects at all to illumine. It is only the Light of Consciousness reflected in the mind-intellect* that becomes the special beam of light, the intelligence, in which alone the sense-objects become illumined. That is why, very often, when we are thinking intensively on some problem, even if some of our friends come in front of us and talk to us, we neither see, nor hear them. The image of the object has already fallen on the retina of the eye, and the sound of the speaker has made the necessary vibrations on the tympanum of the ears, and yet, we see or hear nothing, because the conscious mind is turned elsewhere. Therefore, using the mind along with each sense separately, the individualised ego (*Jiva*) the dweller in the body enjoys the sense-objects such as sound, form, touch etc.

IF THE CONSCIOUSNESS WHICH IS ETERNAL AND PERFECT IS SO INTIMATELY PRESENT IN EVERY EXPERIENCE OF MAN, HOW IS IT THAT WE, WHO ARE LIVING THROUGH VIVID AND REAL EXPERIENCES AT EVERY MOMENT OF OUR EXISTENCE, FAIL TO RECOGNISE THIS DIVINE PERFECTION, WHICH IS SO CONSTANTLY WITH US AT ALL TIMES AND EVERYWHERE? THE SELF IS VISIBLE ONLY TO THE EYE-OF-KNOWLEDGE.

10. *Him, who departs, stays and enjoys, who is united with GUNAS, the deluded do not see; but they do behold Him, who posses the 'eye-of-knowledge'.*

उत्क्रामन्तं स्थितं वापि भुञ्जानं वा गुणान्वितम् |
विमूढा नानुपश्यन्ति पश्यन्ति ज्ञानचक्षुषः || १० ||

utkrāmantaṁ sthitaṁ vāpi bhuñjānaṁ vā guṇānvitam
vimūḍhā nānupaśyanti paśyanti jñānacakṣuṣaḥ 10.

* Refer *Atmabodha* – stanza 25

It is true everywhere that a common man, though observing an object does not fully and correctly understand it. The better understanding of things is always reserved for the man-of-knowledge.

Everybody can read a great piece of literature, but a man of letters alone can come to comprehend and enjoy fully the vision expressed in and through the artistic design of the piece.

Only a jeweler can really estimate the quality and worth of jewel, even though all can look at it.

Everyone can hear music, but only a musician can judge and experience the subtle beauties in a mastery recital.

Similarly, every one of us, so long as life resides in us, can perceive, feel and think and yet, it is only the 'wise' man who can come to recognise and live the Infinite Essence of Life Itself.

The Infinite Self is at all times present and never is there a time when It is not. When LEAVING the body, the subtle-body is vitalised by the presence of the Spirit. While the body is EXISTING, the Self is illuminating all experiences. While ENJOYING the pleasures of life, it is the light-of-Consciousness that illumines for us all our mental experiences and our intellectual judgements. At moments, our entire mental climate change from peaceful calmness (*sattva*) to riotous agitations (*rajas*), or sinks into a dull inertia (*tamas*), and all these moments, whatever be the nature of the climate within, are experienced only by the light-of-Consciousness. And yet the unintelligent one perceives not his Conscious Knowledge that is constantly making him aware of his moment-to-moment experiences.

An average man is so much preoccupied with the details of experiences that, he, clinging to his desires for enjoying the outer beauty of things and situations, comes to overlook and fails to recognise the steady light-of-Consciousness in him, in the presence of which alone can any experience be ever possible. Those who have got the necessary detachment from the minor details of the outer field-of-experience[1] alone come to recognise and live the joys of the Pure Self - the subject.

This special vision available to the man-of-Perfection is called the 'EYE-OF-WISDOM' in the stanza. This is not any special inner organ as such; it only represents an extra faculty that develops in the spiritual seeker, with which he comes to perceive the deeper significances and subtler suggestions in the superficially chaotic play of plurality. Those who do not have this intuitive perception necessarily fail to have this vision of the play of the Immortal Divine in and through the day-to-day activities and happenings. The same idea is more artistically stressed by Sri Shankara elsewhere.[2] This 'EYE-OF-KNOWLEDGE' cannot be developed unless the disciplines of Self-perfection are properly practised. The subjective technique of self-integration (*Yoga*) can be successfully brought about only when complete integration of personality at the outer levels has taken place.

A FEW ONLY ULTIMATELY COME TO EXPERIENCE THIS SELF, WHILE OTHERS, EVEN THOUGH STRIVING, FAIL TO HAVE THIS REALISATION. WHY?

11. *The seekers striving (for Perfection) behold Him dwelling in the Self; but, the unrefined and unintelligent, even though striving, see Him not.*

यतन्तो योगिनश्चैनं पश्यन्त्यात्मन्यवस्थितम् ।
यतन्तोऽप्यकृतात्मानो नैनं पश्यन्त्यचेतसः ॥ ११ ॥

yatanto yoginaścainaṁ paśyantayātmanyavasthitam
yatanto'pyakṛtātmano nainaṁ paśyantyacetasaḥ 11.

[1] Refer *Geeta* Chapter XIII – *Kshetra*–the items that constitute the 'Field-of-experience' have been enumerated in Stanzas 5 and 6.

[2] *Atmabodha* – stanzas 47 and 65

Those who are successful in their attempts at stilling their mind and cleaning their intellect of its disturbing attachments and desires, come to recognise the glory of the Self and experience Its Infinite Beatitude. But it is also true that all those who mechanically but in plenty of self-effort (*Yoga*) do not necessarily succeed. Hundreds are those who complain that though they were regular in their spiritual programme for years, no appreciable amount of self-development has come to them. One may wonder why this should be so.

This moot point is being answered here very logically. "THOUGH STRIVING, THOSE OF UNREFINED MIND AND DEVOID OF WISDOM, PERCEIVE HIM NOT." Two conditions are unavoidable if meditation is to ultimately yield its promised result: (a) The purification of the mind is generally defined as removal of agitations (*Vikshepa*) created by one's false egocentric attachment to sense-objects; (b) Also, the intellect is to be tuned up properly to a correct understanding of the nature of the Self, and thus all doubts of the misty mind (*Avarana*) that veil its right perception are also to be removed through study, reflection and practice. If these two adjustments are not properly accomplished, through practice of devotion (*Bhakti Yoga*) and service (*Karma Yoga*), all attempts of meditation in the path-of-Knowledge can only end in failure.

In short, the stanza emphasises that those whose minds have not been properly regenerated through practice of self-control of the senses, and who have not renounced and abandoned their evil ways of looking at things from limited egocentric standpoint, whose pride has not yet been subdued -such seekers, however sincerely and ardently they may meditate, have little or no chance of unfolding themselves into their diviner possibilities; 'THEY BEHOLD HIM NOT'. Though the Self is the nearest, and therefore, most easily perceivable, yet, all do not see Him, because of their complete slavery to the enchantments of the sense-objects.

So far the Self has been indicated as: (1) That, which cannot be illumined by the known phenomenal sources of light, such as the Sun, the Moon and the Fire; (2) That having reached which, none returns from that state-of-Perfection; (3) That, of which the individual entities (*Jivas*) are as though only a part.

Hereafter, in the following four stanzas the Immanence of the Lord (a) as the All-illumining light-of-Consciousness, (b) as the All-sustaining Life, (c) as the subjective warmth of Life, in all living organisms and (d) as the Self in all the hearts is being described.

TO SHOW THIS VERY GOAL AS THE ESSENCE OF ALL AND THE REALITY BEHIND ALL THESE EXPERIENCES, KRISHNA PROCEEDS TO GIVE A SHORT SUMMARY OF THE LORD'S IMMANENCE, IN THE FOLLOWING FOUR VERSES:

12. *That Light which is residing in the Sun and which illumines the whole world, and that which is in the moon and the fire - know that Light to be Mine.*

We, who are familiar with the modern scientific observations, must necessarily get rattled a bit when we read the meaning of the stanza. But without losing our balance, if we were to quietly ruminate over the statement, we shall realise that our confusions are only because of the limitation of our own intellect – which we have cultivated by the study of intellectually limited sciences. In the early classrooms we are told, very scientifically, that the earth is a portion of the Sun

---

यदादित्यगतं तेजो जगद्भासयतेऽखिलम् ।
यच्चन्द्रमसि यच्चाग्नौ तत्तेजो विद्धि मामकम् ॥ १२ ॥

yadādityagataṁ tejo jagadbhāsayate'khilam
yaccandramasi yaccāgnau tattejo viddhi māmakam 12.

that has got detached from it and got held within the web of mutual attraction of the planets, and which has now cooled to its present temperature. But if we ask the question where the Sun itself came from, the teacher of science is not only uncomfortable, but also positively tickled to a justifiable bad temper! Science can move only in a field where it can gather the necessary data to calculate and to prove.

But philosophy seeks to satisfy the questionings of the human intellect regarding the Ultimate Source of all things, even if the necessary scientific data for such an attempt may not be available in the laboratory. There is a definite frontier at which the intellect and its observations, its logic and conclusions, its reasoning and assertions, must necessarily exhaust themselves and cry halt. And yet, the question is not fully answered, for we find an honest intellect still left wondering: Why! How!! What!!! There science is silent. Where science has fulfilled itself, and from where onwards its light fails to illumine the path, there philosophy starts its pilgrimage towards the Absolute satisfaction.

Here, the stanza says that the very light which emerges from the Sun and which illumines the whole world, is the Light that is emerging from Me, the Infinite Consciousness. Nay, the light that comes from the moon, the light that emanates from the fire, are all expressions of the Infinite Reality, When It expresses through the moon and the fire.

The manifestations are different because the equipments are different; the LIGHT in the bulb, the HEAT in the furnace, the MOVEMENT in the fan, are all indeed different manifestations, because the bulb, the furnace, and the fan are dissimilar equipments; but the energy called electricity is one and the same. In brief. Consciousness expressed through the Sun manifests sunlight, expressed through the moon is the moon-light, and expressed through the dry fuel is the fire --

and yet, all of them are, in reality, nothing but the Infinite Itself, in Its varied glorious manifestations. The Infinite manifests Itself, in Its varied glorious manifestations. The Infinite manifests Itself in order to create the conducive environment, in which the world can exist, and wherein, as the Lord, He can come to express Himself and play His game of plurality!!

MOREOVER:

13. *Permeating the earth I support all beings by (My) energy: and having become the liquid moon, I nourish all herbs.*

PERMEATING THE EARTH I SUPPORT ALL BEINGS WITH MY ENERGY—Long before artificial manure was discovered, the earth had, no doubt, a long history; and some of those eras in the bygone days were, perhaps, more over-populated than the present. And yet, the earth continued to sustain life. The capacity of the earth to sustain life and nourish it, the warmth and the mineral contents, are all, says the Lord, "MY OWN VITALITY" meaning, the same Consciousness which, through the Sun became the necessary warmth of the atmosphere, while expressing through the earth, became the 'potential fertility' of the soil and the 'life-giving secret capacity' of the earth.

HAVING BECOME THE MOONLIGHT I NOURISH ALL THE PLANTS—The same Eternal Consciousness, while functioning through the moon expresses Itself as moon light and fills each plant with its 'essence' content. If this passage was rejected by members of a previous generation, children of the

---

गामाविश्य च भूतानि धारयाम्यहमोजसा ।
पुष्णामि चौषधीः सर्वाः सोमो भूत्वा रसात्मकः ॥ १३ ॥

gāmāviśya ca bhūtāni dhārayāmyahamojasā
puṣṇāmi cauṣadhīḥ sarvāḥ somo bhūtvā rasātmakaḥ 13.

modern scientific knowledge will not dare to question it. Modern agriculaural science proves that the planetary organisation, especially the moon, has got some strange connection with the expected productivity in agriculture! Recent experiments have been reported where tomato seedling sown on the full-moon day and plucked again on a full-moon day were found to yield better crop.

Indeed, it is accepted everywhere that the paddy preserved for seeds is not only to be dried in the Sun, but it must also lie exposed to the moon. The naturopaths keep some of their preparation – as also the *Ayurvedic* physicians – exposed to the moon for a certain number of days, and they claim that the medicines gain certain curative power thereby.

All those above facts, touched upon lightly here, should prove that the declaration in the stanza is not totally unscientific.

The Sun, the moon and the fire are the cosmic sources of all energy in the world, and the very Source of the energy, from where it flows through these phenomenal expressions, is the Infinite Consciousness. The Consciousness functions through the earth and gives to the field their special capacity to sustain and nourish the vegetable world, and when the flora grows up, it is again the same Consciousness, functioning through the moon and manifesting of moonlight that falls (Vitamins).

14. *Having become (the fire) VAISHVAANARA, I abide in the body of beings, and associated with PRANA and APANA digest the four-hold food.*

ABIDING IN THE BODY OF LIVING BEINGS AS *VAISVAANARA*—The same Supreme Consciousness

---

अहं वैश्वानरो भूत्वा प्राणिनां देहमाश्रितः ।
प्राणापानसमायुक्तः पचाम्यन्नं चतुर्विधम् ॥ १४ ॥

ahaṁ vaiśvānaro bhūtvā prāṇināṁ dehamāśritaḥ
prāṇāpānasamāyuktaḥ pacāmyannaṁ caturvidham 14.

expresses Itself as the warmth-of-life in all living creatures. That physical structure, from which all warmth has gone, is dead. Metabolism creates the body-heat and the functions of the inner organisms continue automatically without any conscious effort on the part of the individual, so long as LIFE is pulsating in the body.

Here, the Eternal Reality is indicated as that mighty LIFE, which, when pulsating through the body, manifests Itself as the 'digestive fire' (*Vaishvaanara*), which assimilates all the food taken in.

I DIGEST THE FOURFOLD FOOD—The digestive power in a healthy living organism assimilates all types of food. The entire variety of human diet is classified under four heads in Sanskrit as food that should be (i) masticated, (ii) swallowed, (iii) sucked, and (iv) licked. Under these four types, we can embrace all kinds of food, vegetarian and non-vegetarian, prepared and unprepared, raw and ripe. All things consumed by the mouth are digested, assimilated and absorbed because of the digestive system and the power in the digestive system is nothing but a manifestation of the All-present Life Principle.

ASSOCIATED WITH *PRANA* AND *APANA* — The two physiological functions of 'perception' and of 'excretion' in all living creatures are called *Prana* and *Apana*. Here, however, these terms can be considered in their broadest general sense. Not only does the Consciousness, as the 'digestive fire', assimilate the food that has reached the stomach, but is again Life manifested as the peristaltic movement (*Prana*) that receives and rolls down the food swallowed, through the oesophagus into the stomach. After digesting, assimilating and absorbing food, it is again the same divine spark of Life that gives the intestines its capacity to throw out (*Apana*) the undigested and unnecessary by-products. In short, it is the Lord that helps us to swallow the food, it is the Lord that assimilates the food, and it is the Lord again that presides over the function of eliminating the by-products.

MOREOVER:

15. *And I am seated in the heart in the hearts of all, from Me are memory, knowledge, as well as their absence. I am verily that which has to be known in all the VEDAS; I am indeed the author of VEDANTA, and, the "knower of the VEDAS" am I.*

I AM SEATED IN THE HEARTS OF ALL—If there be thus an Infinite Omnipotent Power that manifests Itself as the different things in the world, how can a seeker make his pilgrimage towards It and meet this Great Divine? Lord Krishna says that He lives in the Hearts of all living creatures. Here the HEART does not mean the physiological 'heart', but it is the metaphysical HEART. The term HEART, in philosophy, means "minds which have been trained to entertain constantly the positive qualities of love, tolerance, mercy, charity, kindness, and the like". A peaceful, joyous settled in tranquillity, alert and vigilant to receive higher intimations, is called the 'heart'.

The Infinite 'DWELLS IN THE HEART' means, though He is present everywhere the Lord is most conspicuously self-evident, during meditation, in the HEART of the mediator.

सर्वस्य चाहं हृदि संनिविष्टो
मत्तः स्मृतिर्ज्ञानमपोहनं च ।
वेदैश्च सर्वैरहमेव वेद्यो
वेदान्तकृद्वेदविदेव चाहम् ॥ १५ ॥

sarvasya cāhaṁ hṛdi sanniviṣṭo
mattaḥ smṛtirjñānamapohanaṁ ca
vedaiśca sarvairahameva vedyo
vedāntakṛdvedaideva cāham 15.

FROM ME COME MEMORY, KNOWLEDGE, AS WELL AS THEIR ABSENCE—The Consciousness Divine has been declared above as revelling in the heart of every living creature. The light-of-Life seems to have no particular justification to exit since all perceptions are through the body, all feelings are through the mind, all thoughts are through the intellect. The *Geeta* here declares what exactly is then the special grace of Consciousness. It is the light of Consciousness that illumines all our experiences in life. From this Supreme alone all memories, knowledge, as well as forgetfulness, come to us. Memory is constituted of our experiences of the past, stored away in our understanding which guides our present and future activities. All education and knowledge that we have at this moment are memories from the past. Unless we are aware of these memories, they will not be available in our present life. Reacting properly to the present sets of stimuli and thereby gaining fresh and vivid experiences, is the process of widening our field of knowledge. And all these processes are possible only in the light of Life.

Acquisition of new knowledge presupposes our capacity to give up our earlier false notions. Imperfect knowledge gets weeded out when a person is cultivating new knowledge. A capacity to forget is an essential prerequisite in acquiring fresh knowledge. This stanza explains that all these subjective activities, mental and intellectual, arise from and are maintained by the Conscious Principle, the Lord-Himself.

IT IS I THAT IS TO BE KNOWN BY ALL THE *VEDAS*—In all the scriptures of the world, including the various portions of all the *Vedas* in India, Krishna says, this Infinite Consciousness is the one common factor that has been extolled and adored. To realise this is to reach the goal-of-life, the fulfilment of existence. The Consciousness that revels in the hearts of all living creatures is the non-dual Immortal Reality, the All-pervading and It is the only substratum for the pluralistic world of experiences.

I AM INDEED THE AUTHOR OF *VEDANTA*, AS WELL AS THE KNOWER OF THE *VEDAS*—Since Consciousness alone is the Eternal Reality, and everything else is a projection upon it, the very essence in everything, as expressed in the *Vedas* also, is this Consciousness. The seeker who listens to the *Vedas*, reflects upon their wisdom, and ultimately comes to experience the fulfilment of his life, is also at no stage anything other than the same Consciousness.

In short,* it has been said that the Consciousness is the Light in the sun; it is the same Consciousness that fertilises the earth; the Consciousness as moonlight, supplies food-value to the plant-kingdom; it is Truth Itself, as the body-warmth that presides over the assimilation of the food within the body, and supervises the process of life's transactions with the world outside; and it is the same light of Consciousness that makes it possible for us to gain experiences, to store away knowledge, and to replace ignorance with better knowledge.

The Eternal Principle which thus expresses Itself as the phenomenal power – which, with their activities make it possible for life to exist on the surface of the earth, and which helps the higher life to grow and expand into wisdom - is the very theme indicated in the *Vedas* as the Eternal Reality, and to know it and to bring It under our experience is to know the Infinite.

Till now the earlier verses have enumerated the glories of *Narayana*, the Blessed Lord, as manifested through the various vehicles such as the sun, the moon, the earth, the body, the mind and the intellect. Now, in the following verses,

---

* That is to summarise the previous four stanzas.

Lord Krishna points out the True Nature of the Infinite as the unconditioned (*Niru-padhika*), All pervading (*Sarva gatah*) and Eternal (*Nityah*). This Infinite Reality transcends all intellectual concepts, such as the finite and the infinite -- as the perishable and the imperishable.

CONSIDERING THE RELATIVE WORLD OF EXPERIENCE, BHAGAWAN SAYS:

16. *Two 'PURUSHAS' are there in this world, the Perishable and the Imperishable. All beings are the Perishable and the 'KOOTASTHAH' is called the Imperishable.*

Earlier, in Chapter XIII, we had an exhaustive discussion of the field-of-Matter and the Knower-of-the-field. The discussion we had so far in this chapter must prove that the sun, the warmth in the atmosphere, the earth, its potentialities, the plant-kingdom, and man and his capacities – all of them together constituting the field-of-Matter, are nothing other than the Supreme Itself.

When the Infinite Consciousness becomes the light and heat of the sun, the fertility of the earth, the essence in the plant, the Consciousness in the heart, the faculties of knowing and remembering, etc., they are all different forms of Consciousness alone.[1] Thus, the fact that the field-of-Matter is nothing other than the Spirit Itself was already demonstrated. The only difference is that the Spirit, when It has assumed the form of Matter, looks as though It is subject to change and destruction. Thus the realm-of-Matter is indicated in this stanza as the Perishable (*Kshara*) *Purusha*.[2]

द्वाविमौ पुरुषौ लोके क्षरश्चाक्षर एव च ।
क्षरः सर्वाणि भूतानि कूटस्थोऽक्षर उच्यते ॥ १६ ॥

dvāvimau puruṣau loke kṣaraścākṣara eva ca
kṣaraḥ sarvāṇi bhūtāni kūtastho'kṣara ucyate 16.

In the relative field of experience, when we talk with reference to the inert and perishable world-of-Matter, the Spirit is indicated as the Conscious Principle, which is Imperishable. With reference to one's wife alone is one called a husband; when I have a son I will become a father. Similarly, with reference to the perishable and the changing Matter-envelopments, the Consciousness is indicated as the Imperishable and the Changeless. The body changes; from childhood to youth, from youth to old age; the mind changes in its quality of feelings and emotions; the intellect expressing differently with each added knowledge and experience is ever in a state of change. But one is constantly AWARE OF all these changes. This Consciousness which is constantly recognising and illumining all changes, at all levels, all through the individual's life, is necessarily changeless. This Conscious Principle is called *Akshara* only with reference to and as a contrast with the Perishable, the (*Kshara*).

This Immutable and Imperishable principle of life is the Self, common in all living creatures at all times. That this Self, in the midst of change remains changeless and that all changes can take place only in contact with it are both indicated by the metaphor suggested by the term used here *Kootasthah*.*

DISTINCT FROM THESE TWO – THE PERISHABLE AND THE IMPERISHABLE – UNTAINTED BY THE IMPERFECTIONS OF THESE TWO RELATIVE CONDITIONS, IS THE HIGHEST SPIRIT:

---

[1] If a goldsmith, in order to make a chain, beats out a piece of gold into a bar, draws it out into lengths of wire, cuts it into bits, knocks each bit into rings, and solders them together to form a chain, and if the chain ultimately is made of gold, all through the intervening process it must have been gold only. The bar, the wire, the bits and the rings are all different forms of the same gold.

[2] In Sanskrit, the Life Principle is called *Purusha* because it dwells in the cityof the physical body (*Purishayat* – resting in the body).

17. *But distinct is the Supreme PURUSHA called the Highest Self, the Indestructible Lord, who, pervading the three worlds (waking, dream and deep-sleep), sustains them.*

But distinct from all these is the Highest Spirit spoken of as the Supreme Self. With reference to my own children alone am I really a father. With reference to my duty or status I may have yet another name. Similarly, the Imperishable is a status and a dignity gained by the Spirit only with reference to the field of the perishables around and about It, through which It manifests as the various expressions of Life. When my children have died, or I am dismissed from my job, I am no more a father, nor can I any more claim my erstwhile official dignity. But that does not mean that I am, in the absence of children or work, an absolute zero, a total non-entity! No. I will exist as 'the son of my father' or in my individual capacity, though devoid of all my special status and dignity born out of my relationship with my profession, or with my children.

When the perishable (*Kshara*) is transcended, what remains is not Imperishable (*Akshara*) but that which played as the *'Perishable-Purusha'* as well as the *'Imperishable-Purusha'*. This Pure Spirit *(Purusha)* is spoken of as the Supreme Self, who PERVADES AND SUSTAINS THE THREE WORLDS: 'World'

उत्तमः पुरुषस्त्वन्यः परमात्मेत्युदाहृतः ।
यो लोकत्रयमाविश्य बिभर्त्यव्यय ईश्वरः ॥ १७ ॥

uttamaḥ puruṣastvanyaḥ paramātmetyudāhṛtaḥ
yo lokatrayamāviśya bibhartyavyaya īśvaraḥ 17.

Koota means 'anvil' of the blacksmith; *Sthah* means 'to sit'; *Kootasthah* means 'that which remains like an anvil' of the blacksmith, which allows every iron piece to change its shape but itself remains changeless.

in Sanskrit means 'realm of experience'. The three realms of experiences in which we eke out our life's returns are the states of waking, dream, and deep-sleep. The same Self is the illuminator of the experiences in all the above three states of Consciousness.

There are not three different types of *Purushas;* according to the limitations and conditions around, It, the Spirit, appears different in Its manifestations. A pot is in a room; now the pot-space is a lesser part of the room-space, and the room-space is only a negligible portion of the total-space. At the same time pot-space minus the pot, if understood as 'space', is the same space as the infinite-space. Now, in the above example, pot-space and room-space are something other than the outer-space, is as much as, conditioned as they are, they have gathered unto themselves certain limitations, but the unconditioned pot-space and the room-space are nothing but the infinite-space; break the pot, pull down the walls, the space that was pot-space and the space that was the room-space have both become one with the Infinite-space!

The Infinite Consciousness is Itself the perishable-field in another form, and as the Knower-of-the-Field, the same Consciousness is the Imperishable Reality in the perishable conditionings, But when these conditionings are transcended, the same self is experienced as the Supreme Self - *Paramatman.*

SHOWING THE ETYMOLOGY OF THE VERY TERM *PURUSHOTTAMA,* THE LORD SHOWS HOW HE IS REALLY THE SUPREME:

18. *As I transcend the perishable and I am even Higher than the Imperishable, I am declared as the PURUSHOTTAMA (the Highest-PURUSHA) in the world and in the VEDAS.*

Explaining the very word *Purushottama*, Lord Krishna says that Pure Consciousness is HIGHER than both the Perishable and the Imperishable. The Perishable can continue its processes of change only against the Imperishable Truth. It is a scientific fact that no change is perceptible without reference to a changeless factor. If two trains are both moving at the same speed no movement is recognised by perceivers in both the trains. If the changes in the world of Matter – the body, the mind and the intellect are recognised, then there must be steady principle that illumines all these different changes. This constant factor among the Perishing is called the Imperishable.

This illumining factor gathers its status as the Imperishable only with reference to the Perishable realms. Once the perishable realms are transcended, the Imperishable amidst them Itself comes to shine forth as the Pure Infinite, which is the *Purushottama.* Since the Truth, *Purushottama*, is experienced only on transcending both the *Perishable* and the *Imperishable,* It is known by the term the Highest-Spirit - *Purushottama*. This term is used to indicate the Supreme-most Self, both by the ancient sacred volumes *(Vedas*), and by the poets and writers of the world.

NOW THE LORD SPEAKS OF THE FRUITS GAINED BY ONE WHO REALISES THE SUPREME TRUTH AS DESCRIBED ABOVE.

यस्मात्क्षरमतीतोऽहमक्षरादपि चोत्तमः ।
अतोऽस्मि लोके वेदे च प्रथितः पुरुषोत्तमः ॥ १८ ॥

yasmātkṣaramatīto'hamakṣarādapi cottamaḥ
ato'smi loke vede ca prathitaḥ puruṣottamaḥ 18.

19. *He who undeluded, thus knows Me, the Supreme PURUSHA, he, all-knowing, worships Me with his whole being, O Bharata.*

'Undeluded' means, one who has totally detached oneself from one's wrong identifications with body, mind, and intellect, and therefore, also from the world of perceptions, feelings, and thoughts, which these vehicles provide.

THUS KNOWS ME—To 'know' here is not a mere intellectual comprehension, but a deep subjective spiritual apprehension. That the undeluded one thus experiences himself that he is the *Purushottama*-principle Itself, seems to be the suggestion here.

Such a man who has fully identified himself with the Infinite 'Me' alone is a true devotee, who 'WORSHIPS ME WITH ALL HIS BEING'; such a one is the greatest of devotees, declares the *Geetaacharya.* Identification with the beloved is everywhere the measure of love; the greater the love, the greater is our identification with the object of our love. Therefore, arithmetically, total identification should be the maximum love or devotion.

The Highest Spirit, *Purushottama*, being the Infinite Consciousness, it is the 'All-knower', inasmuch as whenever anything is known perception, feeling, or thought, it is the Principle of Consciousness that illumines it. One who has transcended one's matter-equipments and has successfully sought and discovered one's spiritual nature as the Infinite Consciousness, that individual, as the Supreme Awareness, indicated here as the 'All-knower' *(Sarvavit).*

यो मामेवमसंमूढो जानाति पुरुषोत्तमम् ।
स सर्वविद्भजति मां सर्वभावेन भारत ॥ १९ ॥

yo māmevamasammūḍho jānāti puruṣottamam
sa sarvavidbhajati māṁ sarvabhāvena bhārata 19.

THE KNOWLEDGE OF THE TRUE NATURE OF THE LORD IS THE THEME OF THIS CHAPTER AND THE FOLLOWING CONCLUDING VERSE KRISHNA EXTOLS THIS THEME, WHICH GIVES LIBERATION TO MAN FROM ALL HIS FLESH-BORN SORROWS, MIND-BORN AGITATIONS AND INTELLECT-BORN RESTLESSNESS:

20. *Thus, this most secret science (teaching), has been taught by Me, O sinless one. On knowing this (a man) becomes 'wise' and all his duties are accomplished, O Bharata.*

In this concluding verse Krishna says that He has taught in this chapter THE MOST SECRET SCIENCE. The spiritual science *(Brahma-vidya)* is termed as 'secret', not in the sense that it should not be given out to anybody, but that it is a knowledge which cannot, of its own accord come to anyone, unless one is initiated into it by a 'Knower of Reality'.

O SINLESS ONE—'Sin' means an act, a feeling or thought, which having been perpetrated, entertained, or thought of, comes back after a time to agitated our bosom with its insulting taunts and helpless regrets. In short, SIN is the result of the past that comes to demean our Self-estimate and creates in us a lot of mental storm and consequent dissipation. One who has thus an inner personality which carries disturbing memories of undignified acts and cruel schemes, has indeed, a bosom that is ever agitated and restless. Such a mind-intellect-equipment cannot consistently apply itself to any serious and deep investigation into subtle realm of the Pure

---

इति गुह्यतमं शास्त्रमिदमुक्तं मयानघ ।
एतद्बुद्ध्वा बुद्धिमान्स्यात्कृतकृत्यश्च भारत ॥ २० ॥
iti guhyatamaṁ śāstramidamuktaṁ mayānagha
etadbuddhvā buddhimānsyātkṛtakṛtyaśca bhārata 20.

Awareness that lies beyond the frontiers of the intellect. Therefore, the term 'sinless' in the context here only means "O STEADY-MINDED, ALERT AND VIGILANT STUDENT".

He who has realised this *PURUSHOTTAMA*-state of Consciousness becomes 'wise', for he cannot thereafter make any error of judgement in life and thereby create confusions and sorrows for himself and for other around him.

The second of the benefits accrued by entering the *Purushottama*-state is the enjoyment of complete sense of fulfilment *(Krita-Krityataa)* -- a total and overwhelming joy that comes to a man when he realises that he has fully accomplished what is expected of him. This is promised here in this verse as the reward for the realisation of the *Purushottama-state.*

Thus, in the UPANISHADS of the glorious Bhagawad-Geeta, in the Science of the Eternal, in the Scripture of YOGA, in the dialogue between Sri Krishna and Arjuna, the fifteenth discourse ends entitled:

The *Yoga* of the Supreme Spirit

Om Om Om Om Om

ॐ तत्सदिति श्रीमद् भगवद् गीतासूपनिषत्सु ब्रह्मविद्यायां
योगशास्त्रे श्रीकृष्णार्जुनसंवादे पुरुषोत्तमयोगो नाम
पञ्चदशोऽध्याय:

Oṁ tatsaditi śrīmadbhagavadgītāsū ūpaniṣatsu brahmavidyāyāṁ yogaśāstre śrī kṛṣṇārjuna saṁvāde puruṣottamayogo nāma pañcadaśo'dhyāyaḥ

XVI

Divine and Devilish Estates
Introduction

Every system of ethics catalogues a series of virtues and vices, and strangely enough all such systems read the same although their Prophets belonged to different times and places. Irrespective of clime, creed, race and tongue, a good man is a good man. No doubt, there are slight differences between faith and faith, but such differences are found only in the Prophets' emphasis on the peoples' abstinence from certain vices and/or cultivation of certain virtues. And their special advice and appeals to the people are obviously determined by the sort of life lived by the majority of the people in their respective eras and areas.

The very same qualities accepted as virtues some three thousand years ago, are still regarded as virtues, and even today, those who live them are considered virtuous and noble. Strangely enough, we find that human beings are the same in this uproarious present as they were in the peaceful past. In this chapter, the entire mankind, of all times and of all ages, has been classified under three types: (a) the Divinely Good (*Devas*) (b) the Diabolically Fallen (*Asuras*) and (c) the Incorrigibly Indifferent (*Rakshasas*). However, the *Rakshasic* type is not taken up for discussion in the following stanzas, most probably because, for that type, no conscious self-development programme is ever possible unless it is broken, recast and molded again by the relentless hand of adversity.

Earlier, (in Chapter IX) we had a discussion in which Krishna explained the three kinds of nature of the sentient beings, *Prakritis*. Later on (in Chapter XIII) the Field-of-Experience (*Kshetra*), and the Knower-of-the-Field (*Kshetrajna*) were discussed in detail. In conclusion, it was established that the Subject, the 'Knower', is one in all 'Fields'.

The natural question of a brilliant intellect, at this stage of discussion, could only be how and why the experiences are so varied from individual to individual, even though the 'Subject' is one and the same. It was explained (in Chapter XIV) that the 'Field', being under the influence of different temperaments (*gunas*), no two individuals can experience a given field of happenings in the same fashion. After thus discussing exhaustively, how the Fields-of-Experience differs from one another under changing temperaments, we had a discourse from the *Geetaacharya*, (in Chapter XV) on the essential nature of the Infinite and Eternal 'Subject', the Knower-of-the-Field. This *Purushottama* had been ably painted therein as the transcendental state of Perfection and as Pure Knowledge.

Naturally, therefore, in the logical development of thought in the *Geeta*, this chapter discusses the types of manifestations that are available in the living world when the same 'Knower', the one Eternal Spirit, expresses Itself through various 'Fields'. The logic of the Sixteenth Chapter can generally be a bit confusing to all hasty students; and there are daring critics who have come to the conclusion that, more often than not, 'the Divine Song of the Lord is a rambling poem'. This is very unfair. The sequence in the thought development in Chapter Sixteen is from the ideas not yet concluded in Chapter Nine and from the ideas merely touched upon during the explanations in the preceding three chapters.

Another severe criticism generally levelled against Hindus is that as believers in the Non-dual Reality, the *Brahman*, they have no respect for moral and ethical values. Some critics compare the devotional religions, semetic or otherwise, with *Vedanta*, and desperately strive to establish an unsubstantiated superiority for themselves. But here a lie is given to this criticism; how consistently *Vedanta* insists upon the moral virtues, as a prerequisite even for entering its portals, is evident from the chapters of the *Geeta*. And this chapter will reveal how exhaustively the *Rishis* had pointed out the mental contents of the good as compared with those of the bad.

The anxiety of the *Geeta* is not to classify mankind as good and bad, to promise a paradise to the good and to curse the bad to endless damnation in hell. The qualities enumerated here are the result of scientific observations made in the physical, mental and intellectual behaviours, when life, the 'Knower', pulsates through a DISCIPLINED 'Field', and an UNDISCIPLINED 'Field' of experience.

The Blessed Lord said:

1. *Fearlessness, purity of heart, steadfastness in the YOGA-of-Knowledge, alms-giving, control of the senses, sacrifice, study of the SHASTRAS, and straightforwardness ...*

As we read the opening stanza we are reminded of the twenty VALUES of life, that were described earlier by Lord

---

श्रीभगवानुवाच
अभयं सत्त्वसंशुद्धिर्ज्ञानयोगव्यवस्थितिः ।
दानं दमश्च यज्ञश्च स्वाध्यायस्तप आर्जवम् ॥ १ ॥
śrībhagavānuvāca
abhayaṁ sattvasaṁśuddhirjñānayogavyavasthitiḥ
dānaṁ damaśca yajñaśca svādhyāyastapa ārjavam 1.

Krishna in His Divine discourse (XIII – 8 to 12). Herein we find an almost exhaustive list of the noble TRAITS in a cultured man living the spiritual way-of-life; a life wherein he accepts and lives those twenty VALUES of life, while meeting the work-a-day world. And in the enumeration of these qualities, FEARLESSNESS (*Abhayam*) comes first. Fear is generated in one, only when one is in a field which is clouded by 'ignorance'. Fear is the expression of *Avidya*. Where there is Knowledge there is fearlessness. By placing this quality of fearlessness at the head of the list, with the unsung music of sheer suggestiveness, the divine *Acharya* is indicating that true ethical perfection in one is directly proportional to the spiritual evolution attained by the individual.

PURITY OF HEART—No amount of external discipline can supply the student the positive dynamism that is the very core in all moral living. The *Geeta* preaches a dynamic religion, militant in both theory and practice. The Divine Charioteer is not satisfied by a tame generation of passive goodness. He wants the members of the perfect Hindu society not only to live among themselves the highest values of life, but also to burst forth with the positive glow of righteousness and bathe the entire generation of men in the light of truth and virtue – virtue that implies honesty of intentions and purity of motives.

STEADFASTNESS IN THE *YOGA*-OF-KNOWLEDGE—this ethical purity at the level of the heart cannot be brought about when the human mind is turned outward to the flesh. Only when the mind is constantly in unison with the Infinite Song of the Soul, can it discover in itself the necessary courage to renounce its low appetites, clinging attachments and the consequent foul motives GURGLING from within itself. Devotion to Knowledge

(*Jnana Yoga*) is thus the positive way to persuade the mind to leave all its low temptations. When a child is playing with a delicate glass curio, to save the precious object, the parents generally offer it a piece of chocolate, and the little child, anxious to get at the chocolate, drops the precious thing down. Similarly, a mind that is awakened to the serener joys of the Self-will, naturally, never hang on to sensuous objects and their fleeting joys.

ALMS-GIVING (CHARITY), CONTROL OF THE SENSES AND SACRIFICE—These three are now the techniques by which an individual successfully tunes up his inner instruments of knowledge in order to discover the required amount of 'steady devotion to Knowledge'. Charity must come from one's sense of abundance. Charity springs only from a sense of oneness in us - oneness between the giver and the recipient. Unless one is able to identify oneself with others, one will not feel this noble urge to share all that one has with others who do not have it. Thus *Daana* is born out of a capacity to restrain one's instincts of acquisition and aggrandisement, and to replace them with the spirit of sacrifice, and it consists in sharing with others the objects of the world that one possesses.*

If charity (*Daana*) develops in one the capacity to detach oneself from the wealth that one possesses and share it with others who are poorer, then we can say that control of the sense-organs (*dama*) is the application of the same spirit of sacrifice in one's personal life. To give a complete licence for indulgence to

---

* This does not mean that we are to disregard the charity of the level of the heart and the head. In fact to share with others our sympathy and kindness and to distribute one's knowledge are considered by our *Smritis* as great charities (*Vidya-daana*, etc.).

the sense-organs is to waste, unproductively, the total human vitality. To economise in the expenditure of energy through the sense-organs in the fields of sense-objects is to discover an extra amount of untapped energy. This energy can be made use of as the motive power behind the mind and intellect that is set on a flight to the higher realms of meditation. To keep the mind tuned up to the Self, a subtle energy is called forth, and it will be discovered within ourselves when we control our sense excesses. Without *dama* and *Daana* the pilgrimage to Truth is merely a dream.

In the *Vedic* period, SACRIFICE (*Yajna*) was the day-to-day devotional ritualism that the average man of spiritual seeking diligently practised. Without this regular prayer-cum-*puja*, which is the substitute for *Yajna* available for us, control of the sense-organs will be impossible, and without this control, the spirit of charity cannot come. In the absence of both *Daana* and *dama*, spiritual experience of the Self, recognition of the Divine within us, is impossible. It is interesting to note that each subsequent term in this list is logically connected with the one indicated immediately before.

STUDY OF THE SCRIPTURES (*Swaadhyaaya*) — traditionally, this term indicates regular study of the scriptures. Study of scriptural literature daily, in measured quantities, will provide the necessary inspiration to live the divine life in our day-to-day existence. But, scriptural study is indicated here by a very significant term,* which in Sanskrit suggests that the study of the scriptures should not be merely an intellectual appreciation, but as the student reads the textbooks, he must be able,

---

* *Swaadhyaaya* = *Swa* + *adhyaaya* – Self-study.

simultaneously, to observe, analyse and realise the truth of what he is studying within his own life. Regular studies, coupled with regular practice (*Yajna*), will give us the courage to live in self-control of the sense-organs, which in its turn will supply us with steadiness in meditation for realising the Highest.

ASCETICISM (*Tapas*)—All conscious self-denials at the body level, whereby an individual reduces his indulgences in the world outside, gains more and more energy within himself, and applies the new-found energy for the purpose of self-development, are called *tapas*.

UPRIGHTNESS (*Arjavam*)—Crookedness in thought, emotion and general conduct has a self-destructive influence upon the personality. Actions belying one's own true intentions and motives, convictions and aspirations, realisation and discrimination will result in the crookedness of one's personality. He who is indulging in this way-of-life will thereby develop in himself a split personality and will soon lose the glow of efficiency and be impoverished in the powers of personal grit.

In short, in this very opening stanza of the chapter, while enumerating the qualities of a 'Divinely good' man, we find a definite scientific connection among them. Ethical values and moral beauties described in Hinduism are not arbitrary declarations of an imaginative Saint or a melancholy prophet. They are built on the rocky foundations of reason and experience. Sincerely pursued and consciously lived, they contribute to a better expression of the diviner possibilities in man which generally lie dormant. Ethics in India are not, by themselves, a passport to heaven, but are a preparation for a fuller unfoldment of the divine contents in the bosom of man.

MOREOVER, HERE ARE LISTED THE MENTAL CONTENTS OF THE GODLY:

2. *Harmlessness, truth, absence of anger, renunciation, peacefulness, absence of crookedness, compassion to beings, non-covetousness, gentleness, modesty, absence of fickleness ...*

Continuing, Lord Krishna enumerates the mental contents of the godly type of men.

HARMLESSNESS (*Ahimsa*)—it does not consist so much in not causing bodily injury to beings in the physical world, as in not harming any living creature in the world around from the realm of thought. Physical *ahimsa* is simply impossible. To continue living, some kind of physical harm or the other has to be brought about; it is unavoidable. But even while bringing about unavoidable disturbances around ourselves, if our motives are pure and clean, the harm so wrought is not regarded as causing injury.

TRUTH (*Satyam*)—We have already discussed this virtue while explaining the last term in the previous stanza 'uprightness'.

AN EVEN TEMPER (absence of anger-*Akrodha*)—Sometimes it is rendered as 'angerlessness' which is not very happy. A better rendering would be the capacity to check, at the right time, waves of anger as they mount up in our bosom, so that we do not manifest anger in our actions. It will be almost unnatural to expect the mind to become incapable of anger. But

---

अहिंसा सत्यमक्रोधस्त्यागः शान्तिरपैशुनम् ।
दया भूतेष्वलोलुप्त्वं मार्दवं ह्रीरचापलम् ॥ २ ॥

ahiṁsā satyamakrodhastyāgaḥ śāntirapaiśunam
dayā bhūteṣvaloluptvaṁ mārdavaṁ hnīracāpalam 2.

* Especially when they, by their thought, word or deed come to injure our interest, or insult our own self-evaluation.

no emotion should be allowed to overwhelm us to such a degree as to render us almost impotent. This anger arises out of an insufferable impatience with others.* In short, *Akrodha* does not mean 'without anger' but only keeping, as far as possible, an 'even temper'.

SPIRIT OF RENUNCIATION (*Tyaga*)—in this stanza also we find, as we noticed in the previous stanza, that there is a sequential order strictly followed in the development of thought from term to term. If without respect to Truth, we cannot live in the spirit of *ahimsa*, so also without the spirit of renunciation an even temper is but a vain hope.

PEACEFULNESS (Quietude-*Shanti*)—If a seeker is capable of living, conscious of Truth, harming none, keeping an even temper, in a spirit of renunciation, in spite of all disturbing environments and happenings around, then he is the one who shall come to experience peace and quietude in himself. Even in the midst of a stormy life and outrageous circumstances, such an individual can successfully keep his inward balance and intellectual poise.

ABSENCE OF CROOKEDNESS (Unmalicious tongue-*Apaishunam*)—the ugliness or beauty of the tongue is ordered by the personality behind it. A shattered entity will seek self-gratification in malicious scandal mongering, and the soft, fleshy tongue can often become more devastating than the most destructive missile. A seeker who is trying to reach a fuller and more exhaustive self-expression should develop such an inward harmony that his speech should echo the fragrance of his soul. A speech with softness of tone, clarity of expression, honesty of conviction, power of bringing a clear picture in the listener's mind with no veiled meaning, overflowing with sincerity, devotion and love, becomes the very quality of the autobiography of the speaker's personality. To develop, therefore, a habit of such speech would be unconsciously training many aspects in ourselves which are all necessary for the perfect disciplining of the inner equipments.

COMPASSION (TENDERNESS) TOWARDS BEINGS —in the society in general, it is not reasonable for a seeker to expect that all will keep up to the ideal that he himself entertains. There will be imperfections around. But to recognise, in and through those imperfections, the Infinite beauty of life expressed, is the secret of enduring tenderness in all Saints and Sages. Love alone can discover an infinite amount of tenderness in us. Unless we train ourselves to see the beauty of life pulsating through even wretched hearts and ugly characters, we will fail to bring forth tenderness to sweeten life within and without.

NON-COVETOUSNESS (*Aloluptvam*)—in the subjective life, to live 'without covetousness' means controlling our sense-organs from extreme indulgence in sense-enjoyments. An average man has an endless thirst and an insatiable hunger for sense indulgence. To remain in self-control without endless sense-hunger is meant by the term non-covetousness.

GENTLENESS AND MODESTY—these are not so much the particular disciplines of the individual, as the resultant beauty and harmony which an individual brings forth as the fragrance of his culture, in his contacts with the world outside. These two qualities are best seen in one who has established himself in all the above-mentioned noble qualities. The conduct of such a disciplined man will be both gentle and modest.

ABSENCE OF FICKLENESS-NOT UNNECESSARILY MOVING THE LIMBS (*Achaapalam*)—Restlessness of mind and unsteadiness of character are reflected in the physical movements of a person. The body shadows the condition of the mind. A constant restlessness, a sudden outburst of activity, an immodest shaking of the body and voluptuous tossing of the limbs are all noticed only in individuals who have not yet cultivated a steady character and a purposeful personality. These can be seen in a child and there they are even considered as enhancing its beauty. But as an individual grows, the beauty in him is his mastery over himself as declared by his movements.

Shankara explains this as 'NOT TO SPEAK OR MOVE HANDS AND LEGS IN VAIN'. This is an extension of the meaning of this term, and implies the promptitude and economy of all physical energy in any efficient activity. Unnecessarily exhausting the muscles with indecisive movements and thoughtless exertions are signs of weakness in the personality. Such individuals are extremely imaginative and miserably weak in their intellectual calibre and emotional vitality. To avoid such movements, therefore, is to cure many simple weaknesses at the various facets of any given personality.

MOREOVER, CONTINUING THE LIST OF DIVINE QUALITIES:

3. *Vigour, forgiveness, fortitude, purity, absence of hatred, absence of pride -- these belong to the one born for the Divine Estate, O Bharata.*

VIGOUR – BRILLIANT GLOW (*Tejas*)—this is not a mere physical glow of complexion produced by good food and ample rest. Nor is it just an exterior beauty arising out of careful tending of the physical structure and planned nourishing of the pads of flesh around the sage. The glow of spirituality is not literally a

---

तेजः क्षमा धृतिः शौचमद्रोहो नातिमानिता ।
भवन्ति संपदं दैवीमभिजातस्य भारत ॥ ३ ॥

tejaḥ kṣamā dhṛtiḥ śaucamadroho nātimānitā
bhavanti sampadaṁ daivīmabhijātasya bhārata 3.

painted halo around him, glimmering as a ring-of-fire. The brilliance of his intellect, the twinkling joy in his eyes, the thrilling fragrance of peace around, the serene poise in his activities, the dalliance of his love for all, the light of joy that ever shines forth from the innermost depths of his being – these constitute their irresistible attraction of the personality of the sage, who, with abundant energy, serves all and discovers for himself a fulfilment in that service.

FORGIVENESS-PATIENCE (*Kshamaa*)—the context in which the word is used here should increase the depth of its meaning. It is not merely 'a capacity to patiently live through some minor physical or mental inconvenience, when insulted or injured by others'. It is a subtle boldness that is shown by a man in facing the world around with an unruffled serenity even in the face of the most powerful opposition and provoking situations.

FORTITUDE (*Dhriti*)—When an individual daringly meets life he cannot expect, all the time, happy situations, favourable circumstances and a conducive arrangement of chances in his field of activity. Ordinarily, a weak man suddenly feels dejected and is tempted to leave his field of work when it is only half done. Many lose their chances of achieving the Highest, and desert the field of action, almost at the moment when, perhaps, victory is round the corner! In order to stick to his guns, man needs a secret energy to nurture and nourish his exhausted and fatigued morale, and this sacred energy welling up in his well-integrated personality is FORTITUDE. Strength of faith, conviction in the goal, consistency of purpose, vivid perception of the ideal and a bold spirit of sacrifice cultivated diligently -all these form the source from which fortitude trickles down to remove exhaustion, fatigue, despair and so on.

PURITY (*Shoucham*)—the word indicates not only the inner

purity - purity of thoughts and motives - but it also suggests, the purity of environments, cleanliness of habit and personal belongings. As a result of an over-emphasis on subjective purity, today, we find in our society, an utter neglect of external purity. Clean clothes and civic-habits have both become rare in our society. Even the devotee-class is unmindful about these, although our religion emphasises that purity and cleanliness are unavoidable disciplines for a seeker.

ABSENCE OF HATRED (*Adroha*)—Harmlessness (*Ahimsa*) was a virtue explained in the previous stanza. Here the same virtue is repeated not only for the purpose of emphasis but also to indicate a slightly different shade of meaning. The term here should mean more than ABSENCE OF HATRED. Just as an individual will never have, even in his dream, any idea of injuring himself, a true seeker, in his recognition of the Oneness in all living creatures, must come to feel that to injure anyone is to injure himself.

ABSENCE OF OVER-PRIDE (*Na-ati-maanitaa*)—To leave off one's exaggerated notions of self-honour is, immediately to relieve oneself from thousands of avoidable excitements and responsibilities. Life is as light as a feather to one who has renounced his over-exaggerated pride while to a Coriolanus; life becomes a heavy cross, to be carried painfully, as it mercilessly cuts through the living flesh on his shoulders.

The twenty-six qualities described above give us a complete picture of the nature of a man of 'Divine Estate'. These qualities are enumerated to serve as a guide to all those who thirst to become 'perfect'. To the extent we are able to reorganise our way-of-life and change our vision of the world around us on the above lines, to that extent we shall economise our energies that are often wasted in idle pursuits. To respect and live these twenty-six values of life completely is to assure ourselves of a right way-of-living.

HERE FOLLOWS A DESCRIPTION OF THE DEMONIC (*ASURIC*) NATURE:

4. *Hypocrisy, arrogance and self-conceit, anger and also harshness and ignorance, belong to one who is born, O Partha, for a demoniac-Estate.*

The dark features of the ugly personalities in the world were never before so strikingly brought within the embrace of a simple stanza. All the *satanic* forces that can ever come to express in the bosom of man have been brought together under some all-comprehensive 'types' of devilish-ness, as indicated here. To know them would be a sufficient warning of what we must avoid and what all traits, in us, we must carefully weed out from our mental composition, so that the greater energy that is available to a well-developed man, may, without any obstruction, flow out of our bosom.

HYPOCRISY (Ostentation-*Dambha*)—'Pretending to be righteous but living unrighteous ways of life' is the meaning that Sankara gives to this term. Hypocrisy is, certainly, one of the cheapest poses assumed by the vicious. To them, all their superficial glow of goodness and purity, of religiosity and sincerity are but attractive hoods to cover their deadly motives and ugly intentions.

ARROGANCE (*Darpa*)—Endless pride of learning, or of wealth, or of social status, or of family connections, gives to an

---

दम्भो दर्पोऽभिमानश्च क्रोधः पारुष्यमेव च ।
अज्ञानं चाभिजातस्य पार्थ संपदमासुरीम् ॥ ४ ॥

dambho darpoabhimānaśca krodhaḥ pāruṣyameva ca
ajñānaṁ cābhijātasya pārtha sampadamāsurīm 4.

individual a kind of insufferable uppishness, and he looks at the world and the happenings around him through this misinterpreting and self-deluding medium and lives in a world of imagined self-importance resulting in an arrogance that drives away all inward peace. Such an individual gets exiled from the love of the community around. An arrogant man is a lonely creature in the world and his only companions are his own imagined self-importance and dreams of his glories which none but he can see. And naturally he becomes highly self-conceited (*Abhimanah*).

ANGER (*Krodha*)—When such a self-conceited, arrogant, hypocrite looks at the world around him and finds that the world's estimate of him is totally different from his own estimate of himself, he revolts within and hence his wrath (*Krodha*) at everything around him. And once such an individual gets worked up with anger, in his speech and action, there must necessarily be a disconcerting insolence (*Parushya*).

Such arrogance, self-conceit, wrath and insolence – arise from his own self-delusions (*ajnanam*). He knows not himself, that he is ignorant of the scheme of the world around him, and consequently, he is blind to the right relationship that he should maintain with the world around him. In short, he is extremely egocentric and he expects the world to be what he wants it to be, and, in his delusion, he supplies a mad blueprint prescribing how the world of healthy beings is to behave and act in his field of actions. This ignorance of oneself and one's relationship with the things and beings around is the secret cause that generally forces one to revolt against the environments and act quixotically.

Such people are termed here by Krishna as the 'Diabolically Fallen', the *Asuric*. Such a spectacular contrast provided by the picture of the *Asuric*, as given here, gloriously brings out the earlier picture of the 'Divinely Good' – the *Daivic*, in relief.

THE EFFECTS OF THE TWO NATURES - THE DIVINELY GOOD AND THE DIABOLICALLY FALLEN - ARE SPOKEN OF AS FOLLOWS:

5. *The divine nature is deemed for liberation, the demoniacal for bondage; grieve not, O Pandava, you are born with divine qualities.*

On hearing such an exhaustive enumeration of the qualities in the good and the bad hearts, it will be natural for every sincere student of the *Geeta* to feel a despair not knowing whether he himself belongs to the latter or the former category. Generally, one would find it easier to consider oneself bad rather than feel the confidence that one belongs to the good. Arjuna must have felt the same despair and, perhaps, reading this in his face, Krishna consoled him: "GRIEVE NOT, O PANDAVA! YOU ARE BORN OF THE DIVINE ESTATE". That a seeker has the necessary interest and perseverance to read the *Geeta* up to this chapter, itself shows that he belongs to the 'DIVINELY-GOOD' category!

Both the ethical beauties and the non-ethical ugliness are painted here not for the purpose of sending the good to an eternal heaven and of damning the vicious to a perpetual hell! Here, the theme is taken up on a more scientific basis. Ethical virtues are the intelligent ways of reviving man's exhausted energies and fatigued spirit to live. By living these healthy values of a righteous life, the individual unshackles his psychological

---

दैवी संपद्विमोक्षाय निबन्धायासुरी मता ।
मा शुच: संपदं दैवीमभिजातोऽसि पाण्डव ॥ ५ ॥

daivī sampadvimokṣāya nibandhāyāmurī matā
mā śucaḥ sampadaṁ daivīmabhijāto'si pāṇḍava 5.

personality from its self-made entanglements: 'THE DIVINE ESTATE LEADS TO RELEASE'. As a contrast to this, the negative tendencies cultivated by the 'Diabolically Fallen' are self-made shackles that chain a man to a realm of confusions and sorrows, forbidding him to grow into the ampler fields of his own inner possibility: 'THE DEVILISH TO BONDAGE'.

GRIEVE NOT (*Maashuchah*)—To become sentimental and desperate or to exhaust oneself in self-pity, or self-condemnation, is a psychological malady, and one suffering from it can never discover in oneself, the energising cheer, the sustaining confidence and the steady will that are required for an intelligent self-diagnosis and an effective self-cure. To a seeker, living the ethical values is, in itself, a kind of treatment to cure him of some of his personality-diseases. To the Hindus, a sinner is not a dangerous mental leper, or a failure of the Omnipotent Lord. To a *Vedantin*, Satan is not a perpetual challenge to God.

The good, contaminated by weakness and 'ignorance', is the evil. And the evil, when cured of 'ignorance,' itself becomes the good. A looking glass covered with dust, cannot reflect light, and mirror properly the objects in front of it. This is not because the glass has lost its capacity to reflect, but because its effectiveness has got veiled at present by the accumulated dust, which is essentially something other than the glass. To wipe it clean is to bring forth from it more clarity and light for the reflection. A 'Diabolically Fallen' one has also the same Infinite Light of Pure Wisdom - but alas, extremely dimmed by false values and wrong concepts in his bosom.

TAKING UP THE 'DIABOLICALLY FALLEN', KRISHNA SCIENTIFICALLY ANALYSES THEIR MENTAL CONTENTS, AND THEY ARE SEPARATELY OBSERVED AND STUDIED IN THE FOLLOWING STANZAS:

6. *There are two types of beings, in this world, the 'divine' and the 'demoniacal;' the divine have been described at length; hear from Me, O Partha, of the demoniacal.*

According to Krishna the entire creation falls under two categories: the 'Divinely Good' (*Daivic*) and the 'Diabolically Fallen' (*Asuric*). But in fact, there is yet another group, the 'Incorrigibly Indifferent' (*Rakshasic*), about whom the Lord is serenely silent. This silence regarding them is perhaps more eloquent than all his eloquence regarding the other two groups! Religions and the techniques of self-development are addressed only to the former two groups and not to the *Rakshasic* type of men. They have not yet sufficiently grown in their evolution; they are still in the hands of the molding Nature and they have yet to be properly baked in the furnace-of-life and its scorching experiences. As they grow up sufficiently, they come under the category of the 'Diabolically Fallen', and religion can come forward to lift them to the status of the 'Divinely Good'. From then onwards it can show them the way to experience and realise the Absolute Goodness which is the Eternal Reality.

If all about the *Asura* type was given in a broad sketch earlier, (XVI-4) the details are being filled in elaborately in the following stanzas.

In almost all religious textbooks of the world, the positive qualities of goodness and righteousness are glorified. But they rarely paint, exhaustively, the negative tendencies in a devilish personality. Some critics of Hinduism are jubilant in discovering

---

द्वौ भूतसर्गौ लोकेऽस्मिन्दैव आसुर एव च ।
दैवो विस्तरशः प्रोक्त आसुरं पार्थ मे श्रृणु ॥ ६ ॥

dvau bhūtasargau loke'smin daiva āsura eva ca
daivī vistaraśaḥ prokta āsuraṁ pārtha me śṛṇu 6.

this tendency in our scriptural texts as a great weakness in our prophets and seers. This criticism against Hinduism was levelled mainly by the critics of the nineteenth century. They are very silent nowadays because of the results of the twentieth century psychological researches and the success of some of the psychiatric methods. To become poignantly aware of the negative tendencies in one's own personality-structure and to become consciously disgusted with those vulgar urges, are the ways of easily eradicating such wrong tendencies from one's inner nature. Be aware of a weakness; it readily disappears from our character – says the modern psychiatrist.

The bad is not merely an opposite of the good. It can never be that the good has certain urges and the bad has another type of urges. Human urges are always typical, and both the good and the bad are expressions of man's heart. Bad is only 'GOOD MISCONSTRUED'. Therefore, in the enumeration of the qualities of the bad, we do not have to meet with a sapless list of the opposites of the previous enumeration which pointed the good. As we discover the contents of the bad mind, we shall discover that they are all the very same as those of the good, but mis-applied under a wrong enthusiasm created as a result of some false evaluations. Virtue, poisoned with ignorance is evil; evil, treated and cured of its poison, when it regains its health, becomes virtue.

THUS THE VERY FIRST STANZA WHICH PAINTS THE *ASURIC* TYPE OPENS, AS IT WERE, WITH AN APOLOGY FOR THE 'DIABOLICALLY FALLEN', ALONG WITH A POWERFUL SUGGESTION ELICITING OUR MOST TENDER KINDNESS TOWARDS THEM:

7. *The demoniac know not what to do and what to refrain from; neither purity, nor right conduct, nor truth is found in them.*

WHAT TO DO AND WHAT TO REFRAIN FROM—the men of *Asuric* nature know not either 'action' or 'inaction'.* Here 'action' means any intelligent piece of work undertaken and pursued with a right motive so as to gain for ourselves a better inner satisfaction.

Religious acts, selfless work and dedicated service are all examples of right actions whereby the individual gains not only immediate profits, but also the ultimate inner heightening of culture; for he will then be working without losing sight of his Higher Goal. 'Inaction' here means forbidding ourselves from striving in the right channels, and that can bring about only restlessness for ourselves and for others. The list enumerating the negative tendencies of the 'fallen' starts with the idea of 'ignorance'. This is very significant. If any one commits a crime in 'ignorance', though justice may not accept it as an excuse, the heart of the society will readily discover a tender forgiveness for the erring soul.

NEITHER PURITY NOR RIGHT CONDUCT NOR TRUTH IS FOUND IN THEM—Outer cleanliness is, to a large measure,

---

प्रवृत्तिं च निवृत्तिं च जना न विदुरासुराः ।
न शौचं नापि चाचारो न सत्यं तेषु विद्यते ॥ ७ ॥

pravṛttiṁ ca nivṛttiṁ ca janā na vidurāsurāḥ
na śaucaṁ nāpi cācāro na satyaṁ teṣu vidyate 7.

* The terms *'pravritti'* and *'nivritti'* used here have been differently interpreted by different commentators; (a) they are taken in their technical senses as 'the coming forth' and the 'return' of the manifested world and then the rendering becomes 'neither creation', nor its end'; (b) others take 'action' to mean 'the pursuance of religious and moral objects by a course of work' and 'inaction', the pursuance of the same ends by ascetic withdrawal from the work of the world' – *sannyasa*.

a reflection of the inner condition. A disciplined man with education and culture alone can, in fact, maintain a systematic order and cleanliness around him.

One who is incapable of deciding the actions to be pursued as well as those to be avoided by him, has no harmony within; and therefore, there is no inner purity, or outer cleanliness (*shaucha*), for such an individual. If the mind is indiscipline there cannot be a decent and well-regulated life, since outward behaviour (*Achara*) is nothing but an expression of the mind. Therefore, Krishna indicates that in them good conduct is conspicuous by its absence.

He who is confused about 'action' and 'inaction', who has no purity, or external cleanliness, and who fails in good conduct, cannot maintain TRUTHFULNESS in his words. All through, if you read these terms very carefully in the spirit in which the Divine Charioteer has given them out you will find in them a divine tenderness for such 'Diabolically Fallen' folks. There is no revengefulness for the sinner anywhere, even hinted at, in the entire length of the *Geeta*. It is a logical conclusion that such a man must necessarily be untruthful in words, not because he is deliberately pursuing dishonesty, but because by temperament he is incapacitated to be honest.

MOREOVER:

8. *They say, "the universe is without truth, without (moral) basis, without a God; not brought about by any regular causal sequence, with lust for its cause; what else?"*

असत्यमप्रतिष्ठं ते जगदाहुरनीश्वरम् ।
अपरस्परसंभूतं किमन्यत्कामहैतुकम् ॥ ८ ॥

asatyamapratiṣṭhaṁ te jagadāhuranīśvaram
aparasparasambhūtaṁ kimanyatkāmahaitukam 8.

In the description of the 'Diabolically Fallen', we recognise the picture of an utterly sceptical materialist who looks at life from his own limited intellectual standpoint, and who, naturally, fails to recognise any final purpose or permanent substratum for this seemingly confusing array of illogical happenings. Such materialists, however, have stalwart intellects and are capable of original and independent thinking, but they have to be a wee bit trained, to see something beyond what their general observation and analysis can discover for them. The materialist viewpoint of life and the world are explained in the stanza.

WITHOUT TRUTH (*Asatyam*)—even when they are very scientific in their observation and analysis, the materialists fail to recognise the Truth that upholds the Universe. They recognise change, and the constant change itself is accepted by them as the world, without having for it any steady and changeless substratum. At the same time, scientists admit that change is a relative phenomenon and without a changeless, constant foundation, change cannot take place and give us the impression of continuity. Without a screen, steady and motionless, a running film cannot be projected; without a constant bed, the waters of the rivers cannot flow continuously. The ever-changing universe cannot give us a constant APPEARANCE without its having a steady and changeless 'foundation'. This eternal and unchanging Reality behind the ever-changing Universe is called the Truth. According to the materialist, "the Universe is without Truth (*Asatyam*)".

WITHOUT A LORD (*An-Ishwaram*)—there is no substratum; at least, is there a commanding intelligence that orders, regulates, and generally guides the happenings in the world? According to the materialist there is no such Director of Events, no Architect of Happenings. There is no Creator, no Sustainer.

NOT BROUGHT ABOUT IN REGULAR SEQUENCE—The entire universe of beings and things is formed only as a result of mutual combinations of the great elements and the sole ruling factor that determines Creation is 'chance'; and the only deciding urge, propelled by which beings are born, is nothing but 'lust'. Even modern psychologists insist that the sex urge alone is the mother urge because of which everything is happening, every achievement is gained and every profit is made everywhere in life.

AFTER DESCRIBING THUS, THE POINT OF VIEW OF THE PURE MATERIALIST, KRISHNA SYMPATHISES WITH THE LOT OF SUCH MEN AND TRACES THEIR INSTINCTIVE DEEDS:

9. *Holding this view, these ruined souls of small intellect and fierce deeds, come forth as the enemies of the world, for its destruction.*

HOLDING THIS VIEW—Holding the view, as described in the previous stanza, that the world has no substratum, that there is no controlling power, and that the world continues to exist and procreate by itself, if a society were to live, giving full vent to animal nature, it will only achieve restlessness and strife, disaster and destruction for itself.

RUINED SOULS—a balanced personality can only be for the individual who has, to begin with, a clear conception and a correct judgement of himself. Whenever an individual forgets himself, he acts in a manner unbecoming to the dignity of his birth, education, culture and social status, like a mad man or a

---

एतां दृष्टिमवष्टभ्य नष्टात्मानोऽल्पबुद्धयः ।
प्रभवन्त्युग्रकर्माणः क्षयाय जगतोऽहिताः ॥ ९ ॥
etām dṛṣṭimavaṣṭabhya naṣṭātmāno'lpabuddhayaḥ
prabhavantyugrakarmāṇaḥ kṣayāya jagato'hitāḥ 9.

drunken fool. When a materialist thus works in ignorance of his own divine status, he, naturally, behaves as though he is an animal - insulting the divine status of his own evolution.

OF SMALL INTELLECT (*Alpa-Buddhayah*)—once an individual refuses to recognise the 'Divine Presence of Truth', embracing and underlying life, he will function in life as a self-centred, selfish entity, endlessly striving to eke out his own personal satisfaction from the material world. Seeking complete fulfilment in the gratification of his sensual urges, he strives hard but discovers only a carping disappointment, a burning hunger and a sense of defeat in life. Krishna, in his infinite kindness, sympathises with such men and calls them MEN OF SMALL INTELLECT.

FIERCE DEEDS—if a materialist does not want to believe in the Eternal Reality, and if others must believe in some Permanent Truth, why not allow equal freedom to both—the believers and non-believers? This is a natural question that will arise in any man, if he be truly democratic and tolerant in his point-of-view. Anticipating such a doubt in a sincere student, Krishna says, in the second line of the stanza, that when an individual loses his faith in the Higher Reality, he becomes licentious at all levels of his expression. Prompted by his selfish urges to seek and discover his fulfilment in life, he would, perhaps, ultimately bring about irremediable disasters to his era. Historically, the world to-day is going through the same predicament as declared and anticipated in the *Geeta*!

Materialists, who do not recognise the Truth, seeking its expression through life's happenings, will unconsciously, bring about such a discordant note of disharmony in the community that it will plunge the world into a bloody mire of disastrous wars.

THE VIEWPOINT OF THE LIFE OF A MATERIALIST AND HIS MOTIVES IN HIS EVERYDAY LIFE, ARE BEAUTIFULLY DESCRIBED IN THE FOLLOWING STANZAS:

10. *Filled with insatiable desires, full of hypocrisy, pride and arrogance, holding evil ideas through delusion, they work with impure resolves.*

The gruesome ugliness of the inner nature of a pure materialist, as he struts about in the fields of his achievements, cannot be better expressed than what Vyasa has accomplished in this stanza. For a more vivid and thorough depiction of the mental contents of the 'Diabolically Fallen', for a clearer description of the quality and texture of his activities in society, one has to go ransacking the entire existing literature of all the languages in the world, only to fail to find a parallel to this pregnant verse.

FILLED WITH INSATIABLE DESIRES—Activities are not at all possible unless they are instigated by desires. Where desires have ended, the expression of dynamic life in achievements is impossible. And yet, to remain as victims of desires, is to be some horrid machines of activity, vomiting out into the world our inner poison of ego and egocentric passions. To sustain life only for the satisfaction of desires is unintelligent; for they have a knack of multiplying themselves as we go on satisfying them one after another. They are 'hard to appease'. Filled with insatiable desires, when a man uses his intelligence,

---

कामामाश्रित्य दुष्पूरं दम्भमानमदान्विताः ।
मोहाद्गृहीत्वासद्ग्राहान्प्रवर्तन्तेऽशुचिव्रताः ॥ १० ॥

kāmamāśritya duṣpūraṁ dambhamānamadānvitāḥ
mohādgṛhītvāsadgrāhānpravartante'śucivratāḥ 10.

abilities and knowledge, he naturally brings about an endless stream of disturbances in and around him.

FULL OF HYPOCRISY, PRIDE (CONCEIT) AND ARROGANCE—Desire is but an expression of the ego when the seeker seeks a permanent satisfaction and infinite fulfillment through sense enjoyments. When he is thus deluded in the misconception of his ego-vanity, negative tendencies such as hypocrisy, pride (conceit), and arrogance will naturally rise up, and smothered by them, he ceaselessly strives to satisfy the unending demands of his own unbridled desires.

VICTIMS OF DELUSION—Desire cannot come to the all-fulfilled.* Desire can come only to him who fails to feel his own Infinitude and expresses himself as a limited ego (*Jiva*). Forgetting his own divine nature, in his identification with the unreal things and values of life, he develops in himself a hunger to enjoy peace and happiness. Naturally, numerous desires arise in him and seeking fulfilment of all such desires, he indulges in sense-gratification.

THEY WORK WITH IMPURE RESOLVE—The mental biography of the 'Diabolically Fallen' (*Asuras*) is complete in its sequence when the stanza says that the ego, desperately struggling to gain inner peace, must necessarily forsake all consideration for others, ignore all noble values-of-life, and enter into the fields of activity, shamelessly intolerant, inconsiderate and even brutal. Drunk with passions, opiated with his own desires, he works in the world as a maniac, hurling blood and acid, death and disaster all around him in the community!

---

* '*Aptakamasya ka spriha*': To the all-fulfilled, how can there be desire-prompted

The picture, viewed microcosmically, shows a materialist, building his life upon the restless waves of his desire-tossed mind. The same word-painting, when looked at macrocosmically, portrays vividly the ugliness of materialistic communities and nations. Life's beauty depends upon the beauty of the philosophy upon which it is built.

If the foundations are false, the edifice, however strongly built, will prove to be no better than a card-castle. The economic break-up, social evils, political upheavals, and general restlessness that are found all over the world are all thoroughly discussed in this stanza, if we know how to read them all into it.

It is also interesting to note how Krishna, while explaining the 'Diabolically Fallen' (*Asuras*), without directly saying so, is painting the picture of a materialist, who by nature, is an atheist in thought and a tireless hunter of pleasure in action. In this age of materialism, don't we prove ourselves faithful to the type just now discussed?

PAINTING THE CONCEPT OF LIFE IN A CONFIRMED MATERIALIST, KRISHNA CONTINUES:

11. *Giving themselves over to immeasurable cares ending only with death, regarding gratification of lust as their highest aim, and feeling sure that, that is all (that matters).*

ENDLESS CARES—wedded to anxiety and care, such desperate men drag their life of futile endeavours along the corridors of sobs and sorrows to the silent courtyard of death.

चिन्तामपरिमेयां च प्रलयान्तामुपाश्रिताः ।
कामोपभोगपरमा एतावदिति निश्चिताः ॥ ११ ॥

cintāmaparimeyāṁ ca pralayāntāmupāśritāḥ
kāmopabhogaparamā etāvaditi niścitāḥ 11.

In an ordinary life, cares besiege the citadel of peace and joy, especially when hosts of powerful desires conquer the individual. The struggles in acquiring (*Yoga*) and anxieties in preserving (*Kshema*) the acquired objects-of-desires are the contents of all cares of life. To waste an entire lifetime in such anxieties, and in the end to realise how miserably one had failed is indeed a tragedy.

SATISFACTION OF LUST AS THE HIGHEST (*Kama-upabhoga-parama*)—Consistent effort either in the field of the good, or in the field of the vicious, put forth without a philosophy of life that sustains the continuity of an individual's activities, is a haphazard endeavour, ignoble and futile.

The philosophy of life that is accepted by the 'Diabolically Fallen' is invariably the same wherever they are. The philosophy of the (*Charvakas*) atheists* has been hinted at herein. To them, satisfaction of their lusty nature is the goal of life and there is nothing beyond it.

ASSURED THAT IS ALL—generally, such materialists are no fools; they have an ample share of a rough and ready intellect. They do realise that a life dedicated to an endless hunt after sense-gratifications is a tragic way of living, and that in such a scheme of existence the individual is called upon to pay an exorbitant price for relatively insignificant gains. And yet, they continue, seeking satisfaction of their uncontrolled lust. If you question them, their answer is that life is nothing but a series of such strifes. They know not of any life, the contents of which are peace and joy. They are generally pessimistic, and since they scrupulously avoid seriously thinking about life, they invariably

---

* The atheistic philosophy of the *Charvakas* is summarised in their *Darshana* as:
'Yavad jeevet sukham jeevet; Rinam Kritva ghritam pibet;
Bhasmee-bhutasya dehasya punara-gamanam kutah' –
Brihaspati Sutra declares that desire is the supreme end of man;
'Kama-eka-eva-purusharthah.'

come to express suicidal tendencies and homicidal temperaments. According to them, sorrows and care alone constitute the fabric of life. They fail to discover any harmony or rhythm underlying the superficial disturbances in life. Entertaining no hope, either for themselves or for the world, they live with embittered hearts, revengefully meeting the happenings around them in the world. In unproductive exertions, they waste their powers only to die a miserable death; exhausted, wearied, disappointed.

THE EXPRESSION OF THE ABOVE PHILOSOPHY IN THE LIFE OF THE INDIVIDUAL IS DESCRIBED IN THE FOLLOWING STANZA:

12. *Bound by a hundred ties of hope, given to lust and anger, they do strive to obtain, by unlawful means, hoards of wealth for sensual enjoyments.*

BOUND BY A HUNDRED TIES OF HOPE, LUST AND ANGER—bringing vividly to the mind of the student, the picture of such a materialist, Krishna records in this stanza, the activities of such an individual. Entangled by hundreds of desires, his mental and intellectual energies get dissipated. Such an individual becomes restless and impatient with things that happen around him, and soon loses his balance of mind – his sense of judgement. Irritated and constantly unhappy with himself and his environments, such a man is seen in life 'GIVEN TO YEARNINGS AND ANGER'. Wherever desire is throttled, anger is natural. Since he is devoted to desires he pursues sense-fulfilments, and since in the world of competition, desire-

---

आशापाशशतैर्बद्धाः कामक्रोधपरायणाः ।
ईहन्ते कामभोगार्थमन्यायेनार्थसञ्चयान् ॥ १२ ॥

āśāpāśaśatairbaddhāḥ kāmakrodhaparāyaṇāḥ
īhante kāmabhogārthamanyāyenārthasañcayān 12.

fulfilments often get throttled, his lusty urges get transformed into wild and passionate anger.

THEY DO STRIVE, no doubt, they do tirelessly and diligently strive to satisfy their ever-increasing urges. To secure their quota of sensual enjoyments, they must necessarily acquire and procure objects of sense-satisfaction from the world without. They are not seeking happiness as such or peace as such; theirs is the anxiety to quench a nameless thirst which they are constantly feeling; a strange hunger they are chronically suffering from. They have not the mental equipoise to investigate into their urges, and analyse and judge them properly. Madly they strive on to acquire and possess, and in their desperate anxiety to indulge and to enjoy, they lose sight of the divine principles of existence and the noble dictates of their conscience. THEY DO STRIVE, day and night, to satisfy their inexhaustible passion, with wealth acquired and hoarded by all known unjust means.

Though written some five thousand years ago, strangely enough, this portion of the description of the 'Diabolically Fallen' reads as though it were a bitter, but honest, criticism of our own age!! Thus, if students of the *Geeta* were to judge our era of brilliant scientific knowledge, material prosperity, secular achievements and political freedom, they will have to classify our era as of this 'Diabolically Fallen' type. Amidst the bleating sirens of our booming industries, the horrid thuds of our modern missiles, the devastating powers of nature that we have discovered and released for our own destruction, we may not give our ears to the thundering truth declared by the 'wise' men of such a distant past; but sincere students of the *Geeta* cannot but perceive the unquestionable veracity in them, and must come to feel sad for the world and age.

CONTINUING, THE LORD PAINTS THE ATTITUDE OF SUCH PEOPLE TO LIFE:

13. *"This has to-day been gained by me"-- "this desire I shall obtain"*
"this is mine" -- and "this wealth shall also be mine in future".

There is not much in this stanza that calls for explanation, for the average man of the world to-day lives, exactly the life suggested here. The most successful man in a competitive world is the one who lives in constant consciousness of what he has already acquired, and remembers and sweats for his day-to-day ambitions, to acquire and possess, more and more of the wealth of the world. And the laughable paradox in the philosophy of possession is that the more one has, the more one craves for. No material-wealth hunter has ever declared, "I have this much now that will do". On the other hand, when one gets drunk with the vanity of possession, one's shameless cry is only; "I HAVE THIS MUCH, AND THIS WEALTH SHALL ALSO BE MINE".

The game of desires is an endless gamble. The more one possesses the more one is tempted to strive to possess more. Each time a man strives to acquire something; his desire is to feel his full share of satisfaction. But, invariably, his experience is that he is not fully satisfied, and in his disappointment, he thirsts for more and more possessions. Earlier in the *Geeta,* it is said that "he who has disciplined and controlled himself to such an extent that the world of stimuli cannot create in him even a ripple of reaction, alone knows what peace is and not the desirer of desires".*

इदमद्य मया लब्धमिमं प्राप्स्ये मनोरथम् ।
इदमस्तीदमपि मे भविष्यति पुनर्धनम् ॥ १३ ॥

idamadya mayā labdhamimaṁ prāpsye manoratham
idamastīdamahi me bhaviṣyati punardhanam 13.

---

* *Geeta* Chapter II-70: Description of the 'Man of Steady-Wisdom'.

THIS STANZA POINTED OUT THE MATERIALIST'S ATTITUDE TO THE PHYSICAL THINGS AROUND HIM; THE FOLLOWING STANZA GIVES US HIS ATTITUDE TOWARDS THE WORLD OF BEINGS:

14. *"That enemy has been slain by me" -- "and others also shall I destroy" -- "I am the Lord"-- "I am the enjoyer" -- "I am perfect, powerful and happy".*

The translation of this stanza is itself its commentary. And it is a commentary on the lives of all of us too! All businessmen in the world, unknown to themselves, constantly chant this stanza in their heart-of-hearts. "I destroyed one competitor in the market, and now I must destroy the remaining competitors also. ... In fact, what can those poor men do to stop me from doing what I want?... Because there is none equal to me in any respect ... I am the Lord. I enjoy, I am the most successful man. I am strong in influence, among political leaders, in my business connections, and in my bank balance. I am strong and healthy...." This, in short, is the ego's SONG OF SUCCESS that is ever hummed in the heart of a true materialist. Under the spell of this Satanic lullaby, the higher instincts and the diviner urges in man go into a sleep of intoxication.

WHAT IS THE INTELLECTUAL ESTIMATE OF A MATERIALIST ABOUT HIMSELF? LISTEN:

असौ मया हत: शत्रुर्हनिष्ये चापरानपि ।
ईश्वरोऽहमहं भोगी सिद्धोऽहं बलवान्सुखी ॥ १४ ॥

asau mayā hataḥ śatrurhaniṣye cāparānapi
īśvaro'hamahaṁ bhogī siddho'haṁ balavānsukhī 14.

15. *"I am rich and well-born" -- "who else is equal to me?" -- "I will give (alms, money)" -- "I will rejoice". Thus are they, deluded by 'ignorance'.*

Deluded by misconceptions of himself, such a man of sickly, bloated conceit looks at the world through a mind distorted by vanity, and wrongly judges the world and his own relationship with it. He feels happy and congratulates himself on his high birth and breed, on his belongings and wealth, and fails to find anyone equal to him. Self-exiled from society, he lives in a false castle of vanity, suffering innumerable psychological privations. He gloats that he will, by his ritualism, even order the gods to serve him --that he shall, with his gifts, purchase the whole world. And thus glorified by the world, served by the gods, "I shall rejoice in the world..." Such are some of the maddest ravings of his restless heart, in the dark depths of his utter 'ignorance'.

SUMMARISING THE THREE PREVIOUS STANZAS, IT IS SAID:

आढ्योऽभिजनवानस्मि कोऽन्योऽस्ति सदृशो मया ।
यक्ष्ये दास्यामि मोदिष्य इत्यज्ञानविमोहिता: ॥ १५ ॥
āḍhyo'bhijanavānasmi ko'nyo'stisadṛśo mayā
yakṣye dāsyāmi modiṣya ityajñānavimohitāḥ 15.

16. *Bewildered by many a fancy, entangled in the snare of delusion, addicted to the gratification of lust, they fall into a foul hell.*

BEWILDERED BY MANY A FANCY—when an egocentric individual, who has thus sold himself to sense-indulgence, spends his time seeking gratification from the world-of-objects, his mind becomes ever unsteady. The mind of an indulgent sensualist soon learns to empty its powers of concentration and exhausts itself in its own hallucinations, fancies and imaginations. ENTANGLED IN THE SNARE OF DELUSION—if the individual's mind, as a result of its false philosophy, gets dissipated in sapless dreams, his intellect also is in a sad condition. His power of judgement and discrimination is caught up in a web of delusions and false values. His intellect, cut off from its permanent moorings, has thereafter no platform of its own to spring from and come to a correct judgement and evaluation of life. It fails to recognise the permanent harmony of life, but recognises only its own ego-centric vanities. Life looked at through such a disturbing equipment naturally gives a distorted view.

ADDICTED TO GRATIFICATION OF LUST—when an individual's intellect is clouded, his mind gets agitated, and his sense-organs, which are the vehicles through which the mind-intellect has to express itself, certainly behave erratically. When a driver is drunk, the car cannot move properly. Naturally,

---

अनेकचित्तविभ्रान्ता मोहजालसमावृताः ।
प्रसक्ताः कामभोगेषु पतन्ति नरकेऽशुचौ ॥ १६ ॥

anekacittavibhrāntā mohajālasamāvṛtāḥ
prasaktāḥ kāmabhogeṣu patanti narake'śucau 16.

therefore, such an individual becomes a victim of lust and sense-gratifications.

THEY FALL INTO A FOUL HELL—We need not be great philosophers to understand that such an individual, tired physically, confused mentally, and upset intellectually will live here in a self-created hell, distributing his own personality-contents of woes to others around him. A man can make a heaven of hell, and a hell of heaven, by the harmony or discord in himself. A subjectively shattered personality cannot find peace or fulfilment in any situation. Even if the environments are conducive, he discovers, in himself, methods of unsettling them by his own inner sufferings.

If a single individual, who has these false values, discovers for himself but a sad world of sorrow even in the midst of happy surroundings, we can very well understand what would be the condition of the world when a good majority of us are having, in varying degrees, the above qualities. Hell and heaven are determined by the amount of discord or harmony that we successfully bring about in our inner makeup.

WHAT THEN ARE THE CHARACTERISTICS OF SUCH PEOPLE, AND HOW DO THEY PERFORM THEIR *YAJNAS*?

17. *Self-conceited, stubborn, filled with pride and drunk with wealth, they perform sacrifices in name (only) out of ostentation, contrary to scriptural ordinance.*

आत्मसंभाविताः स्तब्धा धनमानमदान्विताः ।
यजन्ते नामयज्ञैस्ते दम्भेनाविधिपूर्वकम् ॥ १७ ॥

ātmasambhāvitāḥ stabdhā dhanamānamadānvitāḥ
yajante nāmayajñaiste dambhenāvidhipūrvakam 17.

* Undertake any national, social, or communal work.

Yajna need not necessarily be considered as the elaborate ritualism described in the *Vedas*. But it can be interpreted, in the *Geeta* style (Ch III) as 'A CO-OPERATIVE ENDEAVOUR IN WHICH EACH INDIVIDUAL POURS HIS BEST INTO THE ACTIVITY OF LIFE, AS AN OBLATION TO PROPITIATE THE POTENTIAL GOODNESS IN EXISTENCE, AND WHICH, WHEN INVOKED, IS TO BE DISTRIBUTED EQUALLY TO ALL'. This spirit of selfless effort in the service of mankind was described by Krishna as the greatest *Yajna*; WORK IS WORKSHIP.

SELF-CONCEITED, STUBBORN, FULL WITH PRIDE AND DRUNK WITH HIS OWN POSSESSIONS AND WEALTH— When an individual enters the fields of social work or national service, he does not always do so with a true *Hanja*-spirit only. In spite of very many of the leaders and workers striving hard for the upliftment of their country, we find that the world of our age is falling away from peace, plenty, and prosperity. When a man of the 'Diabolically Fallen' type reaches any field of activity, in spite of his vociferous claims of selfless service, he is incapable of it, because of the very nature of his personality and character. Such friends of society can perform a *Yajna** in name only. Unconsciously, their actions will be poisoned by their vanity, coloured by their sensuality, distorted by their arrogance, and generally polluted by their false philosophy. As a result of all their actions, sorrow alone will be the result.

SUCH LOW MEN CONTINUE FALLING LOWER AND LOWER EACH DAY:

18. *Given to egoism, power, haughtiness, lust and anger, these malicious people hate Me in their own bodies, and in those of others.*

Once egoism takes possession of an individual, he steadily sinks to the ugliest depths of animalism. Drunk with passions, he abdicates from all the dignity of a cultured man and behaves as an ineffectual beast, strutting about precariously on its hind legs! Such a biological freak, who is physiologically a man but temperamentally an animal, is the type that is now being discussed as the 'Diabolically Fallen' (*Asura*).

Enumerating the inner contents of such an individual, Lord Krishna says that he is "FULL OF EGOISM, BRUTE STRENGTH, ARROGANCE, PASSION AND ANGER". Any one of these is sufficient to pull one down to the depths of depravity, but the Lord characterises the *Asura* -- type of man as having all these qualities, all at once. Not only does he have these qualities – and who does not have? – But, unlike an evolver, the *Asuric* man comes to pin his faith on these qualities, and he struggles to discover his fulfilment only in the expression of these tendencies.

What is the harm if an individual lives these values? This is a question that is often asked by an indulgent youth, when he is advised by his elders not to live yielding readily to his low urges and ugly temptations. The *Geetacharya* here explains that the consequence of disrespecting all cultural values, and living an uncultured egocentric existence of passions and desires would be nothing short of total destruction of life.

अहंकारं बलं दर्पं कामं क्रोधं च संश्रिता: ।
मामात्मपरदेहेषु प्रद्विषन्तोऽभ्यसूयका: ॥ १८ ॥

ahaṁkāraṁ balaṁ darpaṁ kāmaṁ krodha ca saṁśritāḥ
māmātmaparadeheṣu pradviṣnto'bhyasūyakāḥ 18.

Persons, who are entertaining the above-mentioned attitudes, would ignore the sanctity of life, and without any compunction whatsoever, desecrate it. They will grow malignant, and in order to satisfy the low urges of egoism, would come to "HATE ME IN THEIR OWN BODIES AND IN THOSE OF OTHERS". The Sacred Life, the *Paramatman*, does not come out to express Its full play when blanketed by the low sensuous urges. Ethical values are disciplines of the thought-life, whereby a mind so tuned up becomes the right instrument to serve faithfully the seeker of the Self. Unethical values and immoral intentions choke the great Melody of Life and reduce it to a discordant, purposeless noise, shattering peace and contentment within one's own and in another's bosom.

THE FALL IN EVOLUTION SUFFERED BY SUCH THOUGHTLESS MATERIALISTS AS A RESULT OF THEIR OWN FALSE VALUES AND FOUL ACTIONS IS BEING TRACED IN THE FOLLOWING STANZAS:

19. *These cruel haters, worst among men in the world, I hurl these evil-doers for ever into the wombs of the demons only.*

Specimens of the 'Diabolically Fallen' type of men are characterised here, in a spirit of loving despair by the Lord, "AS THE MOST DEGRADED OF MEN IN THIS WORLD. THEY ARE MALICIOUS AND CRUEL"—malicious against the dignity of themselves, and cruel to the living beings around. They are, says the Lord, "THROWN BY ME PERPETUALLY INTO THE WOMBS OF DEMONS". Here Krishna is identifying Himself

---

तानहं द्विषतः क्रूरान्संसारेषु नराधमान् ।
क्षिपाम्यजस्रमशुभानासुरीष्वेव योनिषु ॥ १९ ॥

tānahaṁ dviṣataḥ krurānsaṁsāreṣu narādhamān
kṣipāmyajasramaśubhānāsurīṣveva yoniṣu 19.

with the Law of Action and Reaction -- wrong action leaves wrong tendencies behind, and, propelled by such negative tendencies, the personality in an individual, after his death in this physical structure, demands an appropriate field of existence. An *Asuric* individual should necessarily discover his fulfilment only in an *Asuric* environment. Therefore the Law of Action and Reaction orders that such cruel men, again and again, reach similar wombs until the sheer horror of their experiences brings home to them a sudden realisation of the follies and futilities in following such a low tempo of life. The idea of reincarnation suggested herein has already been exhaustively discussed earlier in our discourses (VIII-6).

CONTINUING:

20. *Entering into demoniacal wombs, and deluded, not attaining to Me, birth after birth, they thus fall, O Kaunteya, into a condition still lower than that.*

Tracing the line of fall of an *Asura* type of man, Krishna says that an individual having repeatedly reached, as a result of his previous life, the same *Asuric* environment, life after life, fails to realise the Infinite joys of the Self. They never climb the heights of cultural beauty but slowly sink lower and lower to reach the bottom grades of beings.

So far we had a vivid review of two types of men: the 'DIVINELY GOOD' and the 'DIABOLICALLY FALLEN'. A majority of us, in varying degrees, belong to the latter class. As a spiritual seeker is never satisfied merely with the theoretical explanations and descriptions, Krishna now advises the entire

---

आसुरीं योनिमापन्ना मूढा जन्मनि जन्मनि ।
मामप्राप्यैव कौन्तेय ततो यान्त्यधमां गतिम् ॥ २० ॥

āsurīṁ yonimāpannā mūḍhā janmani
māmaprāpyaiva kaunteya tato yantyadhamāṁ gatim 20.

mankind, through Arjuna, on how even he who has fallen so hopelessly to the *Asura* level, can learn to climb up and steadily progress in his spiritual evolution. None is eternally condemned, nor does anyone deserve a perpetual hell – such a view is illogical, unphilosophic, and stupid.

DESCRIBING THE TECHNIQUE OF HASTENING ONE'S EVOLUTION, THE DIVINE CHARIOTEER SAYS:

21. *These three are the gates of hell, destructive of the Self - lust, anger and greed; therefore, one should abandon these three.*

The Lord indicates here that there are three gateways to reach HELL. Earlier in a stanza, in the very same chapter, He described that HELL and HEAVEN are conditions created by the mind only; they are merely subjective experiences in life, and the three false values mentioned here are the main causes of the former.

DESIRE, ANGER, GREED—the main theme of the entire chapter is to call man away from a life of sense-gratification into the ampler fields of desireless actions and egoless perfections.

Where there is desire, anger is a natural corollary. The constant flying of an individual's thoughts towards an object of gratification is called 'desire' and when the steady flow of these thoughts of aggrandisement and possession are deflected by some obstacle, the refracted thoughts are called 'anger'. When

---

त्रिविधं नरकस्येदं द्वारं नाशनमात्मनः ।
कामः क्रोधस्तथा लोभस्तस्मादेतत्त्रयं त्यजेत् ॥ २१ ॥

trividhaṁ narakasyedaṁ dvāraṁ nāśanamātmanaḥ
kāmaḥ krodhastathā lobhāstasmādetattrayaṁ tyajet 21.

disappointed in desire-gratifications, a storm of revolt rises in the mind, as a consequence of which anger soars up to toss, wreck and sink the boat of life.

If ANGER is thus the thought-storm arising in our mind at the disappointment of a desire, GREED is the erosion of our mental strength and inner peace when desires are more and more satiated. When a desire gets fulfilled, an insatiable thirst for more and more joy holds the individual, and this endless appetite ruins the mental strength and saps dry the personality-vitality in the individual. Greed is a sense of dissatisfaction constantly pursuing and poisoning the sense of satisfaction that we have already experienced. In an undisciplined man, there can be no satisfaction at any time; even when his desires are satisfied he is unhappy, because his appetite for enjoyment is thereby sharpened and he hungers for more; if the desires are throttled, the disappointment brings into him anger, and he suffers the consequent wretchedness.

If this logic about the action and interaction between desire, anger, and greed is accepted, then we are forced to accept Krishna's conclusion in this stanza: "THEREFORE ONE SHOULD FORSAKE THESE THREE".

HERE FOLLOWS THE PRAISE OF THE RENUNCIATION OF EGO, ANGER AND GREED:

22. *A man who is liberated from these three gates to darkness, O Kaunteya, practises what is good for him and thus goes to the Supreme Goal.*

एतैर्विमुक्तः कौन्तेय तमोद्वारैस्त्रिभिर्नरः ।
आचरत्यात्मनः श्रेयस्ततो याति परां गतिम् ॥ २२ ॥
etairvimuktaḥ kaunteya tamodvāraistribhirnaraḥ
ācaratyātmanaḥ śreyastato yāti parāṁ gatim 22.

Those who are avoiding all the three gateways to hell are complimented here. It is promised that those who avoid derailing themselves into any of these dangerous by-paths of self-exploitation and self-ruination, will steadily progress on the straight path to their life's goal. To wander into fields of desire, anger and greed is to dissipate our energies. Devoid of the divine vitality of a fully grown and well-balanced human personality, the seeker feels fatigued and not strong enough to meet the terrible challenges that arise from within himself. To overcome the strong temptations of the sense-objects, the mind and intellect should recharge the individual's inner abilities with which the individual can strive hard and effectively achieve self-expansion. He who is avoiding THESE THREE GATES OF DARKNESS – which are sure to lead him into deeper and deeper confusions and despairs and ultimately take him to the sub-human level of existence – will be, it is promised here, practising WHAT IS GOOD FOR HIM.

The term '*Shreyas*' has no equivalent word of the same import in English. It does not merely mean 'good' but it has a deeper and wider import in Sanskrit. *Shreyas*, when practised, not only brings happiness to the practitioner, but also contributes much to the wellbeing of the people around him.

Progressing thus in the right direction, the individual "GOES TO THE GOAL SUPREME". Cultural unfoldment cannot be a miraculous overnight development. The bud should grow, open and bloom, under the careful nourishment of steady discipline, vigorous study and perfect understanding. The unfoldment is more delicate than that of a flower.

This stanza explains to the seeker what is to be avoided by him and indicates how he will thereby have a positive development and inner growth. But it may be asked how a POSITIVE growth can be effected as a result of a NEGATIVE act of denial. Avoiding bad food can preserve health but it cannot give the positive joy of taking a healthy full dinner. Similarly, avoiding the dissipation of our energies through desire, anger and greed, would, perhaps, end all our agitations caused by these three. But how can that create any positive development in ourselves? The *Geeta* preaches a positive way-of-life; and the stanza, as it stands, suggests this positive achievement when it says that such an individual 'PRACTISES WHAT IS GOOD FOR HIM'.

WHAT IS THE POSITIVE PRACTICE?

23. *He who, having cast aside the ordinance of the scriptures, acts under the impulse of desire, attains neither perfection, nor happiness, nor the Supreme Goal.*

The Divine Teacher of the *Geeta* explains that when the ruinous expenditure of vitality, both psychological and intellectual, is stopped and energy is conserved, it has to be applied in the right direction. If again the energy is misused, the chances are that the seeker would dash himself down with a mightier bump to the depths of a miserable life. Ravana and such other mighty *Asuras* of the *Puranas* are typical examples of personalities that performed fierce *tapashcharya* (penance), accumulated inner dynamism, and yet achieved but a thorough self-destruction! So mighty was their strength that they made their own generation rock, crumble and bite the dust. To avoid such a calamity to the individual, as well as to the world around

---

यः शास्त्रविधिमुत्सृज्य वर्तते कामकारतः ।
न स सिद्धिमवाप्नोति न सुखं न परां गतिम् ॥ २३ ॥

yaḥ śāstravidhimutsṛjya vartate kāmakāearataḥ
na sa siddhimavāpnoti na sukhaṁ na parāṁ gatim 23.

him, a severe warning must necessarily be given; and these two closing stanzas contain such a warning.

HE WHO DISOBEYS THE *SHASTRAS* AND ACTS UNDER THE IMPULSE OF DESIRE—such a man stands to gain no benefit at all. Here the term *shastra* need not necessarily be understood as a bundle of ritualistic injunctions, strictly followed and sacredly insisted upon by the fanatic orthodox. The textbooks discussing the theory of Truth (*Brahma-Vidya*) and the technique of self-perfection (*Yoga*) are called *shastras*, while other subsidiary books which explain and throw light upon the *shastras* are called *Prakarana* texts; the latter explain the categories in the Science of *Vedanta*. Since the *Geeta* is a philosophical poem, exhaustively explaining the theory and practice of God-realisation, IT IS CONSIDERED AS A *SHASTRA*.

UNDER THE IMPULSE OF DESIRE—the theme developed in the previous two stanzas is that a seeker of the Higher, should of necessity renounce desire, anger and greed. We have explained earlier that ANGER is a product when desire is throttled, and GREED is a logical consequence when a passionate heart gains some fulfilment of desires. Therefore, desire is the root cause. Naturally, Krishna contrasts the way-of-life advocated in the *Geeta* with our ordinary way-of-life, wherein the main impulse is desire. The seekers are advised not to disobey the commands given in the *Geeta Shastra* and live under the impulse of their baser appetites and lower instincts.

ATTAINS NEITHER JOY NOR SUCCESS, NOR GOAL—what exactly would be the harm if one did not implicitly live the way-of-life advocated in the *Geeta*? The consequences of such an unintelligent and naughty disregard of the right way-of-life is clearly indicated here. Propelled by desires, coaxed by greed, torn by anger and constantly dancing to the changing tunes of the lusty flesh, an individual comes to live a life of restless agitations and tyrannical passions. Such a man cannot feel any happiness or attain any cultural development.

THEREFORE THE NATURAL CONCLUSION IS:

24. *Therefore, let the Scriptures be your authority, in determining what ought to be done and what ought not to be done. Having known what is said in the commandments of the Scripture, you should act here (in this world).*

THEREFORE—Because of the line of argument given in the last three stanzas, the seeker of an ampler life must necessarily follow the authority of the Scriptures in planning his way-of-life. The right conduct in life can be determined only when the individual has correct knowledge of WHAT IS TO BE PURSUED AND WHAT IS TO BE AVOIDED. The grand road to Truth is the same for all. It cannot be determined by each pilgrim according to his own whims and fancies. *Shastras* are declared by those, who had travelled the road many a time. And when the *Rishis* supply us with a map of the road-to-Perfection, we, the humble pedestrians, must pursue the path faithfully and come to bless ourselves.

HAVING KNOWN—Therefore, before setting out on a pilgrimage to that Goal, every seeker is required to study intelligently the scriptures, which are the reports left for our guidance by those who successfully walked the 'Path' earlier. A correct knowledge and a clear intellectual vision of the Goal

---

तस्माच्छास्त्रं प्रमाणं ते कार्याकार्यव्यवस्थितौ ।
ज्ञात्वा शास्त्रविधानोक्तं कर्म कर्तुमिहार्हसि ॥ २४ ॥

tasmācchāstraṁ pramāṇaṁ te kāryākāryavyavasthitau
jñāatvā śāstravidhānoktaṁ karma kartumihārhasi 24.

* For the word meaning of *'Sankalpa Vakya'* please refer to our notes at the end of chapters I and II.

and of the direction in which It lies, and perhaps, of the possible difficulties en route – are the unavoidable pre-requisites for a seeker.

YOU SHOULD ACT HERE—Ninety per cent of the seekers, perhaps, 'know' the s*hastra* exhaustively, in all detail as explained above, but alas, how few of them discover in themselves the courage to live, the will to pursue, and the patience to wait till the Supreme is realised within themselves. Naturally, Lord Krishna closes the chapter with the injunction that man should act, without desire, anger or greed. This is the right way of action as exhaustively discussed in the third chapter on *Karma Yoga.*

*Thus, in the UPANISHADS of the glorious Bhagawad Geeta, in the Science of the Eternal, in the scripture of YOGA, in the dialogue between Sri Krishna and Arjuna, the sixteenth discourse ends entitled:**

The Divine and the Devilish Estates

Om Om Om Om Om

ॐ तत्सदिति श्रीमद् भगवद् गीतासूपनिषत्सु ब्रह्मविद्यायां
योगशास्त्रे श्रीकृष्णार्जुनसंवादे दैवासुर सम्पद्विभागयोगो नाम
षोडशोऽध्यायः

Oṁ tatsaditi śrīmadbhagavadgītāsū ūpaniṣatsu brahmavidyāyāṁ yogaśāstre śrī kṛṣṇārjuna saṁvāde daivāsura sampad vibhāgayogo nāma ṣodaśo'dhyāyaḥ

XVII

The Threefold Faith

Introduction

THE concluding two verses of the last chapter introduced an idea that the *shastra* is the final court of appeal in all doubts, and for the power of discrimination in us to arrive at all its moment-to-moment judgements. But it is very difficult for the average person to develop that amount of proficiency in the spiritual codes. Thus we cannot get a ready-reckoner which will easily guide us in our life's pilgrimage. Now, Arjuna's appetite to live the Higher-life more intensely has been fully whetted and he is mentally planning to give Krishna's philosophy a fair trial. As a man of action, when he mentally plans to live the *Geeta* way-of-life, he finds it hard, because of its insistence upon the knowledge of the *shastras*. At the same time, he is confident that he has developed in himself a sufficient 'faith' (*shraddha*) in the nobler way of life, as enunciated in this sacred scripture.

This chapter opens with these doubts; is it sufficient if one lives with 'faith' a life of good conduct and noble aspirations, or is it necessary that he must 'know' the *shastra* and work with 'faith' implicitly obedient to the injunctions laid down in the *shastra*?

Earlier also in the *Geeta*, on more than one occasion, (IV-39; XVI-23). 'faith' (*shraddha*) has been prescribed as the fuel required for the seeker to soar higher. The emphasis and importance given to *shraddha* are almost equal to those given to the *shastra*, and therefore, Arjuna has every right to raise the question whether, even without the knowledge of the *shastras*, blind-faith alone can take the seeker far!

The special capacity of the human intellect, not only to know and appreciate the *shastra*, but also, to absorb and assimilate the noble ideals, so completely as to bear upon all one's actions, is called '*Shraddha*'. It is that powerful, impelling force which springs forth spontaneously from within, and propelled by which, all layers of personality in an individual act in their appointed fields. Faith is the content and the very essence of the equipments of man's whole being. Faith gives the direction, the dash, and provides a destination for one's determination.

Instead of directly answering the question, the philosopher in Krishna takes this opportunity to give a thorough exposition of 'faith' as seen in the various fields of man's endeavours -- his physical indulgences (*ahara*), his dedicated activities (*yajna*), his self-denials (*tapas*), and his charities (*daana*).

In the scheme of this discourse, the Lord first of all explains that *shraddha* is of three kinds, according to the nature of the temperament (*gunas*) which the individual entertains in himself. The three classifications under which the temperaments fall are (1) balanced joy (*sattva*), (2) ambitious and feverish activities (*rajas*), (3) vegetative existence and heedlessness (*tamas*). Earlier this topic of the three *gunas* governing and controlling the mental and intellectual life of men was exhaustively dealt with.* How men, under the influence of these *gunas* in varying proportions, would come to live the religious values, and strive for spiritual unfoldment is now being discussed. From a close study of this discourse, we can direct our activities away from the influence of the lower urges and guide our spiritual practices consistently on the royal path of sure success.

* XIV – The threefold *gunas*.

Arjuna said:

1. *Those who, setting aside the ordinances of the scriptures, perform sacrifice with faith, what is their condition, O Krishna? Is it SATTVA, RAJAS or TAMAS?*

In the very opening stanza, Arjuna takes up the discussion where it was left in the previous chapter and gives it a definite push forward, making Krishna expound exhaustively the most profitable and dynamic way of spiritual life, clearly distinguishing it from the unprofitable and self-dissipating channels of misconceived spiritual endeavours.

SETTING ASIDE THE ORDINANCES OF THE *SHASTRA*—The injunctions of scriptural texts are not generally available for all people, and even when they are made available, very few will have the intellectual capacity to understand them. In the excitement of life's activities around, and the confusions and anxieties within, very few of us can hope to plan the 'paths' of our life according to the *shastra*-provided blue-print. But a sincere seeker might have a great 'faith' in the Higher way-of-life and a deep devotion to the ideals preached and propounded generally by all the scriptures of the world. Hence this question.

PERFORM ACTIONS (*Yajantah*)—The term (*Yajna*) used here need not be understood as indicating the *Vedic* sacrifices and ritualistic performances only. The *Geeta* is quite a complete scripture, and as such, it has its own definitions of terms. The

---

अर्जुन उवाच
ये शास्त्रविधिमुत्सृज्य यजन्ते श्रद्धयान्विता: ।
तेषां निष्ठा तु का कृष्ण सत्त्वमाहो रजस्तम: ॥ १ ॥

arjuna uvāca
ye śāstravidhimṛtsṛjya yajante śraddhayānvitāḥ
teṣāṁ niṣṭhā tu kā kṛṣṇa sattvamāho rajastamaḥ 1.

term *Yajna* has been earlier (in Chapter III) defined to include all selfless cooperative endeavours of every individual in a society, undertaken to bring forth to manifestation, the latent wealth and prosperity that are in that community. Therefore, all acts done by an individual during his life, in a spirit of selfless dedication to the general well-being can come under this term. Without knowing the serene harmony that throbs behind life, can one, who is striving hard in the world in a spirit of detachment and selflessness, hope to avoid agitations? What would be his condition (*Nishtha*)? And in a parenthetical clause Arjuna adds what he wants to know; "whether such actions of men fall under the category of 'unactivity' (*sattva*), or of 'activity' (*rajas*), or of 'inactivity' (*tamas*)."

The Blessed Lord said:

2. *Threefold is the faith of the embodied, which is inherent in their nature -- the SATTVIC (pure), the RAJASIC (passionate) and the TAMASIC (dull, dark). Thus thou hear of it.*

As a preface to his discourse, the Lord says that 'faith' (*shraddha*) itself is of three kinds; the divine, the undivine, and the diabolic. *Shraddha* determines the texture of our impressions (*vasanas*) in us, which, in their turn, command our view-of-life. Our desires, thoughts, and actions are charted by our view-of-life. Naturally, an individual's physical activities, psychological behaviours, and intellectual make-up are all ordered by the type

---

श्रीभगवानुवाच
त्रिविधा भवति श्रद्धा देहिनां सा स्वभावजा ।
सात्त्विकी राजसी चैव तामसी चेति तां श्रृणु ॥ २ ॥

śrībhagavānuvāca
trividhā bhavati śraddhā dehināṁ sā svabhāvajā
sāttvikī rājasī caiva tāmasī ceti tāṁ śṛṇu 2.

of *shraddha* he has come to maintain in himself. And, if the *shraddha* is of the wrong type, the entire expression of his personality, in all walks of life and in every field of endeavour, can only be ugly. As his inner disposition, so will be the man. The more an individual identifies himself with his physical sheath, the more crystallised becomes his ego, under the influence of his inner disposition. The temperaments that rule the behaviours of the human are three in number,* the 'Good' (*sattvic*), the 'Passionate' (*rajasic*) and the 'Dull' (*tamasic*).

WHY SHOULD WE TAKE INTO CONSIDERATION THESE TEMPERAMENTS AT ALL, AND TRY TO UNDERSTAND THE TYPES OF FAITH AND THEIR PLAY IN LIFE? THESE ARE EXPLAINED IN THE FOLLOWING:

3. *The faith of each is in accordance with his nature, O Bharata.*
Man consists of his faith; as a man's faith is, so is he.

ACCORDING TO ONE'S OWN NATURE (*Sattvaanuroopa*)—The type of faith that feeds and nourishes each bosom is, we notice, vastly different from that of another. The more we observe the differences the more we are led to inquire why it should be so. The Lord, in the *Geeta*, explains that the 'faith' in each heart is ordered by its own nature. It is very difficult to say whether 'faith' prescribes the nature or the nature prescribes the 'faith'; each is intimately wedded to the other, each obeys the other most faithfully, indeed.

However, the *Geeta* declares that it is the nature in an individual that rules his FAITH; although, if 'faith' can be broken

---

सत्त्वानुरूपा सर्वस्य श्रद्धा भवति भारत ।
श्रद्धामयोऽयं पुरुषो यो यच्छ्रद्धः स एव सः ॥ ३ ॥

sattvānurūpā sarvasya śraddhā bhavati bhārata
śraddhāmayo'yaṁ puruṣo yo yacchraddhaḥ sa eva saḥ 3.

* For a detailed discussion of these, refer Chapter XIV.

and remoulded, as it can be, sometimes, at the irresistible compulsion of painful experiences, the nature of that one does faithfully obey the new *shraddha*. But, generally speaking, the 'faith' in each man takes the hue and quality from the stuff of his being – the predominant temperament in him. The essence of 'faith' lies in the secret energy of the ego with which it holds on to its convictions, to reach a definite, chosen end, by well thoughtout and entirely self-planned means.

Man's potentiality determines his 'faith' to a given end, and this 'faith' then reacts upon his potentiality, determining his future course, and moulds the being in the man. Both act and react upon each other. That the nature of man is determined by the preponderance of any one of the *gunas* over the others, has been already discussed (XIV-10). As a result of previous conservation of a particular tendency, one of the 'qualities' gains a preponderance over the other two, even from one's childhood. This is indicated here by the term *sattva*, according to which (*Anuroopa*) is the 'faith' entertained by the individual.

SHRADDHA IS THE INDIVIDUAL—Man is constituted of and exists in his *shraddha*. Each devotee ultimately reaches the seat of his devotion, if he consistently, and with sufficient intensity, devotes himself to its attainment (VII-20 to 23).

AS A MAN'S FAITH SO IS HE (*Yo yat shraddhah sa eva sah*) Man is verily what his 'faith' is. The type of personality and its effectiveness or otherwise are all determined by the 'faith' under which it functions. That the achievement of life, is ever coloured by the type of 'faith' with which the individual pursues his activities,* is very well known and realised by all men of action. In the very language of the *Geeta* this idea is already explained in an earlier chapter (IX-23).

4. *The SATTVIC, or 'pure' men, worship the gods (DEVAS); the RAJASIC or the 'passionate', the YAKSHAS and the RAKSHASAS; the others -- TAMASIC people, or the 'dark or dull' folk, worship the ghosts (PRETAS) and the hosts of BHUTAS, or the nature / spirits.*

SATTVIC MEN WORSHIP *DEVAS*—Every man in life brings his entire devotion and offers it at one altar or another, and seeks fulfilment from the benefits that accrue from the invocations. In scriptural language this is called WORSHIP. This need not indicate only the ritualistic worship of some God or deity. The term WORSHIP here embraces a wider implication. Every one of us is a WORSHIPPER at some altar chosen by him; even atheists are worshippers ... perhaps they devote themselves to the alter of sense-objects, or of wealth, or of power. In this ampler meaning, if we are to read the stanza, the meaning becomes very clear indeed. Men of *sattvic* temperament, because of their serene composure and tranquil disposition, seek their fulfilment at an altar of divinity indicating the Higher impulses and the nobler qualities of their being. Naturally, they seek and come to adore such a divine Godly altar.

YAKSHAS AND *RAKSHASAS* BY THE *RAJASIC*—Men of 'passionate nature' (*rajas*) are those who have extreme ambition and are constantly restless in their self-chosen fields of activity. They are said to be worshipping and propitiating demi-gods

---

यजन्ते सात्त्विका देवान्यक्षरक्षांसि राजसाः |
प्रेतान्भूतगणांश्चान्ये यजन्ते तामसा जनाः || ४ ||
yajante sāttvikā devānyakṣarakṣāṁsi rājasāḥ
pretānbhūtagaṇāṁścānye tajante tāmasā janāḥ 4.

* 'Such are the trends of our desires and the nature of our souls, just such each of us becomes' - Plato 'Earnestness alone makes life eternity' -- Goethe

(*Yakshas* and *Rakshasas*).* The idea here is that the choice of the altar will depend upon the silent demands of the heart of the devotee. One will never go to a bookstall to purchase some dress. So too, the active and the passionate type of men can feel an admiration for, and can appreciate, only an equally active and passionate (*rajasic*) demi-god or deity.

THE *TAMASIC* MEN (WORSHIP) THE *PRETAS* AND *BHUTAS*—The dead 'spirits' and such other low and vicious powers are invoked by the men of 'inactivity' (*tamas*) for the satisfaction of some of their low urges for vicious sense-gratifications. Men of low moral calibre and false education, generally, would try to fulfil their pernicious ambitions with the help of the wretched vengeful scum of the society (*Pretas*, *Bhutas*), who, though physically alive, are dead to all sweetness and goodness in life. These hired *goondas* (thugs), generally chosen from professional jailbirds, are the fit powers to be invoked in order that low and criminal ambitions of the *tamasic* can be fulfilled.

The same import has been brought out in many earlier stanzas (VII-20 to 23; IX-23 to 25). The modern man would be rather curious to know whether there really exist such powers and deities as *pretas* and *bhutas*. It is in fact immaterial for the purpose of studying this portion of the *Geeta* whether such powers really exist or not. They are indicative of certain types of powers which are available in this world of ours.

---

* It is interesting to note that *Yakshas* are described as 'the brothers of *Kubera*', the minister in charge of Finance in Heaven, and the *Rakshasas* as 'beings of strength and power'. All men of action ambitious of success and achievement would necessarily seek the friendship of only BROTHERS OF RICH MEN AND MEN OF POWER AND STRENGTH. Now, turn wherever you will, and you can find the truth of this principle amply illustrated in the present-day world.

'The help gained from good friends', the 'protection invoked from the rich and the powerful', and the 'enormous strength gathered from the low thoughtless men of criminal intentions' – these are the different types of 'altars' at which men of serenity (*sattvic*), of ambition (*rajasic*), of heedlessness (*tamasic*), generally seek their individual satisfaction. From the nature of a man's field-of-activity, we can, to a large extent, understand to what type he belongs.

THAT THE SPIRIT OF DEVOTION IN MEN, EVER REMAINING THE SAME, EACH WILL SELECT ACCORDING TO THE TYPE OF HIS '*SHRADDHA*', HIS OWN ALTAR OF DEVOTION, HAS BEEN SHOWN IN THE ABOVE. THE WRONG WAY OF STRIVING IS PAINTED BELOW:

5. *Those men who practise terrible austerities, not enjoined by the scriptures, given to hypocrisy and egoism, impelled by the force of lust and attachment ...*

6. *Senselessly torturing all the elements in the body, and Me also who dwells within the body -- you may know these to be of 'demoniacal' resolves.*

अशास्त्रविहितं घोरं तप्यन्ते ये तपो जनाः ।
दम्भाहंकारसंयुक्ताः कामरागबलान्विताः ॥ ५ ॥

aśāstravihitaṁ ghoraṁ tapyante ye tapo janāḥ
dambhāhaṅkārasaṁyuktāḥ kāmarāgabalānvitāḥ 5.

कर्षयन्तः शरीरस्थं भूतग्राममचेतसः ।
मां चैवान्तःशरीरस्थं तान्विद्ध्यासुरनिश्चयान् ॥ ६ ॥

karśayantaḥ śarīrasthaṁ bhūtagrāmamacetasaḥ
māṁ caivāntaḥ śarīrasthaṁ tānviddhayāsuraniścayān 6.

Over-enthusiasm can produce only a physical exhaustion, and an inward fatigue. No spiritual unfoldment can be expected from unintelligent expenditure of energy in wrong channels merely because it is undertaken in the name of religion. The majority of seekers mis-apply their energies and come to suffer. Therefore, Krishna considers it easier to paint the picture of the false seekers and ridicule their unintelligent methods.

Physical restraints and self-denials are, no doubt, sometimes prescribed for some sturdily-built types, for some limited period. At the same time it is not proper or correct to believe that any kind of self-denial would constitute an austerity, and that by following it, creative unfoldment of the inner personality-structure could be successfully brought about. The austerities must be scientific, and therefore, not against the injunctions laid down in the sacred books that discuss this subject.

Some people generally undertake severe austerities only as a show. Men GIVEN TO OSTENTATION AND EGOISM are not fit for austerity. They remain mentally unfit for *tapas* as long as they are lusty and extremely attached to the world-of-objects around. Such individuals cannot practice austerities.

Even when such people practise austerities and develop some inward dynamism as a result of their *tapas*, their intentions being gross, they will only misuse the newfound strength in wrong channels, and in the end, bring about their own self-destruction—the famous examples of *Rakshasas* in the *Puranas* are illustrative enough. Such people, practising austerities, regardless of the correct injunction of the *shastras*, belong to the *Asuric* type.

ME, DWELLING IN THE BODY—Such unintelligent austerities not only oppress the elements constituting the physical frame but also the Sacred and the Divine Lord within. Life gets choked as it were in such an individual – meaning, Life cannot express its fullest beauty through such a broken form. Extreme *tapas* is stupid and is condemned* here. Intelligent control is *tapas*, not cruel self-torture!

THE THREE KINDS - THE *SATTVIC*, THE *RAJASIC*, AND THE *TAMASIC* – OF FOOD, OF WORSHIP, OF AUSTERITY, AND OF GIFT ARE DISCUSSED IN THE FOLLOWING STANZAS:

7. *The food also which is dear to each is threefold, as also sacrifice, austerity and alms-giving. You may now hear the distinction of these.*

Introducing the theme that is to follow, Lord Krishna enumerates the topics that He is going to discuss. The temperamental influences that govern the mind and its thought-life express themselves in all departments of activity in which the individual employs himself. His choice of food, of friends, of the type of emotions in his bosom, of the view-of-life that he will be entertaining are all indicative of the type to which the seeker belongs. As a matter of fact, everyone living on the surface of the earth expresses himself in one of these classifications, due to the preponderance of one or the other of the three temperaments (*gunas*).

Yajna, Tapa, Daana—In the choice of 'food', in the type of 'sacrifices' which he would feel inspired to make, in the texture

---

आहारस्त्वपि सर्वस्य त्रिविधो भवति प्रिय: ।
यज्ञस्तपस्तथा दानं तेषां भेदमिमं श्रृणु ॥ ७॥

āhārastvapi sarvasya trividho bhavati priyaḥ
yajñastapastathā dānaṁ teṣāṁ bhedamimaṁ śṛṇu 7.

* *Gautama Buddha* warns his disciples: 'The habitual practice of asceticism or self-mortification, which is painful, unworthy and unprofitable, is not to be followed.'

of his 'self-denials', and in the quality and quantity of his 'charity', he will declare himself as belonging to one or the other of the three types.

Here follows a detailed analysis of one's inner nature, and naturally, one's outward expressions, when one is under the irresistible influence of any one particular *guna*. These verses are not to be misconstrued as ready-reckoners TO CLASSIFY OTHERS. Hinduism, in its essential beauty, is a subjective science for bringing about a fuller unfoldment of the dormant potentialities in AN INDIVIDUAL'S OWN PERSONALITY. In unravelling the beauties of the soul and in exploiting the strength of the heart, each one will have to purify himself from the dullness of *tamas*, and from the agitations of *rajas*, and keep oneself in the creative alertness and spiritual glow of *sattva*.

HEREUNDER, WE FIND ENUMERATED A SERIES OF SYMPTOMS BY WHICH WE CAN CORRECTLY CLASSIFY OURSELVES:

8. *The foods which increase life, purity, strength, health, joy and cheerfulness (good appetite), which are savoury and oleaginous, substantial and agreeable, are dear to the SATTVIC (Pure).*

In describing the natural taste for some particular types of food in good men of spiritual urges (*sattva*), it is said that they like only such diet which increases the vitality (*Aayuh*), and not sheer bulk; which supplies the energy for meditative purposes (*Veerya*); which discovers for them a secret strength (*Bala*) to resist the temptations for the sense-objects; which provide health

---

आयु:सत्त्वबलारोग्यसुखप्रीतिविवर्धना: ।
रस्या: स्निग्धा: स्थिरा हृद्या आहारा: सात्त्विकप्रिया: ॥ ८ ॥
āyuḥsattvabalārogya sukhaprītivivardhanāḥ
rasyāḥ snigdhāḥ sthirā hṛdyā āhārāḥ sāttvikapriyāḥ 8.

(*Aarogya*) so that they may not often fall ill and suffer a break in their regular *sadhana*. Such people will have a natural inclination to take food which will augment joy (*Preeti*) and inner cheerfulness (*Sukha*). In short, such creative men, by their own choice, enjoy only food that is clean and wholesome with no chance for them, when consumed, to putrefy within.

All the different types of food eaten by man in the world have been classified and brought under four types on the basis of their physical properties. They are the savoury, the greasy, the firm and the cordial types of food. Men of purity instinctively like all these types of foods when they have the above-mentioned effects upon the consumers – when they (the consumers) have digested and assimilated them.

No doubt, food has certain effects upon the eater. Generally, an eater is, to some extent, conditioned by the type of diet he eats. Not only is our inner nature built by the type of food consumed, but the inner nature, in its turn, commands our tastes; and we find very often that we have developed an irresistible appetite for certain types of food.* In the case of animals it is noticed that sometimes they change their diet, according to their physical need in life; dogs and cats are often seen eating grass, cows licking salt-slabs, etc., children eating sand, and pregnant women manifesting different tastes at different periods of their pregnancy.

EXPLAINING THE *RAJASIC* TYPE OF MEN AND THEIR TASTE IN FOOD, THE LORD SAYS:

* There are some who translate these terms as "the sweet, the soft, the nourishing and the agreeable types of food that are dear to the 'God' (*sattvic*)".

9. *The foods that are bitter, sour, saline, excessively hot, pungent, dry and burning, are liked by the RAJASIC, and are productive of pain, grief and disease.*

Men of energy, the 'passionate', desire such food (*Rajasasya ishtaah*) that have strong flavour and dense taste. Bitter, sour, saltish, very hot, pungent, harsh, burning tastes are to the liking of all vigorous men, restlessly striving to fulfil their uncontrolled passions and desires (*rajasic*).

Such a diet, no doubt, creates in an individual brilliant energies, but in their wildness, they are, to a degree, uncontrollable; and therefore, in their final reactions they lead the eater towards a life productive of PAIN, GRIEF AND DISEASE.

A student of these discussions in the *Geeta* is not justified, if he considers that, by a control of diet the thought-discipline in himself will also be brought about. From these stanzas, we have to understand that, when the texture of thought improves, the individual finds himself changing his tastes: even his choice of food which would give him full satisfaction is totally revolutionised.

WHAT TYPE OF FOOD WOULD MEN OF DARKNESS (*TAMAS*) CHOOSE?

10. *That which is stale, tasteless, putrid and rotten, refuse and impure, is the food liked by the 'TAMASIC'.*

कट्वम्ललवणात्युष्णतीक्ष्णरूक्षविदाहिन: ।
आहारा राजसस्येष्टा दु:खशोकामयप्रदा: ॥ ९ ॥
kaṭvamlalavaṇātyuṣṇatīkṣṇarūkṣavidāhinaḥ
āhārā rājasasyeṣṭā duḥkhaśokāmayapradāḥ 9.
यातयामं गतरसं पूति पर्युषितं च यत् ।
उच्छिष्टमपि चामेध्यं भोजनं तामसप्रियम् ॥ १० ॥
yātayāmaṁ gatarasaṁ pūti paryuṣitaṁ ca yat
ucchiṣṭamapi cāmedhyaṁ bhojanaṁ tāmasapriyam 10.

(*Yaata-yaamam*)—A day is divided, in our old calculations in the *shastras,* into eight *Yaamas,* wherein a period of three hours constitutes a *Yaama*. Therefore, food cooked three hours earlier, 'gone cold' is that which is considered as spoiled. In these days of canned food, preserved fruits, stored vegetables and refrigeration facilities, almost a substantial majority of us have come to love stale food.

TASTELESS (*Gata-rasam*)—In South India, we find a peculiar hunger for taking rice that has been kept soaked in water the previous night. The next morning, it becomes both stale and tasteless. I suppose, in the north, some like old *roti*.

FOUL-SMELLING (*Pooti*)—Men of inertia have a natural liking for stinking food that has an insufferable smell for others. The *pulav* of the modern tables perhaps belongs to this category; so too, prawns -- we can multiply examples. 'Men of purity', however, would instinctively revolt against a diet that has any stink about it, e.g., seafood.

STALE (*Paryushitam*)—Food that has been cooked overnight, or that has been kept for days together. Here we can include all the fermented drinks, which the *tamasic* people love to drink. All drinks are fermented and the 'kick' in them increases as the time after preparation increases.

Unsanitary and unclean food seems to attract the taste of all despicable men of insufferable ignorance and low culture. They love to eat 'refuse' (*Ucchishtam*) that is left over, and impure (*Amedhyam*) filthy food that is not fit for human consumption. The above-enumerated list is a comprehensive report on the base and disgusting tastes of *tamasic* men of low culture and dull discrimination.

WHAT TYPE OF SACRIFICES THESE THREE CLASSES OF MEN WOULD THEMSELVES ENGAGE IN, CHEERFULLY?

11. *That sacrifice which is offered by men without desire for fruit, and as enjoined by ordinance, with a firm faith that sacrifice is a duty, is SATTVIC or 'pure'.*

After exhausting the classification of the temperaments as determined by tastes exhibited by different people in the world, the *Geeta* continues to indicate how, in the very type of activities undertaken; there is an unmistakable declaration of the temperamental beauty, or ugliness, of the individual.

PERFORMED BY MEN DESIRING NO FRUIT— Sacrifices undertaken by men of purity are always executed in a spirit of selflessness. We have already explained, earlier in the *Geeta,* that a burning anxiety for the fruits-of-action is an unprofitable channel of dissipation of the sacred and vital human energy. Fruits belong to future periods of time, and to waste the present in anxiety over the future is indeed an unintelligent policy of existence.

AS REQUIRED BY ORDINANCES—Actions in the world fall under four categories, according to ancient *Vedic* lore. Of them 'desire-ridden' (*Kamya*) and positively self-insulting, and therefore 'forbidden' acts (*Nishiddha*) are the two types that are to be studiously avoided. The other two classes: (a) the 'daily duties' (*Nitya*), and (b) the 'special duties' on special occasions (*Naimittika*) are the types of actions that should not be avoided but must be most diligently pursued. These two types – *Nitya* and *Naimittika* together constitute what the *shastra* terms as the 'unavoidable' or 'obligatory duties'. These actions and duties are indicated here as those required by ordinance. This term is

---

अफलाकाङ्क्षिभिर्यज्ञो विधिदृष्टो य इज्यते ।
यष्टव्यमेवेति मनः समाधाय स सात्त्विकः ॥ ११ ॥
aphalākāṅkṣabhiryajño vidhidṛṣṭo ya ijyate
yaṣṭavyameveti manaḥ samādhāya sa sāttvikaḥ 11.

used here in contrast with the *tamasic* type of activity, 'wherein no ordinance is observed' and men are always devoid of 'faith' (XVII-13).

SACRIFICE IS OUR DUTY—This is the motive that propels the 'good' to act in life. He suffers no dissipation of his inner energies either through anxieties to drive himself to a particular goal or through his restlessness in herding the environments to settle themselves into a preplanned and preconceived system of harmony. His mind is ever at rest in its own native satisfaction. He is consciously happy that he is pursuing a line of action which is most conducive to the welfare of all. Such actions are classed under the *sattvic* type of sacrifices.

12. *The sacrifice which is offered, O best of the Bharatas, seeking fruit and for ostentation, you may know that to be a RAJASIC YAJNA.*

WITH A VIEW TO GAINING FRUIT—In order to gain a chosen result, some people act in the world, and naturally, while in the field of activity, they are much too preoccupied with their anxieties and worries. They grow more and more nervous at their own imaginary fears – they ever live in an atmosphere of fear as to whether they will gain a particular chosen goal or not.

FOR OSTENTATION—There are others in the world who act, ever so vigorously, not necessarily for gaining any predetermined goal, but merely for satisfying their vanity by exhibiting their wealth or knowledge, thus proving themselves to be the show of society. Ordinarily, there are many who work

---

अभिसन्धाय तु फलं दम्भार्थमपि चैव यत् ।
इज्यते भरतश्रेष्ठ तं यज्ञं विद्धि राजसम् ॥ १२ ॥

abhisandhāya tu phalaṁ sambhārthamapi caiva yat
ijyate bharataśreṣṭha taṁ yajñaṁ viddhi rājasam 12.

in the world and make such sacrifices. These do not constitute divine acts, nor can they ever be expected to yield a reward of cheerfulness or inner peace.

Such sacrifices undertaken by men who are anxious to reach a particular goal and who work for satisfying their vanity in the community, are to be understood as *rajasic*.

THE *TAMASIC* TYPE IS NOW TAKEN UP FOR DISCUSSION:

13. *They declare that sacrifice to be TAMASIC which is contrary to the ordinances, in which no food is distributed, which is devoid of MANTRAS and gifts, and which is devoid of faith.*

Disobeying all the prescriptions laid down in the scriptures and acting against all *Vedic* injunctions – contrary to all the principles laid down by the science of right living -- the sacrifices performed become of the lowest type. Such a sacrifice cannot at all bring about happiness either to the performer, or in its final analysis, to his generation.

WITHOUT DISTRIBUTION OF FOOD—The utter necessities of life are, in the vocabulary of the modern age, indicated by the familiar phrase 'food-clothing-shelter'. In the scriptural language of Hinduism, the term 'food' indicates all these necessities of life. A man of sacrifice and right action cannot expect any inner development because of his actions, unless they are accompanied by a mental development and an expansion in love which makes him share whatever he has with the have-nots.

विधिहीनमसृष्टान्नं मन्त्रहीनमदक्षिणम् ।
श्रद्धाविरहितं यज्ञं तामसं परिचक्षते ॥ १३ ॥
vidhihīnamasṛṣṭānnaṁ mantrahīnamasakṣiṇam
śraddhāvirahitaṁ yajñaṁ tāmasaṁ paricakṣate 13.

Apart from the above-mentioned two, when rituals are conducted without mantra or without distribution of reward for the educated (*Dakshina*), those sacrifices are classified as *tamasic*.

IN ORDER TO CLASSIFY THE THREE TYPES OF *TAPAS*, PURSUED BY THE DIFFERENT TYPES OF PEOPLE, HERE WE HAVE THREE CONSECUTIVE STANZAS DEFINING AND EXPLAINING WHAT *TAPAS* REALLY MEANS:

14. *Worship of the gods, the twice-born, the teachers and the 'wise'; purity, straight-forwardness, celibacy, and non-injury; these are called the 'austerity of the body'.*

WORSHIP OF THE *DEVAS*, THE TWICE-BORN, THE *GURU*, AND THE WISE—To maintain an attitude of attunement with a Higher-ideal, whereby the meditator develops in himself the qualities of the meditated, is called 'worship'. All cultural development, moral growth and ethical unfoldment can be accomplished only through these processes implied in 'worship'. It is almost like 'the touch method' of magnetisation.[1] One who is trying to come away from one's inner personality-encumbrances must necessarily have an attitude of devotion and reverence towards the ideals represented in the *Deva*, the DEITY, worked out and lived by the TWICE-BORN, preached by the *Guru* and recommended by the WISE.

TWICE-BORN (*Dwija*)—The term indicates the *Brahmins*; and the term *Brahmin* means one who has realised the Self. Born

---

देवद्विजगुरुप्राज्ञपूजनं शौचमार्जवम् ।
ब्रह्मचर्यमहिंसा च शारीरं तप उच्यते ॥ १४ ॥

devadvijaguruprājñapūjanaṁ śaucamārjavam
brahmacaryamahiṁsā ca śārīraṁ tapa ucyate 14.

[1] A soft-iron piece is repeatedly rubbed with a horseshoe magnet whereby the iron-bit so treated gains to itself the magnetic properties.

as we are from the wombs of our mothers, we are all born as humans with certain intellectual beauties, no doubt, but also with many moral defects. Born out of the womb all right, but we are yet in the womb-of-matter! To hatch ourselves out of our matter-identifications and to emerge into the joy-of-Perfection is to grow into the Divine Estate of Godmen. This is conceived in our philosophy as the 'second birth', and one who has accomplished it is called the 'twice-born': once born from the womb, and for a second time grown out of all the limitations suffered by the Spirit in Its seeming identifications with matter.

PURITY AND STRAIGHT-FORWARDNESS—The importance of these two has been discussed earlier.[1] External cleanliness, not only physical but also environmental, is an unavoidable qualification for a true aspirant. Unless a seeker diligently practises straight-forwardness in his dealings with others he will be developing in himself a split-personality, which will drain away all his composure, tranquillity and mental vitality.

Brahmacharya—Constant revelling in the contemplation of the Supreme *Brahman* is called *Brahmacharya*.[2] This is not possible unless our nature is turned away from bodily indulgences in sense-objects and our minds are trained to turn inward to the Spirit. Therefore, all mental disciplines, by which we come to develop in us this introspection, are together comprehended by the term '*Brahmacharya*'. Likewise, a medical college student is called a doctor, because he is applying himself to the direct means for becoming one, and the means are not far from the end.

---

[1] 'Purity' – refer XVI – 1,2,
'Straight-forwardness' – XVI - 1

[2] *Brahmani Charati iti Brahmachari.*

NON-INJURY—This term has already been discussed many times very exhaustively. Refraining from bringing about any harm to others in society with the mind is called 'non-injury'. Physically, it is impossible for us to continue our existence without bringing, even unconsciously, some sort of injury to others, but our attitude can be changed, so that the seemingly unavoidable harm itself can bring about a great blessing to the world. A doctor ripping open a patient's abdomen with a sharp knife, though doing an act of injury, can ultimately bring about a cure for the patient's illness. Diligently avoiding all acts of injuring others from our emotional and intellectual realms is the strictest 'non-injury' that can be practised in life.

All that has been so far explained[1] constitutes bodily asceticism: physical austerity (*Shaareeram Tapas*).

Austerity (*tapas*) is not a life of brutal self-denial only. On the other hand, it is an intelligent method of living in right relationship with the world-of-objects, thereby avoiding all unnecessary dissipations of our vital energies. The energies that are so economised and conserved are thereafter directed and employed in cultivating creative fields. This scheme of discovering precious new energies, conserving them intelligently, and directing them into more profitable fields of spiritual enquiry is called *tapas*, self-control. Conservation of energy, and redirection of the same to fertilise fresh fields of cultivation within one's own bosom are all meant herein, and the stanza concludes with a clear endorsement that this is true *tapas* intelligently pursued at the body level.

TAPAS IN SPEECH IS NOW DESCRIBED:

---

[1] Worship of the *Devas*, the twice-born, the *Guru* and the wise, purity, straightforwardness, *Brahmacharya*, and non-injury.

15. *Speech which causes no excitement, and is truthful, pleasant and beneficial, and the practice of the study of the VEDAS, these constitute the 'austerity of speech'.*

Speech is a powerful vehicle in man and it reflects the intellectual calibre, the mental discipline and the physical self-control of the speaker. Unless he is well-formed at all these levels, his words will have no force – no magic about them. Again, speech is the constant activity of all and it is an outlet through which the greatest amount of one's energies is wasted. To control and conserve this unproductive waste of energy would constitute a great inner wealth indeed for the seeker.

This does not mean that one must keep a self-ruining, disgustingly irritating, silence (*Mouna*). The power of speech must be made use of for integrating the personality of the seeker. There is an art of using this power in the right way, beneficial to the aspirant as well as to others. The technique of employing speech in the most profitable way is being indicated here in this stanza. The idea suggested in the previous stanza is being more and more deepened by the clear suggestions contained in this stanza that *tapas* is not a diabolic act of breaking and destroying oneself but it is a benevolent scheme for remaking and rediscovering oneself.

SPEECH THAT CAUSES NO SHOCK—The words spoken must be such that they bring no disturbance to others; they 'should neither be irritating nor obscene'. The real touchstone to know whether we are speaking the right words or not is the reaction of the listeners, which is expressed so unmistakably on

---

अनुद्वेगकरं वाक्यं सत्यं प्रियहितं च यत् ।
स्वाध्यायाभ्यसनं चैव वाङ्मयं तप उच्यते ॥ १५ ॥

anudvegakaraṁ vākyaṁ satyaṁ priyahitaṁ ca yat
svādhyāyābhyasanaṁ caiva vāṅmayaṁ tapa ucyate 15.

their faces. But generally, people speak with their eyes shut, or even when they are open they are as though blind. Many a miserable man has failed in his efforts in life, and lost all his friends and relatives merely because of the bitterness of his tongue, the harshness of his words, and the stink of his indiscreet thoughts!

TRUE, AGREEABLE AND BENEFICIAL (*Satyam-priyam-hitam*)—Words uttered to express the truth in an agreeable style for the blessing of others constitute 'speech', which, when properly handled and made use of, will bless the speaker himself. In telling a lie, a lot of energy is wasted and this waste is avoidable if one adopts the policy of truthfulness in his expression. Words that harmoniously bring forth the exact shade of ideas in the intellect are 'truthful' expressions, and those that deliberately distort the intentions and meanings of the intellect are called falsehood. In the name of truthfulness one can become a disagreeable creature in society. This is not allowed in a seeker. The *Geeta* accepts only that speech as truthful WHICH IS ALSO AGREEABLE. By unsaid words the Lord's Song seems to say that when a truth is disagreeable to others, the speaker is required to maintain a discreet silence!

It is not sufficient that the words in the speech should be honest and agreeable, but they should also be beneficial. Speech should not be wasted. Unprofitable talking is a great drain upon man's energies. Talk only when you want to express agreeable ideas of permanent values, which will be useful to the listeners. Those who are respecting these qualities in their day-to-day vocal activities can be considered as men performing AUSTERITY IN SPEECH.

REGULAR STUDY OF THE SCRIPTURES—Control of speech certainly does not mean entering into a state of inert and lifeless silence of the grave. Investing the energies of speech in self-profiting and self-creative channels of endeavour is considered by Krishna as '*tapas* in speech'. *Swadhyaya* is a technical term used in our sacred literature to indicate the careful study of and deep reflections upon the theme of the scriptures. The vital energy so economised in daily life through a policy of 'speaking only that which is beneficial, agreeable and truthful', is invested in chanting, in reflecting upon, and in meditating over the *mantras* of the *Upanishads* and other scriptures.

This stanza is complete in its explanation of the technique. The first line indicates the channels of economy possible in the daily expenditure of energy. The second line shows the avenues of investment wherein the seeker can expect to gain for himself a greater dividend of a fuller joy. Both the schemes so suggested completely indicate the 'AUSTERITY IN SPEECH'.

TAPAS OF THE MIND IS NOW TAKEN UP FOR DISCUSSION:

16. *Serenity of mind, good-heartedness, silence, self-control, purity of nature -- these together are called the 'mental austerity'.*

If the five noble values-of-life enumerated herein are lived, they, in their aggregate, effectively produce the *tapas* of the mind. SERENITY OF MIND can be gained only when our relationship with the world at large is put on a healthier basis of understanding, tolerance, and love. One who is an uncontrolled sensualist can have little serenity or composure. Mind runs out

---

मन:प्रसाद: सौम्यत्वं मौनमात्मविनिग्रह: ।
भावसंशुद्धिरित्येतत्तपो मानसमुच्यते ॥ १६ ॥

manaḥ prasādaḥ saumyatvaṁ maunamātmavinigrahaḥ
bhāvasaṁśuddhirityetattapo mānasamucyate 16.

through the sense-organs into the sensual fields to eke out its satisfactions.

The driving force that sets the mind on its endless errands is an intellect, ever seething with desires. Quietude of the mind can be gained only when it is protected from both the inflow of the stimuli from the tempting sense-objects of the outer world, and the whipping desires that march out from the intellect to drive the mind out into the fields-of-enjoyment. In fact, a seeker who has discovered for himself a divine ideal; in the contemplation of which his mind forgets to run about, or his intellect overlooks to send out new desires; alone can hope to win the serenity of the mind (*Manah-prasada*).

KINDNESS (*Soumyatwam*)—That warm feeling of affection for all, which readily rises in a heart of true devotion and love, is kindness. And that kindly seeker who lives in this divine attitude towards all things and beings around, will have no chance of entertaining the feeling that he is outrageously molested by, or even temporarily upset with his environment.

SILENCE (*Mouna*)—We have already noted that 'not speaking' is not *'Mouna'*. In this stanza, while enumerating the 'austerities of the mind', Lord Krishna speaks of 'silence'. It is neither a contradiction, nor a mistake. Silence of speech must arise from the relative silence of the mind. Thus *Mouna* means that noiseless inner calm, which one comes to experience when corroding passions and exhausting desires are no more building up in one's mind. *'Mouna'* (silence) can also mean the state of *Muni*, implying the state of constant contemplation.

SELF-CONTROL—The three above mentioned qualities; serenity of composure, constant kindness towards others, and unbroken, calm silence within -- are impossible unless we are able to control our inner nature deliberately. The animal in us is generally very powerful, and unless we are ever vigilant, the lower nature in us may upset our inner balance and equanimity.

HONESTY OF MOTIVE—Self-control is not possible unless our motives are pure and serene. Without any definite goal in life, without planning our onward march towards the ideal, we are apt to fall a victim to the various temptations en-route, and exhaust ourselves in the by-lanes of life. To stick constantly on to the grand road to success is to assure for ourselves a happy pilgrimage to Truth. The urge in us that motivates all our mental activities must be inspiring and divine, or else the chances are that we will be undermining our own perfections and ruining our own chances of making life a great success.

The above three stanzas thus give us a clear picture of what is true *tapas*, in our bodily contacts with the world outside, in our speech and in our mental life. The very same *tapas* is pursued by different people, and even when they do so, with equal faith, each of them is observed to gain different results. This is not accidental. The people who do *tapas* (*tapaswins*) are of different temperaments: the 'good' (*sattvic*), the 'passionate' (*rajasic*) and the 'dull' (*tamasic*). According to their governing temperaments they act differently, with different tempo and with different emphasis, so that they come to reap diverse results from the different types of *tapas* performed by them.

IN THE FOLLOWING STANZAS, THE THREE TYPES OF '*TAPASWINS*' AND THE NATURE OF THEIR *TAPAS* ARE INDICATED:

17. *This three-fold austerity, practised by steadfast men, with the utmost faith, desiring no fruit, they call 'SATTVIC'.*

श्रद्धया परया तप्तं तपस्तत्त्रिविधं नरैः ।
अफलाकाङ्क्षिभिर्युक्तैः सात्त्विकं परिचक्षते ॥ १७ ॥

śraddhayā parayā taptaṁ tapastattrividhaṁ naraiḥ
aphalākāṅkṣabhiryuktaiḥ sāttvikaṁ paricakṣate 17.

When men practise austerities of body, speech and mind, steadily 'with no clinging attachment to, or anxiety for, the fruits thereof', their *tapas* falls under the type: the *sattvic*. The 'good' are those integrated men who refuse to worry about the future, because they know that, in the harmony in nature, the future is the resultant of the total past modified by the present.* Since the perfection and efficiency of the PRESENT activities determine and command the FUTURE results, it is certainly unintelligent to worry over the FUTURE and spoil the very quality of the PRESENT activities. Thus the 'good', desiring no fruit, but all the same practising, with great sincerity, the threefold *tapas* as explained above, come to reap a large dividend from their austerities.

18. *The austerity which is practised with the object of gaining good reception, honour and worship, and with hypocrisy, is here said to be RAJASIC, unstable, and transitory.*

Penance that is performed with a view to gaining respect, honour and reverence is said to be of the *rajasic* type, performed generally by men of 'passionate' nature. Self control and self-application pursued not for the purpose of one's own inner development, but only for hood-winking the world and getting cheap respect, reverence or worship, is indeed, one of the basest deceits that a man of culture can ever practise. Earlier *Shri Bhagawan* Himself (III-6, 7) called such men hypocrites. Seekers

---

सत्कारमानपूजार्थं तपो दम्भेन चैव यत् ।
क्रियते तदिह प्रोक्तं राजसं चलमध्रुवम् ॥ १८ ॥

satkāramānapūjārthaṁ tapo dambhena caiva yat
kriyate tadiha proktaṁ rājasaṁ calamadhruvam 18.

* The continuity of the past MODIFIED by the present is the future, since times flows from the 'past' through the 'present' to become the 'future'.

belonging to this group perform austerities mainly for their propaganda value, and hence, *Bhagawan* says that their *tapas* is 'with ostentation' (*Dambhena*).

One may wonder what harm is there in practising this type of *tapas*? After all *tapas*, as we observed, 'is economy of thought-forces and the intelligent reinvestment of the economised energy into more creative fields of self-development'. And yet, the *Geetacharya* condemns those who perform *tapas* with this wrong motive, and declares that such *tapas* is UNSTABLE AND TRANSITORY.* Any intelligent self-effort, ordinarily, has a time-lapse, before it can produce its results. Self-application must be constant and continuous in order that it may produce substantial results. When *tapas* is performed with such a low motive as of winning respectability in society, it cannot even gather the necessary amount of intensity and thus, *tapas* of the 'passionate' can only end in a lot of unproductive and painful self-denials.

THE DULL-WITTED PURSUE THE *TAMASIC* TYPE OF *TAPAS*:

19. *That austerity which is practised with self-torture, out of some foolish notion, for the purpose of destroying another, is declared to be TAMASIC.*

Tapas undertaken with a foolish obstinacy by means of self-torture, and 'austerities' indulged in for the sake of destroying others are of the lowest type. A *tapaswin* must have clear notions

मूढग्राहेणात्मनो यत्पीडया क्रियते तपः ।
परस्योत्सादनार्थं वा तत्तामसमुदाहृतम् ॥ १९ ॥
mūḍhagrāheṇātmano yatpīḍayā kriyate tapaḥ
parasyotsādanārthaṁ vā tattāmasamudāhṛtama 19.

* *'Chalam-Adhruvam'* is the phrase used in the verse for 'Unstable and transitory'.

as to why he undertakes the *tapas*. And also, he should know what is *tapas* and how to do it. Without a correct knowledge of the technique, no seeker can independently walk the 'path' of inner integration and gain spiritual fulfilment.

When the *Vedic* notion of *tapas* is misconstrued, the seeker will, at best, be only torturing himself. Self-torture cannot bring about any unveiling of the true beauty of the Soul; it can only create a ludicrous caricature of the Perfection in us. Twisted and torn into a disfigured personality, perverted in its emotion and unclean in its ideals -- this alone can be the outcome of any unintelligent austerity.

And when these misconceived and wrongly practised austerities are undertaken by any one for bringing about sorrow and discomfort to others, such *tapas* is considered as *tamasic*.

CHARITY ALSO CAN FALL UNDER THREE KINDS:

20. *That gift which is given, knowing it to be a duty, in a fit time and place, to a worthy person, from whom we expect nothing in return, is held to be SATTVIC.*

The gift which is given to someone because of one's conviction that 'it is an act that is to be done', is the right type of charity. The recipient should be one who can do no service in return (*anupakari*). The right type of charity expects the benefactor to make no discrimination against the recipients of his charity. A gift is always to be offered, in a fit place and time, to a worthy person. Such charity, made with RIGHT faith, to

---

दातव्यमिति यद्दानं दीयतेऽनुपकारिणे ।
देशे काले च पात्रे च तद्दानं सात्त्विकं स्मृतम् ॥ २० ॥

dātavyamiti yaddāna ṁ dīyate'nupakāriṇe
deśe kāle pātre ca taddānaṁ sāttvikaṁ smṛtam 20.

the RIGHT person, at the RIGHT time and place is of the *sattvic* type.

There is a school which believes that charity must be given just as a tree gives its fruits. The fruits on a tree are available to all who come under its shade – irrespective of their race, status or sex. They argue that as the trees do not make any discrimination between one enjoyer and the other, so too man should, without making any discrimination between one recipient and another, share his possessions freely.

Many will find it difficult to believe in, and live up to, this principle. The *Geeta* insists, and rightly so, that man must use his faculty of discrimination and see whether his charities are reaching the deserving members in the community.

THE *RAJASIC* TYPE IS DESCRIBED BELOW:

21. And that gift which is given with a view to receiving in return, or looking for fruit again, or reluctantly, is held to be RAJASIC.

That which is given in charity with a hope of receiving in return some benefit, be it in any form – perhaps at a different time and place – is of the 'passionate' type. And also, a charity that is done reluctantly, not conscientiously, is of the same *rajasic* type. In our everyday worldly activities, many of our gifts fall under this category.

THE DULL TYPE OF CHARITY IS BEING DESCRIBED NOW:

यत्तु प्रत्युपकारार्थं फलमुद्दिश्य वा पुनः ।
दीयते च परिक्लिष्टं तद्दानं राजसं स्मृतम् ॥ २१ ॥

yattu pratyupakārārthaṁ phalamuddiśya vā punaḥ
dīyate ca parikliṣṭaṁ taddānaṁ rājanaṁ smṛtam 21.

22. *The gift that is given at a wrong place and time, to unworthy persons, without respect, or with insult, is declared to be TAMASIC.*

Gifts that are made at an improper time, and those made at the wrong place, to an unworthy person, without respect, or with contempt, are charities of the dull-witted, and they are called the *tamasic*.

Charity must come from within, as an expression of an irrepressible urge of one's own heart. Intelligent charity must spring from the abundance felt within the individual. He who feels impoverished by his giving has not done a charity by the mere physical act of giving away.

THE FOLLOWING INSTRUCTIONS ARE GIVEN WITH A VIEW TO PERFECTING SACRIFICES, GIFTS, AUSTERITIES, ETC.:

23. *"OM TAT SAT" -- this has been declared to be the triple designation of BRAHMAN. By that were created formerly, the BRAHMANAS, VEDAS and YAJNAS (sacrifices).*

OM TAT SAT—This is being declared as the triple designation (*Nirdesha*) of *Brahman*. A *Nirdesha*, generally given in ritualism, is that by performing which any defects that are in

---

अदेशकाले यद्दानमपात्रेभ्यश्च दीयते ।
असत्कृतमवज्ञातं तत्तामसमुदाहृतम् ॥ २२ ॥
adeśakāle yaddānamapātrebhyaśca dīyate
asṛtkṛtamavajñātaṁ tattāmasamudāhṛtam 22.
ॐतत्सदिति निर्देशो ब्रह्मणस्त्रिविधः स्मृतः ।
ब्राह्मणास्तेन वेदाश्च यज्ञाश्च विहिताः पुरा ॥ २३ ॥
om tatsaditi nirdeśo brahmaṇastrividhaḥ smṛtaḥ
brāhmaṇāstena vedāśca yajñāśca vihitāḥ purā 23.

the sacred worship are all removed. Each action, no doubt, has its fruit, but the fruit depends not only on the action as such, but also on the purity of the intentions and motives entertained by the performer. However diligent the performer of the sacred acts may be, if the motive behind such acts be foul, they are rendered too ineffective to yield rich dividends. Actions performed by all of us, may appear similar, but the results thereof would vary from individual to individual, according to the essential quality of their intentions.

The brilliance and glory of our intentions can be heightened by the remembrance of the Lord. Dissociation of oneself from one's Matter-envelopments is at once one's awakening and identification with the Lord. To the extent the sacred activity is selfless; to that extent its rewards are pure. To liquidate the ego, the individual must gain the consciousness of his spiritual status.

'Om Tat Sat' is a sentence of three words, each denoting one aspect or the other of the Reality. *Om* represents the Transcendental and the Pure Self, the Absolute and the Unborn, which is the Infinite Substratum upon which the projections of the body, mind and intellect are maintained. The term *Tat* is used in our scriptures to indicate the Eternal Goal, the Changeless and the Ever-perfect. In the famous grand declaration of the *Vedas, 'Tat-twam-asi'*, the term *'Tat'* indicates that from which everything has come, in which everything exists and into which everything merges back in the end. *Sat* means 'existence'. The 'Principle of Existence' functioning through all things; perceived, felt, and thought of in our everyday life; is called *Sat*.

Thus, to invoke the thoughts of *Om*, which express the TRANSCENDENTAL ABSOLUTE, or to invoke *'Tat'*, the UNIVERSAL TRUTH, or to cherish the concept of *'Sat'*, the

REALITY, is to tune up our instruments of action and thereby chasten all our activities in the world outside.

The Eternal Reality, indicated in the triple designation of *Brahman 'Om Tat Sat'*, is the Source from which all castes, the *Vedas* and the sacrifices proceeded, even at the time of Creation. All super-impositions can only arise from, exist in and disappear into that which is their own substratum.

All human activities and endeavours can be classified under the heads: (a) activities (*Ahaara*) undertaken for the maintenance of the body, and (b) activities (*Niyata*) that nourish the culture by all cooperative activities pursued with a spirit of dedication (*Yajna*), all charities (*Daana*), and all intelligent methods of self-control (*Tapas*).

WHEN ARE WE TO USE THE TERM *'OM'* ?

24. *Therefore, with the utterance of 'OM' are begun the acts of sacrifice, gifts and austerity as enjoined in the scriptures, always by the students of BRAHMAN.*

The term *OM* is uttered while acts of sacrifice, gift and austerity are undertaken by the followers of higher life. To cherish in our minds the divine awareness and the absolute supremacy of the Infinite, as expressed in *OM*, is to add purpose and meaning to all our acts of sacrifice, charity and austerity. To invoke in our minds the divine concept of the Absolute is to free our personality from its limited fields of egocentric attachments. When a mind is thus liberated from its limitations, it becomes more efficient in all austerities, more selfless in all *Yajnas*, and more liberal in all charities.

तस्मादोमित्युदाहृत्य यज्ञदानतप:क्रिया: ।
प्रवर्तन्ते विधानोक्ता: सततं ब्रह्मवादिनाम् ॥ २४ ॥

tasmādomityudāhṛtya yajñadānatapaḥkriyāḥ
pravartante vidhānoktāḥ satatam̐ brahmavādinām 24.

WHEN IS *'TAT'* USED?

25. *Uttering 'TAT' without aiming at the fruits, are the acts of sacrifice and austerity and the various acts of gift performed by the seekers of liberation.*

THOSE WHO ARE SEEKERS OF LIBERATION—He, who is thus trying to 'liberate' himself from his own attachments, selfish desires, self-centredness, and the consequent agitations, should undertake to perform all his activities in such a way that the causes that generate these disturbances (*vasanas*) in him are not thereby nourished, but are deliberately extinguished. The stanza is providing a tip to the seekers on how this subtle result can be achieved through actions performed with the right mental attitude.

WITH THE UTTERANCE OF THE *'TAT'* ALONE, THE ACTS OF SACRIFICE, PENANCE AND GIFT ARE UNDERTAKEN BY THE SEEKERS OF FREEDOM,[1] WITHOUT EXPECTATION OF ANY REWARD. *'Tat'* indicates, as we have already explained, the 'Universal Truth' and it declares 'the oneness of all living creatures'. To remember the larger interests of the family is to forget our own self-interest; to work for the community is to obliterate our own family-interests; to work for the national redemption is to overlook the limited community benefits; and to work for the world and humanity is to sink our national interests. Thus, to work in the field of

तदित्यनभिसंधाय फलं यज्ञतपःक्रियाः ।
दानक्रियाश्च विविधाः क्रियन्ते मोक्षकाङ्क्षिभिः ॥ २५ ॥

tadityanabhisandhāya phalaṁ yajñatapaḥkriyāḥ
dānakriyāśca vividhāḥ kriyante mokṣakāṅikṣabhiḥ 25.

[1] Freedom from the limitations of personality.

yajna or *tapas* or *daana* with a mind that is tuned up to Tat, 'the universal oneness of the Spiritual Truth', is to work with no ego, and consequently, redeem ourselves from the thraldom of the flesh, from all the limitations of Matter.[1]

WHAT IS THE SIGNIFICANCE OF REPEATING *'SAT'*? WHAT ARE ITS IMPLICATIONS?

26. *The word 'SAT' is used in the sense of Reality and of Goodness; and also, O Partha, the word 'SAT' is used in the sense of an auspicious act.*

Sat is used to mean both REALITY and GOODNESS. It is also used for all praiseworthy actions. In our everyday contact with the world, we live in a realm of RELATIVE REALITY and a seeker is apt to take the world perceived, felt and thought of -through the play of his body, mind and intellect equipments - as ABSOLUTELY REAL. Therefore, the term *Sat* is often used to remind us that all these RELATIVE REALITIES have the self-same substratum *Sat*, the Absolute Reality.

THE USE OF THE DESIGNATION *'SAT'* FOR *BRAHMAN* IS GIVEN AS FOLLOWS:

सद्भावे साधुभावे च सदित्येतत्प्रयुज्यते ।
प्रशस्ते कर्मणि तथा सच्छब्द: पार्थ युज्यते ॥ २६ ॥

sadbhave sādhubhāve ca sadityetatprayujyate
praśaste karmaṇi tathā sacchaydaḥ pārtha yujayate 26.

[1] The existing *vasanas* are exhausted and no new *vasanas* are created – Ch. III.

27. *Steadfastness in sacrifice, austerity and gift is also called 'SAT' and also, action in connection with these (for the sake of the Supreme) is called 'SAT'.*

The term *Sat* is used to indicate a man's faith and devotion in sacrifice, austerity and gift. Thus *Sat* registers one's faith in the principles underlying *Yajna, Daana* and *Tapas* and also in his various acts of sacrifice *(Yajna)*, charity (*Daana*) and austerity (*Tapas*).

In short, even acts of sacrifice and austerity, when they are not of the *sattvic* type can be rendered 'good', when they are pursued with this required inner attunement which is gained by invoking in the performer's bosom the concept of -- the Supreme (*OM*), the Universal (*Tat*), and the Real (*Sat*) -- the Infinite *Brahman*. If these chantings are undertaken with faith and sincerity the seeker's mind expands and gives up all its selfishness and arrogance. Ego and egocentric desires bring about attachments, which, in their turn, destroy the freedom of the individual to grow into the ampler field of joy of the Spirit.

To cut off these shackles which are forged in the fields of activity, we have to re-enter the very 'realm-of-action' and persuade ourselves to perform such 'right' *Karmas* as will liquidate the bad reactions (*Karma-Phala*), of the 'wrong' actions of the past.* This unwinding of the *vasanas*, the very creators of our psychological imperfections, can be effected only in the field-

---

यज्ञे तपसि दाने च स्थितिः सदिति चोच्यते ।
कर्म चैव तदर्थीयं सदित्येवाभिधीयते ॥ २७ ॥

yajñe tapasi dāne ca sthitiḥ saditi cocyate
karma caiva tadarthīyaṁ sadityevābhidhīyate 27.

* Right and wrong : those actions which leave behind in our mind a storm of regrets are called 'wrong' and those which leave behind a great peace and sense of fulfilment, are classified as 'right'.

of-activity. This is accomplished by an intelligent, right adjustment of our mental attitude all along, when we are at work. The required changes are brought about by the remembrance of the Infinite Reality as indicated by the three terms *'OM-TAT-SAT'*. The fundamental principle is that the actions can leave behind only such reactions as are ordered by the type of motives and attitudes of the performer.

ALL THESE ACTS BECOME PERFECT ONLY WHEN DONE IN FULL FAITH. THEREFORE:

28. Whatever is sacrificed, given or performed, and whatever austerity is practised without faith, it is called 'A-SAT', O Partha; it is not for here or hereafter (after death).

In this thundering negative statement, we have an indication that faith is man, and an individual without faith, even if he performs a most glorious act, "IT IS NOT FOR HERE OR HEREAFTER". Action can create only such effects as are ordered by the ardour of faith and conviction of the performer, together indicated here as 'steadfastness' (*Sthiti*). The intellectual values entertained by the seeker will supply the glow in his actions, and since the results of his actions always depend upon the sincerity and ardour with which the actions are undertaken, the good or the bad effects of his actions directly depend upon the 'strength of faith' with which the actions are undertaken or performed.

Herein, we have a conclusive statement that whatever sacrifice is made, whatever penance is performed, or whatever charity is given, it is called *'Asat'*, if it is undertaken 'without

---

अश्रद्धया हुतं दत्तं तपस्तप्तं कृतं च यत् ।
असदित्युच्यते पार्थ न च तत्प्रेत्य नो इह ॥ २८ ॥
aśraddhayā hutaṁ dattaṁ tapastaptaṁ kṛlaṁ ca yat
asadityucyate pārtha na ca tatpretya no iha 28.

faith'. Unreality or non-existence, in Sanskrit, is called *Asat*. From the unreal, nothing real can ever emerge. From the unreal activity, no real result can come. Therefore, devoted actions, spiritual or religious, when undertaken WITHOUT FAITH, fail to produce any result. By so saying, the Lord is indicating that *shraddha* is unavoidable, and that without it no progress or evolution can ever take place.

HEREAFTER—It is not only in the realm of the Spirit that this law holds good but also in the material world of our day-to-day activities. This is a unique, and unquestionable, rule of life. Without 'faith', no one can come to shine in any field of activity. No one can hope to gather any profit at all out of any activity, if he has no faith in it. Both in the secular activities of the market-place and in the sacred performance of religious acts, the factor that determines the quality and quantity of the result is our 'faith' in our own efficiency and goodness, and in our field of activity.

SUCH ACTS PERFORMED WITHOUT 'FAITH' BECOME BARREN – '*ASAT*' – SAYS LORD KRISHNA.

Thus, in the UPANISHADS of the glorious Bhagawad-Geeta, in the Science of the Eternal, in the scripture of YOGA, in the dialogue between Sri Krishna and Arjuna, the seventeenth discourse ends entitled:

The Three-Fold Faith

Om Om Om Om Om

ॐ तत्सदिति श्रीमद् भगवद् गीतासूपनिषत्सु ब्रह्मविद्यायां
योगशास्त्रे श्रीकृष्णार्जुनसंवादे श्रद्धात्रयविभागयोगो नाम
सप्तदशोऽध्यायः

Oṁ tatsaditi śrīmadbhagavadgītāsū ūpaniṣatsu brahmavidyāyāṁ yogaśāstre śrī kṛṣṇārjuna saṁvāde śraddhātrayavibhāgayogo nāma saptadaśo'dhyāyaḥ

XVIII

Liberation Through Renuciation
Introduction

The *Geeta* is a piece of art of strange beauty and it stands apart from everything else, in a class all by itself. It is liquid poetry, expounding solid philosophy. In the fluidity of its metre, it crystallises some of the rarest gems of moral and spiritual values. Its breezy discourses have a firm style. The fluidity of its eloquence falls like merciful rain upon every broken personality, making it whole by its magic touch. It is not a book of science, and yet, it is very scientific in its approach to the theme. It has not the airy nothingness of familiar philosophical discourses, and yet, all philosophies seem to meet within its ample stretch.

It is the duty of science to DESCRIBE life; it is the purpose of philosophy to EXPLAIN life. Science describes the natural structures and processes; philosophy attempts their explanations. Thus viewed, the *Bhagawad Geeta* is an enchanting impossibility; it is at once a science and a philosophy, and yet, strangely enough, it is neither a scientific philosophy nor a philosophical science. In its eighteen chapters, it explains a philosophy of living, and while doing so, it also expounds and demonstrates the science of living.

This closing chapter of the *Geeta* is, in fact, a summary of the entire Song of the Lord. If the second chapter, as we found earlier, is a summary of the *Geeta* in anticipation, the eighteenth chapter is a report on the *Geeta* in retrospect* It is already proved that, everywhere, the One Eternal Spirit functions through matter, and It expresses Itself in this pluralistic world of phenomena. The multiple world of plurality is extremely variegated; in the nature, behaviour and quality of the individuals, variations are noticed in thousands of shades.

On the basis of temperaments, the *Geeta* indicated three types of personalities: The 'Good' (*sattvic*), the 'Passionate' (*rajasic*) and the 'Dull' (*tamasic*). In this chapter we have an elaborate and exhaustive discussion on how these three temperaments, in their variations, create differences among individuals, in sacrifice, in wisdom, in actions, in fortitude and in happiness.

Also in the *Geeta*, two familiar terms, 'renunciation' (*Sannyasa*) and 'abandonment' (*Tyaga*) were very often used in different contexts with seemingly different imports. The terms have to be redefined in order to remove all confusions, as an ambiguity in a science is dangerous to true understanding.

This concluding chapter opens with a direct question from Arjuna as to what constitutes 'renunciation' and what the contents of 'abandonment' are. Lord Krishna takes up the theme and starts defining these two terms; 'but', some students of *Geeta* complain, "The *Geetacharya* has drifted away into a rambling discourse on various other topics unconnected with the main question". In fact, this is no fair criticism. Having defined what is *Sannyasa*, the Lord explains *Tyaga* and shows how, through the latter alone, the former can be achieved and

* Serious students, who had so far been following these discourses very carefully, would do well now, to go back to the beginning of the text and kindly read the 'introduction' that is given at the opening of each of the preceding seventeen chapters.

fully lived. Unless we discover in ourselves, the capacity to banish from our mind its various unhealthy relationships with the world outside and reeducate it to be continuously vigilant and alert to live in a healthy, intelligent spirit of detachment (*Tyaga*), the total withering away of the false ego and its endless desire-promptings, *Sannyasa* can never be achieved. Abandonment is the true content of the status of renunciation – *Sannyasa* without *Tyaga* spirit is but an empty show; it is a false crown with no kingdom of joy within for it to lord over.

The endless, minute details given here, all true to life, analysing and classifying the tendencies, urges, emotions, actions etc., are pointers that help each one to understand himself. They are so many 'instruments' on the 'dash-board' of our bosom within, which can, by their indications, give us a true picture of the condition of the personality-mechanism working within us. Just as a driver of a car can understand the condition of the engine and the nature of its performance by watching the play of the 'pointers' in the meters on the dashboard in front of him – heat, pressure, oil, charge, speed, fuel, mileage, ignition and what not – a seeker is asked to check up at similar definite 'pointers' within and note their readings. If all are indicating the safe-sign, *sattvic*, a smooth life of maximum efficiency and definite progress in cultural evolution is promised. If we can classify ourselves in our tendencies and actions only as *rajasic*, we are advised to take note and be cautious. If the tendencies declare a definite *tamasic* temperament, better halt the vehicle and attend to the ENGINE. This seems to be the advice of this concluding chapter.

The giving up of these lower impulses of the 'Passionate' (*rajasic*) and the 'Dull' (*tamasic*) in our moment-to-moment contacts with life, is 'abandonment' (*Tyaga*), which will give us sufficient mastery over ourselves, ultimately to give up the very ego-centre which causes all these deflections. And this final giving up of the perception of the finite in the acquired wisdom of the Infinite is the fulfilment of life, indicated here by the term 'Renunciation' (*Sannyasa*).

Arjuna said:

1. *I desire to know severally, O mighty-armed, the essence or truth of 'Renunciation', O Hrishikesa, as also of 'Abandonment', O slayer of Keshi (Krishna).*

The chapter begins with Arjuna's question, demanding of Lord Krishna a precise definition, and an exhaustive explanation, of the two terms used by the Lord in the *Geeta*, off and on, here and there. 'Renunciation' (*Sannyasa*) and 'Abandonment' (*Tyaga*) are the two technical terms used more than once in the *Geeta*. Though the question is asked in a spirit of academic interest, Krishna takes up the question in all seriousness. When a disciple expresses his doubt, he invariably fails to express his exact difficulty. However, it is the duty of the teacher to discover the difficulty of the student and clear his doubt, as even the Lord of the *Geeta* does here.

The logic of the entire chapter revolves around the meanings of 'Renunciation' and 'Abandonment'. *Sannyasa* without the spirit of *Tyaga* is incomprehensible, and if at all it is ever so practised, it can only be a sham pose. The bulk of the chapter maps out the tendencies, urges, impulses and motives, that are to be

---

अर्जुन उवाच
संन्यासस्य महाबाहो तत्त्वमिच्छामि वेदितुम् ।
त्यागस्य च हृषीकेश पृथक्केशिनिषूदन ॥ १ ॥
arjuna uvāca
sannyāsasya mahābāho tattvamicchāmi veditum
tyāgasya ca hṛṣīkeśa pṛthakkeśiniṣūdana 1.

abandoned, so that true 'Abandonment' of the undivine personality can effectively take place. We must read the chapter in this spirit, or else it will surely fail to influence us.

SLAYER OF KESHI (*Keshi-nishudana*)—*Keshi* was a *Daitya* who attacked Krishna in the form of a horse. Krishna killed him by tearing him into two halves.

DEFINING THESE TERMS AND INDICATING THE ENTIRE SIGNIFICANCE OF THEIR CONNOTATIONS, KRISHNA SAYS:

The Blessed Lord said:

2. *The Sages understand SANNYASA to be "the renunciation of works with desire"; the wise declare "the abandonment of the fruits of all actions" as TYAGA.*

"Totally giving up all desire-prompted activities" is RENUNCIATION, and ABANDONMENT is "giving up of all anxieties for enjoying the fruits-of-action". As they stand, both of them read almost the same to the uninitiated; for, all desires are always for the fruits of our actions. Thus, 'renouncing desire-motivated activity' and 'renouncing our anxiety for the fruit' would read the same for those who see only their superficial suggestions.

No doubt, both mean giving up desire, but *Tyaga* is slightly different from *Sannyasa*; and yet, 'abandonment' has an integral relationship with 'renunciation'. Action is an effort put forth in

---

श्रीभगवानुवाच
काम्यानां कर्मणां न्यासं संन्यासं कवयो विदुः ।
सर्वकर्मफलत्यागं प्राहुस्त्यागं विचक्षणाः ॥ २ ॥
śrībhagavanuvāca
kāmyānāṁ karmaṇāṁ nyāsaṁ sannyāsaṁ kavayo viduḥ
sarvakarmaphalatyāgaṁ prāhustyāgaṁ vicakṣaṇāḥ 2.

the present, which, in its own time will, it is hoped, fulfil itself into the desired fruit. And, the fruit is what we reap later on as a result of the present action. A desireless action, therefore, belongs to the PRESENT, while the anxiety to enjoy the fruit (desire) is a disturbance of our mind regarding a FUTURE period of time. The fruit comes after the action; the fruit is the culmination of an action undertaken in the present.

Desire and agitation bring about restlessness, and the deeper the desire, the greater is the amount of dissipation of our energies within. A dissipated man cannot execute any piece of work with steady efficiency and true ardour. Also, it is to be noticed, desire is always ordered by the ego. Elimination of the ego is at once the sublimation of the individuality and the ascension of the individual from the lower realms of consciousness to the uppermost stratum of the effulgent Universal Awareness, the One Eternal God.

The tragedy of life becomes complete if a desire-ridden individual comes under the endless persecution of steady anxiety to enjoy the fruits of his actions. Fruits-of-actions belong to the FUTURE and they are always ordered by the quality and quantity of the action in the PRESENT moment, and also by the circumstances available in the chosen field of activity. Naturally, without the 'Abandonment' (*Tyaga*) of our clinging attachment to the expected FRUITS OF OUR ACTIONS, we will not discover the full potentialities of our own personality. Without this, our activities will naturally become ineffective, and ineffective activities can never provide for us enjoyable fruits.

In short, 'Renunciation' is the goal to be reached through the process of 'Abandonment' of our moment-to-moment anxiety to enjoy the fruits. 'Abandonment' (*Tyaga*) is the means to reach the goal of 'Renunciation' (*Sannyasa*).

Both *Sannyasa* and *Tyaga* are disciplines in our activities. Krishna is never tired of emphasising the importance of work. Neither of these terms indicates that work should be ignored; on the other hand both of them insist that WORK WE MUST. Work, however, can gain a total transmutation by the removal of the things that clog our efficiency, and thus every piece of work can be made to yield its fullest reward. Snapping the chains that shackle us with the past and the future, and working without being hustled by anxieties or henpecked by desires, in the full freedom and inspiration of the present, is the noblest way to perform actions. To a large extent, we can say that the definition of these two terms in the *Geeta* is more broad-minded and tolerant than the implications of these two words as we read in the *Vedic* lore.

SHOULD THE 'IGNORANT' PERFORM WORK OR NOT?

3. *All actions should be abandoned as evil, declare some philosophers; while others (declare) that acts of sacrifice, gift and austerity should not be relinquished.*

In the previous stanza it was conclusively declared that ABANDONMENT is the 'way' and total RENUNCIATION is the 'goal'. On this theory of abandonment there is a school of philosophers, the *Sankhyas*, who declare: "ACTION SHOULD BE ABANDONED AS EVIL". According to them, all actions are productive of *vasanas* which cloud the realisation of the Self; and therefore, without exception, all actions should be

---

त्याज्यं दोषवदित्येके कर्म प्राहुर्मनीषिण: ।
यज्ञदानतप:कर्म न त्याज्यमिति चापरे ॥ ३ ॥

tyājyaṁ doṣavadityeke karma prāhurmanīṣiṇaḥ
yajñadānatapaḥkarma na tyājyamiti cāpare 3.

renounced. Some commentators upon the *Sankhyan* philosophy point out that 'WORK IS NOT TO BE ABANDONED, EXCEPT WHEN IT IS GOING IN WRONG CHANNELS, MOTIVATED BY DEMONIC URGES LIKE PASSION, GREED, AND DESIRE ETC'.

The philosophers not only indicate that all seekers should avoid unhealthy activities which have, in their reactions, a deadening influence upon the spiritual beauty in man, but also advise that every man should engage himself in creative, character-moulding, moral-rebuilding work that can aid the individual's personality-integration. This latter school of thinkers recommends that 'sacrifice' (*Yajna*), 'charity' (*Daana*) and 'austerity' (*Tapas*) should never be abandoned.

As students of the *Geeta*, we should know that Krishna wants Arjuna only to renounce all evil activities, and perform worldly work in a spirit of dedicated, selfless devotion. Krishna's *Geeta* calls upon man to make work itself the greatest homage unto the Supreme; this is SPIRITUAL *Sadhana*.

THE LORD'S DECREE IS THAT THE 'IGNORANT' SHOULD PERFORM WORK. NOW, AS TO THESE DIVERGENT VIEWS:

4. *Hear from Me the conclusion or the final truth, about this 'abandonment', O best of the Bharatas; 'abandonment', verily, O best of men, has been declared to be of three kinds.*

Lord Krishna is now promising Arjuna that he will scientifically explain what constitutes *Tyaga* and under what headings this spirit of 'abandonment' can be considered.

निश्चयं श्रृणु मे तत्र त्यागे भरतसत्तम ।
त्यागो हि पुरुषव्याघ्र त्रिविध: संप्रकीर्तित: ॥ ४ ॥

niścayaṁ śṛṇu me tatra tyāge bharatasattama
tyāgo hi puruṣavyāghra trividhaḥ samprakīrtitaḥ 4.

For a mortal mind, GIVING UP is no easy task; acquisition and aggrandisement are the very life-breath of man's mind. Naturally therefore, Krishna has to invoke the best in Arjuna by addressing him as the 'best among *Bharatas*' (*Bharata-Sattama*) and as a 'tiger among men' (*Purusha-Vyaaghra*).

'Abandonment' (*Tyaga*), for purposes of study and understanding, is threefold. All through the *Geeta* this threefold classification is followed, and everywhere we find that it is classed as the 'pure' (*sattvic*), the 'passionate' (*rajasic*) and the 'dull' (*tamasic*).

WHAT THEN IS THE FINAL DECREE? THE LORD SAYS:

5. *Acts of sacrifice, charity and austerity should not be abandoned, but should be performed; worship, charity, and also austerity, are the purifiers of even the 'wise'.*

What has been said earlier has been accepted and emphasised. Practice of worship (*Yajna*), charity (*Daana*), and austerity (*Tapas*) should not be abandoned. We have already found, in the previous chapter, that these, when properly pursued, bring about a brilliant discipline within and create conditions under which alone, the highest spiritual unfoldment and the final experience of the Infinite are possible. Krishna says here that these can 'purify even thoughtful men'. Men of evolutionary tendencies, who seek freedom from their personality-obsessions must, with devotion and the right attitude of mind, perform *Yajnas*, *Daana* and *Tapas*. Thereby they can discover an endless amount of inner peace and balance.

यज्ञदानतप:कर्म न त्याज्यं कार्यमेव तत् ।
यज्ञो दानं तपश्चैव पावनानि मनीषिणाम् ॥ ५ ॥

yajñadānatapaḥ-karma na tyājyaṁ kāryameva tat
yajño dānaṁ tapaścaiva pāvanāni manīṣiṇām 5.

OBLIGATORY DUTIES SHOULD BE PERFORMED WITHOUT ATTACHMENT:

6. *But even these actions should be performed leaving aside attachment and the fruits, O Partha; this is my certain and best belief.*

Even these actions, namely, 'Sacrifice' (*Yajna*), 'Charity' (*Daana*) and 'Austerity' (*Tapas*) should be performed LEAVING ATTACHMENTS AND FRUITS. The term 'attachment' in the *Geeta* has a peculiar flavour, and throughout, this term has been used to indicate the spirit in which an egocentric personality will come to work in any field of activity, while fulfilling its own egocentric desires. Thus, an ego and its desires are the component parts of attachments. When an ego strives to fulfil its own burning desires, it comes to live in a certain relationship with the world of things and objects around – this wrong relationship is called 'ATTACHMENT'.*

Once an individual starts working under the poison of 'attachment', he comes to entertain an unintelligent, self-destructive anxiety to gain and enjoy the results of his actions. Long before the actions are completed, one's hope and hunger for their fruits can present themselves to weave a charm of their own, benumbing one's efficiency in the field of the action undertaken.

एतान्यपि तु कर्माणि सङ्गं त्यक्त्वा फलानि च ।
कर्तव्यानीति मे पार्थ निश्चितं मतमुत्तमम् ॥ ६ ॥

etānyapi tu karmaṇi saṅgaṁ tyaktavā phalāni ca
kartavyanīti me pārtha niścitaṁ matamuttamam 6.

* The arithmetic of attachments in the *Geeta* is that
Ego + Egocentric desires = Attachment (*Sanga* or *Raga*).

The idea that CHARITY, SACRIFICE and AUSTERITY must be performed in an attitude of 'detachment', 'renouncing all anxieties for the enjoyment of the fruits' is, Krishna admits, his own personal opinion (*matam*). It is not, however, purely an original Krishna-creed, but is perfectly in line with the technique of selfless action as advised in all the Hindu scriptures.

To be rid of attachment and to be free from anxieties regarding the fruits that are yet to present themselves as a reward for the work undertaken in the present, are the main limbs of the Krishna-creed in the *Geeta*. To live this Krishna-way of action is to assure for ourselves a healthy inner equipment, which can tenderly guide us to the peaks of Super manhood. The loving term used here by Krishna in addressing Arjuna has its own appeal to the Prince. It recommends to him the Krishna-theory of 'abandonment' (*Tyaga*) as explained in this stanza.

THEREFORE, FOR A SEEKER OF SPIRITUAL LIBERATION, WORK IS UNAVOIDABLE; AND WITH A PROPER SPIRIT OF '*TYAGA*', WORK CAN HELP HIM ON HIS PATH. THE '*TAMSIC TYAGA*' IS:

7. *Verily, the renunciation of 'obligatory actions' is not proper; the abandonment of the same from delusion is declared to be TAMASIC (dull).*

Abandonment of obligatory duties is considered by the Lord as the lowest and the darkest. Every individual has his own obligations to himself and to others in society. They include

---

नियतस्य तु संन्यासः कर्मणो नोपपद्यते ।
मोहात्तस्य परित्यागस्तामसः परिकीर्तितः ॥ ७ ॥
niyatasya tu sannyāsaḥ karmaṇo nipapadyate
mohāttasya parityāgastāmasaḥ parikīrtitaḥ 7.

both the unavoidable DAILY DUTIES, as well as the SPECIAL DUTIES that arise on special occasions in the life of an individual, and in the society of the times. Therefore, as long as an individual is a member of the society, enjoying the social life, and demanding protection and profit from the society, he has no right, according to the Hindu code of living, to abandon his 'obligatory duties'.

Even if one abandons one's moral duties in ignorance, one is not excused; for, as in the civil laws of the modern world and in the physical laws of the phenomenal world, so in the spiritual kingdom also, 'ignorance of the law is no excuse'. Out of ignorance and lack of proper thinking, if an individual ignores his obligations and refuses to serve the world he is living in, that 'abandonment' is considered as 'dull' (*tamasic*).

THE *RAJASIC TYAGA* IS:

8. *He who, because of fear of bodily trouble, abandons action because it is painful, thus performing a RAJASIC (passionate) abandonment, obtains not the fruit of 'abandonment'.*

Someone may come to give up his individual obligatory duties BECAUSE THEY ARE PAINFUL or THROUGH FEAR OF BODILY SUFFERING. The 'relinquishment'* thus practised falls under the 'passionate' type (*rajasic*).

This clearly shows in its unsaid suggestions that a man of action and passion (*rajas*) will readily undertake to act and fulfil his obligatory duties if they are not painful, and are not too

दुःखमित्येव यत्कर्म कायक्लेशभयात्त्यजेत् ।
स कृत्वा राजसं त्यागं नैव त्यागफलं लभेत् ॥ ८ ॥

duḥkhmityeva yatkarma kāyakleśabhayāttyajet
sa kṛtvā rājasaṁ tyāgaṁ naiva tyāgaphalaṁ labhet 8.

* Relinquishment or Abandonment.

fatiguing. To become a man of action, fulfilling all obligations and performing all duties without sacrificing one's own personal comforts, is no heroic life at all. Such actions have no special reward. In fact, Krishna says: "HE SHALL ATTAIN NO FRUIT WHATSOEVER OF HIS ABANDONMENT".

Performance of one's obligatory duties is itself the most glorious of all forms of *Tyaga*, and it can be considered doubly so, when it involves a certain amount of sacrifice of one's own personal convenience and bodily comfort. Arjuna himself was hesitating to fight the battle which was his obligatory duty. Arjuna's 'relinquishment' of this duty could be considered as falling under this category of *Rajasic Tyaga*.

Real abandonment should always lead us on to the ampler fields of self-expression, push us into the fuller ways of living, and introduce us to the greater experiences of joy. A bud ABANDONS itself to become a flower, the flower GIVES UP its soft petals and its enchanting fragrance and gains for itself the richer status of a fruit. Every real ABANDONMENT should haul us up into a nobler status of fulfilment.

WHAT THEN IS THE *SATTVIC* ABANDONMENT?

9. *Whatever 'obligatory action' is done, O Arjuna, merely because it ought to be done, abandoning 'attachment and also fruit', that abandonment is regarded as SATTVIC (pure).*

Those who execute thoroughly all their obligatory duties 'because they are to be done' (*karyam iti*), because to remain without accomplishing them is almost death to them – fall under

---

कार्यमित्येव यत्कर्म नियतं क्रियतेऽर्जुन ।
सङ्गं त्यक्त्वा फलं चैव स त्यागः सात्त्विको मतः ॥ ९ ॥

kāryamityeva yatkarma niyataṁ kriyate'rjuna
saṅgaṁ tyaktavā phalaṁ caiva sa tyāgaḥ sāttviko mataḥ 9.

the *sattvic* (pure) variety. They believe that certain acts of 'relinquishment' MUST be done, for otherwise, according to them, it is just insufferably indecent. When such persons, under these inspiring ideas, come to serve the community, or work in any field, they provide us with examples of the *sattvic* type of 'relinquishment'.

Activities have certain unavoidable encumbrances. All that the Lord says in the *Geeta* amounts only to this; that we must act on without these encumbrances curtailing and limiting our freedom of action. Thus, the *Tyaga* of the good (*sattvic*), or real *Tyaga*, means doing actions with the correct mental attitude. This may seem strange, but those who have carefully gone through these three stanzas explaining the true type of *Tyaga*, must have understood that all these discussions were not so much on what is to be 'relinquished' but as to HOW we must 'abandon', and in WHICH FIELD we must act. In short, Lord Krishna's concept of *Tyaga* condemns abandonment of the world and our duties in it. To the Lord in the *Geeta*, *Tyaga* is a subjective renunciation of all inner selfishness and desire, which limit the freedom of the individual in his field of activity. It is something like the abandonment that everyone practises in his dining room; renunciation of hunger by positively taking the food!

In these three stanzas the abandonment (*Tyaga*) discussed is not the 'ABANDONMENT of actions' but 'ABANDONMENT of such things within our subjective personality that block the free flow of our own possibilities'. *Tyaga* makes an active man a more potential worker in the world.

Acting in the world outside, renouncing both the ego and the egocentric desires, an individual comes to exhaust his *vasanas*, and grows in his inward purity.

HOW DOES SUCH A PURE MAN, PURIFIED THROUGH '*SATTVIC TYAGA*', GAIN THE HIGHEST SPIRITUAL EXPERIENCE?

10. *The abandoner, soaked in purity, being intelligent, with all his doubts cut asunder, hates not disagreeable action, nor is he attached to an agreeable action.*

The previous stanza would, at the outset, look as an impossible thesis to any strong man of action and adventure. Perhaps the royal heart of Arjuna could not comprehend such a person who fulfils his obligatory duty 'only because it ought to be done' (*karyamiti*) renouncing attachment and fruit. As though answering the look of surprise on Arjuna's face, which faithfully registers his failure to appreciate the idea, Krishna gives in this stanza a more elaborate picture of such an individual.

A man established in *sattvic* abandonment never hates, nor does he ever feel attached. He is not miserable in disagreeable environments nor does he get attached to the circumstances and schemes of things which are agreeable to his taste. He does his duties under all circumstances agreeable or disagreeable, without feeling elated when he finds himself on the 'peaks', or feeling dejected when he discovers himself in the 'pits' of life.

He is overwhelmed neither by extreme joy, nor by extreme sorrow; equanimity becomes his essential nature. He stands as a rock, ever at ease, and watches with an unbroken balance of vision, the waves of happenings rising and falling all around him at all times. He is, in short, independent of the happenings in the outer world around him.

न द्वेष्टयकुशलं कर्म कुशले नानुषज्जते ।
त्यागी सत्त्वसमाविष्टो मेधावी छिन्नसंशयः ॥ १० ॥

na dveṣṭyakuśalaṁ karma kuśale nānuṣajjate
tyāgī sattvasamāviṣṭo medhāvī chinnasaṁśayaḥ 10.

When, to such a man of *Sattvic Tyaga,* impulses such as jealousy, anger, passion, greed etc. come, he does not get involved in those impulses, as we do in our attachments and identifications with them. That is, a man of abandonment (*Tyaga*) readily discovers in himself a secret faculty to abandon his identification with the false, the lower instincts in himself. He does not become a victim of his own mental impressions (*vasanas*); he stands ever free and surely apart from the tumults of his mind.

Such a man is said to be an educated and cultured man. An uncultured man is like a dry leaf that is tossed hither and thither by every passing breeze; is like a reed upon the bosom of the sea, rising and falling in the mad revelry of the tireless waves. It is the privilege of the animal alone to get faithfully coloured by its own instincts and act according to the dictates of its impulses. It is only man, the inheritor of an intellect, who can enquire into the nature of the rising waves of impulses, judge them in the light of the ideal he holds onto in himself, and, if need be, stand apart from them and allow them to die away.

But ordinarily, an individual finds it impossible to stand apart and live, to act independently of his impulses. According to the *Geeta,* this is because man has allowed his faculty of 'abandonment' (*Tyaga*) to die away. A *Tyagi* is he who has cultivated this habit to live intelligently in life, practising from moment to moment the 'abandonment' of all the animal whisperings in himself, and following diligently the Melody of the Soul. Such a man is established in *Sattvic Tyaga.*

In order that one may come to judge correctly and renounce the false, one must have a very clear and steady picture of the Perfect in oneself. *Medha-shakti* is not merely the intellect's power of understanding or reasoning, but it is also the intellect's

FACULTY TO MEMORISE AND RETAIN THINGS. A cultured man of unbroken equipoise and steady understanding must have a constant memory of: (1) the constituents of the field of his activity, (2) the instruments through which he contacts the world outside, (3) his own essential infinitely divine nature, and (4) his exact relationship with the world-of-objects when he is contacting it through his senses. Such a person is called *Medhaavee*, "A MAN OF FIRM UNDERSTANDING". And in case his knowledge be spotted with patches of doubts or slightly poisoned by traces of false knowledge, there will be in him endless confusions, which in their turn will bring about wrong judgements. Therefore, Krishna indicates that a man of *Sattvic Tyaga* is one whose DOUBT IS CLEFT.

The highest type of *Tyaga* is not, perhaps, abundantly found except in a minority who have accomplished their detachments from all their matter vestures completely. But to the majority, identification with the body-mind-intellect equipment is so natural that they have the SENSE OF AGENCY and come to live in the world, conditioned by the happenings around.

SUCH AN AVERAGE MAN, WHO WORKS WITH AN EGO AND ATTACHMENT, MUST LEARN TO WORK, AT LEAST RENOUNCING THE FRUIT. KRISHNA EXPLAINS:

11. *Verily, it is not possible for an embodied being to abandon actions entirely, but he who relinquishes the fruits-of-actions is verily called a 'relinquisher' (Tyagi).*

न हि देहभृता शक्यं त्यक्तुं कर्माण्यशेषत: ।
यस्तु कर्मफलत्यागी स त्यागीत्यभिधीयते ॥ ११ ॥

na hi dehabhṛtā śakyaṁ tyaktuṁ karmāyaśeṣataḥ
yastu karmaphalatyāgī sa tyāgītyabhidhīyate 11.

Actions we have to perform. Without action no living organism can continue living. Existence itself is the manifestation of life's activities. To remain without doing anything is itself an action, and the physiological and psychological actions continue up to the grave. Anything that has a body, even a unicellular organism, can never hope to abandon ALL activities. Actions are the insignia of life. It is the fragrance in the flower of existence. Where there is no action, there life has ended; there existence has withered away – the substance has dried up – stinking death has come.

Since all of us are embodied, and therefore, cannot abandon all activities as long as we live, the only choice left to us is to direct and discipline all our actions in such a way as to bring a harmony into our inner life and a dynamic rhythm into our outer duties.

If *Tyaga* of the *Sattvic* type is not possible for all of us due to our attachments to the world of matter, certainly we can practise the 'abandonment' of at least our clinging attachments and anxieties for the fruits of our actions. Action cannot be completely abandoned by one who is conditioned by the gross, subtle and causal bodies. Such an individual – and most of us at this stage of our evolution fall under this category – is advised by Krishna to abandon his anxiety to enjoy the fruits of his actions which are yet to come in a future period of time and act diligently, entirely, and enthusiastically in the present. A man who thus abandons the thirst to enjoy the fruits of his action is called a *Tyagi*.

NOW WHAT IS THE BENEFIT WHICH COMES FROM '*TYAGA*'? THE LORD ANSWERS:

12. *The threefold fruit-of-action, evil, good and mixed-accrues, after death, only to those who have no spirit of 'abandonment'; never to total relinquishers.*

The results of all actions depend; it is said, upon the quality of the actions. Abandonment (*Tyaga*) has already been described as belonging to three different categories. Here we have a discussion of the different types of reactions that would accrue when the different types of *Tyaga* are practised.

Projection of a wilful desire in the world outside is an action, and according to the purity of the motive and the serenity of composure of the actor, a psychological reaction is left behind at the end of every activity. The mind has an instinctive habit of repeating itself. Future thoughts faithfully follow the footprints left by the past thoughts. Thus, actions in the world determine the 'thought tendencies' of the human mind, and these tendencies (*vasanas*) condition the mental equipment and order our reactions to the things that are happening around.

The fruit-of-action, in philosophy, is not only its manifested results in the material world, but also the subtle constitutional changes it leaves in the thought-personality of man.

The total reactions gained by the mind's working in the world, according to Lord Krishna, fall under three distinct types: (1) the disagreeable or the calamitous; meaning those that are positively bad; (2) agreeable or non-calamitous; meaning positively good; (3) the mixed type of balanced or average; wherein the tendencies are balanced equally between the good and the bad.

अनिष्टमिष्टं मिश्रं च त्रिविधं कर्मणः फलम् ।
भवत्यत्यागिनां प्रेत्य न तु संन्यासिनां क्वचित् ॥ १२ ॥

aniṣṭamiṣṭaṁ miśraṁ ca trividhaṁ karmaṇaḥ phalam
bhavatyāgināṁ pretya na tu sannyāsināṁ kvacit 12.

In the constant flow of time, the PRESENT determines the immediate FUTURE, and therefore, these tendencies, in their different textures, must necessarily determine our reactions to our environments in the IMMEDIATE future. If we extend this theory to the very last moment of our days in this embodiment, it becomes amply evident that, after the departure from here through death, our next embodiment and the general type of environment that we will find ourselves in, would be determined by the type of tendencies produced by our actions. This is what is called the 'reincarnation theory' in the *Sanatana Dharma*.

If the *vasanas* are good (*sattvic*), then a joyous field of prosperity and happiness would be the only realm wherein such a mind would discover its destiny. Those who are entertaining and deliberately cultivating the low animal-*vasanas* in themselves will find for themselves a complete fulfilment only by appearing in the lower strata of life. When the 'tendencies' for good and bad are almost equal (*mishram*), then we enter into this world of action – the world in which we are now living – the world of the intelligent man. No doubt, in each of us there is a call of the 'higher' constantly leading us towards an undetermined and indeterminable ideal, but there are also the barkings and the brayings, the hissings and the roars, of the 'lower' in us, constantly confusing and systematically distracting our vision of the ideal.

If an individual were to identify himself with the higher and live up to the ideal as best as he can, the 'higher' *vasanas* will multiply and ultimately silence the 'lower' completely. If, on the other hand, as is the fashion in the modern world, we allow ourselves to be tempted by the 'lower' and identify with the animal-impulses in us, they will multiply and make us a caricature of the Divine that we really are. In short, in the tug-of-war between the 'higher' and the 'lower', the determining factor is the individual's own personality.

Both these *vasanas* grow, be they good or bad, and in either case, there is still a manifestation as birth in the realm of pangs and perils. The transcendence of the experiencer – personality is possible only when the conditionings have totally ended and the *vasanas* are rendered powerless to hold the Pure Spirit, seemingly, at ransom.

To explain further the difference between 'abandonment' (*Tyaga*) and 'renunciation' (*Sannyasa*), the Lord says here that for a man-of-renunciation there is no reaction either to the actions done in the PAST or to actions undertaken by him in the PRESENT.

This idea clearly brings out the subtle difference that the *Geeta* makes between *Tyaga* and *Sannyasa*. Earlier we found that *Tyaga* is that capacity in us with which, from moment to moment, we withdraw ourselves from the impulses of our mind; while *Sannyasa* is the total renunciation of the entire 'tendencies', both good and bad – from their crystallisation as the 'ego'.

The *Geeta*-technique for the rehabilitation of man's personality, so beautifully elaborated and exhaustively discussed, when briefly put would be: (a) the seeker first gets detached from the lower sensuous cravings and passions by identifying himself with the nobler ideals of self-control and moral-perfection; (b) a mind so conditioned becomes tamer than a mind goaded by sensuality. This purified mind develops in itself the required amount of subtle powers of thinking, of consistent self-application and of steady contemplation; (c) on realising the Pure 'Be'-ness, all becomings end. To the pure Self there is no becoming; the 'tendencies' of the mind (*vasanas*) cannot shackle the Spirit. Its subtle Presence cannot but be ever Immaculate and Unconditioned.

The 'pleasant', the 'unpleasant' and the 'mixed' types of reaction (*Karma Phala*) reach only those who have an egocentric sense of identification with the actions as well as their resultant reactions. Those who abandon (*Tyagee*) both the sense of ego and the anxiety for the action-results are not caught in the clutches of reactions-actions. Memories of the past are the fertile fields where desires are cultivated and it is only in the future that the fruits are borne by the trees of actions. Renouncing our indulgence with the inheritance of the past and leaving all our anxieties for the future, to serve the world as a service to the Lord is abandonment – T*yaga*.

AFTER THUS HANDLING THE THEME OF 'ABANDONMENT' IN GENERAL, KRISHNA NOW TAKES UP A CLOSER EXAMINATION OF IT, DISSECTING THE VERY COMPONENT PARTS THAT CONSTITUTE WORK:

13. *Learn from Me, O mighty-armed, these five causes for the accomplishment of all actions, as declared in the SANKHYA (UPANISHAD) system, which is the end of all actions.*

When Arjuna was thus told conclusively that action could be performed without egocentric desires and clinging attachment to the fruits, as an intelligent enquirer, he had every right to ask: "What constitutes an action?" To lay bare the inner essence of action, Krishna analyses the anatomy of work; the external structure of action, and the physiology of action, the inner inspirations, motives and urges in work.

पञ्चैतानि महाबाहो कारणानि निबोध मे ।
सांख्ये कृतान्ते प्रोक्तानि सिद्धये सर्वकर्मणाम् ॥ १३ ॥

pañcaitāni mahābāho kāraṇani nibodha me
sāṅkhye kṛtānte proktāni siddhaye sarvakarmaṇām 13.

Addressing Arjuna as mighty-armed, Krishna declares that, for the real accomplishment, fulfilment or achievement of an action, five aspects of action are necessarily to be disciplined and marshalled. These five are the 'limbs of action' without which no action is ever possible. When these five aspects work in happy coordination, the undertaking is assured of the greatest success, be it secular or sacred, material or spiritual. The term 'Mighty-armed' is used to invoke the adventurous heroism in Arjuna, for, a large share of daring courage, consistency of purpose, faith in oneself and intellectual heroism are necessary, if one is to discipline one's actions and successfully accomplish a thorough cultural development within.

In this stanza, the *Geetaacharya* confesses that this enumeration of the aspects that constitute an action is not his own original contribution, but it is exactly what is said in the *Sankhyan* philosophy. The *Sankhyan* philosophy as a separate text no longer exists ... perhaps, here; the word *Sankhyan* indicates only the *Upanishads*. The existing *Sankhyan* books do not mention these fivefold categories. It is reasonable to suppose that at the time of Vyasa there might have been some books discussing this topic which are now lost to us. However, one thing is clear: that this fivefold division, which the Lord discusses in the following stanzas, faithfully follows the philosophy of the *Geeta* as discussed so far. The *Geeta* has declared that all actions cease when the knowledge of the Self dawns, so that the *Advaita* commentator concludes: "*Vedanta*, which imparts to us knowledge, is THE END OF ACTIONS".

HEREIN THE LORD ENUMERATES FIVE FACTORS WHICH ARE THE CONSTITUENT PARTS IN ALL ACTIONS:

14. *The 'seat' (body), the doer (ego), the various organs-of-perception, the different functions of various organs-of-action, and also the presiding deity, the fifth.*

The promise made in the previous stanza is being fulfilled herein and Lord Krishna enumerates the five component parts that go into the constitution of any 'action'. We have already discussed that the enumeration as it stands today in this stanza does not correspond to the *Sankhyan* declaration. Commentators interpret these terms, each slightly differently from the others, and this fivefold division being rather obscure, the various explanations of the commentators are not very helpful to a practical student. However, we can see in these five terms the twenty-four fold division of *Prakriti*, which the *Sankhyans* hold and follow.

Every work is undertaken with the help of the 'body' (*Adhishthanam*), for the body is the gateway for the stimuli to enter as well as for the responses to exit. A body in itself can neither receive the world nor react to it unless there is the 'ego' (*Karta*) functioning in and through it. There must be an intelligent personality, presiding over its own desires, wanting to fulfil them and thus constantly seeking a fulfilment through its body activities. The ego sets the body in continuous activity. When an ego, thus riddled with its own desires, wants to seek its fulfilment in the world of objects outside, it certainly needs 'instruments' (*Karanam*) of perception. Without these, the inner personality cannot come to contact the field of enjoyment and find satisfaction in it.

अधिष्ठानं तथा कर्ता करणं च पृथग्विधम् ।
विविधाश्च पृथक्चेष्टा दैवं चैवात्र पञ्चमम् ॥ १४ ॥
adhiṣṭhānaṁ tathā kartā karaṇaṁ ca pṛthagvidham
vividhāśca pṛthakceṣṭā daivaṁ caivātra pañcamam 14.

The term 'function' (*Cheshta*) here has been commented upon by Sankara as the physiological activities, known as *Prana, Apana*, etc. No doubt it is sufficiently explanatory to all students who have a knowledge of the traditions in *Vedantic* thought. But to a lay student this explanation might be rather confusing. As a result of the physiological activities (*Prana, Apana* etc.) the health of the body gets toned up and it must flow out in its own vigour and enthusiasm through the organs-of-action. Thus, for our understanding of these enumerations, we can directly take the term 'function' (*Cheshta*) used here as indicating the organs-of-action.

The organs-of-perception are presided over by the five great elements.[1] These presiding deities are technically called *Devas*, and they indicate particular functions and faculties in the sense-organs, such as the 'power of vision' of the eye, the 'power of audition' in the ears etc. i.e., the sense-organs must have their full vigour and must function properly in order to play their part in any field of work.

Stripping off all these details of explanations, if we reread the stanza, it merely enumerates the constituent parts of every action. They are: (1) the body, (2) the ego,[2] (3) the organs-of-perception, (4) the organs-of-action and, (5) the five elemental forces. The stanza is dedicated merely to enumerating these five aspects without which no egocentric activity is ever possible.

HOW CAN THESE FIVE BECOME THE COMPONENT PARTS IN EVERY HUMAN ACTIVITY?

---

[1] The eye by Fire, the ear by Space, the tongue by Water, the skin by Air and the nose by Earth.

[2] In Sri Shankara's commentary it is clearly defined as the 'enjoyer', meaning the Spirit that has identified itself with an intellectual and mental demand for any gratification (*Upaadhi-lakshana-bhoktaa*).

15. *Whatever action a man performs by his body, speech and mind - - whether right, or the reverse -- these five are its causes.*

The items listed above must all come into full play in order to accomplish any work, and therefore, these five component parts are called the causes of all actions. To show that there is no exception, the Lord says that whatever action a man might undertake, be it by his body, speech or mind, and that too, whether right or wrong, in every expression of action there is the play of all these five essential parts.

These five constitute the equipment of action, and the Spirit, the eternally Actionless, conditioned by the intellectual desires, behaves AS THOUGH it is an ego (*Jiva*); and this individualised personality, forgetting its own state-of-Perfection demanding satisfaction through sense gratifications, making use of the faculties of sense-enjoyment, strives in the world-of-objects to achieve, to gain, to aggrandise. Here we should not forget, in our haste, to grasp clearly that the fivefold division is the description of the 'engine under the bonnet' and not of the 'petrol'; and yet, 'petrol' in itself cannot make the travel pleasant and successful – nor can the 'engine' move without the 'petrol'.

A motor vehicle becomes an automobile only when 'petrol' plays through the 'engine', and when the driver can, by his faculties; take the vehicle to its destination, which is determined by the demand or the desire of the owner of the vehicle. If this

---

शरीरवाङ्मनोभिर्यत्कर्म प्रारभते नरः ।
न्याय्यं वा विपरीतं वा पञ्चैते तस्य हेतवः ॥ १५ ॥

śarīravāṅmanobhitkarma prārabhate naraḥ
nyāyyaṁ vā viparītaṁ vā pañcaite hetavaḥ 15.

analogy is understood, we can correctly evaluate this portion of Krishna's enumeration, and can truly appreciate what the Lord means when he says 'these five are the causes' of all work.

ALL THESE ENUMERATIONS AND EXPLANATIONS OF THE LAST TWO STANZAS ADD UP TO THE CONCLUSION THAT THE 'SENSE-OF-AGENCY' OF THE SELF IS AN ILLUSION:

16. *Now, such being the case, verily he who -- owing to his untrained understanding -- looks upon his Self, which is 'alone' (never conditioned by the 'engine'), as the doer, he, of perverted intelligence, sees not.*

In the previous stanzas we found that action belongs to the realm of matter, no doubt IN THE PRESENCE of the Spirit. Failing to discriminate thus between the equipments of action and the actionless Spirit, which, in an unhealthy combination between them, comes to manifest as the 'actor' (doer), the poor egocentric personality so born comes to pant and sigh at its own disappointments and failures, or dances and jumps at its own joys and successes. The moment an individual becomes aware of these inner mechanisms and their play, the delusory egocentric individuality ends as it becomes a mere myth of the mind, a delusory phantom of a midsummer, mid-day dream.

THIS BEING THE CASE (*Tatra evam sati*)—In all such actions, whether good or bad, as undertaken by the body, speech or mind, the essential component parts are the body, ego, organs-

---

तत्रैवं सति कर्तारमात्मानं केवलं तु यः ।
पश्यत्यकृतबुद्धित्वान्न स पश्यति दुर्मतिः ॥ १६ ॥
tatraivaṁ sati kartāramātmānaṁ kevalaṁ tu yaḥ
paśyatyakṛtabuddhitvānna sa paśyati durmatiḥ 16.

of-perception, organs-of-action and the elements; thus all actions belong to matter. But the Spirit, which is the essential nature, in identifying Itself with the matter-vestures, comes to live through the disturbing destinies as the ever-changing man. All pangs and joys, all failures and successes, all imperfections and impediments, belong to the ego, which is the Spirit considering Itself as conditioned by these components of action. The Supreme Pure Self (*Kevalam Aatmaanam*) is misunderstood by the ordinary man to be the actor (*Kartaram*), and in the consequent ego-sense, the divinity is forgotten and the individual comes to despair. The causes of this misunderstanding have been indicated here. Untempered reason (*Akrita Buddhi*) and perverted mind (*Durmati*) are the maladjustments in an individual, because of which, right recognition of one's own divinity is not constantly maintained within. The implication of the statement is that, if a seeker can integrate himself – through the process of disciplining his reasoning faculty and guiding his mind away from his intellectual perversities – that individual will come to experience within himself that it is only the fivefold components made up of matter that are indulging in the agitations of the outer activity.*

ELUCIDATING THE FOREGOING IDEAS MORE VIVIDLY, THE LORD CONTINUES:

Even while they are all dancing around, Krishna, the Spiritual Truth, remains motionless in the centre of the ring of the dancing crowd, untouched by the *Gopis*, moving in their ecstatic trance. The divinely sweet maidens of *Vraja* dance in thrilled ecstasy because of the maddening music of the Flute-bearer, who, by His breath draws out the 'melody of existence'. To identify ourselves with the Centre is to be the master of the situation; to play among the whirls of dancers is to suffer the fatigue and exhaustion, the thrills and sorrows of the milkmaids of Vrindavana... This is *Raasa-Kreedaa*.

17. *He who is free from the egoistic notion, whose intelligence is not tainted (by good or evil), though he slays these people, he slays not, nor is he bound (by the action).*

So far we have been told that the realm-of-matter is the field of all activity, and the weeds of sorrows and agitations can grow only therein. The Spirit, the farmer, has an existence independent of this field and yet the farmer, in his identification with the self-projections on the field, feels happy or unhappy according to the condition of the field at any given moment.

Similarly, it is our unhealthy contact created by our self-projections on to the matter-envelopments around us that has given rise to the 'ego', which in its turn comes to suffer the buffetings of life. Therefore, Krishna says that "HE WHO IS FREE FROM THE SENSE OF EGOISM" and whose "INTELLIGENCE IS NOT TAINTED" by false values of possession, acquisition, aggrandisement, etc., does no action even though activities take place all around and even through him; "THOUGH HE SLAYS THESE PEOPLE, HE SLAYS NOT".

This does not mean that a man-of-Wisdom, who has withdrawn from his false evaluation of matter, will no longer act in the world. He will not remain like a stone statue. The statement only means, that even while he is acting in the world, to him it is all a self-entertaining game. It is always our egocentric clinging that leaves impressions (*vasanas*) in our mind and thus actions of the past come to goad us on to more and more activities. A man-of-Perfection who has the necessary discriminative intellect, learns to detach himself and act, and

---

यस्य नाहंकृतो भावो बुद्धिर्यस्य न लिप्यते |
हत्वापि स इमाँल्लोकान्न हन्ति न निबध्यते || १७ ||

yasya nāhaṅkṛ bhavo buddhiryasya na lipyate
hatvāapi sa imām̐llokānna hanti nibadhyate 17.

therefore, in him the footprints of the past activities cannot beat out any deepening footpath.

Krishna says: "THOUGH HE KILLS, HE KILLS NOT; NOR IS HE BOUND". If we were to compare the results of the lusty, passionate acts of some self-seeking murderer, with the honourable heroic activities of some devotedly dedicated warrior championing the cause of his country's freedom and independence, we shall easily understand the above assertion of the Lord. The murderer develops *vasanas*, and propelled by his tendencies, he again and again commits heinous crimes and disturbs the society, while the hero on the battlefront, though he too kills many, returns from the battlefront as a more educated, noble, and refined personality. In the former, there is the 'ego', and therefore, the foul *vasanas* get registered; while in the latter, the soldier's mind was fixed in his love for the country, and therefore, the murderous activity on the battlefront could not leave in him any ugly mental residue. Once the ego is surrendered in the consciousness of the Divine, the "BONDAGE OF *VASANAS* CAN NO MORE REMAIN IN HIM".

AFTER THUS DESCRIBING THE 'CONSTITUENTS THAT MAKE UP ANY ACTION', THE *GEETAACHARYA* DESCRIBES THE 'IMPULSES TO *KARMA*' AND 'THE BASIS OF *KARMA*':

18. *Knowledge, the known and knower form the threefold 'impulse to action'; the organs, the action, the agent, form the threefold 'basis of action'.*

ज्ञानं ज्ञेयं परिज्ञाता त्रिविधा कर्मचोदना ।
करणं कर्म कर्तेति त्रिविधः कर्मसंग्रहः ॥ १८ ॥

jñānaṁ jñeyaṁ parijñātā trividhā karmacodanā
karaṇaṁ karma karteti trividhaḥ karmasaṅgrahaḥ 18.

In the scientific treatment of the subject-matter, Lord Krishna had already explained the constituent parts that make up an action and also indicated that the entire assemblage is of matter only. Continuing the theme, he is now trying to explain the threefold impulses that propel activity (*Karma-Chodana*) and also the basis of action (*Karma-Sangraha*).

The 'impulse to action', according to Krishna, is a threefold arrangement made up of KNOWLEDGE (*Jnanam*), THE KNOWN (*Jneyam*) AND THE KNOWER (*Parijnaata*). These three are called technically in *Vedanta* as the 'Triputi'; indicating the 'experiencer', the 'experienced' and the resultant 'experience' – the 'knower', the 'known' and the 'knowledge'. Without these three no knowledge is ever possible, as all 'impulses to act' arise out of a play of these three. The EXPERIENCER, playing in the field of the EXPERIENCED, gains for himself the various EXPERIENCES; and these constitute the secret contents of all actions.*

The 'impulse to action' can spring either from the 'experiencer', in the form of a DESIRE, or from the 'experienced', in the form of TEMPTATION, or from the 'experience' in the form of similar MEMORIES of some past enjoyments. Beyond these three there is no other 'impulse to action' (*Karma-Chodanaa*).

The 'impulse to action', when it has arisen, must also find a field to act in; and the 'basis for action' (*Karma-Sangraha*) is constituted of the 'instruments', the 'reaction' and the 'agent' (the actor). This 'sense of agency' expressed by the ego, can maintain itself only as long as it holds a vivid picture of the 'fruit of its action' which it wants to gain. Fruit, meaning the

* Here we can also use the term 'knowledge' and say 'The knower' playing in a field of the 'known', gains to himself the various bits of 'knowledge'.

* That which is sought after, that which is finally reached through action by the agent is *Karma* here.

profit or the gain that is intended to be gained by the action, is indicated here by the term 'work' (*Karma*). According to Sri Sankaraacharya '*Karma*' here means the end.*

When a desirer, the agent, encouraged by this constant attraction towards a satisfying end, wants to achieve it, he must necessarily have the instruments-of-action *(Karanam)*. These instruments include not only the organs-of-perception and action, but also the inner equipments of the mind and the intellect. It cannot be very difficult for a student to understand that: (1) an AGENT having a desire, (2) maintaining in his mind a clear picture of the END or the goal, (3) with all the necessary instruments to act thereupon, would be the sum total contents of any activity (*Karma-Sangraha*). If any one of the above three items is absent, action cannot take place. These three (*Karanam, Karta* and *Karma*) are together designated as the parts of the '*Karma*-assembly', the 'basis of all *Karmas*' – (*Karma-Sangraha*).

Thus having roughly indicated in this stanza the threefold 'impulses of action' and the threefold 'basis for action', Krishna continues to explain in His Song why different people act so differently under different impulses and obey different basis in their actions. He divides each one of them under the three categories of human nature; the 'good' (*sattvic*), the 'passionate' (*rajasic*), and the 'dull' (*tamasic*).

THE LORD NOW PROCEEDS TO SHOW THE THREE-FOLD DISTINCTIONS IN EACH ONE OF THE ABOVE, ACCORDING TO THE THREE PREDOMINANT NATURES – THE 'GOOD', THE 'PASSIONATE' AND THE 'DULL':

19. *'Knowledge', 'action', and 'actor' are declared in the science of temperaments (gunas) to be of three kinds only, according to the distinctions of temperaments; hear them also duly.*

As an introduction to what is to follow immediately, here it is said that 'knowledge', 'action', and the 'actor' (agent), all the three because of the difference of the temperament in the individuals, at the given time of observation, fall under a threefold division. This classification is being exhaustively explained in the following stanzas.

Guna is the preponderance of a given type of temperament in one's inner nature. The human mind and intellect function constantly, but they always come to function under the different 'climatic conditions' within our mind. These varying climates of the mind are called the three *gunas;* the 'good', the 'passionate' and the 'dull'.

Under each of these temperaments the entire human personality behaves differently, and, naturally therefore, the permutations and combinations of the varieties make up the infinite types that are available in the world; even within the biography of one and the same personality we find different moods and behaviours at different periods of time, depending entirely upon the occasion, the type of the situation, the nature of the problem and the kind of challenge the person is called upon to face.

According to the science of the *gunas*, as enunciated in Kapila's *Sankhya Yoga*, 'Knowledge', 'Action' and 'Actor' are each classified under these three categories. They are being

---

ज्ञानं कर्म च कर्ता च त्रिधैव गुणभेदत: ।
प्रोच्यते गुणसंख्याने यथावच्छृणु तान्यपि ॥ १९ ॥

jñānaṁ karma ca kartā ca tridhaiva guṇabhedataḥ
procyate guṇasaṅkhyāne yathāvacchṛṇu tānyapi 19.

enumerated here and Krishna invites the students of the *Geeta* to LISTEN ATTENTIVELY TO THEM. It is meaningless, in fact, to ask Arjuna to listen to the discourses, because he was all the time listening to the Lord. The implication must be that the teacher is attracting the special attention of the student because of the importance of the theme.

HERE FOLLOWS THE THREEFOLD TYPE OF 'KNOWLEDGE':

20. *That by which one sees the one indestructible reality in all beings, undivided in the divided, know that 'knowledge' as SATTVIC (Pure).*

Inasmuch as the constituents of action, namely 'knowledge', 'work', and the 'ego', are under the influences of different moods, each one of them can fall into the three types. We fluctuate among these three *gunas* and the different proportions in which they are mixed in our bosom determine the innumerable types of individuals that we are.

These detailed descriptions of the different types of 'knowledge', 'action' and 'actor' are given here not for the purpose of judging and classifying others, but for the seeker to UNDERSTAND HIMSELF. A true student of culture and self-development must try to maintain himself as far as possible, in the *sattvic* temperament. By self-analysis, we can diagnose ourselves, and immediately remedy the defects in us.

In this stanza, we have the description of the *sattvic* type of 'knowledge'. The 'knowledge' by which the One Imperishable

---

सर्वभूतेषु येनैकं भावमव्ययमीक्षते ।
अविभक्तं विभक्तेषु तज्ज्ञानं विद्धि सात्त्विकम् ॥ २० ॥

sarvabhūteṣu yenaikaṁ bhāvamavyayamīkṣate
avibhaktaṁ vibhakteṣu tajjñānaṁ viddhi sāttvikam 20.

Being is seen in all existence, is *sattvic*. Though the forms constituted by the different body-mind-intellect equipments are all different in different living creatures, the *sattvic* 'knowledge' recognises all of them as the expressions of one and the same Truth, which is the Essence in all of them.

Just as an electrical engineer recognises the SAME electricity flowing through all the bulbs, a goldsmith recognises the ONE metal 'gold' in all ornaments, and every one of us is aware of the SAME cotton in all shirts, so also, the intellect that sees the screen upon which the play of life and the throbs of existence are projected as the Changeless One is the 'knowledge' that is *sattvic*.

UNDIVIDED IN THE DIVIDED (*Avibhaktam Vibhakteshu*)— Even if there are a hundred different pots, of different shapes and colour, and different sizes, the 'space' is the ONE undivided factor in all these different pots. Bulbs are different but the current that is expressing through them all is the ONE electricity. Waves are different, and yet the SAME ocean is the reality and the substance in all the waves. ... Similarly, the one LIFE throbs in all, expressing itself differently as Its different manifestations, because of the different constitution in the matter-arrangements. The 'knowledge' that can recognise the play (*vilasa*) of this One Principle of Consciousness in and through all the different equipments, is fully *sattvic*.

WHAT TYPE OF AN INTELLECT DOES THE 'PASSIONATE' POSSESS?

21. *But that 'knowledge' which sees in all beings various entities of distinct kinds, (and) as different from one another, know that knowledge as RAJASIC (Passionate).*

After having found a description of the 'good', we have herein an equally complete description of the 'knowledge' that is 'passionate' (*rajasic*).

The 'knowledge' that recognises plurality, by reason of separateness, is *rajasic* in its texture. The 'knowledge' of the 'passionate', ever restless in its energy, considers various entities as different from one another; to the *rajasic* 'knowledge', the world is an assortment of innumerable types of different varieties; the intellect of such a man perceives distinctions among the living creatures, and divides them into different classes – as the animal, the vegetable and the human kingdoms – as men of different castes, creeds, races, nationalities etc.

WHAT THEN IS THE NATURE OF 'KNOWLEDGE' OF THE DULL?

22. *But that 'knowledge', which clings to one single effect, as if it were the whole, without reason, without foundation in truth and narrow, that is declared to be TAMASIC (Dull).*

पृथक्त्वेन तु यज्ज्ञानं नानाभावान्पृथग्विधान् ।
वेत्ति सर्वेषु भूतेषु तज्ज्ञानं विद्धि राजसम् ॥ २१ ॥

pṛthaktavena tu yajjñānaṁ nānābhāvānpṛthagvidhān
vetti sarveṣu bhūteṣu tajjñānaṁ viddhi rājasam 21.

यत्तु कृत्स्नवदेकस्मिन्कार्ये सक्तमहैतुकम् ।
अतत्त्वार्थवदल्पं च तत्तामसमुदाहृतम् ॥ २२ ॥

yattu kṛtsnavadekasminkārye saktamahaitukam
atattvārthavadalpaṁ ca tattāmasamudāhṛtam 22.

* Shankara comments upon this world and declares it to mean 'NOT FOUNDED ON REASON'. The knowledge of the dull recognises only the effects, but ignores their unavoidable causes.

An intellect that has got fumed under the dulling effects of extreme *tamas* clings to one single 'effect' as though it were the whole, never enquiring into its 'cause.' The 'knowledge' of the dull is painted here as that belonging to the lowest type of spiritual seekers. They are generally fanatic in their faith and in their devotion, in their views and values in life. They never enquire into, and try to discover, the cause of things and happenings; they are unreasonable (*ahaitukam*).*

Looking through such a confused intellect loaded with fixed ideas, the dull not only fail to see things as they are, but invariably project their own ideas upon the world and judge it all wrongly. In fact, a man of *tamasic* intellect views the world as if it is meant for him and his pleasures alone. He totally ignores the Divine Presence, the Infinite Consciousness. The 'knowledge' of the dull is thus circumscribed by its own concept of self-importance, and thus its vision becomes narrow (*alpam*) and limited.

To summarise, the 'knowledge' of the 'good' (*sattvic*) perceives the oneness underlying the universe; the comprehension of the 'passionate' (*rajasic*) recognises the plurality of the world; and the understanding of the 'dull' (*tamasic*) indicates a highly crystallized, self-centred ego in him, and his view of the world is always perverted and ever false.

It must again be noted that in this chapter we shall come across similar threefold divisions in the various aspects of our personal inner life and they are not meant to serve as reckoners to classify OTHERS, but they are meant to help us to SIZE OURSELVES UP from time to time.

THE THREEFOLD NATURE OF 'ACTION' IS NOW DESCRIBED IN THE FOLLOWING STANZAS:

23. *An 'action' which is ordained, which is free from attachment, which is done without love or hatred, by one who is not desirous of the fruit, that action is declared to SATTVIC (pure).*

Having so far explained the three types of 'knowledge', Krishna now classifies 'actions' (*Karma*) under the same three heads. A *sattvic* 'action' is the best, productive of peace within and harmony without in the field of activity, and therefore, it is the purest of the three types of 'action'. It is an obligatory action (*Niyatam*), a work that is undertaken for the work's own sake, in an attitude that work itself is worship. Such activities chasten the personality and are ever performed in a spirit of inspiration. Inspired activities naturally surpass the very excellence the actor or the doer is ordinarily capable of. Such an activity is always undertaken without any attachment (*Sanga-rahitam*) and without any anxiety for gaining any definite end. It is a dedicated activity of love,* and yet, it is not propelled by either love or hatred.

The missionary work undertaken by all prophets and sages are examples in point. We too, can recognise the same type of work, which we unconsciously perform on some rare occasions. A typical example that can at this moment be remembered is an individual nursing his own wounded limb. As soon as, say, your left toe strikes against some furniture in the house and gets wounded, the entire body bends down to nurse it. Herein, there is neither any special love for the left leg nor any particular

---

नियतं सङ्गरहितमरागद्वेषतः कृतम् ।
अफलप्रेप्सुना कर्म यत्तत्सात्त्विकमुच्यते ॥२३ ॥

niyataṁ saṅgarahitamarāgadveṣataḥ kṛtam
aphalaprepsunā karma yattatsāttvikamucyate 23.

* An act of love, not merely an act of law; an act of grace, and not a simple act of obligation.

extra attachment for it, as compared with other parts of the body. To an individual the whole body is himself, and all parts are equally important; he pervades his whole body.

In the same fashion, an individual with a *sattvic* intellect that has recognised the All-pervading One, lives in the Consciousness of the One Reality that permeates the whole universe, and therefore, to him the leper and the prince, the sick and the healthy, the rich and the poor are so many different parts of his own spiritual personality only. Such an individual serves the world in a sense of self-fulfilment and inspired joy.

Summarising, a *sattvic Karma* is a humane action, performed without any attachment, and not motivated either by likes (*Raga*) or dislikes (*Dvesha*), and undertaken without any desire to enjoy the results thereof. The 'action' itself is its fulfilment; a *sattvic* man acts, because to remain without doing service is a choking death to him. Such a man of *sattvic* 'action' alone is a true *Brahmana*.

WHAT IS *RAJASIC* ACTION?

24. *But that 'action' which is done by one, longing for desires, or gain, done with egoism, or with much effort, is declared to be RAJASIC (Passionate).*

The 'action' of the 'passionate' (*rajasic*) is that which is undertaken to fulfil one's desires with an extremely insistent 'I-

---

यत्तु कामेप्सुना कर्म साहंकारेण वा पुनः ।
क्रियते बहुलायासं तद्राजसमुदाहृतम् ॥ २४ ॥

yattu kāmepsunā karma sāhaṅkāreṇa vā punaḥ
kriyate bahulāyāsaṁ tadrājasamudāhṛtam 24.

* For even these can easily fall into the type of the 'dull' (*tamasic*) which the next stanza will describe. Here we specifically say 'when they are at their best'.

act' mentality. Always such undertakings are works of heavy toil involving great strain, and all the consequent physical fatigue and mental exhaustion. The individual is impelled to act and struggle by a well-defined and extremely arrogant ego-sense. He works, generally under tension and strain, since he comes to believe that he alone can perform it and nobody else will ever help him. All the time he is exhausted with his own anxieties and fears at the thought whether his goal will ever be achieved, if at all. When an individual works thus with an arrogant ego, and with all its self-centredness, he becomes restless enough to make himself totally exhausted and completely shattered. Such 'actions' belong to the category of the passionate (*rajasic*).

All activities of political leaders, social workers, great industrialists, over-anxious parents, fanatic preachers, proselytising missionaries and blind money-makers, when they are at their best,* are examples of this type.

THE CHARACTERISTIC FEATURES OF ACTIONS OF THE 'DULL TYPE' ARE DESCRIBED HEREUNDER:

25. *That 'action' which is undertaken from delusion, without regard for the consequence, loss, injury, and ability, is declared to be TAMASIC (dull).*

The 'actions' (*Karma*) of the 'dull' type (*tamasic*) are performed without any consideration for the consequences thereof, without any regard for their loss of power or vitality. Such actors never care for the loss or injury caused to others by their actions, nor do they pay any attention to their own status and ability, when

---

अनुबन्धं क्षयं हिंसामनवेक्ष्य च पौरुषम् ।
मोहादारभ्यते कर्म यत्तत्तामसमुच्यते ॥ २५ ॥

anubandhaṁ kṣayaṁ hiṁsāmanavekṣya ca pauruṣam
mohādārabhyate karma yattattāmasamucyate 25.

they act. All such careless and irresponsible 'actions' (*Karmas*) undertaken merely because of some delusory misconception of the goal, fall under the *tamasic* type. Habits of drinking, reckless gambling, corruption, etc., are all examples of the dull (*tamasic*) 'actions'.

Such people have no regard for the consequences of their actions. Ere long, they lose their vitality, and injure all those who are depending upon them. They surrender their dignity and status, their capacities and subtle faculties -- all for the sake of their pursuit of a certain delusory goal in life. All they demand is a temporary joy of some sense gratification and a tickling satisfaction of some fancy of the hour.

'Actions' of this type (*tamasic*) immediately provide the performer with a substantial dividend of sorrow. *Rajasic* 'action' comparatively takes a longer time to bring its quota of disappointments and sorrows, while *sattvic* 'action' is always steady and blissful.

THE THREE KINDS OF 'DOERS' (ACTORS) ARE DESCRIBED IN THE FOLLOWING STANZAS:

26. *An 'agent' who is free from attachment, non-egoistic, endowed with firmness and enthusiasm, and unaffected by success or failure, is called SATTVIC (pure).*

So far we have a description of the three types of 'knowledge' and 'action'. The third of the constituents that goes into the make-up of an action is the 'Doer', the ego that has the desire to do. Since the three *gunas* come to influence the

---

मुक्तसङ्गोऽनहंवादी धृत्युत्साहसमन्वित: ।
सिद्धयसिद्धयोर्निर्विकार: कर्ता सात्त्विक उच्यते ॥ २६ ॥

muktasaṅgo'nahaṁvādī dhṛtyutsāhasamanvitaḥ
siddhayasiddhayornirvikāraḥ kartā sāttvika ucyate 26.

psychological life and the intellectual perception of all of us, the doer-personality in each one of us must also change its moods and temperaments according to the preponderant *guna* that rules the bosom at any given moment of time. Consequently, the 'ego' also is classified under three kinds. With this stanza starts the discussion on the three types of 'actors' (*Karta*) who act in the world outside.

A *sattvic* 'Actor' is the one who is free from attachment to any of his kith and kin (*Mukta-sangah*), and non-egoistic (*Anaham vadin*). He is one who has no clinging attachment to the things and beings around, as he has no such false belief that the world outside will bring to him a desirable fulfilment of his existence. He sincerely feels that he has not done anything spectacular even when he has actually done the greatest good to mankind, because he surrenders his egocentric individuality to the Lord, through his perfect attunement with the Infinite.

When such an individual – who has destroyed in himself his ego-sense and the consequent sense of attachment – works in the worldly fields of activities, he ever acts with firm resolution (*Dhriti*), and extreme zeal (*Utsaaha*). The term '*Dhriti*' means 'fortitude' – the subtle faculty in man that makes him strive continuously towards a determined goal. When obstacles come his way, it is this faculty of '*Dhriti*' that discovers for him more and more courage and enthusiasm to face them all, and to continue striving towards the same determined goal. This persevering tendency to push oneself on with the work until one reaches the halls of success, unmindful of the obstacles one might meet with on the path, is called '*Dhriti*'; and '*Utsaha*' means untiring self-application with dynamic enthusiasm on the path of achievement, while pursuing success.

Lastly, a *sattvic* 'actor' is one who ever strives unperturbed, both in success and in failure, both in pleasure and in pain. At this moment I can only think of one example of this type of 'actor' (*Karta*); the nurse in the hospital. She has generally no attachment to the patient; she has no ego that she is curing the patient, because she knows that there is the ability of the doctor behind every successful cure. She has fortitude (*Dhriti*) and enthusiasm (*Utsaaha*) – or else she will not be able to continue efficiently in her job. And lastly, she is not concerned with success or failure; she does not rejoice when a patient walks out fully cured, nor does she moan for every patient that dies. She cannot afford such an indulgence. She understands the hospital to be an island of success and failure, of births and deaths, and she is there only to serve.

An 'actor' (or agent) of the above type is one who suffers the least dissipation of his energies, and so he successfully manages to bring into the field of his actions the mighty total possibilities of a fully unfolded human personality. The *sattvic* 'agent' strives joyously in *sattvic* 'actions', guided by his *sattvic* 'knowledge'; his is the most enduring success, and the world of beings is benefited the most by the inexhaustible rewards of the love-labour of such prophets.

A *sattvic Karta* realises that in all his actions, his body, mind and intellect come into play and serve the world only because the Spirit, the Infinite, is in contact with them. The equipments of matter are as helpless as a broomstick left in a corner. Whenever the body functions, the mind-intellect-equipment throbs and heaves in its pursuit of the new ideals and achievements. And this is because of the Life which thrills them into their respective expressions.

The faculties of the intellect, the beauties of the heart, the vitality of the body, are all vehicles for the sacred will of the Spirit to sing through. If the vehicles are not properly disciplined, and if they do not come to surrender totally to the Infinite, the Lord, they get broken and shattered.

A *sattvic* 'doer' is one who is ever conscious of the touch of the Infinite Light in all his activities.

WHO IS THE *RAJASIC* 'DOER'?

27. *Passionate, desiring to gain the fruits-of-actions, greedy, harmful, impure, full of delight and grief, such an 'agent' is said to be RAJASIC (passionate).*

A 'doer' belonging to the PASSIONATE type is being exhaustively painted here. He is full of desires, passions and attachments, and he tenaciously clings on to some wished-for gain or goal. He is swayed by passion (*raga*) and eagerly seeks the fruit of his work. He is ever greedy (*Lubdhah*) in the sense that such a *rajasic* 'doer' is never satisfied with what he gains and greedily thirsts for more. His thirst is insatiable because his desires multiply from moment to moment.

When a man, full of desires and passions, works with mounting greed, he naturally becomes very malignant (*Himsatmakah*) in his programmes of pursuit. He never hesitates to injure another, if such injury were to win his end. He is blind

---

रागी कर्मफलप्रेप्सुर्लुब्धो हिंसात्मकोऽशुचिः ।
हर्षशोकान्वितः कर्ता राजसः परिकीर्तितः ॥ २७ ॥

rāgī karmaphalaprepsurlabdho hiṁsātmako'śuciḥ
harṣaśokanvitaḥ kartā rājasaḥ parikīrtitaḥ 27.

to the amount of sorrow he might bring to others; he is concerned only with the realisation of his ulterior motives. When a man of this type (with the above qualities) becomes maliciously resolved to gain his own ends, it is but natural that he becomes impure (*ashuchih*), meaning 'immoral.'

Even unrighteous methods and vulgar immoralities are no ban to such a 'doer' and he will pursue them, if his particular desire can be fulfilled thereby. He may ordinarily be quite a moral and righteous man, but the beauty of his composure and the steadiness of his morality, expressed during his quieter moments, all fly away as brilliant splinters when the sledge hammer of his greed and passion, vengeful plans and malignant schemes, thuds upon his heart.

It is but natural that such a PASSIONATE 'doer', when he acts in his blinding desires, comes to live, all through his embodied existence, a sad life of agitations, moved by joys and sorrows, 'full of delight and grief', (*Harsha-Shoka-Anvitah*). This completes the picture of a man who is a 'passionate' (*rajasic*) 'doer'.

AND HOW DOES A *TAMASIC* 'DOER' FUNCTION IN THE FIELD OF ACTIVITY?

28. *Unsteady, vulgar, unbending, cheating, malicious, lazy, despondent, and procrastinating, such an 'agent' is said to be* TAMASIC (Dull).

Here we have a description of a *tamasic* 'doer' pursuing his

---

अयुक्तः प्राकृतः स्तब्धः शठोऽनैष्कृतिकोऽलसः ।
विषादी दीर्घसूत्री च कर्ता तामस उच्यते ॥ २८ ॥

ayuktaḥ prākṛtaḥ stabdhaḥ śaṭho naiṣkṛtiko'lasaḥ
viṣādī dīrghasūtrī ca kartā tāmasa ucyate 28.

* He maintains a malicious attitude towards anybody who tries to come and interfere in the way of his desire gratification.

work motivated by his *tamasic* 'knowledge' and expressing himself through his *tamasic* 'actions'.

UNCONTROLLED (*Ayuktah*)—A 'doer' who has no control over himself, and therefore, is ever unsteady in his application, is of the *tamasic* type. He becomes unbalanced in his activities, because his mind does not obey the warnings of his intellect. A *yukta*-mind is one which is obedient to and perfectly under the control of the intellect. A *tamasic* man is uncultured inasmuch as he acts in the world, spurred by the impulses and instincts of his own mind. The glory of a cultured man comes out only when he brings the impulsive storms of his mind under the chastening control and intelligent guidance of his intellect. He is *Ayuktah* who behaves with no control over his own animal impulses and low instincts. When such an individual acts in the world, he cannot but behave as a vulgar man (*prakrita*).

If shown an intellectual mirror, he will never admit the reflected vulgarities as his own, nor will he acknowledge his way of living as base and licentious. He is arrogant and obstinate (*stabdhah*) and in his stubborn nature he will not lend himself to be persuaded to act more honourably.*

DISHONEST (*Shathah*)—He becomes dishonest. He becomes extremely deceitful. Herein the dishonesty, or deceitfulness, arises out of his incapacity to see any point-of-view other than the false conclusions he has arrived at. Such an individual is not a dependable character, for he conceals his real motives and purposes and secretly works out his programmes which generally bring about a lot of sorrow to all around him.

MALICIOUS (*Naishkritikah*)—The term describes, according to Sankara, one who is bent upon creating quarrels and disputes

---

* Ravana the mighty represents the *Rajasic Karta* and Vibhishana, the devout, is an example of the *Sattvic Karta*.

among people. With a vengefulness, such a person pursues his adversary to destroy him.

INDOLENT (*Alasah*)—The 'dull doer' is a very indolent man spending his time in over-indulgence. He is an idler, for he avoids all creative endeavours and productive efforts, if by deceit or cunning, he can easily and readily procure enjoyable chances and pleasure-goods. He pursues such a path, however immoral it may be. He is a social parasite; he enjoys and consumes without striving and producing. He puts forth no effort; drowsiness of intellect that renders him incapable of correct thinking is a typical feature. The three brothers, from Lanka, in fact, represent these three types of 'doers'. Of them, Kumbhakarna, who sleeps six months and wakes up only to spend the rest of the six months in eating, is symbolic of a *tamasic* 'doer'.*

DESPONDENT (*Vishadi*)—He is one who will not meet the challenge of life squarely. He has neither the vitality nor the stamina to stand up against the challenges of life. This is because his over-indulgent nature has sapped up all his vitality and courage to meet life. Invariably, he spends his time complaining of men and things around him and wishes for a secure spot in the world, where he can be away from all obstacles so that he may peacefully continue satisfying his endless thirst for sensuous enjoyments.

PROCRASTINATOR (*Deergha-sootree*)—An individual so benumbed in his inner nature, slowly gathers within himself an incapacity to arrive at any firm judgement. Even if he comes to any vague decision, he has not the will to continue the consistent pursuit of his judgement. Indolent as he is by nature, more often than not, he postpones the action until it is too late. This procrastinating tendency is natural to a *tamasic* 'actor'. The term *deergha-sootree* has been interpreted by some commentators as 'harbouring deep and long (*deergha*) vengeance against others (*sootra*)', which is also not inappropriate in the context of the thought development in this stanza.

Thus, one who is unsteady, vulgar, arrogant, deceitful, malicious, indolent, despondent and procrastinating belongs to the 'dullest' type of agents available in the fields of human endeavour. This and the two preceding stanzas provide us with three beautifully framed mental pictures, bringing out in all details the *sattvic*, the *rajasic* and the *tamasic* types of 'doers' available in the world. As we have already emphasised, these pictures are NOT yardsticks to classify OTHERS, but are meant for the seekers to observe themselves. Whenever a true seeker discovers symptoms of *tamas* and *rajas* growing in him he should take notice of them at once and consciously strive to regain his *sattvic* beauty.

ACCORDING TO THE PREDOMINATING *GUNA*, 'UNDERSTANDING' AND 'FORTITUDE' ALSO CAN FALL UNDER A THREEFOLD CLASSIFICATION – SAYS KRISHNA:

29. *Hear (you) the threefold division of 'understanding' and 'fortitude' (made) according to the qualities, as I declare them fully and severally, O Dhananjaya.*

'Work', no doubt, is constituted of the three factors: the 'knowledge', the 'action' and the 'actor'. Each of these three factors was shown to fall under a threefold classification and all these classifications were described in the foregoing NINE

बुद्धेर्भेदं धृतेश्चैव गुणतस्त्रिविधं श्रृणु ।
प्रोच्यमानमशेषेण पृथक्त्वेन धनञ्जय ॥ २९ ॥

buddherbhedaṁ dhṛteścaiva guṇatastrividhaṁ śṛṇu
procyamānamaśeṣeṇa pṛthaktavena dhanañjaya 29.

STANZAS. When an actor, guided by his knowledge, acts in the world, no doubt, manifestation of work takes place.

But underlying these three, are TWO FACTORS which supply the fuel and the motive force in all sustained endeavours. They are 'understanding' (*Buddhi*) and 'fortitude' (*Dhriti*).

Buddhi, or 'understanding, means 'the intellectual capacity in the individual to grasp what is happening around him'. 'Fortitude' (*Dhriti*) is 'the faculty of constantly keeping one idea in the mind and consistently working it out to its logical end; consistency of purpose and self-application, without allowing oneself to be tossed about hither and thither like a dry leaf at the mercy of a fickle breeze, is called 'fortitude'.

Every action is controlled and guided by our intellectual capacity of 'understanding', and faithful consistency of purpose, 'fortitude'. This stanza is an introduction to a scientific discussion of these two faculties (*Buddhi* and *Dhriti*) and their threefold classification.

WHAT IS *SATTVIC* UNDERSTANDING?

30. *That which knows the paths of work and renunciation, what ought to be done and what ought not to be done, fear and fearlessness, bondage and liberation, that 'understanding' is SATTVIC (pure), O Partha.*

The intellect may be considered as having the best type of 'understanding' if it can readily discriminate among beings and situations in its field of activity. The intellect has various functions – observing, analysing, classifying, willing, wishing,

---

प्रवृत्तिं च निवृत्तिं च कार्याकार्ये भयाभये ।
बन्धं मोक्षं च या वेत्ति बुद्धिः सा पार्थ सात्त्विकी ॥ ३० ॥

pravittiṁ ca nivṛttiṁ ca kāryākārye bhayābhaye
bandhaṁ mokṣa ca yā vetti buddhiḥ sā pārtha sāttvikī 30.

remembering and a host of others – and yet, we find that the one faculty essential in all of them is the 'power of discrimination'. Without 'discrimination', neither observation nor classification, neither understanding nor judgement, is ever possible. Essentially, therefore, the function of the intellect is 'discrimination', which is otherwise called the faculty of 'right understanding'.

An 'understanding' (*Buddhi*) which is capable of clearly discriminating between the RIGHT field of pursuit and the WRONG field of false proposition, is the highest type of 'understanding'. The individual must have the nerve to pursue the right path and also the heroism to defect from all wrong fields of futile endeavour. In short, true 'understanding' has a ready ability to discriminate between actions that are to be pursued (*Pravritti*) and actions that are to be shunned (*Nivritti*).

An intellect that can discriminate between the true and the false types of work must also be able to function in judging correctly WHAT IS RIGHT AND WHAT IS WRONG. Every moment, we are called upon to decide what responses should be made to the flux of happenings and challenges that continuously take place around us. A *sattvic Buddhi* always helps us to arrive at the correct judgement. A person in a mood of anger or with a wounded vanity suddenly resigns his job only to regret thereafter, the folly of his action. His capacity to judge rightly was mutilated by his bad temper of the moment, or by his exaggerated vanity, and so he comes to regret. Arjuna himself had come to a state of mental hysteria when he complained that his power of judgement had been lost, mainly because of his inordinate attachment to his kith and kin.

WHAT IS TO BE FEARED AND WHAT IS NOT TO BE FEARED (*Bhaya-abhaya*)—"Fools rush in where angels fear to tread". Men of indiscrimination, in their false evaluation of the sense-world, hug on to delusory objects and things, fearing nothing from them, and yet, they fear to read and understand philosophy, to strive and to experience the Infinite. A true intellect must have the right understanding to discriminate between what is to be feared and what is not to be feared.

BONDAGE AND LIBERATION (*Bandham-Moksham-cha*)

If the 'understanding' is clear, we can easily recognise the tendencies in our make-up that entangle the Higher in us, and curtail its fuller play. To observe and analyse ourselves with the required detachment, and to evaluate critically our psychological behaviours and intellectual attitudes in life is not easy; it is possible only for those who are endowed with a well-cultivated *sattvic* 'understanding'. If we cultivate *sattvic* 'understanding', it can not only diagnose for us the false values and wrong emotions that work in us, but also intuitively discover the processes of unwinding ourselves from these cruel *vasanas*, and help us to regain our personality-freedom from these subjective entanglements.

To summarise; the *sattvic Buddhi* is defined as one which makes known to us what type of work is to be done, and what type of work is to be renounced, which distinguishes the right from the wrong, which knows what is to be feared and what is to be faced fearlessly, which shows us the causes of our own present ugliness in life and explains to us the remedies for the same.

Proper 'understanding' can make a garden in a desert; can churn out pure success from every threat of failure. Without 'understanding' and 'fortitude', even the best of chances will become utter disaster. Right 'understanding' can convert the greatest of tragedies into chances for ushering in a prosperous destiny.

WHAT IS *RAJASIC* UNDERSTANDING?

31. *That by which one wrongly understands DHARMA and ADHARMA and also what ought to be done and what ought not to be done, that intellect (understanding), O Partha, is RAJASIC (passionate).*

The 'understanding' of the passionate (*rajasic*) comes to judge the righteous (*Dharma*) and the unrighteous (*Adharma*), what is to be done and what is not to be done, in a slightly perverted manner (*Ayathavat*). Such a *rajasic* 'understanding' cannot reach right judgements, because it is invariably coloured by its own preconceived notions and powerful likes and dislikes.

WHAT IS *TAMASIC* 'UNDERSTANDING'?

32. *That which, enveloped in darkness, sees ADHARMA as DHARMA, and all things perverted, that intellect (understanding), O Partha, is TAMASIC (dull).*

The type of 'understanding' which brings sorrow to everyone including the individual himself is the 'understanding' of the 'dull' (*tamasic*). Actually it is no 'understanding' at all; it

---

यया धर्ममधर्मं च कार्यं चाकार्यमेव च ।
अयथावत्प्रजानाति बुद्धिः सा पार्थ राजसी ॥ ३१ ॥

yayā dharmamadharmaṁ ca kāryaṁ cākāryameva ca
ayathāvatprajānāti buddhiḥ sā pārtha rājasī 31.

अधर्मं धर्ममिति या मन्यते तमसावृता ।
सर्वार्थान्विपरीतांश्च बुद्धिः सा पार्थ तामसी ॥ ३२ ॥

adharmaṁ dharmamiti yā manyate tamasāvṛtā
sarvārthānviparītāṁśca buddhiḥ sā pārtha tāmasī 32.

can, at best, be called only a chronic bundle of misunderstandings. Such an intellect runs into its own conclusions, but unfortunately, it always lands up with wrong conclusions only. It has such a totally perverted 'understanding' that it recognises *'Adharma'* as *'Dharma'*, the 'wrong' as 'right'. This faculty of coming to wrong judgements is amply seen in the dull, because their entire reasoning capacity is enveloped by complete darkness and egoistic drunkenness.

DISCUSSING THE THREE TYPES OF 'FORTITUDE', LORD KRISHNA CONTINUES:

33. *The unwavering 'fortitude' by which, through YOGA, the functions of the mind, the PRANA and the senses are restrained, that 'fortitude', O Partha, is SATTVIC (pure).*

In this section of three stanzas we get a description of the three types of 'fortitude' (*Dhriti*).

Dhriti is that power within ourselves by which we constantly see the goal we want to achieve, and while striving towards it, *Dhriti* discovers for us the necessary constancy of purpose to pursue the path, in spite of all the mounting obstacles that rise on the way. *Dhriti* paints the idea, maintains it constantly in our vision, makes us steadily strive towards it, and when obstacles come, *Dhriti* mobilises secret powers within us to face them all courageously, heroically, and steadily. We shall use the term 'fortitude' to indicate all the above-mentioned suggestions implied in the term *Dhriti*.

धृत्या यया धारयते मन:प्राणेन्द्रियक्रिया: ।
योगेनाव्यभिचारिण्या धृति: सा पार्थ सात्त्विकी ॥ ३३ ॥

dhṛtyā yayā dhārayate manaḥ prāṇendriyakriyāḥ
yogenāvyabhicāriṇyā dhṛtiḥ sā pārtha sāttvikī 33.

This secret fire in man that makes him glow in life and rockets him to spectacular achievements is not generally found in those who have no control over themselves and are voluptuously indulging in sensuous fields. A dissipated individual, who has drained off his energy through wrong-thinking and false-living, shall discover no *Dhriti* in himself. The subtle faculty of 'fortitude' is being analysed and classified here, under the three main heads: the 'good' (*sattvic*), the 'passionate' (*rajasic*) and the 'dull' (*tamasic*). But in all of them, it is interesting to note, *Dhriti* stands for 'the constancy of purpose' with which every individual pursues his field of endeavour chosen for him, with his own 'understanding' (*Buddhi*).

The constancy with which one steadily controls one's mind and sense-organs and their activities, through single-pointed attention and faithful concentration upon a given point-of-contemplation, is the *Dhriti* of the *sattvic* type.

Mind alone can control the organs-of-action (*Karma-Indriyas*) and the organs-of-perception (*Jnana-Indriyas*). To dissuade the organs-of-action and perception from their false pursuits of the ephemeral joys and the consequent dissipations, the mind must have some fixed source to draw its energies and satisfactions from. Without fixing the mind upon something nobler and higher, we cannot detach it from its present pursuits. Therefore, Krishna insists that *Yoga* is unavoidable.

With faithful contemplation upon the Self, the mind gains in steadiness and equipoise, peace and satisfaction, and therefore, it develops a capacity to rule over the sense-organs. But all these achievements are possible only when the inward personality can constantly supply a steady stream of *Dhriti*. Constancy in endeavour and consistency of purpose or 'fortitude' that is expressed in any field of activity becomes *sattvic Dhriti* when constituted as described above.

WHAT IS *RAJASIC 'DHRITI'*?

34. *But the 'fortitude', O Arjuna, by which one holds to duty, pleasure and wealth, one of attachment and craving for the fruits-of-actions, that 'fortitude', O Partha, is RAJASIC (passionate).*

The constancy with which a person holds on to duty (*Dharma*), wealth (*Artha*) and pleasure (*Kama*), encouraged by his growing desire to enjoy the fruit of each of them, is the steadiness or 'fortitude' of the *rajasic* type. It is interesting to note that in the enumeration Krishna avoids *Moksha* and only takes the first three of the 'four ends of man' (*Purushartha*), for, a *rajasic* man is satisfied with the other fields of self-effort and has no demand for spiritual liberation.

The constancy of pursuit of such an individual will be in these three fields of duty, wealth and pleasure, and he will be pursuing one or the other of them with an extreme desire to enjoy the resultant satisfactions. He follows *Dharma*, only to gain the heavens; he pursues *Artha* so that he may have power in this life; and he pursues *Kama* with a firm belief and faith that sensuous objects can give him all satisfactions in life.

The steadiness with which one with such an 'understanding' would strive and work in these fields is classified as *Rajasic Dhriti*.

यया तु धर्मकामार्थान्धृत्या धारयतेऽर्जुन ।
प्रसङ्गेन फलाकाङ्क्षी धृतिः सा पार्थ राजसी ॥ ३४ ॥

yathā tu dharmakāmārthāndhṛtyā dhārayate'rjuna
prasaṅgena phalākāṅkṣī dhṛtiḥ sā pārtha rājasī 34.

WHAT IS *TAMASIC DHRITI*?

35. *The 'constancy' because of which a stupid man does not abandon sleep, fear, grief, depression, and also arrogance (conceit), that 'fortitude', O Partha, is TAMASIC (dull).*

In this stanza we have the description of the dull type of 'fortitude', and it is not very difficult to understand it because a substantial majority of us belong to this type! The steadiness-of-purpose with which one DOES NOT give up one's dreams and imaginations, fears and agitations, griefs and sorrows, depressions and arrogance, is the *Dhriti* of the *tamasic* type.

The term dream (*Swapna*) is used here to indicate fancied imaginations thrown up by a mind that is ALMOST drowned in sleep. To see things which are not there but are delusorily projected by one's own fancy, is called a dream. The dull personalities project upon the world of objects a dream-like value of reality and false joy, and then laboriously strive to gain them.

FEAR (*Bhaya*)—Such men of delusion will have many a fancied fear of the future, which, of course, may never come to pass, but it can efficiently destroy the equilibrium and balance, poise and peace in the individual's life. There are many among us who have experienced such fears by the hundreds in the past. Some fear that they are going to die, but each following day a healthy man wakes up to face the world! Psychologically, they are victims of a fear-complex. And it is interesting to note with what great tenacity these men hug on to such complexes.

यया स्वप्नं भयं शोकं विषादं मदमेव च ।
न विमुञ्चति दुर्मेधा धृतिः सा पार्थ तामसी ॥ ३५ ॥

yayā svapnaṁ bhayaṁ śokaṁ viṣādaṁ madameva ca
na vimuñcati durmedhā dhṛtiḥ sā pārtha tāmasī 35.

GRIEF, DEPRESSION AND ARROGANCE (*Shokam, Vishadam, Madam*)—These again are great channels through which human vitality gets dissipated. A man of extreme 'dullness' will constantly keep these three within his bosom and thereby suffer a sense of self-depletion and inner exhaustion. 'Grief' (*shokam*) is, in general, the painful feeling of disappointment at something that has already happened in the PAST; while 'depression' (*vishadam*) generally reaches our bosom as a result of our despair regarding the FUTURE; and 'arrogance' (*madam*) is the sense of lusty conceit with which a foolish man lives his immoral, low life in the PRESENT.

He who follows these five values of life is called by Krishna a fool (*Durmedha*), and the constancy with which such a fool follows his life of dreams and fears, griefs and despondencies, arrogance and passion, is indicated as the *Dhriti* of the *tamasic* type.

'PLEASURE' ALSO IS THREEFOLD ACCORDING TO THE PREDOMINANT *'GUNA'* IN THE INDIVIDUAL; HERE FOLLOWS THE THREEFOLD DIVISION OF 'PLEASURE', WHICH IS THE EFFECT OF 'ACTION':

36. *And now hear from me, O best among the Bharatas, of the threefold 'pleasure,' in which one rejoices by practice, and surely comes to the end of pain.*

In the logical thought development in this chapter, hitherto we found the three factors that constitute the 'impulse of all

---

सुखं त्विदानीं त्रिविधं श्रृणु मे भरतर्षभ ।
अभ्यासाद्रमते यत्र दु:खान्तं च निगच्छति ॥ ३६ ॥

sukhaṁ tvidānīṁ trividhaṁ śṛṇu me bharatarṣabha
abhyāsādramate yatra duḥkhāntaṁ ca nigacchati 36.

actions': (1) the knowledge, (2) the actor and (3) the action. Afterwards, the very motive forces in all activity – which not only propel activity, but intelligently control and direct it – the *Buddhi* and the *Dhriti*, have also been shown severally, in their different types.

Every 'actor' acts in his field, guided by his 'knowledge', ruled by his 'understanding' (*Buddhi*), and maintained by his 'fortitude' (*Dhriti*). The dissection and observation of 'work' is now complete since we have understood the 'anatomy and physiology' of work. The Psychology of work is now being discussed: why does man act? In fact, every living creature acts propelled by the same instinct, namely, the craving for happiness.

With the three constituents of action – namely, 'knowledge', 'agency' and 'action' – helped by the right type of 'understanding' (*Buddhi*) and 'fortitude' (*Dhriti*), every living creature from the womb to the tomb continues acting in the world. To what purpose? Everyone acts for the same goal of gaining happiness, meaning, a better sense of fulfilment.

And though the goal be thus one and the same (viz., happiness), since different types of constituents go into the make-up of our actions, and since we are so different in the texture of our UNDERSTANDING and FORTITUDE, the path adopted by each one of us is distinctly different from those adopted by all others. In and through the variety of actions in the universe, all people – the good, the passionate, and the dull – seek their own sense of satisfaction.

Since each of the five component parts that make up an 'action' is of the three different types, it follows that 'happiness' that is gained by the different types must also be different in its texture, perfection and completeness. Here follows a description of the three types of 'happiness'.

THROUGH PRACTICE (*Abhyasat*)—Through a familiarity of this complete scheme-of-things within, an individual can, to a large extent, come to diagnose himself and understand the why and the wherefore of all his miseries. He can thus learn to readjust and re-evaluate his life and thereby come to end his sorrows totally, or at least, alleviate them to some extent.

WHAT IS *SATTVIC* (PURE) 'HAPPINESS'?

37. *That which is like poison at first, but in the end like nectar, that 'pleasure' is declared to be SATTVIC (pure), born of the purity of one's own mind, due to Self realisation.*

That 'happiness' which, in the beginning, is like poison and very painful, but which, when it works itself out, fulfils itself in a nectarine success, is the enduring 'happiness' of the 'good' (*sattvic*). In short, 'happiness' that arises from constant effort is the 'happiness' that can yield us a greater beauty and a larger sense of fulfilment. The flimsy 'happiness' that is gained through sense-indulgence and sense-gratification is a joy that is fleeting, and after its onslaught there is a terrific undercurrent that comes to upset our equilibrium and drag us into the depths of despondency.

The joy arising out of inner self-control and the consequent sense of self-perfection is no cheap gratification. In the beginning its practice is certainly very painful and extremely arduous. But one who has discovered in oneself the necessary courage and heroism to walk the precipitous 'path' of self-purification and

---

यत्तदग्रे विषमिव परिणामेऽमृतोपमम् ।
तत्सुखं सात्त्विकं प्रोक्तमात्मबुद्धिप्रसादजम् ॥ ३७ ॥

yattedagre viṣamiva pariṇāme'mṛtopamam
tatsukhaṁ sāttvikaṁ proktamātmabuddhiprasādajam 37.

inward balance, comes to enjoy the subtlest of happiness and the all-fulfilling sense of inward peace. This 'happiness' (*sukham*), arising out of self-control and self-discipline, is classified here by the Lord as *sattvic* 'happiness'.

BORN OUT OF THE PURITY OF ONE'S OWN MIND (*Atma Buddhi Prasada-jam*)—By carefully living the life of the 'good' (*sattvic*) and acting in disciplined self-control, as far as possible in the world, maintaining the *sattvic* qualities in all their 'component parts', one can develop the *'Prasada'* of one's inner nature. The term *'Prasada'* is very often misunderstood in ritualistic language.

The peace and tranquillity, the joy and expansion, that the mind and intellect come to experience as a result of their discipline and contemplation, are the true *'Prasada'*. The joy arising out of spiritual practices, provided by the integration of the inner nature, is called *'Prasada'* which is the *sattvic* 'happiness', *Prasada-jam*. In short, the sense of fulfilment and the gladness of heart that well up in the bosom of a cultured man, as a result of his balanced and self-disciplined life of high ideals and divine values of life, are the enduring 'happiness' of all men-of-Perfection, of all true men of religion.

WHAT IS *RAJASIC* (PASSIONATE) 'HAPPINESS'?

38. *That pleasure which arises from the contact of the sense-organs with the objects, (which is) at first like nectar, (but is) in the end like poison, that is declared to be RAJASIC (passionate).*

That happiness which arises in our bosom when the appropriate world-of-objects comes in contact with our sense-

---

विषयेन्द्रियसंयोगाद्यत्तदग्रेऽमृतोपमम् ।
परिणामे विषमिव तत्सुखं राजसं स्मृतम् ॥ ३८ ॥

viṣayendriyasaṁyogādyattadagre'mṛtopamam
pariṇāme viṣamiva tatsukhaṁ rājasaṁ smṛtam 38.

organs is indeed a thrill that is nectarine in the beginning, but unfortunately, it vanishes as quickly as it comes, dumping the enjoyer into a pit of exhaustion and indeed into a sense of ill-reputed dissipation.

Rajasic 'happiness' arises only when the sense-organs are actually in contact with the sense-objects. Unfortunately, this contact cannot be permanently established; for the objects are always variable. And the subjective mind and intellect, the instruments that come in contact with the objects, are also variable and changing. The sense-organs cannot afford to embrace the sense-objects at all times with the same appetite, and even if they do so, the very object in the embrace of the sense-organs withers and putrefies, raising the stink of death. No man can FULLY enjoy even the passing glitter of joy that the sense-organs give him, for even at the moment of enjoyment the joy-possibility in it gets unfortunately tainted by an anxiety that it may leave him. Thus, to a true thinker, the temporary joys of sense-objects are not at all satisfactory, since they bury the enjoyer, ere long, in a tomb of sorrow.

This sort of 'happiness' is classified as the *rajasic* type of 'happiness' and is generally pursued by men of passion.

WHAT IS *TAMASIC* (DULL) 'HAPPINESS'?

39. *The pleasure, which at first and in the sequel deludes the Self, arising from sleep, indolence and heedlessness, is declared to be TAMASIC (Dull).*

यदग्रे चानुबन्धे च सुखं मोहनमात्मनः ।
निद्रालस्यप्रमादोत्थं तत्तामसमुदाहृतम् ॥ ३९ ॥

yadagre cānubandhe ca sukhaṁ mohanamātmanaḥ
nidrālasyapramādotthaṁ tattāmasamudāhṛtam 39.

* Refer Swamiji's Discourses on *Mandukya-Karika*, Chapter IV.

The 'happiness' of the 'dull' (*tamasic*) is that which deludes the Higher in us, and vitiates the culture in us; and, when the pursuit of such 'happiness' is continued for a length of time, it gives to the intellect a thick crust of wrong values and false ideals, and ruins the spiritual sensitivity of the personality.

This type of *tamasic* 'happiness' satisfies mere sense-cravings; for such *tamasic* 'happiness' arises, according to the Lord, from sleep (*Nidraa*), indolence (*Aalasya*) and heedlessness (*Pramada*).

SLEEP (*Nidra*)—It is not the psychological condition of the everyday sleep that is meant here. Philosophically, the term 'sleep' stands for the non-apprehension of Reality,* and the incapacity of the dull-witted to perceive any permanent, ever-existing goal of life. This encourages one to seek simple sense-gratifications at the flesh level.

INDOLENCE (*Aalasya*)—It is the incapacity of the intellect to think out correctly the problems that face it and come to correct judgement. Such an inertia of the intellect makes it insensitive to the inspiring song of life, and a person having such an intellect is generally tossed here and there by the passing tides of his own instincts and impulses.

HEEDLESSNESS (*Pramada*)—As every challenge reaches us and demands our response to it, no doubt, the Higher in us truly guides our activities; but the lower, indolent mind seeks a compromise and tries to act, heedless of the voice of the Higher. When an individual has thus lived for some time carelessly ignoring the Voice of the Higher, he becomes more and more removed from his divine perfections. He sinks lower and lower into his animal nature.

When such an individual, who is heedless of the higher calls, indolent at his intellectual level and completely asleep to the existence and the play of Reality, seeks 'happiness', he only seeks a 'happiness' that deludes the soul, both at the beginning and at the end. Such 'happiness' is here classified by Krishna as 'dull' (*tamasic*).

HERE FOLLOWS A STANZA WHICH CONCLUDES THE SUBJECT OF OUR PRESENT DISCUSSION:

40. *There is no being on earth, or again in heaven among the "DEVAS" (heavenly beings), who is totally liberated from the three qualities, born of PRAKRITI (matter).*

With the above stanza the exhaustive description of the three *Gunas* as impinging upon the personality of all living organisms, is concluded. On the whole, this section of the chapter has given us a psychological explanation for the variety of men that we meet with, in the world-of-plurality, not only in their personality-structures but also in their individual-behaviours. The three types of beings have been described exhaustively --by an analysis of 'knowledge', 'action', 'agent', 'understanding' and 'fortitude'. This is only for our guidance so that we know where we stand in our own inner nature and outer manifestations.

If we detect, with the above-mentioned slide-rule of personality, that we belong to the *tamasic* or the *rajasic* types, we, as seekers of cultural expression and growth, are to take warning and strive to heave ourselves into the *sattvic* state. Remember, and I repeat, REMEMBER, these classifications are given NOT TO CLASSIFY OTHERS but to provide us with a ready-reckoner to help us in our constant and daily self-analysis and self-discipline.

न तदस्ति पृथिव्यां वा दिवि देवेषु वा पुनः ।
सत्त्वं प्रकृतिजैर्मुक्तं यदेभिः स्यात्त्रिभिर्गुणैः ॥ ४० ॥

na tadasti pṛthivyāṁ vā divi deveṣu vā punaḥ
sattvaṁ prakṛtijairmuktaṁ yadebhiḥ syāttribhirguṇaiḥ 40.

These three *gunas* have been described because there is no living organism in the world, 'NO CREATURE EITHER ON EARTH OR AGAIN AMONG THE GODS IN HEAVEN' who is totally free from the influence of these three *gunas;* no living creature can act or work beyond the frontiers provided by these three *gunas*. Nature (*Prakriti*) itself is constituted of these *gunas;* the play of these three *gunas* is the very expression of *Prakriti.*

But at the same time, no two creatures react to the world outside in the same fashion, because the proportion in which these three *gunas* come to influence each one is different at different times. These three *gunas* put together are the manifestation of *'Maya'*. Individuals differ from one another because of the different textures of the *gunas* that predominantly rule over them; it is this *Maya* that gives them their individuality. An individual cannot, at any time, exist without all these three *gunas*, whatever be their relative proportion.

No sample of 'coffee' is possible without its three ingredients, the decoction, the milk, and the sugar; but at the same time, the proportion in which they are mixed together may be different from cup to cup according to the taste of the partaker. He who has transcended the three *gunas* comes to experience the very plurality in the world as the play of the One Infinite. So, let us introspect and evaluate ourselves every day, every minute. Let us avoid the lower *gunas* and steadily work ourselves up towards the achievement of the *sattvic* state. Only after reaching the status of the good (*sattvic*) can we be ushered into the State of Godhood – Perfection Absolute.

With these three measuring rods – the qualities (*gunas*) Krishna classifies the entire community of man under three distinct types. The criterion of this classification is the texture of man's inner equipments which he brings into play for his achievements in his fields of activity. Accordingly, the Hindu scriptures have brought the entire humanity under a four-fold classification. So, its applicability is not merely confined to India - BUT IS UNIVERSAL.

Certain well-defined characteristics determine the types of these four classes of human beings; they are not always determined by heredity, or accident of birth. They are termed, in our society, as: the *Brahmanas* – with a major portion of *sattva*, a little *rajas* and with minimum *tamas*; the *Kshatriyas* – mostly *rajas* with some *sattva*, and a dash of *tamas*; the *Vaishyas* – with more *rajas*, less *sattva* and some *tamas*; and the *Shudras* – mostly *tamas*, a little *rajas*, with only a suspicion of *sattva*.

This fourfold classification is universal and for all times. Even today it holds good. In modern language, the four types of people may be called: (1) the creative thinkers; (2) the politicians; (3) the commercial employers; and (4) the labourers (the proletarians). We can easily recognise how each subsequent classification holds in awe and reverence the previous higher class – the employees are afraid of the employer, the commercial men are suspicious of the politicians and the politicians tremble at the courageous, independent thinkers.

In the following stanzas, by the discussions contained in them, in the immediate context of the Krishna-Arjuna summit talks, the Lord is only trying to make Arjuna understand that his inner equipment is such that he can be classified only as a *Kshatriya*. Being a *Kshatriya*, his duty is to fight, championing the cause of the good, and thus establish righteousness. He cannot, with profit, retire to the jungle and meditate for self-unfoldment, since he will have to grow, first of all, into the status of the *sattvic* personality (*Brahmana*) before he can successfully strive on the path of total retirement and a life of rewarding contemplation. Therefore, with the available texture of mind and intellect, the only spiritual *sadhana* left for Arjuna is to act vigorously in the field of contention. Thereby he can exhaust his existing *vasanas* of *rajas* and *tamas*.

IN THE FOLLOWING VERSES THE DUTIES ORDAINED BY ONE'S NATURE, '*SWABHAAVA*', AND ONE'S STATION IN LIFE, '*SWADHARMA*', ARE LAID OUT WITH THE THOROUGHNESS OF A LAW BOOK:

41. *Of scholars (BRAHMANAS), of leaders (KSHATRIYAS) and of traders (VAISHYAS), as also of workers (SHUDRAS), O Parantapa, the duties are distributed according to the qualities born of their own nature.*

After dealing with the various *gunas* in the preceding stanza, Krishna now applies them to the social fabric of humanity and thus intelligently classifies the entire mankind under four distinct heads: the *Brahmanas*, the *Kshatriyas*, the *Vaishyas* and the *Shudras*.

Different types of duties are assigned to each of these classes of individuals depending upon their nature (*Swabhava*), which is ordered by the proportion of the *gunas* in the make-up of each type of inner equipment. The duties prescribed for a particular type depend upon the manifestation of the inner ruling *gunas*, as expressed in the individual's contact with the world and his activities in society. The good and bad are not diagnosed by merely examining the texture of the person's skin or the colour of his hair; an individual is judged only by his expressions

ब्राह्मणक्षत्रियविशां शूद्राणां च परंतप ।
कर्माणि प्रविभक्तानि स्वभावप्रभवैर्गुणैः ॥ ४१ ॥

brāhmaṇakṣatriyaviśāṁ śūdrāṇāṁ ca parantapa
karmāṇi pravibhaktāni svabhāvaprabhavairguṇaiḥ 41.

* The type of a man's 'action', the quality of his 'ego', the colour of his 'knowledge', the texture of his 'understanding', the temper of his 'fortitude', and the brilliance of his 'happiness' will determine his 'caste' (*Varna*).

in life and by the quality of his contacts with the world outside. These alone can reflect one's inner personality - the quality and texture of the contents of one's mind-intellect.

After testing and determining the quality of the inner personality, the individuals in the community are classified, and different types of duties are prescribed for each. Naturally, the duties prescribed for a *Brahmana* are different from those expected of a *Kshatriya*; and the work of the *Vaishya* and the *Shudra* should necessarily be different from that of the *Brahmana* and the *Kshatriya*. The *shastra* enjoins duties, by pursuing which the preponderant *tamas* can be evolved into *rajas*, which, in its turn, can grow to become *sattva*. And, even then, the seeker must wait for the sublimation of *sattva*, when alone the final experience of the Infinite is gained.

By observing a person* one can conclude as to which class he belongs to -- whether to the *Brahmana*, the *Kshatriya*, the *Vaishya* or the *Shudra*. In this context, when we say a man is *sattvic*, it only means that the *sattvic* qualities are predominant in him; even in the most *sattvic* of persons, at times, the *rajasic* and the *tamasic* qualities can and will show up; so too, even in the most *tamasic* man, *sattva* and *rajas* will necessarily show up sometimes. No one is exclusively of one *guna* alone.

Today, as they are now worked out in India, these four classifications have lost much of their meaning. They signify merely a hereditary birthright in the society, a mere physical distinction that divides the society into castes and sub-castes. A true *Brahmana* is necessarily a highly cultured *sattvic* man who can readily control his sense-organs, and with perfect mastery over his mind, can raise himself, through contemplation, to the highest peaks of meditation upon the Infinite. But today's *Brahmana* is one who is claiming his distinction by birth alone and alas! he gets no reverence, because he has not striven to deserve it.

ANSWERING THE FOUR TYPES OF NATURE, AS DETERMINED BY THEIR PSYCHOLOGICAL CHARACTERISTICS, THERE ARE FOUR KINDS OF SOCIAL LIVING, EACH HAVING A DEFINITE FUNCTION IN SOCIETY: THEY ARE DESCRIBED BELOW:

42. *Serenity, self-restraint, austerity, purity, forgiveness and also uprightness, knowledge, realisation, belief in God -- are the duties of the BRAHMANAS, born of (their own) nature.*

Herein we have a detailed enumeration of the duties of a *Brahmana* born out of his own predominantly *sattvic* nature. Serenity (*shama*), is one of his duties. *Shama* is controlling the mind from running into the world-of-objects seeking sense-enjoyments. Even if we shut off the world-of-objects by carrying ourselves away from the tumults and temptations of life into a quiet, lonely place, even there our minds will stride forth into the sense-fields through the memories of our past indulgences. To control consciously this instinctive flow of the mind towards the sense-objects is called *shama*.

SELF-CONTROL (*Dama*)—Controlling the sense-organs, which are the gateways through which the external world of stimuli infiltrates into our mental domain and mars our peace, is called *dama*. A man practising *dama*, even if he be in the midst

---

शमो दमस्तपः शौचं क्षान्तिरार्जवमेव च ।
ज्ञानं विज्ञानमास्तिक्यं ब्रह्मकर्म स्वभावजम् ॥ ४२ ॥

śamo damastapaḥ śaucaṁ kṣāntirārjavameva ca
jñānaṁ vijñānamāstikyaṁ brahmakarma svabhāvajam 42.

of sensuous objects, is not disturbed by them. A true *Brahmana* is one who practises constantly both *shama* and *dama*, serenity and self-control.

AUSTERITY (*Tapas*)—Conscious physical self-denial in order to economise the expenditure of human energy so lavishly spent in the wrong channels of sense-indulgence, and conserving it for reaching the higher unfoldment within is called *tapas*. By the practice of *shama* and *dama*, the *Brahmana* will be steadily controlling both the mad rush of his senses and his mind-wandering. This helps him to conserve his inner vitality which would have been otherwise spent in hunting after sense-joys. This conserved energy is utilised for higher flights in meditation. This subjective process of economising, conserving, and redirecting one's energies within is called *tapas*. It is a *Brahmana's* duty to live in *tapas*.

PURITY (*Shaucham*)—The Sanskrit term used here includes external cleanliness and internal purity. Habits of cleanliness in one's personal life and surroundings are the governing conditions in the life of one who is practising both *shama* and *dama*. The practice of *tapas* makes him such a disciplined person that he cannot stand any disorderly confusion or state of neglect around and about him. A person living in the midst of things thrown about in a disorderly manner is certainly a man of slothful nature and slovenly habits. It is the duty of the *Brahmana* to keep himself ever clean and pure.

FORBEARANCE (*Kshanti*)—To be patient and forgiving and thus to live without struggling even against wrongs done against one, is 'forbearance' – the duty of a *Brahmana*. Such an individual will never harbour any hatred for anyone; he lives equanimously amidst both the good and the bad.

UPRIGHTNESS (*Arjavam*)—This is a quality which makes an individual straightforward in all his dealings, and his uprightness makes him fearless in life. He is afraid of none, and he makes no compromise of the higher calls with the lower murmurings.

Cultivating the above six qualities – serenity (*shama*), self-control (*dama*), austerity (*tapas*), purity (*shaucham*), forbearance (*kshanti*), and straightforwardness (*Arjavam*) – and expressing them in all his relationships with the world outside is the lifelong duty of a *Brahmana*. The above-mentioned six artistic strokes complete the picture of a *Brahmana* on the stage of the world when he deals with things and beings in the various situations in life. The Lord enumerates, in the stanza, three more duties of a *Brahmana* which are the rules of conduct controlling his spiritual life.

KNOWLEDGE (*Jnanam*)—The theoretical knowledge of the world, of the structure of the equipments-of-experience and their behaviour while coming in contact with the outer world, of the highest goal of life, of the nature of the spirit - in short, knowledge of all that the *Upanishads* deal with - is included in the term *Jnanam*.

WISDOM (*Vijnanam*)—If 'theoretical knowledge' is *Jnanam* then 'personal experience' is *Vijnanam*. Knowledge digested and assimilated brings home to man an inward experience, and thereafter, he comes to live his life guided by this deep inner experience called 'wisdom'. Knowledge can be imparted, but 'wisdom' is to be found by the individual in himself. When a student discovers in himself the enthusiasm to live the knowledge gained through his studies, then from the field of his lived experience arises 'wisdom' – *Vijnanam*.

FAITH (*Aastikyam*)—Unless one has a deep faith in what one has studied and lived, the living itself will not be enthusiastic and full. This ardency of conviction which is the motive-force behind one, who lives what he has understood, is the secret sustaining power that steadily converts [2]KNOWLEDGE into 'wisdom'. This inner order, this intellectual honesty, this subtle unflagging enthusiasm, is called 'FAITH'.

To grow and steadily cultivate knowledge, wisdom and faith are the sacred duties of a *Brahmana* in his spiritual life.

WHAT ARE THE DUTIES OF A *'KSHATRIYA'*?

43. *Prowess, splendour, firmness, dexterity, and also not fleeing from battle, generosity, lordliness -- these are the duties of the KSHATRIYAS, born of (their own) nature.*

The *Kshatriyas* have a greater dose of *Rajoguna* in the composition of their personality. A *Kshatriya* is not defined by Lord Krishna as the lawful son of another *Kshatriya*. He enumerates a series of qualities and behaviours noticed in a truly *Kshatriya* personality. In the *Geeta*, the four 'castes' are described in terms of their manifested individuality when coming in contact with the world-of-objects – the field of expression. In all these descriptions we meet with details of the individual's mental and intellectual reactions to his moral life.

PROWESS AND BOLDNESS (*Shauryam* and *Tejah*)—These mean the vigour and constancy with which he meets the challenges in his life. He who has the above two qualities, heroism and vigour of pursuit, certainly becomes a commanding personality.

शौर्यं तेजो धृतिर्दाक्ष्यं युद्धे चाप्यपलायनम् ।
दानमीश्वरभावश्च क्षात्रं कर्म स्वभावजम् ॥ ४३ ॥

śauryaṁ tejo dhṛtirdākṣyaṁ yuddhe cāpyapalāyanam
dānamīśvarabhāvaśca kṣātraṁ karma svabhāvajam 43.

FORTITUDE (*Dhriti*)—This is already explained in earlier stanzas. Herein, as applied to a *Kshatriya*, it is the powerful will of the personality, who, having decided to do something, pursues the 'path' and discovers in himself the necessary drive and constancy of purpose to meet, and if necessary, break down all the obstacles until he gains victory or success.

PROMPTITUDE (*Dakshyam*)—The Sanskrit equivalent for the army parade-ground command 'Attention' is '*Daksha*' This quality of alertness and smart vigilance is, indeed, *Dakshyam*. In the context here, it means that a *Kshatriya* is prompt in coming to decisions and in executing them. Such an individual is industrious and has an enviable amount of perseverance, however hazardous may the field of his activity be.

NOT FLEEING FROM BATTLE—One who has all the above qualities can never readily accept defeat in any field of conflict. He will not leave any work incomplete. Since Krishna is here generally classifying all human beings according to the *gunas* predominant in them, these terms should be understood in their greatest amplitude of suggestion. No doubt, a true warrior should not step back in any field of battle; but such literal interpretation is only incomplete. The field-of-battle should include all fields of competition wherein things and situations arrange themselves in opposition to the planned schemes of a man of will and dash. In no such condition will a true *Kshatriya* feel nervous. He never leaves a field which he has entered; if at all he leaves, he leaves with the crown of success!

GENEROSITY (*Danam*)—Governments or kings cannot be popular unless they loosen their purse strings. Even in modern days every government budget in all democratic countries has amounts allocated under heads which are not discussed and voted. A man of action cannot afford to be miserly since his success will depend upon his influence on a large number of friends and supporters. The glory of a prince is in his compassion for others who are in need of help.

LORDLINESS (*Ishwara-bhava*)—As a rule, without self-confidence in one's own abilities one cannot lead others. A leader must have such a firm faith in himself that he will be able to reinforce other frail hearts around him with his self-confidence. Thus, lordliness is one of the essential traits in a *Kshatriya*. He must waft all around a fragrance of brilliance and dynamism, electrifying the atmosphere around him. A king is not made by his golden robes or bejewelled crown. The crown, the robe and the throne have a knack of electing for themselves a true wearer. Lordliness is the hallmark of *Kshatriya*.

These eight qualities – bravery, vigour, constancy, resourcefulness, promptitude, courage in the face of the enemy, generosity and lordliness – are enumerated here as the duties of a *Kshatriya*, meaning that it is the duty of a true man-of-action to cultivate, to maintain and to express these traits in himself. In no society can leaders of men and affairs claim to be at once the spiritual leaders of the people. Secular heads cannot be spiritual guides. But a true leader is one who has the subtle ability to incorporate the spiritual ideals of our culture into the work-a-day life and maintain them in the community in all its innumerable fields of activity.

THE DUTIES OF THE *VAISHYAS* AND *SHUDRAS* ARE DESCRIBED IN THE FOLLOWING:

44. *Agriculture, cattle-rearing and trade are the duties of the VAISHYAS, born of (their own) nature; and service is the duty of the SHUDRAS, born of (their own) nature.*

कृषिगौरक्ष्यवाणिज्यं वैश्यकर्म स्वभावजम् ।
परिचर्यात्मकं कर्म शूद्रस्यापि स्वभावजम् ॥ ४४ ॥

kṛṣigaurakṣyavāṇijyaṁ vaiśyakarma svabhāvajam
paricayārtmakaṁ karma śūdrasyāpi svabhāajam 44.

Since each mind-intellect equipment is governed and ruled over by its predominating quality (*guna*), each equipment has its own nature to reckon with. A vehicle that can efficiently work in one medium of transport cannot with the same efficiency work in another medium, a car is efficient on the road – but on water? The *rajasic* mind cannot fly into meditation and maintain its poise as easily and as beautifully as the *sattvic* mind can. Similarly, in the field in which a *Kshatriya* can outshine everybody, a *Vaishya* or a *Shudra* cannot. To rise to the highest station in social life all men cannot have IDENTICAL opportunities. A social system can only give 'equal opportunities' for all its members to develop their gifts in and through life. In order to prove this thesis, the various duties are prescribed that will help to mould the personalities of the different types of men.

AGRICULTURE, BREEDING AND TENDING CATTLE, TRADE AND COMMERCE—These are three fields in which a *Vaishya* can function inspiredly and exhaust his imperfections. These are duties towards which he has an aptitude because of his own nature. Work in a spirit of DEDICATION AND SERVICE IS THE DUTY OF A *SHUDRA*.

The mental temperament of a man determines what class he belongs to and each class has been given particular duties to perform in the world. If a man who is fit temperamentally for one type of work is entrusted with a different type of activity, he will bring chaos not only into the field but also in himself. For example, if a *Kshatriya* were asked to fan someone in a spirit of service, he may condescend to do so, but one will find him ordering somebody else, almost instinctively, to fetch a fan for him! So too, if a man of commercial temperament, a *Vaishya*, comes to serve as a temple-priest, the sacred place will become, ere long, worse than a trading centre; and again, let him become the head of any government, he will, out of sheer instinct, begin doing profitable 'business' from the seat of governmental authority; people call it corruption!!

We must analyse and discover the type of *vasanas* and temperaments that predominate in each one of us and determine what types of men we are. None belonging to the higher groups has any justification to look down with contempt upon others who are of the lower types. Each one serves the society as best as he can. Each one must work in a spirit of dedication for his own evolution and sense of fulfilment. When each one works thus according to his *vasanas* and fully devotes his attention to his prescribed duties, it is said here that he will develop within himself and attain, in stages, the ultimate Perfection.

When a person works devotedly, in the proper field and in the environment best suited to him, he will be exhausting the existing *vasanas* in him. And when the *vasanas* are reduced he will experience tranquillity and peace within and it will become possible for him to discover more and more concentration and single-pointed contemplation.

WITH THESE FACULTIES IN HIM MAN CAN ULTIMATELY REACH THE STATE OF PERFECTION -- THE LIFE IN THE SELF - HOW?

45. *Devoted, each to his own duty, man attains Perfection. How, engaged in his own duty, he attains Perfection, listen.*

EACH DEVOTED TO HIS DUTY, MAN ATTAINS PERFECTION—By being loyal to our own level of feelings and ideas, to our own development of consciousness, we can evolve into higher states of self-unfoldment.

The truth of this classification of mankind may not be very obvious, if we observe it only superficially. But the biographies of all great men of action declare repeatedly the precision with which this law-of-life works itself out in human affairs. A tiny Corsican boy who was asked to tend sheep refused to do so and reached Paris to become one of the greatest generals the world had ever seen – Napoleon. A Goldsmith or a Keats would rather compose his metres in a garret than take up a commercial job, courting prosperity and a life of comfort. Each one is ordered by his own *swabhava*, and each can discover his fulfilment only in that self-ordered field of activity.

By thus working in the field ordered by one's own *vasanas*, if one can live surrendering one's ego and egocentric desires to enjoy the fruits, one can achieve a sense of fulfilment; and a great peace will arise out of the exhaustion of one's *vasanas*. The renunciation of the ego and its desires can never be accomplished unless there is a spirit of dedication and a total surrender to the Infinite. When unbroken awareness of the Lord becomes a

---

स्वे स्वे कर्मण्यभिरतः संसिद्धिं लभते नरः ।
स्वकर्मनिरतः सिद्धिं यथा विन्दति तच्छृणु ॥ ४५ ॥

sve sve karmaṇyabhirataḥ saṁsiddhiṁ labhate naraḥ
svakarmanirataḥ siddhiṁ yathā vindati tatchṛṇu 45.

constant habit of the mind, dedication becomes effective, and man's evolution starts.

Such an intelligent classification of human beings on the basis of their physical behaviour, psychological structure and intellectual aptitude is applicable not in India only. This four-fold classification is universal, both in its application in life and its implication in the cultural development of man.*

HOW CAN ONE, DEVOTED TO ONES OWN DUTY, ATTAIN PERFECTION? "THAT DO THOU HEAR" SAYS LORD KRISHNA:

46. *From all beings arise, by Whom all this is pervaded, worshipping Him with one's own duty, man attains Perfection.*

In this chapter the fourfold classification of men and the duties of the individuals belonging to each classification are given. When a man acts according to his 'nature' (*swabhava*) and station-in-life (*swadharma*), his *vasanas* get exhausted. This exhaustion of the load of *vasanas* and the consequent sense of joy and relief can be gained only when he learns to work and achieve in a spirit of total self-surrender.

By constantly remembering the higher goal towards which we are working our way, if we do our work efficiently, this

---

यत: प्रवृत्तिर्भूतानां येन सर्वमिदं ततम् ।
स्वकर्मणा तमभ्यर्च्य सिद्धिं विन्दति मानव: ॥ ४६ ॥

yataḥ pravṛttirbhūtānāṁ yena sarvamidaṁ tatam
svakarmaṇā tamabhyarcya siddhiṁ vindati mānavaḥ 46.

*As Gerald Heard says: "The *Aryan-Sanskrit* sociological thought, which first defined and named its four-fold structure of society, is as much ours as India's."

Vasana-exhaustion takes place. The goal to be constantly remembered is indicated in this stanza: "HE FROM WHOM ALL BEINGS ARISE AND BY WHOM ALL THIS IS PERVADED". The three equipments – the body, the mind and the intellect, that flutter out into activity, are all in themselves inert matter with no consciousness in themselves. It is only at the touch of the Light-of-Life that inert matter starts singing its *vasanas* through the various activities.

To remember constantly, this Consciousness, the *Atman* – the *Atman* that lends, as it were, Its dynamism to the Matter that invests It in its activities – is to stand apart from all agitations in the field of strife. Just as a musician, constantly conscious of the background drone, sings his songs easily in tune, just as a dancer dances effortlessly to the rhythm of the drum, such a man is never caught on the wrong foot ever in life. A new glow of tranquil peace and dynamic love comes to shine through all his actions, and his achievements radiate the shadowless light of Perfection, unearthly and Divine.

Work can thus be changed into worship by attuning our minds all through our activity to the consciousness of the Self. A self-dedicated man so working in the consciousness of the Supreme pays the greatest homage to his Creator. This subtle change in attitude transforms the shape of even the most dreary situation. Even the most dreadfully unpleasant field of activity is converted into a sacred chamber of devotion – into a silent hall of prayer – into a quiet seat of meditation!

By thus setting one's hands and feet to work in the field-of-objects with one's mind and intellect held constantly conscious of the Divine Presence, one can attain 'THROUGH THE

PERFORMANCE OF ONE'S OWN DUTIES THE HIGHEST PERFECTION'. Work results in self-fulfilment, apart from its legitimate 'fruits'. The inner personality gets integrated, and such an integrated person grows in his meditation and evolves quickly.

"AND YET, WHY SHOULD I NOT GO AND MEDITATE?" SEEMS TO BE THE HONEST DOUBT IN ARJUNA'S MIND. KRISHNA ANSWERS:

47. *Better is one's own duty (though) destitute of merits, than the duty of another well-performed. He who does the duty ordained by his own nature incurs no sin.*

The opening line of this stanza has been exhaustively discussed earlier (III-35). To work in any field ordered by one's own *vasanas* is better, because in that case, there is a chance for exhausting the existing *vasanas*. When an individual strives in a field contrary to the existing *vasanas*, he not only fails to gain any exhaustion of the existing *vasanas*, but also creates a new load of *vasanas* in his temperament. Hence, it is said here: "BETTER IS ONE'S OWN *DHARMA* THOUGH IMPERFECT THAN THE *DHARMA* OF ANOTHER WELL-PERFORMED".

By performing "duties ordained by one's own nature" (*Swabhava-Niyatam-Karma*) the individual comes to no evil – meaning, the individual has no chance of imprinting any new

---

श्रेयान्स्वधर्मो विगुण: परधर्मात्स्वनुष्ठितात् ।
स्वभावनियतं कर्म कुर्वन्नाप्नोति किल्बिषम् ॥ ४७ ॥
śreyānsvadharmo viguṇaḥ paradharmātsvanuṣṭhitāt
svabhāvaniyataṁ karma kurvannāpnoti kilbiṣam 47.

impressions on his mind – the impressions which, in their maturity, might force him to strive, to seek, to achieve and to indulge.

This closing chapter of the *Geeta* is a peroration of the beautiful discourse of the inspired Divine, and it is, naturally therefore, a summary of the whole *Geeta*. Hence, we find here a reiteration of almost all the salient ideas which have been discussed earlier, and which are very important for the cure of the 'Arjuna-disease'.[1]

Anyone can appreciate the logic of it[2] if he considers the following: (1) the deadly poison in the fangs of a serpent never kills the serpent; (2) living organisms crawling in fermented wine never get drunk; (3) the malarial germs in the mosquitoes do not attack them with shivering fevers. THE *SWABHAVA* OF EACH ONE CANNOT DESTROY HIM! If the poison is drawn from the fangs and wine is poisoned, the crawling organisms die. Similarly, if the *Kshatriyas* were to perform the duties prescribed for the *Brahmana*-type of equipment, they would be only doing *harakiri*. Arjuna was a *Kshatriya*; hence retiring from the battlefield to a jungle for meditation would have destroyed him.

In short, it is no use employing our minds in fields which are contrary to our nature. Everyone has a precise place in the scheme of created things. Each one has his own importance and none is to be despised, for, each can do something which the others cannot do so well. There is no redundancy in the Lord's creation; not even a single blade of grass, anywhere, at any time, is unnecessarily created!

Refer 'General Introduction' to the *Geeta*.

[2] The logic behind the assertion in the stanza is this, that they performing one's own duties ordained by one's own nature, the individual comes to no evil.

Everything has a purpose. Not only the good but the bad also are His manifestations and serve His purpose. The Pandavas' glory is, no doubt, great, but the manifestation of the wickedness in the Kauravas is also the glory of His creation. Without the latter, the history of the former would not have been complete. Nothing is to be condemned; none to be despised. Every thing is He. And He alone IS.

BUT IF THE DUTY TO WHICH WE ARE BOUND IS RIDDLED WITH EVIL, ARE WE TO FOLLOW IT? KRISHNA ANSWERS:

48. *One should not abandon, O Kaunteya, the duty to which one is born, though faulty; for, are not all undertakings enveloped by evil, as fire by smoke?*

After explaining this much about the nature (*swabhava*) and the corresponding station-in-life (*swadharma*), Krishna builds up the idea to a subtle climax. His advice is general and it is meant for all people, of all times, in all situations. Even when the work so ordained by the existing *vasanas* (*sahajam karma*) is full of evil (*sadosham*), Krishna's advice is that one should not relinquish it (*na-tyajet*).

Superficially reading this declaration in a hurry, one is apt to think that this is not spirituality. But to a careful thinker, the term 'born with' (*sahajam*) solves the riddle. There is an ocean of difference between the meanings of the phrases 'BORN WITH' and 'BORN INTO'.

सहजं कर्म कौन्तेय सदोषमपि न त्यजेत् ।
सर्वारम्भा हि दोषेण धूमेनाग्निरिवावृता: ॥ ४८ ॥
sahajaṁ karma kaunteya sadoṣamapi na tyajet
sarvārambhā hi doṣeṇa dhūmenāgnirivāvṛtāḥ 48.

There are two forces that control and guide, define and determine, our actions: (i) the impulses brought forth by the pressure of the mental temperaments within; and (ii) the pressure of environments that tickles new temptations in ourselves. One is to follow faithfully, the subjective *vasanas*, even if they be defective. But at the same time, we must courageously renounce all the demands that the objective world makes upon us from without.

The *vasanas* one is BORN WITH are to be lived through, without ego and desire; while the *vasana*-creating atmosphere INTO which one is born should not be allowed to contaminate one's personality. Krishna is very careful in indicating that a spiritual seeker must constantly strive hard to stand apart from the shackling effects of the environments. According to the *Geeta,* man is the master of circumstances. To the extent he comes to assert this mastery, to that extent he is evolved.

IN FACT, 'ARE NOT ALL ACTIONS (WORKS) CLOUDED BY DEFECTS, AS FIRE IS BY THE SMOKE?' Here the term used to indicate 'work' (*arambha*) is very important. This Sanskrit term *Arambha* means 'beginning'. The term was used earlier (XII-16) where also we were asked to 'RENOUNCE THE SENSE OF AGENCY IN ACTIVITY'. When there is an egocentric sense of self-arrogation, the "I-am-the-self" arrogation, the "I-am-the-doer" sense, there is, invariably, creation of new *vasanas* and therefore, it is full of defects (*dosha*).

This defect is as unavoidable as the appearance of smoke in fire. The more an oven is ventilated in the atmospheric air, the less smoky becomes the fire burning therein. The more our inner bosom is ventilated with the Consciousness Divine, the less will the ego assert, and therefore, no defects can pollute the actions. If there be an influx of wrong *vasanas* within, the earlier we exhaust them through 'action' – without any ego or egocentric desire of enjoying their fruits – the quicker shall the load of existing *vasanas* be lifted from our personality.

WHAT IS THE BENEFIT OF THUS ACTING ACCORDING TO THE TEMPERAMENTS WITH WHICH ONE IS BORN?

49. He whose intellect is unattached everywhere, who has subdued his self, from whom desire has fled, he, through renunciation, attains the Supreme State of Freedom from action.

It must be remembered, that the entire *Geeta* is addressed to Prince Arjuna standing confused at the immensity of his duty. He wants to run away into the jungle and live in a spirit of what he understands as 'renunciation'. Lord Krishna's thesis in the entire *Geeta* is that a MERE running away from life and its duties is not *sannyasa* nor is it renunciation. Here, in the stanza, the Lord is defining the state-of-Actionlessness (*Naishkarmya-Siddhi*). This state is reached when we do not identify ourselves with the equipments of matter which are the instrutments of perception, the three instruments of false interpretation of Truth (Body, Mind and Intellect). To regain our life in Pure Consciousness is the Supreme State.

असक्तबुद्धिः सर्वत्र जितात्मा विगतस्पृहः ।
नैष्कर्म्यसिद्धिं परमां संन्यासेनाधिगच्छति ॥ ४९ ॥

asaktabuddhiḥ sarvatra jitātmā vigataspṛhaḥ
naiṣkamryasiddhiṁ paramāṁ sannyāsenādhigacchati 49.

* Ego is the perceiver, the feeler, the thinker, who is the produce of the past experiences, at the body, mind, and intellect levels.

When we forget our spiritual dignity, the misconception of the ego* arises; we lose our real personality and come to believe that we are merely the limited ego. Such self-forgetfulness can be observed in any drunken reveller. He forgets his individual personality and status in life and assumes to himself a false identity and continues to be in it as long as he is in a state of intoxication. In his false concept of himself the drunken fool acts, disgracing his education and station in life.

The ego arises when we are ignorant and forgetful of our spiritual nature. When this 'ignorance' is ended, there is the experience of the Infinite Bliss of the All-Full-Consciousness. Naturally, there is no want felt, and therefore, no desire can arise. When desires are absent, the thought-breeding end. When thoughts are dried up, actions, which are the parade of thoughts, marching out through the archway of the body, are no more. This state is called 'ACTIONLESSNESS' – *Naishkarmya Siddhi*.

The Supreme state described so elaborately in the *Upanishadic* literature and indicated here by the technical term '*Naishkarmaya-Siddhi*', is that 'WISE' state-of-being wherein there is no 'ignorance'. DESIRES are the children of 'ignorance'; THOUGHTS arise from desires; ACTIONS are thoughts expressed in the outer world. In the spirituo-psychology of *Vedanta* we may thus say that 'knowledge' of the Spirit, ends 'ignorance', and in that state, thoughts and actions cannot be. This is the state of Full Awakening, and with reference to its

---

* Hence the symbolism of clean-shaven head in *Sannyasa*. There is also a symbolism in keeping a tuft on the crown of the head before a *Brahmana*-boy is taken near (*Upanayana*) a teacher; the *Brahmachari* has snapped off all his other endless attachments, and maintains only single faithful attachment to the Supreme.

previous conditions as expressed and manifested through the body, this condition is indicated as 'ACTIONLESSNESS' or 'THOUGHTLESSNESS' or 'DESIRELESSNESS'.

The *Geetacharya* , in this stanza, declares that this state-of-Perfection, defined as the state-of-Actionlessness, cannot be gained by a cheap and ignominious escape from the fields of life's activities. Making use of the fields, we must gain in purity by getting rid of the existing *vasanas*, through selfless activities, which are prescribed to each one of us according to the type to which we naturally belong. Arjuna being a *'Kshatriya'*, his duty is to fight; and by fighting alone will he exhaust his *vasanas*. By the exhaustion of the *vasanas* alone can one hope to reach the Supreme state of Pure Awareness.

AN INTELLECT UNATTACHED EVERYWHERE (*Asakta-Buddhih Sarvatra*)—An intellect that is attached to sensuous things of the world outside knows no peace within itself. It gets agitated and the frail body gets shattered as the fuming mind escapes through it in its hunt for satisfaction among the sense-objects. A 'clean-shaven' intellect',* devoid of all the cobwebs of attachments with the equipments of perception, feeling and thinking, and the equipment of perceptions, feeling and thinking, and their respective objects perceived, felt or thought of, is the vehicle that stands dissolved, revealing THAT which pulsates through them all. This is the true state-of-Actionlessness and a man who has earlier disciplined his intellect alone can attain it.

In the case of Arjuna, his tall talks of detachment and renunciation were false urges of escapism paraded as an angelic urge. His *Sannyasa* arose out of his 'attachment' to his kith and kin, while true *Sannyasa* must arise out of 'detachment'.

ONE WHO HAS SUBDUED HIS EGO (*Jitatma*) – An intellect of complete detachment is an impossible dream. The seeker subdues his heart which ever seeks its flickering joys in sense-gratifications. This self-mastery of the mind is impossible as long as there are even the minutest traces of desire in him. One from whom all desires have fled (*Vigatasprihah*) alone can subdue the mind, and such a seeker alone can accomplish the state of complete detachment of his intellect from the world of sense-objects.

Mind is the seat of all vanities of agency, like "I am the doer" sense (*kartritwa-bhavanaa*). The intellect is the seat of all false arrogations that "I-am-the-enjoyer" (*Bhoktritwa- bhaavana*). These two together make up the ego, and it is fed, nurtured and nourished by its clinging attachments (*spriha*) to the joy that is in the objects of the world outside. By correct analysis and investigations, when the '*spriha*' is dried up, both the senses of enjoyership and doership will get steadily sublimated, leaving behind the Infinite experience of the Self. The *Geeta* is never tired of repeating that self-restraint and freedom from desire are the unavoidable prerequisites for spiritual growth. Herein, we have a beautiful example of explaining the Supreme Goal, not in achieving any Higher state, but as the state of complete detachment from the lower urges.

FREEDOM FROM ACTION IS A CONDITION IN WHICH ALONE THE EXPERIENCES OF THE SUPREME BEING CAN RUSH IN. HOW? LEARN THIS FROM ME IN BRIEF:

50. *How he, who has attained perfection, reaches BRAHMAN (the Eternal), that in brief do you learn from Me, O! Kaunteya, that Supreme state-of-knowledge.*

Here we are told how to get detached from the wrong tendencies in life, and how, to that extent, we attain serenity and composure. Detachment from matter-hallucinations itself is the rediscovery of the spiritual beauty. The following few stanzas make a beautiful section of this chapter which refreshingly reminds us of the various descriptions of a man-of-Perfection that were given earlier, throughout the Lord's Song. When we thus get purified, meaning, when the intellect becomes free from its attachments, and the mind and body come well under the control of the intellect, then alone are we fit for the path-of-Meditation, which is the process of accomplishing and fulfilling renunciation of the lower, base, ego-sense.

It is not possible to renounce all attachments completely, unless one experiences the Truth, and thereby becomes the Infinite Self. Our attempt now is to reduce our attachments to the irreducible minimum, leaving but the thinnest film of 'ignorance' veiling the Supreme. Krishna says here, "LEARN THAT FROM ME IN BRIEF,* O, son of Kunti, how to remove this last lingering film of 'ignorance' and thereby get permanently established in that Supreme God-consciousness, which is the Self:"

सिद्धिं प्राप्तो यथा ब्रह्म तथाप्नोति निबोध मे |
समासेनैव कौन्तेय निष्ठा ज्ञानस्य या परा || ५० ||

siddhiṁ prāpto yathā brahma tathāpnoti nibodha me
samāsenaiva kaunteya niṣṭhā jñānasya ya parā 50.

THE TECHNIQUE-OF-MEDITATION IS BEING DESCRIBED NOW; THIS AND THE FOLLOWING TWO STANZAS EXPLAIN WHAT SHOULD BE THE CONDITION OF THE EQUIPMENTS OF PERCEPTION, FEELING, AND THINKING AT THE TIME OF PERFECT MEDITATION:

51. *Endowed with a pure intellect; controlling the self by firmness; relinquishing sound and other objects; and abandoning attraction and hatred;*

ENDOWED WITH PURE UNDERSTANDING—An intellect that has grown to remain without *vasanas*.* An intellect that has thus purified itself of all its tendencies of joy-hunting is indicated here as pure (*Vishuddha*) understanding.

CONTROLLING THE MIND AND THE SENSE WITH FORTITUDE—These two sabotage the harmony and balance in a meditator when he is at his seat of meditation. At that moment the sense-organs receive a rush of stimuli with which they can disturb the music of meditation in the mind; or, often the mind can topple down from its steady concentration, by itself remembering its own experiences of the past. By controlling both these, which were earlier described as *shama* and *dama*, the

---

बुद्ध्या विशुद्धया युक्तो धृत्यात्मानं नियम्य च।
शब्दादीन्विषयांस्त्यक्त्वा रागद्वेषौ व्युदस्य च ॥ ५१ ॥

buddhayā yukto dhṛtyātmānaṁ niyamya ca
śabdādīnviṣayāṁstyaktavā rāgadveṣau vyudasya ca 51.

* The Lord promises here that He is going to explain this aspect of Self-knowledge (*Adhyatma Vidya*) in brief, because, this technique of Meditation for the final release was exhaustively explained earlier in Chapter V and VI.

* *Vasanas* – meaning 'tendencies' of acquiring, possessing and enjoying sense-objects, that had once supplied a sort of satisfaction.

seeker comes to tune himself up properly. He becomes invulnerable to all such attacks.

The idea of controlling the mind and sense-organs described in the earlier epithet is clearly elucidated in the second line of the stanza. RENOUNCING SENSE-OBJECTS – controlling the sense-organs means allowing none of the stimuli such as sound, form, touch, taste or smell to infiltrate through their respective gateways of ears, eyes, skin, tongue and the nose. When thus a complete wall-of-understanding has been built around the mind, protecting it from any onslaught from the outer world, the mind can, of its own accord, either dance in some REMEMBERED joy, or sob in grief at some EXPECTED sorrow – because of its likes and dislikes, loves and hates. Therefore, these instinctive impulses of the mind are also to be controlled.

To summarise, a meditator is one who has: (1) an intellect purified of all its extrovert desires; (2) a mind, together with the sense-organs, brought well under the control of this intellect, so purified; (3) the sense-organs no more contacting the sense-objects; and (4) a mind that has given up its ideas of likes and dislikes. It is this individual who becomes a successful meditator.

AGAIN:

52. *Dwelling in solitude; eating but little; speech, body and mind subdued; always engaged in meditation and concentration; taking refuge in dispassion;*

विविक्तसेवी लघ्वाशी यतवाक्कायमानस: ।
ध्यानयोगपरो नित्यं वैराग्यं समुपाश्रित: ॥ ५२ ॥

viviktasevī laghvāśī yatavākkāyamānasaḥ
dhyānayogaparo nityaṁ vairajyaṁ samupāśritaḥ 52.

* Mentioned and exhaustively explained by us in ibid., Verse 51

DWELLING IN SOLITUDE (*Vivikta-Sevee*)—A seeker who has developed all the above-mentioned* physical, mental and intellectual adjustments, must now seek a sequestered spot of loneliness. This does not mean that he must move out of a town to a jungle. The term indicates only a spot 'wherein there is the least disturbance'. Even in the midst of a market there are moments when it is deserted and quiet. If the seeker is sincere, he can discover such moments of complete solitude under his own roof.

EATING BUT LITTLE—Over-indulgence and stuffing oneself with highly nutritive food is fattening the body and thickening the subtlety of one's intellectual activities. Temperance is the law for all spiritual students (VI-17).

CONTROLLING SPEECH, BODY AND MIND—The mind cannot be subdued unless the body is brought under its command. The body is constituted of the sense-organs of perception and action. The grossest manifestation of the mind is action, and to control action is to discipline the mind. The term SPEECH used here indicates all sense-organs-of-action and their functions; and the term BODY represents the organs-of-perception and all their activities of perceiving their respective objects. Unless these two sets of organs are controlled, the mind cannot be subdued.

In fact, the mind ITSELF, at the body-level, becomes the sense-organs, and the mind projected away from the body is the great universe of sense-objects. When the mind, playing through the body, identifies itself with its own projections - the objects – it is called PERCEPTION; and when it comes in contact with the world-of-objects seeking satisfaction and entertainment, it is called ACTION. Disciplining action and regulating perception - in short, eliminating the egocentric attitude in all our perceptions, in all our relationships with the world-of-objects, is what is advised here.

EVER ENGAGED IN MEDITATION—Controlling the actions and perceptions of the mind is not possible as long as the mind is constantly flowing out through the sense-organs towards the sense-objects. Seeking sense-gratifications, the mind is in a constant state of agitation. To quieten such a mind, it is necessary that we must give it some point-of-contemplation wherein, as it engages itself more and more, it shall discover consummate happiness and get sufficiently disengaged from everything else. Diverting the mind from the world of sense-objects and maintaining it in a steady flow towards contemplation of the Lord in an utter attitude of identification, is called MEDITATION. To be steadily in a state of such an all-consuming dedication unto a nobler and higher ideal is the method of cooling down the mind's boiling lust for sense-enjoyments.

POSSESSED OF DISPASSION—Dispassion is *vairagya*. It is not a mere self-denial of any object of enchantment, but it is a state when the mind rebounds upon itself from the objects as a result of its discovery that the objects contain no glow of happiness. The essence of dispassion is not in our running away from the object; from a truly dispassionate man, the objects run away in inexplicable despair.

When the old interests of a person die away and when he is ordered by new intellectual visions, new interests rise up in his mind; then the old world-of-objects around him suddenly retires, yielding place to the new set of things that he has willed around him by his newly developed mind. As long as I was a vicious man, sensuous friends and pleasure-seekers crowded my drawing room; when I changed my way-of-life and took to serious social work and political activities, the group of idlers went away yielding their places to politicians and social workers. After a time I grew in my mental make-up, and so, in my spiritual interests, even these politicians with their power-politics, and the social workers with their unspeakable jealousies and rivalries retired, yielding their places to men of thought and spiritual benediction. This is a typical example of how, as a mind grows, it leaves its old toys behind and enters totally into a greater field of the nobler gains of life.

To sum up, a true seeker of the Higher Life must seek solitude, live in temperance, subdue his speech, body and mind, and must live in a spirit of dispassion, a true life of aspiration to heave himself towards the ideal.

THESE EFFORTS CAN BUILD UP A TEMPLE OF SUCCESS ONLY WHEN THE INNER PERSONALITY HAS A DEEP FOUNDATION UPON CERTAIN ENDURING VALUES OF LIFE. THESE ARE ENUMERATED IN THE FOLLOWING:

53. *Having abandoned egoism, power, arrogance, desire, anger and aggrandisement, and freed from the notion of 'mine', and therefore peaceful -- he is fit to become BRAHMAN.*

If the preceding verse indicated things that are to be acquired and brought about in the relatively outer surfaces of the meditator's personality, here we have a list of things which are to be renounced from the inner core of the meditator's personality. Here are the enduring values of life a meditator must learn to live.

अहंकारं बलं दर्पं कामं क्रोधं परिग्रहम् ।
विमुच्य निर्ममः शान्तो ब्रह्मभूयाय कल्पते ॥ ५३ ॥

ahaṅkāraṁ balaṁ sarpaṁ kāmaṁ krodhaṁ parigraham
vimucya nirmamaḥ śānto brahmabhūyāya kalpate 53.

The items enumerated in the stanza are not, in fact, so many different items, but they are all different manifestations of one and the same wrong notion, namely the "I-act-mentality" (*Ahamkara*). When this 'sense-of-agency' develops, egocentric vanities intensify within our bosom, and they manifest as 'power' (*Balam*) – the 'power' to strive and struggle, sweat and strain, to fulfil passions and desires. A powerful ego will, with each success in the sensuous world, gather to itself more and more 'pride' or 'arrogance' (*Darpam*).

To an individual personality, working under the influence of both power and arrogance, lust and anger (*Kama* and *Krodha*) are but natural, and thereafter, he becomes a mad machine of restlessness within and of disturbances around, ever anxiously bearing himself down upon the society in order that he may, by means fair or foul, acquire, possess and aggrandise the objects of his fancy, indicated here by the term 'aggrandisement' (*Parigraha*).

The six items listed above are nothing but manifestations of the sense-of-agency – the "I-act-mentality" (*Ahamkara*). Krishna asks the meditator to forsake these and thus to immediately become egoless (*Nirmamah*) and peaceful (*Shantah*). This is not the peace of the grave nor the quiet of the desert; this is the peace that arises out of the fullness of 'wisdom', out of our absolute satisfaction experienced in the Realm-of-Perfection.

All restlessness is caused by the ego and its onward rush towards finite objects, seeking among the ephemeral, a

---

[1] Otherwise explained as the "I-do-mentality" (*Kartritwa-Bhaavana*).

[2] This is the secret psychology behind such *Sadhakas* or monks, who, after an initial period of renunciation and divine seeking, suddenly come to leave their life of self-control or the sacred robes, to live a sensuous life. The "I-enjoy-mentality" of the ego has not been fully transcended by them during their spiritual practices.

satisfaction and joy that are permanent and enduring. When this sense-of-agency and endless seeking of sense-gratifications have been renounced, the seeker (*sadhaka*) experiences a relative quiet within his bosom. He who is tuned thus, through understanding and discipline, can discover in himself the required balance and equipoise to rocket his total personality into the higher climbs of 'conscious unfoldment'. The stanza does not say that such an individual has reached Perfection, but it definitely says that "HE IS FIT TO BECOME BRAHMAN". The above is but a preliminary preparation for the final realisation.

WHAT THEN IS THE NEXT STAGE OF DEVELOPMENT? THE *GEETA* EXPLAINS:

54. *Becoming BRAHMAN, serene in the Self, he neither grieves nor desires; the same to all beings, he obtains a supreme devotion towards Me.*

After liquidating the ego and its manifestations– enumerated in the preceding stanza as power, pride, lust, passion and sense of possession – the seeker comes to experience a relatively greater peace within, as he is released from all the confusions generally created by the psychological maladjustments and intellectual false evaluations of life. This newly discovered inner tranquillity, no doubt artificially propped up for the time being by severe self-discipline, should be positively reinforced by definite efforts and constant vigilance.

ब्रह्मभूत: प्रसन्नात्मा न शोचति न काङ्क्षति ।
सम: सर्वेषु भूतेषु मद्भक्तिं लभते पराम् ॥ ५४ ॥

brahmabhūtaḥ prasannātmā na śocati na kāṅkṣati
samaḥ sarveṣū bhūteṣu madbhaktiṁ labhate parām 54.

With constant self-effort, relative peace in the mind is to be maintained for longer periods of time and zealously guarded. Joys and sorrows will be constantly reaching our bosom from the outer world; we are helpless before them. For, even when the sense-of-agency[1] has been renounced, the other aspect of the ego, "I-enjoy-mentality" (*Bhoktritwa-bhaavana*) will assert itself and poison the mind of the meditator. A worm cut into two pieces becomes two separate, independent living worms ere long. So too, if one aspect of the ego, the "I-do-mentality" is conquered, we must equally attend to the destruction of the other aspect of the ego, the "I-enjoy-mentality"; or else, the surviving part will revive within a very short time and we shall discover a healthier ego, potentially more powerful, dangerously rising out of the seemingly dead individuality.[2]

One who has read well, reflected upon and understood the theme of the Absolute Reality as discussed in the scriptures, is indicated here by the term '*Brahma-Bhootah*' This word employed in this verse should not be construed as 'one who has become *Brahman*'. It can only mean "one who has convinced oneself of the existence and nature of the Reality as discussed in the Scriptures". Once this Spiritual Truth is understood, the student necessarily becomes less agitated, because, all disturbances enter our life through our identification with the equipments-of-experiences only. To the extent an intellect realises the existence of the diviner aspect in it, and so automatically withdraws its all-out clinging to the matter-realm, to that extent it is not disturbed by the objects of perception, feeling and thought. Thus it discovers a growing tranquillity (*Prasannatma*) within itself.

A seeker who has gained the 'knowledge' of *Brahman* through STUDY, and makes it his own through REFLECTION, gains the tranquillity of composure as a result of his understanding, and therefore experiences a partial liquidation of his ego-sense. Thereby he discovers in himself the courage to stand apart, both from grief and desire. He grieves not (*Na shochati*) because he feels no incompleteness in himself, as he used to feel in the earlier days of his arrogant ego. Since there is no sense of imperfection, his intellect no longer spins new and novel plans for satisfactions and temporary gratifications, which are called desires. Naturally, one who grieves not in life desires not (*Na Kankshati*) for the possession of anything to make his happiness complete.

A tranquil seeker—who, in his understanding, comes to desire nothing and has developed an independent source of happiness which is free from the presence or the absence of any external environment -- lives in the world, with a totally new set of values of life, in which, according to him, there is nothing but the constant experience of the Divine presence. Naturally, he develops an equanimity of vision (V-18, 19 and 20).

THIS TYPE OF AN INDIVIDUAL ATTAINS SUPREME DEVOTION UNTO ME—Earlier, an entire chapter has been devoted to the discussion on devotion (Ch. XII) wherein we found that, according to the Scripture, devotion is measured by our sense of identification with the Higher Ideal. In order to identify with the Infinite Truth, the seeker must have a definite amount of detachment from his usual channels of dissipation, both in the outer world and the realms within.

The previous verse indicated the methods of detachment and it was said that he who has accomplished them in his inner composition is the only one who is capable of striving for and succeeding in a true identification with the play of the Infinite in and through the finite. The expansiveness of vision, the catholicity of love and the release from sense preoccupation – all these are necessary in order to produce in the seeker, supreme love for the Lord. There is yet another stage in one's pilgrimage to Truth.

WHAT THEN IS THE NEXT STAGE?

55. *By devotion he knows Me in Essence, what and who I am; then, having known Me in My Essence, he forthwith enters into the Supreme.*

BY DEVOTION HE COMES TO KNOW ME—Devotion, as we have explained, is 'love for the Supreme'. Love is measured by the degree of identification the lover maintains with the beloved. When an egocentric individuality, having made all the above adjustments, increasingly seeks and discovers its identity with the Self, it comes to experience the true nature of the Self more and more clearly. Such a seeker comes to understand "WHAT AND WHO I AM".

In the entire *Geeta,* the first person singular is used by the Lord to indicate the Supreme Goal. It is not Lord Krishna, as an individual person who is indicated by the terms 'I' and 'Me' as used in these discourses. Remember, this is the Lord's own Song, sung to revive His devotees, and the pronouns used here represent the *Paramatman*. To know the Self means to know both Its nature and identity. These are the topics in all scriptures. But the scriptural study gives us only an intellectual comprehension of Truth and not its Essence (*Tattwatah*), a

---

भक्त्या मामभिजानाति यावान्यश्चास्मि तत्त्वतः ।
ततो मां तत्त्वतो ज्ञात्वा विशते तदनन्तरम् ॥ ५५ ॥
bhaktayā māmabhijānāti yāvānyaścāsmi tattvataḥ
tato māṁ tattvato jñātvā viśate tadanantaram 55.

spiritual apprehension of Truth as a lived experience.

THEN, HAVING KNOWN ME IN ESSENCE—When this experience comes through a slow and steady unfoldment of the light-of-Consciousness, through the dropping of the veils of 'ignorance' created by our identifications with the body, we come to apprehend, IN TOTO, the Infinite. The individuality or the ego, ends and "HE THEREAFTER ENTERS ME".

The ENTRY mentioned here is not like that of a man entering a structure, a house separate from himself. There is no ego to enter into the plane of God-consciousness. The term ENTRY is used here exactly in the same fashion as 'the dreamer ENTERS the waking state'. The dreamer cannot retain his own individuality when he ENTERS the waking world, but he himself becomes the 'waker'. Similarly, when the ego ENTERS God-consciousness, the individuality cannot retain itself as such. The misconception that he is an individual ends and he rediscovers, becomes or awakens to, the Infinite *Brahmanhood* – the State of Krishna-Consciousness.

DEVOTION FOR THE LORD IS NEVER COMPLETE WITHOUT SERVICE TO THE LIVING WORLD OF CREATURES:

---

* *Mad-bhaktim Labhate Param* – Stanza 54
Maam Vishate tad-anantaram – Stanza 55
Aapnoti Shashwata Padam Avyayam – Stanza 56

56. *Doing all actions, always taking refuge in Me, by My grace he obtains the Eternal, Indestructible State or Abode.*

The philosophy of the *Geeta* is extremely dynamic. The Song of the Lord is an innocent-looking magazine of power which can be detonated by correct understanding. The warmth of living makes it explode, blasting the crust of ignorance that has grown around the noble personality and its divine possibilities in the student.

Devotion to the Lord (*Bhakti*), in the *Geeta,* is not a mere passive surrender unto the ideal, nor a mere physical ritualism. Lord Krishna insists, not only upon our identification with the Higher through an intelligent process of detachment, from both the senses, of AGENCY and ENJOYMENT, but also upon the understanding and the inner experience positively brought out in all our contacts with the outer world, in all our relationships.

Religion, to Lord Krishna, is not fulfilled by a mere withdrawal from the outer world of sense objects, but in a definite comeback into the world, bringing into it the fragrance of peace and joy of the yonder, to brighten and beautify the drab, inert objects that constitute the world. Therefore, after describing one who can be considered as the higher devotee, in this stanza, Krishna now adds another condition to be fulfilled by all seekers.

The *Geetaacharya* never wants to receive any devotee at His gate, nor will He give an audience to anyone, unless the seeker

---

सर्वकर्माण्यपि सदा कुर्वाणो मद्व्यपाश्रयः ।
मत्प्रसादादवाप्नोति शाश्वतं पदमव्ययम् ॥ ५६ ॥

sarvakarmāṇyapi sada kurvāṇo madvayapāśrayaḥ
matprasādādavāpnoti śāśvataṁ padamavyayam 56.

carries the passport of selfless service to society – "PERFORMING CONTINUOUSLY ALL ACTIONS, ALWAYS TAKING REFUGE IN ME".

In order to serve without the 'sense-of-agency', the practical method is "TAKE REFUGE IN ME". Such a seeker, who is constantly working in fulfilling his obligatory duties to society and towards himself has 'My grace' (*Mat prasada*).

The Supreme has no existence apart from His Grace; He is His Grace, His Grace is He. The Grace of the Self, therefore, means more and more the play of divine Consciousness in and through the personality layers in the individual. In an individual, to the extent his mind and intellect are available, in their discipline to be ruled over by spiritual truth, to that extent he is under the blessing of His Grace.

HE ATTAINS THE ETERNAL IMMUTABLE STATE— When thus working in the world, without the sense of agency and enjoyment, the existing *vasanas* become exhausted and the ego gets eliminated. Awakening thus from the delusory projections of the ego, the individual attains the state of Pure Consciousness and comes to live thereafter the Eternal, Immortal State -- THE KRISHNA-STATE OF PERFECTION.

In the preceding three stanzas the 'Paths' of Knowledge, Devotion and Action are indicated, and in all of them the same goal of realising the seeker's oneness with the Supreme has been indicated.* Integral *sadhana* is the core of the *Geeta* technique. To synthesize the methods of Work, Devotion and Knowledge is at once the discipline of the body, mind, and intellect. For, all disciplines PURSUED AT THE BODY LEVEL, in order to control the mind and turn it towards the ideal, are called *Karma Yoga;* all methods of channelising emotions in order to DISCIPLINE

THE MIND to contemplate upon the Higher are called *Bhakti Yoga* and all study and reflection, detachment and meditation, PRACTISED AT THE INTELLECTUAL LEVEL, whereby, again the mind is lifted to the realm of the silent experience of its own Infinitude are called *Jnana Yoga*. To practise all the three during our life is to discipline all the three layers in us. Thus, the philosophy of total spiritual transformation of the perceiver, the feeler and the thinker, all at once, is the prime contribution that the *Geeta* has to make to the timeless tradition of the Hindu culture, as available for us in the *Upanishads*.

THEREFORE:

57. *Mentally renouncing all actions in Me, having Me as the Highest Goal, resorting to the YOGA-of-discrimination, ever fix your mind in Me.*

RENOUNCING MENTALLY ALL DEEDS TO ME—Both the ego and the egocentric anxieties for enjoying are to be renounced at the altar of the Lord, and thus to act in the world is the 'path', through which a man of action reaches the greater cultural climes. This idea of surrender has been discussed earlier,

---

चेतसा सर्वकर्माणि मयि संन्यस्य मत्परः ।
बुद्धियोगमुपाश्रित्य मच्चित्तः सततं भव ॥ ५७ ॥

cetasā sarvakarmāṇi mayi sannyasya matparaḥ
buddhiyogamupāśritya maccittaḥ satatam bhava 57.

* Refer commentaries on the most crucial stanza in the *Geeta* (III-30)

* II-39, wherein we have exhaustively described *Buddhi Yoga*.

* This statement is often misunderstood by the hasty generation that the 'laws of religion' are tyrannical. A little thought will clear this misunderstanding. If the scientific discoveries in the world have brought the forces of nature to serve man's needs, it is only because the scientists have discovered the laws that govern them, and the generation has condescended to follow these laws implicitly.

very exhaustively.* This spirit of surrender can come only when the student has infinite courage to maintain a steady aspiration for "HAVING ME AS THE HIGHEST GOAL". The mind needs a positive hold upon something, before it can be persuaded to leave its present props.

RESORTING TO *Buddhi Yoga*—The intellect's main function is discrimination. To discriminate the false from the true, and to fix ourselves on the path of seeking the true, is called *Buddhi Yoga*. Controlling life and regulating its movements through discrimination is *Karma Yoga*. And thus the term *Buddhi Yoga* is an original coined-word, met with only in the *Geeta*, to indicate in essence the path of Selfless-Action. It has been used in the very early portions of the *Geeta** and there it has been very exhaustively explained.

PLEASE EVER FIX YOUR MIND UPON ME—One who has fixed Krishna-*Tattwa* as the goal of his life, one who surrenders himself mentally at all times at this altar, and serves all His creatures, one who ever discriminates and avoids all undivine thoughts and egocentric self-assertions; such a one alone can naturally come to fix his thoughts constantly upon the Lord.

It is an eternal law of mental life that "AS WE THINK SO WE BECOME". A devotee who has thus come to live all his activities in dedication to his goal, the Krishna-Consciousness, must necessarily come to live as Krishna, and experience the Eternal, Immutable, state of the Self.

SUPPOSING ONE REFUSES TO FOLLOW THIS SEEMINGLY ARDUOUS 'PATH,' WHAT WOULD BE HIS CONDITION? LISTEN:

58. *Fixing your mind upon Me, you shall, by My grace, overcome all obstacles, but if, from egoism, you will not hear Me, you shall perish.*

Lord Krishna, in essence, says: "By your thoughts, renounce all your activities in Me". All activities in the world are only expressions of the Divine Consciousness flashing Its brilliance through the body. In all activities be conscious of the Lord, without Whom no action is ever possible. Keep Him as your Goal.

Make your intellect constantly aware of this Lord of all actions. Gradually, the mind and the body will begin to work under the command of such an inspired intellect.

How will this constant remembrance of the Lord help? This is now being answered. Krishna says: "HE, WHO HAS COMPLETELY FIXED ALL HIS THOUGHTS UPON ME, WILL CROSS OVER ALL DIFFICULTIES BY MY GRACE". Most of our obstacles in life are imaginary; created by false fears and deceitful anxieties of our own confused mind. The 'grace' referred to here is 'the result accrued in our mind when it is properly tuned up to and peacefully settled in contemplation upon the Infinite'. It does not mean any special consideration shown by the all-loving Lord to some rare persons of His own choice. The Grace of the all-pervading is present everywhere because Grace is His form. Just as the ever-present sunlight on a bright day cannot illumine my room as long as the windows

---

मच्चित्तः सर्वदुर्गाणि मत्प्रसादात्तरिष्यसि ।
अथ चेत्त्वमहङ्काकारान्न श्रोष्यसि विनङ्क्ष्यसि ॥ ५८ ॥

maccittaḥ sarvadurgāṇi matprasādāttariṣyasi
atha cettvamahaṅkārānna śroṣyasi vinaṅkṣyasi 58.

are closed, so too, the harmony and joy of life of the Infinite cannot penetrate into our life, as long as the windows of discrimination in us are tightly shut. To the extent the windows of my room are opened, to that extent the room is flooded by the sunlight; to the extent a seeker pursues his *sadhana* and brings about the above-mentioned adjustments, to that extent the Grace of the Self shall flood his within.

In the second line of the verse, the Lord warns against all those who, in their utter ignorance, disobey this Law-of-Life. Natural laws are irrevocable; they have neither eyes, nor ears. They just continue in their own rhythm and that man is happy who discovers the law and obeys it implicitly.*

BUT IF, FROM EGOISM, YOU WILL NOT HEAR ME, YOU SHALL PERISH—This is not a threat hurled down upon mankind by a tyrannical power, to frighten the human beings into obedience. This is not comparable with the threat of hell held out by other religions. This is a mere statement of fact; even if Newton himself were to jump from the third floor balcony of his house, the gravitational force would indeed, act upon him also! There is an inevitability in nature's laws. Man is free to choose freedom or bondage. The path of freedom is described above, and in this open and sincere statement, the Lord is only showing great anxiety, not to mince matters, but to be callously frank in His expressions.

Guidance to this true way-of-life always comes to us from the depth of our nature, expressed in the language of the soft, small voice of the within. But man's ego and egocentric desires force him to disobey the ringing voice of the Lord and such a

---

* And hence the name of India is 'Bharata'.

one pursues a life of base vulgarity, seeking sense-gratification and ultimately bringing himself down to be punished by his own uncontrolled emotions and unchastened ideas. Hence the warning: "YOU SHALL PERISH".

TO WEAVE THE IDEA INTO THE VERY WARP AND WOOF OF ARJUNA'S LIFE, THE LORD SAYS:

59. *Filled with egoism, if you think, "I will not fight", vain is this, your resolve; (for) nature will compel you.*

General statements of truth are too volatile to be retained in one's understanding permanently. But the general statements of life's principles, when woven into the texture of one's own experiences, remain as one's own earned 'knowledge', and they become permanent WISDOM. Therefore, Krishna is trying to bring the philosophical contents of his discourse into the very substance of Arjuna's own immediate problem.

If, due to a sense of self-importance, the self-conceited Arjuna were to think "I WILL NOT FIGHT", he shall be thinking so in vain! The temperament of Arjuna must seek its expression, and being a *Kshatriya* of 'passionate' nature, his *Rajoguna* will assert itself; "NATURE WILL COMPEL YOU". One who has eaten salt must feel terribly thirsty, ere long. The false arguments raised by Arjuna for not fighting the battle are all compromises made by his ego with the situation which he is compelled to face in the crush of events around him.

यदहंकारमाश्रित्य न योत्स्य इति मन्यसे ।
मिथ्यैष व्यवसायस्ते प्रकृतिस्त्वां नियोक्ष्यति ॥ ५९ ॥

yadahaṅkāramāśritya na yotsya iti manyase
mithyaiṣa vyavasāyaste prakṛtistvāṁ niyokṣyati 59.

Even if he were to follow his temporary attitude of escapism and desist from fighting, it is a law of nature that his mental temperament would assert itself at a later period, when, alas! he may not have the field to express himself in and exhaust his *vasanas*.

ALSO BECAUSE OF THE FOLLOWING REASON, "YOU MUST FIGHT".

60. *O son of Kunti, bound by your own KARMA (action) born of your own nature, that which, through delusion you wish not to do, even that you shall do, helplessly.*

Continuing, the Lord, in effect, says: "I am asking you to fight, not because I have no personal sympathies for you, but because that is the only course left for you. You have no other choice. Though you now insist that you 'WILL NOT FIGHT', it is merely an illusion. You will have to fight, because, your nature will assert itself."

The actions we do are propelled by our own *vasanas* and they shackle our personality. Arjuna is essentially of the *Rajoguna* type, and therefore, he must fight. The Pandava Prince cannot, all of a sudden, pose to have the beauties of the *sattvic* nature of heart and retire to a solitary place to live a serene life of steady contemplation and come to experience the consequent self-unfoldment.

स्वभावजेन कौन्तेय निबद्धः स्वेन कर्मणा ।
कर्तुं नेच्छसि यन्मोहात्करिष्यस्यवशोऽपि तत् ॥ ६० ॥
svabhāvajena kaunteya nivaddhaḥ svena karmaṇā
kartuṁ necchasi yanmohat kariṣyasyavaśo'pi tat 60.

* *'Samashti-Kaarana-Shareera-Abhimaani – Ishwarah.'*

Because of wrong thinking and miscalculations, Arjuna feels that he does not like war, and therefore, he is not ready to face it. But in spite of his determination, he will be compelled to fight by his own nature, ordered by the existing *vasanas* in him. This is the irrevocable law of life.

He who has no control over his mind becomes a victim of circumstances. He gets thrown up and down by the whim and fancy of things around him. But he who gains inner mastery over the mind and stands firmly rooted and unshaken by the circumstances is the one who will revel (*Rati*) in the Pure Light (*Bha*) of wisdom;* and the country that recognises this culture has acquired its immortal name 'Bharata'.

In the previous two or three stanzas, we are told by Krishna, "REMEMBER ME CONSTANTLY". What does this mean? How should we remember? Does it mean meditating upon the Lord? What should be our relationship with Him? Are we to remember Him as a historical event, or remember Him as intimately connected with us as a 'Presence' expressing Itself at all times in and through us?

ALL THESE QUESTIONS ARE APT TO RISE UP IN THE MIND OF ANY SERIOUS STUDENT. THEY ARE ANSWERED IN THE FOLLOWING:

61. *The Lord dwells in the hearts of all beings, O Arjuna, causing all beings, by His power of illusions, to revolve, as if mounted on a machine.*

ईश्वरः सर्वभूतानां हृद्देशेऽर्जुन तिष्ठति ।
भ्रामयन्सर्वभूतानि यन्त्रारूढानि मायया ॥ ६१ ॥

īśvaraḥ sarvabhūtānāṁ hṛddeśe'rjuna tiṣṭhati
bhrāamayansarvabhūtāni yantrārūḍhāni māyayā 61.

The advice given by the Lord is clear and beyond all shades of doubt. "Remember the Lord", says the *Geetaacharaya*, "as the One who organises, controls and directs all things in the world and without Whose command nothing ever happens. In His 'presence' alone everything can happen; therefore remember Him as *Ishwara*". The steam functioning in the cylinder of the engine is the Lord of the engine, and without it the piston can never move. It is the steam which provides the locomotion and renders the train dynamic.

Do not remember the Lord as merely a personified Power, as *Shiva* in *Kailas*, as *Vishnu* in *Vaikuntha*, as the Father in Heaven etc., but recognise Him as one who dwells in the heart of EVERY CREATURE. Just as the address of a person is given, in order that the seeker of that person may locate the individual in a busy town, so also in order to seek, discover and identify with the Lord, His 'Local address' is being provided here by *Bhagawan* Krishna!

When we say that "THE LORD DWELLS IN THE HEART OF ALL LIVING BEINGS", we do not mean the physical heart. In philosophy the use of the word 'heart' is more figurative than literal.

RESIDING THUS IN THE HEART—meaning, in the mind of one who has cultivated the divine qualities such as love, kindness, patience, cheer, affection, tenderness, forgiveness, charity etc. The Lord lends His Power to all living creatures to

---

* As a contrast to the sceptic, the atheist is one so dull and underdeveloped in his evolution, that the poor man lives a mere animal-life even though he has the physical form of a man. His goal in life is mere satisfaction in momentary joys, gained while he gratifies and soothens his nerve-tips. He has not yet an awakened heart or head, to feel the majesty and glory of life, or to think and question the existence of faith and its basis.

act on. He energizes everyone. Everything revolves around Him - like the unseen hand that manipulates the dolls in the marionette-play. The puppets have no existence, no vitality, no emotions of their own; they are only the expressions of the will and intention of the unseen hand behind them.

It is not the matter in us that moves or becomes conscious of the world of transactions; or else the cucumber and the pumpkin, the corn and the tomato of which our bodies are made, will also have locomotion or Consciousness. When the same vegetables are consumed as food and are digested and assimilated to become part of our physical body, the matter, in contact with the Life-Principle in us becomes vibrant and dynamic, capable of perceiving, feeling and thinking. The spark-of-Life presiding over the body, the Pure Eternal Consciousness, is that which, as it were, vitalises inert matter. Pure Consciousness in itself does not act; but in Its Presence the matter envelopments get vitalised, and then they SEEM to act.

The *Atman*, conditioned by the body, mind and intellect, expresses dynamism and action, and creates what we recognise as the manifested individuality. "The Supreme functioning through the total bodies as the cause of all action" is called *Ishwara*.* Life functioning in each one of us is the master, the controller, the director and the Lord of our individual activities.

The essential Life in all of us is one and the same; therefore, the total Life functions through and manifests as the entire universe, energising all existing equipments. Thus expressing through all activities, is the Lord of the Universe, *Ishwara*. With this understanding, if you read the stanza again, you will comprehend the metaphor employed herein.

IF THERE BE THUS A LORD WITHIN, MEANING A POWER THAT RULES OVER AND GUIDES ALL MY ACTIVITIES, WHAT ARE MY RESPONSIBILITIES AND DUTIES TOWARDS HIM?

62. *Fly unto Him for refuge with all your being, O Bharata; by His grace you shall obtain Supreme Peace (and) the Eternal Abode.*

Such an elaborate description has been given of the Spiritual Presence which vitalises the world-of-matter around man, only to bring about ultimately an evolutionary self-development in the student. The very core of this *Geeta*-philosophy is the theme that is indicated in the opening stanza of the *Ishavasya Upanishad*. "The Infinite Truth pervades everything in the world, and therefore, renouncing all the multiplicity, enjoys the Infinitude, and covet not anybody's wealth."

Recognition of the body through our abject identifications with it creates a false sense of individuality, and it is this 'ego' that suffers and sighs.

The one commandment that has been repeated all through the Divine Song with great insistence is; "Renounce the ego and act". The ego is the cause for all our sense of imperfections and sorrows. To the extent we liquidate this sense of separateness and individuality, to that extent we climb into an experience of greater perfection and joy within ourselves.

Krishna has been advising surrender of the 'ego' unto the Lord by developing a devoted attitude of dedication. Arjuna,

---

तमेव शरणं गच्छ सर्वभावेन भारत ।
तत्प्रसादात्परां शान्तिं स्थानं प्राप्स्यसि शाश्वतम् ॥ ६२ ॥

tameva śaraṇaṁ gaccha sarvabhāvena bhārata
tatprasādatparāṁ śāntiṁ sthānaṁ prāpsyasi śāśvatam 62.

like a true intelligent skeptic, asks: "To which Lord should I renounce all my action; and dedicate all my activities at which altar? Krishna has defined the Infinite Lord in the previous verse, and now, here He advises Arjuna to surrender his 'ego' unto HIM. "FLY UNTO HIM FOR REFUGE WITH ALL YOUR WILL".

Ours is an age of scepticism. The Arjuna of the *Geeta* is rather like a typical representative of our own age in this respect. A sceptic is one who questions the existing beliefs; he wants to be intellectually convinced of the logical grounds upon which the existing beliefs stand.*

Earlier, Krishna has explained to Arjuna what is indicated by the term *Ishwara*. Now the call of the *Geeta* to Arjuna is to surrender himself unto the Lord. The *Geeta* requires all of us to live and act with our hearts resting in self-dedicated surrender to the Consciousness, the harmonious oneness of Life that pulsates everywhere through all equipments. In short, we are asked to identify ourselves with the Spirit rather than the vehicles of Its expression. He who has thus surrendered totally (*Sarva-bhavena*) gains an intellect fully awakened, and thereafter, external circumstances cannot toss and crush his individuality.

The body and mind of such an individual who has learnt ever to keep the refreshing memory of the present cannot make any foolish demands. And when one brings such a brilliant intellect into the affairs of life, all his problems wither away and carpet his path to strive progressively ahead.

To the extent we identify ourselves with Him, to that extent His light and power become ours, and they are called 'His Grace' (*Prasada*). Ere long, as a result of this 'grace' accumulated within, through the integration of the personality and constant surrender of the ego, the individual shall obtain THE SUPREME PEACE, THE ETERNAL RESTING PLACE.

WITH ALL ONE'S BEING (*Sarva-bhavena*)—This surrender unto the Lord should not be a temporary self-deception. We must grow into a consciousness of the Presence of the Divine in all the planes of our existence. To illustrate such a total devotion, we have the examples of Radha, Hanuman, Prahlada, and others. Without bringing all the levels of our being, and all the facets of our personality, into our love for Him, we cannot drown our finite ego-sense into the joyous lap of the Infinite Lord. Thus, a true devotee must reorientate his being and must surrender himself as a willing vehicle for His expression. Then and then alone, all the delusions end, and the mortal gains divine experience, and comes to live fully the State of Immortality of the Godhood.

IN CONCLUSION KRISHNA ADDS:

63. *Thus, the 'Wisdom' which is a greater secret than all secrets, has been declared to you by Me; having reflected upon it fully, you now act as you choose.*

This can be considered as THE CLOSING VERSE of the *Geeta* discourses on the battlefield of Kurukshetra. The word 'thus' (*Iti*) is generally used in Sanskrit to indicate what we mean nowadays, by the phrase 'quotation closes'. The Lord has ended His discourses here.

इति ते ज्ञानमाख्यातं गुह्याद्गुह्यतरं मया ।
विमृश्यैतदशेषेण यथेच्छसि तथा कुरु ॥ ६३ ॥

iti te jñānamākhyātaṁ guhyādguhyataraṁ mayā
vimṛśyaitadaśeṣeṇa yathecchasi tathā kuru 63.

A GREATER SECRET THAN ALL SECRETS (*Guhyat-Guhyataram*)—A secret can be so called only as long as it is not divulged. The moment we come to know of a thing it is no longer a secret at all. The spiritual truth and the right way-of-living as discussed in the *Geeta* are termed as 'THE SECRET OF ALL SECRETS' in the sense that it is not easy for one to know the *Geeta* way of dynamic life and the *Geeta* vision-of-Truth, unless one is initiated into them. Even a subtle intellect, very efficient in knowing the material world, both in its arrangement of things and their mutual interaction, must necessarily fail to feel the Presence of this Subtle, Eternal and Infinite Self.

Guhyam—This is a term that has gone into much misuse and abuse in India in our recent past. The term was misconstrued to mean that the spiritual knowledge, which is the core of our culture, is a great secret to be carefully preserved and jealously guarded by the privileged few against anybody else coming to learn it. This orthodox view has no sanction in the scriptures if we read them with the same large-heartedness of the *Rishis* who gave them to us. No doubt, there are persons who have not the intellectual vision, nor the mental steadiness, nor the physical discipline to understand correctly this great Truth in all its subtle implications, and therefore, this is kept away from them lest they should come to harm themselves by falsely living a misunderstood philosophy.

REFLECT OVER IT ALL—Any amount of listening cannot make one gain in 'wisdom'. The knowledge gained through reading or listening must be assimilated and brought within the warp and the woof of our understanding; then alone can knowledge become wisdom. Therefore, Arjuna is asked not to tamely accept Krishna's Song of Life as truth, but he has been asked to independently think over all that the Lord has declared. To put the ideas between the mind and the intellect and to chew them properly is 'reflection'. Each one will have to get his own individual confirmation from his own bosom.

HEREAFTER ACT AS YOU PLEASE—Krishna ultimately leaves the decision to act, the will to live the higher life, to Arjuna's own choice. Each one must reach the Lord by his own free choice. There is no compulsion; for, spontaneity is an invaluable requisite for all new births. Having placed before him all the facts and figures of life, principles and methods of living, Krishna rightly invites Arjuna to make his own independent decision after considering all these points. Spiritual teachers should never compel. And in India there has never been any form of indoctrination.

DEVOTION TO THE LORD IS THE SECRET OF SUCCESS IN '*KARMA YOGA*'. THIS IS EXPLAINED IN THE FOLLOWING:

64. *Hear again My supreme word, most secret of all; because you are My dear beloved, therefore, I will tell you what is good (for you).*

When the Lord has concluded His entire discourse with the words, "THE WISDOM HAS BEEN DECLARED BY ME; NOW DO AS YOU PLEASE", Arjuna, who has been all along devotedly and attentively listening to the expounded philosophy, seems

---

सर्वगुह्यतमं भूयः श्रृणु मे परमं वचः ।
इष्टोऽसि मे दृढमिति ततो वक्ष्यामि ते हितम् ॥ ६४ ॥

sarvaguhyatamaṁ bhūyaḥ śṛṇu me paramaṁ vacaḥ
iṣṭo'si me dṛḍhamiti tato vakṣyāmi te hitam 64.

to register an expression of confusion on his face. Arjuna wants to get some more instructions. The Pandava Prince, perhaps, feels that he has not fully assimilated the deep and intimate philosophy of life as expounded by the Lord. Therefore, Krishna continues, "AGAIN I WILL REPEAT THE PROFOUNDEST 'WISDOM'; PLEASE, ARJUNA, LISTEN ONCE AGAIN TO THIS SUPREME WISDOM".

The motive force behind every teacher coming out into the world to preach, to explain and to expound is his abundant love for mankind. Krishna repeats here the salient factors of his philosophical goal and the means of realising it, to Arjuna, "BECAUSE YOU ARE DEAR CLOSE OF ME" meaning "YOU ARE MY BEST FRIEND". For this reason, Krishna tries to recapitulate his scheme of right living and noble endeavour in brief.

Arjuna is by temperament a soldier; and a soldier's intellect has no patience with a dialectical discourse. What he can best appreciate is only a cut-and-dried order shouted at him, and he has been trained by his vocation always to follow it implicitly. Arjuna is expecting Krishna to recast the whole philosophy into a precise, definite, decisive commandment. Understanding this silent demand of the soldier's heart, Krishna promises here that He shall now declare the truth which is "the most secret of all" (*Sarva-guhya-tamam*).

WHAT IS IT?

65. *Fix your mind upon Me; be devoted to Me; sacrifice for Me; bow down to Me; you shall come, surely then, to Me alone; truly do I promise to you, (for) you are dear to Me.*

Four conditions are laid down for a successful seeker; and to those who have accomplished them all in themselves, an assurance of realisation, "YOU SHALL REACH ME", is given here. When a philosophy is summarised and enumerated in a few points, it has a deceptive look of utter simplicity, and a student is apt to take it lightly, or ignore it IN TOTO. In order to avoid such a mistake, the teacher invariably endorses his statement that it is indeed all Truth: I PROMISE YOU TRULY.

To add a punch to this personal endorsement, Krishna guarantees the motive behind His discourses: "YOU ARE DEAR TO ME". Love is the correct motive force behind all spiritual teachings. Unless a teacher has infinite love for the taught there is no inspired joy in teaching; a professional teacher is, at best, only a wage earner. He can neither inspire the student nor, while teaching, come to experience within himself the joyous ecstasy of satisfaction and fulfilment, which are the true rewards of teaching.

A substantial part of the philosophy and the 'Path' declared herein have already been taught in an earlier chapter (IX-34). And the same thing is repeated here with the endorsement that

---

मन्मना भव मद्भक्तो मद्याजी मां नमस्कुरु ।
मामेवैष्यसि सत्यं ते प्रतिजाने प्रियोऽसि मे ॥ ६५ ॥
manmanā bhava madbhākto madyājī māṁ namaskuru
māmevaiṣyasi satyaṁ te pratijāne priyo'si me 65.

what He is declaring is no pleasant compromise but the total unadulterated truth.

WITH THE MIND FIXED ON ME—Meaning "ever remembering Me, ever devotedly identifying with Me" through the process of dedicating all your activities unto Me, in an attitude of reverence unto the All-pervading Life, if you work in the service of the world, the promise is that you will reach the Supreme Goal.

In all other religions the Goal is other than the Prophet; only in the *Geeta* the Supreme Himself is advising the seeker, and therefore, He has to declare: "YOU WILL REACH ME".

Looking up to Vasudeva alone as your aim, means and end, "you shall reach Me". Knowing that the Lord's declarations are true, and being convinced that liberation is a necessary result of devotion to the Lord, one should look up to the Lord as the highest and the sole refuge.

The maladjusted 'ego' in us has, by its own false concepts and imaginations, spooled us all up into cocoons of confusion and has tied us down with our own self-created shackles. Now, it is up to us to snap these cords that bind us and gain freedom from them all. The All-perfect Supreme has been as though shackled by our mind and intellect, and now the same mind and intellect must be utilised to unwind the binding cords. If we lock ourselves up in a room, it is left to us only to unlock its doors and walk out into freedom. *Vasanas* are created by our egocentric activities (*Sa-kama-Karma*) and by selfless work (*Nish-kama-Karma*) alone can these *vasanas* be ended. Therefore, Krishna advises us: "Act on with mind fixed on Me. Devotedly work for Me. Dedicate all your activities as a sacrifice, as an offering unto Me".

An attitude of reverence to the Supreme is necessary in order to reincorporate into the texture of our own life, the qualities of the Supreme. Like water, knowledge also flows only from a higher to a lower level. Therefore, our minds must be in an attitude of surrender to Him in utter reverence and devotion.

When you work in the world with such an attitude, Krishna says, "YOU SHALL REACH THE SUPREME".

ACCORDING TO SHANKARA, "HAVING TAUGHT, IN CONCLUSION, THAT THE SUPREME SECRET OF *KARMA YOGA* IS IN REGARDING THE LORD AS THE SOLE REFUGE, KRISHNA NOW PROCEEDS TO SPEAK OF THE INFINITE KNOWLEDGE, THE FRUIT OF *KARMA YOGA*, AS TAUGHT IN THE ESSENTIAL PORTIONS OF ALL THE *UPANISHADS*":

66. *Abandoning all DHARMAS, (of the body, mind, and intellect), take refuge in Me alone; I will liberate thee from all sins; grieve not.*

This is the noblest of all the stanzas in the Divine Song and this is yet the most controversial. Translators, reviewers, critics and commentators have invested all their originality in commenting upon this stanza, and various philosophers, each maintaining his own point of view, has ploughed the words to plant his ideas into the ample bosom of this great verse of brilliant

---

सर्वधर्मान्परित्यज्य मामेकं शरणं व्रज ।
अहं त्वा सर्वपापेभ्यो मोक्षयिष्यामि मा शुचः ॥ ६६ ॥
sarvadharmānparityajya māmekaṁ śaraṇaṁ vraja
ahaṁ tvā sarvapāpebhyo mokṣayiṣyāmi mā śucaḥ 66.

* We have met with the same idea in chapter VI-25, when after explaining the ways of developing concentration, the Lord advised: *'Na kinchidapi chintayet'* 'thereafter start no new thought disturbances'.

import. To Sri Ramanuja, this is the final verse (*Charama-Shloka*) of the whole *Geeta.*

Most often used, and yet in no two places having the same shade of suggestion, the term, '*Dharma*' has become the very heart of the Hindu culture. This explains why the religion of India was called by the people who lived in the land and enjoyed its spiritual wealth as the '*Sanatana Dharma*'.

Dharma, as used in our scriptures is, to put it directly and precisely, THE LAW OF BEING. That because of which a THING continues to be the THING itself, without which the THING cannot continue to be that THING, is the *Dharma* of the THING. Heat, because of which fire maintains itself as fire, without which fire can no more be fire, is the *Dharma* of fire. Heat is the *Dharma* of fire; cold fire we have yet to come across! Sweetness is the *Dharma* of sugar; sour sugar is a myth!

Every object in the world has two types of properties: (a) the essential, and (b) the non-essential. A substance can remain itself, intact, when its 'non-essential' qualities are absent, but it cannot remain ever for a split moment without its 'essential' property. The colour of the flame, the length and width of the tongues of flame, are all the 'non-essential' properties of fire, but the essential property of it is heat. This essential property of a substance is called its *Dharma*.

Then what exactly is the *Dharma* of man? The colour of the skin, the innumerable endless varieties of emotions and thoughts – the nature, the conditions and the capacities of the body, mind and intellect – are the 'non-essential' factors in the human personality, as against the Touch of Life, the Divine Consciousness, expressed through them all. Without the *Atman* man cannot exist; it is TRUTH which is the basis of existence.

Therefore, the 'essential *Dharma*' of man is the Divine Spark of Existence, the Infinite Lord.

With this understanding of the term *Dharma*, we shall appreciate its difference from mere ethical and moral rules of conduct, all duties in life, all duties towards relations, friends, community, nation and the world, all our obligations to our environment, all our affections, reverence, charity, and sense of goodwill – all that have been considered as our *Dharma* in our books. In and through such actions, physical, mental and intellectual, a man will bring forth the expression of his true *Dharma* – his Divine status as the All-pervading Self. To live truly as the *Atman*, and to express Its Infinite Perfection through all our actions and in all our contacts with the outer world is to rediscover our *Dharma*.

There are, no doubt, a few other stanzas in the *Geeta* wherein the Lord has almost directly commanded us to live a certain way-of-life, and has promised that if we obey His instructions, He will directly take the responsibility of guiding us towards HIS OWN BEING. But nowhere has the Lord so directly and openly expressed His divine willingness to undertake the service of His devotee as in this stanza.

He wants the meditator to accomplish three distinct adjustments in his inner personality. They are: (1) Renounce all *Dharmas* through meditation; (2) surrender to My refuge alone; and while in the state of meditation, (3) stop all worries. And as a reward Lord Krishna promises: "I SHALL RELEASE YOU FROM ALL SINS". This is a promise given to all mankind. The *Geeta* is a universal scripture; it is the Bible of Man, the Koran of Humanity, the dynamic scripture of the Hindus.

ABANDONING ALL *DHARMA* (*Sarva-Dharman Parityajya*)—As we have said above, *Dharma* is the law-of-being and we have already noted that nothing can continue its existence when once it is divorced from its *Dharma*. And yet, Krishna says, "COME TO MY REFUGE, AFTER RENOUNCING ALL *DHARMAS*". Does it then mean that our definition of *Dharma* is wrong? Or is there a contradiction in this stanza? Let us see.

As a mortal, finite ego, the seeker is living, due to his identification with them, the *Dharmas* of his body, mind and intellect, and exists in life as a mere perceiver, feeler, and thinker. The perceiver-feeler-thinker personality in us is the 'individuality' which expresses itself as the 'ego'. These are not our 'essential' *Dharmas*. And since these are the 'non-essentials', RENOUNCING ALL *DHARMAS* means ENDING THE EGO.

To renounce, therefore means 'not to allow ourselves to fall again and again into this state of identification with the outer envelopments of matter around us'. Extrovert tendencies of the mind are to be renounced. "Develop introspection diligently" is the deep suggestion in the phrase RENOUNCING ALL DHARMAS.

COME TO ME ALONE FOR SHELTER (*Mam-ekam Sharanam Vraja*)—Self-withdrawal from our extrovert nature will be impossible unless the mind is given a positive method of developing its introvert attention. By single-pointed, steady contemplation upon Me, the Self, which is the One-without-a-second, we can successfully accomplish our total withdrawal from the misinterpreting equipments of the body, mind and intellect.

Philosophers in India were never satisfied with a negative approach in their instructions; there are more 'DO's than

'DONTS' with them. This practical nature of our philosophy, which is native to our traditions, is amply illustrated in this stanza when Lord Krishna commands His devotees to come to His shelter whereby they can accomplish the renunciation of all their false identifications.

BE NOT GRIEVED (*Ma shuchah*)—When both the above conditions are accomplished, the seeker reaches a state of growing tranquillity in meditation. But it will all be a waste if this subjective peace, created after so much labour, were not to form a steady and firm platform for his personality to spring forth from, into the realms of the Divine Consciousness. The springboard must stay under our feet; supply the required propulsion for our inward dive. But unfortunately, the very anxiety to reach the Infinite weakens the platform. Like a dream-bridge, it disappears at the withering touch of the anxieties in the meditator. During meditation, when the mind has been persuaded away from all its restless preoccupations with the outer vehicles, and brought, again and again, to contemplate upon the Self, the Infinite, Lord Krishna wants the seeker to renounce all his ANXIETIES TO REALISE.* Even a desire to realise is a disturbing thought that can obstruct the final achievement.

I SHALL RELEASE YOU FROM ALL SINS—That which brings about agitations in the bosom and thereby causes dissipation of the energies is called 'sin'. The actions themselves can cause subtle exhaustions of the human power, as no action can be undertaken without bringing our mind and intellect into it. In short, the mind and intellect will always have to come and control every action. Actions thus leave their 'foot prints', as it were, upon the mental stuff, and these marks which channelise the thought-flow and shape the psychological personality, when our mind has gone through its experiences, are called *vasanas*.

Good *vasanas* bring forth a steady stream of good thoughts as efficiently as bad *vasanas* erupt bad thoughts. As long as thoughts are flowing, the mind survives – whether good or bad. To erase all *vasanas* completely is to stop all thoughts i.e. the total cessation of thought-flow viz. 'mind'. Transcending the mind-intellect-equipment is to reach the plane of Pure Consciousness, the Krishna-Reality.

As a seeker renounces more and more of his identifications with his outer envelopments through a process of steady contemplation and meditation upon the Lord of his heart, he grows in his vision. In the newly awakened sensitive consciousness, he becomes more and more poignantly aware of the number of *vasanas* he has to exhaust. BE NOT GRIEVED, assures the Lord, for, I SHALL RELEASE YOU FROM ALL SINS – the disturbing, thought-gurgling, action-prompting, desire-breeding, agitation-brewing *vasanas*, the 'sins'.

The stanza is important inasmuch as it is one of the most powerfully worded verses in the *Geeta* wherein the Lord, the Infinite, personally undertakes to do something helpful for the seeker in case the spiritual hero in him is ready to offer his ardent co-operation and put forth his best efforts. All through the days of seeking, a *sadhaka* can assure himself steady progress in spirituality only when he is able to keep within himself a salubrious mental climate of warm optimism. To despair and to weep, to feel dejected and disappointed, is to invite restlessness of the mind, and naturally, therefore, spiritual unfoldment is never in the offing. The stanza, in its deep imports and wafting suggestions, is indeed a peroration in itself of the entire philosophical poem.

HAVING CONCLUDED THE ENTIRE DOCTRINE OF THE *'GEETA-SHASTRA'* IN THIS DISCOURSE, AND HAVING ALSO BRIEFLY AND CONCLUSIVELY RESTATED THE DOCTRINE IN ORDER TO IMPRESS IT MORE FIRMLY, THE LORD NOW PROCEEDS TO STATE THE RULE THAT SHOULD BE BORNE IN MIND WHILE IMPARTING THIS KNOWLEDGE TO OTHERS:

67. *This is never to be spoken by you to one who is devoid of austerities or devotion, nor to one who does not render service, nor to one who desires not to listen, nor to one who cavils at Me.*

In almost all scriptural texts we find, in their closing stanzas, a description of the type of students to whom this knowledge can be imparted. Following faithfully this great tradition, here also we have this enumeration of the necessary qualifications for a true student of the *Geeta*. These are not so many fortresses raised round the treasure-house of the *Geeta* in order to protect some interests and provide some people with a kind of monopoly in trading upon the wealth of ideas in these discourses. On the other hand, we shall find that these qualifications are essential adjustments in the inner personality of the student. And a bosom so tuned up is the right vehicle that can daringly invest that knowledge in living one's life and thus earn the joy of 'wisdom'.

THOSE WHO DO NOT LIVE AN AUSTERE LIFE—Those who do not have any control over their body and mind; who have dissipated their physical and mental energies in the wrong

---

इदं ते नातपस्काय नाभक्ताय कदाचन ।
न चाशुश्रूषवे वाच्यं न च मां योऽभ्यसूयति ॥ ६७ ॥
idaṁ te natapaskāya nābhaktāya kadācana
na cāśuśrūṣave vācyaṁ na ca māṁ yo'bhyasūyati 67.

direction and have thus become impotent bodily, mentally and intellectually – to them "NEVER IS THIS TO BE SPOKEN BY YOU"; for, it will not be beneficial to them. There is not a trace of prejudice in this stanza. It is equivalent to saying '"please do not sow seeds upon rocks" for, the sower will never be able to reap, as nothing can grow on rocks.

THOSE WHO HAVE NO DEVOTION—That is, those who do not have the capacity to identify themselves with the ideal that they want to reach. If one cannot sympathise with an ideal one can much less absorb or assimilate it. An ideal, however well understood intellectually, cannot yield its full benefit unless it is expressed in life. To hug on to the ideal, in a clasp of love, is devotion.

THOSE WHO DO NOT RENDER SERVICE—We have seen earlier, almost in all chapters, Krishna again and again insisting that selfless activity is not only a means for the *sadhaka*, but it is at once also the field where the perfect masters discover their fulfilment. Seekers who are not able to serve others, who are selfish, who have no human qualities, who have never felt a sympathetic love for others – such persons are merely consumers and not producers of joy for others, and they invariably fail to understand or appreciate or come to live the joys of the Krishna way-of-life.

THOSE WHO CAVIL AT ME—Those who murmur against Me. If we do not respect and revere our teacher we can never learn from him. The first person singular used in the *Geeta* is identical with the Self, the Goal, and therefore, it means, "those who are not able to respect philosophy". Forceful conversion may enhance the numerical strength of a faith, but self-development and inner unfoldment cannot come that way. Religion should not be forced upon anyone. One who has mentally rejected a philosophy can never, even when one has understood it, live up to it. Therefore, those who are entertaining a secret disrespect for a philosophy should NOT BE FORCED to study it.

Stanzas like this in a *shastra* are meant as instructions for the students on how to attune themselves properly so that they can make a profitable study of the *shastra*. None should expect an immediate result from his study of the *Geeta*. Personality readjustments cannot be made overnight. There is no miracle promised in the *Geeta*.

Indirectly, the stanza also gives some sane instructions by its suggestions. If a student feels that he cannot satisfactorily understand the *Geeta*, he has only to sharpen his inner nature further by the above subjective processes. Just as we cleanse a mirror to remove the dimness of the reflection, so too, by properly readjusting the mind-intellect-equipment its sensitivity to absorb the *Geeta*-philosophy can be increased.

NOW THE LORD PROCEEDS TO STATE WHAT BENEFITS WILL ACCRUE TO HIM WHO HANDS DOWN HIS KNOWLEDGE TO OTHERS IN SOCIETY:

68. *He who, with supreme devotion to Me, will teach this supreme secret to My devotees, shall doubtless come to Me.*

The stanza under review and the following one are both glorifications of a teacher who can give the correct interpretation of the *Geeta* and make the listener follow the Krishna way-of-

---

य इमं परमं गुह्यं मद्भक्तेष्वभिधास्यति ।
भक्तिं मयि परां कृत्वा मामेवैष्यत्यसंशय: ॥ ६८ ॥

ya imaṁ paramaṁ guhyaṁ madbhakteṣvabhidhāsyati
bhaktiṁ mayi parāṁ kṛtvā māmevaiṣyatyasaṁśayaḥ 68.

life. "Fight the evil down, whether it be within or without" is the cardinal principle that Krishna advocates to Prince Arjuna. In order to impart such a culture, it is not enough that the teacher be a mere scholar, but he must have the Krishna-ability. Hence the glorification. The Lord's Song has a special appeal to those who have the mysterious spiritual thirst to live a fuller and more dynamic life. Hence it is said: "This deeply profound philosophy" (*Paramam Guhyam*) must be imparted to "My devotees" (*Mad-bhakteshu*). Devotion to the Lord (*Bhakti*) means the capacity to identify with the ideal, and therefore, the philosophy of the ideal way-of-life can profitably be imparted only to those persons who have a capacity to identify themselves with the ideal and thereafter live up to it.

It is not sufficient that the student alone has this capacity to identify himself with the higher ideal, but the teacher also must have (*Bhakti*) 'perfect attunement' with the Supreme Krishna-Reality. Such an individual, who is himself rooted in his attunement, and who tries to impart this knowledge to others and thereby constantly occupies himself in reflections upon the philosophical ideals of the *Geeta;* "shall certainly (*Asamshayah*) come to Me alone".

An educated man should, in his gratitude, feel much indebted to the men-of-Wisdom. In fact, this indebtedness is actually called, in our tradition, *Rishi*-indebtedness (*Rishi-Rinam*), to absolve ourselves from which, we are asked to study their works and preach their ideas everyday.

Philosophy is the basis of every culture. The Hindu culture can revive and assert its glory only when it is nurtured and nourished by the philosophy of India which is contained in the *Upanishads*. The fathers of our culture, the great *Rishis*, knowing this secret, urged the students of the scriptures not to keep this knowledge to themselves, but to impart it freely to others. In this way alone the culture can be successfully brought into the dim-lit chambers of people's lives.

If a student, who has understood even a wee bit of our cultural tradition, does not convey it to others, it means that there is no mobility of intelligence or fluidity of inspiration in him. He who is thus capable of conveying the truths of the *Geeta* to others is complimented here with the promise of the highest reward: "HE SHALL DOUBTLESS COME TO ME".

NOT ONLY THIS, BUT THE LORD EXPRESSES THAT HE LOVES SUCH A TEACHER MUCH MORE THAN ANYBODY ELSE:

69. *Nor is there any among men who does dearer service to Me, nor shall there be another on earth dearer to Me than he.*

Krishna again takes up, in this stanza, the glorification of the teacher who teaches the *Geeta*-knowledge. Herein, Krishna explains how such a man can reach Him easily, as declared in the previous verse. The *Geetaacharya* emphasises that such an individual is "DEAREST TO MY HEART, AS I FIND NONE EQUAL TO HIM IN THE WORLD". Not only is there none to compare with him amongst the present generation, but there

---

न च तस्मान्मनुष्येषु कश्चिन्मे प्रियकृत्तमः ।
भविता न च मे तस्मादन्यः प्रियतरो भुवि ॥ ६९ ॥
na ca tasmānmanuṣyeṣu kaścinme priyakṛttamaḥ
bhavitā na ca me tasmādanyaḥ priyataro bhuvi 69.

* FAITH – "Faith is the bird that feels the light and sings when the dawn is still dark." – Tagore.

SHALL never be (*Bhavita-Na-Cha*) anyone, even in future times, so dear to Him, the Lord says, as such an individual who spends his time in spreading the knowledge of what little he has understood from the *Geeta.*

Earlier, in the *Geeta,* a great psychological truth has been hinted at, which is often repeated throughout the entire length of the Divine Song, and this cardinal secret is that he who can bring his entire mind to the contemplation of the Divine, to the total exclusion of all dissimilar thought-currents, will come to experience the Infinite Divine. A student of the *Geeta,* who is spending his time in serious studies and in deep reflection upon them, and in preaching what he has understood, comes to revere the knowledge and thus reach an identification with an inner peace that is the essence of truth. Therefore, Krishna says: "THERE CAN NEVER BE ANY OTHER MAN MORE DEAR TO ME THAN SUCH A PREACHER; FOR, HE IS DOING THE GREATEST SERVICE TO ME BY EARNESTLY AND DEVOTEDLY TRYING TO CONVEY THE IMMORTAL PRINCIPLES EXPOUNDED IN THE *GEETA*".

It is not necessary in this context, that we must first ourselves become masters of the entire *Geeta*-Knowledge. Whatever one has understood one must immediately, with an anxious love, give out to those who are completely ignorant. Also, one must sincerely and honestly try to live the principles in one's own life; "SUCH A MAN IS DEAREST TO ME".

NOT ONLY THE PREACHER BUT ALSO EVEN THE SINCERE STUDENT IS CONGRATULATED IN THE FOLLOWING STANZA:

70. *And he who will study this sacred dialogue of ours, by him I shall have been worshipped by the 'sacrifice-of-wisdom', such is My conviction.*

Having thus glorified all teachers of the *Geeta* who carry the Wisdom of the sacred discourse to the masses, the *Geeta*, here, is glorifying even the students who are studying this sacred text of the Lord's Song. The great philosophy of life given out here as a conversation between Krishna -- the Infinite, and Arjuna -- the finite, has such a compelling charm about it, that even those who read it superficially will also be slowly dragged into the very sanctifying depths of it. Such an individual is, even unconsciously, egged on to make a pilgrimage to the greater possibilities within himself, and naturally, he comes to evolve through what Krishna terms here as '*Jnana Yajna*'.

In a *Yajna*, Lord Fire is invoked in the sacrificial trough and into it are offered oblations by the devotees. From this analogy, the term *Jnana Yajna* has been originally coined and used in the *Geeta.* Study of the scriptures and regular contemplation upon their deep significances kindle the Fire-of-Knowledge in us and into this the intelligent seeker offers, as his oblation, his own false values and negative tendencies. This is the significance of the metaphorical phrase *Jnana Yajna*. Therefore, here the Lord admits but a truth in the Spiritual science when He declares that those who study the *Geeta;* contemplate upon its meaning, understand it thoroughly; and those who can, at the altars of

---

अध्येष्यते च य इमं धर्म्यं संवादमावयोः ।
ज्ञानयज्ञेन तेनाहमिष्टः स्यामिति मे मतिः ॥ ७० ॥

adhyeṣyate ca ya imam dharmyaṁ saṁvādamāvayoḥ
jñānayajñena tenāhamiṣṭaḥ syāmiti me matiḥ 70.

their well-kindled understanding, sacrifice their own egocentric misconceptions about themselves, and about the world around them, are certainly the greatest devotees of the Infinite.

When a rusted key is heated in fire, the rust falls off and the key regains its original brightness. So too, our personality, when reacted with the knowledge of the *Geeta*, is chastened, since our wrong tendencies, unhealthy *vasanas* and false sense of ego which have risen from false-knowledge (*Ajnana*), all get burnt up in Right-Knowledge (*Jnana*).

AFTER THUS EXPLAINING THE GLORY OF THE TEACHER AND THE BENEFITS OF THE STUDY SO FAR, KRISHNA INDICATES IN THE FOLLOWING STANZA, THAT EVEN 'LISTENING' TO THE *GEETA* DISCOURSES IS BENEFICIAL:

71. *That man also, who hears this, full of faith and free from malice, he too, liberated, shall attain to the happy worlds of those righteous deeds.*

A student of the *Geeta* cannot stand apart from his textbook, and merely learn to appreciate the theme of the Lord's Song. An all-out, ardent wooing of the *Geeta* by the student at all levels is necessary, if the study of the *Geeta* is really to fulfil the student's spiritual unfoldment. Consequently, Krishna indicates here two conditions, fulfilling which alone can one profitably listen to the *Geeta* discourses and hope to gather a large dividend of joy and perfection.

श्रद्धावाननसूयश्च श्रृणु यादपि यो नरः ।
सोऽपि मुक्तः शुभाँल्लोकान्प्राप्नुयात्पुण्यकर्मणाम् ॥ ७१ ॥
śraddhāvānanasūyaśca śṛṇuyadapi yo naraḥ
so'pi muktaḥ śubhām̐llokāmprāpnuyātpuṇyakarmaṇām 71.

ONE OF FAITH (*Shraddhavan*)—The term *shraddha* in Sanskrit, though usually translated as 'faith', actually means much more than what it indicates in the English language and in the Western tradition. *Shraddha* has been defined as 'that faculty in the human intellect which gives it the capacity to dive deep into and discover the subtler meaning of the scriptural declarations, and thus helps the individual to absorb that understanding into the warp and the woof of his own intellect'.*

Therefore, that faculty in the intellect, (1) to understand the subtle import of the sacred words, (2) to absorb the same, (3) to assimilate, and (4) to make the student live up to those very same ideals, is *shraddha*. Naturally, listening to the Lord's discourses can be fruitful only to those who have developed this essential faculty in themselves.

FREE FROM MALICE (*Anasooyah*)—They alone who are free from malice against the teachings of the *Geeta* can undertake, with a healthy attitude of mind, a deeper and detailed study of it. No doubt, Hinduism never asks any student to read and study a philosophy with an implicit and ready faith. But the human mind, as it is, will grow dull and unresponsive when it has idle prejudices against the very theme of its study.

The intellect can receive the ideals preached in the *Geeta* only through the sense-organs, and these ideas must reach the intellect, filtered through the mind. If the mind contains any malice towards the very philosophy or the philosopher, the arguments and the goal indicated therein can never appeal to the student's intellect. No doubt, the student should bring in his own constructive criticism of an independent judgement upon what he studies, but he must be reasonably available to listen patiently to what the scripture has to say. In short, a student of religion must learn to keep an open mind and not condemn the philosophy before understanding what it has to say.

Such an individual who has attentively listened to the *Geeta,* who has intellectually absorbed, and assimilated the knowledge, 'he too', says the Lord, 'gets liberated' from the present state of confusions and sorrows, entanglements and bondages in his personality, and reaches a state of inner tranquillity and happiness.

JOY IS AN INSIDE JOB—The kingdom of joy lies within all of us. Heaven is not somewhere yonder; it is HERE AND NOW. Happiness and sorrow are both within us. To the extent we learn and live the principles of right living, as enunciated in the *Geeta,* to that extent, we shall come to gain a cultural eminence within ourselves and live an ampler life of greater achievements.

It is the duty of a teacher to see that the student understands the great Goal and the 'Path' completely. If the 'Path' advised is found to be inadequate to bless the student, it is the duty of the teacher to find out ways and means of making the student discover his own balance.

HENCE IN THE FOLLOWING STANZA WE FIND KRISHNA ENQUIRING WHETHER ARJUNA HAS UNDERSTOOD WHAT HE HAS EXPOUNDED IN THESE EIGHTEEN CHAPTERS:

72. *Has this been heard, O son of Pritha, with single-pointed mind? Has the distraction, caused by your 'ignorance', been dispelled, O Dhananjaya?*

Here, we find Lord Krishna, the teacher of the *Geeta*, putting a leading question to his disciple, Arjuna, giving him a chance to say how much he has benefited from the discourses. Of course, Krishna had no doubt about it; but it is only like a doctor, who, confident of his own achieved success, looks at the beaming face of the revived patient and enquires "how are you feeling now?" This is only to enjoy the beaming satisfaction that comes to play on the face of the relieved patient.

HAVE YOU BEEN LISTENING WITH AN ATTENTIVE MIND?—The very question implies that if you have been attentive you must have understood sufficiently the logic in the things, beings and happenings around, and therefore, your relationship with them also. The study of *Vedanta* broadens our vision, and we start RECOGNISING, in a new light, the same OLD SCHEME OF THINGS around us, and then its previous ugliness gets lifted as though by magic.

HAS YOUR DISTRACTION OF THOUGHT, CAUSED BY 'IGNORANCE', BEEN DISPELLED?—The false values that we entertain distort our vision of the world and our judgement of its affairs. The delusion of mind was expressed by Arjuna in the opening chapters of the *Geeta* (I-36 to 46, and II-4 and 5).

Amputating a septic toe to save the body is no crime; on the contrary it is a life-giving blessing; it is not a toe destroyed, but it is a body and its life saved. The CULTURAL CRISIS of

---

कच्चिदेतच्छ्रुतं पार्थ त्वयैकाग्रेण चेतसा ।
कच्चिदज्ञानसंमोहः प्रनष्टस्ते धनञ्जय ॥ ७२ ॥

kaccidetacchraṁtaṁ pārtha tvayaikāgreṇa cetasā
kaccidajñānasammohaḥ pranaṣṭaste dhanañjaya 72.

those times had egged the Kauravas on to rise up in arms against the beauty of the spiritual culture of the land. Arjuna was called upon by the era to champion the cause of the righteous. It was indeed a false reading of the situation that perverted the judgement of the Pandava Prince, as a consequence of which he became utterly broken down, and came to entertain a neurotic condition in himself. The fundamental cause of all confusions was his own NON-APPREHENSION OF REALITY called in *Vedanta* philosophy as 'ignorance' (*Ajnana*). When this 'ignorance' is removed by the APPREHENSION OF REALITY, termed as 'knowledge' (*Jnana*), the entire by-products of 'ignorance' are all, in one sweep, eliminated. Hence the logic of this enquiry from the teacher.

True 'knowledge' expresses itself in one's own dexterity in action and it should fulfil itself in the splendour of its achievements in the service of society. In case Arjuna has understood the philosophy of the *Geeta* he will no more hesitate to meet the challenges as they reach him. This seems to be the unsaid idea in the heart of the Lord.

ARJUNA CONFESSES THAT HIS CONFUSIONS HAVE ENDED:

Arjuna said:

73. *Destroyed is my delusion, as I have now gained my memory (knowledge) through your grace, O Achyuta. I am firm; my doubts are gone. I will do according to your word (bidding).*

अर्जुन उवाच ।
नष्टो मोहः स्मृतिर्लब्धा त्वत्प्रसादान्मयाच्युत ।
स्थितोऽस्मि गतसन्देहः करिष्ये वचनं तव ॥ ७३ ॥

arjuna uvāca
naṣṭo mohaḥ smṛtirlabdhā tvatprasādānmayācyuta
sthito'smi gatasandehaḥ kariṣye vacanaṁ tava 73.

Somewhat like one who has suddenly awakened from an unconscious state, Arjuna, with a regained self-recognition, assuredly confesses that his confusions have ended -- not because he has unquestioningly swallowed the arguments in the discourses of the *Geeta,* but because, as he himself says, "I have gained a RECOGNITION of my Real Nature. The hero in me has now become awakened, and the neurotic condition that had temporarily conquered my mind has totally ended".

Such a revival within and a rediscovery of our personality are possible for all of us if only we truly understand the significance of the *Geeta* philosophy. The Infinite nature of Perfection is our own. It is not something that we have to gain from somewhere by the intervention of some outer agency. This Mighty Being within ourselves is now lying veiled beneath our own egocentric confusions and abject fears. Even while we are confused and confounded, and helplessly suffering the tragic sorrows of our ego, we are IN REALITY, none other than our own Self. When the dream ends, the confusions also end, and we awaken to our Real Nature. So too, in life. This awakening of the Divine in us is the ending of the beast within.

In this newfound equilibrium, born out of Wisdom, he experiences an unshakable balance established upon firm foundations. All vacillations of the mind, doubts and despairs, dejections and hesitations, fears and weaknesses have left him (*gata sandehah*).

With such a revived personality, when Arjuna reevaluates the situation, he finds no difficulty at all in discovering what exactly his duty is. He openly declares, "I WILL DO ACCORDING TO YOUR WORD" for in the *Geeta,* Lord Krishna stands for the Divine-Spark-of-Existence manifested as 'pure-intelligence'.

All students -- who have thus fully understood the *Geeta*, have a clear picture of the goal-of-life, who know what 'Path' to follow and how to withdraw from the false by-lanes of existence -- will surrender themselves, each to his own integrated inner personality. To surrender ourselves to our own 'higher intellect' and to declare confidently and with faith, "I SHALL DO THY BIDDING" is the beginning and the end of all spiritual life.

SANJAYA GLORIFIES THE *GEETACHARYA* AND HIS DIVINE SONG, THE *GEETA*:

Sanjaya said:

74. *Thus have I heard this wonderful dialogue between Vasudeva and the high-souled Partha, which causes the hair to stand on end.*

In the previous stanza, when one carefully understands the full significance of the assertion made by the rediscovered, and therefore, revived Arjuna, one cannot avoid remembering a parallel declaration made by another teacher of the world, when he revived from his temporary confusion (*Arjuna-sthiti*). When he regained his spiritual balance, which he, as it were, lost temporarily while carrying the cross through the taunting crowd, Jesus also cried: THY WILL BE DONE. Here Arjuna, revived

---

सञ्जय उवाच
इत्यहं वासुदेवस्य पार्थस्य च महात्मनः ।
संवादमिममश्रौषमद्भुतं रोमहर्षणम् ॥ ७४ ॥

sañjaya uvāca
ityahaṁ vāsudevasya pārthasya ca mahātmanaḥ
saṁvādamimamaśrauṣadbhutaṁ romaharṣaṇam 74.

* Read Discourse on *Geeta* Chapter II – Stanza 9.

by the Grace of Krishna, similarly cries, "I SHALL ACT ACCORDING TO YOUR WORD (*Karishye Vachanam Tava*)". In both cases we find that the statements are almost identical.

Earlier, at the opening of the *Geeta*, the Pandava Prince said to Govinda: "I SHALL NOT FIGHT"* and became despondent; it is the same Arjuna, now entirely revived and fully rehabilitated, who declares: "I shall abide by Thy will". The cure is complete and with this the *shastra* also ends.

THUS HAVE I HEARD THIS DIALOGUE BETWEEN VASUDEVA AND THE HIGH-SOULED ARJUNA—In the context of the Vyasa-literature, the conversation between Vasudeva, Lord Krishna, and the son of Pritha, Arjuna, is but a silent mystic dialogue between the 'higher' and the 'lower' in man, the 'Spirit' and the 'Matter'. Vasudeva means the Lord (*Deva*) of the *Vasus*; the eight *Vasus* (*Ashta-vasu*) together preside over Time. Therefore, Vasudeva, in its mystic symbolism, stands for the Consciousness that illumines the 'concept of Time' projected by the intellect of man. In short, Vasudeva is the *Atman*, the Self. Partha represents matter (earth) which is capable of shedding itself, sheath by sheath to emerge as the pure Eternal Spirit, the Supreme. This act of understanding himself as different from his matter vestures is man's highest art, the Art of unveiling the Infinite through the finite. The technique of this art is the theme of the *Geeta*.

WONDERFUL (*Adbhutam*)—This philosophy of the *Geeta*, listened to so far by Sanjaya, is reviewed by him as 'miraculous', as 'wonderful'. Every philosophy, no doubt, is a marvel of man's intellect and represents its subtle visions and powers of comprehension. But the philosophy of the *Geeta* was indeed a shade more marvellous and wonderful to Sanjaya, because, it revived the BLASTED personality of Arjuna into a DYNAMIC WHOLE. Because of this practical demonstration of its powers to bless man, the *Geeta* philosophy has acquired the marvellous lustre of the rare.

It has proved, beyond all doubt, that every average human being is endowed with potential power with which he can easily conquer all the expressions of life in him and command them to manifest exactly as he wants. He is the Lord of his life, the master of the vehicles, and not a victim of some other mightier power that has created him, only to be endlessly teased by the whims and fancies of his own body, mind and intellect. When this truth is revealed, it is but human for Sanjaya, in ecstasy, to exclaim: "Oh! what a marvellous revelation! What a stupendous demonstration!! *Adbhutam*!!!"

HIGH-SOULED PARTHA—In the stanza Arjuna has been glorified and not Lord Krishna, the *Parthasarathi*. The Pandava Prince, Arjuna, had the courage and heroism to come out of his mental confusions, when he gained the right knowledge from his Master's teachings. Certain acts of a child call forth our admiration, but the same acts performed by a grown-up person, look perhaps ridiculous and childish. To the omnipotent Lord, the declaration of the whole *Geeta* itself is but a love-play. But, for the confused Arjuna to understand the philosophy, and heroically walk out of his confusions is indeed an achievement, worthy of appreciation. Thus Krishna, the All-perfect, is almost ignored, but Arjuna, the mortal, who has understood the art of living as expounded in the *Geeta*, and has actually revived himself by living it, is heartily congratulated and glorified!

Sanjaya's sympathies were with the Pandavas; but as an employed minister, he was eating the salt of Dhritarashtra, and it was not *Dharma* for him to be disloyal to his master. At the same time, in the context of the politics of that time, Dhritarashtra was, perhaps, the only one who, even then, could stop the war. Diplomatically, Sanjaya tries his best, in these stanzas, to bring into the blind man's heart the suggestion of a peace treaty. He makes the blind king understand that Lord Krishna has revived and re-awakened the hero in Arjuna. The blind king is reminded of what the consequences would be: the death and disaster to his hundred children, the pangs of separation in his old age, the dishonour of it all -- all these are brought home to Dhritarashtra. But the tottering king's 'blindness' seems to be not only physical but also mental and intellectual, for Sanjaya's beseeching moral suggestions fall on the deaf ears of the blind elder.

SANJAYA OPENLY ACKNOWLEDGES HIS INDEBTEDNESS TO *SHRI* VEDA-VYASA:

75. *Through the grace of Vyasa I have heard, this supreme and most secret YOGA, directly from Krishna, the Lord of YOGA, Himself declaring it.*

Before the great battle started, Vyasa had approached Dhritarashtra to offer him the 'power of vision' to witness the war; however, the weak-hearted king had not the courage to accept the offer. The king had then suggested that if this power could be given to Sanjaya, the king could, through the faithful minister, listen to a running commentary of what was happening on the Kurukshetra battlefield. It was thus from Vyasa that Sanjaya, sitting in the carpeted chambers of the Kaurava palace, gained the special faculty of witnessing all that happened and listening to all that was said at the distant battle-field. Grateful to Shri Veda-Vyasa for having given him this wonderful chance of listening to this "Supreme and most profound *Yoga*" Sanjaya is mentally prostrating to the incomparable poet-sage, the author of the Mahabharata.

व्यासप्रसादाच्छ्रुतवानेतद्गुह्यमहं परम् ।
योगं योगेश्वरात्कृष्णात्साक्षात्कथयतः स्वयम् ॥ ७५ ॥

vyāsaprasādācchraṁtavānetadguhyamahaṁ param
yogaṁ yogeśvarātkṛṣṇātsākṣātkathayataḥ svayam 75.

DIRECTLY FROM KRISHNA HIMSELF (*Yogeshwarat Krishnat*)—The suggestion is NOT that Sanjaya had never heard the philosophy of the *Upanishads* ever before, and that the novelty of the revelation had stunned him; but that his joy is due to the fact that he got a chance to listen to the Eternal Knowledge of the *Upanishads* directly from the Lord-of-all-*Yogas*, Shri Krishna Himself (*Sakshat*), from His own sacred lips.

Here also we can see how Sanjaya is sincerely trying to make the blind Dhritarashtra realise that it is not Krishna, the son of Devaki, nor the cowherd boy, but it is the Lord Himself the *Yogeshwarah* who has revived Arjuna, and who is serving His devotee as his charioteer. The blind king is reminded that his children, though they have marshalled a large army, stand doomed to destruction, since they have to face the Infinite Lord Himself in their enemy ranks.

THE DEEP IMPRESSION CREATED BY THIS IRRESISTIBLE PHILOSOPHY ON THE DEVOTED HEART OF SANJAYA IS VIVIDLY PAINTED:

76. *O King, remembering this wonderful and holy dialogue between Keshava and Arjuna, I rejoice again and again.*

Herein we have a clear statement of Sanjaya's reactions to his listening to the Lord's Song. He says, "THIS DISCOURSE BETWEEN KRISHNA AND ARJUNA" – between God and man, between the Perfect and the imperfect, between the 'higher' and the 'lower' – is at once 'WONDERFUL AND HOLY'.

राजन्संस्मृत्य संस्मृत्य संवादमिममद्भुतम् ।
केशवार्जुनयोः पुण्यं हृष्यामि च मुहुर्मुहुः ॥ ७६ ॥

rājansaṁsmṛtya saṁsmṛtya saṁvādamimamadbhutam
keśavārjunayoḥ puṇyaṁ hṛṣyāmi ca muhurmuhuḥ 76.

The vision and impression created in his heart by the philosophy that was heard are so deep and striking, that Sanjaya admits how irresistibly the memory of those words rises up again and again in his bosom, giving him 'the thrill of joy' (*Harsham*).

Indirectly, Vyasa is prescribing the method of study of the *Geeta.* It being a handbook of instruction on the Art of Living, it has TO BE READ AGAIN AND AGAIN, REPEATEDLY REFLECTED UPON AND CONTINUOUSLY REMEMBERED, until the inner man in us is completely re-educated in the way-of-life that the *Geeta* charts out for man. The reward for such a painstaking study and consistency of application has also been clearly pointed out.

One rejoices when one comes to recognise a definite purpose in the otherwise purposeless pilgrimage of man, from the womb to the tomb, called 'life'. The study of the *Geeta* gives not only a purpose to our every-day existence but also a positive message of hope and cheer to the world. The *Geeta* picks us up from the by-lanes of life and enthrones us as the sovereign power that rules, commands and orders our own life within.

Thus the *Geeta* is an infinite fountainhead of inspiration and joy. It provides our mind with a systematic scheme of re-education whereby it can discover a secret power in itself to tackle intelligently the chaotic happenings around us which constitute our world of challenges. The *Geeta*-educated man learns to RECOGNISE A RHYTHM, to SEE A BEAUTY, and to HEAR A MELODY in the ordinary day-to-day life – a life which was till then but a mad death-dance of appearances and disappearances of things and beings.

SANJAYA CONFESSES THAT NOT ONLY DOES THE PHILOSOPHY ENCHANT HIS MIND, BUT EVEN THE MEMORY OF THE LORD'S WONDROUS FORM AS THE TOTAL MANIFESTED UNIVERSE HAS A MAGIC OF ITS OWN WHICH WARMS UP HIS HEART:

77. *Remembering and again remembering, that most wonderful Form of Hari, great is my wonder, O king; and I rejoice again and again.*

AS I OFTEN REMEMBER REPEATEDLY THAT MOST WONDERFUL FORM OF HARI—Lord Krishna, the charioteer, gave the vision of His Cosmic-Form (*Vishwaroopa*) in an earlier chapter;[1] it is that Form that is indicated by Sanjaya here. The Cosmic-Form of the Lord is as impressive to the man-of-heart, as the philosophy of the *Geeta* is unforgettable to the man-of-intelligence. The concept of the Lord's 'Total-Form' is staggering in the *Vedas*, and no doubt, highly impressive in the *Geeta*. But it need not necessarily be a mere poetic vision of the great Vyasa; there are many others whose experiences are almost parallel.[2]

If the philosophy of the *Geeta*, as it reveals to us the glorious purpose in life, inspires and thrills the thinking aspect in man, the vision of the smiling Lord of Vrindavana BEHIND EVERY NAME AND FORM, BENEATH EVERY EXPERIENCE, UNDER

तच्च संस्मृत्य संस्मृत्य रूपमत्यद्भुतं हरेः ।
विस्मयो मे महान्राजन्हृष्यामि च पुनः पुनः ॥ ७७ ॥
tacca saṁsmṛtya saṁsmṛtya rūpamatyadbhutaṁ hareḥ
vismayo me mahān rājanhṛṣyāmi ca punaḥ punaḥ 77.

[1] Refer the description of the Lord's Cosmic-Form as given in Chapter XI, Stanza 5 to 47

[2] See 'Studies in the History and Method of Science' edited by Charles Singer (1937).

EVERY SITUATION, adds a life-giving joy and a maddening ecstasy to the drunken heart of love.

Given the freedom, I suppose, Sanjaya would have written a full length Sanjaya-song on the Lord's Divine Song! When the head is thrilled with the silence of understanding, and the heart is intoxicated with the embrace of love, man gets transported into a sense of inspired fulfilment.

TO EXPRESS THAT SATISFACTION, LANGUAGE IS A FRAIL VEHICLE; THEREFORE, WITHOUT DILATING MUCH UPON WHAT IS UPPERMOST IN HIS MIND, SANJAYA SUMMARISES THEM ALL INTO A DECLARATION OF HIS BURNING FAITH, IN THIS CONCLUDING STANZA OF THE *BHAGAWAD GEETA*:

78. *Wherever is Krishna, the Lord of Yoga, wherever is Partha, the archer, there are prosperity, victory, happiness and firm (steady or sound) policy; this is my conviction.*

This is the closing stanza of *SRIMAD BHAGAWAD GEETA,* which contains altogether seven hundred and one verses. This concluding verse has not been sufficiently thought over and commented upon by the majority of commentators of the *Geeta.* The superficial word-meaning of the verse, in fact, can only impress any intelligent student, at its best, as rather drab and dry. After all Sanjaya is expressing his private faith in and his personal opinion about something which the readers of *Geeta* need not necessarily accept as final. Sanjaya, in effect, says: "Where

---

यत्र योगेश्वरः कृष्णो यत्र पार्थो धनुर्धरः ।
तत्र श्रीर्विजयो भूतिर्ध्रुवा नीतिर्मतिर्मम ॥ ७८ ॥

yatra yogeśvaraḥ kṛṣṇo yatra pārtho dhanurdharaḥ
tatra śrirvijayo bhūtirdhravā nitirmatirmama 78.

there is Krishna, the Lord of *Yoga*, and Arjuna, ready with his bow, there prosperity (*Sree*), success (*Vijaya*), expansion (*Bhooti*), and sound policy (*Dhruva-neeti*) will be; this is my sure faith".

After all, a student of the *Geeta* is not interested in Sanjaya's opinion, and it almost amounts to a foul and secret indoctrination, if Sanjaya means, diplomatically, to inject into us his own personal opinion. The *Geeta,* as a Universal Scripture would have fallen from its own intrinsic dignity as the Bible of man had this stanza no Eternal Truth to suggest, which readily invokes a universal appeal.

The perfect artist, Vyasa, could never have made such a mistake; indeed, there is a deeper significance in which an unquestionable truth has been expounded.

KRISHNA, THE LORD OF *YOGA* (*Yogeshwarah Krishnah*)— All through the *Geeta,* Krishna represented the Self, the *Atman*. This spiritual core is the Ground upon which the entire play of happenings is staged. He can be invoked within the bosom of each one of us through any one of the *Yoga*-techniques expounded in the *Geeta*.

ARJUNA, READY WITH HIS BOW (*Partho-Dhanurdharah*)— Partha represents, in this textbook, "the confused, limited, ordinary mortal, with all his innumerable weaknesses, agitations and fears". When he has thrown down his 'instrument' of effort and achievement, his bow, and has reclined to impotent idleness, no doubt, there is no hope for any success or prosperity. But when he is READY WITH HIS BOW, when he is no more idle but has a willing readiness to use his faculties to brave the challenges of life, there, in that man, we recognise a PARTHA READY WITH HIS BOW.

Now putting these two pictures together—Lord Krishna, the *Yogeshwarah*, and Arjuna, the *Dhanurdharah* - the symbolism of a way-of-life gets completed, wherein, reinforced with spiritual understanding, man gets ready to exert and pour in his endeavours, to tame life and master prosperity. In such a case, there is no power that can stop him from success. In short, the creed of the *Geeta* is that spirituality CAN be lived in life, and true spiritual understanding is an asset to a man engaged in the battle-of-life.

Today's confusions in society and man's helpless insignificance against the flood of events -- in spite of all his achievements in science and mastery over matter -- are seen, because the *Yogeshwarah* in him is lying neglected, uninvoked. A happy blending of the sacred and the secular is the policy for man as advised in the *Geeta*. In the vision of Sri Veda-Vyasa, he sees a world-order in which man pursues a way-of-life, wherein the spiritual and the material values are happily wedded to each other. Mere material production can, no doubt, bring immediately a spectacular flood of wealth into the pockets of man, but not peace and joy into his heart. PROSPERITY WITHOUT PEACE WITHIN IS A CALAMITY, GRUESOME AND TERRIBLE!

The stanza at the same time refuses to accept the other extreme; *Yogeshwarah* Krishna could have achieved nothing on the battlefield of Kurukshetra without the Pandava Prince, Arjuna, ARMED AND READY TO FIGHT. Mere spirituality without material exertion and secular achievements will not make life dynamic. I have been trying my best to bring out, as clearly as I can, this running vein of thought throughout the

Geeta, which expounds the PHILOSOPHY OF HARMONY and explains its plan for man's enduring happiness.

Krishna, in the *Geeta,* stands for the MARRIAGE BETWEEN THE SECULAR AND THE SACRED. Naturally, it is the ardent faith of Sanjaya* that when a community or nation has its masses galvanized to endure, to act, and to achieve (Partha, the bow-man) and if that generation is conscious of and has sufficiently invoked the spiritual purity of head and heart in themselves (Krishna, the Lord-of-*Yoga*), in that generation, prosperity, success, expansion, and a sound and sane policy become the natural order.

Even in the arrangement of these terms – prosperity, success, expansion and sound policy – there is an undercurrent of logic which is evident to all students of world history. In the context of modern times and the political experiences, we know that without an intelligent and STEADY POLICY, no government can lead a nation to any substantial achievement. With a sound policy, EXPANSION of all the dormant faculties in the community is brought out, and then only the spirit of co-ordination and brotherhood in the fields of achievement comes to play. In this healthy spirit of love and cooperation, when a disciplined people work hard, and when their efforts are intelligently channelised by the sound policies of the government, SUCCESS cannot be far away. Success thus earned, as a result of national endeavour, disciplined and channelised by a firm, intelligent policy, should necessarily yield true PROSPERITY. A saner philosophy we cannot find even in modern political thought!!

Enduring prosperity must be that which arises from successful endeavour, that is the result of cooperative and loving effort and this cannot yield any success unless it is nurtured and nourished, guarded and protected, by an intelligent and sound policy.

It now becomes quite clear that it is not only Sanjaya's faith, but it is the ardent conviction of all men of self-control and disciplined mind (Sanjayas), trained to think independently.

There are some commentators of the *Geeta*, who draw our attention to this concluding word in the *Geeta*, 'my' (*mama*), and to the opening word in the *Geeta*, '*Dharma*'.* Between these two words the seven hundred stanzas are hung together as a garland of immortal beauty, and so these commentators summarize the meaning of the *Geeta* as 'MY *Dharma*' (*Mama Dharma*). The *Geeta* explains the nature of man, 'MY *Dharma*', and the nature of Truth, 'MY *Dharma*' and how the true life starts when these two are in harmony and come to play in one single individual. The ideal nature of all true students of the *Geeta*, therefore, should be a glorious synthesis of both the SPIRITUAL KNOWLEDGE expressed in their equipoise and character, and the DYNAMIC LOVE expressed through their service to mankind and their readiness to sacrifice.

Thus, in the UPANISHADS of the glorious Bhagawad Geeta, in the Science of the Eternal, in the scripture of YOGA, in the dialogue between Sri Krishna and Arjuna, the eighteenth discourse ends entitled:

The *Yoga* of Liberation Through Renunciation

The closing chapter is entitled as "Liberation through Renunciation (*Moksha-Sannyasa-Yoga*)". This term is very closely reminiscent of the *Asparsa-Yoga* of the *Upanishads*, and the definition of *Yoga* as given by Krishna Himself in an earlier chapter.* To renounce the false values of life in us is at once to rediscover the Divine nature in each one of us which is the essential heritage of man. To discard the beast in us (*Sannyasa*), is the Liberation (*Moksha*) of the Divine in us.

OM TAT SAT

MAMA SADGURU TAPOVANA CHARANAYOH

"At The Feet Of My Master Tapovanam"

Om Om Om Om Om

ॐ तत्सदिति श्रीमद् भगवद् गीतासूपनिषत्सु ब्रह्मविद्यायां
योगशास्त्रे श्रीकृष्णार्जुनसंवादे मोक्षसंन्यासयोगो नाम
अष्टादशोऽध्याय:

Oṁ tatsaditi śrīmadbhagavadgītāsū ūpaniṣatsu brahmavidyāyāṁ yogaśāstre śrī kṛṣṇārjuna saṁvāde mokṣasannyāsayogo nāma aṣṭādaśo'dhyāyaḥ